FROMMER'S

BUDGET TRAVEL GUIDE

Eastern Europe on $30 a Day

5th Edition

Albania, the Czech & Slovak Republics, Hungary, Poland, Slovenia & Romania

by Adam Tanner

with Ian Watson, Zachary Schrag, and Andrew Kaplan

MACMILLAN • USA

ABOUT THE AUTHORS

Adam Tanner was formerly a correspondent for *The Moscow Times,* in Moscow, Russia. He has written the Frommer's guide to Eastern Europe since 1987, and has contributed to two editions of *Frommer's Europe on $50 a Day.* Before his stint in Moscow, Mr. Tanner worked as a staff writer at the Nashville *Tennessean,* and as a freelance writer researching articles in five continents for newspapers and magazines.

Ian Watson, Zachary Schrag, and Andrew Kaplan are Americans of Eastern European descent. After graduating from Harvard University, the three crisscrossed Eastern Europe as tourists, caterers, journalists, photographers, and telecommunications consultants. Mr. Watson, who contributed to the Albania, Hungary, and Slovenia sections of this guide, is also the author of *The Baltics and Russia Through the Back Door.* Mr. Schrag researched the latest sections on Bulgaria and Poland, and Mr. Kaplan updated the Czech Republic, Romania, and Slovakia.

MACMILLAN TRAVEL
A Prentice Hall Macmillan Company
15 Columbus Circle
New York, NY 10023

ISBN 0-02860092-4
ISSN 1044-7792

Design by Michele Laseau
Maps by Geographix Inc. and Ortelius Design

SPECIAL SALES

Bulk purchases (10 or more copies) of Frommer's Travel Guides are available to corporations at special discounts. The Special Sales Department can produce custom editions to be used as premiums and/or for sales promotion to suit individual needs. Existing editions can be produced with custom cover imprints such as corporate logos. For more information write to: Special Sales, Prentice Hall, 15 Columbus Circle, 15th Floor, New York, NY 10023.

Manufactured in the United States of America

Contents

List of Maps

What the Symbols Mean

★ **Frommer's Favorites** Hotels, restaurants, attractions, and entertainments you should not miss.

$ **Super-Special Values** Really exceptional values.

Abbreviations in Hotel and Other Listings

The following symbols refer to the standard amenities available in all rooms:

A/C air conditioning
MINIBAR refrigerator stocked with beverages and snacks
TEL telephone
TV television

The following abbreviations are used for credit cards:

AE American Express
CB Carte Blanche
DC Diners Club
DISC Discover
ER enRoute
EU Eurocard
JCB Card
MC MasterCard
V Visa

Trip Planning with this Guide

USE THE FOLLOWING FEATURES:

What Things Cost To help you plan your daily budget

Calendar of Events To plan for or avoid

Suggested Itineraries For seeing the regions or cities

What's Special About Checklist A summary of each region's highlights

Easy-to-Read Maps Walking tours, city sights, hotel and restaurant locations—all referring to or keyed to the text

Fast Facts All the essentials at a glance: currency, embassies, emergencies, safety, taxes, tipping, and more

OTHER SPECIAL FROMMER FEATURES

Did You Know . . . ? Offbeat, fun facts

Famous People The country's greats

Impressions What others have said

Invitation to the Readers

In researching this book, we have come across many fine establishments, the best of which we have included here. We're sure that many of you will also come across recommendable hotels, inns, restaurants, guesthouses, shops, and attractions. Please don't keep them to yourself. Share your experiences, especially if you want to comment on places that we have covered in this edition that have changed for the worse. You can address your letters to me:

Adam Tanner
Frommer's Eastern Europe on $30 a Day, 5th Edition
c/o Macmillan Travel
15 Columbus Circle
New York, NY 10023

Disclaimer

Readers are advised that prices fluctuate in the course of time and travel information changes under the impact of the varied and volatile factors that affect the travel industry. The authors and the publisher cannot be held responsible for the experiences of the readers while traveling. Readers are invited to write to the publisher with ideas, comments, and suggestions for future editions.

Safety Advisory

Whenever you're traveling in an unfamiliar city or country, stay alert. Be aware of your immediate surroundings. Wear a moneybelt and keep a close eye on your possessions. Be particularly careful with cameras, purses, and wallets, all favorite targets of thieves and pickpockets.

1

Introduction to Eastern Europe

Welcome to the new, improved, democratic Eastern Europe! The Berlin Wall is gone, the Cold War is over, and Eastern Europeans are now enjoying democratic freedom for the first time in more than 50 years.

In 1989 the downfall of Communism in the region was one of the dramatic historical moments of this century. Although the euphoria of the first days of democracy has faded, the ongoing political evolution makes it an especially fascinating time to visit.

Facing economic reform, growing unemployment, and spiraling prices, the Eastern Europeans realize what herculean tasks confront them in transforming their unproductive economies and developing truly democratic political and social institutions. But visit the region and you'll gain confidence that Eastern Europeans, especially the young, are up to the task; they possess in abundance the talent, energy, and ingenuity to weather this painful transition. You can watch students enthusiastically putting up posters in free elections, window-washers polishing the storefronts of businesses that put the customer first, and locals crowding around newsstands to buy papers finally free of government control.

WHAT TO SEE

For travelers unfamiliar with Eastern Europe, the demise of the Iron Curtain unearthed a dazzling ancient treasure from a rotting casket. The area we call Eastern Europe was long part of Central Europe's political, cultural, and artistic traditions, and in the past only politics kept people away.

What is there to see in Eastern Europe? Well, from Roman ruins in Bulgaria to shining new private businesses run by proud Polish entrepreneurs, there is as great a range of cultures, as many layers of history, and as stunning a collection of natural wonders as in the western part of the continent:

Prague, the beautiful 18th-century capital of the Czech Republic, which managed to emerge unscathed from the two world wars as the most splendidly preserved capital in Europe.

Kraków, Poland, a truly magical city with winding medieval streets where the great Wawel Castle and cathedral still dominate the Old Town.

Budapest, strategically situated on the Danube, which still boasts the lively sidewalk cafés and baroque buildings that recall the glory days of the Austro-Hungarian Empire.

Bulgaria's small towns, where 19th-century houses are preserved as museums but horsecarts and grape arbors are still in daily use.

And Romania's unforgettable 16th-century monasteries, unique treasures whose brilliant-colored exterior frescoes have miraculously withstood the ravages of four centuries.

Very low prices also make Eastern Europe a natural magnet for budget travelers. A liter of some of the finest beer in the world for 50¢? Sounds incredible, but come to Bohemia in the Czech Republic, home to the original Budweiser (Budvar). How about a double room within five minutes of Prague's glorious Old Town Square for $30? Or a complete three-course steak dinner for $2 in Bucharest? Or a rousing orchestral rendition of Beethoven's Fourth Symphony for 75¢? Take your seat at Sofia's Palace of Culture.

Of course, all of Eastern Europe's problems have not been eliminated, and plodding bureaucratic traditions have a strong hold on society, even after the demise of Communism. In several of the countries you'll find that amenities and service standards fall considerably short of those you may be used to at home. Rather than lament these shortcomings, consider them part of the travel adventure.

1 A Brief History

The geographical term "Eastern Europe" came into use only after World War II, when the area, to all appearances, was unified under Communism. In reality, broad cultural and historical differences have always separated the peoples of this area.

The Czech Republic, Hungary, Poland, Slovakia, and Slovenia claim with some reason to be more central than eastern, especially as they renew old economic and cultural ties to Germany and Austria. Albania, Bulgaria, and Romania, which have never been as westernized, form a southeastern group. You can debate the question endlessly, but the term "Eastern Europe" distinguishes those countries whose main objective today is to recover from 45 years of Soviet puppetdom and economic catastrophe.

ANCIENT EASTERN EUROPE The Romans conquered much of Eastern Europe—from what is now Hungary down to the Mediterranean Sea—by the first century B.C. In A.D. 106, the empire occupied the province of Dacia, in present-day Romania. The Dacians married Roman soldiers and colonists, adopted the Roman language, and became the ancestors of today's Romanians. The Roman Empire also swallowed up Albania, although the Albanians, who had already lived there for at least a thousand years, kept their own language intact. To the north of Roman lands, in what is now Poland, Bohemia, and Slovakia, lived an assortment of Germanic, Slavic, and Celtic tribes.

The empire broke up in the 400s amid a stream of barbarian invaders. On the heels of the Huns and the Goths, the Slavs pushed south and east until they were stopped by the mountains that still separate the Czech Republic from Germany, Slovenia from Italy, Serbia from Albania, and Bulgaria from Greece. The Byzantine Empire, which had inherited the Roman lands in southeastern Europe, was shaken by these Slavic and Turkic advances but managed to reassert control over the Balkans during the 800s. In the 860s, the brothers Cyril and Methodius (both later canonized as saints) were sent out from Byzantium to Christianize the Slavs, bringing the Cyrillic alphabet with them.

To the north, the Poles and Czechs united into medieval Christian kingdoms and began an epic struggle to define their western borders with Germany. They were kept linguistically and geographically apart from the South Slavs by the Avars, a Turkic tribe that had settled in modern-day Hungary. Charlemagne destroyed the Avars, but Magyar horsemen invaded from the Asian steppes in 896, settling the old Avar lands in Hungary, subduing Slovakia, and pressing further west.

MEDIEVAL EASTERN EUROPE Holy Roman Emperor Otto I defeated the Magyars at Lech in 955; this had a quieting effect on these eastern nomads and gave Europe a bit of peace. But his Germans were thrown back by the great Slav revolt of 983, and Poland became the first great Slav empire, while the Byzantines endured in the Balkans.

In the 13th century, the Mongols, having swept through Russia, conquered Hungary, but were unable to continue farther west for lack of grassy plains on which to feed their ponies. Serbia had its heyday in the mid-14th century, only to be crushed in 1389 by the Ottoman Turks, who went on to conquer Bulgaria in 1393 and

Byzantium itself at Constantinople in 1453. Meanwhile, to the north, Poland, Bohemia, and Hungary (not coincidentally the same areas now most eagerly seeking closer economic and political ties with Western Europe today) evolved into Western-style kingdoms with strong monarchies, royal courts, and universities. But these states were threatened by the Teutonic Knights, Austrians, and Turks.

The Turks made their move in the 1520s, annexing Hungary and unsuccessfully besieging Vienna. The Turks besieged Vienna once more in 1683 only to be driven back again. With Ottoman power clearly in decline, affairs in the region began to be dominated by Hohenzollern Prussia, Habsburg Austria, and Romanov Russia. These empires partitioned Poland and dismembered the Ottoman Empire piece by piece, until all four empires destroyed each other in the inferno of World War I.

MODERN EASTERN EUROPE The peace treaties after World War I recognized a sovereign Poland, Czechoslovakia, Hungary, Romania, Bulgaria, Albania, and Yugoslavia on the lands of the former imperial provinces. In preparation for independence, Eastern Europeans split into Soviet Socialist and conservative camps. From 1918 into the early 20s, the war effectively continued as these groups fought both for control among themselves, and along disputed borders between each country. Conservative forces generally prevailed in the governments of Eastern European nations—except in the Soviet Union itself—but during the depression of the 1930s, these governments tended to degenerate into authoritarianism. World War II brought vast destruction to Eastern Europe; after the war, the area was occupied by Soviet troops.

The Soviets quickly set up puppet Communist governments, and by the late 1940s dissent was brutally repressed. The region had fallen behind an Iron Curtain.

Although many Eastern Europeans collaborated in ways big and small with their governments, the Communist system was largely detested. Periodically, popular uprisings broke out, most notably in East Germany in 1953, in Poland and Hungary in 1956, in Czechoslovakia in 1968, and in Poland during 1980–81. On each occasion, the actual use or threat of Soviet military force restored Communist order.

When antigovernment sentiment started to bubble over in 1989, the Soviet Union under Gorbachev apparently decided that it would no longer intervene militarily to maintain Communist rule in Eastern Europe. Perhaps Gorbachev hoped that Moscow's laissez-faire policy would result in the emergence of reformist Communists like himself. Yet given a taste of freedom, the local populations wanted nothing more to do with Communism.

Poland led the region with the first partially free elections in June 1989, which resulted in a landslide victory for the opposition Solidarity. In September 1989, Hungary decided to allow East Germans to flee their country via Hungary. In desperation, the East German government responded by opening the Berlin Wall in November 1989. With its most repressive control valve released, the East German Communist government collapsed. In the next few weeks, popular revolt brought the downfall of one Communist government after another in Eastern Europe. The revolutions in Slovenia and Albania, because of their special conditions, did not happen until 1991. By 1994, all the countries covered in this book had experienced—to varying degrees—free elections, free speech, resurgent nationalism, political reform, corruption scandals, a nascent free-market economy, raging inflation, open borders, unemployment, Western investment, and all the other hallmarks in the bumpy process of decommunization.

Eastern Europe

2 Recommended Books & Films

ALBANIA

An amusing look at Communist Albania is Jon Halliday's *The Artful Albanian: The Memoirs of Enver Hoxha* (Chatto & Windus, 1988) with a wry introduction; this competently annotated selection contains the best bits of the late dictator's writings on Stalin, Mao, Tito, Khrushchev, and his own small country. It may be hard to find, but check your library. Edith Durham's *High Albania* (Beacon), originally published in 1909 but recently reissued in paperback, is not only a classic of travel-literature but also gives an unparalleled view of northern Albania before modernization. Bill Hamilton's *Albania: Who Cares?* (Grantham, 1992) in a British journalist's slightly dramatized report on Albania today. A number of new English translations of Ismail Kadare's novels have also come out recently; I've recommended some titles in Chapter 4.

BULGARIA

The dedicated reader might tackle *The Balkans Since 1453* by L. S. Stavrianos (Rinehart and Co.), a hefty 850-page history of the region. Another erudite study is R. J. Crampton's *A Short History of Modern Bulgaria* (Cambridge University Press). For serious sightseeing in Bulgaria, consider Nagel's 500-page *Bulgaria*, filled with maps, diagrams, and in-depth information, for about $30. Philip Ward's *Bulgaria: A Travel Guide* (Pelican, 1990) is less detailed than a guidebook without being flashy enough to be a travelogue, but it does cover the country in depth.

THE CZECH & SLOVAK REPUBLICS

For fiction, I'm a big fan of Milan Kundera, whose novels graphically capture the flavor of Czechoslovak life, often against the background of the oppressive former Communist government. Perhaps his best-known work is *The Unbearable Lightness of Being*, which later received critical acclaim as a film. (If you get a chance before leaving, rent the video of *The Unbearable Lightness of Being*, a romance set against the backdrop of the 1968 uprising in Prague.) I've also enjoyed Kundera's *Book of Laughter and Forgetting* (Penguin) and *Farewell Party* (Penguin). He has also written several other novels and a play, *Jacques and His Master* (Harper and Row).

Czechoslovakia's most prominent author is clearly Václav Havel. His works include *Largo Desolato* (Grove Press) and *Temptation* (Grove Press). For insight into the man, consider *Disturbing the Peace* (Knopf), a book-length interview with Havel that reflects on his life and times, and *Václav Havel, Living in Truth* (Faber and Faber), a collection of his essays and tributes from friends and admirers.

Other favorites are Franz Kafka and Jaroslav Hašek, whose *Good Soldier Schweik* is a satire on war.

On politics, you might consider Mlynář Zdeněk's serious *Nightfrost in Prague: The End of Humane Socialism* (Karz) about the Prague Spring of 1968. For information on the early years of the country, try *History of the Czechoslovak Republic, 1918–1948* (Princeton University Press), edited by Victor Mamatey and Radomir Luza. You'll probably find these two books only in libraries. *Munich: The Price of Peace* by Telford Taylor (Vintage) is a detailed diplomatic history of Europe's appeasement of Hitler in 1938, which resulted in the occupation of Czechoslovakia.

I strongly recommend *Baedeker's Prague* (Simon & Schuster). It has an excellent detailed map attached to the back, and its descriptions of sights and additional maps make this guidebook very useful.

HUNGARY

John Lukács' *Budapest 1900* (Weidenfeld & Nicolson, 1988) exquisitely captures the feeling of imperial Budapest at the turn of the century. In *Between the Woods and the Water* (Penguin, 1986), British travel writer Patrick Leigh Fermor recounts in lyrical, romantic prose his walk across Hungary in 1933 on his way from London to Constantinople. He visited many Hungarian aristocratic homes not unlike the mansion hotels you can stay in today, hit several village festivals, and enjoyed himself thoroughly.

For history, try *A History of Hungary* (Indiana University Press, 1990), edited by Peter Sugar, or István Lázár's *Hungary: A Brief History* (Corvina, 1989). *Hungary and the Soviet Bloc* (Duke University Press, 1986), by Charles Gati, is a serious look at Communist-era politics. On the 1956 revolution, read *Thirteen Days That Shook the Kremlin*, edited by Tibor Meray (Praeger, 1959).

If you're interested in Hungarian booking, Charlotte Slovak Biro's *Flavors of Hungary* (101 Productions) is an excellent place to start.

You may want to postpone any serious book-buying until you reach Budapest, where the Bestsellers English-language bookstore has an excellent selection of titles, including many of the above.

POLAND

God's Playground: A History of Poland, by Norman Davies (Columbia University Press), in two volumes, is perhaps the best, if lengthy, history of Poland; another good history is Norman Davies's *Heart of Europe: A Short History of Poland* (Oxford). *The Polish Way* by Adam Zamoyski (Franklin Watts, 1988) covers the period from the 14th century to the end of World War I particularly well. For a description of life in Poland between the wars, read Ron Nowicki's *Warsaw: The Cabaret Years* (Mercury House, 1992). There are many narratives of the Nazi occupation and the Holocaust. I recommend *Maus: A Survivor's Tale* (Pantheon, 1991, 2 vols.) in which cartoonist Art Spiegelman presents his father's story, and *Survival in Auschwits*, by survivor Primo Levi (Macmillan, 1961). Neal Ascherson's *The Polish August* (Penguin Books) is an absorbing postwar history that culminates in the rise of Solidarity in the early 1980s. Stewart Stevens's *The Poles* (Collins/Harvill) gives a good picture of life in Poland under Communist rule; a similarly readable account is Janine Wedel's *The Private Poland* (Facts on File). Timothy Garton Ash's *Polish Revolution: Solidarity* (Scribner's, 1983) contains an eyewitness account of the Solidarity movement of 1980-81, as well as a perceptive analysis of the conditions that brought it about.

Perhaps the most engaging and insightful accounts of recent events are *Mad Dreams, Saving Graces: Poland, A Nation in Conspiracy* by Michael T. Kaufman (Random House, 1989) and *Unquiet Days: At Home in Poland* by Thomas Swick (Ticknor & Fields, 1991). Andrew Nagorski's *The Birth of Freedom: Shaping Lives and Societies in the New Eastern Europe* (Simon & Schuster, 1993) is an excellent, anecdotal account of recent Poland by *Newsweek*'s longtime Warsaw correspondent; it touches somewhat on Czech and Hungarian affairs as well.

If you don't like formal history books, try James Michener's *Poland* (Random House, 1983), a novel that chronicles Poland's dramatic history in light, readable form.

There has also been some more serious fiction written by and about Poles. If you only read one novel about Poland prior to visiting, a good choice would be *The Beautiful Mrs. Seidenman*, by Andrzej Saczypiorski (Vintage, 1991). Set in Warsaw in 1993, it focuses on a small number of characters, while incorporating enough flashbacks and flashforwards to encompass an operation sweep of history. Four Polish-born writers have won the Nobel Prize for literature: Henryk Sienkiewicz, Wladyslau Reymont, Isaac Bashevis Singer, and Czeslaw Miloss. Many of Singer's stories, set in the Jewish communities of prewar Poland, are written for children.

For an in-depth guide to the country—especially the southeastern part—try *Poland Travel Guide* by Marc Heine (Hippocrene Books), or the rambling but detailed travelogue *Polish Cities* by Philip Ward (Pelican, 1989).

Poland, People to People by David Stotler lists the addresses, telephone numbers, and interests of Poles who would like contact with English-speaking foreigners. It's published by Canongate Press PLC in Edinburgh, Scotland; in the U.S., it can be ordered from Zephyr Press, 13 Robinson St., Somerville, MA 02145, for $10.

Andrej Wajda is Poland's most famous filmmaker, with such noteworthy credits as *A Generation, Ashes and Diamonds, Man of Marble,* and *Man of Iron.*

ROMANIA

For absorbing background reading about the time between the two world wars when Bucharest reached its heyday as a fashionable city, read Hannah Pakula's engaging biography of Queen Marie, *The Last Romantic* (London: Weidenfeld and Nicolson, 1984). Marie of Edinburgh, the beautiful and eccentric half-British, half-Russian granddaughter of Queen Victoria, married King Ferdinand to become Queen of Romania and the darling of European café society.

For a sinister account of international intrigue, try *Red Horizons* (Regnery Gateway) by Ion Pacepa, the former head of the Romanian secret police; this book gives a fascinating account of the inner machinations of Communism under Ceauşescu. *The 25th Hour* by Virgil Gheorghiu (Pocket Books) tells the story of a Romanian peasant in World War II. *Journey to Freedom* by Nicholas Dima (Selous Foundation Press) is a first-person account of life under Romanian Communism and an escape to the West. A number of books about recent historical events in Romania have appeared, including *Romania: The Entangled Revolution* (New York: Praeger, 1991) by Nestor Ratesh, former head of Radio Free Europe's Romanian Broadcasting Department. Andrei Codrescu's wry book *The Hole in the Flag* (New York: William Morrow, 1991) is the poet-journalist's account of his return to his homeland during the December 1989 events, based in part on his compelling eyewitness reports aired on National Public Radio. Recent books about the rise and fall of the Ceausçescus are George Galloway's *Downfall: The* Ceauşescu*s and the Romanian Revolution* (London: Futura, 1991) and the very readable *Kiss the Hand You Cannot Bite* (Villard Books, 1991), full of revelations and scandals, by Edward Behr. *Mad Forest, a Play from Romania* by the Englishman Caryl Churchill is a dramatized depiction of the events in Timisoara leading up to the 1989 Revolution (London: Nick Hern Books, 1991).

Many scenes in Olivia Manning's novel *The Balkan Trilogy* (Penguin) portray life in Bucharest before and during World War II when it was a sophisticated European capital.

Several recent travelogues feature Romania. *Stealing from a Deep Place* by Brian Hall (Hill and Wang, 1988) records a cyclist's observations about the people and politics of Romania, Bulgaria, and Budapest. *Danube* by Claudio Magris (Farrar, Straus & Giroux) discusses a journey along the length of the Danube River, from its source in Germany to the Delta on the Romanian Black Sea Coast. Georgina Harding's *In Another Europe: A Journey to Romania* (London: Hodder & Stoughton, 1990) is a sensitive, insightful account of her solo journey by bicycle from Vienna to Istanbul through northern Hungary and remote parts of central Romania.

SLOVENIA

In the United States, there is almost nothing up-to-date that discusses Slovenia as a separate entity from the former Yugoslavia. An exception is the thorough discussion of Slovene independence in Lenard J. Cohen's *Broken Bonds: The Disintegration of Yugoslavia* (Westview, 1993). Coffee-table books on the Slovene architect Jože Plečnik include the notable *Jože Plečnik, Architect* (MIT Press, 1989) and Peter Krecic's *Plečnik, The Complete Works* (1993). Otherwise, I suggest you wait until you reach Ljubljana, where you'll find a fair selection of guidebooks and picture books on sale locally.

GENERAL EASTERN EUROPE

New books on Eastern Europe are continually coming out. Here are a few books that may be among the more enduring.

The Columbia History of Eastern Europe in the Twentieth Century (Columbia University Press, 1992), edited by Joseph Held, provides concise, readable histories of the region's different countries, covering approximately 1918–91.

Timothy Garton Ash's *The Magic Lantern: The Revolution of '89 Witnessed in Warsaw, Budapest, Berlin and Prague* (Vintage, 1990) is a firsthand account by a British journalist who was particularly involved in the Velvet Revolution in Prague. Misha Glenny, the longtime Central European correspondent for the BBC, writes his account of the events of 1989 in *The Rebirth of History: Eastern Europe in the Age of Democracy* (Penguin, 1990). Both of these books are available in paperback.

Ruth Ellen Gruber's *Jewish Heritage Travel: A Guide to Central and Eastern Europe* (Wiley, 1992) has extensive listings of sites of Jewish interest.

Without Force or Lies: Voices from the Revolution of Central Europe in 1989–90, edited by William M. Brinton and Alan Rinzler (Mercury House) is an important anthology of essays, speeches, and eyewitness accounts, including an essay by Sakharov, Vaclav Havel's speech to the U.S. Congress in February 1990, and Gorbachev's address to the Soviet Communist Party in 1990 calling for the advent of political pluralism.

PHRASE BOOKS & AUDIO TAPES

One of the biggest challenges for a traveler in Eastern Europe, or anywhere for that matter, is communicating with the local people in their language. You might invest in phrase books before you go—they're difficult to find in Eastern Europe.

Perhaps the best-known publisher of phrase books is Berlitz, which offers Hungarian, Czech, and Polish books. Few bookstores carry these titles, but you can order them directly from Berlitz, P.O. Box 305, Riverside, NJ 08075 (☎ toll free **800/526-8047**). (The cost is $5.95 plus $1.50 shipping.)

I found the handy pocket-size *Lonely Planet Eastern Europe Phrasebook* in a travel bookstore only after I had carted around several dictionaries and phrase books on my travels. This 380-page book has useful Czech and Slovak, Polish, Hungarian, Bulgarian, and Romanian phrases and terms. You can have your local bookstore order it, or you can write to Lonely Planet Publications, Inc., P.O. Box 2001A, Berkeley, CA 94702. (The price is $6.95.)

If you're interested in learning to speak an Eastern European language with more fluency, I recommend the cassette courses produced by Audio Forum. They offer courses in Czech, Slovak, Albanian, Bulgarian, Romanian, Hungarian, and Polish, among others. In each course, you listen to native speakers on a cassette and follow along with a textbook. Prices range from $20 to $235. You can contact Audio Forum for their catalog at 96 Broad St., Guilford, CT 06437 (☎ toll free **800/243-1234**).

If you don't want to tackle an Eastern European language, you could try to learn a bit of German, which is becoming ever more important in Central Europe.

3 Enjoying Eastern Europe on a Budget

The $30-a-Day Budget

As I was preparing this guidebook, many friends asked incredulously whether it was really possible to spend only $30 a day and travel well in Eastern Europe? Sure it is—in fact, in many cases you can spend even less than $30 a day! This sum allows for about $10 a day for food and $20 for accommodations, but excludes transportation, museum fees, and other expenses. However, with Eastern European museums and cinemas entrance fees so low (just pennies in Romania) and domestic transportation only a few dollars for lengthy journeys, you can often spend less than a total of $30 a day. How easy it will be to do this depends on the following three factors:

Where you go. In Bulgaria and Poland you should have the least problem staying within the $30-a-day budget. The Czech Republic, Hungary, and Slovenia demand the most vigilance. Also, the capital city of each country is always more expensive, particularly Budapest and Prague, where you may feel more comfortable on a budget of $35 to $40 per day if you want to stay in a hotel.

What kind of accommodations you stay in. It's not hard for couples to stay in hotels and keep within the $30-a-day budget, but you do have to keep to the less expensive establishments like those listed in this book. Renting a private room in someone's house—a very common option in Eastern Europe—rarely costs more than $15 for one or $20 for two people. Staying in private accommodations will bring you in under $30 virtually anywhere in the region.

Whether you bring a friend. Everywhere in Eastern Europe you can save a lot of money by traveling with a companion. Most hotels have double rooms only, and charge the same for a room whether it's occupied by one guest or two. Solo travelers may have to stay in private rooms or the few hotels that have singles to keep within the $30-a-day budget.

Note: For specifics on how to save money on accommodations, restaurants, and shopping, consult the chapter on planning a trip to each individual country, as well as the tips given the individual city and regional chapters.

Of course, prices do go up over time. Consider, for example, the 1903 complaint of Lee Meriwether in *A Tramp Trip: How to See Europe on Fifty Cents a Day:* "I was finally forced to content myself with a bed in the attic of a second-rate inn," he lamented about Budapest, "having to pay therefore the extortionate price of one gulden—forty cents—the highest price I had yet paid in Europe." With Eastern Europe making the difficult transition from Communism to free enterprise, price changes will be abrupt and unforeseen in the coming years. I've provided up-to-date rates, but remember that prices will change somewhat by the time you visit.

A Note on Price Overcharges

If you disagree with a waiter, a hotel clerk, a cab driver, or anyone else over a bill, settle the matter then and there. Be aware that in Eastern Europe, as in many other countries across the globe, some people see Americans as prime targets to earn extra money. In a restaurant, ask to have every item on the bill matched up with the menu if you think something is wrong. In a hotel, ask to see the price chart that all hotels have. If the disagreement continues, you can ask to see the manager, but often this is an administrative bureaucrat unsympathetic to your plight. Hold your ground and try to reach a compromise.

I recently stayed in an American hotel that boasted "We guarantee you will be completely satisfied with your stay—or you don't pay." That policy is about the mirror opposite of much of Eastern Europe: "You pay no matter what you think of the place." Even with the dramatic political changes of the last few years, the adage "the customer is always right" remains alien to most of the region. Unfortunately, in the end there's little you can do to fight petty overcharges. If you've been overcharged a gross sum of money, you can turn to the local legal system, but a resolution will probably take a long time.

I don't mean to worry you about all transactions. Very few at most will result in the unpleasant situations described above. I mention them because it's best to be informed and prepared for any eventuality.

A Few Caveats

No restaurant, inn, hotel, guesthouse, or shop paid to be mentioned in this book. What you read are personal recommendations—in many cases, the managers never knew their establishments were being appraised.

A Word of Warning: Unfortunately, prices change, and they rarely go down.

Always, when checking into a hotel, inquire about the price—and agree on it. This policy can save much embarrassment and disappointment when it comes time to settle the tab. Under no circumstances can you invariably demand to be charged the price quoted in this book.

It is impossible to predict if, and by how much, prices will rise by the time you read this. Since Eastern European currencies tend to inflate against the U.S. dollar, the dollar prices included in each listing will probably stay more stable than their local-currency counterparts. But Eastern Europe's transition from state-controlled Communism to free-market democracy is unprecedented, and nobody really knows how things will turn out in the coming years. As a traveler, you should be prepared for occasional abrupt changes in rules or prices. The currency rate could change radically overnight, or the nation's hotel prices could jump unexpectedly.

One reader recently wrote me and asked why a certain ice-cream parlor in Poland that I had recommended didn't have ice cream when he visited. Well, things change from day to day in Eastern Europe, often without apparent logic. In the case of the ice-cream parlor, supplies just ran out on the day he visited.

This sort of frustration also extends to getting around, obtaining information, seeing the sights, and using the phone. I've tried to sort things out as best as possible, but remember that particularly in Albania, Bulgaria, and Romania, you'll need an additional dose of patience and a good sense of humor; otherwise you may wind up regretting that you ever came. When you're in a country where it's hard to buy a map of the town you're in, where the only way to get around is by bus and they don't run on time, where tourist officials are not well briefed, and where the phones don't work—if you write out a list of everything you want to see and then get upset each time something doesn't work out, you'll have a coronary before your second week. But if you make up your mind in advance to roll with the punches and make them into good stories to tell at home, you'll be okay. Improvise, and the surprises and rewards that await you in the new, dynamic Eastern Europe will make it all worthwhile.

2

Before You Leave Home

THE PATH TO SMOOTH TRAVELS IN EASTERN EUROPE BEGINS AT HOME. RESEARCH on the countries you plan to visit will make your journeys more worthwhile—and may save you some money. This chapter lists some tips and general information to make your planning easier.

1 Passports & Other Documents

PASSPORT You'll need a passport to travel in each country listed in this book. If you don't have one, or you need to renew it, go to or write to your nearest passport office several months in advance so that you'll have enough time to procure the necessary Eastern European visas. For more information on passports, call the U.S. Department of State's comprehensive recorded message (☎ **202/647-0518**).

When in Eastern Europe, carry your passport with you at all times. You'll need it to check into hotels, to exchange Western money for local currency, and to reserve certain services at tourist offices. When you check into a hotel, your passport will usually be held by the hotel for a few hours (during which time you'll be unable to exchange money; if you need local currency, exchange money as you check in). Except for these few hours, try to keep this important document with you in a secure place at all times. Be carefulyour passport is a very valuable document and should be closely guarded. Be sure to have a photocopy of the pages with your photo and signature and carry this separately from the passport. Keep any separate visa papers with your passport, as you may occasionally be asked to show them as well.

VISA At press time, Americans could enter every country in this book without a visa, except Romania. British citizens are treated slightly less favorably, Canadians and the Irish even less so, and Australians and New Zealanders require a visa to visit most of the countries in this book. See the individual country chapters for details. Since visa regulations can change quickly, it is wise to double-check before you go. Some countries will issue visas at the border, but this is risky, and usually impossible if you come by train. If you just need to travel *through* a country on your way to another, ask about a transit visa, which generally costs less than a regular visa.

To apply for a visa, first ask the national tourist office or embassy to send you the visa form. After filling it out, go to the post office. Purchase a money order to pay for the visa charges; then send it by registered mail (which costs about $5) to the embassy, along with your passport and a self-addressed return envelope (with enough postage for return registered mail). If you are able to go to the embassy or consulate in person you'll save the mail costs. Just to be sure, allow several weeks to be granted a visa.

For complete details on the visa requirements of each country in Eastern Europe, refer to Section 1, "Information, Entry Requirements, and Money," of the "Planning a Trip to …" chapter for each country in this guide.

After you enter some countries in Eastern Europe, part of the visa paper remains in your passport—it serves as an exit visa. If you lose this paper, you will be required to pay a fine or remain in whatever country you're in until an exit visa is reissued.

DRIVER'S LICENSE It's a good idea to bring along both your national (or state) driver's license and an international driver's license. Only Poland and Hungary officially require the international driver's license in addition to your national or state license, but in Eastern Europe two documents are always better than one. You can easily obtain an international driver's license from your local American Automobile Association (AAA) or other U.S. auto clubs upon presentation of your state license, two passport-size photos, and $10.

ISIC (International Student Identity Card) Eastern Europe offers many attractive discounts for students with the correct documentation. All you need is the ISIC available to all high school and college or university students at your local student office.

FIYTO (Federation of International Youth Travel Organizations) If you are not a student but are less than 26 years of age, then the FIYTO card is the next best thing to a student card. Available in the West at your local student office, the FIYTO card offers young people discounts at select hotels, at museums, and on certain forms of transportation.

Anyone who plans on staying in youth hostels should invest in a **youth hostel card,** which offers discounts at youth hostels across Eastern Europe. The card costs $25 for those aged 18 to 54, $10 for those 17 and younger, and $15 for those over 55. You can buy this card from accredited student offices or from Hostelling International, P.O. Box 37613, Washington, DC 20013-7613 (☎ **202/783-6161**). This office also sells the *Guide to Budget Accommodation,* Volume 1, *Europe and the Mediterranean,* a sage investment as it includes a listing of all of Europe's youth hostels for $13.95, including shipping.

A Note of Caution

In societies still reliant on lots of paperwork, you'll want to be sure that nothing happens to your passport, visas, and other documents. But just in case, you can save some hassle and lost days by photocopying your passport, visa, driver's license, etc., before you go and putting these in a safe place in your luggage. I suggest that you also record your passport and visa numbers in another secure place, away from the original documents. These photocopies will expedite the process of replacing your passport and/or visa in case of loss or theft abroad.

INSURANCE If you want extra medical coverage abroad or have a chronic medical problem that you fear might flare up while you travel, there are at least half a dozen reputable companies that have numerous comprehensive one-week to three-month plans that cover everything from accidents, sickness, and medical evacuation to legal assistance and lost or stolen luggage. Two such companies are the Travel Insurance Pak Co., 1 Tower Sq., 15 NB, Hartford, CT 06183 (☎ toll free **800/243-3174**); and HealthCare Abroad (MEDEX), 107 W. Federal St., Suite 13, P.O. Box 480, Middleburg, VA 22117-0480 (☎ toll free **800/237-6615**). Contact them for full details.

2 What to Pack

HEALTH CONSIDERATIONS

When traveling to any of the countries, it's a good idea to bring all toiletry supplies you are going to need, except perhaps soap, and any specific prescription medications—you may have difficulty finding them in Eastern Europe. Some Western medicines are available in Eastern Europe, but you're best off if you carry the pharmaceuticals you might need—starting with aspirin. (It's also a good idea to bring the prescription with the generic name of the drug, in case you lose your medication.)

If you wear contact lenses, be sure to bring enough cleaning solution, as well as a spare set of lenses or a pair of glasses.

For those prone to stomach upset or diarrhea when changing diets or environments, bring along the appropriate medication.

GENERALLY FOR EASTERN EUROPE

In general, pack lightly. In past editions, I wrote that you only need to take along your most basic clothes and that people dress casually in Eastern Europe; but now with markets opening up, many Eastern Europeans have rediscovered smart-looking and fashionable clothes, and perhaps you'll be quite surprised at some of the outfits in Warsaw, Varna, and Bucharest.

Some useful items you might consider bringing along include:

Calculator Many travelers find it useful to figure out foreign-exchange rates (and metric conversions) on a calculator. Feed the local exchange rate into the memory, and every time you want to translate local prices, enter the price, then divide by the memory, and out pops the dollar equivalent. A credit-card calculator, which fits snugly into your wallet or purse, or a digital watch with a built-in calculator are the most compact and convenient.

Camera/Film If you run out of film, you can easily obtain Western film and camera batteries in the major cities of the Czech and Slovak Republics, Hungary, Slovenia and Poland; camera supplies are scarcer in Albania, Bulgaria, and Romania. **Note:** Eastern European film brands are of inferior quality and can be hard to develop in the United States.

If you plan to travel through any Eastern European airports, I highly recommend Filmshield, a small, lead-lined, malleable pouch that prevents powerful x-ray machines from ruining your film. Without such a device the film may look foggy when developed.

Avoid carrying expensive-looking camera bags, as this immediately marks you as a target for the growing number of thieves and hustlers.

Electric-Current Transformer/Adapter If you bring any appliances, remember that the electricity in Eastern Europe is 220 volts AC, not the standard 110 volts of North America. A 110-volt appliance will soon burn out when attached to an unconverted 220-volt plug. Rather than mess with heavy, clumsy transformers or converters, I'd advise investing in dual-voltage hairdryers, electric razors, etc., and using them with the appropriate foreign outlet adapter plugs (there are only three styles and they're pounds lighter and much less expensive than converters). Be advised that some budget hotels don't have electrical outlets in some rooms, so check for them *before* you check in.

For more information on the topic, call the Franzus Company at **203/723-6664** and ask for their short pamphlet "Foreign Electricity Is No Deep Dark Secret."

Gifts I suggest T-shirts with athletic, college, music, or professional logos; car decals; souvenir key chains; and fabric patches—these have become status symbols of direct contact with the West or a Westerner. Music cassettes always make good gifts. East Europeans are still crazy about stickers and decals of all kinds—advertising is a new medium there. For those who read English, copies of recent magazines (any variety) and the latest paperback best-seller are appreciated.

Liquid Soap If you're planning to stay in private accommodations and budget hotels, liquid soap is another useful item to have. I suggest soap in a plastic container because it's less messy than a bar of soap.

Money Belt/Neck Pouch This is essential for carrying your money, passport, and other essential documents. Look for something that can fit as unfolded airline ticket.

Overnight Bag/Day Pack You'll find that a lightweight fold-up bag or small day pack that fits easily into your luggage is very handy for hikes and short trips, shopping at outdoor markets, and bringing home those breakable gift souvenirs you simply couldn't resist.

Plastic Bags For wrapping wet bathing suits, damp laundry, and leaky bottles, and storing food.

Pocketknife A Swiss army-type pocketknife with scissors, toothpick, and corkscrew serves innumerable purposes.

Postcards Postcards or photos of your hometown are great to carry around to show people curious about the West.

Sewing Kit Your kit should include not only the usual mending necessities, but several large safety pins and a large needle and heavy-duty thread for emergency luggage and purse repairs.

Short-Wave Radio News junkies who don't want to lose touch with what's going on back home will enjoy a short-wave radio. Tuning to the BBC or the Voice of America will keep you up-to-date in these exciting times of change in Eastern Europe. A useful book in finding the right frequencies at different times of day is the *World Radio TV Handbook,* available from Watson-Guptill Publications, 1515 Broadway, New York, NY 10036 (☎ **908/363-5679**), for $19.95.

Slippers These are especially good if you are planning to spend a lot of time in private homes, since Eastern Europeans often remove their shoes at the door.

Toilet Paper A roll or two can come in handy, especially when staying in private accommodations (the newspaper in the bathroom isn't always for reading) or in southeastern Europe. Check your local camping store for compact rolls without a hollow core.

Travel Alarm Many hotels don't have a wake-up service, and so for the traveler following a schedule, a small, reliable alarm clock is a necessity.

Women's Hygienic Needs Bring an adequate supply of tampons or pads. Local products are poor imitations and hard to find; Western brands, when available, are very expensive.

Woolite Powder Coin-operated laundries are rare in Eastern Europe, so you may need to hand-wash smaller items of clothing. I recommend Woolite powder in small packets. Hotel sinks may lack stoppers, so also bring a flat rubber bathtub stopper that can plug any size drain.

Writing Materials A pocket-size loose-leaf notebook is extremely useful in any country where you don't speak the language. You can write down the names of unpronounceable streets or sights, show the notebook to local people, and then let them indicate directions in your notebook. You can write down the departure times, destinations, and classes of trains that you want and show it to clerks at the railroad.

SPECIFICALLY FOR . . .

ALBANIA Bring a flashlight to help negotiate Tirana's potholed streets after dark.

BULGARIA You'll want to take along your bathing suit, sunscreen, and a hat if you'll be spending any time at Bulgaria's coastal resorts. Or, if the mountains delight, bring hiking boots and a canteen.

THE CZECH & SLOVAK REPUBLICS You might pack a good pair of walking shoes for the ancient cobblestone streets of Prague or hiking boots for the mountains of the High Tatras.

HUNGARY You might want to bring your bathing suit, either for summer swimming in Lake Balaton, or for a visit to one of Budapest's many thermal bath houses at any time of year.

POLAND Anyone familiar with northern Europe knows that you need to bundle up for much of the year. My advice is to dress warmly; even in summer you'll often need a sweater, especially in the evening, and if you plan on going to the mountains in the Zakopane area, you may need both a sweater and a jacket. Also, bring along sufficient rain gear (such as a waterproof jacket, galoshes, and an umbrella) because it rains frequently, particularly from May to September.

ROMANIA You'll want to bring especially warm clothes for any wintertime travel, with boots, heavy overcoat, gloves, and a hat. For summer travel, dress lightly as it can get hot, especially in July and August, and air conditioning is rare. It's always quite a bit cooler in the mountains.

3 Receiving Mail & Messages Abroad

Most Eastern European postal systems, although improving, are not as efficient as their Western counterparts. Nonetheless, you can receive mail c/o the American Express offices or their representatives in five capital cities—Budapest, Ljubljana, Prague, Tirana, and Warsaw—if you wish. (For full addresses, see the "Fast Facts" sections in the chapters dealing with these cities). Allow 10 days to two full weeks for mail delivery to these offices, more than 10 days to Tirana. Note that American Express cannot receive registered mail. Since the Bulgarian and Romanian postal systems have terrible reputations and American Express has not opened full service offices in their capitals yet, I'd advise against having any mail sent there. American Express cardholders and checkholder receive their mail for free; others pay a nominal fee.

If you need to receive crucial documents or important mail abroad, you might consider having them sent to you at your hotel or the American Express office via the U.S. Post Office's International Express Mail Service. It's relatively inexpensive ($13 for up to eight ounces) considering that the mail reaches the destination country within two or three days. I've used it extensively within Eastern Europe and elsewhere in the world and find it almost foolproof.

If you want to avoid postal systems altogether, fax machines are becoming an increasingly popular means of communication in Eastern Europe. At least one public fax service has been opened to date in all the Eastern European capitals, except Tirana.

3

Traveling to Eastern Europe

GETTING TO EASTERN EUROPE ON A LIMITED BUDGET REQUIRES SOME ADVANCE preparation and planning. Many of my specific suggestions on getting there are given in each country's introductory chapter, but below is a general overview of some of the transportation choices you have.

The one good piece of advice that applies to all transportation is this: Plan ahead of time whenever possible to take advantage of cheaper advance-purchase fares, to avoid last-minute ticket lines, and to ensure yourself a seat. This is especially true for travel within Eastern Europe.

1 Getting There

BY PLANE

Austrian Airlines has frequent service from New York, Chicago, and Western Europe to Vienna, a city whose proximity and historical connections to Central Eastern Europe make it a good choice for the starting or ending point of a trip to the region. With Vienna as its gateway city, Austrian Airlines also serves every capital city in this guide (except Ljubljana), as well as Timisoara in Romania and several cities in the former Soviet Union. In the U.S., call toll free **800/843-0002** and ask for their brochure, "Welcome Guide Eastern Europe."

Other Western airlines with connecting flights into Eastern Europe include Lufthansa, Swissair, Delta, British Airways, Alitalia, and KLM. Each country listed in this guide also has its own national airline or airlines. Some Eastern European airlines, such as Poland's LOT, the former Czechoslovakia's ČSA, and Hungary's MALÉV, have recently improved their service to a level that's not quite on par with Western carriers but is perfectly satisfactory for flights within Europe.

As a rule, whenever you call an airline, always ask if there are any discounted specials being offered, since reservations clerks don't volunteer the information unless specifically asked.

BUCKET SHOPS When shopping around for the best fares, be sure to check with discount travel agencies, sometimes known as "bucket shops." In recent years it has become increasingly easier to find lower fares to Eastern Europe through bucket shops. Airlines often sell groups of tickets at a large discount to travel agents or consolidators to ensure that seats don't go unused; these agencies then pass along the savings to the traveler. Restrictions often apply, so make sure to ask the travel agent.

To find these discount travel agencies, check your local newspaper's travel section for the tiny ads often hidden at the bottom of the page. Work your way through all the ads of the Sunday travel section until you find the best deal. Inquire about any restrictions, refund possibilities, special routing, payment conditions, "frequent flier" miles (are they credited or not with the ticket you get?), and air carrier.

BY SEA

If you like the romance of ship travel, you can sail to Poland by ferry from Scandinavia, to Albania by ferry or hydrofoil from Italy, or take a hydrofoil from Vienna to Bratislava, Slovakia, or Budapest, Hungary. See the description in the chapters on these countries for full details. At present, no regularly scheduled boats service the Black Sea coast of Romania and Bulgaria.

BY TRAIN

Trains connect all of Western Europe's major cities to Eastern Europe's capitals. Going by rail gives you an opportunity to see the countryside while traveling in a relaxed manner. There are many routes to choose from; for example, a train from Berlin takes about nine hours to Warsaw, or about seven hours to Prague. From Vienna a train takes five to six hours to Prague or three to four hours to Budapest.

Many routes feature day as well as night service. Be aware that on overnight trains—where you sleep away your traveling hours in a couchette—when you cross international frontiers, passport and customs officials will wake you several times.

In 1991 Eastern Europe established a regional first-class rail pass good in the Czech and Slovak Republics, Hungary, Poland, and Austria. It costs $185 for 5 days of travel over a 15-day period, or $299 for 10 days of travel over a month's time. As train travel is very inexpensive in Eastern Europe, this option, called the European East Pass, may cost you considerably more than if you buy individual tickets. It's most worthwhile for those who plan extensive travel in Austria, where trains are more expensive, or for travelers who just can't bear to wait even a few minutes for train tickets at local stations. For information about this pass, as well as price quotes for all routes, contact Rail Europe, 230 Westchester Ave., White Plains, NY 10604 (☎ toll free **800/438-7245**).

BY BUS

Although the bus is a common means of transportation in many Eastern European countries, generally speaking it's not a practical means of getting there. Exceptions are the Vienna–Bratislava (in the Slovak Republic) bus route, and bus connections between Turkey and Romania and Bulgaria.

BY CAR

Until very recently, car rentals generally cost more in Eastern than in Western Europe, in some cases substantially more. Now that these countries are all moving toward free-market economies, some with more vigor and success than others, car-rental prices are falling in all of them except Poland. The best rates run around $175 per week or $600 per month for the smallest car class.

Although you can sometimes find a competitive rate from locally based car-rental firms in Eastern Europe, it makes more sense to shop around the major multinational agencies before you leave home. Rates often vary from agency to agency within a certain country (or from country to country within a certain agency), so call as many as you can. You may find it cheaper to pick up a car in Austria or Germany and drive it into Eastern Europe, but only some agencies will let you do this. Budget (☎ toll free **800/537-0700**); Avis (☎ toll free **800/331-1212**); Hertz (☎ toll free **800/654-3001**); Dollar, called Interrent abroad (☎ toll free **800/421-6868**); and National, called Europcar abroad (☎ toll free **800/328-4567**), each operate in several of the countries covered in this guide. Europe By Car (☎ toll free **800/223-1516**) will lease you a car out of Germany, which can be driven into the East, at a favorable monthly rate.

Poland imposes certain special restrictions on car rentals, such as mandatory collision-damage insurance, and you will often find that a car rented elsewhere in Europe cannot be driven into Poland.

Usually drivers must have had their license for at least a year to rent a car.

Eastern Europe Rail Map

— Main Rail Lines

0 270 km / 166 mi N

Baltic Sea
LITHUANIA
RUSSIA
Kaliningrad
Vilnius
Gdańsk
Olsztyn
Minsk
Białystok
Toruń
BELARUS
Berlin
WARSAW
Poznań
POLAND
GERMANY
Łódź
Wrocław
Lublin
Karlovy Vary
CZECH REP.
Częstochowa
Katowice
PRAGUE
Plzeň
Ostrava
Kraków
Lviv
Mariánské Lázně
České Budějovice
Žilina
Zakopane
UKRAINE
Poprad
Brno
Košice
Banská Bystrica
SLOVAKIA
Vienna
BRATISLAVA
Miskolc
Eger
AUSTRIA
Sopron
Győr
Debrecen
BUDAPEST
Szombathely
Suceava
Iași
HUNGARY
MOLDOVA
Lake Balaton
SLOVENIA
Szeged
Chișinau
Sighișoara
Pécs
Cluj-Napoca
LJUBLJANA
Zagreb
Timișoara
Sibiu
Brașov
CROATIA
ROMANIA
Tulcea
BOSNIA-HERCEGOVINA
Belgrade
BUCHAREST
Constanța
Sarajevo
Ruse
Adriatic Sea
YUGOSLAVIA
Varna
Veliko Turnovo
SOFIA
BULGARIA
Burgas
Stara Zagora
Rila
Plovdiv
Black Sea
Skopje
MACEDONIA
ITALY
To Istanbul
Durrës
TIRANA
ALBANIA
Thessaloniki
Gjirokastër
TURKEY
GREECE
Athens
Mediterranean Sea

Drive with caution in Eastern Europe. In many cases the major "highway" will be a two-lane road crowded with horsecarts, tractors, and other slow-moving vehicles. Patience is the watchword. You must wear seat belts, and drinking while driving is forbidden. Try to keep the tank topped off—gas stations are sometimes scarce, and may not always carry unleaded gas (which your car will probably require).

If you bring your own car, buy Green Card insurance, which provides full insurance coverage in foreign countries (inquire at your insurance agency). If you rent a car, you can get insurance at the rental agency.

Car-theft insurance is especially recommended these days, as there has been a tremendous increase in car theft in Eastern Europe.

Eastern Europe Road Map

4

Getting to Know Albania

ALBANIA ISN'T A COUNTRY FOR IDLE TOURISM, BUT IT'S NO LONGER A COUNTRY TO avoid. After hitting rock bottom in 1991—a year when images of young Albanians escaping on rusty boats to Italy were flashed on nightly television newscasts—the country has crept slowly upward. Its cities are rough and poor but are calm again. Plenty of foreign businesspeople, missionaries, aid workers, and academics have begun to visit the country. This chapter aims to help these travelers and also those visitors who are curious about a country that for 45 years was as isolationist as North Korea. Although Albania boasts stunning mountain scenery and a beautiful coastline, you'll enjoy the country most if you are not a tourist but a sort of Eastern Europe junkie. That means you'd find ruins and beaches less interesting than Albania's peculiar history or its current economic agonies.

1 Geography, History & Politics

GEOGRAPHY

Albania consists of a narrow coastal plain surrounded by some of the highest mountains in the Balkans. At the geographic center of Albania is the city of Durrës. Across dry, lofty mountain passes are the Serbian-speaking Yugoslav republic of Montenegro to the north, the Albanian-speaking but Serbian-governed province of Kosovo to the northeast, the former Yugoslav republic of Macedonia to the east, and Greece to the south and southeast. To the west, Italy is as little as two hours away by hydrofoil across the Adriatic Sea.

The cultures of northern and southern Albania differ greatly. Before Communism, southern Albania was a feudal society with a landowning nobility, while northern Albania (including Kosovo) was a tribal society where disputes rose to blood feuds. The Tosk dialect, which is the basis for the modern standard Albanian language, is spoken in the south; northerners speak the Geg dialect. Southern Albanian Christians are Orthodox; those in northern Albania are Catholic. The south has always been more open to foreign cultural influences than the north. Southern Albania served as the gateway for Albanians emigrating to America. Later the south was the cradle of the Communist movement. Northern Albania is still the most remote and backward part of the country, and southerners still tend to consider northerners rude and unwashed.

HISTORY & POLITICS

The Albanians are descended from the Illyrians, one of the minor peoples of the ancient Mediterranean—whose greatest claim to fame is their cameo appearance in Shakespeare's *Twelfth Night.* Like the Greeks, the Illyrians spoke an Indo-European language. The Illyrians probably migrated south into the Balkan peninsula shortly before the beginning of written historical records. Greece colonized Illyria between the 700s and 500s B.C. In 229 B.C., with the Greek world in decay, the Romans invaded. You can see modest archeological remains of both empires in Albania today.

After the partition of the Roman Empire in 395 A.D., Albania became part of Byzantium and was ruled from Constantinople. When the Christian church split in A.D. 1054, however, northern Albania remained loyal to Rome, which accounts for the fact that even today northern Albanian Christians are Catholic while those in southern Albania are Orthodox.

The power vacuum left by the collapse of Byzantium was filled by the Serbs in 1347. The Ottoman Turks, however, were hard on the heels of the Serbs, and their famous victory over Serbia at Kosovo Polje in 1389 helped bring Albania under their sway as well. The four centuries of Turkish rule that ensued were Albania's time of stagnation. The Turks imposed a heavy tax on Christians that eventually spurred 70% of Albanians to convert to Islam. Turkish influence is still evident: Modern Albanians drink strong coffee out of small cups, eat Turkish delight, and bear first names such as Ismail and Mustafa. Some Albanian women wore veils until they were outlawed in 1937.

As the Ottoman Empire decayed in the late 19th century, Albanian nationalist agitation began among the country's small group of intellectuals. In the fall of 1912 when the First Balkan War broke out between Serbia, Greece, Montenegro, Bulgaria, and Turkey, Albanians decided it was time to go it alone and proclaimed independence. The first real Albanian government was soon overthrown by the dictatorship of the self-styled "King" Ahmed Zog, a chieftain from the north. Although Zog did his best to modernize the country, he was desperately in need of foreign exchange, for which he unfortunately turned to Fascist Italy and Benito Mussolini. One thing led to another, and eventually Mussolini occupied and annexed Albania in April of 1939.

As World War II drew to an end and the Axis powers withdrew from Albania, Communists led by Enver Hoxha gained power in November of 1944. Albanian Communism was homegrown and independent, not a product of Soviet meddling. The Red Army had never occupied Albania. Communism promised literacy, electric power, railroads, industry, and health care to the most backward country in Europe. By the time of Hoxha's death in 1985, Albania did have all these things, but it was still the most backward country in Europe. Albania had found a series of wealthier patrons in the Communist world, but had rejected each in turn, claiming their Communism was not pure enough—Yugoslavia in 1948, Russia in 1961, and China in 1978. After breaking with China, Albania had become fiercely isolationist. The country readied itself for an imagined foreign invasion by planting thousands of ugly concrete bunkers across the countryside. The secret police, the prison camp system, and the Hoxha-centered cult of personality rivaled Stalin's in Russia.

The riots and demonstrations that toppled Communism in Albania, though they were not notably bloody, did manage to destroy much of what little economic potential the country had left. The revolution in Albania was more drawn-out and excruciating than in other Eastern European countries. It lasted from June of 1990, when thousands of Albanians sought refuge in Tirana's Western embassies for the first time, to March of 1992, when nationwide elections finally brought in a democratic government. Most factories were destroyed, either by protestors out to erase every vestige of Communism, or by bitter Communists out to show the people that without industry there would be no bread or electricity.

Since 1991, conditions in Albania have steadily improved, and many refugees have returned home. Privatization has brought life to the agricultural sector. Light

Did You Know . . . ?

- Mother Teresa is an ethnic Albanian from Kosovo?
- The American poet Henry Wadsworth Longfellow once published a poem based on the exploits of the Albanian hero Skënderbeg?
- Albania is the only country in Europe officially classified by the United Nations as part of the third world?
- Albanians traditionally marry when the groom is about 30 and the bride about 20?

industry is still paralyzed. Heavy industry—in particular, chromium mines and oil fields—operates at only a fraction of capacity. Although the new government has not been as enlightened or democratic as hoped—major corruption scandals have emerged and there's been only limited freedom of the press—the relative political calm has attracted tempered interest from investors, brought in a modest amount of foreign aid, and encouraged Albanians to build their own small businesses. Travelers to the country no longer hazard food shortages or violence, but should prepare for Albania as for a trip to any third world country that's been shattered by unrest and poverty. Including Albania on your tour is an excellent way to learn about developing nations without leaving Europe. If you don't have patience for periodic interruptions in heating, electricity, and hot water, and if you're fazed by the sight of burned-out buildings and mud and ignorance and squalor, stay out of Albania. But if you can rough it a little, and if you follow the recommendations below, you can spend your time here very pleasantly.

2 Cultural Notes

Albania's only literary figure of note is Ismail Kadare, who enjoyed a privileged position under the Communist government before he fled to exile in Paris in 1990. Although some Albanians revile him for his complicity with Enver Hoxha, Kadare's works straddle the fence; sometimes his writing seems to support the old regime, sometimes it tentatively speaks against it. Kadare's best-known novels are *Chronicle in Stone,* an autobiographical story of boyhood in Gjirokastër during World War II, which mixes comedy, nationalism, and lament; *The Palace of Dreams,* banned after its publication in 1981, in which Kadare conjures up a Kafka-style Ottoman bureaucracy in veiled criticism of the Communist system; and *Broken April,* a straightforward, suspenseful narrative of a blood feud. These three books have recently been retranslated and reissued in Britain and the U.S.

Albanian literature is also enriched by a strong oral tradition, closely bound up with the country's ancient system of blood feuds. Once on a bus ride in southern Albania I heard an old woman pass away the trip by singing an ancient ballad in the traditional style.

Albania's musical tradition is modest and its artistic tradition even more so; art and culture have suffered over the past few years, and the supposedly regular folk festival in Gjirokastër has not been held since 1984.

3 Food & Drink

Albanian home cooking shares common elements with the surrounding Balkan nations. Eggplant, peppers, olives, and tomatoes are used ubiquitously in Albanian cuisine. The quality of bread (*bukë*) is improving as more and more private bakeries open. Potatoes are consumed in large quantities. Meat (*mish*) is generally available and of adequate quality. Coarse, salty white cheese (*djathë e bardhë*) is common. Fruit stands are stocked full of produce, and towns generally have a small fruit market that offers the best selection. Kiosks sell candy, soda, and Western snacks at Western prices. The city of Tirana has the only well-stocked grocery stores.

Albanian wines are a mixed bag. Some are pleasant, but others can be sickeningly sweet or startlingly pungent. If you're a guest in an Albanian home, you'll most likely be served Turkish coffee and raki, which is a clear, strong spirit. Candied fruit and Turkish delight (*llokumë*) are also part of Albanian hospitality traditions.

5

Planning a Trip to Albania

1 Information, Entry Requirements & Money

SOURCES OF INFORMATION

Albania does not have tourist offices abroad. **Kutrubes Travel,** 328A Tremont St., Boston, MA 02116 (☎ **617/426-5668** or toll free **800/878-8566**), is the best American source of information on traveling to Albania. The staff at Kutrubes Travel makes both group and individual arrangements and will know if there are any special airfares available.

ENTRY REQUIREMENTS

American, Canadian, British, and Irish citizens require only their passport to visit Albania for up to one month. Citizens of Australia and New Zealand require a visa, but will have to get it during their travels, as there is no Albanian consulate in either country. In the U.S., the Albanian Embassy is located at 1511 K St. NW, Suite 1010, Washington, DC 20005 (☎ **202/223-4942**). An embassy in London was just opening as this book went to press. There are also Albanian embassies in other European capitals including Athens, Paris, Rome, Berlin, Vienna, Prague, Budapest, Ljubljana, Sofia, and Istanbul.

MONEY

CASH/CURRENCY The official currency of Albania is the **lek,** made up of 100 rarely seen **qindarka.** Notes come in denominations of 1, 3, 5, 10, 50, 100, 200, 500, and 1,000 leks. Many notes in circulation are very worn, but everyone accepts them anyway. The prices quoted here reflect an exchange rate of $1 = 100 leks. Many places of business will also accept American dollars.

Please note—especially if you learn numbers in Albanian—that in speech only Albanians quote prices as if there were an extra zero at the end. If something costs 100 leks, an Albanian will say it costs *një mijë lekë* (1,000 leks). This is never done, however, in writing. This strange habit is the remainder from a 1964 devaluation. To confuse things further, Albanians usually quote the price *without* the extra zero (correctly, from my point of view) when speaking English. Ask people to write prices down if you have any problem understanding.

Exchanging Money You can exchange money at banks, hotels, and at a few exchange booths in central Tirana. Both banks and the police seem to condone—and even encourage—black-market traders, who offer up to two or three more leks per dollar than most official exchange bureaus. However, the small savings isn't worth the impropriety and the risk of getting swindled.

TRAVELER'S CHECKS The best place to cash traveler's checks is at the State Bank on Skënderbeg Square in Tirana, which will convert them into dollars for a 1.5% commission. You can then go and change the dollars at more competitive rates elsewhere. See also the listing for "American Express" under Fast Facts: Albania/Tirana below.

CREDIT CARDS A few of Tirana's hotels and restaurants accept American Express.

2 When to Go

CLIMATE Summers in the Albanian lowlands, including Tirana, are sunny and very hot. May, September, and October are more comfortable times to travel. In November, it starts to snow in the mountains and rain in Tirana, and by December it's *cold*, everywhere. Bring warm clothing if you come after November 1, since buildings in Albania lack central heating—or at times have no heating at all.

HOLIDAYS Parliament was about to vote on new holiday dates as this book went to press, and the only dates I could be sure of were January 1, May 1, Easter, Christmas, and November 28 (when Albanian independence was proclaimed in 1912).

3 Getting There

BY PLANE Austrian Airlines (☎ toll free **800/843-0002**) flies three times a week from Vienna to Tirana. Their afternoon flights are well timed for connections from the U.S. to Albania, and are convenient for connections from other cities in Europe.

Other airlines with reliable service to Albania include MALEV (two to three flights per week from Budapest, with youth fares as low as $80 one-way, but at inconvenient times), Adria Air from Ljubljana (five flights per week, also at very inconvenient hours of the day); Balkanair from Sofia; Alitalia from Rome; and Swissair from Zürich.

BY BUS It's possible to take a scheduled bus to Albania from Greece, Bulgaria, or Istanbul, but these overnight trips are long, uncomfortable, and expensive. The Greek Railways bus from Athens (about $30) is perhaps the nicest of these, although it lacks an on-board bathroom; Magic Bus, at 20 Filellinon St. in Athens (☎ **30-1/323-7471**) has complete fare and schedule details.

BY TRAIN The railway link to Podgorica (formerly Titograd) in Montenegro does not carry passenger traffic.

BY SHIP At last report at least four companies were sailing to Durrës and Vlora from various ports on the Adriatic. The most reliable deal is on **La Vikinga,** a Norwegian-built hydrofoil managed by a Norwegian-Swiss-Albanian joint venture. The cleanest of all the ships to Albania, it sails from Durrës to Bari, Italy, and back (a 3½-hour trip) five times a week, usually leaving Durrës about 9am and Bari about 4:30pm. Fares are about $100 one-way or $180 round-trip; students receive a 25% discount. You can reserve by calling the La Vikinga offices in Tirana (☎ **042/27665**) or Durrës (☎ **052/23544**), or their agents in Bari (☎ **+39 (80) 521-416**). Unless you plan to stay in Durrës, be sure to ask about transfer buses from the port to Tirana.

If you have a car, you can bring it to Albania on a ferry run by **Adriatica Navigazione,** which has two overnight sailings a week from Bari to Durrës and back. Passenger fares start at $70 one-way and $90 round-trip; cabins and cars cost extra. You can reserve in Italy at **+39 (41) 781-611.** Other Adriatica Navigazione ferries sail from the Italian ports of Ancona and Trieste, but the fare is more expensive.

It's also quite easy to reach Albania by sailing from the Greek island of Corfu to the southern Albanian port of Saranda. Several companies run ferries on this route, schedules are unpredictable, but there is generally at least one ferry a day. You can stay overnight in the Hotel Butrinti in Saranda and leave for Tirana by bus the next morning (an all-day trip), or continue directly to Gjirokastër (two hours by bus).

4 Getting Around

Albania has the worst public transportation of all Europe. Train and bus travel are both rickety and smelly. Although the hour-long trip from Tirana to Durrës is bearable for most travelers anything longer is only for the adventurous. On the bright side, trains run on fixed schedules (posted at the stations), cost slightly less than the bus, are easy to move around in and avoid smokers, and can be more comfortable if you are with a group of people who can commandeer an entire compartment or pairs of facing seats. But buses are usually faster, go to more destinations, and are more comfortable for single travelers or groups of two or three. The price difference between buses and trains is negligible. If you are uncomfortable with crowds, shoving, and general mess, you should avoid trains and buses altogether.

BY TRAIN Albania's train system is like a set of spokes radiating outward and uphill from the port city of Durrës to major towns including Tirana, Elbasan, Pogradec, Shkodër, and Vlora. Seven trains a day make the hour-long trip from Tirana to Durrës for 24 leks (24¢). The longest run is from Tirana to Pogradec via Durrës (seven hours). The rolling stock is a collection of Chinese cars and hand-me-downs from Italian State Railways, pulled by Czech engines.

BY BUS The average Albanian bus is a dilapidated vehicle from the 1970s, retired after many years of service somewhere like Greece or the former Czechoslovakia, but on the road are some comparatively new and comfortable Mercedes. There are rarely any printed schedules, but there is a certain predictability to Albanian bus travel. Go to the bus station (preferably between 6 and 8am for longer trips), look for your destination on a placard in the front window, confirm it with the driver of the bus, and then board. Sometimes the sign also lists the departure time, but usually the bus just leaves when it fills. Once it gets going, you will pay the conductor according to a nationally regulated fare structure (for example, Tirana–Gjirokastër costs 250 leks or $2.50). Luggage space is rarely adequate, and you may want to try to buy an extra seat for your bags, though this doesn't always work. Drivers are usually skilled, but when two buses need to pass on a narrow mountain ledge it can be hair-raising. Most passengers are men. You can try to ask your neighbors not to smoke, but cigarette fumes are the least of the unpleasant smells and sights you may encounter.

BY CAR • Car Rentals Under the Hoxha regime, private cars were banned, and 90% of the traffic on Albanian roads was on foot, bicycle, or pulled by four-legged beasts. Since the downfall of Communism, traffic has soared, but the roads are just as narrow and unlit and hairpinned as before. The thousands of new drivers lack experience and judgement; for instance, they'll often pass on blind curves while tooting their horn to warn oncoming traffic. Driving in Albania is recommended to only extremely skilled, alert, and confident drivers. The only rental agency in the country is a Hertz shed at Rinas Airport. You can reserve in advance through their international computer network, but rates are high. In 1993, diesel fuel was easily available in Albania for about 25 leks (25¢) per liter; other fuels were scarce and expensive.

• Chauffeur Hire The cost of hiring a car and driver is not much more expensive than a car rental. Most of the travel agencies on Rruga e Durrësit in Tirana will be happy to arrange this for you for about $70 to $80 a day. The best deal is the black stretch Mercedes offered by Skënderbeg Travel on Rruga e Durrësit

(☎ **23946**) for $80 per day, which includes the driver's food and lodging. It can carry four passengers comfortably and seven in a pinch.

BY BOAT The most scenic way around northern Albania is by riverboat along the Drin River, which has been dammed into lakes to produce hydropower.

Suggested Itineraries

If You Have 3 Days

Base yourself in Tirana, but make at least one day trip to Berat, Kruja, Lake Ohrid, or Durrës.

If You Have 1 Week

Base yourself in Tirana and allot three or four days for day trips to Berat, Kruja, Lake Ohrid, or Durrës and/or an overnight trip to Gjirokastër.

5 Enjoying Albania on a Budget

Since Albania's domestic economy is so depressed, most of what you can buy is imported, and will cost the same as it would in Italy or Greece. Prices in the better restaurants, hotels, and food shops are similar to those in the West. The only bargains are on transportation (since Albania produces some of its own diesel fuel) and on locally produced food (such as what you might get for breakfast if you stay in a private home).

Still, it is not difficult to live on $30 a day in Albania if you take advantage of the less expensive accommodations and restaurants listed in Chapter 6. However, a $10 meal here compared to a $7 meal, or a $60 double compared to a $35 double, is a small step up in price but a great leap in comfort and quality.

TIPPING Formerly forbidden, tipping is now common. Add about 10% to restaurant bills; give less or nothing if you've received poor service.

Fast Facts: Albania/Tirana

American Express The Ada Air office at Rr. e Durrësit 11 (☎ and fax **32035**), a couple minutes' walk from Skënderbeg Square on the left, represents American Express in Albania. They can issue traveler's checks for cash or against a charge on your card, cover check and card replacement, hold client mail, and were at last report awaiting permission to cash traveler's checks into leks. Open daily (including weekends) from 8am to 8pm.

Business Hours Typical business hours are from Monday through Saturday from 8am to 1pm and from 4 to 7pm. Many offices open only in the morning during the week and are closed on Saturday and Sunday.

Camera/Film Film is available at a few shops in Tirana.

Doctors/Dentists Do not travel to Albania if you are in poor health. If you get sick, your embassy can recommend a doctor. You'll probably have to leave the country for any treatment that's out of the ordinary.

Drugstores Several private drugstores in central Tirana stock Western medication. Ask your host or your hotel's staff where the nearest one is.

Electricity The electric power is 220–240 volts, 50 cycles, A/C.

Embassies/Consulates Citizens of Australia, Canada, Ireland, and New Zealand should contact the British *chargé d'affaires.*

- **United Kingdom:** Rr. Skënderbeg 12, inside the French Embassy (☎ **34054**).
- **United States:** Rr. e Elbasanit 103 (☎ **32875** or **33520**) American Citizen Services regular hours are Monday through Friday from 1 to 4pm.

Etiquette As in Bulgaria, Albanians nod to say "no" and shake their head to say "yes."

Language Although Albanian forms its own isolated branch of the Indo-European language family, it has borrowed many words from its Slavic and Latin neighbors. You will be able to decipher some signs and menu items; any knowledge of a Romance or Slavic language will make things easier. Albanians are, given the circumstances, surprisingly proficient linguists. Almost everyone in Tirana and western Albania understands Italian after years of tuning into TV programs from across the water. A respectable number of Albanians speak English as well. French is also useful, Russian is spoken by many older Albanians, and German is becoming more popular. Greek helps in southern Albania, since many people there either are ethnic Greeks, have worked in Greece, or watch Greek TV.

Laundry/Dry Cleaning Ask your host or your hotel's staff.

Maps The reception desk at the Hotel Dajti, the newsstand in front of the Hotel Tirana, and many travel agencies sell maps of Albania and Tirana for 100 to 500 leks ($1 to $5).

Newspapers/Magazines All the major Western newspapers and periodicals are available from the stands inside the Hotel Dajti and (in good weather) in front of the Hotel Tirana. The morning edition of the *International Herald Tribune* usually arrives from Rome by early afternoon.

Post Office The post office in Tirana is on the southwest corner of the intersection of Rruga Dëshmorët e 4 Shkurtit and Rruga Shyqyri Bërxolli, one block west of Skënderbeg Square, behind the State Bank (Banka e Shtetit Shqiptar). It's the most reliable place in the country to send mail abroad. Postcards and letters to Europe cost 18 leks (18¢); postcards to America or Australia cost 38 leks (38¢), while letters cost 51 leks (51¢). Open daily from 7am to 7pm.

Safety Your greatest danger in Albanía is getting hit by a car. Be extremely careful crossing streets. Since private automobiles were forbidden under Communism, Albanians associate cars with power and status, and Albanian drivers generally expect pedestrians to yield the right of way to them. Moreover, do not assume that drivers are in full control of their cars. Many have been behind the wheel only a few months. Always carry a flashlight at night to guard against dark streets and power outages. As in other Mediterranean countries, anger and intimidation are important to social interaction in Albania, especially among unemployed young men. If you find yourself in a threatening situation, the most important thing is to remain calm and to do absolutely nothing that might escalate the matter.

Women may feel uncomfortable traveling alone in Albania, more so on intercity buses, less so in downtown Tirana. Traveling with a companion of either sex would be a smart idea.

Sports Albania has good beaches. The developed ones are a little dirty and the undeveloped, clean beaches are inaccessible. In winter you can ski in the mountains near Korca or in northern Albania. Excellent possibilities for hiking and mountain climbing exist, but no trails are marked.

Telephones There are virtually no pay phones in Tirana. You can usually make local calls from hotel reception desks for a rather steep 12.5 leks (13¢) per minute. To make an intercity call, dial the city code (which begins with 0) and then the local number. Unfortunately, getting through, for example from Tirana to Elbasan, can take dozens of tries. It is possible to dial abroad from many hotel and private phones in Albania. An outpost of the Italian telephone system is located in Tirana in a trailer in the park next to the statue of Skënderbeg in Skënderbeg Square. The lines here are always long. Calls to America cost 132 leks ($1.32) for the first minute and 120 leks ($1.20) per minute thereafter; the trailer is open daily from 6am to 1:30pm and from 2 to 9:30pm.

Calling Albania from abroad is generally not too difficult. The country code is 355. Remember to drop the initial zero of the city code.

Time Albania is in the same central European time zone as Paris, Rome, Prague, and Budapest. It's one hour ahead of London and six hours ahead of New York.

Water In most Albanian cities, the municipal water supply flows only three times a day. Most Albanian apartments have small reservoir tanks, which allow showering and washing between these times as well. Native Albanians drink the water just about everywhere, especially when it comes from the high mountains. For travelers, it's safer to stick to bottled water, at least in the major lowland cities, where it's available at better markets and restaurants.

6 Tirana

MOST OF TIRANA DATES FROM 1920, WHEN IT BECAME THE CAPITAL OF ALBANIA. It's been fashionable to disparage Tirana as the least historically interesting city in Albania, but Tirana is currently the most interesting place in the country. Both the legacy of Albanian Communism and the revolutionary economic changes that have followed its demise are most palpable here. On a summer evening, Tirana's main boulevard is the nicest place in Albania to take a stroll. You are virtually guaranteed to meet interesting, English-speaking people, both Albanians and foreigners. One day in Tirana, I was stopped by a wiry middle-aged man who, seeing that I was a foreigner, introduced himself as the world champion for keeping a soccer ball going in the air using only his feet. From his briefcase, he whipped out his *Guinness Book* certificate to prove it. Then he invited me to watch him train the next day at Dinamo Stadium. This is not an unusual experience.

Tirana (pop. 300,000) is the only city in Albania where visitors are assured of decent accommodations, tasty and healthy food, well-stocked shops, and good transportation. Although it's true that there are few tourist sights here, visitors who can amuse themselves by checking out shops and trying to understand a developing economy will have no trouble spending several pleasant days here.

1 Orientation

ARRIVING

BY PLANE Rinas Airport is about 40 minutes' drive northwest of Tirana. After going through passport control, you'll find your baggage laid out in an adjacent room; occasionally, customs officials will want to look through it. If there is no one to meet you, you have three options. You can ask a fellow passenger for a ride into town; Albania is still so untraveled that foreigners feel a sense of camaraderie. You can take the bus, which usually meets every flight and costs 35 leks (35¢). Or you can take a taxi from the parking lot. You may want to haggle with the drivers and attempt, bring them down to $5 per trip (not per person), although you may have to settle for $10.

BY TRAIN OR BUS The train station and the bus stations are all within walking distance of the center of town. If you can't carry your luggage, you may have problems since very few taxis wait at the stations.

TOURIST INFORMATION

Tirana has no tourist office. However, decent maps, as well as a helpful yellow pages–style booklet with an indexed map in the back, are available at the Hotel Dajti, Hotel Tirana, and from the travel agencies along Rruga e Durrësit.

CITY LAYOUT

MAIN ARTERIES & STREETS It's helpful to orient yourself from Skënderbeg Square, named for the national hero (1403–67) famed for his guerrilla fighting against the Turks. The square is home to the Hotel Tirana, the National Historical Museum, the State Bank, the Palace of Culture, a number of yellow-painted ministry buildings, along with a small park with beautiful cedar trees, a fountain, and an equestrian statue of Skënderbeg himself. North and south from the square runs Bulevardi Dëshmorët e Kombit (Martyrs of the Nation Boulevard), Tirana's main street, with the railroad station at the north end and the university at the south.

Other important arteries radiate from Skënderbeg Square: Rruga e Durrësit runs northwest towards the airport and Durrës, Rruga e Kavajës runs west toward the town of Kavaja, and several other streets run eastward into a part of town that is less important for tourists. Tirana is circled on its western side by a ring road (the *unaza*). On Tirana's southern side (halfway between Skënderbeg Square and the university) runs the Lena River, which is so small and so tamed that it seems more like a canal.

FINDING AN ADDRESS

Finding your way around Tirana can be very confusing, since street names are only sometimes posted and house numbers, almost never. A good map is essential (see "Tourist Information," above). You should know the following words: *rruga* (street); *pallati* or *lagia* (building); *shkalla* (stairway); and *apartament* (apartment). Asking locals is not always helpful, since they navigate by landmarks and popular names (like "the restaurant where the Chinese specialists used to eat") rather than by official names and numbers.

Some of Tirana's street names were changed in 1993, but the old names will probably stick around for a few years. Rruga Kongresi i Përmetit is now Rruga e Durrësit; Rruga Konferenca e Pezës is now Rruga e Kavajës; Rruga Bajram Curri is now Rruga e Dibrës; Rruga Labinoti is now Rruga e Elbasanit; Bulevardi Marsel Kashen is now Bulevardi Zhan D'Ark; and Bulevardi Shqiperia e Re is now Bulevardi Bajram Curri.

2 Getting Around

BY BUS Tirana is serviced by public buses, which were donated by the European Community and display the community's logo on the side. Since there are no bus numbers, schedules, or marked stops, a local's help is necessary.

BY TAXI The only two spots where it's easy to get a taxi are in front of the Hotel Tirana and the Hotel Dajti. Fares around town should run you to 100 to 200 leks ($1 to $2), although drivers will usually quote you a starting price of 150 to 300 leks ($1.50 to $3).

ON FOOT Tirana is a small city, and with the aid of a map it's possible to walk just about everywhere. Traffic is dangerous, but European Community–donated stop lights on Bulevardi Dëshmorët e Kombit have made things easier for pedestrians.

3 Where to Stay

PRIVATE ROOMS

You often get the most value for your money in Tirana if you stay in a private room in someone's apartment, or if you rent an entire unoccupied, furnished apartment. However, not just any private room will do. Many apartments have only a squat toilet (i.e., a hole in the floor) and intermittent running water. Insist on an apartment with a reservoir, which ensures water whenever you want it; a built-in water heater; and—unless you're used to third world conditions—a real toilet. A private room like this can be preferable to a hotel; not only do you have the secure feeling of being hosted, but some Albanians go to a lot of trouble to make their living space welcoming and their bathrooms dignified, whereas the staff of state-run hotels often don't care if your hot water is running or not.

Private rooms will cost you $6 to $15 per person per night, depending on the quality of the facilities. An entire apartment will run $20 to $30 per night. The travel agencies on Rruga e Durrësit can usually make arrangements; contact the Ada

Air/American Express office (☎ and fax **042/32035**), Skanderbeg Travel (☎ and fax **042/23946**), or Albania Travel & Tours (☎ and fax **042/32983;** fax 042/33981) in advance. You must arrive early in the morning if you want to find a private room through these agencies after you arrive, since most proprietors have no telephone and it takes time for the office to track them down.

You can also find a private room by asking at the Hotel Tirana; most of the staff have apartments (or friends with apartments) that they will be happy to show you on the spot. On my most recent visit I stayed in the home of Ilir Gjata at Rr. Myslym Shyri, p. 56, shk. 2, ap. 13. Mr. Gjata, who can be reached by phone (☎ **042/32733**) at work at the Albafilm studios on weekday mornings from 9am to noon, speaks excellent English, has one of the nicest bathrooms in Tirana, and charges about $15 for one person with breakfast or $20 for two.

HOTELS

Hotel Arbëria, Bul. Dëshmorët e Kombit. ☎ **042/42813.** 90 rms (55 with bath), 4 suites with one double bed (all with bath). **Directions:** Walk north from Skënderbeg Square; it's on the left.

Rates (including breakfast): 1,750 leks ($17.50) single without bath, 2,300 leks ($23) single with bath; 2,300 leks ($23) double without bath, 3,500 leks ($35) double with bath; 4,600 leks ($46) suite.

The Arbëria was the third best of Tirana's hotels under Communism and hosted the remaining foreign tour groups that somehow didn't make it into the Dajti or the Tirana. The lobby is spartan but not uncomfortable, the rooms are shabby but respectable, and the bathrooms are clean. When I visited, there was water (hot and cold) every day from 6 to 8:30am, 2:30 to 3:30pm, and 7:30 to 9pm. All things considered, the rooms with bath are one of the best deals in town—though remember, this is Tirana. Rooms without bath are only suitable for the hardiest travelers, as the public showers are broken and the public toilets not particularly appealing. There's a restaurant downstairs—they have no printed menu—as well as a bar and nightclub.

Armstrong Motel, Rr. Jeronim de Rada 83. ☎ **042/25733.** 3 rms (none with bath). **Directions:** Follow the signposts from the corner of Rruga Elbasani and Rruga Jeronim de Rada, near the canal.

Rates: $40 double; $45 triple. Breakfast $3 per person. **Parking:** $3 per car per night.

Jazz enthusiast Agush Gina runs this odd little establishment that's located on a tiny back street of old one-story houses in the center of town. Mr. Gina, who speaks English, named it after one of his musical heroes, Louis Armstrong. It's a small and homey place with one large, clean bathroom, a common sitting room, and an enclosed courtyard through which you enter. Mr. Gina plans to expand to five rooms and to install private bathroom facilities in each one.

Hotel Dajti, Bul. Dëshmorët e Kombit. ☎ **042/33326, 32172,** or **27860.** Fax 042/32012. Telex 2148. 84 rms (78 with bath). TEL **Directions:** Walk from Skënderbeg Square to the canal; it's on the left.

Rates (including breakfast): 3,500–4,000 leks ($35–$40) single with bath, 2,400 leks ($24) single without bath; 6,000–7,500 leks ($60–$75) double with bath, 3,000 leks ($30) double without bath. AE (both credit cards and traveler's checks). **Parking:** Free.

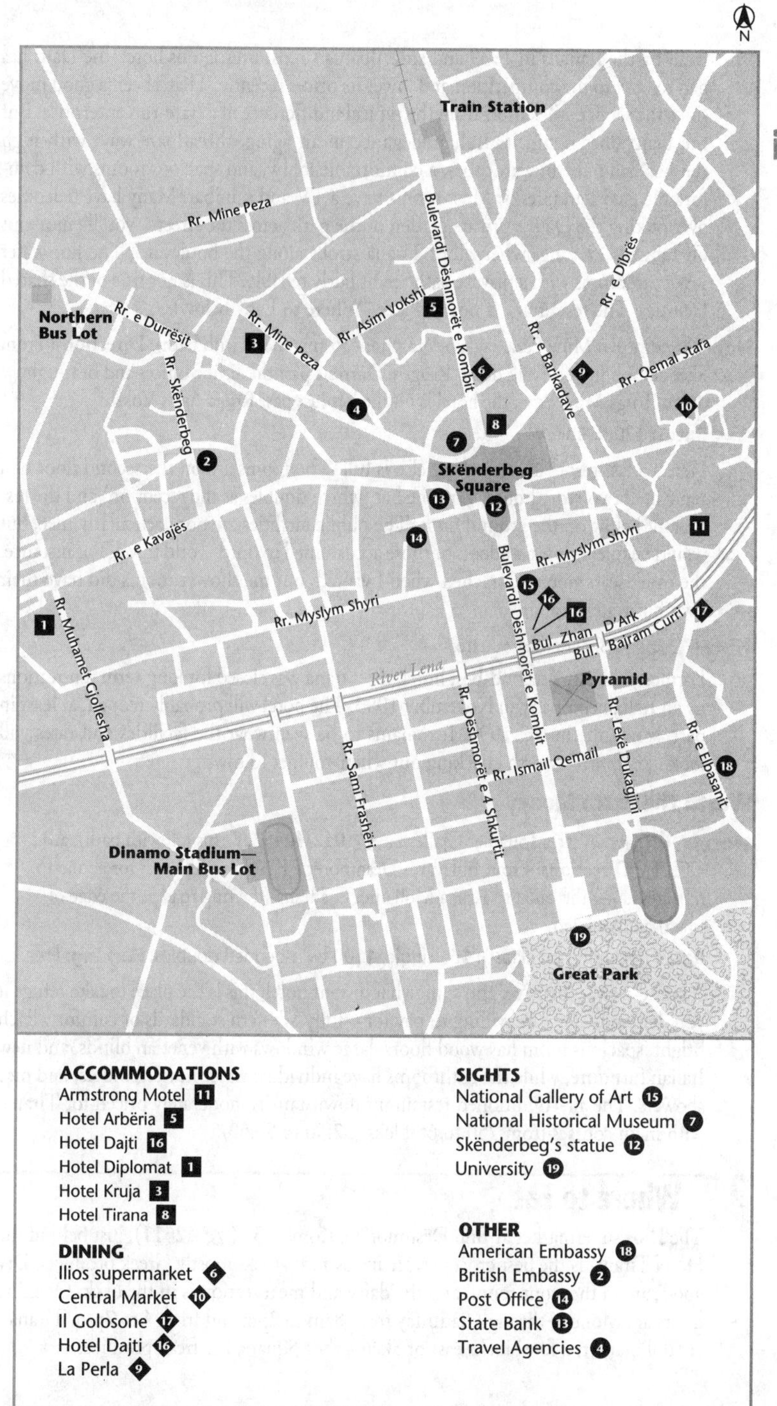
N
Train Station
Rr. Mine Peza
Bulevardi Dëshmorët e Kombit
Rr. e Dibrës
Rr. Asim Vokshi
Northern Bus Lot
Rr. e Durrësit
Rr. Mine Peza
Rr. Skënderbeg
Rr. e Barikadave
Rr. Qemal Stafa
Skënderbeg Square
Rr. e Kavajës
Rr. Myslym Shyri
Rr. Myslym Shyri
Bulevardi Dëshmorët e Kombit
Rr. Muhamet Gjollesha
Bul. Zhan D'Ark
Bul. Bajram Curri
River Lena
Pyramid
Rr. Dëshmorët e 4 Shkurtit
Rr. Lekë Dukagjini
Rr. e Elbasanit
Rr. Sami Frashëri
Rr. Ismail Qemail
Dinamo Stadium—Main Bus Lot
Great Park
ACCOMMODATIONS
Armstrong Motel 11
Hotel Arbëria 5
Hotel Dajti 16
Hotel Diplomat 1
Hotel Kruja 3
Hotel Tirana 8
DINING
Ilios supermarket 6
Central Market 10
Il Golosone 17
Hotel Dajti 16
La Perla 9
SIGHTS
National Gallery of Art 15
National Historical Museum 7
Skënderbeg's statue 12
University 19
OTHER
American Embassy 18
British Embassy 2
Post Office 14
State Bank 13
Travel Agencies 4

Built by the Italians in 1939 and still Albania's most prestigious hotel, the Dajti has had to bow to the competition and lower its prices recently. That's been a good move since the service still suffers from the typical indifference of a state-run enterprise. But the Dajti does retain its Italian elegance in an aging, threadbare way, with high ceilings, tall built-in wardrobes, a comfortable lobby, and spacious rooms with comfortable chairs and desks. Most rooms have a TV and minibar. Many have balconies overlooking the Dajti's private garden or the park across the street—you'll enjoy this on summer evenings when all of Tirana strolls along the boulevard. The hot-water service in rooms with a private bath seems fairly reliable. This is not true of the shared facilities. The restaúrant is not bad (see "Where to Eat," below).

Hotel Kruja, Rr. Mine Peza, lagja 5. No phone. 5 rms (none with bath). **Directions:** From Skënderbeg Square, walk down Rruga e Durrësit past the airline offices and bear right down Rruga Mine Peza; the hotel is on the left just past Rruga Asim Vokshi.

Rates: $20 double.

Here's a last resort if everywhere else is full. The rooms are on the second floor of a renovated two-story house, with the bar (which doubles as the reception) and the restaurant below on the ground floor. The public facilities are not particularly nice, but would be tolerable for students or those accustomed to third-world travel. For instance, the toilet seats weren't attached when I visited, but the shower rooms did have their own hot water heaters.

Hotel Tirana, Skënderbeg Square.

Formerly the city's second-best hotel, the Tirana was closed for long-term renovations by an Italian company in November 1993. The hotel will probably reopen, at least in part, sometime in late 1994. It remains to be seen what the facilities and rates will look like, but it's worth checking out when you get to town.

Worth the Extra Money

Hotel Diplomat, Rr. Mohamet Gjallesha. ☎ **042/42457.** 7 rms (all with bath). A/C TEL TV **Directions:** From Bulevardi Dëshmorët e Kombit, walk west for about 15 minutes along the canal to Rruga Mohamet Gjallesha (the ring road at the edge of town) and look left.

Rates (including breakfast): $65 single; $100 twin-bedded doubles. **Parking:** Free.

A brand-new, expensive, and somewhat distant hotel, this is the place to take refuge if you demand—and are willing to pay for—fully Western standards of comfort. Each bright, spacious room has wood floors, large windows with venetian blinds, and new Italian furniture, while the bathrooms have individual water heaters, biders, and nice showers. The air-conditioned restaurant downstairs is moderately priced for Tirana, with main courses from 250 to 650 leks ($2.50 to $6.50).

4 Where to Eat

The **Ilios** supermarket at Bul. Dëshmorët e Kombit 34 (☎ **42511**), just behind the Hotel Tirana, is the best grocery store in town. It stocks mostly Greek products. Dry goods are in the front room, and the dairy and meat section is in the back. Opening hours are Monday through Saturday from 8am to 2pm and from 4 to 7pm. Tirana's central market, a few blocks east of Skënderbeg Square, has fresh produce.

Il Golosone, Rr. Elbasani 31.

Cuisine: ITALIAN. **Directions:** Look for the orange storefront just across the Rruga Labinoti bridge.
Prices: Pizzas 450–600 leks ($4.50–$6); pasta dishes 350–700 leks ($3.50–$7).
Open: Mon–Sat 7am–10pm.

Although you can find better food elsewhere, this restaurant is reliable and relatively inexpensive. The pizzas satisfy one large or two small appetites. Servers are friendly. There's also a take-out section where cheaper, less tasty pizza goes by the slice.

Hotel Dajti, Bul. Dëshmorët e Kombit. ☎ **33326, 32172,** or **27860.**

Cuisine: ALBANIAN. **Directions:** Walk into the lobby and turn right down the hall.
Prices: Main courses 120–1,050 leks ($1.20–$10.50).
Open: Breakfast daily 6am–9:30am; lunch daily 12:30–3:30pm; dinner daily 6:30–10:30pm.

The Dajti is one of Tirana's most reliable dining choices and offers food in a wide variety of price ranges. Not everything on the large menu is available, but the spaghetti with sauce is a good bet and costs only 120 leks ($1.20). You might also order a bottle of mineral water or some salty Albanian cheese (*djathë e bardhë*) with bread. In the summer you can eat on a terrace overlooking the Dajti's garden, which exudes a colonial ambience; music is provided by an unobtrusive three-piece band. In the winter, life retreats to a quiet, elegant indoor dining room lit by chandeliers and windows that stretch from the floor up to the lofty ceiling.

La Perla, Rr. Kostandin Kristoforidhi 84. ☎ **42951.** Fax 32516.

Cuisine: ITALIAN. **Reservations:** Recommended in summer. **Directions:** One block east of Skënderbeg Square is a row of distinctive nine-story, three-winged apartment buildings; the restaurant is in an alleyway behind the northernmost of these.
Prices: Antipasto buffet 250–500 leks ($2.50–$5); pasta dishes 400–550 leks ($4–$5.50); meat dishes 700–850 leks ($7–$8.50).
Open: Lunch daily 12:30–4:30pm; dinner daily 7:30pm–12:30am.

La Perla serves excellent Italian food in an attractive and brightly lit basement room. The centerpiece is the antipasto buffet. The most mouthwatering sight in Tirana, it's a spread of cold meats, fruits, cheeses, and vegetables such as grilled eggplant or cauliflower fried in batter. You can take as much as you can heap onto your plate. Excellent bread comes free, and there is a good selection of Italian wines. The menu is in Italian only, but the waiters can help you decipher anything on the menu you can't figure out on your own.

5 Attractions

You may enjoy Tirana most by wandering around outdoors, rather than by heading to any particular tourist sights. The highlight of a visit in summer is **strolling hour** around 7pm, when all of Tirana seemingly congregates on Bulevardi Dëshmorët e Kombit near the canal to enjoy the evening air. Other sights that you can take in without an entry ticket include Skënderbeg Square (the south side is attractive, with cedar trees, Skënderbeg's statue, and Italian colonial architecture), the mosque nearby; the Vatican (formerly Cuban) Embassy just down Rruga e Durrësit on the left; Tirana's main open-air market, a few blocks to the east; the complex of university and government buildings at the south end of Bulevardi Dëshmorët e Kombit; and the expansive park on the hillside south of the main university building.

The National Historical Museum (Muzeu Historikë Kombëtar) is located in the big building with the mosaic on the northwest corner of Skënderbeg Square (☎ **23446**). It is air-conditioned, but the $3 admission price for foreigners (Albanians pay just a few leks) isn't really worth it unless you have an Albanian with you to help explain the monolingual displays. There are occasional temporary exhibitions in a hall to the right of the lobby. The museum is open Wednesday through Saturday from 9am to noon and from 4 to 7pm, and on Sunday from 9am to 1pm. Along Bulevardi Dëshmorët e Kombit on the north side of the Hotel Dajti, it's worth checking to see if there's anything interesting in the **National Gallery of Art** (Galeri Kombëtar e Arteve)—although when I last visited, only one small exhibition was open. A few private art exhibitions have also been open now and then in Tirana.

Try to check out the huge pyramid-shaped building across the canal from the Hotel Dajti. Originally built to house a museum of Enver Hoxha and his personal possessions, it has been transformed into Tirana's International Culture Center—this after a brief stint as a disco in 1991. Inside the south entrance is a café popular with students from the university nearby. Go in the east entrance and you'll find the **American Culture Center** (Qendra Kulturës Amerikan), where there's a U.S. Information Service library open Monday through Friday from 9am to 3pm (☎ **33246**). Always packed with Albanian university students, it's a heartwarmingly worthwhile use of U.S. tax dollars, as well as a cool and quiet refuge on a hot summer day.

6 Moving On—Travel Services

Tirana's travel agencies are clustered along Rruga e Durrësit near Skënderbeg Square and on Rruga Mine Peza, which branches off Rruga e Durrësit. You can take care of almost all your travel needs along these few blocks.

BY PLANE The Austrian Air/Swissair office (☎ **32011**) is on the second floor of the building at the corner of Bulevardi Dëshmorët e Kombit and Skënderbeg Square behind the National Historical Museum; the entrance is off Bulevardi Dëshmorët e Kombit. It's open Monday through Friday from 8am to 6pm, and on Sunday from 10am to 2pm. The Adria Air, MALÉV, Alitalia, and Balkanair offices are all near the corner of Rruga e Durrësit and Rruga Mine Peza. Beware that some of these offices do not accept credit cards; bring U.S. dollars in cash if you need to buy a ticket in Tirana, but try to come with a prepaid return ticket.

The cheapest way to get to Rinas Airport is by bus, which leaves from the corner of Rruga e Durrësit and Rruga Mine Peza in connection with every flight. A ticket costs 35 leks (35¢). Schedules are posted in the window of the Albtransport office a few doors down Rruga Mine Peza. Many flights leave just around daybreak; for these there's usually a bus at 4:30am. A taxi to Rinas Airport from the Hotel Dajti or Hotel Tirana should not cost more than $15.

At the airport you must pay a departure tax of $10, preferably in cash U.S. dollars. Other Western currencies are accepted, but leks are not.

BY TRAIN The train station is a few minutes' walk from Skënderbeg Square at the north end of Bulevardi Dëshmorët e Kombit. The ticket windows (*biletaria*) are in front of the station to the right, and schedules are posted on the station wall nearby.

BY BUS Frequent buses to Durrës leave from in front of the train station. Buses to northern Albania leave from a station at the end of Rruga e Durrësit, where it meets Tirana's ring road. Buses to southern Albania leave from a parking lot on the west side of Dinamo Stadium, which is located a block south of the canal on the southwestern side of Tirana. From Skënderbeg Square, to Dinamo Stadium, it's a 15- to 20-minute walk.

BY SHIP La Vikinga is the only ferry agency with an office in Tirana, at Rruga e Durrësit (☎ **27665**). It's open Monday and Wednesday through Saturday from 8am to 6pm, and on Tuesday from 9am to 2pm.

7 Easy Excursions from Tirana

Durrës

25 miles W of Tirana

GETTING THERE • By Bus, Train or Taxi You can reach Durrës by train from Tirana (there are seven per day) for 24 leks (24¢); by bus for 40 leks (40¢); or by taxi for anywhere from 600 to 1,000 leks ($6 to $10).

• By Ship Numerous ferries run to Durrës from Brindisi, Bari, and other Adriatic ports. In Durrës, the La Vikinga office (☎ **052/23544**) is on Bulevardi Kryesor, located a half block west of the mosque. It's open daily from 7am to 6pm. The Adriatica Navigazione office is in the Porti Detar at the seaward end of Bulevardi Kryesor. It's open in connection with ferry sailings.

Note: The Porti Detar is not the same as the ferry docks, which you reach by walking toward the sea from the train station.

ORIENTATION Durrës Beach is along a turnoff from the main Tirana road about 4 km (2¹/₂ miles) south of the center of town, and can be reached via taxi from the train station for 150 leks ($1.50) or by city bus for 3 leks (3¢). The train station and long-distance bus lot are on a square where the Tirana road meets the center of town; the ferry docks are five minutes' walk away, and can be reached by cutting across the disused tracks and wasteland in the direction of the loading docks. If you walk out of the front door of the train station and continue straight a couple blocks, a left turn along Bulevardi Kryesor will quickly take you past the city bus stop to Durrës's central square, mosque, and amphitheater, Continuing through the square and along Bulevardi Kryesor brings you past the La Vikinga office to the sea, the Porti Detar and the Adriatica Navigazione office.

Durrës is Albania's main port city. It's not somewhere you'd probably like to spend a lot of time, but it is worth a day trip from Tirana or a few hours' exploration on your way to and from the ferries that dock here.

WHAT TO SEE & DO

The highlight of a visit to Durrës is the huge Roman amphitheater built into the hill behind the mosque. Only rediscovered this century, it's still not completely excavated. You can wander through it for free. Nearby are some old walls and a tower (with a bar inside) still standing from the city's fortification system. Atop the hill is a palace formerly used by King Zog, but it's closed to the public. Along the sea nearby not far from the resistance monument is the Muzeu Arkeologjik, which displays local relics in an attractive garden. The museum is open Tuesday through Sunday from 9am to 1pm. Admission is 100 leks ($1). On hot summer days, people from Tirana flock to Durrës Beach to swim in the Adriatic, although the water could be cleaner.

WHERE TO STAY

If you're going to stay in Durrës, you might as well enjoy yourself, since there's good value for less money than you'd have paid in Tirana. When I last visited, a hotel and small restaurant was opening in a new three-story building along Rruga Nako Spiru between the amphitheater and the sea. It didn't yet have a name, but the telephone number is **052/24149.** Its six apartments, all with bath and kitchen, will most likely cost about $60 a night. If you don't mind the isolation of Durrës Beach, you can stay in the Hotel Adriatik (☎ and fax **052/23612**). Built in 1957, it's almost as elegant as the Dajti in Tirana. Most rooms open onto a common seaside terrace and the bathrooms are okay, but don't expect hot water or great food in the restaurant. Doubles cost 5,140 leks ($51.40), including breakfast. If these two choices are full, there are a number of cheaper hotels along the beach next to the Hotel Adriatik.

OTHER DAY TRIPS FROM TIRANA

A trip to the small town of **Kruja** is a good alternative to visiting Durrës. Only 20 miles north of Tirana, Kruja is home to Skënderbeg's imposing, reconstructed castle; a small ethnographic museum; some streets of old houses; and a *teqe,* or minaretless mosque, used by members of the Bektashi sect of Islam (the most numerous in Albania after the Sunni).

If you want to see the best in Albanian architecture without the hassle of a trip to Gjirokastër, head to **Berat** for the day. Berat's narrow streets and houses with large windows wind their way up a hillside topped with a castle and a museum of icons by the medieval Albanian painter Onufri. Berat is 76 miles south of Tirana along relatively flat roads.

More ambitious day-trippers, who have a car and are willing to make an early start, could make the three-hour drive to **Pogradec** on Lake Ohrid, 87 miles over spectacular roads from Tirana. Depending on your car insurance, it may be possible to cross into Macedonia for a lunch of rare Ohrid trout at the monastery of Sveti Naum, just a few minutes' drive across the border from Pogradec. On the way to Pogradec from Tirana, you'll pass through the city of **Elbasan,** where you can gape at the massive, defunct "Steel of the Party" metallurgical combine, which was built under the direction of Chinese specialists in the 1970s. Elbasan has an interesting old quarter, found inside the square walls of a fortress that dates to Roman times. Elbasan's Hotel Scampa is probably the best state-run hotel in Albania; it's a reasonable alternative if lodgings in Tirana are full.

Gjirokastër & Southern Albania

144 miles S of Tirana

GETTING THERE • By Bus Gjirokastër is a long six-hour bus ride south of Tirana. Tickets cost 250 leks ($2.50), and the best time to catch a bus is from 7 to 7:30am at Dinamo Stadium in Tirana. When you arrive in Gjirokastër, don't get off along the main road at the bottom of town but at Sheshi Çerçiz Topulli, the square at the center of the upper town. For the return trip, buses from Gjirokastër to Fier (from where you can connect to Tirana), as well as Saranda, Korça, and other destinations generally leave from the Sheshi Çerçiz Topulli square at about 6:30am; there's also a direct bus to Tirana, but it leaves at 4am.

Gjirokastër is Albania's most appealing city and one of its most historic as well. It sprawls down a steep slope among the high mountains in the far south of Albania, not far from Greece. It's a center for Albania's Greek minority, although that's not particularly evident as you wander around town. The most striking aspect of Gjirokastër is its architecture. Houses are mostly two-story constructions in which the first floor contains the entryway and storage space, while the kitchen and bedrooms are on the overhanging upper floor. This design was originally intended as a defensive tactic by feuding families, and overall it gives Gjirokastër the look of a forest of miniature fortresses stacked in terraces up the mountainside. On a steep rise at the very center of town towers a vast, dark, and imposing castle.

WHAT TO SEE & DO

When I last visited Gjirokastër, its museums were closed, apparently a consequence of disputes about returning houses and land to their prewar owners. In the case of the Enver Hoxha Museum, there were straightforward political reasons. But just hiking around town is more than interesting enough. You can walk up to and around the castle for a spectacular view. If you knock at the castle's iron gate, the caretakers might give you a personal tour of the dungeonlike tunnels, the military museum, and a downed American spy plane. The base of the monument to Enver Hoxha outside the house where he was born is still there, although the statue is gone. One of the most intriguing sights in Gjirokastër is the crowd that forms around the Greek consulate as visas are distributed; a consular worker calls out the names of visa recipients and tosses each passport out the window to its owner in the crowd below. Reading Ismail Kadare's *Chronicle in Stone,* a tale of childhood in wartime Gjirokastër, may deepen your appreciation of the town considerably.

Gjirokastër is a two-hour bus ride across the pass from Saranda, Albania's southernmost port city. Although Saranda itself is a dump, it does have a decent hotel (the Butrinti), and daily ferries to the Greek island of Corfu. Saranda is also close to Albania's best-preserved classical site, the Roman city of Butrint.

WHERE TO STAY

The best place to stay in Gjirokastër is in the home of **Drago Kalemi;** this is a traditional Gjirokastër house in the center of town at Lagja Parto 26, on Rruga Karafil Bello (☎ **0726/3724;** fax 0726/3730). Mr. Kalemi, an English teacher at a nearby high school, can sleep up to six people at $10 per person per night. He's hoping to renovate the bathroom, which only has a squat toilet but does have a water reservoir and a hot-water heater. You can always stay at the **Hotel Çajupi,** on the main square, Sheshi Çerçiz Topulli (☎ **0726/3626**), where doubles with bath cost 3,500 leks ($35). The Hotel Çajupi is pretty run-down and unattractive and has hot water only occasionally. When I visited, the hotel had the only open restaurant in town. Although that will probably change soon, you'd be well advised to bring some food from Tirana.

Elsewhere in Albania

Northern Albania is the most wild, backward, mountainous, inaccessible, and dangerous part of the country, and many say it's the most interesting. Traveling to far north towns—like Valbona, Tropoja, Bajram Curri, and Theth—requires near expedition-style preparation and preferably a local guide. You can get a taste of the north, however, by going to the large city of Shkodër, a three-hour ride north of Tirana, staying overnight there, and then in the morning going by bus or taxi to the village of Koman, from where you can make a round-trip day trip on one of the ferries that ply the Drin River basin. The river runs between high cliffs and has been dammed to form a narrow lake to generate hydroelectric power. The trip along the Drin is magnificent. Between Tirana and Shkodër, it's possible to eat at, or stay in, a hunting lodge near the town of **Lezhë** that was originally built for Mussolini's son-in-law.

The city of **Korça,** in southeastern Albania near Lake Ohrid and the Greek border, is considered by some the intellectual capital of Albania. It was also the center of Albanian migration to America. It takes about five hours to reach Korça from Tirana by car. There's also a route from Gjirokastër via Përmet, which takes 10 hours by car, that is one of the most beautiful drives in Albania.

Near the town of **Fier** in south central Albania are two important historical sites: The Greek center of Apollonia is on a hillside a short way south of Fier, while the monastery and church of Ardenica are between Fier and the town of Lushnja.

7

Getting to Know Bulgaria

FEW AMERICANS VISIT THIS SMALL COUNTRY OF NINE MILLION, BUT THOSE WHO DO discover surprise after pleasant surprise. Bulgaria is a land of great natural beauty and a nation rich in ancient and recent historical monuments. Its pristine mountainous regions offer spectacular hiking and excellent inexpensive skiing. The golden beaches of its Black Sea coast stretch for miles, dotted with romantic unhurried fishing villages and lively modern resorts. Ancient ruins and fortresses dating back thousands of years, dozens of lovingly restored monasteries and museum villages like Koprivshtitsa, old cities of great charm like Plovdiv and Veliko Turnovo with their age-old ruins and 19th-century Bulgarian Renaissance architecture—all speak of a long and stormy history.

Bulgaria is less industrialized than much of the former East Bloc, and you can still see horse-drawn wagons carrying produce right down the main streets of its cities. This relative lack of heavy industry has been something of a blessing; the countryside has not been ravaged by industrial pollution, and a strong agricultural sector has cushioned the ongoing transition to capitalism. But although Bulgaria is not a third-world country, you can expect some third-world style glitches, like poor maps, late buses, and the occasional lack of hot water. As long as you are willing to accept these things with a sense of humor and adventure, Bulgaria offers low prices, magnificent scenery, and lots of sunshine.

1 Geography, History & Politics

GEOGRAPHY

Located in southeastern Europe, in the center of the Balkan Peninsula, Bulgaria borders Romania to the north, Yugoslavia and the former Yugoslav republic of Macedonia to the west, Greece to the south, and Turkey to the southeast. To the east is a 234-mile coastline along the Black Sea that constitutes the largest tourist attraction in this region. With 42,800 square miles and about 9 million people, Bulgaria has roughly the area and population as the state of Ohio.

The country has several major mountain ranges: the Stara Planina range (with its Sredna Gora and Balkan branches) stretching east-west across the entire country, the Rhodopes along the border with Greece, and south of Sofia, two of the most popular hiking areas in the country, the Rila mountains and farther south, the Pirin Massif. Rila's Musala Peak, at 9,594 feet, is the highest peak between the Alps and the Caucasus Mountains.

The Danube River forms Bulgaria's northern border with Romania while all the rail lines from the capital follow the other major rivers: north to the Danube along the Iskar, south to Greece along the Struma, and southeast to Turkey along the Maritsa.

The capital city, Sofia, has a population of about a million people, followed by Plovdiv, Varna (under half a million), and Ruse and Burgas (under 200,000). The Turks, about three-quarters of a million in number, form Bulgaria's largest ethnic minority.

IMPRESSIONS

The women here do almost all the work . . . they wear silver rings almost on every finger, bracelets of black and white beads or shells upon their wrists, and great collars of silver coins about their necks.

—Robert Bargrave, *Journal*, 1648–52

HISTORY & POLITICS

Recent archeological finds show that highly skilled goldsmiths and metalworkers practiced their crafts in Bulgaria as early as 4000 B.C. In ancient Greek times, Bulgaria was inhabited by the Thracians, who, according to the ancient Greek historian Herodotus, "would be invincible and by far the most powerful of peoples" if only they were united by a strong leader. Instead they fought among themselves and were soon conquered by Philip II of Macedonia and his son, Alexander the Great. By the 1st century A.D. the area was incorporated by the Romans into their empire. As Rome fell apart in the 4th century, the area came under Byzantine rule.

Invading Slav tribes began peaceably settling as farmers. In A.D. 681 Khan Asparukh—the leader of a conquering tribe, the Bulgars—united them to create the First Bulgarian Empire. By the mid-13th century Bulgaria reached the height of its power in the area, controlling most of present-day Albania, half of Greece and Romania, and parts of Serbia and Turkey. It fell increasingly under Turkish domination and fell to the Ottoman Turks by 1396. In 1878 a combined force of Bulgarians, Romanians, Russians, and Serbians defeated the Turks, and Bulgaria became an autonomous kingdom within the Ottoman Empire.

Bulgaria was granted more than half of the Balkan Peninsula, but soon lost most of it during the Balkan Wars of 1912–13. Led by its elected German-born king, Alexander of Battenberg, and disenchanted with these losses, Bulgaria sided with Germany, Austria-Hungary, and Turkey during World War I only to lose even more land in defeat. The attempt to regain this territory prompted Bulgaria to side with the Germans in 1941, but by 1942 there was an underground resistance movement and in August 1944 the Bulgarians declared neutrality rather than fight the advancing Soviets. They fought on the Allied side until the end of the war. The Soviets nonetheless declared war on Bulgaria and again "liberated" the country, ushering in Soviet-style Communism.

During Bulgaria's Communist years the country closely followed the Soviet Union, earning Bulgaria the reputation as Russia's most faithful ally. Georgi Dimitrov was the first Communist leader, and until recently was revered as the modern father of the nation. In 1954 Todor Zhivkov took over as ruler. Despite years of oppression Bulgarians enjoyed relative

Dateline

- **4th century B.C.** Philip of Macedonia conquers Thrace.
- **1st century A.D.** Romans seize Thrace.
- **6th century A.D.** Bulgar horsemen from central Asia settle on the Danube.
- **681** Slavs and Bulgars unite to found first Bulgarian kingdom.
- **863** Cyril and Methodius create the alphabet.
- **870** Under King Boris, Bulgaria becomes an Orthodox Christian country.
- **1018** Byzantine conquest.
- **1185** Second Bulgarian kingdom.
- **1396** Ottoman Turks conquer Bulgaria.
- **1878** Russia helps liberate Bulgaria from the Turks.
- **1908** Bulgarian independence.
- **1912–13** The Balkan Wars; Bulgaria loses half its territory.
- **1914–18** Bulgaria allies with Germany in World War I.
- **1935** King Boris declares dictatorship.
- **1941** Bulgaria joins Nazis in World War II, but refuses to fight the Soviet Union.
- **1944** Soviets invade Bulgaria.
- **1946** Communism established.
- **1989** Zhivkov ousted in Communist coup.
- **1990** Zhivkov jailed; first free elections in 45 years elect a Communist government.
- **1991** Parliamentary elections won by UDF, the anti-Communist coalition.

➤

Dateline

- 1992 Zhelyu Zhelev elected president in first direct presidential elections.

economic prosperity and never rose up against Communism as did the peoples of Poland, Hungary, East Germany, and Czechoslovakia.

After ruling for 35 years, Zhivkov was toppled in an internal Communist shake-up in November 1989, just one day after the Berlin Wall collapsed. In February 1990 the 78-year-old leader was put on trial for murder, corruption, and abuse of power. He was sentenced 18 months later, in September 1992, to seven years' imprisonment for embezzling $26 million from the state.

Bulgaria's first free elections in 45 years were held in June 1990 with the renamed communist party winning a majority. But by October 1991, voters favored the anti-Communist coalition in parliamentary elections. In January 1992, Zhelyu Zhelev was elected president and Blaga Dmitrova, a leading writer, as vice-president, in Bulgaria's first direct presidential elections. As Bulgaria shifts to a market-oriented economy, many minor restrictions have eased and reforms continue.

2 Famous People

Orpheus Figure of Greek legend from the Rhodope Mountains of present-day Bulgaria, Orpheus was famous for his beautiful lyre playing—his music was so magnificent that all nature stopped to hear him. The son of Apollo and Calliope, he is the most noted musician and poet of Greek mythology.

Spartacus (1st century A.D.) Thracian born near the present-day town of Sandanski, he was captured by the Romans and brought to Rome. There he led a legendary slave revolt that lasted two years and threatened Rome before he was killed and the uprising defeated.

Zaharl Zograf (1810–53) Great icon and fresco painter, and an important figure in the National Revival period in the 19th century, when Bulgarian culture re-emerged from five centuries of Ottoman domination. His work is found in the Rila, Bachkovo, Troyan, and Preobrazhenski (Transfiguration) Monasteries. His visage graces the new 100-leva note.

Georgl Dimitrov (1882–1949) Communist who headed the Comintern (Communist International), the Soviet-controlled assembly that officially sought to spread Communism around the globe, from 1924 until its dissolution in 1944. He was arrested by the Nazis for his alleged complicity in the Reichstag fire of 1933, and his witty self-defense against cross-examinations by Hermann Goering earned international attention; he was eventually acquitted. He later became the postwar leader of Communist Bulgaria and served until his death in 1949. His achievements were glorified and he became a sort of Bulgarian Lenin with his body displayed in a large mausoleum at the center of Sofia. In 1990, in the spirit of recent political transformations, his body was removed.

Christo Javacheff (1935–) An artist-engineer famous for wrapping buildings and objects in plastic and other materials, Christo made his career in the West. His larger works involving interior and exterior spaces usually exist for only a short period of time, causing some to classify Christo's work as "events" or "spectacles." Among his many projects, Christo has wrapped Australia's coastline and islands off Florida and has erected thousands of umbrellas in California and Japan.

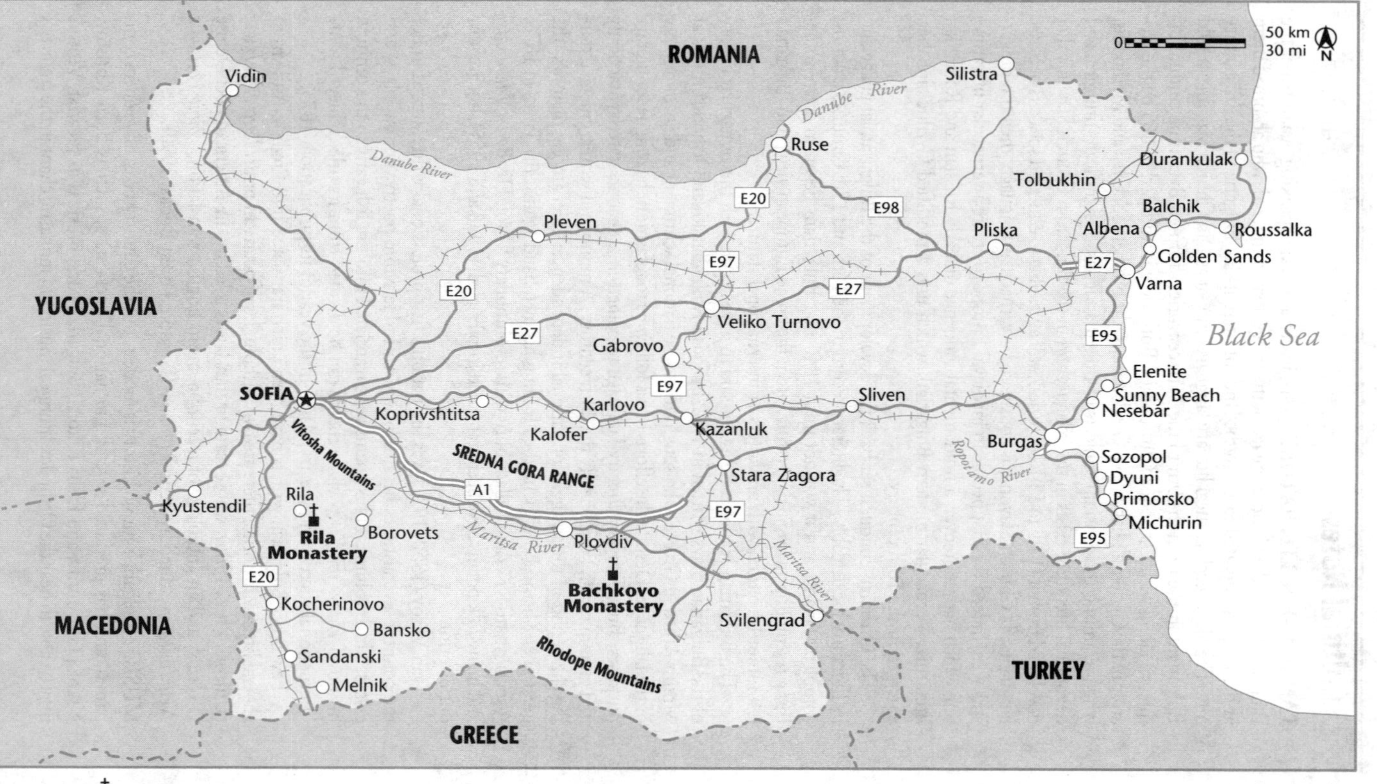
ROMANIA
YUGOSLAVIA
MACEDONIA
GREECE
TURKEY
Black Sea
0
50 km
30 mi
N
Vidin
Silistra
Danube River
Danube River
Ruse
Durankulak
Tolbukhin
Balchik
Albena
Roussalka
Golden Sands
Varna
Pliska
Pleven
E20
E98
E97
E27
E20
E27
E27
Veliko Turnovo
Gabrovo
E95
Elenite
Sunny Beach
Nesebăr
SOFIA
E97
Karlovo
Sliven
Koprivshtitsa
Kalofer
Kazanluk
Burgas
Vitosha Mountains
SREDNA GORA RANGE
Stara Zagora
Sozopol
Dyuni
Primorsko
Michurin
Ropotamo River
Kyustendil
Rila
A1
Rila Monastery
Borovets
Maritsa River
Plovdiv
E97
E95
Bachkovo Monastery
Maritsa River
E20
Kocherinovo
Bansko
Svilengrad
Sandanski
Melnik
Rhodope Mountains
Monastery
Railway
Bulgaria

3 Cultural Notes

LANGUAGE & LITERATURE Originally a Turkic-speaking Asian tribe, the Bulgars adopted the Slavic language of the tribes they conquered, who absorbed them as the Bulgars migrated east into the lands of present-day Bulgaria in the 7th century A.D. The Slavic ecclesiastical literary language known as Old Church Slavonic or Old Bulgarian, in use from the 9th to the 11th centuries, diffused Byzantine cultural influence along with Orthodox Christianity. Both were introduced in 865 by the creators of the Cyrillic alphabet, two Greek monks, the brothers SS. Cyril and Methodius, who are among the constant subjects of Bulgarian icons. A significant liturgical and devotional literature exists in this tongue, and in the Bulgarian Church Slavonic that developed from it (12th to 15th centuries), still accessible to educated speakers of Slavic languages. If Church Slavonic is considered a vernacular language, then the Bulgarians were indeed the first people in medieval Europe to create a vernacular literature, one which had, moreover, a fundamental influence on early Russian and Romanian literature. Vernacular modern Bulgarian, which uses a modified Cyrillic alphabet, emerged in the 16th century.

The Ottoman conquest set back the development of the Bulgarian language and its literature incalculably. The literary record in the 16th and 17th centuries is almost completely blank, and it was not until 1840 that Bulgarians began to create something resembling an original literature. From the broad European viewpoint, Bulgaria's is a minor literature, with no writers of international stature.

The Bulgarian National Revival is said to have begun with the vernacular history of the Bulgarian Slavs written in 1762 by Paisii Khilendarski, an Orthodox monk at Mount Athos in Greece, who sought to arouse national sentiment and encourage use of the language. Despite the efforts of his followers to refashion the tongue for literary purposes, Bulgarian as a literary language remained in a chaotic state (syntactically and grammatically) until nearly the 20th century. A number of writers emerged during the period of the struggle for national independence; chief among them was the great poet Khristo Botev, who died leading his own band against the Turks in 1876. A socialist, his lyrics and ballads burn with revolutionary fervor. His *Borba, Mehanata,* and many folk poems have been translated into English (1948 and 1955), but are now out of print.

Ivan Vazov (1850–1921) was the nation's first professional writer, forced to flee the country several times because of his work. He wrote poetry, fiction, plays, and essays. Three volumes of his poems were translated into English early in this century; his novel *Under the Yoke,* whose theme can be divined from its title, achieved some international success and was translated in the year of its publication, 1873.

Few other Bulgarian writers have been much translated into English. Aside from general literary histories, there are two anthologies of poetry in print: *Poets of Bulgaria* (Unicorn Press, 1985), whose team of translators is led by the American poet Denise Levertov, and an anthology of recent poems in English translation, *Young Poets of a New Bulgaria,* edited by Belin Tonchev (London: Forest Books, 1990).

MUSIC Bulgaria's music history is modest, but the country boasts five opera companies, and has produced several international opera stars, such as Boris Khristov, Nikolai Ghiaourov, and Elena Kikolai. Bulgaria's vocal music is its greatest. Visitors may be able to hear the Orthodox liturgical music and monastic chant in the country's churches and monasteries. The nation's folk song and dance troupes have garnered international acclaim. Three recordings by the Bulgarian State Radio Women's Chorus, recently issued under the title "Le Mystère des Voix Bulgares" (The Mystery of the Bulgarian Voices; Elektra/Nonesuch), have stimulated great interest in traditional Bulgarian singing throughout Europe and America. Many listeners find the exotic technique—a vibratoless polyphonic texture featuring sustained dissonant intervals (2nds, 9ths, 11ths)—of an unearthly beauty. Three of the choir's leading soloists have recorded as the Trio Bulgarka; the success of "Le Mystère" has opened up a market for all types of traditional Balkan and East European music.

ARCHITECTURE Like its neighbor Romania, Bulgaria once had a rich heritage of Byzantine churches and monasteries, though little of much importance remains. Many buildings have been lost to earthquakes (including many fine churches in Turnovo), and some of the most famous, such as the Rila Monastery near Sofia, have been rebuilt centuries after their original construction, of which there are few remnants.

The Rila Monastery has long been among the country's most famous structures. Founded on a magnificent mountainous site in the 10th century, it was ruined by fire many times, most recently in 1833, but rebuilt, restored, and expanded at the end of the 19th century. Today it rises like a fortress, its walls pierced by tiny windows. Inside the walls, the five-domed Byzantine-style basilica is painted throughout the interior, including the domes' drums and cupolas; the standard of craftsmanship and preservation is high.

The National Revival of the late 18th and 19th centuries contributed a distinctive style of domestic architecture. Two-story houses were built, the second story of wood overhanging the first, which was often of stone; the wooden parts were often whitewashed. Such houses also had wooden oriels (projecting bay windows) and broad overhanging eaves in several characteristic designs; many are decorated with elaborate polychromed wood carving or murals. The design allowed for increased living space in crowded towns and lower property taxes; usually the ground floor was used for storage. Clusters of National Revival houses may be seen in Tryavna, Plovdiv, Veliko Turnovo, Koprivshtitsa, Nesebar, the Trimontium section of Plovdiv, and at the Rila Monastery. The Balkantourist brochure "Museum Towns and Villages" is a good guide to such architecture in these and other cities.

Twentieth-century architecture in Bulgaria has followed along Russian and Soviet lines. In the capital, the flamboyant Cathedral of Sofia, Alexander Nevsky (1904–13), was designed by the Russian architect Pomerantsev to honor the Russian liberators of 1878. Both exterior and interior are decorated in the Byzantine tradition; the interior is entirely painted with biblical scenes, in styles ranging from traditional iconic formality to modern realism. Also designed by a Russian in Sofia is the much smaller Russian Church of St. Nikolai (1913), whose gilt onion domes and slender steeple recall the Kremlin cathedrals. After 1945 Stalinist architecture lumbered into Sofia, as in the buildings surrounding Sveta Nedelya Square, or the Stadium, modeled on Moscow's Palace of Congresses.

ART Some of the most beautiful art collections in Bulgaria are not Bulgarian at all, but belong to the ancient civilization of Thrace. The Thracians lived in the Balkan peninsula from at least the late Chalcolithic Era (3500–3000 B.C.) through the Iron Age (ca. 500 B.C.), in a vast territory bounded by the Carpathians, the Prut and Dnestr

Rivers, the Aegean, and northwestern Asia Minor—Herodotus called them "the biggest nation in the world, after the Indians." Some scholars have speculated that the Thracians were the original Indo-Europeans who migrated west into Europe in the late Chalcolithic, though this remains to be substantiated archeologically (and is nigh impossible to prove linguistically, since Thrace had no written language). Bulgaria is extraordinarily rich in Thracian artifacts, with more than 500 burial mounds and 750 dolmens and other megalithic structures. The Bronze Age Thracians were extremely skilled in silver and gold metalwork, of which there are huge collections in Bulgaria, which have traveled worldwide. Sofia's National Museum of History and the municipal museum of Varna have especially fine displays.

Post-Byzantine art in Bulgaria is the humblest and least developed of the Balkans partly because of its relatively low level of development before the Ottoman conquest and its subservient position vis-à-vis the dominant Hellenic culture of the Byzantine period. Most important, the decay of the Ottoman Empire, which set in around 1800, led in Bulgaria to a period of anarchy, followed by war, revolution, and a postliberation reconstruction mania, which spread across the country during the wholesale rebuilding of Sofia. Innumerable churches, mosques, and synagogues, many of them centuries old, along with all the artworks they contained, were thoughtlessly razed, including most of the surviving monuments from the First and Second Bulgarian Empires. Even in this century many important buildings have simply disappeared without trace or explanation.

Like all Orthodox countries, Bulgaria has a venerable tradition of icon painting. Sadly, examples from the First and Second Bulgarian Empires (9th to 14th centuries), during which fine icons were painted in abundance, are few, and for the first century of Turkish rule almost none were made. From 1550 to 1730, however, icon painting flourished. In this period, monasteries were the only centers of culture and learning in the country; accordingly, it is monastery churches that have the finest pieces, especially at Bachkovo, Rila, and Nesebar, which has Bulgaria's best-preserved collection of icons. Many churches of this period are also festooned with colorful murals, which serve the same function as stained-glass windows in Western Europe; Arbanassi and Nesebar have particularly fine examples.

The National Revival, dating from about 1750, was also a great period for icons. Influenced by Western Europeans, icon artists began replacing the highly stylized Byzantine images with more realistic figures.

By the 1890s, which saw the opening of the State Art School and the publication of the first art journal, a wave of genre painting (folkloric customs, market scenes, popular holidays, etc.), based on half-assimilated European academicism and impressionism, marked a final break with the past. Bulgaria had passed from the medieval to the modern without a Renaissance.

The major icon collections in Sofia are in the National Art Gallery, National Archeological Museum, and National History Museum; and in the Alexander Nevsky Memorial Church and the museum of the Holy Synod of the Bulgarian Orthodox church. Other major collections are in the district museums of Veliko Turnovo, Varna, and Pleven; the art galleries of Plovdiv and Burgas; and the monasteries mentioned above, as well as the Rozhen Monastery and St. Athanasius Church in Melnik.

Did You Know . . . ?

- Bulgaria supplies 70% to 90% of the rose attar on the international market.
- In the 13th century, Bulgaria was the superpower of the Balkans, controlling most of present-day Albania, half of Greece and Romania, and parts of Serbia and Turkey.
- During World War II, Bulgaria was one of few European nations to spare its Jews—even though it was allied with Nazi Germany.
- Although 85% to 90% of Bulgarians were illiterate in 1878, almost the entire population can read today.
- Sofia may be the only capital whose center is paved with yellow bricks.
- Bulgaria is the world's second-largest exporter of cigarettes and one of the world's five leading exporters of both red and white wines.
- Bulgarians nod their heads to say "no" and shake their heads from side to side to say "yes."
- Todor Zhivkov once asked Soviet leader Nikita Khrushchev to make Bulgaria the 16th Republic of the USSR.
- Nikita Khrushchev reputedly suggested that the Black Sea coast be developed as a tourist area, but the huge population of snakes inhabiting the area had to be destroyed before Golden Sands, the coast's biggest international resort, was opened in 1956.

4 Food & Drink

FOOD • Restaurants Bulgaria's standard of living is simply not high enough to support many full-scale restaurants. Instead, it seems like every available patch of sidewalk in the country has been turned into a café, where for a few leva customers can enjoy espresso, soft drinks, beer, or a light snack and linger while watching the passersby. A *sladkarnitza* is a place that serves a variety of cakes. Also popular is the *mekhana*, a tavern serving drinks and grilled meats.

Restaurants with somewhat varied menus and full meals are often state-owned operations. In the past—and still to some extent—these restaurants depended on the patronage of relatively wealthy foreigners, so the menus have often been translated into English. Throughout Bulgaria, new, privately owned restaurants are challenging older hotel and other government operations. The level of elegance, creativity, and service in these newcomers can be astonishing.

Service in any Bulgarian eating establishment has a leisurely pace and may seem inattentive by Western standards, but there is much to be said for being left in peace. It's usually not too hard to get the server's attention when you want to pay.

In addition to sit-down establishments, Bulgarian cities often have a large number of hamburger stands, as well as street vendors with an array of carbohydrate goodies, from bagellike *gavretsi* to fried dough. Western fast-food chains have yet to tap the Bulgarian market, but no doubt that's coming soon.

• The Cuisine While not the most interesting cuisine in Eastern Europe, Bulgarian food is very cheap and hearty. Grilled meats and meat stews, bread and potatoes, sheep's cheese, yogurt, and a few vegetables form the mainstay of the average diet. Greek, Turkish, and Central European cuisines have influenced Bulgarian cooking. As in other Eastern European countries, the Bulgarian diet emphasizes hearty meat dishes such as lamb, pork, sausages, and meatballs; and, as in Greece and Turkey, these meats are generally grilled or prepared on a skewer (like a shish kebab). Unlike Turkish cuisine, Bulgarian dishes rarely include a sauce to break the monotony.

Among Bulgarian meat dishes are such specialties as kebapcheta, grilled minced pork and veal rolls; and vreteno, a rolled and stuffed meat "spindle." For a choice cut of meat, look for a filet called kareta. Grilled lamb on a spit is a special treat. Kavarma and gyuvech are both stews of pork, beef, or lamb slowly cooked with onions, vegetables, and spices in clay pots, the latter with eggs on top. Eggs often crown a clay casserole of rich sheep's cheese, tomatoes, and green peppers known as sirene po shopski. Seafood is rarely to be found except on the Black Sea coast. Fish is too often fried beyond recognition, so order in grilled (*po skara*). Other nonmeat dishes include tarator, a cold yogurt-and-cucumber soup; banitsa, a pastry filled with cheese or spinach; fasul, white beans in tomato sauce; and the ubiquitous shopska salad, a mixed salad of cucumbers, tomatoes, and onions, sprinkled with grated sheep's cheese. Outside Sofia, non-Bulgarian cuisine is rare, though one can occasionally find good pizza. Yogurt, which reputedly originated in Bulgaria, is getting harder to find in restaurants.

For dessert, a wide variety of delicious fresh fruit is available at some restaurants and at outdoor markets in the summer. For anyone accustomed to the myriad flavors of ice cream in the West, the few local varieties seem pale. Baked desserts—largely variations on Turkish and Hungarian sweets, like baklava, palachinka with jam, and Garasch torte—tend to be rich and very sweet.

DRINK While Bulgarian restaurants may not serve enough fresh vegetables, they always have plenty of very good, inexpensive wine. Wine production in Bulgaria is an ancient art, going back to the 9th century B.C. in Thrace. The prices are so low that you can sample many local varieties and keep well within your budget. The best-known export to America is the Trakia label, but local red varieties that are especially good with grilled meats include rich merlots and mavruds, and lighter cabernets and gamzas. The selection of white wines is extensive: miskats, chardonnays, traminers, and muskats. Be sure to try the Euxinograd white, miskat vratsa, a delightfully aromatic white wine that's fruity yet dry. Full-bodied Melnik reds are also quite interesting. Bulgarian wines have been gaining popularity in Western Europe recently, particularly in England.

Beer has become widely available and some of the best labels are Stara Gora, Shumensko pivo, and Haskovo (the only one in cans; "Astika" is its export label). Most beer is 4.5% alcohol; *lux* or *spetsialni* is 12%.

If you like stronger drink there are two local brandies: rakiya (grape) and slivova (plum).

If you don't drink alcohol, look for the sometimes difficult-to-find bottled fruit juices (especially apricot and peach) in shops—they're cheap and superb. Espresso and cappuccino, as well as variants like eis-caffe (coffee and vanilla ice cream), can be found at Bulgaria's myriad cafés.

8

Planning a Trip to Bulgaria

IN SPITE OF SOME MAJOR CHANGES IMPROVING TOURISM SINCE THE SWEEPING EVENTS of late 1989, Bulgaria still poses more travel challenges than most other countries of Eastern Europe—with the exception of Albania and Romania. The travel industry is still heavily bureaucratized, not service-oriented, and strongly biased in favor of pre-paid group travel. This situation can be frustrating for the individual budget traveler who has not done some careful advance planning. This chapter will help you identify and tackle major planning issues before you go.

1 Information, Entry Requirements & Money

SOURCES OF INFORMATION

IN THE U.S. Currently there is only one major source of up-to-date information: **Balkan Holidays Ltd.,** 41 E. 42 St., New York, NY 10026 (☎ **212/573-5530;** fax 212/573-5538); they are open Monday through Friday from 9am to 6pm. They promptly send out colorful brochures and maps; they will book tours and hotel, airline, and car reservations. Recently privatized, they're more interested in selling their travel packages than in answering too many questions or dealing with individual budget itineraries. Unless you're booking a package tour, reserving hotels through this office is no longer a great money-saving strategy as their prices are no longer competitive. They also do not deal with many of the smaller budget hotels listed in this guide.

IN THE U.K. There is a Balkan Holidays office at Sofia House, 19 Conduit St., London W1R 9TD (☎ **071/491-4499;** fax 071/491-7068).

IN CANADA Contact the Tourist Department, Bulgarian Consulate, 100 Adelaide St. W., Suite 1410, Toronto, ON M5H 1S3 (☎ **416/363-7307;** fax 416/696-8019).

IN BULGARIA Most towns and cities in Bulgaria have a branch of Balkantourist, a state-run tourist agency. These offices can book you a hotel or a private room (see "Enjoying Bulgaria on a Budget," below). But don't expect them to speak English, provide maps, hand out brochures, answer questions about transportation, or do anything that tourist offices in most of Europe do. Instead, try to be creative. The lobby of the best hotel in town is often a good place to find maps, English speakers, and working public telephones. Museums also often sell maps and, in more visited towns like Plovdiv and Nesebar, English-language guides to the city.

ENTRY REQUIREMENTS

Passports are required of all visitors to Bulgaria. Americans can visit up to 30 days without a visa—plenty of time for the most comprehensive itinerary.

Visas are still required for non-U.S. citizens. Contact the Bulgarian Embassy in your home country. Non-U.S. citizens residing in the U.S. can obtain an entry or transit visa from the consular office of the Bulgarian Embassy, 1621 22nd St. NW, Washington, DC 20008 (☎ **202/483-5885;** fax 202/234-7973). It costs $20 and is valid for 30 days. Package-tour companies arrange visas for their travelers. In Canada, the address is 325 Steward St., Ottawa, ON K1N 6K5 (☎ **613/232-3215;** fax 613/232-3215). There is also a Bulgarian Consulate General at 100 Adelaide St. W., Suite 1410, Toronto, ON M5H 1S3 (☎ **416/363-7307** or **363-7308**). In the United Kingdom the Bulgarian Embassy is at 188 Queen's Gate, London SW7 5HL (☎ **584-9400;** fax 584-4948).

Upon arrival, all foreigners are required to fill out a small white "statistical card" which must be stamped at hotels and private-room bureaus. Upon departure, this card must be turned in at the passport-control booth. Perhaps this useless holdover from the days of strict bureaucratic controls will be scrapped by the time you visit. Until that day, take good care of the card. If you lose it, you can be charged a whopping $50 to $100 fine.

MONEY

CASH/CURRENCY The monetary system is one of the many areas in which Bulgaria is undergoing reform. The official currency of Bulgaria is the **lev,** or **leva (lv)** in the plural, made up of 100 **stotinki.** Coins used to come in denominations of 1, 2, 5, 10, 20, and 50 stotinki, and 1, 2, and 5 leva; and notes were issued in 1-, 2-, 5-, 10-, and 20-leva denominations. There will be changes over the next few years as the National Bank withdraws old notes and coins from circulation and introduces new ones. Although currency reforms began in March 1991, you'll still see some old money in circulation. Coins of 1, 2, and 5 stotinki will be withdrawn by 1995 and new coins will be valued at 10, 20, and 50 stotinki. Bills of 1, 2, 5, and 10 leva will continue to be withdrawn slowly until 1996, and will be replaced by 1, 2, 5, and 10 leva coins.

Prominent Bulgarian cultural figures and symbols grace new 20-, 50-, 100- and 200-leva notes; Communist heros like Georgi Dimitrov have been scrapped along with their monuments.

While the National Bank sets the basic rate of currency exchange, market forces have been playing more of a role in determining the dollar/leva exchange rate for the past two years. The prices I quote reflect the exchange at the time of writing: $1 = 28 leva; or 1 lv = 3.6¢, 10 lv = 36¢, and 100 lv = $3.57.

Exchanging Money You can exchange money at banks, hotels, Balkantourist offices, and the numerous private exchange bureaus that have sprung up everywhere. The best place to change money is at a commission-free private exchange bureau. These bureaus offer fairly uniform rates. Avoid changing money with individuals on the street (who are probably swindlers), or at hotels (which often have poor rates), or at bureaus that charge commissions. It's still forbidden to import or export Bulgarian currency.

TRAVELER'S CHECKS Traveler's checks are not as popular in Bulgaria as cash. Most places engaged in currency exchange will charge a stiff 5% commission rate to turn traveler's checks into leva. Biochim Bank on Sveta Nedelya Square in Sofia (open Monday through Friday from 9am to 3pm) is one of the few places in Bulgaria that will convert traveler's checks into dollars. They charge a commission of $5 per check up to the amount of $2,500, regardless of denomination, and a 2% commission fee over this amount.

CREDIT CARDS Credit cards are not widely accepted in Bulgaria except in upscale hotels, shops, and restaurants in Sofia and on the Black Sea coast. This will no doubt change as tourism increases in the future.

Note: Assume that restaurants and hotels do not accept credit cards unless I've listed the cards they accept.

What Things Cost in Bulgaria	U.S. $
Taxi from Sofia's airport to the city center	10.00
Tram from the train station to city center	.10
Local telephone call	.01
Double room, with bath, at Sofia's Hotel Serdika (moderate)	56.00
Double room, with bath, at Veliko Turnovo's Etur (budget)	30.00
Private room for two people in Varna	7.00
Lunch for one, without wine, at Nesebar's Kraibrezna (moderate)	2.50
Lunch for one, without wine, at Veliko Turnovo's Hotel Yantra (budget)	2.00
Dinner for one, without wine, at Varna's Gerana (moderate)	4.25
Dinner for one, without wine, at Sofia's Krim (budget)	3.50
Pint of beer	.43
Bottle of Coca-Cola	.18
Cup of espresso	.10
Admission to the National Museum of History, Sofia	.90
Concert at the Sofia Palace of Culture	1.00

2 When to Go

CLIMATE Most of inland Bulgaria experiences hot, dry summers and cold, damp winters. In Sofia the Voice of America (VOA) broadcasts news briefs and weather reports continuously through the day.

Vacationers will be especially interested in the weather at the Black Sea resorts: The coast has mild winters and sunshine an average of 240 days a year. Temperatures there average in the 70s in May, June, September, and October, and in the 80s in July and August. For up-to-date information, Radio Varna broadcasts the weather and news in the summertime in five languages, including English. The broadcast times change, so check at Balkantourist.

Sofia's Average Daytime Temperatures

	Jan	Feb	Mar	Apr	May	June	July	Aug	Sept	Oct	Nov	Dec
Temp. (°F)	29	33	40	51	60	66	70	69	62	52	42	33
Temp. (°C)	-2	1	4	11	16	19	21	21	17	11	6	1

HOLIDAYS Bulgarian holidays include January 1 (New Year's Day), March 3 (Liberation Day from the Ottoman Empire), Greek Orthodox Easter Sunday and Monday (about a week following the Western Easter), May 1 (Labor Day), and May 24 (Day of Slavonic Literacy, Education, and Culture).

Bulgaria Calendar of Events

January to June

- **International Spring Fair of Consumer Goods** (May), Plovdiv.
- **International Biennial of Humor and Satire in the Arts** (mid-May), Gabrovo. A unique week-long festival.
- **Annual Festival of Roses** (May), Kazanluk and Karlovo. From late in May through the first week in June, events associated with the rose harvest, including dancing, music, and crowning of the Rose King and Queen.
- **International Chamber Music Festival** (June), Plovdiv. Concerts performed in churches and houses across old Plovdiv.
- **Summer International Music Festival** (mid-June), Varna. Symphony, ballet, opera, and chamber music performances; lasts until mid-July.
- **Golden Orpheus International Festival of Bulgarian Pop Songs** (June), Sunny Beach.

July to December

- **International Ballet Contest** (July), Varna. Held every other year.
- **Koprivshtitsa Folklore Festival** (Aug), Koprivshtitsa. Dances, songs, and shows performed in traditional dress; held every five years (next in 1996).
- **Festival of Arts in Old Plovdiv** (Sept), Plovdiv. Theater, opera, and ballet in the oldest part of town; to October.
- **Apollonia Festival of the Arts** (Sept), Sozopol. Celebrates drama, music, and film with the local artistic community for two weeks.
- **International Autumn Fair of Machinery and Technology** (Oct), Plovdiv. The largest business fair in the Balkans; lasts about a week.

Sofia Calendar of Events

January to June

- **New Bulgarian Music Review** (Feb). Performances of recent music, ballet and other artistic works.
- **Sofia Music Weeks** (May–June). Concerts performed by orchestras, soloists, and dance groups from all over the world. A broad spectrum of classical music is presented.

July to December

- **Rock Ring** (Aug), Akademik Stadium. Concerts by Bulgaria's favorite rock bands.
- **World Film Panorama** (Nov), Palace of Culture. Film series and world premieres.
- **New Year's Music Festival** (Dec), Palace of Culture. Concerts continue into early January.

3 Alternative Travel

FOR STUDENTS Students and other budget travelers who want to make hotel arrangements before they leave the U.S. should contact **AD Travel,** a wing of Arts Development, 136 Lawrenceville-Pennington Rd., Lawrenceville, NJ 08648

(☎ **609/896-9330;** fax 609/896-3450). They are specialists in Eastern European travel with over 15 years' experience and working primarily with groups, but they try to accommodate individual travelers at whatever level they wish to spend. AD Travel reserves rooms in hotels run by Orbita, the national youth organization, as well as other hotels. After you prepay the room, you'll get a voucher to present at your hotel when you arrive. A single in a two- or three-star hotel costs $30 to $56 and a double costs $34 to $80. Fees for faxes and reservations are already included in the price. You can pay less if you wait until you get to Bulgaria, but you'll save some headaches by having everything already arranged and reserved before you arrive. However, if you change dates you probably won't be able to get a refund. AD Travel can help with moderately priced flights to Bulgaria, and they can also book domestic flights.

They have an extremely knowledgeable, helpful, and friendly staff and will most benefit those travelers who like their schedule prearranged and prepaid. Travelers more inclined to improvise their itineraries might consider booking a room their first night in an unfamiliar country to use as a base before exploring the accommodation scene on their own.

Once in Bulgaria, **Orbita,** the national student organization, runs a number of moderately priced but decent-quality hotels in most major Bulgarian destinations, most with private bathrooms in the rooms.

Students with the International Student Identity Card (ISIC) receive a 25% discount on train travel to other Eastern European countries and a discount of 30% on some Balkan Air flights. Whether foreign students qualify for discounts at museums is up to the discretion of the ticket seller.

Orbita runs a variety of special-interest tours around the country focused on instruction in Bulgarian folk music and dance, or in folk crafts; training programs in sports combined with hiking trips; an ecologically oriented trip to forest and botanical reserves; as well as more touristic sightseeing trips around the country. Contact them for information at their Sofia office at 48 Khristo Botev Blvd., 1000 Sofia (☎ **02/87-91-28;** fax 88-58-14). The office sells the ISIC Monday through Friday from 9:30am to 12:30pm and 1:30 to 4:30pm for 150 lv ($5.35) upon presentation of proper student identification.

GROUP TOURS For those who'd prefer a packaged introduction to Bulgaria, contact Balkan Holidays about their seven-day land package tours of the entire *country*— "The Classic Bulgaria Tour," which costs a reasonable $450 during the high season, or the "Discover Bulgaria Tour," which adds a look at the Black Sea.

SPAS For those who believe in "taking the waters" to treat their ailments, Bulgaria offers a choice of about half a dozen spa treatment centers well known since ancient times for the curative properties of their environments, hot mineral springs, and mud deposits.

Spa holidays tend to be one to three weeks long and must be booked and paid in advance. Prices vary according to hotel class and range of therapies required. Arrangements can be made through Balkan Holidays abroad or in Sofia for several Black Sea coast spa hotels which include: Hissarya in the Valley of Roses, 25 miles north of Plovdiv; Kyustendil, 54 miles west of Sofia; and the new Austrian-built spa for foreigners in Sandanski, in the foothills of the Pirin Mountains, 105 miles south of Sofia.

SKIING Mountainous Bulgaria has several major downhill skiing resorts, including Mt. Vitosha (just outside of Sofia), as well as Borovetz (43 miles from Sofia),

Pamporovo (about 50 miles from Plovdiv), and Bansko (60 miles from Sofia). The skiing season lasts from December to March. In the past, lift tickets have been fairly cheap by world standards. Hotels near the slopes are usually booked up months in advance, so don't go without reservations (Vitosha is the exception as you can sleep in Sofia). Balkan Holidays in London arranges ski packages.

4 Getting There

BY PLANE Balkan Airlines, the Bulgarian national carrier, connects Sofia and New York twice a week and Sofia and London four times a week. The carrier also flies weekly to 35 other destinations in Europe and around the world. Reservations are handled by Balkan Holidays offices (see "Sources of Information" at the beginning of this chapter).

Austrian Airlines has connecting flights from Vienna to Sofia six times a week, with easy transfers in Vienna to other European and American cities. Several other European airlines also serve Sofia. Depending on your itinerary, another option is to fly to Istanbul, a city very much worth seeing, before proceeding overland to Bulgaria.

BY TRAIN Trains connect Sofia with Vienna, Dresden, Munich, and Athens in the West, and in the East, Bucharest, Prague, Budapest, and Istanbul. You can reserve your seat and pay for your ticket in the West through **Rail-Europe** (☎ toll free **800/345-1900**). Sample fares: Vienna–Sofia (16 hours) costs $161 in first class, $106 in second class; Sofia–Istanbul (12 hours), $59 in first class, $39 in second class; Sofia–Bucharest (11 hours), about $50 in second class if you pay for it in the West, but a mere $20 if you purchase it in Sofia (expect delays on this route, no matter where you buy your ticket).

Trains are a terrific way to travel in Eastern Europe, but unfortunately, recent reports show that foreign tourists are getting robbed more frequently on trains and at train stations, so take extra precautions.

BY BUS For those travelers improvising their itineraries as they go, there are now a few convenient, inexpensive express buses run by new private bus lines connecting Munich, Vienna, Prague, Budapest, and Sofia. As a rule, Eastern European buses and trains are much less expensive than those in the West. One bus originates in Sofia and goes to Warsaw with stops in Belgrade, Budapest, and Prague, arriving an exhausting 36 hours later, but it costs only $45! It returns from Warsaw along the same route the next day. Check locally at tourist information centers and travel agencies in these cities, as these tickets can only be bought directly in these cities and schedules vary seasonally.

There are overnight bus connections from Thessaloniki and Athens to Sofia a few times a week. Check with **Appia Tours** in Thessaloniki (☎ **+30 31/22-24-53;** fax +30 31/28-74-47) or **Mihail Tours** in Athens (☎ **+30 1/524-57-62**). The buses usually go to major hotels where Greek tour groups stay.

If comfort matters to you on a long bus trip, inquire about or try to see the type of bus you'll be traveling on; they can vary tremendously. Some inexpensive ones are comfortable, even luxurious; others are decrepit and unpleasant. Some drivers will drop you off anywhere you ask, if it's on their route—it always pays to explore your options in the newly privatizing Balkans. Anywhere in this part of Europe, expect a lot of cigarette smoke on the bus.

BY CAR Although you can drive to Bulgaria from any point in Europe, East or West, some countries (such as Turkey) may forbid the use of their rental cars in Bulgaria. Make sure that the company you rent from outside Bulgaria allows travel into Bulgaria before you plan a tour by car.

BY SHIP Very few luxury cruise liners dock in Bulgaria, and no regularly scheduled ferryboats service the coast.

There are week-long luxury cruises originating in Vienna down the Danube with stops in Budapest, Belgrade, and Cernavoda (near Constanta, Romania's main port on the Black Sea). But currently they are hardly budget-oriented—cruises start at $1,295. Balkan Holidays has full details.

5 Getting Around

BY PLANE Domestic flights on Balkan Air from Sofia to Varna, Burgas, and a few other Bulgarian cities are no longer the travel bargain they used to be. It now costs about $65 for a flight from Sofia to Varna. Contact Balkan Holidays abroad (see "Information, Entry Requirements, and Money," above in this chapter) for flight schedules and other details.

BY BUS & BY TRAIN New express buses and standard express trains are the most convenient and the most inexpensive forms of transportation between major cities in Bulgaria. Buses and trains are equally inexpensive, but they can get very crowded, especially on weekends, and are not always comfortable or clean.

Trains cost 25 lv (.90¢) per 62 miles (100km) on the average and come in three types: express (*ekspressen*), fast (*brzi*) and local (*putnichki*). Unless you're specifically traveling for local color, stick with the express trains.

Try to purchase train tickets a day or two beforehand if possible, and always arrive with plenty of time to spare before departure. In small towns, train ticket offices open 30 minutes before the train's departure, and close 3 minutes before that (no last-minute rush at the ticket counter!). In larger cities you can also buy train tickets at special train ticket offices; some are listed in the individual city descriptions.

For longer night-train trips you can sleep away the journey. A bed in a sleeper (*spalen vagon*) with three beds in a compartment costs 60 lv ($2.15) and a bed in a couchette with six beds to a sleeping car costs 50 lv ($1.80). Seat reservations (*zapazheni mesta*) cost are required on express trains and cost 5 lv (18¢).

Because Bulgaria only has two east-west cross-country rail lines, you will have to rely on buses in the southwest and along the coast. Bulgarian buses vary greatly—from the sleek private lines that run between Sofia and the Black Sea in the summer to rickety old crates, full of frisky schoolchildren, that wind their way, often behind schedule, through the Pirin Mountains. Always check the schedule of bus departures as soon as you arrive in a town. Plan to travel between towns before 8am, when buses are most frequent. Some Bulgarian buses can be a bit cramped, but they cost next to nothing and the scenery is superb.

BY CAR • Car Rentals Car-rental rates are still quite high in Bulgaria averaging from $375 to $400 a week for unlimited mileage, plus $15 a day for insurance. **Hertz** (☎ toll free **800/654-3001** in the U.S.) rents Peugeot 205s and **Europcar,** Renault 5s.

Note: Car theft is becoming a major problem in the capital city of Sofia, with foreign rental cars a prime target. If you're thinking of renting a car, I recommend that you find out if your car insurance policy covers you abroad or whether you need to purchase additional theft insurance from the car-rental agency. In case of theft, if you aren't insured, you may be liable for the entire cost of the vehicle.

If you're flying into Sofia, you can pick up your car at Sofia Airport. Hertz, Europcar, and Avis have offices there as well as in the major cities of Sofia, Plovdiv, Varna, and some Black Sea resorts like Golden Sands and Nesebar. Hertz at the airport is (☎ **79-60-41**) open daily from 9am to 7pm. Europcar is available at Interbalkan's airport office; it's open daily from 8am to 9pm.

• **Gasoline** Gas costs 15 lv (50¢) per liter ($2 per gallon) of regular leaded gasoline. Gas stations are located about every 20 to 25 miles on major roads and on the outskirts of large cities. They are usually open Monday to Friday from 7am to 9pm; there is usually one 24-hour station open in every major city. Regular 86, super 93, and premium 96 octanes are available; unleaded gas is found less frequently, mostly at border crossings, on major highways, and at major seaside and mountain resorts. Be sure to obtain a map with gas stations indicated. A local driver estimates that highway driving requires about 8.5 liters per 100km (62 miles) while city driving uses 10 liters per 100km.

• **Driving Rules** All you need to drive in Bulgaria is your national (or state) driver's license. However, you must have "civil liability" insurance (the Green Card), which you can buy at the border if you drive into Bulgaria from another country.

Speed limits are 120 kmph (80 m.p.h.) on Bulgarian highways, 80 kmph (50 m.p.h.) outside cities, and 60 kmph (37 m.p.h.) in populated areas. Generally two-lane and narrow, roads abound with signs indicating horse-drawn-cart traffic, water sources, villages' boundaries, and gas stations.

Don't risk being stopped for driving under the influence of more than a pint of beer or 50 grams of stronger drink, as the penalties are severe: Either your license will be taken away from you or you will be escorted back to the nearest border. For roadside assistance, call the **Union of Bulgarian Motorists** (☎ **146**). In case of an accident, don't leave the scene; have someone call the police.

BY BOAT Along the Black Sea coast, fast boats provide the most enjoyable way, though not the most reliable way, of getting around. See Chapter 11 for details.

HITCHHIKING The ongoing civil war in the former Yugoslavia has rerouted an increased number of trucks through Bulgaria. This may be a boon to hitchhikers hoping to catch a ride on main highways, as some curious drivers are eager to meet foreigners and to share the long hours on the road. It's not advisable for women to hitchhike alone, as crime is on the rise. If you insist on hitchhiking, it's better to travel in pairs.

Suggested Itineraries

City Highlights

Sofia, the repository of the country's greatest treasures, including 6,000-year-old gold in the Museum of National History, and sacred ancient icons in the Alexander Nevsky Cathedral.

Plovdiv, site of a charming 19th-century neighborhood of typical Bulgarian houses, as well as a stunningly well-preserved Roman theater.

Veliko Turnovo, former capital of Bulgaria situated on hills overlooking a beautiful valley, a city of panoramic views; also the site of a huge fortification hill and several museums.

Varna, an ancient city on the Black Sea coast, with a number of Roman baths and an important archeological museum.

Planning Your Itinerary

If You Have 7 Days

Days 1 and 2 Settle into your room, get some maps, and explore Sofia, the Bulgarian capital.

Day 3 Take a day trip to the stronghold of Bulgarian Christianity, the Rila Monastery, which is nestled in the Rila mountains south of Sofia.

Day 4 Continue on to either of the ancient cities of Plovdiv or Veliko Turnovo.

Days 5 and 6 Spend two days exploring quiet fishing towns or the lively resorts on Bulgaria's Black Sea coast. Nesebar with its medieval churches and the romantic Sozopol are small towns that are especially picturesque.

Day 7 Visit Koprivshtitsa, a magnificently restored 19th-century museum village full of charm and beauty. Or if you're traveling in early June, plan a day trip to the Rose Festival Harvest in Kazanluk, the heart of the rose-growing region of central Bulgaria.

If You Have 10 Days

Add another day on the seacoast, and spread the other two days between Plovdiv and Veliko Turnovo. Or take a spur to the Pirin mountain towns—Bansko, Sandanski, and Melnik—of the Southwest.

If You Have 14 Days

Consider more time on the Black Sea coast visiting smaller towns such as Balchik and other romantic resort spots listed in Chapter 11 on the Black Sea; or visit more sights such as Etur, the Bulgarian Williamsburg; and Gabrovo, home to the unique House of Humor.

And if you have never been to Istanbul, consider taking a train from Sofia or Plovdiv or a bus from Varna or Burgas to this incredible city that for centuries held sway over Bulgaria and the rest of the Balkan peninsula. For information, contact the Turkish Tourist Office, 821 UN Plaza, New York, NY 10017 (☎ **212/986-5050**).

6 Enjoying Bulgaria on a Budget

THE $30-A-DAY BUDGET

Bulgaria is a veritable budget traveler's dream. Although inflation over the past four years has more than doubled prices for Bulgarians, the purchasing power of Western currencies remains strong in view of the devaluation of the lev. Public transportation costs pennies, museum fees and concert tickets are remarkably cheap, taxis are still quite affordable, and most meals cost only $3 to $4. If you stay in private accommodations (which are available throughout most of Bulgaria) you could spend as little as $15 a day on food, a room—and even a bottle of wine! Hotels have higher prices for foreigners, making them considerably more expensive than meals and public transportation, but still far less than in the West. Staying in a hotel will bring your budget closer to $30 a day. Nonetheless, you must plan ahead to get the best deals on hotel rooms (especially in Sofia), so make sure to read "Saving Money on Accommodations," below. Sofia is the most expensive city in the country, followed by the Black Sea coast, and you'll probably spend between $25 and $40 a day there if you prefer a hotel to a private room.

SAVING MONEY ON . . .

ACCOMMODATIONS • Hotels Hotels are rated by the government on a one- to five-star system. As a point of reference, think of two-star hotels as the standard Class B hotels of other Eastern European countries, except that in Bulgaria they are equipped with private bathrooms. Most hotels listed in these chapters have two or three stars. One-star hotels are usually for the more adventurous, backpacking traveler; they lack private bathrooms, and the facilities, especially public bathrooms, may not be very clean.

The pricing system for accommodations in Bulgaria was always complex and unpredictable. The move toward privatization and the breakup of Balkantourist, the state travel monopoly, into autonomous regional tourist offices has complicated matters even further, particularly for the individual budget traveler. While the following guidelines were up-to-date at the time of writing, the situation is volatile and readers are cautioned to double-check prices by letter or fax before making firm plans.

In the past, prepaid advance bookings through Balkan Holidays in New York and London guaranteed the traveler large discounts on the steep walk-in rates charged by hotels, particularly in Sofia. Increased competition is making it possible to get lower rates than those offered by Balkan Holidays abroad, which now charges $40 for singles and $60 for doubles in two-star "standard" hotels and only minor discounts on three-star hotels. Given plenty of lead time you may be able to get good discounts by booking through the new private travel agency, **SunnyTours Travel** of Sofia, which you can contact at Lulin 7, Bld. 740 A, Apt. 32, 1336 Sofia (fax 02/27-41-32).

If you don't prebook from abroad, you run the risk of not being able to stay in the hotel of your choice when you arrive or having to pay much higher rates. However, you do have the option of taking an inexpensive private room anywhere in the country, or, in Sofia, the additional option of staying in an inexpensive private mini-hotel in the suburbs.

Hotels in inland cities such as Plovdiv or Veliko Turnovo are less costly to begin with, so the savings of prebooking is reduced; still, prebooking guarantees a place.

If you arrive at some resorts on the Black Sea coast without advance reservations, you must go to the Balkantourist office, which will find you a room.

Remember that all these rules and discounts can change at a moment's notice as Bulgaria revamps its economy, so double-check the whole system when you arrive. How? Call ahead to a hotel to learn their latest tariff, and then see what Balkan Holidays and SunnyTours are charging for the same hotel.

• Private Rooms Private rooms in a Bulgarian home are the country's best budget accommodation buy, typically about $8 to $10 in Sofia and $5 to $8 elsewhere for a double room. Private accommodations are divided into three categories and priced according to location and facilities. My own experiences with private accommodations in several towns and on the Black Sea coast have proved rather pleasant as I stayed in clean, centrally located apartments with clean communal bathrooms. Of course when you stay in a private room, you lose some privacy but in general you will be given your own key so you can come and go as you please. Moreover, you will have the opportunity to see how Bulgarians live, and if you are lucky, you may get a friendly host who will tell you far more about his town than you could learn otherwise. It's cheapest to arrange a private room when you arrive in a town rather than from abroad.

In smaller Bulgarian towns, the staff at the tourist bureau that rents out private rooms rarely speak any Western language. To tell them you want a private room, say: "Bich iskal chasna kvartira za [number of nights you want to stay] noshti."

MEALS Restaurants are remarkably inexpensive, and you can eat in almost any restaurant in any part of the country and still live on $30 a day. Mekhanas (taverns) and cafeterias are cheaper still. The only danger is being overcharged occasionally, since some waiters still try to pad the charges. Ask (if necessary, insist) to have the check added again in front of you if you're in doubt. Be aware that the establishment may try to add potatoes, carrots, salad, or other garnishes to your main course even if you didn't specifically order them, and then charge you. If you don't want garnishes, let the waiter know when you order.

SIGHTSEEING & ENTERTAINMENT You won't need to do much planning to receive good values on museums and incredible prices for cultural events. Museum entrance fees are 20 to 25 lv (70¢ to 90¢), with discounts for students. Concerts and other cultural events usually cost 15 to 30 lv (55¢ to $1.10), astonishing as that may seem to the traveler from the West.

SHOPPING Folk art provides solid shopping value, and each town has a few good stores to choose from. Favorite tourist buys include embroidered tablecloths, place mats, and napkins; lace; wines; rose oil; ceramics; and dolls in national costumes.

TRANSPORTATION Domestic buses and trains are remarkably inexpensive, so you can go as far and as frequently as you want without ever worrying about the price.

TIPPING Although Bulgarians have not been big tippers in the past, rampant inflation and the new push for privatization is changing attitudes. Tip the rare porter in a hotel at least 10 lv (35¢). Add 10% to 15% to your check in restaurants, unless a service charge has already been figured in. If the service has been poor, don't tip.

MONEY EXCHANGE As mentioned previously, private exchange bureaus are most likely to give you the most favorable rates without commission rates, but always check, as this may change.

Fast Facts: Bulgaria

American Express American Express's representative in Bulgaria is Megatours, 1 Levski St., 1000 Sofia (☎ **02/88-04-19;** fax 02/87-25-67; telex 25241). See "Fast Facts: Sofia" in Chapter 9.

Business Hours Most offices are open Monday through Friday from 8 or 8:30am to 5pm, with a break for lunch. Stores are usually open Monday through Friday from 9am to 12:30 or 1pm, then anywhere from 2 to 4pm until 6 or 7pm, with shorter hours on Saturday. Most shops are closed Sunday, except on the coast in the summer.

Camera/Film Fuji and Kodak film are now more widely available in major cities and tourist areas on the Black Sea coast, but for maximum savings you still might want to bring your own supplies from home.

Customs Officially, you are allowed to bring in two liters of wine and one liter of alcohol, 250 grams of cigarettes or tobacco, as well as personal possessions. Careful scrutiny is typical at border crossings from Romania and Turkey because of drug trafficking. Luggage is rarely checked either coming into or going out of the country by air. However, if you're buying valuable antiques or large items, be sure to check with your embassy about any requirements, duties, or unusual restrictions.

Doctors/Dentists In Sofia, check with your embassy for an English-speaking doctor or call the Bulgarian Medical Academy Institute for the Treatment of Foreign Citizens (ITFC) (☎ **74-60-15**), located at 1 Acad. Pavlovski St. Elsewhere in the country, ask your hotelier for help.

Electricity The electric power is 220-240 volts, 50 cycles, AC.

Embassies/Consulates Citizens of Australia, Canada, and New Zealand should contact the British Embassy for assistance.

- **United States** The embassy is at Suborna 1, Sofia (☎ **02/88-48-01** or **88-48-02**). The American Consular Office is at 1 Kapitan Andreev St., Sofia (☎ **02/65-94-59;** 24-hour answering machine **02/65-31-31**). See "Fast Facts: Sofia" in Chapter 9 for more details.
- **United Kingdom** The embassy is at Vasil Levski Blvd. 65, Sofia (☎ **02/87-83-25** or **88-53-61**).

Emergencies In case of **fire,** call **160;** for the **police,** call **166.** If you need **emergency auto repairs,** call **146.** The number to call **for help** throughout Bulgaria is **150,** but they don't speak English.

Etiquette To avoid misunderstandings, be aware of the Bulgarian custom of nodding to say "no" and shaking the head from side to side to show agreement. Photographing the insides of churches and museums is often forbidden or requires a special fee; always ask before you snap your shutter.

Language Bulgarian is a close cousin to Russian and both use the Cyrillic alphabet. Most Bulgarians over age 25 speak at least some Russian; and in a crowd of this age group, you are likely to find a German speaker, but younger Bulgarians know less Russian and more English. The most expensive hotel in any town is likely to employ English speakers at the desk who can help you in a pinch. But if you don't speak Bulgarian, Russian, or German, be prepared for a lot of pointing and gesturing. Road signs are often written in Roman as well as Cyrillic lettering; larger hotels often have English menus in their restaurants. However, for the most part, English and Roman lettering are rare, so learning the Cyrillic alphabet (see Appendix A at the back of the book) is crucial.

Inexpensive English-Bulgarian phrase books and dictionaries are sold by street vendors in many Bulgarian cities. Unfortunately, these books usually don't have phonetic pronunciations for the Bulgarian phrases, so you will need to know Cyrillic.

Laundry/Dry Cleaning There are no coin-operated laundries in Bulgaria. Besides doing your laundry by hand, you might ask about laundry services at your hotel or speak with your host if you're renting a room. The cost is usually quite minimal.

Maps English-language maps of varying quality are usually available for major cities, but keep in mind that street names are often transliterated differently from the Bulgarian in various publications. On the whole these differences are small and usually not overly confusing. Note that streets named after people are sometimes, indexed by first name.

What can still be confusing are the changes in street names. Some Bulgarian cities are adopting new street names more slowly than others. Some maps and street signs may not reflect these recent changes, nor will all local residents necessarily be informed about them.

Movies Foreign films are generally subtitled, and cost 15 lv (55¢) depending on the theater. Seats are assigned, so buy your tickets early for the best view. Look for foreign film festivals, held every three or four months in cities like Sofia and Varna, to catch up on films you've missed at home.

Newspapers & Magazines Western publications like *Newsweek* and others are now more readily available in major tourist centers. You can pick them up at upscale hotels and at newsstands and kiosks with the letters RP in Cyrillic.

Registration If you stay in a hotel, tourist office–sponsored private room, or campground, your statistical card will be stamped to account for every day in Bulgaria. If you stay in private homes not set up by a local tourist bureau (such as a friend's house), make sure your host knows the latest regulations about registering your stay with the local police. Many such restrictions are easing up, and this rule may soon be eliminated.

Restrooms Many public bathrooms charge 1 to 2 lv (4¢ to 7¢). Should you forget to pay as you walk in, an attendant will loudly remind you.

Safety Although Bulgaria is safer than most Western European countries, it's a generally acknowledged fact that the crime rate has been steadily rising since the collapse of the police state. Recently, organized-crime groups have stepped up their operations of foreign car theft and break-ins.

Shoe Repair Ask the reception desk at your hotel or your private room host where to find the nearest shoe repair shop.

Sports Bulgaria offers year-round opportunities to engage in sports and recreational activities. During the summer, several excellent ski resorts (see "Alternative Travel," above), attract hikers, climbers, and campers who enjoy the woods, mountain air, and pleasant chalets. Hunting and fishing trips can be arranged through Balkan Holidays.

The Black Sea coast has long been a magnet for both Eastern and Western European vacationers in search of sun and fun at very reasonable prices. Water-sports equipment can be rented at many resorts.

Telephone Domestic telephone service has not improved much in the past few years. Public phones are often hard to find and many, especially in Sofia, are broken; even those that look functional will require several attempts before a good local connection is made.

Some pay phones take 20-stotinki coins, others utilize 50-stotinki.

There are two systems of telephone cards in Bulgaria. Post offices sell phonocartes in denominations of 7 to 100 lv, plus a 10-lv deposit. These cards can be used for local (1 lv per call), long-distance, or intra-European calls. In general, phones accepting these cards can only be found in post offices, and they are very frequently out of order.

BETKOM cards, good for long-distance and intra-European calls, are more expensive, but it is easier to locate a working phone that takes them. BETKOM phones can be found in better hotels and in many post offices. BETKOM cards can be purchased, for 100 to 400 lv, at hotel reception desks.

To call another continent you will have to go to the post office and have your call dialed for you. Calling the United States costs 50 lv ($1.80) per minute. Note that when calling Bulgaria from abroad the zero at the beginning of the city area code is dropped.

Television/Radio Satellite TV broadcasts (like CNN and German TV) are available in some hotels, private restaurants, and pubs. In Sofia, Voice of America (VOA) broadcasts news and weather reports continuously throughout the day on the radio.

Time Bulgarian time is two hours ahead of London time and seven hours ahead of eastern standard time. Daylight saving goes into effect the last week in September and ends the last week in March.

Water There are drinking fountains along principal roads all over the country. Mountain water remains largely as yet unpolluted. Mineral water from the Balkan mountains, some of which gets exported, is quite cheap, at about 25¢ for 1.5 liters. Ask for *mineralna voda* at a grocery or sidewalk stand.

9

Sofia

MODERN-DAY SOFIA BECAME BULGARIA'S CAPITAL AS RECENTLY AS THE TURN OF THE century, although it was inhabited for thousands of years. Its first recorded inhabitants were the Thracians (who called it Serdica), followed by the Romans and the Byzantines, then the Slavs and the original Bulgar tribe (who called it Sredets, "the middle"). Its present name, acquired in the 14th century, means "wisdom" in Greek, and the city's motto is "Grow, but not old."

At the time of liberation from the Turks in 1878, Sofia was only a provincial town in the Ottoman Empire with a population of fewer than 15,000 people. Its population has grown to over a million, but in spite of its grand buildings and the increasing traffic around it, the center of Sofia retains its pleasant, somewhat provincial, unhurried air. Its parks, large squares, and traffic-free streets paved with yellow bricks that link its great sights and museums make it ideal for strolling and pausing at outdoor cafés in the summer.

Most of Sofia's memorable architecture, like the splendid Alexander Nevsky Cathedral, dates from the beginning of this century, and although the traces of ancient times abound, they're not as numerous as they are in Plovdiv, Veliko Turnovo, and Nesebar. Nearby is the magnificently wooded Mount Vitosha, a fine place for summer hikes and excellent winter skiing, just a half-hour ride from the center of the city.

1 Orientation

ARRIVING

BY PLANE On arrival, you'll be required to fill out a small "statistical card" before you proceed to passport control. Exactly how long you'll have to wait for your luggage will depend on how many flights came in at the same time yours did. The airport can be very crowded and chaotic, and you may have a long wait. Passing through customs is no longer the ordeal it used to be—you'll probably just be waved through.

If you haven't made reservations for a hotel room from abroad and want the least expensive lodgings in downtown Sofia, go to the Private Accommodations Desk in the small airport lobby, where doubles cost $13.

Several taxi drivers will approach you, asking for hard currency to drive the 7½ miles into town. For maximum savings, take bus no. 84 or 284, leaving every 15 to 20 minutes, for 3 lv (10¢).

If you want to check your luggage, you must go to the domestic terminal across the street, where a service counter is open daily from 6am to 10pm.

BY TRAIN Sofia's main train station has a huge arrivals hall divided into two major levels. On the lower level, you can buy tickets for trains to the southern half of Bulgaria and deposit luggage to the right after leaving the tracks (you'll see a sign in French, CONSIGNE DES BAGGAGES). Open daily from 6am to 11pm, the office charges 3 lv (10¢) plus 2% of declared value per day. Thus a $50 bag costs $1.10 per day.

On the upper (street) level of the train station you can buy tickets to destinations in the northern half of the country at Windows 1 to 8. Tickets to southern cities are sold downstairs, while sleeping-car tickets are sold at their own window, to your right as you face away from the tracks. For shorter lines and more polite service, go downstairs to the Rila Bureau, where all types of tickets—domestic, international, and

What's Special About Sofia

Churches

- Alexander Nevsky Cathedral, an impressive neo-Byzantine structure.

Culture

- Some of the lowest-priced concerts and cultural performances in Europe.

Monuments

- A yellow-brick road connecting the sights and museums at the very center of town.

Museums

- National Museum of History, with some of the oldest and finest ancient gold objects in the world.
- National Archeology Museum, an impressive collection of ancient sculptures and relics.
- National Art Gallery, showing Bulgarian painting of the 19th and 20th centuries.

Natural Spectacles

- Splendid Mount Vitosha, with hiking trails and skiing just a half hour south of downtown Sofia.

Shopping

- A variety of shops and open-air bazaars selling art and folk objects.
- A large and colorful produce market.

sleeper—are sold. To buy an international ticket, you will need to show your passport. To the right of Window 8 is a post office and telephone bureau, open Monday through Friday from 7am to 9pm and on Saturday and Sunday from 7am to 12:30pm and 1 to 7pm. Trams depart from this level.

To get from the train station to town, simply follow the signs to the tram station and take tram no. 1, 7, or 15 for four stops south across the river to Sveta Nedelya Square. These trams also head toward Balkantourist's Accommodations Office at 37 Dondukov Blvd. If you walk, it won't take more than 20 minutes east and then south along Maria Luisa Boulevard until you reach Sveta Nedelya Square.

BY BUS The international bus station is at 23 Hristo Mihailov Blvd. (☎ **52-50-04**). If you're arriving by private bus, before you disembark try to get directions from someone on board on how to get to the center of town or to your hotel.

TOURIST INFORMATION

The Balkantourist office at 1 Vitosha Blvd. (☎ **87-51-92**) has a helpful, if not always well-informed, English-speaking staff. You can buy maps of Sofia and Bulgaria or hire an English-speaking guide ($6 for one hour, $8 for two hours, $20 for a day, more for out-of-town trips). The office organizes English-language guided tours to Rila Monastery on Wednesdays, Saturdays, and Sundays (eight hours, $19). The office may add more tours to other destinations. They are open Monday to Friday, 8am to 8pm (7:30pm in winter), Saturday 8:30am to 1:30pm.

The English-language *Sofia City Info Guide*, published monthly, is well worth its 25-lv (90¢) price. It contains a handy centerfold map of downtown, a calendar of performances and gallery shows, restaurant listings, and several hundred potentially useful telephone numbers. Look for it at the airport, the Sun Hotel, and Orbita.

CITY LAYOUT

MAIN BOULEVARDS & SQUARES Surrounded by mountains, Sofia is roughly in the central axis of Bulgaria and not far from its western border. The city is bounded by the small Vladajska Reka (river) to the north and by an extensive range of parks to the south. The cultural center of the city is located between Maria Luisa Boulevard/ Vitosha Boulevard on the westernmost edge and Vasil Levski Boulevard on the southeast. Tsar Osvoboditel Boulevard runs through the heart of town from Alexander Battenberg Square near Maria Luisa Boulevard, passing along a large yellow-brick pedestrian area around what used to be Georgi Dimitrov's Mausoleum, then past Plac Narodno Sabranie, all the way to Vasil Levski Boulevard. All the major sights are within easy walking distance of Tsar Osvoboditel Boulevard.

The showplace street of Sofia is Vitosha Boulevard, the continuation of Maria Luisa Boulevard south of Sveta Nedelya Square. It's so developed that it looks quite Western—except for the low prices. No cars are allowed (only trams and delivery vehicles) on the street, so it's a good place for a stroll. Sveta Nedelya Square itself provides an easy point of reference in finding your way across town: It's home to the huge Sheraton Hotel. About 15 blocks south of Sveta Nedelya Square on Vitosha is the massive and modern Palace of Culture.

FINDING AN ADDRESS Most street names in Sofia associated with Communist figures and dates have been changed or are in the process of being changed, but some of the maps sold abroad are out of date and don't reflect these changes. Adding to the confusion is the fact that not all the old street signs in Sofia have been replaced with new ones. The following list of main downtown street-name changes may help you decipher old maps of Sofia (alphabetized by the first letter of former name): Georgi Dimitrov Blvd. = Kn. Maria Luisa Blvd.; Lenin Square = Sveta Nedelya Square; 9 Septemvri Square = Alexander Battenberg Square; Ruski Blvd. = Tsar Osvoboditel Blvd.; Sofiiska Kommuna = ul. Alexander Battenberg; Marshal Tolbuhin Blvd. and Volgograd Blvd. = Vasil Levski Blvd.; Vasil Kolarov = Solunska.

Maps New English-language maps of Sofia are available at the Balkantourist office at 1 Vitosha Blvd. for 25 lv (90¢).

2 Getting Around

BUSES & TRAMS All public transportation in Sofia—and throughout most of Bulgaria—costs 3 lv (10¢) per ticket, and each ticket is good for one ride on a bus or tram. With prices likely to climb again in the future, check the latest fare when you arrive. You pay on the honor system by perforating your ticket in small metal boxes on the buses and trams; if you transfer you must use another ticket. If you ride without a ticket, you could be fined. (You won't see many people cancelling their tickets, since most people buy weekly or monthly passes for their daily commuting.) Tickets are sold in the small booths or newsstands located near major stops. It's best to stock up if you plan to use the mass-transit system all day. The system operates daily from 5am and stops running at about midnight for buses and 1am for trams and trolleybuses.

TAXIS You can get a taxi at hotels, train or bus stations, marked taxi stands, on the street, or by calling **142.** Prices for taxis are astonishingly low, starting at 10 lv (35¢) and rising by 4.50 lv (16¢) per kilometer. At night, fares start at 10 lv (35¢) and increase by 6 lv (20¢) per kilometer. Most daytime rides in the city center cost as little as 55 lv ($2). Of course, the fares can't stay this low forever, so inquire as to new rates when you arrive.

In addition to state taxis, many private taxis cruise the streets, some driven by professional Bulgarians who moonlight. Note, however, that although they charge the same fares, the private taxis do not have meters. Rather, they gauge the fare *based on their odometer.* Make sure the driver sees you checking the odometer before you begin the ride, perhaps by leaning over the front seat and jotting down the kilometer number.

ON FOOT One of the pleasures of discovering Sofia is strolling along its wide boulevards, provided the day's not too smoggy. Most of the sights are tightly clustered around Alexander Battenberg Square, a large pedestrian square, so walking is the easiest, most enjoyable, and simply the most sensible way to discover Sofia. (See "Walking Tour—Downtown Sofia," below.)

BY CAR Rent a car to explore the mountains, for overnight trips, or to drive cross-country to the seacoast, but *not* to see Sofia. Since most of Sofia's sights are well within walking distance and traffic is getting congested downtown, you'll only be adding to the traffic and increasing the already-noticeable pollution. Besides, there has been a rash of foreign car theft in Sofia recently.

For car rentals in Sofia, the **Hertz** office at 41 Vitosha Blvd. (☎ **83-34-87**) is open daily from 8am to 8pm. If you haven't prebooked in the U.S. in order to receive a 15% discount, you'll have to pay about $350 to 400 for their most economical model. **Europcar (☎ 68-12-06)** is located next to the main Balkantourist office at 1 Vitosha Blvd., and their rates are roughly the same. (See "Getting Around" in Chapter 8 for more details.)

Fast Facts: Sofia

American Express American Express's representative in Bulgaria is Megatours, 1 Levski St., 1000 Sofia (☎ **88-04-19;** fax 87-25-67; telex 25241), just east of the mausoleum on Boulevard Tsar Osvoboditel. They will replace lost traveler's checks, hold client mail, and cash traveler's checks into dollars or leva for a 4% to 4.5% commission. They are open Monday to Friday from 9am to 6:30pm, Saturday from 9am to noon.

Area Code Sofia's telephone area code is 02.

Business Hours Generally, offices are open Monday through Friday from 8 or 8:30am to 5pm, with a break for lunch. Stores are usually open Monday through Friday from 9am to 12:30 or 1pm, then anywhere from 2 to 4pm until 6 or 7pm, with shorter hours on Saturday and usually closed Sunday. On major shopping streets such as Vitosha, stores generally don't close for lunch.

Camera/Film There's a Konica shop next to the Balkantourist Office at 1 Vitosha Blvd., open Monday through Friday from 10am to 2pm and 3 to 7pm. At the south end of Vitosha is a Fuji shop. There is also a counter selling Kodak products in the Central Department Store.

Sofia

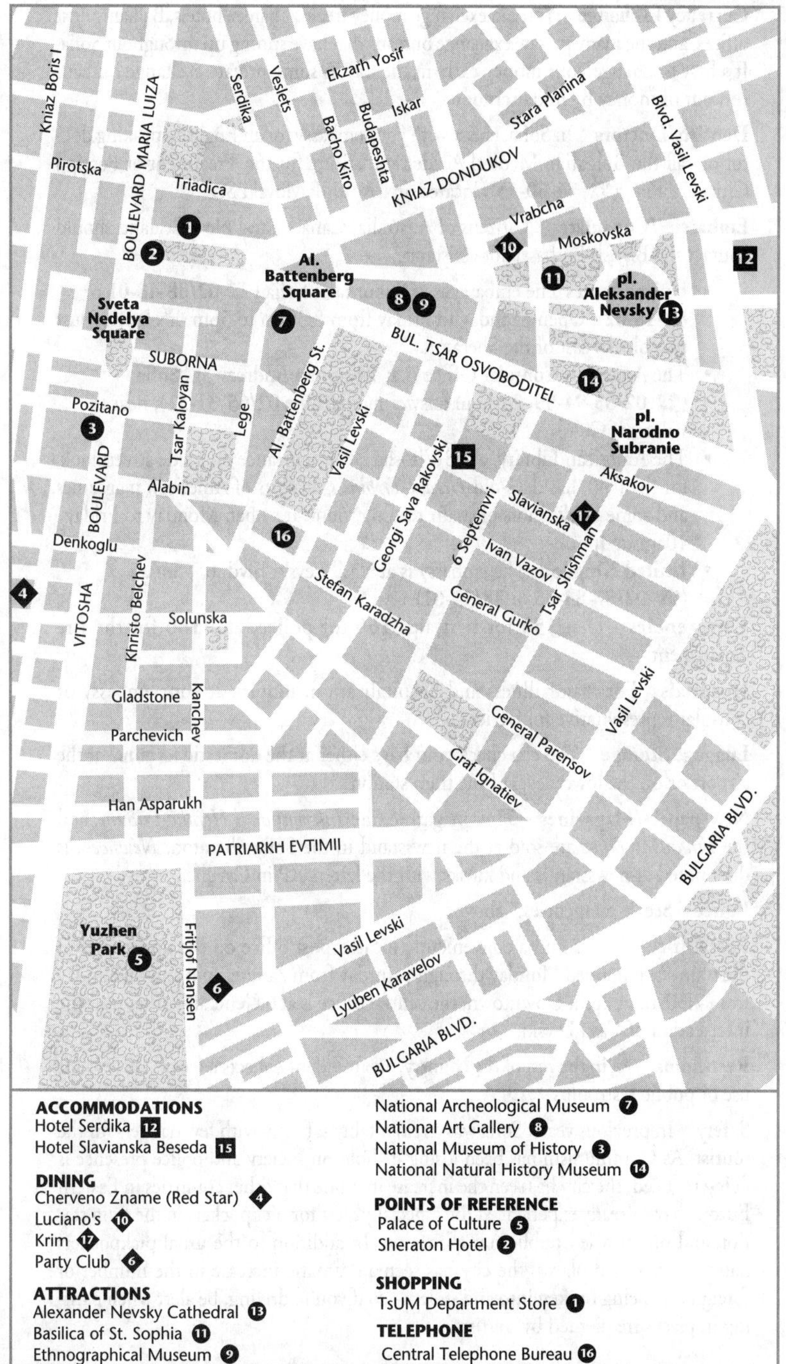
0
200 m
220 y
N
Kniaz Boris I
BOULEVARD MARIA LUIZA
Serdika
Veslets
Ekzarh Yosif
Iskar
Bacho Kiro
Budapeshta
Stara Planina
Blvd. Vasil Levski
Pirotska
Triadica
KNIAZ DONDUKOV
Vrabcha
Moskovska
Al. Battenberg Square
Sveta Nedelya Square
pl. Aleksander Nevsky
SUBORNA
BUL. TSAR OSVOBODITEL
Pozitano
Tsar Kaloyan
Lege
Al. Battenberg St.
Vasil Levski
pl. Narodno Subranie
Georgi Sava Rakovski
Aksakov
BOULEVARD
Alabin
6 Septemvri
Slavianska
Denkoglu
Ivan Vazov
Tsar Shishman
Stefan Karadzha
General Gurko
VITOSHA
Khristo Belchev
Solunska
Gladstone
Kanchev
Parchevich
General Parensov
Vasil Levski
Graf Ignatiev
Han Asparukh
PATRIARKH EVTIMII
BULGARIA BLVD.
Yuzhen Park
Fritjof Nansen
Vasil Levski
Lyuben Karavelov
BULGARIA BLVD.
ACCOMMODATIONS
Hotel Serdika 12
Hotel Slavianska Beseda 15
DINING
Cherveno Zname (Red Star) 4
Luciano's 10
Krim 17
Party Club 6
ATTRACTIONS
Alexander Nevsky Cathedral 13
Basilica of St. Sophia 11
Ethnographical Museum 9
National Archeological Museum 7
National Art Gallery 8
National Museum of History 3
National Natural History Museum 14
POINTS OF REFERENCE
Palace of Culture 5
Sheraton Hotel 2
SHOPPING
TsUM Department Store 1
TELEPHONE
Central Telephone Bureau 16

Currency Exchange You can exchange money freely at banks, hotels, Balkantourist offices, and the many private exchange bureaus that have sprung up throughout Sofia. It's best to change your money early in the day as some private exchange bureaus run out of money by midafternoon.

Dentists/Doctors In Sofia, check with your embassy for an English-speaking doctor or call the Bulgarian Medical Academy Institute for the Treatment of Foreign Citizens ITFC (☎ **74-60-15**), located at 1 Acad. Pavlovski St.

Embassies/Consulates Citizens of Australia, Canada, and New Zealand should contact the British Embassy for assistance.

- **United States** The embassy is at Suborna 1, Sofia (☎ **02/88-48-01** or **88-48-02**). Open Monday to Friday from 8:30am to 5pm, it's located just two blocks east of the Sheraton.
- The American Consular Office is at 1 Kapitan Andreev St., Sofia (☎ **02/65-94-59,** 24-hour answering machine **02/65-31-31**), near the Palace of Culture.
- The American Library, at 18 Vitosha Blvd. (entrance on a side street; look for the flag), has days-old *Herald Tribunes,* all sorts of American magazines, and some books in its pleasant reading room. It's open Monday to Friday 10am to 4pm.
- **United Kingdom** The embassy is at Vasil Levski Blvd. 65, Sofia (☎ **02/87-83-25** or **88/53-61**).

Emergencies Dial **150** for first aid, **166** for police, and **160** for the fire department.

Hospitals For major illness and hospitalization, inquire at your embassy or consular representative for advice.

Luggage Storage You can check your bags either at the domestic terminal at the airport or on the lower level of the train station.

Newspapers/Magazines *Time* magazine, the *International Herald Tribune,* and the *Financial Times* are sold at the newsstand in the Sofia Sheraton. *Newsweek* is distributed at newsstands and kiosks with the letters RP in Cyrillic.

Police See "Emergencies," above.

Post Office You'll find a conveniently located post office on the upper level of the train station, open Monday through Saturday from 7am to 7pm and on Sunday from 7:30am to 2pm. Downtown, the central office is at 6 General Gurko, near the intersection of Vasil Levski.

Restrooms As in the rest of the country, an attendant collects a fee of 2 lv (7¢) for use of public restrooms.

Safety In previous years, Sofia was a remarkably safe city with few dangers for the tourist. As Communism has been losing its hold on society and police presence is being reduced, the city has seen the increase in crime that other countries in Eastern Europe have already experienced. Be especially alert for pickpockets in the train station and on crowded public transportation. In addition to the usual pickpockets haunting crowded places, the city has seen a dramatic increase in the number of foreign cars being broken into and stolen—so if you're driving, be alert when parking in places frequented by tourists.

Telephone To make long-distance telephone calls, go to the Central Telephone Bureau at 6 Stefan Karadzha, one block south of Gurko Street. The three-story yellow plastic and glass office is open 24 hours a day.

3 Where to Stay

PRIVATE ROOMS The Balkantourist office at 27 Stamboliiski Blvd. (☎ **88-44-30**), rents reasonably priced private rooms—$10 per person. Balkantourist stays open daily from 8am to 8pm. You pay directly here, and they'll give you the address and keys to the apartment.

Hotels

Sofia does not have a good range of budget hotels, and a complex bureaucratic reservations system ensures that only the most informed travelers pay reasonable prices. You may save by booking hotel rooms from the Balkantourist office at 27 Stamboliiski Blvd. or through SunnyTours Travel from abroad. Their rates for better hotels as well as budget rooms in Sofia are sometimes lower than walk-in rates.

Failing advance preparations, you can stop by Balkantourist when you arrive in Sofia or you can try to reach SunnyTours Travel on the phone (☎ **02/27-41-32**).

IN THE CENTER

Hotel Hemus, 31 Georgi Traikov Blvd. ☎ **02/6-39-51.** Fax 02/66-13-18. Telex 22684. 248 rms (all with bath). TEL **Tram:** 2 or 9 toward Mount Vitosha.

Rates (including breakfast): Walk-in rates, $40 single; $60 double; $80 suite. AE, DC, JCB, MC, V.

Although not centrally located, the Hemus is as close as you'll come to an inexpensive, comfortable, modern hotel in Sofia. This large high-rise is a 10-minute tram ride from downtown. It has large pleasant rooms, some with splendid views of Mount Vitosha. Bathrooms are clean with freshly tiled enclosed showers. The clientele is mixed—mostly foreigners from the Middle East as well as natives. The large lobby attracts many people to its shops and bars; on warm evenings there are lots of young people milling about its entrance.

Hotel Serdika, 2 Janko Sakazov Blvd. (on Levsky Sq.). ☎ **02/44-34-11.** 171 rms (all with bath). TEL **Tram:** 1 or 7 from the train station to the third stop, and then switch to tram no. 3 or 4 and get off at the third stop.

Rates (including breakfast): $39 single; $56 double. AE, DC, MC, V.

The Serdika is a rarity in Sofia: a reasonably priced, centrally located and well-maintained hotel. The rooms on the fifth floor have been recently renovated with dark-wood paneling, clean white stucco walls, new tiling in the bathrooms, and real shower stalls. Older rooms are attractive but have unenclosed showers. Ask for one of the quiet rooms near the back of the hotel. When I visited, several families were making good use of one of its best features: sunny, large lobbies on every floor with attractive rugs, huge couches, and coffee tables. On the first floor you'll find the restaurant Berlin with vaguely German food, a small bar, and a gift shop. It may be difficult to get a room in the summer, so try to make reservations well in advance by writing the Balkantourist office. You'll enjoy the international clientele and the proximity of the Alexander Nevsky Cathedral and Sofia University.

Hotel Slavianska Beseda, 2 Slavianska St. ☎ **02/88-04-41.** 60 rms (all with bath). **Tram:** 12 from the train station to Georgi Rakovski Street, then walk north four blocks.

Rates: $30 single; $40 double, $50 apartment.

Here you pay for location—this hotel is surrounded by theaters and is in walking distance from major sights. Other than that, the hotel has little going for it. Its privatization in April 1992 hasn't done much to raise its comfort level. Ugly, stained carpets, lumpy wallpaper, and dim, graffiti-marred hallways won't lift your spirits if you're depressed. But if all you want is a clean bed in the center of town, this is a reasonable choice.

Worth the Extra Money

Sun Hotel, 89 Maria Luisa Blvd. ☎ **02/83-36-70** or **83-18-33.** Fax 02/83-53-89. 16 rms (all with bath). TV TEL MINIBAR **Tram:** 1, 7, or 15 from the train station.

Rates (including breakfast): $65 single; $85 double; $120 suite. AE.

The Sun is a brand-new 75-year-old hotel. The 1920 hotel is situated at the intersection of the two prominent boulevards; its ornate facade was intended to mark the way from the train station into the center of the capital of the still young Bulgaria. Under Communism, it was used for government offices. But the wheel has turned again, and in 1993 the refurbished Sun opened as a foreign-owned luxury hotel. Its owner says he intends to rival the Sheraton in comfort but not in prices. Certainly you will be taken care of. The rooms are a joyous escape from state-owned drabness, with stylish bedspreads, intriguing wallpaper, and brass doorknobs. Everything you could want, except shower curtains. English is spoken at the desk.

IN THE SUBURBS

Another inexpensive option is the **mini-hotels** in the suburbs of Sofia at the foot of Mount Vitosha, which can cost as little as $5 a night and as much as $20 a day with full board. Although some distance from downtown (four or five miles), these are large country homes and villas that have been converted into bed-and-breakfasts or full-board mini-hotels. Two villages that abound in mini-hotels along the route to the skiing complexes in the higher elevations of Mount Vitosha are Dragalevtsi and Simeonovo. You might like to escape the heat and pollution of the city for the fresh air, serenity, and beautiful mountain hiking trails this area offers. You can hike to the 14th-century Dragalevtsi Monastery or, on a clear day, take the cable-car ride up the mountain for a stunning view of Sofia.

Dragalevtsi

To get to Dragalevtsi (travel time 35 to 40 minutes, less by taxi) take tram 2 or 9 up Cherni Vrah Boulevard to the final stop (Khladilnika) and catch bus no. 64 (they run about every 15 minutes) up the mountain. Get off the bus near the small town square (fifth stop). You'll see little signs (in Latin script) everywhere for the dozens of private hotels like the Hotel Darling, the Hotel Orkhideya, the Edelweis, and the Hotel Emily (below). The going rate is about 100 to 150 lv ($3.60 to $5.35) per bed. Terms are negotiable if a common language can be found.

Hotel Emily, Pl. Karnobatski Prokhod 6-a (at the corner of Paprat St.). ☎ **02/67-14-75.** 5 rms (none with bath). **Directions:** Ask at the town square.

Rates: $5 per bed.

This is a large three-story, spotlessly maintained home. Emily, the owner's daughter, speaks passable English and is glad to practice it. There are two well-furnished double rooms upstairs with a shared bath and kitchen; the three singles downstairs are more simple and share a small bathroom. Owner Petr Georgiev and his wife are friendly and have had many foreigners stay here.

Simeonovo

To get to Simeonovo, take tram 14 or 19 to the bus terminus (Pl. Velcheva Zavera) and then bus no. 67; the trip takes about an hour. A taxi ride will cost about $5 one way. To book a mini-hotel in Simeonovo, it's best to call **Sunny Tours** in Sofia (☎ **02/27-41-32**). Lyuben Markov speaks good English and arranges for rooms at the best mini-hotels, like the Hotel Kitka, the Hotel Bor, the Hotel Zdravets, the Bojour, and the Krystal (English spoken). A double room costs about $25.

Where to Eat

Sofia offers excellent budget dining opportunities. You'll find quite a number of very inexpensive cafés, fast-food stands, and self-service bistros in town, but with prices so low in restaurants as of this writing (often less than $2 to $3), I have concentrated on listing the best food values in town.

A Word of Warning: As any Bulgarian will tell you, regard Sofia's waiters with caution and keep a very watchful eye on the tab. If need be, ask for the menu again when the check comes to double-check prices, or keep it with you the entire meal. Don't worry about the small amounts—there are lots of hidden surcharges—but any large discrepancies should be brought to the attention of the waiter, or manager if necessary.

Cherveno Zname [Red Star], 16 Vitosha St. ☎ **88-05-19.**

Cuisine: BULGARIAN/ITALIAN. **Reservations:** Recommended for dinner. **Directions:** Walk two blocks up Vitosha Boulevard from the National History Museum; enter from the side street.

Prices: Soups and salads 20–25 lv (70¢–90¢); pasta 40 lv ($1.40); main courses 45–60 lv ($1.60–$2.15). AE, DC, MC, V.

Open: Lunch daily noon–3pm; dinner daily 6:30–11:30pm.

A nice change from grilled meats if you miss pasta—but don't expect the real thing and you won't be disappointed. The real Italian pasta chef packed his bags and went back to Italy in 1990. The intriguing-sounding "spaghetti on wood" turns out to mean "forest style" and turns out to have a few mushrooms and a weak tomato sauce. One tasty specialty of the house is "fonduta," a steak with ham and cheese smothered in white sauce. Broiled mushrooms sprinkled with cheese and herbs are a treat in winter if you miss vegetables. The ambience is pleasant and the location is very convenient, on the second floor overlooking Vitosha Boulevard. (Take note: There's no sign on the door except COOP, which refers to the pâtisserie on the first floor.) There's piano music in the evenings and an English-language menu. The "Coop café" on the first floor has the best coffee and pastries in downtown Sofia. For 15 lv (55¢) each; it's open 8:15am to 3pm and 3:30pm to 10pm.

Garden Club [Bulgartsvet], 99 Kniaz Boris St. ☎ **55-30-84.**

Cuisine: BULGARIAN. **Reservations:** Recommended for lunch. **Directions:** Walk two blocks west from Vitosha Boulevard; it's on the corner behind the National Museum of History.

Prices: Soups and salads 20–50 lv (70¢–$1.80); main courses 65–100 lv ($2.30–$3).
Open: Daily noon–12:30am.

Don't be turned off by a rather forbidding entrance: The exterior is a dirty, dull orange, and you may have to push past a man selling laundry detergent to get to the dining room, but the interior is quite nice, with polished granite, brass, and floral upholstery—all combined to create a vaguely deco atmosphere. The menu, which is more or less translated into English, has simple fare that ranges in quality. The untranslated daily specials can be more imaginative.

Krim, 2 Dobroudja. ☎ **87-01-31.**

Cuisine: RUSSIAN. **Reservations:** Recommended. **Directions:** From Ploshtod Plac Narodno Sabranie, walk two blocks south and then turn right.
Prices: Soups and salads 25–30 lv (90¢–$1.10); hot and cold appetizers 25–45 lv (90¢–$1.60); main courses 70–80 lv ($2.50–$2.85); desserts 20–25 lv (70¢–90¢).
Open: Lunch Mon–Sat noon–3pm; dinner Mon–Sat 6–11pm.

The food here is nothing special, but the location is very convenient for a downtown lunch, and the prices are lower than average for a sit-down meal. Moreover, you have two great choices of where to eat: inside the glittering 1910 building or in the shady garden. The menu is in English and several other languages.

★ **Luciano,** 29 Moskovska St. ☎ **87-06-42.**

Cuisine: COFFEE/DESSERTS. **Directions:** From Alexander Nevsky Cathedral, walk north to Moskovska Street and turn left.
Prices: Coffees 10–60 lv (35¢–$2.10); crêpes and waffles 35–50 lv ($1.25–$1.75), ice-cream creations 65–70 lv ($2.25–$2.50).
Open: Daily 10:30am–11pm.

Lace curtains, crystal chandeliers, and a lot of mauve justify this establishment's claim to be a "Viennese salon." But don't expect anything as prosaic and refined as a Sachertorte. Instead, the menu is filled with exuberant combinations of fruit, chocolate, nuts, and ice cream. They are creative, delicious, and large enough to serve as a decadent lunch. The location, just a block or so from the cathedral, the art museum, and the ethnographic museum makes this place a good choice for an elegant interruption of your sightseeing. Or come by in the evening to listen to live piano music.

★ **Party Club,** 3 Vasil Levski Blvd. ☎ **81-43-43.**

Cuisine: ASIAN. **Reservations:** Recommended, especially on Sun. **Tram:** 6 or 9 to the Palace of Culture, then walk east one block on Vasil Levski.
Prices: Salads 45–80 lv ($1.60–$2.80); appetizers 75–100 lv ($2.60–$3.50); main courses 80–190 lv ($2.80–$6.75); desserts 45 lv ($1.60). AE, DC, EU, JCB, MC, V.
Open: Daily noon–midnight.

A long and varied menu, available in English, includes entries from China, Taiwan, Vietnam, as well as Bulgaria. Fortunately the cooking traditions are kept separate, so you won't find yogurt spilling onto your spring rolls. The battered eggplant is crisp not greasy and is served with a tasty sauce. The wrappers of the meat rolls are properly flaky, although the meat filling is a bit dry and could use a dipping sauce. The snazzy dining room doubles as an art gallery—you'll get a price list along with your menu—and triples, on Sunday evenings, as a venue for local jazz bands.

5 Attractions

Ideally, you need at least two days to enjoy the attractions of Sofia. It has a number of museums, churches, and art galleries with low admission fees. Here are some highlights, and a 1$^1/_2$-hour walking tour of the downtown area.

GUIDES If you're a history or art buff and want to get the maximum from visits to museums and monasteries, hire an English-speaking guide for a few hours to accompany you, because most of the inscriptions in museums are in Bulgarian. Inquire at the tourist office at 1 Vitosha Blvd. about making arrangements before you set off to your destination.

Suggested Itineraries

If You Have 1 Day

Follow the walking tour described below, with visits to the National Museum of History and the National Archeological Museum. In the late afternoon, walk along Vitosha Boulevard.

If You Have 2 Days

Follow the same walking tour, but spend more time in the dazzling National Museum of History and add the National Art Gallery, the Ethnographic Museum, the Basilica of St. Sophia, and more strolling and shopping. Attend a concert or cultural event for bargain prices in the evening.

If You Have 3 Days

Ride the cable car up Mt. Vitosha for fresh air, hiking, and panoramic views (see "Easy Excursions," below), or take a day trip to Rila Monastery (see Chapter 10).

If You Have 5 Days or More

You should definitely visit the alluring sights outside Sofia in Koprivshtitsa, Plovdiv, or Veliko Turnovo (see Chapter 10); or spend a few days relaxing on the beaches of the Black Sea coast (see Chapter 11).

THE TOP ATTRACTIONS

Alexander Nevsky Cathedral, Alexander Nevsky Sq.

This cathedral is the heart of Sofia—and perhaps all of Bulgaria. It's a monument to the 200,000 Russian soldiers who died in the war to free Bulgaria from Turkish domination. Built at the turn of the century, the cathedral was designed by a Russian architect in the Byzantine style of the grandest cathedrals in Russia. The huge cupola, extensive giltwork, rich frescoes, and three massive altars (one done by a Czech, one by a Russian, and one by a Bulgarian) contribute to the awesome sense of sacrifice the structure enshrines. Times may have changed, but the Alexander Nevsky Cathedral embodies a debt that many Bulgarians feel is owed to the Russian people, and it remains a symbol of their enduring friendship.

The cathedral, always well known for its choir, is also the center of new religious expression in Bulgaria. On Christmas, Easter, and other major holidays the church is crowded with worshipers, and the services are now televised as well.

A museum of religious art in the church crypt was closed for repairs at press time. When open, it houses a superb collection of icons painted in fresco, on wood, and in mosaic dating back to the medieval period. Enter the gallery from the left side of the facade. You can buy recordings of Church Slavonic music, as well as postcards and slides at the entrance to the cathedral.

Admission: Cathedral, free; icon museum in the crypt, 45¢.

Open: Cathedral, daily 7:30am–7pm, to 5:30pm in winter; crypt, Wed–Mon 10:30am–7pm, to 5:30pm in winter. **Directions:** Walk two blocks north from Ploschad Narodno Sabranie.

★ **National Museum of History,** 2 Vitosha Blvd. ☎ **88-41-60.**

This vast museum will surely impress you with one of the richest collections of ancient gold artifacts and archeological pieces in all of Europe. Housed in the former Judicial Building right off Sveta Nedelya Square, it contains important relics from every major site across Bulgaria. Here are the highlights:

Room 1: 4th-millennium B.C. gold objects found in graves without bodies as a tribute to the sun god. Archeologists suggest that the bodies were missing because either the graves represent those who died in foreign lands, or they are offerings made to living priest-kings.

Room 2: 13th- or 15th-century B.C. gold treasures of the Thracian king.

Room 3: The Panagurishte Treasures, the most famous Bulgarian gold drinking vessels from the 3rd century B.C., shaped like human and animal heads and adorned with scenes from Greek mythology. Their use was reserved for only the kings and the gods themselves.

Room 5: The Preslav Treasure from the 10th century A.D., including a necklace worn by the queen and four small gold objects that probably adorned the king's crown.

Room 6: Displays on SS. Cyril and Methodius, who created the Cyrillic alphabet used by Bulgarians, Russians, and some other Slavs; manuscripts and stone inscriptions from the 10th and 11th centuries A.D.

Room 7: Art and objects from the second Bulgarian kingdom in the 13th and 14th centuries.

Central Hall of the Ground Floor: Roman-era 1st- to 4th-century A.D. black-and-white floor mosaics from southeastern Bulgaria.

Upstairs: Here the collection continues chronologically with magnificently carved doors from Rila Monastery, religious art from across the country, and weapons from Veliko Turnovo.

It's a very large museum with a lot to see, and you can easily spend a long afternoon here. You may be able to arrange for an English-speaking guide in the summer at the entrance. As the museum descriptions are only in Bulgarian, you'll find much use for one.

Admission: 25 lv (90¢) adults, 10 lv (35¢) students.

Open: Tues–Sun 10:30am–6:15pm; Nov–Apr: Mon–Fri 9:30am–5:15pm. Last entry 45 minutes before closing. **Directions:** From the Sheraton Hotel on Sveta Nedelya Square, walk a block south on Vitosha.

National Archeological Museum, off Alexander Battenberg Sq. ☎ **88-24-05** or **88-24-06.**

Located in the former Great Mosque (Buyak Djamia) from the 15th century, this museum displays Bulgarian archeology from prehistoric times to the Middle Ages. Highlights include jewelry from the Roman era; Greek vases from Sozopol; frescoes of the Thracian, Macedonian, and Roman eras; and ancient funeral monuments. On the circular balcony overlooking the central floor is a collection of medieval icons and paintings.

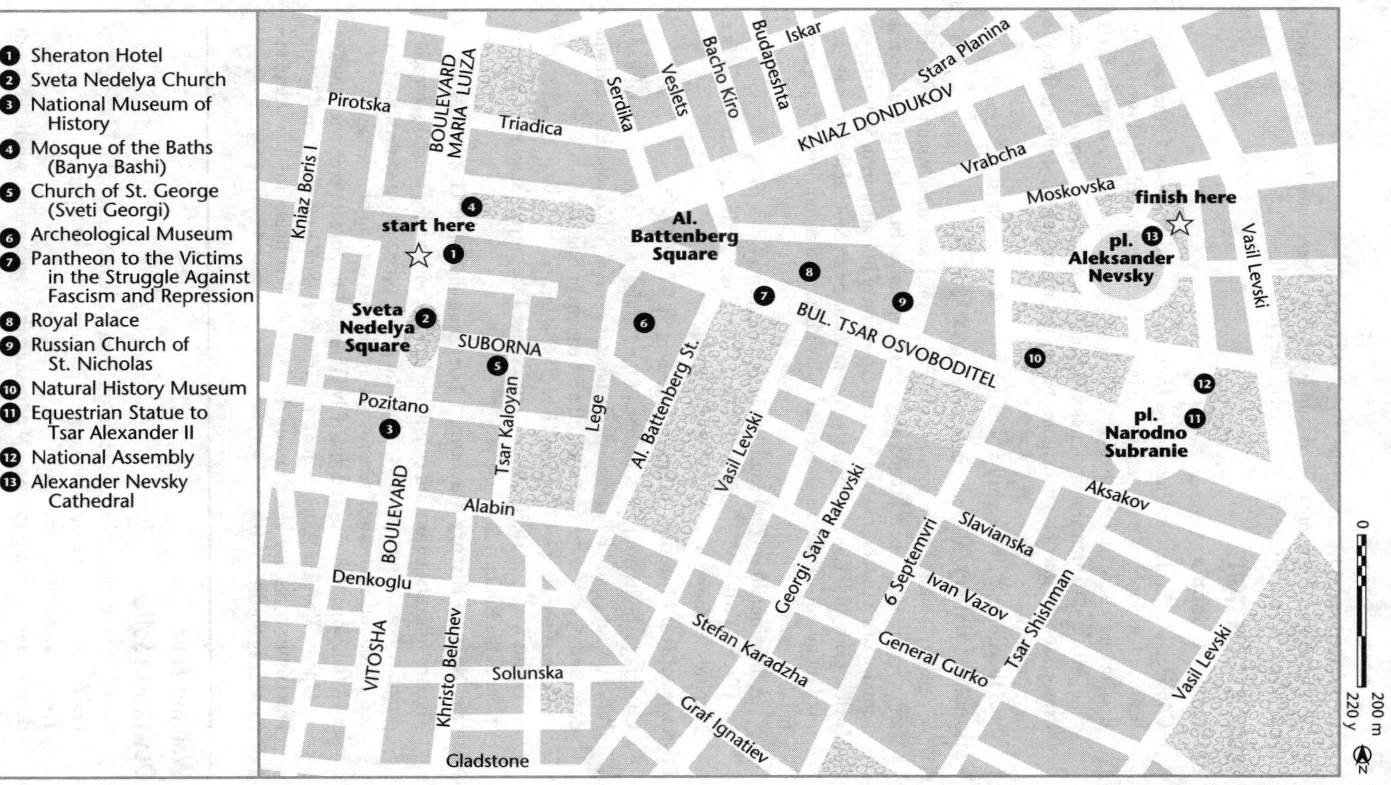

Walking Tour—Downtown Sofia

Admission: 20 lv (70¢) adults, 10 lv (35¢) students.

Open: Tues 10am–noon, Wed–Sun 10am–6pm. **Directions:** From the National Art Gallery, walk a block to the right and then turn left.

MORE ATTRACTIONS

Basilica of St. Sophia, Alexander Nevsky Sq.

Considerably smaller, and just across from the Alexander Nevsky Cathedral, the basilica of St. Sophia was originally built in the 6th century on the site of two smaller Roman churches. Under Ottoman rule, it was converted into a mosque for a time. Much of the remaining church has been reconstructed to repair earthquake damage, and the interior is undergoing repairs that are expected to continue into the next century.

Directions: Walk west half a block from the Alexander Nevsky Cathedral.

National Art Gallery, Alexander Battenberg Sq. ☎ **88-35-59.**

The gallery is located in the former Royal Palace, which was initially built as Turkish army headquarters. The collection highlights Bulgarian art from the National Revival period of the 19th century—the first real expression of Bulgarian art in 500 years—as well as many 20th-century paintings. Also noteworthy are some of the rather elegant royal rooms, such as the massive central hall with its brass chandeliers and long array of tall mirrors.

Admission: 20 lv (70¢) adults, 10 lv (35¢) students.

Open: Wed–Mon 10:30am–6:30pm. **Directions:** Walk opposite the former Dimitrov Mausoleum, and take the left staircase up.

Ethnographical Museum, Alexander Battenberg Sq. ☎ **88-51-17.**

Changing exhibits from the collection of the National Art Gallery in the old Royal Palace display typical Bulgarian folk costumes, models of houses, old doors and windows, and peasant crafts typical of different regions of Bulgaria.

Admission: 20 lv (70¢) adults, 10 lv (35¢) students.

Open: Wed–Sun 10:30am–6pm. **Directions:** Take the right staircase at same entrance as the National Art Gallery.

National Natural History Museum, 1 Tsar Osvoboditel Blvd. ☎ **88-51-15.**

The largest natural history museum in the Balkans, with stuffed alligators, ostriches, penguins, bears, bison, monkeys, lions, and zebras; collections of spiders, scorpions, and all your other favorite insects; as well as a large collection of minerals.

Admission: 20 lv (70¢) adults, 10 lv (35¢) students; free for everyone Thurs.

Open: Wed–Fri 9am–noon and 1–6pm, Sat–Sun 9am–noon and 3–6pm. **Directions:** Walk one block east on Tsar Osvoboditel Boulevard from Alexander Battenberg Square.

Walking Tour

Downtown Sofia

Start In front of the Sheraton Hotel on Sveta Nedelya Square.
Finish Alexander Nevsky Cathedral on Alexander Nevsky Square.
Time About 1½ hours.
Best Times During the day, Wednesday through Sunday, when the major museums are open.
Worst Times Monday, when most museums are closed.

On the east side of Sveta Nedelya Square is an icon of American capitalism, the:

1. **Sheraton Hotel.** In the late 1980s Sheraton revamped an older hotel here at a cost of $60 million. Although the Stalinist Gothic facade remains, inside you'll find modern comfort unusual for Bulgaria. To recoup their investment, Sheraton requires all guests, including Bulgarians, to pay in hard currency.

   At the center of the square you'll see the small:

2. **Sveta Nedelya Church,** where several churches have stood since the earliest days of Bulgarian Christianity. Half a block farther south is the must-see:
3. **National Museum of History,** the treasure chest of Bulgaria's past. One block to the north you'll see the:
4. **Mosque of the Baths (Banya Bashi),** built in 1576 by the Ottoman Turks.

   Now head back to the Sheraton and walk east down Suborna, a major street with many travel offices and stores, and take the first left to reach the:

5. **Church of St. George (Sveti Georgi),** in the courtyard of the Sheraton. Formerly a Roman bathhouse from the 2nd to 3rd century A.D., it was converted into a church centuries later. In the 15th century the red-brick rotunda was made into a mosque, only to be changed into a church again. In front of the church you can still see the remains of a Roman street. The church is undergoing restoration and is rarely open to the public.

   Exit the square to the east and you'll reach the:

6. **Archeological Museum,** in the former Great Mosque of the 15th century (see "The Top Attractions," above). Continue a few steps north and you pass by Alexander Battenberg Square, the political center of the Bulgarian capital, lined with yellow bricks. Near the entrance of the museum is a stairway leading down into an underpass that runs beneath the busy Kniaz Dondukov Boulevard. Descend the steps and enter the passage to see sections of the ancient city walls of Serdika, which were discovered when the underpass was being tunneled. Then exit the way you entered.

   A block away you'll reach the:

7. **Pantheon to the Victims in the Struggle Against Fascism and Repression.** Until 1990 the structure served as the showplace of Bulgarian Communism, and displayed the embalmed body of Bulgarian Communist leader Georgi Dimitrov. During important socialist holidays, Bulgarian party leaders viewed parades from its summit. In 1990 Bulgaria's leaders decided to bury Dimitrov after 49 years of lying in state, and rededicated the monument to all those who fell in past struggles for liberty and democracy.

   Across the street is the former:

8. **Royal Palace.** Once used as their army headquarters by the Ottoman Turks occupying Bulgaria, it was taken over by the Bulgarian royal family in the late 19th century. Today it houses the National Art Gallery and the Ethnographic Museum.

Refueling Stops

You can eat well in the **Krim Restaurant,** a few blocks away off Tsar Osvoboditel Boulevard. For dessert, try Luciano (see "Where to Eat," above) or the lively café in the **Grand Hotel Bulgaria,** at the beginning of Tsar Osvoboditel Boulevard. Several good restaurants within a 10-minute walk (in the direction you're headed) are the mezzanine restaurant of the **Grand Hotel Sofia,** off Narodno Sabranie Square, or if you want to go back to Vitosha Boulevard, the **Garden Club Restaurant** (see "Where to Eat," above) behind the National Museum of History.

Continuing east, you'll pass the distinctive gold domes of the:

9. **Russian Church of St. Nicholas,** and then the:
10. **Natural History Museum,** to the left. Just past the museum is Narodno Sabranie Square. At the center stands the:
11. **Equestrian Statue to Tsar Alexander II,** perhaps the only such monument to a prerevolutionary Russian leader in all of Eastern Europe. Bulgaria honors him for his role in liberating the country from the Turks in 1877–78. On the north side of the square is the:
12. **National Assembly.** From this square, walk north a block and a half to reach the impressive:
13. **Alexander Nevsky Cathedral** (see "The Top Attractions," above) and the end of our tour.

6 Savvy Shopping

The new economic climate has stimulated a great deal of entrepreneurial activity on Sofia's once-sedate streets. Street vendors now clutter Vitosha Boulevard selling items once impossible for Bulgarians to buy except in tourist shops with hard currency, like imported chocolates, cigarettes, liquors, cosmetics, Turkish jeans—items of minor interest to visiting Westerners. Of more interest are the good buys in Bulgarian folk art such as embroidered table linens, tooled leather, carved wooden articles, rugs, and copper utensils, as well as antique silver articles.

These items are sold in boutiques along main shopping streets like Vitosha Boulevard (the Fifth Avenue of Sofia) and Tsar Osvoboditel and Rakovski Boulevards, as well as in less expensive open-air art markets. Zadruga, 14 Vitosha, is a particularly well stocked crafts store. It's open Monday to Friday from 10am to 7pm and on Saturday from 10am to 2pm. The new marketplace is operating at a feverish pitch, with shops opening and closing at an alarming tempo. Despite this instability, you can be sure that there are more shops now than ever before. The center of town is also small enough that you'll have many opportunities to shop on your walking tour of Sofia's main sights.

Traders and artisans display their wares along the walks of the small Kristal park, diagonally across from the Russian Church of St. Nicholas and in the large square near the Alexander Nevsky Cathedral. In addition to a large selection of embroidered items and jewelry, you'll find modern paintings, copies of icons, Russian caviar (it's highly perishable, so be sure you know how old it is), antique cameras and fountain pens, old silver cigarette cases and watches, and elaborate Bulgarian filigree belt buckles and jewelry at good prices. You can also pick up low-cost wood folk crafts and other tourist items here.

Another open-air shopping area featuring handcrafts like ornamental carved wooden plaques and copies of icons is located in the passageway between TsUM (the Central Department Store) and the Sheraton Hotel. TsUM is Bulgaria's largest department store, a relatively well stocked place with everything from clothing to food.

If you haven't much time to shop, but want to pick up a few inexpensive folk items like carved wooden boxes, dolls, and pottery, there's a Bulgarian souvenir department on the ground floor. It's open Monday through Friday from 8am to 8pm and on Saturday from 9am to 5pm.

If bargaining at outdoor markets is not your style, you can find select antique items at two small shops at no. 4 and no. 6 (on the second floor) Tsar Osvoboditel Blvd., open Monday through Saturday from 10am to 6pm. And don't overlook the shops in several of Sofia's museums, especially the ethnographic museum (see "Attractions," above).

If you love outdoor food markets, you'll want to visit the stalls of Sofia's colorful main open market (Zhenski pazar) along Stefan Stambolov Boulevard (formerly Georgi Kirkov). This is where Bulgarians buy their fresh produce, household items, and clothing. There's plenty of excellent fresh fruit here in the summer.

7 Evening Entertainment

Aside from loud derivative rock music at a few discos and floor shows with Russian striptease artists (the groups have incongruous names like the "Pushkin Ballet") performed in the large upscale hotels, Sofia's nightlife is quite tame compared to that in the West. However, Sofia's serious cultural life is of high quality and very lively, especially during the month-long **Sofia Music Weeks** (from the last week in May through most of June), when international chamber groups and soloists, choral groups, and dance troupes perform at the Bulgaria Concert Hall.

The **Bulgaria Concert Hall** is at 1 Aksakov St. For information about concerts, call **87-76-56;** for tickets, stop by the concert bureau at 2 Tsar Osvoboditel Blvd. (☎ **87-15-88**). Tickets are remarkably inexpensive: 25 to 35 lv (90¢ to $1.25). Note that the Sofia Philharmonic does not play here during the summer.

Bulgarian opera stars are known throughout the world. You can hear them performing classics at the **Sofia Opera** at 55 Dondukov Blvd. (☎ **87-13-66**); ballets are performed here as well. The opera's company sings as the choir at the Alexander Nevsky Cathedral, so you may want to attend a service there.

On a lighter note, operettas are performed at the **Stefan Makedonski State Music Theater,** at 4 Levski Blvd. (☎ **44-19-79**). For the young at heart, there's the **Central Puppet Theater** at 14 Gurko St. (☎ **88-54-16**). Tickets cost a pittance by Western standards. Plays are so inexpensive and the performances so good that it's worth going to a classic by Shakespeare or Brecht that you know well, even if you don't understand a word of Bulgarian. Tickets are available at the **Ivan Vazov National Theater,** at 5 Levski St. (not Blvd.) (☎ **80-24-10**), near the City Garden. Many concert performances begin early, at 7pm.

For a schedule of performances, refer to the *Sofia City Info Guide* (see "Tourist Information," above).

The Palace of Culture, 1 Bulgaria Sq. (☎ **5-15-01**), at the south end of Vitosha Boulevard, offers a tremendous variety of cultural programs in its 14 performance halls, all under one huge modernistic roof, at extraordinarily low prices: 25 to 35 lv (90¢ to $1.25), arguably the lowest concert prices in all of Eastern Europe. Programs span a wide range of interests and include chamber music, piano soloists, modern jazz groups, folklore ensembles, ballets, musicals, theater, and film festivals! There are also discos for young people. The box office is open daily from 8am to 7pm.

8 Networks & Resources

FOR STUDENTS The national student travel agency, Orbita has an office in Sofia at 48 Khristo Botev Blvd. one block south of Al. Stamboulski (☎ **87-91-28** or **80-01-02**; fax 88-58-14; telex 22381). They sell maps and the *Sofia City Info Guide.* The staff will book hotel rooms and English-speaking tours throughout Bulgaria, including special-interest tours centered on sports, nature, and folk culture. Students from any country can buy the ISIC card here for 150 lv ($5.35).

9 Easy Excursions

The most worthwhile sights near Sofia are of the lengthy day trip or overnight variety. The most interesting are: Rila Monastery, the cradle of Bulgarian Christianity, about two hours away; Plovdiv, home to a charming 19th-century National Revival neighborhood and some important Roman ruins, about two hours away by express bus or train; and Koprivshtitsa, a charming 19th-century museum village about two hours away by express train. See Chapter 10 for more detailed information.

For good tips on shorter outings in the vicinity of Sofia, ask at the Balkan Holidays office in New York or London for the new brochure, "In and Out of Sofia."

MT. VITOSHA NATIONAL PARK The best escape from Sofia's often oppressive air pollution is to head for Mt. Vitosha, which sits broodingly just south of the city. An Austrian-built gondola lift (8 lv—30¢—each way) takes about 30 minutes to travel the 3 1/2 miles up the mountain (there are two intermediate stops; don't get off until you've crossed the river of boulders just before the summit). The ride is great fun and gorgeously scenic, especially in fall when the leaves change color.

Once at the top (7,200 feet), you can eat lunch at a small restaurant at the lift station. Or better yet, do as the Sofians do and bring a picnic. There are numerous hiking trails, both wooded and clear. The views of Sofia are astounding because of the density of the smog that lingers in a great brown smudge over the capital and all but obscures the mountains beyond the city.

From December to March, Vitosha is covered with snow, and several ski lifts operate at the top. You can rent skis and buy lift tickets near the gondola's top station.

To get to the base station from the city center, take tram 14 or 19 to the VTLI stop, just before the end of the line. Then take bus 122 or 123 to the last stop: Lifta Simeonovo. Because getting to the lift and ascending the mountain take time, it's best to start early and budget most of the day for Vitosha.

10 Moving On—Travel Services

The best place to get information on both domestic and international travel is the Transportation Center in the basement of the Palace of Culture on Vitosha Boulevard (☎ **59-71-86** or **59-71-87**), open Monday through Friday from 7am to 7pm and on Sunday from 8am to 2pm. Different counters here provide information and sell tickets for planes, buses, and trains.

BY PLANE Balkan Airlines has offices at 12 Narodno Sabranie Sq. (☎ **87-57-24** or **88-06-63**) and 10 Kniaz Al. Battenberg St. (☎ **88-44-36**), open Monday through Friday from 7:30am to 7:30pm and on Saturday from 8am to 4pm. You can also book tickets at Interbalkan, with offices across town, including on the lower level of the train station (☎ **32-31-90**), open Monday through Friday from 8am to 7pm.

For airport information, dial **72-24-14** for domestic flights, **45-11-13** for international flights.

BY TRAIN If you want to buy international train tickets, go to the Rila Railway Bureau, 5 Gurko St. (☎ **87-07-77** for information or **87-23-45** for purchases), open Monday through Friday from 8 to 11:30am and noon to 7pm, and on Saturday from 7am to 2pm. English is spoken there.

To buy an international ticket, you will have to show your passport and any necessary visas. There are also Rila offices in Sofia's train station and the Palace of Culture.

For domestic train information, call **87-57-42;** you can also go in person to the offices at either 23 Maria Luisa Blvd. (☎ **87-02-22**) or 1 Slaveikov Sq. (☎ **87-57-42**).

BY BUS Three main bus terminals serve all of Bulgaria. Buses to Plovdiv and Svilengrad leave from the South Terminal (☎ **72-00-63**) on Samokov Boulevard south of the Park Hotel Moskva; to get there, take tram no. 14 from Sveta Nedelya Square. Buses to Blagoevgrad, Melnik, Sandanski, and the Rila Monastery leave from the West Terminal on Boulevard Tsar Boris (☎ **55-50-85**); to get there, take tram no. 5. The Podujane Bus Terminal near Pirdop Square (☎ **45-30-14**) serves all of northern Bulgaria; take bus no. 12, 14, 16, 17, 90, 100, 117, 118, or 216 past the railroad tracks.

You can buy tickets up to 10 days ahead in the basement Transportation Center of the Palace of Culture (☎ **59-31-06**).

For current information in English on schedules, prices, and departure points for new private express bus lines, call or drop in at the Balkantourist office at 1 Vitosha Blvd. (☎ **87-51-92**).

10

Bulgaria's Inland Cities

BULGARIA'S INLAND CITIES OFFER VISITORS A WEALTH OF HISTORIC MONUMENTS: THE remains of ancient kingdoms, beautifully restored monasteries, and picturesque old towns. At the Rila Monastery, to the south of Sofia, you can follow Bulgarian Christianity from its earliest roots in the 10th century. Veliko Turnovo, the medieval capital of Bulgaria, has the remains of fortifications that once protected the heart of a great empire. In Koprivshtitsa, Veliko Turnovo, and Plovdiv you can admire charming neighborhoods showing off the picturesque architecture of the 18th and 19th centuries, the period of Bulgaria's "National Revival" after 500 years of Turkish domination. Bansko, Sandanski, and Melnik perch in the beautiful Pirin Mountains, a region where the scarcity of Western tourists can translate into lower prices and greater hospitality.

Overall, Bulgaria's inland cities have such a wealth of historic and artistic sights that they should not be left out of your visit to the Balkans.

SEEING THE INLAND CITIES

Rila Monastery can be visited as a day trip or an overnight trip from Sofia, or you can continue from the monastery down to Sandanski or Bansko. But if you plan to continue eastward, you are better off returning to Sofia rather than trying to get from Rila to Koprivshtitsa or Plovdiv.

Plovdiv is on the main international rail line to Istanbul, so if you plan to arrive or depart by rail to Turkey, stop here. Otherwise you can also continue by rail from Plovdiv to the Black Sea coast, or to points to the north of the country.

Start your explorations of north-central Bulgaria from Veliko Turnovo. From there you can visit Gabrovo, Etur, Kazanluk, and then Koprivshtitsa en route back to Sofia; alternatively, you can continue from Veliko Turnovo to Varna on the Black Sea coast (see Chapter 11).

1 The Rila Monastery

75 miles S of Sofia

GETTING THERE • By Train You can take the train south to Kocherinovo and then switch to a bus for the last 15 miles to Rila Monastery.

• By Bus As of this writing, in summer two buses leave daily at 6:30am and 2:30pm from Sofia's Western Bus Terminal, arriving three hours later at the Riletz Hotel; a ticket costs 30 lv ($1.05). Buses return from Rila Monastery to Sofia at 10:20am and 5:40pm.

The easiest way to see the monastery is an English-language guided bus tour organized by the Balkantourist office at 1 Vitosha Blvd. in Sofia. The tour departs on Wednesdays, Saturdays, and Sundays and lasts eight hours. The cost is $19.

• By Car Take the Sofia-Athens highway to the town of Kocherinovo, and then continue up a well-marked winding road for about another 18 miles; the journey takes over two hours.

Hitchhiking to Kocherinovo is a possibility, but traffic through the valley is sparse.

ESSENTIALS Make your way immediately to the monastery, which contains all the museums and sites listed below. Keep in mind that the town of Rila is a good 12 miles from the monastery, so don't get off the bus too soon. Behind the monastery, on the side farthest from the bus stop, there are several restaurants offering lunch to the crowds of visitors.

What's Special About Bulgaria's Inland Cities

Ancient Monuments

- Remarkably well preserved 3rd-century B.C. Roman Theater in Plovdiv.
- Two Byzantine basilicas, still under excavation in Sandanski.

Churches

- Rila Monastery, the cradle of Bulgarian Christianity.
- Arbanassi's Church of the Birth of Christ, with frescoes from the 16th and 17th centuries completely intact.
- Rozhen Monastery, with its beautiful icons and stained glass.

Museums

- Tsarevets, the 12th- to 14th-century fortifications once at the center of the Bulgarian kingdom in Veliko Turnovo.
- Historical Museum in the Rila Monastery with the Rila Cross, with 140 biblical scenes carved on a cross less than 16 inches tall.
- Gabrovo's House of Humor, the only museum dedicated to comedy and satire in the world.

Natural Spectacles

- The Melnik Pyramids, unworldly sandstone formations carved by erosion into fantastic shapes.
- The Valley of the Roses, source of 70% to 90% of the world's output of rose attar.
- The spectacular views over hills and valleys in Veliko Turnovo and Koprivshtitsa.

Museum Towns and Neighborhoods

- Trimontium, picturesque neighborhood of 19th-century houses in Plovdiv.
- Koprivshtitsa, a museum town that's an architectural gem of the Bulgarian "National Revival" style.
- Etur, the Bulgarian Williamsburg, where artisans demonstrate traditional crafts in a charming 19th-century village setting.

The monastery is located in some of Bulgaria's most beautiful mountain terrain and is a good starting point for hikes to the seven Rila lakes and Malyovitsa peak. The monastery gift shop has maps of the area.

Rila Monastery, 3,785 feet high amid the bare, granite faces of the Rila Mountains, has been important since the earliest days of Bulgarian Christianity. Founded near the site where John of Rila (Ivan Rilski), a hermit, lived and prayed in a cave, the monastery was well established as a colony of hermits by the 10th century. By the time of the first Bulgarian kingdom, it was already an acknowledged center of learning and church power; 134 precious manuscripts dating from the 10th through the 19th century survive.

When you first arrive, the complex may appear more like a fortress than a traditional monastery, but such construction was common in the Middle Ages. As the wealth of the monasteries attracted bandits and foreign invaders, the monasteries were obliged to protect themselves, and Rila's fortifications proved crucial to its survival. Even during the Ottoman conquest, the monastery was able to maintain quasi-independence, and as a result, parts of Rila Monastery standing today date back to the 14th century. The rest of the complex was thoroughly reworked in the colorful 19th-century National Revival style and restored in this century.

WHAT TO SEE & DO

Church of the Blessed Virgin, in Rila Monastery.

The five-domed green-and-gold monastery church was rebuilt in the National Revival style in 1833–34, and features a fantastic array of frescoes inside and out, many painted by Zahari Zograf. Monks still practice here, following the monastic tradition of St. John of Rila who lies buried inside. Also inside are four lavishly decorated ceremonial guest rooms, each named after the town that helped refurbish it: Koprivshtitsa, Teteven, Samokov, and Chirpan. Outside, the **Tower of Hrelyu,** dating from the monastery's inception, soars above the church. Inside this tower is a small chapel decorated with 14th-century frescoes.

Admission: Free.

Open: Daily 6am–6pm. **Directions:** Walk to building at the center of the monastery.

Historical Museum, in Rila Monastery. ☎ **22-08.**

Features a collection of objects connected with the monastery's thousand-year history, including jewelry, coins, weapons, and a bishop's inlaid throne. One highlight of the collection is the original monastery charter granted by the last king of the second Bulgarian kingdom in 1378. Written on leather in Old Bulgarian, the document carries the signature of the king and his gold seal.

The most spectacular object here, however, is the famous ★ **Rila Cross,** in the last room of the ground floor. Less than 16 inches high, it contains 140 biblical scenes with over 1,500 human figures with faces no larger than a grain of rice. The cross took monk Raphael 12 years (1790–1802) to carve with a needle and eventually blinded him. Hold onto your museum entrance ticket, which also allows you entry into a few reconstructed monks' chambers and communal rooms around the main courtyard.

Admission: 50 lv ($1.80) adults, 20 lv (70¢) students.

Open: Daily 8am–5pm. **Directions:** Walk straight to the right of the church facade.

WHERE TO STAY

Riletz Hotel, Rila 2630. ☎ **09076954/21-06.** 70 rms (all with bath). **Directions:** Walk about 20 minutes from monastery, or hitch a ride.

Rates: $20 single; $32 double. AE, DC, MC, V.

The best place in town, this charming five-story chalet-style hotel offers some magnificent views of forests and hills. The rooms are fairly new, well lit, and nicely decorated with blond wood and white plaster walls. Singles have double beds and a pinewood desk, and all rooms have terraces. In the past this hotel mainly housed large groups of East European youth hiking groups. When I last visited it was up for auction by the state, which is not interested in renovating it. There's good skiing nearby. The hotel has a day bar, a nightclub, and video games. The restaurant, with very large windows, serves average Bulgarian fare. A three-course meal costs $1.50 to $2 here. Open daily from 7am to 11pm, with music in the evening.

2 Koprivshtitsa

80 miles E of Sofia

GETTING THERE • By Train Trains running from Sofia to Burgas stop at the Koprivshtitsa station 12 miles away from town (19 lv/65¢). An express train takes 1½ hours, and a regular train takes; 2¼ hours. Koprivshtitsa can be a day trip from Sofia; catch the 7:05am express, which arrives at the Koprivshtitsa station at 8:40am.

From the station, a bus (5 lv/18¢) will take you into town. Return bus schedules are posted at the town bus station.

• By Bus From Sofia, it takes three hours.

ESSENTIALS Koprivshtitsa is a peanut-sized town so you shouldn't have much trouble finding your way around. Your first stop should be at the museum ticket office. The telephone area code is 997184.

SPECIAL EVENTS Once every five years Koprivshtitsa hosts a folklore festival, with locals in traditional dress and folk dance and music performances. The next festival is scheduled for August 1996.

To see how Bulgarians lived a century ago just as they were emerging from Turkish occupation, don't miss Koprivshtitsa, a well-preserved museum town. The street layouts, homes, and monuments remain largely as they were in the time of the Bulgarian National Revival of the 19th century.

Nestled in a spectacular valley in the Sredna Gora mountain range, Koprivshtitsa (pop. 2,000) emanates a serenity and storybook charm that mask its turbulent past and the pivotal role that it played in the 19th century as the hotbed of conspiracy against five centuries of Turkish oppression. The revolt against the Ottoman occupation began here in April 1876 when two revolutionaries, Todor Kableshkov and Georgi Benkovski, organized and led fellow patriots to storm Turkish headquarters in the town. Their homes and those of other patriots—the poet Dimcho Debelyanov, the writer Lyuben Karavelov, the merchant Oslekov, and other notables in Bulgarian society of the period—have been carefully restored and are open to the public.

Koprivshtitsa shows off not only the Bulgarian artistic revival of the time, but also its economic growth. An important craft (especially textiles) center, Koprivshtitsa helped form the basis for a Bulgarian economy after the Turks were driven out in 1878.

WHAT TO SEE & DO

After you arrive, buy your tickets (which allow you admission to all sights for a day—for the astonishing price of 5 lv/15¢) at the museum ticket office at the entrance to the Old Town, open Tuesday through Sunday from 8am to noon and 1:30 to 5:30pm. A map showing all the historic houses costs another 20 lv (70¢). The ticket office can be difficult to find as it's poorly signed; look for a building facing the main square with a stone first floor and a cobalt blue upper story. The ticket office is in this building in a low wing to the left.

After buying your ticket, walk up the hill to the **House of Oslekov,** a splendid example of the National Revival style unique to Koprivshtitsa, with slender cypress-wood columns supporting its marvelously painted facade. The frescoes on the front are thought to have been inspired by the great cities of Constantinople and Venice, where Oslekov had traveled; when he returned home, he described what he had seen to the local artist. The interior is equally stunning, with its incredible carved-wood ceiling, sumptuous couch coverings, and weavings.

Oslekov, a rich merchant and tax collector, was one of many citizens hung by the Turks for aiding the rebels who rose up in revolt. A group of more fortunate merchants managed to save their lives and Koprivshtitsa from destruction by bribing the troops called in to quell the uprising.

There are several more houses you can enter with unique, multicolored facades, sunny balconies, and richly decorated interiors. Most have lovely gardens in their courtyards hidden behind high timber-and-stone walls. It's such an enchanting place to wander that you may fall under the spell of Koprivshtitsa's village charm and may want to stay overnight.

WHERE TO STAY

Hotel Koprivshtitsa, on other side of the river from the town museums.

☎ **0997184/21-82.** Telex 22998. 30 rms in the hotel (all with bath), 25 rms in old-style houses (7 with bath). **Directions:** From the museum area of town, cross the river and head slightly uphill. Look for street lamps with red and white globes.

Rates: In the hotel, 254 lv ($8.95) single, 502 lv ($17.90) double; in old-style houses, $12 double without bath, $30 double with bath.

This attractive budget hotel is surrounded by hills and offers attractive, clean hotel rooms with blond-wood furniture, as well as traditional rooms with wooden ceilings, attractive curtains, dark-wood furniture, and attractively painted walls. Although the regular hotel rooms have alluring views across the valley, I prefer the old-style rooms located in separate wooden houses down the hill from the main hotel. No English is spoken at the hotel, but the staff are friendly. There's a restaurant and bar in the hotel. The hotel also arranges private rooms in town for 150 lv ($5.35) per person.

WHERE TO EAT

Diado Liben Cafe, across the river from the main square.

Cuisine: BULGARIAN. **Directions:** Cross the bridge from the museum ticket office.
Prices: Salads 12–18 lv (45¢–65¢); main courses 30–60 lv ($1.10–$2.15).
Open: Lunch daily noon–3pm; dinner Tues–Sun 7:30pm–11:30pm.

To complete your experience of this historic Bulgarian museum village, have a meal in this authentic National Revival–period inn. The atmosphere is friendly and a live orchestra accompanies your evening meal from May to October. The menu features Bulgarian specialties such as kavarma and mixed grill, and the ubiquitous shopska salad of cucumbers and tomatoes. The service can be slow, but the atmosphere is delightful.

3 Veliko Turnovo

150 miles NE of Sofia, 119 miles NE of Plovdiv, 141 miles W of Varna

GETTING THERE • By Plane Veliko Turnovo is serviced by the airport in Gorna Orechovitza, almost five miles away. Flights from Sofia are not very regular and take 45 minutes.

Buses into Veliko Turnovo usually connect up with arriving flights.

• By Train From Sofia, take the train ($4^1/_2$ hours) to Gorna Orechovitza, about five miles away on the primary international route, for 78 lv ($2.80) in first class, 55 lv

($1.95) in second class. Express trains are 30 minutes faster and cost 9 lv (30¢) more. There's bus service from Gorna Orechovitza to Veliko Turnovo.

From the train station at Gorna Orechovitza, go out the main entrance and walk straight ahead; keep to the right past a small market to the first intersection with a main road—not more than a 5- to 10-minute walk. To your right you'll see the bus stop where you'll buy your 3 lv (10¢) ticket and board bus no. 10 to the middle of Veliko Turnovo, about a 40-minute ride. Buses leave every 20 minutes from 5:40am to 10:40pm.

There are also a few direct trains from Sofia to Veliko Turnovo, but they're painfully slow (about 6½ hours) as the train meanders through the hills.

• **By Bus** In the summertime, new private bus lines run convenient and inexpensive daily expresses from Sofia to Varna that stop in Veliko Turnovo. The journey takes about four hours and costs about 35 to 40 lv ($1.10 to $1.55). Consult the Balkantourist office in Sofia for the precise schedule.

• **By Car** Veliko Turnovo is approximately in the center of Bulgaria, but because of steep slopes only one north–south highway runs through town. Parking can be difficult; park either by the 16-story Hotel Etur on Ivailo Street, or at the train station and take the bus into town.

ESSENTIALS Veliko Turnovo's telephone area code is 62.

INFORMATION The **Yantra Tourist Agency,** located in the same building as the Hotel Etur at 2 Ivailo St. (☎ **21-5-45**), is Balkantourist's privatized successor. It's open Monday to Friday from 9am to noon and from 1:30 to 6pm. Yantra's staff rents private rooms, sells maps, and provides guide services and excursions to neighboring towns that you might like to visit, like Arbanassi, Gabrovo, and Etur. If you happen to be in Veliko Turnovo in early June and wish to take in a day during the Rose Festival in Kazanluk (about 64 miles away), you can book a day excursion here. Ask them about the schedule of buses to Sofia and to Varna on the Black Sea coast.

TRAVEL SERVICES The Balkan Airlines office is in the Hotel Etur at 2 Ivailo St. (☎ **21-545**), open Monday through Friday from 8am to 8pm and on Saturday from 8am to 4pm.

There's a post office and phone bureau at 1 Khristo Botev St., open Monday through Friday from 7am to 9pm and on Saturday and Sunday from 8am to noon and 1:30 to 8pm.

CITY LAYOUT The early Bulgarians who founded Veliko Turnovo chose a well-protected site for the castle and town walls, on a piece of land that's almost entirely surrounded by steep cliffs bordering the Yantra River. The rest of Veliko Turnovo expanded west from the Old City and spreads over what little valley bottom there is.

Think of the town as a sideways S, with the main commercial district on the west side of the S. As you move east, you pass the main park, restaurants, the older part of town, and ancient fortification sights. The main street running through town is called Vasil Levski, which turns into Georgi Dimitrov (which will be renamed); then for a short distance it becomes Dimitur Blagoev, and finally Nikola Pikolo. Parallel streets above and below this main street are connected to it by staircases built into the hillside.

GETTING AROUND One of the great charms of Veliko Turnovo is the 30-minute walk on this winding main street across town or one of the streets below, for you frequently have sweeping panoramas of the hills. If, however, you're in a hurry to get from one part of town to the other, you can take any bus along the main street. The buses run from 4am to midnight. Taxis congregate by the war memorial near the post office.

Veliko Turnovo (pop. 50,000) is one of Bulgaria's most pleasant towns, with quaint streets and cafés and stunning panoramic views of mountains and valleys. Capital of Bulgaria during the greatest years of the Bulgarian Empire (1185–1396, known as the second Bulgarian kingdom), the city boasts some of the most important medieval fortifications in the country, a charming collection of 19th-century buildings, and a large student population.

Veliko Turnovo has a long history of opposition to foreign invaders. In 1185 the brothers Piotr and Assen began a successful insurrection against the Byzantine Empire; two years later the state of Bulgaria was reestablished in the Second Bulgarian Empire.

In 1393, Veliko Turnovo unsuccessfully battled the Ottoman Turks, who then began almost 500 years of subjugation. One cannot view the town fortifications and the broad expanse of cliffs without immediately noticing the immense difficulties any attacker would have faced. The three-month Ottoman Turk siege of 1393 was a brutal one, and after its capture, Veliko Turnovo was burned to the ground.

WHAT TO SEE & DO

 **Tsarevets [Castle of the Tsar],** on Tsarevets Hill. ☎ **38-848** for the guide office, **37-868** for the church.

First fortified in the 6th century by the Byzantines, who knew a commanding position when they saw one, Tsarevets Hill became the royal center of the Second Bulgarian Kingdom in 1185. It housed the royal family and the nation's highest clergy until 1393, when the Turks destroyed the castle and the kingdom along with it. Although archeological excavations began in the 1930s, lack of money has left them still incomplete. But the fortifications—some restored, some still in ruins—and the sweeping mountaintop panoramas make the hill well worth a visit.

Near the summit is the **Holy Assumption Patriarchal Church,** once the religious center of the royal compound. This ancient church has been completely restored based on original plans and drawings. The interior is embellished with a set of haunting, expressionistic murals, painted from 1962 to 1986 by artist Teofan Sokerov.

Also on the fortifications hill to the southeast is the restored **Baldwin Tower,** named after Baldwin of Flanders, a Crusader who died here after his capture in 1205. To the north is **Execution Rock,** from which prisoners, traitors, and even a church patriarch were thrown to their deaths.

Near the entrance you can hire an English-speaking guide for 30 to 50 lv ($1.10 to $1.80).

A second important, but not extensively restored, defensive ridge across from the Tsarevets in Veliko Turnovo is the **Trapezitza,** with ruins of palaces and chapels of the boyars, the Bulgarian nobility who shared this hill with merchants and artisans when the tsars ruled from Tsarevets.

Admission: 50 lv ($1.80) adults, 25 lv (90¢) students.

Open: Apr–Oct, daily 8am–noon and 1–7pm; Nov–Mar, daily 9am–noon and 1–4:40pm.

Museum of the National Revival and Constituent Assembly, on Saedinenie Sq. ☎ **29-8-21.**

Bulgaria's answer to Independence Hall, this former town hall witnessed in 1879 both the signing of Bulgaria's first constitution and the first session of its National Assembly. On the upper floors, a reconstruction of the assembly chamber and displays of documents commemorate these events. But the greatest attraction of the museum is downstairs, where hundreds of 17th- and 18th-century icons—taken from monasteries near Veliko Turnovo—show the great range of styles used by Bulgaria's artists. There are also cases of jewelry and tools from the National Revival period.

Admission: 25 lv (90¢).

Open: Daily 8am–noon and 1–5pm. **Directions:** From the Hotel Yantra, follow Velcho Dzamdshiyata and then Ivan Vasov to the square.

WHERE TO STAY

For maximum savings, rent a private room at the **Yantra Tourist Agency,** in the Hotel Etur at 2 Ivailo St. (☎ **21-5-4**), open daily from 8am to 6pm. They'll find you a double room for $3.50 per person in the summer and $3.80 in the winter.

$ **Etur Hotel,** 2 Ivailo St. ☎ **062/21-838.** 108 rms (72 with bath), and 12 apartments. TEL **Directions:** Walk down the main street to Khristo Botev and then turn left on Ivailo, the side street.

Rates: $8 single without bath, $15 single with bath; $16 double without bath, $30 double with bath; $34 apartment. DC, JCB, V.

Despite its somewhat run-down condition, this best budget hotel in town has many advantages. The rooms are quite large, there's a tourist information agency and an exchange bureau in the lobby, and the bus on the Sofia–Varna route stops here. Some English and German are spoken. All the rooms in this 16-story glass-and-concrete tower are basically the same. The bathrooms in the rooms have a toilet and sink with a shower hose attached, but there's no shower stall to allow you to take areal shower. The hall bathrooms have showers mounted on the walls. The apartments are only slightly more spacious than the ordinary doubles, but the beds are placed side-to-side rather than toe-to-toe.

Try to get a room on one of the upper floors—the views are terrific. It's lively, with lots of young people. There's an inexpensive restaurant and outdoor café in the summer.

Hotel Belitza, 2 Gurko St. ☎ **062/22-5-17.** 5 rms. 1 apartment (none with bath).

Rates: 180 lv ($6.50) single; 320 lv ($11.20) double; 420 lv ($15) triple; 460 lv ($16.50) apartment.

This small private hotel is in an old building on lovely, cobblestoned Gurko Street, close to the main street. The rooms, furniture, and common areas are all very well maintained and up to Western European standards. The apartment has two beds and a separate sitting area with a TV. Like some of the other rooms, the apartment commands a view of the river. The manager speaks French and Russian.

Hotel Yantra, 1 Velchova Zavera Sq. ☎ **062/20-3-91.** Fax 062/21-8-07. 75 rms (all with bath). **Bus:** 15 from the train station, then bus no. 7.

Rates: $12 single; $20 double.

A notch or two above the Etur in both condition and location; this hotel has rooms that are tidy and in good shape, if a bit small and drab. Some of the rooms have spectacular views of the surrounding steep hills. The bathrooms are cramped and have hand-held showers. The restaurant terrace has terrific views and only decent food. You can get a view of the action on Old Town Square from the coffee shop where the windows were the cleanest I've seen anywhere in Bulgaria.

Turisticheski Dom Trapezitsa, 79 Stefan Stambolov. ☎ **062/22-0-61.** 30 rms (all with bath).

Rates: 260 lv ($9.25) single; 350 lv ($12.75) double; 400 lv ($14.25) triple; 550 lv ($19.50) quad. A bed in a shared room, hostel-style, costs 176 lv ($6.25), with a discount for holders of hostel cards.

A large youth-hostel sign (a cabin with a fir tree) in front draws in students, who compose this hotel's core clientele. The location on Veliko Turnovo's main street is a mixed blessing: It's very convenient but can be a bit noisy. The rooms are Spartan and the mattresses are saggy. But wood furniture adds some charm, and many of the rooms have great views of the river. The bathrooms are clean, with curtainless showers. Russian and German are spoken at the reception.

In Arbanassi

★ **Hotel Zagorie,** in Arbanassi, two miles from Veliko Turnovo. ☎ **062/30-1-33.** Fax 062/23-5-60. 4 rms. 2 apartments. **Directions:** Take a bus from Iskra Square or a taxi to the hotel.

Rates: $30 single; $60 double; $70 apartment.

To stay in this unique and popular private hotel, you must make reservations (get in touch from abroad by writing or faxing well in advance). It's situated in a beautiful setting with spectacular views and is open year round. It was highly recommended to me by several foreigners who stayed there. It used to be a summer residence for Ministry of the Interior officials (the Bulgarian KGB) and was one of the first hotels to be privatized (acquired by auction and renovated) in Bulgaria. Its pleasant rooms have blond furniture and clean tiled bathrooms. The apartments have two bedrooms, with two beds, and a drawing room. There's a day bar, a pool room, and an open terrace garden in the summer. The restaurant features good home-cooked food.

Off-season, you might try booking and arranging transportation through their textile shop on Velchova Zavera Square in Veliko Turnovo (☎ **2-20-83**).

WHERE TO EAT

Hotel Yantra, 1 Velchova Zavera Sq. ☎ **20-391.**

Cuisine: BULGARIAN. **Bus:** 7 or 11 stops nearby.
Prices: Salads 5–9 lv (18¢–30¢); main courses 10–50 lv (35¢–$1.80); desserts 4–16 lv (14¢–60¢). AE, DC, MC, V.
Open: Daily 8am–11pm.

Have lunch on the outdoor terrace for its fabulous views of the Tsarevets's Hill and Trapezitsa Hill. The menu (with English translation) is large and features daily specials (only in Bulgarian) such as kavarma kebab (meat stew in a clay pot), steak with egg, and pork with mushrooms. While the food is not spectacular, the views from the terrace are. A large and filling lunch can be enjoyed here for under $2. It's a very busy place, but the service is efficient.

$ **Sukhindol,** 14 Marmarchev St. ☎ **34-7-94.**

Cuisine: BULGARIAN PUB. **Directions:** From the Hotel Yantra at Pl. Velchova, walk up the steps to the tiny Marmarchev Street.

Prices: Salads 8–10 lv (29¢–35¢); main courses 13–28 lv (50¢–$1).

Open: Lunch Mon–Fri 11:30am–2pm; dinner Mon–Fri 5:30–10pm.

We found this place full of university students and locals by following some well-heeled Bulgarians down into a smoky basement pub. It's a lively, cavelike stone tavern with rough-hewn wood pillars and beamed ceilings; the tables look a bit dirty thanks to heavily stained table linen. The menu, available in English, offers a small selection of grilled meat dishes, red wines, and good beer. A full lunch with garnishes and strong beer runs less than $2.

A Coffee Bar

Umbria, 15 Vasil Levski St.

Cuisine: DESSERT.

Prices: Espresso 4 lv (14¢); fancy coffees 6–12 lv (21¢–40¢); tortes 12–19 lv (40¢–70¢); sundaes 20–45 lv (70¢–$1.60).

Open: Daily 8am–10pm.

The spacious interior of this jazzy Italian café is enlivened by large green plants and mirrors embellished with colorful hand-drawn patterns. Coffees and tortes (which sell for half price after 9pm) are tasty and artfully presented. Picture windows and outdoor seating both provide good opportunities for people-watching.

SHOPPING

After you've seen the major sights in town, take a walk along Manarchev Street and its continuation, Rakovski Street, a cobblestone lane lined with charming 18th- and 19th-century houses, which begins near the Yantra Hotel at Velchova Zavera Square. Here you can watch artisans like potters, goldsmiths, and weavers engage in traditional crafts as they have for hundreds of years. Their work is for sale and makes wonderful gifts. At Rakovski 19, a small antique shop sells coins, medals, and all sorts of jewelry, including 19th-century betrothal bracelets. The shops open their wooden shutters Monday through Friday from about 9am to 6pm and sometimes on Saturday mornings.

At the end of Rakovski, you can marvel at the scenery from the outdoor terrace of the café Busco, a good spot for viewing the surrounding hills.

For prints by instructors at Veliko Turnovo's art school, inquire at the shop in the art museum, located on the peninsula formed by the river's bend, across the bridge from the Hotel Veliko Turnovo. The art museum, itself, is worth a look.

NEARBY EXCURSIONS

ARBANASSI When visiting Veliko Turnovo, don't miss Arbanassi, two miles away, a beautiful little hilltop village of restored white stone homes. It was first settled in the 15th century by Albanian immigrants who were trying to escape from the Turks.

Arbanassi thrived as a commercial center in the 16th and 17th centuries, and 50 houses from this era remain. Two of these have been restored and furnished with original pieces and—along with two churches from the same era—are open to visitors. Of these buildings, the most remarkable is the ★ **Church of the Birth of Christ.** Built from 1632 to 1649 during Muslim rule, the exterior is intentionally inconspicuous. But inside is a small Chartres, with hundreds of colorful frescoes blanketing the walls and ceilings, depicting thousands of saints.

The museum buildings are open from April through October. On Tuesdays and Wednesdays, one church and one house are open. These buildings close on Wednesdays and Thursdays, while the other church and house open. All four museum buildings are open on Saturdays and Sundays.

To get to Arbanassi, take the bus leaving about every half hour from Iskra Square in Veliko Turnovo. A small kiosk in the center of town sells admission tickets: 25 lv (90¢) for all the sites in the village. It's open Tuesday through Sunday 9am to noon and 1 to 5:30pm, until 6pm in the summer. You can arrange for an English-language tour of the town by calling **30-2-29.** For food or lodging, head to the Hotel Zagorie (see "Where to Stay," above).

GABROVO Gabrovo is home to one of the most unusual museums in Eastern Europe, the **House of Humor,** 68 Brianska (☎ **27-229**). The museum displays paintings, cartoons, photos, prints, and other art portraying satirical and humorous images.

How is it that Gabrovo came to host this museum? "Gabrovans were famous in the past for their inventiveness in saving money, which resulted in many jokes," says museum director Stefan Furtunov. The museum was originally founded to catalog these jokes, and then rapidly expanded.

During odd-numbered years, the museum sponsors the **International Biennial of Humor and Satire in the Arts,** a week-long festival in mid-May with some 3,000 international participants displaying humorous images, the best of which are displayed in the museum until the next Biennial.

The museum is open Tuesday through Sunday from 9am to noon and 1:30 to 5:30pm; admission is 25 lv (90¢), 2 lv (7¢) for students. At the gift shop downstairs you can buy various practical jokes made of pottery (such as a spoon with a hole at the center so that a penurious host offering coffee or tea can save money on sugar), as well as a book of jokes in English called *Gabrovo Anecdotes.*

Buses leave every hour from Veliko Turnovo 31 miles away and take about 45 minutes.

ETUR Built only in 1964, Etur is a remarkable tourist attraction—a re-creation of a typical 19th-century village. Many of the houses here function as traditional workshops, with artisans using 19th-century techniques, similar to Colonial Williamsburg, Virginia. You can see metalworking, weaving, hat making, copper bell forging, carpentry, and other crafts. You can also buy some of the goods at various shops. It's very popular with tourists in the summer, so be prepared for crowds.

To get here from Gabrovo, five miles away, take trolleybus no. 32 to the last stop and then change to bus no. 7 or 8. It's open daily from 8am to noon and 12:45 to 6pm. Admission is 30 lv ($1.05) for adults 1 lv (4¢) for students, free for everyone on Mondays. Call **42-927** or **42-023** for information.

4 Plovdiv

97 miles SE of Sofia, 119 miles SW of Veliko Turnovo

GETTING THERE • By Train An express from Sofia takes about two hours, at a cost of 50 lv ($1.80) in first class, 37 lv ($1.30) in second. An express from Burgas takes about four hours.

From the train station on the south side of town, take trolley no. 2 or bus no. 26 into town.

• **By Bus** A deluxe express bus from Sofia gets you to Plovdiv in less than two hours for 25 lv (90¢). It leaves from the Balkantourist office at 1 Vitosha Blvd. daily at 7am and 4pm, and returns the same day at 10am and 7pm.

ESSENTIALS Plovdiv's telephone area code is 032.

INFORMATION Balkantourist, at 19 Noyemvri Square (☎ **55-38-48**), in an arcade above the Roman Stadium, will book rooms and provide some information about the town. They are open in summer daily from 8am to 5pm and from Monday through Friday the rest of the year. There is another Balkantourist office at 106 Bulgaria Blvd. (☎ **55-28-07;** fax 55-51-42), across the river from the Old Town. English-language maps and brochures are sold in many of the city's museums and by some street vendors in Trimontium.

TRAVEL SERVICES For a taxi, call **5-27-36** or **142.** For train tickets, go to the Rila Bureau of Voyage in the center of town at 13 Gourko, at the corner of Alexander I (☎ **22-27-29**). Bulgarian Airlines is at 4 Vazrazhdane Blvd. (☎ **23-30-81**). The post office and telephone bureau, open daily from 6am to 7pm, is located off Vazrazhdane Blvd. at the beginning of Alexander I Street.

CITY LAYOUT The Maritsa River divides Plovdiv into a modern section to the north and the historic section to the south. Vazrazhdane Boulevard is a major thoroughfare that connects the two sections across a bridge. On the south side of town, the charming traditional district Trimontium lies to the east of Vazrazhdane Blvd. (and partly over it, as Vazrazhdane runs through a tunnel), or to your right when facing the river. You'll notice that Trimontium really is located on three green hills, so you'll have to hike up to find Plovdiv's most interesting section. Two blocks parallel to Vazrazhdane Blvd. to the west lies Alexander I Street, the town's main shopping mall and promenade, which is usually crowded, especially in the evening. Alexander I is bounded to the north by 19 Noyemvri Square, site of the Roman stadium, and to the south by Central Square, site of the central post office and fragments of an ancient Roman forum.

Finding an Address The old street signs in Plovdiv don't reflect the new street name changes. The following list of main downtown street and square name changes may help you decipher old maps (alphabetized by the first letter of former name): Georgi Dimitrov Boulevard = Vazrazhdane Boulevard; Moskva Boulevard = Bulgaria Boulevard; 9 Septemvri Square = Central Square; Sacho Dimitrov Street = Gladston Street; Vasil Kolarov Street = Alexander I Street; and Maxim Gorki Street = Suborna.

SPECIAL EVENTS The city hosts two international trade fairs: in May, the International Spring Fair of Consumer Goods and in October, the International Autumn Fair of Machinery and Technology.

The annual calendar is filled with numerous art and music festivals. During June and September the International Chamber Music Festival features performances in churches and houses across old Plovdiv. In June, September, and October there's the Festival of Arts in Old Plovdiv, with theater, opera, and ballet performances in Trimontium. Operas are performed in the Roman theater with its unique atmosphere and extraordinary acoustics. Additionally, concerts are held in the garden in front of the Ethnographic Museum in June and September.

Plovdiv (pop. 390,000) ranks as Bulgaria's second city in size, and in economic and cultural importance. Straddling the Maritsa River and the seven hills that rise out of the vast, agriculturally significant Thracian valley, Plovdiv is also a very ancient city. Some archaeologists claim that it's one of the oldest cities in Europe—a primitive settlement dating back 7,000 years has been unearthed there. Philip of Macedon, Alexander the Great's father, made the settlement a city, which he modestly named Philippopolis. Under Roman rule for several centuries, it was the prosperous city of Trimontium (Three Mountains); one ancient inscription called it "the most brilliant metropolis in the province of Thrace."

Situated on a crossroad between the Danube and the Aegean, and an important trade route linking Europe with Asia, it developed as a significant trade and cultural center. It continues to be, hosting two major annual trade fairs and several music and arts festivals. An area blessed by a mild climate, this valley is Bulgaria's most fertile farming region.

Once you reach ★ **Trimontium,** the historic heart of Plovdiv, you'll be able to trace several major historical periods in its remarkable monuments. Antiquity, the Middle Ages, and the period of the Bulgarian National Revival (18th and 19th centuries) coexist here in picturesque harmony. Its Roman ruins include a stunningly well preserved marble theater unearthed about 20 years ago as well as a stadium. Cobblestone streets, mostly free of automobiles, wind their way up three hills lined with elaborately embellished Bulgarian Renaissance period houses and churches, creating an altogether charming and peaceful atmosphere. And along Suborna (formerly Maxim Gorki), some of the most pleasant cafés in Bulgaria offer refreshment and calm in their enclosed gardens.

But Trimontium is by no means merely an exquisite open-air architectural museum with excellent restaurants. More than 4,500 people live in it and many of the houses have been turned into studios for artists and performers. There's an art school and a branch of the Bulgarian Academy of Music here.

WHAT TO SEE & DO

A Stroll Through Plovdiv

Begin on Central Square, site of the central post office, the large Trimontium Hotel, and the Forum of Philippopolis, which shows off scattered 3rd-century A.D. Roman ruins. Then continue up Alexander I, a pedestrian avenue at the heart of modern Plovdiv, filled with stores, shoppers, and strollers. At the end of the street is 19 Noyemvri Square, site of a fragment of the Roman stadium, which you'll see far below the current ground level at the center of the square. On the right side of the square is a Turkish mosque.

From there, turn right on Suborna and head up into Trimontium, where streets are lined with typical Bulgarian homes of the 19th century with the second floor overhanging the ground floor and sometimes the third overhanging the second. This enabled builders to create more living space on narrow streets and the homeowner to pay less in taxes, for the government levied property taxes according to the size of the land below. On the first floor you'll observe large stones cemented together, and on the second, painted stucco facades in such colors as pale yellow or dark gray. The houses of the more affluent are recognizable by the ornate patterns or decorations on the second floor.

When wandering in Trimontium, visit the Museum of the National Revival and the National Liberation Struggles, the Balabanov House, and the Ethnographic

Museum. From the Ethnographic Museum, head north on Chomakov Street to the hilltop (Nebet Tepe) overlooking all of Plovdiv. Here you'll also see 6th- to 2nd-century B.C. ruins from an early settlement in Plovdiv.

Leaving the best for last, go to the southernmost part of Trimontium and finish with a visit to the stunning Roman theater.

Museums and Other Sights

 **Roman Theater,** on Djoumaya Sq. in Trimontium.

Don't miss this stunning 3rd-century marble Roman theater, one of the best preserved of its kind. The theater was only uncovered about 20 years ago, helping account for its remarkable condition. Located on the edge of a hill in Trimontium, high above the entrance to the Vazrazhdane tunnel below, the seats have a fine vantage point over the surrounding area as well as the stage. Concerts are frequently held here in June and September, and locals say that the acoustics are remarkable.

Admission: Free.

Open: Daily 24 hours. **Directions:** Walk down Tsar Ivailo Street in Trimontium.

Roman Stadium, 19 Noyemvri Sq.

Located at the end of Plovdiv's most bustling pedestrian promenade, this 2nd-century Roman ruin is oddly displayed at the center of a busy modern square. It's far below the current street level and a bit hard to see, but it's still exciting if you can imagine that a Roman city once existed around it.

Admission: Free.

Open: Daily 24 hours. **Directions:** Walk to the end of Alexander I.

Ethnographic Museum, 2 Doctor Chomakov, in Trimontium. ☎ **22-56-56.**

Housed in an ornate structure from 1847, this museum displays mostly 18th- and 19th-century Bulgarian National Revival art and folk objects. The collection includes ceramic bowls, pots, tools, costumes, shepherd's bells, farming tools, musical instruments, and paintings of old Plovdiv. A few rooms illustrate typical living conditions of the 19th century. In summer, concerts are held in the garden in front of the museum.

Admission: 20 lv (70¢) adults, 5 lv (18¢) students.

Open: Tues–Thurs and Sat–Sun 9am–noon and 2–5pm, Fri 2–5pm. **Directions:** Walk north up Suborna Street in Trimontium.

Archeological Museum, 1 Suedinenie Sq. ☎ **22-43-39.**

A small museum of just four rooms, with objects from ancient Greece and Rome. Unfortunately, the star attraction, the Panagurishte gold treasure, a wine set from the 3rd century B.C. illustrating scenes from Greek mythology, is a 1973-made replica; the not-to-be-missed original is in Sofia. The other rooms have some ancient Greek vases, but in all the collection is a bit pale in comparison to Sofia's stunning National Museum of History. Unfortunately, the museum descriptions are only in Bulgarian.

Admission: 20 lv (70¢) adults, 5 lv (18¢) students.

Open: Tues–Thurs and Sat–Sun 9am–12:30pm and 2–5:30pm, Fri 2–5pm. **Bus:** 37 from Central Square.

Balabanov House, 57 Stamat Matanov St., in Trimontium. ☎ **23-70-82.**

A typical Bulgarian house of a 19th-century merchant, it serves today as an art gallery with works by some of Bulgaria's best 20th-century artists; part of the museum accommodates changing exhibitions.

Admission: 20 lv (70¢) adults, 5 lv (18¢) students.

Open: Daily 9am–noon and 1–4:30pm. **Directions:** Walk one block west from the Ethnographic Museum.

WHERE TO STAY

PRIVATE ROOMS **Balkantourist** (see "Information," above), rents private rooms for $6 single and $8 double, plus a $1 heating charge from October 15 to April 15. Private rooms really are the best alternative in Plovdiv, especially if you can get one in Trimontium, since most of the two-star hotels are below standard and quite uninviting, while the upscale ones are expensive, with minimal discounts available. A note of advice: Avoid going to Plovdiv during the Spring and Fall International Trade Fairs, unless you're specifically interested in attending them, because accommodations are difficult to find and much more expensive during these times.

Hotels

Hotel Leipzig, 70 Ruski Blvd., Plovdiv. ☎ **032/23-24-70.** Fax 032/45-3160. 130 rms (all with bath). TEL **Directions:** Bus no. 12 or 16 from the train station, or walk four blocks north on Ruski Boulevard.

Rates (including breakfast): 650 lv ($23.25) single; 900 lv ($32.15) double.

A 15-minute walk to Trimontium and a 10-minute walk from the train station, the eight-story Leipzig offers small rooms with large wall-to-wall windows, desks with mirrors, and showers in the bathrooms. The singles were recently renovated and in general the rooms are in good condition. There's also a hotel restaurant with evening music and a bar, entered around the corner. English is spoken at the desk.

Hotel Bulgaria, 13 Patriark Evtimii Blvd. ☎ **032/22-60-64.** Fax 032/22-62-64. 78 rms, 3 apartments (all with bath). TEL **Directions:** From Central Square, walk two blocks north on Alexander I and turn right.

Rates (including breakfast): $25 single; $38 double; $40 apartment. AE, DC, MC, V.

The Bulgaria is a plain 50s-style hotel with equally plain but adequate rooms with small showers. Its best feature is its central location facing the large town square, off Alexander I, the main traffic-free shopping street, a beehive of activity. (If the Bulgaria is full, you might try one of the lesser-known two-star hotels along this street.) A clean lobby with lots of plants greets you here, and the halls are light and airy. For more room, more light, side-to-side beds, and other comforts, rent an apartment. English is spoken at the desk.

WHERE TO EAT

The Puldin, 3 Knyaz Tseretelev St., in Trimontium. ☎ **23-17-20.**

Cuisine: BULGARIAN. **Reservations:** Recommended. **Directions:** From 19 Noyemvri Sq., walk up Suborna Street and take the third right.

Prices: Salads 25–40 lv (90¢–$1.40); main courses 45–180 lv ($1.60–$6.40); desserts 35–40 lv ($1.25–$1.40). AE, DC, MC, V.

Open: Lunch daily 11am–3pm; dinner daily 6:30–11:30pm.

One of the most memorable restaurants in all of Bulgaria. Named after the early Slavic version of one of Plovdiv's many names, the Puldin is built on the ruins of the 2,000-year-old Roman fortress walls that once encircled ancient Trimontium. Whether you have dinner by candlelight on a balcony overlooking the ruins and the large mural in the main dining hall, or have lunch outdoors in the summer garden, you'll be eating in a unique setting. In the evenings, the excellent piano-and-violin duo play everything from Chopin waltzes to jazz tunes. The English-language menu lists only typical Bulgarian veal and pork specialties, but when I last ate there, a blackboard near the entryway listed several fish and chicken dishes. The choice of local wines is excellent, including a 1986 mavrud from Assenovgrad for $1.50. If all you're in the mood for is a strong cup of Turkish coffee with dessert, visit their Turkish café and try the baklava. In the evenings there's also a disco and a bar.

★ **Ritora (Wine Vessel),** Tsar Ivailo St. ☎ **22-20-93.**

Cuisine: CAFE/BULGARIAN. **Directions:** Walk north from the Roman amphitheater.
Prices: Sandwiches and snacks 15–20 lv (55¢–70¢); main courses 30–100 lv ($1.10–$3.50); desserts 30–50 lv ($1.10–$1.80)
Open: Daily 11am–8pm.

Located in a finely restored house typical of the ornate Plovdiv National Revival style, this restaurant is beautiful inside and out. It's furnished with comfortable elegant couches and padded chairs, and adorned with brass light fixtures and a tile floor on the inside, while the exterior is embellished with ornamental stenciled frescoes. It's altogether lovely to sit in the flower-filled courtyard sipping something, especially on summer evenings when chamber music is played. It isn't just visually pleasing: the light sandwiches of cheese and ham, the ice-cream sundaes, and coffee are fresh and tasty. A very continental spot and a most delightful change from the usual heavy lunch fare.

Worth the Extra Money

★ **Restaurant Philipopol,** 56B Stamat Matanov St., in Trimontium. ☎ **22-52-96.**

Cuisine: BULGARIAN. **Reservations:** Recommended. **Directions:** From the Balabanov House, walk north (toward the river) to the very end of the street.
Prices: Salads 50–60 lv ($1.40–$2); main courses about 120 lv ($4.25), more for items like salmon; desserts 40–50 lv ($1.40–$1.75).
Open: Daily 11am–2am.

This privately owned restaurant, opened in 1991, is a standout. When I sat in the whitewashed courtyard or on one of the terraces of this beautiful retreat, I felt as if I were in Florence. The setting is elegant down to the smallest detail: wicker chairs, soft lighting, and a good scattering of geraniums and other plants. The menu, available in English, has superb versions of Bulgarian dishes. The *burik* (a red pepper and white cheese fritter) was as good as it gets. The food is garnished as if it were competing for the cover of a cooking magazine, and it tastes as good as it looks.

EASY EXCURSIONS

BACHKOVO MONASTERY Second in importance and size after Rila, this monastery is situated on the bank of the Chepelarska River about 17 miles (28km) from Plovdiv. Originally founded in 1083, it was destroyed during the Ottoman conquest of Bulgaria in the early 15th century and rebuilt by the end of the 16th century. It contains many treasures: icons, manuscripts, embroidered vestments, and, notably, the first recorded frescoes of the great National Revival painter, Zahari Zograf. His *Last Judgment,* over the doorway of the Church of St. Nicholas, is remarkable for its frank contents of a social nature, including portraits of local sinners—Plovdiv's uncivic-minded merchants and known ladies of leisure.

You might want to hire an English-speaking guide (30–50 lv/$1.10–$1.80 per hour) in Plovdiv for your visit to the monastery; there is little material for sale in English (although that may change by the time you arrive). If you're traveling with several people, you might want to share a guided excursion for $25; call Puldin Tours for details (☎ **55-28-07**). To get there on your own, take the bus headed to Smolyan, which runs every half hour or so from the South Bus Station (near the train station). Buses tend to be very crowded on Friday and weekends during the summer. Be sure to find out how late the buses run for your return to Plovdiv or you'll have to beg the monks to put you up for the night in the monastery.

On the way to Bachkovo or back, stop in for lunch at the **Vysokata Pesht (Tall Kiln) Restaurant,** a few miles from the monastery. Ask the bus driver to let you off. If you're driving, it's near Assenovgrad, some 15 miles from Plovdiv. Uniquely housed in a renovated lime kiln, this three-story privately run restaurant is quite popular and crowded on weekends. The food and service here are terrific, and the prices low (although the owner told us candidly that prices have recently gone up 100% for food and 25% for wine, and will probably rise again). Two of us ate a delicious roast rack of young lamb with cold rice and salad, complemented by a superb local 1982 mavrud from Brestnik, all for a total of $5 for the meal!

KAZANLUK, THE VALLEY OF THE ROSES There's an annual festival unique to Bulgaria held in Kazanluk during the last days of May through the first weeks of June. It's the **Rose Festival,** celebrating a tiny heavenly scented rose that grows in the Valley of the Roses between the Balkans and the Sredna Gora range. This valley is the source of 70% to 90% of the world's production of rose attar, a vitally important ingredient in perfume making. It takes about 2,000 of these tiny petals to make a gram of attar; a pound of extract requires 3,000 to 4,000 *pounds* of petals!

The Turks were the first to harvest roses here, using them to perfume the harems of Constantinople. Since then, dozens of villages around the area have dedicated themselves to growing roses. They pick their valuable crop at the end of May and in the first half of June. The harvest culminates in the annual Festival of Roses, with parades, songs, dancing in national costume, and the coronation of the Rose King and Queen.

Since there are few hotels in the area and the existing ones are usually crowded with Rose Festival participants, it's best to come to the festival on a day trip from Plovdiv (50 miles), Veliko Turnovo (64 miles), or the Black Sea coast resorts. The excursions usually depart very early in the morning in time for rose-picking ceremonies. They are arranged by Balkantourist or local tourist agencies and cost $30 to $50, depending on the distance.

5 Bansko

60 miles S of Sofia, 69 miles SW of Plovdiv

GETTING THERE • By Bus Bansko has direct service from Sofia, three hours away, several times per day. There is also one bus per day from Plovdiv and frequent service from Blagoevgrad.

ESSENTIALS The telephone area code is 07443.

ORIENTATION From the main entrance of the bus station, walk up the steps to the road, turn left, and walk one block. Follow the signs to the skiing center and you will be walking south on Todor Alexandrov. This street will take you to Ploshad Demokratsia, the center of town.

INFORMATION Elena Ltd. (see "Where to Stay," below) sells an English-language brochure called "Bansko: the Best Kept Secret of Bulgaria" for 40 lv ($1.40). It contains a map of town, a trail map of the Pirin Mountains, and advertisements for local restaurants.

GETTING AROUND In the ski season, buses run from the bus station to the slopes. Off-season, you will probably have to take a taxi (find one at the station or call **26-21**) to get to the entrance of the park, about 250 lv ($8.75) each way.

Situated just outside the mountainous Pirin National Park, Bansko (pop. 12,000) serves as a base for hikers and, from December through March, downhill skiers. The town thrived in the 19th century, thanks to its location on the main land route between Greece and the rest of Europe. Its wealthy merchants supported Rila and other monasteries, and were patrons of local artists and writers, such as the four generations of Vishanovs who became icon painters. Bansko was also a center of Bulgarian nationalism, with a reputation for violence that deterred Turkish governors from even visiting.

Today, when it isn't overrun by skiers, Bansko is a quieter place, where old women congregate on the sidewalks to comb wool together. The air is scented by grapes ripening in small arbors, and almost everything shuts down from noon to 2pm. The central part of town is quite handsome, with tidy pavements, wooden signs, and numerous cafés, all left over from a facelift prior to the town's hosting the 1989 winter Balkan Games.

WHAT TO SEE & DO

In town, there are a few memorials of Bansko's past, including a **museum** in honor of Nicola Vaptsarov, a local poet and revolutionary who won international acclaim. The **Holy Trinity Church,** built in 1835, is richly decorated inside, with an iconostasis bearing works by the Vishanov family (open Saturday through Thursday from 9am to noon and 2 to 5pm). On Tsar Simeon Street, just off Ploshad Demokratsia, there is a gallery selling craft goods, all made by hand by Bansko women, and works by local artists. It is generally open Monday through Friday from 9am to noon and 2 to 5pm; if not, inquire at the Vaptsarov house on the main square.

WHERE TO STAY

Elena Ltd. (☎ **07443/51-02,** after hours **07443/28-49,** 2 Pl. Demokratsia; open Monday through Friday from 9am to noon and 2 to 6pm and Saturday from 9am to noon) arranges **private rooms**. Singles cost $8 during ski season, $6 off-season. Doubles are $15 in-season, $10 off-season. Elena Ltd. also changes money at reasonable rates and can arrange for English-speaking mountain and ski guides.

Hotel Tipis, 15 Todor Alexandrov. ☎ and fax **07443/47-64.** 10 rms (1 with bath).

Directions: The hotel is located between the bus station and the center of town.

Rates: Ski season (including breakfast) $10 single, $16 double, $21 triple. Off-season 100 lv ($3.60) per person.

Opened in 1991, this private hotel is a three-story house on a quiet residential street. The rooms are sunny, with firm mattresses, warm blankets, and flowers on the windowsills. The owner is probably one of the few people in Bansko who speaks English. Downstairs is a café that also functions as the reception.

WHERE TO EAT

Dedo Pene Inn, Al. Buynov. ☎ **50-71.**

Cuisine: BULGARIAN. **Directions:** From Ploshad Demokratsia, walk uphill and turn left at the Holy Trinity Church.

Prices: Salads 12–15 lv (40¢–90¢); main courses 30–80 lv (50¢–$2.75).

This 1820 inn achieves a rustic atmosphere—the walls are decorated with farming implements that may not be as obsolete as they appear in this not very mechanized land. On the menu are a few local specialties, like *sudzhuk* (a grilled sausage resembling an Italian sweet sausage).

6 Sandanski

78 miles S of Sofia

GETTING THERE • By Bus Direct buses from Sofia to Sandanski run five times per day. The trip takes about four hours and costs 35 lv ($1.25).

• By Train Arriving in Sandanski by train from Sofia is less convenient, since the station is a good distance outside of town and you will have to take a bus or taxi to get to the center.

ESSENTIALS The telephone area code is 0746.

ORIENTATION The main axis of Sandanski is tree-lined Svoboda Street, which feeds into the central Ploshad Bulgaria and then continues north as Makedonia Street.

Less than 10 miles, as the crow files, from the Greek border, Sandanski enjoys milder winters and suffers hotter summers (up to 110°F) than most of Bulgaria. The town's warm climate and reputedly therapeutic hot springs have attracted visitors for decades.

The town is fairly small. Here prices are low, English is rare, and Americans are something of a curiosity, but images of Mickey Mouse and the Teenage Mutant Ninja Turtles decorate local eateries.

WHAT TO SEE & DO

At the north end of Makedonia Street is the four-star Hotel Sandanski, a favorite of Scandinavians fleeing their harsh climate. In front of the hotel is a fountain, where 176°F water bubbles up from underground and is collected in plastic bottles by city residents who are eager to benefit from its alleged healthful properties.

Surrounding the hotel is an extensive park. Playgrounds, fountains, benches, rickety footbridges, and modern sculptures give the park an air of whimsy.

At 2 Makedonia St. is the **Archeological Museum** (☎ **31-81**) where a Byzantine basilica (ca. A.D. 400–600) was discovered in 1960. Even before the site had been excavated, the town built the museum around it. Excavations are ongoing, so you'll walk across a dirt floor with half-unearthed mosaics sticking up from the surface. Picks and wheelbarrows lurk in the corners, while upstairs fragments of buildings lie around, waiting to be pieced together. This place highlights the drama of archeology.

Just around the corner from the archeology museum, is another active dig of an even richer basilica that was discovered in 1989. An unearthed, ancient street is visible from Makedonia Street, near the museum. Archeologists are still searching for the forum.

At the far end of Svoboda Street at the southern edge of town, an enormous monument to Spartacus rises out of a hillside. Spartacus, who was born nearby, led a 71 B.C. slave revolt against the Roman Republic. Under Communism the gladiator was presented as a role model for youth. This monument, mostly a series of marble steps ascending the hill, was built in 1980 to commemorate the Moscow Olympics. Since then it has suffered from decay and vandalism. At the top is a massive statue of the rebel himself—bulky and ponderous.

WHERE TO STAY

The Balkantourist staff at the Hotel Spartak (see below) arranges **private rooms** Monday through Saturday from 7am to 7pm. The charge is 60 lv ($2.10) per person per night.

Hotel Spartak, Pl. Bulgaria. ☎ **0746/24-05.** 75 rms (all with bath).

Rates: 355 lv ($12.50) single; 480 lv ($17) double.

Although it's classified as a three-star hotel because of its private baths, the Spartak offers drab rooms with scuffed furniture and rickety chairs. Broken tiles in the small bathrooms add to the worn atmosphere. But the mattresses are fine, and the location—about two blocks from the bus station and right in the center of town—is excellent.

WHERE TO EAT

El Camino, Hristo Smirnenski St. 3.

Cuisine: SPANISH/BULGARIAN. **Directions:** From the Archeological Museum, walk downhill on Hristo Smirnenski Street.

Prices: Soups and salads 15–40 lv (50¢–$1.40); main courses 35–80 lv ($1.25–$2.75); wine 40 lv ($1.40) per bottle.

Open: Daily 7:30am–midnight.

Vastly outnumbered by Bulgarian dishes the Spanish entries on the menu are worth a sampling. *Riba po ispanski* (fish Spanish-style) is tender chunks of fish served with a sauce of mushrooms, celery, and peas. The atmosphere both inside the restaurant and outdoors is quite pleasant. Recorded Spanish singing plays.

7 Melnik

7 miles E of Sandanski

GETTING THERE • By Bus Two buses (three Tuesday through Thursday) per day run from Sandanski to Melnik. You can take in Melnik as a day trip from Sandanski, but only if you catch the 5:45am bus. The trip costs 10 lv (35¢) and lasts between 45 minutes and two hours, depending on how many villages the bus stops at en route.

ESSENTIALS There is no direct-dial area code for the town.

ORIENTATION/INFORMATION The bus stops at Melnik's tiny bus station/information bureau/accommodations office, open Tuesday to Saturday from 3 to 7pm (☎ **259;** after hours **200**). From there, walk in the same direction the bus was going to reach the foot of Melnik's main street.

Melnik lies at the mouth of a sandstone gorge, and millions of years of erosion has carved the soft stone into a strange and wonderous pattern of cliffs, ridges, and pyramids. Melnik is now Bulgaria's smallest town with only 284 inhabitants. During the

17th and 18th centuries, Melnik's population, which reached a peak of 20,000, prospered from tobacco trading and producing Melnik wine. Gleaming white houses from the town's boom years and new buildings that harmonize with the old stand against the impressive natural setting.

WHAT TO SEE & DO

While several interesting sandstone formations can be seen in Melnik itself, the **pyramids of rock formations** only grow more fantastic as one goes east, up the often dry riverbed, out of town. The main trail follows the riverbed into a wooded area, where rock formations on each side tower above the trees. Eventually, about two miles outside of town, the trail climbs out of the ravine and up onto one of the ridges. The resulting panorama is as unique and breathtaking as the Swiss Alps or the Grand Canyon (though if you've been to Göreme, Turkey, it may look a bit familiar). Boulders perch on slender pillars of stone, and impossibly sharp ridgelines separate wooded vales. If you climb high enough, you can see into the next valley—not a good thing if you are afraid of heights.

The path is steep and dusty, so bring water, snacks, and good shoes or hiking boots. Unfortunately, the trail is blazed only by a couple of cairns and some litter, so it is quite easy to get diverted onto a dead-end goat trail and have to turn back, while staying on course to the monastery is hard. The early morning is a particularly good time to start, giving you plenty of time and cool morning air, while the low sun sends the rock formations into sharp relief.

In town the itself, a few buildings bear witness to Melnik's glory days. The **Kordopoulov House** (☎ **291**), near the eastern, uphill end of town, was built in 1754 for a wealthy wine merchant. His affluence found expression in such features as Venetian glass windows, several staircases, and elaborately carved ceilings. Below the house were the foundations of his wealth; you can wander through wine cellars cut right into the sandstone. The museum is open Tuesday to Sunday from 8am to noon and 1 to 5pm. Admission is 20 lv (70¢).

WHERE TO STAY

Hotel Evdokia Gurvano. ☎ **309.** 2 rms (none with bath). **Directions:** The entrance is across from the Hotel Melnik, which was closed for repairs at press time. Look for a sign in English reading SLEEPING ROOMS.

Rates: 100 lv ($3.60) per person.

This "hotel" consists of two spare rooms belonging to a very engaging woman who speaks only Bulgarian. The rooms are bright, sunny, spacious, and cheerful, with such personal touches as a large photomural of a nonsandstone mountain.

WHERE TO EAT

There are several small taverns and one restaurant in town, none particularly noteworthy. A sign reading DOMASHNO VINO means that the owner's own wine is served.

Nameless Wine Shop.

Cuisine: WINE. **Directions:** As you walk uphill, look to your left for a sign reading VINO in Cyrillic.
Prices: House wine 3 lv (10¢) per glass; various bottled vintages 30 lv ($1) per bottle.

When asked what the name of his wine shop was, the owner replied, "the shop." It's a small town, so you'll probably stumble upon it as you walk uphill. No food is served here, but this is a good place to sample the full-bodied, refreshing red wine unique to this town. Your glass is filled right out of one of the enormous barrels along the wall. The dark, cool interior of the shop will protect you from the strong midday sun.

A NEARBY EXCURSION

Three-and-a-half miles in the next valley from Melnik lies the Rozhen Monastery. Originally founded around 1300, the monastery now houses religious art in several media—wood carving, icon painting, calligraphy, and even stained glass. While it's possible to hike to the monastery from Melnik, the lack of trail markings makes this a somewhat unreliable route. If you want to be certain of reaching the monastery, take a bus from Melnik or Sandanski to the town of Rozhen. From there it is about a one-mile walk to the monastery.

Bulgaria's Black Sea Coast

11

A LONG STRETCH OF FINE SAND BEACHES WARMED BY A MEDITERRANEAN SUN, THE Bulgarian coast gives travelers to Eastern Europe the chance to add a bit of beach to their itineraries. About a fifth of the coast is occupied by big resorts like Golden Sands and Sunny Beach. Comprised of clusters of large hotels built close to the water, these towns were built after World War II. For a brief period after the fall of Communism, these resorts offered tremendous bargains, and even budget travelers could afford to stay in hotels once reserved for the ruling elite, or even in a Club Med. But the resorts are getting more expensive each year, and, already overbuilt, they aren't getting any nicer. Still, they do have their merits, and they tend to attract large group tours of Western Europeans eager for organized water sports and evening entertainment for less money than one would pay in Spain or Portugal.

Far more alluring are the many peaceful, undeveloped areas where small towns like Sozopol and Balchik still exist pretty much as they did before World War II. In a number of these villages, fishermen still take out their boats to sea in the early morning, and in the afternoon you can see them at the docks untangling their nets. A number of these seaside towns also offer art museums, from the medieval churches and 19th-century architecture in Nesebar to the ruins of Roman baths in Varna.

Although the locals debate the merits of the various beaches, those north of Varna are arguably some of the most beautiful, with dramatic cliffs and clear waters. The south holds a special appeal for those who prefer the more deserted strands and rocky coves. Singles or young people might prefer the resort towns of Albena or Sunny Beach. Families and couples may find the more secluded and modern Dyuni and Elenite holiday villages an appealing option.

You might be able to save considerably by reserving a package ahead of time, from Balkan Holidays overseas or in Sofia. If you're coming from England, Balkan Holidays Ltd. offers a round-trip flight from London to Varna, a week's hotel stay, and full board at very reasonable rates. Contact them for their "Balkan Summer Holidays" brochure at Balkan Holidays Ltd., Sofia House, 19 Conduit St., London W1R 9TD, England (☎ **071/491-4499;** fax 071/491-7068; telex 2629331).

Keep in mind that from October to about April most of the hotels and restaurants along the coast are closed, especially in the resort towns.

SEEING THE BLACK SEA COAST

GETTING THERE • By Plane The easiest way to reach the Black Sea coast is the 40-minute airplane flight from Sofia to Varna.

Call Balkan Airlines in Sofia for details (see "Travel Services" in Chapter 7). You can also fly directly via charter from London, contact Balkan Holidays in New York or London.

• By Train The train from Sofia to Varna takes 8 to 10 hours and costs 144 lv ($5.15) in first class, 100 lv ($3.50) in second class. A comfortable sleeping berth costs 50 to 60 lv ($1.80 to $2.15) more.

• By Bus Currently there's a private bus line that runs a daily bus between Sofia and Varna in the summer. It leaves from several convenient points in Sofia like the Hotel Serdika and from the Hotel Odessa in Varna. The trip takes about eight hours and costs about $3. Check at Balkantourist in Sofia or Varna about the schedule and tickets.

What's Special About Bulgaria's Black Sea Coast

Ancient Monuments
- Roman baths in Varna, Bulgaria's largest monument from antiquity.

Architectural Highlights
- Medieval churches and 18th- and 19th-century houses in Nesebar.
- Gardens and a small royal villa in Balchik.

Beaches
- Large resorts such as Albena, Sunny Beach, and Golden Sands.
- Quieter, more romantic beach villages at Elenite and Dyuni.
- Traditional fishing villages such as Sozopol and Balchik.

Museums
- Museum of History and Art in Varna, with a large collection of ancient finds and an original burial chamber.
- Naval Museum in Varna, which includes ship models and actual ships in indoor and outdoor displays.

GETTING AROUND • **By Bus** The best and most economical way to get around the coast is by bus. Frequent service connects the major coastal cities in summer, but buses fill up quickly and standing room is limited. If the bus originates at the town you're in, it's a good idea to buy your tickets as soon as possible (the day before departure in summer, earlier that day in winter). In smaller towns, however, they only sell tickets after the bus arrives and the driver announces how many seats are available.

• **By Hydrofoil** In past summers, hydrofoils and fast boats have whisked passengers between Balchik, Varna, Nesebar, Burgas, and Sozopol. The routes and schedules change each year, and it is not at all certain that this service will last much longer; you can inquire at the ferry terminals in these cities. Buses are a more reliable means of getting around.

• **By Train** A train links Varna and Burgas to the south, but the route is circuitous, taking about five hours. After Varna and Burgas the line veers inland, so it's not an option for other towns along the coast.

WHEN TO VISIT The best time to visit the Black Sea coast is in June or September, when it's sunny with temperatures averaging the mid-70s. Try to avoid July and August, when it's really crowded, but even then the enterprising traveler can find a quiet beach outside the major resorts. May and October are pleasant as well, with temperatures around 65°.

1 Varna

282 miles E of Sofia

GETTING THERE • **By Plane** The frequent flights from Sofia take only 40 minutes and cost $65 one way.

From the airport take bus no. 50 to the center; it costs 1 lv (4¢) and takes 20 to 25 minutes.

• **By Train** From Sofia the train takes 8 to 10 hours and costs 144 lv ($5.15) in first class, 100 lv ($3.50) in second class. A sleeping berth costs an additional 50 to 60 lv ($1.80 to $2.15).

To reach the center from Varna's train station (☎ **22-25-51** or **22-25-52**), exit Slavejkov Square (in front to the northeast) and walk for about 10 minutes down Vaptsarov Street (ask to make sure you're on the right street). After two blocks, Vaptsarov veers slightly to the left; continue walking along this street to reach Musala Street (site of Balkantourist) and then Kniaz Boris Boulevard.

• **By Bus** An express bus from Sofia takes about eight hours and costs $3. Vans to nearby destinations like Balchik and Golden Sands stop across the street from the cathedral, where a large concrete lean-to shelters waiting passengers. Long-distance buses to Sunny Beach, Burgas, and Sofia stop at the bus station, at the intersection of Stroga and Vladislav Varnenchick (formerly Karl Marx). Local bus 1 connects the train station, cathedral, and bus station; bus 50 also runs from the cathedral to the bus station.

ESSENTIALS Varna's telephone area code is 052.

INFORMATION Varna's most central information office remains Balkantourist, at 3 Musala St. (☎ **52/22-55-24**), a side street off Kniaz Boris (formerly Lenin) Boulevard, near Pobeda (formerly 9 Septemvri) Square. The office is open May to September, daily from 8am to 8pm; in September and October, daily from 8am to 6pm; the rest of the year, Monday through Friday from 8am to 6pm. The staff can also help you find private rooms. This office provides free, easy-to-read maps that unfortunately show the old, Communist street names. For newer maps, try the Cherno More Hotel.

TRAVEL SERVICES The Balkan Airlines office is at 15 Kniaz Boris Blvd. (☎ **22-29-48** or **22-54-08**), open daily 8am to 7pm. For flight arrival and departure information, you can also call the airport (☎ **4-42-13**).

If you're going westward by train, there are several places to buy tickets: Go to the Rila Bureau at 3 Shipka St. (☎ **22-62-88**), just across from Balkan Airlines, for international railway tickets, open Monday through Friday from 8am to 4:30pm and on Saturday from 8am to 1pm. For domestic tickets, try 27 (Dvadeseti Sedmi) Juli St. no. 13 (☎ **22-11-37**), open Monday through Friday from 8am to 5pm, or the bureau at Avram Gachev (☎ **22-30-51** or **22-30-52**), open daily from 7am to 8pm.

You can check your bags across the street from the train station at 13 Slaveikov Sq., open daily from 6am to 10:30pm with two half-hour breaks during those hours. Next to this office at 16 Slaveikov Sq. is a private rooms bureau (☎ **22-22-06**) (see "Where to Stay," below, for details).

CITY LAYOUT The streets in the center of old Varna resemble a mosaic, but thanks to a number of large avenues framing this mosaic of streets it's possible to orient yourself without too much trouble. The city borders the Black Sea, and the train and boat stations are near the main port.

Primorski Boulevard runs along this port in the center of town. If you walk about a dozen blocks down Primorski Boulevard from the train station, you'll come to Slivnitsa Boulevard (to your left), a wide pedestrian avenue perpendicular to the sea. Follow Slivnitsa Boulevard for four blocks; a lively pedestrian mall continues to the left on Kniaz Boris Boulevard. Varna's major museums, hotels, tourist agencies, and stores are all situated on and around these three major avenues.

Street signs abound, and in this cosmopolitan port they're in Latin letters as well as native Cyrillic. Main street-name changes include: Chervenoarmeiski = Primorski; Dimitar Blagoev = 8 (Osmi) Primorski Polk; Georgi Dimitrov = Slivnitsa; Karl Marx = Vladislav; Lenin = Kniaz Boris; Ploshad 9 Septemvri = Ploshad Pobeda; and Vasili Kolarov = Tsar Osvoboditel.

GETTING AROUND Buses service some of the center, but you'll do best on foot.

SPECIAL EVENTS In May you can enjoy the Choral Music Festival. From mid-June to mid-July Varna hosts the Summer International Music Festival, with symphony, ballet, opera, and chamber music performed. In July every other year is the International Ballet Contest.

Travelers to the Black Sea coast are likely to begin their visit in Varna (pop. 340,000), a lively port town that has been an important trade center for thousands of years. It was first inhabited around 600 B.C. by Greek settlers who called it Odessos. In the 4th century A.D., the Romans took over and commanded much of their regional trade from this port. Under Bulgarian rule, medieval Varna handled much of Bulgaria's foreign trade to Constantinople, Venice, and Dubrovnik. In A.D. 1393 the Turks captured Varna and used the port as a major military installation for hundreds of years.

Today Varna is a favorite for vacationers both for its rich history and for its excellent transportation connections to the rest of the Black Sea coast. The city's museums, including the Museum of History and Art and the Naval Museum, display many relics from Varna's long history. Other monuments in town include the Roman baths from antiquity. Aside from its tourist sights, Varna offers a lively holiday resort atmosphere, bustling with visitors from all the world, everyone from Albanian sailors to Vietnamese exchange students. A pedestrian shopping area runs through the center of town.

A Trivia Tidbit: In 1949 Varna was renamed "Stalin," and it was not until 1957, four years after the Soviet leader's death, that the town regained its old name.

WHAT TO SEE & DO

★ **Museum of History and Art,** 41 8 Primorski Polk near the intersection of Slivnitsa Blvd. ☎ **23-70-57.**

Varna's foremost museum, with 40,000 archeological objects, is located in a former girls' high school. This collection highlights settlements in Varna from the earliest inhabitants in the Paleolithic era until the end of Ottoman Turkish rule in the 19th century. It includes a striking 10,000-year-old burial chamber with jewelry scattered across a real skeleton. Other highlights include a remarkable gold jewelry collection, Roman-era statues of such heroes as Heracles, Roman-era marble tombstones with bas-reliefs, and 2nd- to 3rd-century marble bas-reliefs of Thracian horsemen. Upstairs there's an icon collection and frequently changing art exhibits.

Admission: 20 lv (70¢) adults, 5 lv (18¢) students; free for everyone Thurs.

Open: Tues–Sun 10am–5pm. **Directions:** Walk to the intersection of 8 Primorski Polk and Slivnitsa Boulevards, then continue across the small park area to the large institutional building.

★ **Roman Public Baths,** a city-block-wide area with its entrance at the intersection of Han Krum St. and San Stefano St.

Varna was once under the administration of Rome, and the building housing these baths is the largest public building in Bulgaria from ancient times. Coins found in the sewers date the *thermae* back to the 2nd to 3rd centuries A.D. During those years the baths served not only as a place to wash, but also as a central meeting point for the town's citizens. Today you can tour the remains of the dressing and bathing rooms, and at one point actually descend to the original level of the baths. There is some printed material in English for sale at the entrance.

Interestingly, modern housing covered this entire area until 1959; a decade-long effort ending in 1971 brought the ruins to light for the first time in centuries. There is a second set of remains of Roman baths at 15 Primorski Blvd., which is visible from the sidewalk.

Admission: 20 lv (70¢) adults, 2 lv (7¢) students; free for everyone Thurs.

Open: Tues–Sun 10am–5:30pm, Tues–Sat in winter. **Directions:** Walk to the intersection of Han Krum Street and Kap. Parvi Rang Dobrev Street.

Museum of the Bulgarian Renaissance, 27 Juli no. 9. ☎ **22-35-85.**

Because of Turkish rule, Bulgaria's Renaissance, the revival of its national consciousness was held back for centuries, but it produced some marvelous architecture, writing, and art. Here, at the first Bulgarian school in Varna after the end of Turkish rule, you'll see a church area with icons, old textbooks, newspapers, journals, and documents. On the second floor is a collection of Bulgarian watercolors depicting scenes of everyday life. The building is designed in the National Revival style and dates back to 1861. There's a lovely small garden in the courtyard.

Admission: 20 lv (70¢).

Open: Tues–Sun 10am–5pm. **Directions:** Walk half a block from Kniaz Boris Street toward the sea on 27 Juli.

Naval Museum, 2 Primorski Blvd. ☎ **22-26-55.**

This museum highlights the history of the naval forces of Varna from ancient to modern times, both merchant and military. Displays include a section on the Russo-Turkish War of 1877 and the Serbian-Bulgarian War of 1885. Bulgarians are particularly proud of the outdoor exhibit of the ship *Druzky* (Intrepid), which blew up a Turkish ship during the Balkan War in 1912. Other outdoor displays include artillery guns, torpedoes, missiles, a massive searchlight, and even a helicopter. The exhibit has not been changed much since the collapse of Communism; revolutionary sailors and their mutinies are lauded, while Bulgarian participation in two world wars against Russia receives scant attention. Ask for the binder with detailed English-language descriptions at the entrance to the museum.

Admission: 20 lv (70¢) adults, 5 lv (18¢) students.

Open: Daily 8am–5pm. **Bus:** 4, 6, or 12 to the intersection of Primorski Boulevard and Koloni Street; then walk south three blocks.

WHERE TO STAY

PRIVATE ROOMS The best accommodations values in Varna are private rooms; they are incredibly inexpensive and can be booked at the **Balkantourist** office located at 3 Musala St. (☎ **052/22-55-24**), for 150 lv ($5.35) per person. Open May to September, daily from 8am to 8pm; in September and October, daily from 8am to 7pm; and the rest of the year, Monday through Saturday from 8am to 6pm.

You can also rent private rooms across from the train station at 16 Slaveikov Sq. (☎ **22-22-06**), next door to the luggage-check office. It's open Monday through Friday only, from 8am to noon and 12:30 to 4:30pm.

Hotels in the Center

As for budget hotels, Varna offers few choices. If the following picks don't appeal to you, consider finding a hotel in a nearby resort and visiting Varna on a day trip.

Musala Hotel, 3 Musala St. ☎ **052/22-39-25.** For reservations, contact the Varnaski Bryag firm at fax 25-30-83. 48 rms (none with bath).

Rates: 400 lv ($14) single; 600 lv ($21) double.

Located in the same turn-of-the-century building as the Balkantourist office, this budget hotel is quite central and clean. The rooms are pleasant, with solid furniture and fresh paint. Some have balconies, but since they overlook a noisy street, they aren't much of an asset. Although the hall bathrooms are in fairly good shape, there's just enough grime to make this distasteful for finicky travelers. English is spoken at the desk.

Hotel Odessa, 1 Slivnitsa Blvd. ☎ **052/22-53-12** or **22-83-81.** 96 rms (all with bath). TEL **Bus:** 4, 6, or 12 from the train station; enter from Primorski Blvd.

Rates (including breakfast): 950 lv ($34) single; 1360 lv ($49) double for two.

The Odessa is yet another banal concrete-and-glass hotel, but it's comfortable and its location is terrific—at the end of a pedestrian mall across from the lively Varna Cultural Center and overlooking the Sea Garden, a large well-maintained park along the shore.

The rooms are spacious and adequately lit, with mediocre furniture, lumpy mattresse and makeshift closets. The bathrooms are tiny but clean, with real shower curtain. Many rooms have enclosed private balconies, but if you don't like the heavy coastal boulevard traffic, the raucous seagulls, or loud evening disco music, ask for a room facing the back. The moderately priced restaurant has a designer menu with English translations and serves decent food at pleasant outdoor tables.

Hotel Orbita, 25 Tsar Osvoboditel Blvd. ☎ **052/22-51-62.** Telex 77200. 60 rms (all with bath). TEL **Bus:** 6 or 12 from the train station.

Rates (including breakfast): $30 single; $50 double. Additional beds $9 extra.

This hotel is run by Orbita, the youth travel organization, known for its budget rates, but singles are on the pricey side here. The location is good, overlooking a park, a few blocks from the central intersection of Kniaz Boris and Slivnitsa Boulevards. It's very spacious, light, and airy, and all rooms are the same—clean, with decent beds. It's often full in the summer.

WHERE TO EAT

If you're tired of eating in sit-down restaurants and want a quick lunch, try one of the many fast-food stores and stalls lining Kniaz Boris Street or along the mall between the Odessa Hotel and the Cherno More Hotel. Better yet, have a picnic. Varna is a good place to eat picnic style. There are many shops where you can get fresh bread, olives, and juices, and several outdoor markets selling delicious ripe tomatoes, cherries, and peaches. There's a good charcuterie (cold-cuts shop) on the corner of Kniaz Boris and Anton Ivanov featuring German specialty wursts. Find something that looks appealing and ask for the amount in grams or the number of slices you'd like (use sign language if necessary). Take it all down to the Sea Garden or the beach.

Paraklisa, Primorski and Parashkava Nikolau St. ☎ **22-34-95.**

Cuisine: OLD-FASHIONED BULGARIAN. **Directions:** The restaurant is just across Primorski Street from the Naval Museum.

Prices: Soups and salads 20–40 lv (70¢–$1.40); main courses 100–125 lv ($3.50–$4.40); desserts 20–30 lv (70¢–$1).
Open: Daily 11am–midnight.

The dining room and terrace at the Paraklisa are quite pleasant and comfortable, making this a good place to sit and eat a leisurely meal for an hour or two. The salads are particularly attractive, colorful blends of cabbage, roasted peppers, and olives. The main courses, while tasty, are not as exciting. There's more emphasis on sauces and more attention to presentation here than at most Bulgarian restaurants. The menu has not been translated into any other language besides Bulgarian.

★ **Restaurant Gerana,** 1 Sofroni Vrachanski St. ☎ **25-72-64.**
Cuisine: INTERNATIONAL/BULGARIAN. **Reservations:** Recommended. **Directions:** From the Balkantourist office on Musala Square, bear right on Preslav until you reach Vrachanski Street; turn right and walk one short block.
Prices: Soups 8–15 lv (30¢–55¢); salads 17–25 lv (60¢–90¢); main courses 52–82 lv ($1.85–$2.90); desserts 20–30 lv (70¢–$1.10).
Open: Daily noon–11pm.

Gerana is tucked away in the cozy cream-colored basement of an elegant renovated pink-and-white mansion not far from Kniaz Boris, the lively pedestrians-only shopping street. Owner Gianni Sharkov, who has extensive experience in the world of tourism, opened it in 1991 "to set an example of what a good restaurant in Bulgaria could be." He has done a splendid job. The decor is tasteful, the live music subtle, and the food superb.

The staff, taught by a Singapore-trained cook turns out delicious and unexpected dishes reminiscent of Indian and Oriental cuisines, a far cry from the standard unchanging Bulgarian menu. They offer an enormous selection of hot and cold appetizers and such exotic items as shrimp salad, "Tahiti" chicken salad, and Thai spring rolls. The ingredients are very fresh—this is as close as you'll get to nouvelle cuisine in the Balkans. And as with nouvelle cuisine elsewhere, the portions are a bit small. The wide assortment of main courses includes chicken, beef, fish, and pork in sauces richly spiced with fruits, wine, or curry. Here you can order wine by the glass and, if you absolutely must indulge in dessert, a banana split. As for prices—they couldn't be more reasonable, considering the high quality of the food and service.

NEARBY EXCURSIONS

About five miles north of Varna the first tsar of modern Bulgaria, Tsar Ferdinand I, had this summer residence, **Château Euxinograd,** built on the site of St. Dimitrius Monastery in 1891. An avid botanist, the tsar himself helped design and plant the château's beautiful gardens. From 1944 it served as an exclusive summer residence and conference center for Bulgarian political leaders and their foreign guests. After the political changes of 1989, it was remodeled and opened to the public in 1990.

Today the large estate consists of a neo-Baroque château, a lovely 120-acre park in both English and French styles with over 200 native and exotic plants from 30 countries, a small world-renowned winery producing vintage wines and brandies, holiday villas and restaurants, and facilities variously outfitted for recreation and business. The wine cellar was built in 1891 by French specialists and still uses its original and beautiful old technology, producing magnificent wines and a limited vintage of 10- and 20-year-old brandies.

The park and grounds can now be toured from May through December, Wednesday through Sunday. Excursions start at 10am and 2pm and cost 40 lv ($1.40) for adults, 20 lv (70¢) for children. Call ahead to see if there's a tour in English scheduled (☎ **86-12-41,** ext. 432). If the palace is in use, you probably won't be able to see the interior. Large foreign groups come here for excursions in the summer from nearby Varna, Albena, and Golden Sands.

2 Golden Sands [Zlatni Pyassutsi]

11 miles NE of Varna

GETTING THERE • By Bus City buses, private buses, and minivans—all marked no. 9—run north along the coast from Varna. The fare is 10 lv (35¢), 15 lv (50¢) after 10pm. The buses run every 20 to 30 minutes from 5am to midnight, and the ride takes about 30 minutes. Bus no. 9 stops in front of the Balkantourist office in Golden Sands.

ESSENTIALS The telephone area code for Golden Sands is 52.

Completed in 1956, Golden Sands is the largest and most popular resort town on the northern half of the Bulgarian coast. It has always attracted more Western Europeans than other Black Sea resorts and is especially popular with Germans and Americans.

Though less built up than Sunny Beach, its rival to the south, Golden Sands is still very developed. Its two-mile stretch of sand is interrupted by ditches, jetties, and other artificial intrusion. Just about any frolicking you do will take place beneath hundreds of hotel balconies. The resort's 80 hotels and 128 restaurants (capacity: 15,000 visitors) are more diverse and imaginative architecturally than those of Sunny Beach. It offers good recreation facilities (best tennis courts on the coast) and all kinds of water-sports equipment for rent. A yacht club that rents out sailboats opened in 1992.

WHERE TO STAY

For less hassle, reserve rooms through Balkan Holidays overseas or at the Hertz office in Sofia. They charge $40 for a single and $60 for a double in a two-star hotel, $58 for a single and $78 for a double in a three-star hotel. If you arrive without a reservation, go to Balkantourist, located right on the main road that goes up the coastline (☎ **52/85-56-81** or **85-51-84** to **85-51-88**), open from May to September, daily from 7:30am to 7:30pm; the rest of the year, Monday through Friday from 8:30am to 5:30pm. As with most of these beach villages, you aren't allowed to choose hotels here; you just decide how much you can pay. Rooms in three-star hotels with private bathrooms and breakfast cost $35 per person.

3 Albena

18 miles N of Varna

GETTING THERE • By Bus Buses depart every half hour in summer from the bus station across the boulevard from Varna's cathedral; the ride takes almost an hour. Buses from Golden Sands cost 10 lv (35¢). The bus station (☎ **28-60** or **20-40**) is off the main road past the Hotel Dobroudzha heading out of town.

ESSENTIALS For tourist information, call **23-12, 21-52,** or **29-30.** For the police, dial **20-02**; the fire department is at **160**, and for medical emergencies, dial **23-06.**

While many of Bulgaria's other resorts attract families, Albena is very popular with young singles from Eastern Europe. With only 42 hotels, almost half as many as in Bulgaria's largest resorts, and a five-mile-long beach, Albena allows a little more space to move around in, and almost everything is accessible on foot.

Another attraction of Albena is its proximity to isolated beaches. Just to the north, quiet beaches welcome the serious sunseeker in search of a tranquil place to rest by the seaside for the day.

WHAT TO SEE & DO

Albena also offers a wide variety of recreation and sports. For example, a tennis game at the Hotels Kaliopa, Kardam, Prague, Zvezda, and Ralitsa; parasailing (a boat pulls you while you're suspended in midair by parachute) outside the Dorostar and Gergana Hotels; or water sports, renting surfboards, waterskis, and boats at many beachfront hotels.

At the south bazaar across from the Dorostar Hotel, you can rent a bike cheaply for the day. Many hotels also rent roller skates, flippers, snorkels, and masks.

WHERE TO STAY

As at other resorts, you can book ahead through Balkan Holidays overseas or the Hertz office in Sofia. If, however, you arrive without accommodations, you *must reserve the room* through the main Balkantourist office (☎ **21-52, 23-10,** or **23-12;** telex 74453), located half a block away from the Dobroudzha Hotel. Again, you choose by price rather than individual name. Rates for three-star hotels are $50 for a single and $76 for a double. Prices include breakfast. Major credit cards are accepted.

4 Balchik

28 miles NE of Varna

GETTING THERE • **By Bus** Buses leave frequently from Albena for 10 lv (35¢).

First settled in the 5th century B.C. by Greek traders, then by Romans who called it Dionysopolis, Balchik today is a pleasant, typically Mediterranean-looking old seacoast town under white chalk cliffs. There are few places to stay, so come here on a day trip by bus from Varna (28 miles away) or Albena (10 miles away).

WHAT TO SEE & DO

Aside from wandering about the old section of the seaside town itself, the major attraction of Balchik is **Quiet Nest (Tenka Yava),** the villa and lovely gardens of the well-known Romanian queen, Marie Sarovetz. Local lore has it that she had an Oriental-style villa built here in 1931 for her Turkish lover when Romania owned this part of the coast called Dobruja (1913–40). The modest palace was apparently intended as an ecumenical symbol of the union of the cross of Christianity and the minaret of Islam, and the queen lived in it from 1931 to 1938. Queen Marie was not only the darling of European café society in the '20s but she became known for her conflict-resolution efforts—and there is a legend that she was mortally wounded when she threw herself between her two sons as they were dueling over a woman.

Throughout the six levels of the extensive gardens descending to the sea, there are hidden love seats, Roman baths, a minaret, a silver well, and an enormous collection of shrubs, flowers, and cacti, albeit somewhat neglected. These grounds are now part of Balchik's **Botanical Gardens** and can be visited daily from 8am to 7pm. The admission to the park is 10 lv (35¢); the palace is occasionally open when local artwork is displayed and sold inside. Call **0579/25-66** or inquire at the local tourist agency.

5 Sunny Beach [Slunchev Bryag]

59 miles S of Varna, 4 miles N of Nesebar

GETTING THERE • By Bus Frequent buses run from Varna and Burgas.

ESSENTIALS Sunny Beach's telephone area code is 0557. Within Sunny Beach, a mini-train runs from the center at the Hotel Kuban to both ends of the resort from May to October for 1 lv (4¢).

SPECIAL EVENTS In early June, Sunny Beach hosts the Golden Orpheus International Festival of Bulgarian Pop Songs.

If you love to see lots of people and be seen, or if you want a place with child-care facilities so you can have some time to relax during your vacation, this is your kind of resort. Sunny Beach (Slunchev Bryag) is a mammoth place, Bulgaria's largest and most popular resort, with more than 100 hotels and restaurants—enough to accommodate 25,000 people. This leaves little room for charm, but there's plenty of that in the small fishing towns. This is the best beach resort for family vacations; there are scores of recreational facilities for children: kiddie castles, a puppet theater, playgrounds, water slides, and best of all, child-care facilities as well, so parents can relax. Or maybe finally take some time for sailing, riding, or tennis lessons. A great variety of recreational activities and evening entertainment are available.

WHERE TO STAY

Apply the usual rule of thumb for traveling in Bulgaria: Make advance reservations for substantial discounts. As with most of the beach towns, if you arrive without reservations you must go to Balkantourist (☎ **0557/23-12**), near the Kuban Hotel off the main highway into town, where you will only be able to specify how much you want to pay, not what hotel you prefer. Rooms generally run $30 single and $40 double for a basic two-star hotel with breakfast. Little English, if any, is spoken here. Open daily: mid-May to the end of September, daily 24 hours; in winter, from 8am to 6pm.

WHERE TO EAT

Chuchura [Water Source], Sunny Beach. ☎ **29-50.**

Cuisine: BULGARIAN. **Reservations:** Recommended in summer. **Directions:** Head about three miles on the main coastal road to Nesebar; the bus driver will let you out if you can make yourself understood.
Prices: Main courses 25–30 lv (90¢–$1.10), somewhat higher in summer.

At this very spacious and modern-looking new private restaurant, the interior is reminiscent of a Scandinavian ski lodge, with low round tables and benches, bright-blue woven tablecloths, and blond-wood walls decorated with folk objects. The menu is small, but printed in English, French, and German, and the food is well prepared and very reasonably priced. Specialties of the house include pork kavarma with mushrooms, homemade sausage, and *kaiser pastyrma* (dried goat meat). The fries, salad, local Burgasko beer, and apricot juice are good, too.

6 Elenite

6½ miles N of Sunny Beach

GETTING THERE • By Bus A bus leaves every 30 minutes from Sunny Beach and costs 10 lv (35¢).

Northeast of Sunny Beach at the end of a dead-end road is the resort of Elenite, a favorite of Western Europeans on the coast for comfortable facilities and a peaceful setting.

WHERE TO STAY

 **Elenite Holiday Village,** ☎ **0554/24-23,** ext. 607. Fax 0554/51-47. 511 rms (all with bath, 220 also with kitchen).

Rates: Including breakfast, $24 per person in a villa room without a kitchen, $26 with a kitchen; $22 per person double in the Hotel Emona. Including half board, $30 per person in a villa room without a kitchen, $32 with a kitchen; $28 per person double in the Hotel Emona. AE, DC, MC, V.

Unlike the mass of hotels across the Bulgarian coast, Elenite is an imaginative modern complex built by Finns and opened in 1985. Villas with two to four rooms spread out on a hill overlooking the seaside account for most of the lodgings here; there's also a conventional hotel with 46 rooms. Villa rooms are decorated with terra-cotta tiles and blond-wood furniture, and have large balconies. Half the villa rooms have small kitchenettes with sinks and fridges but no stoves.

It's now possible to book accommodations a few weeks in advance directly by fax from abroad or by calling from within Bulgaria when you arrive, but check with Balkan Holidays to see if they offer a discount rate. It's a bit of a splurge, but with full board, prices are quite reasonable for the holiday fun you get.

Facilities: Several food stores, restaurants, and discos operate in the village complex. At the hotel's private beach you can rent Windsurfers and umbrellas. There's also a gym, swimming pool, sauna, and tennis court. A variety of excursions can be booked from the office in the main lobby, such as an all-day excursion to Sozopol including lunch for $20; all-day trips to Bulgarian villages such as Kotel or Zheravna or to the Rose Festival in Kazanluk for $30; and an evening (5 to 10pm) wine-tasting trip to Pomorie (15 miles away) to sample some of Bulgaria's finest wines and brandies for $17.

7 Nesebar

4 miles S of Sunny Beach, 27 miles N of Burgas

GETTING THERE • By Bus From Sunny Beach, buses leave about every 15 minutes from 5:30am to midnight. From Burgas, buses leave every 30 minutes from 6am to midnight.

ESSENTIALS Nesebar's telephone area code is 099554.

In sharp contrast to the modern resort developments built along the Black Sea coast in the last 30 years, Nesebar is one of the Bulgarian coast's most ancient and interesting towns. The Greek settlers who founded a trading center in 513 B.C. on this small rocky peninsula connected to the mainland by a narrow isthmus called it Mesembria. It soon became so prosperous that it was minting its own gold currency. Roman conquest plunged it into decline in the 1st century B.C., but it flourished again in the 5th and 6th centuries A.D. under Byzantine rule when it became an episcopal center. Some of the 42 churches, 8 of which still stand today, were built then.

A prize passed back and forth between Bulgarian and Byzantine rulers, Nesebar declined into obscurity during the Ottoman conquest in the mid-1400s. It was revived yet again during the Bulgarian Renaissance when many of its quaint stone-and-wood dwellings were built. Crowds from Sunny Beach flock to Nesebar, but fishing vessels still outnumber tour buses. As you move away from the neck of the peninsula, the postcard vendors thin out a little, and a picturesque Bulgarian town is revealed.

WHAT TO SEE & DO

In Nesebar, the most interesting sights are the medieval churches that managed to survive the 500-year Turkish occupation. Starting in the 10th century, 40 churches were built in Nesebar, and today 8 remain (the Turkish invasions and an earthquake in 1913 destroyed the others). Several of these churches are now used as art galleries.

Sveti Stefan, the town's principal church since the 15th century, still has many of its mosaics and wonderful frescoes, including the painted wooden altar. It's located just off Ribarska Street, open daily from 9am to 1pm and 2 to 6pm, for 15 lv (55¢) admission.

Also of interest are the typical 18th- and 19th-century homes in Bulgarian National Revival style, in which the second story of wood overhangs the first of stone. The first floor was used for storage (often fishing nets) and the second story as living quarters.

A booklet called *Ancient Nesebar,* written in both Bulgarian and English, contains descriptions and photographs of the town's most notable buildings, as well as two helpful maps. Several museums and some street vendors sell it for 40 lv ($1.40).

WHERE TO STAY

Private Rooms The **Messambria** bureau (☎ **099554/28-55**) arranges private rooms for 200 lv ($7) per person. This office sometimes runs out of rooms in summer, so it is best to reserve in advance. The staff speaks English, and they sell maps and change money. The office is halfway between the isthmus gate and the ferry port; as you enter the peninsula, veer right past the food stands. It's open daily in summer from 8am to 8pm, in winter from 8am to noon and from 1 to 5pm.

You can also rent a room directly from **Zoya Marcova,** who lives in the heart of town at 35 Mitropolitanska (☎ **099554/21-50**). Her 150-year-old house is a charming typical wooden Nesebar house. Zoya is a landscape architect who speaks English and is very friendly, so give her a call before arriving in town. She charges 100 lv ($3.50) per person. If she has the time, she'll give you a tour of her hometown for $2 per person.

Hotels

The only hotel in old Nesebar, the Mesembria, is booked solid by groups all summer, but new mini-hotels are springing up in the newer section of Nesebar on the mainland to accommodate the huge influx of vacationers. Try the following:

Hostel Mistral, coastal highway, Nesebar. ☎ **099554/30-48.** Fax 099554/29-33. 25 rms (most with bath). **Directions:** Take the bus from Sunny Beach; it stops a few paces away, next to the post office. The hotel is located a few blocks before the causeway into the old section of town.

Rates: 100 lv ($3.50) per person. Price are a bit higher June–Aug.
Open: 7:30am–11pm.

An unassuming place that looks like a small apartment building, the Hotel Mistral has very basic lodgings in the new part of town. The palm-flanked entrance leads into the pleasant outdoor terrace of a modest restaurant. Try to get a room on the fourth floor with a view of the bay. Many rooms share a sunny balcony, most rooms have a bathroom with shower. Mattresses are only in fair shape, but the public facilities are clean.

WHERE TO EAT

Nesebar has become such a popular tourist destination that scores of new restaurants, bistros, and cafés have opened to cater to the multitudes of summer visitors. I'm listing only two—a fresh new place on the west side and an old favorite near the marina—as a sampling of the great range of choices. As you wander through the tiny town you'll see numerous eateries with menus prominently displayed, featuring three-course fixed-price meals for $2 to $4. Pick the one that suits your fancy; they don't differ that much in price. There are also many small stalls along the southside promenade selling fast food, snacks, and drinks as well as jewelry, small leather items, and other crafts.

Restaurant Kraibrezna, 1 Kraibrezna St. ☎ **29-17.**

Cuisine: BULGARIAN. **Directions:** Go left past the fortress ruins and walk a short distance along the western shore.
Prices: Meals $1.50-$4.
Open: Summer only, daily noon–midnight.

One of many new private restaurants on the west side with brisk service by friendly young servers. The babble of many foreign languages gives it a lively atmosphere. There's no set menu: It varies according to the fresh catch and produce of the day. It's inexpensive, but my waitress cautioned me that prices double at the height of the summer season. Tastefully decorated in an updated Nesebar Revival style with arches, marble floors, and carved-wood ceilings, Kraibrezna's three stories include a billiard room downstairs, a cocktail bar, and an outdoor terrace on the top floor with a superb view of Sunny Beach and Elenite.

Kapitanska Sreshta (Captain's Rendez-Vous), Chaika St. ☎ **34-29.**

Cuisine: BULGARIAN/FISH. **Reservations:** Recommended in summer.
Prices: Main courses 70–100 lv ($2.50–$3.50); bottle of wine 80 lv ($2.85).
Open: Daily 10am–11pm.

An old tourist favorite with nautical decor and furniture from the original old house near the ferry station it now occupies. Waiters wear naval outfits, enhancing its already-theatrical air. In the summer, tour groups fill the upstairs banquet halls. The menu is mainly fish: grilled bluefish, breaded fish filet, fried pike-perch, mackerel; the house specialty is "baked fish on tile with spices." It's especially nice to have a drink out on the terrace overlooking the marina at sunset. A guitar, accordion, and violin trio play Greek and Bulgarian folk and pop tunes, and there are folklore shows outside on the terrace in the summer. The manager, Dancho, is very friendly and promises he'll assist you in finding a private room if you can't find one.

8 Burgas

27 miles S of Sunny Beach, 83 miles SW of Varna

GETTING THERE • **By Plane** Daily flights from Sofia take 45 minutes to 1¼ hours and cost $65. From the Burgas airport (☎ **28-31**), bus no. 15 leaves for the train station in downtown Burgas every hour from 5:30am to midnight.

Balkan Airlines has its office at 2/4 Aleksandrovska St. (☎ **45-605** or **45-685**).

• **By Train** The train from Sofia takes about seven hours and costs 75 lv ($2.70) in first class and 67 lv ($2.40) in second class. The circuitous route from Varna takes about five hours.

There's a baggage check outside the train station near the bus station, open daily from 6am to 10pm. For train information in Bulgarian, call **45-022**.

• **By Bus** From Sunny Beach, buses leave every 30 minutes from 6am to midnight. Buses also leave from Varna to the north and Sozopol to the south. The central bus station (☎ **45-631**) is in front of the train station. The overnight bus to Istanbul takes 10 hours and costs $18. Tickets are sold at Balkantourist; the bus leaves from the Hotel Primorets (see "Where to Stay," below).

ESSENTIALS Burga's telephone area code is 056.

ORIENTATION The old downtown section of Burgas sits on the end of a promontory between two large lakes and the sea. This area is at the center of a large bay and is roughly circular in shape. The train, bus, and hydrofoil stations are all conveniently next to each other facing the port off Garov (formerly Kolarov) Square. Most visitors spend little time in Burgas, using it as a transit point for points south. One of the main avenues, Aleksandrovska (formerly Parvi Mai), a bustling pedestrian mall, begins here. It's lined with cafés, shops, street stalls, and shoppers, and is a good place to have a bite to eat or just have a stroll while waiting for transportation connections.

Intersecting Aleksandrovska at the Hotel Bulgaria is Bogoridi Street (formerly Lenin), another pleasant street lined with cafés and bars, with an open-air movie theater at its end. For beach-lovers, there's a long strip of black-sand beach and a large pleasant Sea Garden that form the eastern edge of the old part of town.

Burgas is the youngest city on the Bulgarian seacoast, a fishing town which developed rapidly into a commercial port at the turn of the century after the railway line from Sofia was completed. Now a modern industrial port dominated by huge shipbuilding cranes and oil refineries, Burgas has little to recommend it in terms of tourist sights.

However, Burgas may be a good base from which to make day trips to the rarely visited beaches to the south. Apart from the Dyuni Holiday Village to the south, Burgas marks the last cluster of hotels on the south coast.

WHERE TO STAY

PRIVATE ROOMS The best deal in this town is a private room. The Balkantourist office, opposite the train station at 2 Alexander I (☎ **056/4-55-53** or **4-72-75**), can find you a double room for 200 lv ($7) per person. The day I stopped in, the woman on duty was knowledgeable and spoke good English. The office hours are daily 8am to 6pm year-round.

Hotels

Hotel Primorets, 1 Battenberg St. ☎ **056/2-27-87.** Fax 056/4-29-34. 122 rms (97 with bath), 4 apartments. TEL **Directions:** From the train station, walk across Garov Square in front and exit to far right of the square onto Battenberg Street; the hotel is about five minutes from there.

Rates (including breakfast): 560 lv ($19.75) single; 780 lv ($27.50) double; 920 lv ($32.40) apartment. AE, DC, EU, JCB, MC, V.

A recent renovation has left this hotel a good bit cheerier than the typical Balkantourist establishment. Even the singles are relatively spacious, with enough room for a few padded chairs and a desk. The bathrooms are ugly—a poor choice of tile—but clean and in excellent condition. The Primorets is a few minutes from the busy train station in a quiet area near the sea. Rooms with balconies in the back overlook the sea and the attractive sea garden.

WHERE TO EAT

$ **Pizzeria Grand'italia,** 4–6 Yaborov St.

Cuisine: PIZZA.

Prices: Salads 20 lv (70¢), pizza or pasta 40–50 lv ($1.40–$1.75), gelato 3–6 lv (10¢-20¢) per scoop.

Open: Daily 9am–midnight.

This pizzeria is located in what used to be the local headquarters of the Pioneers, the organization that once instilled the ideals of Lenin in children. Now diners chat and munch in the graceful interior or beneath enormous canvas umbrellas outdoors. The pizzas are fantastic—huge slaps of crisp, thin crust, topped with cheese and various combinations of meat and vegetables. The gelato, both ices and creams, makes a fine ending to a meal or is reason enough to stop by for dessert. On the second floor there is a bar that serves as a disco on weekends.

9 Sozopol

19 miles S of Burgas

SOUTH OF BURGAS • Orientation The 45 miles of coast south of Burgas have long been a favorite of campers. However, it's harder to get around here than in the north: There is less frequent public transportation and roads that are not as well maintained as those in the north. The restaurants serve simpler fare than those in the north; and with the exception of Dyuni Holiday Village, the hotels are usually unsuitable.

The south coast is for the traveler who is not seeking comfort, but wants to soak in the sun during the peak season of July and August on sparsely populated beaches. You can find these isolated seaside villages with coves and beaches by walking, public bus, or hitchhiking.

If you travel south of Dyuni to explore the lovely beaches near Kiten, note that English is as rare here as Bulgarian is in Alabama. The southbound bus is the only transportation, and aside from the traveler on a stray Eastern European tour bus, you'll probably be one of the few Western tourists around.

GETTING THERE • By Bus Buses from Burgas run every hour from 6am to 9pm for 16 lv (55¢). Private vans also cover the same route, making service more frequent.

ESSENTIALS Sozopol's telephone area code is 05514. Balkantourist is in the new part of town at 28 Ropotamo (☎ **05514/251**), open daily from 8am to 8pm.

SPECIAL EVENTS The **Apollonia Festival of Arts** (music and drama) is held in Sozopol during the first half of September.

Sozopol was called Apollonia by the Greek colonizers who founded it in 610 B.C. as a trading center. As old and charming as Nesebar, it possesses few ruins and attracts fewer tourists. But this small fishing village has long attracted a community of artists who like to spend their summers here. Much of its charm comes from its picturesque narrow cobblestone streets lined with two-story timber-and-stone houses. High walls shelter courtyards fragrant with roses and honeysuckle, fig trees, and grape arbors; fishing nets are hung out to dry in the sun; women sell lace to passersby. A small but gorgeous beach, framed by rocky cliffs, has water so clear you can see the soft, sandy bottom several feet deep. Altogether, it's a lovely seacoast town to wander through for an afternoon or to retreat to for a few days.

WHERE TO STAY

You can rent a private room or an entire apartment from **Balkantourist,** at 28 Ropotamo (☎ **05514/251**), for $4 to $8. The office is open daily from 8am to 8pm in the summer (but often closed on Sunday); the rest of the year, Monday through Friday from 8am to 5pm. They are located in the new part of town about two miles from the old quarter where the coastal bus lets you off (there's no place to check your bags either), so get a local bus marked UL. ROPOTAMO in Cyrillic or get a taxi. More conveniently located is **Sozopol Ltd.** (☎ **05514/17-84;** fax 05514/316), amid the vendors' stalls in Han Krum Square, near the bus station.

WHERE TO EAT

Depending on the ambience and view you desire, you can take your pick of several good restaurants serving mainly fish for $2 to $3: the Sozopol Mekhana, the largest and most touristy on Apollonia, the main street; the Old Captain, in an alley next to it; and the Vyaturna Melnitsa, on Morski Skali, near the old lighthouse. The Druzhba is a restaurant on a boat moored by the town dock. Here you can eat the catch of the day and take in great views of the tiny, colorfully painted wooden fishing boats. There's also a large open-air market in the summer where you buy some picnic fare and take it down to the nice wide stretch of beach on the east side of town.

---

10 Dyuni

Just eight years ago Dyuni was just a barren stretch of coast; today it offers one of Bulgaria's best-organized and most architecturally interesting tourist facilities, the Dyuni Holiday Village (see below). Dyuni is 25 miles south of Burgas and 5 1/2 miles south of Sozopol; the buses from Sozopol to Michurin pass in front of the "mini-villages" resort complex.

WHERE TO STAY

Dyuni Holiday Village. ☎ **056/20-442.** Telex 83584. 230 rms in the Pelican Club, 100 rms in the Marina Club, 1,000 beds in Zelenika (all with bath). TEL **Directions:** Take the intercity bus to the complex entrance.

Rates: $40 single, $60 double in hotel; $75 for one or two persons in villa.

This family-oriented complex is designed in "mini-villages," each with its own bar, café, and shops. The accommodations in the hotel areas feature a reception area that is separate from the stairs leading up to the rooms, creating the feeling that you're in someone's home. The hotel units are all doubles with big couches so that children can stay without additional beds, and most have large balconies.

Other lodgings in the complex are diverse in their levels of comfort and architectural style; they include four-star fisherman's huts, Sozopol-style houses, and modern villas with design elements reminiscent of Bulgarian monasteries. All are set into the gently sloping dunes, and a forest of young pines has been planted to divide the three main sections. The Marina Club village is located just off the beach; the other facilities are set back from the beach by a major highway.

You can now make reservations directly by writing to Dyuni Village, Dyuni (that's all you need, it will get there) or by calling at least two or three days in advance. Or you can book through Balkan Holidays.

Facilities: The beach is fine (but not the best since the highway runs behind it) and offers waterskiing, parasailing, sailing, and windsurfing. Land-sport facilities include three swimming pools, seven tennis courts, bicycling, volleyball, and table tennis. Inexpensive lessons are also available for a variety of sports.

NEARBY ATTRACTIONS

Just nine miles south of Dyuni flows the **Ropotamo River,** an unspoiled area with very lush, almost tropical vegetation. Boats take travelers to the sea and back on a one-hour tour of this beautiful and quiet area for 20 lv (70¢) per person. Boats leave whenever they have 10 to 20 riders. Departures are daily from 7 or 8am until 6 or 7pm May to August, and about 8am to 3pm in April and September and October.

If you're coming by car from the north on the E87 highway, take the first left after the bridge. This will bring you down a dirt road to the boats.

If you'd prefer something more organized, you can join a small group for a half-day excursion-picnic or fishing trip to the river organized by Dyuni Holiday Village. The cost is $6 to $8 for a minimum of five or six people.

It's only 43 miles to the Turkish border from here.

12

Getting to Know the Czech & Slovak Republics

WHEN CZECH-BORN DIRECTOR MILOŠ FORMAN WANTED TO CAPTURE THE SPIRIT of 17th-century Europe to film *Amadeus,* he didn't construct elaborate sets. Rather, he filmed on location in Prague. He made the right choice, for few cities can rival the opulence and splendor of the Czech capital.

What about the rest of the former Czechoslovakia, a name once synonymous for all that is unknown and distant? Let the secret be known: this land is a virtual living museum and of vast natural beauty. Wars have not ravaged its architecture here for hundreds of years, accounting for a unique state of preservation in modern Europe. Buried deep in pine forests and serviced by sleepy little spur rail lines, timeless Czech and Slovak hamlets remain practically unchanged. Seemingly on every hilltop or mountain pass stands a castle or fort. The number of historical monuments intact rivals that of any other country in Europe, with over 2,500 castles, manors, and palaces.

Most of the beer consumed throughout the world today is a light brew called pilsner. This golden, flavorful drink originates in the town of Plzeň. Take time to put down your beer glass and explore the incredible natural wonders of the High and Low Tatra Mountains (as well as the Little Fatra). Snowcapped peaks, glittering waterfalls, and some of the wildest, most mountainous country in Eastern Europe lies in Bohemia and Slovakia. So varied and many are the Czech and Slovak Republic's sights that you'll be hard-pressed to see them all in one visit.

1 Geography, History & Politics

GEOGRAPHY

If you travel through Eastern Europe, you'll probably have to cross the Czech and Slovak Republics at least once. They're in the center of Central Europe, a gateway bounded by Germany and Poland to the north and west, Austria and Hungary to the south, and Ukraine in the east.

There are three geographic regions of the former Czechoslovakia: Bohemia, Moravia, and Slovakia. In the 10th century the Hungarians controlled Slovakia, while the German-dominated empires to the west controlled Bohemia and Moravia. This division led to a distinct difference between the two cultures and languages. Today, of a total population of 15.5 million people, 64% are Czech and 31% are Slovak, with a scattering of Hungarians, Polish, Germans, Ukrainians, and other minorities. Over half of the Czech population lives outside urban areas or in small villages of 5,000 people or less.

Most of Slovakia is mountainous, with the High Tatras the largest mountain range in the region. Some low mountains ring the western edge of Bohemia, but the terrain is far flatter than in Slovakia. The major rivers are the Vltava, which runs through Prague, and the Danube, which goes through Bratislava and forms a small part of Slovakia's border with Hungary.

HISTORY & POLITICS

THE FORMER CZECHOSLOVAKIA CAME into existence after World War I in 1918. Yet the history of the Czechs and the Slovaks who inhabit these lands dates back to the 5th century A.D. when Slavic tribes settled in the region. The Czechs formed the Kingdom of Bohemia in the 10th century and ruled until the 16th century.

Dateline

- **5th century** Slavic tribes settle in area of today's Czech and Slovak Republic.
- **10th century** Moravia begins to adopt Roman Catholicism.

Dateline

- 1346 Charles IV ushers in Prague's Golden Age, opening the first university in Central Europe, establishing a bishopric, and erecting hundreds of buildings.
- 1403 Jan Hus becomes rector of the University of Prague, and launches antichurch crusade.
- 1415 Jan Hus burned at the stake, beginning decades of religious warfare.
- 1434 Hussite armies defeated in the Battle of Lipany.
- 1526 Habsburgs gain control of Bohemia, following the Battle of Mohacs.
- 1618 Bohemian revolts, igniting Thirty Years' War.
- 1620 Austrian Habsburgs defeat Czech uprising at the Battle of the White Mountain.
- 1918 The state of Czechoslovakia is formed following World War I.
- 1938 Munich Pact cedes the Sudetenland to Hitler's Germany.
- 1939 Hitler absorbs the rest of Czech lands; puppet Slovak Republic established.
- 1945 Soviet army occupies Prague; Ruthenia forcibly ceded to the Soviet Union.
- 1946 Communists win 38% of vote in free elections and enter a coalition government.
- 1948 Communists take over the entire government in a coup.
- 1967–68 Alexander Dubček becomes the first

➤

Under Charles IV (the Holy Roman Emperor from 1346 to 1378) Prague was transformed into a great European political, cultural, and religious center. A lavish patron of the arts and a devout Roman Catholic, Charles secured an archbishopric for Prague with St. Vitus Cathedral as its seat. He established the first university in Central Europe in 1348—appropriately named Charles University. Especially significant in this period of artistic expansion was the evolution of the typical Bohemian architectural style that graces the skyline of Prague to this day.

Charles's rapid introduction of Catholicism in Bohemia aroused strong opposition from Jan Hus (1369–1415). Hus was eventually burned at the stake, but his followers (the Hussites) fought Catholic armies until the Battle of Lipany in 1434.

From 1620 until 1918 the Austrian monarchy ruled over the Czechs, following their victory at the Battle of the White Mountain. The collapse of the Austrian monarchy in 1918 allowed the Czechs, along with the Slovaks (who had been subjugated by the Hungarians for 1,000 years), to form their own independent state.

Between 1918 and 1938 the former Czechoslovakia was a parliamentary democracy, a unique example in Eastern Europe. However, the Great Depression, compounded by difficulties with the country's Germans, who made up 22% of the population in the Sudetenland (in Bohemia and Moravia), created turmoil during these years. Hitler insisted that all territories with a population more than 50% German be ceded to him, promising that "the Sudetenland is the last territorial claim I have to make in Europe." Fearing another world war, Britain, France, and Italy, at the Great Powers conference in Munich (August 29–30, 1938), agreed to Hitler's demand. The Great Powers' appeasement of Germany was fruitless. On March 15, 1939, Hitler invaded Czechoslovakia.

In many ways the Czechs responded to this war as they responded earlier in World War I. With the exception of a few isolated incidents, the Czech people again used passive resistance against their occupiers. However, Hitler was determined to completely "assimilate" Czechoslovakia into Germany and proceeded with a systematic and brutal suppression in Bohemia and Moravia. He played upon Slovak desires for an independent state, and during the war Slovakia existed as a quasi-independent part of the Third Reich. By the end

Dateline

secretary of the Communist Party and ushers in liberal reforms; Soviet army invades Czechoslovakia to crush reforms.

- **1977** Czechoslovak dissidents form Charter 77 to protest suppression of human rights.
- **1989** Antigovernment protests erupt in Prague shortly after the opening of the Berlin Wall in November; Communist government resigns; Parliament nominates playwright Václav Havel as president: he seeks to transform country to free market economy.
- **1990** First free elections in 44 years elect Havel and his allied political forces.
- **1993** Czechoslovakia divides into the Czech Republic and the Slovak Republic.

of the war more than 250,000 Czechoslovaks had died as a result of the Nazi occupation. After the war, Czechoslovakia expelled 2.5 million Germans from their land to ensure that a "Munich" would never be repeated.

In 1946, in a rare example of fair elections, the Communists won 38% of the vote, the highest (nonrigged) percentage in postwar Eastern Europe. The Communists shared power in a six-party coalition, but with Soviet prodding and assistance, they took full power in a 1948 coup. Although most of Czechoslovakia's vast industrial capacity was still intact at the end of the war, mismanagement and extensive Soviet "reparations" led to inflation, low productivity, and social discontent in the 1950s.

In 1968 Communist Party Secretary Alexander Dubček introduced dramatic political and economic reforms to create "socialism with a human face." Censorship was eased, political prisoners were rehabilitated and released, and industry was decentralized. Known as "The Prague Spring," this rapid liberalization eventually displeased Czechoslovakia's mighty neighbor to the east. On August 20, 1968, Soviet troops and a few token brigades from other Warsaw Pact forces crossed the Czechoslovakian frontier and entered Prague, ending the Czechoslovak experiment in applied socialism.

In the two decades that followed, the Czechoslovak government was one of the more rigidly dogmatic in the Warsaw Pact. Waste, mismanagement, and the worsening economic situation left the Czechoslovakian economy in a sad state, and the country resisted Gorbachev-style perestroika in the latter half of the 1980s.

Communism in Czechoslovakia started to unravel during the "Velvet Revolution" of late November 1989, just weeks after the opening of the Berlin Wall. When police brutally dispersed a large demonstration in Prague on November 17, protests swelled, and soon prompted the resignation of the Communist leadership. By December 10, the departing Communist president swore in the first cabinet without a Communist majority in 41 years. By December 29, the Parliament nominated as president the playwright Václav Havel, who had been in prison for antigovernment dissent until May 1989. The new government began implementing a free-market economy and negotiated the departure of Soviet troops from Czechoslovakia.

In June 1990, Havel and his Civic Forum Party, allied with the Public Against Violence Party in Slovakia, won the first free elections in Czechoslovakia since 1946. Havel declared the task ahead as follows: "To lead in the transition from

IMPRESSIONS

Your government, my people, has returned to you.
—Václav Havel, 1990

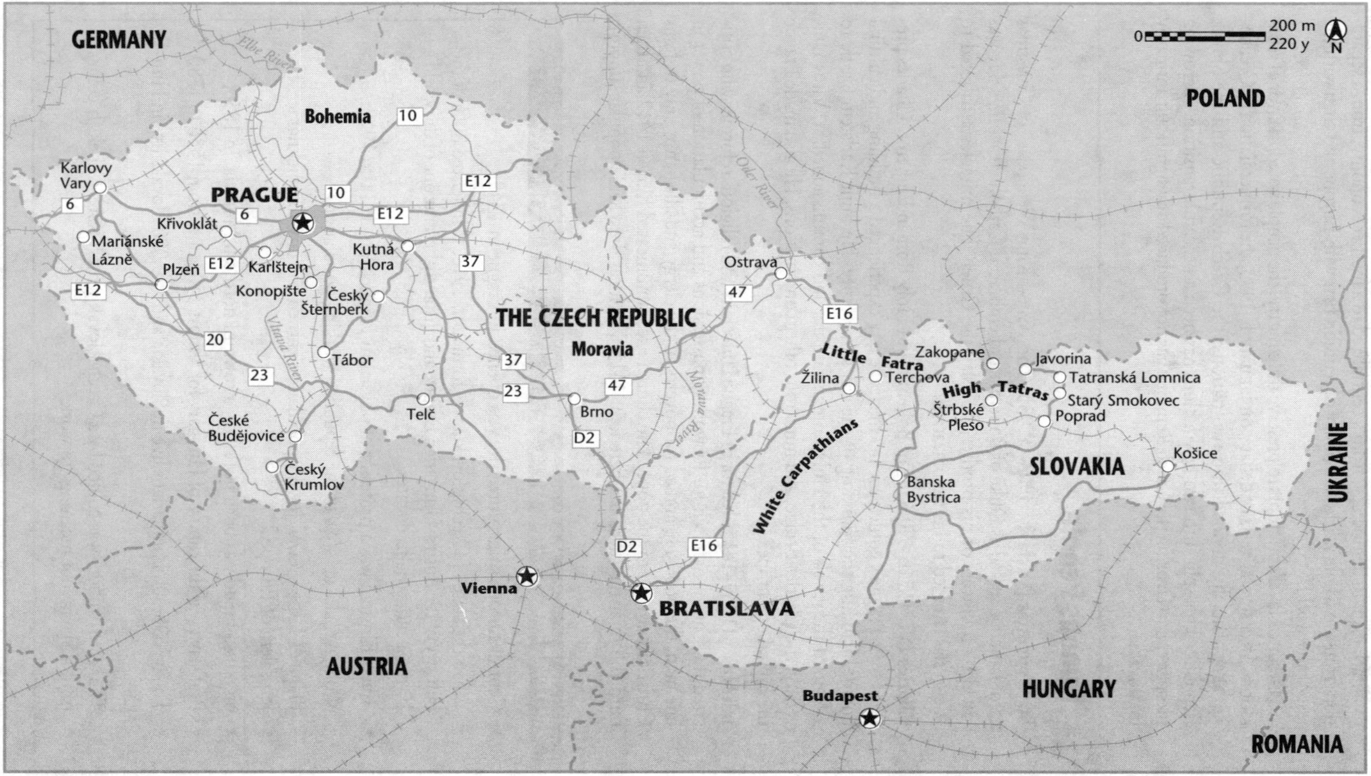

Major Railways

The Czech & Slovak Republics

totalitarianism to democracy, from a centralized to a market economy, from a separation from the whole world to a policy of reunion first with Europe and then with the rest of the world."

Despite Havel's attempts to preserve the country, the people voted in favor of separation. After several years of debate, on January 1, 1993, the former nation of Czechoslovakia officially divided into two nations: the Czech Republic and the Slovak Republic. This split into two new nations has been a peaceful transition. A growing prosperity gap favoring the Czech Republic has not produced any significant antipathy in Slovakia.

2 Famous People

St. Wenceslas [Václav] (903-ca. 935) The "Good King Wenceslas" of Christmas carol fame, he served as Duke of Bohemia and embraced Catholic teachings. He was killed by followers of his brother, Boleslav the Cruel. The miracles attributed to Wenceslas later led to his canonization.

Charles IV (1316–78) King of Bohemia and Holy Roman Emperor, Charles presided over Prague's golden age in which the city experienced a building and cultural boom, including the founding of the city's university. He built Karlstein Castle to safeguard the jewels of the Holy Roman Empire, and commissioned St. Vitus University, the Charles Bridge, and numerous other constructions. He also made Prague the capital of Europe.

Jan Hus (1369–1415) Rector of Prague University and religious reformer who criticized the Catholic church for its worldly possessions and accumulation of power in one man, the pope. He argued for poverty in the clergy and allegiance only to Jesus Christ rather than to the pope. The church excommunicated him in 1412 and then burned him at the stake as a heretic in 1415. His ideas drew wide popular support,

Did You Know . . . ?

- Central Europe's first university was opened in Prague in 1348.
- When the state of Czechoslovakia was formed in 1918. It inherited 80% of the industry of the Austro-Hungarian Empire and instantly became one of the world's 10 most industrialized states.
- Albert Einstein was a professor of physics in Prague from 1911 to 1912.
- Women make up 45% of the republics' working population.
- Prague's large prewar Jewish population earned the city the nickname "The Jerusalem of Europe."
- Sigmund Freud was born in Pribor, a town in northern Moravia, in 1856.
- Bratislava was the capital of Hungary for almost 250 years, from 1536 to 1780.
- Today, 690,000 Hungarians live in Slovakia and 110,000 Slovaks live in Hungary.
- The word "robot" was coined by a Czechoslovak writer, Karel Čapek. It comes from a Slavic root meaning "to work."

and, after his death, sparked a revolution of his followers against the church and emperor, a conflict known as the Hussite Wars. The Hussite Wars came to an end in 1436, but Hus's ideas were later reflected in Martin Luther's teachings of the reformation.

Bedřich Smetana (1824–84) Composer of both operas and symphonies, often incorporating elements of local folk music into his scores. His best-known opera is *The Bartered Bride* (1886), and his other work includes *Ma Vlast* (My Country).

Antonín Dvořák (1841–1904) Composer best known for his Symphony no. 9, *From the New World.* In addition to writing nine symphonies, he also composed operas, songs, and orchestral works. He headed the National Conservatory in New York from 1892 to 1895.

Tomáš Garrigue Masaryk (1850–1937) A former Charles University philosophy professor, Masaryk is considered the founder of the Czechoslovak state. He spent the World War I years lobbying abroad for its creation, and building bridges at home between the Czechs and Slovaks who would constitute its main ethnic groups. A true Renaissance man, Masaryk served as the republic's first president (1918–37). Ahead of his time, he took his wife's maiden name—Garrigue—as his own middle name.

Franz Kafka (1883–1924) Prague-born author whose works grappled with themes of human fate in a brutal world. Only his short stories, including *Metamorphosis* (1912), were published during his lifetime. He received enduring acclaim for his novels published posthumously: *The Trial, The Castle,* and *America.* He is buried in Prague's New Jewish Cemetery.

Václav Havel (1936-) The Czech Republic's president and most prominent playwright. Prior to the demise of Communism in 1989, Havel was one of the country's leading dissidents and a founding member of Charter 77, a dissident group. In 1979 the Communist government sentenced him to 4½ years in prison; he was also imprisoned on several other occasions. He is the author of plays noted for their absurdist humor, including *Largo Desolato, Temptation,* and *The Memorandum*—which were banned in Czechoslovakia from 1968 until the revolution in 1989. "God—I don't know why—wanted me to be a Czech," he has said. "It was not my choice. But I accept it, and I try to do something for my country because I live here." Havel was elected to a five-year term as president of the Czech Republic in 1993.

3 Cultural Notes

ARCHITECTURE Prague escaped the destruction of World War II, and this "city of a hundred spires" is a vast museum of the Gothic and baroque. Unfortunately, under the Communist regime many buildings were allowed to decay, suffering the lack of necessary restoration.

Romanesque A number of Romanesque castles and churches were built in the Czechoslovakian lands from the 10th century on, but most exist now only as fragments incorporated in later Gothic structures—for example, the cathedral of the Hradčany in Prague, which replaced two earlier churches. The castle itself retains some Romanesque elements; more important is the Basilica of St. George, which dates from 1142, still Romanesque inside despite the baroque facade and 19th-century restorations.

Gothic This style of architecture was introduced into Bohemia by the monastic orders. Sadly, most of the early Gothic monuments were gravely damaged or destroyed during the Hussite Wars; consequently, most remaining medieval Czech buildings are in the "Caroline" High Gothic style, dating from the 14th to the 16th century, when Bohemia dominated the cultural life of Central Europe. Gothic architecture in Bohemia is especially praised for its daring use of "collective polygonal shafts" (sort of aggregate columns), otherwise unknown outside of France, and for the integration of paintings and sculpture into the architectural fabric.

Prague is the center of the Bohemian Gothic. The finest Gothic building in the country is St. Vitus's Cathedral on the Hradčany, which was completed by Peter Parléř of Cologne. Parléř also designed the Charles Bridge, which leads to the Hradčany, a great technical achievement for the period; and the St. Bartholomew Cathedral at Kolín. The castle-palace on the Hradčany is noted for its interior decoration, partly by another great figure of the era, Benedikt Rejt (especially the unusual swirling, interlaced vaulting). Also important are the Powder Tower, the Old and New Town Hall, and the Tyn Church, another great Parléř building, with a baroque interior.

Renaissance The Renaissance came late to the Czechoslovak lands, and the social turmoil of the era left few buildings. Exceptions are Emperor Ferdinand's Royal Summer Palace in Prague, influenced by Brunelleschi, and the Archbishops's Palace, which has a later rococo interior. The town of Tábor, south of Prague, has several Renaissance houses on its market square. České Budějovice's marketplace retains some Renaissance buildings too, in an ensemble spanning several centuries.

Baroque Czechoslovaks, to put it mildly, embraced the baroque with enthusiasm. At first there was a strong Italian influence, then a brief period of French dominance, which gave way in the late 17th century to Viennese and Bavarian ideas. Fine baroque buildings exist all over the country, in secluded hamlets as well as in Prague.

Modern In the 20th century the country followed an Austrian lead, indulging in many fine art nouveau shops and houses, of which the Hotel Europa is considered the best. Czechoslovakia was also in the vanguard of modern architecture, with many fine buildings in the 1920s, such as the Prague Sample Fairs Palace, an early example of glass curtain walls. Czech architects also invented a unique adaptation of cubist structural ideas with a style known as "rondocubism," which combined an analytical faceting of surfaces with elements of Czechoslovak vernacular architecture. Noteworthy buildings are Pavel Janak's office buildings at the corner of Národní Street and Jungmannova Street, and Novotný's hostel just off Bilkova Street.

ART The reign of Rudolf II is often compared to the glorious period under Charles IV—the twin peaks of Bohemian cultural history. A passionate hoarder of art and curios, Rudolf assembled one of the greatest private collections of paintings in the history of the world—now much dispersed. His court welcomed great painters from all over Europe; Prague was called Europe's "artistic treasure house." Tragically, most of the works by native Czechoslovak artists inspired by this intense creative activity and many architectural monuments were lost during the Thirty Years' War.

Czechoslovakia did not develop an important tradition of easel painting and freestanding sculpture until the late 19th century. The glories of Czechoslovakian art are mainly in churches, or in collections of church art (especially the National Museum in Prague). Bohemian sculptors are specially praised for their crucifixions filled with pathos, and a number of original ways of showing the Madonna, particularly the so-called "Lion Madonnas," which show the Virgin trampling the Devil underfoot.

From 1900 to 1945 Prague enjoyed one of the most vital modernist "scenes" in Europe, which has only recently begun to find the recognition it deserves in the West. Though the painting of the era is in many ways broadly derivative of trends originating elsewhere in Europe (impressionism, symbolism, expressionism, cubism), Czechoslovakia's achievements in photography and film are of undeniable international importance. The Czechoslovak cinema began in 1896, only a few years after the Lumière brothers' first exhibitions in Paris; Czechoslovakian film of this period is much cherished by lovers of the avant-garde—experimental work flourished alongside a successful film entertainment industry. The first systematic film theory and criticism originated in Prague, in the work of Václav Tille, enlarged upon by the Čapek brothers. There was in addition a thriving bohemian (in both senses of the word) cabaret/street theater, with wild absurdist, anarchist multimedia experiments, which enriched the whole atmosphere.

A new museum of 20th-century art has been planned for Prague. In the meantime, art lovers might look in the national collections for the work of the painters Kupka, Preissig, Filla, Kubišta, Josef Čapek, Zrzavý, Štyrský, Toyen, and Rykr; the sculptors Gutfreund and Rešánek; photographers Mucha, Vobecký, Valter, Zykmund, Drtikol, Sudek, Funke, Teige, and Rössler. Those interested in knowing more about Czech film directors, beyond the familiar names of Miloš Forman and Jiři Menzel, may consult the national film archive, the ČSFÚ-FA. An institution of great international prestige, it preserves commercial and experimental Czech films from the modernist period through the work of the directors of the Communist era—often heroic in their resistance to state censorship—to the present.

CZECH LITERATURE Until about 1400 Czech literature consisted of devotional and hagiographical works in Old Church Slavonic (including the 10th-century legends of St. Wenceslas) and Latin chronicles and religious drama, as well as hymns, chivalric tales, and verse romances in Czech. Increased national self-awareness nourished poetic growth in the 15th century; in particular, the linguistic reforms introduced by the religious reformer and martyr Jan Hus while he was rector of Prague University helped forge a strong Czech literary language for the Renaissance. The glory of the age was the Kralice Bible, translated by the Czech Brethren (1579–93).

The Thirty Years' War wrought the utter destruction of Czech literary works and fierce national repression. The great educational reformer known as Comenius (Jan Amos Komensky; 1592–1670) was forced to work in exile, while Czech dwindled to little more than a peasant dialect. The language was revived in the 18th and 19th centuries by many writers, including Jan Kollár, leader of the Pan-Slavic movement; the Romantic Karel Hynek Mácha, considered the nation's greatest poet; and playwright Josef Kajetán Tyl.

From the 1880s on, Czech literature was the most cosmopolitan of the Slavic literatures between the wars; the first Czech writers to achieve world renown, in the 1920s, were the dramatists Josef and Karel Čapek (*R.U.R.*, *The Insect Comedy*, among others, widely available in English). Another fine playwright, František Langer, even had a great Broadway success (with *The Camel Through the Needle's Eye*, 1923; translated in 1932); his *Periferie* has twice been rendered in English, as *The Ragged Edge* and *The Outskirts* (all out of print, but available in libraries). In the same period, Jaroslav Hašek created one of the most famous works of Czech fiction, *The Good Soldier Schweik*, a classic satire of war (though many Czechs in the 1920s, and even today, considered the cunning Schweik immoral and bad for the national image). Before 1945, when the expulsion of three million Germans from the country put an end to the old German-Czech society, there were two separate-but-equal literary cultures in Prague, Czech and German; Franz Kafka is, of course, not merely the finest writer to emerge from the latter, but one of the greatest artists of this century, and one of the many Jews who flourished in the Czech-German literary scene.

The official doctrine of Socialist Realism produced only sterile works in Czechoslovakia, as throughout the East Bloc, while intellectuals were humiliated and imprisoned, but some important writers did emerge during the thaw of the 1960s and since, including the nation's much-beloved president, playwright Václav Havel, whose absurdist plays are related to those of Ionesco and the Pole Sławomir Mrozek. Many of Havel's works are now available in English, including the famous *Letters to Olga*, written to his wife from prison (Holt), and the plays *Largo Desolato, The Memorandum*, and *Temptation* (Grove Press). Other contemporary Czech novelists have found international success: Milan Kundera, especially with *The Unbearable Lightness of Being* (Harper & Row) and *The Book of Laughter and Forgetting* (Penguin); Bohumil Hrabal, with *I Served the King of England* and *Too Loud a Solitude* (Harcourt Brace); Josef Skvorecky, who now lives in Canada, with *The Bass Saxophone, The Engineer of Human Souls* (both Washington Square Press), *Dvořák in Love* (Norton), and *Talkin' Moscow Blues* (Ecco), among others; Ivan Klima, author of numerous books, including two short-story collections available in translation, *My Merry Mornings* and *My First Loves*; and Ludvik Vaculik, author of the allegorical *The Guinea Pigs*, among other works.

SLOVAK LITERATURE The earliest documents in Slovak date from the 15th century, but the literary language was not finally standardized (using the central Slovakian dialect as its basis) until the turn of the 19th century. There are many important Slovak writers in the 19th and 20th centuries; unfortunately, almost nothing has been rendered into English. Those who can read Czech or German might look for poets Samo Chalupka, Ján Botto, Janko Král, Andrej Sládkovič, Svetpzár Vajanský, Pavel Országh-Hviezdoslav (the greatest Slovak poet), Ján Smrek, and Andrej Zarnov, who inspired a whole generation of writers; and novelists Ján Kaliincak, Martin Kukučin, Elena Marothy-Soltesova, Josef Hronsky, and Milo Urban.

MUSIC The musical culture of Bohemia and Moravia has deep roots. The Cathedral of St. Vitus in Prague has been a musical center since the 13th century. Like the Lutherans and Calvinists 150 years later, whom they anticipated, the Hussite reformers had a profound influence on religious music (including the adaptation of secular tunes and the use of the vernacular in hymn singing), which can be traced through Germany to England and then to America, in the music of the Moravian, Methodist, Anglican, and even the Catholic churches. Choral-singing societies flourished in Bohemia more than anywhere else in Europe; there were still a hundred of them in the late 18th century.

"All Bohemians Are Musicians" The Prague court of Rudolf II, who was not only king of the Czech lands but of Hungary, and Holy Roman Emperor, was home to musicians from all over Europe; Rudolf's example inspired many nobles to hire bands of musicians for their castles or town houses. By this time musical culture had spread to all levels of society; an English writer traveling in Bohemia in 1772 noted that music was a vital part of the education of every peasant child in every country schoolhouse throughout the kingdom—he called Bohemia "the conservatory of Europe." Bohemian musicality became proverbial (it was said that "All Bohemians are musicians") due mainly to this national reverence for musical education. In the 18th century it had become common for aristocrats to insist that every member of their families, and every servant from the stable boy on up, be trained to play an instrument or at least to sing, and Bohemian virtuosos filled the orchestras of Europe. This period of "Bohemian classicism" also produced a number of composers, widely admired in their day.

Opera Prague has always been open to new music from all over Europe as well: Mozart visited the city in 1787 to give the premiere of *Don Giovanni*, following the wild success of *The Marriage of Figaro* there; later the great German composer Carl Maria von Weber was director of the German Opera House (1813–16). Opera indeed has always enjoyed a great popular audience in Prague, since it was always performed at public, rather than court, theaters. Schoenberg's solo opera *Erwartung* was also premiered in Prague.

Folk Music The Romantic movement in Bohemia stimulated a nationalistic interest in the native folk music, as it did throughout Europe, and many collections of Czech folk songs were published after the 1820s. Folk dance music was also very vital—the polka is a Bohemian folk dance form that at one time in the 19th century became a world-wide craze. The first operatic performances in Czech translation were given in 1823; the first composer of operas in Czech was Franz Škroup (1801–62). The Romantic period also gave the nation its first composers of permanent international stature, Bedřich Smetana (1824–84) and Antonín Dvořák (1841–1904), both of whom tried to express the national "folk soul," often through the use of folk-musical materials. Among the Czech modernists are three other great composers, Leoš Janáček, Gustav Mahler (of German-Bohemian extraction), and Bohuslav Martinu.

4 Food & Drink

FOOD Czech and Slovakian food is typically hearty, and pork specialties abound. Prague ham is justly world famous, and you'll consider yourself lucky if you ever have the opportunity to sample the farm-fresh sausages from a local butcher. Cheese making is an ancient part of Bohemian culture and the Slovaks pride themselves on their fine sheep and goat cheeses. Dumplings, crêpes, cakes, and gingerbread are a few of the delicious baking specialties.

Prague ham, Slovak sausages, Moravian smoked meats, liver sausage, and pâtés are just part of the traditional pork dishes. These are often accompanied by knedle or knedliky (dumplings, or round, flat lumps of fried bread) or, in Slovakia, halušky (bits of homemade pasta). Creamy Roquefort-type cheese from Tábor, oštiepok, brynza, and parenica (Slovakian sheep's cheese) are just a few of the famous cheeses. Goose and duck are also important dishes on the Czech menu. They are sometimes served in their own juices with dumplings and cooked in special ovens to make them light but not greasy. An array of pickled gherkins, onions, sauerkraut, peppers, and most often, cucumbers accompany each meal. There is usually a choice of strudels, cakes, and pastries, as well as the traditional gingerbread (occasionally) to round off your meal.

In general the Czech and Slovak diets rely heavily on meat, so vegetarians may have a bit of difficulty, especially in smaller restaurants or beer pubs where only a few dishes—usually pork—are served. Fresh vegetables other than cucumbers are given little prominence on the Czechoslovak table.

DRINK Sóda is soda water, which is sometimes strongly effervescent. Minerálna voda, also called minerálka, is mineral water, occasionally with an overpowering sulfur taste. Imported soft drinks are often available as well.

Beer Czech beer is among the world's finest, and Slovak beer isn't far behind. The best-known brew comes from the Bohemian city of Plzeň: Plzeňský Prazdroj, known to the world as Pilsner Urquell. Gambrinus, another Plzeň beer, is popular throughout the Czech and Slovak Republics as well. Budvar—the original Budweiser—comes from Česke Budejovice, in southern Bohemia. Prague's most popular brews are Staropramen and Velkepopovický Kozel. Wherever you go in this land, though, you're likely to find obscure locally produced beers which are among the best you've ever tasted. The variety is numbing, and the quality always excellent. The beer, moreover, can often be sampled in a beer hall (*pivnice*) on the premises of the local brewery.

A degree number, signifying proof, is found on all beer labels. The alcohol content is roughly half this number. The most common are 10° and 12° (12° is the proof of choice for most Czechs and Slovaks).

Wine The Czechs also grow good grapes. The number of quality local burgundies from Bohemia has steadily increased since Emperor Charles IV introduced grapevines to this region. Favorite white wines include the dry Limbasský Silvaň, the medium Nitrianske Knieza, and the light sweet Raoiansky Výder. A favorite red is Sviečka. There are many other decent wines; ask around for other suggestions.

Liqueurs/Mead There are also numerous fruit liqueurs such as the herb-based Becherovka, but the rarest drink can only be found at traditional Moravian weddings. The father of the groom will carefully broach a cask of mead that he has been carefully tending since the bridegroom was born. The wedding party will sample the mead—the drink, according to legend, that gave the ancient Slavs their strength.

13

Planning a Trip to the Czech & Slovak Republics

Although the Czech and Slovak Republics pose fewer problems for the traveler than some other Eastern European countries, seeing these beautiful countries (with the exception on Prague) is still not as simple as touring through Western Europe. Therefore, additional care in planning will pay off handsomely. This chapter is devoted to the where, when, and how of your trip—the advance-planning issues required to get it together and take it on the road.

1 Information, Entry Requirements & Money

SOURCES OF INFORMATION

IN THE U.S. The Czech Travel Bureau, **Čedok** (pronounced "*Chay*-dauk") is a commercial travel agency that will make hotel and car-rental reservations only through travel agents. Čedok will also provide information and brochures. Čedok has an office at 10 E. 40th St., Suite 1902, New York, NY 10016 (☎ **212/689-9720;** fax 212/481-0597). [**Note:** The telephone lines are often busy.] Čedok clerks rarely volunteer information or services that you do not request. Be inquisitive, persistent, and—above all—friendly, and you will find people going out of their way to help you.

The Slovak portion of Čedok spun off into a new business entity, the Slovakia Travel Service **Satur**. Like Čedok, Satur is a commercial travel agency that makes reservations, arranges tours, and provides information. Satur's New York office is in the same building as Čedok's, at 10 E. 40th St., Suite 3601 (☎ **212/213-3865**).

IN THE U.K. Čedok has an office at 17–18 Old Bond St., London W1X 4RB (☎ **071/629-6058**).

ENTRY REQUIREMENTS

American citizens need their passport to enter the Czech and Slovak Republics but do not need visas. For further information, contact the consular sections of their embassies. The Embassy of the Czech Federal Republic, is at 2900 Linnean Ave. NW, Washington DC 20008 (☎ **202/363-6315**); its hours are Monday through Friday from 8:30am to 11:30am.

The Embassy of the Slovak Federal Republic is at 2201 Wisconsin Ave. NW, Suite 3180, Washington, DC 20007 (☎ **202/965-5160**); hours are Monday through Friday from 9am to 5pm. Or contact the Czech or Slovak embassy in your home country.

MONEY

CASH/CURRENCY The Czech currency is the **koruna** (abbreviated as Kčs); it's known in English as the crown. Each koruna is worth 100 haléřú (abbreviated as **h**), known in English as the heller. The koruna is circulated in notes of 50, 100, 500, and 1,000 Kčs. Coins come in denominations of 5, 10, 20, and 50 haler, and 1, 2, 5, 10, 20, and 50 Kčs. The prices in the chapters devoted to the Czech Republic were calculated at 28 Kčs equaling $1. Thus, 1 Kčs = 3.57¢, 10 Kčs = 36¢, and 100 Kčs = $3.57, $10 = 280 Kčs, and $100 = 2,800 Kčs.

The Slovak is the **Slovak koruna** (abbreviated as Sk), known in English as the Slovak crown, or simply crown. Each Sk is, like the Czech crown, worth 100 haléřú. Bills come in denominations of 20, 50, 100, 500, and 1000 Sk. Coins come as 1, 2, 5, 10, 20, and 50 h. The rate of Slovak crowns to the dollar was calculated at 31 Sk equaling $1. Thus, 1 Sk = 3.23¢, 10 Sk = 32¢, and 100 Sk = $3.20, $10 = 310 Sk, and $100 = 3,100 Sk.

What Things Cost in the Czech & Slovak Republics	U.S. $
Taxi from Prague's airport to the city center	20.00
Metro from the train station to Můstek in Prague	.14
Local telephone call	.04
Double room, with bath, at Prague's Hotel Paříž (deluxe)	200.00
Double room, with bath, at Prague's Hotel Axa (moderate)	89.00
Double room, with bath, at Žilina's Hotel Polom (budget)	28.00
Lunch or dinner for one, without wine, at U Modré Růžé, in Prague (deluxe)	14.10
Lunch or dinner for one, with beer, at Deminka, in Prague (moderate)	3.60
Lunch or dinner for one, without wine, at Másne Krámy, in České Budějovice (budget)	2.00
Pint of beer	.55
Coca-Cola	.40
Cup of coffee	.35
Admission to Prague's European Art Museum	1.40
Movie ticket	.85

Exchanging Currency Generally, the best place to exchange money is in banks, where the commission is usually from 1% to 2%. Banks are generally open Monday through Friday from 8am to 5pm, and are rather tourist friendly. If you must exchange money after banking hours, try the exchange bureaus of larger hotels. Avoid the private exchange offices generally found in tourist areas—their commissions are often as high as 10%.

The black market in hard currency, which once offered the highest rates for the dollar, is all but defunct. You'll get only a 2% to 5% better rate, and risk being ripped off. A popular trick these days involves giving the unsuspecting tourist a stack of worthless old crown notes, which were moved out of circulation in 1993.

If you stay in a private room, your host may wish to buy dollars from you; such transactions, of course, involve no middle man and you don't pay a commission.

TRAVELER'S CHECKS You may exchange traveler's checks at almost all banks, as well as other exchange bureaus.

CREDIT CARDS On the whole, credit cards are not readily accepted by the budget hotels and restaurants, although some of the more upscale places do accept them. Assume that restaurants and hotels do not accept credit cards unless they are mentioned specifically in the listing.

A Note on Prices

Some prices in the following chapters are given in German marks (DM) or Austrian schillings (AS). Because Western currencies are more stable than the Czechoslovakian crown, some businesses choose to base their prices on the daily exchange rates of either the German mark or Austrian schilling. The dollar amount of those prices is based on the following exchange rates: $1 = 1.60 DM, and $1 = 11.70 AS. If the dollar rises, some hotel costs could be lower than those cited in this book; if it falls, the reverse could be true.

2 When to Go

CLIMATE The best time of year to visit is from May to September. Keep in mind that during other times of the year, it frequently rains, so bring good raingear and warm clothing. The highest average summer temperature in Prague is in late July or early August, and the lowest average winter temperature is in January. Of course, if you do come in the off-season, you'll have the advantage of avoiding the crowds that swarm in Prague in summer.

Prague's Average Daytime Temperatures

	Jan	Feb	Mar	Apr	May	June	July	Aug	Sept	Oct	Nov	Dec
Temp. (°F)	27	29	37	46	55	61	64	63	57	47	38	31
Temp. (°C)	–3	–2	3	8	13	16	18	17	14	8	3	–1

HOLIDAYS National holidays include: January 1 (New Year's Day), Easter Monday, May 1 (Labor Day), May 9 (end of World War II), July 5 (the Coming of SS. Cyril and Methodius), July 6 (observed only in Bohemia and Moravia, in honor of Jan Hus), October 28 (Republic Day), and December 24–26 (Christmas).

Czech & Slovak Calendar of Events

January to March

- **Winter Amusement of the Czech Nobility Festival** (Jan) in Český Krumlov.
- **Jazz Festival** (Mar) in Karlovy Vary.

April to June

- **International Music Festival** (May; sometimes held in June) in Mariánské Lázně.
- **Bratislava Lyre** (May), a festival of popular music.
- **Dvořák Singing Contest** (June), in Karlovy Vary.
- **Chamber Music Festival** (June), where concerts are performed in period costumes on original instruments inside Český Krumlov Castle.
- **Janaček Music Festival** (June), in Brno.

July to December

- **International Film Festival** (July) every even year in Karlovy Vary.
- **American Independence Day Parade** (July 4), in Mariánské Lázně.
- **International Folklore Dance Festival** (July), three-day festival in Východná, Slovakia, with dance, song, food, and carnival fun.
- **Bratislava Summer,** a continuing program of cultural events in July and August.
- **Chopin Festival** (Aug), in Mariánské Lázně.

- **Dvořák Autumn Music Festival** (Sept), in Karlovy Vary; continues until October.
- **Brno International Music Festival** (Sept), continuing until October.
- **Bratislava Jazz Days** (Oct).

Prague Calendar of Events

January to June

- **Prague City of Music Festival** (Mar), with concerts around town.
- **Prague Spring Music Festival** (May), with music and cultural events in Prague's major concert halls; continues until June.
- **Concertino Praga** (June), with classical music events across town.

July to December

- **Prague Marathon** (Oct), a major footrace through the city.
- **Prague City of Music Festival** (Nov), with concerts around town.

3 Alternative/Adventure Travel

SPAS Beer isn't the only liquid resource with which the Czech and Slovak Republics are blessed. Underground mineral springs give the land more spas than practically any other European country. The spa town of Karlovy Vary (Karlsbad) and Mariánske Lázně (Marienbad) have been resorts and recuperation centers for centuries, and the Czechs have restored and modernized the old resorts. The mineral waters are for drinking as much as for bathing. If you're serious about "taking the waters," reserve a hotel and treatment package ahead of time. See "Karlovy Vary" in Chapter 15 for more details. Travel agencies in the U.S. that specialize in the Czech Republic and Slovakia can also often make spa reservations, as can Čedok.

HIKING The Czech and Slovak regions offer excellent hiking opportunities on numerous trails and nature reserves. Two areas are featured in this guide, the Little Fatra or Malá Fatra (see "Žilina and the Little Fatra" in Chapter 16) and the High Tatras (see "The High Tatras" in Chapter 16), the latter steep enough for challenging climbs for experienced mountaineers. Detailed hiking maps are available in the regions where hiking is popular. They usually cost 10 to 25 Sk (30¢ to 80¢) each.

4 Getting There

BY PLANE The Czechoslovak national airline, **ČSA** offers direct flights to Prague from New York and Chicago (via Toronto) and Montréal (two to four times a week) at highly competitive fares. Their New York office is at 545 Fifth Ave., New York, NY 10017 (☎ **212/682-5833,** or toll free **800/223-2365**). There are also offices in Chicago (☎ **312/201-1781**), Toronto (☎ **416/363-3174** to **3176**), Montréal (☎ **514/844-4200** or **844-6376**), and London (☎ **071/255-1898**).

You can fly to Prague on several experienced European air carriers that connect to Prague from the cities they serve in Western Europe. Among them, I recommend Austrian Airlines (☎ toll free **800/843-0002**) for reliable, professional service at competitive prices. They offer daily flights to Prague from Vienna. Their office in Prague is at Revoluční 15 (☎ **231-33-78** or **231-18-72**).

Before flying any carrier, I strongly suggest that you look for bargain flights in your local newspaper travel section—often listed on Sunday. If direct flights are too expensive, consider flying to Berlin or Vienna and then connecting by train.

BY TRAIN Many tourists take the six-hour train ride from Vienna to Prague. The train usually leaves from the Franz Josef Station, northwest of the city center. The cheapest way to travel by train from Vienna to Prague is to buy an Austrian ticket to Bratislava, and then transfer to a Czechoslovak train to Prague.

Another convenient route is from Berlin, which takes six or seven hours. Dresden is only four hours from Prague.

BY BUS You can take a bus to Bratislava or Brno from Vienna's Mitte station. The bus journey to Bratislava (1¼ hours) is far quicker than the train.

BY CAR All the major routes into the Czech Republic center on Prague: the E15 from Berlin to Budapest via Prague and Bratislava, and the E12 from Warsaw to Nürnberg and Munich.

BY SHIP You can get from Budapest or Vienna to Bratislava by boat. See "Bratislava" in Chapter 16 for details.

5 Getting Around

The trains may be a little slow and the roads narrow, but whichever route you take, you'll pass through some of Europe's most beautiful scenery.

BY PLANE The national carrier, **ČSA,** offers rather inexpensive domestic flights, connecting Prague to Bratislava, Košice, Ostrava, Pieštány, and Poprad; and connecting Bratislava to Prague, Košice, Poprad, and Pieštány. Children under 2 fly for 90% off the normal fare, and children between 2 and 12 get 50% off. ČSA's Prague office is at Revolučni 1 (☎ **2/231-7395**), near the Náměsti Republiky metro station.

BY TRAIN Czech and Slovak trains seem slower than many of the other Eastern European national rail services. In most cases, buses will be preferable for short hauls.

Trains travel at three speeds: express (*expresný*), fast (*rýchlik*), and ordinary (*osobný*). Avoid all the ordinary trains if possible; at one point I was certain that a farmer and his horse, plowing the fields next to the tracks, were making better time than our local train.

Tickets for domestic trains generally cannot be bought in advance. One-way tickets for trips of less than 200km (134 miles) are valid for only one day; tickets for trips of over 201km (135 miles) are valid for only two days. Since ticket prices are based solely on rail kilometers traveled, no discounts are gained by buying round-trip tickets, which also have very short validity periods. For trips up to 50km (30 miles), the ticket is valid one day; for trips of 51 to 200km (31 to 134 miles), it's valid for two days; and for trips over 201km (135 miles), it's valid for three days. You are therefore advised to buy only one-way tickets, and to buy them on the day you plan to travel.

You are allowed to interrupt your trip, but only within the above validity limits.

Seat reservations are required when an R with a box around it appears on the timetable; they are available but optional when an R without a box around it appears on the timetable. Reservations cost, but, annoyingly, sometimes must be purchased at a different window.

On overnight domestic train routes, couchettes and sleepers are available at very low prices—by all means you should buy one. A first-class couchette costs 80 Kčs

($2.85), a second-class couchette costs 50 Kčs ($1.80), and a sleeper costs 30 Kčs ($1.05).

Children under 6 ride free, and those under 16 get half-price tickets.

ČSD, the national rail company, offers a special pass good for 2,000km (1,340 miles) of rail travel in the Czech and Slovak Republics. Called the Kilometriká Banka, it costs only 490 Kčs ($17.50) and is valid for a year. What makes it really special is that more than one person can share a single pass, enabling a couple or a group who would not ordinarily amass 2,000km of domestic rail travel to use one card together. You are required at the time of purchase to write in the names of those who will be using it. It's not valid for trips of less than 70km (43 miles) or more than 700km (430 miles). Inquire at the information office of Prague's Hlavní nádraží.

The Interrail Pass is valid in the Czech and Slovak Republics, but the Eurailpass, alas, is not.

BY BUS You may end up taking more buses than you normally do elsewhere in Europe, as many of the castles and smaller villages are only accessible by road, and buses are often faster even to towns serviced by train. Most buses leave in the morning, so the earlier you start the more connections are available.

If you are boarding a bus at its city of origin (almost all buses leaving Prague or Bratislava, for example, originate there), then you may buy your ticket as much as a month in advance. It's a good idea to buy it a day or two ahead—you'll have a guaranteed seat number printed on the ticket. If you're boarding a bus that has originated elsewhere, which you will need to do if you're traveling at all in the smaller towns, you must pay the driver directly as you board, and hope that there's an empty seat.

Each bus station has a posted schedule, with red to indicate express lines and black for normal buses. If you're taking a long-distance bus, say, from Prague to Bratislava, make sure to get the express.

A Note About Bus and Train Stations In almost every city in the Czech and Slovak Republics, the train and bus stations are located either just next to each other or within easy walking distance. This makes travel much easier since you can look into two options for connections to your destination.

BY CAR • Car Rentals With many of its fascinating sights and castles outside the major cities, this is an excellent place to splurge on an auto. Though the big international car-rental firms now serve the Czech and Slovak Republics, the best deals are available from smaller, local firms. It's not as easy, however, to confirm reservations with these firms, which you should definitely try to do since their fleets are considerably smaller than those of the international agencies.

The local agency that seems to offer the best rates is **A Rent Car,** located at Opletalova 33, Prague 1 (☎ **24-22-98-48** or **24-21-15-87;** fax 24-21-20-32), as well as at the airport. The cheapest rental with unlimited mileage costs 1,552 Kčs ($55.45) per day for one to two days, 1,163 Kčs ($41.55) for each of three to six days, and

Tips for Students

Students with an ISIC (International Student Identity Card) receive a range of discounts from cheaper museum admissions to reduced travel fares on both domestic and international travel.

1,013 Kčs ($36.20) for seven or more days. The collision damage waiver (CDW) adds 169 Kčs ($6.05) per day or 1,011 Kčs ($36.10) per week. The company accepts credit cards (AE, DC, EC, JCB, MC, and V) and has offices in Karlovy Vary, České Budějovice, Brno, Bratislava, Žilina, Košice, and Poprad. Other competitive companies are **CS Czechocar,** which operates from Čedok offices, and **ESUCAR,** Husitská 58, Prague 3 (☎ **2/691-2244**).

Local agencies rent Czechoslovak Škodas, perfectly adequate no-frills cars. The larger firms charge a lot more, even for the same cars, than local agencies do. The large firms all seem to offer similar rates; check with the American offices to see if any are offering a special deal at the moment in Prague. If you're unable to confirm reservations with the above small companies in Prague, then you can easily make reservations through Hertz, Avis, National, or Budget offices in your home country or in Prague. Their main Prague offices are: **Avis,** Opletalova 33, Prague 1 (☎ **2/26-74-17** or **22-23-24;** fax 2/22-30-94; telex 123 153); and **Europcar** (National's affiliate in Europe), Pařižska 26, Prague 1 (☎ **2/31-34-05;** fax 2/31-02-78; telex 12-27-26). **Hertz,** Na Fišerce 24, Prague 6 (☎ **2/311-6354;** fax 2/311-4144; telex 123 162); and **Budget,** Kompas Tourism, Národni 17/IV, Prague 1 (☎ **2/232-2916;** fax 2/32-52-24; telex 123 149). All four also have counters at the airport.

• **Gasoline** Two grades of gasoline are available: Special (ninety one octane) and Super (ninety six octane). Gasoline is subjected to a 23% tax.

• **Driving Rules** Roads are generally two-lane and narrow, and often have many different kinds of nonmotorized traffic—including horse-drawn vehicles and foot traffic. The speed limit is 110 kmph (80 m.p.h.) on highways, 90 kmph (55 m.p.h.) on major roads, and 60 kmph (35 m.p.h.) through villages, whether posted or not. The driver and front-seat passengers must wear seatbelts; for back-seat passengers it's optional. The police levy on-the-spot fines.

All cars with non-Czechoslovak plates need to have proof of international insurance (the "Green Card"). If you plan to rent a car in another country and drive to the Czech and Slovak Republics, make sure you get that card from the rental agency. International driver's licences are not required.

BY LOCAL BUS & TRAIN Public transport systems rely on the honor system. You have to buy tickets from newsstands or nearby ticket machines, and cancel them when you get on board. If you ride without a ticket you could get hit with a fine, which you'll rarely see coming since inspection personnel do not wear uniforms. As of this writing, most tickets cost only 4 Kčs (14¢). In Prague and Bratislava, one-day and multiday passes are available for an extremely low price.

HITCHHIKING This is a common way of getting around, though, as always, women traveling alone should exercise extra caution.

BY FOOT When reading maps, searching for addresses, or navigating your way around, you should know that ulice (ulica in Slovakia; abbreviated "ul.") means "street," třida means "avenue," náměsti (námestie in Slovakia; abbreviated "nám.") is a "square" or "plaza," and nábřeži (nábrežie in Slovakia) means "quay." Cesta, a word used more often in Slovakia, means "road." None of these words is capitalized, and in addresses, street numbers follow the street name (for example, Václavské náměstí 25). Also, keep in mind that in the last few years many street names have been changed back to their pre-Communist names.

Suggested Itineraries

There are more worthwhile palaces, museums, parks, galleries, and picturesque villages in the Czech and Slovak Republics than two weeks of touring can do justice to:

CITY HIGHLIGHTS

Prague is the glorious capital of Eastern Europe, untouched by war for centuries, and an unrivaled relic of old Europe. The city's charms overwhelm just about everybody who visits. I rate it the most interesting city in Eastern Europe.

Elsewhere in Bohemia, to the west of Prague, are the 18th- and 19th-century Austro-Hungarian spa towns of Karlovy Vary (Karlsbad) and Mariánské Lázně (Marienbad), each well worth a day's visit. Plzeň, nearby, is well known as the hometown of Pilsner-Urquell beer.

Bohemia, south of Prague, is perhaps the most beautiful area in all of the Czech Republic, with the beautiful baroque and Renaissance towns of Tábor, the old Hussite stronghold, and České Budějovice. One of my favorite towns for old-world charm is just south of České Budějovice at Česky Krumlov, home to the second-largest castle in Bohemia.

In Moravia, the Czech Republic's central region, visit beautiful and sleepy Telč, with a Renaissance castle and Old Town Square. With an early start, you can get to it by bus from Tábor or České Budějovice and in the afternoon you can go from Telč to Brno, the major city of Moravia. Although Brno suffered heavy damage during World War II, several interesting museums and historic sites make for an enjoyable visit. One of the only superhighways in the Czech and Slovak Republics makes the trip from Brno to Prague (or vice versa) especially convenient.

Bratislava, the capital of Slovakia, is about two hours south of Brno on that same superhighway. An enjoyable collection of small museums and a recently restored historic center make Bratislava an alluring draw. Bratislava is also a good place to end your trip, as it's just over an hour by bus from Vienna. If, however, you want to continue your travels elsewhere in Slovakia, head to Žilina and the Little Fatra Mountains, or to the dramatic heights for hiking and climbing in the High Tatras, about two hours farther on the same train line.

If you plan extensive travels in Slovakia, consider exiting the region into Hungary through its northeastern border.

Planning Your Itinerary

If You Have 1 Week

Days 1–4 Spend at least four days in Prague. Though some people may try to pack most of the major sights into three one-day programs, it's an exhausting endeavor.

Days 5 and 6 While based in Prague, visit some of the impressive sights in the vicinity of the city. These might include the magnificent castles Karlštejn, Konopiště, and Český Šternberk; Kutná Hora, a Gothic silver-mining town; as well as Lidice, the symbol of the suffering endured during World War II.

Day 7 Leave a day for Český Krumlov, spending the night either there or in České Budějovice.

If You Have 2 Weeks

Give Prague and its surrounding castles a full week. Use the extra time to begin to really see the city. If a street calls to be explored, explore it. If a restaurant door stands invitingly ajar, peek in to see if it's open. When you have time in Prague, do as the Praguers do—follow your heart.

Spend your second week with a day each in Česky Krumlov, Česke Budějovice, and Tábor in Bohemia, and swing past Telč en route to Brno, with a night or two there depending on how much time you spend in Telč. Then proceed to Bratislava for two days, or consider a journey to the High Tatras.

If You Have 3 Weeks

Add visits to Karlovy Vary and Mariánské Lázné in Bohemia, consider a day in Plzeň, spend two nights in Brno, and add time to the High Tatras and/or the Little Fatras.

6 Enjoying the Czech & Slovak Republics on a Budget

THE $30-A-DAY BUDGET

Lovely Prague will stretch your $30-a-day budget, especially with its expensive accommodations. But in the rest of the country you'll have no problem staying within the budget. Domestic rail and bus fares are still incredibly low; see the individual city sections for sample fares.

SAVING MONEY ON . . .

ACCOMMODATIONS It is becoming increasingly necessary to pre-book hotel rooms in the Czech and Slovak Republic. At the very least, book your first night in Prague. You can personally contact some of the hotels or room-rental agencies listed in this guide, or you can rely on one of the following U.S.-based travel agencies.

- **Adventure International Travel Service,** 14305 Madison Ave., Lakewood, IL 44107 (☎ **216/228-7171;** fax 216/228-7170), can book hotel rooms, plane tickets, and spa visits. Ask for Paul Hudak or Priska Merai.
- **Tatra Travel,** 1489 Second Ave., New York, NY 10021 (☎ **212/486-0533**), charges a $25 service fee for hotel bookings.
- **AD Travel,** at Arts Development (☎ **609/896-9330;** fax 609/896-3450), can reserve private rooms in Prague as well as hotel rooms throughout the country. Reserve one month in advance, a private apartment for two in central Prague costs $85.
- **Benyo World Wide Travel,** 240 McLean Ave., Yonkers, NY 10705 (☎ **914/968-0175,** or toll free **800/872-8925;** fax 914/963-1329), will book hotel rooms without a service fee, but only if you also arrange your flight through them.
- You can also contact the U.S. number of **Prague Suites** (☎ toll free **800/426-8826**), the Prague-based agency which rents out private apartments in Prague, and also sends someone to meet your flight.
- Or ask your local travel agent to contact **Čedok** for you—though you will probably end up in the most expensive hotels.

Though advance reservations are recommended, particularly for overcrowded Prague, if you don't reserve ahead you can always take advantage of Eastern Europe's cheapest accommodations option—private rooms. These are *never* completely filled, even in Prague.

Once in the Czech and Slovak Republics, you can make reservations in the next town you're going to visit (or for your whole stay) through **Čedok.** This is useful for it allows you a flexible schedule but ensures that you don't have much difficulty finding a room (and difficulties do happen in Eastern Europe). Use this book to target hotels and ask for them in order of your preference. If one Cĕdok won't help you (and this does occur), then go to another one.

In the Czech and Slovak Republics, you can also book hotels through **Slovakoturist,** Panská 13, 81615 Bratislava (☎ **32-50-78;** fax 33-34-66). They are especially strong in the High Tatras and the rest of Slovakia, but they can reserve hotels anywhere in the two Republics. They have an office at Siroká 9, 11000 Prague (☎ **231-9148** or **232-4116**).

Hotel prices do tend to change abruptly in the Czech and Slovak Republics especially in Prague, as old hotels are privatized and renovated—placing them, unfortunately, outside the budget range.

MEALS Restaurants are very reasonably priced, almost all within range of the budget traveler (of course, prices could dramatically rise in the future as state subsidies end and the economy becomes more capitalistic). The main problem comes in Prague, where unscrupulous waiters have done just about everything they can to mar the image of the city's tourism industry. Generally, waiters elsewhere in the country are far more honest, but always monitor the bill with a careful eye to guard against "errors."

SIGHTSEEING & ENTERTAINMENT Museums and entertainment are very inexpensive in both Slovakia and the Czech Republic—with the occasional exception in Prague. Major Prague sights can total up to as much as $10 a day in admission fees. An option is to buy a **Prague Card,** a three-day transportation pass that also grants free admission to more than 60 of Prague's major sights. Pick it up at the American Express office, Cĕdok, and Pragotur for 360 Kčs ($12.85), or 260 Kčs ($9.29) for students.

SHOPPING Bohemian crystal is far and away the favorite shopping item for visitors. What's the difference between crystal and glass? Crystal has at least 24% lead in it, allowing for intricate designs of sharp lines and decorations worked into the glass and plates. Crystal also reflects more light than glass, and typically costs double the price of comparable glassware. Crystal in the Czech and Slovak Republics costs considerably less than it would at a store back home. Moreover, if you shop with your credit card, you'll generally avoid having to pay the 20% duty that's tacked on to the advertised price.

Folk arts and crafts such as leatherwork, folk costumes, and ceramics are also souvenir favorites. Classical records and CDs, garnets and costume jewelry, and art and coffee-table books are good buys.

Duty-Free Shopping You are allowed to export 500 Kčs ($17.85) of gifts duty free. Above this limit, there's a 20%-of-value duty, although border controls are lax. For more information, you can contact any Czech or Slovak consulate or Cĕdok office.

Shopping Etiquette Note that almost all stores expect you to bring your own plastic bag with you—they just don't give out bags. Many stores, such as grocery or bookstores, have baskets in front that you're supposed to take even if you don't intend to buy anything. If there are no available baskets, you'll see a line in front of the store with people waiting for other customers to exit and leave their baskets.

SERVICES Leave 5% to 10% of the bill in restaurants, strictly according to the level of service. Locals just round off the bill to an even number, often leaving less than 5%. Give a bellhop 20 Kčs (70¢). A bartender will appreciate 5% or 10%.

Fast Facts: The Czech and Slovak Republics

American Express There's an American Express office in Prague at Václavské nám. 56, Prague 1, 11000-1 (☎ **2/24-22-98-89;** fax 2/24-22-77-08), open Monday through Friday from 9 am to 6 pm and on Saturday from 9 am to noon. The 24-hour emergency number is **0044/273 571600** or **235-74-00.** All American Express services—from client mail to card replacement—are handled here.

Business Hours Government offices are open from 8am to 5 or 6pm Monday through Friday. Shops open around 9am and close at 6pm Monday through Friday, with late hours to 7 or 8pm on Thursday; on Saturday they may be open until noon. Food stores open at 7am and close at 6pm Monday through Wednesday and Friday, and 8pm on Thursday, and are usually open on Saturday until noon or 1pm. Many stores in Prague now keep longer business hours. Some are even open on Sunday.

Camera/Film All your photographic needs can be met in Prague and Bratislava, though you may not be able to find the type of film or batteries you want in smaller towns.

Drugstores Ask for a *Lékárna* in Bohemia and Moravia, or a *Lekáren* in Slovakia. Each pharmacy posts a list of local 24-hour drugstores. Sometimes the all-night pharmacies appear closed, but ring the bell outside and someone will come to the door.

Electricity The electric current is 220 volts, 50 cycles, AC.

Embassies/Consulates Citizens of New Zealand should contact the British embassy for assistance.

- **Australia** The embassy is at Hotel Praha, Susicks 20 (☎ **24-31-00-70**).
- **Canada** The embassy is at Mickiewiczova 6, Prague (☎ **24-31-11-08**).
- **United Kingdom** The embassy is at Thunozská 14, Prague (☎ **24-51-04-39**).
- **United States** The embassy is at Tržiště 15, Prague (☎ **24-51-08-47**).

Emergencies For the **police,** call **158;** for an **ambulance,** call **155.** Everyone is entitled to emergency first aid in the Czech and Slovak Republics although unless your insurance specifically covers it, you may have to pay for any such treatment.

Etiquette Try to remember that Czechs are people from Bohemia and Moravia, and Slovaks are from Slovakia.

Language Czech and Slovak are two closely related and mutually intelligible Slavic languages. German is spoken by many of the older people in Bohemia and in the northern part of Moravia. English is widely understood in Prague, less so in other Czech towns. Russian is perhaps widely understood throughout the Czech Republic, but most conversants ignore it. Slovaks, on the other hand, speak relatively little German and English but will communicate in Russian without discomfort.

Liquor Laws Bars don't serve those under 18. Drinking and driving is forbidden.

Luggage Lockers Since taxis in the smaller towns are rare (and inexpensive), consider packing a day-pack with your toiletries and a change of clothes, and taking advantage of the luggage-storage facilities in the railway stations.

Mail To North America it costs 9 Kčs (32¢) and up for airmail letters, and 6 Kčs (21¢) for postcards. Generally the mail services are reliable, with delivery to the U.S. in two or three weeks. Post offices are usually open Monday through Friday from 8am to 6pm. Anything sent airmail must be given to a post office clerk. If you just drop it into a mailbox, it may go with surface mail and take much longer.

Maps With only a few exceptions, good maps are available throughout the Czech and Slovak Republics.

Movies Foreign films are shown with either subtitles (*titulky*) or dubbing (*dabing*); ask at the theater which is used. Movies cost 10 to 18 Kčs (35¢ to 65¢), though they're about 25% more expensive in Prague.

Newspapers/Magazines The *International Herald Tribune, USA Today*, assorted British newspapers, and a variety of English-language newsweeklies are widely available throughout central Prague and Bratislava. They're more difficult to come by in other towns; check in the luxury hotels. In addition, Prague has two English-language newspapers which are indispensable to the visitor: the weekly *Prague Post* and the biweekly *Prognosis.*

Restrooms Many public restrooms cost 2 Kčs (7¢), and if you don't remember to leave the attendant a coin, she'll loudly remind you. You'll do well to bring toilet paper to public restrooms as well, although it is sometimes available.

Safety As elsewhere in Eastern Europe, crime has increased with the demise of Communism and the police state. And as in other major European destinations, thieves prey on the most vulnerable-looking tourists, especially in Prague. Don't get dizzy with the beauty of Prague and forget to keep an eye on your wallet or pocketbook. Be especially aware on crowded streets and public transport in Prague. Smaller towns have far fewer safety problems.

Telephone/Telex/Fax Coin-operated telephones are being replaced by phonecard-operated machines in Prague. Telekarts are available in prices that range from 105 to 294 Kčs ($3.70 to $10.50). They are available in *tabak* shops and at Windows 20 and 36 of Prague's post office.

For **local calls** on the coin-operated machines, place a 1-Kčs (4¢) coin on the coin holder; it will fall in when the connection is completed. A long buzzing tone means the line is ringing; two very short tones indicate the line's busy. Once your call gets through, you can talk for as long as you'd like.

For **long-distance calls** within the country, go to larger gray boxes and insert 1-, 2-, or 5-Kčs coins as fast as you can. You'll hear a warning tone just before you're to be cut off. Yellow or orange boxes are for local calls only.

You have several options for **international calls.** To contact an ATT or MCI operator, use a gray telephone box or go to the local telephone office, usually in the post office. A 2-Kčs coin (later returned) enables you to connect with an international operator, through which you can either bill a call to your calling card or call collect. The MCI access number is **00/42-000112;** the ATT access number is **00/42-000101.** You can also call Canada direct by dialing **00/42-000151,** and the U.K. by dialing **00/42-004401.**

If you choose to make your call from the telephone office and pay directly for your call in Czech currency, one minute costs 74 Kčs ($2.65) to the U.S., Canada, Australia, or New Zealand.

To reach **information** in Prague, dial **120;** for the rest of Czechoslovakia, dial **121.**

You can send **telexes** and **faxes** conveniently from the main post office in Prague (60 Kčs/$2.15 per minute outside of Europe) as well as from the business centers of major hotels.

Time The Czech and Slovak Republics are on Central European standard time, which is six hours ahead of eastern standard time in the U.S. The Czech and Slovak Republics change to daylight saving time at roughly the same time as the U.S.

Water Usually you can drink the tap water. Occasionally you'll see a pictogram of a glass of water with an "X" over it, in places such as train stations or parks. This water is only for washing. In parts of Slovakia the drinking water, direct from the mountains, is delicious.

14

Prague

IF YOU CAN VISIT ONLY ONE CITY IN EASTERN EUROPE, MAKE IT PRAGUE (POP. 1,200,000), the capital Thomas Mann called "one of the most magical cities on earth." The "city of one-hundred spires" beguiles like a walking dream, emerging from morning mists as if from drowsy layers of sleep. Sprawling over seven hills, the city gradually rises to the Gothic spires of Prague Castle and St. Vitus Cathedral, the royal refuge resting halfway between earth and firmament.

The Staré Město (the Old City) below the castle is an arched, cobble-stone mystery; its old churches, buildings, and fountains are time-worn but intact—almost untouched by the passage of centuries. Between the castle and the Staré Město flows the Vltaya (Moldau). Delicately framing the river with 14th-century spans is the Charles Bridge, the very symbol of Prague.

Because of its precious beauty and state of preservation, Prague has been transformed from a placid monument to a go-go hotspot. The "Velvet Revolution" of 1989 thrust the city, so long weighed down by Nazi and Communist tyranny, onto the international stage. The pent-up potential for tourism exploded, and visitors from all over the world began showing up on the city's fabled ramparts. Writers who were used to viewing this repressed city as a character in an absurdist comedy have been forced to adapt to a new round of clownish occupiers, toting Nikons not AK-47s and wearing star-spangled leisure shirts not uniforms with red Soviet stars. Cobbled-stoned streets ring with the likes of Andean pan-flute musicians, peddlers hawking trinkets, and tourists lining up to buy gummi bears from sidewalk kiosks.

Perhaps the most startling element of Prague's recent cosmopolitan potpourri is the large contingent of young Americans who have settled here. Invited by Havel himself, as many as 30,000 teach English, run restaurants, practice street theater, or just hang out. They have left a deep mark on the city that some residents decry but most welcome. For many residents, they've become a symbol of Prague's rebirth.

1 Orientation

"Prague is a golden ship majestically sailing on the Vltava," wrote Guillaume Apollinaire (1880–1918), a French poet of Polish descent. Once you're in the city center many views include the wide Vltava River that cuts through the center of the city. The mighty Prague Hrad (Castle) and St. Vitus Cathedral on the west bank and the Church of our Lady of Týn and the Staroměstské náměstí (Old Town Square) on the east bank could almost be the bulkheads of some mighty ship.

ARRIVING

Prague is one of the primary transportation hubs of Central Europe, and it's the logical point to begin any tour of the Czech and Slovak Republics.

BY PLANE Prague's **Ruzyně Airport** (☎ **334, 36-77-60,** or **36-78-14**) is about 12 miles from the city center at Praha-Ruzyně. In the main hall after Customs you'll find several car-rental offices, a money-exchange desk, and a telephone and post office (open Monday through Saturday from 8am to 9pm and on Sunday from 8am to 1pm). There's also a Čedok office that theoretically can reserve hotel rooms in town, but it's quite disorganized and unlikely to offer you this service.

The Czechoslovak airline ČSA operates buses into town every 20 or 30 minutes from 7:30am or 7:40am until 7:40pm for only 15 Kčs (55¢). The bus arrives after about 45 minutes at a square in the Old Town immediately south of the Švermuv

What's Special About Prague

Monuments

- Old Town Square, one of Europe's most attractive, combining Gothic, Renaissance, baroque, and rococo architecture.
- Charles Bridge, Prague's oldest bridge and the symbol of the city.

Castles

- Prague Castle (Hrad), dating from Prague's golden age in the 14th century, dominating the west side of the Vltava River.
- Karlštejn, 45 minutes from Prague, a well-preserved structure from 1348, built to house the crown jewels of the Holy Roman Empire.

Buildings

- Royal Palace, home of Bohemian kings and princes from the 9th to the 16th century.
- Old Town Hall, from the 11th century, with its 14th-century tower.
- Powder Tower, a 140-foot-tall tower, the only one remaining from Prague's medieval fortifications.

Museums

- European Art Museum, with one of Central Europe's finest collections.
- National Museum, with a collection recalling the nation's archeological and historical past, ensconced in a neo-Renaissance building.
- Czech National Gallery, with a major collection of Bohemian painting and sculpture.
- St. Agnes Convent, housing within its Gothic halls a gallery of 19th-century Czech art.
- National Technical Museum, with a spectacular photographic collection including several original daguerreotypes.

Places of Worship

- St. Vitus Cathedral, a massive 14th-century Gothic structure containing the tombs of Saints Vitus and Wenceslas (of Christmas carol fame).
- Týn Church, with its twin 260-foot spires, where Jan Hus first heard Reformation sermons.
- St. Nicholas Church, one of the world's most opulent baroque churches.
- Old New Synagogue, Europe's oldest remaining Jewish house of worship.

Parks/Gardens

- Letná Park, with its Renaissance gardens and Royal Summer Palace.
- Wallenstein Palace Gardens, surrounding the first baroque palace in Prague.

Events/Festivals

- Prague Spring Music Festival, in May and June, with music and cultural events performed in Prague's major concert halls.
- Prague City of Music Festival, in November, with concerts around town.

most (bridge), at Revoluční ulice 25, about five blocks from the náměsti Republiky metro stop. The bus stops in front of a ČSA reception office, which offers information, a luggage-check service, and bathrooms.

Public bus no. 119 goes from the airport to the Dejvická metro station, where you can easily connect to all points in Prague. The cost of the ticket is 4 Kčs. (15¢).

Avoid the overpriced Čedok bus from the airport. Either of the two above buses is fine.

An honest taxi ride into town should cost around 200 Kčs ($7.10), though first you should read "Getting Around" "By Taxi," below.

BY TRAIN If you're arriving in Prague by train, you will pull in at one of several principal stations:

Main Train Station Prague's main train station *(Praha hlavni nádraží)*, on Wilsonovciz třída (☎ **24-22-32-26**), renamed Woodrow Wilson station in 1990 after the American president, is a modern, well-laid-out building resembling an airport terminal. From the train platform you'll walk down a flight of steps and through a tunnel before arriving at the first large hallway, where you'll find the train information office; ticket and seat reservation windows; money-exchange bureaus (some open 24 hours); bathrooms; a few newsstands selling good maps and metro and bus tickets; food vendors; and offices for several accommodations services (see "Where to Stay," below).

If you continue walking straight ahead down another flight of stairs, you can check your luggage in either lockers for 4 Kčs (15¢) per day or a baggage-check service, open 24 hours daily, for 5 Kčs (20¢). From another area of this level you can also descend into Prague's convenient metro system. You can also make telephone calls or mail letters from the post office, open Monday through Friday from 8am to 8pm and on Saturday from 8am to 1pm. On the left side of this level is a small tourist information office, with maps and some information as well as English-speaking officers, open Monday through Friday from 6am to 8 pm, on Saturday from 7am to 7pm, and on Sunday from 8am to 4pm. They charge 20 Kčs (70¢) for a shower and a clean towel. You can also get a manicure or have your hair cut here.

The rarely visited upper level of the train station is a huge dome, built in 1907, in an interesting art deco style.

To get into town from the station take metro Line C, which connects with Line A one stop south or with Line B one stop north. If you don't have exact change for the metro, buy tickets at the newsstand near the entrance. Alternatively, walk northwest for about 15 minutes to Staroměstské náměstí (Old City Square).

Holešovice If you arrive from northern Europe (Berlin or Dresden) or from the Balkans you might pull into Prague at this station north of the city center (☎ **80-75-05**). The station has a baggage-check service, an information window, and a room-finding travel agency.

This station connects with the northern terminus of metro Line C, at nádraží Holešovice. You can connect to Line B after two stops at Florenc, or to Line A after four stops at Muzeum.

Masaryk If you're traveling from elsewhere in the Czech and Slovak Republics, especially Bohemia, but also Brno and Bratislava, you might arrive at Masaryk Station, on Hybernská ulice, 5 or 10 minutes on foot from the main train station. You'll find a baggage-check service here charging 5 Kčs (20¢) and lockers off Track 7. You can catch metro Line B from the náměstí Republiky stop by exiting on the right side of the station. You can also walk to town center in just a few minutes.

Smíchov Station Mostly commuter trains from southern and western Bohemia (such as Mariánské Lázně, Plzeň, and Karlštejn) arrive and depart from this station on Nádranžní ulice, although an occasional international train pulls in. There's a 24-hour baggage-check service here, as well as a post office and an international train bureau to the left as you exit. From here you can connect to metro Line B at the Smíchovské nádraží stop.

BY BUS Prague's major bus station, **Florenc,** is on Wilsonova třída (☎ **22-14-45/9**), a few blocks north of the main railroad station. You can check luggage here in lockers. The station connects up to the Florenc station of metro Lines B and C.

Ticketing for buses isn't as centralized as it is for trains. For domestic routes, you must purchase tickets at the station itself. The ticket office is open Monday through Friday 6am to noon and 12:40 to 6pm, Saturday from 6am to 12:30pm; and on Sunday from 8:30am to noon and 12:30 to 6pm.

BY CAR If you arrive by car, you should be aware that central Prague around the Staré Město (Old Town) is closed to all cars unless you have accommodations there.

Parking is generally not a problem as there are several parking lots on the outskirts of the Staré Město.

TOURIST INFORMATION

General Information Prague has a superb tourist information office called **Pražská Informační Služba (PIS),** at Na Příkopě 20 (☎ **54-44-44**), just two minutes from the Powder Tower. You can pick up brochures on upcoming cultural events and get sightseeing and concert information. In summer, they work Monday through Friday from 8am to 7pm and on Saturday and Sunday from 9am to 3pm. In winter, hours are scaled back to 8am to 6pm weekdays and 8am to noon on Saturday.

There are also PIS branches as in the Old Town Square (Staroměstské Nám. 22), under the castle (Valdštejnské náměstí), and in the main railway station (see "Arriving" "By Train," above).

You can pick up detailed maps of the Prague Castle at the **Castle Information Office,** to the right as you enter the castle's second courtyard (☎ **33-37** or **33-38**). Although they specialize in information about the buildings in the castle area, they can also help you with general information about Prague. Open Tuesday through Sunday: April to September from 9am to 5pm and the rest of the year from 9am to 4pm.

The **American Hospitality Center,** at Na Můstku 7 (☎ **236-7486;** fax 26-97-38), is just a block from the foot of Weneslaus Square and is open daily from 9am to 10pm from April through October, 9am to 8pm in the off-season. Staffed by Czech and American students, this not-for-profit center provides advice, American newspapers, and brochures for all travelers and maintains a message board for friends meeting in Prague. They also sell tickets to all kinds of events in Prague. It's connected to an American-style coffee shop.

The main **Čedok office** is at Na Příkopě 18, and is open Monday through Friday from 8:30am to 6pm, and on Saturday from 8:30am to 12:30pm. This office is the domain of Umberto Boffi. If no one else in town can answer your question, odds are he can. He's on your left as you enter, at the "Information" desk.

Transportation Information In the main train station on the same level where you buy train tickets you can get information on the local transportation network and pick up a free transportation map. This window is open Monday through Friday from 7am to 6pm.

You can also dial **235-5850** for transportation information.

Private Guides If you want to hire a private guide, go to the guides' office of Pražská Informačni Služba (PIS) at Panská 4 (☎ **22-34-11, 22-43-11, 22-60-67,** or **22-61-36**). Give them a few hours' notice and later that day you'll have a private guide for 1,000 Kčs ($35.70) for three hours any day of the week.

For a guided tour of Josefov, Prague's Jewish Ghetto, contact Eva Feiglova, Sládkovičova 1306, Box 69, 142 00 Prague 4 (☎ **2/471-9081**). A Hebrew scholar and Prague native, she leads lively and informative two-hour tours, charging 20 DM ($12.50) for one or two people, and 10 DM ($6.25) for each additional person in the group.

CITY LAYOUT

NEIGHBORHOODS IN BRIEF There are five major parts of the city center of primary interest to tourists: Hradčany, the castle district atop a hill on the left bank of the Vltava River; Malá Strana, the lower or lesser town at the foot of Hradčany, also on the west bank of the Vltava; Staré Město, the Old Town on the right bank of the river; Josefov, the old Jewish ghetto immediately north of Staré Město; and Nové Město, the New Town (at least it was new in the 14th century when it was built), located south and east of Staré Město.

The magnificent Hradčany includes St. Vitus Cathedral dominating the skyline. St. Nicholas Church as well as hundreds of other architecturally important structures nearby grace the streets of Malá Strana. The Staré Město is one of the largest and most beautiful in Europe, where you'll find Charles Bridge, Týn Church, and the Old Town Hall.

MAIN ARTERIES & STREETS The Vltava River divides Prague, with the Hradčany (castle district) on the left or west side and the Old Town (Staré Město) on the right or east side of the river.

Hradčanské náměstí lies at the center of the Hradčany (castle district), just west of the actual entrance to the large Prague Castle. Loretánská ulice, farther west, connects the square to the Loreto Church. Southeast of Hradčanské náměstí is a long stairway, Zámecké schody, leading to the central thoroughfare of Malá Strana, Mostecká ulice (Bridge Street). Mostecká ulice is appropriately named as it connects with Prague's most famous bridge Karlův most (Charles Bridge).

Across the Vltava are the twisted narrow streets of the Staré Město (Old Town). From the Karlův most, Karlova ulice leads directly to Prague's most important square, Staroměstské náměstí (Old Town Square). Several important streets exit from Staroměstské náměstí. Pařížská ulice, a street with a number of travel agencies, leads toward Josefov, the Jewish Quarter, to the north.

Celetná ulice, exiting east from the square, leads to Prague's major shopping areas. Follow the street until you reach the tall Powder Tower (Prašná brána) off náměstí Republiky. Then make a sharp right to Na Příkopě, home of Prague's main information office and Čedok's international ticket office. After several blocks you'll reach Václavské náměstí, the central boulevard of modern Prague, filled with hotels, stores, and restaurants—and the center of the 1989 democratic revolution.

Finding an Address When reading maps, searching for addresses, or navigating your way around Prague and the rest of Bohemia and Moravia, you should know that ulice (abbreviated "ul.") means "street," třída means "avenue," náměstí (abbreviated "nám.") is a "square" or "plaza," and nábřeží means "quay." In Czech none of these words is capitalized and in addresses, street numbers follow the street name (for example, Václavské náměstí 25).

The city is zoned into 10 districts. Nine districts radiate around district 1, the city center and the location of most of the sights listed in this chapter. There are also hotels, restaurants and attractions in district 2 (the neighborhoods of Vysehrad and Vinohrady) to the southeast of district 1; district 3 (Žižkov) to the west; district 5 (Smíchov) in the southwest; and district 7 (Holešovice), due north. Districts are given in the addresses throughout this chapter.

Because Prague is so large, with small, winding streets, you'll want to bring a detailed map along with you on your explorations. Fortunately, most maps available in Prague are cross-referenced on the back.

Maps A number of good maps of the city are readily available at the tourist offices and newsstands across town. Most cross-reference the streets and give the addresses of the major sights, museums, and concert halls, and include bus and metro routes. The best is the one with the yellow and purple cover put out by Kartografie Praha. An average map should cost 30 to 50 Kčs ($1.05 to $1.80).

The Prague transit authority prints a map without streets but with all the metro, tram, and bus routes; it's available free of charge from the transportation information office at the central train station.

Check any of the bookstores in the center for a good selection of maps of Prague, other Czech and Slovak cities, and other European cities and countries. Buy locally made rather than Western-made maps; you get basically the same quality for a much lower price.

2 Getting Around

BY METRO, BUS & TRAM Getting around Prague is easy, thanks to three metro lines serving almost all of "tourist Prague," complemented by an extensive bus and tram network. The system closes a few minutes after midnight except for a few night tram and bus lines (which leave every 40 minutes), and reopens shortly before 5am.

All public transport in Prague requires the same 4-Kčs (15¢) tickets, which can be bought in tobacco shops, newsstands, or from machines (which require exact change) in most metro stations. The honor system is used, with each passenger responsible for validating his/her own ticket. Inspectors do occasionally fine ticketless riders 200 Kčs ($7.15).

If you plan to be using public transport with any frequency it makes sense to buy day passes, which are quite cheap and allow you to ignore the hassle of constantly buying and validating tickets. A one-day pass costs 30 Kčs ($1.05), a two-day pass is 50 Kčs ($1.80), a three-day pass costs 65 Kčs ($2.15), and the best deal of all, a five-day pass, costs 100 Kčs ($3.55). These passes are available in central Prague at tobacco kiosks and from ticket windows in some of the busier metro stations.

Another option is to get a **Prague Card,** a three-day transportation pass that also gains the user free admission to over 60 of Prague's major sights and museums. It's

Telephone Number Advisory

Prague's Communist-era telephone system is under renovation, and many phone numbers will change during the lifetime of this book. Eventually, all Prague numbers will have eight digits, but until then, some will also do with five, six, and seven digits. In Prague, you can check numbers in the biannually updated yellow pages.

available at the American Express office, Čedok, and Pragotur (see "Where to Stay," below) for 360 Kčs ($12.85), or 260 Kčs ($9.30) for students.

Three lines make up Prague's metro system, with the most important sightseeing destinations along Line A. The five most important stops on this line (in order of appearance) are: Muzeum, at the top of Václavské náměstí, site of the National Museum; Můstek, at the other end of Václavské náměstí, near many of Prague's favorite shopping streets as well as the central Prague information office and Čedok; Staroměstská, just a few blocks from the Old Town Square; Malostranská, the nearest stop to the Prague Castle (but still a 10-minute walk up a long series of stairs); and Hradčanská, the next stop in the castle district (Hradčany), which offers the possibility of changing to tram no. 22 to Keplerova ulice, and then walking *downhill* to the castle.

Signs in the Prague metro—though totally inadequate—are color-coded: Line A is green, Line B is yellow, and Line C is red.

On most Prague maps it's very difficult to make out the actual metro lines among all the other jumbled information on the map. The handiest metro map is available in postcard form for 3 Kčs (10¢) from some metro ticket windows.

The convenience of the public transportation system renders taxis all but unnecessary in Prague.

BY TAXI Taxis are increasingly expensive in Prague. Moreover, Prague's taxi drivers are the most seasoned hustlers in all of Eastern Europe—and given the unscrupulous practices of some of Eastern Europe's cab drivers, this is really a dubious distinction. Here are some tips on how to avoid being ripped off:

- If you get into a taxi and the driver doesn't turn on the meter immediately (a common trick), remind him to turn it on by showing him this phrase: "Zapněte taxameter prosím" ("Please turn on the meter"). Profi Taxi is reputedly the cheapest, at 10 Kčs ($36¢) per kilometer.
- Make sure that the meter is visible. If it's covered with a newspaper, the driver's hat, or anything else, ask the driver to remove the item so that you can see the meter. Drivers sometimes keep meters running after their passengers leave so that the next fare starts at a high price.
- If the driver tells you that the meter is broken (which is almost always a lie) or refuses to turn it on, he will be breaking Czech law, which requires that all taxis have a working meter. You can confront such a driver in several ways: by immediately exiting his taxi, by agreeing on a fare right away (although the fare will be inflated), or by saying nothing until you arrive at your destination.

If you try the feistier latter course, you can exit the car and then, through the window, hand the driver what you think a normal metered fare would have cost; as the driver has broken the law, he ultimately must accept whatever you offer him—including nothing at all—although he may become aggressive. Alternatively, you can ask him how much he wants and then insist on a receipt, which he is obliged to furnish, complete with name, time of service, area traveled, and taxi number. Show this phrase: "Prosím dejte mi potvrzení" ("Please give me a receipt"), and then "Bez potvrzení nemohu zaplatit" ("Without a receipt, I cannot pay"). As a receipt could be used as evidence of illegal unmetered driving, the cabbie will probably refuse (another illegality), so again you have the right to pay whatever you want or just leave altogether, although be prepared for a dose of the driver's hostility.

You can either hail a taxi, wait for one at a taxi stand, or dial **20-39-41** to **20-39-49** or **20-29-51** to **20-29-59.**

ON FOOT With a seemingly endless array of beautiful buildings and charming neighborhoods, Prague is a great city for walking. As cars are banned from several of the most important areas of the city, you'll have to walk inside the large castle (Hrad), on many streets of the Old Town (Staré Město), and on Charles Bridge.

BY CAR Driving in Prague can be a hassle and is definitely not recommended for sightseeing purposes. You may want a car, however, for day or overnight trips to nearby towns. For car-rental information, see "Getting Around" in Chapter 13.

Most car-rental agencies produce materials that list parking places and gasoline stations throughout the city.

Fast Facts: Prague

American Express There is an office at Václavské nám. 56, 11000 Prague 1 (☎ **24-22-98-89;** fax 24-22-77-08). It's open Monday through Friday from 9am to 6pm, and on Saturday from 9am to noon. The local emergency number is **235-74-00** daily 6am to 3am. All American Express services—from client mail to card replacement—are handled here.

Area Code Prague's telephone area code is 2.

Bookstores Prague has a wide variety of bookstores, many of them selling guidebooks to the Czech and Slovak Republics in English. I especially recommend two guides published by Olympia, one titled just *Prague,* and the other *Czechoslovakia/Prague.* You'll find them in bookstores across the Old Town. *Prague Naturally,* written by four American expatriates, is a guide to healthy food, medical facilities, and recreation facilities in Prague.

The city has two notable English-language bookstores for stocking up on serious reading. The **Globe Bookstore/Coffeehouse** at Janovského 14 in Prague 7 (metro: Vltavská) is fast on its way to becoming legendary. Not only does the Globe have Eastern Europe's best selection of mostly used and some new English-language books, it's a scene. Hours are 10am to midnight daily. (Also see listing in "Where to Eat," below.) The **International Bookstore,** at Pařížská 25 in Josefov, has a poorer selection than the Globe but more new books. It's open 10am to 8pm daily.

Currency Exchange Avoid the high-commission private exchange offices and exchange money instead in banks, where the normal commission is 1% to 2%. Banks are generally open Monday through Friday from 8am to 5pm. Some conveniently located are at Na Příkopě 5, 14, 20, 28, and 42, and Václavské nám. 42. The Komerční Banka at Na Příkopě 42 is the place to reexchange crowns into hard currency before leaving the country. Naturally, you need your exchange receipts. Cash advances on credit cards can be obtained at the Živnostenská Banka at Na Příkopě 20. The Obchodní Banka at Na Příkopě 14 will cash international bank checks. Čekobank at Na Příkopě 10 is open until 11pm Monday through Friday, and Komerčni Banka at Na Příkopě 3–5 has Saturday hours from 8am to 11am.

If you absolutely must change money after banking hours, try some of the large hotels on Václavské náměstí.

Dentist A clinic at Vladislavova 22 (☎ **26-13-74**) provides emergency dental work for foreigners.

Doctors See "Hospitals," below.

Drugstores For a pharmacy with night service, visit Na Příkopě 7 (☎ **22-00-81**).

Embassies/Consulates The **U.S. Embassy** is at Tržiště 15 (☎ **24-51-08-47** or **24-51-08-48**). The **Canadian Embassy** is at Mickiewczova 6 (☎ **24-31-11-08** or **24-31-02-94**), and the **Embassy of the U.K.** is at Thunovská 14 (☎ **24-51-14-43** or **24-51-04-39**).

Emergency For **emergency, medical aid in English,** dial **29-93-81;** for the **police,** dial **158;** for an **ambulance,** dial **155;** for the **fire department,** dial **150.**

Hospitals For medical difficulties, call your embassy for advice. Foreigners are usually treated at the **Faculty Polyclinic,** Karlovo nám. 32.

Laundry/Dry Cleaning The project of a few expatriots' zeal for clean clothing, Laundry King (☎ **312-37-43**) has been profiled by so many visiting journalists that it has achieved a weird celebrity. The world's first post-Communist self-serve coin-op does magical things with travel-soiled clothing for 100 to 120 Kčs ($3.55 to $4.30) per load. From metro Hradčanská in Prague 6, walk one block north to Dejvičká; the store is another block away at Dejvičká 16. Hours are Monday through Friday 6am to 10pm, Saturday and Sunday 8am to 10pm.

Luggage Storage/Lockers You can store luggage at a number of places in Prague, including at the ČSA airport bus terminal at Revolučni ulice 25, immediately south of Švermův most (bridge); at every train station; and at Florenc bus station. The average charge is 5 Kčs (20¢) per day.

Lost Property Don't hold out much hope of success, but there's an official lost-property office at Bolzanova 5 (☎ **236-8887**).

Newspapers/Magazines The *International Herald Tribune, USA Today,* assorted British papers, and numerous foreign weeklies are available throughout central Prague. Prague has two English-language newspapers, the weekly *Prague Post* and the biweekly *Prognosis,* which provide detailed cultural schedules as well as more general tourist information. They are also very useful for those who are interested in what's going on in local politics. Each costs 20 Kčs (70¢) and is widely available in central Prague.

Photographic Needs All your photographic needs can be met in Prague, as well as in smaller towns of the Czech and Slovak Republics.

Police In an emergency, phone the police at **158.**

Post Office The main post office at Jindřišská 14 (☎ **26-41-93** or **26-48-41**), off Václavské náměstí is open 24 hours. This branch can send and receive faxes, and even has a special window for stamp collectors. Other conveniently located post offices are: on the lower level of the main train station, open Monday through Friday from 8am to 8pm and on Saturday from 8am to 1pm; inside the castle across from St. Vitus Cathedral, open daily from 8am to 7pm; and at the airport.

Restrooms In Prague, as elsewhere in the Czech and Slovak Republics, you should have a few spare 1-Kčs (4¢) coins to give to attendants at public restrooms; 2 Kčs (7¢) should do. The cleanest restrooms in the city are at McDonald's, Vodičkova 15—and they're free.

Safety Crime has risen in Prague since the fall of Communism, especially along the major tourist streets. Watch your wallet or bag when on crowded streets around the castle area or Old Town Square, at the various train stations, and on crowded public transportation.

Telephones/Telegrams/Telex Local calls require a 1-Kčs (4¢) coin. To reach Prague information, dial **120;** for the rest of the country it's **121.**

You can make international calls or send faxes 24 hours a day from the post office at Jindřišská 14 (☎ **26-48-41**). Other phone offices include the post office in the Hrad (castle) just in front of St. Vitus Cathedral, open daily from 8am until 7pm, and another on the lower level of the main train station, open Monday through Friday from 8am to 8pm and on Saturday from 8am to 1pm. See "Telephone/Telex/Fax" in "Fast Facts: The Czech and Slovak Republics," in Chapter 13, for rates to the U.S. and other countries.

3 Where to Stay

Prague is the hardest city in Eastern Europe in which to find an affordable hotel room—or even an unaffordable one! This was the case even in the "bad old days," and is even more so now; fully half the budget hotels recommended in previous editions of this guide have been privatized, renovated, and moved upscale. If you're lucky enough to get a room in a hotel (or thoughtful enough to have booked ahead), the price you pay will likely shatter your $30-a-day budget.

The cheapest accommodation option is a bed in a hostel—these are available to anyone, not just students. Almost as inexpensive and far more comfortable is a room in a private home—the price of the nicest private room undercuts that of the ugliest hotel room in a seedy neighborhood. Agencies that arrange such rooms (as well as hotel rooms) have proliferated recently to handle the tourist overflow. Guests usually share an apartment with the host, often receiving the largest and most comfortable room. Most hosts have rented their places for years. Agencies screen rooms and hosts. All rooms are easily accessible by public transportation. Rooms in the center and castle district cost more than those on the periphery. At a higher cost, you can rent an unoccupied apartment.

Most hotels and room agencies lower prices between mid-October and February.

RESERVATION AGENCIES

- **Prague Suites,** Melantrichova 8, is a block west of the Old Town Square (☎ **2/24-22-99-61** or **24-23-04-67;** toll-free **800-426-8826** in the U.S.; fax 2/24-22-93-63). Open 24 hours. This classy operation excels at booking private apartments, hotels, and pensions. You must pay a one-time booking fee of $35. No credit cards are accepted. A minimum of a two-night stay is required. It's best to reserve accommodations three to four weeks in advance. The following are approximate daily prices: a studio apartment costs $99, a one-bedroom apartment goes for $149, and a two bedroom apartment is $199.

- **The Čedok Accommodations Office,** at Panská ulice 5 (☎ **2/24-21-35-94;** fax 2/24-22-23-00). Čedok has access to thousands of rooms, both in hotels and private residences. The office is open Monday through Friday from 9am to 8:45pm, Saturday 9am to 4pm, Sunday 9am to 2pm. Their private hotel rooms are pricey ($50 and up for a single), and rooms in private pensions only a little less so. Rooms in private homes are the best deal: a single in the center costs 630 Kčs ($22.50), 550 Kčs ($19 .65) on the periphery; doubles in the center go for 1,000 Kčs ($35.70) and 850 Kčs ($30.35) outside. This office controls the largest number of rooms in town and is the least likely to run out. Minimum stay is two nights. Credit-card payment (AE, MC, V) is possible.
- **Čedok** operates another accommodations office at Rytířská 16, one street parallel and northwest of Na Příkopě (☎ **2/26-36-97;** fax 2/26-63-10). Hours are Monday through Friday 9am to 9pm, Saturday 9am to 4pm, and Sunday 9am to 2pm. Winter closing is an hour earlier. Private rooms here are less expensive than at the main branch, but they control many fewer and may run out. Rooms in the center cost 480 Kčs ($17.15) per person. Other Čedok services are handled here as well, from tours to ticketing. Hours are Monday through Friday 9am to 6pm, Saturday 9am to 2pm.
- **Pragotur,** at U Obecniho 2, just off náměstí Republiky (☎ **2/24-81-09-43** or **2/232-51-28;** fax 2/24-81-16-51). They are open from April to October 8am to 9pm and November to March 8am to 6pm. Private rooms with one or two beds are available in the center for 900 Kčs ($32.15) per day, outside the center for 600 to 700 Kčs ($21.43 to $25). Prices are 100 Kčs ($3.55) lower from November to March. There is no minimum stay. The agency also books tours and serves as an information center for cultural events. Pragotour is one of Prague's oldest accommodations agencies.
- **Top Tour,** at Rybná 3 (☎ **2/232-10-77** or **231-40-69;** fax 2/24-81-14-00), one block west of náměstí Republiky off Celetna. This agency prides itself on being more upscale than others, providing apartments, suites, and private rooms with high levels of amenity and decor. A double with private bath and toilet costs 1,611 Kčs ($57.55), or 1,321 Kčs ($47.20) for single use. A double with shared bath is 1,050 Kčs ($37.50), or 833 Kčs ($29.75) for single use. Suites are also available with dining room and kitchen. Prices go up 10% for each of the following conditions: one-night stays; location in the center; and stays during special holiday periods, including Christmas and New Year's. Add 91 Kčs ($3.25) per day to include breakfast. They take reservations far in advance by phone or fax.

READERS RECOMMEND

*This past summer we found a GREAT B&B in Prague for $30 a night for two! The lady who owns it, Alena Peslova, will pick you up at the station, help you any way she can (she got me a job!), speaks beautiful English, and is a lovely and charming person to be around. Her address is: Strakonicha 15, 150 00 Praha (☎ **2/535-92-54**). You'll love her! P.S. We had almost canceled our trip to Prague because of the outrageous hotel prices.* —Pamela Resch, San Jose, Calif.

If you're arriving in Prague by train and don't have a place to stay, you can make arrangements at the agencies listed below, which are conveniently located in or near the main train station, Hlavni nádrazí.

- **AVE Travel,** on the middle level of the railway station (☎ **2/236-2560**). Open daily from 6am to 11:30pm. This agency arranges the gamut of accommodations options: hotels, pensions, apartments, and rooms in private homes. They have contracts with 70% of Prague's hotels, including several listed in this guide. In addition, they can arrange accommodations in other towns of Bohemia and Moravia. A room in a private home in the center, quite a broad area as defined by the agency (including Prague 1, Prague 2, and part of Prague 3), goes for 500 Kčs ($17.85) as a single, 800 Kčs ($28.55) as a double. Rooms farther afield are 350 Kčs ($12.50) for a single, 600 Kčs ($21.45) for a double. Credit cards are accepted (AE, DC, JCB, MC, V), and reservations can be made by phone.
- **Vesta,** in the railway station (☎ **2/24-22-57-69;** fax 2/24-22-57-90). Open Monday through Saturday 8:30am to 7:30pm and Sunday 8:30am to 4:30pm. Vesta handles booking for hotels, rooms in private homes, and youth hostels. Rooms in private homes in the center (Prague 1 and Prague 2) run for 600 Kčs ($21.45), doubles for 900 Kčs ($32.15). Rooms in the "near center" are 500 Kčs ($17.85) for singles, 800 Kčs ($28.55) for doubles. They have photographs of some of the rooms. A bed in a hostel will cost 250 to 300 Kčs ($8.95 to $10.70).
- **Universitas Tour,** just outside the station at Opletalova ulice 38 (☎ **22-35-33**). This agency is connected with the Charles University and has access to more than 1,000 youth hostel beds. (See "Youth Hostels" below for more information.)

Hotels

DOUBLES FOR LESS THAN $30

In Motol

Hotel Tip, Za Opravnu 420, 15123 Prague 5. ☎ **2/55-86-65** or **55-89-48.** 115 rms (all with bath). **Tram:** 4 or 9 to Motol; then walk 200 yards along the highway away from the city until you see it on the right.

Rates (including breakfast): 650 Kčs ($23.20) with bath shared by one other room; 700 Kčs ($25) with private bath.

Traveler Advisory

In the train stations or in front of some of the above listed agencies, you may be approached by people offering you a room. These are generally honest people out to make a little extra money by renting out a room in their home. Use caution and your best judgment before striking a deal with these people. Prices are negotiable, and you should not go with anyone until a deal has been made and you see on the map where you'll be staying. Once you arrive at the room, if you don't like it, feel free to back out of the arrangement.

Ave Travel 10
Čedok Accommodations Office 8
Pragotur 4
Prague Suites 2
Universitas Tour 9
Vesta 10

ACCOMMODATIONS

CKM Junior Hotel 16
Hotel Axa 5
Hotel Balkán 15
Hotel Belvedere 1
Hotel Brno 6
Hotel Julian 12
Hotel Juliš 7
Hotel Kafka 11
Hotel Tip 14
Hotel Ungelt 3
Kavalír 13
Zotavona 17

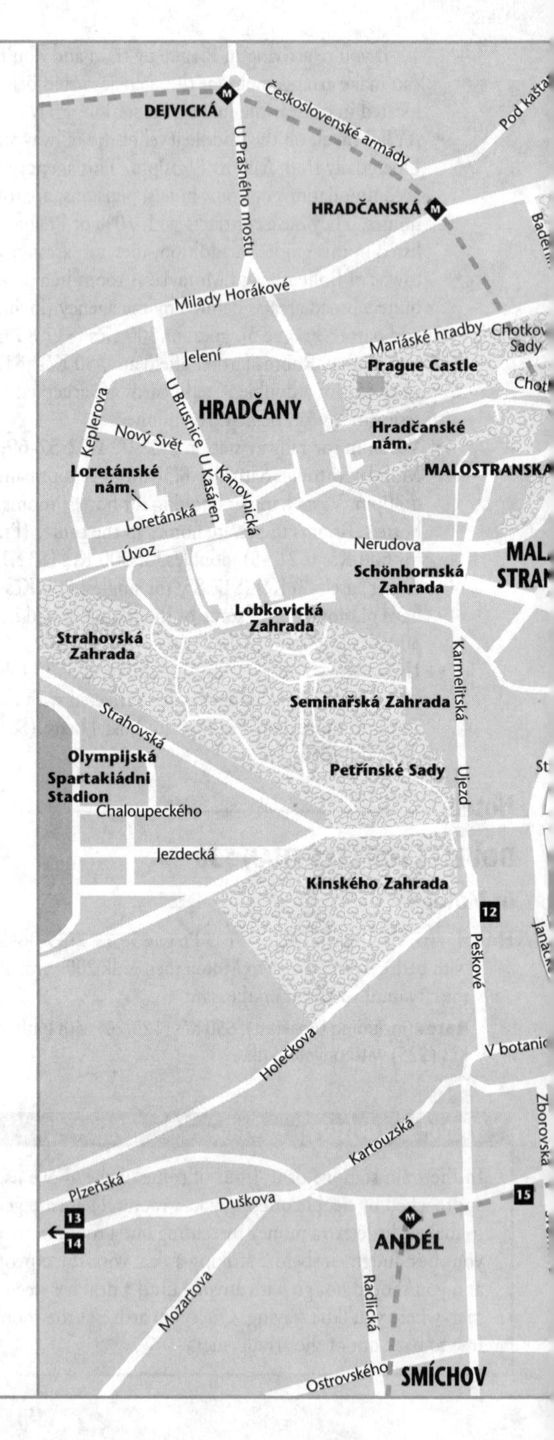

9023

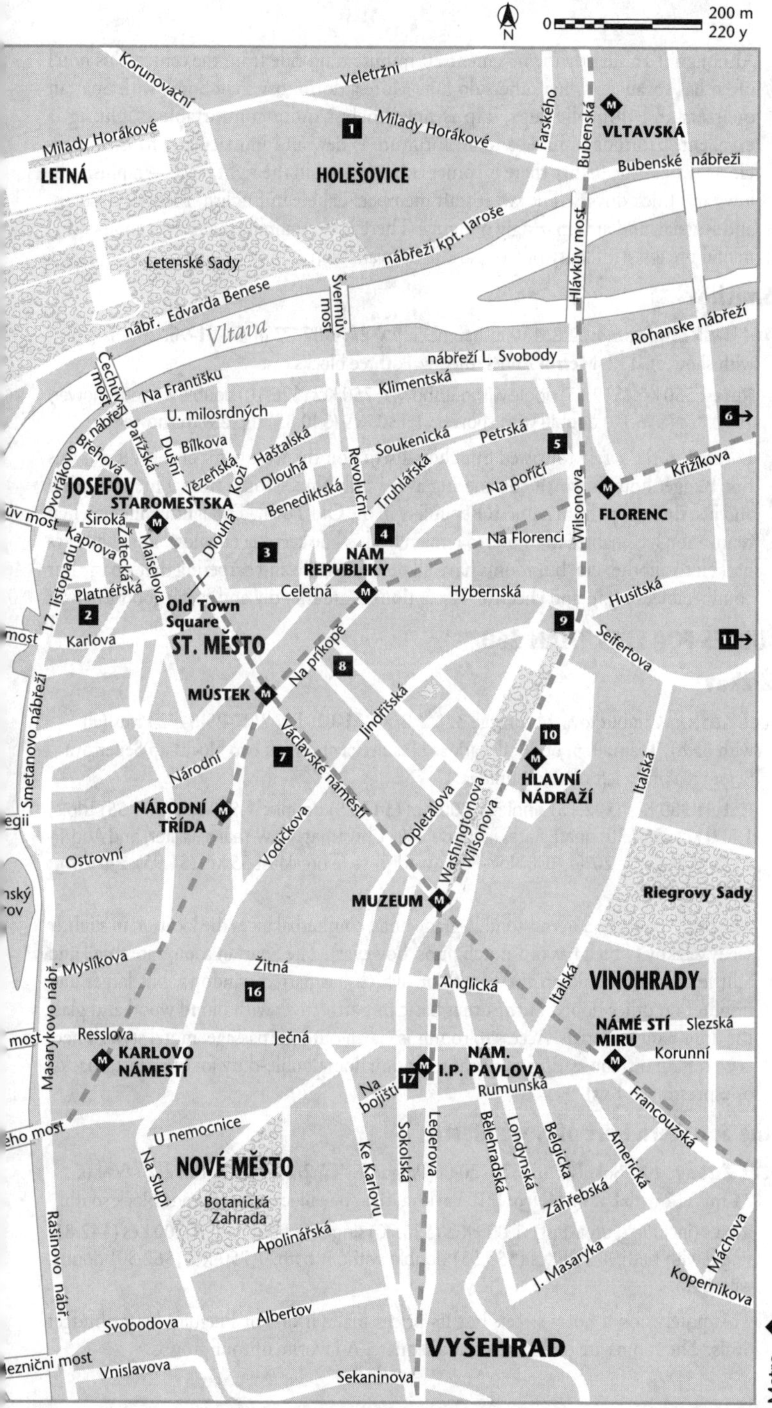
200 m
220 y
N
Korunovační
Veletržni
Milady Horákové
LETNÁ
HOLEŠOVICE
Farského
Bubenská
VLTAVSKÁ
Bubenské nábřeži
Letenské Sady
nábřeži kpt. Jaroše
nábř. Edvarda Benese
Vltava
Švermův most
Hlávkův most
Rohanske nábřeži
Čechův most
nábřeží L. Svobody
Na Františku
Klimentská
U. milosrdných
Bílkova
Haštalská
Soukenická
Petrská
Dvořákovo nábřeži
Břehová
Pařížská
Dušni
Vězeňská
Kozi
Dlouhá
Revoluční
Truhlářská
Na poříčí
Křižíkova
JOSEFOV
STAROMESTSKA
Benediktská
Wilsonova
FLORENC
Široká
Kaprova
Žatecká
Maiselova
Dlouhá
NÁM REPUBLIKY
Na Florenci
17. listopadu
Platnéřská
Old Town Square
Celetná
Hybernská
Husitská
Karlova
ST. MĚSTO
Seifertova
Na příkope
MŮSTEK
Jindřišská
Smetanovo nábřeži
Národní
Václavské náměstí
HLAVNÍ NÁDRAŽÍ
Italská
NÁRODNÍ TŘÍDA
Opletalova
Washingtonova
Wilsonova
Vodičkova
Ostrovní
MUZEUM
Riegrovy Sady
Myslíkova
Žitná
Anglická
Italská
VINOHRADY
Resslova
Ječná
NÁMĚ STÍ MIRU
Slezská
Korunní
KARLOVO NÁMESTÍ
NÁM. I.P. PAVLOVA
Masarykovo nábř.
Na bojišti
Rumunská
Francouzská
U nemocnice
Sokolská
Legerova
Bělehradská
Londynská
Belgicka
Americká
Na Slupi
NOVÉ MĚSTO
Ke Karlovu
Záhřebská
Botanická Zahrada
Rašínovo nábř.
Apolinářská
J. Masaryka
Máchova
Kopernikova
Svobodova
Albertov
VYŠEHRAD
Vnislavova
Sekaninova
Metro

Although it's a slightly inconvenient 20-minute tram ride from the center, this hotel often has vacancies when others do not. More a dormitory than hotel, with Spartan quarters and thin-pile rugs, Tip is nevertheless quite comfortable. Lighting is excellent, bathrooms shine, and all furniture is new and immaculate. Most importantly, what little luxury there is comes concentrated in the right place—in plush pillows and thick duvets. The sweet staff members dabble in English, French, German, and Russian and are amazingly obliging. There is a restaurant that serves good continental breakfasts. Plenty of free parking is available.

In Smíchov

Hotel Balkan, Svornosti 28, 15000 Prague 5. ☎ **2/54-07-77** or **54-01-96.** 26 rms (15 with shower). TEL **Metro:** Anděl; then walk three blocks east.

Rates: 550 Kčs ($19.65) single without shower; 750 Kčs ($26.10) double without shower, 1010 Kčs ($36.10) double with shower; 1,130 Kčs ($40.35) triple with shower.

Located in the rarely touristed Smichov district on the west bank of the Vltava, this fine budget hotel is worth considering as it's only three blocks from a metro station and just three stops from náměstí Republiky in the Old Town. Thoughtful, incremental renovation has enabled this hotel to remain fresh while keeping rates low. Dim hallways harken to another era, but rooms have all new furniture and carpeting that's basic but comfortable, bright, and cheerful. Receptionists are friendly and speak good English.

DOUBLES FOR LESS THAN $60

In Žižkov

Hotel Kafka, Cimburkova 24, Prague 3. ☎ **2/27-31-01.** Fax 2/27-29-84. 23 rms (all with bath). **Tram:** 9, 5, or 26; debark at Husinecka and walk two blocks up Seifertova before making a left on Cimburkova.

Rates: 900 Kčs ($32.15) single; 1,200 Kčs ($42.85) double; 1,500 Kčs ($53.55) triple; 1,800 Kčs ($64.30) quad. Rates increase 20% Christmas, New Year's, Easter, and Aug 1–21, and decrease 20%–40% Nov–Feb. Swedish-style breakfast 55 Kčs ($1.95). **Parking:** 50 Kčs ($1.80).

The fresh renovation of this solid B-grade hotel counterbalances the location in slightly seedy Žižkov (which has top-notch pubs, however). The Spartan rooms are small and a little claustrophobic on the first floor, which has barred windows, but larger and brighter on other floors. Furniture is basic but attractive, with blond wood and glass the dominant materials. Access to rooms is via an outdoor passage, motel style. There is no restaurant; the seating area near reception does double-duty for breakfast, snacks, or espresso (10 Kčs).

In the Southern Part of Nové Město

Hotel Zotavona, Sokolská ul. 33, 120 00 Prague 2. ☎ **2/29-11-18.** Fax 2/20-66-86. 24 rms (14 with bath). **Metro:** I. P. Pavlova, then one block west and one block south.

Rates (including breakfast): 1,000 Kčs ($35.70) single without bath, 1,200 Kčs ($42.85) single with bath; 1,500 Kčs ($53.55) double without bath, 1,750 Kčs ($62.50) double with bath.

This hotel is on a noisy street, but its prices make it one of Prague's better budget deals. The rooms are pedestrian but adequate. A favorite of tour groups.

Near Křižíkova Metro Stop, East of Staré Město

Hotel Brno, Thámova 26, 186 00 Prague 8. ☎ **2/24-81-18-88.** Fax 2/24-81-04-32. 40 rms (all with bath). **Metro:** Křižíkova; the hotel occupies the same pedestrian island as the metro stop.

Prices (including breakfast): 1,150 Kčs ($41.10) single; 1,700 Kčs ($60.70) double; 1,800 Kčs ($64.30) triple. Off-season prices are 10% less. AE, MC, V.

This fine, freshly renovated European-style budget hotel is conveniently located at a metro stop just two stations from náměstí Republiky. New furniture resplendent in reds and browns is plump, overstuffed, and comfortable in the manner of a 1970s rec room. All rooms enjoy an extra layer of security from the lockable anterooms that separate bedrooms from the main corridor. Parking is available.

Near the Florenc Metro Stop, East of Staré Město

Hotel Axa, Na poříčí 40, 11000 Prague 1. ☎ **2/232-72-34.** Fax 2/232-21-72. 134 rms (109 with bath). **Metro:** Florenc; then walk two blocks northwest.

Rates (including breakfast): 1,000–1,400 Kčs ($35.70–$50) single without bath, 1,500 Kčs ($53.60) single with bath; 1,400–1,800 Kčs ($50–$64.30) double without bath; 2,500 Kčs ($89.30) double with bath; 3,100 Kčs ($110.70) triple with bath. Rates Nov–Mar are 15%–30% cheaper. AE, DC, MC, V.

Gorgeous renovation has transformed this hotel east of Staré Město into something sleek and modern as a German kitchen appliance. All furniture and fixtures are new and tastefully color-coordinated in chrome and shades of black, white, or teal, down to the digital clocks in each room. Beds are comfortable and firm. New color TVs get MTV as well as Czech and German programming. Also on the premises: a restaurant, exchange office, laundry service, and a health club.

DOUBLES FOR LESS THAN $80

In Malá Strana

Hotel Julián, Elišky Peškové 11, Prague 5. ☎ **2/53-51-37.** Fax 2/54-75-25. 29 rms (all with bath). TV TEL **Tram:** 6 or 12 to náměstí Kinských, and then walk a half block south along El. Peškové.

Rates (including breakfast): 1,170 Kčs ($41.80) single; 1,940 Kčs ($69.30) double; 2,200 Kčs ($78.60) triple. Extra bed 700 Kčs ($25). Rates are 35% lower Oct–Feb. **Parking:** 100 Kčs ($3.55).

The limpid green-white paint scheme of this art nouveau building illuminates the street in a charming section of Malá Strana, only a short walk from the Charles Bridge. Reconstructed in 1993, it features tasteful, simple decor that complements and enhances the beauty of the architecture. Details in the sparkling white lobby and landings such as wrought-iron grating, arched partitions, and the wafting smell of espresso from the reception convey luxury the moment you step in. The bedrooms are less enchanting but still comfortable and new, featuring muted gray-on-white furniture and cotton-candy-pink bedclothes. Breakfast is served Swedish style in a radiant dining room. Management has not finalized pricing, so the above quotes may change significantly.

In Smíchov

Hotel Kavalír, Plzeňská 177, 150 00 Prague 5. ☎ and fax **2/52-44-23.** 49 rms (all with bath). TEL **Tram:** 4, 9, or 7; get off at Kavalirky.

Prices (including breakfast): 1,900 Kčs ($67.85) single; 2,200 Kčs ($78.55) double; 3,500 Kčs ($125) double plus one. Off-season prices (mid-Oct to Feb) are 15% lower. AE, MC, V. **Parking:** Covered garage 200 Kčs ($7.15).

This beautiful hotel in a placid residential district is served by a very convenient tramline and is just 15 minutes from the center. As yet undiscovered by boisterous tour groups, it offers a peaceful stay. Visitors shuttle through a narrow, glossy lobby up to rooms attractively decorated in various shades of crimson. Gorgeous bathrooms with elegant fixtures and ornamental tiles set this renovation job apart from that of other Prague hotels. Attention from the well-trained staff is personal. Breakfast is served Swedish style in the spacious dining room.

In Holešovice

Hotel Belvedere, M. Horákové 19, 17000 Prague 7. ☎ **2/37-47-41** to **37-47-49** or **37-03-55.** 119 rms (62 with bath). TV TEL **Metro:** Vltavská; then walk six blocks east. Tram: 8 from the Florenc bus station.

Rates (including breakfast): 1,700 Kčs ($60.70) single without bath, 2,250 Kčs ($80.35) single with bath; 2,200 Kčs ($78.60) double without bath, 2,950 Kčs ($105.35) double with bath. Extra bed 700 Kčs ($25). Rates Nov 11–Dec 29 are 50% less. Peak period rates, including Easter, Christmas, and New Year's, are 10% more. AE, EU, MC, V.

The Belvedere offers a modern lobby with English-speakers at the reception desk, and clean, comfortable rooms with white walls and a huge bank of windows. About 90% of the rooms are taken by groups, but if you're lucky you might find a vacancy—usually a room without a private bathroom. The Technical Museum is a few blocks away, but in general the location north of the Vltava River in Holešovice is a bit inconvenient. The nearest metro stop is about six blocks away.

Youth Hostels

To secure a bed in one of Prague's youth hostels, go to **Universitas Tour** at Opletalova ulice 38 (☎ and fax **2/22-35-43**), near Hlavní nadraží, the main railway station. Exit the station and walk right for 1½ blocks. They have replaced CKM as the main youth-hostel agency in town. Their hours are daily from 8am to 9pm in July and August, and daily from 9:30am to 6pm the rest of the year. There's a youth hostel on the premises with 400 beds. They also do bookings for about 10 other hostels throughout the city, with an additional 600 to 700 beds. Hostel addresses are not listed here because you must book the room through Universitas Tour. A bed costs 250 to 350 Kčs ($8.90 to $12.50), usually including breakfast. While the hostels are open to all comers, ISIC cardholders receive rooms at a discount for 125 Kčs ($4.45). You can also book private rooms through Universitas Tour for 25 to 50 DM ($15.60 to $31.20) per person.

CKM Junior Hotel, Žitná 12, 12105 Prague 2. ☎ **2/29-29-84.** Fax 2/24-22-39-11. 22 rms (all with bath). TV TEL **Metro:** Karlovo náměstí.

Rates (including breakfast): 980 Kčs ($35) single; 1,260 Kčs ($45) double; 1,540 Kčs ($55) triple.

Run by the Czech Republic's youth travel agency, this hotel offers nice rooms with dark-wood paneling, clean walls and bedspreads, older carpets, and small tiled bathrooms. Every two rooms share a balcony. Downstairs are an attractive café and a restaurant. Although mostly young people stay here, it's open to travelers of all ages. Unfortunately, it's often booked solid. It's located about a five-minute walk from Václavské náměstí.

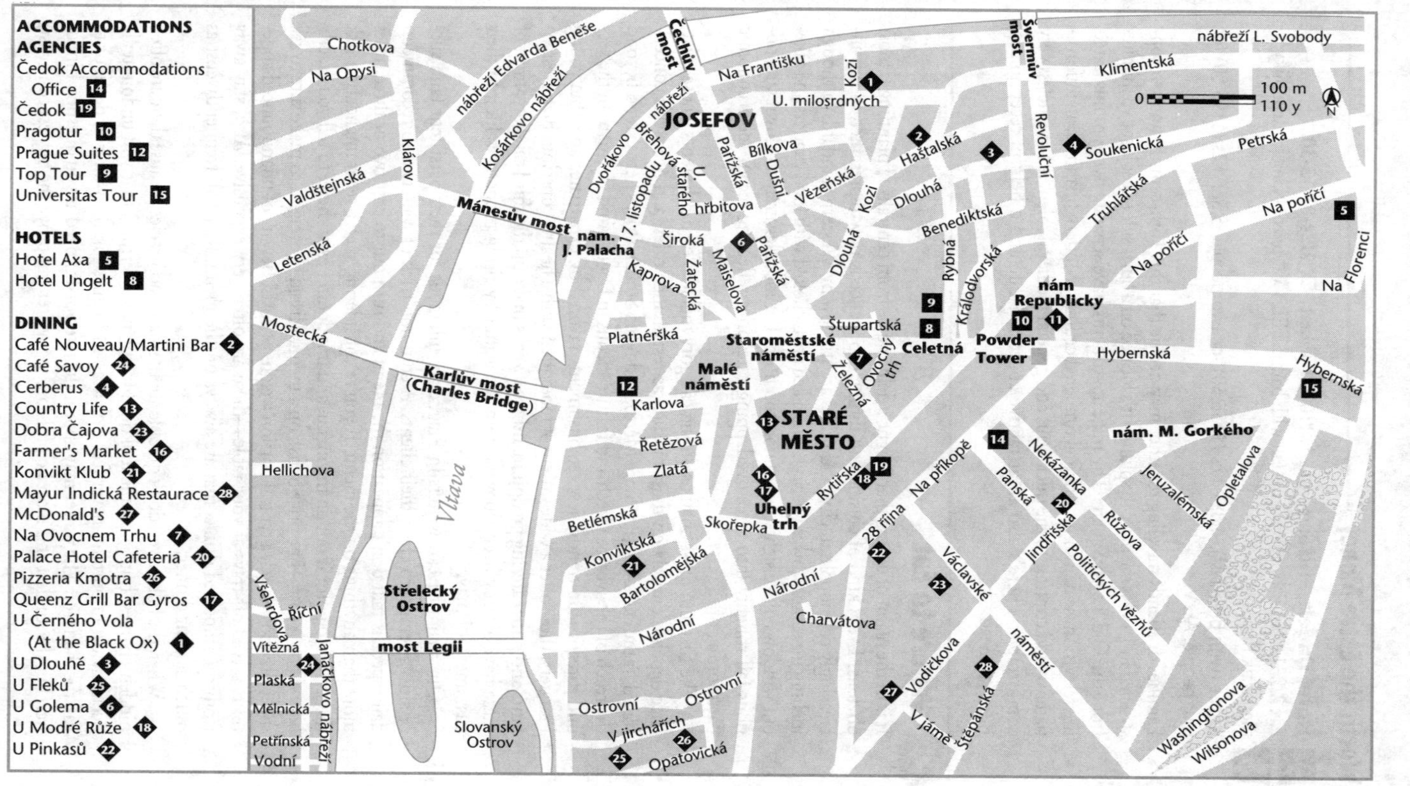

Old Town Accommodations & Dining

Worth the Extra Money

Hotel Ungelt, Malá Štupartská 1, 11000 Prague 1. ☎ **2/24-81-13-30.** Fax 2/231-95-05. 10 apartments (all with bath). TEL TV **Metro:** Náměstí Republiky; then walk three blocks west.

Rates (with breakfast): 4,382 Kčs ($156.50) for two people, 5,566 Kčs ($198.80) for four people. AE, V.

Families or friends traveling together may decide that this 16th-century house reconstructed in 1989 is the place to splurge. It's located on a quiet side street just two minutes from the Old Town Square. The huge apartments have separate living rooms, satellite television, and in some, original timbered ceilings. Modern furniture, an unfortunately bland contrast to the thick walls and general medieval mien, is nonetheless very comfortable. There's also an attractive courtyard café and a helpful receptionist. Reserve ahead.

4 Where to Eat

It is in the realm of dining that Prague's deliverance from centralized planning is most obvious. Every kind of cuisine and dining experience is now represented in this increasingly cosmopolitan city, and prices are still low by Western standards (although inching inexorably toward parity). Touristed areas choked with food vendors and take-out windows make sightseeing a nonstop nosh. For more leisurely sit-down fare, options fall roughly into three overlapping categories reflecting recent socioeconomic partitioning of the city.

The first and most obvious dining category includes establishments whose existence depends entirely on tourism, such as restaurants, cafés, and beer halls concentrated in the castle district, Staré Město, and Malá Strana. Prices here extend beyond the reach of the average Czech and feature menus in English and German. In the second category are trendy new establishments favored by expatriates and chic young Praguers; these offer a wide variety of food often with a health-conscious bias. Restaurants and pubs catering predominantly to Czechs make up the third category; most of these have already been elbowed from the center by rising property values, to their customers' dismay.

One major caveat; waiters in Prague are infamous for their persistent (and successful) attempts to cheat their clients. A common trick of waiters is to recommend daily specials that don't appear on the menu and turn out to cost two or three times more than anything on the menu. If you're considering such a recommendation, ask the waiter to point it out on the menu, and if it doesn't exist there, to tell you exactly how much it costs. The price of fish on a menu is listed by weight, so make sure to ask the waiter how much a typical portion weighs or costs. Beware of unannounced appetizers served off trays at your table—these are often very expensive. Also, stay away from the imported drinks that are always on the menu; they will frequently cost as much as your dinner.

When the bill arrives, don't quibble about small inaccuracies because there are often hidden charges, but be on the lookout for the major "errors" that will undoubtedly occur. Most important, never feel embarrassed to question the waiter in detail or to call the manager. The waiter may appear flustered or annoyed as you question him or her, but the kindest and most helpful-looking waiter can prove the biggest con artist.

One reader, Janet Burstall of Sydney, Australia, who learned from painful experience, summed up a good restaurant strategy for Prague: "*Never* order food or drink without a menu or the price at least being known first. *Always* order only *exactly* what is on the menu. *Never* accept anything that you did not order specifically."

There are three main areas where you'll find the most restaurants: Staré Město, Malá Strana, and Hradčany. There are many good restaurants in other areas, but these three districts have the greatest concentrations.

You'll also find a list of health-oriented restaurants in *Prague Naturally,* a book written by four American expatriates. In addition, *Prognosis* and the *Prague Post,* the two English-language newspapers, frequently review new Prague restaurants.

STREET FOOD

For eats on the run, there are three places among the countless options in Staré Město that merit your attention for a healthy bite. **Country Life**, at Melantrichova 15, just off Malé náměstí, churns out tasty little salads of julienned vegetables with a yogurt dressing for 22 Kčs (80¢). (Open Monday through Thursday 10am to 7pm, Friday 10am to 2:30pm.) A bit farther down Melantrichova, which opens up onto Havelská, there is a **farmer's market** with fresh fruit and vegetables, dried fruit, and nuts, and fountains in which to wash them. (Open Monday through Saturday 10am to 5pm, roughly.) **Queenz Grill Bar Gyros**, at Havelská 12, sells superlative falafel sandwiches for 25 Kčs (90¢). (Open daily 10am to 10pm.)

MEALS FOR LESS THAN $3

$ **FX Cafe,** Bělehradská 120, Prague 2. ☎ **25-12-10.**

Cuisine: VEGETARIAN/INTERNATIONAL. **Reservations:** Not accepted.
Metro: I.P. Pavlova, and walk two blocks west to Bělehradská and two blocks north.
Prices: Soups 30 Kčs ($1.05); salads 45–55 Kčs ($1.60–$1.95); main courses 65–85 Kčs ($2.30–$3.05).
Open: 11:30am–5am; Sun brunch 10:30am–3pm.

Part of a complex that includes a club, art gallery, and record store, this hip expatriate creation serves tasty vegetarian food in big portions to a youngish, fashionable crowd. The menu features burritos, pastas, padthai, salads, pizza, and other staples of the gourmet vegetarian diet. Decor is spare and arty, tinctured with postmodern moments like pieces of Greek statuary poking out from the walls and lamps deconstructed to look torn from the rafters. The cafe is always a bit crowded, but you can lounge in the adjoining art gallery until your number comes up.

Mayur Indická Restaurace, Stěpánská 61. ☎ **236-9922.**

Cuisine: INDIAN. **Reservations:** Recommended for dinner.
Prices: Café, average meal 50–70 Kčs ($1.80–$2.50). Restaurant, average meal 90–140 Kčs ($3.20–$5).
Open: Daily noon–11pm.

The same good Indian food is served in the restaurant and in the more casual café next door. Prices in the café, however, are considerably lower. Vegetarians can easily build a meal out of several appetizers. The lentil soup is particularly savory. An English menu is available.

Palace Hotel Cafeteria, Panská 12. ☎ **235-7556.**

Cuisine: CZECH. **Directions:** From Václavské náměstí, walk northeast on Jindřišská and turn left on Panská.

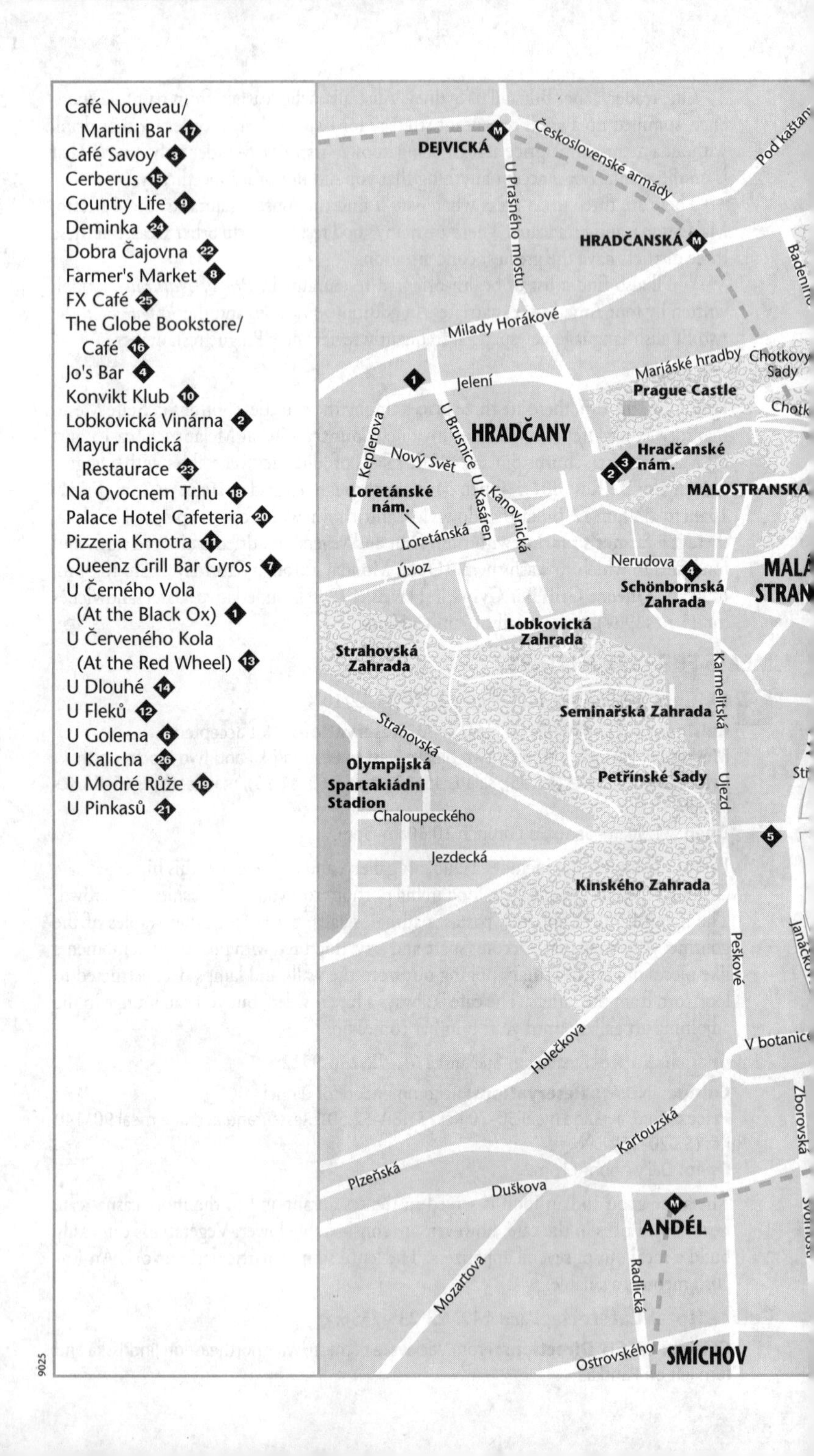

Café Nouveau/ Martini Bar 17
Café Savoy 3
Cerberus 15
Country Life 9
Deminka 24
Dobra Čajovna 22
Farmer's Market 8
FX Café 25
The Globe Bookstore/ Café 16
Jo's Bar 4
Konvikt Klub 10
Lobkovická Vinárna 2
Mayur Indická Restaurace 23
Na Ovocnem Trhu 18
Palace Hotel Cafeteria 20
Pizzeria Kmotra 11
Queenz Grill Bar Gyros 7
U Černého Vola (At the Black Ox) 1
U Červeného Kola (At the Red Wheel) 13
U Dlouhé 14
U Fleků 12
U Golema 6
U Kalicha 26
U Modré Růže 19
U Pinkasů 21
DEJVICKÁ
Československé armády
Pod kaštany
U Prašného mostu
HRADČANSKÁ
Milady Horákové
Mariáské hradby
Chotkovy Sady
Prague Castle
Jelení
Keplerova
U Brusnice
HRADČANY
Nový Svět
Hradčanské nám.
MALOSTRANSKA
Loretánské nám.
U Kasáren
Kanovnická
Loretánská
Úvoz
Nerudova
Schönbornská Zahrada
Lobkovická Zahrada
Strahovská Zahrada
Karmelitská
Seminařská Zahrada
Strahovská
Olympijská Spartakiádni Stadion
Petřínské Sady
Újezd
Chaloupeckého
Jezdecká
Kinského Zahrada
Peškové
Holečkova
V botanice
Zborovská
Kartouzská
Plzeňská
Duškova
ANDĚL
Mozartova
Radlická
Ostrovského
SMÍCHOV

9025

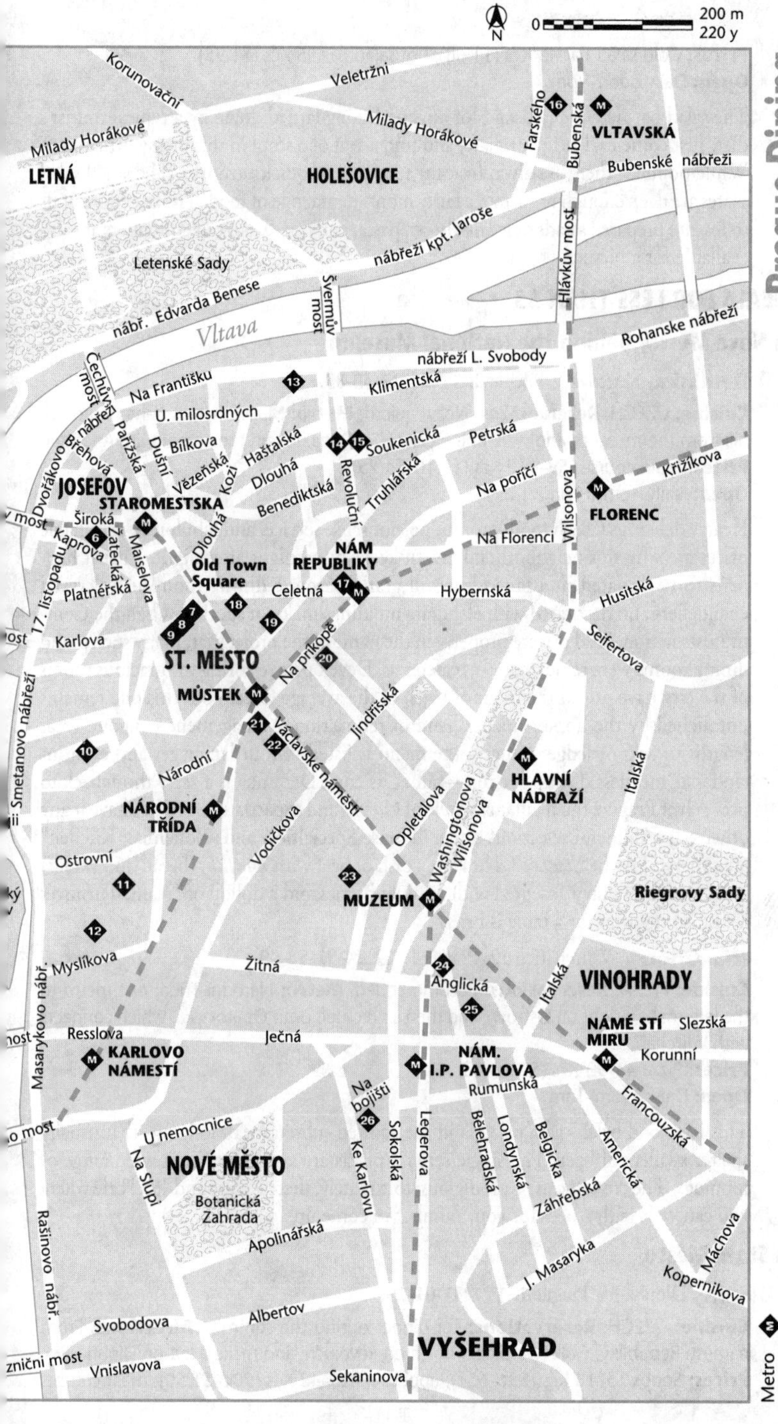

N
0
200 m
220 y
Korunovační
Veletržni
Milady Horákové
LETNÁ
HOLEŠOVICE
Farského
Bubenská
VLTAVSKÁ
Bubenské nábřeži
Hlávkův most
nábřeži kpt. Jaroše
Letenské Sady
Švermův most
nábř. Edvarda Benese
Vltava
Rohanske nábřeži
nábřeží L. Svobody
Čechův most
Na Františku
Klimentská
U. milosrdných
Dvořákovo nábřeží
Břehová
Pařížská
Bílkova
Dušní
Haštalská
Soukenická
Petrská
Věžeňská
Kozí
Dlouhá
Revoluční
Truhlářská
Křižíkova
JOSEFOV
STAROMESTSKA
Benediktská
Na poříčí
Wilsonova
FLORENC
Široká
Kaprova
Žatecká
Maiselova
Na Florenci
17. listopadu
NÁM REPUBLIKY
Old Town Square
Celetná
Hybernská
Husitská
Platnéřská
Karlova
Seifertova
ST. MĚSTO
Na příkopě
MŮSTEK
Jindřišská
Smetanovo nábřeží
Václavské náměstí
Národní
HLAVNÍ NÁDRAŽÍ
Italská
NÁRODNÍ TŘÍDA
Vodičkova
Opletalova
Washingtonova
Ostrovní
MUZEUM
Riegrovy Sady
Myslíkova
Žitná
Anglická
VINOHRADY
Masarykovo nábř.
Resslova
Ječná
NÁMĚ STÍ MIRU
Slezská
KARLOVO NÁMESTÍ
NÁM. I.P. PAVLOVA
Korunní
Rumunská
Na bojišti
Francouzská
U nemocnice
Sokolská
Legerova
Bělehradská
Londynská
Belgicka
Americká
Na Slupi
NOVÉ MĚSTO
Ke Karlovu
Botanická Zahrada
Záhřebská
Apolinářská
Máchova
Rašínovo nábř.
J. Masaryka
Kopernikova
Svobodova
Albertov
VYŠEHRAD
Vnislavova
Sekaninova
Metro

Prices: Cold salad bar 45 Kčs ($1.60); hot salad bar 55 Kčs ($1.95).
Open: Daily noon–9pm.

The salad bar here is a godsend for anyone feeling larded down by a typical tourist's diet. Just come in, load your plate, and find a seat or a stool in this brassy little room. While popular, there are always vacant seats due to quick turnover. The small salad plates are deep enough to sustain a fairly monumental pile of food. The selection tends to feature prepared salads of lentils, beets, pasta, and rice. Take-out containers are also available for a picnic.

MEALS FOR LESS THAN $5

In Nové Město, behind the National Museum

Deminka, Škrétova 1, Prague 2. ☎ **24-22-33-83.**

Cuisine: CZECH. **Reservations:** Not required. **Metro:** Muzeum; exit behind and uphill from the museum and walk one block to Škrétova, it's on the corner with Anglická.
Prices: Main courses 59–119 Kčs ($2.10–$4.25).
Open: Daily 4pm–11pm.

Hearty delicious Czech food, prompt no-nonsense service, and fabulously reasonable prices are why this neighborhood tavern keeps busy, night after night. That it happens to be situated in a faded but still grand baroque dining room lit by crystal chandeliers and decorated with elaborate moldings makes it special. When the Communists nationalized private property in the name of the proletariat, many such grand dining rooms were reincarnated as cafeterias. Developers restoring the gracious rooms of the city have priced them out of reach of the average Czech, but this one remains untouched by the homogenizing hand of renovation. Management *has* gone great lengths to acknowledge change—the menu is listed in four languages and even includes a "meatless dishes" section—but at its core, Deminka is a zesty throwback to pre-Velvet Prague; the regular clientele of Czechs and expatriates wouldn't have it any other way. All menu selections under "House Specialties" and "Bohemian Kitchen" are superb. Try the *Svičkové,* a heavenly dish of beef with *knedliky* (bread dumplings) in a citrus-beef gravy accented with juniper berries and a dollop of cream. Turnover is fast, so the wait for a table is brief.

Pizzeria Kmotra, V Jirchářích 12, Prague 1. ☎ **24-91-58-09.**

Cuisine: PIZZA. **Reservations:** Recommended. **Metro:** Národní Třida; exit metro to the left, make a right on Ostrovní and then a quick left onto Opatovická, which connects with V Jirchářích.
Prices: Pizza 44–93 Kčs ($1.55–$3.30).
Open: Daily 11am–1am.

This is a good brick-oven pizzeria in the vaulted subterranean lodgings that usually shelter swillers of beer. The single-serving pizzas are available with a wide range of toppings. The crowds can be prodigious; fortunately, there is a ground-level café where you can wait with a beer for your number to come up.

In Staré Město

U Dlouhé, Dlouhá 35, Prague 1. ☎ **231-61-25.**

Cuisine: CZECH. **Reservations:** For dinner during the summer. **Directions:** From náměstí Republiky, walk two blocks north on Revolučni and make a left on Dlouhá.
Prices: Soups 15–18 Kčs (55¢–65¢); appetizers 25–42 Kčs (90¢–$1.50); main courses

52–135 Kčs ($1.85–$4.80); desserts 22–43 Kčs (80¢–$1.55). Cover charge 5 Kčs (18¢). AE, MC, V.

Open: Mon–Friday 11am–11pm, Sat–Sunday 11am–10pm.

Traditional Czech food is served without pretension at this bright and lively restaurant. Come for the wild game—duck, venison, rabbit, and boar—although classic pork- and beef-based Czech dishes and goulashes also command the respect of a nicely mixed clientele of tourists and locals. Buried somewhat on the menu are fish, chicken, and three vegetarian dishes. The recently renovated decor of hearty stained wood furniture and wainscoting with whitewashed walls does not have the patina of more venerable establishments, but the food here is superior. Take care with the tip, which may be included on the bill.

U Golema, Maislova 8. ☎ **232-8165.**

Cuisine: CZECH. **Reservations:** Recommended. **Directions:** Exit from the northwest corner of the Old Town Square past the church facade; then walk north up Maislova.

Prices: Main courses 81–137 Kčs ($2.90–$4.90); complete meal 300–500 Kčs ($10.70–$17.85). Cover charge 10 Kčs (35¢). AE, DC, MC, V.

Open: Mon–Fri 11am–10pm, Sat 5–11pm.

Located in the heart of the old Jewish ghetto, this restaurant is named for the Golem, a mythical being supposedly created nearby by a medieval rabbi. Aside from the plastic statue representing the Golem, a funky dark ambience is the restaurant's signature feature—a product of burnished wood walls and ceiling and subdued lighting from lamps shaped like menorahs. The limited menu features carp, trout, and several beef dishes; they also serve delicious crispy french fries. Three varieties of lavish complete meals are also offered, with drinks included. The restaurant is located minutes from the Old Town Square, making it a great choice for a lunch break while sightseeing.

MEALS FOR LESS THAN $10

In Staré Město

Cerberus, Soukenická 19, Prague 1. ☎ **231-09-85.**

Cuisine: CZECH/INTERNATIONAL. **Reservations:** Recommended for dinner. **Directions:** From naměstí Republiky, walk two blocks north on Revolučni and make a right on Soukenická.

Prices: Soups 50 Kčs ($1.80); appetizers 70–150 Kčs ($2.50–$5.35); main courses 60–340 Kčs ($2.15–$12.15), with most around 160 Kčs ($5.70). AE, EU, V.

Open: Daily noon–midnight.

This highly evolved restaurant combines Czech staple foods such as pork and game with seasoning and preparation informed by an enlightened awareness of current culinary trends. Which is to say, the food is excellent and original, sometimes evincing French-style devotion to cream sauces and Provençal herbs, at other times staking out ground of what may someday be called Czech nouvelle. All dishes, from a veal roll au jus, to the duck à la bolognaise, to the divine stewed rabbit, come with a halo of vegetables. The several vegetarian options feature vegetables and homemade pasta. The decor—a somewhat confused mix of booths, tables under a skylight, and a windowless subterranean wine cellar—does not detract from the experience, which you can sear into memory with a postprandial Cuban cigar, sold by the bar.

In the Zizkov Region, East of the Old Town

Myslivna, Jagellonská 21, Prague 3. ☎ **627-02-09.**

Cuisine: CZECH/GAME. **Reservations:** Recommended. **Metro:** Jiřího z. Poděbrad; walk two blocks east on Vinohradská and three blocks north on Milesovská to reach Jagellonská.
Prices: Soups 28–41 Kčs ($1–$1.45); main courses 95–285 Kčs ($3.40–$10.20), specialties on the high end. Cover 20 Kčs ($70¢). AE, EU, MC, V.
Open: Daily noon–4pm and 5pm–midnight.

If you're game for game—venison, boar, quail, pheasant—but a little leery of eating wild animals, this restaurant makes it easy. What the menu lays out in plain English, the kitchen produces with unexpected refinement. For maximum gaminess, go for the boar slices with juniper berries and quail eggs, although stag goulash comes close. The setting is rustic and comfortable, with muted lighting, half-timbered walls, and a few hunting trophies. No need to dress up anything but your appetite.

In the Southern Part of Nové Město

U Kalicha, Na bojišti 12, Prague 1. ☎ **29-19-45** or **29-07-01.**

Cuisine: CZECH. **Reservations:** Recommended. **Metro:** I.P. Pavlova; then walk two blocks to the southwest.
Prices: Soups 20 Kčs (70¢); main courses 150–300 Kčs ($5.35–$10.70). AE, DC, JCB, V.
Open: Lunch daily 11am–3pm; dinner daily 5–10pm.

U kalicha is visited by the "Good Soldier Schweik" in the novel of the same name by the Czech writer Jaroslav Hašek. In commemoration of this popular novel, the walls of one room boast drawings of characters from the book. Another novelty is a seven-foot-high music box that plays martial music while you eat. The music, drawings, and good wine and beer translate into one of Prague's most popular restaurants with a lively crowd—which gets louder as the evening goes on. The kitchen at U kalicha features traditional though undistinguished Czech specialties such as pork and beef, although carp, roast chicken, and roast goose are also served. They have a menu in English.

WORTH THE EXTRA MONEY

In Malá Strana

Lobkovická Vinárna, Vlassaká 17, Prague 1. ☎ **53-01-85.**

Cuisine: CZECH. **Reservations:** Required, days ahead of time. **Directions:** From Malostranské náměsti, walk half a block south and then turn right onto Tržiště, which leads into Vlassaká.
Prices: Main courses from 300 Kčs ($10.70).
Open: Lunch daily noon–3pm; dinner daily 6:30pm–1am.

Practically in the park, this elegant, romantic restaurant was originally officers' quarters, and 200 years ago it shook to the tramp of imperial boots. Now the subdued lighting and the cosmopolitan English-speaking headwaiter complement the excellent food. A limited but very appealing menu is featured, offering four excellent varieties of steak and two pork dishes—the only main courses. Before the meal you might wish to try some of the delicious locally grown mushrooms, served in a variety of ways. It's a fairly formal place attracting many embassy officials; dress accordingly. You should come here only for a full meal; one reader recently wrote that he was rudely asked to leave after ordering only light refreshments.

In Staré Město

U Červeného Kola ("At the Red Wheel"), Anežská 2. ☎ **24-81-11-18.**

Cuisine: CZECH. **Reservations:** Highly recommended, especially for dinner. **Directions:** From the Old Town Square, walk north up Dlouhá, which changes its name and continues north for about five blocks; at the small square with a church, walk around to the other side.

Prices: Main courses 230–490 Kčs ($8.20–$17.50); desserts 40–85 Kčs ($1.40–$3.05). AE, DC, EU, JCB, MC, V.

Open: Lunch daily 11am–3pm; dinner daily 5–11pm.

This is one of my favorite restaurants in town, even though some of the waiters are not scrupulous in preparing the bill. It's a quiet place with several small intimate dining rooms with only two or three tables in each room. There's a lovely, very quiet garden out back for al fresco dining—a rarity in Prague. The delicious specialties are beefsteak with mushrooms and beefsteak with cranberries. The only nonmeat offering is trout.

U Modré Růže, Rytířská 16, Prague 1. ☎ **26-38-86** or **26-10-81.**

Cuisine: CZECH/INTERNATIONAL. **Reservations:** Required. **Directions:** From Na Přikopě, cross over to Rytířská, which is parallel to it.

Prices: Appetizers 75–95 Kčs ($2.70–$3.40); main courses 195 Kčs ($6.95); desserts 95 Kčs ($3.40); deluxe prix-fixe menu 395 Kčs ($14.10); pretheater (5:30–8pm) prix-fixe menu 295 Kčs ($10.50). AE.

Open: Daily noon–3pm and 5:30–11pm.

This wine cellar ranks as one of Prague's finest restaurants, mixing the formality of starched linen place settings and old-school service with the coziness of a vaulted stone cellar in a 600-year-old building. The intimate dining room is lit by bulbs set into planted pots, wreathing the ceiling in an arbor of shadows. A belt-high partition in paneled dark wood separates the room into upper and lower dining areas through which the formally attired waitstaff glides as though on skates, accompanied by gentle strains from the pianist. The menu specializes in simple, delicious preparations of highest-quality beef, chicken, duck, or rabbit, presented beautifully in large (the crucial difference between Czech and French haute cuisine) portions. There is no dress code, although you may feel uncomfortable without a jacket or in jeans.

SPECIALTY DINING

Beer Halls

A word about beer-hall etiquette: You can sit in any free seat, even one at "someone else's" table. There's no such thing as a private table, but you should politely ask first if the seat is free. Don't signal the waiter; simply place a coaster in front of you. The waiters come around with armloads of mugs and distribute them to those who appear ready for one. In most halls you run up a tab, which usually appears in the form of a scrap of paper the waiter puts in front of you and ticks off every time he brings you a beer. Incidentally, you'll usually be given a fresh mug the moment you finish the one you're drinking (sometimes, even *before* you have finished), even if you haven't "asked" for it. To quit, signal your desire to pay while you still have at least half a mug in front of you; the waiter will bring no more beer after you have settled your tab.

Jo's Bar, Malostranské nám. 7, Prague 1.

Cuisine: MEXICAN **Reservations:** Not accepted. **Directions:** Walk behind the Church of St. Nicholas in Malostranské náměstí.

Prices: Mexican food 55–135 Kčs ($1.95–$4.80); sandwiches 55–65 Kčs ($1.95–$2.30).
Open: Daily 10am–2am; Sun brunch 11am–3pm.

Well located in the epicenter of Mala Straná, this is not a beer hall but a straightforward bar, run by Canadian expatriates. Robust Gambrinus 12° served in bottles may seem like heresy in the usual Prague drinking establishment—but no more so than the excellent Mexican food served here instead of pub grub. This is a favorite watering hole among Prague's foreign population and the atmosphere is festive most nights.

Konvikt Klub, Konviktská 22, Prague 1. ☎ **24-21-28-81.**

Cuisine: BEER HALL. **Reservations:** Not accepted. **Directions:** From the east side of Charles Bridge, walk one block east and turn right down Liliova, which leads into Betlémské náměstí. Konviktská leads into the square on its southeast side.
Prices: Main courses 24–90 Kčs (85¢–$3.20); half liter of beer 16 Kčs (55¢). AE.
Open: Mon–Fri 11am–1am, Sat 2pm–1am, Sun 5pm–1am.

A classic Czech pub tucked in the basement of a residential building, this jolly, smoky place serves Prazdroj 12° and Gambrinus 12°. The street is reputedly haunted by a "Hairy Ghost" (not to be confused with the "Smelly Monster" or the "Fiery Skeleton" who also roam these parts) who lives in the Vltava but rages on Konviktská.

Na Ovocnem Trhu (At the Fruit Market), Ovocný trh 568/17, Prague 1.

Cuisine: BEER HALL. **Reservations:** Not accepted. **Directions:** From náměstí Republiky walk down Celetná and turn left on Ovocný trh.
Prices: Cold dishes 16–54 Kčs (55¢–$1.95); hot dishes 48–85 Kčs ($1.70–$3.05); half liter of beer 14.60 Kčs (50¢).
Open: Daily 10am–midnight.

While its location in the middle of the tourist district pretty much determines the clientele, this pub is an archetypal Czech drinking spot in every other respect, down to the rollicking behavior it promotes. The high ceiling keeps the smoke level manageable.

U Pinkasů, Jungmannovo nám. 15. ☎ **26-57-70.**

Cuisine: BEER HALL. **Reservations:** Not required. **Metro:** Můstek; then walk half a block.
Prices: Hot and cold dishes 36–50 Kčs ($1.30–$1.80); half liter of beer 14.80 Kčs (55¢).
Open: Daily 9am–3pm and 4pm–midnight.

The seven tables downstairs are packed to a boisterous degree (12°, Prazdroj, to be exact) with mostly Czech tipplers. This was the first establishment in Prague to tap the famed Prazdroj (Pilsener Urquell) beer. Excellent ventilation keeps smoke levels low. The upstairs room has more tables and a reputation for bilking foreigners. If you order food, be sure to get a menu with prices.

U Černého Vola [At the Black Ox], Loretánské náměstí. ☎ **53-86-37.**

Cuisine: BEER HALL. **Reservations:** Not accepted. **Directions:** From Hradčanské náměstí, walk east to Loretánské náměstí.
Prices: Main courses about 85 Kčs ($3); half liter of beer 16.60 Kčs (60¢).

Come here to quench your thirst after a hard day's sightseeing at the castle and Loreto. At the top of a hill, this old-fashioned beer hall serves snacks at long wooden tables and benches. The building was built in the 1500s, though the pictures of beer steins and hunting horns on the walls were painted by a local only about 20 years ago.

U Flekû, at Křemencova 11. ☎ **29-32-46.**

Cuisine: BEER HALL. **Reservations:** Not accepted. **Tram:** 21 from Václavské náměstí.
Prices: Main courses 99 Kčs ($3.55); half liter of beer 29 Kčs ($1.05).
Open: Daily 9am–11pm.

Originally a brewery dating back to 1459, this is Prague's most famous beer hall, a huge place with many rooms and a large courtyard attracting hundreds of revelers at all hours. Restorations have tried to create such details of the past as a decorated medieval wood ceiling in one room or a courtyard surrounded by columns in another area. U Flekû still produces its own brew, a dark beer, but only enough to service its own restaurant, so you're in for a special treat; the cuisine, on the other hand, is undistinguished. You can drink to the strains of an open-air oompah band from 6 to 9pm on Wednesday, Friday, and Saturday, and 4 to 9pm on Sunday.

Cafés and Bistros

In Prague, to linger is to live. Sit back and drink up at any of the following.

Cafe Nouveau/Martini Bar, Obecní Dům, nám. Republiky 5. ☎ and fax **24-81-10-57.**

Cuisine: INTERNATIONAL. **Metro:** náměstí Republiky, next to the Powder Tower.
Prices: Soups 30 Kčs ($1.05); salads 50–80 Kčs ($1.80–$2.85); main courses 70–90 Kčs ($2.50–$3.20).
Open: Daily 11am–midnight.

After years of being just a pretty face, this landmark café is finally under management committed to supplementing its good looks with substance. A wide variety of drinks and a modest menu of fresh and tasty bistro food will sustain you, while jazz every night beginning at 7:30pm (no cover) will entertain you. However, it is the room—a triumphant testament to style for its own sake—that will move you. This is a smashing place to conclude a day of sightseeing with a late meal, a drink, and some people-watching.

The Martini Bar (open 6pm to midnight) occupies the balcony, close to the ornate ceiling and in a cloud of cigarette smoke from the gloomy-chic types who frequent it. The tremendous drink list includes many a whimsical offering. During happy hour, from 6 to 9pm, drinks are two for the price of one.

Café Savoy, Vítězná 1, Prague 5. ☎ **53-97-26.**

Cuisine: CAFE. **Tram:** 6, 9, or 22 to the first stop past the river into Malá Strana; walk one block east.
Prices: Cold dishes 15–40 Kčs (55¢–$1.45); hot dishes 86–100 Kčs ($3.10–$3.55).
Open: Daily noon–midnight.

The murals and ornate ceiling of this rejuvenated café confer class and elegance on all who sit below, and the low table density apportions it exclusively. All manner of drinks are available, as well as snacks, fresh fruit, and a few light main dishes. Swing jazz on the sound system and a pile of newspapers encourage you to do the natural thing: linger.

Dobra Čajovna, Václavské nám. 14, Prague 1.

Cuisine: TEA. **Reservations:** Not accepted. **Metro:** Můstek, and walk up the right side for two or three blocks.

Prices: Tea and snacks 20–55 Kčs (70¢–$1.95).
Open: Mon–Sat 10am–9pm, Sun 3–9pm.

Secreted in a little alley off the main drag, this serene and fragrant space pungent with potpourri and hushed tones is a temple of tea. The staff restricts customers beyond the number of available seats, but once in, you won't want to leave (and won't be asked to either). The tea menu (with an English translation) describes 56 varieties of green, half-green, white, and black teas from Taiwan, China, Vietnam, Japan, Hong Kong, India, Sri Lanka, and Paraguay. The subtlety and moderation of the place—snacks such as candied ginger come in tiny ramekins—make this an anti-*pivnice.* Just the place to rejuvenate after fervently exploring the city. There is no smoking, of course.

The Globe Bookstore/Café, Janovského 14, Prague 7.

Cuisine: INTERNATIONAL. **Tram:** 1, 5, 8, 12, 14, 17, 25, or 26 to Strossmayerova náměstí; walk east one block on Milady Horákové to Janovského, and then north two or three blocks.
Prices: Drinks 8–30 Kčs (30¢–$1.05); food 25–45 Kčs (90¢–$1.60).
Open: Daily 10am–midnight.

This bookstore-café is home base for an expatriate community of radical chic anarcho-syndicalist neobeatnik nipple-piercing tattoo-mapped English-major types. It's also a holistic haven for a committed band of litterateurs, who publish the thick quarterly *Trafika*—an international compendium of prose, poetry, and criticism with an Eastern European cant. Browse the bookstore's wonderful selection of used and new books, or pull up a chair in the café, where tipplers hash over Kafka and Kurt Cobain or play board games. The food is good, too, with homemade baked goods, delicious soups, healthy salads and sandwiches, and outstanding Velkopopovice Kozel 12° on tap.

5 Attractions

Prague escaped the destruction that most of Europe has periodically suffered over the past centuries. The precious little warfare or vandalism since the 17th century to besmirch the city is the paradoxical product of war itself. The city was the powerful capital of an aggressive feudal coalition in the 14th and 15th centuries, but when the reformist minister Jan Hus was burned at the stake in 1415, a bloody internecine religious war broke out. By the time of its culmination at the Battle of Lipany in 1434, all chances that the squabbling Bohemian nobility might cobble together a nation state had evaporated. Trade routes that once centered on Prague moved elsewhere, and neighboring nobles gobbled up contiguous territory. But as political and economic gravity shifted away from Prague to other cities, fighting and strife went with it. From the early 17th century onward, Prague enjoyed a peace that only its diminished significance could have brought.

Prague's long history and succession of self-aggrandizing royal patrons has enabled it to collect buildings from every significant era in the history of architecture. The first golden age came during the 14th-century reign of Charles IV. Upon returning from his education in Paris, he found his 11th-century castle a sorry wreck—no match for the splendor of the French court to which he had grown accustomed. His subsequent building spree enlarged the city and gave it its most significant Gothic structures, including St. Vitus Cathedral, the Charles Bridge, and the castle walls. Habsburg rule ushered in the Renaissance style, which supplanted some Gothic structures and was grafted onto others. Subsequent baroque, rococo, art nouveau, and constructivist eras deposited buildings on Prague as well, leaving the city with the most fantastic architectural heritage of any Eastern European city.

Museums for all tastes complement the architectural monuments. Check with Prague Information Service for *Museums and Art Galleries in Prague,* a booklet listing all museums and their opening and closing times.

Note: Students receive a 50% percent discount on most museum charges. The purchase of a **Prague Card** buys three days of transportation and free admission to most of Prague's top sights and museums. (See "Getting Around: By Metro, Bus, and Tram," above.)

Suggested Itineraries

If You Have 1 Day

If you have the bad fortune of having only a mere day in Prague, you should begin your tour at one of two points: Staroměstské náměstí (Old Town Square) in the heart of the Staré Město, or the Hradčanské náměstí (Castle Hill Square) in the center of the Hradčany (castle district). Between these two points lie most of Prague's important sights.

I suggest starting up at the castle and working your way down the hill, hitting the highlights of the Walking Tours to the Prague Castle and the Old Town (see below).

If You Have 2 Days

Take the Walking Tours to the Prague Castle and the Old Town on separate days, allowing ample time for sights such as St. Vitus Cathedral and the Royal Palace on one, and the Old Town Hall and Tower and Týn Church during the other. Also add the European Art Museum, just outside the Prague Castle gates.

If You Have 3 Days

Visit the sights mentioned above and add the Loreto and Strahov Monastery west of the castle, the Church of St. Nicholas and the Malá Strana bridge tower in Malá Strana, and the Powder Tower and the old Jewish ghetto in the Old Town area.

If You Have 5 Days or More

There's still plenty to see! Consider the Czech National Gallery for Czechoslovak paintings, the Bethlehem Chapel, the National Museum, the Museum of Applied Arts, St. Agnes Chapel, one of Prague's parks, the Military History Museum, the National Technical Museum, or the three music museums, dedicated to Mozart, Smetana, and Dvořák.

If you have still more time, you'll enjoy day excursions from Prague to some of the nearby castles like Karlštejn or Konopiště, or the silver-mining town of Kutná Hora. As you can see, there's so much to do in Prague and its environs that it's easy to spend a week without a dull moment.

THE TOP ATTRACTIONS

In Prague Castle

St. Vitus Cathedral, in Prague Castle.

The center of Prague's religious life and its largest church, St. Vitus dates its foundations to A.D. 926 when it was first constructed as the court church of the Přemysl princes. It was named after St. Vitus, a 4th-century Sicilian who was tortured to death

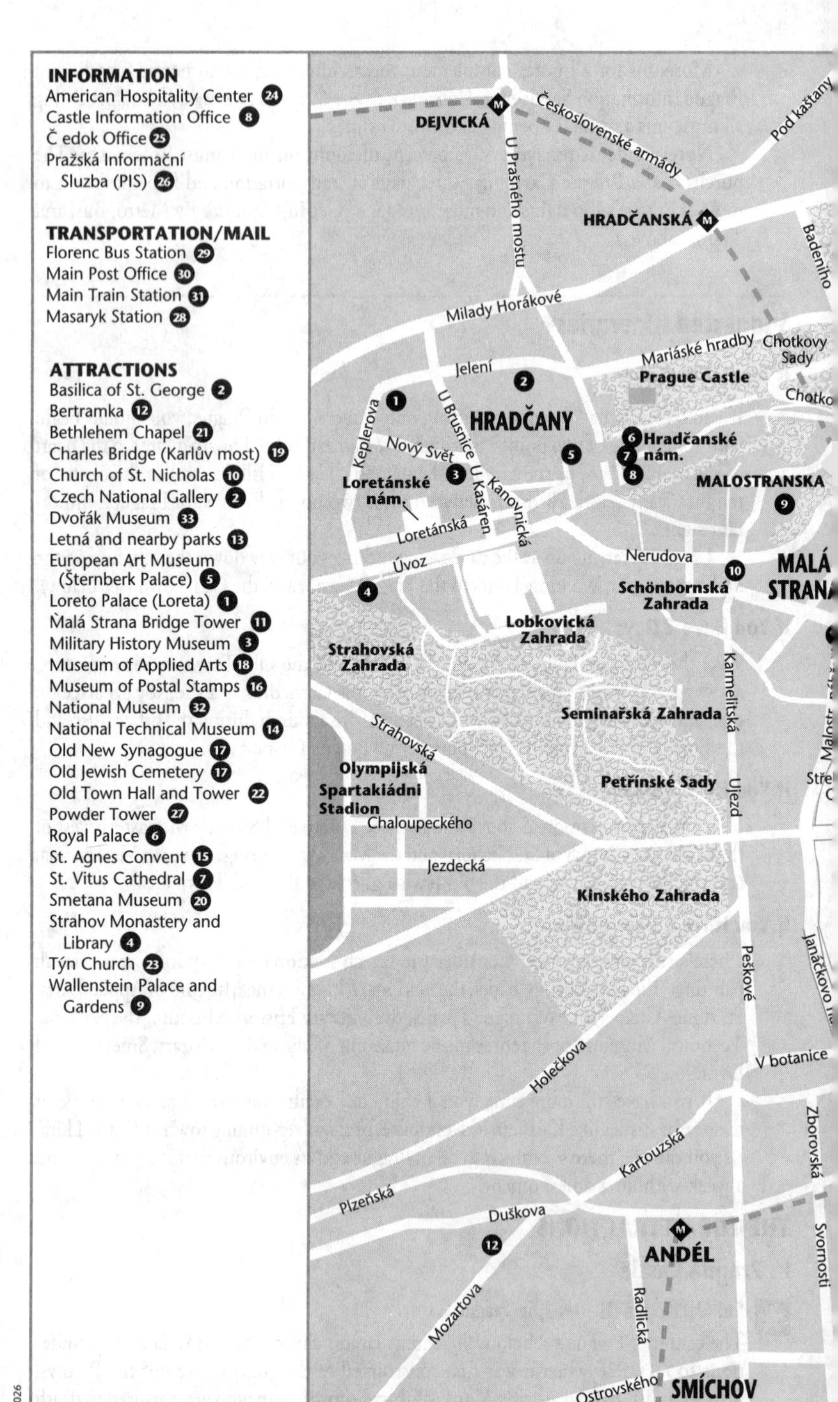
INFORMATION
American Hospitality Center 24
Castle Information Office 8
Č edok Office 25
Pražská Informační Sluzba (PIS) 26
TRANSPORTATION/MAIL
Florenc Bus Station 29
Main Post Office 30
Main Train Station 31
Masaryk Station 28
ATTRACTIONS
Basilica of St. George 2
Bertramka 12
Bethlehem Chapel 21
Charles Bridge (Karlův most) 19
Church of St. Nicholas 10
Czech National Gallery 2
Dvořák Museum 33
Letná and nearby parks 13
European Art Museum (Šternberk Palace) 5
Loreto Palace (Loreta) 1
Malá Strana Bridge Tower 11
Military History Museum 3
Museum of Applied Arts 18
Museum of Postal Stamps 16
National Museum 32
National Technical Museum 14
Old New Synagogue 17
Old Jewish Cemetery 17
Old Town Hall and Tower 22
Powder Tower 27
Royal Palace 6
St. Agnes Convent 15
St. Vitus Cathedral 7
Smetana Museum 20
Strahov Monastery and Library 4
Týn Church 23
Wallenstein Palace and Gardens 9
DEJVICKÁ
Československé armády
Pod kaštany
U Prašného mostu
HRADČANSKÁ
Badeniho
Milady Horákové
Mariáské hradby
Chotkovy Sady
Jelení
Prague Castle
Keplerova
U Brusnice
HRADČANY
Nový Svět
Hradčanské nám.
Loretánské nám.
U Kasáren
Kanovnická
MALOSTRANSKA
Loretánská
Úvoz
Nerudova
MALÁ STRANA
Schönbornská Zahrada
Lobkovická Zahrada
Strahovská Zahrada
Karmelitská
Seminařská Zahrada
Strahovská
Olympijská Spartakiádni Stadion
Petřínské Sady
Újezd
Chaloupeckého
Jezdecká
Kinského Zahrada
Janáčkovo
Peškové
V botanice
Holečkova
Zborovská
Kartouzská
Plzeňská
Duškova
ANDĚL
Svornosti
Mozartova
Radlická
Ostrovského
SMÍCHOV
9026

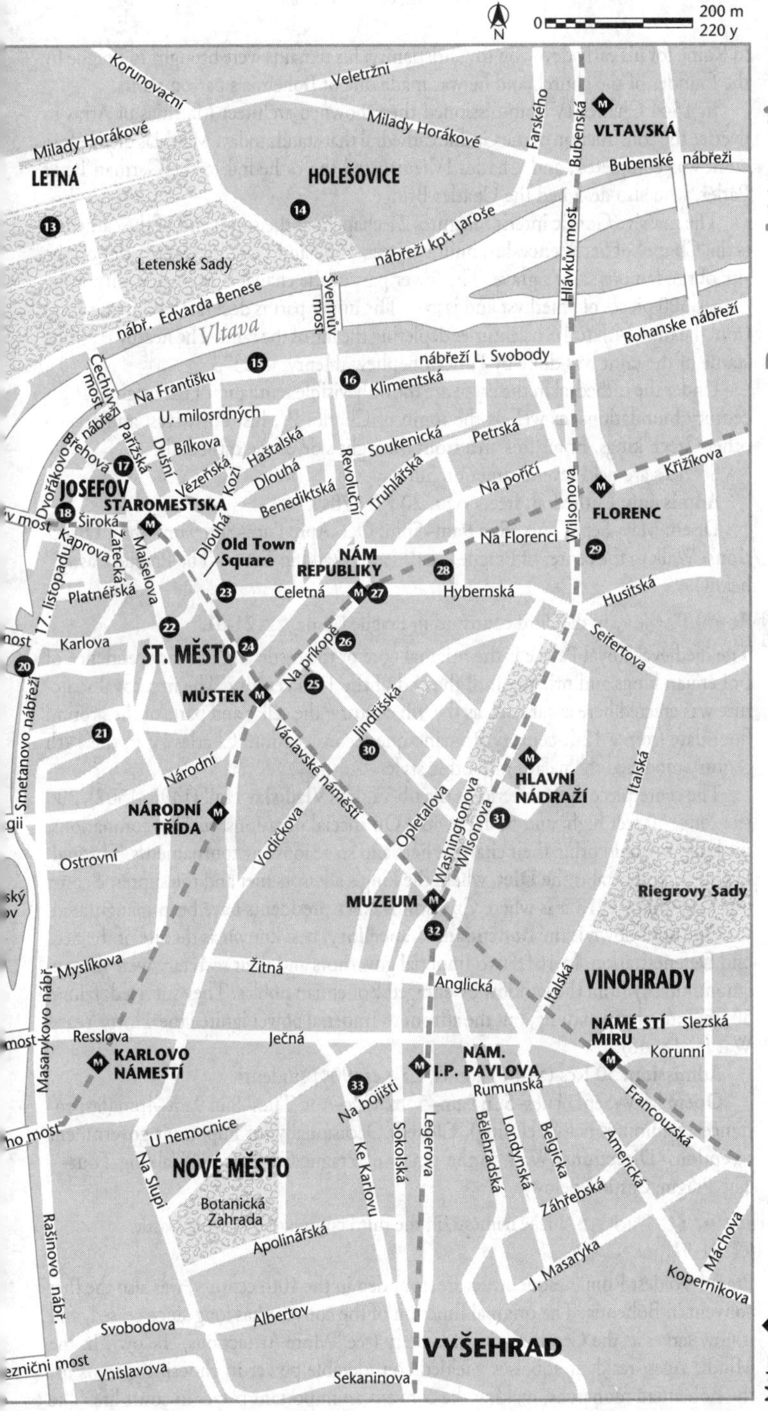
N
0
200 m
220 y
Korunovační
Veletržni
Milady Horákové
LETNÁ
HOLEŠOVICE
Farského
Bubenská
VLTAVSKÁ
Bubenské nábřeži
Letenské Sady
nábřeži kpt. Jaroše
Hlávkův most
Švermův most
nábř. Edvarda Benese
Vltava
Rohanske nábřeží
nábřeží L. Svobody
Čechův most
Na Františku
Klimentská
U. milosrdných
Bílkova
Haštalská
Petrská
Soukenická
Revoluční
Truhlářská
Dvořákovo nábřeží
Břehová
Pařížská
Dušní
Vězeňská
Kozí
Dlouhá
Benediktská
Na poříčí
Křižíkova
Wilsonova
JOSEFOV
STAROMESTSKA
FLORENC
Široká
Kaprova
Žatecká
Maiselova
Dlouhá
Old Town Square
NÁM REPUBLIKY
Na Florenci
17. listopadu
Platnéřská
Celetná
Hybernská
Husitská
Karlova
ST. MĚSTO
Na příkopě
Seifertova
Smetanovo nábřeží
MŮSTEK
Jindřišská
Národní
Václavské náměstí
HLAVNÍ NÁDRAŽÍ
Italská
NÁRODNÍ TŘÍDA
Opletalova
Washingtonova
Wilsonova
Vodičkova
Ostrovní
MUZEUM
Riegrovy Sady
Myslíkova
Žitná
Anglická
Italská
VINOHRADY
Resslova
Ječná
NÁMÉ STÍ MIRU
Slezská
Korunní
KARLOVO NÁMESTÍ
NÁM. I.P. PAVLOVA
Rumunská
Masarykovo nábř.
Na bojišti
Francouzská
U nemocnice
Sokolská
Legerova
Bělehradská
Londýnská
Belgická
Americká
NOVÉ MĚSTO
Na Slupi
Ke Karlovu
Záhřebská
Botanická Zahrada
Apolinářská
Rašínovo nábř.
J. Masaryka
Máchova
Kopernikova
Albertov
Svobodova
VYŠEHRAD
Vnislavova
Sekaninova
Metro
13
14
15
16
17
18
20
21
22
23
24
25
26
27
28
29
30
31
32
33

in Rome for his early devotion to Christianity; his remains were brought to Prague by the founder of the church and he was made one of Bohemia's patron saints.

In 1344 Charles IV commissioned the renowned architect Matthias of Arras to oversee the construction of the Gothic cathedral that stands today. Matthias died before work was completed, and Charles IV entrusted the cathedral to the German Peter Parléř, who also designed the Charles Bridge.

The massive Gothic interior features 21 chapels; at the south end of the cathedral is the **Chapel of St. Wenceslas,** built between 1362 and 1364 by Peter Parléř on the site of the famous saint's grave. The lower part of the chapel is encrusted with more than 1,300 pieces of amethyst and jasper. The upper part is decorated with paintings from the mid-14th to 16th centuries depicting the life of the saint. The nearby ragstone statue of the saint was done by Parléř's nephew, Henry, in 1373.

Under the cathedral in the crypt are the only visible remnants of the original 10th-century foundations, as well as the tomb of Charles IV, his four wives, and several other Czech kings. Enter this area from the right side of the cathedral.

Services are held several times on Sunday.

Admission: Cathedral, free; crypt, 20 Kčs (70¢).

Open: May–Sept, Tues–Sun 9am–5pm; Oct–Apr, Tues–Sun 9am–4pm. **Directions:** Walk to the center of Prague Castle (see "Walking Tour—The Prague Castle," below).

★ **Royal Palace,** in the third courtyard in Prague Castle. ☎ **21-01.**

The medieval Royal Palace is the original core of the castle and primary residence of Bohemian kings and princes until the end of the 16th century. The first royal structure was erected here as far back as the 9th century; the cellar and parts of the ground floor date from a 12th-century Romanesque reconstruction. Charles IV in the 14th century modified the palace in Gothic style.

The centerpiece of the interior is the rib-vaulted **Vladislav Hall** (1493–1502), 200 feet long, 50 feet high, and 50 feet wide. On special occasions, such as coronations, the knights would bring their chargers here and stage jousting tournaments. Through the northern portal is the **Diet,** where the king's advisors met and the supreme court was held. Since 1918 it is where Czechoslovakia's presidents have been inaugurated.

One floor down is the **Bohemian Chancellory,** best known as the site of the Second Defenestration. In 1618 two Imperial governors and their secretary were thrown ignominiously from the window by enraged Bohemian nobles. They survived, falling 50 feet into a heap of dung, but the affront to Imperial power ignited the Thirty Years' War (1618–48).

Admission: 50 Kčs ($1.80) adults, 25 Kčs (90¢) students.

Open: May–Sept, Tues–Sun 9am–5pm; Oct–Apr, Tues–Sun 9am–4pm (last entrance 15 minutes before closing). **Closed:** Occasionally for important government receptions. **Directions:** Walk to the center of Prague Castle (see "Walking Tour—The Prague Castle," below).

Basilica of St. George, Jiřské náměstí, in the third courtyard in Prague Castle. ☎ **21-01.**

Prague's oldest Romanesque structure, founded in the 10th century, was also the first convent in Bohemia. The original function of the convent has long since ceased, and it now serves as the Czech National Gallery (see "More Attractions," below). In the Middle Ages, resident abbesses wielded considerable power in choosing queens for the Bohemian monarchs, making the convent an important player in court life. The bright-red facade dates to a baroque reconfiguration in 1670, but the interior retains a stone Romanesque construction. The smooth flat walls and tremendous vault lend acoustic clout to the concerts held here frequently.

Admission: 10 Kčs (35¢) adults, 5 Kčs (18¢) students.

Open: May–Sept, Tues–Sun 9am–5pm; Oct–Apr, Tues–Sun 9am–4pm. **Directions:** Walk across from the east side of St. Vitus Cathedral inside Prague Castle.

Castle Treasury, in the second courtyard of Prague Castle. ☎ **21-01,** ext. 3380.

Located in the former 18th-century Chapel of the Holy Cross is this collection of royal jewelry, reliquaries, monstrances, and relics of Bohemian patron saints. These include the cassock of St. Wenceslas, St. Stephen's sword, and other objects from the 8th to the 19th century. Unfortunately, descriptions are only in Czech. The best time to visit is toward the end of the day when crowds are smaller.

Closed: Until further notice. **Directions:** Walk to the second courtyard of Prague Castle from Hradčanské náměstí (see "Walking Tour—The Prague Castle," below).

West of Prague Castle

European Art Museum, Hradčanské náměstí 15. ☎ **35-24-41** to **35-24-43** or **53-44-57.**

Housed in the 18th-century Šternberský (Šternberk Palace) just outside the Prague Castle is one of Central Europe's finest art museums. French 19th- and 20th-century art is featured on the ground floor, and European masters (including Lorenzo Lotto, El Greco, Tintoretto, Canaletto, Tiepolo, Guardi, Rubens, Van Dyck, Rembrandt, Monet, Cézanne, Renoir, Gauguin, van Gogh, Matisse, and Chagall) are on the first. Highlights include Dürer's *Festival of the Rosary* with the Madonna and Child surrounded by important contemporary figures; and some important early Picassos from the first decade of the 20th century.

Admission: 40 Kčs ($1.40) adults, 10 Kčs (35¢) students and children, 60 Kčs ($2.15) family; free for everyone Thurs.

Open: Tues 9am–7pm, Wed–Sun 10am–6pm. **Directions:** With your back to Prague Castle on Hradčanské náměstí, go to the building on the right, and follow the cobblestone street to the ticket desk.

Loreto Palace [Loreta], Loretánské náměstí 7. ☎ **536-6228.**

Named after the town of Loreto, Italy, where the dwelling of the Virgin Mary was reputedly brought by angels from Palestine in the 13th century. After the Catholic Habsburgs defeated the Protestant Bohemians at the Battle of White Mountain in 1620, the Loreto cult was chosen as the device for the re-Catholicization of Bohemia. More than 50 copies of the Loreto church were constructed, the most famous being this one in Prague, built between 1626 and 1750.

As you walk in, you come into a large courtyard with the **Santa Casa,** the Virgin Mary's House, at the center. The interior has frescoes in fragmentary form—exactly as they appear in the original in Italy. Behind this stands the **Church of the Nativity of Our Lord,** one of Prague's most beautiful baroque churches, with elaborate interior decorations and ceiling frescoes. Concerts are held here from time to time.

The highlight of the visit, however, is upstairs in the ★ **Loreto Treasury,** a fabulous collection of 17th- and 18th-century jewelry, reliquaries, and monstrances. The most impressive item in the treasury is a lethal-looking Viennese monstrance (1699) of gold-plated silver studded with more than 6,200 diamonds. You can also buy a detailed English-language guidebook at the entrance.

Across from the Loreto sits the Ministry of Foreign Affairs, in the former Černín Palace built between 1669 and 1687.

Admission: 30 Kčs ($1.05) adults, 20 Kčs (70¢) students.

Open: Tues–Sun 9am–1pm and 1:30–4:30pm (to 6pm July–Aug). **Directions:** Walk for about seven minutes straight ahead away from the Prague Castle gates, then turn right on the large square Loretánské náměstí.

In Malá Strana

Just down the hill from the Hradčany is Prague's second-oldest quarter, the Malá Strana (Lower Town). Founded by Otakar II in 1257, the Malá Strana was an exclusive section of town. Damaged in the fighting between local Bohemians in the Malá Strana and the Imperials in the Hrad in 1419, it has remained otherwise intact since the 16th century. After the Battle of White Mountain (1620) the Habsburgs moved in and built the many beautiful baroque buildings—at the expense of equally beautiful Renaissance Bohemian structures—that are here today.

★ **Church of St. Nicholas [kostel sv. Mikuláše],** Malostranské náměstí.

As St. Vitus Cathedral represents Gothic architecture in Prague, the Church of St. Nicholas represents the pinnacle of the baroque Counter-Reformation. One of the most opulent baroque structures in existence, it was begun in 1703 and work continued for almost 60 years (1760). The ceiling fresco alone took 9 years to complete. Covering almost 4,275 square feet and resplendent in trompe-l'oeil technique, it's one of the largest single frescoes in Europe. The overall interior marks an interesting transition between the pastel colors of the later rococo and the splendor of the baroque. The church also attracted Mozart during his stay in Prague—he played the church organ here. Ask for the English-language description as you enter.

Admission: 20 Kčs (70¢) adults, 10 Kčs (35¢) students.

Open: May–Sept, daily 9am–6pm; Mar–Apr, daily 9am–5pm; Oct, daily 10am–5pm; Nov–Feb, daily 9am–4pm (last entrance 30 minutes before closing). **Directions:** From the west side of Charles Bridge, walk west down Mostecká to Malostranské náměstí; enter from the rear of the square.

★ **Malá Strana Bridge Tower [Mostecká Věz],** Mostecká ullce.

After hiking up many wooden stairs inside this former medieval defensive tower, you'll be rewarded with views over the Old Town in the distance and Charles Bridge below, as well as the castle looming on the other side. It's a great spot for photos.

Admission: 20 Kčs (70¢) adults, 10 Kčs (35¢) students.

Open: May–Sept, daily 10am–6pm; Apr and Oct, daily 10am–5pm (last entry 30 minutes before closing). **Closed:** Nov–Mar. **Directions:** Walk to the west side of Charles Bridge.

In the Old Town

★ **Old Town Hall and Tower,** Staroměstské náměstí. ☎ **28-38-71.**

Every hour after the chiming of the Astronomical Clock (see "Walking Tour—The Old Town," below) you can go on a guided tour of the Town Hall. Originally built in the 11th century, this seat of the Town Council added a tower and the distinctive Gothic portal in the 14th century. The highlight of the interior tour is the **Old Council Chamber,** which remains as it was in 1470 with a richly decorated Renaissance wooden ceiling, 46 colored emblems of Prague on the wall, and a 1410 sculpture of Christ.

Several other official rooms are included on the tour, including the **King George Room,** which has fragments of medieval frescoes, and the **Brožik Hall,** the largest in the Town Hall. The whole tour takes about 30 minutes.

After the tour you can visit the Town Hall chapel on your own. Built in 1381 by Peter Parléř, it has Gothic rib-vaulting and 14th-century frescoes. From there you can climb up to the top of the tower for a great view over the Old Town and all of Prague.

Admission: Town Hall, 20 Kčs (70¢) adults, 10 Kčs (35¢) students; chapel, 20 Kčs (70¢) adults, 10 Kčs (35¢) students; tower, 10 Kčs (35¢) adults, 5 Kčs (20¢) students.

Open: Closed for restoration as of this writing. **Directions:** Walk to the southwest side of the Old Town Square.

★ **Týn Church,** Celetná 5.

Long the bastion of Hussite religion (1415–1621), Týn Church was where Jan Hus first heard the fiery reformist oratory of Konrád Waldhauser and Jan Milič that inspired his struggle with the Roman Catholic church. Founded in 1365 on the site of several earlier churches, the Týn Church received numerous alterations over the centuries. The fantastic 260-foot towers were added in the second half of the 15th century, and other portions were designed by Parléř, Rejsek, and others. Of historical interest is the tomb next to the high altar of the famous Danish astronomer Tycho de Brahe (1601), court astronomer to Emperor Rudolf II.

Admission: Free.

Open: Closed to tourists for restoration although open for mass, Mon–Fri 4pm, Sat 1pm, Sun 11:30am and 9pm. **Directions:** Walk east down Celetná from the Old Town Square and through the small courtyard at no. 5.

Powder Tower, náměstí Republiky.

The only remaining tower from Prague's Old Town city fortifications, this 140-foot-tall stone structure stored gunpowder for hundreds of years. It's the late Gothic masterpiece of Matěj Rejsek, built in honor of the Polish king Vladislav Jagellon, who in 1475 brought peace in the wake of the Hussite Wars. In addition to its military functions, it served as the main gate on the king's route entering Prague from his foreign journeys. Today you can enjoy a nice view from the top, although not as impressive as the tower at Charles Bridge. Ask for the English-language description as you go in.

Open: Closed for restoration as of this writing. **Metro:** Náměstí Republiky.

In Josefov

Josefov is home to the State Jewish Museum, which includes eight different sites: see "Walking Tour—Josefov" below, for a complete list. All are open Sunday through Friday.

Old New Synagogue, Červená 2. ☎ **231-0681.**

The Gothic Altneuschul is the oldest synagogue in Europe. Its physical situation—sunk several feet and many historical strata below street level—is an apt metaphor of its continued survival. Constructed from 1270 to 1280 by builders of the nearby St. Agnes Monastery, who were conveniently on hand from France, it was called "new" to distinguish it from an older (now gone) synagogue. Hebrew inscriptions on the simple interior walls are phrases and acronyms from psalms and blessings. Setting an appropriately obeisant tone, the inscription on the left wall reads, "Know before whom you are standing," and on the right, "I am ever mindful of the LORD's presence."

The banner at the back, made in 1716, is marked with the symbol of Prague's Jewish community, given by Emperor Ferdinand III in 1648. The Swedish cap in the middle of the Star of David symbolizes the emperor's gratitude for help defending against a Swedish invasion.

Admission: 30 Kčs ($1.05) adults, 15 Kčs (55¢) students.

Open: Sun–Fri 9:30am–5:30pm. **Directions:** From Old Town Square, walk three blocks down Pařižská and then turn left.

★ **Old Jewish Cemetery,** U st. hřbitova ulice.

Dating back to 1439, this is Europe's oldest Jewish burial ground, located one block from the Old New Synagogue. The walled-in grounds pitch and roll under a jagged maw of thousands of gravestones. Due to the limited available space in the Jewish settlement, the ghetto inhabitants buried their dead in layers. Gravestones from earlier strata were unearthed and placed alongside the new markers. The resulting 12,000 gravestones stand over an estimated 100,000 graves in 10 to 12 layers. Vertical interment continued until 1787 when Emperor Joseph II closed the cemetery. Reliefs on some stones represent the family names of the deceased, such as a lion for the Löws and a carp for the Karpeles. The most celebrated buried here are Rabbi Avigdor Kara, the poet and first resident of the cemetery; Rabbi Löw, the philosopher whose renown in life generated myths after his passing, including the story of the clay golem he created to guard the ghetto; and Mordecai Maisel, whose enormous wealth and philanthropy built two synagogues and renovated much of the Jewish town. The pebbles and rocks piled on tombstones, instead of flowers, represent a Jewish tradition that dates back to the wanderings of Jewish tribes in arid Canaan. The dead were buried under rocks, and stones piled on the spot marked their resting place. A more recent tradition involves mourners addressing notes to the dead and leaving them under the stones, a posthumous honor most often bestowed at the grave of Rabbi Löw.

Admission: 30 Kčs ($1.05) adults, 15 Kčs (55¢) students. The ticket to the cemetery also entitles you to enter the nearby Ceremonial Hall and an exhibit of children's drawings from the Terezín Ghetto (same hours). You can, however, buy a single pass good for entrance to all the sites of the State Jewish Museum (except the Old New Synagogue, for which it is invalid) for 80 Kčs ($2.85) for adults, and 30 Kčs ($1.05) for students.

Open: Sun–Fri 9am–5:30pm. **Directions:** From Old Town Square, walk three blocks down Pařížská and then turn left.

MORE ATTRACTIONS

In or near Prague Castle

Czech National Gallery, Jiřské nám. 33, in the third courtyard in Prague Castle. ☎ **53-52-40** or **53-52-46** to **53-52-49.**

Formerly the convent of the adjacent Basilica of St. George, this structure now houses Bohemian painting and sculpture from the 14th to the 18th century. The most common subject portrayed is the Virgin Mary.

Admission: 40 Kčs ($1.40) adults, 10 Kčs (35¢) students, 50 Kčs ($1.80) family; free for everyone Thurs.

Open: Tues 9am–7pm, Wed–Sun 10am–6pm (last entrance 30 minutes before closing). **Directions:** Walk next door to the Basilica of St. George inside Prague Castle.

Strahov Monastery and Library, Strahovské nádvoří.

The second-oldest monastery in Prague, from 1143, Strahov is a favorite tourist destination for its beautiful ornate libraries with almost a million volumes. The **Philosophical Library** boasts a 46-foot-high ceiling covered by a huge 18th-century fresco; the adjacent 17th-century **Theological Library** is also lavishly decorated in carved wood and ceiling frescoes. The pair juxtapose early baroque and late classicist styles. The most valued book of the collection is the 9th- or 10th-century *Strahov Evangeliarium*, a Latin work in gold lettering.

Downstairs is the **Museum of Czech Literature,** with old printing presses, books, and other displays of Czech literary greats. There's also a small exhibition of famous photographs.

Admission: 20 Kčs (70¢) adults, 5 Kčs (20¢) students.

Open: Tues–Sun 9am–12:15pm and 1–5pm. **Directions:** From Hradčanské náměstí, walk west down Loretánská, which leads into Pohořelec; at 9 Pohořelec, climb the covered stairway and continue straight ahead.

In the Old Town

Bethlehem Chapel [Betlémská Kaple], on Betlémské náměstí.

This church was where Jan Hus from 1402 to 1413 preached his revolutionary ideas about challenging the Roman Catholic church. Even after Hus's death, the church remained a center of revolutionary activity. Following the Battle of White Mountain the Jesuits bought the chapel. In 1786 it was practically demolished and turned into an apartment building. After World War II a painstaking reconstruction, finished in 1954, restored the church to its Hus-era form.

Admission: 20 Kčs (70¢) adults, 10 Kčs (35¢) students.

Open: Apr–Sept, daily 9am–6pm; Oct–Mar, daily 9am–5pm. **Directions:** From the east side of Charles Bridge, walk one block east and turn right down Lillová, which leads into Betlémské náměstí after two blocks.

National Museum [Národní muzeum], Václavské nám. 68. ☎ **26-94-51.**

A massive museum in the neo-Renaissance building that framed the Velvet Revolution in the viewfinders of the world's news media, its collection is massive and eclectic. One section is dedicated to the history of Czechoslovakia until World II, showing documents and objects such as Nazi posters. Another exhibit shows archeological remains such as ancient pottery, bones, etc. The third floor is devoted to natural history, with stuffed animals from bats to bears and insects and fish. Unfortunately, museum descriptions are only in Czech.

Admission: 20 Kčs (70¢) adults, 10 Kčs (35¢) students.

Open: Daily 9am–6pm. **Metro:** Muzeum on Line A or C.

★ **Museum of Applied Arts,** 17 listopadu 2. ☎ **232-0051.**

This is a museum not so much about art as it is about beauty. The collection includes tapestries, carved furniture dating back as far as the 16th century, vases, grandfather clocks, porcelain, bookcovers, elaborate beer steins, glass, and other examples of applied art. You'll also see a collection of 19th-century dresses. The neo-Renaissance museum building, which appears to have once been a palace, actually serves the purpose for which it was originally built in 1885.

Admission: 30 Kčs ($1.05) adults, 10 Kčs (35¢) students.

Open: Tues–Sun 10am–6pm. **Metro:** Staroměstská; then walk west two blocks and north two blocks.

St. Agnes Convent [Anežský klášter], Anežská ulice. ☎ **231-4251.**

Formerly a convent established in 1233, St. Agnes today houses a wing of the Czech national gallery. Displayed here are 19th-century Czech landscapes and portraits in classicist, post-Romantic, and realistic styles. As you view the collection, you'll pass through the original convent halls and see Gothic spires and other details of Bohemia's first Gothic structure. The convent was founded by Princess Agnes, the sister of King Wenceslas I. Concerts are also held here on occasion.

Admission: 40 Kčs ($1.40) adults, 10 Kčs (35¢) students.

Open: Tues–Sun 10am–6pm. **Directions:** From the Old Town Square, walk north up Dlouhá, which changes its name and continues north for about five blocks; at the small square with a church, walk around to other side.

Museum of the City of Prague, Sady Jana Švermy 1544. ☎ **236-2449.**

If you have a lot of time to see Prague, you should consider this modest museum with displays on the city's history from the 9th century to the present. Highlights include a scale model of Prague in 1826 (with Josefov intact) as well as old statues, emblems, guns, and photos. Temporary exhibitions are also held; on my last visit there was one on the 1968 uprising.

Admission: 10 Kčs (35¢) adults, 5 Kčs (20¢) students.

Open: Tues–Sun 10am–6pm. **Metro:** Florenc.

PARKS & GARDENS

Letná and Nearby Parks, northeast of Prague Castle.

After sightseeing in the castle area, you might want to relax in the late afternoon and take some photos of the Old Town with the river and several bridges in the foreground. I suggest the vantage point at the **Hanavský Pavilion** at the southwest corner of Letná Park. After that, you can enjoy a drink outside an 1897 art nouveau building.

To the west of this park is the **Royal Summer Palace** (Královský letohrádek), also called the Belvedere. Built between 1538 and 1563 for Queen Anne, wife of Ferdinand I, it's a remarkably pure example of Italian Renaissance architecture. The Renaissance garden in front is also a wonder, with the Zpívající fontána (Singing Fountain) in the very center. Unfortunately, the palace is closed for repairs as of this writing, but the gardens are open and are quite peaceful and shaded, with a great view over Prague.

Admission: Free.

Open: Parks, 24 hours daily. **Tram:** 18 from Staroměstská or 22 from Malostranské náměstí; get off after it climbs the hill.

Wallenstein Palace and Gardens [Valdštejnská Zahrada], off Letenská ulice.

The first baroque palace in Prague, the Wallenstein Palace was built between 1624 and 1630 for a nobleman, Albrecht Václav Eusebius of Wallenstein, who spared no expense in his desire to rival the castle up the hill. A virtual galaxy of Italian masters worked on his palace at one time or another. Although the palace now serves as a government building and is closed to the public, you'll enjoy a stroll around its attractive park in front.

Admission: Free.

Open: Palace, closed to the public. Park, May–Sept, Tues–Sun 8am–7pm; Oct–Apr, Tues–Sun 10am–6pm. **Directions:** From Malostranské náměstí, walk northeast up Letenská, and then take the first left into the gardens.

SPECIAL-INTEREST SIGHTSEEING

For the History and Science Buff

Military History Museum, Hradčanské nám. 2. ☎ **53-64-88.**

Located across the square from the European Art Museum, the Renaissance Schwarzenberský palác (Schwarzenberg Palace) today houses the Czech and Slovak Republics' oldest military museum. The first floor starts with armor, clubs, and crossbows of the 10th to the 15th century. The second floor chronicles various conflicts since the 16th century, including the Thirty Years' War, Austrian conflicts with Prussia and the Ottoman Empire, the Revolution of 1848, and World War I. A highlight is a 19th-century model of the battlefield of the Battle of Austerlitz, a gift of Napoleon himself.

Prague also has a second military museum with modern weaponry in the Žižkov section of town east of the Old Town, at U památníku 2.

Admission: 20 Kčs (70¢) adults, 10 Kčs (35¢) students.

Open: May–Oct, Tues–Sun 10am–6pm. **Closed:** Nov–Apr. **Directions:** With your back to Prague Castle on Hradčanské náměstí, look for the striking black-and-white facade on the left side of the square.

National Technical Museum, Kostelní 42. ☎ **37-36-51.**

Rarely visited by tourists, this museum boasts an extraordinary collection of inventions, including locomotive trains, old cars, motorcycles, and actual planes. One of the automobiles is said to be the most valuable race car in the world: a 1938 Mercedes-Benz that could accelerate up to 195 m.p.h. One investor recently offered $20 million for the battered vehicle—which the museum declined.

Another part of the museum boasts one of the best history of photography and film collections in the world. Some of the earliest photographs ever taken are here, including five daguerreotypes, one-of-a-kind photos developed on sheets of silver from 1839 to 1855. Of the seven existing daguerreotypes taken by French inventor Louis Daguerre himself, two are displayed here: *Metternich* and *Palace Royal.* You'll also see one of the earliest attempts at 3-D photography from 1910.

The museum also has a large collection of old timepieces and astronomical devices.

Admission: 30 Kčs ($1.05) adults, 5 Kčs (20¢) students.

Open: Tues–Sun 9am–5pm. **Bus:** 125 from the south side of Švermův most near St. Agnes Convent; exit after the tunnel.

For the Music Lover

Bertramka, Mozartova 169. ☎ **54-38-93.**

A villa in a lovely quiet park in southwestern Prague, Bertramka was Wolfgang Amadeus Mozart's home on several occasions in 1787, 1789, and 1791. During one stay he completed *Don Giovanni* before personally presiding over its 1787 premiere in Prague. Today the museum honors his stays here with the clavier he used, documents about Mozart, and original period furniture. As you tour the house, taped Mozart music plays. Ask for the English-language description at the entrance.

Admission: 50 Kčs ($1.80) adults, 30 Kčs ($1.05) students.

Open: Daily 9:30am–6pm. **Metro:** Anděl; then a 10-minute walk west. **Bus:** 123, 130, 132, 167, 191, or 217. **Tram:** 9 to "Bertramka."

Smetana Museum, Novotného lávka 1. ☎ **26-53-71.**

Fans of the composer Bedřich Smetana can view copies of his musical scores, his piano, his letters, and other documents from his life in a neo-Renaissance building in Nové Město that also houses the bustling nightspot Lavka. Ask for the English-language description at the entrance.

Admission: 10 Kčs (35¢) adults, 5 Kčs (20¢) students.

Open: Wed–Mon 10am–5pm. **Directions:** From the east side of Charles Bridge, walk a block south and then a few steps west onto a small spit of land over the Vltava.

Dvořák Museum, Ke Karlovu 20. ☎ **29-82-14.**

Located in the 18th-century "America" villa, this museum established in 1932 honors Czech composer Antonín Dvořák. You'll see many pictures, prints, clothes, a walking stick, a piano, and other objects associated with the composer best known for his symphony *From the New World.* As you walk about you'll also hear taped Dvořák music. Make sure to ask the front desk for the English-language museum description.

Admission: 10 Kčs (35¢) adults, 5 Kčs (20¢) students.

Open: Tues–Sun 10am–4:30pm. **Metro:** I. P. Pavlova.

For the Kafka Fan

Kafka's Grave, New Jewish Cemetery (Židovské Hřbitovy), Nad Vodovodom ulica.

Pilgrims from around the world come to pay their respects to Prague's great scribe. Kafka is buried in the "new cemetery," still in use today.

Admission: Free.

Open: Summer, Sun–Thurs 8am–5pm; winter, Sun–Thurs 9am–4pm. **Metro:** Line A to Želivského.

For the Stamp Lover

Museum of Postal Stamps [Muzeum Poštovních Známek], Nové mlýny 2. ☎ **231-2060.**

Czechoslovakia is famous among stamp collectors for its beautiful stamps, thousands of which can be seen at this small museum. History lovers, too, can see stamps featuring the various "rulers" of 20th-century Czechoslovakia: Masaryk, Hitler, Gottwald, Stalin, Novotný, and Havel among them. An English-language documentary is shown on request.

Admission: 10 Kčs (35¢).

Open: Tues–Sun 9am-5pm. **Metro:** Náměstí Republiky; then walk a few blocks toward the river.

Walking Tour

The Prague Castle

Start Hradčanské náměstí.

Finish Malostranská metro stop.

Time Allow approximately two hours, not including museum stops; a half or full day with museum stops.

Best Times 9am to 5pm Tuesday through Sunday, when the museums are open.

Worst Times Monday, when all the museums are closed.

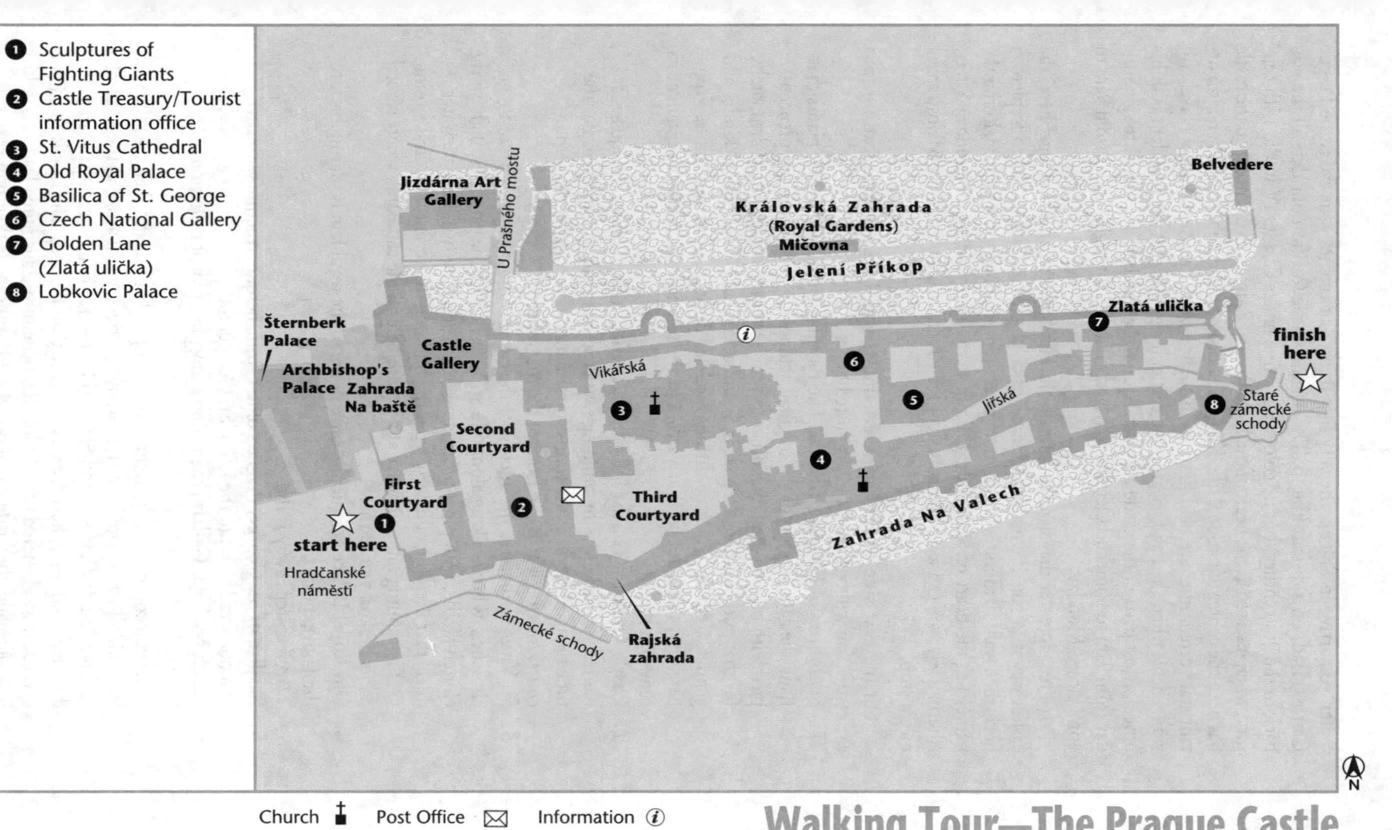

Walking Tour—The Prague Castle

When you arrive in Prague, the very first thing that catches your eye is the Prague Castle (Hrad) on a distant hilltop. The original castle fortifications date all the way back to the 9th century, but its golden age came under Charles IV in the 14th century, when it served as the heart of the Holy Roman Empire. Ever since then the castle has been the center of national life. Kings, archbishops, and nobles lived here; important state ceremonies are held here; to this day, Czech President Václav Havel still works here (when the flag flies atop the castle, it signifies that the president is in his office). Most parts of the castle are open April to September, Tuesday through Sunday from 9am to 5pm; and October to March Tuesday through Sunday from 9am to 4pm; closed Monday.

It's best to enter the castle complex from Hradčanské náměstí. To get here, the easiest way is to take the metro to Hradčanská, change to tram no. 22 to Keplerova ulice, then walk 10 minutes east. A more pleasant route, however, is from Malostranské náměští at the heart of Malá Strana. From here, simply walk up Nerudova Street. Alternatively, you can walk up many steps for 10 minutes from near the Malostranská metro stop.

On the east side of Hradcanské námêstí you'll see the gate leading into the castle. You will pass two soldiers posted beneath two:

1. **Sculptures of Fighting Giants,** "The Battling Titans." The nude giants that flank the gate, replicas of the originals sculpted in 1768, seem too preoccupied with bludgeoning each other to watch over the castle entry. Fortunately, for that purpose there are guards, in uniforms that are noticeably "kinder and gentler" than the fearsome threads modeled during Communist times. From here, pass through two courtyards. Off the second (which has a fountain at its center) is the:
2. **Castle Treasury/Tourist information office,** to the right of the square. It has been closed until the building's weak security can be improved. For the time being, it serves as the tourist information center. After the second courtyard, you'll arrive in front of the magnificent:
3. **St. Vitus Cathedral,** the nucleus of the castle and the largest of all of Prague's churches. When walking alongside St. Vitus, notice the gargoyles, high on the church facade, with pipes protruding from their mouths. These are water ducts that keep the rain away from the building to prevent structural erosion.

   Continuing on, you arrive at a square behind the cathedral, where several doors beckon you to the:
4. **Old Royal Palace,** a structure once home to the royal family, dating back to the 16th century.

   A few steps away is the:
5. **Basilica of St. George,** Prague's oldest Romanesque structure with a red baroque facade, and to the left of St. George, the:
6. **Czech National Gallery,** the nation's most prominent collection of Czechoslovak art.

   If you continue to the right of St. George's Basilica and then take the first left and follow the curves to the end of the street, you'll arrive at the magical:
7. **Golden Lane (Zlatá ulička).** Here 16 Lilliputian houses, each painted a different bold color, have facades no taller than five feet. The lane is so named because it was believed that Rudolf II's alchemists transmuted lead into gold here. Actually, the castle gunners and goldsmiths made their homes in this

curious narrow lane. One of the houses later served as Franz Kafka's home in 1913–14. Today, several are souvenir shops.

If you backtrack from the Golden Lane to the main street inside the castle (Jiřská ulice) and turn left, you'll pass the:

8. **Lobkovic Palace,** which displays an interesting collection of objects from Czech history such as St. Wenceslas's helmet and the coronation jewels. If you continue past here and through a covered passageway, a long series of steps runs down to the Malostranská metro stop.

Walking Tour
The Old Town

Start Charles Bridge.
Finish Wenceslas Square.
Time Allow approximately three hours, not including museum stops.
Best Times Tuesday to Sunday, when most museums are open.
Worst Time Monday, when most museums are closed.

The oldest section of Prague, the Staré Mêsto (Old Town) dates back to sometime in the 10th century. A hundred years later it included a Jewish settlement and a German merchant quarter. In A.D. 965 the Arab-Jewish chronicler Ibrahim Ibn Jacob spoke of the Staré Mêsto as a busy, growing trading center where food and goods were inexpensive. By the turn of the next century Prague was permanently on the map, with numerous public buildings and a stone bridge across the Vltava (Moldau). The Staré Mêsto increased in importance with the Hussite Wars and continued to be the dominant section of the city until the Bohemian defeat at the hands of the Habsburgs at the Battle of White Mountain.

Begin your tour of the area at:

1. **Charles Bridge (Karlův most),** the oldest standing bridge in the city, and the symbol of Prague. Commissioned by Charles IV, work began in 1357 under the supervision of the 27-year-old Peter Parléř and was not completed until the end of the century. Standing almost 1,500 feet long and 30 feet wide, the bridge is built of sandstone blocks and is designed as both a major thoroughfare and an aspect of the city's defense, hence the two towers at either end. The bridge became one of the focal points of life in Prague—a marketplace, a law court, a theater, and even tournaments were organized on the bridge. Even today young people still gather at the bridge to play music and vendors sell arts and crafts. In 1620 the crushed remnants of the Bohemian army retreated across it after the debacle at White Mountain; 18 years later heavily armored Swedes hacked their way across to finally occupy the former imperial bastion of the Hrad. In the late 17th century the wonderful baroque statues that adorn the sides were added; the most recent addition was in 1938. Notice the odd contrast between the luxuriant baroque statuary and the severe Gothic lines of the bridge itself.

On the castle (west) side of the bridge you can climb the:

2. **Malá Strana Bridge Tower** or Mostecká věž, just opposite the U tří pštrosu Hotel.

If you walk east of Charles Bridge for about five minutes, you'll reach Prague's:

3. **Old Town Square (Staroměstské náměstí),** one of the great squares of Europe. At the heart of the Old Town, this magnificent piazza shows old Europe at its very best by fusing the Gothic, Renaissance, baroque, and rococo art styles. Each facade on the square sports a different pastel color, each immaculately painted, complete with such details as crests above the windows. Statues watch over the roofs of several of these buildings.

   Dominating the square off to the side is a:

4. **Statue of Jan Hus,** who was burned at the stake in 1415. The statue was unveiled in 1915 to mark the anniversary of his death.

   On the southwestern side of the square you'll see the Town Hall Tower, adjacent to the:

5. **Town Hall.** Visitors to Prague love to gather hourly beneath the Astronomical Clock on the southern facade of the Town Hall to watch the procession of figures of Christ and the Apostles above the clock faces. At exactly two minutes after the hour (a delay to accommodate stragglers, one guide told me, a mechanical defect according to another), the figure of Death rings a bell, as if to announce "Everybody has to die, everybody has to die." Next to Death you'll see a musician, and on the other side a rich man with his money, and a vain man with a mirror. The upper part of the 15th-century clock shows the movements of the sun and moon, and the time of day. The clock below shows the signs of the zodiac.

   On the north side of the Town Hall you'll notice that part of the structure facing the main square ends abruptly; Nazi bombardment and subsequent fires during World War II destroyed this wing, a rare example of war damage in Prague. A park stands today where the building once extended.

   Towering over the east side of the square is:

6. **Týn Church,** the largest structure by far on the square, which is actually set back off the square by buildings. You enter the church from Celetná ulice, which runs east from the Old Town Square.

   If you continue down Celetná, you'll arrive at the:

7. **Powder Tower (Prašná brána),** a structure that once stored gunpowder, about five minutes away on náměstí Republiky. The Powder Tower and Celetná were part of the Royal Route the king took upon entering Prague. After going under the gate and down Celetná ulice, the king proceeded through the Old Town Square, across Charles Bridge, and then all the way up to the castle (Hrad).

   From the Powder Tower, make a sharp right down:

8. **Na Příkopě,** one of Prague's main shopping streets and home of the Prague Information Service. After five minutes the street leads to:

9. **Wenceslas Square (Václavské náměstí),** which looks more like a large avenue than a traditional square. At the south end of the square is an equestrian statue of St. Wenceslas. The modern history of Czechoslovakia has been closely associated with this square and the statue. In 1948 Czechoslovakia's Communist leader Klement Gottwald announced the birth of Communist rule here. In 1968, 20 years later, protesters faced Soviet tanks that came to crush the "Prague Spring." Then, in 1989, anti-Communist protests again swelled in the square around the statue, this time resulting in the overthrow of the long-despised Communist government.

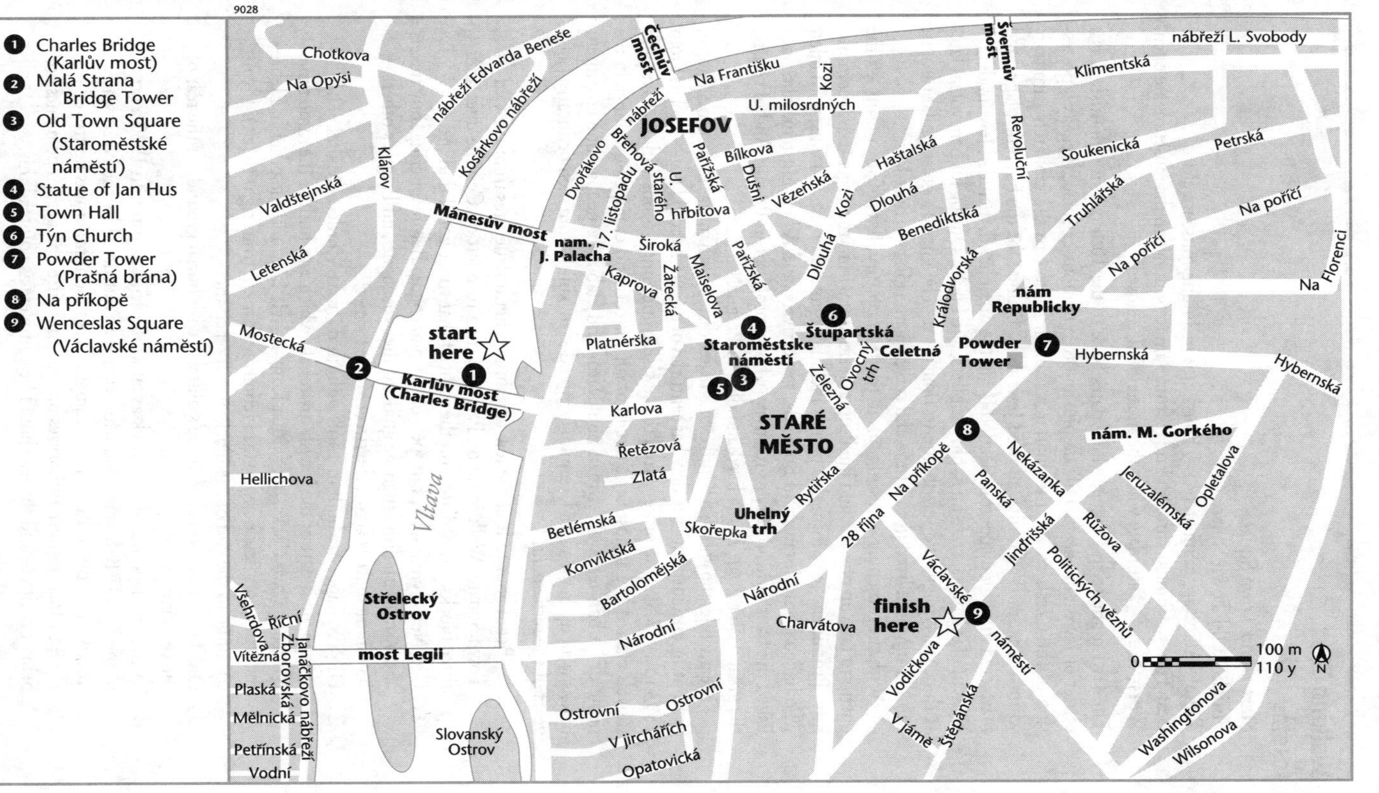

Walking Tour — The Old Town

Walking Tour

Josefov

Start Old Town Square.
Finish Old Town Square.
Time Allow approximately 1½ hours, not including museum stops.
Best Times Sunday through Friday from 9am to 5pm, when the museums are open.
Worst Time Saturday, when the museums are closed.

The Jewish ghetto in Prague, which dates back to the 10th century, flourished as a center of Jewish intellectual life despite an often tenuous existence. Legally a possession of the Czech crown, the quarter was often subject to the monarch's arbitrary whims. Charles IV, for one, allowed Jews to be blamed for the bubonic plague and massacred in a bloody pogrom. Rudolf II, on the other hand, included Jews under his big tent of scientists, craftsmen, philosophers, and kooks. During his benevolent late-16th-century reign, the Jewish ghetto flourished. The ghetto's great philanthropist Mordecai Maisel lived in this time and served as the king's "court Jew."

With the loosening of restrictions in the 19th century, Jews of any means left the ghetto to take up physical and intellectual residence within the larger Czech community. Prominent Jews from this period include Sigmund Freud and Gustav Mahler, who hailed from Moravia and Bohemia, respectively, and Albert Einstein, who published the basis of his theory of relativity while a professor in Prague. And of course, the great writer Franz Kafka lived and died in Prague.

Meanwhile, the ghetto fell into even greater disrepair than was its historical norm, prompting city authorities to do what centuries of monarchs could not—level it. From 1893 to 1917, despite protest from the Jewish community, teams with pickaxes and shovels cleared the atmospheric tangle of tiny streets and cramped dwellings in the name of "urban renewal." Broad boulevards and elaborate neobaroque apartment blocks went up in their stead, seemingly intended to banish from memory nearly 1,000 years of the settlement.

Begin your tour of the few remaining ghetto structures from the Old Town Square. Walk north on Pařízska, then turn left on Cervená ulice after three blocks. Immediately on the right of that street you'll find the:

1. **Old New Synagogue,** Europe's oldest synagogue. Before entering, buy tickets and a small English-language guide to the synagogue and Prague's other Jewish memorials across the street at the former:
2. **High Synagogue,** built in 1568 with funds from Mordecai Maisel. The synagogue is part of the Jewish town hall, which was built at the same time. Notice the two clocks, one with a Roman-style face, and the other in Hebrew that runs counterclockwise (as Hebrew is written, from right to left). If you continue to the end of the block, you'll reach the:
3. **Old Jewish Cemetery,** Europe's oldest Jewish burial ground. At the rear of the cemetery is the:
4. **Pinkas Synagogue,** dating back as far as the 13th century. In 1960 a list of the 77,297 Bohemian and Moravian Jews murdered by the Nazis was inscribed on the walls of the synagogue. This monument was destroyed in 1968 by Communist authorities due to "moisture damage." The names are being rewritten, and the list should be complete as you read this.

Walking Tour—Josefov (The Jewish Quarter)

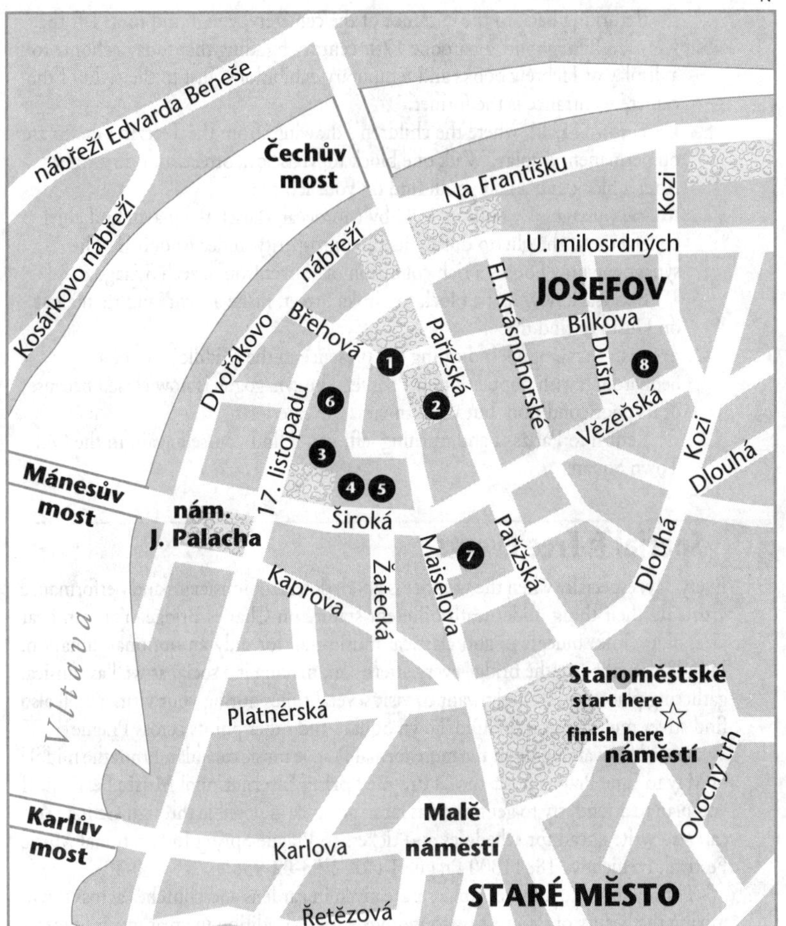

1. Old New Synagogue
2. High Synagogue
3. Old Jewish Cemetery
4. Pinkas Synagogue
5. Klausen Synagogue
6. Ceremonial Hall
7. Maisel Synagogue
8. Spanish Synagogue

Returning back to the entrance of the cemetery, you'll find to its left the:

5. **Klausen Synagogue,** a baroque 17th-century building that today is home to a display of Hebrew books and temporary exhibitions. Just to the right of the cemetery entrance is the former:
6. **Ceremonial Hall,** where the children's drawings from the Terezín Ghetto are on permanent display. Walk one block to Maiselova Street, and turn right. After a block and a half you'll find on your left the:
7. **Maisel Synagogue,** built in 1592 by Mordecai Maisel, the mayor and chief benefactor of the ghetto during its brief prosperity under Rudolf II. The synagogue now houses a rich collection of "Silver from Czech Synagogues."

   Backtrack now half a block to Široká Street, make a right, and then a left on Dušni to find the:
8. **Spanish Synagogue,** indicating the presence in the Middle Ages of a Sephardic Jewish population in Prague. The synagogue is now closed because of its poor condition, but you can view the exterior.

   Return to Pařížská and, turning left, you'll find yourself again in the Old Town Square.

6 Special & Free Events

Every day, especially when the weather is good, dozens of musicians and performance artists do their thing underneath different statues on Charles Bridge. You can hear jazz, blues, folk, bluegrass, and classical music—all for only an optional donation. Hundreds gather on the bridge every afternoon, making it a social as well as musical gathering place; you'll surely want to visit several times during your visit. You'll also find street musicians on the Old Town Square and other points across Prague.

Several festivals highlight the more formal Prague music calendar. From the middle of May to June Prague hosts the ★ **Prague Spring International Music Festival.** If you plan to attend, try to get tickets as far in advance as possible through Čedok. You can also write ahead for schedules and tickets to Prague Spring International Music Festival, Hellichova 18, 11800 Prague 1 (☎ **2/53-02-93;** fax 2/53-60-40).

Throughout the summer concerts are given in gardens and churches across town, mixing the beauty of Prague's surroundings with its tradition in great music. Tickets are usually quite inexpensive. Inquire at Prague's Tourist Information Service for further information.

7 Sports & Recreation

SWIMMING There are a number of public pools in Prague. One popular—and crowded—outdoor and indoor pool complex that I visited was the **Plavecký stadión,** at Podolská nábřeží 74/43 (☎ **43-91-51**), across from the Botel Racek along the riverfront in the southern part of the city. Admission to the outdoor or indoor pool is 10 Kčs (35¢); the sauna is 33 Kčs ($1.20). Lawns and bleachers surround the outdoor pool, and there's a snack bar. To get there, take tram no. 3 from Václavské náměstí, or tram no. 17 from the National Theater. The pools are open daily from 6am to 10pm, and you can bake in the sauna daily from 10am to 7pm.

TENNIS The Czechs are avid tennis players, and they've produced such champions as Ivan Lendl and Martina Navrátilová. Today's stars, such as Petr Korda, Helena Suková, and Jana Novotná train regularly at the **Czechoslovak Tennis Center** (☎ **231-1270**), and you can play here, too. The center boasts Prague's most distinguished tennis courts—the crème de la crème and also the most expensive—located on a small island in the Vltava River called Ostrov Štvanice, a five-minute walk south across the bridge from the Vltavská metro stop. The courts are open to the public daily from 6am to 1am. From 6am to 8am and 11pm to 1am, a court costs 150 Kčs ($5.35) per hour; and from 8am to 11pm, it's 275 Kčs ($9.80) per hour. To rent a racquet costs 15 Kčs (55¢).

Other tennis courts are listed in the "Prague" booklet.

Other Sports Information on horse-racing, golf, minigolf, bowling, and other sports and recreational options is available at the Prague Information Service office.

8 Savvy Shopping

BEST BUYS Intricately designed Bohemian crystal is the favorite shopping item for visitors. Most stores selling crystal accept credit cards, use of which exempts you from paying duty. Other favorite souvenirs include street art and photographs of Prague. Some stores offer hand-worked leather and wooden craft items from the country's villages, as well as handmade jewelry and cloth. Classical records/tapes and books are also a good value.

THE SHOPPING SCENE Many of my favorite shops are located near each other, so you might want to devote a few hours to a small shopping tour of Prague. From the Old Town Square, proceed down Celetná, a picturesque pedestrian street with record, book, crystal, and souvenir stores. Once you reach the Powder Tower, turn right onto Na Příkopě, which leads to Václavské náměstí, another major shopping avenue.

Throughout Prague, you'll find artists and craftspeople selling their wares, jewelry, prints, and handcrafts. They're concentrated on Charles Bridge, in the Old Town Square, and on Na Příkopě.

Crystal

Bohemia Moser, Na Příkopě 12. ☎ **22-18-51** or **22-18-52**.

Named for this country's most famous crystal, this store dates back to 1857. After World War II, the state took over the enterprise—the Moser family had fled the Nazis—and still managed to offer good quality crystal. Today the still state-owned store exudes an inimitable old-world splendor. Even if you're not buying come to browse. All major credit cards are accepted; and by using your credit card you avoid the 20% duty tacked onto the displayed price. The shop is open Monday through Friday from 9am to 7pm and on Saturday from 9am to 1pm.

Karlovarský Porcelán, Pařížská ulice 2. ☎ **231-7734.**

If nothing appeals to you in Moser, try this store; the quality is good and the variety fair. They accept all major credit cards. Open Monday through Friday from 10am to 7pm, on Saturday from 10am to 3pm, and on Sunday from 10am to 2pm. To get there, walk to the north side of Old Town Square.

Department Stores

Prior Kotva, Náměstí Republiky 8. ☎ **235-0001** to **235-0010.**

Prague's largest department store, with several floors offering a variety of goods. Open Monday through Wednesday and Friday from 8am to 7pm, on Thursday from 8am to 8pm, and on Saturday from 8am to 2pm. Metro: Náměstí Republiky.

K-Mart, Národní 26. ☎ **26-23-41.**

Previously Prior Máj. Open Monday through Wednesday and Friday from 8am to 7pm, on Thursday from 8am to 8pm, and on Saturday from 8am to 2pm. Metro: Můstek.

Jewelry and Watches

Soluna, Maiselova 16. ☎ **231-8447.**

In the heart of the old Jewish ghetto, this small shop sells antique watches and clocks, as well as porcelain, crystal, antique typewriters, and a variety of other collectibles. They're open Monday through Friday only, from 9am to noon and 1 to 5pm (10am to noon and 2 to 5pm in June and July). To get there exit the Old Town Square past the church on the northwest corner and continue north up Maiselova.

Prints

Antiquariat [Antikvariat], ul. 28 Října 13. ☎ **26-80-58.**

Located just half a block from the Mustek metro stop at the beginning of Václavské náměstí, this specialty shop sells old prints and books. Open Monday through Friday from 10am to 6pm. Metro: Můstek.

9 Evening Entertainment

For information on concerts, theater, and opera, consult *Prognosis* or the *Prague Post,* these are Prague's two English-language newspapers. The people at the American Hospitality Center (see "Information" in "Orientation," above in this chapter) are very helpful regarding cultural events, and you can also buy tickets from them. Another reliable ticket agent is the Prague Information Service (PIS) (see "Information" in "Orientation," above).

You may notice that most Prague box offices charge foreigners more than what a native would pay for the same ticket. This is an officially tolerated practice that you can avoid by having a Czech friend purchase your ticket.

THE PERFORMING ARTS

THEATER As you would think in a country where a playwright has become president, theater is a significant cultural force. The plays of Václav Havel are frequently performed in Prague, but usually in Czech. An accessible form of theater for foreigners is **black theater,** named for the pitch-black stage background. In this art form, stagehands, who are dressed completely in black so as to be invisible to the audience, manipulate props around the stage to tell a story. These genuinely entertaining performances combine elements of vaudeville, pantomime, and ballet. Another popular theater company is the **Laterna Magika (Magic Lantern),** which produces multi-media shows involving images and recorded songs along with live performers. All performances are given at the New Stage.

CLASSICAL MUSIC Despite its smaller population, Prague boasts more symphony orchestras than New York or London. Concerts are performed in many venues, including at the National Theater and the Smetana Hall at the Municipal House (listed below). Concerts are also given in St. George's Basilica and the Lobkovic Palace in Prague Castle, as well as St. Nicholas church in Malá Strana. Almost all concert tickets are very reasonably priced.

In each of the following three concert/performance halls, tickets cost about 200 to 300 Kčs ($7.15 to $10.70) for foreigners.

National Theater [Národní divadlo], Národní 2. ☎ **20-53-64.**

A striking neo-Renaissance building from 1883 by the riverfront, the National Theater is Prague's major hall for drama, opera, and ballet. The main season is from September to June.

You can buy tickets from a window in the covered passageway of the New Stage next door, across from the New Stage's restaurant. The box office (☎ **20-53-64**) is open Monday through Friday from 10am to 6pm and on Saturday and Sunday from 10am to noon. You can also buy tickets 30 minutes before show time at the entrance to the theater as they reserve seats ahead and then sell them to you.

To get here, walk about 10 minutes south along the river from the east end of Charles Bridge.

New Stage [Nová Scéna], Národní 4. ☎ **20-62-60.**

A modern glass structure, this theater presents only drama. The Magic Lantern theater company performs here as well. You can buy tickets from a window near the National Theater window in the covered passageway across from the restaurant. The box office is open Monday through Friday from 10am to 6pm and on Saturday and Sunday from 10am to noon. Like the National Theater, it's about 10 minutes south along the river from the east end of Charles Bridge.

Smetana Hall at the Municipal House, náměstí Republiky 5. ☎ **232-5858.**

Home of the Czech Philharmonic Orchestra, this building has one of the most distinctive art nouveau facades (1906–12) in town. You can buy tickets around the corner from the FOK bureau at U Prašné brány (☎ **232-5858**), open Monday through Friday from 9am to noon and 1:30 to 4:30pm (from 3pm in winter), and on Saturday from 9am to noon and 1:30 to 3pm. Metro: Náměstí Republiky.

THE JAZZ SCENE

Prague's jazz clubs are perennially popular with visitors. **Reduta,** Národní třída 20 (☎ **20-38-25**), is the city's original jazz hotspot. Concerts are Monday to Saturday from 9:30am to midnight. Admission is 80 Kčs ($2.85). Take the metro to Můstek. The **AghaRTA Jazz Centrum,** Krakovská 5, just off Václavské náměstí (☎ **22-45-58**), is a cool spot showcasing jazz nightly from 9pm to midnight. The cover charge is 40 Kčs ($1.45). Wonderful but less intimate is the jazz experience at **Cafe Nouveau** in náměstí Republiky (see "Where to Eat," above). The nightly jazz begins at 7:30pm and is free of charge.

ROCK & DANCE CLUBS

There are vibrant rock 'n' roll and dance club scenes in Prague, with new venues constantly popping up and others closing down. Recent hotspots include the **Repre Rock Klub,** náměstí Republiky (☎ **24-81-10-57**); **Radost F/X,** Belehradská 120 (☎ **25-12-10;** see FX Café in "Where to Eat," above in this chapter); **Mismas,**

Veletrzni 67 (☎ **37-92-78**); and **RC Bunkr,** Lodeská 2. Consult Prognosis for an up-to-date account of the hip and the has-been.

10 Networks & Resources

FOR STUDENTS The **CKM branch office** at Jindřišská 28 (☎ **26-85-32** or **26-86-23**) sells ISIC and IYHF cards. Bring your own passport-size photos—no other requirements. Open Monday through Friday from 10am to 12:30pm and 1:30 to 6pm.

For discount youth tickets (rail, bus, and air), head to the **CKM Travel Office** at Žitná ulice 11 (☎ **20-13-33** or **20-33-80**), across the street from the CKM Junior Hotel. Open Monday through Friday from 9am to noon and 1 to 4pm, this office offers discounts for students and all others under 26. Others may buy tickets here, too, but at no discount. The Interrail pass is also available here.

There are **bulletin boards,** which are popular with Prague's English-speaking community, located in the Globe Bookstore/Café (see "Where to Eat," above), and Laundry King (see "Fast Facts: Prague," above). On these you will find notices for apartments, flight tickets, Czech-language tutoring, guitars for sale, etc. Not only are these boards valuable, they encapsulate expatriate life in Prague.

11 Easy Excursions

Prague is no more than 50 miles from some of the largest and most impressive castles in Europe, and I highly recommend an extra day or two in Prague for day trips to see them. The three most impressive are Karlštejn, Konopiště, and Česky Šternberk, but there are quite a few others of interest as well. And to the east of Prague is the stunning Gothic and baroque masterpiece, the town of Kutná Hora.

In addition, Prague is close to two symbols of wartime suffering, the razed village of Lidice and the "model" Jewish ghetto of Terezin (Theresienstadt). A day trip to either of them is a sobering experience.

Of course, the cheapest way to reach any of these sites is to go by public transportation without an organized tour. Details are provided with each site description below about how this can best be done.

Organized Tours A number of private companies offer castle tours. Čedok, the state travel agency with years of experience, probably remains the best bet. If you prefer to use a private company, shop around; all their offices are in central Prague. Čedok offers full-day tours (including lunch) to Karlštejn and Konopiště for 1,350 Kčs ($48.20), to Kutná Hora and Česky Šternberk for 1,150 Kčs ($41.05), and to Křivoklát and Karlštejn for 1,150 Kčs ($41.05). Full-day tours depart at 8:40am. Čedok also offers half-day tours (also including lunch) to Konopište for 850 Kčs ($30.35) and to Karlštejn for 850 Kčs ($30.35). Half-day tours depart at noon. All Čedok tours are booked at their main office at Na Příkopě 18.

The private agency Wittmann Tours, at Uruguayská 7 (☎ **25-12-35** or **439-62-93**), offers tours to Terezín on Sunday, Tuesday, and Thursday at 10am. The price is 550 Kčs ($19.65) for adults and 450 Kčs ($16.05) for children. Tours leave from Pařížská 28. The half-day Čedok tour to Terezín costs 850 Kčs ($30.35) per person.

You are advised to find your own way to Lidice, since few tour operators go there. Čedok, though, does offer a combined tour to Karlovy Vary and Lidice for 1,350 Kčs ($48.20). It's a full-day tour, including lunch.

Note: All the castles are closed on Tuesday following a Monday holiday.

KARLŠTEJN [KARLSTEIN]

★ Karlštejn was founded in 1348 by Charles IV to safeguard the crown jewels and holy relics of the Holy Roman Empire. Charles often stayed in his palace designed by architect Matthias of Arras, but after the jewels of the Holy Roman Empire were moved elsewhere in 1420, the castle was no longer used for royal habitation (today the jewels of the Holy Roman Empire are displayed in Vienna). Bohemia's royal jewels remained here until 1619, when the advance of gunpowder technology made the castle obsolete. Invading Swedish armies overcame walls as thick as seven meters in places and wreaked great devastation in 1648. In 1887–97 the castle was rebuilt and modified by its Habsburg owners.

Today you can visit this well-preserved structure on a guided tour. You'll see Charles IV's reception rooms, his bedroom, a large collection of medieval Bohemian paintings, and a few pieces of Charles's vast treasures. There are also panoramic views of the countryside from the castle. The Chapel of the Holy Rood, adorned with beautiful 14th century frescoes by Master Theoderik and gilded with more than 2,000 precious stones, will be reopened to the public in 1995 after many years of repair. This was where the jewels of the Holy Roman Empire were kept.

The castle (☎ **0311/94-211**) is open Tuesday through Sunday: 8am to 5pm June to August; 9am to 4pm in April, May, September, and October; and 9am to 3pm in March and December (with a pause from noon to 12:30pm); closed during November. The admission fee is 80 Kčs ($2.85) for adults and 30 Kčs ($1.05) for children. The reception also sells a small English-language guidebook to the castle.

If you want to have lunch in the area, there are several restaurants lining the road that leads up to the castle.

The Karlštejn castle is 17 miles west and south of Prague. Karlštejn is also halfway to the castle of Křivoklát, which will also make a good same-day excursion if you are driving. Seven trains between 8:25am and 12:05pm make the 45-minute journey from Prague's Smíchov station. From the train station, walk right, and then make a left over the bridge. Continue right for seven minutes until you reach the base of a hill; private cars must park here. The walk uphill to the castle is about 20 minutes.

KONOPIŠTĚ

★ Less than 30 miles south of Prague (45 minutes by car) on the E14, lies the 13th-century Konopiště Castle, a favorite hunting lodge of the Habsburgs. In 1887, the castle came into the possession of its last and most notorious lord, Archduke Franz Ferdinand, whose assassination in Sarajevo in 1914 gave the Great Powers an excuse to begin World War I.

Over his 40-year hunting career, Archduke Ferdinand felled over 300,000 animals, an average of 22 per day. The trophies displayed in the house make up only 1% of his total. Each trophy is numbered and dated meticulously, from elephant tusks, to antlers by the hundreds, to a family of badger heads on a single plaque, to leaves used to wipe away blood. Fortunately, the castle also displays beautiful decor, furniture, and objets d'art, including baroque carved furniture, Murano and Meissen glass and porcelain, and a Botticelli painting. There's also an impressive collection of 15th-and 16th-century weapons and late Gothic statuary.

The castle is open Tuesday through Sunday, May through August, from 9am to 5pm; in September it closes at 4pm, and in April and October, at 3pm. It's closed from November through March. The admission fee (including a guide) is 70 Kčs ($2.50) for adults, 30 Kčs ($1.05) for children 6 to 16, free for children under 6. The admission fee without a guide is only 15 Kčs (55¢), but the tour is excellent and well worth the extra cost.

To get here, take the bus from the Florenc station in Prague. It stops about half a mile from the castle and you must walk from there. You can also take an express train from Prague's main station to Benešov (a 50-minute journey) and then catch a local bus (from platform no. 7) directly to the castle.

For a cheap and delicious Czech meal, try Bistro Mydlařká, which is located in a building adjacent to the Benešov bus lot. Open Monday through Friday 7am to 6pm, it's a fun opportunity to rub shoulders with the locals, who make it the most popular lunch spot in town. For more information, call **231-2030** in Prague.

ČESKÝ ŠTERNBERK

Only about another 10 miles off on a side road (head east at the town of Benešov), Český Šternberk was once one of Bohemia's most powerful fortifications. It was built in the first half of the 13th century during the reign of King Wenceslas I, in the late Gothic style. The Habsburgs added baroque elements to the castle and improved the defenses.

You can see the elaborate interior rooms on a one-hour tour. Highlights include the huge main hall and several smaller salons with fine baroque detailing, elaborate chandeliers, wooden furniture, and period art. After the tour, you'll enjoy a stroll amid the lovely, thick forest and streams that surround Český Šternberk—it's a good place to escape the heat on a summer's day.

The castle is open from mid-April through October. In the second half of April and in October it's open only on Saturday, Sunday, and holidays; in May and September, it's open Tuesday through Sunday from 8am to 4:30pm; June through August, Tuesday through Sunday from 8am to 5:30pm. Admission is 15 Kčs (55¢) for adults and 5 Kčs (20¢) for children. English-language guidebooks and tours are available.

You can get here by bus from the southern part of Prague from a subsidiary bus station at the Roztyly metro station on Line C (☎ **795-0481**). The ride takes an hour and 50 minutes. There are also easy trains via Cerčany, of which there are six from Prague's Hlavní Nádraží between 8:04am and 11:23am. Inquire at the Prague Information Service for details.

KŘIVOKLÁT

A royal castle as early as the 11th century, this fortress was rebuilt in the 13th century and several times over the next few hundred years in a variety of Gothic styles. The royal family occasionally stayed here and used the place as a hunting lodge. Charles IV and later his son, Václav II, each spent many childhood days here happily chasing butterflies through the dense Křivoklát forest.

While touring the castle you'll see the 80-foot-long **King's Hall,** the largest interior secular space in the country, with an exhibition of late Gothic sculpture and paintings; the **Fürstenberg Picture Gallery,** lined with portraits of the spooky

Fürstenberg lords who held the castle from 1685 to 1929; one of the largest castle libraries in the country with 53,000 volumes; and the 13th-century **Royal Chapel.** There's also a small, separate **weapons museum** next to the castle.

The castle is open Tuesday through Sunday: in February, March, and October to December, from 9am to 3pm; in September, it's open until 4pm, and from May through August, until 5pm. It's closed daily from noon to 1pm and all of January. Admission (with guide) is 80 Kčs ($2.85) for adults and 30 Kčs ($1.05) for children; without a guide, it's 20 Kčs ($70¢) and 10 Kčs (35¢).

To get here, take the train from Prague's Smíchov station to Beroun, just under an hour's journey, and then switch for the train to Křivoklát, another 40 minutes of travel. Take either the 9:23am or 11:10am train from Prague; you'll have a 20-minute wait in Beroun before the train to Křivoklát departs.

You'll have to walk up a steep hill to the castle. Karlštejn is in the same direction from Prague (west) as Křivoklát, and the two make a good sightseeing pair.

KUTNÁ HORA

★ Short of growing it on trees or alchemically producing it from lead, Kutná Hora's history shows that minting money is perhaps the best way to secure fortune. The 12th-century discovery of silver deposits in the area drew a stampede of miners, tired of digging less profitable lead. The silver they subsequently mined was pressed into the Prague Groschen—an important medieval unit of currency—and bolstered the coffers of the Bohemian kings. Kutná Hora became the second-richest city in the kingdom. Until the mines dried up in the 17th century, the city benefited from its patricians' largesse—a splendid patrimony of Gothic structures overshadows the modest activity of what is now a quiet provincial town.

The bus and train stations are at the southeastern end of town, and St. Barbara's Cathedral lies uphill at the northwestern end, about a 30-minute walk. All sights lie in between the terminals and the cathedral, centered on the scenic Komenského and Palacského squares.

Begin your visit at the top, at the **Church of St. Barbara.** Intended by its builders to rival the splendor of St. Vitus Cathedral, it's the epitome of a more hunkering Gothic style. In terms of detail—the fantastic sum of arches, buttresses, rosettes, pinnacles, and all-important gargoyles—exceeds St. Vitus. The three spires that appear to stretch the roof like the fabric of a circus tent have a uniquely festive, almost whimsical air. Built in spurts between 1380 and 1565, initially by Peter Parléř, it received the baroque interior detail and fantastic spidery vaulting from the Jesuits, who used it from 1626. Children scampering around the grounds attend school in the neoclassical building behind the church. It's open Tuesday through Sunday: April to September from 8am to noon and 1 to 5pm; the rest of the year from 9am to noon and 2 to 4pm. They charge 20 Kčs (70¢) for admission, half that for students. Ask for the English-language description at the church entrance.

From the church, walk downhill to the beautiful late 15th-century **Hradek** (castle), on Barborská (☎ **0327/21-59**), today home to the **District Museum of Mining (Okresní Muzeum).** The collection highlights the history of mining in the town and takes you into an actual, very narrow, 15th-century mine—a journey not for the large or claustrophobic. Although they have no written material about the museum in English, they'll play you an English-language tape describing the history of mining in the region. Admission is 30 Kčs ($1.05); 15 Kčs ($54) for students. Open April to October only, daily from 8am to noon and 1 to 5pm.

From here, walk a few minutes northwest to the Gothic **Italian Court (Vlašský Dvur)** on Havlíčkovo náměstí (☎ **0327/27-01**). Built in 1300 as a royal seat and mint, the building today serves as another town museum. It shows off locally produced silver coins of the 14th to the 18th century, and interior rooms of the building, such as the Session Hall where town meetings were once held, and the chapel built by King Wenceslas IV (now popular for weddings). Ask at the entrance for the English-language description. Open daily: April to September from 8am to 5pm; the rest of the year from 10am to 4pm. Admission is 20 Kčs (70¢) for adults, 5 Kčs (20¢) for students.

Kutná Hora is about 45 miles due east of Prague on Highway 333. Express trains from Prague take as little as an hour. Walk right from the train station; left before the highway underpass, and continue straight. From here, you can continue walking for 25 minutes or take bus no. 1 or 4 into town.

LIDICE

The village of Lidice (pronounced Lee-*deet*-tseh), 20 miles northwest of Prague, for 50 years has been a symbol of Czech suffering under Nazi occupation. On June 10, 1942, two weeks after the assassination of the highest-ranking Nazi in the occupied Czech lands, SS Obergruppenführer Reinhard Heydrich (by Czech paratroopers operating out of England), the Gestapo took their awful revenge, rounding up and killing all the men of Lidice—173 in all. The 203 women and 99 children of the village were sent to concentration camps, from which only half returned. The Germans also leveled Lidice, but the Czech government—with an outpouring of international support—began rebuilding it on neighboring land in 1948. Today the site of the "original" Lidice remains an expanse of empty fields adjacent to the new town.

The **Lidice Memorial Museum** (☎ **0312/923-52**) open Tuesday through Sunday from 8am to 5pm, displays photos of the town's martyred residents, as well as various other artifacts. A 20-minute English-language documentary can be seen (on request only), and a 10-minute cassette can be heard. From the museum, you can look down on the empty fields where the village formerly stood (also visible from the road as you drive in to Lidice). Visitors are welcome to wander the pastoral site of the former village. Memorials in the "old" Lidice include: a wooden cross marking the spot where the executed men were buried in a mass grave (by a group of 30 unlucky Jewish prisoners); Lidice's old and new cemeteries (the old one was desecrated by the Nazi effort to extract gold teeth from dead bodies); and, in front of the museum, a vast series of internationally sponsored rose gardens.

To get to Lidice, take a bus from the stands across from the Diplomat Hotel, near the Dejvická metro station. Take a bus toward Kladno; from stand 1, the ride takes about 35 minutes and Lidice is the 12th stop; from stand 3, the ride takes 25 minutes, with Lidice the 5th stop. A bus leaves about every 30 minutes during the day, costing 7 Kčs (25¢). Confirm with the driver that the bus is going to Lidice.

TEREZÍN

Established in the 18th century as a Habsburg garrison town, Terezín (about 40 miles north of Prague) achieved its worldwide notoriety during World War II, under the German name Theresienstadt, when the entire town was emptied of its residents and converted into a way station for Czech Jews en route from occupied Czechoslovakia to the death camps of Poland and Germany.

Prisoners in Terezín were forced to live in appallingly crowded and unsanitary conditions; though Theresienstadt was not a "death camp" per se, over 30,000 prisoners died there during the years 1941–45. More than 100,000 Jews from the Czech lands were sent to Terezín, of whom 86,900 were eventually deported, mainly to Auschwitz.

In June 1944, in an infamous incident, Nazi authorities duped a visiting Red Cross inspection committee into believing that the awful ghetto way station was actually "an exemplary German camp for the re-education of Jewish citizens." The camp was liberated by the Red Army on May 8, 1945.

Today visitors are free to wander the now-empty grounds of the camp. In addition, you can visit the inappropriately named Memorial of National Martyrdom, the Small Fortress (with crematorium), and the Terezín Ghetto Museum (☎ **416/922-25**), where you can view a chilling documentary. The exhibits are open daily from 9am to 4:30pm.

Terezín can be reached by bus no. 17 or 20 from Prague's Florenc Station; the ride takes about an hour, and costs 29 Kčs ($1.05). You can also reach Terezín from the nearby town of Litoměřice, on the main road between Berlin and Prague. Terežin is a short bus ride or a 30-minute walk from there. Organized day tours are available from Prague. Wittmann Tours is the agency of choice, but Čedok and others also offer tours (see above).

12 Moving On—Travel Services

TRAVEL AGENCIES There are a number of private and semiprivate travel agencies in Prague where rail, bus, and plane tickets are available. Among them are Bohemia Tour at Zlatnická 7, Galatour at Thámova 8, Prago-Via at Kralovodvorská 5, and several clustered together on Senovazné nám.

Elegant Pařížská ulice, just off the Old Town Square, remains home to the travel agencies of the once-fraternal countries of Eastern Europe. There you will find Orbis (Poland), Malév (Hungary), JAT (Yugoslavia), Balkantourist (Bulgaria), Tarom (Romania), and Aeroflot (Russia). Swissair also has an office on this street.

GETTING TO THE AIRPORT ČSA buses leave for the airport every 20 to 30 minutes from 5:20am to 6:40pm Monday through Friday and from 6:30am to 6:30pm on Saturday and Sunday. They depart from the ČSA bus office at Revolučni ulica 25 (☎ **231-7395**), located between the Old Town Square and the Švermův Bridge (this is *not* the same office as the main ČSA ticket office, also on Revoluční ulica, at no. 1). The nearest metro stop is Náměstí Republiky, about three blocks away. On the way to the airport, the bus stops near the Dejvická metro stop to pick up more passengers. From the ČSA office, the price is 30 Kčs ($1.05); from Dejvická, the price is 20 Kčs (70¢). Pay the driver directly.

You can also ride public bus no. 119 to the airport from the Dejvická metro stop. The price is one transit ticket (4 Kčs/15¢) and the bus leaves throughout the day, about every 30 minutes. Stay on until the last stop, even if you think you're passing the airport.

LEAVING BY BUS For national bus information, go to the Čedok office or the Florenc main bus station (Florenc autobusové nádraží) on Wilsonova třída (☎ **22-14-45**).

Some of the travel agencies above may be able to help you with international bus tickets.

LEAVING BY TRAIN All international rail tickets are now sold in Czech currency. You can buy your tickets at Čedok, or directly at the station. It's terribly important that you know which of Prague's several stations your train is departing from. Most—but by no means all—international trains depart from the main station (Hlavní nadraží).

At the main station, international tickets are bought on the middle level from two well-marked windows. You must go downstairs to the lower level to make your seat reservation at a different window.

Students with an ISIC card get 50% off, but only for the portion of the trip in the Czech and Slovak Republics, which generally ends up making little actual difference.

Sample second-class fares for international destinations: Budapest, 377 Kčs ($13.45); Warsaw, 515 Kčs ($18.40); Vienna, 548 Kčs ($19.55); Berlin, 776 Kčs ($27.70); Frankfurt, 2,008 Kčs ($71.70); Bucharest, 3,105 Kčs ($110.90); Paris, 4,293 Kčs ($153.30).

Eurocity (EC) and Intercity (IC) trains carry an additional 30-Kčs ($1.05) surcharge for second class. Seat reservations, when required, cost 6 Kčs (20¢). International tickets are normally valid for two months.

Eurailpass holders should only buy a ticket to the border, if they are traveling to a country where the pass is valid.

When departing by train for destinations foreign or domestic, remember to check which of Prague's many stations you'll be leaving from.

15

Bohemia & Moravia

BOHEMIA AND MORAVIA, THE WESTERN AND CENTRAL PROVINCES OF WHAT WAS Czechoslovakia, contain some important historical sights. Rocky and forested in the north, with broad fertile plains in the south, this area is little explored by Western tourists. Many of the small towns and the wooded countryside remain much as they were in the 18th century.

Moravia is the smaller of the Czech Republic's two regions. Where the Carpathians and the Bohemian highlands meet, the hilly north of Moravia gives way to the smiling plains in the south. Sandwiched between Bohemia and Slovakia, Moravia nevertheless has maintained a distinct identity. The north, known for its mineral wealth and deep forests, had earned the nickname "steel heart" of Czechoslovakia because of the vast smelting complex here.

Southern Moravia is a pleasant fertile land, home to some of the country's most beautiful folk music and the best wines. The fecundity of the land must have inspired even prehistoric inhabitants, as one of Central Europe's earliest fertility symbols, the *Věstonice Venus,* was found in southern Moravia. Castles, forests, vineyards, and friendly people will make any trip to Moravia memorable.

SEEING BOHEMIA & MORAVIA

If you're interested in taking a spa vacation or just passing through some of the spa towns, begin your explorations in Bohemia by bus or train west from Prague to Karlovy Vary or Mariánské Lázně. Otherwise, proceed directly to southern Bohemia, stopping in such towns as Tábor, České Budějovice, and Český Krumlov, which more or less follow in a line.

From here, consider a swing east into Moravia, centered around Brno. On the way I highly recommend a stop in Telč, which is about halfway between Brno and České Budějovice.

When traveling around the region, consider traveling by bus as well as by train. Some cities are not on major rail routes, making train journeys excruciatingly slow. Compare bus and train schedules and then decide which is best for your destination. This will usually be easy since bus and train stations are normally adjacent to one another. If you're boarding a bus at its city of origin (rarely the case in smaller towns) you are advised to buy your ticket a day in advance.

1 Karlovy Vary

75 miles W of Prague

GETTING THERE • **By Train** Avoid the train from Prague, which takes over four hours on a circuitous route; the cost is 120 Kčs ($4.30) in first class and 80 Kčs($2.85) in second class. Karlovy Vary's main train station (☎ **233-77**) is north the center and has a 24-hour baggage-check service; take bus no. 13 from the square in front into town. If arriving from the south, you'll come into dolni station, which is next to the bus station.

• **By Bus** The frequent express buses from Prague's Florenc station take 2$^1/_3$ hours for 59 Kčs ($2.10). Karlovy Vary's bus station is northwest of the town center, on Horakova náměstí. Take bus no. 4 into town, or walk for about 10 minutes.

• **By Car** The car journey from Prague takes over two hours.

What's Special About Bohemia & Moravia

Architectural Highlights

- The perfectly symmetrical old town square in Ceské Budějovice.
- The massive town square in Telč lined by centuries-old Gothic and Renaissance houses.
- Cathedral of SS. Peter and Paul in Brno, a unique fusion of medieval and baroque styles.

Beer Shrines

- Pilsner-Urquell Factory and Beer Museum in Plzeň.

Castles

- Bohemia's second-largest castle, at Český Krumlov, with an impressively decorated interior.
- Kotnov Castle in Tábor, with a museum of the Middle Ages and a great panoramic view over the town.
- The splendid Renaissance interior of the castle in Telč.
- Špilberk Castle in Brno, with a town history museum and a sweeping panorama over the town.

Museums

- Museum of the Hussite Movement, chronicling the radical Hussite past of Tábor.
- Capuchin Cloister in Brno, with well-preserved bodies dating back hundreds of years in open catacombs.

Spa Towns

- Karlovy Vary, a fading 19th-century town with many pedestrian promenades; famous for its curative hot mineral waters.
- Mariánské Lázně, a smaller spa town noted for its cold mineral waters.

ESSENTIALS Karlovy Vary's telephone area code is 017.

INFORMATION There are two "Info-Centrum" booths in Karlovy Vary, one in the train station and the other in a parking lot at the base of Jana Palacha ulica. They don't seem to have regular hours, and are best able to deal with German-speakers, but they can both provide maps, private-room bookings, and various other services. Ask for the not-too-helpful—but free—"Promenáda" brochure. The booth in the parking lot is far more concerned with collecting parking fees than with dispensing information, so use the train station one if you can.

You can also ask in the fancier hotels for information, where English-speakers can usually be found.

ORIENTATION The town of Karlovy Vary is arrayed around its two rivers, which join in the shape of a T. The Ohre runs east–west and forms the crossbar; the Teplá, forming the stem, runs north–south through the steep hills that cradle the town. Most sights and hotels line the Teplá banks along narrow promenades. The bus and dolni train stations lie just southwest of the river juncture. The main train station lies due north of the river juncture.

SPECIAL EVENTS Karlovy Vary hosts a Jazz Festival in March, the Dvorák Singing Contest in June, the Dvorák Autumn Music Festival from September to October, and every even-numbered year the International Film Festival in July.

DEPARTING When leaving Karlovy Vary, buy bus tickets right next to the Hotel Adria, at the intersection of náměstí Republiky and Ul. Západní, about 100 yards from where the bus leaves you off (☎ **243-59**). Buses to Prague depart from Platforms 1 to 3 and stop at Prague's Hradcanská metro stop and the Florenc bus station.

The fabled Habsburg spa and resort town of Karlovy Vary (pop. 58,000) was supposedly discovered by King Charles IV while out hunting. A stag he shot stumbled into a bubbling spring and, the story goes, healed miraculously on the spot. The King named the area after himself—Karlovy Vary means "Karl's boiling place"—Charles built a hunting lodge here and later conferred special privileges on the growing settlement. As a royal asylum dedicated to healing, visitors could not be brought to justice here, nor could they carry weapons. Of no strategic military importance, Karlovy Vary never needed fortification.

Only in the late 18th century did Karlovy Vary, then called Karlsbad by the ruling Habsburgs, earn its stature as a chic playground for the fashionably ailing and the royally invalid. Regulars attempting to outdo each other built fanciful houses, churches, and gardens on the slopes overlooking the town, resulting in an elaborate, frosted appearance that prompted modernist architect Le Corbusier to call Karlsbad a "conference of cakes." European notables who came to "take the cure" (as bathing in and imbibing the waters was termed) included the greatest thinkers, artists, and statesmen of the period. Peter the Great, Bach, Goethe, Paganini, Schiller, Beethoven, Gogol, Chopin, Brahms, Marx, and Freud all had a go in Karlovy Vary's bubbly waters.

Postwar years did not treat Karlovy Vary well, as Soviet overlords allowed much to decay while bestowing several architectural eyesores to boot. Two prime offenders are the Sprudel Colonnade (*née* Yuri Gagarin), the terribly inappropriate glass-and-steel enclosure of the Sprudel spring, and the ghastly Thermal Hotel, which resembles the upended keel of some gargantuan capsized vessel. Fortunately, renewed tourism and the return of many Sudeten Germans, the original administrators of Karlsbad before the Soviet period, are helping renovate and restore some of its splendor.

Spa physician David Becher, who encouraged visitors to drink from the springs as well as bathe in them, introduced 18th-century spa-goers to another medicinal innovation: the intense herb-based Becherovka liqueur, still produced in the town. The nearby Moser crystal factory serves vacationers' souvenir needs now much as it did in the 19th century.

WHAT TO SEE & DO

Spa Cures

Some 80,000 people come to Karlovy Vary annually to "take the waters," most for stays of two or three weeks. All treatment starts with a visit to a physician, who prescribes a regime, which might include mineral baths, massages, wax treatments, mud packs, electrotherapy, and pure oxygen inhalation. After a morning at a sanatorium, guests usually pass the afternoon walking through town and along paths in the nearby forest. The leitmotif of all cures is an ample daily dose of local hot mineral waters.

The minimum spa cure lasts a week, and it must be arranged ahead of time. Information may be difficult to obtain as the spas move toward privatization. You should first contact Cedok or any other agency which deals with the Czech and Slovak Republics (including those recommended in this book). You can also try contacting one of the following: **Lázné III,** Vřídelné ulice, 36001 Karlovy Vary; or **Balnea,** Pařižská 11, 11001 Prague (☎ **017/232-3767;** Telex 122215).

Rates for room, full board, and complete treatment vary from only $35 up to $100 per person per day, depending on the season and comfort of the facilities. Rates are lowest November 15 to February 28, and highest May to September. Some specialized medical techniques are not included in this price.

Of course, you can simply enjoy the waters à la carte. Self-directed treatment may not yield much medical benefit, but sipping from the trademark narrow ceramic tumbler and making genteel stops at various springs for refills is a pleasurable way to promenade. And the bubbly is interesting, almost tasty. Twelve different springs originate one to two kilometers below the surface, collecting minerals, carbon dioxide, and heat before surfacing. Their chemical composition is reputedly therapeutic for a variety of ailments. The springs are enclosed in four colonnades—essentially Victorian roofs over dribbling taps where you can harbor thoughts about how Karl Marx held his little drink cup here almost a century and a half ago. The only non-Victorian colonnade, an ugly Soviet steel-and-glass structure completed in 1975, houses Karlovy Vary's most impressive spring, the Sprudel ("geyser"), which spurts up to 30 feet at a scalding 162°F.

Other Activities

There are about 60 miles of walking paths around the hills and woods surrounding Karlovy Vary, and those taking the cure often enjoy lengthy strolls there. One good place to start is in back of the Grand Hotel Pupp, where a cable car takes you to the top of a hill every 15 minutes from 10am to 6pm daily from April to November. It costs 15 Kčs (55¢).

Karlovy Vary is also a town of many pedestrian promenades, most along the river. Many stores and turn-of-the-century buildings line these streets, and forested hills rise up in the distance, creating a very pleasant environment for relaxation.

From May 15 to September 15 you can enjoy open-air concerts at the Sprudel Colonnade, held Tuesday through Sunday at 4:30pm.

There's also tennis at the Hotel Gejzírpark, Slovenská 5A (☎ **226-62**), south of the city center. They have 14 clay courts, for which they charge 150 Kčs ($5.35) an hour. They're open daily from 9am to 3pm; take bus no. 7 to get here.

WHERE TO STAY

PRIVATE ROOMS In addition to the two "Info-Centrum" offices which rent private rooms (see above), there are two Čedok offices in town which also rent rooms. The closest to the bus station is at Moskevská 2 (☎ **017/222-92** or **222-96;** fax 017/278-35). From the station, walk left to náměstí Republiky and right up Dr. Davida Bechera to where it intersects Moskevská. It is open on Monday and Wednesday from 8am to 5pm; on Tuesday, Thursday, and Friday from 8am to 4pm; and on Saturday from 9am to noon. The centrally located office at Karla IV č. 1 (☎ **017/261-10** or **267-05;** fax 017/278-35) is open Monday through Friday from 9am to 5pm and on Saturday from 9am to noon. Rooms are about 400 Kčs ($14.30) for a single and 600 Kčs ($21.45) for a double.

There are also ZIMMER FREI signs on residential streets, where you can negotiate directly with your "landlord."

Hotels in or near the Center

There are many spa hotels in Karlovy Vary, which administer health treatments as well as provide a bed to sleep in, but there are also enough regular hotels for the private traveler who does not plan to take a cure.

Hotel Adria, Západní Str. 1, 36001 Karlovy Vary. ☎ **017/237-65.** 40 rms (none with bath). **Directions:** It's across the street from the bus station.

Rates: 500 Kčs single ($17.85); 770 Kčs ($27.50) double. Extra bed 100 Kčs ($3.55).

This faded old hotel needs renovation, but for the price and its proximity to the bus station it stands up adequately. Bathrooms and rugs are a bit worn, and the hallways are dim, but neither exceedingly so.

Hotel Atlantic, Tržiště 23, 36062 Karlovy Vary. ☎ **017/252-51.** Fax 017/290-86. 38 rms (6 with full bath, 2 with shower but no toilet). **Bus:** 11 from the train station; or 6 one stop, then 11 from the bus station.

Rates (including breakfast): 39 DM ($24.55) single without bath; 69 DM ($43.45) double without bath, 109 DM ($68.65) double with bath. The hotel is open Apr 1–Nov 1 and Dec 22–Jan 1; Apr 1–29, prices are lower by 15%–20%. At certain peak periods, prices go up 10%–15%. AE, DC, JCB, MC, V.

Now administered by Hotel Central, at Divadelní nám. 17, 150 meters farther down Nová Louka, this centrally located hotel remains clean, well maintained, and quiet. In 1990 they replaced the furniture and added clock radios. Many rooms have balconies overlooking the main promenade in town and the nearby valley.

★ **Ibiza,** Zámecký Vrch 3, 36003 Karlovy Vary. ☎ and fax **017/23-315.** 7 rms (all with bath). TV **Directions:** From the Market Colonnade on the west bank of the Teplá, walk up Tržiště, which becomes Zamecky Vrch.

Rates (including breakfast): 800 Kčs ($28.55) single; 1,240 Kčs ($44.30) double; 1,770 Kčs ($63.20) single and double suite. AE, DC, JCB, V.

If Karlovy Vary is indeed the conference of cakes described by Le Corbusier, then this hotel is its cherry. It's situated on a bluff overlooking the center of town. A 1992 reconstruction transformed the dour 18th-century burgher house into the happiest little inn this side of Candyland. Entry is through an ice-cream café that doubles as the breakfast room. The small rooms with high ceilings are so well illuminated by large windows that they feel simultaneously cozy and spacious. Furniture and bathrooms are all new and modern, and each room has a large color TV with satellite programming. Zealous housekeeping keeps the air lemony. Reserve as far in advance as possible during peak season.

U Tří Mouřenínů, Stará Louka č. 2, 36001 Karlovy Vary. ☎ **017/251-95.** 21 rms (none with bath). **Bus:** 11 from the train or bus station.

Rates: 600 Kčs ($21.45) single; 1,190 Kčs ($42.50) double; 1,770 Kčs ($63.20) triple. Low-season rates are 15% lower.

This centrally located pension, just around the corner from Hotel Puškin and across from Hotel Atlantic, is a classic of 19th-century neobaroque style, done in a paint scheme of salmon and white. A careful renovation has preserved its atmosphere and its management has kept prices low. The ceiling moldings and filigree trimming may not be in marvelous condition, nor does the furniture transcend clunky functionality, but all is new and comfortable. **Note:** The hotel is located at the confusing juncture of Stará Louka and Tržiště, where there is no sign or geographical change to indicate the transition from one street to the next.

Hotel Puškin, Tržiště 37, 36001 Karlovy Vary. ☎ **017/226-46** or **221-93.** 20 rms (all with bath). TEL **Bus:** 11 from the train or bus station.

Rates (including breakfast): 1,105 Kčs ($39.45) single; 1,480 Kčs ($52.85) double; 2,205 Kčs ($78.75) triple. Rates Nov 1–Mar 30 are 10%–20% lower.

The newly freshened facade of this classic Karlovy Vary hotel beams exuberantly with a carnivalesque palette of yellows and ochers. Rooms here have lost the fancy moldings and other belle-époque details that characterize other Karlovy Vary hotels of similar vintage. Instead, renovation has invested rooms with clean, comfortable, modern decor. The ground-floor restaurant enjoys the same airy attractive quality as the rooms.

Hotels outside the Center

Motel Autocamping, Slovenská 9, 36000 Karlovy Vary. ☎ **017/25-10-12.** 24 rms (about half with bath). **Bus:** 7.

Rates: 650 Kčs ($23.20) single, double, or triple without bath; 1,140 Kčs ($40.70) double with bath; 1,485 Kčs ($53.05) triple with bath. Additional bed 350 Kčs ($12.50) extra.

Located near the Hotel Gejzír just outside town, this is basically a campground with motel bungalows. Camping sites—largely utilized by German car campers—cost 80 Kčs ($2.85) per person. There's a restaurant and a bar on the grounds. It's not a quiet place at night, and though close to numerous hiking trails, it's too loud and crowded in the campsite to be called "in the woods."

Hotel Gejzír, Slovenská 5A, 36000 Karlovy Vary. ☎ **017/226-62.** 25 rms (none with bath). **Bus:** 7.

Rates: 350 Kčs ($12.50) single; 720 Kčs ($25.70) double; 950 Kčs ($33.95) triple; 1,100 Kčs ($39.30) quad.

Located in the hills above town, this hotel features 14 tennis courts and easy access to nearby forest walking trails. The receptionist speaks good English, and the rooms are adequate. The rate structure is a curious one, encouraging all travelers to take separate single rooms.

Worth the Extra Money

Grand Hotel Pupp, Mírové náměstí 2, 36091 Karlovy Vary. ☎ **017/221-21.** Fax 017/240-32. Telex 156220. 358 rms (all with shower or bath). TV TEL **Bus:** 2 or 11.

Rates (including breakfast): 136 DM ($85.70) single with shower; 179 DM ($112.75) double with shower, 199 DM ($125.35) double with bath. 25% discounts Nov–Apr (except Christmastime). AE, DC, MC, V.

An impressive sprawl of buildings, begun in 1701 and completed in its present form by 1908, this once-prestigious hotel has served kings, rajahs, and cultural nobility. Renovation is helping it cast off postwar dinginess (as well as its postwar name Moskva), and in spots it shines with splendor. But glitz and garish color for the most part have not been judiciously applied, and the new gaudiness can stun. Nevertheless, the old place, no matter how it's gussied up, has ineffable class. Rooms differ greatly, and so you are advised to look at several before taking one. The awesome gala hall is used mainly for large groups or concerts, but you might ask a staff member to unlock it for a peek.

Dining/Entertainment: Several restaurants and a disco are on the premises.
Facilities: Sauna, fitness center, barbershop.

WHERE TO EAT

Café Elefant, Stará Louka 32. ☎ **234-06.**

Cuisine: CAFE. **Directions:** Head up the main pedestrian promenade from the Sprudel Colonnade.
Prices: Cake 6–29 Kčs (20¢–$1.05); coffee 10–25 Kčs (35¢–90¢); glass of wine 30–60 Kčs ($1.05–$2.15).
Open: Daily 9am–10pm (to 8pm Oct–May).

The most recent incarnation of this Karlovy Vary landmark, in business since 1715, may well be its least elegant. Walls that used to be an extravagant belle-époque pink are now pale yellow and white, and the new carpeting was chosen more for its durability rather than luxury. Still, the excellent selection of coffees, cakes, and wine ensures that Elefant remains a nice place for a break, especially when the outdoor patio on the pedestrian promenade is open.

Linky, Sportovni 28.

Cuisine: DINER. **Directions:** From the juncture of ulice T. G. Masaryka and the pedestrian promenade, cross the bridge; it's on the corner to the left.
Prices: Salad 15 Kčs (55¢); chicken 18 Kčs (65¢) per 100g (about 4 oz.).
Open: Mon–Fri 9am–7pm, Sat–Sun 9am–6pm.

This self-serve diner is notable for its rotisserie-grilled chicken and green salads—healthier and tastier than the usual options for lunch in Karlovy Vary. Next door to Linky is a pizzeria, and next to that, an outlet where you can pick up divine Lazenské Oplatky—delicious wafers produced in nearby Mariánské Lázně.

Krásná Králova (The Beautiful Bride), Stará Louka 48. ☎ **255-08.**

Cuisine: CZECH. **Reservations:** High season. **Directions:** Head up the pedestrian promenade on the west side of the Teplá.
Prices: Appetizers 30 Kčs ($1.05); main courses 32–143 Kčs ($1.15–$5.10), averaging around 90 Kčs ($3.20).
Open: 11am–10pm.

Paneled, furnished, and decorated with wood, this restaurant has clearly done more time serving vacationing Soviet bloc families than Victorian-era notables. With ketchup, soy sauce, and vinegar on each table, it appears that the chef isn't dogmatic, or apparently confident, about the seasoning— this makes the simply excellent food served here a little surprising. Try the Lázeňska Jehia, a skewer of perfectly grilled and seasoned meats and vegetables. The extensive menu includes two vegetable pasta dishes. Staropramen beer is served in peculiar glasses that look like a cross between wine goblets and beer mugs.

SHOPPING

It was in Karlovy Vary that Ludvík Moser first founded his glassware shop in 1857, and this country's foremost name in crystal still has its factory here today: Moser, kapitána Jaroše 19 (☎ **41-61-11**). Located to the west of the town center (take bus no. 1, 10, or 16), the showroom displays copies of crystal made for prewar royalty and VIPs in a museum area, and shows a small room with current crystal for sale. Open

Monday through Friday only, from 7:30am to 3:30pm. There is also a store in town at Stará Louka 40, open Monday through Friday from 9am to 5pm.

EVENING ENTERTAINMENT

If you're all revved up, you can try the bars of the Hotel Central, the Grand Hotel Pupp, or the Hotel Thermal, all of which stay open till 3am.

You might also enjoy a visit to the Casino Karlovy Vary (☎ **231-00**), at Lázně 1 just a block from the Grand Hotel Pupp. It's located inside the former gym of the Imperial Spa from 1895, a splendid space of carved cherry wood covered by large paintings of Olympic sports. Games include roulette and blackjack. It's open Sunday through Thursday from 6pm to 2am and on Friday and Saturday from 6pm to 3am.

If you're looking for something a bit more sedate, you can attend concerts every Friday at Spa (Sanatorium) No. 3, or organ concerts twice monthly at the Grand Hotel Pupp. Other hotels also sponsor music from time to time.

2 Mariánské Lázně

29 miles SW of Karlovy Vary, 100 miles W of Prague

GETTING THERE • By Train The express train from Prague takes just over three hours for 105 Kčs ($3.75) in first class, 70 Kčs ($2.50) in second class. The train takes about an hour and 10 minutes from Plzeň, and 1½ hours through stunning terrain from Karlovy Vary.

The train station in Mariánské Lázně is at Nádražní nám. 292 (☎ **53-21**), south of the center, take trolleybus no. 5 into town.

• By Bus The bus from Karlovy Vary takes 1 hour and 10 minutes and costs 34 Kčs ($1.20). The bus station is next to the train station at Nádražní náměstí; take trolleybus no. 5 into town; pay the driver 2-Kčs (7¢) fare.

ESSENTIALS Mariánské Lázně's telephone area code is 0165.

INFORMATION City Service, at Hlanvní třída 1 (☎ and fax **0165/42-18** or **38-16**), just across the street from the Hotel Bohemia, is the best information source in town. They sell maps, and provide private room and hotel bookings. Hours are Monday through Friday from 9am to 7pm, and on Saturday and Sunday from 9am to 6pm. Winter closing is one hour earlier.

ORIENTATION Mariánské Lázně is situated mostly along one north–south avenue, Hlavní třída. Trolleybuses frequently travel its length. The train and bus stations are on the southern end. At the northernmost point, the avenue makes a sharp right turn, arcing through Mariánské Lázně's spa and mineral water district, centered on the Lázeňska Colonnade, before curling back into the main street. You will notice a á fenced-in patch of land here—the abandoned building site of an unfinished hotel begun in 1985. Town maps are widely available.

Note about Street Numbers: The numbers on Hlavní třída absolutely defy comprehension. The Hotel Corso (no. 41), for example, lies between the Hotel Cristal Palace (no. 61) and the Hotel Palace Praha (no. 67). And it remains a mystery why City Service, smack in the middle of the street's length, is graced with the number 1.

SPECIAL EVENTS Mariánské Lázně hosts an International Music Festival in July, an American Independence Day Parade on July 4, and a Chopin Festival in August.

Famous for its 39 mineral springs, Mariánské Lázně (pop. 18,000), known also by its German name, Marienbad, is more restful than its neighbor Karlovy Vary. Development of the spa lagged behind Karlovy Vary's, but by the mid-19th century, Marienbad's lush gardens and curative waters began drawing its share of famous visitors, counting among the devout the likes of Mark Twain, Thomas Edison, Franz Liszt, Henrik Ibsen, and especially Johann Wolfgang von Goethe. Picturesque woods surround a lone sleepy street frosted with Victorian-era pleasure palaces. There are about 25 sanatoriums for those seeking a health retreat, and tennis courts for sports enthusiasts.

Mariánské Lázně is also famous all over the Czech Republic for its large, thin, round wafers, called *Lázeňské Oplátky,* often fused together with a narrow layer of chocolate. You can buy boxes of them at cafés and food stores throughout town.

Every July 4th, Mariánské Lázně plays host to an American Independence Day parade. This part of the former Czechoslovakia was liberated by American forces at the close of World War II, and with the demise of Communism, the locals have decided to again celebrate their friendship with the U.S.

WHAT TO SEE & DO

City Museum, Goethovo nám. 11. ☎ **27-40.**

The ground floor chronicles the development of Mariánské Lázně from 1805 when its first house was built, and includes a small section on natural history. Upstairs you can see the rooms where Goethe stayed in 1823 as a 74-year-old man consumed with passion for a 17-year-old girl. This floor also has photos and documents of other famous visitors to Mariánské Lázně, including Mark Twain, Thomas Edison, Chopin, and Tsar Nicholas II. If you ask the museum guards, they'll play English-language tapes describing the museum collections in each room. There's also an English-language tapes describing the museum collections in each room. There's also an English-language film on the town's history, which can be viewed on request. Only the German and Czech versions are shown on a regular schedule.

Admission: 15 Kčs (55¢).

Open: Tues–Sat 9am–4pm. **Directions:** Walk one block east from Lázeňska Colonnade.

Lázěnska Colonnade, off Skalníkovy Sady.

A cast-iron-and-glass construction with ceiling frescoes from 1889, this open colonnade propped up by Corinthian columns is the local gathering point. First spa-goers get a cup of mineral waters at the different public fountains inside the colonnade, and then they slowly sip their "liquid health" as they talk with friends. A stage at the center hosts afternoon concerts.

Adjacent to the colonnade on a landscaped patio burbles the singing fountain, a multimedia water sculpture in the spirit of a Victorian-era "amusement." Every two hours from 7am to 9pm, the fountain comes alive for a concert of choreographed aquabatics set to musical selections of Bach, Dvořak, Mozart, and Strauss. Check the schedule posted by the fountain for exact times and music.

Admission: Free.

Open: Daily 24 hours; water distributed free daily 6am–noon and 4–6pm. **Bus:** 3 or 5. **Directions:** Walk east of Hlavní třída on Vrchlického ulice.

Russian Orthodox Church of St. Vladimir, on Ruská.

Built in 1902 by vacationing Russian gentry, this fanciful *sobor* serves the small Russian community still living in Mariánské Lázně. The only thing more edible-looking than its pastel exterior is the fantastic enameled iconostasis inside, which was awarded the Grand Prix de France at the 1900 Paris World's Fair. An English description is available for 10 Kčs (35¢). For a good earful of Russian opinion, ask the woman who staffs the church if Russia is a European country.

Admission: Free

Open: May–Oct, daily 8:30–11:30am and 2–4:30pm; Nov–Apr, daily 9:30–11:30am and 2–4pm. **Directions:** Climb the path behind the pale-yellow apartment building at Hlavní třída 56.

Golf Mariánské Lázně, east of the town center. ☎ **43-00.**

Edward VII was a frequent guest at Mariánské Lázne, and he presided over the opening of this 18-hole, par-72 golf course 88 years ago. Today it's still the largest in the Czech and Slovak Republics. They don't officially rent clubs or sell balls here, but the club workers might arrange a private deal with you if you really want to play. There's also a driving range of sorts, but you must bring your own balls. It's best to call ahead to make reservations.

Admission: 400 Kčs ($14.30) Mon–Fri, 500 Kčs ($17.85) Sat–Sun.

Open: End of Apr until the first snow. **Bus:** 12.

WHERE TO STAY

Hotel Corso, Hlavní třída 41, 35301 Mariánské Lázně. ☎ **0165/30-91** or **30-92.** 24 rms (4 with full bath, 6 with shower but no toilet). TV TEL **Bus:** 5 from the train or bus station.

Rates: 462 Kčs ($16.50) single without bath; 735 Kčs ($26.25) double without bath, 945 Kčs ($33.75) double with shower but no toilet; 1,195 Kčs ($42.70) double with bath. Showers cost a whopping 97 Kčs ($3.45) extra. AE, DC, MC, V.

The creatively decorated rooms of this hotel all feature live plants, reproductions of modern masters on the walls, and purple carpets. Some rooms have balconies out over the street. Furniture and beds are a tad worn but adequate. The fresh and youthful staff is charming.

Hotel Cristal Palace, Hlavní třída 61, 35301 Mariánské Lázně. ☎ **0165/20-56** or **20-57**. Fax 0165/20-58. 94 rms (4 with bath). **Bus:** 5 from the train or bus station.

Rates: 410 Kčs ($14.65) single without bath; 810 Kčs ($28.95) double without bath, 1,300 Kčs ($46.45) double with bath; 1,055 Kčs ($37.70) triple without bath. AE, DC, MC, V.

Located on the main street in town just a few minutes south of the center, the Cristal Palace offers 1950s or 1960s furniture in its rooms, and facilities that are clean and well kept. Some rooms have balconies, and all have double doors against hallway noise. The reception sells cigarettes, sodas, and some sweets, and gives service with a smile.

Juniorhotel Krakonoš, okres Cheb, 35334 Mariánské Lázně. ☎ **0165/26-24** or **23-83.** Telex 156311 101 rms in the main building (22 with shower but no toilet). 127 rms in the chalet building (all with full bath). TV **Bus:** 12 from the Hotel Excelsior in town.

Rates: In the chalet building, 860 Kčs ($30.70) double; 1,100 Kčs ($39.30) triple; 1,320 Kčs ($47.15) quad. In the main building, 580 Kčs ($20.70) single or double without bath, 730 Kčs ($26.05) single or double with shower but no toilet; 730 Kčs ($26.05) triple without bath, 900 Kčs ($32.15) triple with shower but no toilet; 875 Kčs ($31.25) quad without bath, 1,080 Kčs ($38.55) quad with shower but no toilet. Students with ISIC card, 200 Kčs ($7.15) per person. Breakfast 50 Kčs ($1.80) per person extra.

Located in a wooded area three miles southeast of the center, this CKM-run hotel offers accommodations in two different buildings, one a "modern" chalet and the other a grandly decaying, splendid old hotel. The chalet rooms have wood furniture, TVs, and balconies overlooking the countryside. The main building rooms are a bit more worn but large. There are also several dining rooms. The hotel is a good choice for those who want to play sports during their stay in Mariánské Lázně.

Facilities: Tennis courts cost 50 Kčs ($1.80) per hour, with racquet rental an additional 10 Kčs (35¢); minigolf costs 5 Kčs (20¢) an hour; volleyball is free; and horseback riding can be arranged at a nearby stable which is not connected to the hotel.

WHERE TO EAT

Filip, Poštovní 96. ☎ **26-39.**

Cuisine: CZECH. **Reservations:** Not required. **Directions:** From the central information office, cross up to Poštovní, which is parallel to Hlavní třída on the east bank.
Prices: Soups 9–18 Kčs (30¢–65¢); salads 12–27 Kčs (45¢–95¢); main courses 60–105 Kčs ($2.15–$3.75).

A shining light in the inky Mariánské Lázně culinary darkness, this privately owned restaurant is one of the few favored by locals as well as tourists. Long menus in Czech and German feature a broad array of fresh, well-prepared Czech, Slovak, and German dishes, as well as salads and vegetable options. All seating is in comfortable booths that encircle a bar counter, and in the summer there's a beautifully situated outdoor terrace. Try the divine *Slovácka cibulačka* (Slovak onion soup).

SHOPPING

The shopping scene in Mariénske Lázně is far more subdued than in Karlovy Vary, but you can buy the famous "Lázeňské Oplátky" wafers right from the source. The store is at Hlavní třída 122 (across the street and one block north from the information center). Get 'em boxed (26 Kčs/95¢ for chocolate, 23.90 Kčs/85¢ vanilla, eight per box) or in singles hot from the sizzling waffle press (4.40 Kčs/15¢ chocolate, 3 Kčs/10¢, Kčs/10¢ vanilla). It's open Monday through Friday 9am to noon and 2 to 5pm, on Saturday 9am to 1pm.

3 Plzeň

55 miles SW of Prague

GETTING THERE • **By Train** Frequent, fast trains from Prague take just over 1¾ hours and cost 108 Kčs ($3.85) in first class. The train station (☎ **422-33**) has baggage lockers and a luggage-check service, and a post office just to the left outside the main hall.

To get into town, walk from the main hall to the big road in front and turn right, continue half a block, then turn left one block on Moskevská. There you'll find the bus stop; take bus no. 12 or 16 into town.

• **By Bus** The bus from Prague takes two hours, costing 50 Kčs ($1.86). The bus station (Centrální autobusové nádraži) is west of the center at Dělová 1 (☎ **22-37-04**). Take tram no. 2 to náměstí Republiky at the town center, or turn left on Leninovo and walk into town.

ESSENTIALS Plzeň's telephone area code is 019.

ORIENTATION The central core of town is around náměstí Republiky. My recommended hotels, Čedok, and the beer museum are all within a few blocks of here. The Pilsner-Urquell beer factory is located about 10 minutes east of this square on foot.

INFORMATION Čedok, Prešovská 10 (☎ **019/366-48;** fax 019/332-98), is a block away from the main square, open Monday through Friday from 9am to noon and 1 to 5pm and on Saturday from 9am to noon. This excellent Čedok office also rents private rooms (see "Where to Stay," below).

SPECIAL EVENTS Plzeň hosts a Liberation Day celebration, May 4–5, and Pragoexpo, a small consumer-goods show in July.

Many who have enjoyed the beer that bears the town's name agree that Pilsner-Urquell, the original pilsner beer, is the world's finest brew.

The tradition of beer brewing began here hundreds of years ago. In its early years Plzeň's beer was characterized by a bitter, disagreeable taste, but bad beer does not prevent its consumption. By the 16th century, Plzeň had its own guild of beer drinkers. The group preached and practiced the time-honored tradition of "sleeping in the daytime; drinking, playing, loving, and making merry by night."

History dictates, however, that over time even lumpen beer drinkers achieve higher consciousness, and in the 19th century, revolutionary ferment arrived in Plzeň. One rebellious night in 1838, discontent with inferior beer frothed over. A mob of townsmen poured out 36 barrels in front of the town hall. With spilled beer sloshing at his ankles, one of the town's home brewers rose up. In a stentorian voice embodying the collective hopes and dreams of the people, he demanded, "Give us what we want in Plzeň—good and cheap beer!" Once the crowd had settled down somewhat, he continued. "Let the citizens holding boiling privileges join and build a brewery together." The Plzeň (Pilsner) brewery was quickly built, and in 1842 a great beer was born.

The medium-sized town of Plzeň (pop. 175,000) offers few sights other than the Pilsner-Urquell factory. Although the town has a quaint town square and some interesting architecture, Plzeň's World War II damage and years of industry and pollution (as home to Škoda and other industrial enterprises) have grayed much of the beauty. Beer is the best reason to come here, and with excellent train and bus connections to Prague, Plzeň can even be visited as an ambitious day trip.

WHAT TO SEE & DO

The Beer Shrines

Pilsner-Urquell Factory, U Prazdroje. ☎ **019/21-64.** Fax 019/22-72-83.

As the producer of what experts consider the world's greatest beer, the Pilsner-Urquell Factory is the place for anyone interested in the process of brewing beer. Every year this large factory produces 40 million gallons of beer and exports about 40% of it to some 64 different countries—accounting for about 10% of the country's total exports.

Individuals can tour the factory at 12:30pm Monday through Friday; solo travelers meet at the main factory gate for the one-hour tour. The cost is 30 Kčs ($1.05), but includes a pack of 12 beer-oriented postcards, and, if you're lucky, a glass of Plzeň gold after the tour. The tour (and the film) will most likely be in German because majority rules, but the guide may make some comments in English, too, if you are persistent.

The brewery tour begins with a 15-minute movie; then you're off to see the wondrous brewery, most of which has hardly changed since the factory opened in 1842. In the first room, ground malt and water, beer's staple ingredients, are mixed into one of 20 huge copper vats, the start of the long road to brewing smooth beer.

After leaving the factory, stop at the Na Spilce Restaurant, outside the factory gates, for a beer right at the source (see "Where to Eat," below).

Admission: 30 Kčs ($1.05).

Open: Tour Mon–Fri at 12:30pm. **Directions:** Walk east of náměstí Republiky to U Prazdroje.

Beer Museum [Pivovarské muzeum], Veleslavinova 6. ☎ **339-89.**

Inside this former 15th-century malt house you'll learn all you could want to know about the history and evolution of beer. In the first room—once part of a 19th-century pub—the guard will wind up a German polyphone music box from 1887 that plays Strauss's "Blue Danube." Subsequent rooms display the old production tools, mugs, pub artifacts, vats, and other objects associated with beer making and drinking. Make sure to ask for the very detailed museum description in English as you walk in.

Admission: 30 Kčs ($1.05) adults, 15 Kčs (55¢) students.

Open: Tues–Sun 10am–6pm. **Directions:** From náměstí Republiky, walk a block north to Veleslavinova then turn left for a block.

More Attractions

After visiting Plzeň's beer shrines, you'll also enjoy a walk around the symmetrical Old Town centered around the very large square named **náměstí Republiky,** which was founded in 1295. At the center of the square is the **Cathedral of St. Bartholomew,** built between 1320 and 1470, with the tallest steeple in the Czech Republic at 333 feet. The interior has tall columns leading to a ribbed, webbed ceiling.

At nám. Republiky 1 you'll see the 16th-century **Town Hall,** with a brown-and-black, illustrated Italian Renaissance facade. Closed to the public, the building operates as the mayor's office to this day. There are also porcelain, crystal, and other shops on the square.

At the intersection of Prešovská and sady Pětatřicátniků, just outside the town center, stands the soot-blackened, now-unused Synagogue of Plzeň. It's easily the largest building in the neighborhood, but only the faded Star of David indicates its former purpose. It is closed to the public.

WHERE TO STAY

PRIVATE ROOMS • **Čedok,** at Prešovská 10 (☎ **019/366-48**), rents nice private rooms beginning at 320 Kčs ($11.45), usually located outside the center of town.

Open Monday through Friday from 9am to noon and 1 to 5pm, and on Saturday from 9am to noon.

Hotels

Hotel Continental, Zbrojnická ulice 8, 30534 Plzeň. ☎ **019/723-52-92.** Fax 019/722-1746. Telex 154380. 42 rms (34 with bath). TV TEL **Tram:** 1 or 2 from the train station.

Rates (including breakfast): 548 Kčs ($20.85) single without bath or WC; 802 Kčs ($28.65) double without bath or WC; 1,025 Kčs ($36.60) single with shower without WC; 1,528 Kčs ($54.55) double with shower without WC; 1,492 Kčs ($53.20) single with bath; 2,184 Kčs ($78) double with bath. AE, DC, MC, V.

The American-born George Janacek, who covered the Velvet Revolution in 1989 as a photographer for *Life* magazine, didn't expect that visiting a hotel that once belonged to his family would affect him so deeply. The Janacek-Ledecky family ran the Continental until 1946, when the Soviet installation of a Communist government in Czechoslovakia compelled them to flee to the United States. In 1992, after several years of struggling with bureaucratic red tape. Mr. Janacek was able to reacquire the hotel. The heart he has poured into remedying years of neglect is apparent in the restaurant (considered by locals to be one of the town's best), the casino, and in many of the rooms. Some rooms are quite spacious, with beautiful velvet-covered furniture; others make do with far less charming trappings, which Mr. Janacek is steadily replacing. The excellent staff delivers near-Western levels of service.

Hotel Slovan, Smetanovy sady 1, 30528 Plzeň. ☎ **019/22-72-56.** Fax 019/22-68-41. 110 rms (24 with bath). TEL **Directions:** Turn right at the main exit from the train station, then left onto Amerika; after about 10 minutes, turn right at Jungmannova.

Rates (including breakfast): 680 Kčs ($24.30) single without bath, 1,400 Kčs ($50) single with bath; 1,060 Kčs ($37.85) double without bath, 1,800 Kčs ($64.30) double with bath. AE, DC, MC, V.

A hotel for more than 100 years, one of several elegant touches here is an ornate turn-of-the-century staircase leading up to the rooms. Some of the rooms are quite large, with high ceilings and furniture from the 1960s and 1970s; some also have TVs. Double doors shield the room from hallway noise. The reception is friendly and sells souvenirs and a few snacks. The hotel is also well located, just a few blocks south of náměstí Republiky.

WHERE TO EAT

Restaurace Na Spilce, U Prazdroje 1. ☎ **566-11-11.**

Cuisine: BEER HALL. **Directions:** Enter the beer factory and look to the right.
Prices: Soups 9 Kčs (30¢); pub grub 25–45 Kčs (90¢–$1.60); specialties 48–121 Kčs ($1.70–$4.30); half liter of beer 15 Kčs (55¢).
Open: Daily 11am–10pm.

This enormous beer hall, the last stop on the brewery tour, couldn't come a moment too soon. The reward is, of course, lovely Pilsner-Urquell, which can be accompanied with good and inexpensive pub fare.

4 České Budějovice

92 miles S of Prague, 86 miles SE of Pizeň

GETTING THERE • By Train The three-hour express ride from Prague costs 114 Kčs ($4.05) in first class. The train station (☎ **233-33**) has a luggage-check service as well as baggage lockers. There's also a post office and telephone office a block to the right of the station, open Monday through Friday from 7am to 8pm and on Saturday from 8am to noon.

• By Bus The bus from Prague costs 78 Kčs ($2.80).

ESSENTIALS České Budějovice's telephone area code is 38.

ORIENTATION The circular Old Town is surrounded by a river and parks where its fortifications once stood, and is centered on the huge náměstí, Přemysla Otakara II. Most points of historical interest are within easy walking distance of here.

From the railroad and bus stations, located side by side on Nádražni ulice, walk west for 10 minutes along Rudolfovská to the central square, náměstí Přĕmysla Otakara II.

INFORMATION The best source of tourist information is at **Turistické Informační a Mapové Centrum**, at the southwest corner of the main square (☎ **594-80**), open Monday through Friday 9am to 12:30pm and 1 to 5:30pm, Saturday 9:30am to 6pm, and Sunday 9 to 10:30am and 4 to 5:30pm. They supply information and maps, speak English, and arrange private accommodations (see "Where to Stay," below). Inquire here about tours of the Budvar brewery, offered for 95 Kčs ($3.40), Monday through Thursday 8:30am to 4pm, Friday 8:30am to noon.

Čedok is also on the main square at nám. Přemysla Otakara II 39 (☎ **38/322-79**), open May 15 to September 13, Monday through Friday from 9am to 6pm and on Saturday from 9am to noon; the rest of the year, Monday through Friday from 9am to 5pm and on Saturday from 9am to noon.

Make sure to buy the standard town map available in all bookstores. It locates all hotels, as well as points of interest.

Useful Telephone Numbers The emergency number (for the whole country) is **158.** For auto accidents, call **344-80.** For a taxi, call **233-17.**

SPECIAL EVENTS České Budějovice hosts a two-week music festival at the end of August that honors Emmy Destinn, a turn-of-the-century opera singer who lived her last years in České Budějovice. Also in August is an International Agricultural Show.

A quintessential Bohemian town, České Budějovice, near the mouth of the Vltava (Moldau) River, was founded by King Otakar II in 1265 to protect the approaches to southern Bohemia. Wealth flowed into the town in the form of wine and salt extracted from Austria in the south.

Despite the name of its main square (after Žižka, a Hussite commander), České Budějovice was a bastion of Catholic reaction to the Hussites in the north. The town's golden age came during the Renaissance when local silver mines and a mint funded the construction of numerous edifices and the huge marketplace. The catastrophic Thirty Years' War (1618–48) later flattened the town, and a 1641 fire nearly finished off what was left. In the 18th century, under the Habsburgs, České Budějovice was reconstructed in beautiful baroque style. In 1832 České Budějovice became the starting point of Europe's first horse-drawn railroad.

Today the pace is relaxed and slow for tourists. Still, the town is noted for its industry, including the Budvar brewery (better known as the original Budweiser) and the Koh-i-noor pencil factory. In all, České Budějovice is a pleasant spot to pass through, and a good place to launch an expedition to Telč en route to Brno, or to Český Krumlov just to the south.

WHAT TO SEE & DO

The Main Square

The Old Town of České Budějovice is small enough to be comfortably seen in a day. At the center of town is the broad náměstí Přemysla Otakara II, one of the largest squares in Central Europe. Unlike many piazzas in Europe, this one is actually a geometrical square, 430 feet long and 430 feet wide.

At the very center of the square is the ornate Fountain of Sampson, built in 1727 and once the town's principal water supply. On one side of the square is the Town Hall, originally a Renaissance building and later rebuilt in a baroque style in 1731.

More Attractions

Cerná Věž [Black Tower], U Černé věže. ☎ **386-38.**

The symbol of České Budějovice, this 232-foot-tall tower was built in the 16th century as a watchtower and belfry of the adjacent St. Nicolas Church. Badly damaged in the Thirty Years' War, it was later restored, and today it still commands an excellent view of the surrounding countryside—which you'll see after climbing 255 steps.

Admission: 6 Kčs (20¢) adults, 4 Kčs (15¢) students.

Open: Mar–June, Tues–Sun 10am–6pm; July–Aug, daily 10am–7pm; Sept–Nov, Tues–Sun 9am–5pm. **Closed:** Dec–Feb. **Directions:** Walk beyond the northeast corner of náměstí Přemysla Otakara II.

Church Of St. Nicolas, U Černé věže. ☎ **98-967.**

Perhaps the most important sight in České Budějovice, this 13th-century church was built around the time the city was founded. It's the symbol of the town's adherence to Catholicism in the face of the Hussites. The interior reflects a 17th-century baroque style with a white-and-cream interior, flamboyant pulpits, and a large organ.

Admission: Free. **Directions:** Walk beyond the northeast corner of náměstí Přemysla Otakara II, next to the Black Tower.

Jihočeské Museum, Dukelská 1. ☎ **374-61** or 372-52.

A potpourri of exhibits of past and present life in Bohemia. Part of the collection shows the fish, flora, and fauna of the region starting with early fossils, and then moves up to the first human habitation of the region with ancient pottery and jewelry. Medieval weapons, crests, and manuscripts continue the human saga in the 14th century, and the more recent centuries are represented by objects as varied as furniture, weaving looms, crystal, glass, farm tools, and even 20th-century postcards.

Admission: 16 Kčs (55¢) adults, 8 Kčs (30¢) students.

Open: Tues–Sun 9am–noon and 1–5:30am. **Directions:** Exit the main square east on Karla IV; take the first right and continue a block and a half.

WHERE TO STAY

The Turistické Informační a Mapové Centrum, at the southwest corner of the main square (☎ **594-80**), can arrange accommodations at hotels, pensions, or very inexpensively (250 to 400 Kčs—$8.95 to $14.30) in superbly located private homes. They are open Monday through Friday 9am to 12:30pm and 1 to 5:30pm, Saturday 9:30am to 6pm, Sunday 9 to 10:30am and 4 to 5:30pm.

Hotel Zvon, Přemysla Otakara II náměstí, 37042 České Budějovice. ☎ **38/353-61.** 70 rms (35 with bath). TV TEL **Directions:** Walk to the east side of the main square.

Rates: Old hotel: 540 Kčs ($19.30) single without bath, 850 Kčs ($30.35) single with bath; 850 Kčs ($30.35) double without bath, 1,450 Kčs ($51.80) double with bath, 1,750 Kčs ($62.50) double with bath and view. Use of hallway baths or showers costs 50 Kčs ($1.80) extra. New hotel: 950 Kčs ($33.95) single with bath; 1,350–1,640 Kčs ($48.20–$58.55) double with bath, 1,750–1,900 Kčs ($62.50–$67.85) double with bath and view.

Location is everything here—right on the main square with great views from some rooms. Old hotel rooms are typical B-grade, for the most part clean with new furniture and rugs and good light. The A-grade rooms in the new hotel, on the other hand, have been renovated to a very high Western standard. The effect of stepping from B-grade to A-grade sections of the hotel is like seeing Dorothy's arrival in Oz from black-and-white Kansas. Pristine white walls, color-coordinated decor, and gorgeous bathrooms rank with those of any Sheraton.

Dining/Entertainment: The hotel also has an attractive restaurant on the second floor, with heavily carved wooden ceilings and high-backed wooden chairs. The service is friendly and courteous, and the prices are standard, as is the food.

Hotel Grand, Nádražní 27, 370 01 České Budějovice. ☎ **38/365-91.** Fax 38/522-68. 67 rms (all with shower or bath). TEL **Directions:** Cross the street from the train station.

Rates (including breakfast): 580 Kčs ($20.70) single with shower, 640 Kčs ($22.85) single with bath; 835 Kčs ($29.80) double with shower, 920 Kčs ($32.85) double with bath.

Recent renovations have given this conveniently located hotel a clean, albeit utilitarian look, marked principally by the wood-grain linoleum that clads most surfaces. The furniture is comfortable, and high ceilings lend a spacious feeling. The shower-only rooms have showers that are little more than booths of prefabricated fiberglass set up in the corners—a little slapdash in appearance but perfectly serviceable. WCs in the hallways are immaculate. Rooms with bath boast proper tiled facilities. Reception serves up all manner of supplies, including 18 Kčs (65¢) espressos. Avoid street-facing rooms if you are sensitive to traffic noise.

Hotel Bohemia, Hradební 20, 370 01 České Budějovice. ☎ and fax **38/562-63.** 10 rms (all with shower or bath). TV/TEL **Directions:** Exit the northern side of the main square from Placheho and walk two blocks.

Prices (including breakfast): 1,290 Kčs ($46.05) single, 1,590 Kčs ($56.80) double. Prices Nov–Mar 20%–30% lower. AE, MC, V.

This restful private inn, crafted from a burgher house, lies on a quiet corner near the old citadel walls. Rooms have tasteful decor that mixes dark wood with pristine white-washed walls and heather-colored carpets. Every room has satellite television, art nouveau Mucha prints on the walls, and sleek new furniture. Rooms differ in size and shape, with those on the top floor graced by skylights. The wonderful receptionist brims with hostful charm and speaks German and a little English.

WHERE TO EAT

Masné Krámy, Krajinská 29. ☎ **329-57** or **326-52.**

Cuisine: CZECH. **Directions:** Exit the main square from the northwest corner and walk a block.
Prices: Main courses 27–158 Kčs (95¢–$5.65); half liter of beer on tap 13.90 Kčs (50¢).
Open: Sun–Thurs 10am–11pm, Fri–Sat 10am–midnight.

Just off the northwest side of náměstí Přemysla Otakara II, Masné Krámy is the unofficial beer church of the Budvar brew. Devotees drink in little "apses" that branch off a long nave. The food is typical pub fare—cheap and filling, leaning heavily on pork, but with duck, trout, and a few other offerings on the poorly mimeographed menu. A few small sandwiches are also offered behind a counter to the left as you walk in. The atmosphere is boisterous and lively.

Huang Jin, Hroznová 18. ☎ **52-327.**

Cuisine: CHINESE. **Reservations:** Not required. **Directions:** Walk one block north of the main square to Hroznová.
Prices: Appetizers 68–110 Kčs ($2.45–$3.95); main courses 70–200 Kčs ($2.50–$7.15); three-course fixed-price meals 48–98 Kčs ($1.70–$3.50). Cover charge 10 Kčs (35¢).
Open: Daily 11am–10:30pm.

For a break from heavy Czech fare, indulge in some heavy Chinese fare. Situated in a typical Gothic burgher house, the dining room is, to put it mildly, eclectically decorated, replete with pagoda lamps hanging from medieval wood-beam ceilings and prints of rice-paper landscape paintings on the thick whitewashed walls. The food, which leans heavily on sweet sauces and MSG, will be tasty and familiar to anyone who knows the classic Chinese food of the American suburb. The Chinese staff speaks no English, but have no fear, the menu is translated into English. The fixed-price meals, consisting of soup, a stir-fry dish on rice, and tea, are an excellent deal.

5 Český Krumlov

12 miles SW of České Budějovice

GETTING THERE • **By Train** The slow train from České Buděejovice costs 22 Kčs (80¢) in first class and 15 Kčs (55¢) in second class. The station is a fair distance north of the town center but convenient shuttle buses synchronized with the train schedule take passengers from the train to the bus station, from which it is an easy walk to the center.

• **By Bus** Bus is the best way to go from České Budějovice. It takes 40 minutes and costs 14 Kčs (50¢). The bus station (☎ **34-15**) is about 15 minutes east of the main square by foot; follow signs over the bridge to Rožmberk.

ESSENTIALS Český Krumlov's telephone area code is 337.

ORIENTATION The bus station is situated just north of the two kernels of old Český Krumlov. Separated from one another by the tight coils of the Vltava River, the kernels are, north to south, Latrán and the Old Town. The castle saddles a rocky ridge that rises up between the two, gainable by a bridge. At the center of the Old Town is náměstí Svornosti, site of the town hotel.

INFORMATION The best source of information in town is the Služby Turistum (Tourist Service), located on the street leading up to the castle entrance, at Zámek 57 (☎ and fax **337/46-05**). It's open daily from 9am to 6pm, with a break for lunch. The English-speaking staff sells maps and guidebooks, books private rooms, books local and regional tours, and gives general information.

There are several other small private information agencies along Latrán ulica, where private rooms can be rented. Čedok is at Latrán 79 (☎ **337/21-89** or **34-44;** fax 337/20-62).

SPECIAL EVENTS Český Krumlov hosts the Winter Amusement of the Czech Nobility Festival in January, the Festival of the Rose in mid-June, with music and folklore, and the Chamber Music Festival in late June, when concerts are performed inside the castle in period costumes with original instruments.

All but the most hurried travelers should try to visit Český Krumlov (pop. 14,000), one of the most charming towns in the country. Český Krumlov's fairy-tale features include a Lilliputian city center situated within a tight kink of the Vltava River, closely built buildings capped in red terra-cotta tiles, and the stupendous castle—the second largest in Bohemia—perched high above.

Wonderful structures, for which Český Krumlov has been named one of the 300 most beautiful cities in the world by UNESCO, reflect the influence of the powerful noble families that once ruled it. The region's lack of mineral wealth helped the town escape monstrous industrial developments. Its thriving community of artists and a major exhibition and performance space are establishing present-day Český Krumlov as a major cultural center.

WHAT TO SEE & DO

The Castle. ☎ **20-75.**

The largest castle in Bohemia after the Prague Castle, this structure was first built in the 13th and 14th centuries as part of a private estate and then rebuilt in Renaissance style in the 16th century. It has had several private owners, including the Rožzmberk family, the largest landholders in Bohemia.

Today you can visit the castle after passing over a bridge high above a moat where live bears guard against unwanted intruders. You can see the interior only on a guided tour. The tour starts at the rococo **Chapel of St. George,** and then passes through the **Renaissance Hall** filled with family portraits. You'll see the royal family **apartments,** with lovely ornate furniture including 19th-century Biedermeier pieces, Flemish wall tapestries, and Dutch and other European paintings. One highlight is the rococo **Mirror Room,** the old ballroom decorated in a trompe-l'oeil style alongside panels of mirrors.

Visitors are only permitted to enter on tours, which last one hour. English-language tours for groups should be booked ahead of time. Individual travelers may luck out by finding an English-language group to join but more likely they will have to join a Czech or German group.

After touring the castle, you can explore the magnificent gardens behind it.

Admission: Tour, 80 Kčs ($2.85) adults, 40 Kčs ($1.40) students.

Open: May–Aug, Tues–Sun 8am–noon and 1–5pm; Sept, Tues–Sun 9am–noon and 1–5pm; Apr and Oct, Tues–Sun 9am–noon and 1–3pm (last entrance one hour before closing). **Closed:** Nov–Mar. **Directions:** Walk north of náměstí Svornosti, across the bridge, and to the left.

Town Museum, Horní ul. 152. ☎ **20-49.**

The town history and art museum surveys the region's past from 100,000 B.C. to the present day. Highlights include a reconstructed apothecary of a few hundred years ago, a big model of the town, old regional clothing and furniture, and some local art of Český Krumlov and other subjects. Start on the third floor and work your way down; ask for the English-language description at the entrance.

Admission: 20 Kčs (70¢) adults, 10 Kčs (35¢) students.

Open: May–Sep, daily 10am–12:30pm and 1–6pm; Feb–Apr and Oct–Dec, Tues–Fri 9am–noon and 12:30–5pm, Sat–Sun 1–5pm. **Closed:** Jan. **Directions:** Walk two blocks east of náměstí Svornosti.

Church of St. Vitus, Kostelní ulice.

The most important building of the inner-city core, this late Gothic church was constructed between 1407 and 1439. Inside, you'll see tall Gothic arches and a series of wall paintings.

Admission: Free. **Directions:** Walk a block east of náměstí Svornosti.

Schiele Centrum, Široká 70–72. ☎ **42-32. Fax 28-20.**

Viennese artist Egon Schiele experienced many of the rare happy moments of his brief troubled life in Český Krumlov. Named for him, this cultural center is housed in a classy 16th-century building that used to serve as the town brewery. It's dedicated to the study and celebration of visual art, theater, and music. Stop by for the calendar of special events and excellent temporary exhibits.

Admission: 100 Kčs ($3.55).

Open: Daily 10am–6pm. **Directions:** From náměstí Svornosti, head west two blocks until you reach Široká.

WHERE TO STAY

$ **Hotel Krumlov,** náměstí Svornosti 14, 38101 Český Krumlov. ☎ **337/20-40.** 33 rms (5 with bath, 16 with shower but no toilet). TV TEL **Directions:** Follow the bus station directions to the center.

Rates: 390 Kčs ($13.95) single without bath, 550 Kčs ($19.65) single with shower but no toilet; 550–650 Kčs ($19.65–$23.20) double without bath, 600 Kčs ($21.45) double with shower but no toilet, 1,100 Kčs ($39.30) double with bath. AE, DC, MC, V.

Well located right on the main square in town and a few minutes' walk to the castle, this hotel is ideal for those who want to spend the night in town. The rugs are a bit aged, however, and the public bathrooms run-down. Perhaps this is understandable, as the building dates from 1309 and is the oldest preserved house in town!

The restaurant downstairs, open from 7am to 11pm daily, is a good choice for lunch or dinner.

Pension Ve Věži [In the Tower], Latrán 28, 38101 Český Krumlov.

☎ **0337/52-87** or **49-72.** 4 rms (none with bath). **Directions:** Follow Latrán all the way to the Český Krumlov brewery; the tower is across the street from the brewery.

Rates (including breakfast): 450 Kčs ($16.05) single; 900 Kčs ($32.15) double. Prices are 25% cheaper Nov–March. **Parking:** Free.

This tiny, private pension is in a renovated medieval tower just five minutes by foot from the castle. You should definitely take a room here if any are available; advance reservations are highly recommended, though rooms are sometimes available on the spot. Although there are no private bathrooms, there are full facilities on each floor, shared by just two rooms. The rooms are tastefully furnished in sturdy blond wood.

WHERE TO EAT

Konvice, Horní ul. 144. ☎ **41-80.**

Cuisine: CZECH. **Directions:** Walk one block east from náměští Svornosti along Horní ulice.

Prices: Soups 14–25 Kčs (50¢–90¢); main courses 54–169 Kčs ($1.95–$6.05); desserts 15–49 Kčs (55¢–$1.75).

Open: Daily 10am–11:30pm.

A rare restaurant that manages to be all things to all people, Konvice is a chic café, a mellow restaurant, a rowdy beer hall, and an outdoor bistro with the the best al fresco terrace in the city. The menu is in Czech and German and features a typical variety of continental fare at reasonable prices. The dessert list is extensive and includes gelato, tira misu, and strudels. This is a fine place to sample the local brew, Eggenberk. Popular with tourists and locals alike, the atmosphere froths during the later hours.

Rybářská Bašta/Krčínův Dům (Krcin's House), Kájovská 54. ☎ **671-83.**

Cuisine: FISH. **Directions:** Exit náměstí Svornosti on the southwest side and walk a block until the street widens into a small square.

Prices: Soup 20 Kčs (70¢); fish 82–230 Kčs ($2.95–$8.20). V.

Open: Daily 11am–10pm.

The namesake and original tenant of this house, Krčín, who managed the Rožmberk family's considerable land holdings, is portrayed in the 16th-century fresco on the west wall. The monkey opposite him is believed by historians to symbolize his predilection for booze. Inside, it's a different story, a dark and romantic little tavern serving fresh fish from nearby ponds in a variety of preparations. Trout, carp, eel, and pike can be had crumbed, grilled, lemoned, amandine, gypsy style, or novo-hrady style. The only soup on the menu is an outstanding fish chowder. A couple of venison dishes are offered as well. The sound system pipes in country-western music, which somehow strikes a fitting tone.

6 Tábor

55 miles south of Prague, 37 miles N of České Budějovice

GETTING THERE • **By Train** Tábor is at least 1½ hours by express train from Prague, or almost 1 hour from České Budějovice. From Prague it will cost 48 Kčs ($1.70) in first class, 32 Kčs ($1.15) in second class.

• **By Bus** The 1½-hour express bus ride from Prague costs 34 Kčs ($1.20). The 1-hour bus trip from České Budějovice costs 33 Kčs ($1.15).

ESSENTIALS Tábor's telephone area code is 361. The Staré Město (Old Town) of Tábor is situated around the large square Žižkovo náměstí, site of the town church and Hussite museum. The entire town core is surrounded by medieval walls, with the Kotnov Castle, now one of the town's museums, at the southwest corner.

The Old Town is about a 20-minute walk from the train and bus station. Walk the length of the park and bear right at its farthest corner to walk along the main drag, 9 května třida, into town. Buses nos. 11 and 12 also traverse the route. Most hotels are located here.

INFORMATION Čedok (☎ **361/222-35** or **235-63**) is located next to the Hotel Palcát on 9 května třída. Open Monday, Tuesday, Thursday, and Friday from 8:30am to 4pm, on Wednesday from 10am to 6pm, and on Saturday from 8 to 11am. They have some information, sell bus but not train tickets, and also rent private rooms: Doubles cost 570 to 713 Kčs ($20.35 to $25.45).

Tábor, the center of the Hussite movement, was founded in 1420 and named by the Hussites after the biblical Mount Tábor. Hard as it is to believe today, a relatively small group of people (maybe 15,000 soldiers) decided in 1420 that they had been commanded by God to break the temporal power of the Catholic church. The Táborites, as this sect of the Hussites was known, were led by the legendary Jan Žižka and they routed the combined papal forces for over 16 years.

Needless to say, Tábor has quieted down in the intervening 573 years. The main sights, including several beautiful Renaissance houses, are clustered around the old town center.

WHAT TO SEE & DO

Museum of the Hussite Movement, Žižkovo nám. 1. ☎ **222-42.**

The late Gothic (1440–1515) Town Hall now chronicles the movement that put Tábor in the history books with an interesting collection of Hussite relics. Under the marketplace and extending around the old town is a complex of tunnels. The tunnels were actually just cellars of local buildings dating back to the 15th century, but in 1946 they were linked up underneath the entire main square. Initially they were used to store beer and food, but they gradually became shelters used during fires. They also housed prisoners, and, as my guide put it, "quarreling and wrangling women."

A guide will lead you through the tunnels, in which you traverse about a third of a mile at depths of 22 to 39 feet chilled at a steady temperature of 46°F. You exit the tunnel tour at the other side of the square.

Near the exit you can visit the principal Gothic church on the square, which has a Renaissance gable (added in the middle of the 16th century), a Gothic ribbed wooden altar, and stained-glass windows.

Admission: 20 Kčs (70¢) adults, 10 Kčs (35¢) students.

Open: Apr–Oct, Tues–Sun 8am–4:30pm (last entrance at 4:15pm); Nov–Mar, Tues–Sun 9am–4pm (last entrance at 3:45pm). **Directions:** Walk to the west side of the main square.

Kotnov Castle, Klokotská ulice. ☎ **227-88.**

A 14th-century castle with a big round tower, this defensive structure forms the southwest corner of the town walls that still exist today. The castle interior displays a well-organized collection on the Middle Ages, with old farming tools, armor, weapons, uniforms, and other artifacts. After viewing the museum collection, climb the tower for a great view over the town.

Admission: 20 Kčs (70¢) adults, 10 Kčs (35¢) students.

Open: Tues–Sun 8am–4:30pm. **Directions:** Exit Žižkovo náměstí on the west side of the square and stay left for about 10 minutes until you reach Klokotská.

WHERE TO STAY & EAT

Hotel Bohemia, Husovo nám. 591, 39002 Tábor. ☎ **361/228-28** or **228-27.** 30 rms (21 with bath). TV TEL **Directions:** Walk across from the train station.

Rates (including breakfast): 600 Kčs ($21.45) single without shower, 1,000 Kčs ($35.70) single with shower, 800 Kčs ($28.55) double without shower, 1,200 Kčs ($42.85) double with shower. Use of hallway showers costs 50 Kčs ($1.80). AE, DC, MC, V.

Convenient to train and bus stations, the Bohemia is frequently full. That's unfortunate because this is a clean and cheerful hotel. Some rooms have views of the square in front of the train station, and some have phones. All are attractively furnished. Very well managed.

Dining/Entertainment: The hotel restaurant does Czech cuisine in very attractive modern surroundings at low prices; (main courses cost 19 to 28 Kčs (70¢ to $1).

Hotel Palcát, 9 května třída, 39001 Tábor. ☎ **361/229-01** or **229-03.** 68 rms (all with bath). TV TEL **Bus:** 11 or 12 from the railroad station.

Rates: 1,030 Kčs ($36.80) single; 1,580 Kčs ($55) double. Prices from Oct to Apr are 14%–23% lower. Breakfast 70 Kčs ($2.50) per person extra.

The most expensive hotel in town is the Palcát, a modern building with clean, if unexceptional, rooms. Some rooms have sofas, and the ones on the higher floors have views over the town. The white-tiled bathrooms are small but modern.

Hotel Slovan, 9 května třída 678, 39001 Tábor. ☎ **361/234-35** or **236-97.** 24 rms (all without bath). TV **Directions:** From the train station, walk the length of the park and bear right at the farthest corner; continue about 5-10 minutes down 9 kvetna třída.

Rates (including breakfast): 590 Kčs ($21.05) single; 950 Kčs ($33.95) double; 1,021 Kčs ($36.45) triple. Rates are 100 Kčs ($3.55) lower Nov–Mar. A bath or shower costs 44 Kčs ($1.55) extra.

A modern attractive lobby in this familiar 13-floor concrete bunker greets visitors and suggests a more upscale hotel. The rooms are typical B category, with a radio and TV, blond-wood furniture, and rugs that are a bit old. There's an attractive restaurant downstairs. The price makes this hotel the number one recommendation for Tábor.

Bistro Nipo, Pražska 157. ☎ **320-17.**

Cuisine: CZECH. **Directions:** Exit Žižkovo náměstí on the southwestern side.
Prices: Lunch 25–40 Kčs (90¢–$1.45); dinner 35–100 Kčs ($1.25–$3.55).
Open: Mon–Fri 9am–8pm, Sat 9am–7pm, Sun 10:30am–3pm.

This attractive little café just off náměstí Žižkovo is an overachiever with imaginative food and a stylish environment. Selections include grilled carp and trout dishes, kung pao chicken, and the traditional pork and beef dishes, smartly prepared. There are also daily specials. The menu is in Czech and German, but a few of the waiters speak English.

7 Telč

77 miles SE of Prague. 53 miles W of Brno, 50 miles NE of České Budějovice

GETTING THERE • By Train Train connections are poor. From České Budějovice you must take a two-hour express to Kostelec u Jihlavy, and then change lines for Telč, a 40-minute journey. There's also an express direct from Tábor to Kostelec u Jihlavy, a 1½-hour journey.

You can leave your luggage in storage at Telč's train station, if it's open.

• By Bus Direct buses from Prague's Florenc station take about three hours and cost 78 Kčs ($2.80). Several buses a day between České Budějovice and Brno stop at Telč, a 2-hour ride from either direction costing 52 Kčs ($1.85).

• By Car Telč is located about halfway between České Budějovice and Brno on the main road running through southern Bohemia, Route 23.

ESSENTIALS Telč's telephone area code is 96.

ORIENTATION The center of Telč is shaped somewhat like a trapezoid, with lakes to the north and south. At the center is a very large, triangular square, náměstí Zachariáše z Hradce. On the northwest corner of the square is the town castle.

The castle and town square of Telč are about 10 minutes from the bus station on A. V. Slavika. To get to town, go out the back entrance of the station, turn right on Tyřsora, and then left on the major street, Masarykovo. Follow it as it bears left and then turn right at the second or third small alley to your right. Find Na Müstku and follow it into the square.

INFORMATION There is no permanent information office. A temporary office is always set up somewhere on the main square, usually just in advance of the tourist season. If you cannot find it, ask at the front desk of U Černého Orla hotel. For private accommodations, look for ZIMMER FREI signs in and around the old town.

The old town core of delightful Telč is a diamond in the rough. Built on an outcropping of land surrounded by gentle ponds that once served as a defensive perimeter, very little has changed since Zacharias of Hradec gussied up the Gothic town with a Renaissance skin in the late 16th century. The town outside the walls offers a different kind of pleasure, a dusty quiet so uncorrupted by tourism (despite a few conspicuous exchange offices) that even drowsy little dogs sleeping in doorways pay little notice. It's a great place to stop off when traveling between České Budějovice or Tábor and Brno.

WHAT TO SEE & DO

The main sight in Telč is the huge town square ✪ **náměstí Zachariáše z Hradce,** actually an elongated triangle bordered by two- and three-story burgher houses whose unbroken fascia of Renaissance facades lends the piazza the flat pictorial quality of a stage set. The natty Renaissance tailoring of the square's original Gothic underpinnings was the 16th-century inspiration of Zacharias—scion of the ruling Hradec family—after he returned from touring in Genoa. The thick Gothic arches and vaulting of the pedestrian arcades date back to the 14th century. A wavelet of baroque restyling visited Telč in the 18th century, visible in the facades of several houses and in the coiled baroque column at the southern end of the square, constructed in 1718 and dedicated to the Virgin Mary.

The Renaissance ★ **Telč Castle,** on náměstí Zachariáše z Hradce at the northeast corner of the town square (☎ **28-21**), was built in the 16th century on the site of a former Gothic castle. It's noted for its spectacular interior rooms with painted ceilings and inlaid furniture and wood paneling, which you can see on a 50-minute tour. Highlights include the Africa Hall with rhino heads, tiger skins, and other exotica from 1903–14 hunting expeditions in Africa; the Marble/Knights' Hall with a nice collection of armor with a wood ceiling decorated with bas-reliefs from 1570; and the Golden Hall, where balls and ceremonies were once held. Ask for the useful English-language castle description at the admission desk.

Admission to the castle is 25 Kčs (90¢) for adults and 10 Kčs (35¢) for students and children. It's open Tuesday through Sunday: May to August from 8am to noon and 1 to 5pm, and in April, September, and October from 9am to noon and 1 to 4pm (last entrance is one hour before closing). It's closed from November to March.

After enjoying the old town, spend some time walking its leafy periphery. The placid ponds dotted with ducks and bordered by gardens hardly suggest the defensive role they once played.

WHERE TO STAY & EAT

Tourservis Spol. S.R.O., Štěpnická 409, 58856 Telč. ☎ **066/96-24-31.** 29 rms (all with shower but no toilet). **Directions:** Exit the main square at its northern end, behind the castle; continue straight to Štěpnická, the main road through town, and bear right.

Rates: 300 Kčs ($10.70) single; 550 Kčs ($19.65) double; 750 Kčs ($26.80) triple.

This well-maintained but spartan hotel is located just five minutes on foot from the main square. The rooms are relatively comfortable, with double doors and actual double beds.

U Černého Orla, nám. Zachariáše z Hradce 7, 58886 Telč. ☎ **96/22-20** or **22-22.** 27 rms (3 with bath, 24 with shower). **Directions:** Walk south across nám. Zachariáše z Hradce from the castle.

Rates: 430 Kčs ($15.35) single; 580 Kčs ($20.70) double; 490 Kčs ($17.50) single with shower; 750 Kčs ($26.80) double with shower; 1,040 Kčs ($37.15) triple with shower.

This is the nicest hotel in town, and the only one on the square. It has a beautiful facade with a café in front and a simply decorated, attractive lobby. The medium-sized rooms have recently been redone, and the bathrooms, while not modern, are clean. Some of the rooms have views over the square, and a painting on two of the walls.

Dining/Entertainment: The hotel also houses a competent restaurant despite a somewhat modest appearance. The food is quite good and the service is efficient. Trout from the surrounding fish ponds is assuredly fresh, and the pork schnitzel is good, too. Soup costs 9 to 15 Kčs (30¢–55¢) and main courses run 35 to 130 Kčs ($1.25 to $4.65). It's often packed at lunch, but you're invited to squeeze in where you can. Open daily from 7am to 10pm (closed Monday from October to May).

U Zachariáše, nám. Zachariáše z Hradce 33. ☎ **96-26-72.**

Cuisine: CZECH. **Directions:** Walk to the southwest end of the main square.
Prices: Soups 12–14 Kčs (45¢–50¢); main dishes 35–140 Kčs ($1.25–$5).
Open: Sun and Tues–Thurs 10am–11pm, Mon 10am–10pm, Fri–Sat 10am–midnight.

Food has been served here since the 17th century, when it was a mess hall for castle clerks and an occasional soup kitchen for the poor, legendary for its "sweet gruel." The present-day food isn't memorable, despite a reputation as being the best in town. The wide menu accompanies the expected schnitzels and goulash with dishes of chicken, duck, and pike and perch from nearby ponds. Try the delicious regional brew Bohemian Regent here.

8 Brno

140 miles SE of Prague, 86 miles NW of Bratislava

GETTING THERE • **By Train** The express train from Prague takes as little as 3¼ hours, costing 144 Kčs ($5.15) in first class, 96 Kčs ($3.40) in second class. Many of these trains depart from Prague's Masaryk Station, although some leave from the Central Station. The best express trains from Bratislava take about two hours.

From Brno's train station (☎ **42-21-48-03** or **42-21-48-05**), walk straight ahead into town, about a 10-minute walk, or take tram no. 4 from in front of the station. You can check bags 24 hours a day at the station.

• **By Bus** The nonstop express bus from Prague's Florenc station is the best bet to reach Brno, taking only 2½ hours, for 73 Kčs ($2.60).

Brno's bus station (☎ **33-79-26**) is a few minutes northeast of the train station, just about a five-minute walk into town.

• **By Car** The drive from Prague takes about two hours.

ESSENTIALS Brno's telephone area code is 05.

ORIENTATION Brno is a rather large city, but fortunately most of the sights of interest are concentrated in the old city core. At the center is Svobody náměstí (Liberty Square), the oldest square in town, which connects via Masarykova ulice to the train station in about 10 minutes on foot. Just west of Masarykova ulice is Zelný trh (Cabbage Market), the largest square in town and home to a vegetable market. Kapuchínské náměstí is adjacent to Zelný trh to the south. Špilberk Castle is on a hilltop surrounded by a park just west of the center.

No cars can enter the Old Town, but tram no. 4 runs right through it north to south.

INFORMATION Located in the main hall of the train station, Taxatour (☎ **05/42-21-33-48** or **42-21-33-56**) is a new private 23-hour tourist office, offering services ranging from private accommodations (see "Where to Stay," below) to rides to other European cities (see "En Route to Other Destinations," below). The office is open daily 1am to midnight.

The main office of Čedok is at Divadelni 3 (☎ **05/231-79**)—walk up Benešova třída from the train station to get there. This office is well organized and a good place to make hotel reservations in other cities. Čedok is open April to October Monday through Friday from 9am to 6pm and on Saturday from 9am to noon. The office closes an hour earlier from November to March.

There's a post and telephone office just to the left as you exit the main train station, open Monday through Friday from 7am to 8pm, on Saturday from 8am to 3pm, and on Sunday from 8am to 2pm.

SPECIAL EVENTS Brno hosts an International Food Show in March, the International Consumer Goods Trade Fair in April, the Janáček Music Festival in June, the International Engineering Trade Fair in September, and the Brno International Music Festival in September and October. There are about a dozen other trade fairs a year as well.

Brno (pop. 388,000), the historical and cultural center of Moravia, initially does not appear to be one of the Czech Republic's lovelier cities, because of the heavy damage suffered in World War II. Yet if you spend a relaxed day here, the beauty of the old city center will gradually unfold. Explore the Špilberk Castle and the Gothic Cathedral of SS. Peter and Paul, take a walk down the main streets, survey the town museums, and spend time in the lush parks.

Not far from Vienna, Brno is located at the confluence of the Svratka and Svitava Rivers. The city, first mentioned in documents in 1091, enjoyed its golden age in the 14th century, when the city walls and the Špilberk Castle were built. Today Brno is one of the Czech Republic's largest trade centers, with frequent fairs displaying everything from high-tech electronics to pedigreed dogs.

WHAT TO SEE & DO

Špilberk Castle, in Staré Brno, off Husova.

Built in the 13th century by Czech King Přemysl Otakar II, Špilberk Castle has kept very busy over the centuries staving off invading armies. Defensive highlights include resistance of Hungarian King Matthias Corvinus in the 15th century, a three-month stalemate against superior Swedish forces in the 17th century, and an 18th-century affront to invading Prussian King Frederick II. The castle's many masters have included 15th-century Hussites, Swedes during the Thirty Years' War, and the Nazis, who executed 80,000 people in the castle dungeons. In 1742, the castle was transformed into a prison, with an extensive network of casemates added to the castle fortifications. A reputation for hideous torture—which may or may not have been deserved—attended Špilberk during Habsburg rule.

After being closed for renovation for several years, the casemates are the only reopened portion of the castle, featuring a well-designed exhibit on the Habsburg-era prison, replete with torture instruments. An exhibit on the history of Brno is scheduled to open soon. The excellent view from the castle merits the hike alone.

Telephone Number Advisory

Brno's telephone system is being updated, and I have made every effort to provide updated telephone numbers. However, many will likely change during the lifetime of this book. Eventually, all Brno numbers will have eight digits, but until then, numbers with five, six, and seven digits will also be used. If a number with fewer than eight digits does not work, it has been changed. Check the Brno yellow pages for the new listing.

Open: Tues–Sun 10am–4pm (last entrance 30 minutes before closing). **Directions:** From Husova, on the west side of the old town, take any of the surrounding paths and follow your nose until you reach the top.

Cathedral of Ss. Peter and Paul, Petrov ulice.

On a hilltop site once home to the old Přemyslid castle, this church was built in the late 11th and early 12th centuries. It was rebuilt in the baroque style in 1743, but later re-Gothicized just before World War I. Today it's one of the more architecturally interesting and unique of the Czech Republic's cathedrals as it fuses a Gothic style with baroque touches. The exterior appears pure Gothic, with tall, narrow lines, including two steeples added in 1905. The interior consists of soaring Gothic arches with baroque designs in between. There's a modern organ above the entrance into the church.

Admission: Free.

Open: Mon–Wed and Fri–Sat 6:30am–6pm, Thurs 6:30am–7:30pm, Sun 8:30am–6pm. **Directions:** From Zelný trh, walk west up Petrská, then turn left to the church.

Old Town Hall, Radnická 8.

The oldest secular building in Brno, from the 13th century, this structure is a hodgepodge of Gothic, Renaissance, and baroque styles. On the second floor you can see a meager selection of armor, coins, and photos inside the room where the town council met from the 13th century until 1935. Don't miss the locally famous Brno Dragon and Brno Wheel. You can also climb to the top of the Town Hall tower for a somewhat impressive vantage point on the old town.

Admission: 10 Kčs (35¢) adults, 5 Kčs (20¢) students.

Open: Tues–Sun 9am–5pm (last entrance 15 minutes before closing). **Directions:** Walk a block north down Radnická from Zelný trh.

Capuchin Monastery [Kapucínsky Klášter], Kapucinské náměstí.

The Capuchin Cloister is famous for its catacombs in which either an act of God or the unique ventilation has preserved bodies of famous Brno citizens, including Moritz Grimm, the architect who rebuilt the cathedral in the 18th century, and several members of his family. The bodies are displayed in open coffins, and skin and clothing are still visible. To see this unusual sight, enter the church door marked KAPUCÍNSKÁ HROBKA.

The church stands on a square that once housed Brno's coal market.

Admission: 10 Kčs (35¢) adults, 5 Kčs (20¢) students.

Open: Tues–Sat 9am–noon and 2–4:30pm, Sun 11–11:45am and 2–4:30pm. **Directions:** From Zelný trh, walk a block south.

Moravian Museum, Zelný trh 6. ☎ **222-41.**

A well-presented collection of stuffed birds, fish, deer, bears, and other animals. The museum is inside the Dietrichštejn Palace, a 17th-century early baroque structure where Russian Marshal Kutuzov prepared for the Battle of Austerlitz.

Admission: 8 Kčs (30¢) adults, 4 Kčs (15¢) students.

Open: Tues–Sun 9am–6pm. **Directions:** Exit Zelný trh from the southwest corner.

Ethnographic Museum, Kobližná 1. ☎ **262-82.**

Photos and displays on typical regional homes, costumes, painted Easter eggs, musical instruments, pottery, and other relics of Moravian culture.

Admission: 6 Kčs (20¢).

Open: Tues–Sun 9am–6pm. **Directions:** Walk to the northeast corner of Svobody náměstí.

WHERE TO STAY

PRIVATE ROOMS Good inexpensive hotels are seriously lacking in Brno, especially during trade shows, so it is fortunate that there are many private rooms available at the following agencies.

Taxatour, in the train station (☎ **05/42-21-48-03** or **42-21-48-05**), offers private rooms for 200 Kčs ($7.15) per person on the periphery, 350 Kčs ($12.50) per person in the center.

Čedok, at Divadelni 3 (☎ **05/231-79**), offers rooms starting at 350 Kčs ($12.50) per person.

Hotels

Hotel Astoria [formerly the Hotel Morava], Novobranská 3, 66221 Brno. ☎ **05/225-41** or **237-83**. 89 rms (6 with bath). TEL **Directions:** Take tram no. 1 or 18 one stop from the train station; or walk three blocks northeast from the train station, or one block from the bus station.

Rates (including breakfast): 510 Kčs ($18.20) single without shower, 595 Kčs ($21.25) single with shower, 680 Kčs ($24.30) double without shower, 1,020 Kčs ($36.45) double with shower, 1,060 Kčs ($37.85) double with bath. AE, DC, JCB, V.

Groups of guests often crowd the marble-lined lobby here in evening, many on their way to the hotel restaurant. The rooms themselves may not stir as much excitement, as they feature mismatched decor and furniture that was probably new in 1975. Yet despite poor hall lighting, some stained rugs, and areas that want for new paint, upkeep is generally good, and the location, just a block from the bus station, convenient.

Hotel U Jakuba, Jakubskí nám. 6, 66221 Brno. ☎ **05/42-21-07-95.** Fax 05/42-21-07-97. 37 rms (all with shower or bath, only 10 of which have toilets). TEL **Tram:** 4 from the train station.

Rates (including breakfast): 756 Kčs ($27) single with shower but no toilet; 932 Kčs ($33.30) double with shower but no toilet, 1,115 Kčs ($39.80) double with shower and toilet, 1,184 Kčs ($42.30) double with bath and toilet.

This hotel offers fair-sized, slightly worn rooms in which a curtain separates the bed from the rest of the room. Each room also has a one-channel radio, padded green doors, and older carpeting and couches. The communal toilets are clean, and the reception staff speak English and are friendly. The hotel is in the center of the Old Town, just across from the St. Jacob Church and two blocks from the Ethnographic Museum.

Hotel Avion, Česka 20, 60200 Brno. ☎ **05/277-97.** 55 rms (all with shower, only 1 with toilet). TV TEL **Tram:** 4 from the train station.

Rates: 615 Kčs ($21.95) single with shower but no toilet; 990 Kčs ($35.35) double with shower but no toilet, 1,625 Kčs ($58.05) double with shower and toilet.

After years of rather indifferent service to East Bloc guests, the Avion is having a bit of difficulty adjusting to the new budget travelers from the West. Despite the mediocre reception, the hotel boasts an excellent location, just a block and a half north of Svobody náměstí, within 10 minutes of most sights in town. The rooms are standard

B category, with the shower not far from the bed, separated by only a curtain. Unfortunately, the public bathrooms here are just passable.

WHERE TO EAT

Pegas, Jakubská 4. ☎ **42-21-01-04.**

Cuisine: BEER HALL. **Directions:** Exit náměstí Svobody north on Rašínova, walk one block, and take a right on Jakubská.
Prices: Soups 9–11 Kčs (30¢); main courses 48–134 Kčs ($1.70–$4.80).
Open: Daily 9am–midnight.

This "minipivovar"—a microbrewery that serves its product only on the premises—gets back to the roots of Czech beer tradition, the house brewery. Dominating the center of the convivial wood- and brass-decorated room, guarded like a queen bee by an arc of beer-quaffing locals, tourists, and trade-show attendees, are two enormous copper kettles, one for each of the two Pegas brands, dark and light. The menu, available in English, serves usual pub fare as well as some unusual dishes, like baked trout with caraway seeds, potato-meat-sausage soufflé, and "Chinese style" stir-fry. All go splendidly with smooth and snappy Pegas beer, which, you may agree with regulars, holds its own against other Czech beers.

Cérný Medvěd [Black Bear], Jakubské nám. 1. ☎ **42-21-45-48.**

Cuisine: CZECH. **Reservations:** Recommended. **Directions:** From Svobody náměstí, walk a block north and then take the first right.
Prices: Soups 27–30 Kčs ($1–$1.10); main courses 77–177 Kčs ($2.75–$6.30).
Open: Mon–Fri 11am–11pm, Sat 11am–midnight.

The Black Bear is a plush marriage of food and atmosphere—a dark and intimate spot where the candles on the tables and the flare of desserts flambéed are the only light. The service is excellent for a Czech restaurant, although only German and Czech are spoken. Make sure to reserve ahead.

En Route to Other Destinations

Taxatour operates a service that connects passengers with private automobile drivers who are going to the same destination. Sample prices (all far cheaper than normal train or bus fares) include: Vienna, 120 Kčs ($4.30); Kraków, 250 Kčs ($8.90); Berlin, 400 Kčs ($14.30); Copenhagen, 500 Kčs ($17.85); Frankfurt, 600 Kčs ($21.40); Zurich, 850 Kčs ($30.35); Paris or Rome, 1,200 Kčs ($42.85); and London, 2,000 Kčs ($71.40).

The office is open 23 hours and all the clerks speak at least some English.

16 Slovakia & the Tatra Mountains

GRACED WITH GENTLE ROLLING PLAINS IN THE WEST AND RUGGED MOUNTAINS IN the central and eastern regions, Slovakia comprises the eastern third of what was formerly Czechoslovakia. Since the Hungarians invaded Slovakia in A.D. 896 it has shared little history—or language or popular culture—with Bohemia and Moravia.

It was not until after World War I that the Czechs in Bohemia and Moravia and the Slovaks merged to create Czechoslovakia. Relations between the two peoples were not always smooth, and Slovaks often complained that Czechs have dominated the country. But Slovak demands for increased power and economic prosperity played an essential part in the reforms of 1968. After the Soviet invasion, reforms permitting Slovakia equality in a federal Czechoslovak state were the only significant changes allowed to remain from the Prague Spring. On January 1, 1993, the former country of Czechoslovakia divided into two republics: the Slovak Republic and the Czech Republic. The transition has been peaceful and borne with goodwill by both countries.

Czechs and Slovaks alike agree that nature has endowed Slovakia with some of its best. Two large mountain ranges, the Little Fatra and the Tatras, with peaks over 8,500 feet high, crown Slovakia. The forested, sparsely populated region east of the mountains is called Slovak's Paradise. Elsewhere in Slovakia you'll find untouched peasant hamlets and mountain folk who try to keep the old village ways alive. Slovakia is also home to Bratislava.

SEEING SLOVAKIA

Bratislava, the Slovak capital, is just across the border from Vienna, so I strongly suggest at least a quick stop in Vienna, either on your way to or from Slovakia. The Little Fatra around Zilina are easily accessible from Bratislava or Brno, but if you are willing to go a few hours further, you'll be rewarded with delicious alpine peaks in the High Tatras. Slovakia shares the Tatras with Poland, and if you have a Polish visa (not necessary for U.S. citizens) you should consider a visit to Zakopane (see "Zakopane and the Tatra Mountains," in Chapter 28 for a description).

In much of the region buses are faster than trains; see "Getting There" in the individual city descriptions for comparisons.

A Note on Accommodations

Privatization has come more slowly to Slovakia's tourist industry than to the Czech Republic's. Even though tourists are far less likely than during Communist years to join large package tours, tourist services remain highly group-oriented, and agencies such as Satur (formerly Čedok), Slovakoturist, and Tatratour continue to control most hotels. The agencies also often retain the sole right to offer discounts, resulting in the odd situation where a tourist will pay more by negotiating with the hotel directly than if by using a booking agent. An added frustration is the two-tier pricing system, with rates that rarely reflect the value of services; rates for Slovaks are set artificially low, whereas for foreigners they are artificially high. A sweep of liberalization and privatization could reorder the environment in a flash, but until then, consider using the large state-controlled booking agencies for most reservations. One benefit of this system is that you can order rooms in advance, through any Satur or Slovakoturist agency—whether in Prague, Bratislava, or elsewhere. Beware that agencies will attempt to book you in the more expensive hotels. You can specify hotels from this book to get around that.

What's Special About Slovakia & the Tatra Mountains

Castles

- Bratislava Castle, a political center for over 1,000 years, once home to the Hungarian monarchy.

Churches

- Bratislava's St. Martin's Cathedral, where Hungarian kings and queens were crowned for centuries.

Museums

- Town Hall Museum in Bratislava, with displays on Slovak history and original rooms, including intact dungeons.
- A diverse assortment of small museums in Bratislava, with exhibits ranging from medieval weapons to natural history and from clocks to folk art.

Mountain Resorts

- Stunning alpine peaks with ski slopes and hiking paths in the High Tatras, and more modest mountains closer to Prague and Bratislava in the Little Fatra.

1 Bratislava

225 miles SE of Prague, 86 miles SE of Brno

GETTING THERE • By Plane You can fly from Prague in about 50 minutes. One-way seven-day advance fares are 2,350 Kčs ($83.95). Take bus no. 24 from the airport into town.

• **By Train** Vienna is only 1½ hours away by train, and Budapest is 3 hours away. The express train from Prague takes 5 hours and costs 206 Kčs ($7.35) in first class and 137 Kčs ($4.90) in second class.

Bratislava's Main Train Station (Hlavná Stanica) is at Predstaničnénám. (☎ **482-75**). The station has a post office open 24 hours for telephone calls, and Monday through Friday from 6:30am to 9:30pm, on Saturday from 7am to 8pm, and on Sunday from 9am to 8pm for letters. There's also a 24-hour luggage check off Platform 1. To get into town, take tram no. 1 or 13.

Some domestic trains, especially from the southeastern part of the country, arrive and leave from Bratislava Nové Město, northeast of the center at Tomásikova (☎ **607-48**). Take tram no. 6 into the town center.

• **By Bus** The express bus from Prague's Florenc station is faster than the train at 4 hours and 40 minutes, at a cost of 180 Kčs ($6.45). The 2- to 2½-hour journey from Brno costs 98 Kčs ($3.50).

The bus station (☎ **632-13** or **21-22-22**) is east of central Bratislava on Mlynské Nivy, across from the Ondrejský Cintorín (a cemetery). You can check your bags at the station daily from 5am to 10pm, or in lockers daily around the clock. There's a post office just to the left of the main exit, open Monday through Friday from 7:30am to 6pm and on Saturday from 7:30 to 10am. To get to the center, take bus no. 53 or 57 or trolleybus no. 210 or 211. If you prefer to walk, it will take you about 20 minutes heading west down Dunajská.

• **By Boat** The boat from Vienna's Reichsbrücke station (near Mexicoplatz) departs twice daily from mid-April through mid-October, costing 210 AS ($17.95) one way or 330 AS ($28.20) round-trip. The trip takes 1¼ hours.

From Budapest, boats depart the Vigado tér landing on Tuesday, Wednesday, Friday, and Saturday from early May through early September. The fare is 830 AS ($70.95) one way and 1,200 AS ($102.60) round-trip. The trip takes 3½ hours.

Children under 6 travel free, and those between 6 and 15 receive a 50% discount. The fares are payable in the local currency, based on the daily AS or DM exchange rate, or, if you prefer, you may pay directly in hard currency.

Boats arrive at Bratislava's Danubius Station at Fajnorovo nábreži 2 (☎ **36-22-58, 36-22-62,** or **36-22-66**). You can either walk northwest into the town center, or take tram no. 13.

SPECIAL EVENTS There are a number of festivals in Bratislava, including: the Bratislava Lyre, a festival of popular music in late May; the Istropolitana Festival of student theater from late June to early July; the Bratislava Summer, a series of cultural programs in July and August; the Bratislava Classical Music Festival in late September to early October; and Bratislava Jazz Days, in October.

CITY LAYOUT Bratislava is a large city with many residential districts, but the town center is compact, located just north of the Danube River. You can get your bearings by locating the castle (Hrad), perched on a hill at the southwest corner of town, just off the Danube River—the town center lies immediately east.

At the foot of Castle Hill is the north-south Staromeská, a highway running south to the most SNP, the Slovak National Uprising Bridge. The Old Town streets immediately east of Staromeská are somewhat haphazardly arrayed and hard to remember, but the major squares include Hviezdoslavovo námestie, a long piazza with a small park at the center; and Hlavné námestie, site of the Old Town Hall and the main square of old Bratislava, where markets and executions once took place. Most of the streets in the Old Town core are closed to traffic.

Immediately north of the Old Town core is námestie SNP, with a small pedestrian mall, Poštová ulica, running north of it. Southeast of námestie SNP is a large traffic intersection at Kamenné námestie, site of Prior, the town's largest department store. To the south of this square is Štúrova ulica, another large avenue leading toward the river.

GETTING AROUND • By Bus and Tram Local buses and trams cost 5 Sk (15¢). Tickets must be bought at newsstands before boarding; most stops have yellow automatic machines that sell tickets for 5-Sk coins. A day pass valid for all public transport can be bought at selected kiosks and tobacco shops in the town center for 20 Sk (65¢), as well as at the DPHMB public transportation office, inside the passage under Mierove námestie, near Hotel Forum. You can also buy a public transportation map here.

• **By Taxi** Taxis are cheaper than in Prague, but the efficiency of the public transportation system affords you the option to avoid them altogether. Rates are the same day and night, seven days a week. A crosstown taxi should cost about 90 Sk ($3.20). Three of the best taxi services are VIP Taxi (☎ **30-11-11**), Paladio Yellow Express (☎ **31-31-31** or **49-79-78**), and Unitax (☎ **72-72-41**).

ESSENTIALS Bratislava's area code is 07.

INFORMATION Unfortunately, none of Bratislava's entry points is equipped with tourist information. The best source of information is the Bratislava Information

Service (BIS), at Panská 18 (☎ **07/33-37-15** or **33-43-25;** ☎ and fax 07/33-43-70). In addition to the normal tourist information services and tour bookings, they also book hotel and private rooms, and have information about Bratislava youth hostels. Make sure to ask them for a copy of *Kam V Bratislava*, a monthly Slovak publication sold here. It has a comprehensive listing of concerts, films, art exhibitions, and other events in town.

BIS is open June to September, Monday through Friday from 8am to 6pm and on Saturday from 8am to 1pm; from October to May, Monday through Friday from 8am to 4:30pm and on Saturday from 8am to 1pm.

BIS has a 24-hour computerized information terminal on the street in front of the office; it provides addresses and directions to various hotels and restaurants.

Slovakoturist, at Panská ul. 13 (☎ **33-50-78** or **33-34-66**), is less well equipped to provide services within Bratislava than either BIS or Satur. However, as they control many hotels throughout Slovakia, they are very useful in helping plan further travel into the country. They are open Monday through Friday from 9am to 6pm, and on Saturday from 8am to noon.

TRAVEL SERVICES • Airline Office The main ČSA office is at Štúrova 13 (☎ **07/31-12-17** or **31-12-06**). It's open Monday through Friday from 7am to 7pm, and on Saturday from 8am to noon.

• Car Rental BIS sells a list for 5 Sk (15¢) of 46 agencies that rent cars. Favorit Car, at Pri vinohradoch 275 (☎ **28-41-52**), and Slovcar, at Prievozská 30 (☎ **624-27**), are recommended as especially inexpensive. Other proven agencies are Auto Danubius, Trnavská 31 (☎ **670-96**); Karol Hučka, Uderníсka 6 (☎ **35-25-25**); and Pilárik, Jaskovy rad 205 (☎ **37-52-39**). More expensive options include Hertz, in the Hotel Forum (☎ **34-81-45**), and Europcar, at letisko Ivanka (☎ **22-02-85**).

Fast Facts: Slovakia & the Tatra Mountains

American Express A full-service agent is soon scheduled to open up at Tatratour, Františkanske nám. 3 (☎ **33-50-12**). At present, services for cardholders available through Tatratour include issuance, exchange, and replacement of lost traveler's checks and cards. Hours are Monday 9am to 4pm; Tuesday, Wednesday, and Friday 9am to 4:30pm; and Thursday 9am to 6pm.

Consulates A number of countries now have consulates in the Slovak capital, including those of Eastern European countries, where you can make visa inquiries.

- **United States,** Hviezdoslavova nám. 4 (☎ **33-08-61**)
- **Great Britain,** Grősslingová 35 (☎ **36-44-20**)
- **Bulgaria,** Kuzmányho 1 (☎ **31-53-08**)
- **Romania,** Fraňakrál'a 11 (☎ **49-16-65**)
- **Russia,** Godrova 4 (☎ **31-34-68**)
- **Ukraine,** Radvanská 35 (☎ **31-26-51**).

Currency Exchange The two downtown branches of Všeobecna Uverová Banka, at nám. SNP 19 or Dunajská 24, offer exchange at standard rates, charging only a 1% commission on traveler's checks and no commission at all on cash. The exchange windows are open Monday through Friday from 7:30 to 11:30am and noon to 5:30pm, and on Saturday from 8am to noon. Satur, BIS, and others charge higher commissions.

Dry Cleaning You can get 24-hour service at Hviezdoslavovo nám. 23 (☎ **33-38-11**), open Monday through Friday: in winter from 6am to 7pm, and in summer from 11am to 7pm.

Newspapers Several newsstands in Bratislava carry a good selection of English-language newspapers and magazines, including the *International Herald Tribune, USA Today,* a variety of British dailies, *Time,* and *Newsweek.* They also carry Prague's two English-language papers, *Prognosis* and the *Prague Post.* One newsstand, Interpress Slovakia, at Laurinská 9 (open Monday to Friday 6am to 6pm, Saturday 6am to 1pm), is just up the street from BIS. Another is on the pedestrian bridge at the north end of Michalská. Some of the larger hotels also carry Western papers and magazines.

Post Office and Telephone The main post office is at the corner of námestie SNP and Uršulínska. You can also make telephone calls 24 hours a day at the central train station, and send letters there Monday through Friday from 6:30am to 9:30pm, on Saturday from 7am to 8pm, and on Sunday from 9am to 8pm. There's also a post and telephone office at the bus station, open Monday through Friday from 7:30am to 6pm and on Saturday from 7:30 to 10am.

You can make international telephone calls 24 hours a day at Kolárska ulica 12, off Kamenné. They also have Italian, Austrian, and Czechoslovakian telephone directories here. The telephone room at nám. SNP 36 is open Monday through Friday 7am to 9pm, Saturday 7am to 5pm, and Sunday 7am to 2pm.

Just 35 miles east of Vienna, Bratislava (pop. 444,000) is the capital and largest city of the Slovak Republic.

Archeological finds indicate that the area was inhabited as long ago as 4000 B.C. The Romans fortified the area around Bratislava from the 1st to the 4th century A.D. because it was an important location on the Amber Route, which went north to the Baltic Sea. By the 5th and 6th centuries the first Slavs had migrated here.

In A.D. 906 the Hungarian Arpád dynasty conquered Bratislava, and the city remained a part of Hungary until 1918. After the Turks threatened Budapest in the 16th century, Bratislava became Hungary's capital from 1536 to 1784. During these years some 19 Hungarian coronations took place here. In 1918 the victorious Allied powers, drawing up a postwar Europe, incorporated Bratislava and the rest of Slovakia into the new state of Czechoslovakia.

With rapid reconstruction and growth in the postwar period, the city known to Hungarians as Pozsony and to Germans as Pressburg gave way to a clearly Soviet Bratislava. The principal monuments of that period—the unfortunate Danube bridge and highway, bifurcating the old town into unnatural halves; the smokestacks and housing blocks that compete for control of the horizon—remind one that the Slovak capital's history has rarely been determined by Slovaks.

Independence has at last given the city control of its lease, and with that, an odd fascination that museum-piece Prague, tidily hidden behind the petticoats of historical irrelevance for 300 years, cannot boast. Where Prague obsesses about eternity, Bratislava seems to teeter on the precipice of dramatic change. With the mishmash of historical reminders everywhere, there is a feeling that the city's fortunes could change suddenly, either for better or for worse. Prague, by comparison, seems only able to grow cafés. Such precipitous possibility, and with that the possibility of relevance and transformation, give Bratislava a gutsy charm.

WHAT TO SEE & DO

The Top Attractions

Bratislava Castle [Bratislavsky Hrad], on the hilltop west of the town center. ☎ 31-14-44.

First mentioned in documents in A.D. 907, the Bratislava Castle fought off attacks by the Tartars, the Turks, and the Czech Hussites. When Bratislava was the capital of Hungary, the castle housed both the Hungarian Parliament and the nation's most valuable crown jewels.

The rather plain exterior is the result of frequent restorations. In 1811 a fire destroyed much of the castle, and from 1953 to 1962, the regime renovated with its usual heavy cement hand. Today, it serves as the executive office of the president of Slovakia and the meeting place for the Slovak National Council, continuing over a millennium of political activity in the castle.

The castle's archeological and historical exhibits, which used to occupy the third and fourth floors, have been closed for yet another spate of renovation. There are plans to permanently move the collections to an adjacent building, to be called the History Museum of Bratislava. For the time being, you can visit the castle treasury, directly to the left as you enter the castle courtyard.

Admission: 8 Sk (25¢) adults, 4 Sk (15¢) students, free for children under 6.

Open: Tues–Sun 10am–noon and 2–4pm. **Trolleybus:** 210, 213, or 217.

★ **Town Hall [Mestské Muzeum],** Primaciálne nám. 1. ☎ **33-46-90.**

The 14th- to 15th-century Old Town Hall contains one of Bratislava's more interesting museums on the town's history. Highlights include displays on famous residents of the past, archeology of the region (including a piece of bread 5,000 years old!), objects associated with the Hungarian coronations that took place in Bratislava, and Mozart's first piano from when he was 6 years old. Many of the rooms show the original Town Hall decorations, such as the **Law Room,** with an elaborate ceiling fresco—an allegory of justice—and the **Pompeii Room** with more ceiling frescoes. Downstairs, you can walk through the dungeons where prisoners were executed.

Admission: 10 Sk (30¢) adults, 3 Sk (10¢) students.

Open: Tues–Sun 10am–5pm (last entrance at 4:15pm). **Directions:** From Bratislava's information office, walk a block north and then take the first right down a block.

More Attractions

Medieval Weapons Museum, in St. Michael's Tower, Michalská 24. ☎ **33-30-44.**

A 14th-century tower once part of the city walls, this structure now contains medieval swords, armor, uniforms, 18th-century rifles and gunpowder horns, and other weapons. The tower was originally built in medieval style, but redone in the early 16th century with Renaissance styling. You can enjoy a view over the Old Town from the top of the tower.

Admission: 8 Sk (25¢) adults, 2 Sk (6¢) students.

Open: Wed–Mon 10am–5pm. **Directions:** From the BIS tourist office, walk two blocks northwest and turn right onto Michalská.

Pharmaceutical Museum [Expózicia Farmácie], Michalská 26. ☎ **33-35-96.**

Located adjacent to the Medieval Weapons Museum, this genial collection, stuffed with all manner of jars, flasks and vials, re-creates the look of a pharmacy from about 250 years ago. The building itself used to house one of Bratislava's oldest pharmacies,

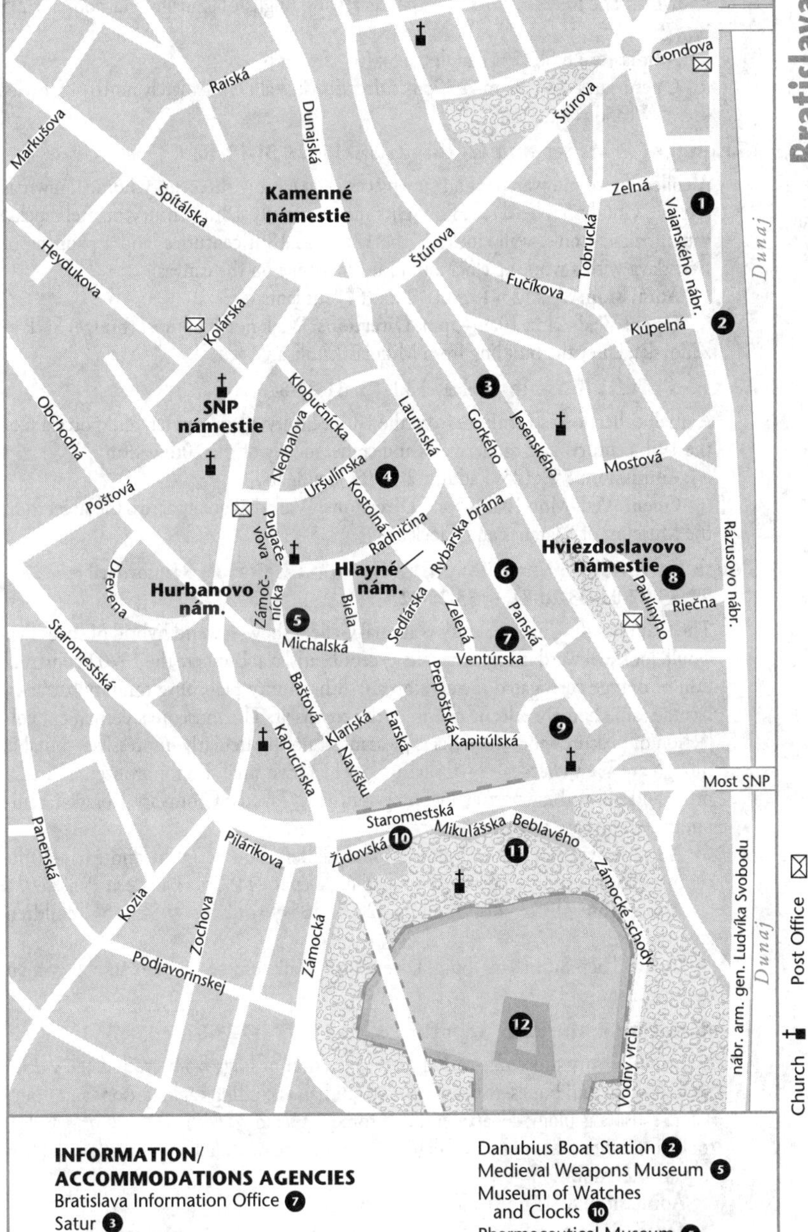

INFORMATION/ ACCOMMODATIONS AGENCIES

Bratislava Information Office 7
Satur 3
Slovakoturist 6

ATTRACTIONS

Arts and Crafts Museum 11
Bratislava Castle 12
Danubius Boat Station 2
Medieval Weapons Museum 5
Museum of Watches and Clocks 10
Pharmaceutical Museum 5
Slovak National Gallery 8
Slovak National Museum 1
St. Martin's Cathedral 9
Town Hall 4

known as The Red Crab. Ask for the interesting English-language tour book for 2.5 Sk (7¢).

Admission: 8 Sk (25¢) adults, 2 Sk (6¢) students.

Open: Tues–Sun 10am–4:30pm. **Directions:** Walk immediately north of the Medieval Weapons Museum.

Museum of Watches and Clocks, Židovská 1. ☎ **31-19-40.**

A collection of old watches and timepieces inside a tiny three-story home known as "At the Good Shepherd's." Highlights include lovely 18th-century mantel clocks, watchmakers' tools, wall clocks of the 17th and 18th centuries, and a painting of Bratislava with a working clock built into the scene on the canvas.

Admission: 8 Sk (25¢) adults, 2 Sk (6¢) students.

Open: Wed–Mon 10am–5pm. **Directions:** Walk north of most (bridge) SNP to Židovská; enter the building from Mikulášska ulica.

Arts and Crafts Museum, Beblavého 1. ☎ **31-27-84.**

A small collection of furniture from the 18th century, glass, pewter, and porcelain of the 19th century, and modern arts and crafts, mostly of the 20th century.

Admission: 8 Sk (25¢) adults, 2 Sk (6¢) students.

Open: Wed–Mon 10am–5pm. **Directions:** Walk diagonally across the street from the Museum of Watches and Clocks.

Slovak National Gallery [Slovenská Narodná Galéria], Rázusovo nábrežie 2. ☎ **33-07-02, 33-20-81,** or **33-20-82.**

The main building of the Slovak National Gallery shows a weird hybrid of styles that would look awkward in any other city except Bratislava. But here the 1970's construction of orange corrugated metal, atop an 18th-century Habsburg military barracks, has the same homely eclectic charm of the city itself. The museum's permanent collection of obscure modern works is pleasant, if not particularly impressive—notable though are a few charcoals by Oskar Kokoschka, two small Rodin bronzes, a Picasso print, and a disturbing portrait by Hungarian artist Tivodar Csontvary-Kosztka. Temporary exhibits are consistently excellent, however.

Another wing of the Slovak National Gallery houses 19th- and early-20th-century Slovak art in the newly renovated belle-époque **Palffy Palace** at Panská 9.

Admission: 40 Sk ($1.30) adults, 20 Sk (65¢) students, 5 Sk (15¢) children and seniors.

Open: Tues–Sun 10am–6pm. **Directions:** Walk across from the Hotel Devin on the riverfront.

Slovak National Museum, Vajanského nábrežie 2. ☎ **33-29-85** or **33-07-91.**

A natural-history museum, with a huge collection of bugs from around the world, human skulls and bones, fish, and stuffed animals including eagles, bison, and bears. There's also a geology department, and some archeology, with early armor, jewelry, tools, and other relics of human habitation in the region. Walk up to the fourth floor to start the exhibition.

Admission: 8 Sk (25¢) adults, 2 Sk (6¢) students.

Open: Tues–Sun 9am–5pm. **Directions:** Walk across the Danubius boat landing off the river.

St. Martin's Cathedral, Rudnayovo námestie.

When Hungary ruled Bratislava, its kings and queens were crowned in this 14th-century Gothic cathedral. At the center you'll see a steeple 275 feet tall, with a clock on its facade. Inside is a rare lead equestrian statue of St. Martin. Next to the church is a fragment of the original town fortifications, running beside the highway.

Admission: Free.

Open: Mon–Fri 8am–noon and 1–4pm, Sat 8am–noon, Sun for services only. **Directions:** From the BIS information office, walk two blocks southwest.

Slavin Monument, in Horský park.

A tribute to the Soviet effort in World War II, this monument shows a statue of Victory in the form of a Soviet soldier. From the monument you have a fine panorama of all of Bratislava.

Built in 1960 to celebrate the 15th anniversary of the Red Army liberation of Slovakia, this monstrous piece of socialist realism is one of the best examples of that genre still extant in the country.

Admission: Free.

Open: Daily 24 hours. **Trolleybus:** 216 or 217.

Observation Deck, most SNP (bridge).

This garish, showpiece bridge was built in the 1960s. Erected on what was the Jewish district of the city, the bridge divides the Old Town Center into two pieces, which are extremely difficult to pass between. The observation deck, an errant flying saucer lodged atop the bridge's only suspension tower, provides a wonderful panoramic view of Bratislava and its environs. You need not eat in the overpriced restaurant which occupies the entire deck. The tower does tend to sway a bit in the wind, so those with weak stomachs should note the weather before ascending.

Admission: 10 Sk (30¢).

Open: Mon 1–10pm, Tues–Sun 10am–10pm.

Recreational Activities

If you want to take a break from sightseeing, consider a visit to **Zlaté Piesky** (☎ **65-170**), the ever-popular lake on the outskirts of Bratislava, where all Slovakia seems to gather on hot summer afternoons. You can take a refreshing swim, rent a pedalboat, play minigolf or tennis, or just relax. Admission to the lake area is 14 Sk (45¢) for adults, half price for children. There's a 140-Sk ($4.50) charge per hour for tennis. The complex is open daily from 9am to 6 or 7pm. To get here, take bus no. 110 to the end of the line, or bus no. 32, 35, 106, 108, or 114.

WHERE TO STAY

Accommodations Agencies

BIS (the Bratislava Information Service) at Panská 18 (☎ **33-37-15** or **33-43-25**) books both private rooms and hotels. They are open June to September, Monday through Friday from 8am to 6pm and on Saturday from 8am to 1pm; from October to May, Monday through Friday from 8am to 4:30pm and on Saturday from 8am to 1pm.

The private rooms cost about 500 Sk ($16.15) per person per night in the center, 300 Sk ($9.70) on the periphery. In July and August several university dormitories are converted into youth hostels; these locations change from year to year, so are not listed here (one permanent summer hostel, however, is listed; see "Youth Hostels," below). Beds cost about 150 to 200 Sk ($4.85 to $6.45) per night, with ISIC cardholders paying at the lower end of the scale. BIS is the best source of information about the locations of these summer youth hostels.

Satur (formerly Cedok) at Jesenského 5 (☎ **36-77-28** or **36-76-24**), handles both private room and hotel reservations. Hotel rooms cost from 750 to 2,500 Sk ($24.20 to $80.65) for a double room, depending on location. Private rooms cost 320 Sk ($10.30) for singles, 520 Sk ($16.75) for doubles. This office is immense, occupying nearly a city block. Go to Door 3 for all accommodations bookings. Satur is open Monday through Friday from 9am to 5pm, and on Saturday from 9am to noon; in July and August, the weekday hours are extended to 6pm.

Slovakoturist, at Panská 13 (☎ **33-34-66** or **33-50-78**), books only hotel rooms, but can also book rooms anywhere else in Slovakia. They're open Monday through Friday from 9am to 6pm, and on Saturday from 8am to noon.

Hotels

Hotel Krym, Šafárikovo nám. 7, 81102 Bratislava. ☎ **07/32-54-71** to **32-54-73.** 42 rms (1 with bath, 8 with shower but no toilet). TEL **Tram:** 13 from the train station. **Bus:** 23 from the bus station.

Rates: 650 Sk ($20.95) single without bath, 830 Sk ($26.75) single with bath; 930 Sk ($33.20) double without bath, 1,160 Sk ($37.40) double with shower, 1,610 Sk ($51.95) double with shower and toilet; 1,440 Sk ($46.45) triple without bath, 2,010 Sk ($64.85) triple with shower and toilet.

Located two blocks north of the river, this is the only budget hotel within reasonable walking distance of the center. Despite its rather scuffed furniture and socialist-era decoration, it manages to be quite cheerful, with colorful carpet runners in the halls and framed prints and radios in each room. Some rooms have TVs. Those in the front face the clatter of frequent trams and may be too noisy for light sleepers. The hotel fills up very quickly in the summer.

Hotel Dukla, nám. Dulovo 1, 82108 Bratislava. ☎ **07/21-29-07** or **21-31-81.** 80 rms (all with bath). TV TEL **Bus:** 23 from the train station. **Directions:** Walk east for about five minutes from the bus station.

Rates (including breakfast): 1,320 Sk ($42.60) old double, 1,700 Sk ($54.85) new double. AE, DC, EU, JCB, MC, V.

The "old" doubles have themselves been fairly recently renovated, decorated with dark-red rugs, prints on the wall, and radios. New rooms share the lobby's swoopy, modern, deco-ish look with color-coordinated decor all around, tasteful furniture, and large televisions. Many rooms overlook a square, which, if not particularly beautiful, is quiet. The hotel is east of the town center, a 15-minute walk into town.

Junior Hotel Sputnik, Drieňová 14, 82101 Bratislava. ☎ **07/23-80-84** or **23-43-40.** Telex 92144. 95 rms (all with bath). TEL **Bus:** 22 from the train station or 38 from the bus station.

Rates: 850 Sk ($27.40) single; 1,350 Sk ($43.55) double; 1,800 Sk ($58.05) triple. Visitors with an ISIC card pay 400 Sk ($12.90) per person. AE, MC, V.

The Sputnik, which opened in 1982, is a large, modern six-story building, with a garish, spacey indoor atrium where young people meet at a bar on the first floor at all hours. Rooms have prints on the walls, dark-wood furniture, and hand-held showers. Lighting is a bit dim, but wall-to-wall windows allow a lot of light by day. The hotel is a short bus ride west into town, located on the banks of a small lake, which, unfortunately, is polluted so you can't swim in it.

Dining/Entertainment: Budget restaurant (open daily from 7am to 9pm), day bar, disco club in the basement.

Hotel Bratislava, Urxova 9, 82663 Bratislava. ☎ **07/23-90-00.** Telex 092336. 344 rms (all with bath). TEL **Tram:** 9 or 12, about 10 stops from the city center.

Rates (including breakfast): $46 single; $62 double. AE, DC, MC, V.

Unless you have a car, leave this as your last pick, for it's fairly far from the center in the eastern part of town. Almost indistinguishable from the hulking housing blocks around it, this hotel is a throwback to the bureaucrat's utopia of 1977. Rooms, while fairly modern, are a bit seedy with age, an impression reinforced by their shocking orange upholstery. Because of its remote location, tour groups often stay here.

Dining/Entertainment: Atrium courtyard café with skylight, hanging plants, and a fountain at the center; there's also a casino.

Youth Hostels

Youth hostels are open only in July and August, and since the locations tend to change from year to year, you are advised to check at BIS for the current addresses. That said, it seems that at least one location (see below) is used every summer for a youth hostel:

Youth Hostel Bernolák, Sd. J. Hronca, Bernolákova 1, 81107 Bratislava. ☎ **07/25-70-03** or **279-64-96.** Hundred of rooms (all with shower and toilet). **Tram:** 2, 3, 8, or 14 from the train station. **Trolleybus:** 210 or any from the train or bus station. **Bus:** 22, 23, or 24 from the bus station; or 24, 37, or 57 from the airport.

Rates (including breakfast): 180 Sk ($5.80). ISIC cardholders get about a 25% discount.

Run by an extremely friendly group of mostly English-speaking Slovak students, this youth hostel has beds for very low prices. Friends arriving together can get a room together; otherwise you are put with other travelers. This hostel, like all others, is in a university dormitory, and the rooms are consequently well worn. There's sometimes access to a swimming pool, a sauna, and a fitness room. There is also a bar and a disco on the premises.

WHERE TO EAT

Vináreň U Čierneiio Orla/Café Amadeus, Obchodná ul. 11. ☎ **33-53-58.**

Cuisine: SLOVAK. **Tram:** 1, 6, 7, 9, or 13. **Directions:** Walk to the west end of námestie SNP, and make a right onto Obchodná.

Prices: Soups 10–16 Sk (30¢–50¢); main courses 40–105 Sk ($1.30–$3.40); half liter of beer 13.60 Sk (45¢).

Open: Vináreň, Sun–Thurs 10am–midnight, Fri–Sat 10am–2am; café, daily 7am–11pm.

This excellent restaurant is good enough to challenge any prejudice against Central European food. Soups, meat dishes, and turkey dishes are all interestingly seasoned and well prepared. *Slovenska pochutna* ("Slovak pocket")—a heavenly rendering of meat with mushrooms and onions in a husky potato pancake—is highly recommended. The atmosphere, a conflation of wine cellar and beer hall, is elegant but informal, convivial and not rowdy. Three different subterranean rooms supply a measure of intimacy while assuring plenty of seating. Cafe Amadeus upstairs has the same menu but the atmosphere and clientele of a beatnik watering hole. Stein, the local malt beverage, packs a wallop.

Vinaren Velkí Františkani, Františkánske námestie 10. ☎ **33-30-73.**

Cuisine: SLOVAK. **Reservations:** Recommended. **Directions:** Walk a block north of the Old Town.
Prices: Soup 12–18 Sk (40¢–60¢); main courses 59–173 Sk ($1.90–$5.60). Cover charge for music 50 Sk ($1.60). AE, DC, MC, V.
Open: Dinner only, daily 5pm–1am.

This romantic restaurant dating from 1347 has three different dining areas: an indoor restaurant, a cellar with Gypsy band music, and a small courtyard in warm weather. A Gypsy band plays in the cellar, and the headwaiter will appear at your table to collect the music fee as soon as you sit down.

Only beef and pork are served; specialties include *prešporska pochútka obložená* (hot pork with pepperoni) and *hovädzie filé obložené* (beefsteak in tomato sauce with paprika and cheese). Unfortunately, the menu is only in Slovak and nobody here seems to speak English, despite a large number of tourist groups.

★ **U Mamičky,** Michalská 9. ☎ **33-46-18.**

Cuisine: MACEDONIAN. **Reservations:** Recommended. **Directions:** From St. Michael's Tower, walk one block south.
Prices: Salads 30–40 Sk (95¢–$1.30); main courses 100–150 and 250 Sk ($3.25–$4.85 and $8.05); desserts 40 Sk ($1.30).
Open: Daily 11am–11pm.

This is a distinctive and elegant dining experience, one that perhaps reflects Bratislava's true nature as a cosmopolitan crossroads. Macedonian cuisine, from the former Yugoslav Republic of Macedonia, is marked by its reliance on Mediterranean vegetables and legumes, grilled meats, and intensely sweet Turkish-style desserts. All main dishes, featuring fresh cuts of pork, beef, chicken, or veal, are charcoal-grilled over an open range. Vegetarians can assemble a meal from among the bean appetizers, salads, and grilled vegetables listed on the English menu. The pristine whitewashed dining room features linen tablecloths, heavy flatware, and Turkish touches such as hanging kilims, straw screens between tables, and a general airiness throughout.

The snack bar at the front of the restaurant is an excellent lunch spot, offering the same menu but in smaller portions and prices.

Flauta, Ventúrska 10.

Cuisine: VEGETARIAN. **Reservations:** Recommended Sat–Sun. **Directions:** Walk to the rear left-hand side of the Mozart House courtyard.
Prices: Main courses 30–50 Sk (95¢–$1.60).
Open: Thurs–Tues 11am–11pm.

This vegetarian tea house is located in the back left side of the Mozart House courtyard. There's a wide selection of herbal teas and a small but enticing selection of well-prepared dishes. The menu is basically vegetarian, but duck is available in season, and some dishes include bacon.

British Council Café and Reading Room, Panská 17. ☎ **33-10-74,** ext. 28.

Cuisine: CAFE. **Directions:** Across the street from BIS.
Prices: Coffee 8–28 Sk (25¢–90¢); snacks 20–39 Sk (65¢–$1.25).
Open: Mon–Thurs 10am–8:30pm, Fri 10am–6pm.

A pretty little place rimmed by black marble-top counters, this is an excellent place for a midday meal. A delicious homemade soup of the day, salads, all manner of coffee drinks, and, on occasion, Indian specialties are offered.

Across the hall is a public reading room abundantly supplied with newspapers, magazines, and reference tomes, also operated by the British Council.

Restaurant Stará Sladovna ["Mammoth"], Cintorínska 32. ☎ **36-16-20.**

Cuisine: SLOVAK/ITALIAN. **Directions:** From the south side of the Hotel Kyjev, walk east on Cintorínska to the end of the street.

Prices: Salads 25–60 Sk (80¢–$1.95); pizza and pasta 55–100 Sk ($1.80–$3.25); main dishes 30–164 Sk (95¢–$5.30); desserts 8–11 Sk (25¢–35¢); half liter of beer 20 Sk (65¢).

Open: Daily 10am–10pm (garden opens at noon).

Equal parts country-western bar and Slavic beer hall, "Mammoth" or "Mamout" as the locals call it, may spawn a whole new genre of watering hole. Eastern Europe's largest beer hall, with 1,600 seats, it's located in a converted hops warehouse (in use from 1872 to 1976). Two separate restaurants, a billiards hall, a dance floor, and nightly live music ensure a three-ring-circus of revelry.

Slovak and Czech specialties are prepared on the first floor, Italian specialties on the second, and grilled foods are offered in the garden to the right. The food is better than in most beer halls I've been to, and offered in great variety—100 different dishes. The Stará Sladovna is a lively place, with the Revival Jazz Band playing from 6 to 10pm on Thursday; folk music on Wednesday, Saturday, and Sunday; and on Friday, good lord, country music.

Note: Check your bill. If you're sure your bill is mistaken, the waiters will eventually lower it accordingly.

EVENING ENTERTAINMENT

For information on cultural events, go to **BIS,** at Laurinská 1 (☎ **33-44-15**). They sell *Kam V Bratislava,* a monthly Slovak publication listing concerts, films, art exhibitions, and other events in town; there's a small English-language section in the center of the magazine.

The main performance halls are the **Slovak National Theater,** Hviezdoslavovo námestie (☎ **552-28**), for opera and ballet, where tickets usually cost 150 Kčs ($5.35); and the **Reduta,** Palackého 2 (☎ **333-351**), seat of the Slovak Philharmonic Orchestra, which sells tickets from 1 to 6pm for 40 to 150 Kčs ($1.40 to $5.35).

For other concert or film tickets, go to the **BIS ticket office** on Nedbalova ulica (☎ **33-40-59**), open Monday through Friday from 8am to noon and 2:30 to 4:30pm.

Other evening activities in Bratislava center largely around long, leisurely dinners, or pub crawling in Bratislava's old town.

NETWORKS & RESOURCES

For information on the student scene in Bratislava, visit **UNIA,** the Union of Slovak Students, on the first floor at Leškova 5 (☎ **49-71-46** or **49-73-09**). Open Monday through Friday from 9am to 5pm, the office is staffed by friendly students who are pleased to meet foreigners. If you're unable to find out anything about summer youth hostels through BIS, you can try asking someone here, though this is definitely not an accommodations office.

The main office of **CKM,** the Czechoslovak student agency, at Hviezdoslavovo nám. 16 (☎ **33-16-07**), sells ISIC and IYHF cards, as well as Interrail passes, but doesn't give information on youth hostels or student housing. They're open Monday through Friday from 9am to noon and 1 to 4pm.

MOVING ON

BY TRAIN All train tickets, domestic and international, can be bought in crowns at the train station. Frequent trains depart for Budapest, Vienna, Prague, and numerous other destinations.

BY BUS The four daily buses to Vienna cost 75 AS ($6.40). In theory it's still necessary to pay in hard currency, but that may not be enforced. The once-weekly (Friday) Hungarian bus to Budapest bases the fare on the Hungarian forint, though you can also pay in crowns or hard currency; it's likely to cost about $14 to $18. Ask at Satur or the bus station for more information.

In addition to these and other international routes, of course, buses depart Bratislava for all corners of the Czech and Slovak Republics.

BY BOAT See "Getting There: By Boat" above in this chapter for schedules and fares. Though fares are based on the Austrian schilling, Czech crowns may be used in purchasing the tickets. Boats leave from the Danubius Station at Fajnorovo nábreži 2 (☎ **595-27, 595-16,** or **595-22**).

2 Žilina & the Little Fatra

125 miles NE of Bratislava, 245 miles SE of Prague, 88 miles W of Poprad

GETTING THERE • By Train The express train from Bratislava takes about 3 hours and costs 155 Sk ($5) in first class, 103 Sk ($3.30) in second class. The express from Prague takes about 6½ hours, for 225 Kčs ($8.05) in first class, 150 Kčs ($5.35) in second class.

The train station (☎ **313-04**) is northeast of the center of Žilina. To get into town, walk straight ahead down Národná ulica.

• By Bus Žilina's bus station (☎ **209-50**) is a block east of the train station on Hviezdoslavova ulica. To get into town, walk a block west to the train station, then turn left up Národná ulica.

ESSENTIALS Žilina's telephone area code is 089.

ORIENTATION The pedestrians-only Národná ulica leads west from the bus and train stations to a large square Andrej Hlinku, which has a K-mart on the corner. Beyond this square continuing west up the gradient, past the two-steepled Parish Church of the Holy Trinity, lies Zilina's historic core, Mariánske námestie, with several restaurants and the Tatratour office. Due south of Mariánske námestie is a larger, more modern square, námestie L. Šturá, where Satur (formerly Čedok) and Slovakoturist are located.

INFORMATION For information on Žilina or the Little Fatra, first try Tatratour, at Mariánske nám. 21 (☎ **200-71** or **475-29**). It's open Monday through Friday 9am to 6pm, and on Saturday from June through August 9am to noon. In addition to arranging tours and accommodations (occasionally, private rooms from 100 Sk—$3.25—per person) for the Fatras and Tatras, Tatratour provides basic American Express services, such as check issuance, cashing, and replacement. If you have no luck with Tatratour, you can try Slovakoturist, next door to the Hotel Slovakia on námestie L. Stúra (☎ **089/483-39** or **483-60**). Hours are Monday through Friday from 9am to 4:30pm. Satur (☎ **089/485-11** to **485-13;** telex 75202), also on námestie L. Stúra, is another option. It's open Monday through Friday from 9am to 6pm and on Saturday from 9am to noon.

A good map of Žilina is available at Tatratour.

After a fast-paced tour in Prague and other large cities in Eastern Europe, consider a visit to the Little Fatra in northwestern Slovakia. Though not as a awesome as the Tatra Mountains, the Little Fatra offer beautiful, quiet scenery and excellent hiking opportunities.

Žilina (pronounced "*Zhi*-lee-na") serves tourists mainly as a transit point to the Little Fatra. But because mountainside accommodations are usually booked far in advance, you may have to base your Fatra excursions from accomodations in town. Fortunately, Žilina has more than its share of diversions. A sprinkling of interesting architecture, many heartening signs of private entrepreneurial activity, a marvelous situation amid rolling hills, and a pedestrian zone that covers nearly the whole city center assure a pleasant stay. One unexpected pleasure—Žilina's cafés and *cukrárnen* serve truly superior pastries and sweets.

WHERE TO STAY

Hotel Slovan, Šafárikova 2, Žilina 01001. ☎ **89/205-56, 208-74,** or **230-83.** Fax 89/223-09. 14 rms (all with bath). TV TEL **Directions:** Exit the train station and walk right down I. P. Hviezdoslavova, then make a left on Šafárikova.

Rates (including breakfast): 660 Sk ($21.30) single; 800 Sk ($25.80) double; 1,000 Sk ($32.25) triple. EU, MC, V.

This privately owned inn, a five-minute walk from the train station, is easily the top choice for Žilina. It's new and clean throughout, with new carpeting, attractive blond-wood furniture, and sparkling bathroom fixtures. You can take comfort for granted here. Art on the walls is by local hero Joseph Zovadski.

Hotel Polom, Olomoucká 1, 01001 Žilina. ☎ **089/211-51** or 211-52. Fax 089/217-43. 56 rms (all with bath). TV TEL **Directions:** Walk across the street a few steps to the right from the train station.

Rates (including breakfast): 750 Sk ($24.20) single; 1,150 Sk ($37.10) double. MC, V.

Despite a recent renovation, Polom remains a somewhat shabby hotel. It's decor and cleanliness are not up to the rates charged. Rooms are smallish, bathrooms are ugly, and the showers are hand-held units. Some rooms, however, enjoy striking views of the mountains that surround the town. The receptionists are helpful and speak English. The location, across the street from the train station, can't be beat for those who want an early headstart to the mountains. Reserving in advance through Satur, Slovakoturist, or Tatratour may get you a better price.

WHERE TO EAT

★ **Eve Vegetariánska Reštaurácia,** Mariánske námestie 11. ☎ **220-14.**

Cuisine: SLOVAK VEGETARIAN. **Directions:** Walk to the corner of Mariánske nám., next door to the CKM office.

$ **Prices:** Soups 8 Sk (25¢); main courses 25–30 Sk (80¢–95¢).

Open: Mon–Fri 9am–9pm, Sat–Sun 10am–9pm.

Refreshingly inexpensive, this small, tastefully decorated restaurant is a good example of the new, private places that are just beginning to emerge in Slovakia. Even if you're not a vegetarian, the food here is delicious. It's conveniently located in one of Žilina's main squares.

China Restaurant, Šturová ul. ☎ **483-25.**

Cuisine: CHINESE. **Reservations:** Recommended. **Directions:** Exit Mariánske námestie on the south side.

Prices: Hors d'oeuvres 19–78 Sk (60¢–$2.50); soups 14–61 Sk (45¢–$1.95); main courses 37–190 Sk ($1.20–$6.15), although most cost around 100 Sk ($3.35). Cover charge 5 Sk (15¢).

Open: Daily 10am–10pm.

This popular private restaurant uses a lighter hand with the MSG, corn syrup, and paper-pagoda decor than most of the other Asian restaurants listed in this book. Although the menu is in Czech or German, the waiters speak a little English to help you along (enough to point you to the many meatless dishes, if you so desire). Old favorites such as kung pao chicken and moo shu pork are competently prepared. A favorite spot among locals celebrating a special occasion, this place affords great people-watching opportunities.

Excursions in the Little Fatra

WHAT TO SEE & DO

The reason tourists come through Žilina is to continue on to the Little Fatra, a modest-sized but bucolic mountain range not far to the southeast. If you arrive in winter you can ski the Little Fatra slopes; in summer you can ride the chair lifts, breathe the fresh air, and take in the mountains and forested landscape on hikes.

From Žilina, take the bus to the last stop in Vrátna (at the Hotel Vrátna), in the heart of the mountains. Buses leave every 45 minutes or so from 6am to 6pm for 23 Sk (75¢), and take 50 minutes. From here you can take a cable car up 2,500 feet in 12 minutes to Chleb Mountain to admire the beautiful landscape. From the chair-lift landing at the summit, you can set your sights on one of several hiking destinations: Chalet pod Chlebom, 30 minutes away, a mountain lodge with a restaurant; Medziholie, about 3 hours away (you'll find the Chata pod Rozsutcom there); or Zazrivá, the site of another tourist chalet 7 3/4 hours away.

The chair lift (☎ **952-35**) up Chleb Mountain operates from 7:30am to 7pm and costs 50 Sk ($1.60) round-trip. From the first part of October until Christmas and for three weeks around Easter the chair lift closes down for maintenance and repairs.

Alternatively, you can ask the bus driver from Žilina to let you off at Vrátna-Rázcestie, where a chair lift will whisk you up Grúň Mountain. From here you can begin a series of more modest hikes to Starý Dvor (1 hour), Starý Dolina (45 minutes), Štefanová (45 minutes), and Poludňový Grúň (1 1/4 hours). The Chata na Grúni (see below) is just a few minutes from the chair-lift summit.

This chair lift (☎ **951-04**) operates from 7am to 7pm daily, and takes 15 minutes to get to the top for 50 Sk ($1.60) round-trip. For April, October, and November the lift closes down.

Before setting out on your exploration of the area, I suggest purchasing the *Vrátna-Martinské hole* detailed map of the mountain area. Remember, also, that the weather can be brisk in the mountains, even in July, so dress warmly and bring hiking shoes.

WHERE TO STAY

If you plan to stay in the mountains, be sure to visit Tatratour, Slovakoturist, or Satur in Žilina. Note that all the hotels below list a Terchová postal address, but they're all located in different areas of the hills.

On or Near Grúň Mountain

Hotel Boboty, near the Nový dvor bus stop, 01306 Terchová. ☎ **089/962-27** to **962-29.** Telex 075314. 100 rms (all with shower but no toilet). TV TEL **Directions:** Take the bus from Žilina to "Vrátna cez Štefanová" (*cez* means "via") and tell the driver "Boboty"; from the bus stop, walk up this midsize hill.

Rates: 20 DM ($32) single; 30 DM ($48) double. There's a 2 DM ($3.20) minimum charge for board. AE, DC, MC, V.

This fairly modern B* hotel located on a hillside offers a sauna, swimming pool, restaurant, and disco. The rooms feature balconies overlooking the hills, a shower in the room separated only by a curtain, and a slightly worn couch. Most rooms share a toilet with the adjacent room. The hotel also operates a folk-style restaurant. In all, it's a good choice for those looking for a bit of relaxation in the Little Fatra. It's not far from the chair lift up Grúň Mountain.

Chata Na Grúni, on Grúň Mountain, 01306 Terchová. ☎ **089/953-24.** 8 hostel rms (none with bath). **Directions:** Take the bus from Žilina to Vrátna-Rázcestie; then take the chair lift up Grúň Mountain, turn left, and walk five minutes.

Rates: 100 Sk ($3.25) per person.

This two-story wood house is for outdoor types only, as it offers hostel-style rooms sleeping four to six people. The bathroom is an outhouse and there are no showers. They also have a restaurant open daily from 7:30am to 8:30pm, specializing in very cheap Slovak fare such as sausages. It's located in a tranquil area free of roads 3,200 feet above sea level where sheep are more common than humans. Make sure to reserve ahead at Satur, Slovakoturist, or Tatratour in Žilina, as they speak no English here in the hills.

In Vrátna

Hotel Vrátna, at the foot of Chleb Mountain in Vrátna, 01306 Terchová. ☎ **089/952-23.** 20 rms (none with bath). **Directions:** Take the bus from Žilina to the last stop.

This popular wood-and-stone hotel, 2,500 feet above sea level, offers quaint wood-cabin-style rooms and a decent restaurant downstairs. It's located next to the cable car up Chleb Mountain, making it a convenient place to begin mountain walks. Unfortunately, the place is always full, so you have to reserve months in advance. In addition, both the reception staff and the manager are unusually curt.

3 The High Tatras

334 miles SE of Prague, 203 miles NE of Bratislava, 88 miles E of Žilina.

GETTING TO POPRAD Poprad, a modern town at the center of the High Tatras, is the major transportation hub servicing the region. Once there, you can easily make onward connections to the mountain resorts. The train and bus stations are adjacent to each other, just a five-minute walk from the town center.

By Plane You can fly from Prague to Poprad in an hour and 25 minutes for 3,410 Kčs ($121.80) seven-day advance fare.

By Train The 375-mile ride from Prague to Poprad takes eight or nine hours by express train, costing 260 Kčs ($9.30) in first class and 173 Kčs ($6.20) in second class. You might want to get a couchette on a night train to sleep away the long journey. Zilina and the Little Fatra are only two hours and 96 Sk ($3.10) away by express train.

By Bus The bus from Žilina to Poprad takes about 2½ hours and costs 75 Sk ($2.40). There are also buses from Budapest, Hungary, to Poprad, taking just under 7 hours; and from Zakopane, Poland, to Poprad, taking 2½ hours.

GETTING TO THE MOUNTAIN RESORTS • By Bus The bus is the fastest way to get from Poprad to the mountain resorts. From Poprad the bus goes first to Starý Smokovec in 17 minutes, and then stops in Tatranská Lomnica after 27 minutes. Another line travels from Poprad to Štrbské Pleso in 46 minutes.

You can also catch a bus from Žilina directly to Štrbské Pleso, a journey of 2 hours and 55 minutes.

In addition to links with Poprad, the Tatra resort towns have extremely good bus and rail connections with each other.

• By Narrow-Gauge Railway From Poprad, a narrow-gauge railway winds its way up to Starý Smokovec (35 minutes) and Štrbské Pleso (1¼ hours). Another line connects Starý Smokovec with Tatranská Lomnica in just 15 minutes.

• By Cable Car and Chair Lift At each of the major resorts, several chair lifts and cable cars shuttle tourists up the mountainsides.

ESSENTIALS The telephone area code for the Tatra region is 0969.

INFORMATION The best source of information is the Starý Smokovec Satur office (☎ **0969/27-10;** fax 0969/32-15), the main Čedok branch in the Tatras. Located just above the train and bus stations, it's open Monday through Friday from 8am to 4pm and on Saturday from 8am to noon (in July and August, Monday through Friday from 8am to 6pm). They book rooms in selected hotels (including several recommended here) and also arrange various tours. **Slovakoturist** runs an office in Horný Smokovec, a 10-minute walk or single narrow-gauge train stop toward Tatranská Lomnica from Starý Smokovec (☎ **20-31** or **28-27;** fax 24-82). While less organized and less generally helpful with advice or materials than the Satur office, they control a wider range of beds in the area (see "Where to Stay," below). Hours are Monday through Friday 8am to 5pm and Saturday 9am to 2pm (October to December 22 and April and May, Monday through Friday 8am to 4pm).

There's a tiny Satur office in Štrbské Pleso (☎ **0969/928-46**), where considerably less information is available. Located next door to the train station, it's open Monday through Friday from 9am to 3pm.

In Tatranská Lomnica, information is available from the tiny Tatra Turist office just off the lobby of the Hotel Družba, and from the Hotel Slovakia reception.

AREA LAYOUT The three main resort towns of the High Tatras (Vysoké Tatry) are Štrbské Pleso, Starý Smokovec, and Tatranská Lomnica; they run roughly diagonally from the southwest to the northeast for 15 miles.

These three towns are northwest of Poprad, the main transportation center in the Tatra region. As Poprad itself is unexceptional and at the foot of the mountains, you'll want to continue from Poprad pretty much as soon as you pull into town. Poprad's train station (☎ **228-09**) and bus station (☎ **233-90**) are just across the street from each other.

The Tatras are an international mountain range, and an overly ambitious hike can accidentally put you inside Poland. Border officials are used to this sort of thing, however, and will simply point you back in the right direction toward your hotel and your host country.

Don't go without a map! *Vysoké Tatry: Letná Turistická Mapa* shows the main roads and hiking paths in the region, and *Tatranské Strediská* (Centres of the High Tatras) illustrates the individual streets of the main Tatra villages, which is especially useful since there are no street addresses in the Tatra area.

The High Tatras don't dally with foothills. They rise sharply from the plain, without so much as a covering of evergreens—these are the most jagged mountains in Slovakia. And with peaks that top out at more than 8,600 feet, they are second in Europe only to the Alps. Accordingly, the Tatras have an enchanting effect on the legions who flock to their slopes all year round for a fest of hiking, climbing, skiing, and mountain biking.

Much of the area was settled by Saxons, who defended the western provinces from Tartar attacks and mined the mountains. They stayed in this vicinity and formed a semi-independent province in the 13th century. Tourism had already begun by the late 18th century; twice in the early 20th century Vladimir Lenin is reputed to have climbed one of the local mountains, a rare recreational outing for the rather dour revolutionary.

Alas, such grandeur isn't cheap, as popularity coupled with the relatively small number of mountainside beds (the Tatras are protected as a natural park and have been spared overdevelopment) keep prices and occupancy relatively high.

WHAT TO SEE & DO

With more than 200 miles of hiking trails, smashing slopes, and grand views all around, the Tatras offer a feast of outdoor activity. Lifts ferry skiers, hikers, and walkers up the mountains year-round, closing only for May and the period from mid-October to Christmas. A lift pass for a day of skiing costs 200 Sk ($6.45).

The best place to get fitted for mountain sports is at **Tatrasport Adam,** in Starý Smokovec right next to Satur (☎ **21-10;** fax 35-52). They rent mountain bikes for 200 Sk ($6.45) per day, ski equipment for 150 to 250 Sk ($4.85 to $8.05) per day, snowboards for 150 Sk ($4.85) per day, and sleds for 30 Sk (95¢) per day. The voluble owners are a great source of information about biking, hiking, and skiing routes. Hours are daily 8am to 8pm in the summer, 8am to 6pm in winter. They also run a store in Tatranská Lomnica, located in the train station.

Before doing any serious hiking, you would do well to check in at **Horská Služba,** next door to Satur in Starý Smokovec (☎ **28-20** or **28-55**). They provide guide service, maps, and advice about hiking routes. These services will soon be available in the Satur office next door. Hours are Monday through Friday 8am to 6pm and Saturday 9am to 1pm.

In Štrbské Pleso

Home to ski-jump competitions, Štrbské Pleso (4,375 feet above sea level) comes alive in winter with cross-country skiing and ice skating. From here you can head up into several major valleys with shimmering mountain lakes (including Štrbské Pleso lake itself, just a few minutes from the bus and train stations), or begin a mountain journey.

A good starting point for expeditions is the chair lifts across from the Hotel Fis. One goes to **Mount Solisko** for 40 Sk ($1.30) round-trip; buy your tickets near the main entrance to the Hotel Fis. You can also take a chair lift to near the top of the ski-jump platform for 25 Sk (80¢). Both chair lifts operate from 9am to 4:30pm daily, with a month off in spring and autumn for repairs.

You can also hike from Štrbské Pleso to a lodge and restaurant at the lake at **Popradské Pleso** (4,825 feet), up the slope about three miles away.

In Smokovec

Smokovec (3,262 feet above sea level), the largest town and the center of the High Tatra resort area, actually includes several smaller towns that have merged together for all practical purposes. With several hotels and the main railway station, Starý Smokovec is the main village in this grouping, and a good place to begin any exploration of the Tatras. Since it's in the center of the mountain range, you have the greatest choice of hiking routes in the summer and cross-country skiing trails in the winter.

You can begin your hike in back of the Grand Hotel, where a cable car climbs up to **Mount Hrebienok** (4,080 ft.) in just 7 minutes for 10 Sk (30¢); it runs from 6:10am to 7:45pm daily. There's a waterfall 20 minutes from here, various hiking paths, and several food and lodging chalets in the area.

You can also take a plane ride over the area for one hour, if 10 others want to join you. Inquire at the Grand Hotel for details. The cost is about 2,000 Sk ($64.50).

In Tatranská Lomnica

At the other end of the Slovakian Tatras is the town of Tatranská Lomnica (2,745 feet above sea level), with the best winter skiing, as well as bobsled runs and ice skating. In the summer you can take a 25-minute cable-car ride to the top of the peak at **Skalnaté pleso** (8,632 feet) for a fantastic view of the surrounding countryside and most of the Tatra range. You can also get off halfway up the mountain at **Štart.** The cable car operates Wednesday through Monday from 7am to 8pm. To the top it costs 40 Sk ($1.30) for adults and 20 Sk (65¢) for children. Tickets to Štart (halfway up) are half the above prices. The cable car closes for two weeks in spring and autumn.

From Skalnaté pleso you can continue farther by cable car to **Lomnický štít.**

WHERE TO STAY

It remains difficult at times for individual travelers to find accommodations in the High Tatra region. Slovakoturist and other agencies continue to lease entire hotels for group packages. You should therefore consider reserving rooms in advance, at least during peak periods, which are Christmas and the ski season (December 22 to March 15) and summer (June through August). Room rates fluctuate widely over the course of the year, going from quite expensive during Christmas to very reasonable in October and November. All prices quoted here are from the booking agencies and lower than those charged by the hotels directly.

If you haven't booked a room in advance, your best bet might be to pay a visit to the Satur or Slovakoturist offices in Starý Smokovec. In addition to its conventional hotels, **Satur** can also arrange rooms in chalets in the nearby towns of Nová Lesná and Stará Lesná, which are served by the narrow-gauge railway. All beds are within a 10-minute walk of the train stop and cost 300 Sk ($9.70) per head. If you prefer a more rugged Tatra experience, **Slovakoturist** operates four mountain huts strung out along the range's favorite hiking routes. With from 18 to 48 dorm-style beds in each and hot hearty meals included, these huts, at 350 Sk ($11.30) per person, represent your most thrilling option for enjoying the mountains. Slovakoturist also arranges private accommodations in Nová Lesná, Stará Lesná, and Ždiar for 225 Sk ($7.25) per person.

In Štrbské Pleso

Štrbské Pleso has three hotels: one right across from the narrow-gauge rail and bus station (Hotel Panoráma), the second between the station and the chair lifts into the mountains (Hotel Patria), and the third next to the chair lifts (Hotel Fis). You can walk between these hotels in no more than 20 minutes. Check luggage at the lockers at the bus station if you don't want to carry all your belongings to your hotel.

Hotel Fis, 05985 Štrbské Pleso. ☎ **0969/922-21** or **923-01.** 67 rms, 10 bungalows (all with bath). TV TEL **Directions:** Bus or narrow-gauge railroad to last stop in Štrbské Pleso; then a 15- to 20-minute walk north.

Rates (including breakfast): 800 Sk ($25.80) double; 1,525 Sk ($49.20) bungalow for four. Booking is handled by Slovakoturist. **Parking:** Free.

Built for the world skiing championship in 1970, the Fis has remained a favorite of skiers ever since, and many groups stay here. The rooms are a bit small, with toe-to-toe beds, most with a small balcony, but the sporting facilities here are excellent. The hotel also has a pizzeria and another restaurant, making it a center of youthful activity. It's well located just across from the chair lift that takes you up the nearby mountain. Scheduled for renovation by early 1995, Fis may reopen with an entirely new look.

Facilities: Sauna, indoor swimming pool, fairly well equipped weight room, pool table, gym with basketball court, bicycles, therapy center.

Hotel Panoráma, 05985 Štrbské Pleso. ☎ **0969/921-11.** 96 rms (all with shower or bath, some with toilet). TEL **Directions:** Walk across from the bus or narrow-gauge railroad station in Štrbské Pleso.

Rates (including breakfast): June–Aug, 930 Sk ($30) single; 1,470 Sk ($47.40) double. Sept–Dec 22, 400 Sk ($12.90) single; 660 Sk ($21.30) double. Dec 23–Jan 2, 1,190 Sk ($38.40) single; 1,870 Sk ($60.30) double. Jan 3–Mar, 840 Sk ($27.10) single; 1,330 Sk ($42.90) double. Apr–May, 600 Sk ($19.35) single; 900 Sk ($29.05) double. AE, DC, JCB, MC, V. Reservations are arranged by Slovakoturist.

Of the three listed here, this hotel shaped like a narrow step-pyramid is the easiest to reach from the train and bus stations in Štrbské Pleso, but also the farthest from the lifts into the mountains. There's a shopping center and post office nearby. The rooms offer real showers rather than the hand-held units found all too often in Slovakia, and stunning mountain views. There's a restaurant, café, and disco in the hotel, often filled with an international crowd. Guests can also use the sports facilities in the Patria Hotel about 15 minutes away.

Hotel Patria, 05985 Štrbské Pleso. ☎ **0969/925-91** to **925-95.** Telex 678255. 150 rms (all doubles with bath). TV TEL **Directions:** Bus or narrow-gauge railroad to the last stop in Štrbské Pleso; then walk north for 10 minutes.

Rates (including breakfast): June–Sept and Jan 3–Mar, 2,000 Sk ($64.50) double. Dec 22–Jan 2, 2,200 Sk ($70.95) double. Oct–Dec 21 and Apr–May, 1,200 Sk ($38.70) double. Admission to recreational facilities 60 Sk ($1.95). AE, DC, MC, V. Reservations are arranged by Satur. **Parking:** Free.

A nine-story A-frame building of cement-reinforced timber, the Patria is Štrbské Pleso's "upscale" hotel, featuring a handsome lobby with a pianist and an indoor garden, and comfortable rooms with lovely views of either the glacial lake Štrbské or the 2,655-meter Gerlachovský štít. Rooms have couches, radios, blond-wood walls, and toilets and baths in separate little rooms. Priced above our daily budget, it's worth the rate it charges.

Dining/Entertainment: Poolside bar, lobby bar, afternoon café, main restaurant (see "Where to Eat," below).

Facilities: Midsize indoor swimming pool, sauna, fitness center.

In the Smokovec Area

Four towns comprise the Smokovec area: Nový Smokovec, to the west; Starý Smokovec, farther east, the main town of the area; Dolný Smokovec, to the southeast; and Horný Smokovec, immediately north of Dolný Smokovec.

Grand Hotel, 06201 Starý Smokovec. ☎ **0969/21-54** to **21-56.** 85 rms (69 with bath). TV TEL **Directions:** Narrow-gauge railroad to Starý Smokovec and walk two blocks north.

Rates (including breakfast): Jan 3–Mar and July–Sept, 565 Sk ($18.25) single without bath, 1,360 Sk ($50.35) single with bath; 1,283 Sk ($41.40) double without bath, 2,100 Sk ($67.75) double with bath. Apr–Jun 24, 424 Sk ($13.70) single without bath, 908 Sk ($29.30) single with bath, 688 Sk ($22.20) double without bath, 1,429 Sk ($46.10) double with bath. Oct–Dec 21, 328 Sk ($10.60) single without bath, 540 Sk ($17.40) single with bath; 555 Sk ($17.90) double without bath, 880 Sk ($28.40) double with bath. Dec 22–Jan 2, 956 Sk ($30.85) single without bath, 1,565 Sk ($50.50) single with bath; 1,502 Sk ($48.45) double without bath; 2,558 Sk ($82.50) double with bath. AE, DC, MC, V. Reservations are arranged by Satur. **Parking:** Free.

Built in 1908 and long the grand dame of the Tatras, this hotel is still a beautiful, relaxing place to stay even though it may not live up to its prewar standards. The expansive lobby is perhaps its most endearing feature, with separate lounging, reading, and billiards areas that encourage après-ski lounging even in midsummer. Rooms come in a wide variety of shapes, amenities, and trimming, so you are encouraged, if possible, to peruse a few before choosing one. Although some rooms have been renovated, prices for old and new are the same, which is just as well, because each has unique charm. The old rooms are quite large, well kept, and feature live plants and old photos of the Tatras on the white walls; some have porches and porcelain chandeliers. New rooms are considerably smaller but feature totally integrated decor, green patterned velvet upholstery, and new color TVs with satellite hookup. Bathrooms all around are in good condition, and some feature wonderfully large tubs that invite a long posthike soak. The restaurant is one of the town's best (see "Where to Eat," below).

Facilities: Indoor swimming pool, sauna, fitness room, billiards tables.

Hotel Park, 06201 Nový Smokovec. ☎ **0969/23-42.** 96 rms (all with bath). TEL **Directions:** Narrow-gauge railroad to Nový Smokovec and walk across the street.

Rates: May–June 740 Sk ($23.85) single; 1,200 Sk ($38.70) double. July–Sept, 1,050 Sk ($33.85) single; 1,650 Sk ($53.25) double. Oct–Dec 21 and Apr, 540 Sk ($17.40) single; 880 Sk ($28.40) double. Dec 22–Jan 2, 1,350 Sk ($43.55) single; 2,120 Sk ($68.40) double. Jan 3–Mar, 950 Sk ($30.65) single; 1,500 Sk ($48.40) double. AE, DC, JCB, MC, V. Reservations are arranged by Satur. **Parking:** Free.

The five-story C-shaped hotel wraps around a circular courtyard filled with minigolf links. The price you pay for the whimsical shape is a weird-shaped room, which may remind you of sleeping quarters on a flying saucer. Cramped bathrooms aside, the rooms are quite comfortable and cozy, featuring colors and furniture right out of a 1974 Sears catalog and a nifty movable curtain that separates sleeping and lounging areas. Top-floor rooms have the best Tatra views.

Facilities: Minigolf.

In Tatranská Lomnica

Hotel Horec, 05960 Tatranská Lomnica. ☎ **0969/96-72-61.** 33 rms (8 with bath). **Directions:** Narrow-gauge railway or bus to Tatranská Lomnica, then a 15-minute walk (ask for directions).

Rates: June–Sept and Dec 22–Mar, 720 Sk ($23.25) double without bath, 770 Sk ($24.85) double with bath; 800 Sk ($25.80) quad with sink. Oct–Dec 21 and Apr–May, 520 Sk ($16.75) double without bath, 570 Sk ($18.40) double with bath; 600 Sk ($19.35) quad with sink. Extra bed 190 Sk ($6.15). Breakfast 50 Sk ($1.60) per person extra. Reservation arranged by Slovakoturist. **Parking:** Free.

About half a mile from the train station, the Hotel Horec is located well away from the other hotels, but near the chair lift to Skalnaté pleso. Rooms have toe-to-toe beds, floral wallpaper, and prints on the walls, and some have balconies and tiny private bathrooms. The public bathrooms are well kept. You'll have to walk as many as three stories up to your room.

Hotel Slovakia, 05960 Tatranská Lomnica. ☎ **0969/96-79-61.** 50 rms and 8 apartments (all with bath). TEL TV **Directions:** Narrow-gauge railway or bus to Tatranská Lomnica, then walk across the street.

Rates: June–Sept and Dec 22–Mar 15, 680 Sk ($21.95) single without bath or WC; 1,800 Sk ($58.05) double with bath; 4,150 Sk ($133.85) five-person apartment with bath. Oct–Dec 21 and Mar 16–May, 480 Sk ($15.50) single without bath or WC; 1,600 Sk ($51.60) double with bath; 3,950 Sk ($127.40) five-person apartment with bath. Extra bed 470 Sk ($15.15). Breakfast 50 Sk ($1.60) extra per person. AE, DC, MC, V. Reservation arranged by Slovakoturist. **Parking:** Free.

Built in the 1950s as a guesthouse for Communist Party dignitaries, this three-story white building has housed former Nicaraguan leader Daniel Ortega and the chairman of the Slovak Communist Party, among others. Following the "Velvet Revolution," the hotel opened to tourists in 1990. The rooms are sizable, with radios, refrigerators, and balconies large enough for some chairs, and the bathrooms have modern tiling and a bidet. You can snack at a café just off the lobby. Consider reserving ahead through Slovakoturist in Bratislava.

Facilities: Sauna, swimming pool, tennis court. You can also rent mountain bikes from the hotel, for 60 Sk ($1.95) a half day and 120 Sk ($3.85) a full day. You don't need to be staying at the hotel to rent a bike.

Eurocamp FIcc, 05960 Tatranská Lomnica. ☎ **0969/96-77-41** to **96-77-45.**
118 bungalows (all with bath), 46 hotel rms (none with bath), 3,000 camping places. **Directions:** Narrow-gauge train to the Lomnica Eurocamp stop and then walk about five minutes; in July–Aug a bus also comes from the main area of Tatranská Lomnica.

Rates: 450 Sk ($14.50) hotel double; 1,100 Sk ($35.50) bungalow for four; 50 Sk ($1.60) per person camping place. **Parking:** Free.

The largest and most modern camp in the High Tatras, FICC offers several sleeping possibilities. The most expensive option is the oddly shaped bungalows for four, with a bedroom downstairs and a narrow staircase leading up to a second bedroom. The hotel rooms, without private plumbing, are less attractive than some of my other listings here. If you have a tent, you can also take advantage of the camping places, which have access to hot running water and a restaurant and café. The hotel is a bit inconveniently located for those without a car.

Facilities: Sauna.

In Javorina

Hotel Polana, 05956 Javorina. ☎ **0969/991-02.** 30 rms (all with bath). TV TEL
Directions: Drive on the main road north of Tatranská Lomnica, which eventually veers left toward the Polish border.

Rates: 60 DM ($37.50) single; 100 DM ($62.50) double; 150 DM ($93.75) apartment. Reservations arranged by Slovakoturist.

If you have a car and really want to get away from even a modest mountain village, this upscale hotel makes for a perfect retreat. Located near the Polish border about a 30-minute drive northwest of Tatranská Lomnica, this arc-shaped hotel once accommodated the elite of the Communist Party.

The hotel is hard to get to, and built that way to leave the party men in peace, but you're rewarded by lovely surroundings, including extraordinary views from the rooms over a valley and mountains in the distance. The food and service remain excellent, which is a good thing for there are no restaurants around for miles. For a splurge, you can consider one of the huge apartments, with stereos and extra-large balconies.

Located just minutes from the Polish border, this hotel can be approached from either Slovakia or Poland. On the Polish side of the border you can drive to one of my favorite lakes in the area, Morskie Oko, or to Zakopane in about 30 minutes (see "Zakopane and the Tatra Mountains," in Chapter 28).

Facilities: Indoor swimming pool, sauna, very modest exercise room.

WHERE TO EAT

If you go hiking, it's best to stop in one of the stores in Starý Smokovec or Tatranská Lomnica and pick up some bread, cheese, and sausage. The food at the high mountain chalets is quite limited.

In Štrbské Pleso

Hotel Patria Restaurant, in Štrbské Pleso between the Hotels Panoráma and Fis.
☎ **925-91.**

Cuisine: SLOVAKIAN/INTERNATIONAL. **Reservations:** Recommended. **Directions:** Bus or narrow-gauge railroad to the last stop in Štrbské Pleso; then walk north for 15 minutes.

Prices: Soups 15–40 Sk (50¢–$1.30); main courses 35–160 Sk ($1.15–$5.15).
Open: Daily 7–10am, 11:30am–2pm, and 6–9pm.

The "Sunny Restaurant," directly on your left as you enter the Hotel Patria, aims to please with a varied menu in English of pork, beef, fish, and poultry dishes. The large dining room occupies an entire eave of the A-frame hotel, providing one of the nicest eating environments in the Tatras. A broad bank of window glass lets in a beautiful quantity of daylight.

In Smokovec

Grand Hotel. ☎ **21-54** to **21-56.**

Cuisine: SLOVAK. **Reservations:** Recommended during high season. **Directions:** Walk a block north from Satur.
Prices: Soups 30 Sk (95¢); main courses 50–254 Sk ($1.60–$8.20). AE, DC, MC, V.
Open: Daily 7–9:30am, 11:30am–2:30pm, and 6–10pm.

The very pretty dining room, trimmed with green-colored wood and some very lush looking drapes, is large enough that it must once have accommodated whole Communist Party congresses. Only the lethal-looking chandeliers overhead reflect design input of the previous regime. Service is excellent and the food the best in the Tatras. The trout was perfect, and Slovak specialties such as *Živanska ihla* (beef flambéed in gin and garlic) were delicious. Beware that the garnishes accompanying the main course are sometimes priced separately and can run up the bill quickly.

In Tatranská Lomnica

Zbojnícka Koliba, in Tatranská Lomnica. ☎ **30-75-20,** or **96-76-30** for reservations.

Cuisine: SLOVAK. **Reservations:** Recommended. **Directions:** Walk a few minutes west of the Grand Hotel Praha.
Prices: Main courses 38–148 Sk ($1.25–$4.75). Music charge 30 Sk (95¢).
Open: Dinner only, Mon–Sat 4pm–midnight.

A typical folk-style restaurant with live Gypsy musicians pumping out a lively rhythm on violin, bass, and cimbalom, sparking lots of informal singing and dancing. It's a charming place with wooden tables and ceilings. The restaurant is completely surrounded by woods, giving you the sense that you're in the middle of nowhere, which is basically true. The restaurant is known for its grilled specialties, including chicken, sausage, pork, and trout. The small list of offerings is posted on a wooden board on the wall.

SHOPPING

The local folk art is known for its bright colors and excellent craftsmanship. From Zvolen comes delicate lace and embroidery, and nearer to the Tatras are numerous peasant costumes of brilliantly dyed, homespun wool.

17 Getting to Know Hungary

A LAND OF RIVERS AND PLAINS, A HISTORY OF VAST EMPIRES RULED BY THE IRON Magyar horsemen astride their fleet-footed steeds, Christianity tempered by Ottoman Turkish influences, vineyards filled with juicy grapes ripening in the strong southern sun, small towns from the 18th century nestling in green valleys—all this is Hungary.

A small country (35,000 square miles), Hungary has about 11 million citizens, who speak a language unrelated to any other in Europe, except Finnish and Estonian. And along with Poland, Hungary is an eastern outpost of Roman Catholicism, a faith adopted by King (and eventually Saint) Stephen I on Christmas Day in the year A.D. 1000. Today some 67% of the population remains Roman Catholic, with 20% Calvinist and 5% Lutheran.

Hungary boasts beautiful medieval towns in its western provinces, and Lake Balaton, an inland sea and water-lover's paradise nearby. The capital city of Budapest was once the center of the Austro-Hungarian Empire and has a legacy of fine baroque buildings and broad avenues. The Great Hungarian Plain or *puszta,* a short distance east of Budapest, reminds one more of the vast Asian steppes than of Europe's varied geography. Hungarian cooking combines elements of Eastern, Mediterranean, German, and French cuisine to tempt and excite every palate. And all this comes at low cost, possible on a budget of $30 a day.

1 Geography, History & Politics

GEOGRAPHY

Hungary is a mostly flat country located in the Carpathian basin, surrounded by mountainous neighboring countries. The two major rivers cutting through the country are the Danube and the Tisza.

Hungary borders the Czech and Slovak Republics, Austria, Romania, Serbia, Slovenia, Croatia, and Ukraine. Its present-day land area is far smaller than the historic Hungarian nation. Largely because of this, Hungary is an ethnically homogeneous country. Some 93% of the population of 10.7 million call themselves Magyars, descendants of the nomadic plains people. Gypsies make up the largest minority group.

HISTORY & POLITICS

IN THE 3RD CENTURY B.C. CELTIC TRIBES established themselves across much of western Hungary, but it was the Romans who built the first chain of settlements. A few miles from Budapest the Romans built a major legion garrison that later developed into a city called Aquincum. In A.D. 106 Aquincum was made the capital of lower Pannonia, an area incorporating parts of modern Hungary, Yugoslavia, and Romania.

The Magyars, the tribe from which modern Hungarians are descended, entered modern-day Hungary about A.D. 896. The Magyars were skilled horsemen, originally from the Asian side of the Ural Mountains, whose favored offensive tactic was to gallop around enemy forces and shower them with arrows. Led by their chief, Árpád, they easily subjugated the established Slavic tribes. The successful conquest of the Danube

Dateline

- **3rd century B.C.** Celtic tribes move into western Hungary.
- **A.D. 106** Aquincum (today's Budapest) becomes capital of lower Pannonia in Roman Empire.
- **896** Magyar tribes, led by Árpád, conquer Hungary.
- **924** Magyars advance as far as Champagne in present-day France.
- **955** Magyar expansion comes to an end.
- **1000** Hungarians crown first Christian king, Stephen I.

➤

Dateline

- **1241** Mongols invade Hungary.
- **1301** Árpád dynasty ends, followed by a series of foreign-born kings.
- **1389** War with Turks starts.
- **1456** Hungarian noble János Hunyadi leads Christian forces to a victory over the Ottoman Turks in Belgrade.
- **1458** Matthias Corvinus is crowned king of Hungary.
- **1514** Peasant revolt weakens Hungary.
- **1526** Ottoman Turks defeat the Hungarians in the Battle of Mohács.
- **1541** Ottoman armies capture Buda.
- **1686** Habsburg-led army defeats the Ottoman Turks.
- **1703–11** Rebellion against the Habsburgs, led by Ferenc Rákóczi II.
- **1848** War of Independence against the Habsburgs.
- **1867** Dual monarchy of Austria-Hungary established.
- **1914–18** Hungary sides with the Central Powers in World War I.
- **1919** Béla Kun forms a Communist government, which is soon replaced by a conservative regime under Admiral Horthy.
- **1920** Treaty of Trianon gives away two-thirds of Hungary's former land to neighboring countries.
- **1939** Hungary allies with Nazis and Italian fascists.
- **1944–45** Nazi, and then Soviet, forces occupy

➤

Valley bred confidence, and the Magyars began to raid westward. By A.D. 924 they had plundered as far as Champagne in what is now France. German forces finally halted the Magyars in A.D. 955, and in A.D. 1000 Árpád's great-great-grandson accepted Christianity and was crowned as King Stephen I.

In 1241, Odgai, son of Genghis Khan, and his "Golden Horde" (better known as the Mongols) charged through. In the wake of the two-year Mongol rampage, young King Béla IV began to rebuild his newly acquired kingdom. He granted a charter to the fledgling trading town of Pest on the east bank of the Danube. Béla IV also began the serious fortification of Buda Hill, a project that continued until the middle of the 19th century. During his reign, Hungary became increasingly powerful and expanded into neighboring lands.

When the last Árpád king died without an heir in 1301, a series of foreign-born kings held sway over Hungary as enemies slowly whittled down the empire. Hungary went into decline and stagnation until the threat of Ottoman invasion in the middle of the 15th century galvanized the country. A Hungarian noble, János Hunyadi, led the Christian forces to a monumental victory over the Ottoman armies in 1456 near what is now Belgrade. The victory was so important to the defense of Europe that to this day Catholics celebrate it with the joyous pealing of church bells. János Hunyadi's son, Matthias Corvinus, was crowned king in 1458.

Under King Matthias, Hungary experienced a golden age of artistic and intellectual development that lasted until his death in 1490. Many of the beautiful structures that grace Hungarian skylines, in particular the Matthias Church on Buda Hill, were constructed in this period.

After the death of King Matthias, scheming nobles and an unsuccessful peasant revolt in 1514 severely weakened Hungary. The Ottoman armies again swept north up the Danube, and in 1526 routed the Hungarian forces in the Battle of Mohács. The Ottoman armies captured the fortified city of Buda in 1541. An Ottoman pasha reigned in Buda until a Habsburg-led army defeated the Ottomans in 1686. The mosques and many baths that dot the countryside are all reminders of the successful Ottoman Turkish invasion in the 16th century.

After the Habsburg Holy Roman emperors drove out the Turks at the end of the 17th century, put down a rebellion led by Ferenc Rákóczi, and ruled Hungary from Vienna.

Modern History & Politics

The early 1800s saw a renewal of agitation for Hungarian independence from Habsburg Austria, led by figures like Count István Széchenyi (see "Famous People," below). This culminated in the revolution of 1848, which proclaimed a separate Hungarian state and was only put down after the Austrian government received help from Russian troops in 1849. A more stable settlement finally came with the Compromise of 1867, engineered by Ferenc Deák, which recognized Hungary's independent status within the Habsburg Austro-Hungarian Empire. Under the Compromise of 1867, Hungary, and particularly the combined city of Budapest, experienced rapid economic and cultural growth. It all ended with the major social and political upheavals caused by World War I, the defeat of the Habsburgs, and the division of the empire. Under the Treaty of Trianon (Trianon is a palace at Versailles where the accord was signed), two-thirds of Hungary was distributed among Serbia, Croatia, Slovakia, Ukraine, and, particularly, Romania. Ten million inhabitants in these lost territories were non-Magyars who had wanted independence from Hungary just as Hungary had from Austria. However, Trianon also severed three million ethnic Hungarians from their homeland, dooming many to oppression under regimes committed to ethnic homogeneity (notably Ceauşescu's Romania). Even today many Hungarians consider Trianon their great tragedy, and long for a reestablishment of Hungary's imperial borders.

Hungary's woes were compounded by a bloody power struggle between Communist and rightist forces at the end of the war, followed shortly by the Great Depression that spread over Europe. Power fell to a conservative regime under the regency of Admiral Miklós Horthy, whose central policy became the recovery of the territories lost at Trianon. This led to an alliance with Germany (another country that felt ill-treated at Versailles), with Hungary hoping that the Nazis would help return its lost provinces without making Hungarians fight. But Hungary's attempt to have its cake and eat it too failed, and the country was dragged kicking and screaming into fighting for the Axis side. Budapest was the battleground for some particularly brutal last-ditch fighting in early 1945; the Danube bridges, and much of Buda, were blown up.

The country's occupation by Soviet forces after the war led to the formation of a heavy-handed Communist-dominated government in Hungary, but in 1956 reformist currents throughout Eastern Europe encouraged increased Hungarian opposition to its stifling presence. On October 23, 1956, a mass meeting in front of the Budapest radio station was dispersed with gunfire. The result was the 13-day "Hungarian Uprising," which, in the early hours of November 4, was met by an armed Warsaw Pact force composed almost entirely of Soviet troops. About 2,000 people died in the uprising, and an estimated 200,000 Hungarians fled the country. After order was

Dateline

country; bitter fighting leaves Budapest in ruins at the end of World War II.

- **1949** Hungary proclaimed a "People's Republic" and one-party Communist state.
- **1956** Soviet army represses the Hungarian Uprising, killing 2,000; 200,000 flee the country.
- **1968** New Economic Mechanism (NEM) implemented, decentralizing economy.
- **1989** Portions of the barbed-wire frontier with Austria dismantled in May, and Janos Kádár ousted after 33 years; in September, the government lets East Germans flee to the West through Hungary.
- **1990** Communists ousted in April elections.

brutally restored, János Kádár, the new Soviet-supported leader, slowly began a course of reform, which shaped Hungary into one of the most prosperous and liberal of all the Warsaw Pact countries.

Most significant of the reforms was the 1968 introduction of the New Economic Mechanism (NEM), decentralizing many aspects of the economy and encouraging limited forms of private enterprise, a sort of "perestroika" a generation before Gorbachev.

Despite some economic difficulties caused by its large debt and inflation, Hungary continued to lead Eastern Europe in gradual internal Communist reform through the 1980s. In May 1989, six months before the opening of the Berlin Wall, it began dismantling portions of the barbed-wire frontier with Austria, thus becoming the first country to open a hole in the Iron Curtain. Some days later, János Kádár was ousted after 33 years in power. Then in September, with thousands of East Germans gathering in Hungary to flee their repressive hard-line government, Hungary decided to let them emigrate directly to Austria. The decision prompted a flood of some 57,000 East German emigrants through Hungary, and eventually forced a desperate East German government to open the Berlin Wall.

The cascade of political change throughout Eastern Europe that followed prompted the Communists in Hungary to allow the first free elections, in April 1990, since the close of World War II—in which they were soundly defeated. By May Day 1990, traditionally a rousing worker's jubilee, Budapest's Communist Party did little more than operate a single beer stand at the festivities!

Unfortunately Hungary, like its neighbors, is finding life after Communism difficult. Though the shops are full and new businesses booming, people fret about high unemployment and choke on the terrible pollution in Budapest. Relations with Slovakia remain poisoned by the aborted dam project at Nagymáros, and with Romania by ongoing minority issues. Some Hungarians question the government's commitment to freedom of speech; others clamor for the revocation of the Treaty of Trianon, a stance that recalls the specter of racism and fascism from the 1930s. Still, the country now benefits from the freedom to face its problems squarely, and there is plenty of hope for the future.

2 Famous People

Béla Bartók (1881–1945) Hungary's most famous 20th-century composer, Bartók fused elements of folk music within the framework of classical composition. His compositions include the opera *Bluebeard's Castle,* and a series of piano and violin concertos. He was also a longtime professor of music in Budapest.

Zoltán Kodály (1882–1967) Hungarian composer who, along with Bartók, made extensive studies of local folk music. These studies inspired his own creations, including *Háry János, Psalmus Hungaricus,* and *The Peacock.*

Lajos Kossuth (1802–94) Lawyer, politician, and journalist, Kossuth was perhaps the best-known leader of the 1848–49 revolution. He spent the second half of his long life wandering in exile, resolutely refusing to accept the 1867 compromise with the Habsburgs. A giant statue of him graces Kossuth Square in Budapest, site of the Hungarian Parliament.

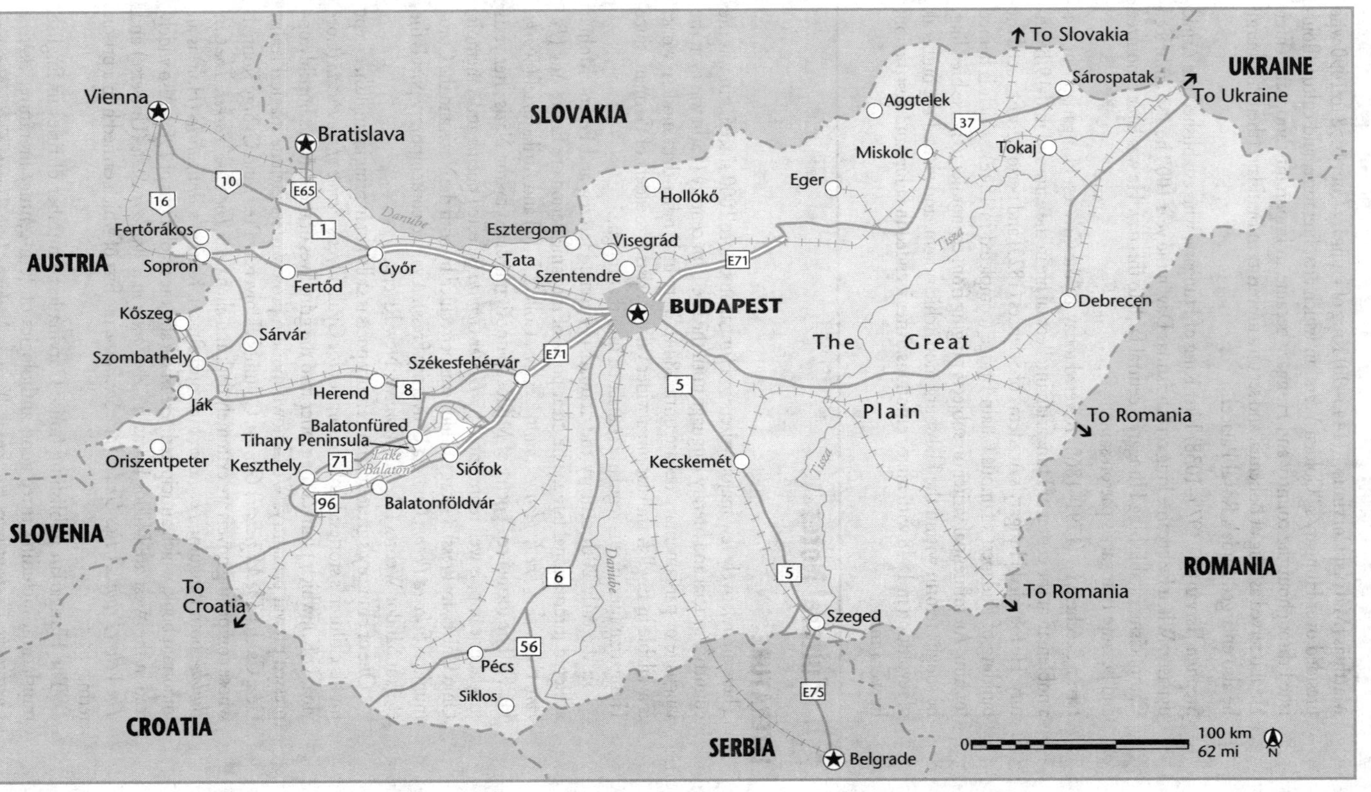
To Slovakia
UKRAINE
To Ukraine
Sárospatak
Aggtelek
37
SLOVAKIA
Vienna
Bratislava
Miskolc
Tokaj
Eger
Hollókő
10
16
E65
1
Danube
Fertőrákos
Esztergom
Visegrád
Tisza
AUSTRIA
Sopron
Győr
Tata
E71
Szentendre
Fertőd
BUDAPEST
Debrecen
Kőszeg
Sárvár
The Great Plain
Szombathely
Székesfehérvár
E71
Herend
8
5
Ják
To Romania
Balatonfüred
Tihany Peninsula
Lake Balaton
Oriszentpeter
Keszthely
71
Siófok
Kecskemét
96
Balatonföldvár
SLOVENIA
6
Danube
5
ROMANIA
To Croatia
To Romania
Szeged
56
Pécs
Siklos
E75
CROATIA
SERBIA
Belgrade
0
100 km
62 mi
N
Railway
Hungary

Matthias [Mátyás] Corvinus (1443–90) King of Hungary from 1458 to 1490 who presided over Hungary's "Golden Years" in which arts, literature, and culture flourished throughout the country and Hungary became an important European center. He also served as king of Bohemia, and set up a university in Bratislava (then Pressburg); he also enlarged Buda's Royal Palace.

Stephen [István] I (975–1038) First King of Hungary, who established the Árpád dynasty. When he became king on Christmas Day in the year 1000 he also embraced Catholicism, establishing Hungary's central faith to this day. He was later canonized and became Hungary's patron saint.

István Széchenyi (1791–1860) Revered today as "the Greatest Hungarian," he was a nobleman at the center of Hungarian intellectual life in the early and mid-19th century. He founded Hungary's Academy of Sciences (1825) and personally financed the building of Budapest's famous Chain Bridge (completed in 1848), which is named for him. An influential writer on subjects ranging from economics to horse breeding, he sought reform within the Habsburg monarchic system, and viewed the outbreak of revolution in 1848 with mixed emotions. After it ended in failure and destruction, he went mad.

3 Cultural Notes

LITERATURE

There are relatively few major writers in Hungarian before 1800 since Latin was the country's official and literary language until the late 19th century (Latin was even the language of parliamentary debate until 1844). Very little other than modern works is available in English translation; a wider variety exists for readers of German, since Hungarian literature is regularly translated into that tongue.

In the early 20th century the dramatists Ferenc Herczeg and Ferenc Molnár achieved international fame. The great poets of the same period are Endre Ady (*Poems,* HCF; also *The Explosive Country,* essays, Collets, U.K.) and Attila József (*Works,* HCF). The tormented poetry of Miklós Radnóti, murdered by the Nazis after years in a labor camp, is well represented by *Under Gemini* (selected poems and a memoir; Ohio University Press). György Faludy was persecuted by both the Nazis and the Communists (*Selected Poems,* Georgia University Press). A valued contemporary poet is the elegant Sándor Weőres (*Eternal Moment,* New Rivers).

One of Hungary's greatest 20th-century poets is sadly not in print in English, except for his children's stories: Look in libraries for Gyula Illyés's *People of the Puszta* (Corvina, U.K.), which plunges the reader into the grim lives of the nation's horribly oppressed prewar peasantry. Well-known modern prose writers include magical realist Géza Csáth (*The Magician's Garden,* Columbia University Press) and György Konrád, whose compelling novels are extremely dark and alienated (*The Case Worker, The City Builder,* both Penguin; *The Loser,* Harcourt Brace). Konrád's *Antipolitics* (Holt) is an important book, which anticipated *perestroika* and the revolutions of 1989. Also widely read in the West are Miklós Haraszti's *A Worker in a Workers' State* (Universe) and *The Velvet Prison: Artists Under State Socialism,* the first of which earned him a prison term.

The Hungarian publishing house Corvina has a number of titles in English translation, including three good anthologies of 20th-century literature: *Present Continuous: Contemporary Hungarian Writing, Nothing's Lost: Twenty-Five Hungarian*

Short Stories, Today: An Anthology of Contemporary Hungarian Literature. Many of Corvina's publications are available at the Bestsellers bookstore in Budapest.

Zsolt Csalog's *Lajos M., Aged 42* (Maecenas, Budapest) is an astonishing tale of life in a Soviet POW camp.

There are some titles published in the U.S., too. They include: *Turmoil in Hungary* (New Rivers), an anthology of 20th-century poetry; the somewhat pricey *Ocean at the Window; Hungarian Prose and Poetry Since 1945* (University of Minnesota Press); and *Modern Hungarian Poetry* (Columbia University Press).

MUSIC

Hungarian musical history is dominated by three great late 19th- and early 20th-century names: Liszt, Bartók, and Kodály.

Ferenc (or Franz) Liszt (1811–86) is a towering figure, one of Europe's greatest piano virtuosos and most successful performers ever. Though born in Hungary his birthplace is now part of Austria, he never spoke Hungarian well, and he lived most of his life elsewhere—he really belongs to the German musical tradition. As a composer, he is known as the inventor of the symphonic poem, and is the very soul of unbuttoned, ivory-chewing Romantic pianism. He was a proud but extraordinarily generous man, who as a conductor or through his influence with publishers launched the careers of many other composers, Brahms, Grieg, and MacDowell among them; he was also a great defender of Wagner. Today he is much more respected as a performer than as a composer, though his influence was vast. About 900 of his 1,300 works were transcriptions of others' work, often hugely ambitious—he even transcribed complete Beethoven symphonies for the piano.

Béla Bartók (1881–1945) is among the most important musicologists and composers of our century. In his earliest years he was a devoted student of Liszt and Wagner,

Did You Know . . . ?

- Rubik's Cube, the popular toy, was designed by Hungarian Ernő Rubik.
- About a million citizens of the U.S. are of Hungarian heritage.
- In 1991, at 15 1/2, Hungarian schoolgirl Judit Polgár became the youngest chess grandmaster ever.
- The first car produced in Hungary since before World War II—a General Motors Opel Astra—rolled off the assembly lines in early 1992 in Szentgotthard.
- In Hungarian, the commonly used greeting of men to women and children to their elders is "I kiss your hand" (*kezet csokolom*).
- The Hungarian word "hello," pronounced almost identically to its English equivalent, is used in saying good-bye.
- The family name precedes the given name in Hungary.
- Among famous Hungarian-born people are Joseph Pulitzer (after whom the prize is named), Arthur Koestler (author of *Darkness at Noon*), Albert Szent-Györgyi (Nobel Prize–winning discoverer of vitamin C), and Edward Teller (atomic physicist).
- Swedish diplomat Raoul Wallenberg, stationed in Budapest, saved thousands of Hungarian Jews from World War II Nazi death camps.

and a brilliant pianist. Later he became a passionate collector, with his friend Zoltán Kodály (1882–1967), of Slovak and Magyar folk music in Romania and Hungary. Bartók realized that what was known as "Hungarian Gypsy music" was really quite recent Hungarian music performed by Gypsy musicians, often embellished beyond recognition. Much older and much more interesting was the true rural Gypsy music, and the authentic Hungarian peasant music, which Bartók and Kodály set out to catalog. Altogether they collected about 7,000 tunes (on 15,000 discs).

Both Bartók (with his *Mikrokosmos,* 153 study pieces for young pianists) and Kodály (with a highly influential system of general music education based on choral singing) made important contributions to music teaching as well as to ethnomusicology.

Gypsies have long had an honored place in national musical life. In 1930 the funeral of Béla Radics, a famed performer, attracted 50,000 people, and was accompanied by an orchestra of 500 Gypsy musicians. A memorial ceremony three months later boasted an orchestra 1,000 strong, and required special trains from all over the country.

ART & ARCHITECTURE

Very little medieval architecture has survived in Hungary, though the Gothic was highly developed, especially in Buda and Visegrád. The only medieval building extant is the Coronation Church of St. Matthias, originally a Romanesque church, Gothicized in the 14th and 15th centuries. After being used as a mosque by the Turks and then as a Jesuit monastery, it was restored by Emperor Franz Joseph. In Esztergom stands one of the earliest extant Renaissance buildings outside Italy. The Chapel of Archbishop Tamás Bakócz, now part of a later cathedral, dates from 1507 and derives from Florentine models. As in Czechoslovakia, Italian artists were brought to Hungary at an early date.

Centuries of political turmoil, war, and the Turkish occupation, which lasted until the early 1700s, severely limited the scope of Renaissance construction, and delayed the adoption of the neoclassical style until the mid-18th century. Buda was expanded and rebuilt following a great fire in 1723, and Pest was extended in the 1770s, yielding a number of notable neoclassical structures, many of which did not survive World War II. Under the Counter-Reformation, the Catholic church built several baroque churches, which show first an Italian, later a Viennese, influence. The greatest is the University Church in Pest (completed 1742) by Mayerhoffer, with a very ornate interior (note the trompe-l'oeil architectural features on the painted ceiling). Mayerhoffer also built the rococo palace at Gödöllő.

The most beautiful surviving baroque palace is the 126-room Esterházy Palace at Fertőd (near Győr), now an agricultural research center, but open to visitors who wish to examine its sweeping, dignified architecture and restrained decoration.

Some of the most important architecture of the 19th century came about because of the replanning of the twin capitals of the Austro-Hungarian Empire, Vienna and Budapest, under the ambitious Franz Joseph. Budapest's 19th-century heritage survived World War II and the Soviet invasion of 1956 better than buildings from previous periods, though much restoration remains to be done. The National Museum

IMPRESSIONS

To be a Hungarian is a permanent joy.
—Joseph Wechsberg, *The Lost World of the Great Spas,* 1979

(1837–47) is in a Romantic-neoclassical fusion style that just predated Franz Joseph. It stands behind the enormous neo-Gothic Parliament (completed 1902), which honors London's Westminster; it's considered an odd but successful stylistic hybrid.

Hungary boasts many 19th-century churches. Among the most renowned are the massive St. Stephen's Basilica in Budapest, a neobaroque design with heavy, intricate interior decoration, and the Esztergom cathedral, which dominates that city's skyline from its proud hilltop site. Its interior gives an impression of lightness, in marked contrast to St. Stephen's.

Before World War I, Hungarian architecture took a heady draught of Viennese Jugendstil (art nouveau), mingling it with the still-prevalent 19th-century eclecticism. One of the best survivors of Budapest's war damage is the IBUSZ headquarters, built in 1909. Since 1945 Hungarians have suffered the indignities of brutal Communist monoliths.

Aside from interior architectural painting and sculpture, folk art is the most vital artistic tradition in Hungary, cherished and protected for over a century by an intelligentsia in search of the Magyar essence. This nationalistic interest has resulted in vast collections of recorded music, dances on film, and all manner of craft objects (especially textiles and pottery) and photographic records, as well as the famous museum villages. The tourist industry has since picked up where the antiquarians left off; if the result is a somewhat "kitschified" folk-art industry, undoubtedly it has enabled various traditions to survive, and beneath the clichés an authentic rural culture does live on.

In this century, Hungary has been distinguished by the modern painter Victor Vasarely (b. 1908), whose geometric designs are familiar worldwide; László Moholy-Nagy (1895–1947), who pioneered abstract photography and experimented with alternative printing methods; and the courageous and flamboyant war photographer Robert Capa (1913–54), born Endre Friedmann, who produced immortal images of the Spanish Civil War and World War II only to be killed by a land mine in Vietnam. All three, however, spent their most productive years outside their homeland.

4 Food & Drink

FOOD Rich and savory soups, stews, and sauces are the highlights of Hungary's distinctive and colorful cuisine. Hungary's renowned *paprika,* the red powder ground from peppers, comes in as many varieties as the peppers themselves. Ranging from sweet (*édes*) to hot (*csípös*), it can be found in countless Hungarian dishes. Butter and bacon drippings are both the leaven and the curse of Hungarian food. Even if you're not trying to eat more healthily, you may find it difficult to stomach a full traditional meal more than every other day.

Lunch, the main meal of the day, begins with soup. *Gyümölcs leves* (a cold fruit soup) is excellent when in season. *Babgulyás* (a hearty bean soup) or *halászle* (a fish soup popular at river and lakeside eateries) can constitute meals in themselves.

The main course is generally a hefty meat dish. Try the *paprika csirke* (chicken cooked in a savory paprika sauce). It's especially good with *galuska* (a pasta dumpling usually made from scratch). *Pörkölt* is a stewed meat dish, which comes in many varieties. *Töltött káposzta* (whole cabbage leaves stuffed with rice, meat, and spices) is another favorite. Vegetarians will mystify waiters throughout Hungary, but would do well to order *lecsó tojással* (eggs scrambled in a thick tomato-onion-paprika sauce), *rántott sajt* (batter-fried cheese with tartar sauce), or *turós csusza tepertő nelkul* (a macaroni-and-cheese dish).

Snack foods include *lángos* (a slab of deep-fried bread served with your choice of toppings: sugar and whipped cream, or garlic sauce and cheese). *Palacsinta* (a paper-thin crêpe stuffed with cheese or draped in hot-chocolate sauce) is a treat that shouldn't be missed. Ice cream (*fagylalt*) is sold by the scoop (*gomboc*). The scoops are small, so order more than one. Ask for the flavors in the order in which you want them put into the cone—few Hungarians get more than one scoop of the same flavor. Fruit flavors are produced seasonally: In the spring try strawberry (*eper*) and sour cherry (*meggy*); in the fall, plum (*szilva*) and pear (*körte*); another summer regular is the delicious cinnamon (*fahéj*).

Hungarian pastries are delicious, so indulge. The light, flaky *retes* are filled with fruit or cheese. *Csoki torta* is a straightforwardly decadent chocolate layer cake and *Dobos torta* is topped with a shiny caramel crust. Pastry made with poppy seed (*mákos*) is a Hungarian specialty. *Gesztenye* (chestnut) is another popular ingredient in coffee-house desserts.

Hungarian bread is baked without preservatives, so people buy just enough for each day. A small paper sticker adorns each loaf, noting the place and day it was baked. There are a number of fine cheeses available in Hungary: *Karavan füstölt* (a smoked cheese), Edámi; and marvány (similar to blue cheese). Picnickers can sample any of Hungary's excellent salamis. In season, produce is delightfully cheap and of the highest quality. You won't find much fresh fruit or vegetables in the winter or in traditional dishes served in restaurants, but there are wonderful open-air markets in every town and city, where, at least in summer, you'll be amazed at the abundance and variety. You might as well be forewarned: Sour cherries (*meggy*) in July are out of this world.

DRINK Hungary does not have a beer culture like the neighboring Austrians, Czechs, and Slovaks, and as a result its beer is unexceptional. The best brand is Dreher, and can be found everywhere in the country. Austrian beer is easily found, but beware—most of it is produced under license in Hungary and tastes suspiciously like the Hungarian beer you should be avoiding.

Hungarian wines, on the other hand, are excellent. The most reknowned are the red Egri Bikavér (Eger Bull's Blood), and the white Tokaj wines, *száraz* (dry) or *édes* (sweet). Soproni wines also enjoy an international reputation.

Unicom, the richly aromatic bitter which some call "Hungary's national drink," is a taste worth acquiring. Pálinka is another variety of Hungarian "fire water" that is often brewed at home and acclaimed for its "medicinal" value.

Most fruit juice sold in Hungary is diluted with water and sweetened with sugar. Pure fruit juice usually carries the notation "100%" somewhere on the box; anything less will say "drink" or "nectar."

18

Planning a Trip to Hungary

ALTHOUGH HUNGARY POSES FEWER PROBLEMS FOR THE TRAVELER THAN SOME OTHER Eastern European countries, seeing this beautiful country is still not as simple as touring through Western Europe. Therefore, additional care in planning will pay off handsomely. This chapter is devoted to the where, when, and how of your trip—things you need to know *before* you go—the advance-planning issues required to get it together and take it on the road.

1 Information, Entry Requirements & Money

SOURCES OF INFORMATION

IN THE U.S. The formerly state-run Hungarian travel agency **IBUSZ** provides tourist information and books hotels; see "Saving Money on Accommodations" in "Enjoying Hungary on a Budget" below in this chapter. IBUSZ has an office at One Parker Plaza, Fort Lee, NJ 07024 (☎ **201/592-8585,** or toll free **800/367-7878;** fax 201/592-8736).

ENTRY REQUIREMENTS

Citizens of the U.S., Canada, the United Kingdom, and Ireland need only their passport to visit Hungary for up to 90 days. Citizens of Australia and New Zealand require a visa. This can normally be issued at the border if you arrive by road, air, or riverboat (*not* by rail), but it is prudent (and cheaper) to get your visa at a Hungarian consulate abroad.

In the U.S., contact the Hungarian Embassy, 3910 Shoemaker St. NW, Washington, DC 20008 (☎ **202/362-6730**), or the Hungarian Consulate, 223 E. 52d St., New York, NY 10022 (☎ **212/752-0661**).
In Canada, contact the embassy at 7 Delaware Ave., Ottawa, ON K2P 012 (☎ **613/232-1711**).
In the U.K., the embassy is at 35 Eaton Place, London SW1X 8BY (☎ **235-7191**).
In Australia, 17 Beale Crescent, Deakirn, ACT 2600, Canberra (☎ **282-3266**). Hungary does not have embassies in New Zealand and Ireland.

The embassy will need your passport, two photos, and $15. Single-entry, multiple-entry, and transit visas are available. Transit visas permit a maximum stay of 48 hours. Regular tourist visas permit stays up to a maximum of 30 days. Visas are valid for six months from the day they're issued. Remember that you must hold onto the visa paper that accompanies the stamp in your passport; it constitutes your permission to exit Hungary.

MONEY

CASH/CURRENCY The official currency of Hungary is the **forint (Ft),** made up of 100 **fillérs.** Banknotes are printed in denominations of 50, 100, 500, 1,000, and 5,000 forints, and there are coins of 1, 2, 5, 10, and 20 forints, and 10, 20, and 50 fillérs. The prices in this book were calculated at 98 Ft = $1. Thus 1 Ft = just over 1¢, 100 Ft = $1.02, and 1,000 Ft = $10.20. Because of inflation of the forint, you may receive more when you visit.

If you have forints left over when you leave Hungary, you may re-exchange back into dollars half the total sum you originally exchanged, up to $100, provided you have the currency-exchange receipts. The best response to this regulation is to exchange only a little bit of money at a time. You're not allowed to export or import more than 1,000 Ft ($10.20) per person.

There are numerous exchange offices now in Budapest, as well as exchange desks in tourist offices throughout the country, but the best rates and lowest commissions can generally be found in banks. Changing outside official offices is forbidden.

TRAVELER'S CHECKS Most official exchange offices happily accept traveler's checks for exchange into Hungarian forints. The state-run OTP and Posta Bank are exceptions. Exchange rates are the same as for cash, but this could change, so compare rates.

CREDIT CARDS Hungary's better hotels, stores, and restaurants accept credit cards; otherwise, you'll need cash.

Any IBUSZ office in the country should be able to give VISA cash advances in forints. American Express cardholders can get cash advances at the American Express office in Budapest (see "Fast Facts" in Chapter 19) or at two cash-advance ATMs in the city: one is just outside the office, while the other is in the main hall of Ferihegy 1, the older airport terminal.

A Note on Prices

Some prices in the following chapters are given in German marks (DM). Because Western currencies are more stable than the "soft" Hungarian forint, some businesses—mainly hotels—choose to base their prices on the daily exchange rate of the mark. The dollar amount of those prices is based on $1 = 1.70 DM. If the dollar rises, some

What Things Cost in Hungary	U.S. $
Airport Minibus from Budapest's airport to the city center	6.10
Metro from Keleti train station to Deák tér in Budapest	.25
Local telephone call	.05
Double room, with bath, at the Budapest Hilton Hotel (deluxe)	191.00
Double room, with bath, at Budapest's Hotel Metro (moderate)	39.30
Double room, with bath, at Sárospatak's Hotel Borostyán (budget)	18.35
Lunch for one, without wine, at Szürkebarát Pinceborozó, in Győr (moderate)	4.75
Lunch for one, without wine, at McDonald's, in Budapest (budget)	2.85
Dinner for one, without wine, at Kikelet Vendéglő, in Budapest (moderate)	8.40
Dinner for one, without wine, at Bohemtanya, in Budapest (budget)	4.50
Half liter of beer	1.05
Coca-Cola	.50
Cup of coffee	.35
Roll of ASA 100 Fujichrome film, 36 exposures	6.90
Admission to the Budapest History Museum	.40
Movie ticket	1.25
Concert at the Hungarian State Opera House, Budapest	5.00

hotel costs could be lower than those cited in this book; if it falls, the reverse could be true.

2 When to Go

CLIMATE The climate in Hungary is very pleasant: cool in winter and warm in summer, with few temperature extremes. The annual mean temperature is 50°F, and summer temperatures rarely exceed 80° to 85°F. There are more than 2,000 hours of sunshine per year in Hungary. January is the coldest month, averaging 30°F. Spring is usually mild and, especially in May and June, wet, and autumn is usually pleasant with mild weather through October.

Budapest's Average Daytime Temperatures

	Jan	Feb	Mar	Apr	May	June	July	Aug	Sept	Oct	Nov	Dec
Temp. (°F)	30	34	38	53	62	68	72	71	63	52	42	35
Temp. (°C)	–1	1	3	12	17	20	22	22	17	11	6	2

HOLIDAYS The official holidays in Hungary are: January 1 (New Year's Day), March 15 (National Day), Easter Monday, May 1 (Labor Day), August 20 (Constitution Day), October 23 (Anniversary of the 1956 Uprising), December 24–25 (Christmas).

Hungary Calendar of Events

January to March

- **Spring Festival** (Mar), in Szentendre. Music and dance, coinciding with the Budapest Spring Festival in the last half of March.
- **Spring Festival** (Mar), in Kecskemét. Held in conjunction with the Budapest Spring Festival, with many street merchants in the town center and open-air dances, concerts, and other events.
- **Spring Festival** (Mar), in Sopron. Street fairs and music in tandem with the Budapest Spring Festival.

April to June

- **Easter** (Apr), in Hollókő. Celebrated in typical folk fashion in a quaint village.
- **Savaria International Dance Contest** (May), in Szombathely. In late May or the beginning of June.
- **Szentendre Theater Performance** (June), in Szentendre. Continues until July.
- **Visegrád Palace Games** (June), in Visegrád. Pageant and equestrian tournaments in period costumes in the old royal castle.
- **Chamber Music Concerts** (June), in Keszthely. Chamber music in the elegant Festetics Palace; continues until August.
- **Pécs Summer Theater** (June), in Pécs. Concerts, folklore performances, ballet, and operetta, held in open-air theaters; continues until August.
- **Győr Music Summer** (June), in Győr. Classical concerts and operas around town in June and July.
- **Sopron Weeks** (June), in Sopron. Concerts, organ recitals, opera performances, folk-art fair, and other cultural events, in late June and about half of July.

- **Savaria Festival** (June), in Szombathely. Concerts in front of the Temple of Isis.

July to December

- **Anna Ball** (Saturday nearest July 26), in Balatonfüred. Highlight of the Lake Balaton social season.
- **Szeged Summer Festival** (approx. July 20–Aug 20), in Szeged. Ballets, dramas, folk dances, concerts, and other events take place on a stage in front of Szeged's Votive Church, as well as throughout the town.
- **Savaria Autumn Festival** (Sept), in Szombathely. Concerts, sports competitions, folk dances, exhibitions, and other cultural events.

Budapest Calendar of Events

January to June

- **Budapest Spring Festival** (10 days at the end of Mar). Festival boasting "100 venues and 1,000 events." Highlights include an outdoor fair on Castle Hill by the Fisherman's Bastion, with folk art for sale and a small performance stage; a concert stage in Vigadó tér for outdoor performances by the Danube; and a rich music program in theaters across town. Simultaneous festivals are held in Sopron, Kecskemét, and Szentendre, making this a great time of year to visit Hungary.
- **Budapest Summer Program** (June–Aug). Accelerated program of cultural events continuing through August, with a special music series on Castle Hill in Buda and in the Dominican Courtyard of the Hilton Hotel. Other events are held in the Margaret Island Open-Air Theater and the Buda Park Theater.

July to December

- **Budapest Art Weeks** (Sept). Concerts; theater, ballet, and dance performances; film premiéres.

3 Alternative Travel

THE SPAS OF HUNGARY Spas are a popular part of Hungarian culture, not just for their curative benefits but also for their social ones. Hungary can boast a second "sea" besides the inland Lake Balaton—the underground sea of mineral water. The thermal and mineral springs are deemed effective cures for a variety of ailments from nervous disorders to gastric complaints. In Budapest alone there are 123 mineral springs, and there are extensive springs at Hévíz, Bük-fürdő, Hajdúszoboszló, and Zalakaros, to name a few.

Although hydrotherapy went out of style in North America while Babe Ruth was still on the Yankees, it remains popular in Central Europe. Whatever actual health benefits spas may or may not have, the thermal bath is a weary traveler's delight. Look for the free "Spas in Hungary" booklet in Budapest's Tourinform office.

SPORTS VACATIONS Surprisingly for a landlocked nation, Hungary offers many water-oriented activities. The fishing is good, with numerous protected and stocked watersheds. Sailing and windsurfing on Lake Balaton are pursued with fervor. There are numerous rivers on which you can go rafting or canoeing, and the Danube is historically the principal artery of communication in Hungary.

You can go hiking almost anywhere you please on the numerous well-maintained trails. Some of the most beautiful areas are the Mátra Mountains in the north, the hills just west of Budapest, and some of the terrain along the northern shore of Lake Balaton.

Hungarian history would have been much different if the Magyars had not been the consummate horsemen that they were. This tradition of horseback riding and breeding horses lives on today. The most exciting place to ride horses is at Hungary's numerous mansion hotels, where you live in an elegant mansion dating back hundreds of years and use the mansion stables. Rentals and lessons are quite reasonably priced. Quite a few mansion hotels are listed throughout the Hungary chapters, with horse-rental prices listed. See "Suggested Itineraries," below, for a tour of my favorite mansion hotels.

Hunting is popular in Hungary, especially among Germans, Austrians, and Italians. About 16,000 people a year try their luck in the Hungarian wilds. For more information, contact Tourinform.

4 Tips for Students

Students in Hungary receive discounts on most international train tickets, regardless of whether tickets are bought through the rail company or an agent. MALÉV, the Hungarian airline, offers some of Eastern Europe's most heavily discounted fares to those under 25 years old, which must be bought directly from the airline no earlier than seven days in advance. Students also receive discounted admission at almost every museum.

The former Communist youth travel agency in Hungary, **Express,** runs a ticket office in Budapest at V, Zoltán u. 10 (☎ **1/111-9898;** fax 1/111-6418), where you can get the latest information on discount train and plane tickets and youth ID cards. If you can, arrange to speak to Judith Sziranyi, a very helpful agent. The office is open Monday through Thursday from 8:30am to 4:30pm and on Friday from 8:30am to 3pm.

5 Getting There

BY PLANE Austrian Airlines (☎ toll free in the U.S. **800/843-0002**) has connecting flights from the U.S. Connections from Vienna to Budapest and back leave three times a day Sunday to Friday (twice on Saturdays).

MALÉV, the Hungarian national carrier (☎ toll free **800/223-6884**), has an extensive European network as well as nonstop flights from New York. Other major American and European airlines also serve Budapest.

BY CAR The Vienna–Budapest expressway is due to be finished in 1995, cutting travel time considerably. The border crossings from Austria and the Czech and Slovak Republics (from which countries most Westerners enter Hungary) are hassle-free; you may be requested to present your driver's license, vehicle registration, and proof of international insurance (the so-called Green Card). If you're driving a rental car, make sure you have that Green Card, which is not automatically given by all rental agencies. In addition, your car should have a decal on it indicating country of registration. Although Hungary requires the International Driver's License (obtainable from any AAA office), I've never been asked to present mine.

BY TRAIN Approximately 10 trains a day arrive in Budapest from Vienna; the journey takes between three and four hours and costs roughly $30. You can also reach Budapest from Bratislava in three hours; from Ljubljana via a seven-hour day train; from Prague in 7 1/2 hours by day or 10 hours overnight; and on overnight trains from Berlin (15 hours), Warsaw or Kraków (12 hours), or Bucharest (16 hours). For more information, pick up a copy of the Thomas Cook European Timetable, or call Rail Europe toll free at **800/848-7245.**

BY BUS From Vienna, there are four buses daily to Budapest (at 7am, 9am, 5pm, and 7pm), departing from the Wien Mitte bus station and stopping at Vienna's airport. You can get tickets and information from Blaguss Reisen, Wiedner Hauptstrasse 15 (☎ **50-18-00**) or from the bus station (☎ **712-0451**). The price of a one-way ticket is 270 AS ($22.50).

BY BOAT An alluring but expensive alternative to travel by bus or train from Vienna from April to mid-October is the daily Danube hydrofoil between Vienna and Budapest. The trip takes 4 1/2 hours downstream and 5 1/2 hours upstream. For reservations and more information in Vienna, contact MAHART, Karlsplatz 2/8 (☎ **505-5644** or **505-3844**); in Budapest, contact MAHART, V, Belgrád rakpart (☎ **118-1704** or **118-1743**). A one-way ticket on the hydrofoil costs 730 AS ($60) from Vienna to Budapest.

You can also book a hydrofoil seat before you leave the U.S. through the Hungarian Hotels Sales Office, 6033 W. Century Blvd., Suite 670, Los Angeles, CA 90045 (☎ **310/649-5960,** or—for travel agents only—toll free **800/448-4321**). The price is the same as you'd pay in Vienna, but unfortunately they don't take reservations directly from individuals; you must ask your travel agent to do it for you (in the likely case that your travel agent doesn't know about these hydrofoils, give him or her the above information). This office can also help reserve certain hotels in Hungary (see "Saving Money on Accommodations" in "Enjoying Hungary on a Budget," below). If you like travelling by hydrofoil, but find the price a bit too high for you, then this is what you should do: Once you arrive in Budapest, ride the incredibly inexpensive hydrofoil up the Danube to Esztergom, taking in the glories of the Danube Bend, Hungary's most scenic stretch of the river. See Chapter 20 for details.

6 Getting Around

BY PLANE There is no domestic air service in Hungary.

BY TRAIN Hungary has a good rail network with many lines extending from Budapest to various destinations across the country. Although the system is excellent for getting from Budapest to most Hungarian cities, it doesn't lend itself to a circular tour of the country, so you may have to take some buses for extensive sightseeing. The state-run rail company is known as MÁV.

Since the country is so small, Hungarians don't make a fuss about domestic train travel. Tickets are just wispy slips of paper, and should not be bought far in advance, as they lose their validity quickly. For one-way trips, tickets for up to 100km must be used on the day of purchase; tickets for 101 to 200km must be used on the day of purchase or within an additional 24 hours; tickets for 201 to 400km must be used on the day of purchase or within an additional 48 hours; tickets for more than 400km must be used on the day of purchase or within an additional 72 hours.

If you choose to buy a round-trip ticket, which, incidentally, will *not* give you any additional savings, another—somewhat simpler—set of restrictions applies.

Round-trip tickets for less than 100km must be used (that is, you must complete the round-trip) on the day of purchase or within an additional 72 hours. Above 101km, they are valid for 30 days.

All trips may be interrupted *once* for any amount of time within the above limits, provided you get your ticket stamped at the station and continue on the same line.

If a train is marked on the schedule with an R in a box (all trains called Expressz or Intercity will be), you need a reservation (*helyjegy*), which costs 38 Ft (38¢) at the ticket window, but 150 Ft ($1.55) on the train.

At all train stations in Hungary the yellow schedules are departures (*induló vonatok*) and the white ones are arrivals (*érkező vonatok*).

A number of discounts are available: children under 4 travel free; children 4 to 14 travel for half price (ask for the *gyerek jegy*); family tickets are available for 33% off (ask about the *csaladi jegy*). Interrail and Eurail passes are valid in Hungary.

For sample fares, see the individual city sections in the following chapters. The Hungary Pass, valid in first class on all domestic trains, is sold outside Hungary in two flavors: five days of free travel during a 15-day period costs $55, while 10 days over a month costs $69. The 10-day pass, in particular, is a good deal if you will be visiting more than four or five cities outside Budapest. You can buy these passes from any railpass vendor, such as Rail Europe (☎ toll free **800/848-7245**) or Europe Through the Back Door (☎ **206/771-8303**).

Nearly every train station in Hungary has a luggage-check office that charges 60 to 120 Ft (60¢ to $1.20) per bag per day, depending on size. At the larger stations, these offices are open 24 hours a day.

Few tourists know about one of MÁV's best services. In certain scenic regions of the country (Lake Balaton, the Danube Bend, the northern hills), you can rent a bicycle from MÁV for an extremely low price. Inquire at Tourinform in Budapest or when you buy your ticket.

BY BUS Buses go almost everywhere in Hungary and although less comfortable than trains, they are a practical alternative to the radial constraints placed on the traveler by a Budapest-centered railway system. So, for example, if you want to go from Pécs to Szeged, two cities in southern Hungary, a bus is your best bet as the train takes a slow, roundabout route. The main drawback to buses is the crowds, especially in the summer and in the mornings and early evenings, and the typical chaos and shabbiness of bus travel.

There are no private bus companies in Hungary; the state agency, Volán, sports a fleet of mustard-yellow buses. Bus fares are roughly equivalent to second-class rail fares (see individual city chapters for sample fares). Although you are theoretically able to buy your ticket in the station (if there's an open ticket window), almost everyone buys tickets directly from the driver when boarding the bus. Only one-way tickets are sold. Children under 4 ride free, and children 4 to 14 ride for half price.

It's a good idea to get departure times as you arrive at the bus station, or ask your hotel to call the station for you, as officials at the station rarely speak English. You can get a schedule and more information at the main bus terminal in Budapest on Erzsébet tér (☎ **117-2562**).

BY CAR Hungary is the easiest country in Eastern Europe in which to rent a car. The terrain makes for easy but still scenic driving, the roads are superior to their Czech and Polish counterparts, and signposting is accurate and consistent. Hungary itself is so small that you can get almost anywhere from Budapest in three hours. Moreover, the nicest places to stay in Hungary are mansion hotels in the deep countryside, virtually inaccessible without your own wheels.

Rental Cars You may rent a car in Hungary if you are 21 or older and have had your driver's license for more than one year. The fee must be paid in hard (Western) currency and includes comprehensive insurance. Most major credit cards are accepted.

The best rates on rental cars in Hungary are available by calling the major multinational companies several weeks in advance from your own hometown and taking advantage of their special discounts. Reserving from abroad is essential; if you show up at their offices in Budapest you will be quoted a much higher figure. For example, **Budget** (☎ toll free **800/527-0700**) offers an excellent off-season rate for their smallest car when you reserve from abroad: $172 for a week's rental with unlimited mileage. Tax is another 25%. Make sure to pick up your car at the Budapest town office rather than at Ferihegy to avoid the extra 7% airport tax. Not all the multinationals have such good prices out of Budapest. Rates out of Vienna are generally lower, and some companies now permit you to drive Western cars into Eastern Europe. If you arrive without finding a good deal, pick up car rental brochures at the airport or at Tourinform. Some smaller local companies have prices not too far above the multinationals' special offers.

Gasoline Gas stations are generally open daily from 6am to 10pm, but in large towns there's usually one 24-hour filling station. Leaded gasoline of several ratings as well as 95 octane unleaded (called by the German term *bleifrei*), and diesel fuels are all available in Hungary. Gasoline is quite expensive in Hungary, equivalent to the average price in Western Europe.

Driving Rules You drive on the right and obey the standard European rules-of-the-road. Hungarians try to keep things interesting by introducing carts, bicycles, pedestrians, even livestock on most of the major roads. Be alert.

The speed limit on limited-access highways is 120kmph (75 m.p.h.); on a few specially labeled sections of dual carriageway, other roads, 80kmph (50 m.p.h.); and in built-up areas, 50kmph (31 m.p.h.). Pedestrians have the right of way in "zebra crossings" (crosswalks) and at road junctions.

A couple of mandatory rules: Three-point (shoulder harness) seat belts must be worn by everyone in the front seat of a vehicle; no children under the age of 6 are allowed in the front seat; all motorcycle riders and passengers must wear crash helmets; in populated areas you may use your horn only to avoid accidents (not if you're in a bad mood).

Unless you want to extend your stay in Hungary indefinitely (in other words, go to jail for a long time), do not imbibe any substance that will affect your ability to drive and then get behind the wheel. Alcohol, sleeping pills, drugs, and medicines of any sort must not be taken by the driver. The Hungarian police are very, very strict in this regard, and keep a sharp eye out for offenders.

In case of accidents involving any injury and/or serious damage, you must notify the emergency service immediately (☎ **07**). Emergency auto repair is handled by the Hungarian Automobile Club. The breakdown service (☎ **088**) operates 24 hours; in a few areas where this toll-free number isn't available, dial **1/115-3620** or **1/252-8000.**

BY BOAT There's an extensive Danube boat system that runs from April through early October, depending on the weather and the depth of the river. Practically every

MAHART Company

large town on the river is in the network, but most tourists use the boats to make stops at Szentendre, Visegrád, and Esztergom. There are also a number of boats and a few ferries connecting various points on Lake Balaton (see Chapter 22 for details). Tickets are available right at the piers.

There are 10 locations on Lake Balaton where you can charter a sailboat from MAHART, the Hungarian state water-transport company. For information, contact the main office in Siófok (☎ and fax **84/310-050**).

BY BICYCLE If you want to see Hungary by bike, contact the Hungarian Bicycle Tourist Association, IX, Kálvintér 9, 1090 Budapest (☎ **1/217-7208**). You can also ask for the free English-language booklet "Cycling Tours in Hungary" at Tourinform.

HITCHHIKING Hitchhiking is reasonably safe and very common in Hungary. As usual, women should not hitchhike alone.

Suggested Itineraries

CITY HIGHLIGHTS

The Capital

Budapest Even a brief excursion to Hungary should include a visit to Budapest, once the other capital of the Austro-Hungarian Empire. I recommend at least three nights in this fascinating city. A brief excursion to Budapest could be made from Vienna.

The Danube Bend

Szentendre Just 40 minutes from Budapest, a charming village of traditional houses and many art galleries along the Danube.

Visegrád A Danube Bend town once the royal seat in Hungary, with remnants of the 14th-century royal palace and medieval citadel.

Esztergom Danube Bend town that is the center of Hungarian Catholicism, with the largest church in Hungary.

Western Hungary

Sopron Traditional Hungarian town with well-preserved town center recalling Europe of centuries ago. The elegant Esterházy Palace of Fertőd is on the way to Sopron from Budapest.

Kőszeg Sleepy yet quaint town near the Austrian border, important in the Hungarian struggles against the Ottoman Turks.

Szombathely Home to the Temple of Isis and other Roman ruins, historically if not visually impressive. The alluring Romanesque Basilica of Ják is also nearby.

Lake Balaton

A paradise for water-lovers and sun-worshipers. Highlights include **Keszthely,** with the most elegant palace on the lake; **Hévíz,** home to the world's second-largest thermal lake; and **Tihany,** a beautiful peninsula jutting into the lake with the oldest church in the country.

Northern Hungary

Eger Town famous for its "Bull's Blood" wine and castle. Also home to the northernmost Turkish minaret in Europe.
Sárospatak Known for its elegant castle surrounded by a moat.
Aggtelek Large cave complex to explore near the Slovak border.
Hollókő Charming Hungarian museum village.

Southern Hungary

Kecskemét Medium-sized town with a number of pleasant museums. It's also near the Puszta, where you can attend Magyar horse shows.
Pécs A town of fine art museums, as well as an impressive cathedral and several important Turkish buildings including the largest mosque in Hungary.
Szeged Southern city that comes alive during its annual summer festival. Also known for its paprika.

Planning Your Itinerary

The following are only suggestions; cater your own visit to the sights that sound most interesting to you.

If You Have 1 Week

Day 1–3 Arrive in Budapest and, after settling into your hotel, see the many sights of the capital.
Day 4 Take a day trip to Szentendre, on the Danube, returning to Budapest for the night.
Day 5 and 6 Head to Pécs, in southern Hungary, to see its fine art museums and Turkish/Muslim and Christian architecture.
Day 7 Return to Budapest.

If You Have 2 Weeks

Days 1–3 Arrive in Budapest and, after settling into your hotel, see the many sights of the capital.
Day 4 Take a day trip to Szentendre, on the Danube, returning to Budapest for the night.
Day 5 Visit Visegrád and/or Esztergom, two old Danube towns, again returning to Budapest for the night.
Day 6 Journey to the well-preserved traditional Hungarian town of Sopron and take in the nearby sights in western Hungary.
Day 7 Travel on to Kőszeg, with perhaps a visit to Szombathely to see the Roman ruins (which would require an extra day in the region).
Days 8 and 9 If it's summertime, visit the resort towns around Lake Balaton; in colder weather, spend Days 6 to 9 visiting Győr, Fertőd, Sopron, Kőszeg, Szombathely, and Ják in western Hungary.
Days 10 and 11 Head south of Lake Balaton to Pécs, in southern Hungary, to see its fine art museums and Turkish/Muslim and Christian architecture.
Days 12 and 13 Travel on to Kecskemét in central Hungary, and take a day trip to the Puszta.
Day 14 Return to Budapest.

If You Have More Time

Add a few days more in western Hungary (to visit the smaller towns and take some side trips) and Lake Balaton (especially if you seek some summertime fun); or visit Hollókő and Eger in northern Hungary, and consider exploring the Aggtelek Caves. If you've exhausted these towns, visit Szeged in the south or Sárospatak in the north.

A Tour Following the Mansion Hotels

One of the most exciting aspects of a visit to Hungary is the many mansion hotels scattered across the country, mostly quite inexpensive as long as you travel with another person. If you decide to tour Hungary by car, you could stay in these hotels in the country and visit the sights by day. Here is one suggested route—not including Budapest—but of course you can pick and choose a myriad different tour routes according to your preferences.

Day 1 Travel to western Hungary and stay in Győr's Hotel Klastrom, a converted religious cloister (see Section 1 in Chapter 21).

Day 2 Stay in the modest dorm facilities of the Esterházy Palace in Fertőd, surrounded by an elegant and royal setting (see Section 2 in Chapter 21). Visit Sopron on a day trip from here.

Day 3 Drive southeast to the Kúria Panzió, a modest mansion hotel where you can ride horses (see Section 3 in Chapter 21). Explore Kőszeg by day.

Day 4 Travel to just outside Szombathely at Uj-Ebergényi Kastély, an elegant mansion with 55 acres of park as well as a swimming pool and tennis (see Section 3 in Chapter 21). Visit Szombathely by day.

Day 5 Drive south to Keszthely on Lake Balaton, and stay in the Festetics Palace Hotel, the most elegant baroque palace in the region (see Section 3 in Chapter 22).

Day 6 Continue on to Nagyvázsony, just north of Lake Balaton, and stay at the Kastélyszálló Hotel, in a mansion from 1750 well known for its stable of fine horses (see Section 1 in Chapter 22).

Day 7 Make the Taurus Kastélyhotel, outside Székesfehérvár, your next home. Spend a day or two enjoying what is perhaps the most elegant mansion hotel in the country (see Section 6 in Chapter 22), and visit Székesfehérvár by day.

Day 8 Bypass Budapest to the north and check in at the Hotel Kastély Szirák, another one of my favorite mansion hotels in the country, with tennis courts and an 18th-century main house (see Section 1 in Chapter 23). Visit the museum village of Hollókő. Consider an extra day here to take a break from the constant travel.

Days 9 and 10 Swing back south to Gerébi Kastélyszálló outside Kecskemét to enjoy swimming, horseback riding, and tennis amid lovely surroundings (see Section 2 in Chapter 24). Consider spending a day or two here to fully explore the area, including Kecskemét and the Puszta.

7 Enjoying Hungary on a Budget

THE $30-A-DAY BUDGET

Here as elsewhere in Eastern Europe, $30 a day means about $20 a day for accommodations and $10 a day for three meals—which is easiest when there are two of you traveling together and allotting $35 to $40 for a double room. In Budapest it's especially difficult to live on $30 a day, so travelers on a strict budget should stay in private rooms. Elsewhere in Hungary, lodgings are less expensive, so it's possible to live on $30 a day staying in hotels as well. More expensive lodgings and restaurants are also listed from time to time for those willing to spend a bit more in their travels.

SAVING MONEY ON . . .

ACCOMMODATIONS You have a wide variety of accommodation choices in Hungary: mansion hotels, regular hotels, pensions, private rooms, private apartments, hostels, and camping sites.

Hotels are ranked by the international system of stars, five stars being the most luxurious. Almost all of the hotels I have listed have two or three stars. These establishments usually have private bathrooms in most if not all rooms, although in more cramped hotels rooms come with private shower and washbasin but share a hall toilet. Most include an unexceptional continental breakfast in the standard room rate. Most rooms are doubles; outside the few hotels that have single rooms, solo travelers usually pay the double room rate minus one breakfast.

The most exciting hotel options in Hungary are mansion hotels (called *kastélyszálló* in Hungarian). These are mostly 18th- and 19th-century private mansions surrounded by beautiful estates that now rent rooms. At the best of these you can play tennis, go horseback riding, or enjoy other activities. Most are located outside small villages and are hard to get to without a car. They are also remarkable values. A sample tour staying in castle hotels is mentioned in "Suggested Itineraries," above.

A pension (*panzió*) is often a large private home converted into a hotel, charging rates lower than hotels. The rooms come in all shapes and sizes, and generally have more character than the average hotel room. The key piece of advice on pensions is that you should (1) always check the room before renting; (2) look at another room if you're unhappy, since rooms are rarely identical; and (3) treat the pension owner as you would a host, not a receptionist—he or she is nearly always very proud of the establishment and cares very much what you seem to think of it. Quite a few new pensions have opened in Hungary over the past few years.

One of Hungary's great money-saving options is private rooms, where you rent a room in a Hungarian home, usually sharing the bathroom with the host family. Private apartments or houses are also sometimes available. Prices vary from town to town and within each town according to location and facilities. You may want to take advantage of private rooms, especially in Budapest where hotel prices are rather high. In each provincial town, you'll usually find two offices that reserve private rooms: one run by IBUSZ and another run by a locally based "tourism company" such as Ciklámen Tourist or Balatontourist. The locals tend to be friendlier and open longer, but at IBUSZ you can normally pay by credit card. Remember that private room rentals of three nights or less cost 30% more than for four or more nights; this is sometimes phrased as a "surcharge" after an agent has quoted you the lower, longer-term rate. In summer, university and college dormitories are converted to youth hostels throughout the country, where beds are available for a very low price.

Travelers on a very limited budget can stay at **campsites** across the country, ranked with one to three stars. A single-star campsite is basically fenced-off, open ground with communal washing and toilet facilities. There are over 100 camping locations in Hungary, open from early May to early October. Tourinform gives out a free, complete list. Most are really only suitable for motor camping, but it's possible to ask locals if you can pitch your tent on their land. Remember, ask first.

Reservations You should know that whatever time of year you plan to arrive in Budapest, you'll be able—on the spot—to take advantage of one of Hungary's greatest bargains: a private room. Still, many travelers opt to prebook hotel rooms for Budapest, particularly in peak season.

For most of the Hungarian hotels listed in this book, the best way to reserve is simply to call before you leave home. But if your tastes run to more expensive hotels, especially those run by Hungary's formerly state-owned hotel chains (HungarHotels, Pannonia, and Danubius), you can prebook rooms in the U.S. Individuals may contact IBUSZ, Hungary's formerly state-owned travel agency, at One Parker Plaza, Fort Lee, NJ 07024 (☎ **201/592-8585,** or toll free **800/367-7878**), but be warned that they do not accept credit cards, so you will have to work well in advance. You can also have your travel agent call the Hungarian Hotel Sales Office, 6033 W. Century Blvd., Suite 670, Los Angeles, CA 90045 (☎ **310/649-5960,** or toll free **800/448-4321**); this office prefers not to deal with individuals.

An important thing to remember about these U.S.-based reservations offices is that they have particular hotels that they are most anxious to sell—and these are usually the largest and most expensive in the country. To get the best value, use this guide to pick hotels that best suit your price range and taste.

INFORMATION Hungary's network of Tourinform offices—official tourist information centers—has recently grown from a single office in downtown Budapest to almost two dozen branches in towns across the country. Friendly, helpful, multilingual, and nonprofit, Tourinform should be your first stop in any town that has one.

MEALS Food in Hungary is generally inexpensive, although over the last few years prices have risen, especially in Budapest. Order with some care to keep costs down. Drinks are taxed at 25%; less alcohol means more savings in Hungary.

Live Gypsy music is a feature of many Hungarian restaurants. A good tip is usually 100 Ft ($1). For 200 Ft ($2.05) they'll play a selection for you; famous tourist restaurants will expect even more from their clients. You can politely refuse. Though the musicians may seem intrusive by Western standards, the attention they give the guests is considered an important part of the Hungarian dining experience.

You may find that the waiter has seemingly disappeared by the time you're ready to pay your bill in a Hungarian restaurant. That's because the customer has to initiate the paying ritual, which goes something like this: Call over your waiter and ask to pay (*fizetni szeretnek*). After handing you the bill, he will stand there, waiting to be paid. Take your time in calculating the tip, and hand him the money, stating the full amount you are paying (bill plus tip). He will give you change on the spot. **Note:** Hungarians *never* leave tips on the table. Such a tip may even be pocketed by the next customer, who would think it was money forgotten by someone. Tips are generally about 10%, and rarely exceed 15%.

A Warning Some restaurants have English-language menus without the prices written in. You may have trouble matching dishes up with the equivalent dishes on the Hungarian-language menu (where prices are, of course, listed) because sometimes everything is in completely different order. This is tantamount to cheating foreign customers, since the waiter can charge anything for a dish with no price next to it. Few, if any, of the restaurants listed here practice this scam, but you may wander into one that does. My advice is to never order a dish without knowing its price in advance.

SIGHTSEEING & EVENING ENTERTAINMENT Museums are very reasonably priced across Hungary; typical admissions are 20 to 80 Ft (20¢ to 80¢). Students and children often enter free.

Cultural events are also very low in cost, with most concerts costing just a few dollars.

SHOPPING The most attractive purchase for most tourists to Hungary is handcrafted items, which consist of everything from hand-painted wood items to delicately dressed dolls. You can also purchase traditional Hungarian folk outfits such as embroidered blouses.

Other popular items include silver, art, and Herend porcelain. The porcelain is sold throughout the country as well as at a special shop outside the factory in the town of Herend. CDs, records, and cassettes of Hungarian composers, like Bartók, and Hungarian folk music (Muzikas is a great group) are a good value.

Though no longer as easy to find (or as cheap) as in the days of the retreating Soviet troops (1990–91), Cold War souvenirs—from military uniforms to lapel pins—are still available in outdoor flea markets around the country.

TRANSPORTATION Public transportation is very inexpensive throughout Hungary. Intercity trains and buses cost just a few dollars (see the individual city chapters for exact prices) and local mass transit runs about 25 Ft (25¢). 35

TIPPING Give honest taxi drivers 10% above the fare or a bit more if the driver carried your luggage around or was otherwise helpful. Tipping in restaurants is also usually 10%. You can add to or subtract from that amount, depending on the service. Always check to see if service charges were added already; all bills are inclusive of taxes. If you feel that the bill is too high, check to see if you've been taxed twice or if there are items on it which you did not have, and always keep a copy of your bill.

Fast Facts: Hungary

American Express There is one American Express office in Hungary, located in Budapest: V, Deák Ferenc u. 10, 1052 Budapest (☎ **1/266-8680;** fax 1/267-2028; telex 22-2124). You can receive mail, replace lost checks and cards, and receive other travel services.

Business Hours Business offices keep about the same hours as in the West, sometimes opening and closing an hour earlier. Stores are generally open Monday through Friday from 10am to 5 or 6pm and on Saturday to 1 or 2pm; closed Sunday. Some stores, particularly in Budapest, have recently started keeping longer hours. Stores with NON-STOP or "0–24" signs are open 24 hours.

Camera/Film Two photographic-store chains have enjoyed a meteoric rise in Hungary in recent years. Sooters and Fotex have stores throughout the country, where all your photographic needs can be filled.

Customs You are allowed to bring no more than 1,000 Ft ($10.20) in cash per person across the border, so don't go buying lots of forints in Vienna. Anything above this limit is unconditionally and automatically donated to the Hungarian Border Patrol. There is no limit to the amount of hard (Western) currency you may bring in. You can import small gift items up to a maximum of 8,000 Ft ($81.65) and you can bring out unlimited food and wine, plus 3,000 Ft ($30.60) of Hungarian goods without receipts. Everything else is subject to duties. "Art" valued at over 1,000 Ft ($12.80) is not exportable unless you buy it in hard-currency stores. If you are uncertain, go in person to Budapest's Customs and Finance Guards, Falk Miksa.

Narcotics, explosives, and firearms are strictly forbidden. Hunting equipment and most advanced electronic equipment—two-way radios (including CBs), radar detectors, etc.—require special permits.

Drugstores Look for the Hungarian word *gyógyszertár,* or *patika.* Hungarian drugstores don't carry many Western medicines, so bring any supplies you need with you.

Electricity The electric current in Hungary is 220 volts, 50 cycles, A.C.

Embassies/Consulates Citizens of New Zealand and Ireland should contact the British embassy for assistance.

- **Australia** The embassy is at VI, Délibáb utca 30, Budapest (☎ **1/153-4233**).
- **Canada** The embassy is at XII, Budakeszi út 32, Budapest (☎ **1/176-7711**).
- **United Kingdom** The embassy is at V, Harmincad u. 6 (☎ **1/118-2888**).
- **United States** The embassy is at V, Szabadság tér 12, Budapest (☎ **1/112-6450**).

Emergencies You can call for assistance at the same telephone numbers anywhere in the country: dial **07** for the **police, 04** for an **ambulance,** and **05** to report a **fire.** The Hungarian Tourist Bureau states that "All foreigners visiting Hungary are entitled to free emergency first aid."

Films *Szinkronizált* means that a film is dubbed in Hungarian; *feliratos* means "subtitled."

Language Hungarian is related only to Finnish and Estonian among European languages, and even there the connection is so ancient that the similarities are only apparent to a trained linguist. The problem, therefore, is that none of the roots are cognate with anything in English, so the glaze of understanding that you have in a Romance or even Slavic language is absent. Just pronouncing Hungarian is easy, though, if you learn a couple of simple rules and go slowly at first, and it's very useful for simple requests such as "telephone card!" Older Hungarians often speak a little German, and younger ones a little English, but with equally modest proficiency. Bring a phrase book if you visit for longer than a week.

Laundry Hungary is not a land of coin-operated laundries, although you will find some stores that do laundry or dry cleaning. I've found the cheapest and most convenient way is to ask the service staff of a hotel or a host of your private room. They usually do a good job and charge very reasonable rates, which you should negotiate beforehand.

Mail Post offices are open Monday through Friday from 8am to 6pm and on Saturday from 8am to 2pm. To receive mail, ask your friends to write you care of American Express (see address above).

Newspapers/Magazines In Budapest, the *International Herald Tribune,* various British newspapers, and Western newsweeklies are widely available. Also useful are the locally published English-language papers. Outside Budapest, some of the above are available, but can be hard to find. Ask in large hotels.

Police In an emergency, dial **07** for the police.

Safety Unfortunately, crime has increased in recent years as Hungary has opened up its borders and dismantled its police state. Many Hungarian towns remain very safe and tranquil, but be prudent in Budapest, where robberies and pickpocketing are frequent occurrences now.

Taxes Tax is already built into the price you see in restaurants, hotels, and stores. Drinks in restaurants and bars are taxed 25% (although food is not). Tourist services such as tours, hotel rooms, and private rooms are taxed 15%.

Telephone/Telex/Fax Be sure to buy a telephone card (*telefonkártya*) if you plan to make any phone calls in Hungary. Though cumbersome coin phones still exist, they are losing favor among tourists and locals alike, and even the smallest villages now have a card phone. Calls are measured in 5-Ft units; cards come in 50- and 120-unit denominations for 250 Ft ($2.55) and 600 Ft ($6.10), respectively. On a local call, one unit buys you three minutes. It helps to dial slowly, as the machines sometimes miss a digit.

For domestic long-distance, you must dial the prefix **06,** wait for the tone, and then dial the city code. The units tick off a little faster, but it's still not expensive. Thus to reach Budapest from the provinces, you dial **06,** wait for the tone, then dial **1** (the Budapest city code), then the seven-digit Budapest number (which always starts with **1** or **2**). City codes outside Budapest have two digits, and local numbers have six digits, almost always starting with **3** or **4.**

For direct-dial international calls, dial the prefix **00** and wait for the tone before you dial the country code. International calls go through pretty well, except to Romania, where it's often faster to book a call at the post office or by calling the international operator at **09.** They cost a lot, however: 66 Ft (66¢) per minute to European countries, 198 Ft ($2) per minute to America or Australia. It helps to use a 120-unit telephone card.

You can reach the various USA Direct services at **00/800-01111** (AT&T), **00/800-01411** (MCI), and **00/800-01877** (Sprint).

Hotels typically add a surcharge to all calls (though some grant free local calls), so use your telephone card.

Television You can watch German-language broadcasts from Austria and Germany in the western part of Hungary. Some hotels (usually upscale) also offer English-language satellite channels.

Time Hungary is six hours ahead of eastern standard or daylight time in the U.S.

Water Most Hungarians drink their tap water, although many prefer the easily available bottled variety.

19

Budapest

BUDAPEST IS ONE OF THE GREAT CAPITALS OF CENTRAL EUROPE, BUILT IN THE GRAND style of Habsburg Vienna itself, the crowning glory of the empire that held the Hungarian people under its sway for so long. "Budapest" is a conglomerate name, signifying the political union in 1873 of the three regions of Buda, Pest, and Óbuda. And the city itself is a conglomeration, carrying the imprint of many masters. Perhaps the most impressive aspect of the Hungarian capital for the modern visitor is how gracefully the various foreign influences have been fused into a bustling modern city.

The Ottoman occupation gave Budapest large public baths and introduced Islamic culture into everything from delicately peaked window frames to the numerous exotic spices found in an authentic Hungarian kitchen. The baths, begun under the Romans and expanded under the Ottomans, harness only some of the 123 mineral springs in Budapest. The volume of "liquid health," as some Hungarians refer to the mineral waters, that bubbles to the surface is so great that it's called "the second river" (after the Danube). The Habsburg era left many of the imposing baroque buildings and stunning parks.

Today Budapest is a vibrant city, complete with an amusement park, dozens of amply supplied markets, restaurants filled with the lively rhythm of Hungarian Gypsy music, busy shopping avenues, and many fashion-conscious people—all of which make a visit there quite exciting. Walk along the waterfront of Pest on a pedestrian mall and admire the Buda castle across the Danube. Stroll through the cobblestone streets of Buda and see houses reconstructed to just the way they were hundreds of years ago. In recent years the city has become even more receptive to foreigners; the unfortunate by-product has been an increase in prices, but it's still far less expensive than the West.

A CAPSULE HISTORY Located on one of Europe's major east-west routes, Budapest has been in the path of most major European invasions. Since Stephen I was crowned King of Hungary on Christmas Day in A.D. 1000, Hungarians have had to defend their country from Europeans, Turks, and Asians. In 1541, following the Hungarian defeat at Mohács, Ottoman armies took the fortified town of Buda. Much of the city was again destroyed when the Habsburgs evicted the Turks in 1686, but reconstruction was swift.

Like most other European capitals, Budapest suffered little physical damage in World War I. However, in the closing days of World War II the Germans demolished all the Danube bridges and fortified Castle Hill. It took the Soviets seven weeks of brutal street fighting to finally take the city. In Budapest more than 80% of all structures were damaged or destroyed.

The 1956 thirteen-day Hungarian Uprising, in which an estimated 2,000 Hungarians were killed by a Warsaw Pact force composed almost entirely of Soviet soldiers, was centered in Budapest. Hundreds of buildings were damaged or even destroyed; thus, not all the bullet marks that can still be seen on side streets are from World War II.

1 Orientation

If you arrive in Budapest from Vienna or elsewhere in Western Europe, you'll find the entire city an immediate relief to your budget. If, however, you're coming from elsewhere in Eastern Europe, you may find it comparatively expensive, but certainly less expensive than the West.

What's Special About Budapest

Architectural Highlights

- Houses of Parliament, a huge structure on the Danube inspired by the Parliament building in London.

Ancient Monuments

- Aquincum, the ruins of a Roman city from 2,000 years ago.

Churches and Synagogues

- Matthias Church, a 15th-century Gothic structure crowning Castle Hill.
- The Great Synagogue, the largest synagogue in Europe.
- St. Stephen's Basilica, a large neo-Renaissance structure in downtown Pest.

Baths

- There are 123 thermal baths across the city, some of them contained in elegant palaces.

Museums

- Hungarian National Museum, with the Crown of St. Stephen and other priceless relics of Hungarian history.
- Museum of Fine Arts, one of Europe's great collection of paintings by the old masters.
- Budapest History Museum, with 2,000 years of local history in the ruins of the former royal palace.
- Museum of Applied Arts, an interesting collection of decorative art.

Natural Landmarks

- The Danube River, the mighty brown body of water that divides the city into Buda and Pest, connected by a series of large bridges.
- Gellért Hill, crowned by a town citadel, with a splendid vantage point over the Danube and the entire town.

Parks

- Városliget Park, the huge city park with a zoo, an amusement park, a boating lake, a Transylvanian castle, a youth center, and more.

Shopping

- Váci utca, the most glamorous pedestrian shopping street in Eastern Europe.
- The Flea Market, with everything from old pocket watches to Soviet military uniforms for sale.

ARRIVING

BY PLANE Hungary's only commercial airport is **Ferihegy International Airport** in Budapest.

Flights on MALÉV (the Hungarian airline) and a few Western airlines such as Lufthansa use the new, efficient **Ferihegy 2** terminal (☎ **157-7000,** for information). All other flights arrive and depart from the older but serviceable **Ferihegy 1** (☎ **157-7155**).

In the arrivals hall at each terminal you'll find currency exchange at reasonable (but not the best) rates, overpriced private-room and car-rental agencies, an information desk, the Airport Minibus desk, and pay phones, for which you'll need to buy a card (try the Airport Minibus desk or the newsstand). You can pick up a Budapest map here, too.

The Airport Minibus service (☎ **157-8555**) is one of the best things about Budapest. For a flat fee of 600 Ft ($6.10) per passenger, courteous, punctual drivers will load your luggage into the back of a white Ford minibus and drop you and several other passengers at the door of your hotel anywhere in the city, at any time of day, even if you're the only passenger. It takes a little longer than a taxi if you're not the first passenger off, but the reliability and honesty of the system is worth it. Simply present yourself at the Airport Minibus desk in the arrivals hall. You can also have the Airport Minibus pick you up at your hotel and drive you out to Ferihegy for the same fee.

There are two cheaper options. Buses marked CENTRUM leave from outside the exit doors at each terminal every half hour from about 6am to 10pm for the Erzsébet tér bus station in the center of Pest. The trip takes 30 to 40 minutes and costs 200 Ft ($2.05). The cheapest way into the city, though, is to spend 50 Ft (50¢) on two bus tickets from the automatic dispensers at each terminal, and ride public bus no. 93 (red, not black) to the last stop, Kőbánya-Kispest. There you transfer to the metro (Blue Line), which takes you into the center.

Do not take a taxi into town. A fair fare is 1,000 to 1,500 Ft ($10.20 to $15.30), but you will almost certainly be overcharged.

BY TRAIN Budapest has three major train stations and a number of smaller subsidiary and suburban stations. Each station has several private accommodations offices (see "Where to Stay," below, for details).

If you arrive by train from the West, you'll normally arrive at **Keleti pu.,** ("pu." is the abbreviation for *pályaudvar,* or train station), located on the east side of Pest. Keleti pu. has two main levels. The *upper level* is constructed in the classic stone and iron-beam manner of older European train stations. Here you find the tracks, international ticket counters, train information booths. You can leave your bags with the 24-hour baggage-check service near the head of Track 5 for 60 to 120 Ft (60¢–$1.20) per bag per day. There are sometimes free luggage carts nearby. Taxis are to the right after exiting the train platform. The *lower level,* a modern plastic-tiled cavern houses domestic ticket windows and the entrance to Metro Line 2 (the Red Line).

The second major train station in Budapest is **Nyugati pu.,** located just north of downtown Pest. The station receives a variety of arrivals, from Szeged in the south of Hungary to Berlin far to the north. The central arrivals hall features a big old-fashioned glass facade. Near the head of Track 10 is the 24-hour luggage-check service. Tram lines depart from directly in front of the station. Down below there's a vast underground area that has several travel offices renting private rooms (see "Where to Stay," below, for details). Metro Line 3 (Blue Line) leaves from this level.

There is also a third major train station, **Déli pu.,** located west of Castle Hill in Buda. Trains from Lake Balaton as well as western and southern Hungary and southern Europe often arrive here. It's at the beginning of the metro's Red Line, which connects with the center of Pest. To reach the 24-hour luggage-check service, go down to the lower level, turn left until you reach the street, then turn right. Luggage carts are available at several points in the station.

BY BUS There are three bus stations in Budapest, each serving a different area of the country.

Buses from western Hungary, the airport, and international destinations arrive at the **Erzsébet tér station** (☎ **117-2562**) in central Pest. It's across the street from the

Deák tér metro station, where the city's metro lines meet. There's a luggage-check office here, but it's only open from 6am to 6pm.

Buses from the towns on the Danube Bend arrive at the **Árpád Híd station** (☎ **129-1450**), by the Árpád Híd metro station (Blue Line).

Buses from anywhere in Hungary east of the Danube arrive at the **Népstadion station** (☎ **252-4496**), by the Népstadion metro station (Red Line).

BY BOAT Boats from the Danube Bend arrive at the **Vigadó tér boat station** (☎ **118-1223**). The Vörösmarty tér metro station (Yellow Line) is two short blocks east.

Boats from Vienna arrive at the **International Boat Station** (Nemzetközi hajóállomás). From here you can take tram 2 north to the metro at Kossuth Lajos tér.

TOURIST INFORMATION

At ★ **Tourinform,** V, Sütő utca 2 (☎ **1/117-9800**), you can get a large selection of English-language travel brochures for Budapest and the rest of Hungary, almost all of them free. The staff is fluent in English and, with only rare exceptions, very friendly and helpful. They provide up-to-date information on cultural events, museums, and accommodations, and book sightseeing tours. You can also telephone Tourinform for information. Open daily from 8am to 8pm.

If you come by in person, make sure to ask them for the monthly *Budapest Panorama* and *Programme in Ungarn/in Hungary,* which lists upcoming cultural events, primarily in Budapest.

This office is near the Deák tér metro station, on a small street between Deák tér and Petőfi Sándor utca.

Tourinform also has a branch along the expressway from Vienna.

CITY LAYOUT

NEIGHBORHOODS IN BRIEF Budapest is actually three historic cities: Buda, Pest, and Óbuda. Because of its excellent defensive location, Buda, on the west side of the Danube (or left on a map), was first a town of forts and castles. Many of its museums and points of historical interest are arrayed along Castle Hill, a mile-long ridge paralleling the Danube. This area has been largely restored to its traditional charm, and should be your first destination in Budapest. The Budapest Castle and the tall Matthias Church provide easy points of reference. The rest of Buda is primarily a residential area with roads that coil and twist around the hills.

On the Danube's east bank (to the right on a map) is Pest (pronounced "Pesht"), the lively city center contained by concentric ring boulevards. The heart of tourist Pest is Vörösmarty tér, which leads to the city's showcase shopping street, Váci utca. Just two blocks from Vörösmarty tér is the Corso, a lovely pedestrian promenade lined by several deluxe hotels along the Danube overlooking Castle Hill. If you walk from Vörösmarty tér two blocks away from the river, you'll come to Deák tér, the transportation center of town where the three metro lines meet. Commercial Pest centers on the Great Ring (Nagykörút)—Ferenc krt., József krt., Erzsébet krt., and Teréz krt.—and the radial streets that intersect it, particularly Rákóczi út and Andrássy út. Budapest's busiest public transport line, trams 4 and 6, run along the Nagykörút, crossing the bridges at either end to Moszkva tér and Móricz Zsigmond körtér (Buda's two major hubs).

Founded on the remnants of the old Roman city of Aquincum, Óbuda is the third major section of Budapest that developed independently. Nowadays it's mostly modern housing for the well over two million inhabitants of Greater Budapest.

THE DISTRICT SYSTEM Budapest, like other Austro-Hungarian cities such as Prague and Vienna, is divided into numbered districts (*kerület*). Maps usually show them in different colors. Addresses in Budapest are always cited with the Roman-numeral district number first, partly because streets in different districts sometimes have the same name, but mostly because every resident of Budapest conceptualizes the city in terms of the districts. For the tourist, it's most important to remember that central Pest is district V, while Castle Hill in Buda is district I.

Maps With a million small streets in Budapest (or so it seems), I suggest buying a detailed, cross-referenced map (with enlargements of Castle Hill and Central Pest) as soon as possible. The best map, light yellow with the city shield on the front, is published by Cartographia; it's well indexed and has all the new street names (180 Ft/$1.85). The blue-covered *Budapest Atlas,* also published by Cartographia, is even more detailed (500 Ft/$5.10). Free maps of central Pest are available in most tourist offices.

Budapest has two stores devoted to maps alone, one, better for domestic city maps, at Bajcsy-Zsilinszky út 37 (☎ **112-6001**), north of the Arany János metro stop (Blue Line), open Monday through Wednesday from 9am to 5pm, Thursday from 9am to 7:30pm, and Friday from 9am to 3:30pm; and the other, better for foreign maps, at Nyár u. 1 (☎ **122-0438**), three blocks east of the Blaha Lujza tér metro stop (Red Line), open Monday through Friday from 9:30am to 5:30pm.

2 Getting Around

Budapest's excellent public transportation network is efficient, safe, and surprisingly comfortable. On all forms of transport, you validate your own ticket, which you purchase in advance from newsstands or from the windows or automatic dispensers in metro stations. On rare occasions, a ticket inspector checks for valid tickets; violators are fined. Tickets for all forms of public transport cost 25 Ft (25¢) each, and entitle you to one ride on one line. This means, for example, that you must punch a new ticket when changing from one metro line to another.

It's worth considering a day pass (*napijegy*) for 200 Ft ($2.05), or a three-day tourist pass (*turistajegy*), a much better value at 400 Ft ($4.10), as you'll go through 25 Ft tickets quickly. Week- and month-long passes are also available, but for these you need to bring a photo and go to one of the metro end stations.

You can also stop by metro station ticket counters to pick up a map called *Budapest Belváros Idegenforgalmi Térképe,* which costs 58 Ft (60¢) and covers public transportation in central Budapest better than the more expensive street maps. Another map covers the suburban routes.

BY METRO Three lines make up the Budapest metro system. Line 1 (the Yellow Line) is the oldest in continental Europe (from 1894), and is located immediately beneath the surface. Major stops include Hősök tere, site of the Museum of Fine Arts; Opera, underneath the State Opera House; Deák tér, the transportation center in downtown Pest; and Vörösmarty tér, heart of tourist Pest. It's sometimes difficult to see the Yellow Line station entrances; look for a modest yellow sign: FÖLDALATTI IRANY: MEXIKÓI ÚT for the metro going toward the Mexikói út station or FÖLDALATTI

IRANY: VÖRÖSMARTY TÉR for metros to downtown Pest. As this example shows, directions inside the metro are given in terms of the end stations, so learn their names.

Line 2 (the Red Line) runs far deeper underground, with major stops at Keleti pu. (the largest train station); Deák tér; Moszkva tér, at the foot of Castle Hill in Buda; and Déli pu., the West railroad station in Buda. The north-south Line 3 (the Blue Line) stops at Deák tér; Kálvin tér, site of the Hungarian National Museum; and Ferenc körút, site of the Museum of Applied Arts. Signs above ground for the Red and Blue Lines are much more visible than for the Yellow Line.

The main shortcoming of the system for tourists is that it has only three stops in Buda and it doesn't go up to the Castle District of Buda Hill.

All three lines merge at Deák tér. If you transfer lines, you must validate a second ticket. The transit network opens daily at 4:30am and closes down at 11:25pm.

BY BUS/TRAM/TROLLEYBUS Above ground, you can take red trolleybuses (buses connected to electric lines), yellow trams, and blue buses, with the system in operation daily from about 4:30am to 11pm, and infrequent service on special routes at night.

The special Várbusz (Castle Bus) connects Moszkva tér to Buda's Castle Hill, departing every two to seven minutes from 5am to 11pm. It's smaller than typical buses, with a blue-and-gray exterior, but requires the same tickets.

If you're switching from the metro to a bus or tram connection, consult the map near the metro exit to find the exact location of the stop.

When visiting Buda, you'll often have to take a bus or tram "from Moszkva tér" or "from Móricz Zsigmond körtér." Moszkva tér (on the metro's Red Line) is the transport hub for Castle Hill, northern Buda, and the residential Buda Hills. Look for the triangular maps that show where the different tram and bus stops are in the square. Móricz Zsigmond körtér is the hub for southern Buda, including Gellért Hill. You can reach it via tram 47 or 49 from Deák tér, tram 61 from Moszkva tér or Déli Station, tram 6 from Nyugati Station, or bus 7 from Keleti Station.

BY CABLE CAR As the metro does not go to Castle Hill and buses take lengthy routes, consider the funicular cable car (Budavári Sikló) from Clark Ádám tér, at the Buda side of the Chain Bridge. It runs between 7:30am and 10pm daily, costing 80 Ft 80(¢) for adults and 60 Ft (60¢) for children, and takes less than a minute. The entrance is just to the left of an imposing large car tunnel with a pair of columns on each side.

BY TAXI Taxi rates in Budapest are similar to those in the West. You can get anywhere in the city by public transportation, so if you're on a budget there's little need for taxis. Moreover, some of Budapest's cabbies have an extremely bad reputation. *Never* take a cab that does not have a company name and logo on the door. Never take a taxi from the airport. Also avoid fancy cars, which charge higher rates. Always call for a taxi if you can't find a fair one locally.

The most reliable taxi company is Főtaxi (☎ **122-2222**), whose cars display a red-and-white checker pattern. Other safe bets are Tele-5 (☎ **155-5555**) and Citytaxi

IMPRESSIONS

Life in Budapest moves to a more rapid rhythm than elsewhere in Europe, as though every moment of the day had unlimited possibilities of emotional excitement.
—Walter Starkie, *Raggle-Taggle*, 1933

(☎ **153-3633**). Try to ask a Hungarian to call for you, as dispatchers rarely speak English.

BY BICYCLE I bicycle frequently in midtown Manhattan's manic traffic, and by comparison I find Budapest even more challenging. Traffic is relentless and there are no shoulders. However, if you're an avid biker, ask Tourinform (see "Tourist Information" in "Orientation," above) for a list of rental shops.

ON FOOT When reading maps, searching for addresses, or navigating your way around Hungary, you should know that *út* means "road," *utca* (abbreviated as "u.") means "street," *körút* (abbreviated as "krt.") means "ring road," *tér* is a square or plaza, and *híd* means "bridge." You may also see the less commonly used *part* and *rakpart* (riverbank), *sor* (row), *fasor* (alley), *sugárút* (avenue), and *köz* (small street).

Fast Facts: Budapest

American Express Hungary's only American Express office is in downtown Pest, at Deák Ferenc u. 10, 1052 Budapest (☎ **1/266-8680;** fax 1/267-2028; telex 22-2124). They provide normal American Express services, like client mail, currency exchange, and traveler's check and credit-card replacement. Hours are Monday through Friday from 9am to 5pm and on Saturday from 9am to 1pm; in June, July, and August, they stay open until 6pm on weekdays. There's an express cash ATM on the street in front. The 24-hour emergency telephone number is **00-44-273-675975** or **571600,** and you can reverse the charges.

Area Code Budapest's telephone area code is 1.

Bookstores Budapest's all-round best English-language bookstore is Bestsellers, V, Október 6 u. 11 (☎ **112-1295**). The store is open Monday through Saturday from 9am to 6pm. It's halfway between the Deák tér and Arany János u. metro stations.

Currency Exchange Banks offer the best rates; those that take traveler's checks often give a better rate than American Express. For instance, the Creditanstalt bank at V, Szervita tér, a block from Tourinform, is particularly convenient and open Monday through Friday from 9am to 5pm. Avoid the numerous change bureaus on and around Váci utca and at the stations; their advertised rate is only available on very large transactions. It's illegal and stupid to trade with black marketeers at Keleti Station or elsewhere.

Doctors/Dentists IMS, an outpatient clinic at Váci út 202 (☎ **129-8423;** 24-hour emergency line ☎ **149-9349**), has a number of English-speaking Hungarian doctors. Many of the American expatriates living in Budapest use this clinic. Váci út is completely different from Váci utca, and is reached via the metro Blue Line to Gyöngyösi utca.

Drugstores These are called *gyógyszertár* or *patika* in Hungarian. Twenty-four-hour pharmacies in Budapest are at I, Szena tér 1 (☎ **202-1816**); II, Frankel Leó út 22 (☎ **115-8290**); VI, Teréz körút 41 (☎ **111-4439**); IX, Boráros tér 3 (☎ **117-0743**); and IX, Üllői út 121 (☎ **133-8947**).

Embassies See "Embassies/Consulates" in "Fast Facts: Hungary" in Chapter 18.

Emergencies You can use the nationwide emergency telephone numbers in Budapest as well: dial **04** for an **ambulance, 05** for the **fire department,** and **07** for the **police.**

Hospitals For advice on hospitals, see "Doctors/Dentists," above, or contact your embassy.

Laundry/Dry Cleaning Look for dry cleaners' shops, which have blue signs saying PATYOLAT. At a few—and I emphasize, only a few—you can also do regular laundry. The most central of these is at Rákóczi út 8, a half block out from the Astoria metro station (Red Line), open Monday through Friday from 7am to 7pm, and on Saturday from 7am to 1pm. A wash plus 30 minutes of drying time costs 407 Ft ($4.50). The no-nonsense women who run the place will yell at you when you do something wrong; they don't speak English, but have a translated instruction sheet near the cash register.

Lost Property For items lost at Ferihegy Airport Terminal 1, call **147-2784** or **157-7690;** for lost and found at Ferihegy 2, call **157-8381** or **157-8108.** If you lose something on the public transportation system, contact VII, Akácfa u. 18 (☎ **122-6613**), open on Monday, Tuesday, and Thursday from 7:30am to 3:30pm, and on Wednesday and Friday from 7:30am to 6:30pm. For general lost and found in town, go to Talált Tárgyak Központi Hivatala, V, Erzsébet tér 5 (☎ **117-4961**).

Luggage Storage/Lockers There are 24-hour luggage-check services at Déli, Keleti, and Nyugati train stations. All charge 60 to 120 Ft (60¢ to $1.20) per bag per day. You can also store bags in the Erzsébet tér bus station in downtown Pest, open daily from 6am to 6pm.

Newspapers/Magazines The *International Herald Tribune,* the major newsweeklies, and assorted British papers are all widely available, especially anywhere near Váci utca. Two English-language weeklies, *Budapest Week* and the *Budapest Sun,* are indispensable for their restaurant and entertainment listings, as well as their current news coverage of Hungary. Most newsstands in the center carry these two as well as the *Budapest Business Journal,* which has the last word on real estate and privatization, and the *Daily News,* the English-language publication of the Hungarian wire service.

Parking If you have a car, you may prefer to find accommodations outside the pollution and congestion of Budapest, and commute in for the day. Most of Budapest's outer metro stations have park-and-ride lots; they're marked with a P+R symbol on the system map posted in each Budapest metro car. Coming from southern Hungary, try the southern Blue Line stations, like Köbánya-Kispest; from the northeast, head for Örs vezér tere; from Balaton or Western Hungary, you could try the lot next to Déli Station, but it's usually full.

Photographic Needs Visit a branch of the Sooters or Fotex chains. There's a Sooters at V, Deák Ferenc u. 23 and a Fotex at V, Petofi Sándor u. 11.

Police In an emergency, you can reach the police at 07, nationwide.

Post Office Budapest's main post office is in Pest at V, Városház utca 18, open Monday through Friday from 8am to 8pm and on Saturday from 8am to 3pm. You can also enter from Petöfi Sándor utca, a block from Váci utca. Budapest also has two 24-hour post offices: one at the Nyugati train station at VI, Teréz krt. 105–107, and another at the Keleti station at VIII, Baross tér 11/c.

Radio Radio Bridge, at 102.1 FM, broadcasts English news on the hour.

Restrooms There are clean-enough public toilets at reasonable intervals throughout the city. There's one at the north end of Castle Hill, on Kapisztrán tér. You can also discreetly dip into any McDonald's or Burger King.

Safety Although Budapest is safer than most Western cities, more purse-snatching and pickpocketing has been reported along the main tourist areas in recent years. Stay alert and be aware of your immediate surroundings, especially at the train station where new arrivals look their most vulnerable. Wear a moneybelt and keep a close eye on your possessions. Be particularly careful with cameras, purses, and wallets, all favorite targets of thieves and pickpockets. Be especially careful walking on dark streets and in parks after dark. Every society has its criminals. It's your responsibility to be alert and aware even in the most heavily touristed areas.

Shoe Repair Services such as shoe repair are usually far less expensive here than in Western capitals. Ask at your hotel or private room for the local *cipész.*

Telephone/Telex/Fax Local and long-distance calls can be made at any coin or card phone; telephone cards (*telefonkártya*) are available from most newsstands. Alternatively, you can visit the modern, pleasant main telephone office at Petöfi Sándor u. 17, a block east of Váci utca. The office is open Monday through Friday from 8am to 8pm, and on Saturday and Sunday from 9am to 3pm. You pay regular rates, but they help you for free.

You can also send and receive faxes and telexes at this office, upstairs. They'll hold faxes for you at 118-9191, or telexes at 225375. Retrieval costs 22 Ft (22¢) per page for telexes, 44 Ft (44¢) per page for faxes. To send a fax, they charge 670 Ft ($6.85) for one page and 900 Ft ($9.20) for two.

The various USA Direct services are at **00/800-01111** (AT&T), **00/800-01411** (MCI), and **00/800-01877** (Sprint).

Water You can drink the water in Budapest, although you may (like many Hungarians) prefer the bottled water (*ásványvíz*) sold at any store.

3 Where to Stay

For single travelers or couples on a tight budget, private rooms are definitely the way to go in a city that lacks centrally located, inexpensive hotels.

PRIVATE ROOMS

You can rent private rooms from a number of agencies in town, centrally located in all three stations and throughout downtown Pest. What you are getting is a room in someone's apartment; usually you share the bathroom (although sometimes you have a private one), and though breakfast is not officially included, the host will often offer it to you for free or a small fee. You also generally have kitchen privileges. Some landlords will greet you when you arrive, give you a key, and seemingly disappear; others will want to befriend you, show you around, cook for you. It is your right to be aloof if you find the landlord too intrusive.

Here are the opinions of two budget-minded visitors I met in Keleti station. Anna Headly of Ann Arbor, Michigan, told me: "We paid 1,900 Ft ($19.40) for a great, airy room, not far from Parliament. There were paintings, tapestries, sculptures—it was like a Hungarian museum!" Kayla S. Stein, from New York City, said: "I stayed in a really cozy room for only 1,000 Ft ($10.20). It was located in a quiet neighborhood, an easy 10-minute metro ride from the center. The family—with a little girl, two cats, and a dog—was very friendly. I plan to keep in touch, and stay with them again next time I'm in Budapest."

When booking a room, make sure the agent shows you the location on the map. Ask for a room in the neighborhood of your choice, but be aware that some neighborhoods (like the Castle District, central Pest, the Buda Hills) will be more expensive. Be sure you understand how to get to the place before leaving the agent. There is no address in Budapest that cannot be reached by public transportation—don't believe anyone who tells you that you must take a taxi. The private rooms in Budapest are never totally booked; in peak season you may need to shop around a bit for the location you want, but you can always find a room.

For single travelers, renting a private room is often the only way to stay within the $30-a-day budget here. Unfortunately, renting a private room in Budapest has a distinctive old-world (that is, pre-1989) flavor. The main agencies like IBUSZ, Budapest Tourist, and Cooptourist were set up during Communist days to milk foreign currency from visitors while providing them with minimum service. Though things have changed here and there, many of the offices still have that state-run feeling: a line of gossiping middle-aged women barricaded behind a dark-wood counter, with an incomplete knowledge of foreign languages and an insecure commitment to providing you with value for your money. If you get frustrated, you may want to head to To-Ma Tour, listed below under "In Downtown Pest," which is Budapest's largest privately operated room-rental agency.

In Keleti Station, you'll probably be approached by people offering private rooms for rent. Use your judgment: Generally they are reliable folk who are registered with the room-rental agencies and are just trying to drum up some business themselves. You should probably get some price quotes from one of the agencies before striking a deal with an individual. If, however, you arrive when the agencies are closed, you should seriously consider listening to reasonable-sounding offers. Remember—all prices are negotiable, especially at night when a room is still unrented.

Below is a list of agencies, organized by location. There are many more that you might chance upon. You will find the best selection and prices at the main downtown branches. The IBUSZ branches accept American Express, VISA, and MasterCard. Note that Tourinform (the tourist office) does not help with private accommodations. Remember also that rates go down significantly the longer you stay; in particular, the rate for a stay of one to three nights is usually 30% more than that for four or more nights, though this may be phrased as a "surcharge" after you've been quoted the four-night rate.

AT FERIHEGY AIRPORT Budapest Tourist's airport offices will rent you a single or double for 2,500 Ft ($25.50). Be aware that especially for singles, you can find a better price downtown or at the train stations. The office in Ferihegy 1 (☎ **157-8670**) is open daily from 8am to 8pm; the office in Ferihegy 2 (☎ **157-8680**) is open daily from 9am to 9pm.

AT KELETI TRAIN STATION Most trains from Western Europe arrive at Keleti pu. The travel agencies are all near each other, in the wing of the building by Track 6.

If you're looking for a single room, head past the moneychangers and down the hall to the left to Express (☎ **142-1772**), where English-speaking Magda Beres rents singles and doubles for 1,000 to 1,200 Ft ($10.20 to $12.25) per person. In July and August, she can book you into one of Budapest's youth hostels for 800 Ft ($8.15). This tiny office stays open daily from 8am to 7pm.

IBUSZ (☎ **142-9572;** fax 121-2619) is usually very crowded; but, on the plus side, they do accecpt American Express, MasterCard, and VISA. Double rooms run 1,400 to 2,400 Ft ($14.30 to $24.50). The office is open Monday through Friday from 8am to 7pm and on Saturday and Sunday from 8am to 5pm; from January to March, Sunday hours are shortened to 10am to 5pm.

Orient Tour, a tiny office without a telephone, advertises singles for 900 to 1,000 Ft ($9.20 to $10.20) and doubles for 2,000 to 2,500 Ft ($20.40 to $25.50). Open Sunday through Friday from noon to 10pm.

Budapest Tourist has an office outside the station and across the square (to the left), at Baross tér 3 (☎ **133-6587**). Rooms cost 1,000 to 1,200 Ft ($10.20 to $12.25) per person. The office is open from May 15 to September 1, Monday through Friday from 8am to 7pm and Saturday from 8am to 1pm; the rest of the year, Monday through Friday from 9am to 5pm and Saturday from 8am to 1pm.

AT NYUGATI TRAIN STATION IBUSZ (☎ **132-7556**), near Track 10, has singles for 1,000 Ft ($10.20) and doubles for 1,500 Ft ($15.30). Open Monday through Friday from 8am to 6pm, and on Saturday from 8am to noon.

Budapest Tourist (☎ **132-4911**), in the underground passage near the metro entrance, has double rooms for 1,900 Ft ($19.40). Open Monday through Friday from 9am to 6pm, and on Saturday from 9am to 1pm.

Cooptourist (☎ **112-3621**), nearby, is open Monday through Friday from 9am to 4:30pm.

AT DÉLI TRAIN STATION IBUSZ (☎ **175-9167** or **156-3684**), downstairs from the platforms, rents singles for about 1,300 Ft ($13.25) and doubles for 2,000 Ft ($20.40). It's open Monday through Friday from 8am to 6:30pm, Saturday from 8am to 3:30pm, and Sunday from 9am to 1pm.

Budapest Tourist (☎ **155-7057**), in the round sunken courtyard, has singles for 1,600 Ft ($16.35) and doubles for 2,300 Ft ($23.45). They're open Monday through Friday from 9am to 5pm and Saturday from 9am to 1pm.

IN DOWNTOWN PEST IBUSZ, at Petőfi tér 3 (☎ **118-5707, 118-3925,** or **118-4842;** fax 117-9099; telex 224941), stays open 24 hours. Near the Inter-Continental Hotel, it's a short walk from Deák tér (the junction of all metro lines). Singles cost 1,100 Ft ($11.20), and doubles go for 1,500 Ft ($15.30). Entire apartments are available for around 2,000 Ft ($20.40).

To-Ma Tour, a friendlier, private agency at Október 6 u. 22 (☎ **153-0819;** telex 227865), rents singles and doubles for an average of 1,500 Ft ($15.30) per room, not per person. Entire apartments start at 2,000 Ft ($20.40). The office is open Monday through Friday from 9am to noon and 1 to 8pm, and on Saturday and Sunday from 9am to 5pm. American Express, Diners, MasterCard and VISA accepted. Október 6 utca is to the north of Deák tér; the Arany János utca metro stop is a little closer.

At Budapest Tourist, along the river at Roosevelt tér 5 (☎ **118-1453;** fax 118-6062; telex 225726), singles cost 1,000 Ft ($10.20), doubles 2,000 Ft ($20.40), and doubles with private bath 3,000 Ft ($30.60). They're open Monday through Friday from 9am to 6pm, and from May 15 to September 15 also on Saturday from 9am to 2pm.

LONG-TERM RENTALS Have a Hungarian help you go through the notices in the most recent edition of *Expressz,* a weekly classifieds broadsheet available at any newsstand. Some of the agencies above will also rent apartments by the week or the month.

HOTELS

The establishments listed below represent the best of a bad lot: Budapest simply doesn't have enough good budget hotels. Travelers with a car may get more value for their money by staying in Szentendre, Székesfehérvár, or the mansion hotels between Budapest and Hollókő, and commuting in for the day.

Doubles for Less Than $25

Citadella Turistaszálló, XI, Citadella sétány, 1118 Budapest. ☎ **1/166-5694.** Fax 1/186-0505. 20 rms (2 with bath, 8 with shower but no toilet, 5 without bath, 5 dorm rms with 10–14 beds). **Bus:** 27 from Móricz Zs. körtér.

Rates: 2,200 Ft ($22.45) double without bath; 2,400 Ft ($24.50) with shower but no toilet; 2,700 Ft ($27.55) with bath; for triple and quad rates, add 500 Ft ($5.10) per person. Dorm 550 Ft ($5.60) per person. **Parking:** Free.

At the top of Gellért Hill inside the 10-foot walls of the 19th-century Citadel, with a remarkable view of Pest, this hotel would be the best value in town if it were better kept up. All the nondorm rooms are clean, large quads with dim lighting and aging furniture. Families would feel comfortable in the rooms with bath or shower, but check the hot water before you hand over your passport. You may be able to eat breakfast in the restaurant downstairs for about 300 Ft ($3.05).

Hotel Express, XII, Beethoven u. 7/9, 1126 Budapest. ☎ **and fax 1/175-3082.** 30 rms (none with bath). **Tram:** 59 from Déli station (two stops) or Moszkva tér.

Rates: 1,650 Ft ($16.85) single or double; 2,090 Ft ($21.35) triple; 2,530 Ft ($25.80) quad. 10% off for youth hostel members.

The Express is one of the cheapest hotels in Budapest and, as a result, is packed with students. The rooms have seen a lot of traffic over the years and the wallpaper is old and peeling. Still, public bathrooms are tolerable and groups of three or four might save money here, though families would probably feel uncomfortable.

Rosella Hotel, XII, Gyöngyvirág u. 21, 1125 Budapest. ☎ **1/175-7329.** Fax 1/155-9565. 26 rms (all with shower but no toilet). **Bus:** 21 from Moszkva tér to Svábhegy, then walk down Diana utca to Gyöngyvirág utca and turn right.

Rates (including breakfast): 2,500 Ft ($25.50) double; 3,000 Ft ($30.60) triple. Prices are 500 Ft ($5.10) lower in winter. **Parking:** Free.

This may be the last inexpensive hotel left in the Buda Hills. Unfortunately, rooms are cramped, the wallpaper is a bit old, and the stairway is narrow. But this high up, the air is clean. Ask for one of the rooms with a balcony and a nice view.

Doubles for Less Than $45

Hotel Délibáb, VI, Délibáb u. 35, 1062 Budapest. ☎ **1/122-8763** or **142-9301.** Fax 1/142-8153. 36 rms (all with bath). **Metro:** Hősök tere.

Rates (including breakfast): 3,000 Ft ($30.60) single; 3,860 Ft ($39.40) double.

This place hasn't seen renovations since Communist days. The rooms are very plain, the bathrooms small and a bit worn. The reception desk's awkward home in the entranceway smacks of irresponsible central planning. There's nowhere to park. Yet the location is great, right on the metro's old Yellow Line and across Heroes' Square from the City Park, Fine Arts Museum, and Széchenyi baths. It's not a disagreeable hotel, just not a charming one, and it would be fine for a short stay if better choices are full.

Hotel Ében, XIV, Nagy Lajos király útca 15-17, 1148 Budapest. ☎ **1/184-0677.** Fax 1/252-3273. 37 rms (20 with bath). TV **Metro:** Örs vezér tere, at the end of the Red Line.

Rates (including breakfast): Apr–Oct, $58 double with bath, $39 double without bath; Nov–Mar, $38 double with bath, $27 double without bath.

Located in outer Pest, this hotel is a 5- to 10-minute walk from the metro and then the ride to Deák tér lasts only 15 minutes. A former worker's hotel, it features petite, clean, but unadorned rooms. The public bathrooms are well kept, and rates tend to be discounted from the above, especially if you pay in forints.

$ **Hotel Medosz,** VI, Jókai tér 9, 1061 Budapest. ☎ **1/153-1700** or **153-1434.** Fax 1/123-4316. Telex 22-7000. 70 rms (all with bath). **Metro:** Oktogon (Yellow Line).

Rates (including breakfast): 2,800 Ft ($28.55) single; 4,100 Ft ($41.85) double. Nov–Mar, about 500 Ft ($5.10) less.

Formerly a trade-union hotel for agricultural workers, the Medosz now offers travelers one of the best values in downtown Pest. Most rooms have TVs and radios, and are fairly utilitarian without much decoration, but the location is excellent with the metro stop just a block away and only four stops to Vörösmarty tér, the heart of tourist Pest. The receptionists speak English, and rooms facing the courtyard are especially quiet. When you arrive at Jókai tér, which lies immediately off Andrássy út, walk to the back of the square with a park at its center.

$ **Hotel Metro,** XIII, Kádár u. 7, 1132 Budapest. ☎ **1/141-4380.** Fax 1/141-4387. 15 rms (all with bath). MINIBAR TEL TV **Metro:** Nyugati pu., then walk a block north and a block left.

Rates (including breakfast): 3,850 Ft ($39.30) double; 4,825 Ft ($49.25) triple; Nov–Mar, 3,150 Ft ($32.15) double, 3,920 Ft ($40) triple.

The Metro occupies the third and fourth floors of a building on a very quiet street. You'll have to push the button to be buzzed in. Right by Nyugati station, a metro stop, and a tram stop, it could hardly be more convenient to public transportation—a good thing since it lacks parking. The calm, carpeted reception area feels liberatingly post-Communist and the staff tries to speak English. Rooms are small but tasteful, with attractive modern furniture and lighting, new telephones, and compact, well-designed bathrooms. It's one of the most hassle-free choices in Budapest and I highly recommend it.

Motel Momini, Beck Ö. Fülöp u. 15, 1124 Budapest. ☎ **1/175-0727.** Fax 1/175-0727. 8 rms (all with bath). MINIBAR **Metro:** Déli pu. (Red Line), then walk 10 minutes south on Alkotás utca, turn right on Tartsay Vilnos utca, make an immediate left onto Beck Ö. Fülöp utca, walk to the end and look right. **Tram:** 61 from Moszkva tér.

Rates (including breakfast): 3,600 Ft ($36.75) single; 4,200 Ft ($42.85) double; 5,000 Ft ($51) triple. In winter, about 25% less. **Parking:** Free, but only five spaces.

This small establishment is one of the few really good deals left in Buda. It's

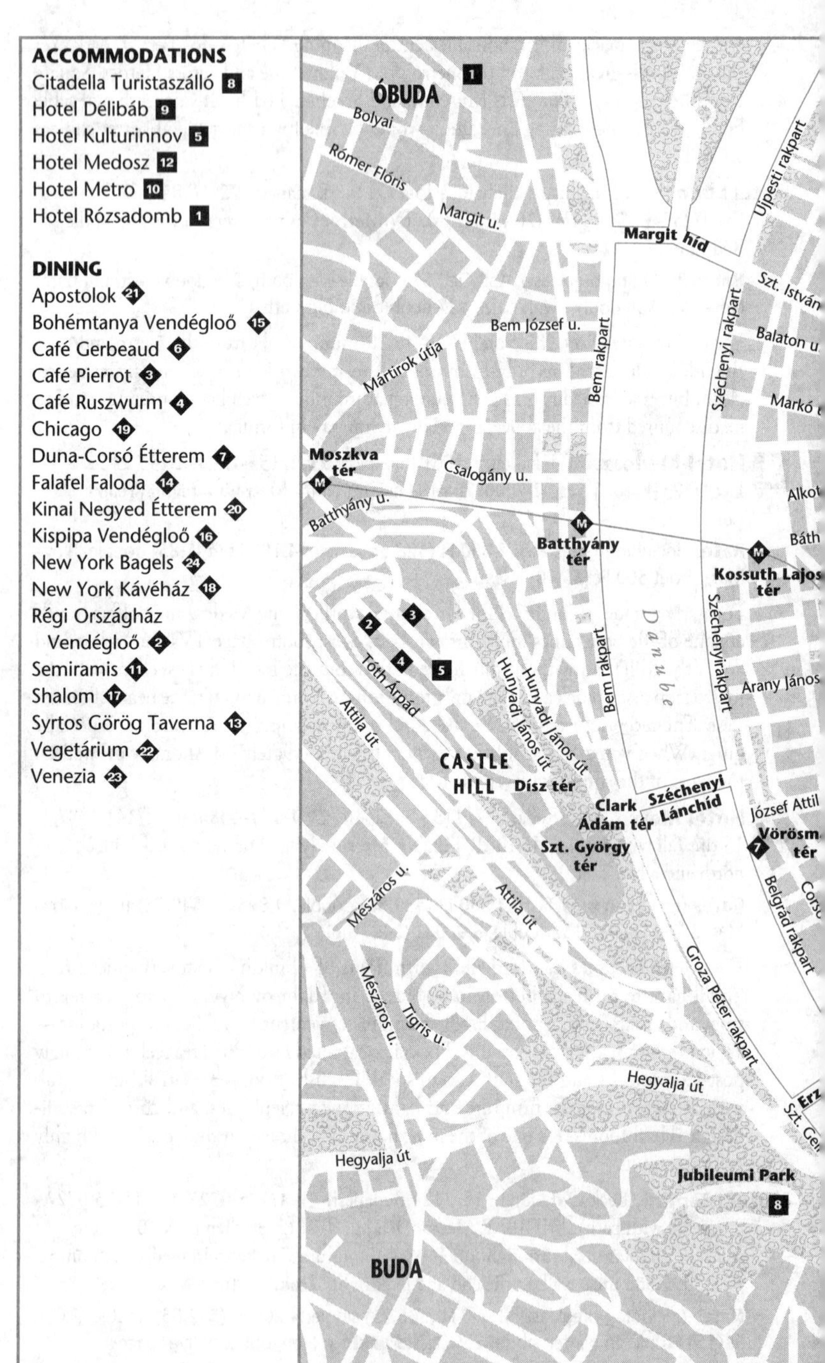
ACCOMMODATIONS
Citadella Turistaszálló 8
Hotel Délibáb 9
Hotel Kulturinnov 5
Hotel Medosz 12
Hotel Metro 10
Hotel Rózsadomb 1
DINING
Apostolok 21
Bohémtanya Vendégloő 15
Café Gerbeaud 6
Café Pierrot 3
Café Ruszwurm 4
Chicago 19
Duna-Corsó Étterem 7
Falafel Faloda 14
Kinai Negyed Étterem 20
Kispipa Vendégloő 16
New York Bagels 24
New York Kávéház 18
Régi Országház Vendégloő 2
Semiramis 11
Shalom 17
Syrtos Görög Taverna 13
Vegetárium 22
Venezia 23
ÓBUDA
Bolyai
Rómer Flóris
Margit u.
Margit híd
Újpesti rakpart
Szt. István
Bem József u.
Mártirok útja
Bem rakpart
Széchenyi rakpart
Balaton u.
Markó
Moszkva tér
Csalogány u.
Batthyány u.
Batthyány tér
Kossuth Lajos tér
Danube
Hunyadi János út
Tóth Árpád
Attila út
Széchenyirakpart
Arany János
CASTLE HILL
Dísz tér
Clark Ádám tér
Széchenyi Lánchíd
József Attil
Vörösm tér
Szt. György tér
Mészáros u.
Belgrád rakpart
Groza Péter rakpart
Tigris u.
Hegyalja út
Jubileumi Park
BUDA
9032

Budapest Accommodations & Dining

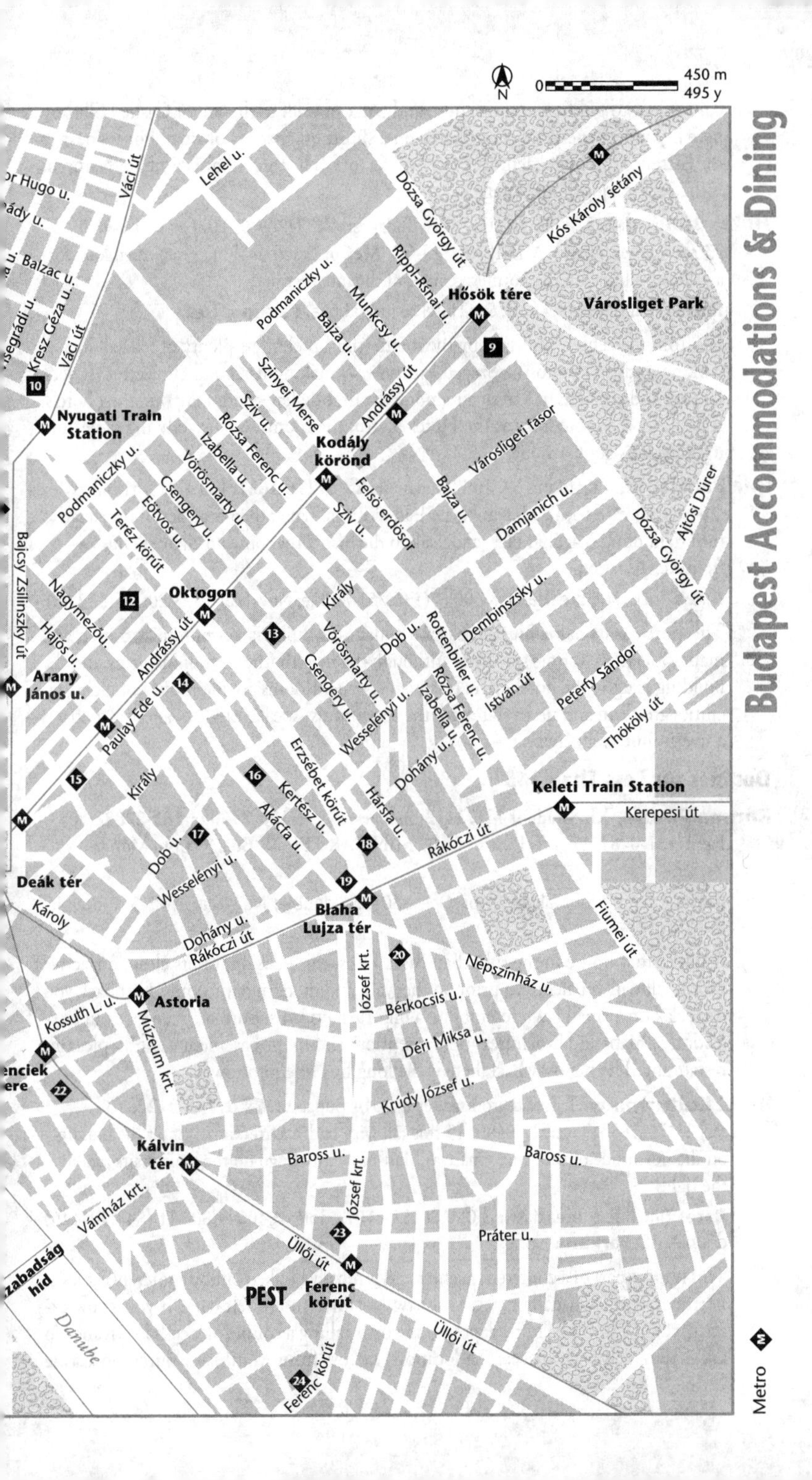

Metro

convenient to public transportation, and you can walk to the top of Castle Hill from here if you feel energetic enough. It's on a short, quiet street of small houses next to the entrance to a huge, defunct eyeglasses factory. The three-flight climb to the rooms is the only major disadvantage.

Hotel Omnibusz, X, Üllői út 108, 1101 Budapest. ☎ **1/269-9510.** Fax 1/269-9870. 23 rms (all with bath). MINIBAR TEL TV **Metro:** Ecseri út (Blue Line); then look for a yellow building on the northern corner of the intersection.

Rates (including breakfast): See Hotel Metro, above. **Parking:** Free.

Far from the center, but right by the metro, this hotel offers plenty of fenced, locked parking and is close to the Szeged expressway, making it a good choice for drivers. Cheery and efficient, it's fresh air among the drab staleness of many Budapest hotels. It's run by the same folks as the Hotel Metro, the rooms look exactly the same, and it's almost as good a value.

Rila Panzió, IX, Vágóhíd u. 62, 1097 Budapest. ☎ **1/216-1621.** Fax 1/215-5184. 26 rms (all with bath). **Metro:** Nagyvárad tér (Blue Line); then walk across the square, turn right down Vágóhíd utca, and walk to the first corner on your right. **Tram:** 24 from Keleti station.

Rates (including breakfast): 3,600 Ft ($36.75) double; Nov–Mar 15, 3,200 Ft ($32.65).

This hotel, as its name hints, is part of Budapest's Bulgarian community center, and many Bulgarian visitors stay here. Although the neighborhood is uninspiring and the building is ugly, the hotel offers reasonable value. Rooms are plain but not tacky, facilities are clean and up to standard, the receptionist speaks English, and the metro is a five-minute walk away.

Doubles for Less Than $65

Korona Panzió, XI, Sasadi út 127, 1112 Budapest. ☎ **1/186-2460** or **181-2788.** Fax 1/181-0781. 17 rms (15 with bath). MINIBAR TEL TV **Bus:** 53 from Móricz Zs. tér.

Rates (including breakfast): Apr–Oct, $50–$55 double; Nov–Mar, $45–$50 double. **Parking:** Free.

A three-story house in the suburban Buda Hills, this pension, offers clean, attractive rooms, all with a balcony, a print on the wall, and modern bathrooms. Out back you can relax on a small lawn resembling a bit of American suburbia. They give out a selection of maps and brochures at the reception, and in the basement there's a pleasant restaurant. The big drawback here is the long bus ride into town.

Hotel Kulturinnov, I, Szentháromság tér 6, 1014 Budapest. ☎ **1/155-0122.** Fax 1/175-1886. Telex 22-6490. 15 rms (all with bath). **Directions:** Enter the building on the north side of the same square as Matthias Church; go up the main stairs and to the right.

Rates (including breakfast): 3,050 Ft ($31.10) single; 4,400–4,800 Ft ($44.90–$49) double. AE. **Parking:** None.

This hotel is part of a conference center and is mostly booked out by conference guests. Fortunately, they usually have at least two or three rooms left over. If you know exactly when you will be in Budapest, it is worth calling a couple of weeks in advance to ask if they will have space. The location—across from Matthias Church on Castle

Hill—is the best spot in Budapest. Inside, the rooms feel slightly dark and plain after the grand stairs and red carpets of the entrance hall, but they're perfectly sufficient.

Hotel Rózsadomb, II, Vérhalom u. 17, 1025 Budapest. ☎ **1/115-0284** to **115-0287.** Fax 1/115-5481. 228 rms (all with bath). MINIBAR TEL TV from Nyugati train station.

Rates (including breakfast): Apr–Oct, 75 DM ($44.10) single; 105 DM ($61.75) double. Nov–Mar, 50 DM ($29.40) single; 70 DM ($41.20) double. AE, DC, MC, V. **Parking:** Free.

Perched on a Buda hilltop north of Castle Hill, this former trade-union hotel is a typical Communist-era pile with one main redeeming feature: dramatic views off private balconies over the Danube, Castle Hill, and Pest from about half its rooms. Rooms are fine; though the decor reflects the year of the hotel's construction—1971. There's a reasonably priced restaurant on the sixth floor, and the neighborhood is nice. Do stress your interest in a room facing the Danube, for it's the view here that makes this place special.

Hotel Ventura, XI, Fehérvári út 179, 1119 Budapest. ☎ **1/182-0308.** Fax 1/182-0307. 64 rms (all with bath). TV **Tram:** 18 from Moszkva tér and 47 from Deák tér stop in front of the hotel.

Rates (including breakfast): Apr–Oct, $63 double; Nov–Mar, $40 double. **Parking:** Free.

Though distant and slightly institutional, this is one of the nicest of Budapest's former worker's hotels. Rooms are carpeted and comparatively spacious, with modern furniture, desks, and plenty of closet space. There's a fairly good Chinese restaurant on the first floor. As at the affiliated Hotel Ében, expect prices to be unpredictably discounted from the above, especially if you pay in forints.

YOUTH HOSTELS

The youth hostel scene in Budapest has been in a state of flux for the last half-dozen years, and it's impossible to predict what will be going on when you arrive in town. The one certain thing is that in July and August throughout Hungary, university and college dormitories are converted into hostels. In Budapest, most of these are on the Buda side, particularly in District XI along the routes of trams 4, 6, and 61. For example, the monstrous dormitory on Irinyi József utca by the Petőfi híd (bridge), near the Muegyetem (Technical University), almost always becomes a summer hostel.

A few buildings are usually run as hostels year-round, but here it's equally difficult to predict the future, with the exception of the Back Pack Guesthouse, below.

The best way to get information is when you arrive. Tourinform, Budapest's tourist office, can give you brochures and advice. Hostels often advertise in the train stations, and sometimes send their staff to meet popular trains and bring back a harvest of hostelers by minibus. In July and August, the Express office in Keleti Station (☎ **142-1772**), open daily from 8am to 7pm, can book you into a hostel for 800 Ft ($8.15). Before checking into a hostel, see whether you might be able to find nicer private rooms for similar prices, especially if you're a group of three or four. Also remember that the Citadella Turistaszálló (under "Hotels," above), has a great view and inexpensive dorms and quads, generally booked up in summer but often deserted in the off-season.

Back Pack Guesthouse, XI, Takács Menyhért u. 33, 1110 Budapest. ☎ **1/185-5089.** 23 beds. **Tram:** 49 from Deák tér to the railroad bridge two stops past Móricz

Zsigmond körtér, then follow Hamzsabégi út alongside the tracks for three blocks. **Bus:** 7 from Keleti Station.

Rates: 550–650 Ft ($5.60–$6.65) per person.

The true international hosteler will want to head straight for this cramped year-round hostel in a tiny private house. It has a dog, cable TV, bunk beds, lots of Australians, plenty of mess, and a friendly communal atmosphere, but you need to reserve ahead since it has so few beds.

4 Where to Eat

Don't come to Budapest expecting a culinary orgy of cold fruit soup, meaty goulash, wild boar in paprika sauce, and chocolate-walnut pancakes, for Budapest's restaurants will disappoint lovers of Hungarian food. If this seems surprising, consider that the city's cosmopolitan young professional class likes to feel sophisticated when they go out to eat, preferring Italian, Middle Eastern, and Chinese cuisine to the dishes their grandmothers made. Restaurants in Budapest these days boast the same diversity of tradition as in any other major European city. For the best in Hungarian food, board the suburban train to the nearby village of Szentendre (see Chapter 20), where there are about a dozen Hungarian restaurants in the pedestrian district alone. Alternatively, save your appetite for the restaurants in Hungary's provincial cities.

The summer tourist presence in Budapest can be overwhelming, so this section tries to emphasize smaller, less pretentious establishments rather than the more hackneyed choices on Castle Hill and in central Pest. Keep in mind that dining on Castle Hill in particular is usually not a good budget option.

Even at the cheaper establishments, though, you'll now need to order with a bit of care to keep costs down. Price categories below assume that you avoid the most expensive items and bill-padders such as alcohol. Except where noted, all of the restaurants I list will give you an English menu on request.

Budapest's English-language newspapers carry reviews of the newest restaurants in town, as will the latest edition of Sam Worthington's *Good Food Guide to Budapest and Hungary.* Note that quite a few restaurants close for a month in summer. You might try calling ahead before setting out to remote destinations.

MEALS FOR LESS THAN $5

In Pest

Bohémtanya Vendéglő [Place of Bohemians], VI, Paulay Ede u. 6. ☎ **122-1453.**

Cuisine: HUNGARIAN. **Reservations:** Recommended. **Directions:** Walk a block north of Deák tér, then turn right onto Paulay Ede utca.

Prices: Large salads 40–130 Ft (40¢–$1.35); main courses 180–480 Ft ($1.85–$4.90). **Open:** Daily noon–11pm.

Bohemtanya proves that you don't need fancy decor for excellent food. Despite the bare walls and tables in wooden stalls, Bohemtanya is a favorite of locals. It's meaty, traditional stuff, with lots of liver, brains, and the like. Not only are prices low, but most main dishes are huge, and they also serve large salads. Don't order what you can't eat. As this is a very popular place, you may have to wait for a table.

Falafel Faloda, VI, Paulay Ede u. 53. No phone.

Cuisine: VEGETARIAN/MIDDLE EASTERN. **Metro:** Oktogon (Yellow Line).
Open: Mon–Fri 10am–8pm.

Just steps from the Oktogon, here's your chance to fill a round of pita bread with falafels and all sorts of healthy vegetables for only 105 Ft ($1.10). Each pita comes in a plastic pita sleeve so you can avoid sticky fingers. Seating is upstairs around small tables. Best for a quick lunch during a day of sightseeing. There's no English menu, but you don't need one.

Kispipa Vendéglő [Little Pipe Restaurant], VII, Akácfa u. 38. ☎ **142-2587.**

Cuisine: HUNGARIAN. **Reservations:** Required in the evening. **Metro:** Blaha Lujza tér, five minutes away. **Directions:** Walk parallel to Teréz körút, three blocks over in the direction of Buda.
Prices: Main courses 200–500 Ft ($2.05–$5.10); complete dinner menus 420 Ft ($4.30).
Open: Mon–Sat noon–1am. **Closed:** July.

This private restaurant is one of everybody's favorites. The piano player (after 7pm) is one of the best nonconcert performers in Hungary, versed in everything from Bach to jazz. There's a delightful and humorous collection of old Hungarian alcohol advertisements on the walls. The evening crowd is a mix of families and couples, both local and visiting. The waiters don't speak much English, but they're friendly and patient, and there's an English menu available.

A house specialty is the fogash fish, served grilled, sautéed, or fried to order, at a very low price. Some of the finer specimens of this delicious fish are on display in the window tank. The complete meals offered on the back page of the menu for less than $5 are the best value here.

New York Bagels, IX, Ferenc körút 20. ☎ **281-7880.**

Cuisine: BAGEL SANDWICHES. **Reservations:** Not accepted. **Metro:** Ferenc körút (Blue Line). **Tram:** 4 or 6 stops at the door; watch for the bright yellow facade.
Prices: Bagel sandwiches 160–310 Ft ($1.65–$3.15); bagel with cream cheese 60 Ft (60¢).
Open: Sun–Thurs 9am–midnight, Fri 9am–1am, Sat 9am–2am.

New York Bagels's inventive sandwiches include salmon with cream cheese, turkey with lettuce and tomato, or ham and Brie, always on your choice of bagel (sesame, cinnamon-raisin, and the like). Or you can get a freshly baked bagel topped with a variety of cream cheese spreads for half the price of a sandwich.

Semiramis, V, Alkotmány u. 20. ☎ **111-7627.**

Cuisine: MIDDLE EASTERN. **Metro:** Kossuth tér (Red Line) or Nyugati pu. (Blue Line).
Prices: Appetizers 85–150 Ft (85¢–$1.55), main courses 200–350 Ft ($2.05–$3.60).
Open: Mon–Sat noon–9pm.

A few blocks from either Parliament or Nyugati pu., this little restaurant is best suited for lunch. Seating is upstairs in a narrow room, tastefully decorated with tapestries and colorful straw trivets. The atmosphere here is casual; the food takes a while to come, but is definitely worth the wait. A safe bet is the diced chicken with spinach *(spenótos csirkemell)*. Vegetarians can easily build a meal out of several appetizers: the yogurt-cucumber salad *(joghurtos saláta)* and the *ful* (a zesty bean dish) are good places to start.

In Buda

Szép Ilona, II, Budakeszi út 1–3. ☎ **155-2851.**

Cuisine: HUNGARIAN. **Bus:** 22 or 158 from Moszkva tér stops right in front of the door. **Tram:** No. 56 stops around the corner.
Prices: Soups 100–240 Ft ($1–$2.45), main courses 175–600 Ft ($1.80–$6.10).
Open: Daily 11:30am–10pm.

This cheerful, unassuming restaurant serves a mostly local clientele. There's a good selection of Hungarian specialties on the menu, as well as a few vegetarian dishes; try the veal paprika with dumplings *(Borjúpaprikás galuskával)*. South-facing windows fill the pink-and-white dining room with sunlight, and there's a small sidewalk-side garden for summer dining.

MEALS FOR LESS THAN $8

In Downtown Pest

Chinatown Restaurant [Kinai Negyed Étterem], VIII, Népszinház u. 15. ☎ **113-3220.**

Cuisine: CHINESE. **Metro:** Blaha Lujza tér (Red Line).
Prices: Soup 100–150 Ft ($1–$1.55), main courses 280–890 Ft ($2.85–$9.10).
Open: Daily 10am–1am.

This is the best combination of quality and convenience among Budapest's many Chinese restaurants. The decor is heavy and ornate; the place is air-conditioned and very clean. Interestingly, the Hungarian waiters here have learned a little Chinese, rather than the other way around. Vegetarian dishes are available.

$ **Schuch & Schuch,** better known as the **Duna-Corsó Étterem,** V, Vigadó tér 3. ☎ **118-6362.**

Cuisine: HUNGARIAN. **Reservations:** Recommended. **Directions:** Walk from Vörösmarty tér toward the Danube.
Prices: Soup 110–160 Ft ($1.10–$1.65); main courses 250–580 Ft ($2.55–$5.90).
Open: Daily noon–midnight.

This is one of Budapest's long-standing popular restaurants both for its convenient location and for its excellent food. The indoor dining room is simply decorated, with bright lighting from hanging circular lamps and well-worn cloth seats. Gypsy music adds to the enjoyment of dining here in the evening. During summer the Duna-Corsó is crowded with Hungarians as well as foreigners, sitting at outdoor tables by the river.

Goose is the specialty, but I enjoyed mushroom soup (very creamy, with chunks of mushrooms and a dab of sour cream) and chicken paprika served with spätzels and condiments much like Italian gnocchi.

Shalom, VII, Klauzal tér 2. ☎ **122-1464.**

Cuisine: HUNGARIAN (KOSHER). **Reservations:** Recommended on summer evenings. **Directions:** Walk to the corner of Dob utca and Nagy Diófa utca, not far from the Great Synagogue.
Prices: Soups 80–150 Ft (80¢–$1.50); main courses 270–550 Ft ($2.75–$5.60).
Open: Daily noon–11pm. Cold dishes only on Fri evening and Sat.

A framed kosher certificate hangs alongside Israeli flags on the dining room wall of this well-lit, friendly restaurant in the heart of Budapest's old Jewish district. Though you can order a few Jewish specialties such as sholet and gefilte fish, the menu is more notable for its vast and multilingually presented range of traditional Hungarian dishes. The prices are on a separate sheet at the back.

Syrtos Görög Taverna, VII, Csengery u. 24. ☎ **141-0772.**

Cuisine: GREEK. **Reservations:** Recommended. **Metro:** Oktogon (Yellow Line).
Prices: Greek yogurt 80 Ft (80¢); main courses 300–500 Ft ($3.05–$5.10); seafood dishes to 900 Ft ($9.20). AE, DC, MC, V.
Open: Daily noon–2am.

Greek students in Budapest dine in this delightful little restaurant. It's tastefully decorated with brick tiles, blue tablecloths, and simple wooden furniture. The clean white walls are decorated with black-and-white photos of Crete peasant life. The owner, György Rezi, is a trained chef who wrote a colorful Greek cookbook (in Hungarian, of course), available for purchase behind the bar. The friendly wait staff and live Greek music nightly make this an enjoyable place.

Vegetárium Étterem, V, Cukor u. 3. ☎ **138-3710.**

Cuisine: VEGETARIAN/MACROBIOTIC. **Reservations:** Recommended in the evening. **Metro:** Ferenciek tere (Blue Line).
Prices: Soups and appetizers 120–220 Ft ($1.20–$2.25); main courses 280–460 Ft ($2.85–$4.70). AE, MC, V.
Open: Daily noon–10pm.

Not far from the south end of Váci utca, Vegetárium is convenient to sightseeing in central Pest. This restaurant doesn't just dabble in vegetarianism; it serves hard-core main dishes such as fried tofu filets with arame alga. Yet the menu preserves a Hungarian accent in items like bean soup, or wheatmeat with paprika sauce and mushrooms. The interior is quiet and soothing, with tasteful paper lanterns hanging from the ceiling and fish tanks and watercolors alternating along the walls. No smoking.

Ristorante Venezia, VIII, József körút 85. ☎ **134-2377.**

Cuisine: ITALIAN. **Reservations:** Recommended. **Metro:** Ferenc körút (Blue Line). **Tram:** 4 or 6 stops at the door.
Prices: Pizza and pasta dishes 250–350 Ft ($2.55–$3.60).
Open: Sun–Thurs 11am–midnight, Fri–Sat 11am–2am.

Some Budapest residents claim that this is the city's best value in Italian food. A real brick oven turns out thin-crusted, savory pizzas. A well-rounded selection of pasta and soups completes the menu. It's convenient to public transport, and the modern interior is a welcoming place to dine.

In Buda

Kikelet Vendéglö [Sunrise Restaurant], II, Fillér u. 85. ☎ **135-5331.**

Cuisine: HUNGARIAN. **Reservations:** Recommended in the evening. **Bus:** 49 from Moszkva tér passes directly in front of the restaurant (five stops).
Prices: 85–165 Ft (85¢–$1.70); main courses 360–680 Ft.
Open: Daily noon–midnight.

The Kikelet reposes at the very top of the hill in one of Budapest's very poshest neighborhoods, surrounded by embassies and the homes of diplomats and the nouveau riche. The restaurant itself is somewhat humbler, and together with the view while you eat and a walk around the neighborhood afterward, it will reward your trip up. The menu is very limited and very Hungarian (vegetarians beware), with typical dishes like veal with creamed mushrooms and fried goose liver.

MEALS FOR LESS THAN $10

In Pest

Apostolok [Apostles], V, Kigyó u. 4–6. ☎ **118-3704.**

Cuisine: HUNGARIAN. **Reservations:** Recommended. **Directions:** From Vörösmarty tér, walk five blocks south on Váci utca, then turn left.
Prices: Soup 130–230 Ft ($1.35–$2.35); main courses 400–1,050 Ft ($4.10–$10.70); bottle of wine 500–850 Ft ($5.10–$8.65). AE, DC, MC, V.
Open: Daily 11am–10pm.

Paintings of the 12 Apostles adorn the walls above the tables in one of the rooms, giving this place its name. Handsomely decorated with fine stained glass, wood paneling, and oak booths, the Apostolok has been a favorite Budapest eatery since 1902. Service can be slow due to heavy demand for this very centrally located restaurant. Austrian beer is available on draft.

Chicago, VII, Erzsébet krt. 2. ☎ **269-6753.**

Cuisine: TEX-MEX. **Reservations:** Accepted. **Metro:** Blaha Lujza tér (Red Line).
Prices: Appetizers 200–365 Ft ($2.05–$3.70); main courses 390–760 Ft ($4–$7.75). AE.
Open: Mon–Sat 11am–midnight, Sun noon–11pm.

This is the place to take the kids when they're sick of European food. It's new, central, and you probably don't need reservations. The restaurant has an identity problem: though decorated fashionably if unimaginatively in a 1920s Chicago theme, they brew beer on the premises (you can see the casks through picture windows), and the menu is all nachos and enchiladas.

On Castle Hill

Régi Országház Vendéglö [Old Parliament Restaurant], I, Országház u. 17. ☎ **175-0650.**

Cuisine: HUNGARIAN. **Reservations:** Recommended. **Directions:** From Matthias Cathedral on Castle Hill, walk north up Országház utca.
Prices: Soup 110–160 Ft ($1.10–$1.65); main courses 160–900 Ft ($1.65–$9.15). AE, DC, MC, V.
Open: Daily noon–midnight.

You can eat better elsewhere in town, but if you're on Castle Hill and want to lunch, this is about as good and reasonably priced as you'll find. The thick walls keep it refreshingly cool in summer, as well as warm in winter. In summer, you can also dine in a small courtyard with a single tree in the middle. Gypsy musicians play in the evening. The menu offers fish, poultry, game, and beef dishes. The decor is total Hungarian, with red and white everywhere, and green trim on the doors and windowboxes.

In the Buda Hills

Aranymókus Kertvendéglö [Golden Squirrel Restaurant], XII, Istenhegyi út 25. ☎ **155-6728.**

Cuisine: HUNGARIAN. **Reservations:** Recommended. **Bus:** 21 (red), two stops from the Moszkva tér metro station.
Prices: Soup 150–300 Ft ($1.55–$3.10), main courses 450–1,200 Ft ($4.60–$12.25) AE, DC, MC, V.
Open: Daily 11am–midnight.

If you're staying nearby, try this pricey but charming restaurant, which has two bearskins on the wall, three rows of tables, and a small bar. There are also some tables outside for summer dining. A self-service salad bar is a treat for many vegetable-starved visitors at 250 Ft ($2.55).

CAFÉS [CUKRÁSZDA]

In Pest

Café Gerbeaud, V, Vörösmarty tér 7. ☎ **118-1311.**

Cuisine: DESSERT. **Metro:** Vörösmarty tér (Yellow Line).
Prices: Coffee from 85 Ft (85¢); pastries 25–160 Ft (25¢–$1.65); ice-cream dishes 150–320 Ft ($1.55–$3.25). AE, CB, DC, MC, V.
Open: May–Aug, daily 9am–10pm. Apr and Sept–Nov, daily 9am–9pm. Dec–Mar, daily 9am–8pm.

The premier café in Budapest, the Gerbeaud retains some of the Habsburg elegance that once graced this city. Its extensive menu offers the finest confections, ice creams, and coffees in all of Hungary. Vast green drapes, polished dark woods, and veined green marble provide just the right atmosphere for midafternoon coffee or a snack. You can take in your dessert at an outdoor table alongside Pest's favorite tourist piazza.

New York Kávéház [also called The Hungária], VII, Erzsébet krt. 9–11. ☎ **122-3849.**

Cuisine: DESSERT. **Metro:** Blaha L. tér (Red Line); then walk a block north.
Prices: Coffee from 100 Ft ($1), pastries 50–200 Ft (50¢–$2.05). AE, DC, MC, V.
Open: Coffeehouse, daily 9am–10pm.

New York, though only a shell of its former self, will give you a taste of how the Habsburg aristocracy lived. The beautiful, baroque interior practically groans under the weight of marble, mirrors, prodigious chandeliers, and exquisite woodwork. Opened in 1894 as the "New York," this was the gathering place of Budapest's fin-de-siècle literati. In 1990, just weeks before elections ousted the Communists from government, the restaurant renamed itself the "New York" after 45 years as the Hungária. You can dine downstairs, but I don't think that the food does justice to the decor, so I'd rather have you buy a drink or a dessert here.

In Buda

Café Pierrot, I, Fortuna u. 14. ☎ **175-6971.**

Cuisine: DESSERT. **Reservations:** Recommended on weekend evenings. **Directions:** From Matthias Church on Castle Hill, walk two blocks north on Fortuna utca.
Prices: Crêpe 190 Ft ($1.95); coffee from 100 Ft ($1). AE, DC, MC, V.
Open: Daily 11am–1am.

Many businesspeople and stylish locals frequent the Pierrot. The decor of subdued lighting, antiques on the walls (such as old dolls, prints, and clocks), and piano music after 8pm all add to an elegant feel. It often fills up after 10pm. You can enjoy crêpes and coffee or mixed drinks such as the Puszta Cocktail, a mix of apricot brandy, Tokaj wine, and a bittersweet liqueur for 290 Ft ($2.95).

Ruszwurm, I, Szentháromság u. 7. ☎ **175-5284.**

Cuisine: DESSERT. **Directions:** Walk half a block west of Matthias Church.
Prices: Pastries 30–130 Ft (30¢–$1.35); coffee 50–80 Ft (50¢–80¢).
Open: Daily 10am–8pm.

Here's another old-time café in Buda. The tiny building, from 1698, has been declared a national monument and is crammed with tourists in the summer because of its proximity to Castle Hill. It's small and not very ornate, nothing like the grand coffeehouses of Pest, but amazingly, it still has fair prices.

FAST FOOD

In a hot, sticky, eclectic city like Budapest, fast food can be an oasis of predictability and comfort. Moreover, the familiar routine and cheerful staff are in marked contrast to the sullenness you find in many Hungarian places of business. Of many **McDonald's** in Budapest, the most convenient are on Regiposta utca, off Váci utca; on Sütő utca next to Tourinform; and next to Nyugati train station. There are **Burger King** restaurants at Moszkva tér, the Oktogon, and Fővám tér. You can also head for **Wendy's, Pizza Hut,** or **Kentucky Fried Chicken.**

Don Pepe's good

5 Attractions

The centers of Buda and Pest are roughly opposite each other across the Danube at the Chain Bridge. Public transportation, however, connects them only at their northern and southern sections. Therefore it's best to do your sightseeing first on one side of the Danube and then move on to the other. The Castle District, both the geographic and historic high point of Budapest, is the traditional starting point. For a more complete list of museums, refer to "Budapest Museums," a pamphlet published by Tourinform.

All museums in Budapest charge extremely low admission fees: just 20 to 80 Ft (20¢ to 80¢). Children, students, and seniors are often entitled to discounts; in some places they enter free of charge. Bring the appropriate ID card, since you may be asked to present it to the cashier. Many museums are open free one day a week, which is listed with the descriptions below; the day, however, is subject to frequent change.

Suggested Itineraries

If You Have 1 Day

Spend the morning on Castle Hill, with visits to the Budapest History Museum and Matthias Church. Wander around some of the charming streets there. In the afternoon, cross the Danube into Pest and visit the Hungarian National Museum. In the late afternoon, stroll along the Danube on the pedestrian Corso and see Budapest's most modern shopping area, Váci utca.

If You Have 2 Days

Spend most of the first day on Castle Hill, taking in the sights more leisurely, and consider taking "Walking Tour—Castle Hill in Buda," described below. On the second day, in addition to the sights listed above, visit the European masters' collection at the Museum of Fine Arts, and if you have time, the Museum of Applied Arts.

If You Have 3 Days

Visit the sights mentioned above. Spend the third day exploring Pest more extensively, following "Walking Tour—Downtown Pest," below. Consider a visit to the Great Synagogue, the Vasarely Museum in Óbuda, or to Gellért Hill for a grand view over Budapest.

If You Have 5 Days or More

There's still plenty to see. Visit the Óbuda section of town to see the Vasarely Museum and the Imre Varga Museum, and if you enjoy Roman history, the nearby ruins at Aquincum. Explore Budapest's Városliget Park. Consider an excursion to the Buda Hills or Margaret Island, visit some other Budapest museums, or take a day trip to the charming town of Szentendre.

BUDA

Buda's mighty Castle Hill (Várhegy), crowned by the former Royal Castle overlooking the Danube, long served as the area's political and religious center. Carefully restored after war damage, it should be your first destination in Budapest. See "Walking Tour—Castle Hill in Buda," below, for a suggested route.

The Top Attractions

Budapest History Museum [Budapesti Történeti Múzeum], I, Buda Castle, wing E. ☎ **175-7533.**

The main museum inside Buda Castle, which served as the royal residence for centuries. Begin your visit on the top floor with ancient remains, and then move down a flight to arrive at medieval Hungary. The most interesting part of the museum is in the lower levels, however, which show the early remains of the Budapest Castle, complete with chapels, library, and dungeon. Some of these early foundations were revealed only after heavy World War II bombing literally blew away the newer castle additions on top. The exhibits down here feature Gothic art as well as a collection of medieval statuary excavated during reconstruction in the 1970s.

Concerts are held in the castle on Sunday at 11:30am.

Admission: 40 Ft (40¢) adults, 20 Ft (20¢) students.

Open: Mar–Oct, Wed–Mon 10am–6pm, Nov–Dec, Wed–Mon 10am–5pm; Jan–Feb, Wed–Mon 10am–4pm. **Directions:** Walk to the southernmost building in the castle.

Matthias Church [Mátyás templom], I, Szentháromság tér 2.

At the center of Castle Hill rises the most striking Gothic edifice of Buda. King Matthias Corvinus (1458–90) built the church for his own wedding to Beatrice of Aragon. The interior is richly ornate and painted, almost Turkish in its design; in fact, with the Turkish invasion and subsequent 150-year occupation, the church was for a time converted into a mosque. The **Loreto Chapel,** in the southwest corner of the church, is known for the red-marble statue of the Virgin Mary. The Turks had walled up the statue, but during the siege of 1686 it was re-exposed. The "miraculous" reappearance of the statue (and certainly also the bombardment that accompanied it) is said to be one of the causes of the Turkish surrender. The church was damaged again during the Hungarian Uprising of 1848–49, but restored quickly. The post–World War II reconstruction took much longer.

On Sunday at 10am the church choir sings (free admission), and from March to October on Friday at 8pm there are organ concerts (300 Ft/$3.10). Part of the church serves as a museum displaying gold works and ecclesiastical treasures.

Admission: Church, free; treasury, 30 Ft (30¢).

Open: Church, daily 7am–7:30 or 8pm; treasury, daily 9am–6pm. **Directions:** Walk north up Tárnok utca from Budapest Castle.

INFORMATION

IBUSZ 13
Tourinform 26

TRANSPORTATION HUBS

Erzsébet tér Bus Station 25
Hev Suburban Rail Station 1
International Boat Station 30
Keleti (Eastern) Train Station 28
Nyugati Train Station 20
Vigadó tér Boat Station 12

ATTRACTIONS

Budapest History Museum 10
Chain Bridge (Széchenyi Lánchíd) 7
Citadella 14
Ferenc Liszt Memorial Museum 21
Golden Eagle Pharmacy 6
Great Synagogue and Museum of Hungarian Jewry 27
House of Parliament 2
Hungarian National Museum 31
Inner City Parish Church 29
Matthias Church 5
Military Museum 3
Museum of Applied Arts 32
Museum of Fine Arts 17
Museum of Hungarian Art 9
Museum of Recent History 8
Musical Instruments Museum 4
St. Stephen's Basilica 24
Transport Museum 19

SPA BATHING

Gellért Hotel Baths 15
Széchenyi Baths 16

EVENING ENTERTAINMENT

Ferenc Liszt Academy of Music 23
Hungarian State Opera House 22
Pesti Vigadó Concert Hall 11
Petőfi Youth Center 18

ÓBUDA
Bolyai
Rómer Flóris
Margit u.
Margit híd
Újpesti rakpart
Szt. István
Széchenyi rakpart
Balaton u.
Bem József u.
Bem rakpart
Mártirok útja
Markó u
Moszkva tér
Csalogány u.
Batthyány u.
Batthyány tér
Kossuth Lajos tér
Alkotr
Báthc
Danube
Bem rakpart
Széchenyirakpart
Arany János
Tóth Árpád
Attila út
Hunyadi Jánosút
Hunyad János út
CASTLE HILL
Dísz tér
Clark Ádám tér
Széchenyi Lánchíd
József Attila
Vörösm tér
Szt. György tér
Mészáros u.
Attila út
Belgrád rakpart
Corso
Groza Péter rakpart
Mészáros u.
Tigris u.
Hegyalja út
Erzs
Szt. Gelle
Hegyalja út
Jubileumi Park
BUDA

9033

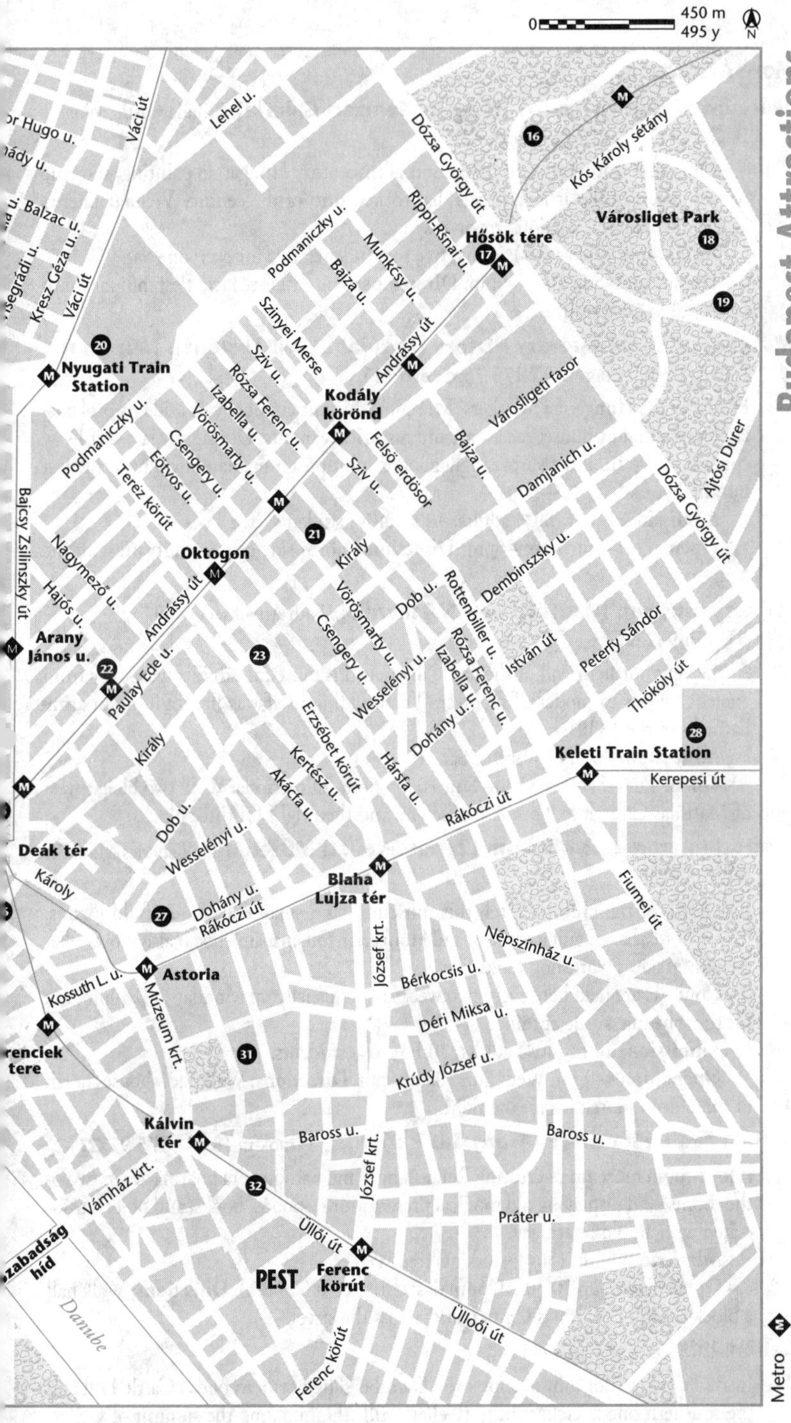

0
450 m
495 y
N
Lehel u.
Váci út
Hugo u.
Balzac u.
Kresz Géza u.
Váci út
Dózsa György út
Rippl-Rónai u.
Podmaniczky u.
Munkácsy u.
Bajza u.
Szinyei Merse
Kós Károly sétány
Városliget Park
Hősök tere
16
17
18
19
20
Nyugati Train Station
Andrássy út
Szív u.
Rózsa Ferenc u.
Izabella u.
Vörösmarty u.
Csengery u.
Eötvös u.
Teréz körút
Podmaniczky u.
Kodály körönd
Városligeti fasor
Felsö erdösor
Szív u.
Bajza u.
Damjanich u.
Ajtósi Dürer
Dózsa György út
Bajcsy Zsilinszky út
Nagymező u.
Hajós u.
Oktogon
21
Király
Dob u.
Rottenbiller u.
Dembinszky u.
Vörösmarty u.
Csengery u.
Arany János u.
22
23
Andrássy út
Paulay Ede u.
Wesselényi u.
Rózsa Ferenc u.
Izabella u.
István út
Peterfy Sándor
Thököly út
Erzsébet körút
Kertész u.
Akácfa u.
Hársfa u.
Dohány u.
28
Keleti Train Station
Kerepesi út
Király
Dob u.
Rákóczi út
Wesselényi u.
Deák tér
Károly
Blaha Lujza tér
Dohány u.
Rákóczi út
27
Fiumei út
Népszínház u.
József krt.
Bérkocsis u.
Astoria
Kossuth L. u.
Múzeum krt.
Déri Miksa u.
31
Ferenciek tere
Krúdy József u.
Kálvin tér
Baross u.
Baross u.
József krt.
Vámház krt.
32
Práter u.
Üllői út
Szabadság híd
PEST
Ferenc körút
Danube
Üllői út
Ferenc körút

M Metro

More Attractions

Museum of Hungarian Art [Magyar Nemzeti Galéria], I, Budá Castle, wings B, C, and D ☎ **175-7533, ext.** 423.

This museum features mostly 19th- and 20th-century Hungarian painting, showing muted effects of the artistic trends that rocked turn-of-the-century Vienna. There's also some medieval religious art on display.

Admission: 80 Ft (80¢) adults, free for students; free for everyone Sat.

Open: Tues–Sun 10am–6pm. **Directions:** The entrance faces Pest, not far south of the cable-car terminus.

Museum of Contemporary History [Legújabbkorii Történeti Múzeum], I, Buda Castle, wing A. ☎ **175-7533, ext.** 145.

Formerly the Hungarian Workers' Museum, this museum has cast aside its proletarian focus and now houses recent art and historical exhibits. During my last visit I saw contemporary art and a surprisingly good exhibit on Hungarian kitchens of the last hundred years.

Admission: 80 Ft (80¢) adults, 40 Ft (40¢) students; free Tues.

Open: Tues–Sun 10am–6pm. **Directions:** north side of the courtyard with the hedges.

Military Museum [Hadtörténeti Múzeum], I, Tóth Árpád sétány 40. ☎ **156-9522.**

At the very northern end of the castle district, this museum exhibits weaponry from ancient swords to modern firepower. The building itself was first built as an army barracks in the 1830s.

Admission: 20 Ft (20¢); free Sat.

Open: Tues–Sat 9am–5pm, Sun 10am–6pm. **Directions:** Walk two blocks west of Matthias Church to Tóth Árpád sétány and then right for three blocks.

Musical Instruments Museum [Zenetörténeti Múzeum], I, Táncsics M. u. 7. ☎ **175-9011.**

Just north of the Hilton Hotel, this museum has a small collection of old pianos, harpsichords, harps, guitars, horns, and Hungarian folk instruments. It also shows what a violin-maker's workshop looks like.

Concerts are held here every two weeks or so, usually on Monday at 7:30pm, ask for the schedule at the entrance.

Admission: 40 Ft (40¢) adults, 20 Ft (20¢) students.

Open: Mon 4–9pm, Wed–Sun 10am–6pm. **Directions:** Walk a few houses north of the Hilton Hotel; it's on the right.

Golden Eagle Pharmacy [Arany Sas Patika], I, Tárnok u. 18. ☎ **175-9772.**

A four-room museum re-creating Renaissance- and baroque-era pharmacies in two of the rooms, and displaying old medical prescriptions, spoons, books, and objects associated with an old pharmacy.

Admission: 50 Ft (50¢); students free Wed.

Open: Tues–Sun 10:30am–6pm (last entrance at 5:30pm). **Directions:** Walk half a block south of Matthias Church and across the street.

Gellért Hill, south of Castle Hill.

In Buda, two major hills overlook the Danube: The northern one is Castle Hill and the southern one is Gellért-hegy (Gellért Hill). Dominating the summit of Gellért Hill is a **Liberation Monument** showing a woman holding a palm leaf high above her head dedicated "To the heroic Soviet liberators from the grateful Hungarian people."

The second attraction up here is the **Citadella** (Citadel). The Citadel was built by the Austrians in 1851 after they put down the Hungarian War of Independence in 1848–49; they wanted to be sure they'd have no more trouble from a restless native population in the empire. Nestled in its 10-foot-thick walls is an overpriced restaurant and an underpriced hotel (see "Where to Stay," above). As you wander about the Citadel, you'll notice many bullet marks inside and outside from heavy World War II fighting.

The **Jubileumi Park** on the hillside immediately south is a popular local place for strolling in summer.

Admission: Citadel 25 Ft (25¢) 8am–5pm when the ticket booth is open.

Open: Daily 24 hours. **Bus:** 27 from Móricz Zs. körtér in Buda (take tram no. 6, 18, 19, 47, or 49 to get to Móricz Zs. körtér).

PEST

Since Pest is the more modern side of the city, it's the place to look for late 19th-century architecture. Many of the sights on this side of the Danube are museums and churches.

The Top Attractions

★ **Hungarian National Museum [Magyar Nemzeti Múzeum],** VIII, Múzeum körút 14–16. ☎ **138-2122.**

The precious Crown of St. Stephen, the symbol of the Hungarian nation, is on exhibit here in a room to the left of the main lobby. The U.S. had taken the crown for safekeeping at the close of World War II, but after it became a major diplomatic issue, it was finally returned in 1978. Also in the museum is a collection of gold and silver chalices, monstrances, and crosses. The curator of decorative arts in New York's Cooper-Hewitt Museum called the collection "extraordinarily beautiful—lush in its use of stones and enamel, with exquisite fillings." The other main attraction is the Hungarian history exhibit; there's also a natural history wing.

Admission: 30 Ft (30¢) adults, 10 Ft (10¢) students.

Open: Mar–Oct, Tues–Sun 10am–6pm. Nov–Feb, Tues–Sun 10am–5pm. **Metro:** Kálvin tér (Blue Line).

★ **Museum of Fine Arts [Szépművészeti Múzeum],** XIV, Dózsa György út 41. ☎ **142-9759** or **142-9336.**

In this museum you'll see antique and Egyptian art on the ground floor, and an impressive collection of European masters upstairs. The collection is especially strong in Spanish paintings of the 17th century, represented by an El Greco series, as well as works of Velázquez and Goya. The museum also boasts a large holding of 17th-century Dutch masters such as van Dyck, Pieter Bruegel, and Rembrandt. The Italians here include Tintoretto, Titian, Veronese, Lotto, Tiepolo, Canaletto, and Gentile Bellini, and the French by Cézanne and Monet. The graphic department boasts 100,000 works in etchings, engravings, woodcuts, and drawings.

The neoclassical 1906 museum building is located on Hősök tere (Heroes' Square), where a tall column honors those who died for Hungary.

Admission: 60 Ft (60¢) adults, free for students.

Open: Tues–Sun 10am–5:30pm. **Metro:** Hősök tere (Yellow Line).

★ **House of Parliament,** V, Kossuth Lajos tér.

Built when Budapest was a part of the Austro-Hungarian Empire, the Parliament, on the Pest bank of the Danube, was one of the largest buildings then in existence, boasting an incredible 691 rooms. The architect, Imre Steindl (1839–1902), must have had the British Parliament building on his mind when he designed this, as the similarity is striking. It remains the center of Hungarian government. The Parliament, Council of Ministers, Presidential Council, and other important government bodies hold their meetings here.

Open: Only with a tour when Parliament is not in session, which is usually in summer; inquire at Tourinform. **Metro:** Kossuth tér (Red Line).

More Attractions

Museum of Applied Arts [Iparművészeti Múzeum], IX, Üllői út 33. ☎ **217-5222.**

This museum presents an overview of 19th-century European decorative art and displays sample rooms in several major home furnishing styles. Check it out if you're interested in European arts and crafts. The building itself is one of Budapest's best art nouveau creations, though ravaged by pollution.

Admission: 40 Ft (40¢) adults, free for students.

Open: Tues–Sun 10am–6pm. **Metro:** Ferenc körút (Blue Line).

St. Stephen's Basilica [Szent István Bazilika], V, Szent István tér.

This neo-Renaissance church is not far from the center of tourist Pest. Started in 1851, the church underwent an extended construction period, and in 1868 its 310-foot-tall dome collapsed; work finished only in 1906. The ornate interior is in need of restoration, although some partial work is currently in progress. During World War II, town planners used the church basement to store valuable art and documents. Art and church garments are displayed in the treasury. Sacred music is played in the church on Sunday.

Admission: 30 Ft (30¢).

Open: Basilica, daily 6am–5pm. Treasury, May–Sept, daily 9am–5pm; Oct–Apr, daily 10am–4pm. **Metro:** Deák tér; then walk two blocks north.

Inner City Parish Church [Belvárosi Plébániatempiom], V, Március 15 tér.

One of the oldest surviving structures in Pest, this church has parts dating from the 12th century. Liszt played the organ here, and his "musical Sundays" concerts were often attended by Richard Wagner. Like many old structures, it has served many masters; the Ottomans carved a prayer niche, or mihrab, facing Mecca on the inside of the church. Many parts of the interior are rather new too, exhibiting a "new age" feel. The exterior dates to the 18th century.

Admission: Free.

Open: Daily 7am–5pm. **Directions:** Walk to the foot of the white Elizabeth Bridge (Erzsébet híd).

The Great Synagogue and Museum of Hungarian Jewry, Dohány u. 2–8, at the intersection of Wesselényi utca. ☎ **142-8949.**

Pest boasts the largest synagogue in Europe, a huge brick structure with two towers from the mid-19th century; seating inside accommodates almost 3,000 people. During World War II the Nazis had planned to blow up the synagogue, but they were driven out of the city just in the nick of time.

Next door, Theodor Herzl, father of Zionism (the advocacy of a separate Jewish state) was born. Today there are no services in the synagogue; it's only a museum of Hungarian Jewry. Budapest's prewar Jewish neighborhood was around this area and the nearby streets, and the current Jewish cultural center is still located in the area. Most of Hungary's approximately 80,000 Jews now live in Budapest. If you're interested in guided tours of Jewish Budapest, see "Organized Tours" below.

Admission: Free; donations accepted.

Open: Synagogue and museum, May–Sept, Mon and Thurs 2–6pm; Tues–Wed, Fri, and Sun 10am–1pm. **Closed:** Oct–Apr. **Metro:** Astoria (Red Line).

Városliget Park

After your visit to the Museum of Fine Arts, explore the Városliget (City Park) park to the east. There are lakes for rowing and swimming, an amusement park, a zoo, various sports facilities, plenty of shade, and even a medieval complex that includes a reconstructed Transylvanian castle (Vajdahunyad vára) from 1896. The castle was one of many structures erected in 1896 to celebrate the existence of the Hungarian state for a millennium.

Admission: Free.

Open: Daily 24 hours. **Metro:** Széchenyi fürdő (Yellow Line).

ÓBUDA & MARGARET ISLAND

Often forgotten by tourists, Óbuda, north of Buda immediately beyond the Árpád Bridge, is the third of the three towns that united with Buda and Pest in 1872 to form Budapest. The historic center of Óbuda is surprisingly charming, with one- and two-story buildings, including several good restaurants, lining the cobblestone streets. On Sunday crafts are sold here. While you're in Óbuda you can also visit a number of art galleries near Fő tér. Consider combining a visit to Óbuda with some time on Margaret Island, a park-island in the middle of the Danube.

The Top Attractions

Vasarely Museum, III, Szentlélek tér 6. ☎ 188-7551.

This handsome and spacious building shelters a definitive collection, on two floors, of works by Hungary's most famous modern artist. It also shows what Vasarely was painting before he developed the geometric style that made him famous.

Admission: 50 Ft (50¢), free on Wed.

Open: Mar 15–Oct, Tues–Sun 10am–6pm; Nov–Mar 14, Tues–Sun 10am–5pm. **Metro:** Árpád Híd (Blue Line), then tram 1 westward to the first stop across the bridge. The museum is the large white building just by the tram stop.

Imre Varga Museum, III, Laktanya u. 7.

Varga is considered Hungary's foremost sculptor. The varied collection here includes life-size bronzes such as a sinister bust of Franz Liszt, and the small but effective Babij Jar, where small crucified Christs are embedded in rock. There's a more pleasant sculpture garden out back.

Admission: 30 Ft (30¢).

Open: Tues–Sun 10am–6pm. **Metro:** Go around the Vasarely Museum to the left, and look for the street with the statue of women holding umbrellas.

Aquincum Museum, III, Szentendrei út 139. ☎ 168-8241.

A short bus or train ride north of Óbuda are the ruins of the original Roman settlement of Aquincum, which began to flourish around the time of Christ. In the 2nd century A.D. it grew to the status of a "colony" in the Roman Empire. Frequent barbarian attacks at the end of the 4th century brought the downfall of the colony.

I suggest a visit to this largely reconstructed outdoor area of ruins to those particularly interested in Roman history. The museum contains ancient glass, keys, and sculpture, and a guidebook you can buy at the entrance has detailed descriptions in English.

Across the road from the Aquincum Museum, the fragmentary 2nd century A.D. **Amphitheater** (Katonai Amfiteátrum) is one of the largest outside the Italian peninsula. Here, up to 16,000 spectators at a time could attend circuses and gladiatorial combat in the arena. Other Roman relics in Óbuda include the **Hercules Villa** and the **Bath Museum.**

Admission: 40 Ft (40¢) adults, 20 Ft (20¢) students.

Open: June–Sept, Tues–Sun 10am–6pm; mid-Apr to May and Sept, Tues–Sun 10am–5pm. **Closed:** Nov to mid-Apr. **Directions:** Suburban rail (HÉV) north from the Batthyány tér metro stop (Red Line), a 15-minute ride. You can also get on at the Óbuda stop.

Margaret Island [Margitsziget].

If it's a nice day, combine a visit to Óbuda with a stop on Margaret Island, Budapest's most placid park, in the middle of the Danube. Here you can stroll through woods and rose gardens, or clamber through the ruins of the Dominican convent where St. Margaret herself lived in the 13th century.

Admission: Free.

Open: Daily 24 hours. **Bus:** 26 from Nyugati pu. or Árpád Híd, both on the metro's Blue Line. **Tram:** 4 or 6 to the south end of the island in the middle of the bridge.

COOL FOR KIDS

At the western edge of Buda you'll see some of the most charming and beautiful countryside in the entire land—right in the backyard of the city. This section of the **Buda Hills** is a huge park, with forests, marked paths, hills, lookout towers, and none of Pest's bus exhaust. A **chair lift** (Libegő) pulls Hungarians and foreigners alike up the 1,735-foot János-hegy (János Hill), and treats them to a fabulous view along the way. To reach it, take the Red Line metro to Moszkva tér, walk up the stairs and cross the street, and catch bus 158, whose last stop is the foot of the lift. From the upper terminus, you can hike another few minutes to the lookout tower at the summit. The chairlift runs daily between 9am and 5pm from May 15 to September 15, and daily from 9:30am to 4pm the rest of the year. A round-trip ticket costs 100 Ft ($1).

The eight-mile **Children's Railway** will bring you right through the heart of the Buda Hills. On this railway, formerly known as the Pioneer Railway after the Communist children's organization similar to the Boy Scouts, everything except the engines is run by schoolchildren. You can reach the railway's Hűvösvölgy terminus by taking tram 56 from Moszkva tér, getting off at the last stop, and following the signs for the *gyermekvasút.* Trains run every hour or so, Tuesday through Sunday from 9am to 4pm; tickets cost 44 Ft (45¢). From the Széchenyi-hegy terminus at the other end, Budapest's **cog railway** will deliver you almost all the way back down to Moszkva tér.

The **Transport Museum** (Közlekedési Múzeum), in the easternmost corner of Városliget park (☎ **142-0565**), is open Tuesday through Friday from 10am to 4pm, and Saturday and Sunday from 10am to 6pm. On Sunday at 11am a film on the history of aviation is shown. After a visit here, children will also enjoy a walk through Városliget park, with perhaps a visit to the amusement park at the northern end of the park or the zoo.

Admission is 20 Ft (20¢) for adults, 10 Ft (10¢) for seniors, and free for students. **Metro:** Széchenyi fürdo (Yellow Line).

FOR THE MUSIC LOVER

Ferenc Liszt Memorial Museum, VI, Vörösmarty u. 35. ☎ **142-7320** or **122-9804.**

Here you'll see the former apartment of the composer best known to us as *Franz* Liszt. His piano as well as notes and personal memos are on display. Note that Vörösmarty utca is not the same as Vörösmarty tér in the heart of downtown Buda; rather it's three blocks west of Oktogon on Andrássy út. Free concerts are given here on Saturday at 11am, except in August.

Admission: 20 Ft 20¢ adults, students free.

Open: Mon–Fri 10am–6pm, Sat 9am–5pm. **Metro:** Vörösmarty utca. (Yellow Line).

Béla Bartók Memorial House, II, Csalán út 29. ☎ **176-2100.**

Here in the Lipótmező district of Budapest, you can see objects and papers associated with another Hungarian musical great, located in his original home. On Friday at 6pm the Bartók String Quartet gives concerts for 200 Ft ($2.05) per person.

Open: Tues–Sun 10am–5pm. **Bus:** 5 from Moszvka tér to Pasaréti tér (the last stop); then a 10-minute walk.

Walking Tour
Castle Hill in Buda

Start Clark Ádám tér on the Buda side of Széchenyi Lánchíd (Chain Bridge).
Finish Hilton Hotel.
Time Two to three hours without museum stops; considerably longer with museum stops.
Best Times When museums are open.
Worst Times Monday and Tuesday, when museums are closed.

Start your tour of the Castle Hill from Clark Ádám tér, named after the 19th-century Scottish engineer who designed the Chain Bridge. From here you can ride the recently reopened:

1. **Funicular cable car (Budavári Sikló),** which dates back to 1870, to Buda Castle atop Castle Hill.

   Situated at the southern end of a hill over a mile long that rises in places to 200 feet is:

2. **Buda Castle (Budai Vár),** which served as the Hungarian royal residence for centuries. King Béla IV built the first defensive works on the hill following the Mongol invasion of 1241. In the 18th century it was rebuilt with more than 200 rooms. Then in World War II the Nazis used it as their command center, and by the war's close it was severely damaged. Today the reconstructed Buda Castle contains several museums and dominates the Buda skyline.

   After you arrive at Szent György tér at the top of the cable-car ride, turn left into a gateway with a big eagle to the side. Here you'll have a sweeping view over the Danube on one side and the facade of the castle on the other. Soon you'll arrive at an:

3. **Equestrian statue of Prince Eugene of Savoy,** who helped liberate Hungary from the Turks. Immediately behind the horse is the entrance to the:
4. **Museum of Hungarian Art,** which is especially strong in 19th-century Hungarian art.

   If you want to pass on this museum for now, walk under a small tunnel just before the statue to reach a beautiful courtyard with statues and sculpted hedges. Then left and you'll reach a large courtyard with the "must see":
5. **Budapest History Museum** at the back of the courtyard. After viewing the museum, backtrack out of the courtyard and to your right you'll have another chance to stop by the Hungarian National Gallery. On the north side of the courtyard is the:
6. **Museum of Contemporary History,** with art and history exhibitions.

   Walk north out of the castle complex, passing Szent György tér where you arrived on the cable car. If you take the street on the left side of this square, Szent György utca, you'll see evidence of the intensity of fighting in World War II. Thousands of bullets have worn away most of a two-story building's stone facade, leaving only brick.

   This street exits into Dísz tér, site of the Korona Café. Take the street to the right where you'll stroll along a cobblestone pavement amid different-colored buildings. Take a look at the pharmacies and stores here, all of which recall a previous era. At Tárnok u. 18 you pass the:
7. **Golden Eagle Pharmacy,** which re-creates a pharmacy from several hundred years ago. A few steps beyond the pharmacy you'll arrive at one of the great highlights of Budapest:
8. **Matthias Church,** an imposing structure dating back to the 15th century. At the center of the square in front stands the:
9. **Holy Trinity Column,** erected in 1713 to ward off a local plague.

   If you're visiting from March to October you'll also see:
10. **Horses and buggies** lined up in front of the church. Drivers in traditional costume offer 15-minute introductory rides on Buda Hill for 500 Ft ($5.10) for adults.

    If you turn right in front of Matthias Church, you'll reach the:
11. **Fisherman's Bastion (Halászbástya).** Built in 1903 in neo-Romanesque style, it's not a reconstruction, but rather a new structure erected to celebrate the 1,000th anniversary of the Hungarian nation. You can climb various staircases onto the bastion, from which you'll enjoy a fine view of the Parliament across the Danube. An equestrian statue of the founder of Hungary, St. Stephen, guards the square in front.

Refueling Stop

For a snack, walk a block west to the famous **Café Ruszwurm.**

From the Fisherman's Bastion, walk three blocks west to Tóth Árpád sétány, a street lined with pastel-colored houses on one side and a sweeping view over the Buda Hills on the other. After 3½ blocks you'll see a series of cannons in front of the:

Walking Tour — Castle Hill in Buda

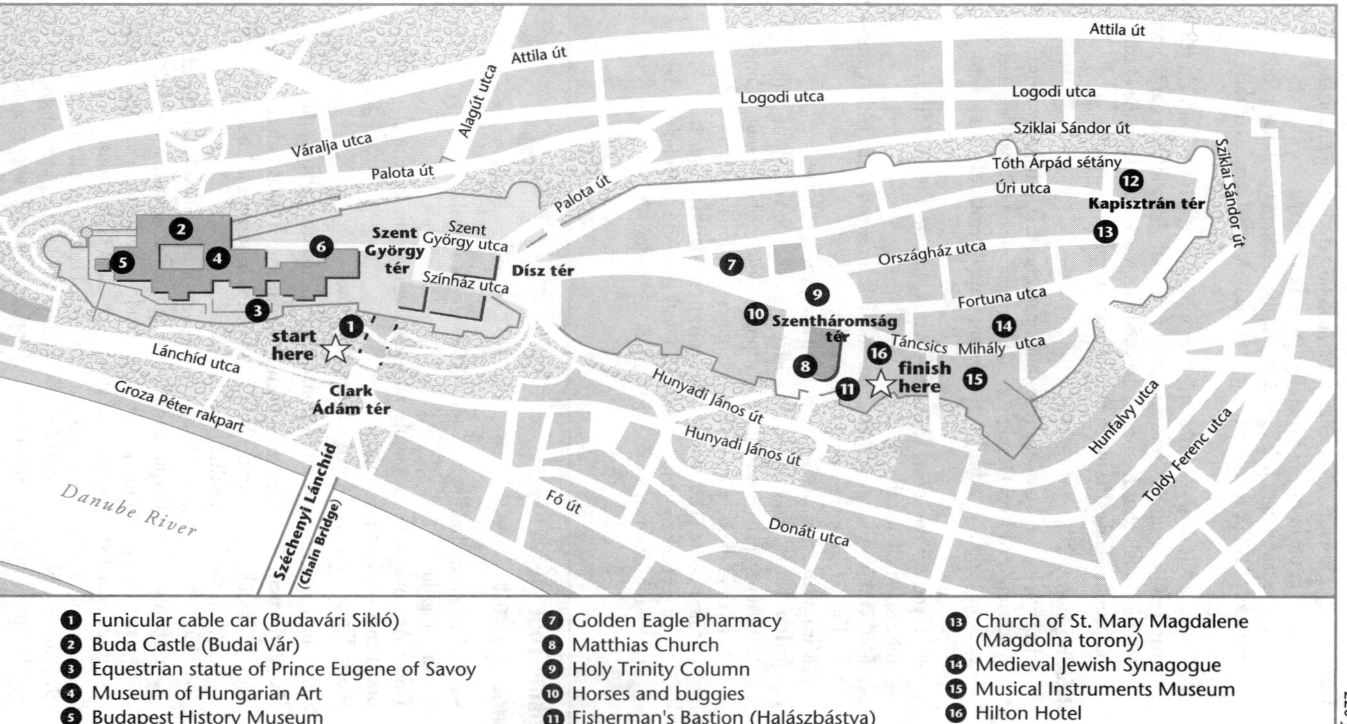

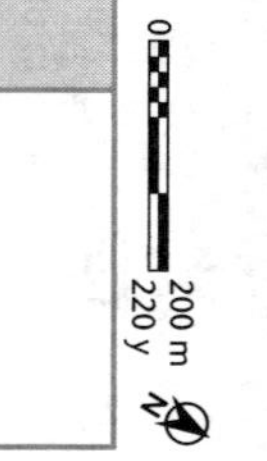

12. **Military Museum,** a former army barracks now chronicling important episodes in the history of the Hungarian armed forces.

If you take a right half a block before the museum, you'll pass a convenient set of public toilets, then arrive at the unadorned remains of the 13th-century:

13. **Church of St. Mary Magdalene (Magdolna torony).** It's the only church that the Ottomans let Christians worship in. Catholics and Protestants prayed together in this church—one of the good things to emerge from the Ottoman occupation. Today the interior serves as an art gallery.

Refueling Stop

Here you have a choice of a restaurant or another café. A block away is the much-touristed **Régi Országház,** on Országház utca. On a parallel street, you can enjoy crêpes or a drink at the elegant **Café Pierrot,** at Fortuna u. 14.

If you exit this square (called Kapisztrán tér) onto Táncsics Mihály utca to the east, you'll pass the:

14. **Medieval Jewish Synagogue** at no. 26, built at the end of the 14th century.

Farther down the street at no. 7 is the:

15. **Musical Instruments Museum.** Soon after, you'll pass the:
16. **Hilton Hotel,** which was built in 1976 upon the ruins of a 13th-century Jesuit abbey, parts of which are incorporated into the hotel design. Concerts are given in the hotel courtyard in summer, and upstairs you'll find the city's foremost casino. The hotel is right across from Matthias Church.

To get back to Pest, you can either walk down the Buda hillside, take the cable car back down, or take the Várbusz to Moskva tér.

Walking Tour
Downtown Pest

Start Parliament Building in Kossuth Lajos tér (Red Line).
Finish Vigadó tér.
Time Approximately three hours, not including museum and church stops.
Best Times When museums are open.
Worst Times Monday, when museums are closed.

Start your tour of downtown Pest from its most distinctive building, the:

1. **Parliament,** a 19th-century structure reminiscent of the British Parliament.

From here, walk to the Danube riverbank to survey the landscape. To the north in the Danube River you'll see:

2. **Margaret Island (Margitsziget),** long a refuge of those weary of the urban rush. About 1 1/2 miles long and several hundred yards wide at the middle, it's green with trees, formal gardens, and meadows. A theater, a stadium, and a gargantuan swimming pool are among the island's attractions.

Walking the south on the path along the Danube, you'll approach the:

3. **Chain Bridge (Széchenyi Lánchíd),** Budapest's oldest and most distinctive bridge. Designed by Adam Clark, a Scottish engineer, it was completed in 1849 and was the first step toward a united Buda and Pest. During the

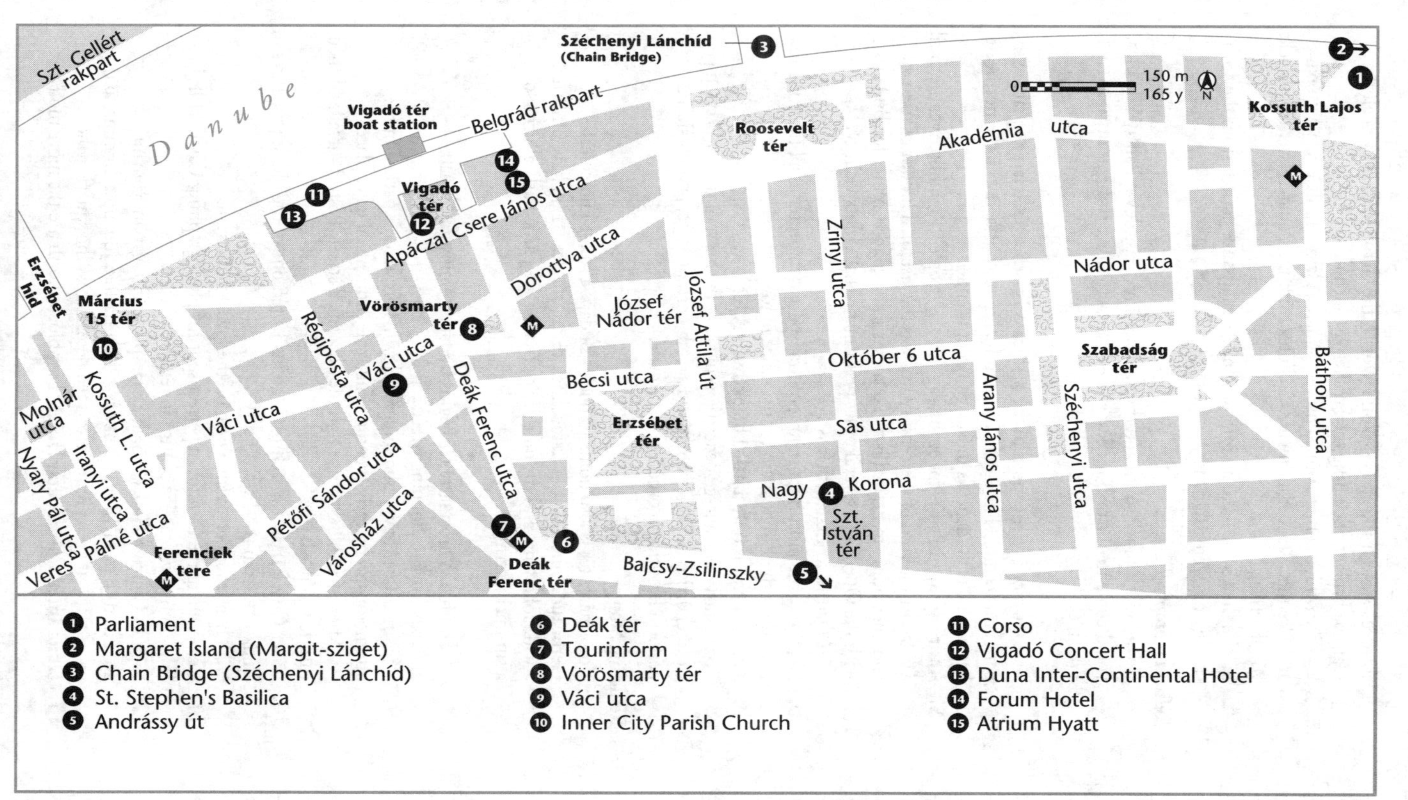

Walking Tour — Downtown Pest

six-week siege at the end of World War II, the Germans destroyed all the Danube bridges, including the Széchenyi Lánchíd.

The bridge connects to Roosevelt Square, a large traffic circle with parks at the center. Walk east down Zrínyi utca from this square. After four blocks you'll arrive at:

4. St. Stephen's Basilica, an imposing neo-Renaissance church from the 19th century on Szent István tér.

Refueling Stop

If you walk a block south and then a block northeast down Paulay Ede utca, you'll come to one of Budapest's finest budget values, **Bohémtanya,** at Paulay Ede u. 6.

One block to the south of the basilica is Erzsébet tér, a large square with a park at its center. The largest bus terminal in town is here. To the northeast begins one of Budapest's most significant avenues:

5. Andrássy út (called Népköztársaság útca, or People's Republic Avenue, until 1990). At the turn of the century this was the fashionable address in town, and once home to Franz Liszt. Today it's still a concert center for Budapest, with the Opera and several other performance halls in its vicinity.

   Adjacent to Erzsébet tér is:

6. Deák tér, the most important local transportation center as all three metro lines meet there. The main tourist office in town:
7. Tourinform, is only a half a block away. A block west is:
8. Vörösmarty tér, a large pedestrian square at the heart of tourist Pest. In good weather artists sell their works and sketch portraits here, and musicians perform in various corners of the square.

Refueling Stop

Vörösmarty tér is also home to one of Budapest's best-known cafés, **Gerbeaud.** Since 1858 its chocolates, cakes, and ice cream have attracted a wide following, and the outdoor café tables are particularly alluring on a summer afternoon.

South of Vörösmarty tér begins Budapest's most fashionable—and expensive—shopping street:

9. Váci utca (see "Savvy Shopping," below). This street is packed in the afternoon and by early evening a full-scale promenade takes place.

   After three blocks, turn right down a small street, Pesti B. utca, and then turn left to reach the:

10. Inner City Parish Church on Március 15 tér, one of the oldest structures in Budapest, from the 12th century.

    Then from here, walk north on the lovely pedestrian:

11. Corso along the Danube, a perfect spot for photographing Castle Hill. In a few minutes you arrive at Vigado tér, site of the:
12. Vigadó Concert Hall, a notable example of Hungarian Romantic architecture from 1859. Franz Liszt, Béla Bartók, Johannes Brahms, and other musical greats have performed here. Across the square is the:
13. Duna Inter-Continental Hotel. Two blocks north are the more modern:

14. Forum Hotel and:
15. Atrium Hyatt, which make easy reference points along the Danube.

Final Refueling Stop

On Vigadó tér you can eat lunch or dinner in one of my preferred restaurants in downtown Pest, the **Duna-Corsó.** Near the Inner City Parish Church is another good choice: **Apostolok,** at Kigyó u. 4–6. And for low-cost Americana, there's always **McDonald's,** on Régiposta utca.

ORGANIZED TOURS

IBUSZ and many of the other tour agencies offer group and private tours of varying lengths by bus, boat, or on foot. These tours are especially worthwhile to see the interior of the Parliament, which is otherwise closed to individual tourists.

Perhaps the best tour value in town is offered by MAHART, the passenger-ship agency. They conduct a 1½-hour ride up the Danube from the center to Margaret Island and back for just 250 Ft ($2.55) per person. Boats leave from the Vigadó tér boat station twice a day from April to mid-October.

In summer only, The Chosen Tours (☎ **122-6527;** fax 268-0498) leads tours to Jewish landmarks in Budapest three days a week. Tours last 2½ to 3½ hours, cost 750 to 1,450 Ft ($7.65 to $14.80), and usually start at 10:30am at the Great Synagogue at Dohany u. 2–8, but call for the current schedule.

6 Thermal Baths

Spa bathing has been a part of Hungary's history since the Roman Empire. Tiberius Nero ordered the first baths built, and they were expanded under Ottoman Turkish control. There are 123 active springs today in the Budapest area. Baths are popular meeting places; some say it was at a bath that the idea to rise against the government in 1956 was first discussed. Here are two favorite baths in town; for a list of others, see the *Budapest Panorama*, or ask at Tourinform for the free pamphlet called "Spas in Hungary."

Gellért Hotel Baths, XI, Szent Gellért tér 1. ☎ **166-6166.**

The best bath in Budapest is available here in the city's most elegant turn-of-the-century hotel. The vast entrance hallway with its long benches, Roman columns, and mosaics was built in 1918. The ambience transports you to another world, and indeed many of those sitting around on the long benches appear to be in perpetual slumber. From this area on, men and women separate and bathe in the nude in hot-spring pools (up to 120°F) and steamrooms. Beyond the bathing rooms, men and women share an indoor and outdoor swimming pool (the outdoor pool has artificial waves). Upstairs, you can enjoy a massage.

Admission: Thermal baths only, 150 Ft ($1.55); baths and swimming pool 300 Ft ($3.10); baths and swimming pool, 170 Ft ($1.75) massage, 170 Ft ($1.75) for 15 minutes; pedicure.

Open: Baths, Mon–Fri 6am–7pm, Sat–Sun 6am–1pm. Pool, May–Sept, daily 6am–7pm; Oct–Apr, Mon–Sat 6am–7pm, Sun 6am–2pm. **Tram:** 47 or 49 from Deák tér; enter from the iron doors around the corner to the right from the hotel facade.

Széchenyi Baths, XIV, Allatkeri út 11, in Városliget park. ☎ **121-0310.**

The biggest thermal bath in Europe, spanning almost five acres in a neoclassical building finished in 1927. There's an outdoor swimming pool here with heated water, open all year long.

Admission: 120 Ft ($1.20). 170

Open: Baths, Mon–Fri 6:30am–7pm, Sat–Sun 6:30am–noon. Pool and sauna, Mon–Sat 6:30am–6pm, Sun 6:30am–3pm. **Metro:** Széchenyi fürdő (Yellow Line). The entrance is hard to find; it's across the street from the circus, and says SZÉCHENYI STRAND above the door.

7 Savvy Shopping

Shopping is one of the great pleasures of Budapest. Begin your walk at Vörösmarty tér (the metro Yellow Line stops on the square), and then continue south on Váci (pronounced "*Vot*-si") utca, the favorite tourist shopping street. Here you'll see a modern pedestrian avenue several blocks long that attracts well-dressed window-shoppers peering in ornately displayed windows. The stores on Váci utca sell everything from china to folk dolls and wine. Several of the side streets off Váci, such as Kigyó utca, are also free of cars and have interesting stores.

Unfortunately, prices have skyrocketed along Váci in recent years, so for bargains you'll have to look elsewhere. Locals prefer the wide boulevards Teréz körút, Andrássy út, and Rákóczi út. Throughout the city you can also find many small open markets selling fruits and vegetables at low cost. The Transylvanian peasants who used to haunt Váci utca, selling their handcrafted wares, have largely been chased away from central Pest by the police. You may still see them at metro stations or along the bridges at night.

Antiques

A quaint antique store in the cellar of the Café Pierrot, Relikvia, Fortuna u. 14 (☎ **175-6971**), has high prices but many interesting things you'll enjoy looking over. It's open daily from 10am to 6pm. To get there, walk two blocks north from Matthias Church on Castle Hill on Fortuna utca.

Department Stores

Skála Metro, Nyugati tér.

A large modern department store opposite the Nyugati train station. Downstairs there's a large supermarket on the same level as the metro, and upstairs, clothing, books, records, electronics, and other goods. Open Monday through Friday from 9am to 7pm and on Saturday from 8am to 3pm. To get there by metro, take the Blue Line to Nyugati pu.

Corvin Áruház [Thing/Commodity House], Blaha Lujza tér.

Another large department store just upstairs from the metro stop. It's open Monday from 10am to 7pm, Tuesday through Friday from 9am to 7pm and on Saturday from 10am to 2pm. Take the metro Red Line to Blaha Lujza tér.

Flea Markets

Ecseri Flea Market, XX, Nagykőrösi út 156.

Located far outside the center, the town flea market offers a wide variety of goods, including coins, pocket watches, clothes, motor parts, and antique signs. Bargaining is essential. The market is most active on Saturday. Open Monday through Friday from 8am to 4pm and on Saturday from 8am to 3pm. Take bus no. 54 (red) or 54 (black) from Boráros tér south of the center of Pest opposite Petőfi bridge; trams nos. 4 and 6 come to this square.

Petőfi Youth Center Flea Market [Petőfi Csarnok Ifjúsági Központ], XIV, Zichy M. utca in Városliget park. ☎ **251-7266.**

This large youth cultural center hosts a flea market on Saturday and Sunday from 6am to 2pm with 3,000 vendors. Admission is 20 Ft (20¢). The metro stop is Széchenyi fürdő (Yellow Line).

Folk Art

Folk Art Centrum, V, Váci u. 14. ☎ **118-5840.**

The largest shop of its kind in Budapest, this is a folk-art supermarket, with rugs, embroidery, and furnishings downstairs, and folk crafts such as carved wood, dolls, napkins, and ceramic goods on the ground floor. The store opens daily at 9:30am, closing at 9pm in July and August and 7pm the rest of the year. American Express, Diners, MasterCard and Visa accepted. The metro stop is Vörösmarty tér.

Éva Dolls, V, Kecskeméti u. 13. ☎ **117-4305.**

Another, though smaller, folk-art shop, on a street not far away in the direction of Kálvin tér. Open Monday through Saturday from 10am to 6pm and on Sunday from 10am to 4pm. The metro stop is Kálvin tér.

Sheet Music

Musicians may want to pick up some sheet music of Béla Bartók or other composers at **Zenei Antikvárium,** V, Múzeum körút 17. A number of other stores in town also sell sheet music. Open Monday through Friday from 10am to 6pm and on Saturday from 9am to 1pm. The metro stop is Kálvin tér.

Souvenirs

★ **Rokiland,** VII, Erzsébet krt. 4.

This shop has an amazing assortment of tiny animals, all handmade from pipe cleaners by the owners; the Tóth family. The best ones are the monkeys. The store is upstairs, and is open Monday through Friday from 10am to 6pm. Metro: Blaha Lujza tér. (Red Line).

Vár-Bazár, I, Ostrom u. 10.

This thrift shop near the north end of Castle Hill has a distinctly Hungarian flavor. Here you can find all sorts of collectables, including hand-painted plates and the occasional piece of Herend china. Two charming women, Márta and Kati, run the shop. They speak no English, but somehow converse with English-speakers anyway. The tiny, subterranean store is open Monday through Friday from 10am to 6pm. Metro: Moszkva tér (Red Line).

8 Evening Entertainment

Budapest's English-language newspapers are the most useful source of cultural information. Two other useful sources are available free of charge from Tourinform, and many other tourist offices and hotels: *Programme in Ungarn/in Hungary* and *Budapest Panorama,* both published monthly.

THE PERFORMING ARTS

In summer, outdoor concerts are performed in several spots around Buda, including at the Fisherman's Bastion and in the courtyard of the Hilton Hotel. A pamphlet available at Tourinform called "Buda Castle Programmes" provides details for events in the current season.

TICKETS In addition to the theater box offices, several agencies in town sell tickets for cultural events. For the Hungarian National Philharmonica and other classical concerts, go to the Philharmonic Booking Office at V, Vörösmarty tér 1 (☎ **117-6222**), the main square at the end of Váci utca. They also have the monthly program ("Koncert Kalendárium") of other classical concerts in Budapest. Open Monday through Friday from 10am to 6pm, Saturday from 10am to 2pm.

The Central Theatre Box Office, VI, Andrássy út 18 (☎ **112-0000**), sells theater, opera, operetta, musical, and occasional concert tickets. Opera tickets generally cost 100 to 600 Ft ($1 to $6.10), although world-famous performers will fetch up to 5,000 Ft ($51). Staffers who speak foreign languages are in short supply in this office and they don't go out of their way to help, but many schedules are posted on the office walls. On the street, you'll see a sign, KÖZPONTI JEGYIRODA, written above the entrance. Open Monday through Thursday from 9am to 6pm, Friday from 9am to 5pm.

Music Mix, V, Váci u. 33 (☎ **138-2237**), sells tickets to rock concerts as well as occasional jazz performances. Open Monday through Friday from 10am to 6pm, on Saturday from 10am to 2pm, and in July and August only, on Sunday from 3 to 7pm.

Major Concert/Performance Halls

Ferenc Liszt Academy of Music, VI, Liszt Ferenc tér 8. ☎ **141-4788.**

Frequent concerts are performed in the main hall, and cognoscenti rate the acoustics better here than at the Vigadó. Unfortunately, there are no concerts in July or August. The box office is open on concert days from 10am to 1pm and 5 to 8pm. Ticket prices start at 300 Ft ($3.05). Metro: Oktogon tér (Yellow Line); enter from Király utca.

Pesti Vigadó Concert Hall, V, Vigadó tér. ☎ **118-9909.**

Built in the last century, this, the oldest concert hall in Budapest, is located inside a fine example of Hungarian Romantic architecture. Brahms, Liszt, Bartók, and other greats have performed here in the past. Metro: Vörösmarty tér (Yellow Line).

Hungarian State Opera House, VI, Andrássy út 22. ☎ **131-2550.**

Opera became popular in Budapest in the 17th century. At that time Italian and German companies performed for the Esterházy princes. Later, Haydn presented his own compositions in Budapest in a small theater he managed. When this opera house officially opened on September 27, 1884, Franz Joseph I, emperor of Austria-Hungary, attended the performance. Today, opera is still very much a part of the city's cultural life, and ballet is also performed here. The box office, located on the side of the building left of the facade, is open Tuesday through Saturday from 11am to 1:45pm and 2:30 to 7pm, and Sundays and holidays from 10am to 1pm and 4 to 7pm. Metro: Opera (Yellow Line).

MOVIES

Budapest will delight film lovers. You can see first-run movies very cheaply here, but even better are the theaters that show a mixture of old and new foreign art films, many of them in English with Hungarian subtitles but no dubbing. Check *Budapest Week* or the *Budapest Sun* for comprehensive, accurate listings; you could find yourself enjoying an old Orson Welles movie one night and Peter Greenaway's latest production the next. The four-screen **Muvész,** two blocks north of the Oktogon at VI, Teréz krt. 30 (☎ **132-6726**), shows the most English-language films. Tickets cost only 100 to 140 Ft ($1 to $1.45).

THE BAR, CLUB & MUSIC SCENE

Fregatt, V, Molnár u. 26. ☎ **118-9997.**

Here is Budapest's premier English-style pub, with beautiful wood decor, dart boards with a clear line of fire, and Guinness (as well as German beer) on draft for 105 Ft ($1.05) per half-liter.

Stuffed, grilled chicken livers are served as well as sausages and pigs' ankles, but there's no formal restaurant dining. Twice a week a blues or country group stops by, and the third Sunday of every month they have Irish music. The place is packed practically every night with trendy, professional Hungarians.

It's open Monday through Friday from 3pm to midnight and on Saturday and Sunday from 5pm to midnight. To get here, walk four blocks south of Március 15 tér to the corner of Molnár and Pintér utca.

Petőfi Youth Center [Petőfi Csarnok Ifjúsági Központ], XIV, Zichy M. u. 14, in Városliget park. ☎ **251-7266.**

A large cultural center for young people in the middle of Városliget park, this place hosts frequent concerts, folk programs, modern dance, fashion shows, theater, and other events, mostly for youth, which means they end by 10pm. Some events are held indoors and others on an open-air stage. They also host a Saturday and Sunday flea market from 6am to 2pm. When there's not much going on at the center, you can always drop by the restaurant and café. Read *Budapest Panorama* or *Programme in Ungarn/in Hungary* or give them a call to learn of upcoming events. Metro: Széchenyi fürdő (Yellow Line).

Picasso Point, VI, Hajós u. 31. ☎ **132-4750.**

Picasso Point is one of Budapest's popular expatriate community hangouts, though it by no means attracts an entirely expat clientele. It's on the ground floor of a typical downtown Pest corner building, not far from the Opera metro station (Yellow Line). The bar—open daily from noon to 4am—has German beer on draft for 125 Ft ($1.30) per half liter, and serves chili at 150 Ft ($1.55) a bowl. There's live jazz every evening from 8 to 10pm, and the airless cellar disco downstairs opens on Fridays and Saturdays.

Young Artists' Club [Fiatal Művészek Klubja], Andrássy út 112. ☎ **131-8858** or **131-5920**.

A good place to meet local artists and learn about their work, this club in a decaying mansion hosts jazz or rock concerts almost daily. I saw a good blues band when I dropped in. You can also view an exhibition of contemporary art in three different rooms, open Monday through Friday from 10am to 6pm. The club is open Monday through Friday from 6pm to 2am, on Saturday and Sunday only for special events. A restaurant downstairs, open only after 8pm, serves Greek and Italian food. Metro: Bajza utca (Yellow Line); then walk half a block. **Admission:** Club and concerts, 100–150 Ft ($1–$1.55); art exhibition, free.

9 Networks & Resources

FOR STUDENTS & OTHERS The Express ticket office at V, Zoltán u. 10 (☎ **1/111-9898**; fax 1/111-6418) is the biggest student and youth travel outfit in town. They sell international youth hostel and ISIC cards, InterRail and other international discounted train tickets, as well as discount airline tickets. The office is near the Kossuth Lajos tér metro station (Red Line). It's open Monday through Friday from 8:30am to 4:30pm, and on Saturday from 8:30am to 3pm.

You can also get discount train tickets straight from the train company if you're under 26 or a student. See "Moving On," below. To connect with people driving to various European destinations, call Liftcentrale, VIII, Kőfarago u. 15 (☎ **138-2019**). A one-way ride to Munich, for example, costs 2,800 Ft ($28.55). The office is open Monday through Friday from 10am to 6pm and on Saturday from 10am to 2pm.

10 Easy Excursions

The most common day trip from Budapest is to the charming village of Szentendre, and many also visit other destinations on the Danube Bend from there. Other places such as Lake Balaton, Eger, or Kecskemét could be visited in an ambitious day outing, and most other towns elsewhere in Hungary are perfect for overnight or several-night jaunts out of the capital. See the chapters that follow for other sightseeing suggestions in Hungary.

11 Moving On—Travel Services

BY PLANE Call **157-8555** at least five hours in advance for the Airport Minibus, which will pick you up anywhere in town at any time and take you to Ferihegy Airport. Be sure to arrive at least an hour before departure.

Budapest's Austrian Airlines office is at V, Régiposta u. 5 (☎ **117-1550**), just off Váci utca. It's open Monday through Friday from 8:30am to 4:30pm. The closest metro is Vörösmarty tér (Yellow Line).

The most central MALÉV office is at Dorottya u. 2 (☎ **266-5616**), on the northwest corner of Vörösmarty tér. It's open Monday from 7:30am to 7pm, and Tuesday through Friday from 7:30am to 5pm. You can make reservations by telephone (☎ **267-4333**) Monday through Friday from 7:30am to 6pm and on Saturday from 7:30am to 2pm. At other times, call or visit the airport office (☎ **157-7211**).

For flight information, call **157-7155** (Ferihegy 1) or **157-7000** (Ferihegy 2).

BY TRAIN Since Budapest has three main train stations, always double-check to make sure you're at the right one. Plenty of visitors have realized their mistake too late.

MÁV, the state rail company, runs a friendly, English-speaking counter (☎ **118-4587**) for international tickets only, inside the MALÉV office at Dorottya u. 2, on the northwest corner of Vörösmarty tér. It's open Monday through Friday from 8am to 4:30pm, and gives all the applicable student and youth discounts. For domestic tickets, you can go to any station or to the central MÁV office at Andrássy út 35 (☎ **122-8056**), near the Opera metro station (Yellow Line). It's open Monday through Friday from 9am to 5pm.

BY BUS To western Hungary, the airport, and international destinations, buses leave from the Erzsébet tér station (☎ **117-2562**), across the street from the Deák tér metro junction.

To the Danube Bend, buses leave from the Árpád Híd station (☎ **129-1450**), by the Árpád Híd metro station (Bus Line).

To anywhere in Hungary east of the Danube, buses leave at the Népstadion station (☎ **252-4496**), by the Népstadion metro station (Red Line; go out the exit away from downtown).

If you don't speak Hungarian, call Tourinform (☎ **117-9800**) for help with schedules.

BY BOAT To the Danube Bend, boats leave from the Vigadó tér boat station (☎ **118-1223**), a yellow building halfway between the white Erzsébet bridge and the Chain Bridge. To reach it, walk towards the river from Vörösmarty tér.

Boats to Vienna leave from the International Boat Station (Nemzetközi hajóállomás), halfway between the green Szabadság bridge and the white Erzsébet bridge. You can reach it on tram 2 from Kossuth Lajos tér.

20

The Danube Bend

ABOUT 25 MILES NORTH OF BUDAPEST THE MIGHTY DANUBE SWINGS ABRUPTLY south. The delightful towns along this "bend" can be easy day trips from the capital as well as longer overnight destinations.

Despite its tranquillity today, this beautiful and strategically located region was once the fulcrum of Hungarian civilization. Under the Roman Empire, the Danube marked the end of "civilized" lands and the main northern line of defense. A millennium later, Hungarian kings dictated to the rest of the country from this natural east–west gateway. The constellation of nobility that inhabited the towns of Esztergom, Visegrád, and Szentendre led the Hungarian Renaissance and built numerous monuments to their power in these towns. Their downfall and the subsequent Ottoman Turkish invasion resulted in an era of decline and devastation that lasted for the 150-year-long occupation. But many of the ruins, castles, and churches still remain, and their proximity to Budapest makes the Danube Bend ideal for a brief visit.

1 Szentendre

12 miles N of Budapest

GETTING THERE • **By Train** Szentendre is virtually a part of Budapest, and the best way to get there is by suburban rail (HEV). Trains leaves every 10 to 20 minutes from Budapest's Batthyány tér metro station, on the Buda side of the Danube across the river from the Parliament. Szentendre is the last stop. The ride takes 40 minutes and costs 64 Ft (65¢), or 39 Ft (40¢) with any Budapest transportation pass; buy tickets before boarding. The first train leaves every morning at about 4am and the last around 11:40pm. One of the stops enroute is near the Roman ruins in Aquincum.

• **By Boat** Boats travel up the Danube from Budapest's Vigadó tér boat station (Hajóállomás) (☎ **118-1223**) from early April until sometime in early October, weather permitting. Three boats a day run from mid-May through August. In early May and after August 31, there's only one 10am departure per day. In April boats only run on weekends. The journey takes about 1½ hours. The price is 135 Ft ($1.40); children under 4 ride free, and those 4 to 14 get 50% off.

ESSENTIALS Szentendre's telephone area code is 26.

ORIENTATION Located on the left bank of the Danube, Szentendre bars vehicular traffic from much of its center, making it a pedestrian paradise. The center of town is Fő tér, half a block from the riverfront. The restaurants and travel agencies listed in this section are within short walking distances of here.

From the bus and train station, right next to each other, it's a 10-minute walk down an underpass and then north up Kossuth Lajos utca (with the Danube on your right) to Fő tér. If you arrive at the boat dock, walk back towards Budapest along the shore about 15 minutes to reach the center of town.

INFORMATION Szentendre's bright, helpful Tourinform office is at Dumtsa Jenő u. 22 (☎ **26/317-965**). It's on the way from the bus and train station to Fő tér, on the right just after you cross the stream. The office is open daily from 9:30am to 5pm.

SPECIAL EVENTS Szentendre hosts the Spring Festival in March, with music and dance, coinciding with the Budapest Spring Festival, and Szentendre Theater performances in June and July.

What's Special About the Danube Bend

Castles

- The 14th-century Royal Castle in Visegrád, once seat of the Hungarian throne.
- The powerful medieval Citadel perched on a hill overlooking Visegrád.
- Esztergom Castle, the oldest royal palace in Hungary, from the 10th century, and the legendary birthplace of St. Stephen.

Museums

- The town of Szentendre itself, made up of charming old Hungarian houses.
- Open-Air Ethnographical Museum in Szentendre, re-creating a traditional Hungarian peasant village.
- Museum of ceremicist Margit Kovács, one of 14 art galleries and museums in Szentendre.

Churches

- Cathedral of Esztergom, the largest in Hungary, center of Hungarian Catholicism and home to a valuable treasury.

Szentendre (which is pronounced "*Sen*-ten-dreh" and means "St. Andrew") has a peculiar history: Serbs settled it in 1690 and made it the center-in-exile of the Serbian Orthodox Church. After the restoration of the Kingdom of Serbia in 1882, most of them left, and Hungarian artists took over their empty houses. The artistic community still thrives today, and fuels a vast tourist industry that somehow doesn't spoil the town's appeal. Szentendre makes a great day trip from Budapest, but you could also think of Budapest as a day trip from Szentendre.

WHAT TO SEE & DO

The most interesting sight of Szentendre is the town itself, and you'll enjoy spending several leisurely hours wandering through the pedestrians-only cobblestone streets. Those with an eye for contemporary art can stop at one of Szentendre's 14 galleries and museums. In addition to art exhibits, there are frequent concerts and other cultural events. Inquire at Tourinform.

Open-Air Ethnographical Museum [Skanzen], Szabadságforrás út, two miles northwest of the town center. ☎ **312-304.**

This museum documents living conditions of Hungarian peasants by showing reconstructions of their houses and working areas.

Admission: 80 Ft (80¢).

Open: Apr–Oct, Tues–Sun 9am–5pm. **Closed:** Nov–Mar. **Directions:** Ask Tourinform for help with bus connections.

Margit Kovács Museum, Vastagh György u. 1.

Beautiful ceramics in an 18th-century house by Margit Kovács (1902–77), who fused traditional Hungarian folk elements with modern art.

Admission: 60 Ft (60¢) adults, 30 Ft (30¢) students.

Open: May–Oct, Tues–Sun 10am–6pm; Nov–Apr, Tues–Sun 10am–4pm. **Directions:** Walk south of Fő tér toward the river.

is the best I had outside Budapest. The specialties change frequently here, but always feature large portions with little touches, like onions braised over charcoal, to make a great meal. There is a detailed English menu.

Régimódi, Futó u. 3. ☎ **311-105.**

Cuisine: HUNGARIAN. **Reservations:** Recommended. **Directions:** Walk on the street immediately south of Fő tér.
Prices: Soup 99 Ft ($1); main courses 250–490 Ft ($2.55–$5). AE, DC, MC, V.
Open: Daily noon–midnight.

A restaurant spread over three floors, this was a private house until 1983, and old family photos still line some of the walls. The restaurant's name means "Old Style," and the decor reflects the classical European style of a century ago, with gold mirrors, embroidered curtains, and carved-wood furniture on the parlor floor; recorded classical music adds to the elegant atmosphere. You can also dine on a terrace with partial views of the Danube. Specialties include paprika chicken, deer soup with tarragon, carp filet, venison goulash, and beefsteak Tartar—raw beef and lots of spices that you mix up with butter to make a sort of pâté.

2 Visegrád

27 miles N of Budapest

GETTING THERE • By Bus The fastest way into town is by the frequent bus service from Árpád híd bus station in Budapest, taking a little over an hour for 142 Ft ($1.45). Ask to get off at the Visegrád boat station (hajóállomás); there are three or four bus stops in town, and the terminus is north of the major sights.

• By Boat From mid-May to August, three boats each morning depart Budapest's Vigadó tér Boat Station for Visegrád. In early May and from September 1 to closedown sometime in early October, there's only one boat a day; in April, boats sail only on weekends, once a day. It is a pleasant three-hour ride, costing 156 Ft ($1.60); children under 4 ride free, and those 4 to 14 pay half price.

ESSENTIALS Visegrád's telephone area code is 26.

ORIENTATION Visegrád is a tiny village, strung out along the main highway from Budapest and the Danube River. One block inland, also parallel to the river, runs Fő utca, site of the Royal Palace. Forested hills begin immediately behind this street, crowned by the Citadel on top.

INFORMATION There is no tourist office in Visegrád, though one may have opened by the time you arrive. Ask local people for directions; it's a small town and everyone knows where everything is.

SPECIAL EVENTS Usually in June, there's Visegrád Summer, with a pageant and equestrian tournament in the castle.

Visegrád, a small village of only 3,000 inhabitants, is set back into the actual bend of the Danube River. The town's size does not match its historical importance. In Roman times Visegrád was a vital strategic point in the Roman frontier fortifications. In 1326 the Hungarian king made Visegrád (which means "High Fortress" in Slavic) the royal capital, and converted the local castle into the royal palace. During the Hungarian Renaissance in the 15th century King Matthias built a new royal palace. This majestic structure attracted political visitors from across the continent—a tribute to the growing Hungarian influence in Europe. Soon after, however, the Turks invaded the region and destroyed whatever came in their path; Visegrád never fully recovered.

WHAT TO SEE & DO

Royal Palace [Mátyás Király Múzeum], Fő u. 29. ☎ **328-026** or **328-252.**

Once the seat of mighty King Matthias, the 14th-century palace features two elegant fountains (one of red marble and the other of white), as well as ornate carvings and coats-of-arms of the royal family. After centuries of war the palace today is largely in ruins; in fact, it was not until World War II that the palace was rediscovered (it had been buried under a landslide). Despite the extensive damage, a dedicated excavation effort has revealed such interesting remains as the steambath; here, coals were heated in an area beneath the floor and then water was thrown on the pavement, not unlike a sauna. After visiting the palace, you will have an idea of the opulent life led by Hungarian royalty.

Admission: 30 Ft (30¢) adults, students free.

Open: Apr–Oct, Tues–Sun 9am–4:30pm; Nov–Mar, Tues–Sun 8am–3:30pm. **Directions:** Enter Fő utca from the main highway near the boat landing and walk about five minutes.

Citadel, high on the hilltop overlooking the Danube.

Better preserved than the Royal Palace, the mighty Citadel is Visegrád's most worthwhile sight. A crucial part of the royal settlement in the Middle Ages and Renaissance, the Citadel in Visegrád hosted important political congresses from the 13th to the 15th century, stored state documents, and served as the center of other political matters. In addition, of course, the Citadel functioned as the town's primary defense against attack. Besides showing off one of the region's most interesting castles, a visit to the Citadel offers a splendid vantage point over the Danube. From the lookout you can see the site of the controversial never-completed Nagymaros Dam; it's a semicircular man-made peninsula at the river's bend.

Admission: 40 Ft (40¢) adults, 20 Ft (20¢) students, 10 Ft (10¢) children.

Open: Daily 9am–5pm. **Directions:** It's a tough half-hour walk to the top of the hill, but look for a red VW van marked CITY BUS VISEGRÁD, which cruises the boat-landing area looking for passengers, at 500 Ft ($5.10) per trip.

WHERE TO STAY

PRIVATE ROOMS Despite the absence of a tourist office, there remains a lively market in private rooms. Look for ZIMMER FREI or SZOBA KIADÓ signs on houses, ask at the Fekete Holló restaurant (see "Where to Eat," below), or look at the list of "szallak" on the map of Visegrád posted by the town parking lot.

Hotels

Hotel Matthias, Fő u. 47, 2025 Visegrád. ☎ **26/328-309.** 14 rms (all with bath).

Directions: From the boat landing, follow the main highway 50 yards to your right to Fő utca and walk another 200 yards; the hotel is on your left, just past the Royal Museum.

Rates (including breakfast): 1,600 Ft ($16.35) single; 2,100 Ft ($21.45) double; 2,600 Ft ($26.55) triple.

4000

There's a restaurant and bar on the premises. The Matthias is conveniently located just minutes from the Royal Museum, but otherwise it's nothing special.

WHERE TO EAT

Fekete Holló Vendéglő [Black Crow Restaurant], Rév u. 12.

Cuisine: HUNGARIAN. **Directions:** From the boat landing, walk 10 minutes west along the waterfront; the entrance is just before Rév utca.
Prices: Soups 65–110 Ft (65¢–$1.10); main courses 220–340 Ft ($2.25–$3.45).

In this appealing restaurant you can eat in either a small vaulted brick dining room or an outdoor lawn area with picnic tables.

3 Esztergom

29 miles NW of Budapest

GETTING THERE • **By Train** Second-class-only trains leave every one to two hours for Esztergom from Budapest's Nyugati station, taking an hour and 45 minutes for 126 Ft ($1.30).

• **By Bus** Buses leave from Budapest's Árpád híd bus station every 30 to 40 minutes, reaching Esztergom after an hour and 15 minutes for 142 Ft ($1.45). About two-thirds of the buses—that's about one per hour—take the riverside highway, so you can get on in Szentendre or Visegrád as well.

• **By Boat** Every day from mid-May to early September, and also on weekends from early April to mid-May and from early September until the end of the season in early October, a boat leaves Budapest at 8am and heads upstream on a five-hour run to Esztergom, arriving at 1pm and returning to Budapest later in the afternoon. Tickets cost 187 Ft ($1.90); children under 4 ride free, and those 4 to 14 get 50% off. On weekends from June to early September, a much faster hydrofoil runs from Budapest to Esztergom each day, taking just 80 minutes for 560 Ft ($5.70); the same discounts apply. All departures are from Budapest's Vigadó tér boat station.

ESSENTIALS Esztergom's telephone area code is 33.

ORIENTATION Astride the Danube River, Esztergom stands at the western entrance to Hungary, the first major Hungarian town you enter if you travel by river.

The town center is at the southern foot of the Várhegy (Castle Hill), home to the cathedral and castle, Esztergom's principal attractions. The Danube River is to the west, shielded by a small island, the Esztergom-sziget, created by a loop of the river. The main street running through town to Castle Hill is Bajcsy-Zsilinszky út.

The bus and train stations are south of the city center. From the train station take bus no. 1 or 6 for four stops. The bus station is within easy walking distance of the city center; walk north on Simor János utca for about 10 minutes. The boat dock is on the Esztergom-sziget, south of the Hotel Esztergom, and within walking distance of the center.

INFORMATION The city of Esztergom runs an information office called Gran Tours at Széchenyi tér 25 (☎ and fax **33/313-756**), across from IBUSZ and on your way from the bus station to the center of town. (Gran is the German name for Esztergom.) They have a brochure rack, sell maps, and can reserve private apartments. Open June to October 15, Monday through Friday from 8am to 5pm and Saturday from 8am to noon; the rest of the year, Monday through Friday from 8am to 4pm and Saturday from 8am to noon.

SPECIAL EVENTS Organ concerts are held in the cathedral from April to October.

Hungary's greatest king, Stephen I, founder of the Árpád dynasty and later canonized, was born, raised, and ruled here in the 10th century A.D. He was not the first to take advantage of Esztergom's excellent location, however; the Romans had built one of the primary bastions of their Trans-Danubian frontier here.

During his reign, in which he converted Hungary to Catholicism in the year 1000, Stephen I also began the construction of a basilica on the Várhegy, the hill where the new basilica now stands. Almost a thousand years later, Esztergom is still the seat of the cardinal-primate of Hungary and the center of Hungarian Catholicism. Unfortunately, the Ottoman Turks ravaged the city and destroyed the old basilica during their occupation.

As important as Esztergom once was, time moves a little slower here now. You'll enjoy cobblestone streets lined with traditional painted houses, and tranquil lanes along the Danube River and its canal. And if you walk into town from the bus station, you pass the heart of local life, the outdoor fruit-and-vegetable market. If you arrive from Budapest, you'll find people markedly more relaxed and friendly.

WHAT TO SEE & DO

★ **Cathedral of Esztergom,** Szent István tér.

You won't want to miss the largest church in Hungary. Begun in 1822, on the ruins of the old basilica dating back to the 11th century, it was completed in 1856. Ferenc (Franz) Liszt presided over the dedication ceremony and conducted his *Gran Festival Mass.* The massive Corinthian columns 70 feet high on the facade recall the Pantheon in Rome; the huge cupola reaches a height of 323 feet.

The altar painting is a copy of Venetian master Titian's *Assumption of the Virgin.* On the southern side of the church is the Renaissance **Bakócz Chapel** from 1506, which was dismantled into 1,600 pieces in the 19th century and then put back together again as part of the newer cathedral. Next to the church are the ruins of the old Royal Palace (see below) as well as ruins from Roman times.

Admission: Free.

Open: May–Oct, daily 7am–6pm; Nov–Apr, daily 7am–5pm. **Bus:** 1, 3, 4, 5, 6, or 7.

Cathedral Treasury [Kincstár], Szent István tér.

Located in a wing of the cathedral are hundreds of stunning gold objects and other regalia. The centerpiece of the collection is the **Corvinus Ceremonial Cross,** also known as the Calvary Cross of Matthias Corvinus, located upstairs in exhibition 13. Fashioned by the premier goldsmiths of Paris, it was originally intended as a New Year's gift in 1402 for the Burgundian noble, Philip the Bold, from his consort. There are also several beautiful drinking horns, including one that may have been used by Corvinus himself, ornate church vestments, and a large model of the cathedral.

Admission: 50 Ft (50¢) adults, 20 Ft (20¢) students.

Open: Mar–Oct, daily 9am–4:30pm; Nov–Dec, Tues–Fri 11am–3:30pm, Sat–Sun 10am–3:30pm. **Closed:** Jan–Feb. **Directions:** Enter through the door to the right of the altar.

Castle Museum [Vármúzeum], Szent István tér. ☎ **311-821.**

Hungary's oldest royal palace, dating back to the 10th century, is the birthplace of King Stephen, who converted the nation to Catholicism. Today you can visit many rooms of the palace as you view a rather sizable collection of old pottery, swords, jewelry, and castle relics, all explained only in Hungarian. One highlight is the **Castle Chapel,** built in the 12th century, with frescoes from various epochs. You can also go up to the rooftop for the best panoramic view around. Outside the castle you'll see a reconstructed stretch of 14th- to 15th-century fortifications.

Admission: 40 Ft (40¢).

Open: May–Oct, Tues–Sun 9am–4:30pm; Nov–Apr, Tues–Sun 10am–3:30pm. **Directions:** Walk across from the cathedral.

WHERE TO STAY

PRIVATE ROOMS The Gran Tours office at Széchenyi tér 25 (☎ and fax **33/313-756**) can find private apartments for up to four people for 1,500 Ft ($15.30) per night. They're open June to October 15, Monday through Friday from 8am to 5pm and Saturday from 8am to noon; the rest of the year, Monday through Friday from 8am to 4pm and Saturday from 8am to noon.

Ibusz, nearby at Lőrinc útja 1 (☎ **33/311-552;** fax 33/311-643), rents doubles for 1,200 Ft ($12.25). Open Monday through Friday from 8am to 4pm, and from June to August also on Saturday from 8 to 11am.

A Splurge Hotel

Hotel Esztergom, Prímás sziget, Nagy-Duna sétány, 2500 Esztergom. ☎ **33/312-883.** Fax 33/312-853. Telex 27765. 34 rms (all with bath). MINIBAR TEL TV **Directions:** Bus 1, 5, or 6 from the train station to the foot of Castle Hill; then walk two blocks east on Bajcsy-Zsilinszky út and turn left over a small bridge. A taxi, about 100 Ft ($1), might be best if you arrive with lots of luggage.

Rates: Apr–Oct, 98 DM ($57.65) double; Nov–Mar, 68 DM ($40) double. AE, DC, MC, V. **Parking:** Free.

For those seeking a bit more comfort in their stay at splurge prices, try this three-star hotel on a small island just across from Castle Hill. A modern tiled lobby with plants matching the green-cloth furniture greets you as you enter. Small balconies in the rooms overlook the Danube in the distance and the parking lot in the foreground. Large windows allow lots of light, illuminating the floral wallpaper and a print above the bed. A Danubius Beta Hotel.

Dining/Entertainment: The summer bar on the roof offers a great terrace view of Castle Hill. There's also a year-round restaurant.

Facilities: Small folk-craft shop in the lobby.

WHERE TO EAT

Alabárdos, Bajcsy-Zsilinszky út 49.

Cuisine: HUNGARIAN. **Directions:** Walk on the street just south of Castle Hill.
Prices: Soup 70–100 Ft (70¢–$1); main courses 350–580 Ft ($3.60–$5.90).
Open: May–Aug, daily noon–10pm; Sept–Apr, Tues–Sun noon–9pm.

The beautiful garden here, open from May to August, makes this my first choice in Esztergom. In poor weather you can eat in a midsize indoor area with a bar at the back.

Szalma Csárda, Nagy Duna sétány 2.

Cuisine: HUNGARIAN. **Directions:** Walk 300 yards past the Hotel Esztergom to the riverboat terminal.
Prices: Soups 50–75 Ft (50¢–75¢); main courses 150–300 Ft ($1.55–$3.10).
Open: June–Sept, daily 10am–10pm, Oct–Nov and Apr–May, daily 10am–4 pm; Dec–Mar, Mon–Fri 10am–4pm.

A quiet breezy place, this *csárda* has an authentic feeling to it, with wooden floors, whitewashed walls, and excellent prices. Photos of the 1991 Danube flooding—the worst in 40 years—are on display.

Western Hungary

21

SMALL VILLAGES TUCKED AWAY AMONG VERDANT HILLS, A BALMY MEDITERRANEAN climate, and a culture dating back to Roman times make western Hungary one of the most attractive regions in the entire country. An abundance of castle hotels and small inns makes the region especially attractive for a brief stay. The region's proximity to Austria also gives it a Western European flavor. If you have some extra time in Hungary, give this charming region strong consideration.

SEEING WESTERN HUNGARY

Győr is an industrial city wrapped around a particularly agreeable medieval core, set on a peaceful riverbank. Nonindustrial Sopron's perfectly preserved Old Town attracts Austrian tourists from just across the border. Kőszeg is a smaller, quieter, and more endearing version of Sopron. Szombathely is marred by ugly socialist architecture, but redeemed somewhat by modest Roman ruins and good transport connections to Kőszeg. In the countryside between these four towns are dozens of Austro-Hungarian aristocratic mansions, built halfway between the social whirlpools of Vienna and Budapest. Many are now hotels, where you can live it up in style and enjoy some recreation while seeing the region—all on a budget. The rest of the region has many attractions, including the religious abbeys of Ják and Pannonhalma and the royal palace at Fertőd.

You can easily get about by train to the region's major cities, although you'll need to connect by bus to the villages. If you want to stay at the mansion hotels, it's most convenient to have a car. If you're traveling from Austria to Hungary, all the towns are on or not far from the main Vienna–Budapest route.

1 Győr

81 miles W of Budapest, 80 miles SE of Vienna

GETTING THERE • By Train Express trains from Budapest take 1¾ hours, costing 627 Ft ($6.40) in first class and 418 Ft ($4.25) in second class. From Vienna, express trains to Győr take less than 2 hours.

ESSENTIALS Győr's telephone area code is 96.

ORIENTATION Rivers frame the northern and western corners of the city center. The main streets in the historic center are closed to vehicular traffic and are centered around the north-south Baross út. A block north, at the end of the street, is Apor Vilmos püspök tere, site of the cathedral, which is just south of the river. Another main square in the historic core is Széchenyi tér, home to Győr's concert hall. Szent István út, a major boulevard, bounds the historic core on the south.

From the train station, just south of the center, walk straight ahead half a block then right one block along Szent István út, and then left (north) on Baross út. From the bus station, behind the train station, walk north over Baross híd, the big bridge crossing the railroad tracks, and then straight up Baross út.

INFORMATION For information or private rooms, visit Ciklámen Tourist, Aradi Vértanúk útja 22, at the intersection of Szent István u (☎ **96/311-557** or **317-601**), open Monday through Thursday from 8am to 4pm, on Friday from 8am to 2pm, and on Saturday from 8am to 1pm. It's opposite the town hall in front of the train station.

What's Special About Western Hungary

Ancient Ruins

- The Temple of Isis and other Roman ruins in Szombathely, the ancient Savaria, once the capital of Pannonia.

Churches

- Győr's cathedral, with the 15th-century gold reliquary of St. Ladislaus.
- Pannonhalma, an important Hungarian religious center dating back 1,000 years.
- Ják's Basilica, one of the best examples of early medieval architecture in the world.

Great Towns

- Sopron, with a town center free of vehicular traffic, preserving the charms of Europe from centuries ago.
- Kőszeg, a sleepy yet very charming town near the Austrian border that played a heroic role in fighting back the Ottoman Turkish invasions.

Mansion Hotels

- Hotel Klastrom, with attractive and modern facilities in a converted religious cloister in the center of Győr.
- Uj-Ebergényi Kastély, just a taxi ride away from Szombathely, with 55 acres of park as well as swimming and tennis in a neoclassical mansion.
- Kúria Panzió near Kőszeg, a good place for horseback riding.

Palaces

- Esterházy Palace in Fertőd, a 126-room royal structure where Joseph Haydn was the court composer for almost 30 years.

Shopping

- Herend, home of the world-famous porcelain factory.

SPECIAL EVENTS In June and July there's the Győr Music Summer, with classical concerts and operas.

Győr (pronounced "Dyuhr"; pop. 160,000) is an industrial city situated astride the confluence of the Mosoni and the Rába rivers, almost exactly midway between Budapest and Vienna. Known as Arrabona by the ancient Romans, the town's rivers now give it the name "city of waters."

As much of the town center is either riverside parkland or pedestrian streets, it's an enjoyable place to stroll around. For many visitors, however, the highlight comes in a side trip to the 10th-century abbey of Pannonhalma, 11 miles away.

WHAT TO SEE & DO

Sitting on a foundation that dates from the 11th century, Győr Cathedral, on Apor Vilmos püspök tere, was destroyed and rebuilt several times. It's the home of one of the greatest masterpieces of Hungarian goldsmithing—the reliquary of (King) St. Ladislaus, who reigned in the latter half of the 11th century. This 15th-century reliquary is much like a gold bust with the stoic face of the king adorned by his symmetrically coiffed hair and beard; it's said to contain a fragment of his skull. You'll find it in the

Héderváry Chapel to your right as you enter. Admission is free. The cathedral is open Monday through Friday from 6:15am to 5:30pm and on Saturday and Sunday from 6:15am to 7pm. To get there, from the north end of Baross út, walk up a winding lane for about another block.

Győr also has an impressive Carmelite church dating from the early 18th century on Bécsihapu tér, and the Old Town Hall at Rákóczi Ferenc u. 1, built in 1562. One of the more elaborate baroque structures in town is the U-shaped newer Town Hall with a 185-foot tower, on Városháza tér across from the train station.

The streets of the Old Town are well preserved and free of cars, with plenty of stores, cafés, and restaurants, which make them a walker's delight. You'll also enjoy a visit to the outdoor market along the riverfront at Dunakapu tér.

WHERE TO STAY

PRIVATE ROOMS Ciklámen Tourist, Aradi Vértanúk útja 22 (☎ **96/311-557** or **317-601**), rents private rooms for 1,000 to 1,300 Ft ($10.20 to $13.25) per person. Open Monday through Thursday from 8am to 4pm, on Friday from 8am to 2pm, and on Saturday from 8am to 1pm.

IBUSZ, at Szent István út 29–31 (☎ **96/311-700** or **314-224**), rents private rooms for about 770 Ft ($7.85) single, and 880 Ft ($9) double. Open Monday through Friday from 8am to 3:30pm.

Hotels

Fehérhajó Hotel, Kiss Ernő út 4, 9025 Győr. ☎ **96/318-050.** 14 rms (3 with bath, 11 with shower and washbasin). **Directions:** Take bus 2 or 14 from the train station.

Rates: 1,500 Ft ($15.30) single with shower and washbasin; 2,000 Ft ($20.40) double with shower and washbasin; 2,500 Ft ($25.50) double with full bath; 2,700 Ft ($27.55) triple with shower and washbasin. Breakfast 150 Ft ($1.55). **Parking:** Free.

This simple hotel is an easy 10-minute walk from the town center, in a sleepy neighborhood across the bridge by the Hotel Klastrom. If you are traveling alone or by car, you will appreciate the lower price for single rooms and the enclosed parking lot out back. Most rooms have a bathroom with only a shower and washbasin, and share a clean toilet off the hotel's single hallway. The restaurant in the basement is plain but inexpensive.

★ **Hotel Klastrom,** Zechmeister u. 1, 9021 Győr. ☎ **96/315-611.** Fax 96/327-030. Telex 24731. 42 rms (a few without private toilet). TV TEL **Directions:** From the train station, walk left half a block, then turn right down Jókai utca four blocks to the riverfront: the hotel is one block farther.

Rates (including breakfast): 4,430 Ft ($45.20) double with shower but no toilet; 5,580 Ft ($56.95) double with bath. AE, DC, MC, V. **Parking:** Free.

I especially recommend this hotel, in a converted religious cloister in the town center. The rooms vary in size but are all charming, with vaulted ceilings and dark-wood furniture. They cost a little extra but are worth it. The reception in the spacious, modern lobby is polite and efficient, and there's also a restaurant and beer cellar downstairs. **Facilities:** Sauna, solarium, restaurant, bar.

$ **Teátrum Panzió,** Schweidel u. 7, 9021 Győr. ☎ **96/310-640.** 10 rms (all with bath). MINIBAR TV **Directions:** Walk down Baross út and then turn right (east) on Arany János utca, which becomes Schweidel utca after a block.

Rates (including breakfast): 2,500 Ft ($25.50) double; 3,000 Ft ($30.60) triple.

A recently refurbished traditional inn, the Teátrum is a good pick of the many pensions in the center of Győr. Several rooms are located under sloping roofs and the facilities are very new and clean. Windows overlook a large square with the garish socialist-realist town theater in front. You can dine in an attractive and popular restaurant on the ground floor.

WHERE TO EAT

Szürkebarát Pinceborozó, inside a courtyard at Arany János u. 20. ☎ **311-548.**

Cuisine: HUNGARIAN. **Directions:** Walk down Baross út to Arany János utca and turn left (west).
Prices: Soup 60–110 Ft (60¢–$1.10); main courses 130–500 Ft ($1.35–$5.10).
Open: Mon–Fri 10am–9pm, Sat 9am–4pm.

For lunch, try this restaurant that specializes in pork steak and goose liver, as well as cold meat appetizers. The restaurant is named after its mixed cold-cut platter (*szürkebarát*) with ham, salami, and turkey, all of which you can assemble onto bread to create several sandwiches; it costs 530 Ft ($5.40) for two and makes a meal in itself. The restaurant is located in two cellar rooms with barrel-vaulted brick ceilings; one of the rooms has game trophies on the wall. The Bécsi Kávéház (Vienna Coffeehouse) across the courtyard is a good spot for pastries and ice cream afterward.

An Excursion to Pannonhalma Abbey

Pannonhalma (☎ **370-022**) was once a powerful Benedictine abbey and still serves as a spiritual and academic center. One of the few remaining examples of early Hungarian monastic architecture, it's also the earliest remaining Gothic church in Hungary, with parts of the abbey over 1,000 years old. The church was transformed into a mosque during the Ottoman Turkish occupation, but generally has been held as a sanctuary. During World War II both the Nazis and the Soviets respected, to a degree, the sanctity of the abbey.

Today you can view an extensive collection of relics, from Stone Age artifacts to carvings taken from beneath the Forum in Rome and given to the abbey by Mussolini's foreign minister. The archives contain over 300,000 volumes, including several priceless 11th- and 12th-century documents, such as a deed for the abbey on the Tihany Peninsula on Lake Balaton. This founding deed, dating from 1055, is important because it's one of the first documents to contain a large number of Hungarian words sprinkled throughout the text. The abbey also commands a magnificent view down the valley and across the surrounding hills.

Organ concerts and other musical events are held here from time to time; inquire at Ciklámen Tourist in Győr.

Pannonhalma is located in the hills about nine miles south of Győr on Highway 82 heading toward Veszprém and Lake Balaton. Buses run every two hours from the main station in Győr, a 20- or 30-minute ride for 60 Ft (60¢). The abbey is open Tuesday through Saturday from 8:30am to 4:30pm, and Sunday from 11:30am to 4:30pm.

2 Sopron

130 miles W of Budapest, 40 miles S of Vienna

GETTING THERE • By Train Sopron is about an hour from Győr by express train, costing 396 Ft ($4.05) in first class and 264 Ft ($2.70) in second class; or three hours from Budapest, for 972 Ft ($9.90) in first class and 648 Ft ($6.60) in second class. Ten trains a day from Vienna's Südbahnhof station take about 1¼ hours; passengers go through passport control in a special wing of the Sopron train station.

• By Bus You can also take a bus from a number of towns in western Hungary.

ESSENTIALS The telephone area code for Sopron, Fertőd, and the surrounding area is 99.

ORIENTATION You might think that Sopron was designed for sightseeing, since most of the sights are within the confines of the Old Town where automobile traffic is barred. The center is shaped like a clenched fist and surrounded by Várkerület, a street that follows the same path as the old moat and town walls that once surrounded Sopron. Inside the Old Town, Fő tér is the main square.

From the railroad station, south of the old city, walk north (the only way you can go) for five blocks on Mátyás király utca to Várkerület. Keep going straight and everything on your left (west) side is the Old Town. Or you can take bus no. 1M, 2, 9, 12, or 12M for three stops.

The bus station is just two blocks west of Fő tér on Lackner Kristóf utca. To get to Fő tér, turn right (east) and walk on Lackner Kristóf utca until you reach Várkerület. It's just a block farther, if you keep to the left.

If you come by car, remember that no vehicular traffic is allowed in the Old Town. Parking lots are conveniently located all around the Old Town off Várkerület.

INFORMATION You can get information on Sopron, as well as Fertőd, Fertőrákos, and a variety of other locations in the area, from Ciklámen Tourist, Ógabona tér 8 (☎ **99/312-040;** fax 99/311-483), right on the corner of Lackner Kristóf utca and Várkerület. They also rent private rooms (see "Where to Stay," below). The office is open Monday through Friday from 8am to 4pm, and or Saturday from 8am to 1pm, and from April 1 to October 15 also on Saturday from 8am to 8pm and on Sunday from 8am to noon.

SPECIAL EVENTS Sopron hosts the Spring Festival in March, with street fairs and music, in tandem with Budapest Spring Festival. In late June and about half of July you can attend a number of concerts and other cultural events during the Sopron Weeks.

One of my favorite towns in western Hungary, Sopron is located on a small spit of Hungarian territory that juts into Austria. It was first settled under the name Scarbantia by the Romans, who established the town's present layout during their 400-year presence. The name Sopron first appeared in documents in the 10th century, when King Stephen founded a municipality here. Unlike every other major town in the rest of Hungary, Sopron was never occupied by the Turks, which helps account for a remarkably well preserved Old Town.

The romantic allure of Sopron today lies in this historic pedestrian center. Many Austrians come on day trips to Sopron (which they call Ödenburg), even though the residents of the town voted not to be part of Austria in a 1921 referendum.

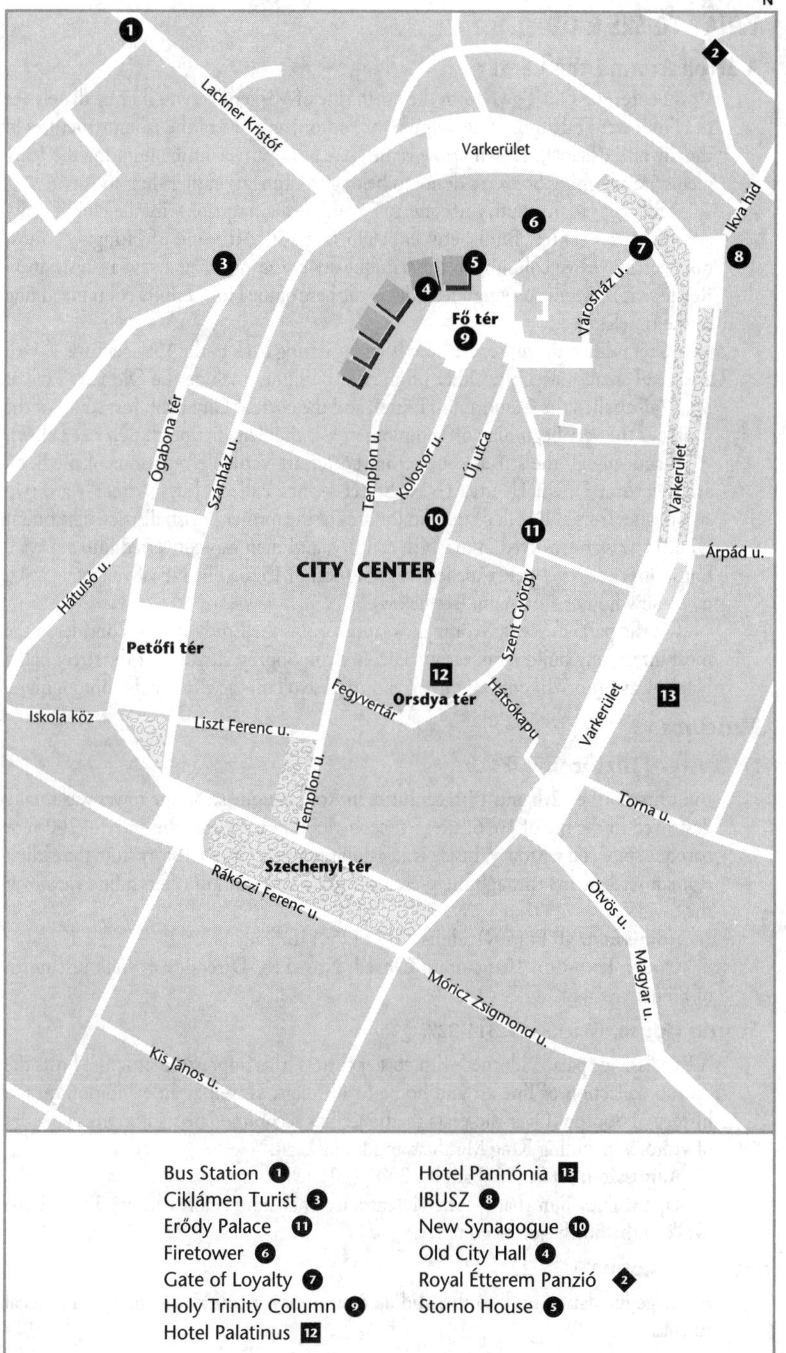
Lackner Kristóf
Varkerület
Ikva híd
Fő tér
Városház u.
Ógabona tér
Szánház u.
Templon u.
Kolostor u.
Új utca
Varkerület
Árpád u.
CITY CENTER
Hátulsó u.
Szent György
Petőfi tér
Fegyvertár
Orsdya tér
Hátsókapu
Varkerület
Iskola köz
Liszt Ferenc u.
Templon u.
Torna u.
Szechenyi tér
Rákóczi Ferenc u.
Ötvös u.
Magyar u.
Móricz Zsigmond u.
Kis János u.
Bus Station 1
Ciklámen Turist 3
Erődy Palace 11
Firetower 6
Gate of Loyalty 7
Holy Trinity Column 9
Hotel Palatinus 12
Hotel Pannónia 13
IBUSZ 8
New Synagogue 10
Old City Hall 4
Royal Étterem Panzió 2
Storno House 5
9037

WHAT TO SEE & DO

A Stroll Around the Center

If you enter the Old Town from the north side of Várkerület, you'll immediately see the Firetower (Tűztorony), the symbol of Sopron, and one of the tallest structures in the town (see below). Down below is the Gate of Loyalty, commemorating the 1921 plebiscite affirming Sopron's desire to belong to Hungary rather than to Austria.

A few steps to the south you come to Fő tér, the main square, with the Holy Trinity column at its center. Built between 1695 and 1701, it's one of Hungary's most noteworthy votive columns in the baroque style. On one visit I saw a musician in Renaissance costume playing a recorder at the base of the Holy Trinity column, adding to the timeless feel.

Fő tér is lined by impressive houses, many dating back to the 15th century, as well as several small museums. Other prominent buildings include the Old City Hall at no. 3 (also called the Gambrinus House), and the current City Hall. Just south of the square at the very beginning of Templom utca is the Benedictine church (see below).

Practically all the streets south from Fő tér are veritable museums of medieval architecture. Down Új utca (New Street—once called "Jews' Street") are two synagogues from the 13th century in the area of the former Jewish district. The one at Új u. 11 was constructed in the 14th century, and then was converted into a private house after the Jews were expelled from Sopron in 1526. The New Synagogue at Új u. 22 now houses a museum (see below).

On the parallel Szent György utca, at no. 16, is the Erődy Palace, considered the most interesting building in early rococo style in Sopron. If you exit the street half a block away onto Várkerület, you can shop and stroll on the city's main thoroughfare.

Museums

Firetower [Tűztorony], Fő tér.

Built first in the 12th and 13th centuries in Romanesque style, the tower was totally destroyed in the fire of 1676; after its reconstruction it became the graceful 200-foot baroque spire you see today. Inside is an exhibition on Sopron's history from the earliest Roman settlements through the present. The tower's summit offers a fine view over the town.

Admission: 40 Ft (40¢) adults, 20 Ft (25¢) student.

Open: Tues–Sun 10am–4pm. **Closed:** Nov–Feb. **Directions:** Walk just north of Fő tér.

Storno House, Fő tér 8. ☎ **311-327.**

A Renaissance palace adorned with corner turrets, this impressive structure hosts the Storno collection of fine art and home furnishings, as well as an exhibition on the history of Sopron. Over the years the house has accommodated an impressive series of visitors, including King Matthias and Franz Liszt.

Admission: 50 Ft (50¢) adults, 20 Ft (20¢) children.

Open: Tues–Sun 10am–5pm (last entrance a half hour before closing). **Directions:** Walk to the north side of Fő tér.

New Synagogue, Új u. 22.

A synagogue dating back to the Middle Ages, today it contains a collection of local Judaica.

Admission: 80 Ft (80¢) adults, 20 Ft (20¢) children.

Open: Mar–Sept, Wed–Mon 9am–5pm; Oct, Wed–Mon 10am–4pm. **Closed:** Nov–Feb. **Directions:** Walk south down Új utca from Fő tér.

Churches

Benedictine Church, Templom utca.

Don't miss the Benedictine church, built between 1280 and 1300 on the south side of Fő tér and popularly called the "Goat Church." According to legend, it was built by a goat herder whose animals came upon a hoard of gold. During the 17th century Hungary held five national assemblies and crowned three kings and queens here.

The interior features a very decorative apse area of sculptured cherubs and angels looking toward the altar painting; rococo and baroque details also flourish on the pulpit and other areas of the church. The Gothic exterior is far less elaborate and features a 155-foot bell tower, which is shorter than the Firetower.

Directions: Walk to the south side of Fő tér.

St. Michael's Church [Szent Mihály Templom], Pozsonyi út.

Out of the Old Town (but not far) to the north is this simple stone-and-brick church dating back as early as the 13th century, though most of the structure was completed in the 16th century. Inside the church are some beautiful wall paintings and sculptures.

Out back in the old cemetery is the **St. James Chapel (Szent Jakab Kápolna)**; built in the early 13th century, it's the oldest building in Sopron. You may also find it interesting to take a quick look in the cemetery, where some graves show large sculptures of figures mourning for the dead.

Directions: Walk under the tower in Fő tér and then north on Pozsonyi út for about five minutes.

Shopping

Since large numbers of Austrians troop across the border on day trips to go shopping, Sopron features many stores with lace, folk objects, and other souvenirs. There are also a number of inexpensive liquor stores, offering Russian champagne, Tokaj dessert wine, Sopron wines, and other popular wines.

WHERE TO STAY

PRIVATE ROOMS For the cheapest accommodations, rent a private room from Ciklámen Tourist, Ógabona tér 8 (☎ **99/312-040;** fax 99/311-483), right on the corner of Lackner Kristóf utca and Várkerület. Double rooms cost 1,300 Ft ($13.25). The office is open Monday through Friday from 8am to 4pm and Saturday from 8am to 1pm, and from April 1 to October 15 also on Saturday from 8am to 8pm and on Sunday from 8am to noon.

You can also rent private rooms from IBUSZ at Várkerület 41 (☎ **99/312-455;** fax 313-281), which has doubles for 1,000 to 1,500 Ft ($10.20 to $15.30). Open Monday through Friday from 8am to 4pm, and on Saturday from 8am to noon.

Hotels

Royal Étterem Panzió, Sas tér 13, 9400 Sopron. ☎ **99/314-481.** 6 rms (all with bath). TEL TV **Directions:** From the north side of Várkerület, walk north on Ikva híd, then turn left to reach Sas tér.

Rates (including breakfast): 4,000 Ft ($40.80) double.

A small two-story house with a red-shingled roof and a stucco first floor, the Royal perhaps attempts to re-create an old European inn. The comfortable rooms have small chandeliers, decorative glass lamps, Persian-style rugs, small blue-tiled bathrooms, and remote control for the TV. The reception doubles as a bar; the owner speaks only German (fragmentary) and Hungarian. Its main attraction is its proximity to the town center.

★ **Hotel Palatinus,** Új u. 23, 9400 Sopron. ☎ **99/311-395.** Telex 24-9146. 30 rms (all with bath). TV **Directions:** From Széchenyi tér immediately south of the Old Town, walk north on Templom utca, then take the first right and turn left on Orsolya tér.

Rates (including breakfast) $40 single; $59 double. AE, DC, MC, V.

If they have a room available, it's worth the bit more you pay. Right in the heart of the Old Town, this hotel is well integrated into the surrounding historical structures. The interior is clean and very well kept, with simple modern furnishings and fixtures. The reception in the modern lobby appears more ready and able to help than at many other hotels of this category.

Dining/Entertainment: The restaurant downstairs serves fine food (see "Where to Eat," below).

WHERE TO EAT

Bécsikapu Borozó, inside the courtyard at Bécsi út 6. ☎ **311-210.**

Cuisine: HUNGARIAN. **Directions:** From the north side of Várkerület, walk north on Ikva híd, then turn left; continue past Sas tér, straight onto Bécsi út.

Prices: Soups 80–100 Ft (80¢–$1); main courses 200–450 Ft ($2.05–$4.60).

Open: Tues–Sun 11am–10pm.

Ten minutes outside the center, you descend the steps to this wine cellar with barrel-vault stone ceilings and ample wine supply, which is the setting for huge portions of hearty and tasty budget fare. The only problem here is the Hungarian- and German-language-only menu; the staff, though friendly, do not speak English.

The chicken Cordon Bleu costs just 320 Ft ($3.25) and wine starts 220 Ft ($2.25) a bottle.

Hotel Palatinus Restaurant, Új utca 23. ☎ **311-395.**

Cuisine: HUNGARIAN. **Reservations:** Recommended for dinner. **Directions:** From Széchenyi tér immediately south of the Old Town, walk north on Templom utca, then take the first right and turn left onto Orsolya tér.

Prices: Soups 95–160 Ft (95¢–$1.65); main courses 320–880 Ft ($3.25–$9); bottle of wine 280–450 Ft ($2.85–$4.60). AE, DC, MC, V.

Open: Daily 7am–11pm.

This small restaurant has brightly colored tablecloths, white walls, dark-wood furniture, and a grid wood ceiling, all helping to achieve a Swiss-chalet feel. In summer you can also eat in a courtyard at the back. A pianist plays here during the evening. If you eat inside, you can watch the chef prepare your meal on a grill on one side of the restaurant.

To start, try the very flavorful oxtail soup, with noodles, vegetables, and meat flavored with pepper and spices, for 160 Ft ($1.65). Then consider the Hungarian paprika veal with gnocchi, richly covered with a tomato-cream sauce, for 420 Ft ($4.30). To finish up this feast, don't resist the palacsinta stuffed with nuts and chocolate sauce for 130 Ft ($1.35).

Excursions

FERTŐRÁKOS

About three miles north of Sopron out Pozsonyi út is the small village of Fertőrákos, most interesting for its now-dormant **quarry,** where limestone has been mined for over 2,000 years. In Roman times the quarry was extremely important, and most of the old city walls of Scarbantia (the Roman name for Sopron) were built with its stone. Concerts are given fairly regularly in the quarry concert hall, which can hold more than 800 people; special performances are given during the Sopron Weeks festival in midsummer. The quarry is on the right as you round a curve coming into Fertőrákos from Sopron. There's a bus stop and restaurant nearby, and the Austrian border is just a few hundred meters away. Past the curve in the center of town is the only public pillory in Hungary, and a little farther on is the mansion hotel.

Twenty buses a day, starting at 7am, run from Sopron's bus station to Fertőrákos for 46 Ft (46¢), so it's feasible to stay here and see Sopron by day.

A Mansion Hotel

$ **Hotel Kastély,** Fő út 153, 9421 Fertőrákos. ☎ **99/355-040.** Fax 99/355-128. 15 rms (3 with bath). **Directions:** Coming from Sopron, the hotel is toward the far end of Fertőrákos village on the right side of the main street.

Rates (including breakfast): 1,000 Ft ($10.20) per person; 650 Ft ($6.65) for children and dogs.

The bishop of Győr formerly summered in this modest palace, which surrounds an enclosed garden. One wing dates from the 1500s, but most of the building is 18th-century. There's an old chapel, and one room is now a small museum. The original interior layout has never been altered or partitioned, so rooms are large—doubles, triples, quads, and two rooms that take up to six. Facilities are neither new nor luxurious, but should be perfectly sufficient.

FERTŐD

About 17 miles east of Sopron, 40 miles west of Győr, and 118 miles west of Budapest is the small town of Fertőd. You can reach it by bus from Sopron for 94 Ft (95¢); there are 15 to 20 buses a day and the ride takes 45 minutes. You can also catch a bus from Győr; the one-hour ride costs 204 Ft ($2.10). Buses into town stop right in front of the palace; ask the driver to let you know when to get off.

What to See and Do

The fantastic ★ **Esterházy Palace** (Esterházy Kastély), Bartók Béla u. 2 (☎ **99/370-971**), was initially built by the Esterházy family in 1720 as a 26-room structure with two major outbuildings. Four architects oversaw the later expansion into a 126-room palace that wasn't finished until the 1780s. In 1788 the baron of Riesbeck, a well-traveled French nobleman, wrote of this palace, "There is, outside of Versailles, no place in France that could be compared with the magnificence of this one." Though damaged in World War II, the palace was skillfully restored and all 126 rooms appear much as they did when the baron visited them.

As you enter the palace grounds, the building's ocher wings surround you. Up ahead is the entrance to the palace museum, where you can see an extensive collection of porcelain, much of it from Herend, and beautiful antique furniture. One part of the museum pays tribute to Joseph Haydn, who was the court composer here for almost

30 years. Musical events are held here on Sundays in summer. Don't miss a stroll through the palace's formal gardens after your visit inside.

Admission is 80 Ft (80¢) for adults and 40 Ft (40¢) for students. The price includes a guide. It's open April 16 to October 15, Tuesday through Sunday from 8am to noon and 1 to 5pm; in winter, Tuesday through Sunday from 8am to noon and 1 to 4pm.

Note: There's not a single sign in town directing visitors to the castle. It's easy to find, as it's on the main road that runs through town; if in doubt, follow the crowds.

Where to Stay

$ **Kastélyszálló,** Bartók Béla u. 2, 9431 Fertőd. ☎ **99/370-971.** Fax 99/370-120. 82 beds in 21 rms (none with bath). **Directions:** Enter the hotel just to the left of the museum admissions desk (follow the SZÁLLÓDA signs).

Rates: 1,000 Ft ($10.20) double; 1,200 Ft ($12.25) triple; 1,400 Ft ($14.30) quad; 210 Ft ($2.15) per person in a 12-bed room.

It's actually possible to sleep in the Esterházy Palace at Fertőd, though finding space may be a problem since many tour groups stay here. Unlike many of Hungary's mansion hotels, this is much more like a dorm or hostel than a hotel. None of the original furnishings is in this part of the palace, but I feel that the price, cleanliness, and the fact that you'll sleep *in* the palace make it worth your while to stay here. Everything is well kept and rooms have views over the palace gardens.

Where to Eat

Haydn Restaurant, Vácim u. l. ☎ **345-977.**

Cuisine: HUNGARIAN. **Directions:** Exit the palace and walk about 600 yards down the main road to the left.

Prices: Main courses 110–460 Ft ($1.10–$4.70). AE, MC, V.

Open: Mon 11am–3pm, Tues–Fri 7am–9pm, Sat–Sun 7am–10pm.

A few minutes from the palace, this restaurant with a small terrace at the back is flanked by a gravel parking lot. Although the food is not particularly distinctive and the menu is only in Hungarian and German, there are a few dishes for vegetarians. The Haydn is often filled with tour groups.

3 Kőszeg

10 miles N of Szombathely, 31 miles S of Sopron, 151 miles W of Budapest

GETTING THERE • By Train From Budapest, take the train to Szombathely, where you can connect to Kőszeg in 30 minutes for 75 Ft (75¢) in first class and 50 Ft (50¢) in second class.

• By Bus You can also take the bus from Szombathely for 80 Ft (80¢), a 30-minute ride, or from Sopron for 188 Ft ($1.90), a 75-minute ride.

ESSENTIALS Kőszeg's telephone area code is **94.**

ORIENTATION Geographically the highest town in Hungary (850 feet above sea level), Kőszeg lies in the easternmost foothills of the Alps. The small town center surrounded by a ring boulevard makes for easy navigation. The main square is Jurisics tér, home of two churches and several museums. The castle is two blocks northwest of here. Just before the entrance to the Old Town is a large square called Fő tér, with two hotels, several travel offices, and the neo-Gothic Church of the Sacred Heart. The area called the Várkör (Castle Circle) starts here and continues along the Old Town walls to the west side of town.

The train station is at the south end of Rákóczi Ferenc utca. To reach the town center, either walk north for about 15 minutes or take any bus three stops.

The bus station is on Liszt Ferenc utca just two blocks from the center. Walk to the end of the street and turn right on Kossuth Lajos utca, then turn left at the end of the street to reach Fő tér.

There's a convenient parking area located just behind the castle at the end of Pék utca.

INFORMATION You can get information about Kőszeg from Savaria Tourist, Várkör 69 (☎ and fax **94/360-238;** telex 37376), open Monday through Friday from 7:30am to 5pm and on Saturday from 7:30am to noon.

SPECIAL EVENTS Although it's a small town, Kőszeg has sponsored an impressive cultural program in years past, including a theater festival in July (in Hungarian), and a wine festival in mid-September.

Kőszeg (pronounced "*Kur*-seg") is another jewel in the crown of western Hungary. It has been inhabited since at least the early Bronze Age, as Celtic remains attest, but it was the Romans who established a settlement here and, among other things, planted vineyards—a tradition that has continued to this day. King Stephen I built a fortress here in the 11th century to protect the border against frequent German attacks. The fortress was built on the hill of Kőszeg, and a village of the same name was founded in the valley. As a border town, Kőszeg changed hands several times in the last millennium, and was also known under the German name Güns.

The town blazed its way permanently into the history books in 1532, when a very small Hungarian garrison under Capt. Miklós Jurisics held off a vastly superior Ottoman Turkish army under Sultan Suleiman II for two to three weeks. To separate fact from legend is not always easy; the number of defenders varies from "around 1,000" down to "Miklós's hundreds," and the attacking Ottoman Turkish force was anywhere from "around 100,000" to "over a quarter of a million." An important battle and a heroic fight, this stand did slow the Ottoman Turks long enough for the Habsburgs to prepare a successful defense of Vienna. Sultan Suleiman II was subsequently defeated at the very gates of Vienna. Later, as a result of the attempted uprising against the Habsburgs in 1710, troops put much of Kőszeg to the torch.

Rebuilt under "German" control, the region regained its fame as a wine-producing area. Never heavily industrialized, the Old Town has changed little since the middle 1700s, as you'll see when you walk through its small but extremely well preserved precincts. At noon the town is serenaded by church bells.

WHAT TO SEE & DO

A Stroll Around the Old Town

Arriving in town, you'll first see the large Fő tér, dominated by a visually striking but historically unimportant Church of the Sacred Heart, a tall, thin neo-Gothic structure. This square is also home to the hotels Strucc and Írottkő, as well as several travel agencies.

From Várkör, enter the Old Town down a small street called Városház utca, just beside the Express office. You'll pass under a five-story tower with a relief of the crucified Christ called the Heroes' Gate, built in 1932 to commemorate the 400th anniversary of the town's struggle against the Turks. Past this gate you enter Jurisics tér, on which practically all the buildings are of historic interest. Straight ahead is the baroque St. Imre Church, built in the early 17th century. Inside you'll see three small baroque altars and a pulpit on the wall to the side.

Immediately behind is the St. James Church (Szent Jakab Templom), built on the site of an ancient Minorite church, which dates from the 13th century. It's one of the most magnificent of Kőszeg's Gothic buildings, with 17th- and 18th-century Gothic frescoes inside.

The other buildings on the square include the Town Hall at no. 8, with a striped red-and-yellow facade on the first floor and oval frescoes on the second, the Pharmacy Museum, and the Miklós Jurisics Museum (see below). In front of the churches you also see the 18th-century town well, and a statue of the Virgin Mary atop a column, at the site of a medieval pillory.

From the square, go left past the church facades, and after a block and a half turn left to reach the famous castle (see below). After a visit to the museum there, exit to the right down Diák köz, to reach a long stretch of town fortifications. Continue to your left along these town walls and then turn left to return to Fő tér.

Museums

Miklós Jurisics Museum, Jurisics tér 4.

Kőszeg's most interesting museum illustrates the past life of the town. One floor recreates traditional artisan shops from a century ago, including an old watch-repair shop, a candy and ice-cream store, a print shop, a locksmith, and a barbershop. From the very top of the museum tower you'll enjoy a great view.

Admission: 30 Ft (30¢) adults, 15 Ft (15¢) students.

Open: Tues–Sun 10am–5pm. **Directions:** Just after passing under the Heroes' Gate, turn sharply to the left.

Pharmacy Museum [Patika Múzeum], Jurisics tér 11.

The highlight is a 250-year-old carved wooden pharmacy cabinet lined from ceiling to floor with jars bearing Latin inscriptions. Other rooms also show off maps, pictures, and canisters of medicines, and ones holding vipers, frogs, and lizards. Upstairs in a large attic room you'll see a display of 18th-century herbs and medicines, which still add a pleasant scent to the air.

Admission: 30 Ft (30¢) adults, 15 Ft (15¢) students.

Open: Tues–Sun 10am–5pm. **Directions:** Walk to the right side of Jurisics tér.

Castle, Rájnis József u. 9.

The most famous of Kőszeg's historical monuments is the castle in which Capt. Miklós Jurisics made his stand against the Ottoman Turks. The two medieval towers (the oldest surviving section of the castle) are flanked by two Renaissance wings, one of which contains a museum detailing the history of the castle and town. Unfortunately, the museum descriptions are only in Hungarian.

Admission: 30 Ft (30¢) adults, 15 Ft (15¢) students.

Open: Tues–Sun 10am–5pm. **Directions:** From Jurisics tér, walk left past the church facades, and turn left after 1½ blocks.

WHERE TO STAY

PRIVATE ROOMS At Savaria Tourist, Várkör 69 (☎ and fax **94/360-238;** telex 37376), you can rent private rooms—singles for 550 Ft ($5.60) and doubles for 1,100 to 1,200 Ft ($11.20 to $12.25). Open Monday through Friday from 7:30am to 5pm and on Saturday from 7:30am to noon.

Hotels in Town

Hotel Strucc, Várkör 124, 9730 Kőszeg. ☎ **94/360-323.** 18 rms (4 with bath, 14 with shower but no toilet). **Directions:** Walk to the south side of Fő tér, just south of the neo-Gothic Church of the Sacred Heart.

Rates (including breakfast): 1,100 Ft ($11.20) single without bath; 1,980 Ft ($20.20) double with shower but no toilet, 2,310 Ft ($23.55) double with bath.

Built in 1663, this has always been an inn or hotel, but because of the ancient construction, most rooms lack toilets. Four rooms feature impressive antique baroque furniture, with the corner Room 7 the best of them all; however, like most of the rooms it has a shower but no toilet. The other rooms are quite plain. With only a total of 18 rooms, this hotel is often full, but by all means stop by and ask, for it's clean and well run.

Hotel Park, Park u. 2, 9730 Kőszeg. ☎ **94/360-363.** Telex 37278. 66 rms (43 with shower but no toilet). **Bus:** 2, for two stops.

Rates: 1,150 Ft ($11.75) double without shower; 1,800 Ft ($18.35) double with shower; 1,500 Ft ($15.30) triple without shower; 2,350 Ft ($24) triple with shower; 1,850 Ft ($18.90) quad without shower; 2,850 Ft ($29.10) quad with shower. Breakfast 150 Ft ($1.55) per person extra.

If things fill up in town, try the Hotel Park, set in bucolic surroundings. Despite its attractive mansionesque facade, inside it's comparable to a clean dormitory. Run by Express, the student travel agency, it attracts many young people. You can inquire about room availability at the Express office, Városház u. 5 (☎ **94/360-247**), next door to Savaria Tourist.

Hotel Írottkő, Fő tér 4, 9730. Kőszeg. ☎ **94/360-373.** Telex 37419. 52 rms (all with bath). TEL **Directions:** Walk to the east end of Fő tér.

Rates (including breakfast): 2,255 Ft ($23) single; 3,850 Ft ($39.30) double. AE, V.

At the renovated Írottkő, conveniently located on Fő tér, everything now looks shiny and clean, starting with the many plants in the huge atrium lobby, which rises the whole height of the building. The rooms are a little institutional, with plain white walls; some have nice views over the square below. This is the largest hotel in Kőszeg and usually has rooms available.

A Nearby Mansion Hotel

More nearby mansion hotels are listed under "Szombathely," below.

Kúria Panzió, Nagy Pál utca 17, 9737 Bük. ☎ **94/358-099.** 6 rms (all with bath). **Directions:** Drive on small roads from Kőszeg to Bük.

Rates (including breakfast): 1,900 Ft ($19.40) double; 2,300 Ft ($23.45) triple.

Horse enthusiasts will enjoy this 19th-century country house made up of three buildings around a lovely garden. The large rooms have white walls and carpets, garden views, new furniture, small chandeliers, and low prices.

Dining: You can eat in a nice restaurant with music. Main courses cost 250 to 660 Ft ($2.55 to $6.75).

Facilities: There's a riding school in back of the estate, with lessons at 500 Ft ($5.10) an hour. The town of Bük is also known for its thermal baths.

WHERE TO EAT

Bécsikapu Söröző, Rajnis József u. 5. ☎ **360-297.**

Cuisine: AUSTRIAN. **Reservations:** Recommended on weekends. **Directions:** Walk from Jurisics tér toward the castle; its entrance is on Diák köz.
Prices: Soup 45–120 Ft (45¢–$1.20); main courses 165–485 Ft ($1.70–$4.95).
Open: Daily 8am–10pm.

Not far from the castle entrance is this excellent, although very Austrian, beer restaurant. The straight-backed wooden chairs in the vaulted cellar won't impede your enjoyment of the old favorite, wienerschnitzel, for 320 Ft ($3.25), usually accompanied by beer (65 Ft/65¢ for a large pilsner). You can also savor a steak for 310 Ft ($3.15), a pizza for 280 Ft ($2.85), or wild boar goulash for 185 Ft ($1.90). In summer they serve in an enclosed garden area. Unlike most restaurants in western Hungary, they have an English menu.

4 Szombathely

142 miles W of Budapest, 10 miles S of Kőszeg

GETTING THERE • **By Train** Szombathely is about 3½ hours from Budapest by train. The ride costs 1,047 Ft ($10.70) in first class and 698 Ft ($7.10) in second class. You can also take a direct train from Győr or Sopron, though these tend to be slow.

• **By Bus** From Sopron it takes two hours for 252 Ft ($2.55).

ESSENTIALS Szombathely's telephone area code is 94.

ORIENTATION One of Hungary's largest pedestrian squares, Fő tér, lies at the heart of town, attracting tourists and locals alike with its stores and cafés. Most of the tourist sights are within walking distance of here.

From the train station, head south (left) on Vasút utca until you reach Szent Márton út, then west (right) and bear to the right (north) for about 10 to 15 minutes until you get to Fő tér. Or you can take bus no. 1, 7, 11, or 15 from the station for two or three stops.

The bus station is on Ady Endre tér, three blocks from Fő tér.

INFORMATION Savaria Tourist, Mártírok tere 1 (☎ **94/312-348**), has information, and also books private rooms (see "Where to Stay," below). Open Monday through Friday from 8am to 5pm and on Saturday from 8:30am to 12:30pm.

SPECIAL EVENTS In late May or the beginning of June Szombathely sponsors the Savaria International Dance Contest, then the Savaria Festival in June, with concerts in front of the Temple of Isis, and in September, the Savaria Autumn Festival.

Szombathely (pronounced "*Som*-bot-hey") is much larger and much less interesting than most of the other towns in western Hungary. Founded in A.D. 48 by Emperor Claudius, the settlement was known as Savaria in Roman times, and served as the capital of Pannonia, the surrounding province. The Roman ruins here are fragmentary, but are almost all Szombathely has to offer. High-rise apartments dominate the town, and Szombathely's chief value to the tourist is as a public transportation gateway to Kőszeg and the mansion hotels in the nearby countryside.

WHAT TO SEE & DO

Roman Ruins

Garden of Ruins [Járdányi Paulovics István Romkert], Szily János u. 1. ☎ **313-369.**

Less striking than the Temple of Isis, the Garden of Ruins has remnants of a Roman road and fragments of the old city walls. A museum nearby has more Roman relics.

Admission: 20 Ft (20¢) adults, 10 Ft (10¢) students.

Open: Apr–Oct, Tues–Sun, 9am–5pm; Nov–Mar, Tues–Sun 10am–4pm. **Directions:** The only entrance is just to the right of the cathedral on Templom tér, just off Berzsenyi tér.

Temple of Isis, Rákóczi Ferenc u. 12.

A 1955 excavation uncovered this 2nd-century sanctuary, which constitutes one of Hungary's most important Roman ruins since it's one of only three surviving Roman shrines in Europe to the goddess Isis. Only two columns still stand, though a partial reconstruction of the temple shows fragments of the original frieze. Adjacent to the temple stands the concrete Szombathelyi Képtar (Szombathely Gallery), producing an odd architectural juxtaposition.

Admission: Free.

Open: Summer only, Tues–Sun 10am–6pm; always visible from the street. **Directions:** Walk south from Fő tér a block and a half.

Houses of Worship

Because Szombathely has long served as a center of Catholicism in western Hungary, its baroque churches constitute the other major category of sights in town. Among these are the Franciscan church on Savaria tér, a 14th-century Gothic building rebuilt in the 17th and 18th centuries in the baroque style; the Dominican church at Szent Márton út 40, a beautiful baroque structure completed in 1670; and the cathedral, on Berzsenyi Dániel tér, one of the most significant buildings from the late 18th century in Hungary. The cathedral interior is remarkably bare, without ceiling decorations, although paintings adorn niches between the large decorative columns.

Szombathely's synagogue (constructed in 1881), now converted into a music school, stands in its 19th-century splendor on Batthyány tér, across the street from the Temple of Isis.

WHERE TO STAY

PRIVATE ROOMS Savaria Tourist, at Mártírok tere 1 (☎ **94/312-348;** fax 94/311-314), rents doubles for 1,200 Ft ($12.25). It's open Monday through Friday from 8am to 5pm and on Saturday from 8:30am to 12:30pm.

Ibusz, at Szell Kálmán u. 3 (☎ **94/314-141**), renting singles for 760 Ft ($7.75) and doubles for 880 Ft ($9), is open Monday through Friday from 8am to 4pm and from June to August also on Saturday from 8am to noon.

Hotels in Town

$ **Hotel Liget,** Szent István Park 15, 9700 Szombathely. ☎ and fax **94/314-168.** 37 rms (15 with shower but no toilet, 22 with bath), 1 apartment. **Bus:** 7 from the train station; the hotel is at the corner of Gagarin utca and Jókai Mór utca.

Rates (including breakfast): 47 DM ($27.65) double with shower but no toilet, 57 DM ($33.55) double with bath; 84 DM ($49.40) apartment. Extra bed 13 DM ($7.65). **Parking:** Free.

This is a one-story establishment not unlike an American motel. Rooms are plain and simple without decoration, but clean. The staff is friendly and patient. It's a 25-minute walk west from the town center, but set in parkland right near the town baths and boating lake. It's also not far from Pásztor Csárda (see "Where to Eat," below).

Hotel Savaria, Mártírok tere 4, 9700 Szombathely. ☎ **94/311-440.** Fax 94/324/532. Telex 37200. 90 rms (31 with bath, 30 with shower but no toilet). TEL **Directions:** Walk a block north of Fő tér.

Rates (including breakfast): 55 DM ($32.35) double without bath, 85 DM ($50) double with shower but no toilet, 95 DM ($55.90) double with bath. AE, CB, DC, MC, V.

This centrally located hotel dates back to 1912, but was renovated in 1985, capturing some of its prewar flair. Rooms feature dark-wood furniture, deep-red carpets, and large mirrors in the bathrooms, with extra space in the corner rooms of each floor. Rooms are usually available in this as yet unprivatized establishment. A HungarHotel.

Dining/Entertainment: There's a restaurant open daily from 6:30am to 11pm.

Nearby Mansion Hotels

Several elegant mansion hotels are sprinkled around the countryside surrounding Szombathely and Kőszeg.

Uj-Ebergényi Kastély, Kossuth Lajos u. 36, 9763 Vasszécsény. ☎ **94/377-340** or **377-023.** Fax 94/377-125. 22 rms (all with bath). MINIBAR TEL TV **Directions:** Drive seven miles south of Szombathely on Hwy. 87 (look for the sign), or take a taxi for about 1,000 Ft ($10.20).

Rates: 3,800 Ft ($38.80) double; 5,200 Ft ($53.05) triple. Breakfast 250 Ft ($2.55) per person extra.

A neoclassical mansion from 1790, this is a great place for a few days of relaxation and a perfect base for seeing Szombathely and other nearby towns. This is what you imagined a mansion hotel would be, complete with iron gates, a tree-lined main drive, and an adjoining peasant village. Surrounded by 55 acres of idyllic park, it also boasts enough recreational facilities to keep you entertained. The rooms are clean and modern with attractive large windows.

Dining: An underground beer cellar with a brick ceiling keeps cool in summer, and has music in the evenings; upstairs there's a more conventional restaurant. Three meals should cost about 1,100 Ft ($11.20) a day.

Facilities: Two tennis courts (racquets and balls available) for free, small playroom for children, large indoor swimming pool beneath a wooden dome and large windows overlooking the property, free sauna. You can also relax in an elegant public meeting room.

Kastélyfogadó Sitke, József A. u. 1, 9671 Sitke. ☎ **60/376-070.** 28 rms (14 with bath, 12 with shower but no toilet). **Directions:** Drive east from Sárvár, take the Papa turnoff, then follow the Kastélyfogadó sign on your right.

Rates (including breakfast): 1,250 Ft ($12.75) double with shower but no toilet, 2,600 Ft ($26.55) double with bath.

A three-story, 300-year-old yellow baroque mansion, this hotel is a relaxing place. Pictures of emblems and shields line the hallways, leading to large rooms with radios and unexceptional bathrooms. Located on a hillside, the rooms overlook the tiny timeless village of Sitke, and in the back you can explore the nearby woods and forests.

Dining: The small restaurant serves meals for 220 to 425 Ft ($2.25 to $4.35).

Facilities: Small outdoor pool (filled roughly June to September). You can drive to Sárvár nearby for horseback riding.

Vadkert Fogadó, Vadkert út vége, 9600 Sárvár. ☎ **94/324-056.** Fax 94/324-210. 24 rms (all with bath). MINIBAR TEL **Directions:** From Szombathely, drive 17 miles east on Hwy. 88.

Rates (including breakfast): 2,800 Ft ($28.60) double; 3,400 Ft ($34.70) triple.

A hunting lodge, this two-story house greets visitors with pelts of animals such as bears and owls on the walls. The rooms are a bit more toned down and cozy, with blond-wood furniture, cloth wallpaper, and windows overlooking the expansive nearby fields and forests.

Dining: A cellar restaurant with antler horns on the walls offers main courses for 180 to 580 Ft ($1.85 to $5.90).

Facilities: Horseback riding costs 610 Ft ($6.20) an hour, lessons 510 Ft ($5.20) a half hour. They also arrange hunting expeditions here, making it a favorite of Germans and Austrians.

Kastélyfogadó Meggyeskovácsi, Petőfi Park, 9757 Meggyeskovácsi. ☎ **94/379-130.** 15 rms (all with shower, some without toilet). 1 apartment. **Directions:** Drive eight miles south of Sárvár.

Rates: 1,800 Ft ($18.35) double with shower but no toilet, 2,700 Ft ($27.55) double with bath; 4,000 Ft ($40.80) apartment.

An attractive two-story yellow building, this is one of the simplest mansion hotels I've listed. The large rooms have wood floors partially covered by rugs, high ceilings, and windows overlooking the bucolic village in the distance. The owners who speaks only a few words of German, keep a veritable herd of St. Bernards.

Dining: The modest restaurant and brick wine cellar have main courses for 240 to 500 Ft ($2.45–$5.10).

WHERE TO EAT

Though these two restaurants are not near the center of town, I think they're worth the ride.

Kispityer Halászcsárda, Rumi út 18. ☎ **311-227.**

Cuisine: HUNGARIAN. **Reservations:** Recommended. **Directions:** Bus no. 1 south to Rumi út; or walk 10 minutes south of Fő tér.
Prices: Soups 90–200 Ft (90¢–$2.05); fish dishes 260–600 Ft ($2.65–$6.10). AE, MC, V.
Open: Tues–Sun 11am–11pm.

No English is spoken at this premier fish specialty restaurant, but there is an English menu, allowing an easier choice among a wide selection of fried fish as well as meat dishes. You can eat at a large open terrace off a quiet residential street that makes for pleasant dining, or in several indoor rooms which include a brick wine cellar. Some of the best Gypsy music in town is played here in the evening.

Pásztor Csárda [Pastor's Inn], Dolgozók útja 1. ☎ **312-884.**

Cuisine: HUNGARIAN. **Bus:** 5 from the center, a 10-minute ride.
Prices: Soups 60–100 Ft (60¢–$1); main courses 180–450 Ft ($1.85–$4.60).
Open: Daily 10am–10pm.

This restaurant on the west side of Szombathely has walls covered with old farm implements, hunting weapons, and deer, fox, and wild goat trophies. The specialty is lamb prepared in a variety of ways. In season you can also sample delicious wild boar stuffed with herbs and served with potatoes, or venison in a burgundy sauce (*szarvascomb burgundi*).

Excursions

BASILICA OF JÁK

About 10 miles southwest of Szombathely, this Romanesque basilica was originally part of a Benedictine abbey. The massive size of the church and the wealth of internal and external detail are in marked contrast to the unpretentious hamlet around it.

Little is known about the family that founded the church. It is believed that its founders stem from the Csák family, descendants of the Szabolcs, a clan second only to the Arpád, the first family of Hungary. Márton, the first recorded founder, appears on deeds dated between 1221 and 1230. He managed to build this fantastic church on his estate around 1220.

Designed to withstand enemy attack, the church has a large central gallery and towers with a single, solidly constructed entrance. The architect set the towers over the first bay and gallery, leaving the nave proper open and airy. The basilica's remote location spared it from the worst ravages of war, and it remains one of the best examples of early medieval architecture in the world.

The ticket office across the street from the church (☎ **94/356-217**) sells an excellent range of postcards and guidebooklets, unfortunately only in German. The monastery is open April to October, daily 8am to 6pm; November to March, daily 11am to 3pm (but call ahead). Admission costs 20 Ft (20¢). Buses leave once an hour from Szombathely's bus station at Ady Endre tér; the cost is 45 Ft (45¢).

HEREND PORCELAIN FACTORY & MUSEUM

Herend is a village of otherwise little note directly between Szombathely and Budapest, also on the way to Lake Balaton. The porcelain factory, opened in 1839, in this sleepy provincial village has become synonymous with fine-quality porcelain, and its goods are sold all over the world. You may not go into the factory itself, but there is a factory store and a museum nearby, where a special porcelain-making show can be seen. Questions can be directed to the factory manager, Mr. Kovács (☎ **88/361-555**), who speaks English.

The factory store, open Monday through Friday from 9am to 4pm and on Saturday from 9am to 1pm, is located near the factory entrance. Major credit cards are accepted.

The museum (☎ **88/361-144**) has a number of fine Herend pieces on display, and also provides some historical background. It's open daily from 8:30am to 4:30pm. Admission is 60 Ft (60¢) for adults and 30 Ft (30¢) for children. Guided tours are available in English. A special technological show on porcelain making can be seen Monday through Saturday only.

From Szombathely, take the train (just over two hours) for 537 Ft ($5.50) in first class and 358 Ft ($3.65) in second class. Exit the station to your right; after a 10-minute walk, you'll see the factory.

From Veszprém, take a bus for 60 Ft ($60¢); the bus station is just two blocks from the factory.

22

Lake Balaton

A LONG, SHALLOW LAKE IN WESTERN HUNGARY, LAKE BALATON SERVES AS THE summer playground for Hungarians, Germans, Austrians, and thousands of other Central Europeans. The attraction for readers of this book is not that it has the bluest waters, the most golden sands, or the least crowded beaches—it doesn't. Its appeal is that it offers good facilities, and it's an enjoyable place to rest for a few days of sightseeing and summertime fun.

Though 48 miles long and quite wide, the lake is rather shallow—even in the center it's only 40 feet deep. Even during the Roman Empire a number of villas were constructed here, but it was not until a railroad was built in the 19th century that Lake Balaton became one of Central Europe's most popular summer destinations. Since then the towns on the lake have grown rapidly and now much of the entire 120 miles of coast has been developed.

Today these modern resort towns offer a full range of summer activities, all at very reasonable prices. For example, for just a few dollars you can rent a bicycle or a water raft for a day, or a windsurfer or a tennis court for an hour. Adding to the fun are a number of excellent restaurants and budget hotels, and you can swim (year-round) in the thermal lake at Hévíz.

The downside is that since 1989, prices have risen faster than quality at Lake Balaton. Boundless bargains have given way to a sense that you get what you pay for. Moreover, so many Austrians and Germans come to Balaton that visitors who speak only English risk feeling besieged by proprietors, waiters, and menus whose only foreign tongue is German. Finally, there's almost no reason to visit Balaton out of season. Except for the thermal lake at Hévíz, the entire region hibernates from sometime in October until sometime in April.

SEEING LAKE BALATON

The northern coast of Lake Balaton outshines the south in physical beauty, with lush, south-facing slopes rising from the shore of the lake. The Tihany Peninsula is everyone's favorite spot on the northern coast, while Balatonfüred is the gateway to Tihany and an important tourist center in itself. Nagyvázsony, over the mountains from Balatonfüred and Tihany, is an excellent horse-riding center. At the northwest corner of Balaton, Keszthely is an alternative center, with the magnificent Festetics Palace in town and the thermal lake at Hévíz a short bus ride away.

By contrast, the south doesn't feature as dramatic a landscape, but it does offer more sports choices, concerts, and general merriment. The two southern-shore towns in this chapter are Siófok (the largest town on Balaton) and its neighbor, Balatonföldvár.

The town of Székesfehérvár, on the train line between Balaton and Budapest, is included in this section more because of organizational convenience than because it forms part of the Balaton area.

Frequent express trains run from Budapest's Deli pu. to the various towns on the lake. Once there, a copious but confusing array of trains, buses, and boats will take you from one town to the next.

In summer, the Lake Balaton passenger-boat network is both extensive and cheap, though it's the slowest form of transportation around. All major towns have a dock with departures and arrivals. Children under 4 ride the boats for free, and those under 14 get 50% off. There's also a car ferry (*komp*) from Tihany-rév, on the north coast, to Szántód in the south, which cuts driving time from Balatonfüred to Balatonföldvár and Siófok. For general ferry information, call the central MAHART office in Siófok at **84/310-050.**

What's Special About Lake Balaton

Beaches

- A wide range of lake beaches, from active sports centers to quieter romantic spots.

Historic Buildings

- Festetics Palace in Keszthely, a baroque masterpiece with an interesting museum of hunting trophies and weapons.
- The Abbey Church in Tihany, the oldest church in the country, where one of Hungary's earliest kings is buried.
- Kinizsi Castle in Nagyvázsony, from the 15th century.
- Fragmentary Garden of Ruins in Hungary's former capital, Székesfehérvár, where 38 Hungarian kings were crowned.

Mansion Hotels

- Taurus Kastélyhotel, perhaps the most elegant mansion hotel in the country, with swimming, tennis, and other luxuries—all affordable for a budget traveler!
- Festetics Palace Hotel, in a swank baroque palace along Lake Balaton, with some of the most dazzling suites in the country.
- Kastélyszálló Hotel in Nagyvázsony, a 1750 mansion that's perfect for avid horse riders.

Natural Spectacles

- The Thermal Lake in Hévíz, the second largest in the world, where you can swim year-round.

If you're coming from Budapest, stop by the Tourinform office there before you leave. They give out excellent free maps and brochures on Balaton. Also, do your best to reserve a hotel or private room at least a few days in advance, since Balaton is crowded and prices are as high as in Budapest.

Be sure to ask for private rooms within walking distance of the lake itself.

1 Balatonfüred

78 miles SW of Budapest

GETTING THERE • **By Train** The express from Budapest's Déli station takes a little over two hours, for 627 Ft ($6.40) in first class or 418 Ft ($4.25) in second class.

• **By Bus** There are frequent connections from other destinations on the north coast.

• **By Boat** From June to mid-September, a boat connects with Tihany, 20 minutes away, and Siófok, 50 minutes away. You can call the boat station at **342-230.**

ESSENTIALS Balatonfüred's telephone area code is 86.

ORIENTATION The main coastal highway through town is Petőfi Sándor utca. The IBUSZ travel office is located on this street just off Vörösmarty utca, and my hotel recommendation is down the street. Jókai Mór utca is the major street perpendicular to this highway. The train and bus stations are located a block from Jókai Mór utca, in the center of town.

INFORMATION Contact one of the travel agencies listed below in "Where to Stay."

SPECIAL EVENTS The highlight of the social season is the Anna Ball on the Saturday nearest July 26.

Balatonfüred has some of the top facilities of all the lakeshore resorts. It has good beaches, and nearby are some of Hungary's best vineyards. Not as provincial as some of the other, smaller spots, Balatonfüred has an active nightlife with bars, live music, and dancing.

WHERE TO STAY

PRIVATE ROOMS The best agency in town is **Balatontourist** at Blaha L. u. 5 (☎ **86/342-822;** fax 86/343-435). In July and August hours are Monday through Saturday from 8:30am to 6:30pm and on Sunday from 8:30am to 12:30pm; the rest of the year, the office is open Monday through Friday from 8:30am to 4pm. Double rooms rent for 1,200 to 1,600 Ft ($12.25 to $16.35). Agnes speaks English and is very helpful and friendly. Ask for a free town map.

IBUSZ, at Petőfi Sándor u. 4/a (☎ **86/342-028;** fax 86/342-251; telex 32343), has double rooms starting at 28 DM ($16.45). Summer hours are Monday through Saturday from 8am to 6pm and on Sunday from 9am to 1pm; the rest of the year, Monday through Thursday from 8am to 4pm and Friday from 8am to 3pm.

A Pension

Korona Panzió, Vörösmarty u. 4/2, 8230 Balatonfüred. ☎ **86/343-278.** 8 rms (all with bath). **Directions:** Walk up Vörösmarty utca from the IBUSZ office.

Rates (including breakfast): June–Aug. 60 DM ($35.30) double; Sept–May, 45 DM ($26.45) double. **Parking:** Free.

This recently opened pension is in a three-story white-and-pink stucco building. There's a pleasant outdoor dining area, with flowers all around. The on-premises restaurant is open from May through October.

WHERE TO EAT

Halászkert Étterem [Fisherman's Garden], Petőfi Sándor u. 2. ☎ **343-039.**

Cuisine: HUNGARIAN. **Reservations:** Recommended in summer. **Directions:** Walk south down Petőfi Sándor utca from IBUSZ and take the second left.
Prices: Soups 60–155 Ft (60¢–$1.60); main courses 195–510 Ft ($2–$5.20). AE, MC.
Open: May–Sept, daily 9am–1am, Apr and Oct, daily 1pm–10pm. **Closed:** Nov–Mar.

Germans make up over 90% of the summer guests at this fish restaurant near the beach. In summer you'll eat outside on a very large terrace. Inside the ceilings are of dark wood and walls are covered with handmade plates, paprika, and other decoration. From May to September Gypsy music plays from 7pm to midnight. Try the grilled pike perch.

Tölgyfa Csárda, Meleghegy utca. ☎ **343-036.**

Cuisine: HUNGARIAN. **Directions:** Located at the top of town; go up Jókai Mór utca to the twin-towered church, then continue up the hill about 2km (1.2 miles).
Prices: Soups 130–150 Ft ($1.35–$1.55), main courses 300–700 Ft ($3.05–$7.15).
Open: Apr–Oct, daily 11am–midnight. **Closed:** Nov–Mar.

The top recommendation in town, this restaurant supplies a gorgeous view over the town and the lake, and the food is certainly some of the best around. Try the pork steak, served with paprika, tomato, onion, and bacon—slightly spicy and delicious.

Baricska Csárda, Baricska dűlő. ☎ **343-105.**

Cuisine: HUNGARIAN. **Reservations:** Recommended for weekends. **Directions:** From the high-rise lakeside Hotel Füred, cross the street and walk past the gas station. **Prices:** Soup 220 Ft ($2.25); main courses 450–850 Ft ($4.60–$8.65). **Open:** Mid-Mar to Oct, daily 11am–11pm. **Closed:** Nov to mid-Mar.

This restaurant has fine food at fairly high prices. It's a huge highway-side place, which can accommodate up to 800 people. A Gypsy band plays in the outdoor dining areas, where leafy vines drape the trellis overhead. The evening view doesn't compare with the Tölgyfa's, but the service—under the watchful eye of the two owners—is superior.

SPORTS & RECREATION

You can play tennis in several places from 6am to 8pm: in the center of Fenyves Park near the beach, at the Marina Hotel on Széchenyi utca, and on Petőfi Sándor utca across from the northeast corner of the park. They charge about 300 Ft ($3.05) an hour.

Miniature golf is available at the FICC Rally Camping spot at the far western end of the beach.

You can rent windsurfing and sailing equipment right in front of the public beach near the Eden Hotel, at the Marina Hotel, or the Kemping area.

An Excursion to Nagyvázsony

For those who want to ride horses or wander through the beautiful countryside north of the Balaton region, the place to go is Nagyvázsony. Inland Nagyvázsony is as pastoral as Balatonfüred is a coastal holiday strip. By car, you can come straight across the ridge from Balatonfüred; the public transportation gateway to this tiny town is, however, through Veszprém, a town north of Balatonfüred. Buses to Veszprém from Balatonfüred are frequent; then change to another bus for the 13 miles from Veszprém to Nagyvázsony. The bus will stop either in front of the Kastélyszálló or at the Vázsonykő Panzió.

WHAT TO SEE & DO

Constructed in 1470, Kinizsi Castle, Kinizsi utca (☎ **88/331-015**), was used to defend the area against the invading Turks; it's named after a famous warrior of the time who helped the king unify the nation. In the 18th and 19th centuries it was used as a prison.

Today, incredibly peaceful in the warm sun, the warlike citadel no longer inspires fears in the Turks as it once did. In fact, when I last visited, a Turkish flag was actually flying from its tower in honor of a school trip from that once-hostile southern neighbor. Inside you'll see an exhibition on the castle's history.

The castle is open daily: June to August, from 7:30am to 7pm; September to May, from 9am to 4pm. Admission costs 50 Ft (50¢).

Just in front of the citadel is a small postal museum. Down the street and just beyond the cemetery you can see the ruins of a small cloister built in medieval times.

WHERE TO STAY

Kastélyszálló, Kossuth u. 12, 8291 Nagyvázsony. ☎ **88/364-109.** 20 rms (all with bath).

Rates: 1,760 Ft ($17.95) single; 3,110 Ft ($31.75) double. Breakfast 250 Ft ($2.55) extra. **Closed:** Dec–Mar.

Built in 1750, this is the former mansion of the Zichy family. The two-story yellow facade appears somewhat weathered, but rooms have new furniture and bathroom accessories. Be certain to call ahead for a reservation.

Facilities: Just to the side of the main house is the riding ring, with the smell of horses! The best way to see the countryside is by horseback. You can rent horses for 800 Ft ($8.15) per hour or 3,500 Ft ($35.70) per day, and a guide is included.

Vázsonykő Panzió, Sörház u. 2, 8291 Nagyvázsony. ☎ **88/364-344.** 8 rms (all with bath).

Rates (including breakfast): 1,500 Ft ($15.30) single; 2,000 Ft ($20.40) double. Nov–Feb.

You could stay here if the Kastélyszálló is full. Rooms are clean and well lit. Downstairs is a mediocre restaurant with an attractive terrace.

2 The Tihany Peninsula

82 miles SW of Budapest, 5 miles S of Balatonfüred

GETTING THERE • **By Bus** Since there are no trains, you'll have to take a bus (from Balatonfüred for instance) to arrive by land from the north side of the lake.

• **By Boat** From the south side of Lake Balaton you can take a car ferry (☎ **86/348-307**) from Szántód-rév to Tihany-rév, which leaves roughly every 40 to 60 minutes from dawn to dusk, from mid-March to mid-December. For a car and a driver, the fare is 250 Ft ($2.55). Fare for each additional passenger is 50 Ft (50¢). The trip takes 10 minutes.

You can also take the passenger boat from Balatonfüred or Balatonföldvár, both 20 minutes away.

ESSENTIALS The telephone area code for the Tihany Peninsula is 86.

ORIENTATION The Tihany Peninsula is a mountainous, oval-shaped projection that almost cuts Balaton in half. In the center of the peninsula nestle two small lakes, Belső-tó and Külső-tó. On the northeastern (Budapestward) side of the peninsula is the town of Tihany. Tihany town is built around the Abbey Church, which caps the rise that divides Belső-tó and Balaton. A couple kilometers downhill at the very tip of the peninsula is Tihany-rév—Tihany Landing—from where the car-ferry across Lake Balaton leaves. There's also a ferry dock near Tihany town, but only the Balaton passenger steamer stops there.

INFORMATION In the center of Tihany town by the Abbey Church is Balatontourist, Kossuth u. 20 (☎ **80/348-519**). From Easter to mid-June and mid-August to mid-October, it's open Monday through Friday from 8am to 4:30pm and on Saturday from 8am to 1pm; from mid-June to mid-August, Monday through Saturday from 8am to 6:30pm and on Sunday from 8am to 1pm; the rest of the year, the office is closed.

ACCOMMODATIONS At Balatontourist, Kossuth u. 20 (☎ **80/348-519**), you can rent private rooms—doubles for 1,500 to 1,800 Ft ($15.30–$18.35).

SPECIAL EVENTS There's a weekend wine festival in mid-September.

Roughly midway along Lake Balaton's northern coast, the Tihany Peninsula boasts the area's best beaches and most beautiful scenery. The allure of Tihany had already been recognized in the Iron Age, when people lived on the peninsula; during the Roman Empire a number of villas were constructed in the Tihany hills. Today, Tihany is one of the Balaton region's most popular, yet most peaceful destinations.

WHAT TO SEE & DO

Abbey Church [Apátsági Templom], Andrássy tér.

The church is part of a Benedictine abbey founded in 1055, and the remaining section of this first church is the oldest in Hungary. You can see the impressive thick stone columns and vaulted ceilings dating back 900 years down in the current church crypt. King Andrew, one of Hungary's earliest kings, has been buried here under a white marble stone since 1060. The monastery's dedication plaque (1055) is the first written example of the Hungarian language. The more modern main section of the church shows baroque frescoed ceilings from the 19th century. The towers in front of the church date back to the 18th century.

In front of the church you can see a 1972 work dedicated to King Andrew by one of Hungary's foremost sculptors, Imre Varga (it's the rock with the metal on it).

Admission: 20 Ft (20¢) adults, 10 Ft (10¢) students.

Open: May–Sept, daily 10am–5:30pm; Oct, daily 10am–4:30pm. **Closed:** Nov–Apr.

Tihany Museum, Andrássy tér. ☎ **348-405.**

The relics of the church, such as a copy of the foundation deed, are displayed in the Tihany Museum next door. The museum also chronicles the history of the Lake Balaton region with a collection of old stones and other objects.

Admission: 30 Ft (30¢) adults, 20 Ft (20¢) students.

Open: May–Sept, Tues–Sun 10am–5:30pm; Oct, Tues–Sun 10am–4:30pm. **Closed:** Nov–Apr.

Echoing Stone, on Echo Hill.

If you walk left from the church, down a winding path overlooking the lake, you'll arrive at the Echoing Stone of Tihany. It's about 15 yards from a restaurant called Echo. If you yell loudly while standing atop this stone, it will return an echo from the side of the church. This stone has given rise to the pejorative tag "like the echo in Tihany" for people who mouth others' ideas.

3 Keszthely

117 miles SW of Budapest

GETTING THERE • **By Train** The express traveling on the south side of the lake from Budapest's Déli station takes three hours, and costs 897 Ft ($9.15) in first class and 598 Ft ($6.10) in second class. On slower trains you may have to change in Balatonszentgyörgy. If you come from the northern part of the lake you must make an inconvenient change at Tapolca.

• **By Bus** Buses arrive daily from Balatonfüred, Veszprém, and other cities.

ESSENTIALS Keszthely's telephone area code is 83.

ORIENTATION Keszthely is situated at the northwesternmost corner of Lake Balaton. Kossuth Lajos utca is the main street in town, which runs through Fő tér

(Main Square) before arriving at the Festetics Palace, the main sight in Keszthely. You'll especially enjoy strolling on the shop-filled pedestrians-only section between Fő tér and the palace. The bus and train stations are next to each other near the shore, about a 15-minute walk from Fő tér, or 5 to 10 minutes from the seaside Hotel Phoenix.

INFORMATION Keszthely's Tourinform office, Kossuth Lajos u. 28 (☎ **83/314-144**), is full of information, maps, and local accommodations brochures. The office is open from June 1 to September 14, Monday through Friday from 9am to 7pm and Saturday and Sunday from 9am to 1pm; from April 1 to May 30 and from September 15 to October 14, Monday through Friday from 8am to 6pm and Saturday from 9am to 1pm; and from October 15 to April 1, Monday through Friday from 8am to 4pm and Saturday from 9am to 1pm.

SPECIAL EVENTS There are chamber music concerts in the Festetics Palace June to August, and organ concerts in the Carmelite church from April to October.

Lake Balaton's second-largest town, on the northwest corner of the lake, Keszthely (pronounced "*Kest*-hay") was once the estate of the Festetics family, from the early 18th century until 1945. In 1745 they built the foremost palace on Lake Balaton, which remains the highlight of a visit. In 1797 Europe's first agricultural college opened here. The combination of historical landmarks and beaches make Keszthely one of the more interesting towns on Lake Balaton.

WHAT TO SEE & DO

Festetics Palace, Kastély u. 1. ☎ **312-190,** ext. 15.

This ornate 1750s baroque structure with an asymmetrical facade and a three-story tower was once home to princes and counts. Today the spacious rooms of the Festetics Palace house a hotel wing, a library with some 94,000 volumes, and a museum of hunting trophies. The museum collection includes lion, tiger, bear, and leopard skins; rhino and elephant tusks; elaborate ivory inlaid guns; and crossbows, muskets, armor, and swords. After your visit indoors you can walk through the spacious sculptured gardens. In June, July and August make sure to inquire about upcoming concerts in the elegant palace concert hall or on the palace grounds. See "Where to Stay," below for information on the hotel rooms inside.

Admission: 250 Ft ($2.55) for adults, 50 Ft (50¢) for students, and 550 Ft ($5.60) for a family. (The admission fee for Hungarians is half of the above.)

Open: July 16–Aug 31, Tues–Sun 9am–6pm; Apr 10–July 15 and Sept 1–30, Tues–Sun 9am–5pm; Oct 1–Apr 9, Tues–Sun 10am–5pm. **Directions:** Walk north on Kossuth Lajos utca from Fő tér.

Balaton Museum, Múzeum u. 2. ☎ **312-351.**

A collection on the geological and natural history of the Lake Balaton region. The ground floor has paintings and views of the lake, some ancient Roman relics from the Balaton region, and modern folk arts and crafts. Upstairs you'll see models on the geology, human settlements, and flora and fauna of the region.

Admission: 50 Ft (50¢) adults, 30 Ft (30¢) students.

Open: June–Aug, Tues–Sun 9am–6pm; Sept–May, Tues–Sun 10am–5pm. **Directions:** Walk about six blocks south of Fő tér on Kossuth Lajos utca.

WHERE TO STAY

PRIVATE ROOMS Zalatours, Fő tér 1 (☎ **83/312-560**), has doubles for 800 Ft ($8.15). The office is open Monday through Friday from 8am to 5pm and on Saturday from 8am to noon.

IBUSZ, Széchenyi u. 1–3 (☎ **83/312-951**), has doubles for 1,700 Ft ($17.35). In Saturday from 8am to 6pm, and on Sunday from 8am to noon; the rest of the year, Monday through Friday from 8am to 3pm. American Express and VISA accepted.

Doubles for Less Than $15

Hotel Amazon, Szabadság u. 11, 8360 Keszthely. ☎ **83/312-248.** 20 rms (8 with bath). **Directions:** Walk half a block south of the Festetics Palace; the entrance is around the corner on Georgikon utca.

Rates (including breakfast): 1,200 Ft ($12.25) single without bath, 1,900 Ft ($19.40) single with bath; 1,400 Ft ($14.30) double without bath, 2,300 Ft ($23.45) double with bath.

The Amazon may remind you of your old university dorm—a crumbling building with dimly lit hallways that are rarely repainted. Rooms are rather large, with prints on the walls. The public toilets are old but clean. The hotel is a 10-minute walk from the beach, a few steps from the Festetics Palace, and a few minutes from a number of restaurants in town. Still, it's not a first choice.

Doubles for Less Than $45

Festetics Palace Hotel, Szabadság u. 1, 8360 Keszthely. ☎ **83/312-190.** Fax 83/315-039. 15 rms (all with bath), 4 apartment. **Directions:** Walk north on Kossuth Lajos utca from Fő tér; enter through the archway and to the right from the museum entrance.

Rates: 3,300 Ft ($33.65) double or triple; 6,600 Ft ($57.35) apartment. Breakfast 250 Ft ($2.55) extra.

Since 1988 tourists have been able to sleep in a wing of the palace. The rooms on the ground floor once belonged to the staff, and are large but a bit bare with little furniture; the windows overlook the palace grounds. The apartments are nothing short of dazzling, with antique wood furniture, elaborate marble fireplaces, huge mirrors, chandeliers, and many windows overlooking the palace grounds. If you can afford the luxury, you'll long remember your stay here. The manager is a member of the Hungarian Parliament.

Hotel Georgikon, Georgikon u. 20, 8360 Keszthely. ☎ **83/315-730.** Fax 83/312-373. 14 apartments (all with bath). TV TEL **Directions:** From the Hotel Amazon, walk three blocks west.

Rates (including breakfast): June–Aug, 3,800 Ft ($38.80) apartment; May and Sept, 3,300 Ft ($33.65) apartment; Oct–Apr, 3,000 Ft ($30.60) apartment.

A two-story, 18th-century ocher building, this hotel offers attractive modern facilities at excellent prices. The rooms feature country-style blond-wood furniture, clean white walls, a desk and small bathrooms, as well as a small kitchenette area with another table and a refrigerator. There's also a hotel restaurant. The only drawback to this fine value is its location—a few blocks away from the town center.

Worth the Extra Money

Hotel Phoenix, Balatonpart, 8360 Keszthely. ☎ **83/312-630.** Fax 83/314-225. 78 rms (all with bath). **Directions:** After exiting the train station, walk 10 minutes to the right.

Rates (including breakfast): July–Aug, 86 DM ($50.60) single; 96 DM ($56.50) double. May–June and Sept, 52 DM ($30.60) single; 61 DM ($35.90) double. Apr and Oct, 34 DM ($20) single; 43 DM ($25.30) double. AE, CB, DC, MC, V. **Closed:** Nov–Mar.

The Phoenix has a large attractive lobby with brick walls and a high blond-wood ceiling that helps create a tropical-beach ambience. The rooms are small, with natural-wood furniture, and all have tiny bathrooms.

WHERE TO EAT

Hungária Gösser Söröző, Kossuth Lajos u. 35. ☎ **312-265.**

Cuisine: HUNGARIAN/GERMAN. **Reservations:** Recommended for summer evenings. **Directions:** Walk on Kossuth Lajos utca just north of Fő tér.

Prices: Soup 70–80 Ft (70¢–80¢); main courses 250–650 Ft ($2.55–$6.65). AE, DC, MC, V.

Open: Sun–Thurs 9am–10pm, Fri–Sat 9am–11pm.

This expansive beer-garden restaurant has a large courtyard and an indoor wood-paneled dining room patronized mainly by Germans and Austrians. Surprisingly for a beer garden, the food here is rather good. They also have good fresh strudels for dessert. There's dance music beginning at 5 or 6pm, except on Wednesdays in winter.

An Excursion to the Thermal Lake in Hévíz

If you're eager to swim outdoors in the spring, fall, or winter, you need not test the cold waters of Lake Balaton; rather, head for the 14-acre ★ **thermal lake** in Hévíz. Throughout the year the lake's temperature remains a stable 86° to 95°F. It's the second-largest thermal lake in the world, after one in New Zealand.

A large square wood-and-glass pavilion sits at the center of the lake, and an enclosed wooden pathway leads you there. Inside, you can change, get a massage, or swim in enclosed areas. You can also swim into this area from the open lake, which could save you some chills on a brisk day. The pavilion also accommodates outdoor deck lounges for sunning and relaxation.

The entrance fee is 140 Ft ($1.45) for three hours, and a massage costs 600 Ft ($6.10). Open daily: May to September from 9am to 6pm, and October to April from 9am to 5pm. The entrance to the lake (TÓ FÜRDŐ) is across from the bus station.

Buses leave Keszthely from Fő tér and from its central bus station every 30 minutes; they cover the four-mile journey to Hévíz in 20 minutes for 34 Ft (35¢). The Hévíz bus station is next to the lake entrance.

WHERE TO STAY

Napsugár Hotel, Tavirózsa u. 3–5, 8380 Hévíz. ☎ **and fax 83/340-472.** Telex 35313. 52 rms (all with bath). TV **Directions:** By taxi, 150 Ft ($1.55) from the Hévíz bus station.

Rates (including breakfast): Apr 1–Oct 15, 69 DM ($40.60) single; 94 DM ($55.30) double; 128 DM ($75.30) quad. Oct 16–Mar 30, 46 DM ($27.05) single; 64 DM ($37.65) double; 102 DM ($60) quad. AE, CB, DC, MC, V.

Located on a hill about 15 minutes on foot from the thermal lake, this hotel offers a kitchenette with a hotplate and a fridge in all rooms. The decor is highlighted by attractive hardwood floors, wall-to-wall windows that let in lots of light, and clean, whitewashed walls. This is the budget best in town, and attracts mostly German and Austrian visitors. A Danubius Beta Hotel.

4 Balatonföldvár

73 miles SW of Budapest

GETTING THERE • By Train The express from Budapest's Déli station takes just under two hours and costs 627 Ft ($6.40) in first class and 418 Ft ($4.25) in second class.

• By Bus You can catch buses from Keszthely, Siófok, or Szántód-rév where the car ferry from Tihany arrives.

• By Boat Passenger boats arrive here from Tihany several times a day in summer. You can call the boat station at **340-304.**

ESSENTIALS Balatonföldvár's telephone area code is 84.

ORIENTATION The town itself is small and consists of only a few rows of streets parallel to the waterfront. An 800-foot pier marks the center of the waterfront; to get to the Siótour office (see "Where to Stay," below), walk south into the town.

Balatonföldvár is across the lake from the Tihany Peninsula and slightly to the south. A wilderness up to the end of the 19th century, it gradually became a favorite of Hungarian aristocracy. Today Balatonföldvár is a popular resort for young people, with excellent sports facilities at its main hotels.

WHERE TO STAY

PRIVATE ROOMS Siótours, near the train station at Hősök u. 9/11 (☎ **84/340-099**), is open Monday through Friday from 8am to 4:30pm. Double rooms are available from 1,200 Ft ($12.25) and villas from 2,500 Ft ($25.50).

Hotels

Hotel Fesztivál, Rákóczi u. 35, 8623 Balatonföldvár. ☎ **84/340-371.** Fax 84/340-380. Telex 227398. 320 rms (all with bath). **Directions:** Walk about 10 minutes west of the pier down Rákóczi utca.

Rates (including breakfast): July 7–Aug 17, 83DM ($48.80) single, 92 DM ($54.10) double. May 28–July 2 and Aug 18–Sep 26, 48 DM ($28.25) single, 64 DM ($37.65) double. May 1–27 and Sept 27–closing 34 DM ($20) single, 44 DM ($25.90) double. **Closed:** Mid-Oct to Apr.

Offering a variety of summer sports, this tall, modern concrete structure on the shore has a long series of balconies with attractive views. You can choose among soccer, badminton, basketball, and volleyball, all free of charge, and tennis and windsurfing at modest rates. It's run by Express, the youth travel agency, and attracts many young people.

$ **Hotel Juventus,** József Attila u. 6. ☎ **84/340-379.** 104 rms (none with bath). **Directions:** Get off the bus on the main coastal road.

Rates (including breakfast): July 18–Sept 5, 2,200 Ft ($22.45) single, 2,400 Ft ($24.50) double, 3,100 Ft ($31.65) triple, 3,300 Ft ($33.65) quad. May 23–July 17, 1,900 Ft ($19.40) single, 2,100 Ft ($21.40) double, 2,700 Ft ($27.55) triple, 2,900 Ft ($29.60) quad. May 1–22 and Sept 6–30, prices about 10% cheaper than above. **Closed:** Oct–Apr.

The cheaper companion hotel run by the Express travel agency, the Juventus is located about 10 minutes away on foot off the main coastal highway. Although the location is less attractive, guests here can use the sporting facilities and beach of the Fesztivál. The rooms have bright-red furniture, bold blue floors, and terraces, but no private bathrooms. There's a disco downstairs, and a restaurant with outdoor tables in an adjacent building.

WHERE TO EAT

Pinter Vendéglő, Táncsics Mihály u. 11. ☎ **340-396.**

Cuisine: HUNGARIAN. **Reservations:** Recommended. **Directions:** Walk about six blocks east of the town pier; enter from Báthóri utca.

Prices: Main courses 350–700 Ft ($3.60–$7.15). **Closed:** Oct–Apr.

This small restaurant with an industrious kitchen attracts huge crowds from all over the Balaton area. Ask to sit in the outside area, shaded by a multicolored canvas that looks like a circus tent. The food, cooked under the owner's supervision, has a loyal following, highlighted by the roast swan "Gypsy style." They have an English-language menu and an English-speaking waiter.

5 Siófok

65 miles SW of Budapest

GETTING THERE • By Train From Budapest's Déli station it takes about an hour and 45 minutes, costing 537 Ft ($5.50) in first class and 358 Ft ($3.65) in second class.

• By Bus Buses arrive from many places north and south of Siófok.

• By Boat Boats arrive from Tihany, Balatonfüred, and other towns. The ride from Tihany takes about an hour and 20 minutes. You can call the boat station at **310-050.**

ESSENTIALS Siófok's telephone area code is 84.

ORIENTATION A resort town spread out parallel to the sea, Siófok has two major roads, Fő utca, the main coastal highway about five blocks inland, and Petőfi sétány, the street alongside the shore lined by large hotels. Both the bus and train station are a block from Szabadság tér, the main square on Fő utca, with several travel agencies nearby.

INFORMATION Siófok's embryonic Tourinform branch has its office at Fő u. 41 (☎ and fax **84/310-117**). During the summer, however, they may operate at the water tower in the center of town.

The largest and most popular resort on Lake Balaton, Siófok (pop. 22,000) is Balaton's undisputed center of activity, offering everything from sports to discos. You'll see people everywhere in Siófok (pronounced "*She*-oh-fok"); this is not the place for privacy. But the crowds of vacationers looking for summer fun create a friendly atmosphere where you can easily meet people.

Siófok's boom dates back to the opening of the southern railway through town in 1861. Since then the town grew rapidly and today Siófok can accommodate thousands of visitors each day during the summer.

WHAT TO SEE & DO

Recreational sports facilities proliferate here. You can rent bicycles for only a few dollars a day, as well as rafts and badminton racquets in the basement of the Balaton Hotel. The four lakefront hotels rent windsurfers at moderate prices.

WHERE TO STAY

PRIVATE ROOMS IBUSZ, Fő u. 174 (☎ **84/311-066;** fax 84/311-481; telex 223797), has doubles for 1,500 Ft ($15.30) and apartments for 2,500 to 3,500 Ft ($25.50 to $35.70). The staff is friendly. It's open June to August, Monday through Saturday from 9am to 6pm and on Saturday from 9am to 1pm; September to May, Monday through Friday from 9am to 4pm.

Siótour, across the street at Szabadság tér 6 (☎ **84/310-900;** fax 84/310-009; telex 224002), offers doubles for 45 DM ($26.45) and apartments for 75 DM ($44.10). The office is open July 8 to August 16, Monday through Saturday from 8am to 8pm; May 4 to July 7 and August 17 to October 1, Monday through Saturday from 8am to 6pm; the rest of the year, Monday through Friday from 8am to 4:30pm.

There are also countless ZIMMER FREI signs in town, and given the above prices, Siófok may be the town to try your luck with them. As always, prices are negotiable.

A Motel

Touring Hotel Fokihegy, 8609 Balatonszéplak-felső. ☎ **84/310-684.** 59 rms (none with bath). **Bus:** 1 or 6.

Rates (including breakfast): July 12–Aug, 1,400 Ft ($14.30) single, 2,800 Ft ($28.55) double; May–July 11 and Sept–Oct 15, 1,300 Ft ($13.25) single, 2,600 Ft ($26.55) double. Half board (at the Piroska Csárda) 600 Ft ($6.10) extra. AE, CB, DC, MC, V. **Parking:** Free. **Closed:** Oct 16–Apr.

Located on Fő utca 2km (1¼ miles) in the direction of Balatonföldvár (west of the town center), this motel offers the best rates in town. Despite its distance from the town center, it's still only a few minutes from the beach. Rooms are small with sinks and large windows. The excellent Piroska Csárda restaurant is next door. A Pannonia Hotel.

WHERE TO EAT

Piroska Csárda, Balatonszéplak-felső, just off Fő utca. ☎ **310-683.**

Cuisine: HUNGARIAN. **Reservations:** Recommended in summer. **Bus:** 1 or 6.
Prices: Soups 100–155 Ft ($1–$1.60); main courses 300–620 Ft ($3.05–$6.35).
Open: Daily 8am–10pm. **Closed:** Oct 16–Apr.

You can't miss this large restaurant built of logs with a straw roof—nor should you. You can dine indoors, in the courtyard, or at a table outdoors in front of the restaurant. This is a lively place, serving really excellent food at moderate prices. There's music every night and a dancing program in the evening. It's 2km (1¼ miles) from the town center. Open for summer season only.

Csárdás, Fő u. 105. ☎ **310-642.**

Cuisine: HUNGARIAN. **Reservations:** Recommended in summer. **Directions:** Walk one long block east of the bus station.

Prices: Soup 60 Ft (60¢); main courses 230–650 Ft ($2.35–$6.65). AE, DC, MC, V.
Open: Daily 11:30am–11pm.

Excellent food is served here under attractive decor. Heavy wooden ceiling beams and low arches are set off by the delicately painted glass lamps and dark-red brick floor. Gypsy music adds to the atmosphere from 6pm to closing. Try the pork with scalloped potatoes, baked in a paprika-and-tomato sauce (Sertésjava magyaróvári módra).

6 Székesfehérvár

37 miles SW of Budapest

GETTING THERE • By Train The frequent trains from Budapest's Déli station take about an hour and cost 294 Ft ($3) in first class and 196 Ft ($2) in second class.

ESSENTIALS Székesfehérvár's telephone area code is **22.**

ORIENTATION From the train station on the south side of town, walk north on Prohászka Ottokár út, which begins to the left of the station. The street eventually turns into Várkörút. After a 15-minute walk you'll see the Hotel Alba Regia; turn left onto a pedestrian street and you'll enter the heart of the Old Town.

The Old Town consists of several pedestrian areas. As you move away from the Hotel Alba Regia, on your right you'll pass the Garden of Ruins, the remains of the former royal basilica. The main square, Városház tér, is just a few steps farther on. From this square begins town's main pedestrian street, Fő utca.

INFORMATION Albatours, the central tourist office with maps and information, is at Szabadság tér 6 (☎ **22/312-494**). Albatours is open Monday and Wednesday through Friday from 9am to 4:30pm, on Tuesday from 9am to 6pm, and on Saturday from 8am to 1pm.

Halfway between Lake Balaton and Budapest. Székesfehérvár (pronounced "*Say*-kesh-fay-hair-var") was the capital of Hungary for over 500 years. From the reign of Stephen I, Hungary's first king, to the 1526 Ottoman Turkish victory at Mohács, Székesfehérvár was the center of coronations and other regal celebrations. The town was totally destroyed by the Ottoman Turks in the 16th century; adding to the previous damage, the city saw heavy Russian-German fighting in the closing days of World War II.

Today the history of Székesfehérvár is better preserved than its sights. The center revolves around a long pedestrian mall, which has a few interesting museums. Outside this area, however, new construction dominates the landscape.

I recommend Székesfehérvár to visitors who want to see a more typical Hungarian town outside Budapest, but who won't have a chance to visit western Hungary.

WHAT TO SEE & DO

Garden of Ruins [Romkert], Koronázó tér.

Here you can see the rather scanty 11th-century remains of the royal basilica where King Stephen and 36 other Hungarian kings were crowned and buried (17 kings were laid to rest here).

Admission: 30 Ft (30¢).

Open: Apr–Oct, Tues–Sun 9am–6pm; visible from the street above at all times.
Directions: Walk half a block east of Városház tér.

King Stephen Museum [István Király Múzeum], Fő u. 6. ☎ **311-465.**

Ancient Roman ruins and other historical and archeological finds are on display here. Interestingly, the Roman ruins in this area of Hungary are in better shape than medieval relics, which were largely destroyed by the Ottoman Turks.

Admission: 50 Ft (50¢) adults, 25 Ft (25¢) students.

Open: Tues–Sun 10am–6pm. **Directions:** From Városház tér, walk two blocks north on Fő utca.

Black Eagle Apothecary [Fekete Sas Patikamúzeum], Fő u. 5. ☎ **315-583.**

In the heart of the Old Town, this 18th-century pharmacy contains original objects from a drugstore of that time. Its rococo interior is well preserved.

Admission: Free.

Open: Tues–Sun 10am–6pm. **Directions:** From Városház tér, walk two blocks north on Fő utca.

WHERE TO STAY

Below I've listed a fine mansion hotel in the surrounding area. The following accommodations are in the center of town.

PRIVATE ROOMS Albatours, at Városház tér 6 (☎ **22/312-494;** fax 22/327-082), has doubles for 1,100 Ft ($11.20), and apartments (minimum of four nights) for 1,400 to 1,600 Ft ($14.30 to $16.35). Open Monday and Wednesday through Friday from 9am to 4:30pm, on Tuesday from 9am to 6pm, and on Saturday from 8am to 1pm.

IBUSZ, Ady Endre u. 2 (☎ **22/311-510** or **313-141;** fax 22/329-393), at the corner of Fő utca, has singles and doubles for 1,000 Ft ($10.30). It's open Monday through Friday from 8am to 4:30pm and on Saturday from 8am to noon.

A Hotel in Town

Hotel Magyar Király, Fő u. 10, 8000 Székesfehérvár. ☎ **22/311-262.** Fax 22/327-788. Telex 21293. 57 rms (all with bath). MINIBAR **Bus:** 33 or 34 from the train station.

Rates (including breakfast): 3,050 Ft ($31.10) single; 3,300 Ft ($33.65) double.

The best-located mid-range hotel in town is at the end of the pedestrian walk in the town center. Completed in 1820 as a count's palace, the hotel has a stone stairway and bold facade that still bespeak aristocratic audacity. The rooms are nothing special, but have recently been furnished with dark-wood furniture and wallpaper, making them clean and very attractive. The bathrooms look a bit older.

A Nearby Mansion Hotel

Taurus Kastélyhotel, 8111 Seregélyes. ☎ **22/365-032.** Fax 22/365-032. 36 rms (all with bath), 5 apartments. MINIBAR TV TEL **Directions:** Székesfehervár is about nine miles away. A bus takes about 30 minutes; a train, about 16 minutes; from either station it's a 15-minute walk.

Rates: May–Oct, 3,900 Ft ($39.80) double; 5,400 Ft ($55.10) apartment. Nov–Apr, 2,900 Ft ($29.60) double; 4,900 Ft ($50) apartment. Breakfast 350 Ft ($3.55) extra. AE, DC, V, but 10% surcharge on credit-card payments.

Built by Count Ferenc Zichy in 1821, this may be Hungary's best mansion hotel. I know of no better place in the country to relax for a few days! In fact, it's also within commuting distance of Budapest for car travelers. It has a very stately facade with four columns in a Greek-style portico. Inside this U-shaped neoclassical mansion, a computer-equipped reception speeds you to your chambers. Some rooms have a spiral staircase leading up to a loft bed, and all rooms have good-looking furniture, large windows, and clean, modern bathrooms. The apartments are similar to the doubles except that they have an auxiliary room with two more beds—perfect for friends traveling together or for a family. Outside are large parks, woods, and a pond. Legend has it that the emperor of Austria and the king of Hungary enjoyed the surroundings so much that Count Zichy built the place just to accommodate a royal hunting trip here! It remains a regal and truly lovely place—my highest recommendation.

Dining/Entertainment: The restaurant serves nice, moderately priced meals and offers an English-language menu; you can also eat in a stone-and-brick wine cellar. There's also a coffeehouse with card-playing tables.

Facilities: Two swimming pools (one for children), playground, billiards, sauna; tennis costs 250 Ft ($2.55) per hour.

WHERE TO EAT

Ősfehérvár Restaurant, Koronázó tér 3. ☎ **314-056.**

Cuisine: HUNGARIAN. **Directions:** Walk across from the Garden of Ruins.
Prices: Main courses 150–455 Ft ($1.55–$4.55). AE.
Open: Mon–Fri 11am–11pm, Sat 11am–midnight.

The best place for lunch is directly in the center of town; the food is plentiful and good. In summer you can dine on a second-floor terrace overlooking the Garden of Ruins. A Gypsy band plays on some summer evenings.

Főnix Étterem És Salátabár, Távirda u. 15.

Cuisine: SALAD BAR. **Directions:** From the Garden of Ruins, walk past the Hotel Alba Regia and turn right on Távirda utca; the restaurant is in the rear of a courtyard.
Prices: Average lunch 150–200 Ft. ($1.55–$2.05).
Open: Daily 8am–midnight.

Although tacky and glittery, this place, suitable for lunch or a late-night snack, offers a refreshingly large range of prepared salads. Seating is primarily in the courtyard. Try the "Turmix," a Hungarian fruit milkshake, for 55 Ft (55¢).

23

Northeastern Hungary

Although the Northern Highlands that rise along Hungary's Slovak border are not very high, a leisurely drive through their broad, uncluttered valleys is a perfect plan for a sunny day. Here you can visit the picture-perfect town of Hollókő, or find traces of the Turkish heritage in Eger, explore caves in Aggtelek, and sample fine wine in Tokaj.

SEEING NORTHEASTERN HUNGARY

Eger, Tokaj, and Sárospatak are more or less one after another on the main rail line from Budapest. The best way to get to the Aggtelek Caves is by bus from Budapest or Eger. To get to Hollókő, you'll need to take a bus. Unless you like socialist industrial nightmare cities, you should do your best to bypass the region's largest urban centers, Miskolc and Ózd.

1 Hollókő

62 miles NE of Budapest

GETTING THERE • **By Bus** Buses leave 6 to 10 times a day from Budapest's Erzsébet tér bus station for Szécsény, a 2½ hour ride for 302 Ft ($3.10). From Szécsény, 10 buses a day (5 on Sundays) run to Hollókő for 60 Ft (60¢).

• **By Train** You can also reach Szécsény by train from Budapest's Keleti Station, though you usually have to change at Aszód.

INFORMATION When you arrive in town, stop first at the tourist information office, Kossuth Lajos út 68 (☎ **Hollókő 4**), open daily from 8 am to 5pm. They provide information on the town's few museums, and can make reservations for accommodations (see below). Unfortunately they speak better German than English.

SPECIAL EVENTS Hollókő celebrates Easter in typical folk fashion, and the Palóc Homespun Cultural Days are held here in August.

Holókő is a medieval town that has been preserved so well it's a veritable museum. The houses—with a little judicious reconstruction—have long outlived the 14th-century castle that made the town important in the Middle Ages. The ruins of the castle are a pleasant walk up the hill, but you can't go inside. The town has been promoted into a major tourist stop, and despite the crowds it's still quite pleasant.

WHAT TO SEE & DO

The tiny (three-room) Village Museum (Falumúzeum), Kossuth Lajos út 82, shows everyday life of a Palóc family at the turn of the century. Displays show typical family rooms with wooden rafters on the ceiling, traditional costumes, agricultural tools, and plates on the wall. The museum is open in summer, Wednesday through Sunday from 10am to 4pm; in winter, on Thursday from 10am to 2pm, on Friday from noon to 2pm, and on Saturday and Sunday from 10am to 4pm. Admission is 20 Ft (20¢). To get there, walk downhill from the tourist information office.

Next door is the Postal Museum, at Kossuth Lajos út 78. It's open only from April to October, Tuesday through Sunday from 10am to 5pm. Admission is 30 Ft (30¢). A little farther down is a weaving workshop and store.

You can eat at either of two restaurants in the center of the village: the Vár Étterem, at Kossuth Lajos út 95, or the Muskátli Vendéglő, at Kossuth Lajos út 61.

What's Special About Northeastern Hungary

An Architectural Highlight

- Turkish minaret in Eger, Europe's northernmost.

Castles

- Eger Castle, which long resisted Turkish attacks, now home to an art and history museum.
- Renaissance Sárospatak Castle, surrounded by a moat, filled with art and historical exhibits.

Mansion Hotels

- Hotel Kastély Szirák, near Hollókő, an elegant 18th-century structure with a tennis court and other facilities.
- Hotel Kastlély Acsa, not far from Budapest, a center for horseback riding.
- Gerébi Kastélyszálló, near Kecskemét, with beautiful grounds offering a swimming pool, horseback riding, and tennis.

Natural Spectacles

- 14 miles of underground caves in Aggtelek.

Villages

- Hollókő, a charming Hungarian museum village.

Wine Centers

- Eger, producer of Egri bikavér (Bull's Blood), where a special street boasts 60 cellars serving local wine.
- Tokaj, producer of Tokaji-Aszu and other renowned wines.

WHERE TO STAY

PRIVATE ROOMS You can stay with local families or rent a traditional-style room or house through the tourist information office, Kossuth Lajos út 68 (☎ **Hollókő 4**), open daily from 8am to 5pm. Private rooms in local family homes are available for 20 to 60 DM ($11.75 to $35.30). And for 100 DM ($58.80) and up, you can rent an entire house with one or two bedrooms.

If you arrive when this office is closed, you can arrange a room through tourist officer Ferencné Bugát, who lives at Petőfi u. 16. If you arrive after dark, it will be hard to find her house since the number is not displayed.

If you expect to arrive late, you can reserve a room through Nógrád Tourist in Salgótarján (☎ **32/316-940** or **310-660**).

Nearby Mansion Hotels

Between Budapest and Hollókő, you can stay at a number of mansion hotels.

Hotel Kastély Szirák, Petőfi u. 26, 3044 Szirák. ☎ **60/353-053.** 4 mansion rms, 4 mansion apts. (all with bath). 17 rms in wings (all with bath). TV (with satellite channels) TEL **Directions:** Take the bus (one per day) from Budapest 59 miles away.

Rates (including breakfast): 5,500 Ft ($56.10) mansion double; 5,000 Ft ($51) wing double; 9,500 Ft ($96.95) mansion apt. AE, DC, MC, V.

You'll know you're arriving somewhere special when you first see this stately, two-story facade dating from 1748, and indeed, the property is one of the nicest in Hungary in any price category. The best rooms are in the main mansion itself, its large doubles furnished with antique chairs and tables, old prints on the walls, refrigerators, and large attractive bathrooms. The mansion apartments here represent a memorable splurge, with old-world splendor spread out over two rooms. The wing rooms to the side have newer furniture, but are also quite large and attractively done. The estate has beautiful gardens with a number of quiet paths. I found the quality of service acceptable, but not of quite the same standard of the property.

Dining/Entertainment: The restaurant downstairs is adequate, but undistinguished. Concerts are held once a month in summer in an elegant conference room in the mansion.

Facilities: Sauna, solarium, bicycles—all free of charge. Horseback riding costs 900 Ft ($9.20) per hour; tennis, 300 Ft ($3.05) per hour; indoor rifle range, 8 Ft (8¢) a shot. There's a small art gallery on the second floor as well as an attractive library (though almost all the books are in Hungarian).

Kastélypanzió Váchartyán, Veres Pálné u. 3, 2164 Váchartyán. ☎ **1/121-1014** in Budapest, for reservations. 7 rms (none with bath). **Directions:** Train from Budapest to Váchartyán, only 20 miles northeast of Budapest, then a 10- to 15-minute walk.

Rates (including breakfast): 600 Ft ($6.10) double.

This 200-year-old building is closer to a youth hostel than a mansion hotel, and has some very low riding prices. The rooms are plain but large, with a few prints on the walls and some carpets over the painted yellow floors. The dining room has a faded ceiling fresco, but like much of the place, is a bit run-down; food prices are normal, with full meals $5 to 6. An hour of riding costs 500 Ft ($5.10). Large fields stretch for a long way out back, but you won't find much to do here other than ride horses.

2 Eger

79 miles NE of Budapest

GETTING THERE • By Train From Budapest's Keleti Station, it's two hours by fast train, costing 717 Ft ($7.30) in first class and 478 Ft ($4.90) in second class. From Eger's train station (pályaudvar), it's a 15-minute walk north on Deák Ferenc út to Dobó István tér, the center of town; if you'd rather not walk, take bus no. 3 for three stops and walk east on Bajcsy-Zsilinszky utca for two blocks to reach Dobó István tér.

ESSENTIALS Eger's telephone area code is 36.

ORIENTATION Eger is roughly oval in shape, with the Old Town centered on Dobó István tér, a large pedestrian square. The castle (Vár) is just a block northeast of this square, over a canal. Most other sights, hotels, and restaurants are also within walking distance of Dobó István tér.

The bus station, on Pyrker tér, is about four blocks west of Dobó István tér.

Eger's network of pedestrian streets and narrow one-way streets (not generally marked as such on maps) makes driving in the center particularly confusing.

INFORMATION The Eger branch of Tourinform, at Dobó tér 2 (☎ **36/321-807**), is particularly friendly and clued in. They have a comprehensive list of accommodations in Eger and the surrounding area, as well as plenty of brochures, maps, and books. They also sell current foreign periodicals, including *Time* and *The Economist.* Open May to September, Monday through Friday from 9am to

7pm, Saturday and Sunday from 10am to 6pm; October to April, Monday through Friday from 9am to 5pm, Saturday and Sunday from 9am to 1pm.

SPECIAL EVENTS Eger hosts a baroque music festival in July, and the Eger Vintage Days around grape-harvest time in early September. Organ recitals can be heard all year in the basilica.

Eger is best known for its regional wines, including the red Egri bikavér (Bull's Blood of Eger). Settled very early in Hungarian history, it was, along with Pécs, one of the first five bishoprics founded by King Stephen I in the 11th century. After the Mongol invasion in 1241, construction began on the castle whose ruins now tower over the town. Before the 16th-century Turkish occupation of Hungary, almost 90% of the population harvested grapes for wine. It's no coincidence that Eger today is one of Hungary's liveliest provincial towns. It also shelters a fine array of baroque and rococo architecture.

WHAT TO SEE & DO

Castle Museum, Vár 1. ☎ **312-744.**

The town's main fortification dating back to the 13th century, this castle successfully resisted a famous Turkish attack in 1552. After the Ottoman Empire finally succeeded in overrunning Eger in 1596, they blew up the castle. Viewing the impressive ruins, reconstructed gun ports, and underground passages, you'll understand how a small force could resist intruders for a long time.

The castle museum chronicles the town and castle history, and is located on the hill in a Gothic building that was once the Episcopal Palace. You'll also see a collection of 16th- to 18th-century European paintings, and a display on the execution and torture methods of old.

Admission: Ruins, free; museum, 60 Ft (60¢) adults, 30 Ft (30¢) students.

Open: Ruins, daily 9am–6pm; museum, Tues–Sun 9am–5pm. **Directions:** The entrance is on the south side of the fortress.

Minaret, Harangöntő utca.

Europe's northernmost minaret provides a reminder of the Ottoman Turkish occupation. The 110-foot-tall, 14-sided structure was once joined to a mosque (destroyed in 1841). You can actually climb to the summit, but the crawl space is claustrophobic. It's a terrifying ascent, definitely not recommended for the weak-kneed or weak-hearted. Those who choose to go up (the narrowness of the staircase prevents turning back partway) are rewarded with an outstanding view.

Admission: 20 Ft (25¢).

Open: Sometimes; pay the man at the booth in front, or if he's not there, inquire at the Hotel Minaret, 10 yards away. **Directions:** Walk across from the Minaret Hotel.

Basilica, on Esterházy tér.

The second-largest church in all of Hungary, the basilica was completely rebuilt in neoclassical style in the early 19th century. In front, a stairway leads to a tympanum resting on Corinthian columns. There are columns on either side of the church and the altar. In the main dome above you'll see a painting of the Revelation, completed only in the 1950s. There are organ recitals from time to time; ask at Tourinform.

Admission: Free.

Open: Daily 6am–7pm. **Directions:** Walk down Bajcsy-Zsilinszky utca from Dobó István tér.

Minorite Church, Dobó István tér 4.

Dominating Eger's main square is a fine example of the baroque architecture for which Eger is famous. The church is dedicated to St. Anthony of Padua.

Admission: Free.

Open: Daily 24 hours. **Directions:** Walk to the southeast side of Dobó István tér.

Wine Museum [Bormúzeum], Városfal u. 1. ☎ **313-812.**

The collection here displays old wine presses and racks in a 500-year-old cellar that reputedly held some of Eger's finest wine. You can also sample some of Eger's best red and white vintages of the 1970s, for 50 to 300 Ft (50¢ to $3.05) a glass.

Admission: Free.

Open: Tues–Sat noon–8pm. **Directions:** Walk two blocks north of the bus station.

EVENING ENTERTAINMENT

Eger is famous for its vineyards. You can sample inexpensive local wines in the 60 cellars lining the road through ✪ **Szépasszony-völgy** (The Valley of Beautiful Women), surrounded by forest southwest of the town center. The street is especially active in the late summer. Cellars open about 4pm and close by 8 or 9pm. A few places also stay open in winter.

WHERE TO STAY

PRIVATE ROOMS You can make room arrangements at IBUSZ, at the back of the small walkway at Bajcsy-Zsilinszky tömb (yard), off Bajcsy-Zsilinszky u. 9, a couple of blocks from Dobó István tér (☎ **36/311-451;** fax 36/312-652; telex 63336). Double cost 975 Ft ($9.95). There are apartments available for 2,300 Ft ($23.45). Open Monday through Friday from 8am to noon and 1pm to 4pm.

Another private-room service, Egertourist, is right on the corner of Bajcsy-Zsilinszky u. 9 at the west end of the foot passage (☎ **36/311-724** or **313-249;** fax 36/311-768, telex 63378). Here, doubles are rented for 800 to 1,100 Ft ($8.15 to $11.20), and apartments go for 1,950 Ft ($19.90). The office is open Monday through Friday from 8am to 4:30pm and on Saturday from 8am to 12:30pm.

Hotels

Hotel Minaret, Harangöntő u. 3–5, 3300 Eger. ☎ **36/410-020.** Fax 36/310-713. Telex 61-63-238. 38 rms (35 with bath, 3 with private bath directly across the hall). TEL **Bus:** 10, 11, or 12 from the train station to the central post office; then walk northwest 5 to 10 minutes to the minaret.

Rates (including breakfast): Mar 15–Oct 31, 2,000 Ft ($20.40) single, 3,000 Ft ($30.60) double. Nov 1–Mar 14, 1,500 Ft ($15.30) single, 2,000 Ft ($20.40) double. AE, DC, MC, V.

Adjacent to Eger's minaret, this hotel offers modern rooms without decoration at fine budget prices. The two-story yellow facade dates back to the 17th century. The English-speaking reception also holds the keys to the minaret.

Hotel Korona, Tündérpart 5, 3300 Eger. ☎ **36/313-670.** Fax 36/310-261. 21 rms (all with bath), 3 apts. MINIBAR TV TEL **Directions:** Walk on the pedestrians-only street, Széchenyi utca, to the point where cars are permitted on it; there make a left on Csiky Sándor utca, and a quick right up Tündérpart.

Rates (including breakfast): Apr–Oct, 3,500–4,400 Ft ($35.70–$44.90) double; Nov–Mar, 2,300–3,700 Ft ($23.45–$37.75). AE, MC, V. **Parking:** Free.

This cozy, new hotel is on an extremely steep, quiet street just steps from the center of town. There's an attractive patio for summer dining, and a wine cellar on the premises. The showers are the best I've found in Hungary. The staff is friendly, and the buffet breakfast is a plus over other Hungarian hotels of this category.

Unicornis Hotel, Dr. Hibay Károly u. 2, 3300 Eger. ☎ **36/312-455** or 312-866. 42 rms (16 with bath but no toilet, 3 with shower but no toilet). **Bus:** 3 from the train station.

Rates (including breakfast): 1,360 Ft ($13.90) double without bath or shower, 1,700–1,900 Ft ($17.35–$19.40) double with shower or bath; 2,450 Ft ($25) triple with bath or shower; 3,000 Ft ($30.60) quad with bath or shower.

From the lone musician playing to an empty dining room to tacky wallpaper in standardized doubles to the displays of imported fruit juice by the reception, the Unicornis is a period piece of Communism. Though more tired and run-down than the two choices above, it is well suited to budget travelers in groups of three or four who can share costs in a large room while taking advantage of the central location.

WHERE TO EAT

Fehérszarvas Vadásztanya [White Stag Hunter's Place], Klapka u. 8. ☎ **313-233.**

Cuisine: HUNGARIAN. **Reservations:** Recommended. **Directions:** Walk a block south on Deák Ferenc út from the basilica and turn left.
Prices: Soups 140–170 Ft ($1.45–$1.75); main courses 250–680 Ft ($2.55–$6.95). AE, DC, MC, V.
Open: Dinner only. Wed–Mon 6pm–midnight.

This restaurant is famous all over Hungary for its game specialties, and has won numerous awards. Selections include wild boar, filet of deer, and venison stew. Dozens of antlers, a large deer head, some old guns, and other hunting gear help maintain a game decor. Generous use of onions, paprika, and other spices in their specialties achieve a memorable, tangy flavor. Ask the waiters to serve you wine from their hunting bottles—they shoot it into your glass, or your mouth, from about a yard away. In the autumn they press fresh grape juice. A piano-and-bass duet play in the evening. The restaurant is next door to the Park Hotel.

Talizmán Vendéglő, Kossuth Lajos u. 23. ☎ **410-833.**

Cuisine: HUNGARIAN. **Reservations:** Recommended. **Directions:** Walk 50 yards south from the castle entrance.
Prices: Soups 85–100 Ft (85¢–$1); main courses 210–450 Ft ($2.15–$4.60).
Open: Daily noon–10pm.

Simple and in a basement, the privately owned Talizmán is decorated with wood paneling and cream-colored vaulted ceilings. A house specialty is Alföldi bojtáravató (270 Ft/$2.75), pork with liver, garnished with dill and served with noodles. The dessert *palacsinta* (pancakes) are also renowned. The menu includes an English translation.

Falafel Sálátabár, Dr. Hibay Károly u. 19. ☎ **320-829.**

Cuisine: MIDDLE EASTERN. **Directions:** Walk from Dobó tér across the bridge and bear right to the first corner.
Prices: Stuffed pita bread sandwiches 120 Ft ($1.20).
Open: Mon–Sat 11am–8pm.

This small, simple, and clean place couldn't be more central. For only 120 Ft ($1.20) you can fill a pita pocket (in a plastic sleeve to avoid mess) with a satisfactory selection of chopped vegetables, sauces, and falafel. Seating is upstairs.

3 Aggtelek

140 miles NE of Budapest.

GETTING THERE • By Bus An express bus leaves Budapest's Népstadion bus station Monday through Friday at 6:15am, stopping in Eger at 8:15am, and reaching Aggtelek about 11:05. The bus returns from Aggtelek to Eger and Budapest at 3pm. The fare is 640 Ft ($6.55) from Budapest and 406 Ft ($4.15) from Eger.

ESSENTIALS Aggtelek's telephone area code is 48.

Aggtelek is famous in Europe for its cave systems. The caves (*barlang,* as they are known in Hungarian) have been inhabited, or at least visited, since Neolithic times, and the remains of early explorers have been found in the main Baradla Cave, in Aggtelek National Park (☎ **48/343-073**). The stalactite cave system continues for 14 miles, 3 miles of which meander into Slovak territory.

Temperatures are a constant 50° to 52° Fahrenheit and it's very damp, so bring appropriate clothing and sturdy shoes. The caves, well lit and safe, can only be seen on a one-hour tour, starting at 10am, 1pm, and 3pm (May to September also at 5pm), which costs 150 Ft ($1.55) for adults and 75 Ft (75¢) for children (free for children under 6). Inquire about longer, more rigorous, more beautiful cave tours, most of which leave from the Josvafu cave entrance on the other side of the mountain, a 6km (3½ mile) bus ride away.

WHERE TO STAY

Hotel Cseppkő, Aggtelek. ☎ **48/343-075.** Telex 64331. 70 rms (all with bath). TEL

Directions: Buses arriving in town park here.

Rates (including breakfast): 2,100 Ft ($21.40) double. AE, V.

Renovated in 1989, this hotel is 300 meters from the caves and convenient for those who want to spend some time exploring the area. The rooms are fairly modern but not extensively decorated. There's a restaurant downstairs.

4 Sárospatak

155 miles NE of Budapest

GETTING THERE • By Train A fast train from Budapest takes 3⅔ hours and costs 748 Ft ($7.65) in second class and 1,122 Ft ($11.45) in first class.

ESSENTIALS Sárospatak's telephone area code is 41.

ORIENTATION The train and bus stations are right next to each other on the northeast side of town. To get into town, simply walk through the park and then turn right on Rákóczi út. You can also take a taxi from the train station into town. Most of the town, including the famous Sárospatak Castle, runs parallel to the Bodrog River.

INFORMATION Borsod Tourist, across from the church at Kossuth Lajos út 50 (☎ **41/323-073**), is open May to September, Monday through Saturday from 8am to 5pm; October to April, Monday through Friday from 9am to 3pm. It gives tourist information but no English is spoken. They also rent private rooms. It's located on a street parallel to Rákóczi út, a block closer to the river.

Since the 16th century Sárospatak, a very small town, has been famous for its Calvinist College, but today the main attraction is its castle. Although it's the sleepiest, most provincial Hungarian town in this book, Sárospatak boasts some very striking modern buildings by Imre Mákovecs, a path-breaking Hungarian architect. Check out the complex between the two department stores in the center of town.

WHAT TO SEE & DO

Rákóczi Castle, Kádár Kata u. 21. ☎ **323-083.**

Dating back to the 11th century, most of the castle has a late Renaissance facade. The oldest remaining part is the six-story Red Tower from the late 15th century, and a moat (now dry) still surrounds the entire structure.

The castle grew in importance after it was taken over by the Rákóczi family in the 17th century. Transylvanian princes, the Rákóczis came to rule Sárospatak by marriage, beginning in 1616. Later, the Habsburgs captured the castle after quashing a rebellion led by Ferenc Rákóczi from 1703 to 1711.

As Transylvania was a principality very rich in art and culture, the castle's museum has a gorgeous exhibition of well-preserved treasures. Highlights include elegant rooms with inlaid wooden cabinets, furniture, guns, glass, coins, and painting. For information on the castle and the rest of the town, be sure to ask at the entrance for the informative booklet in English for 50 Ft (50¢).

Admission: 50 Ft (50¢) adults, free for children.

Open: Apr–Oct, Tues–Sun 10am–6pm; Nov–Mar, Tues–Sun 9am–4pm. **Directions:** Walk five minutes south of the Borsod Tourist office.

Castle Church [Vár Templom], Kádár Kata u.

First built in the 14th-century Gothic style, the Castle Church has accommodated both Catholics and Calvinists, with Jesuits and Calvinists in control twice in its history. There's a small church description posted inside near the entrance. Outside you'll see a statue of St. Elizabeth (on horseback) by Hungary's most noted modern sculptor, Imre Varga.

Admission: 10 Ft (10¢).

Open: Tue–Sat 10am–3pm, Sun noon–3pm. **Directions:** Walk half a block south of the Borsod Tourist office.

WHERE TO STAY

PRIVATE ROOMS Borsod Tourist, Kossuth Lajos út 50 (☎ **41/323-073**), rents doubles for 1,200 to 1,400 Ft ($12.25 to $14.30). Open May to September, Monday through Saturday from 8am to 5pm; October to April, Monday through Friday from 9am to 3pm.

Hotels

Hotel Bodrog, Rákóczi út 58, 3950 Sárospatak. ☎ **41/323-744.** Fax 41/323-527. 50 rms (all with bath).

Rates: 2,200–3,300 Ft ($22.45–$33.65) double. Breakfast 200 Ft ($2.05) per person extra.

A typical concrete Communist leftover, this establishment has large, airy rooms (some with balconies) and a good location, though the bathrooms are old. The restaurant here is not attractive, but it has decent food and is open late in the summer.

Hotel Borostyán, Kádár Kata u. 28, 3950 Sárospatak. ☎ **41/324-611.** Fax 41/323-551. Telex. 62717. 13 rms (5 with bath). TEL

Rates: 1,500 Ft ($15.30) double without bath, 1,800 Ft ($18.35) double with bath.

A two-story stone structure across from the castle, this hotel dates from 1694. Rooms on the ground floor have high arches, dark wood, and white plaster walls, which, combined with the attractive new furniture, make this the top hotel in town, as long as you get a room with bath. The restaurant is satisfactory.

5 Tokaj

145 miles NE of Budapest

GETTING THERE • By Train From Budapest, travel first to Miskolc (2 hours), then change to a train for Tokaj (another 40 minutes). Depending on connection time, the trip takes three to five hours. Tickets cost 1,047 Ft ($10.70) in first class and 698 Ft ($7.10) in second class.

ESSENTIALS Tokaj's telephone area code is 41.

SPECIAL EVENTS There's the Tokaj Harvest Days from mid-September to mid-October.

If you know of Tokaj's centuries-old international reputation for excellent wine ("C'est le roi des vins et le vin des rois," Louis XV once said), you may be surprised to find it just a small peasant town between a hill and a river. The famous vineyards and rich soil of Tokaj lie in the surrounding area.

WHAT TO SEE & DO

Few tourists are ever seen here; visit only if you want to stock up on wine or enjoy the slow pace of a small Magyar town.

Among Tokaj's large wine selection, my favorite pick is Tokaj-Aszu, a delicious sweet dessert wine. A choice place to sample and purchase wine is the massive Rákóczi Pince at Kossuth tér 13, on the main square next to the church.

The Town Museum, across the square at Bethlen Gabor u. 7 (☎ **41/352-636**), chronicles the development of the 900-year-old wine industry in Tokaj, along with some local history. Downstairs there's a small collection of religious art, and upstairs, objects from the town's history. On the third floor you can see old wine presses and vintage bottles of Tokaj's wines. Ask for the short English text that summarizes the museum's collection. The museum is open Tuesday through Sunday from 9am to 5pm; from October to April, it closes at 3pm. Admission is 24 Ft (25¢) for adults and 10 Ft (10¢) for children. You get a free postcard.

WHERE TO STAY

Hotel Tokaj, Rákóczi út 5,3910 Tokaj. ☎ **41/352-344.** Fax 41/352-759. 42 rms (all with bath or shower). **Directions:** Walk to the south end of town.

Rates: 1,800 Ft ($18.35) double with shower, 2,300 Ft ($23.45) double with bath. Breakfast 200 Ft ($2.05) extra.

The town's only hotel is a modern concrete-block construction, and can be easily identified by its distinctive rainbow-colored roof and bubble windows on the top floor. Rooms with a bathtub have a balcony and a view. Downstairs there's a lobby bar and restaurant.

24 Southern Hungary

SOUTHERN HUNGARY IS THE MAGYAR EQUIVALENT OF THE AMERICAN WEST'S WIDE open spaces, yet its major centers lie within three hours' rail travel from Budapest. Many tourists stop in Pécs, which spills down a hillside in the gentle uplands between Lake Balaton and the Danube, to visit its well-preserved Old Town and excellent museums, and to see the remains of the Turkish occupation of Hungary. Kecskemét and Szeged are farther east, in the Hungarian Great Plain. Bugac National Park, near Kecskemét, is the best place to understand the equestrian traditions of the Great Plain, and Kecskemét itself is fairly attractive. Although Szeged is visually rather ordinary, as Hungary's spice capital it's an excellent place to appreciate the country's cuisine. Kecskemét and Szeged are conveniently on the same train route from Budapest. Pécs is on a different line, and Pécs–Szeged train connections are poor—take the bus instead.

1 Pécs

123 miles SW of Budapest

GETTING THERE • By Train Fast trains from Budapest arrive in just over three hours, for 1,047 Ft ($10.70) in first class and 698 Ft ($7.10) in second class.

ESSENTIALS Pécs's telephone area code is 72.

ORIENTATION The center of town is Széchenyi tér, a square with Hungary's largest Turkish mosque as well as the tourist office. The Old Town, with its cafés, stores, and shoppers, surrounds the square, and is itself surrounded by a major ring boulevard.

Pécs's train station, on Indóház tér, is in the southern part of the city at the south end of Szabadság utca. Take bus no. 30, 32, or 33 to the center. The bus station is also on the south side of town at the southern end of Bajcsy-Zsilinszky utca (the extension of Irgalmasok utcája). Take bus no. 30, 32, or 33 north of this street. The bus station has a 25 Ft (25¢) luggage-check service next to the information desk, open daily from 6am to 6pm.

INFORMATION The Pécs branch of Tourinform is at Széchenyi tér 9, on the town's main square (☎ **72/413-315;** fax 72/412-632). From June 16 through August, it's open Monday through Friday from 9am to 7pm, Saturday and Sunday from 9am to 4pm. From September 1 to October 15 and from April 1 to June 15, it's open Monday through Friday from 9am to 5pm and on Saturday from 9am to 4pm. From October 16 through March, opening hours are Monday through Friday from 8am to 4pm.

SPECIAL EVENTS There's the Pécs Summer Theater from June to early August, and also organ concerts in the cathedral April to October.

Pécs (pronounced "Paych") and the surrounding countryside south of Lake Balaton make up a pleasant and fertile region. The temperate climate is one of the mildest in Hungary, with comfortable summers and warm, but not too wet, winters. The major town of the region, Pécs (pop. 200,000) is the fifth-largest city in Hungary.

Although Pécs is a large, fairly cosmopolitan city, its quaint streets suggest smaller villages. Not only does the town have picturesque neighborhoods, but it hosts many museums and churches, making it an important stop on all but the most hurried visits to Hungary.

What's Special About Southern Hungary

Activities

- Horse riding in Bugac, on the Puszta outside Kecskemét.

Architectural Highlights

- Mosque of Pasha Gazi Kassim in Pécs, the largest surviving Turkish building in Hungary.
- Szeged's synagogue, one of Central Europe's grandest.
- Cathedral of Pécs, with foundations dating back to the 11th century.

Museums

- Kecskemét Art Gallery, in a distinctive art deco palace.
- Naïve Art Gallery, in Kecskemét, where local peasant art is shown and sold at moderate prices.
- Toy Museum, in Kecskemét, the largest in Eastern Europe.
- Museum of Jakowali Hassan, in Pécs, showing Turkish-era objects in a former mosque with the minaret still attached.
- Vasarely Museum, in Pécs, at the birthplace of the originator of op art.
- Zsolnay Ceramics Exhibition, in Pécs, featuring the glazed eosine technique.

A Brief History

Pécs was the site of a major Roman settlement, called Sopianae, which was at the junction of several major trade routes. In 1367 Pécs opened the first university in Hungary, the fifth in Europe. From 1543 until 1686 the Ottoman Turks controlled Pécs; during this 143-year period Pécs took on the bustling appearance of a Turkish city as churches were converted to mosques and baths were built.

After the Turkish occupation, Pécs remained an important university center.

WHAT TO SEE & DO

An Orientation Stroll

Begin your sightseeing on Széchenyi tér, the main square dominated by the Mosque of Pasha Gazi Kassim on the north side. At the southernmost end of the square is an eosine ceramic fountain, built on the site of an old Turkish well; it's opposite the elegant Town Hall. Also on the square is an equestrian statue of János Hunyadi, one of Hungary's greatest generals against the Turks. It was raised in 1954, the 500th anniversary of the Battle of Belgrade that forestalled the Turkish conquest by 75 years.

Now go one block north of Széchenyi tér to Káptalan utca. Turn left on this street and you'll pass a succession of museums including the Vasarely Museum and the Zsolnay Ceramics Exhibition (see below).

At the end of this street you arrive at Dóm tér, site of the Cathedral of Pécs on the north side of the square, and the Csontváry Museum near the southeast side (see below).

If you continue west one block from Dóm tér you can see the remains of the old town walls; the circular Barbakán is the best-preserved segment. They were used to repel foreign attack from about the 13th century until the early 18th century and represent some of the best remaining medieval fortifications in Hungary.

Walk south along the fortifications one long block on Klimó György utca and turn left onto Ferencesek utcája. Since medieval times merchants have traded here and even today it's an important shopping street. After a few minutes you'll arrive back at Széchenyi tér.

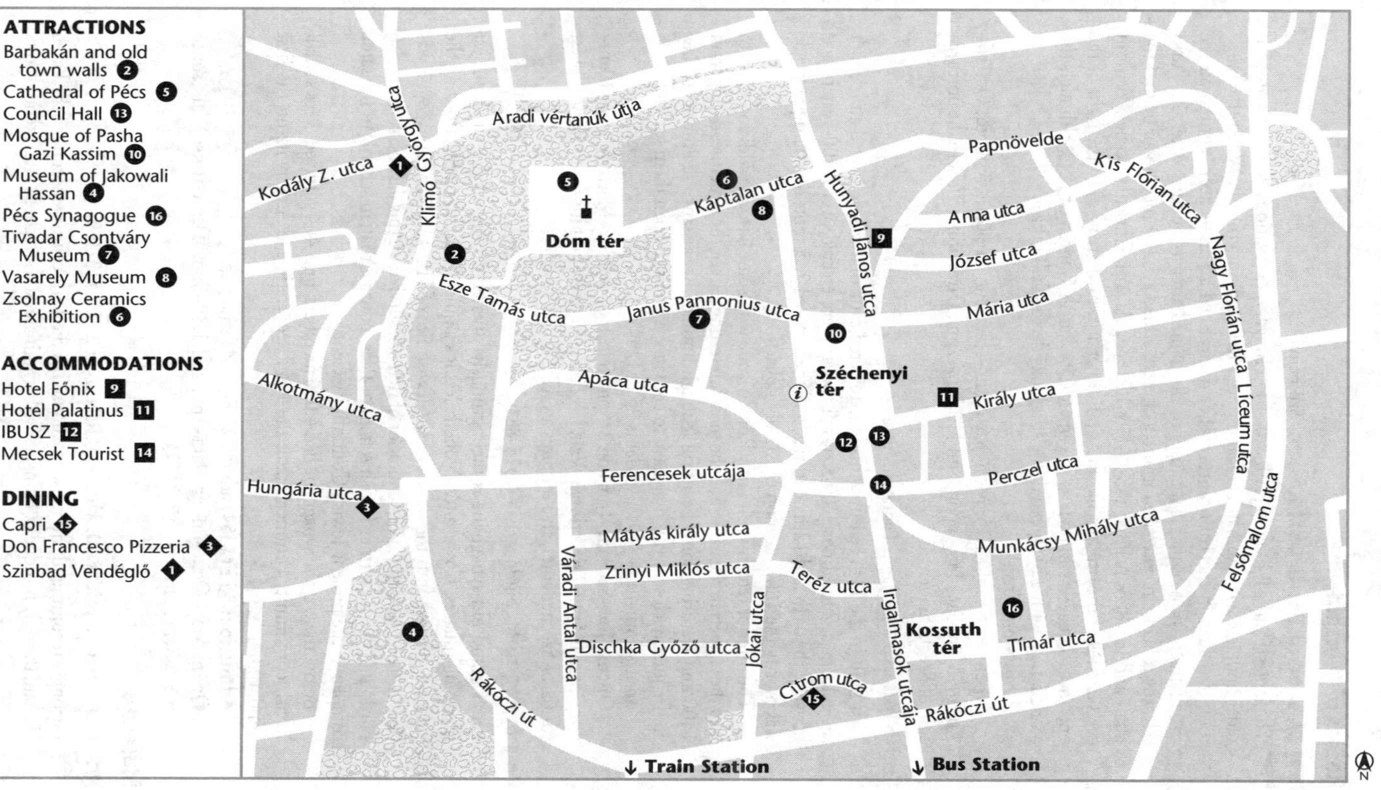
ATTRACTIONS
Barbakán and old town walls 2
Cathedral of Pécs 5
Council Hall 13
Mosque of Pasha Gazi Kassim 10
Museum of Jakowali Hassan 4
Pécs Synagogue 16
Tivadar Csontváry Museum 7
Vasarely Museum 8
Zsolnay Ceramics Exhibition 6
ACCOMMODATIONS
Hotel Főnix 9
Hotel Palatinus 11
IBUSZ 12
Mecsek Tourist 14
DINING
Capri 15
Don Francesco Pizzeria 3
Szinbad Vendéglő 1
Aradi vértanúk útja
Kodály Z. utca
Klimó György utca
Dóm tér
Káptalan utca
Hunyadi János utca
Papnövelde
Kis Flórian utca
Anna utca
József utca
Mária utca
Nagy Flórián utca
Líceum utca
Felsőmalom utca
Esze Tamás utca
Janus Pannonius utca
Széchenyi tér
Apáca utca
Alkotmány utca
Király utca
Ferencesek utcája
Perczel utca
Hungária utca
Mátyás király utca
Munkácsy Mihály utca
Zrinyi Miklós utca
Teréz utca
Váradi Antal utca
Jókai utca
Irgalmasok utcája
Kossuth tér
Tímár utca
Dischka Győző utca
Citrom utca
Rákóczi út
Rákóczi út
Train Station
Bus Station
N
Church
Information

Pécs

Houses of Worship

Mosque of Pasha Gazi Kassim, Széchenyi tér.

The largest Turkish building still extant in Hungary, excavations here show an even older heritage, with Roman-era tombs recently found underneath. When the Turks took over Pécs in the 16th century, they demolished a 13th-century church on the site to erect this mosque; it was supposedly named after its builder. After the Turks left, town planners converted it into a church, added a 3,200-pipe organ behind the altar, and in 1883, painted the 90-foot-high cupola with Christian scenes. You can see sketches of the original mosque and minaret (now destroyed) to the right of the entrance. Today it's known as the Inner City Parish Church of Pécs, although the stone facade with a big green dome still looks decidedly Turkish.

Admission: Free.

Open: Apr 15–Oct 15, Mon–Sat 10am–4pm, Sun 11:30am–3:30pm; Oct 16–Apr 14, Mon–Sat 11am–noon, Sun 11:30am–2pm. **Directions:** Walk to the northern side of Széchenyi tér.

Cathedral of Pécs, Janus Pannonius utca.

First built in the 11th century, this four-towered cathedral was destroyed and rebuilt several times. The almost-200-foot-tall towers were erected over a 100-year period between the 11th and 12th centuries, and the restored 225-foot-long baroque facade was mostly the 1807 creation of Mihály Pollack.

The interior remains primarily Romanesque with some baroque additions. Try to visit the chapels in the cathedral, the most interesting part of the structure, dating from 1400 and featuring some beautiful (though limited) Renaissance sculpture; as they are frequently closed, you may have to convince a priest to open them for you.

Admission: 40 Ft (40¢), students 25 Ft (25¢).

Open: Mon–Sat 9am–1pm and 2–5pm, Sun 1–5pm; Nov–Mar, Mon–Sat 10am–4pm, Sun 1–5pm. **Directions:** Walk left down Janus Pannonius from the northwest corner of Széchenyi tér, five minutes away.

Pécs Synagogue, Fürdő u. 1. ☎ **315-881.**

Pécs's grand old synagogue is incongruously situated on one of the city's busiest shopping squares, Kossuth tér. Nonetheless it's a quiet, peaceful place, affording the visitor a glimpse into the once-vibrant Jewish life of Hungary. The synagogue was built in 1869, and the original interior of rich oak survives to this day. Next door (also Fürdő u. 1) is the former Jewish school of Pécs, now a Croatian school. In the same complex is the present Jewish Community Center.

Before the war the synagogue had 4,000 members; only 464 survived. Pécs's small Jewish community commemorates the 1944 deportation to Auschwitz on the first Sunday after July 4.

Admission: 35 Ft (35¢) adults, 25 Ft (25¢) students.

Open: May–Oct, Sun–Fri 9am–1pm and 1:30–5pm. **Directions:** Walk south from Széchenyi tér.

Museums

Museum of Jakowali Hassan, Rákóczi út 2. ☎ **413-300.**

I strongly recommend this museum, housed in the 16th-century mosque of the Pasha Hassan, the only mosque in Hungary with its minaret still attached. The interior shows off original religious objects that have either been preserved or imported (thanks to a massive gift from the Turks).

Admission: 30 Ft (30¢).

Open: Thurs–Tues 10am–2pm. **Directions:** Walk a few minutes south of the Barbakán down Klimó György utca.

Tivadar Csontváry Museum, Janus Pannonius u. 11. ☎ **310-544.**

Right across from the diminutive statue of Tivadar Csontváry near the Pécs Cathedral you'll find his museum. Csontváry is an international award-winning painter who was a big hit at the Paris World's Fair, and he is credited with early work in expressionism and surrealism.

Admission: 50 Ft (50¢) adults, free for students.

Open: Tues–Sun 10am–6pm. **Directions:** From the Cathedral of Pécs, walk across the small park in front and continue left down Janus Pannonius utca half a block.

★ **Vasarely Museum,** Káptalan u. 3. ☎ **324-822.**

If you're in the mood for modern art, try the lines, boxes, and geometrical squiggles of Hungary's most famous modern artist, Victor Vasarely. The master who originated op art was born in this house in 1908.

Admission: 50 Ft (50¢) adults, free for students.

Open: Tues–Sun 10am–6pm. **Directions:** Walk east from Dóm tér, site of the cathedral.

★ **Zsolnay Ceramics Exhibition,** Káptalan u. 2. ☎ **324-822.**

Zsolnay's brilliance and eccentricity makes this one of the more interesting ceramics exhibits I've seen. World-famous eosine pottery is on display. This kind of pottery has a highly finished glaze polished to a glossy, mirrorlike intensity.

Admission: 50 Ft (50¢) adults, free for students.

Open: Tues–Sun 10am–6pm. **Directions:** Walk across the street from the Vasarely Museum.

WHERE TO STAY

PRIVATE ROOMS Mecsek Tourist, at Széchenyi tér 1 (☎ **72/413-300;** fax 72/412-044), rents doubles for 1,100 Ft ($11.20). It's open Monday through Friday from 8am to 3pm, and on Saturday from 9am to 1pm. American Express and MasterCard accepted.

IBUSZ, at Széchenyi tér 8 (☎ **72/412-176;** fax 72/411-011), rents singles for 800 Ft ($8.15), doubles for 1,100 Ft ($11.20), and triples for 1,600 Ft ($16.35). The office is open Monday through Thursday from 8am to 4pm, and on Friday from 8am to 3pm; and from May through August, also on Saturday from 8am to noon.

Hotels

$ **Hotel Főnix [Phoenix],** Hunyadi János út 2, 7621 Pécs. ☎ **72/311-680.** 14 rms (1 with toilet, 13 with shower but no toilet), 1 apt. MINIBAR TV **Directions:** Exit Széchenyi tér to the northeast and continue a block.

Rates (including breakfast): 2,090 Ft ($21.35) single; 3,040 Ft ($31.55) double; 3,690 Ft ($37.50) triple; 5,190 Ft ($52.95) apt. AE, DC, MC, V. Rooms with toilet cost the same as those without.

I highly recommend this hotel uniquely decorated in revivalist Hungarian art deco. The rooms are all different and designed in odd shapes and angles, but each is spotless, very modern, and a little cramped, and each has a radio and a refrigerator. The apartment, with two huge bedrooms and a living room, has a separate entrance directly off the street and makes a great splurge or place for several friends.

Kertész Panzió, Sáfrány u. 42, Pécs 7620. ☎ **72/327-551.** 5 rms (all with bath), 2 apts. TV **Bus:** 32 or 36 to the MTA Székház stop.

Rates: 2,500 Ft ($25.50) double; 4,400 Ft ($44.90) quad; 3,000 Ft ($30.60) apt. Extra bed 500 Ft ($5.10). Breakfast 200 Ft ($2.05) extra. **Parking:** Free in enclosed lot.

At this small pension in the hills surrounding central Pécs, a quiet, family-run establishment, you can unwind after touring the city. Some of the rooms have balconies, and the quad and apartments are duplexes.

Worth the Extra Money

Hotel Palatinus, Király u. 5, 7621 Pécs. ☎ **72/433-022.** Fax 72/432-261. 88 rms (all with bath), 12 apts. MINIBAR TV TEL **Directions:** Walk down Király utca from Széchenyi tér.

Rates (including breakfast): Apr–Oct, 102 DM ($60) double; 177 DM ($104.10) apt. Nov–Mar, 82 DM ($48.25) single or double; 134 DM ($78.80) apt. AE, DC, MC, V.

This hotel re-creates turn-of-the-century elegance. You encounter a dazzling array of art deco detail in the lobby, and a large marble staircase to the side; even the key chain to your room looks as if it dates back to the 1920s. During that era, Béla Bartók gave concerts in the second-floor hall. The rooms themselves feature clean, modern facilities, all with refrigerators and some with attractive views over the city. The reception offers a range of services such as photocopying and safe-deposit box. A Hungar Hotel.

Facilities: Bowling alley, sauna, massage, solarium (free). You can also use the swimming pool of the Hotel Hullám, 10 minutes away.

WHERE TO EAT

Xavér Söröző, Alkotmány u. 44. ☎ **324-290.**

Cuisine: HUNGARIAN. **Bus:** 33, 35, or 37. **Directions:** Walk west from the Barbakán down Báthory utca; turn left at the end of the street and then right along Alkotmány.
Prices: Soups 40–100 Ft (40¢–$1); main courses 190–380 Ft ($1.95–$2.85).
Open: Mon–Sat 9am–11pm, Sun 10am–4pm.

A few minutes' walk outside the ring road, this budget bargain near the corner of Petőfi Sándor út attracts many students during the school year. The concrete building has an interesting latticework interior and a cool, shaded terrace; at lunch it gets a lot of light from the large windows. Try the tasty turkey filet, very generously topped with cheese. Another plus here are much larger portions than in many of the restaurants in the center. An annex, open Monday through Friday from 11am to 10pm, sells salads by weight.

Szinbád Vendéglő, Kodály Zoltán u. 1.

Cuisine: HUNGARIAN. **Directions:** Walk north on Klimó György utca to the intersection of Kodály Zoltán utca.
Prices: Main courses 200–400 Ft ($2.05–$4.10); complete lunch 160 Ft ($1.65).
Open: Daily noon–midnight.

Across the street from the Barbakán, the Szinbád offers an authentic, inexpensive Hungarian dining experience. It's a cozy neighborhood eatery with a coffee bar and outdoor dining area in summer. The daily "menu" consists of soup, salad, and main course—for 160 Ft ($1.65), this is the quintessential budget meal.

Don Francesco Pizzeria, Hungária u. 3.

Cuisine: PIZZA/HUNGARIAN. **Directions:** Walk west on Ferencesek utcája until it turns into Hungária utca.
Prices: Pizza 130–190 Ft ($1.35–$1.95); pasta 180–420 Ft ($1.85–$4.30); Hungarian main courses 180–230 Ft ($1.85–$2.35).
Open: Mon–Sat noon–1am, Sun noon–midnight.

Pécs's late-night hangout, Don Francesco is reputed to serve the best pizza in town. The entrance looks unwelcoming, but then you descend into a clean, cool beer cellar with two separate dining areas. German beer is available on draft.

For Dessert

Capri, Citrom u. 7. ☎ **319-713.**

Cuisine: ICE CREAM. **Directions:** Walk three blocks south from Széchenyi tér, then turn right.
Prices: 15 Ft (15¢) per scoop.
Open: Coffeehouse, Mon–Sat 10am–9pm; ice-cream parlor, Mon–Sat 10am–8pm.

Enjoy gelato-style ice cream either in an often-crowded take-out section, or in an attractive modern café in a pleasant courtyard. Not worth a special trip.

2 Kecskemét & the Puszta

53 miles SE of Budapest, 52 NW of Szeged

GETTING THERE • **By Train** An express train from Budapest to Kecskemét takes just under 1½ hours and costs 537 Ft ($5.50) in first class and 358 Ft ($3.65) in second class. Szeged is an hour farther south.

ESSENTIALS Kecskemét's telephone area code is 76.

ORIENTATION From the train station, cross the park and walk straight south down Rákóczi út, a boulevard with trees lining a pedestrian path in the middle. At Szabadság tér the street widens into a pedestrian mall at the center of town. About two blocks farther on you'll reach the adjacent Kossuth tér, the main square, with the Town Hall to your left. These two attractive squares form the heart of Kecskemét. Petőfi Sándor utca, a street leading to several museums, begins south of Kossuth tér.

INFORMATION Kecskemét's Tourinform branch is in a corner of the Town Hall building at Kossuth tér 1 (☎ **76/481-065**). They will load you up with brochures and fill you in on events and festivals in Kecskemét. Opening hours from April to September are Monday through Friday from 9am to 6pm, Saturday and Sunday from 9am to 1pm. From October to April they're open Monday through Friday from 8am to 4pm.

SPECIAL EVENTS Kecskemét's Spring Festival in March, in conjunction with the Budapest Spring Festival, brings many street merchants to the center of town and open-air dances, concerts, and other events. There's also Kecskemét Days, an agricultural festival in the beginning of September.

At the center of the Hungarian Great Plain is medium-sized Kecskemét (pronounced "*Ketch*-keh-mayt"), a slow-paced city of wide squares, pedestrian promenades, and green parks. A series of 17th- to 19th-century churches rings the main square, except for the St. Miklós Church, which was built on medieval foundations—part of which poke out into the square itself. Kecskemét also boasts some nice art nouveau buildings, and a sizable collection of museums.

WHAT TO SEE & DO

Town Hall, Kossuth tér.

Built at the end of the 19th century, it's the most noted structure on the main square. Although the interior is otherwise closed to tourists, you'll hear the beautiful carillon bells (called Harangjáték) throughout the day. On the hour from 7am to 11am, 1 to 5pm, and at 7pm they play two folk songs about Kecskemét; at 12:05pm they play the folk tunes plus two works by Zoltán Kodály, the noted Hungarian composer who was born in Kecskemét; at 6:05pm they play the folk tunes as well as works by Handel, Mozart, and Beethoven's "Ode to Joy"; finally at 8pm they ring forth the folk songs plus three folk pieces about the sunset and the stars.

Admission: 10 Ft (10¢).

Open: Mon–Fri noon–4pm, except when meetings are in session. **Directions:** Walk to the southeast side of Kossuth tér.

Kecskemét Art Gallery [Kecskeméti Galéria], Rákóczi út 1. ☎ **321-776.**

Located in the Cifra (Ornamental) Palace, one of Kecskemét's most distinctive art deco facades from 1902, this fairly large museum shows off 19th- and 20th-century Hungarian painting. Inside you'll also see the large ballroom that served as the town casino before 1940. Balls and dancing classes are held in the room today. Directly across the street you'll see the white House of Science and Technology, once the town synagogue.

Admission: 30 Ft (30¢) adults, 15 Ft (15¢) students.

Open: Tues–Sun 10am–5pm. **Directions:** Walk to the northeast corner of Szabadság tér, across from the Reform Museum.

Hungarian Photography Museum [Magyar Fotografiai Múzeum], Katona József tér 12. ☎ **483-221.**

This is Hungary's main photography museum. Exhibits change regularly; on my last visit it had an evocative display of portraits of Hungarians in the 1930s by Sándor Gönci. A small shop sells postcards and photo books.

Admission: 50 Ft (50¢), adults, 30 Ft (30¢) children and students.

Open: Wed–Sun 10am–5pm. **Directions:** Walk a block east of Kossuth tér.

Naïve Art Collection [Naiv Művészeti Galéria], Gáspár András u. 11. ☎ **324-767.**

A gallery of folk-art paintings, wooden sculptures, and other art executed in the last few decades by local artists. Most portray rural life and small towns. In the downstairs gallery you can also buy the works, which range in price from 1,000 to 20,000 Ft ($10.20 to $204).

Admission: 20 Ft (20¢) adults, 10 Ft (10¢) students.

Open: Tues–Sun 10am–5pm. **Directions:** Walk from Kossuth tér south on Petőfi Sándor utca, and turn right behind the first large apartment building.

Toy Museum, Gáspár András u. 11. ☎ **481-469.**

The largest toy museum in Eastern Europe, with a charming collection of old toys, dolls, puppets, books, and dollhouses.

Admission: 20 Ft (20¢) adults, 10 Ft (10¢) students and children.

Open: Tues–Sun 9am–5pm. **Directions:** Walk next door from the Naïve Art Museum.

Reformation Museum, Szabadság tér 7.

A collection of objects associated with the reform Presbyterian church, with old songbooks from Transylvania, chalices, and other church possessions. Many of the objects—which date back hundreds of years—were made by parishioners and given to the church.

Admission: 20 Ft (20¢).

Open: Tues–Sun 9am–5pm. **Directions:** Walk to the northeast corner of Szabadság tér, and around the corner.

WHERE TO STAY

PRIVATE ROOMS You can rent private rooms from the centrally located Puszta Tourist, Szabadság tér 2 (☎ **483-493**), for 1,000 Ft ($10.20) double. It's open Monday through Friday from 7:30am to 4pm.

Prices are similar at IBUSZ, Széchenyi tér 1–3 (☎ **76/322-955**), open Monday through Friday from 7:30am to 4pm.

A Hotel in the Town Center

Hotel Három Gúnár, Batthyány u. 1–7, 6000 Kecskemét. ☎ **76/483-611.** 45 rms (all with bath). 5 apartments. MINIBAR TV TEL **Bus:** 7 from the train station.

Rates (including breakfast): Apr–Oct, 2,750 Ft ($28.05) single; 3,300–3,800 Ft ($33.70–$38.80) double; 4,950 Ft ($50.50) triple or apartment. Nov–Mar, 10% less. AE, CB, DC, MC, V. **Parking:** Free.

This comfortable hotel has an attractive modern lobby and stylishly furnished rooms with small bathrooms. The oddest feature of this hotel is a mini-bowling alley in the cellar (120 Ft/$1.25 per half hour), which makes a bit of noise for rooms on the ground floor. Rooms in the back on the second floor are the quietest. The restaurant is recommended below (see "Where to Eat"), and there's a pleasant bar. The hotel is located two blocks from Kossuth tér in the center of town.

A Nearby Mansion Hotel

Gerébi Kastélyszálló, Alsólajos 224, 6050 Lajosmizse. ☎ **and fax 76/356-045.** 11 mansion rms, 39 motel rms (all with bath). TV **Directions:** Take the train to Lajosmizse and they may pick you up at the station if you call ahead; or take a taxi from Kecskemét, 12 miles away, for about 1,000 Ft ($10.20).

Rates (including buffet breakfast): Apr–Oct, 75 DM ($44.10) mansion room; 60 DM ($35.30) motel room. Nov–Mar, 65 DM ($38.25) mansion room; 50 DM ($29.40) motel room. AE, DC, MC, V.

Surrounded by fields and forests, this mansion was once owned by an important pre–World War I Hungarian economist and is a fine place for a day or two of relaxation. The mansion rooms in the main house have TV, radio, and refrigerator along with wooden ceilings and dark-wood furniture—tasteful but not dazzling. The motel rooms in a nearby annex are simply furnished, with white walls and tiny bathrooms—fairly modest facilities considering the majestic landscape around. Although the landscape and public facilities are great here, the rooms are less regal than in some other mansion hotels; it's especially worthwhile if you won't have a chance to stay in some of these other Hungarian mansions.

Dining: There's a restaurant with live Gypsy music.

Facilities: Outdoor swimming pool, bicycles. Two tennis courts rent for 6 DM ($3.55) an hour including racquets and balls; horseback riding costs 15 DM ($8.80) an hour, riding instruction is 20 DM ($11.75) an hour, coach rides are 55 DM ($32.35) an hour (for up to 15 people), and horse shows cost 12 to 15 DM ($7.05 to $8.80) per person. Hunting is also possible.

WHERE TO EAT

Három Gúnár Fogadó, Batthyány u. 1–7. ☎ **483-611.**

Cuisine: HUNGARIAN. **Reservations:** Recommended. **Directions:** Exit Kossuth tér to the southeast, bear right on Kisfaludy utca, and enter on the other side from the hotel.
Prices: Soups 70–140 Ft (70¢–$1.40); main courses 180–630 Ft ($1.85–$6.45).
Open: Sun–Thurs 6:30am–11pm, Fri–Sat 6:30am–midnight.

Small and very attractive, with large windows, marble floors, and dark-wood columns, this restaurant has a large bar and a modern bistro atmosphere. *Gúnár* in the restaurant's name means "goose," and it appears in several places on the menu. A house specialty is a fine veal chop with goose liver served with rice and potatoes for 400 Ft ($4.10). The sour-cherry soup (in season) makes a delicious appetizer for 80 Ft (80¢).

An Excursion to the Puszta in Bugac

The Puszta (prairie) once covered large sections of the Hungarian Plain, east of the Danube. Formerly a vast wilderness peopled by the legendary Magyar horsemen, the authentic Puszta terrain can now be seen only in a few national parks, like Bugac, where traditional Puszta life—from the tidy villages to the folk costumes—has been re-created. If you're interested in a glimpse at the long-gone Hungary of mythological fame, or trip out into ruggedly beautiful prairie countryside appeals to you, then you should make time for Bugac National Park. If you're fortunate enough to come in late May or early June, you'll see one of Hungary's finest sights—endless fields ablaze with red poppy flowers.

Although buses and even a narrow-gauge train run from Kecskemét to Bugac, they are very inconvenient; you should come here only if you have a car. Head southwest from Kecskemét on Route 54, and turn left at the Bugac signpost after about 20km (12 miles). Continue 10km (6 miles), then turn right, following the signposts for the park, and drive 2km (1.2 miles) to the information booth.

Riding in Bugac costs 800 Ft ($8.15) per hour, with a guide included. A horse-and-cart ride costs 1,300 Ft ($13.25) per hour. There are two restaurants near the park entrance; the Bugaci Csárda is by the riding school, while another is behind the information office. Lunch at either should cost about 600 Ft ($6.10). Bugac Tours in Kecskemét, at Szabadság tér 1/A (☎ **76/321-498;** fax 76/481-643), can give you information and take reservations for all the facilities in the park. They're open Monday through Friday from 8am to 4:30pm, all year. From April to October you can also call the information office in Bugacpuszta at **76/372–688.**

WHERE TO STAY

There are five bungalows by the riding school at Bugac; each has a bathroom and small kitchen and accommodates up to eight people in three rooms. You'll pay 4,000 Ft ($40.80) per bungalow or 1,500 Ft ($15.30) per room. By the information office are small whitewashed houses built in a semitraditional Hungarian style, with slightly larger bathrooms and kitchens, plank floors, and more comfortable furnishings. These cost

3,200 Ft ($32.65) for two people or 6,000 Ft ($61.20) for four. Contact Bugac Tourist for reservations.

3 Szeged

105 miles SE of Budapest

GETTING THERE • By Train An express train takes 2 1/2 hours from Budapest, and costs 897 Ft ($9.15) in first class and 598 Ft ($6.10) in second class.

To get to the center from the train station (☎ **421-821**), take tram no. 1; a little stand just to the left as you exit sells tram tickets. If you prefer a 20-minute walk, go straight for a block and then turn right onto Boldogasszony sugárút.

ESSENTIALS Szeged's telephone area code is 62.

ORIENTATION The Tisza River divides Szeged into two parts, with the historic center—lying Budapest style within a series of concentric ring boulevards—on the left bank. The town's main pedestrian street, Kárász utca, lies parallel to the Tisza, about four blocks in. It's bounded by Széchenyi tér, Szeged's main square, to the north, and Dugonics tér, home of the central university building, to the south. Halfway up Kárász utca is Klauzál tér, home to Szeged Tourist and the popular Virág Cukraszda. The bus station, at Mars tér (formerly Marx tér, and still known to most by that name), is on Szeged's main ring boulevard, about six blocks from the city center.

INFORMATION Szeged's Tourinform office is at Victor Hugo u. 1 (☎ **62/311-711;** fax 62/312-509), near the base of the bridge across the Tisza. From June through August the office is open Monday through Friday from 7:30am to 6pm, and Saturday from 10am to 2pm; the rest of the year, it's open Monday through Friday from 8am to 4pm.

SPECIAL EVENTS Szeged comes alive every year from approximately July 20 to August 20 during the ★ **Szeged Summer Festival.** Ballets, dramas, folk dances, concerts, and other events are staged in front of Szeged's Votive Church.

Famous for its paprika, Szeged (pop. 200,000) is also one of Hungary's most important university towns, as well as the industrial and cultural capital of the Great Plain, or Puszta. The city was largely destroyed by an 1879 Tisza flood, but with help from a number of European cities—Brussels, Berlin, London, Rome, and Paris—was rebuilt in the ring style of the time. Szeged has a few attractive art nouveau buildings, including the town's synagogue, but it's better known for good eating—from spicy fish soup to pastries to sausage to Chinese food.

WHAT TO SEE & DO

If you can't visit Szeged (pronounced "*Se*-ged") during the summer festival, you might try at least to attend one of the frequent organ recitals in the town's impressive church.

Synagogue, Jósika utca, between Gutenberg utca and Hajnóczy utca.

A relic of Szeged's once-numerous Jewish community, this palatial synagogue was completed in 1903 in the art nouveau style of the time. It occupies a full block in a quiet, pleasant residential neighborhood. Inside is a stirring tribute to the local victims of Nazism. Behind the synagogue, at Hajnóczy u. 12, stands the decayed Old Synagogue, built in 1843 and damaged in the flood of 1879.

Admission: Free; donations accepted.

Open: Ostensibly it's open to the public Sun–Fri 9am–noon and 2–4pm. If you find it closed in these hours, you can go to the nearby address posted on the sign and the caretaker will open it for you. **Directions:** From Dugonics tér, walk right on Tisza Lajos körút and turn left on Gutenberg utca.

Votive Church, Dóm tér.

An impressive brick structure with two tall narrow clock towers, the church itself dates back only to 1912, when town fathers fulfilled a pledge to erect a memorial church to celebrate the end of the devastating 1879 flood. The elaborately painted interior in neo-Renaissance style suggests a much older structure and gives a more mysterious appearance than most churches around these parts. Despite the elaborate painting, the work remains incomplete. The interior also houses one of the largest organs in Europe, with over 9,000 pipes; ask at the tourist office for recital details. You'll find an English description of the church posted near the center doorway, although visitors usually come in from the side door.

In front of the church is the **Broken Tower,** a remnant of St. Demetrius Church, the oldest Roman-Gothic relic in southern Hungary; it was first mentioned in a document of A.D. 1099.

The beautiful **Dóm Square,** potentially one of Hungary's finest squares, is unfortunately filled year-round with the grandstand used in the Summer Festival. During that annual festival the church itself becomes the spectacular backdrop to the stage.

Admission: Free.

Open: Mon–Sat 9am–6pm, Sun 9:30–10am, 11–11:30am, and 12:30–6pm. **Directions:** From Széchenyi tér, walk two blocks east on Híd utca and then turn right down Oskola utca.

The Black House [Fekete Ház], Somogyi u. 13. ☎ **312-372.**

Located in an 1857 neo-Gothic house in the town center, this museum chronicles Szeged's history, but with descriptions only in Hungarian. Highlights include wood engravings by artist George Buday, coins and medals, old clocks, an old shoemaker's workshop, posters, crests, and more.

Admission: 12 Ft (12¢) adults, 6 Ft (6¢) students.

Open: Tues–Sun 10am–5pm. **Directions:** Walk west down Somogyi utca from the north end of Dóm tér.

Móra Ferenc Museum, Roosevelt tér 1–3. ☎ **470-370.**

Named after a former director of the museum, this eclectic collection includes Hungarian painting, stuffed animals in a natural history exhibit, gems and minerals, old mining maps and tools, and a room re-creating an old pharmacy.

Admission: 40 Ft (40¢) adults, 20 Ft (20¢) students.

Open: Tues–Sun 10am–5pm. **Directions:** Walk three blocks north of Dóm tér.

WHERE TO STAY

PRIVATE ROOMS Szeged Tourist, at Klauzál tér 7 (☎ **62/321-800;** fax 62/312-928), rents private double rooms for 1,000 to 1,200 Ft ($10.20 to $12.25). The office is open Monday through Friday from 8:30am to 5pm and on Saturday from 9am to noon. Klauzál tér is a block south of Széchenyi tér.

Hotels

Fortuna Panzió, Pecskai u. 8, 6726 Szeged. ☎ **and fax 62/431-585.** 7 rms (all with bath). MINIBAR TV TEL **Bus:** 17 or 71 from Széchenyi tér.

Rates: 2,000 Ft ($20.40) double. Extra bed 600 Ft ($6.10). Breakfast 250 Ft ($2.55) per person extra.

This small family-run private pension is located in the same pleasant New Szeged neighborhood as the Hotel Forrás. The staff speaks English and are happy to help orient you to Szeged.

Hotel Forrás, Szent-Györgyi Albert u. 16, 6726 Szeged. ☎ **and fax 62/430-130.** 178 rms (all with bath). MINIBAR TV **Bus:** 17 or 71 from Széchenyi tér.

Rates (including breakfast): 89 DM ($52.35) double. AE, MC.

If it's luxury you want, head to the Hotel Forrás in Újszeged (New Szeged). Facilities include a sauna, massage parlor, and thermal baths. The hotel, which caters mainly to groups, is in a quiet neighborhood just over the Old Bridge from downtown.

Márika Panzió, Nyíl u. 45, 6722 Szeged. ☎ **and fax 62/313-861.** 9 rms (all with bath). MINIBAR TEL TV **Directions:** From the train station, turn left on Bem utca, and right on Nyíl utca (a 15-minute walk). From the bus station or town center, take bus 74.

Rates: 1,700 Ft ($17.35) single; 2,300 Ft ($23.45) double; 2,850 Ft ($29.10) triple; 3,000 Ft ($30.60) quad. Breakfast 250 Ft ($2.55) extra. AE, DC, MC, V. **Parking:** Free.

A bus ride or 25-minute walk from the town center, the private Márika Panzió is in a pleasant residential neighborhood known as the Alsóváros (Lower Town), two blocks from the pastoral Mátyás tér. The friendly owners speak English.

WHERE TO EAT

Alabárdos, Oskola u. 13–15. ☎ **312-914.**

Cuisine: HUNGARIAN. **Reservations:** Recommended. **Directions:** Walk on Oskola north of Dóm tér.

Prices: Soups 95–110 Ft (95¢–$1.10); main courses 390–850 Ft ($4–$8.65).
Open: Mon–Sat 11:30am–2:30pm and 6pm–2am.

Here is the town's nicest restaurant, with soft lighting and a violin-and-cimbalom duet creating a romantic mood under arched ceilings and white plaster walls decorated with medieval weapons. Try the delicious "Alabárdos Dish," a thin beefsteak with onions, peas, paprika, rice, tomato sauce, and french fries for 680 Ft ($6.95). If you order one of the several flambé dishes, it comes in dramatic fashion: The lights are turned off, the musicians play the musical equivalent of a drum roll, and the waiter emerges from the kitchen with a long shish kebab of flaming meats.

Pagoda Étterem, Zrinyi u. 5. ☎ **312-490.**

Cuisine: CHINESE. **Reservations:** Recommended on weekends.
Directions: Walk one block west of Dóm tér.
Prices: Soups 80–95 Ft (80¢–95¢); main courses 300–600 Ft ($3.05–$6.10). AE.
Open: Daily noon–midnight.

The Pagoda serves what may be the best Chinese food in Hungary, all of it illustrated on the multilingual menu. Vegetarians can easily build a meal out of the underpriced appetizers.

Kiskőrössy Halászcsárda, Felső Tisza-part 336, on the bank of the Tisza River. ☎ **328-410.**

Cuisine: HUNGARIAN. **Reservations:** Recommended. **Bus:** 22, 73, or 73Y to the stadium, then follow the signs down the turnoff.

Prices: Fish soup 160–310 Ft ($1.65–$3.15); main courses 170–440 Ft ($1.75–$4.50). AE, MC.

Open: May–Oct, Sun–Thurs 11am–2am, Fri–Sat 11am–4am; the rest of the year, Sun–Thurs 11am–midnight, Fri–Sat 11am–2am.

Though distant from the town center, this is the best fish restaurant in a town famous for fish soup. The atmosphere is run-down folk style inside, but outside some tables overlook the river and a wooded area. In summer they screen open-air movies here. A organist and Gypsy violinist play inside the restaurant. A lively waiter named Ferenc Muskó speaks English.

For Dessert

Virág Cukrászda, Klauzál tér 1.

Cuisine: DESSERT. **Directions:** Walk across Klauzál tér from Szeged Tourist.

Prices: Pastries and cakes 20–85 Ft (20¢–85¢).

Open: Virág, daily 9am–9pm; Kis Virág, daily 8am–11pm.

This is Szeged's best-known café. In the Virág (which means "flower"), you're surrounded and soothed by antique chairs and potted plants. In the summer, the streetside tables are a favorite meeting point in town. Across the square is the Kis Virág (Little Flower), where a wide selection of pastries, as well as ice cream, is available for take-out.

SAVVY SHOPPING

Szeged is situated within 20 miles of both the Romanian and Serbian borders, and as a result sees both shoppers and vendors from an array of countries. Below are some shopping places that might be of interest to you.

SZEGED SALAMI The famous Pick Salami is produced in Szeged, and the factory runs a small grocery store in the center of town where you can spy on Hungarians exercising their obsession with meat. Visit the Pick Márkahúsáruház, in the Nagy Áruház passage, just off Árpád tér. It's open on Monday from noon to 7pm, Tuesday through Friday from 7am to 7pm, and on Saturday from 7am to 1pm.

THE POLISH MARKET Once largely filled with vendors from Poland, the town's vibrant flea market (Lengyel Piac) is now peopled by Romanians, Russians, Ukrainians, Uzbekis, and others. Here you can buy Russian watches or Romanian dolls, pop-music cassettes, or sausage. No admission charge. It's open Monday through Saturday from dawn to midafternoon, but it's best visited on Saturday. To get there, walk 10 minutes straight from the train station exit. The market is in a dusty field on the corner of Petőfi Sándor sugárút and Cserepessor.

FRUIT & VEGETABLE MARKET Just behind the bus station, on Mars tér, is the town's lively produce market. The vendors are Hungarian farmers from the region around Szeged. Open daily from dawn to midafternoon. Weekends are best, and the earlier you get there the better the variety of goods you'll find.

25

Getting to Know Poland

MOST AMERICAN TRAVELERS STILL HAVEN'T DISCOVERED POLAND, AND THE FEW who have are usually Polish-Americans visiting family and friends. Poland, however, offers travelers a rich array of experiences. Picturesque Kraków in southern Poland stores centuries-old royal treasures in a fairy-tale castle. Gdańsk retains the atmosphere of a medieval trading town, with old cobblestone streets and richly decorated homes. Warsaw, now completely rebuilt after the destruction of World War II, is graced with a charming old market square, not to mention a large museum collection. Nature lovers will enjoy the beauty of the Tatra Mountains in the Zakopane area and the tranquillity of the Mazurian Lake region, with its thousands of lakes and expanses of forest, in the northeast of the country.

1 Geography, History & Politics

GEOGRAPHY

With the Tatra Mountains forming its border with Slovakia to the south and the Baltic Sea to the north, modern Poland also shares borders with Russia, Lithuania, Belarus, Ukraine, the Czech Republic, and Germany. Its borders, too, have shifted countless times over the course of its turbulent history. For instance, at the end of the 15th century, the union of Poland and the Grand Duchy of Lithuania expanded almost to Moscow. However, Poland ceased to exist altogether in 1795 after its neighbors—Prussia, Austria, and Russia—partitioned the entire country. Most recently, Poland's borders were significantly shifted westward after World War II. Although Poland lost such cities as Vilna, Pinsk, Brest, and Łwow in the east, it gained Wrocław and Szczecin in the west.

With a population of 38 million and an area of 120,725 square miles, Poland is the largest and most populous nation covered in this book.

HISTORY & POLITICS

THE POLISH MONARCHY The first polish state was formed in A.D. 965 when Mieszko I of the Piast dynasty was baptized and Poland joined Latin Christendom. The nation was frequently at war, against the Tatars in the east and the Teutonic Knights in the west. But in the 14th century, Poland flourished as an advanced European state, founding a university in Kraków and establishing a strong central monarchy that defeated the Teutons at Grünwald in 1410. But in the following centuries Poland fell behind the rest of Europe. Its famously independent nobles insisted on autonomy and the power of veto—good for liberty but bad for national strength. Poland's elected monarchs were no match for the surrounding absolute sovereigns, and between 1772 and 1795, Russia, Prussia, and Austria divided the country among them so that no

Dateline

- 966 Slavic tribes unify to form Polish state.
- 1226 Teutonic Knights invade East Prussia.
- 1333–70 Kazimierz the Great codifies Polish law, builds cities and castles, and encourages the immigration of large numbers of Jews.
- 1386 Marriage of Polish Queen Jadwiga and Lithuanian grand duke establishes massive union of Poland and Grand Duchy of Lithuania.

➤

IMPRESSIONS

She, like the eagle, will renew her age.
—Thomas Campbell, *Lines on Poland,* 1831

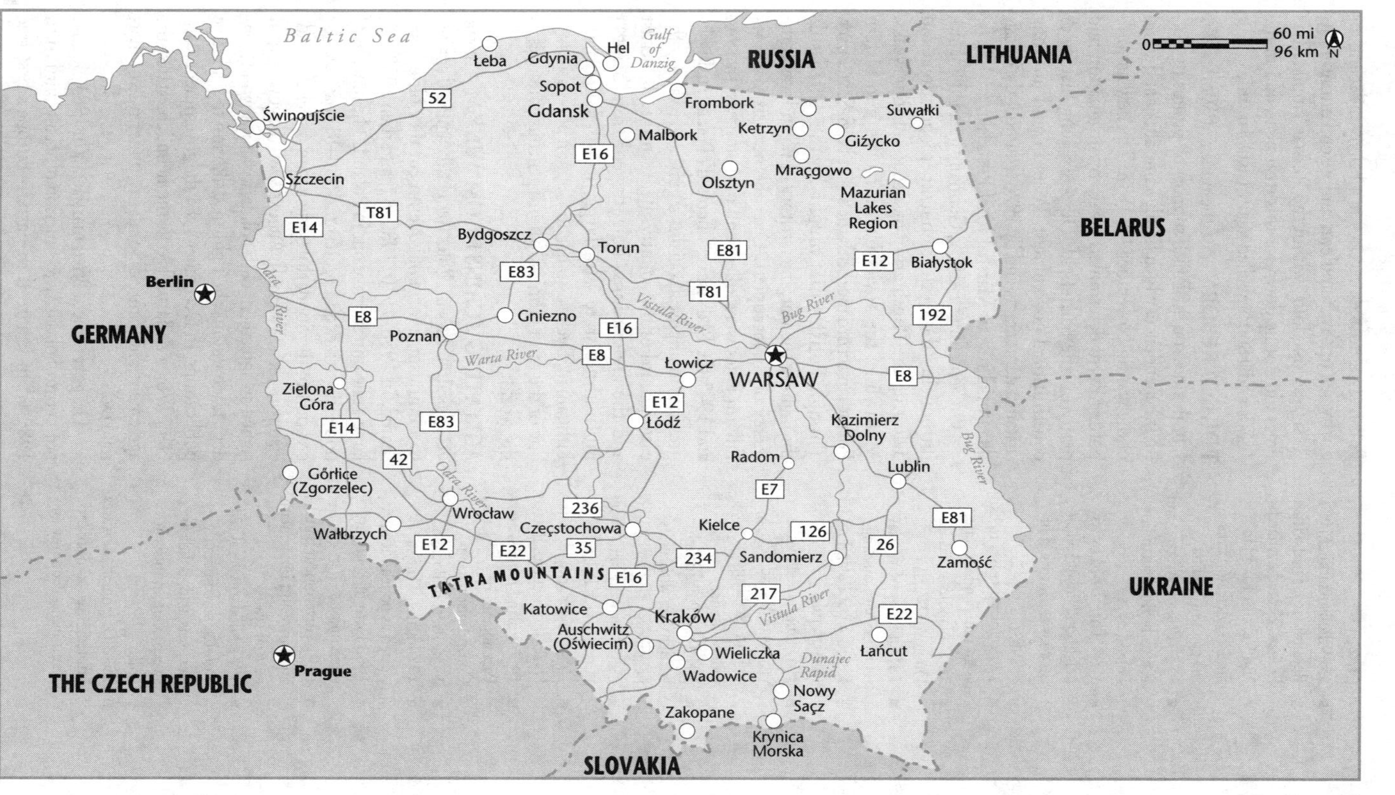

Baltic Sea
Gulf of Danzig
RUSSIA
LITHUANIA
BELARUS
UKRAINE
SLOVAKIA
THE CZECH REPUBLIC
GERMANY
Berlin
Prague
0
60 mi
96 km
N
Łeba
Gdynia
Hel
Sopot
Gdansk
Frombork
Świnoujście
Malbork
Ketrzyn
Giżycko
Suwałki
Mrągowo
Olsztyn
Mazurian Lakes Region
Szczecin
Bydgoszcz
Torun
Białystok
Gniezno
Poznan
Warta River
Vistula River
Bug River
WARSAW
Łowicz
Łódź
Zielona Góra
Kazimierz Dolny
Radom
Lublin
Górlice (Zgorzelec)
Odra River
Wrocław
Wałbrzych
Częstochowa
Kielce
Sandomierz
Zamość
TATRA MOUNTAINS
Katowice
Kraków
Auschwitz (Oświecim)
Wieliczka
Wadowice
Łańcut
Dunajec Rapid
Nowy Sącz
Zakopane
Krynica Morska
52
E16
T81
E14
E81
E12
E83
E8
192
E16
E12
E83
E14
42
E7
236
E81
E12
E22
35
126
26
234
E16
217
E22

Poland

Dateline

- 1569 Polish-Lithuanian Republic is formed with a limited, elected monarchy.
- 1683 Polish King Jan Sobieski defeats Turks at the gates of Vienna.
- 1772 Prussia, Austria, and Russia begin dismantling Poland.
- 1791 Threatened by its neighbors, Poland enacts the first constitution in Europe.
- 1795 Poland ceases to exist as an independent state.
- 1807 Napoléon sets up Duchy of Warsaw.
- 1815 Duchy of Warsaw replaced with quisling Kingdom of Poland under Russian rule.
- 1918 Supported by the victors of World War I, Poland establishes independence.
- 1919–21 Poland fights border wars with all its neighbors.
- 1939 Germany and Soviet Union attack Poland.
- 1944 Soviet army defeats Nazis and occupies Poland.
- 1955 Poland joins Warsaw Pact alliance of Communist nations.
- 1956 Riots in Poznań.
- 1978 Karol Wojtyła elected as pope in Rome.
- 1980 Birth of Solidarity trade union.
- 1981 Government bans Solidarity and implements martial law.
- 1989 Solidarity legalized and free parliamentary elections held; Solidarity sweeps Communists at polls.
- 1990 Draconian measures implemented to dismantle Communist economy and

➤

Polish state existed, except for a briefly independent duchy set up by Napoléon and a semiautonomous "congress kingdom" within the Russian empire. The Poles did not lie down for this treatment, and in the 1830s and 1860s rebelled against Russian rule.

POLAND REBORN At the outset of World War I, both sides sought Polish support by promising Polish independence, which finally came about at the end of the war on November 11, 1918. The new nation's borders were determined partly by negotiation and partly on the battlefield. Despite a long history of constitutional government, Poland could not long sustain a democracy, and by 1926 fell under the quasi-dictatorial rule of Marshal Józef Piłsudski.

On September 1, 1939, Germany invaded Poland, introducing the world to blitzkrieg operations and defeating the Polish army in a space of four weeks. Meanwhile, the Soviet Union moved into eastern Poland, in accordance with the secret Nazi-Soviet pact. Though Polish units fought on the Allied side throughout the war, the territory of Poland was at the mercy of the occupiers. Over the next six years, six million Poles were killed, half of them Jews. In 1944 and 1945 the Red Army "liberated" Poland, using its presence to impose a socialist regime and to annex the eastern third of the country. Between the Holocaust and the annexations, Poland went from being a multiethnic state with large Jewish, Ukrainian, Lithuanian, Byelorussian, and German populations to one of the most ethnically homogeneous countries in the world.

AGITATING AGAINST COMMUNISM In the decades after the war, Poles frequently agitated against Communism, a form of government they bitterly resented. In 1956, 1970, 1980–81, and then 1988–89, large-scale unrest broke out in Poland. The months of domestic strikes and protest in 1980–81 spawned the creation of the Solidarity trade union under the leadership of Lech Wałęsa. In August 1980 the government signed an agreement with Solidarity allowing independent trade unions the right to strike and to print free publications. In December 1981 the government, with Gen. Wojciech Jaruzelski at the helm, abrogated the agreement and banned Solidarity under rule of martial law.

The government lifted martial law in 1983, but did not permit Solidarity to function officially until April 1989 when it agreed to Eastern Europe's first free parliamentary elections in 50 years. Solidarity overwhelmed the Communists in the June 1989 election, and by August, Solidarity journalist Tadeusz Mazowiecki took over as Poland's first non-Communist prime minister since World War II.

Dateline

establish capitalism; Lech Wałęsa elected president of Poland.

TODAY In 1990 the government embarked on a crash program to dismantle the Communist economy. Prices rose dramatically as Poland pushed toward a market-oriented capitalist system. Even this radical approach will take years to improve Poland's quality of life substantially; economic change evolves more slowly than political restructuring in a system previously characterized by economic mismanagement and a moribund bureaucracy. In December 1990, Poles elected former electrician Lech Wał¸esa president.

Virtually all retail business is now in private hands in Poland, and a cornucopia of Western goods has appeared in shops. But in 1993, voters elected legislators who claimed that slowing the pace of reform would soften the blows of transition.

2 Famous People

Nicolaus Copernicus (Mikołaj Kopernik) (1473–1543) The astronomer who postulated that the earth moved around the sun and not the other way around, Copernicus paved the way for modern astronomy. His work *The Revolutions of the Celestial Bodies* also showed that some early Greek writers had proposed a heliocentric universe; it was only after Copernicus, however, that the theory gained wide acceptance.

Jan III Sobieski (1629–96) Polish king who turned back the mighty Ottoman Turkish army from the gates of Vienna in 1683. He had the stunning Wilanów Palace and gardens created as his residence in the late 17th century.

Tadeusz Kościuszko (1746–1817) This patriot served as a general in the American Revolution and helped to achieve victory at Saratoga. In 1794 he returned to his homeland and launched an unsuccessful insurrection by all classes of Polish society against the Russian-led partitions. Defeated and taken prisoner, he died in exile. He is buried in the crypt of Wawel Cathedral in Kraków.

Frédéric Chopin (1810–49) Composer known for his great piano mastery and piano compositions in forms such as études, mazurkas, and polonaises. He only spent his first 18 years in Poland, before emigrating to France where he composed his greatest Romantic works. His birthplace at Zelazowa Wola, 32 miles west of Warsaw, is today a museum. His heart is contained in Warsaw's Church of the Holy Cross.

Joseph Conrad (1857–1924) Born Józef Korzeniowski, Conrad immigrated to England and wrote such works as *Lord Jim* (1900), *Heart of Darkness* (1902), and *Nostromo* (1904) in English.

Maria Skłodowska-Curie (1867–1934) Physicist noted for her research in France on radioactivity. Together with her French husband, Pierre, she discovered two new elements, radium and polonium. For her brilliant research she won two Nobel Prizes, the only woman in history to do so. Her constant exposure to radiation brought on leukemia, which caused her death. Her birthplace in Warsaw is today a museum in her honor.

Józef Piłsudski (1867–1935) To further the cause of Polish independence, he organized Polish Legions in the Austrian army during World War I. Emerging from the war as a hero, he became the first chief of state of the new Polish Republic and led it to victory in the war against the Soviet Union. Then in 1926, he launched a coup d'état against Poland's civilian government and became virtual dictator until his death.

Karol Wojtyla (1920–) Became the first Pole and first Slav in history to serve as Catholic pope (October 1978). Ordained a priest in 1946, and elevated to archbishop of Kraków in 1964 and cardinal in 1978, Pope John Paul II helped inspire the anti-Communist opposition in Poland and bring about the dramatic changes in evidence across Eastern Europe today. He is also known for his conservative positions on many church issues, and for his incredible travel schedule, which has taken him all across the globe. His birthplace in Wadowice is today a pilgrimage museum.

Lech Wałęsa (1943–) Gdańsk Shipyard electrician turned political organizer, Wałęsa spearheaded the rise of the Solidarity trade union in 1980. He negotiated the historic Gdańsk Agreement with the government, allowing independent trade unions the right to strike and to print their own publications. Following martial law in 1981 he was interned until late the next year. He received the Nobel Peace Prize in 1983. He remains the leading voice in Solidarity, and in 1990 was elected president of Poland.

Favorite Haunts: Św. Brygidy Church in Gdańsk on Sunday morning during the "national mass," usually at 11am.

3 Cultural Notes

ARCHITECTURE

A great architectural heritage was intact in Poland until 1939; by 1945 all Polish cities except Kraków were in ruins, with 80% of Warsaw gutted or demolished. Poland was the most devastated country in Europe: Hitler began the war by invading Poland, and Warsaw and Wrocław were among the last cities to see an end to the fighting—between the retreating German and the advancing Soviet forces, little remained standing. The Polish state has slowly undertaken extensive restoration or reconstruction of many buildings since the war, generally with sensitive attention to authentic materials and techniques; nonetheless, Polish architecture, like so much of Polish culture, is marked by a tragic sense of loss.

Did You Know . . . ?

- In 1993, Poland had Europe's fastest-growing economy.
- 98% of Poles over the age of 15 are literate.
- There are 6.5 million Americans of Polish descent.
- Poland is the world's second-largest producer of potatoes, growing even more than the United States.
- Poland has the sixth-largest hog population in the world.
- The Fahrenheit temperature scale is named after Gabriel Daniel Fahrenheit (1686–1736), born in Gdańsk, Poland.
- European bison still run wild in Poland's Białowieski National Park.

Romanesque Vast forests enabled Central Europe to rely on solid timber construction through the Middle Ages (while half-timber techniques predominated in the West); consequently, little of these wooden structures survived. Poland was exceptional, with much Romanesque stone and/or brick construction. However, few buildings escaped later alterations or accretions, and even fewer escaped war damage. Gniezno, the medieval capital and cultural center of north-central Poland, 30 miles southeast of Poznań, was the seat of the country's first archbishopric (A.D. 1000) and a center of the Polish Romanesque. Remains of two Romanesque cathedrals can be seen in the present Gothic Metropolitan Cathedral there; the Collegiate Church of SS. Peter and Paul at Kruszwica and the churches of St. Procopius and of the Holy Trinity in Strelzno (both towns near Gniezno) are better preserved. After 1040, when the Polish king moved from Gniezno to Kraków, a Romanesque castle, church, and walled town were built on the latter's Wawel Hill, some parts of which are extant.

Gothic The Romanesque yielded to the Gothic late in Poland. The new style was introduced by the monastic orders; most Gothic buildings were monastic structures, and brick remained the most common material (examples are the Dominican Monastery of St. Adelbert in Wrocław and the Dominican and Franciscan churches in Kraków, all extensively rebuilt). The German Hallenkirche ("hall church") also became widespread (such as the churches of the Assumption at Chelmo and of St. John in Toruń, and the Collegiate Church of Our Lady in Poznań). Two fine examples in Wrocław (the churches of the Holy Cross and of Our Lady of the Sands) display the unusual Piast vaults, each divided into three sections of three paneled compartments. The cathedrals of Wrocław, Kraków, and Gniezno and the churches of St. Mary in Kraków (the largest Gothic church in the country, and well restored) and Gdańsk are also great monuments of medieval Polish sacred architecture. Of the many medieval castles and fortresses of Poland, among the greatest was the Teutonic Knights' complex, 35 miles south of Gdańsk, called Malbork (originally Marienburg); many of its rooms have been restored since the war, and the whole remains imposing. Kraków was a walled city from the 13th century on; sections of the ancient walls and gates survive, as does the tower of the 14th-century town hall in the Market Place, and parts of the university, founded in 1364.

Renaissance Some of the earliest Renaissance architecture outside Italy was built in Kraków by Italian artists. The royal castle on Wawel Hill was rebuilt after a fire in 1499 in a style blending native Polish and Florentine elements; its palace courtyard set a pattern copied throughout the country. The Zygmunt Chapel attached to the nearby cathedral (1524–33), with its central plan, lantern dome, and rich decoration, also became a prototype. Many of the most beautiful Polish Renaissance buildings, again blending Italian structures with Polish decoration, are in Lviv, today in Ukraine. Well-preserved examples of civic architecture in Poland itself are the town halls of Poznań and Chelmo; influenced more by the German and Flemish Mannerist style than the Italian are many buildings in Gdańsk, including the Armory (1605), which escaped war damage. Few Renaissance town houses are extant—those on Kanonicza Street in Kraków (1550) are fine and fortunate exceptions.

Baroque Italian artists also introduced baroque architecture into Poland, in the late 16th century; the baroque has survived relatively well, and many Gothic and Romanesque churches have fine baroque interiors or exterior additions. The first buildings were erected for the Jesuit and Cistercian orders. In Kraków, the Jesuits built the Church of SS. Peter and Paul, modeled on Il Gesú in Rome; later, in 1689, they built the Church of St. Matthew in Wrocław, whose sumptuous gilded interior features a vaulted ceiling painted all over in a unified design. Wrocław University (begun in 1728) is also an exquisite monument of the Polish Jesuit baroque, which reveals its elegant design when viewed from the University Bridge over the Odra. Other 17th-century Polish baroque churches were influenced variously by German, Flemish, or Italian models. The Church of St. Anthony in Poznań is another modeled on Il Gesú, with an astoundingly ornate interior; in Kraków, the Church of St. Anne contrasts a similarly rich decor with a classically simple exterior. Designs in the 18th century are often more monumental (again, some are in Lviv). The Electoral Chapel was added to the Cathedral of Wrocław in the Viennese baroque in 1716. A late example near the same city is the abbey church at Trzebnica, with a rich white-and-gold interior. Most of the baroque and rococo palaces were wrecked in the war, but the Palace of Wilanów (1677–96), eight miles south of Warsaw, escaped severe damage, except for its interior, now restored; today it's part of the National Museum of Warsaw.

Modern Art nouveau filtered into Poland from Vienna; its influences can be seen throughout Kraków and in the Hotel Polonia in Warsaw. Commercial buildings of this century are much more function-oriented, such as the Prudential headquarters in Warsaw (now the Warszawa Hotel) and the Centrum Department Store in Wrocław. Since 1945 Polish civic architecture has been dominated by the official Soviet-bloc style—pompous, brutal, and ugly. It remains to be seen what new architecture will rise in response to the troubled times since the revolution of 1989. Thus far, much renovation of existing buildings has been under way. The largest completed project to date is the new international airport in Warsaw, which opened in the summer of 1992.

MUSIC

In the 16th century sacred polyphonic music reached a high level of development in Poland, as it did all over Europe; the works of Nicolaj Gomólka (1539–1609), Poland's first great composer, are still performed. Other famous Poles of the period include Nicolaj Zielenski, who composed large-scale works for double choir, two organs, and instrumentalists, and the internationally famed lutenist, Jacob Polak. The first royal opera house was built during the reign of Władysław IV (1632–48), in a period when music enjoyed the patronage of a wealthy aristocracy. Polish music apparently became fashionable in the international musical culture of the 18th century—Bach mentions in a letter that his choir often performed it.

The leading composer at the turn of the 19th century was Joseph Kozlowski, who wrote a vast variety of music, including hundreds of polonaises, one of which became for a time, ironically, the Russian national anthem (he was employed by the Russian court most of his life). King Stanisław August erected a public opera house in Warsaw at the end of the 18th century, where the works of Matthew Kamienski, the first composer of Polish-language opera, were performed. Chopin's teacher, Joseph Elsner, was for a time its director, and a composer in his own right.

Frédéric Chopin himself, of course, is the most monumental figure in Polish music. Born near Warsaw in 1810, he died in Paris only 39 years later, having basically performed himself to death. One of the most idiomatic composers for the piano, and a quintessential Romantic, his lyrical and emotion-filled works are today at the core of the recital literature. While certain Polish folk-dance forms, such as the polonaise and mazurka, had for centuries had a place in the suites of composers all over Europe,

Chopin made them the vehicle for the frustrated heroic patriotism of his oppressed native country, and they are still among his most popular works.

When Poland finally achieved unity and independence, it was a musician, Ignacy Jan Paderewski (1860–1941)—a Romantic composer and pianist who ranks with Rubinstein and Liszt—who became its first prime minister, in 1919. Like Paderewski, the great harpsichord virtuoso and interpreter of Bach, Wanda Landowska (1877–1959), lived most of her career in the West. Other internationally known 20th-century Polish musicians include composers Karol Szymanowski, Witold Lutosławski, Krzysztof Penderecki, and Henryk Gorecki.

LITERATURE

Poland has nourished one of Europe's great literatures, too little known in the West. The modern Polish language emerged in the 16th century, the golden age of Polish literature, in a climate of humanist scholarship and religious reform. Leading figures such as Mikołaj Rej (the "father of Polish literature") and poet Jan Kochanowski wrote for an increasingly sophisticated audience among the gentry. After a period of stagnation, the influence of the French Enlightenment and neoclassicism brought new energy to Polish letters in the mid-18th century; the period is noted for its satire, light drama, and the nation's first journalism. Julian Niemcewicz, a follower of Voltaire, bridged the neoclassical and Romantic movements.

Polish Romanticism, preoccupied with themes of national and personal liberation, is dominated by Adam Mickiewicz (1798–1855), considered Poland's greatest poet. Active in politics from his youth, he was arrested while still in university and deported to Russia; later he organized legions to fight for Polish independence in the Revolution of 1848 and the Crimean War. Among his many volumes of poetry, *Pan Tadeusz,* an epic treatment of the Polish gentry, is considered his masterpiece.

Much 19th-century literature was written by Poles in exile, and after the failed revolution of 1863 was preoccupied by attacks on ignorance and reactionary politics. The historical novels of Henryk Sienkiewicz, a Nobel laureate, achieved international popularity in his day. After independence in 1919 ended generations of partition, Polish literature flowered anew, led by the Skamander urban poets. The German occupation of 1939 devastated Polish cultural life, and the ensuing Communist regime, through its censorship and mandated socialist realism, ensured that authentic literature would, for four decades, have to grow underground. The dilemma of postwar artists and intellectuals is incisively described in Czesław Miłosz's *The Captive Mind* (Random House, 1981).

Miłosz is without question the most famous Polish literary figure of this century. He has published both a *Selected Poems* and a *Collected Poems* (1981 and 1988, both from Ecco Press), a *History of Polish Literature,* and a useful paperback anthology of *Postwar Polish Poetry* (both from the University of California Press, 1983). His exploration of Poland's tragic history and the paradoxes of its search for national identity in *Native Realm: A Search for Self-Definition* and his first novel, *The Seizure of Power* (University of California Press, 1981 and 1983) may be of particular interest to today's traveler.

Miłosz has also collaborated on translations of other major contemporary Polish poets, with Zbigniew Herbert's *Selected Poems* (Ecco Press, 1986) and Aleksander Wat's *With the Skin* (selected poems; Ecco Press, 1988). Also available is Wat's *My Century: The Odyssey of a Polish Intellectual* (University of California Press, 1988). Several volumes of the plays of Slawomir Mrozek, Poland's most admired living dramatist, are available in English, as are more than a dozen books by world-renowned science-fiction writer Stanisław Lem, whose visions of repressive futuristic societies implicitly criticized the Communist regime.

4 Food & Drink

To sample some delicious pastry with a cup of coffee you can slip into a *kawiarnia* (café). For a simple nonmeat meal or snacks try out a *bar mleczny* (milk bar). A *winiarnia* (wine bar) usually serves only wine. Don't be surprised if someone asks to join you if there's an empty seat at your table, for it's customary that all available seats in a restaurant are filled. Your tablemates usually won't engage you in conversation unless you initiate it, and you'll find they are quite friendly if you do.

THE CUISINE • Soup A delicious soup always begins the Polish meal, and favorites include *barszcz,* made of meat broth and beets; *botwina* (a beet soup with young beet greens), *chłodnik* (a cold soup of cucumbers and scallions, or of fruit); and *żurek* (a rich creamy white sour soup with egg and sausage).

• Meat and Fish Providing the staple of the Polish diet are meat dishes, often prepared with rich sauces or garnished with spices. Dill, caraway seeds, mushrooms, and sour cream are prominently featured. Favorite main courses include *bigos* (a sauerkraut dish with either sausage or smoked pork), *kotlet schabowy* (the ubiquitous and savory pork cutlet), roast duckling with apples; lamb or beef *szaszlik* (grilled meat kebabs). Also popular are *pierogi* (dumplings filled with potatoes, blueberries, cheese, or meat) and *golabki* (stuffed cabbage rolls). Pike is likely to be served with a sauce, carp may be jellied, and trout sautéed.

As a side dish, don't miss the buttery and tasty Polish mushrooms. For snacks during the day consider *zapiekanki* (a long slice of garlic bread with cheese, mushrooms, and ketchup on top sold by outdoor vendors).

DRINK Polish drinks include tea, coffee, mineral water, and juices—look for delicious black currant juice. Compote, a fruit drink made with fruit stewed in lots of water, is often served in milk bars and bistros. Lots of American sodas are also widely available.

Poland offers a variety of vodkas, including *Żytnia,* made with rye; *Zubrówka,* flavored with bison grass; *Myśliwska* (Hunter's vodka), and *Wyborowa,* the classic vodka. You may also enjoy Polish beer: *Żywiec, Okoćim,* or *Lech.*

26

Planning a Trip to Poland

POLAND IS EXPERIENCING AN ACCELERATED RENAISSANCE IN TOURISM AND TRAVEL; and on the whole, travel is much easier than in the past. Of course, as the Poles institute economic reforms and privatize the travel industry, there may be glitches that are frustrating to both the traveler and the native. This chapter will help you identify the advance-planning issues you need to tackle before you leave. Additional care in planning your trip should pay off handsomely.

1 Information, Entry Requirements & Money

SOURCES OF INFORMATION

IN THE U.S. Poland's largest commercial travel agency, **Orbis** will make reservations for Orbis hotels and car rentals in Poland. Orbis offers special discounts for advance car-rentals and upscale hotel reservations, and they require payment before you leave for Poland. Unfortunately, Orbis does not deal with most of the smaller budget hotels listed in this guide. Orbis has an office at 342 Madison Ave. Suite 1512, New York, NY 10173 (☎ **212/867-5011;** fax 212/682-4715). Open Monday through Friday, 9am to 5pm.

For tourist information, contact the **National Tourist Office,** 275 Madison Ave., New York, NY 10016 (☎ **212/338-9412;** fax 212/338-9283), open Monday through Friday 9am to 5pm; or at 333 N. Michigan Ave., Chicago, IL 60601 (☎ **312/236-9013;** fax 312/236-1125); open Monday through Friday from 9am to 4pm. Both offices are stocked with a wealth of maps and color brochures covering not only Poland in general but also specific cities and regions and special-interest travel, like sports, national parks, and Jewish sites in Poland. Tell them what you are most interested in, and they will send you what material they have.

IN THE U.K. There is an Orbis office at 82 Mortimer St., London W1N 7DE (☎ **071/637-4971**; fax 071/436-6558).

ENTRY REQUIREMENTS

Passports are required of all visitors to enter Poland. Visas are no longer required for American and citizens of several European countries, including Ireland and the United Kingdom, visiting Poland for up to 90 days. As of this writing, citizens of Australia, Canada, and New Zealand must still obtain visas. Visas are valid for three months, must be used within six months of their issuance, and cost $50 U.S. for Canadians, $32 U.S. for others.

For more details contact the following consulates/embassies:

- **Australia** Polish Embassy, 7 Turrana St., Yarralumla, Canberra, ACT 2600 (☎ **062/273-1211**).
- **Canada** Consulate General of Poland, 2603 Lakeshore Blvd. West, Toronto, ON M8V 1G5 (☎ **416/252-5471**), or 1600 Pine Ave., Montréal, PQ H3G 1B4 (☎ **514/937-9481**).
- **New Zealand** Polish Embassy, 196 The Terrace #D, P.O. Box 10211, Wellington (☎ **04/712-2456**).
- **United Kingdom** Polish Embassy, 47 Portland Place, London, W1N 3 AG (☎ **071/580-4324**).
- **United States** Polish Embassy, 233 Madison Ave., New York, NY 10016

(☎ **212/889-8360**); 2224 Wyoming Ave. NW, Washington, DC 20008 (☎ **202/234-2501**); 1530 N. Lake Shore Dr., Chicago, IL 60610 (☎ **312/337-8166**) and 3460 Wilshire Blvd., Los Angeles, CA 90010 (☎ **213/365-7900**).

MONEY

CASH/CURRENCY Poles conduct their economic affairs in **złoty** (pronounced "zwoty"; "gold" in Polish). Banknotes are issued in 50-, 100-, 200-, 500-,1,000-, 2,000-, 5,000-, 10,000-, 20,000-, 50,000-, 100,000-, 200,000- 500,000- 1,000,000- and 2,000,000- złoty denominations.

For years there have been rumors that the Polish government was about to change its currency—dropping several zeros off the end of all prices, getting coins back into use, and ending the ceaseless debates over who is a national hero by putting cities instead of people on the bills. But this reform is forever around the corner. At the time of writing, $1 = 20,400 złoty. While prices in złotys have soared in past years, prices in dollar terms have stayed more constant. For this reason, prices are listed in dollars in all chapters on Poland. The import or export of Polish złotys is illegal, and Polish currency is not easily obtainable outside Poland; however, this situation will undoubtedly change as Poland's economy improves.

What Things Cost in Poland	U.S. $
Taxi from Warsaw's airport to city center	10.00–25.00
Tram from the Central Station to the Old Town	.20
Local telephone call	.08
Double room, with bath, at Warsaw's Hotel Marriott (deluxe)	330.00
Double room, with bath, at Kraków's Hotel Saski (moderate)	29.50
Double room, without bath, at Toruń's Hotel Polonia (budget)	10.00
Lunch for one, without wine, at Warsaw's Nowe Miasto (moderate)	5.00
Lunch for one, without wine, at Kraków's Chimera (budget)	2.00
Dinner for one, without wine, at Gdańsk's Pod Ło sosiem (splurge)	15.00
Dinner for one, without wine, at Kraków's Balaton (budget)	4.00
Pint of beer	.75
Coca-Cola	.60
Cup of coffee	.30
Roll of ASA 100 Fujichrome film, 36 exposures	5.75
Admission to Kraków's Wawel Castle	2.00
Concert at Warsaw's Chopin Museum	2.25

TRAVELER'S CHECKS Private exchange bureaus do not accept traveler's checks; these rules may change as Poland's economy grows more sophisticated. Currently only the American Express office in Warsaw and the Orbis hotels and travel bureaus in major Polish cities convert traveler's checks into Polish złoty. Many large banks, such as PKO, will cash your American Express traveler's checks into dollars for a $1.50 commission, giving you the opportunity to get the best exchange rate into złoty at a Kantor (a private exchange office), which accepts only cash. Most Orbis desks in Warsaw and throughout Poland will exchange American Express and Thomas Cook traveler's checks into złoty at a lower rate than what Kantors offer for cash, and will charge a 3% commission for the transaction.

CREDIT & CHARGE CARDS You can use credit and charge cards—such as American Express, MasterCard, Diners Club, Eurocard, JCB, and VISA—in hotels, restaurants, travel bureaus, and many shops (Pewex, Balatona, Cepelia, and Desa) in major tourist areas. Always carry some cash with you, in case you are told "We stop taking credit cards at 9pm" or "That sign on the door is only for advertising." (**Note:** If no credit card information is given in my listings, assume that only cash is accepted.)

Lost or stolen credit cards can be reported to PolCard Ltd; their 24-hour number in Warsaw is 022/27-45-13.

2 When to Go

CLIMATE Temperatures average in the 60s in the summer, and in the high 20s in the winter. Winter begins early, toward the end of October or the beginning of November, and lasts until March. From March to May variable weather reigns—in some years warm and in others cool. During the summer the weather can still be cool on occasion. For example, June temperatures average only 63°F in Warsaw and 60°F in Gdańsk, with cooler days sometimes throughout the summer.

Warsaw's Average Daytime Temperatures

	Jan	Feb	Mar	Apr	May	June	July	Aug	Sept	Oct	Nov	Dec
Temp. (°F)	28	26	33	45	55	63	65	64	56	47	37	33
Temp. (°C)	-2	-3	1	7	12	17	18	17	13	8	5	1

HOLIDAYS Polish holidays include January 1 (New Year's Day), Easter Monday, May 1 (Labor Day; this might be eliminated in the future), May 3 (Polish Constitution Day), Corpus Christi (60 days after Easter), November 1 (All Saints' Day), November 11 (Polish National Day), and December 25–26 (Christmas). Often the days after holidays are taken off as well.

Poland Calendar of Events

February

- **Polish Contemporary Music Festival,** Wrocław.

March

- **Ski Racing Competition,** Zakopane. Alpine and nordic races in the Tatra Mountains.
- **Jazz on the Odra,** Wrocław. Jazz festival; sometimes held in April or May.

- **Łódź Operatic Meetings,** Łódź.
- **Polish Festival of Theatrical School Productions,** Łódź.
- **Festival of Polish Violin Music,** Częstochowa.

May

- **Festival of Polish Short Feature Films,** Kraków. Sometimes held in June.
- **Festival of Polish Contemporary Plays,** Wrocław. Continues until June.
- **Łódź Ballet Meetings,** Łódź. Every odd year, next in 1995; sometimes held in June.
- **Festival of Organ and Harpsicord Music,** Wrocław.

June

- **Days of Kraków,** Kraków. Folk music, dancing, and local rock bands.
- **International Trade Fair and St. John's Fair,** Poznań. The latter features medieval stalls in the Old Marketplace and other events.

July

- **St. Dominic's Fair,** Gdańsk. Continues until the beginning of August, with musical events in Main Town and displays of arts and crafts.
- **International Organ Music Festival,** Gdańsk. Concerts on the massive Oliwa Cathedral organ; sometimes held in August.

August

- **Music in Old Kraków Festival,** Kraków.
- **Opera in the Woods,** Sopot. Open-air opera performances in a resort town near Gdańsk.
- **Wrocław Oratorio and Cantata Festival,** Wrocław.

September

- **Tatra Autumn and Festival of Highlanders' Culture,** Zakopane.
- **Wratislava Cantans,** Wrocław. Festival of oratory and cantata music.
- **Wieniawski International Composers' Contest,** Poznań.

October

- **International Textile Triennials,** Łódź. Next held in 1997.

November

- **Jazz Halloween,** Kraków.
- **Jeunesses Musicales International Music Festival,** Częstochowa.
- **Rock Music Festival,** Łódź.

December

- **Nativity Crib Contest,** Kraków.

Warsaw Calendar of Events

May

- **International Book Fair.**
- **Grand Prix du Disque.**
- **Berlin–Warsaw–Prague Bicycle Race.** A big Central European sports event.

June

- **Gold Garter Traditional Jazz Competition.**
- **International Poster Biennials.** Next held in 1995.
- **St. John's Eve** (June 23). Young women celebrate the tradition of floating

candles set in wreaths, with poems addressed to young bachelors on Kupala night. Go down to the Vistula to see the candlelight shimmering on the river.

- **Mozart Festival.** Includes operatic, symphonic, and chamber works of Mozart. Continues through June and July.

September

- **Warsaw Autumn International Festival of Contemporary Music.**

October

- **International Chopin Piano Competition.** Next held in 1995.
- **Jazz Jamboree International Festival.** Oldest jazz festival in Eastern Europe.

November

- **International Theatrical Meetings.**

3 Alternative Travel

EDUCATIONAL/STUDY TRAVEL During July and August, students (with valid ID) and people under 35 can stay at inexpensive student dorms sponsored by Almatur, Poland's youth travel agency, with two to four beds per room. Almatur sells vouchers that can be used for bed and breakfast at any of their university hotels across Poland. Students with an International Student Identification Card (ISIC) pay $7; those under 35 pay $10. Almatur's list of hotels changes from year to year so only some are mentioned in this book. If you don't have vouchers you can still stay at these hotels, and it may even be cheaper. However, special rooms are put aside for those arriving with vouchers before 2pm. Single students should note that most Almatur lodgings are doubles, but sometimes you'll find a room to yourself, especially if you're willing to pay extra.

The **Almatur head office** in Warsaw, at Kopernika 23 (☎ **26-23-56, 26-26-39,** or **26-35-12**), will answer any questions you might have. Other local Almatur offices are listed in the city chapters.

If you haven't already purchased your student ID card (ISIC), you can pick one up at Almatur offices for just $4.15 upon presentation of a photo and proof of academic affiliation.

Students under the age of 26 will also receive a 25% to 40% reduction on train travel to other Eastern European nations by purchasing tickets at the WASTEELS counters of major train stations (no discount on domestic trains, though). Many museums also reduce admission costs by about 50% for students.

4 Getting There

BY PLANE The Polish national airline, **LOT** has direct nonstop flights to Warsaw from New York, Newark, and Chicago. There are also nonstop flights from London to Warsaw, Kraków, and Gdańšk. LOT flies Boeing 767's and offers business and economy classes, as well as a frequent flier program. You can contact LOT at 500 Fifth Ave., Suite 408, New York, NY 10110 (☎ toll free **800/223-0593**).

Austrian Airlines (☎ toll free **800/843-0002**) has daily flights between Vienna and Warsaw, which are scheduled to connect with flights from Vienna to other destinations. Several other airlines serve Warsaw, including KLM, Lufthansa, Delta, and British Airways.

Also check the Sunday travel sections of major newspapers for bargain flights, and be sure to ask reservation agents about any possible flight discounts.

Whichever carrier you choose, you'll be arriving in Warsaw's dazzling new Okęcie International Airport, a vast improvement on the old one.

BY TRAIN Travelers who prefer rail travel can journey to Poland from a number of Western and Eastern European capitals; the connections are good and the fares are reasonable. The *Chopin Express* from Vienna to Warsaw takes about 12 hours and costs $74 in first class, $52 in second class; the 13-hour Prague–Warsaw run costs $62 in first class, $44 in second; the Berlin–Warsaw express takes 12 hours and costs $52 in first class, $37 in second. There are also several trains to choose from not listed by RailEurope (inquire locally abroad for schedules and prices): the Berlin–Gdańsk connection, the Bucharest–Warsaw express, the daily Budapest–Kraków train, and a seasonal train between Varna (on Bulgaria's Black Sea coast) and Warsaw from mid-June to October.

You can try to sleep away the long hours on the train by reserving a couchette on an overnight train, but be aware that border guards have little respect for your slumber and may wake you several times during the night as you cross international frontiers.

Second-class fares on trains leaving Poland from Warsaw are $38 to Berlin, $50 to Budapest, $40.50 to Prague, $50 to Moscow, $125 to Istanbul, and $42.25 to Vienna. Couchettes cost an additional $15 to all these cities—except Istanbul and Moscow, for which the cost of a couchette is included in the fare quoted. Travelers 26 and under can get discounts on all international trains by purchasing tickets at WASTEELS counter in train stations.

BY SHIP A number of ferryboats connect several cities in Scandinavia with Poland's Baltic Coast. Travelers from Copenhagen, Rønne, or the Swedish port of Ystad can sail to the Polish port of Świnoujscie (try to pronounce "Sveen-ow-oo-scheh") near Szczecin. The Copenhagen–Świnoujście trip takes about 9 to 10 hours and costs about $42. There are also boats from Gdańsk to Oxelösund in Sweden and to Helsinki. A new line connects Gdynia with Karlskrona, Sweden. Students with the ISIC card get a substantial reduction on prices. From Świnoujście you can catch an overnight train to Warsaw or Kraków, or take a long day train to Gdańsk.

For sailing times and exact prices, contact one of the following Polferries agents and be sure to ask for a Polferries timetable: **Gdynia America Shipping Lines Ltd.,** 238 City Rd., Passenger Dept., London EC1V 2QL (☎ **071/251-3389;** fax 071/250-3625); or **Vindrose Rejser I/S,** Nordre Toldbod 12A, 1259 Copenhagen K, Denmark (☎ **33-11-46-45;** fax 33-11-95-78).

Perhaps the most unusual way to arrive in Poland is from Great Britain aboard the MS *Inowrocław,* a Polish cargo vessel that has a few passenger cabins. The ship completes a Tilbury–Middlesbrough–Gdynia round-trip once a week, taking about 2 1/2 days to cross the North Sea. The trip costs £108 to £138 per person each way, £60 to £75 from October through March. Contact Gdynia America for details.

5 Getting Around

BY PLANE The Polish national airline, **LOT,** flies from Warsaw to a number of Polish cities, including Gdańsk, Szczecin, Poznań, Wrocław, and Kraków. There are also a few routes directly between Polish provincial cities, such as Poznań–Szczecin. Sample fares are included in the "Getting There" section of the city listings.

BY TRAIN The Polish rail system—known by its initials **PKP**—is one of the pleasures of traveling in Poland. If you are fond of trains and have always wanted to journey by reliable, comfortable, and inexpensive trains, Poland is a good place to indulge your desire.

There are three main types of trains in Poland. Express trains (*epresowy*) are the fastest. To ride these trains, you need, in addition to a ticket, a seat reservation, which you can purchase—usually at a separate ticket window at the train station or at an Orbis office—up to two months in advance for $1.40. IC (intercity) trains are like express trains, but the second-class compartments are less crowded with only six not eight seats. On IC trains, you get a free soft drink and cookie; the seat reservation costs $2.60.

Fast (*pospieszny*) trains, like express trains, are marked in red on departure schedules, usually have cars divided into compartments, and generally run on time to the minute. Unlike expresses, they do not require seat reservations. Tourists travel by fast train most often. Normal (*osobowy* or *normalny*) trains are marked in black on schedules. Normal trains sometimes lack compartments, making the cars noisier and draftier. And since they must move aside to let faster trains past, these trains often run behind schedule. In addition, normal trains often stop at several suburban stations before arriving at the main (*głowny*) station of a city. So if you are taking a normal train, be careful to get off at the correct station.

When plotting your itinerary, consider spending a night or two on sleeper trains, which will save you daylight hours for sightseeing and overnight hotel fare, too. Berths in a six-bed couchette compartment cost only $6.25 plus a second-class ticket. Four-bed couchettes cost $8.50 per person, and very comfortable second-class sleepers (three beds and a sink and closet) are $12.50. First-class sleepers (like second class but with only two beds in a compartment) cost $17.50 plus a first-class ticket.

If you board a train without a ticket and find the conductor right away, you'll pay an additional $1 for the ticket (if he finds you first, he'll fine you $1.25 plus the cost of the ticket).

PolRail Passes allow unlimited travel on all trains within Poland, although you still have to purchase your seat reservation or sleeping berth separately. A first-class pass costs $59 for 8 consecutive days, $69 for 15 days, $75 for 21 days, and $85 for one month. Second-class prices are $40, $45, $50, and $55, respectively. PolRail passes can only be purchased outside of Poland. Orbis sells them, as does RailEurope at 230 Westchester Ave., White Plains, NY 10604 (☎ toll free **800/438-7245**). Depending on how much you travel, these passes can end up saving you money in train fare. They also save you time you'd spend waiting in line for tickets. PolRail passes allow you the freedom to hop on trains without much advance planning.

When checking out departure (*odjazdy*) times in the train station, look for the yellow schedules on the walls. White schedules show train arrival (*przyjazdy*) times. When buying tickets, be certain that you're standing on the correct line. English is not usually spoken, so have your destination, time constraints, and any other concerns written out. Again, if you're not sure that you're in the correct line, ask your neighbor. Carry a phrase book and a pad and pencil—they'll come in handy.

Most Polish rail stations offer a 24-hour baggage-check service, and charge the same fees: 25¢, plus 1¢ per $1 of declared value (for insurance). Thus a bag declared at $50 would cost you 75¢ for the day. The baggage handler will ask you to declare a value as you give him your bag.

If you assign a low value (under $50) to a large bag, the baggage-check clerk may assign a higher insurance value to your bag. If you feel his quote is too high, negotiate by writing your price on a piece of paper. If this fails, try another baggage-check window, as there are several in the station.

A downside of Polish trains is that they are a favorite territory of thieves looking for tourists with big wallets. One popular technique is for a pair of thieves to approach a victim in a narrow corridor from both directions, pinning him in place and searching for valuables, all the while shouting "Excuse me!" as if they were innocently trying to pass. If this happens, hold onto your wallet, camera, and other valuables, and shove your way into a compartment. If you take a sleeper train, lock and bolt or chain the door before going to sleep.

BY BUS Poland operates an inexpensive long-distance bus system known by its initials, **PKS.** However, this form of transportation is very slow and should be avoided whenever possible. Even when the bus is a little faster than the train, the train's superior comfort makes it a better choice. You may have to take a bus to get to smaller towns where trains don't run, especially in eastern Poland where the rail system is less extensive than in the western part of the country.

BY TAXI Official Polish taxis are relatively economical. Short rides in cities usually cost $2 to $3 and a lengthy ride into a nearby suburb costs $4 to $5. The meter starts at 30 złotys, rising by 5 złotys for every kilometer. When you complete your journey, you must pay that amount multiplied by a set figure (about 1,000 when I last visited) depending on the city you're in. *Nightly between 11pm and 5am and on Sunday the price is doubled.*

As a general guideline for Warsaw, official taxis will post their multiplier rate on the dashboard inside their vehicle; many have a yellow and orange stripe on the taxi directly at the windshield level. As a guideline, don't feel obliged to take the first taxi in a line if the fare is unacceptable to you. Check with your hotel when you arrive to see whether rates have risen or the procedure changed.

In previous years, it was often difficult to find a taxi, but now with the worsening of Poland's economic situation, you're likely to see lines of taxis waiting for passengers. Unfortunately, some drivers, rather than treating their rare passengers with more courtesy, occasionally try to cheat tourists by charging considerably inflated rates. Beware, for example, of taxis that wait in front of large hotels or major tourist sights. Keep in mind that the meter should always be turned on *after* you enter the taxi, not before. Always ask to see the fare chart so that you understand what fare multiplier has been used. And it's always a good idea to carry change to avoid any higher rounding-off of the fare by the driver.

BY CAR In a country with some of the most picturesque landscape in Eastern Europe, driving is a pleasure. The price you pay for these memorable sights is narrow roads. Even on many major roads two-way traffic shares two lanes. The driver must exercise extreme caution, especially at night, as roads are usually not lit, making horse-drawn carts and other vehicles difficult to see.

Rentals At time of press, car rentals in Poland were still quite steep (about $450 a week) despite the presence of several major Western car-rental companies. Consider also that collision damage waiver insurance (CDW) of $12 is compulsory in Poland, except for American Express cardholders. For the same reasons, cars rented in other countries cannot be driven into Poland. For maximum savings, it's best to reserve and prepay for your car in the U.S.

Orbis often offer discounted rates. You can contact Orbis at 342 Madison Ave., Suite 1512, New York, NY 10173 (☎ **212/867-5011**).

Hertz (☎ toll free **800/654-3131**) has four offices in Warsaw, as well as offices in Kraków, Łódź, Poznań, Szczecin, Wrocław, and Gdańsk.

Budget Rent-a-Car (☎ toll free **800/527-0700**) has several offices in Warsaw and requires a 48-hour advance reservation.

Gasoline The lines that once characterized most Polish gas stations are now less common, although gas stations are less common on the road than in the United States. Most gas stations are open daily from 8am to 4 or 6pm; some stations stay open 24 hours.

Driving Rules To drive in Poland, all foreigners (with a rented car or their own vehicle) need an international driver's license (issued in the U.S. by the American Automobile Association) and an international insurance card (the Green Card), which can be purchased at the frontier or at any car-rental bureau.

On open roads, the speed limit is 90 kmph (54 m.p.h.), and 60 kmph (37 m.p.h.) within town limits. Other local speed limits are posted. Inside city limits you are not allowed to blow your horn, and wherever you are, drinking and driving is forbidden. Buy road maps at major bookstores, or ask at the local tourist office.

There are several brochures that you can request from The Polish National Tourist Office in the U.S. to help make your travel by car more successful and trouble-free: "Poland: A Tourist Road Map," "By Car to Poland," and "Poland: A Map of Camping Sites." You can also pick them up at any Tourist Information Bureau (PTTK/it) in Poland. Be sure to ask for the latest editions.

Auto Repair The **PZM Automobile Tourism Office,** with its main office at Aleja Jerozolimskie 63, Warsaw (☎ **02/28-62-51**), assists motorists in need, maintaining automobile help stations (*pomoc drogowa*) throughout Poland that will serve you on the spot or tow you to the nearest service station. In most cities you can get **emergency help** by calling **981.** Other regional emergency service numbers are listed in the city chapters.

HITCHHIKING Hitchhiking was a widely accepted and frequently used form of transportation until a few years ago. While it's still officially allowed, it is less widely accepted. If you do decide to hitchhike on freeways, you can only do so at freeway entrances. Penalties for violating this rule range from a scolding to a fine.

Suggested Itineraries

CITY HIGHLIGHTS

Częstochowa Poland's Mecca, where hundreds of thousands of religious faithful visit every year to see the sacred Black Madonna.

Gdańsk A Baltic port and exciting old seafaring town and modern political center.

Kraków Poland's most charming town, a center of art and architecture, as well as one of the few Polish cities to escape World War II destruction.

Toruń A pretty medieval town where Copernicus was born.

Warsaw The Polish capital and a good introduction to the history, politics, and culture of Poland.
Zakopane At the center of the breathtaking Tatra Mountains.

Planning Your Itinerary

If You Have 1 Week

Days 1 and 2 Arrive in Warsaw; use the first day to settle in and recover from your flight and another to see the sights.
Days 3–5 Travel to Kraków. Spend two days in this delightful city, and use a third day to visit the religious shrine of Częstochowa; Łańcut, the beautifully preserved château; or Auschwitz, the Nazi extermination camp. Then take an overnight train to Gdańsk.
Day 6 Tour Gdańsk, a historic port and shipbuilding city, and the home of the Solidarity movement.
Day 7 Return to Warsaw for your international flight.

If You Have 2 Weeks

Days 1–3 Arrive in Warsaw; spend two days seeing the sights of the capital.
Days 4–5 Travel to Gdańsk, the port city, perhaps using your second day for a day trip to Malbork, Frombork, or another nearby town. Then take the night train to Kraków.
Days 6–10 Spend three days in Kraków, using the other two days for side trips.
Days 11–12 Travel to Zakopane for hiking in the Tatra Mountains, then take a night train to Toruń.
Day 13 See the medieval sights of Toruń.
Day 14 Return to Warsaw for your flight.

If You Have More Time

Add more time to your stays in Warsaw or Kraków; or travel to Lublin and some of the smaller towns in southeastern Poland; or journey to some of the towns in western Poland, such as Poznań and Wrocław.

6 Enjoying Poland on a Budget

THE $30-A-DAY BUDGET

It's not overly difficult to eat and sleep for only $30 a day in Poland. Most of that amount will be spent on your hotel room, and dining out in Poland is remarkably inexpensive. If you keep to modest establishments, you can obtain two meals and breakfast for only $10 a day, leaving as much as $20 for your hotel room. If you choose to stay in private rooms and student hotels, you can afford the swankiest privately owned new restaurants in Warsaw, Kraków, and Wrocław. Or combine both strategies and spend less than $30 a day for food and lodging. And of course, if two of you are traveling together it's easier to stay below the $30-target.

SAVING MONEY ON ...

ACCOMMODATIONS • Hotels There are five categories of hotels in Poland: deluxe, four star, three star, two star, and one star. Until very recently Orbis, the Polish national tourist office, held a monopoly on the deluxe and four-star hotels. The best values still remain in the cheaper three-star and lower-rated hotels. (**Note:** Unfortunately, Orbis does not deal with most of the smaller budget hotels listed in this guide, so you must write directly to the hotels.) Some three-star hotels approach the quality of the Orbis hotels, both in the size of their rooms and in staff service. Most two-star hotels are aging and the accommodations are basic. The most noticeable amenity missing in a two-star hotel is a private bathroom (most, however, do have sinks in the rooms). In my descriptions of hotels, I have been careful to describe the state of the shared bathrooms, which range from perfectly clean to those that can be used only by the least fussy traveler.

Note: I recommend that you reserve a hotel room at least for Warsaw, Częstochowa, and Zakopane, because these cities often have large tour groups crowding the hotels.

A smaller Polish travel agency located only in Poland says that it can reserve budget hotel rooms at discounted rates if you contact them ahead of time at **Logos Tours,** ulica Czysta 1, 31–121 Kraków (☎ **012/34-04-11;** fax 012/34-03-25; telex 32-2615), Attn: Jadwiga Deszcz. Ms. Deszcz is fluent in English and is extremely helpful. They deal mostly with a series of teachers' hotels in Poland that provide remarkable value—$20 to $30 per person in doubles with half board. Contact them ahead of time with your specific program, they'll confirm the dates and then ask for a deposit.

One final tip on using hotel services: I have provided telephone numbers of Polish restaurants, organizations, etc., where English may not be spoken. Therefore, ask your hotel receptionist to call for you.

• **Private Rooms** In many Polish towns you can rent spare rooms in private houses, often owned by retired couples or elderly women. These are usually spacious, inexpensive rooms with clean bathrooms, and a boon for all budget travelers! If you intend to stay in private homes in Poland, I recommend that you bring a roll or two of toilet paper, as not every bathroom in Poland is well stocked.

• **Hostels and Camp Grounds** Some 126 youth hostels are open year round in Poland, so budget travelers should buy the *Youth Hostel Handbook,* available from the **Youth Hostel Federation (MTSM** are the Polish initials), at Szpitalna 5 in Warsaw. MTSM has its headquarters at ulica Chocimska 28, Warsaw (☎ **49-83-54**).

Campers can pitch a tent at numerous campgrounds across Poland. A campgrounds map (*Poland: A Map of Camping Sites*) in English is available at PTTK/it offices throughout Poland.

MEALS Although prices for meals in Poland's restaurants have increased in the past few years, they are still much lower than what you would pay for comparable meals in the West. You can dine in a fine restaurant for $4 to $5, and enjoy a more elaborate meal for $8 to $15. A simple lunch or dinner in an unassuming place costs $2 to $3.

Care in ordering, though, will save money. Alcohol, especially imported labels, is expensive and adds enormously to food bills. Limit your consumption of wine and fruit juices, as these are imported items and cost more than local products.

SIGHTSEEING Museums and sights in Poland have fairly low admission fees—most charge between 75¢ and $2.25. Students and children frequently receive a reduction of about 50%.

ENTERTAINMENT It's also relatively inexpensive to keep yourself entertained in Poland. For example, the weekly Chopin concert at Warsaw's Chopin Museum costs only $2.25. Many outdoor concerts are free.

SHOPPING The shopping scene in Polish cities is well on its way to resembling other Western cities; there is an exponentially growing number of stores that carry domestic and imported consumer goods, which range from everyday necessities to luxury items. Goods bought in Poland usually cost less than they do in the West, though this may change as Poland's economy expands. (Pewex, the state-run foreign goods shops, once held the monopoly on imported products. Now that Western items have become available in many shops in major cities, there's no particular advantage in shopping in Pewex stores except for convenience or for the occasional item that's not available anywhere else.) There is talk about imposing a VAT (value-added tax) on luxury items in the future.

Polish craft objects make wonderful gifts—embroidery, wool sweaters and hat, lace, dolls in folk costume, prints and engravings, amber, silver, pottery, and wood carvings. You'll find many of these objects in the national Cepelia shops, but there are also smaller places in cities across the country with good prices.

TRANSPORTATION Domestic train and bus fares have been climbing steadily in recent years; nonetheless, they remain much lower than Western fares. Riding first class on trains is recommended for a more comfortable, less crowded ride. Sample train and airfares are given in the city chapters.

TIPPING I suggest leaving waiters up to 10% of the check, depending on service. Bartenders should get 5%. A bellhop should get a few small złoty notes, and a restroom attendant gets a fixed posted rate of 15¢ to 25¢. Cloakroom attendants in restaurants get 5¢ to 25¢ per article. This amount is often posted, and hanging up one's coat is usually mandatory. Poles do not tip taxi drivers.

EXCHANGING MONEY The best place to change money is through small private exchange offices indicated by signs outside reading KANTOR WYMIANY WALUT, or just KANTOR. You'll see quite a few of these stores in each city you visit. As of this writing, these offices accept only Western cash, and do not charge a commission. Shop around, however, because some offer better rates than others.

Also, be sure to change your money before 5pm Monday through Saturday, since most Kantors close at 5pm. Most Kantors are closed on Sunday and you'll be forced to hunt around for a hotel or casino, which commonly offer significantly lower rates of exchange. Keep your receipts, which will allow you to change your złotys back into Western currency when you leave Poland.

Note: Remember to check all this advice when you arrive, for as Poland continues to adopt free-market ways, rules and regulations will change from month to month.

Fast Facts: Poland

American Express There is an office in Warsaw at Krakowskie Przedmieście 11 (☎ **635-2002;** fax 635-7556). Certain Orbis offices in other Polish cities represent American Express.

Business Hours Most offices and banks open at 8 or 9am and close at 3 or 4pm Monday through Friday; many offices are also open one Saturday a month. Grocery stores are usually open Monday through Friday from 6 or 7am until 6 to 8pm; other stores generally open at 10 or 11am. Many stores now have Saturday hours, generally 10am to 2pm. Most stores are closed on Sunday.

Cameras/Film Many camera shops have opened recently and sell Agfa, Fuji, and Kodak film and other Western camera supplies. Film prices are slightly lower than in the West. Several one-hour photo-developing shops have recently opened in Warsaw, and they're beginning to pop up in other major Polish cities.

Customs When you arrive at the frontier or at the airport, Customs may or may not inspect your bags. You can bring in personal possessions as long as they don't seem to be in excess quantity (like five radios) and gifts as long as their market value doesn't exceed $200. For complete guidelines on what you can take, inquire at the Polish consulate nearest you.

Export regulations change frequently, so if you intend to make any large purchases, I strongly recommend that you ask your embassy for advice first. In general, items can be taken out duty free if their value doesn't exceed $200. Items made or printed before 1945 usually require special permission. If you have to pay duty on an item, the rate ranges from 20% to 300% of the purchase value.

The main Customs office, at ulica Świętokrzyska 12 (☎ **694-35-87** or **694-55-96**), should be able to answer all export questions.

The *Warsaw Voice,* a weekly English-language publication available in many hotels and bookstores, frequently publishes a detailed list of Customs regulations.

Doctors/Medical Care Poland extends free medical care to citizens of Great Britain, but citizens of the United States and other countries must pay for any treatment they receive. If you are ill, call your embassy or consulate for advice (they have a list of recommended physicians), or ask at your hotel. For first aid emergencies, call **999.**

Drug Laws Polish law prohibits the importation, possession, or consumption of narcotics. If you carry medications containing narcotics or other "hard" drugs, bring with you a valid prescription signed by your physician (the same applies for medications injected by syringes).

Drugstores Most common Western medications are now widely available in drug stores (*apteka*) in Poland. There are several 24-hour pharmacies in Warsaw and at least one in major cities.

Electricity The power supply is 220 volts, 50 cycles, AC.

Embassies/Consulates Citizens of New Zealand should contact the British embassy for assistance.

- **Australia** The embassy is at Estonska 3–5, Saska Kepa, Warsaw (☎ **22/617-6081** to **617-6085**).
- **Canada** The embassy is at ulica Matejki 1–5, Warsaw (☎ **22/29-80-51**).
- **United Kingdom** The embassy is at Aleja Róz 1, Warsaw (☎ **2/628-10-01**).
- **United States** The embassy is at Aleja Ujazdowskie 29–31, Warsaw (☎ **22/628-3040**). The consulate in Poznań is at Chopina 4 (☎ **61/52-95-86**). The consulate in Kraków is at Stolarska 9 (☎ **12/22-77-93**).

Emergencies In most cities, for police call toll free **997;** to report a fire, call **998;** and for first aid call **999.**

Etiquette Should you have the pleasure of being invited to a Polish party, it's generally good manners to bring a bottle of something strong to drink; *delikatesy* shops have the best selection and prices. If you must leave early from what looks to be a long and wild affair, you'll need to call upon your best diplomatic skill to extricate yourself.

Information In Poland tourist information offices are identified as **it** (*informacja turystczna*). The staff at it tends to be friendly and helpful, and especially appreciates a genuine interest in local history, sites, and current affairs. You can purchase local maps from it, and also obtain transit schedules and information about festivals, exhibits, and other cultural events. In addition, tourist offices generally have lists of all hotels in town, complete with current prices, and can advise you if any new restaurants have opened.

Language Even if your only language is English, you should not have too much trouble communicating in Poland. Tourist offices generally have at least one English-speaker on duty at all times, as well as brochures in English. Also, most of the hotels listed in this book have English-speakers at the desk, and many restaurants have English translations on their menus, or English menus are available on request. Most important, train schedules, museum prices, and opening hours are posted, so you will have less need to ask spoken questions than, for example, in the Balkans.

Most Poles over 45 speak only Polish. English is a popular second language, as is German, especially in cities like Wrocław and Gdańsk that were inhabited by Germans until 1945. Despite having mandatory Russian in school, the Poles never really took to it, and teachers were not particularly eager to force the occupier's tongue upon their students. If you know any Slavic language, this will help you with numbers, reading, and, in a pinch, conversation.

At first glance, for English-speaking people the Polish language appears impossible to decipher since many consonants have entirely different sounds from the ones they have in English. I have found though that once you learn the sounds of the various letters and consonant clusters, the language becomes progressively easier. You can pick up the phonetic sound of Polish letters through a class or a cassette course. I recommend the eight-cassette course offered by Audio Forum; contact the Foreign Language Dept., 96 Broad St., Guilford, CT 06437 (☎ toll free **800/243-1234**) for a catalogue. *Berlitz Polish for Travellers* is an indispensable aid to help you through all sorts of situations. Only a few stores actually stock it, but you can order it through Berlitz, P.O. Box 305, 1829 Underwood Blvd., Delran, NJ 08075 (☎ toll free **800/526-8047**).

Laundry Poland does not have coin-operated laundries, but the cleaning staff in many hotels will do your wash for a negotiable and often low price. You'll find dry-cleaning stores in many towns; some are listed in the city chapters.

Mail Polish mail is a bit unpredictable; airmail to the United States can take anywhere from one week to three weeks or even ten. But it usually gets there.

Post offices (*poczta*) are usually open Monday through Friday from 8am to 8pm. You can also buy stamps at newsstands. Poland produces some of the world's most interesting stamps, from elegant engravings of Polish kings to hilarious cartoon drawings. For the best selection, head to the philatelic counter of the main post office in a large city.

Maps A firm called PPWK produces maps of every city in Poland. Though not always the absolutely best map of a given town, these maps, which cost about $1 each, are always good, with blowups of the city center, tram and bus lines, a complete street index, and hotels, museums, and other sites marked and labeled in English.

Movies Many movies are shown in the original language with subtitles. Ask first at the theater. Many urban Poles, especially students, are avid moviegoers, and you may be surprised at the number of recently released American films playing in moviehouses in major Polish cities.

Newspapers/Magazines *Newsweek, Time,* and the *International Herald Tribune* are sold in Poland's largest hotels, especially in Warsaw. Two interesting weekly local English-language newspapers are the *Warsaw Voice* and the Solidarity *Gazeta International.*

Photography Aside from military or transportation sites (for example, bridges, train stations, etc.), you can click away freely in Poland.

Police To reach the police, dial **997** (a toll-free call) in most cities.

Restrooms Most public restrooms have an attendant outside who charges a penny or two; it's a good idea to keep small złoty notes for this purpose. A triangle on the door means "men" and a circle means "women."

Safety Recently, crime has markedly increased in Poland, but you'll find Poland safer than most Western European nations. Avoid drunkards, who appear on the street in sizable numbers especially after dark, for they are sometimes combative.

The U.S. Embassy has issued a crime advisory, warning visitors to guard their personal possessions, especially when using public transportation. Americans have filed numerous reports with the embassy and consulates in Poland about the theft of money, passports, and backpacks. Be especially careful along major train routes both domestic and international, as organized crime groups seem to favor them.

Telephone/Telegraph Dial **913** for local information (in Polish), 900 for a long-distance domestic operator, and 901 for an international operator.

Some pay phones in Poland accept tokens—"A" tokens are good for three-minute local calls, and "C" tokens are for longer local calls and for intercity calls. You can buy these tokens (called *żetony*) at newspaper kiosks.

Card phones, which can be used for local, intercity, or international calls, are usually only found in post offices and some train and bus stations. A few card phones can be found on the streets of Warsaw. A city's main post office usually has some card phones that are open 24 hours a day. Post offices and some kiosks sell *karty magnetyczne* in denominations of 50 ($4.25) and 100 ($8.50) "A" token equivalents. A 100-unit card will last for a 6-minute European call or a 3-minute call to North America.

To call another country from Poland, dial "00" followed by the country code, city code, and number.

To call Poland from abroad, dial your international access number (generally 00, 01, or 011), followed by the digits 48 and the city code, dropping the initial zero. For example, to call a number in Kraków from the U.S., you would dial 011-48-12, then the number; to make the same call from Warsaw, you would dial 012, then the number.

Time Polish time is one hour ahead of London time, and six hours ahead of eastern time in the U.S. Poland goes on daylight saving time the last Sunday in March and back to standard time the last Sunday in September.

Water The effects of vast pollution of years past has recently come to light. Initial studies suggest that the water is not as clean as had been officially reported in previous years, especially in the region around Kraków. You might want to stick to bottled mineral water.

27

Warsaw

THE CAPITAL OF POLAND FOR ALMOST 400 YEARS, WARSAW (POP. 1.7 MILLION) offers some of the country's greatest art, architectural, and historical treasures although, truth be told, there is more to see in Kraków. It also continues to be the vibrant intellectual, cultural, and political center of Poland.

According to legend, Warsaw (Warszawa in Polish, pronounced Var-*sha-va*) was founded when a mermaid ordered two fishermen, Wars and Sawa, to form a city. In reality, its position as a bustling trade center established it as an important town in the 15th century; merchants traveling across Europe would usually come through Warsaw.

In 1595 after Poland and Lithuania had united, King Zygmunt III moved the capital from Kraków to Warsaw, so that it would be closer to the geographical center of the realm. But Warsaw, like Poland in general, lacked geographical defenses against invasion. In 1656, the Swedish army completely flattened the city, but it was soon rebuilt. Warsaw escaped foreign rule during the first two partitions of Poland. But after resisting one Russian siege in 1794, it fell to a second, and was awarded to Prussia. The Napoleonic Wars and the Congress of Vienna bounced the beleaguered city back to Russian rule, where it remained until independence in 1918.

Warsaw's darkest days came during World War II, when the Varsovians were crushed by the brutality of the Nazis. From the first day of World War II on September 1, 1939, when the Nazis bombed the city, the Germans continued a policy of terror until Soviet troops entered the city in January 1945. The Poles resisted the Nazi occupation despite great losses and suffering. In 1943, 40,000 Jews in the Warsaw Ghetto rose up against the Nazis but were routed, most sent to concentration camps, and the ghetto was razed. A year later in the Warsaw Uprising, 18,000 soldiers and 150,000 civilians died in 63 days of bitter fighting. After these unsuccessful attempts to overthrow its invaders, Warsaw was systematically devastated by the Nazis, who left only a few facades standing amid the rubble. Over the course of the war, 800,000 Varsovians died and 85% of Warsaw's buildings were completely destroyed.

In the years immediately after the war, town planners gathered old prints, photographs, paintings, and plans, and rebuilt the historic center as it was before the war. This area is surrounded by many examples of gray Stalinist architecture.

1 Orientation

ARRIVING

BY PLANE If you're flying into Warsaw from another country, you'll arrive at the dazzling new **Okęcie International Airport,** at ulica Żwirki i Wigury 1. You can get some Polish złotys after Customs; but as rates are better in town, change only a small amount here.

Note: For international flight information call **46-17-00, 46-91-22,** or **46-98-73.**

Getting to and from the Airport There's a connecting airport minibus to and from the Hotel Marriott in the town center, which leaves every half hour from 6am until 10pm daily. The ride takes from 20 to 30 minutes and costs $3.25. The Airport-City bus runs daily from 6am to 11pm, every 20 minutes Monday through Friday and every 30 minutes on weekends. Tickets cost $1 and can be bought from the driver.

What's Special About Warsaw

Buildings

- Old Market Square, impressively restored from wartime damage to create a 17th- or 18th-century ambience.
- Wilanów Palace, the summer home of Poland's greatest kings, surrounded by lovely gardens.
- The Royal Castle, a reconstructed version with art and furniture from the palace used by centuries of Polish royalty.
- The Citadel, Russian fortress from 1832 where antitsarist Poles were imprisoned and executed.

Museums

- Historical Museum of Warsaw, with screenings of a film showing the city's destruction at the close of World War II.
- National Museum, collection of art from antiquity to modern Polish styles.
- Chopin Museum, celebrating Poland's greatest composer with exhibits and weekly concerts.

Parks

- Łázienki Park, the old royal park with beautiful small palaces and villas throughout.

There's also a slower local bus (no. 175) that goes to and from the Central Train Station and Krakowskie Przedmieście, Warsaw's main street in the town center; it's just 30¢—the best airport to town value in Europe! It runs every 10 minutes between 5:30am and 10:30pm.

A taxi to the town center should cost $5 to $7 with a metered cab—but some drivers will ask for $15 to $20.

Domestic flights arrive in Warsaw at a second airport at 17 Stycznia St. no. 39, which is located near Okęcie International Airport. From here, bus no. 114 will take you to the center of Warsaw. To get to the domestic airport, you can take bus no. 114 from Trzech Krzyz′y Square.

Note: For domestic flight information, call **46-11-43.**

BY TRAIN The central railway station, **Warszawa Centralna,** on Aleja Jerozolimskie (☎ **25-50-50**) is an enormous multilevel building and somewhat confusing in its layout.

Four different levels make up Warszawa Centralna: Trains arrive and depart on Level 1. Level 2 has bus and taxi connections, baggage lockers, and several baggage-check windows. On Level 3, the station's largest area, you can buy tickets (for domestic trains only) and get information. Above Windows 1 to 16 you'll see a giant departure timetable. The Roman numeral next to the departure time indicates the platform number; a boxed Arabic number refers you to special information about the train (such as, what days of the week the train does not run and whether reservations are needed) at the side of the huge timetable. There's also a post office, open daily from 8am to 8pm, on this level. Next to the post office, the WASTEELS counter sells international tickets to people 26 and under; others can buy tickets on Level 4.

Window 1 gives international train information, Windows 2 to 4 sell international tickets for that day only, and Windows 5 to 11 international tickets for up to one month in advance.

Information/Buying Tickets To avoid the often-long lines of Warsaw's train station, make inquiries and purchase tickets at the Orbis offices at ul. Bracka 16 (☎ **27-27-02**) or at the corner of Królewska and Marszałkowska streets, or from the POLRES train office at Al. Jerozolimskie 44 (☎ **24-40-89**).

Buy your tickets for international trains as soon as you can, preferably upon your arrival in town. If you choose to buy your tickets at the station, it's imperative that you write everything down to show the ticket seller: your destination, departure time, type of train (slow, fast, or express), seat class, and request for a seat reservation or sleeping berth.

Note: For train information in Polish, call **20-03-61** to **20-03-69** for domestic trains, or **20-45-12** for international trains.

Arriving trains sometimes make subsidiary stops in Warsaw (at stations such as Warszawa Wschodnia or Warszawa Zachodnia), and often terminate at one of those stations after stopping at Warszawa Centralna. On rare occasions a train may start or terminate at the Warszawa Gdańska station. From there, take tram 15, 31, or 36, or bus A, 116, 122, or 132 to reach the city center.

BY BUS If you take a long-distance bus from Warsaw, you'll probably leave from the main bus terminal (☎ **28-48-11** or **23-63-94**) at the Warszawa-Zachodnia train station on Aleja Jerozolimskie. You can reach this terminal by taking the suburban railway two stops from the central train station. If you're leaving for the northeastern part of Poland, however, you'll depart from the Stadium Coach Terminal on Zamoyskiego (☎ **18-54-73**), which you can reach on tram 7 or 25 from the center. Across the lake from the station is the Stadion Dziesięciolecia (10th Anniversary Stadium), which was built from World War II rubble.

TOURIST INFORMATION

Warsaw's central tourist information office, the **Mufa Agency** (☎ **31-04-64** or **635-18-81**) is conveniently located in Castle Square, at 1/13 Plac Zamkowy, at the entrance to the Old Town. Look for the sign in front that reads "it–Warszawskie Centrum Informacji Turystycznej–Kantor and Guides." It's open Monday through Friday from 9am to 6pm, on Saturday from 10am to 6pm, and on Sunday from 11am to 6pm (summer hours). The staff at Mufa is quite helpful and tries to assist travelers with all their inquiries. They also maintain a list of English-speaking guides.

Maps The best, most up-to-date map of Warsaw is sold here at Mufa, its title is *Warszawa: In Full Administrative Borders–All Streets* ($3). This map is fully indexed and shows all bus and tram lines.

Train Schedules Mufa also posts the latest train schedules; and if you call them (at ☎ **31-04-64**), they will give you departure times in English.

Guidebooks For detailed sightseeing in Warsaw, consider *Warsaw: A Concise Guide* by Wiesław Głębocki and Karol Mórawski. You may also find smaller English-language guides to Łazienski Park, Wilanów, the Royal Way, and other sights in Warsaw on sale at Mufa.

FOR STUDENTS The main youth bureau, **Almatur,** is on a small street parallel to Nowy Świat, at Kopernika 23 (☎ **26-26-39, 26-35-12,** or **26-23-56**). Almatur rents cheap student dorm rooms in July and August to students and those under age

35. In addition they can give you advice on planning your travels and reserve you a room in other summer student hotels across Poland. The office is open Monday through Friday from 9am to 4pm, Saturday from 10am to 2pm.

CITY LAYOUT

Although Warsaw is a large city, it's not overly difficult to find your way around as many of the city's sights are within a compact area. The Old Town (Stare Miasto) is Warsaw's historical center. Its nucleus is the charming Old Town Marketplace (Rynek Starego Miasta), where Poles have traded and shopped for hundreds of years. The Vistula (Wisła) River flows to the east side of the Old Town.

Main Arteries and Streets

You'll learn most of Warsaw's major streets if you walk from the main train station to the Old Town, a 30-minute endeavor. From the train station, walk down Aleja Jerozolimskie, a wide avenue lined with stores. Across this street from the station you'll see the Marriott Hotel, Warsaw's largest and most modern building. A block down, you pass the huge Palace of Culture. It's Warsaw's second-tallest and, according to locals, ugliest building, a gift of "friendship" from the Soviet Union after World War II. Continuing on Aleja Jerozolimskie, you soon pass the tall Forum Hotel on the right side of this noisy, busy street. On the left side is Warsaw's major department store, Centrum. This intersection forms a major public transportation hub, and I'll refer to it later in this chapter.

Three blocks farther along, Aleja Jerozolimskie intersects with Warsaw's principal north–south axis, the Royal Way, which connects the Royal Castle in the Old Town with King Jan Sobieski's residence at Wilanów. At this point, the Royal Way goes by the name of Nowy Świat (pronounced Novi *Svi*-at). Turn left onto this main pedestrian and shopping avenue. Soon the street's name changes to Krakowskie Przedmieście (pronounced Kra-kov-ski-eh Pshed-me-scheh).

After about 15 minutes, the street ends and you arrive at the Old Town. First you enter Plac Zamkowy (Castle Square), site of the Royal Castle and the tourist information office. Walking across the square and then left for a few minutes, you reach the Old Town Marketplace (Rynek Starego Miasta), the heart of the Old Town.

Neighborhoods in Brief

The reconstructed Old Town quarter is a magnet for tourists to Warszawa.

Because of the wholesale destruction of the city in World War II, the joy of discovering architecturally distinct neighborhoods is greatly diminished, for gray modern housing runs almost uniformly across Warsaw.

North of the Old Town is the small New Town (Nowe Miasto), and farther on, Zoliborz, considered a more fashionable address in Warsaw. Across the Vistula you'll find the Praga district. It was the least damaged area of Warsaw during World War II, and largely remains a residential area today.

Maps The most useful map to get is the fully indexed *Warszawa: In Full Administrative Boarders–All Streets;* it has the city's public transportation system fully

IMPRESSIONS

I think one sees more pretty women in five minutes in Warsaw than in half-an-hour in any other European capital, London thrown in.
—Harry De Windt, *From Pekin to Calais by Land,* 1889

demarcated and costs about $3. The common Warsaw maps aren't bad; they have a number of sights on the back that are keyed to the map.

Finding an Address When reading maps, searching for addresses, or navigating your way around Warsaw, you should know that *ulica* (ul.) means "street" (ulica is always lowercased while the following are always capitalized); *Aleja* (Al.) means "avenue"; *Plac* (Pl.) is a "square" or "plaza"; and *Rynek* is the market square. **Note:** In addresses, street numbers follow the street name (for example, ul. Nowy Świat 62).

2 Getting Around

BY BUS & TRAM Warsaw's extensive public transportation system conveniently links the entire city. Tram and bus fare is inexpensive—20¢ a ticket. Currently there are no transfer tickets; a new ticket must be used and canceled for each ride. Ask at the tourist office for an overview on the system, this way you'll avoid any undue surprises in case there have been changes in the system.

Regular daytime lines operate between 5:50am to 11pm. After 11pm, special night buses (designated by three digits beginning with the number six on a dark blue background) run on select lines; these cost 60¢.

Tickets You can buy tickets at newstands, kiosks, and from street vendors designated MZK. If you can't find one, ask someone at the bus or tram stop to sell you a ticket (often, they'll give you a ticket and refuse payment).

Passes Twenty-four hour passes cost 75¢, weekly passes are $3.75, and monthly passes cost $10.

When boarding the bus or tram, be sure to cancel your ticket by pushing it downward in the metal slot boxes to perforate it completely. (You won't see many Varsovians canceling their tickets as they generally purchase monthly passes.) Each bus and tram has its unique design—to crack down on fare beating—and the controller will check your ticket. If there's a discrepancy of design or if you have no canceled ticket, you'll be fined $15 on the spot. [If you don't have the złoty on you, you are within your rights to ask for a bill (*rachunek*) so you can send the payment to the proper agency.] Here, as in Kraków and some other cities, students can ride twice on each ticket, punching only one end of the ticket each ride. Adults must cancel both end, each ride.

BY TAXI Taxis in Warsaw are moderately priced to relatively expensive, depending on the taxi multiplier and where you get your cab. Taxis are very easy to find—in fact you'll see many lined up at taxi stands all around the city. Taxis found near all major tourist areas—train stations, airports, tourist sites—can cost double or even triple the standard fare; beware of rip-offs near Plac Zamkowy (Castle Square) in particular. If you're coming from one of these places, take public transportation, or walk to the next nearest taxi stand and then get the cab. A daytime ride from the Central Train Station to Old Town costs about $4; after 11pm all fares double. If the driver refuses to use the meter, find another. For a radio taxi, call **919;** for complaints, **22-44-44.**

BY CAR You can easily get around Warsaw by public transportation and moderately priced taxis, but if you want to rent a car to explore Poland, it will be easiest to pick up a rental in Warsaw.

Car-rental prices are steep in Poland, in part because collision damage waiver insurance (CDW) is compulsory. Of the major Western car-rental companies, **Budget Rent-a-Car** (☎ toll free **800/527-0700**) offers the best deal in Warsaw—$530 per week with unlimited mileage (with CDW) with a 48-hour advance reservation. However, for maximum savings it's best to reserve and pay for your car in the U.S. with Orbis (☎ **212/867-5011**) which works in conjunction with Hertz (rental must be for a minimum of three days). See "Getting Around" in Chapter 26 for full details.

BY HORSE & BUGGY In the Old Town you can ride much like Warsaw's old aristocrats did—in horse drawn carriages—starting from Rynek Starego Miasta (the Old Town marketplace). One driver quoted me a price of $20 for the 30-minute spin around the Old Town.

Fast Facts: Warsaw

Airlines LOT maintains offices in the Hotel Victoria Inter-Continental, at ul. Królewska 11; and also at the Marriott Hotel at Al. Jerozolimskie 65/67 (☎ **952, 953, 628-10-09,** or **628-75-80**); they are open Monday through Friday from 8am to 8pm and on Saturday from 8am to 5pm. The Austrian Airlines office is at ul. Złota 44/46, 4th floor (☎ **26-11-19**).

American Express There's an office at Krakowskie Przedmieście 11,00069 Warsaw (☎ **635-2002;** fax 635-7556). They cash traveler's checks (American Express checks into złotys at no commission), hold mail, and provide emergency check-cashing (the latter for cardholders only). They're open Monday through Friday from 9am to 5pm and on Saturday from 10am to 2pm. There is also an Express Cash machine outside, open all night.

Area Code The telephone area code for the Warsaw region is 022. It should be noted that recently an extra digit (the number 6) has been added to the beginning of some of Warsaw's telephone numbers. When dialing from outside Warsaw, drop one of the 2's of the usual 022 area code to accommodate the 6.

Bookstores The main tourist office on Plac Zamkowy sells a number of English-language guides to Warsaw and other destinations. With some luck, you can also find good English-language guidebooks, as well as colorful artbooks and biographies of Pope John Paul II, in the many new private as well as government bookstores (called "Dom Ksiazki" in Polish) along the Royal Way and on ulica Jerozolimskie. Panorama, ul. Nowogrodzka 56 (☎ **21-19-28**), near the Marriott Hotel sells a small but varied selection of new English-language paperbacks for only $2 to $2.50 each. It's open Monday through Friday 10am to 6pm. Nearby, Bookland, Al. Jerozolimskie 61 (☎ **625-41-46**), has a slightly better selection and much higher prices (open Monday through Friday 11am to 7pm and Saturday 9am to 1pm).

Cameras/Film Developing Many camera supply shops selling Agfa, Fuji, and Kodak film and other Western camera supplies have opened recently. There are also several one-hour photo-developing services near the train station and the university.

Currency Exchange As elsewhere in Poland, avoid banks and the official Orbis exchange desks as they offer low rates for the dollar. Rather, seek out private money-exchange bureaus, labeled Kantor, for the best rate for Polish złotys. You'll see dozens along the main streets of town; shop around, for the rates do vary. There's an exchange bureau at the Central Train Station that's open 24 hours daily. A few Kantor offices in Warsaw sell the currencies of other Eastern European countries such as the Czech and Slovak Republics, Hungary, Bulgaria, and Romania (rates vary, so check around).

Dentists/Doctors Call the Warsaw Medical Service Information Center (☎ **26-27-61** or **26-83-00**) for a referral, or call your embassy for English-speaking doctors and dentists that they recommend.

Drugstores The Swiss Pharmacy at 2 Al. Róż (☎ **21-32-30** or **628-78-52**), off Aleja Ujazdowskie in the embassy district, is the most reliable pharmacy in Warsaw, with a wide selection of medications and an English-speaking staff. It's open Monday through Friday from 9am to 7pm and on Saturday from 11am to 3pm. There are half a dozen 24-hour drugstores in Warsaw, including one in Old Town at ul. Freta 13 (☎ **31-50-91**). Ask your hotelier for help in contacting one, should you need one in an emergency.

Embassies/Consulates Citizens of New Zealand should contact the British embassy for assistance.

- **Australia** The embassy is at Estonska 3–5, Saska Kepa, Warsaw (☎ **617-6081** to **617-6085**).
- **Canada** The embassy is at ulica Matejki 1–5, Warsaw (☎ **29-80-51**).
- **United Kingdom** The embassy is at Aleja Róż 1, Warsaw (☎ **628-10-01**).
- **United States** The embassy is at Aleja Ujazdowskie 29–31, Warsaw (☎ **628-3040**).

Emergencies For a police emergency, dial **997**. For an ambulance, call **999.**

Hospitals For medical care, ask your embassy or hotel for assistance. In emergencies, you can call an ambulance at **999,** or go to the hospital at ul. Hoza 56 (☎ **628-24-24** to **628-24-27**).

Laundry/Dry Cleaning Usually the cheapest way to have clothes cleaned is to ask the cleaning staff of budget hotels. If you need a dry cleaner, try the one at Krakowskie Przedmieście 6, open Monday through Friday from 9am to 7pm and on Saturday from 9am to 1pm. Near the central train station, you'll find Pralnia-Chemiczna at ul. Chmielna 22, open Monday through Friday from 11am to 6pm.

Luggage Storage/Lockers The second level of Warsaw's Central Train Station (Warszawa Centralna) has baggage lockers, as well as several 24-hour baggage-check services. As in most train stations in Poland, bags cost 25¢ a day to store, plus 1¢ per $1 of declared value for insurance. For more details, see "Getting Around" in Chapter 26.

Maps If you're not staying long, there's an adequate small map of downtown Warsaw in the middle of *Warszawa What, Where, When,* which is available gratis in upscale hotels. Large detailed maps are now sold in travel agencies, bookstores, newsstands, book kiosks, and some hotels; they cost about $3. Be sure to buy the latest edition, and one with good mass-transit information. I recommend *Warszawa: In Full Administrative Borders–All Streets.*

Newspapers/Magazines Foreign newspapers and magazines are sold in most upscale hotel kiosks, International Press and Book Clubs, and selected bookstores. Be sure to look for the local *Warsaw Voice,* a weekly English-language publication available in many hotels. It lists current cultural events, runs features of local and national interest, and often includes a page of useful tourist information. You can also contact their friendly and knowledgeable sales staff Monday through Friday from 10am to 3pm (☎ **37-51-38** or **37-91-45**). There are several free, English-language magazines that are distributed in major hotels and airline offices. The most useful is *Warszawa What, Where, When,* which has short descriptions of all of Warsaw's museums and the latest prices of taxis and stamps.

Photographic Needs See "Cameras/Film Developing," above.

Police In an emergency, dial **997.**

Post Office There are four central post offices: at ul. Świętokrzyska 31/33 (☎ **26-60-01**), the main post office, open 24 hours a day; near the Old Town at Krakowskie Przedmieście 11; in the Old Town Marketplace at Rynek Starego Miasta 15; and in the Warszawa Centralna (the Central Train Station), on the third (main) level, poczta no. 120 (☎ **25-44-16**). The last three post offices are open daily from 8am to 8pm.

Restrooms You'll probably first encounter the pay toilets common throughout Poland in Warsaw's restaurants, museums, and other public places. Keep some small change (5¢ to 25¢) handy; the rates will be posted.

Safety Crime has increased substantially in Warsaw in the last few years. Tourists have been robbed at the train station in daylight hours. Be wary of pickpockets, purse snatchers, and confidence men, especially at Warsaw's train stations, on crowded public transport, and at major tourist destinations.

Shoe Repairs Look for a sign saying NAPRAWA OBUWIA or ask at your hotel. Services such as this are generally very inexpensive in Poland.

Smoking Smoking is prohibited in public buildings and on public transportation.

Telephone/Telegraph/Telex You can place international calls from the main post office at ul. Świętokrzyska 31/33, open 24 hours daily, but you still may have to wait a few hours.

The easiest way to make a long-distance or international call is with a magnetic phone card (see "Fast Facts: Poland" in Chapter 26). An office at ul. Nowogrodzka 45 sells these cards and has several phones that accept them. You can also send a fax at this office. Other card phones appear at post offices, some hotels, and on some downtown streets.

Thomas Cook There's an office at ul. Nowy świat 64 (☎ **26-38-67**), open Monday through Friday from 9am to 4pm. Thomas Cook also sells train tickets to Western countries.

Water Varsovians advise visitors not to drink the tap water in Warsaw—it's reputedly full of heavy toxic metals.

3 Where to Stay

PRIVATE ROOMS For maximum savings, consider private rooms. You won't find a better value for your money. You can rent a basic though centrally located room through the Syrena-Univel Tourist and Trade Corp., located at ul. Krucza 17 (☎ **628-75-40**). They are open Monday through Saturday 8am to 7pm and Sunday 8am to 5pm. A single with bath goes for $9.50; a double with bath for $15. This company is managed by Helena Romaczuk, who speaks good English.

Another excellent source for private rooms is the R & J Agency (☎ **29-29-93**) conveniently located at ul. Emilii Plater 30—just one block from the train station and across the street from the Marriott Hotel. This bed-and-breakfast agency is efficiently run by the enterprising Mrs. Wanda Szymanska, who speaks good English and will find you a single room in a central location for $15 and a double for about $22 a day including breakfast. R & J is open daily from 9am to 7pm. If you're loaded down with luggage, the only drawback is having to climb two flights of steep, old wooden stairs to her apartment (no. 15). You might consider checking your bags at the train station if you're headed to R & J.

FOR STUDENTS During July and August, students and adventurous travelers under age 35 can rent an inexpensive room in a student hotel from Almatur, the main youth bureau. Their office is located at Kopernika 23 (☎ **26-26-39, 26-35-12,** or **26-23-56**), a small street parallel to Nowy Świat. They can also reserve you a room in other summer student hotels across Poland and can advise you on planning your travels. Their hours are Monday through Friday from 9am to 4pm, Saturday from 10am to 2pm.

Youth Hostel, Smolna 30. ☎ **022/27-89-52.** 113 beds. **Tram:** Any from the train station, three stops east, past the Forum Hotel. **Bus:** 158 from the train station.

Rates: $3.70 per person with a hostel card, $4 without. Sheets cost 75¢ for the duration of your stay; a towel is another 25¢. Maximum stay three nights.

Bring your International Youth Hostel card to this very basic but extraordinarily centrally located hostel near the Polish national museum. Rooms have 5 to 16 beds each. You can't stay between 10am and 5pm, and you must return by 11pm. There is a Ping-Pong table, TV room, and kitchen for guests' use.

Another option, with similar arrangements, is the Youth Hostel at ul. Karolkowa 53A (☎ **32-88-29**). Take tram no. 24.

The reception desk at both hostels is open from 5 to 9pm.

Hotels

In Warsaw, budget hotels will not cause you to exceed your $30-a-day limitation. Some budget hotels are a bit shabby with decorations and facilities from 20 to 30 years ago, but many are now being renovated. Most budget hotels offer rooms both with or without a private bathroom. Often you'll save considerably by taking a room without a private bathroom. Have a look at the public plumbing facilities before taking the room—just to make sure they're up to your standards. **Note:** It's helpful to reserve your accommodations, especially during the summer when hotels fill up quickly.

DOUBLES FOR LESS THAN $25

In the Center

$ **Hotel Belfer,** Wybrzeże Kościuszkowskie 31/33, 00-379 Warsaw. ☎ **02/625-05-71.** Fax 02/625-26-00. Telex 816420. 214 rms (60 with bath). TEL **Bus:** 128 from the train station to the intersection of ulica Jaracza and ulica Dobra; the hotel is just a block from there.

Rates: $10.50 single without bath, $18.50 single with bath; $20.50 double without bath, $24 double with bath. $40-$50 apartment.

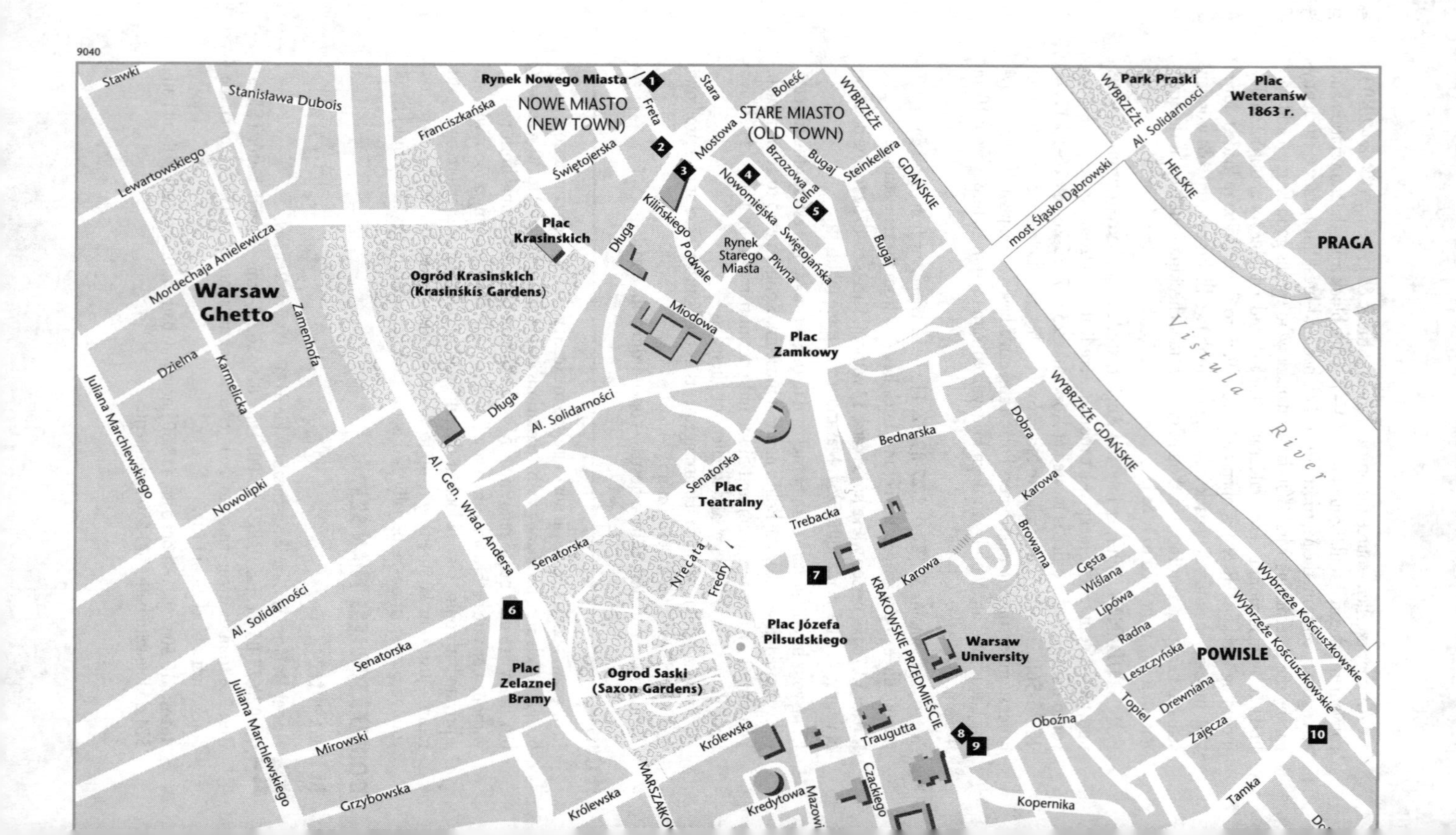
9040
Rynek Nowego Miasta
NOWE MIASTO (NEW TOWN)
STARE MIASTO (OLD TOWN)
Park Praski
Plac Weteranśw 1863 r.
PRAGA
Vistula River
Warsaw Ghetto
Plac Krasinskich
Ogród Krasinskich (Krasinśkis Gardens)
Rynek Starego Miasta
Plac Zamkowy
Plac Teatralny
Plac Józefa Pilsudskiego
Ogrod Saski (Saxon Gardens)
Plac Zelaznej Bramy
Warsaw University
POWISLE
Stawki
Stanisława Dubois
Lewartowskiego
Franciszkańska
Świętojerska
Freta
Stara
Mostowa
Boleść
WYBRZEŻE GDAŃSKIE
Brzozowa
Bugaj
Steinkellera
Nowomiejska
Celna
Kilińskiego
Podwale
Piwna
Świętojańska
Długa
Miodowa
Mordechaja Anielewicza
Zamenhofa
Dzielna
Karmelicka
Julianna Marchlewskiego
Al. Solidarności
Nowolipki
Al. Gen. Wład. Andersa
Senatorska
Niecała
Fredry
Trebacka
Bednarska
Dobra
Karowa
Browarna
Gęsta
Wiślana
Lipówa
Radna
Leszczyńska
Topiel
Drewniana
Zajęcza
Tamka
Oboźna
Kopernika
KRAKOWSKIE PRZEDMIEŚCIE
Traugutta
Czackiego
Królewska
Kredytowa
Mirowski
Grzybowska
most Śląsko Dąbrowski
HELSKIE
Wybrzeże Kościuszkowskie
1
2
3
4
5
6
7
8
9
10

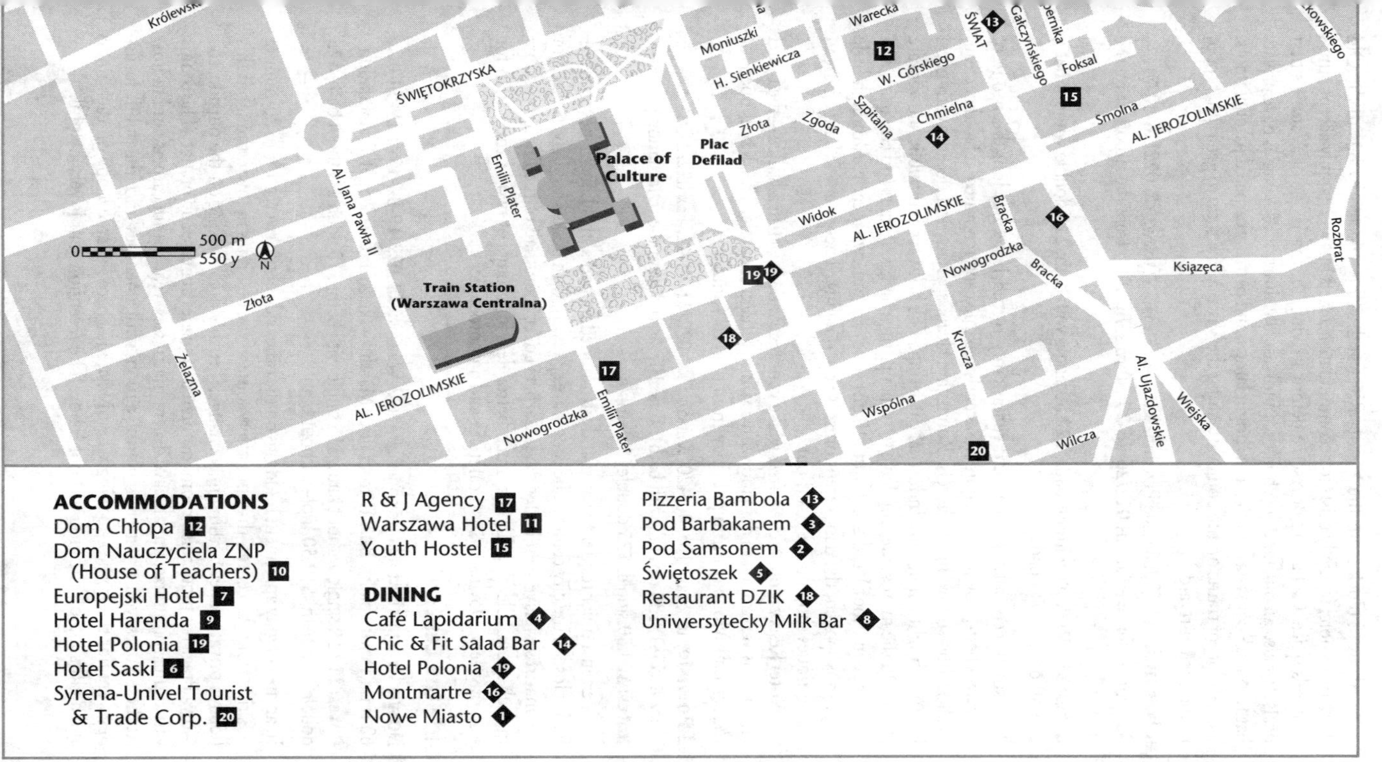

Warsaw Accommodations & Dining

Located just a block from the Vistula River and well connected by bus to the Old Town, this hotel formally exists to accommodate teachers but will happily accept others if there's space. Call ahead or reserve before arriving, for this is one of Warsaw's best deals. It's also an outstanding choice for individual visitors, for 57 singles have private bathrooms. Rooms have fresh paint, bright lamps, and partially carpeted parquet floors. There's lots of traffic on the boulevard along the Vistula River; try to get a quiet room facing the courtyard.

Hotel Harenda, ul. Krakowskie Przedmieście 4/6, 00-333 Warsaw. ☎ **022/26-00-71.** ☎ and fax for reservations **022/26-26-25**. 40 rms. **Bus:** 175 from the airport or train station.

Rates: $17.50 single without bath, $22.50 single with bath; $25 double without bath, $35-40 double with bath.

This small, centrally located, and remarkably priced hotel has long been one of Warsaw's best-known budget hotels. Recently renamed and renovated, it has that clean, fresh feeling so rare in old hotels. Rooms are clean, spartan, and decent, with good lighting, bright colors, and industrial carpeting. The hallways and public showers are clean. On the minus side, you have to walk up three flights of stairs (no elevator), and the check-in (noon) and check-out (10am) times are somewhat early. Although little English is spoken, the desk receptionist is very obliging. There's an exchange bureau and antiques shop on the first floor.

Note: Reservations are *required.* Make your reservations well in advance—the Hotel Harenda is very much in demand with a young foreign clientele. The desk is open for reservations Monday through Friday from 8am to 4pm.

Hotel Powisle, ul. Szara 10a, 00-420 Warsaw. ☎ **022/21-03-41.** Fax 022/21-66-57. Telex 825581. 130 rms (all with bath). **Bus:** 107 or 108 from the train station.

Rates: $24.50 single; $25 double; $30 triple.

Hidden in a quiet residential area and surrounded by parks, this hotel is nevertheless fairly close to the city center. The rooms are spacious, with desks and shelves. Some of the mattresses have seen better days. Carpets cover about half of the linoleum floors in each room. Clearly, this is a much better deal for groups of two or three than for solo travelers. Downstairs is a cafeteria and a photocopier.

Outside the Center

$ **Nowa Praga,** Bertolda Brechta 7, 03-472 Warsaw. ☎ **022/19-82-35** or **19-50-01.** 62 rms (21 with bath). **Bus:** D from ulica Marchlewskiego at the Central Train Station.

Rates: $12.50 single without bath, $15 single with bath; $18 double without bath, $25 double with bath; $19.50 triple without bath.

In an area of gray apartment buildings on the other side of the river, a 15- to 20-minute bus ride from the center, this spot offers some of the best rates in town, though if this hotel is privatized, everything may change. Terribly drab looking on the outside, the Nowa Praga has modernish rooms decorated in shades of beige and orange. The rooms vary quite a bit in size, but all have decent mattresses, veneer-thin carpets, and radios. At these prices, you're better off getting a room with amenities since the public facilities were not the freshest-looking when I visited. There's a large lobby on each floor and a gift shop off the ground-floor lobby. The reception staff is very helpful.

Syrena Hotel, ul. Syreny 23, 01-150 Warsaw. ☎ **022/32-12-57.** 147 rms (36 with bath). **Bus:** B, 109, 155, or 166 from the train station, five to seven stops depending on the line.

Rates: $8.50 single without bath; $15 double without bath, $21 double with bath. A shower costs extra.

The Syrena, named after the mermaid that symbolizes Warsaw, is a seven-story standard hotel in the Wola district, a workers' residential area. The rooms are some of the largest budget doubles in town, with little decoration, but good lighting and huge bathtubs. The lobby restaurant (open 7am to 11pm) serves inexpensive basic Polish fare. You might enjoy walking a dirt path along the tram rails through acres of beautiful residents' gardens cultivated by Varsovians who live nearby; it's a real highlight of the area. Take a bus from Park Mocydło north to the corner of Obozowa and Ksiencia Janusza. But call ahead, because privatization may close this hotel.

DOUBLES FOR LESS THAN $30

In the Center

Hotel Saski, Plac Bankowy 1, 00-139 Warsaw. ☎ **022/20-46-11** to **20-46-15** or **20-27-46.** 103 rms (none with bath). TEL **Tram:** Any from in front of the Centrum department store, three stops north.

Rates (including breakfast): $14.25 single without bath; $18.50 single with shower but no toilet; $22.25 double without bath.

With many single rooms, this hotel is an important option for single travelers. The atmosphere is relaxed, and in the morning you can hear birds sing in the courtyard of this quiet hotel. The simple rooms, some of which are quite small, feature floral-patterned rugs, sinks, and radios. Check the mattresses—they can be poor. There are two clean communal bathtubs and toilets on each floor. Try to reserve at least a week in advance. The lobby has an exchange office, a newsstand, and a restaurant. If you enjoy walking, you might like the 15-minute walk to Old Town along Senatorska at the north end of the Saxon Garden.

DOUBLES FOR LESS THAN $45

In the Center

Dom Chłopa [House of Peasants], Plac Powstańców Warszawy 2, 00-030 Warsaw. ☎ **022/27-92-51.** Fax 022/26-14-54. Telex 816701. 326 rms (200 with bath). **Bus:** 128, 175, or 196 from the train station to the intersection of Aleja Jerozolimskie and ulica Krucza (just after the Forum Hotel); then walk three blocks north on ulica Krucza.

Rates: $20 single without bath, $22 single with bath; $35 double without bath, $40 double with bath. AE, DC, EU, JCB, MC, V.

True to its name, the Dom Chłopa (pronounced Dome *Hope*-a) is where many Polish peasants stay. A double is no bargain here though—just twice the cost of a single. Rooms are small and clean, and singles have a sink without a bath. Public bathrooms are fine. The entrance is obscure and poorly marked; look for an ugly gold mosaic near the main door. The hotel is well located though, just two blocks from Nowy Świat and about a 15-minute walk to the Old Town Marketplace. Groups often book this place solid in summer, so try to reserve at least two weeks ahead.

Warszawa Hotel, Plac Powstańców Warszawy 9, 00-039 Warsaw. ☎ **022/26-94-21.** Fax 022/27-14-72. Telex 813857. 203 rms (124 with bath). TEL **Bus:** 102 from the train station.

Rates: $28 single without bath, $33 single with bath; $33.75 double without bath, $45.50 double with bath.

Right in the middle of town, this hotel has a grave, sober exterior that looks more suited to a tall parking lot or storage facility than a hotel. In fact, in its original incarnation before World War II it served as the headquarters for an American insurance firm; at the time, it was Europe's tallest building. Largely rebuilt after the war, it's just two blocks from Nowy Świat, Warsaw's main shopping street, and a 10-minute walk from the Old Town. Things have an old-fashioned, yet efficient air about them in this hotel, from the brisk, yet polite ladies at the reception desk to the speedy elevator. The rooms I saw were freshly painted and small, but the high ceilings made them seem less cramped. Wood furniture, lace curtains, and enormous pillows make the rooms fairly comfortable. Rooms with bath have tubs and hand-held showers; those without have sinks. Public facilities are very clean. The hotel has a Pewex shop, an exchange bureau, a restaurant, and a pub. Many foreign firms have offices in the building.

Hotel Mdm, Plac Konstytucji 1, 00-647 Warsaw. ☎ **022/21-62-12** to **21-62-19** or **28-25-26.** 134 rms (60 with bath, 74 with toilet but no shower). TEL **Tram:** 4 from the Old Town. **Bus:** 131 from the train station.

Rates (including breakfast): $21 single with toilet but no shower, $29 single with bath; $45 double with bath.

From the outside it looks like a run-down hotel at a noisy traffic intersection. Inside, however, you'll find comfortable rooms in nicely coordinated white and brown colors with shiny wood furniture and radios. Singles are small; some of the mattresses sag quite a bit, but the communal baths are clean. Choose a room facing the quiet courtyard. Higher-priced doubles have two rooms with overstuffed armchairs, a desk with chairs, and large bathtubs. The small, unpretentious lobby is very homey; the staff is helpful, although no English is spoken.

A main shopping district along ulica Marszałkowska begins in this very lively square, and there are numerous places to eat nearby. The American Embassy on Aleja Ujazdowskie is 10 minutes away.

Outside the Center

Hotel Druh, ul. Niemcewicza 17, 00-973 Warsaw. ☎ **022/659-00-11** or **022/659-13-44** for reservations. Fax 22/659-15-07. 59 rms (18 with bath). TEL **Bus:** 127 or 130 southwest from the train station about four stops. **Tram:** 17 or 25.

Rates (including breakfast): $22 double without bath; $29.50 double with bath; $25.50 triple without bath but with sink; $31 quad without bath but with sink.

Despite its dreary-sounding name, this clean hotel attracts a large student crowd. The fairly large rooms feature blond-wood walls, and some rooms overlook a quiet parking lot in back. A few rooms even have refrigerators. The public showers and toilets are clean, though the showers lack curtains. The hotel also has a restaurant, a café, and an exchange bureau. You'll need to use public transportation to get here, since the hotel is located outside the town center. When you arrive, you'll see a four-story gray building with just a small sign that reads BIURO USŁIG TURYTYCZNYCH "ZHP HARCTUR" (Tourist Service Bureau "ZHP Harctur"). Reservations are accepted Monday through Friday only, 8am to 4pm.

DOUBLES FOR LESS THAN $55

Hotel Polonia, Al. Jerozolimskie 45, 00-692 Warsaw. ☎ **02/628-72-41.**
Fax 022/625-30-14. 234 rms. **Directions:** Walk three blocks from the Central Train Station; the hotel is at the intersection of Aleja Jerozolimskie and Marszałkowska.

Rates (including breakfast): $21 single without bath, $28.50 single with bath; $49 double with bath. AE, DC, EU, JCB, MC, V.

If you like to be right in the bustling center of town and you enjoy the illusion of old-world grandeur, this hotel is the right choice for you. It has been in continuous operation since 1913. As the only hotel in Warsaw to survive World War II, it became the center of intrigue right after the war, as diplomats, journalists, profiteers, refugees, spies, and government officials crowded its rooms and restaurants. The staff at the desk are all very experienced and speak several languages. The lobby and hallways are decorated in a high-flown style—wrought-iron staircases, huge mirrors and high ceilings, red plush couches, and lace curtains—but the rooms are on the tacky side. They have good mattresses and good lighting, but the furniture is disappointingly basic and the bathrooms are quite small. Rooms facing the main thoroughfare are very noisy; quieter rooms face the back. The Polonia has an extremely elegant restaurant, with a big menu, that is worth a visit even if you're not staying at the hotel.

WORTH THE EXTRA MONEY

Europejski Hotel, Krakowskie Przedmieście 13, 00-071 Warsaw. ☎ **022/26-50-51.**
Fax 022/26-11-11. Telex 813615. 239 rms (all with bath) TEL MINIBAR TV
Directions: Any tram to Nowy Świat, then any bus going toward Old Town for three stops.

Rates (including breakfast): $50–$60 single; $75–$92 double. AE, DC, EU, JCB, MC, V.

The Europejski has an excellent location, right off one of Warsaw's loveliest streets, and a short walk to Old Town. Over a century old, it claims to be "one of the oldest four-star hotels in Europe." The lobby has grand staircases, marble floors and columns, huge potted palms, and low tables with comfortable armchairs. Hallways are enormous and painted an unusually cheerful pale yellow. Some rooms are very spacious and have soft indirect lighting, very comfortable mattresses, good chairs, and working TVs and radios. The desk staff is very professional and has a good command of English. This is a favorite of many foreigners, particularly Scandinavians.

There's a Polish folk show June through September Sunday through Friday at 8pm ($18.50 with a gala dinner, $6.65 à la carte). If folklore is not your cup of tea, have a drink in the cozy bar or out on the lovely outdoor terrace.

4 Where to Eat

MEALS FOR LESS THAN $3

In the Old Town

Cafe Lapidarium, Nowiemiejska 6.

Cuisine: CAFE/PUB. **Directions:** Walk through the Old Town Marketplace, half a block down Nowiemiejska; it's on the right.
Prices: Salad $1.50; main courses $3; soft drinks or coffee 50¢; beer or wine $1–$3.
Open: May–Sept, Daily 11am–midnight.

Lapidarium has the feel of a popular café in any university town—lively, crowded, and very informal—with an added bit of old-world charm. You pass through an entryway papered with concert and theater fliers into a large courtyard crowded with tables and umbrellas. Join the many young people sipping drinks or order a quick meal of steak or chicken with fries, or a tuna, fruit, or green salad. The student service is fast and friendly. There's a small balcony ideal for people-watching.

$ **Pod Barbakanem,** ul. Mostowa 27/29. ☎ **31-47-37.**

Cuisine: POLISH. **Directions:** Walk north of Barbakan in the Old Town on ulica Freta.
Prices: Soups 20¢–40¢; main courses less than $1.
Open: Mon–Fri 8am–6pm, Sat–Sun 9am–5pm.

This busy cafeteria-style "milk bar" is one of Warsaw's prettiest milk bars, decorated with blue and white tiles. Milk bars are Warsaw's ultimate in budget eating. Everything is very inexpensive, hot, and filling: primarily noodles, potatoes, and soups. This is not a gourmet place; there's a large board listing the daily fare, and you order by crouching down at a small window. Pay the cashier first. Absolutely no English is spoken here so it's best to have your order written out or memorized, especially during the lunch rush. Popular house specialties include *kasza gryczana z pieczarkami* (noodles and mushrooms), *paszteciki* (cabbage-filled crêpes), and *chłodnik* (cold beet-and-vegetable soup).

In the Center

Chic & Fit Salad Bar, ul. Chmielna 11/13. ☎ **27-25-47.**

Cuisine: SALAD. **Directions:** Walk a block north of the main intersection of Aleja Jerozolimskie and Nowy Świat; it's just off Nowy Świat.
Prices: 75¢–$3, depending on salad size and ingredients.
Open: Mon–Fri 9am–6pm.

This little place provides a welcome break from the standard heavy meat 'n' potatoes or the new pizza diet (there are more than 20 pizzerias in Warsaw). Although you'd never suspect it from the antithetical Coke decor, Chic & Fit serves healthy fast food in a small cafeteria-style food bar. Veggie salads, with names like Nordika and Dallas, are all fresh-tasting to go or eat there. The service is fast, and they even have sprouts!

Pizzeria Bambola, Al. Jerozolimskie 111. ☎ **29-16-38.**

Cuisine: PIZZA. **Directions:** Walk east on Aleja Jerozolimskie past the LOT/Marriott building.
Prices: Pizza $1.50–$3.50.
Open: Daily noon–midnight.

Bambola was the first real Italian pizza parlor to open in Warsaw, and many have followed in its wake. This centrally located pizzeria has a simple, pleasant interior of rose-and-beige stucco and attracts pizza-lovers both foreign and native. Poles love to put ketchup on their pizzas!

Bambola has two other locations: Wspólna 27 (☎ **628-31-83**) and Puławska 16 (☎ **49-44-42**). Take-out and delivery service are available.

Uniwersytecki Milk Bar, ul. Krakowskie Przedmieście 20.

Cuisine: POLISH CAFETERIA.
Prices: Soups 30¢–45¢; main courses up to $1.50.
Open: Mon–Fri 7am–8pm, Sat–Sun 9am–5pm.

This centrally located milk bar, just outside the university gates, has kept many a Warsaw University student alive over the years. Unless you're familiar with the standard fare of milk bars, you may have difficulty ordering—the hand-lettered menu in Polish on the wall is not easy to read—so bring along a Polish phrase book, find an English-speaker, or point demonstratively at something in the dining room that appeals to you. The *naleśniki s serem* (New Yorkers know them as blintzes) are especially good here, as are the soups. The decor is on the shabby side, but the food is fresh.

At Wilanów

Wilanów Bistro, ul. Wiertnicza 27.

Cuisine: CAFETERIA. **Directions:** After exiting the palace, turn right to the side of the Wilanów Restaurant.
Prices: Soup 50¢; main courses $1.50–$2; dessert 50¢.
Open: Daily 10am–8pm.

This Orbis-run cafeteria has rough-hewn tables and chairs, and stand-up counters. It's basic and cheap, with mediocre cafeteria food, but there's little else in the area beside the exclusive and pricey Wilanów Restaurant, the touristy and not inexpensive Kuźnia Królewska, and just plain fast-food stalls. Main courses include kielbasa, bigos, roast chicken (the freshest looking), and pork, with lots of mashed potatoes.

MEALS FOR LESS THAN $6

In the Old Town

Nowe Miasto, Rynek Nowego Miasta 13/15. ☎ **31-43-79.**

Cuisine: VEGETARIAN. **Reservations:** Recommend for dinner. **Directions:** Walk to the northwestern corner of the New Town Marketplace.
Prices: Soups and salads $1.50–$3.50; main courses $3–$4. EU, MC, V.
Open: Daily 10am–midnight.

Warsaw's first vegetarian/organic-foods restaurant was founded and is run by an ecologist-professor of philosophy, Bolesłav Rok, who's putting theory into practice. This fresh and imaginative place had just opened when I visited. It's such a refreshing change of pace from the smoky, dark paneled, clubby den atmosphere and decor of so many Polish restaurants—I found it altogether pleasing to the eye as well as to the palate.

High ceilings, Indonesian rattan furniture, and large plants create an airy feeling. Large silk-screened panels lend a predominant color and ambience to three distinct areas: the middle stone room, with a gray marble floor, is done in cool grays and blues, with couches and low tables for drinks; the fire room has narrow red and yellow panels and intimate small tables; the large dining room with a salad bar has earth-toned wood floors and green-blue tree screens. There's a pleasant outdoor terrace overlooking the market square and live harp music in the evenings.

They serve a several mixed salads here—possibly the largest salad you'll ever be served in Poland—with combinations like greens, red cabbage, walnuts, and raisins (under $2.50!). Vegetarians, if you've been missing miso soup with tofu or brown rice and spinach in Europe, you can feast here. You can enjoy stuffed cabbage leaves and crêpes, salmon and tuna salads, and Jakob Gerhardt red and white wines as well.

Pod Samsonem, ul. Freta 3/5. ☎ **31-17-88.**

Cuisine: POLISH/JEWISH. **Directions:** Walk past the Barbakan in Old Town, north along Nowomiejska to Freta; it's on the left.
Prices: Salads 75¢; main courses $2.25–$4. DC, EU, JCB, MC, V.
Open: Daily 10am–10pm.

Delicious home-style cooking at low prices in a very comfortable unpretentious restaurant patronized by local folks in the middle of a major tourist area is a rarity, indeed. Main courses include szaszlyk with fries (*frytki*), chicken cutlet de volaille (breaded chicken breast), and *cielęce v sosie naturalnym* (veal in gravy) with *surowka* (a salad of raw carrots and beets). Prices include potatoes or macaroni, and a salad or vegetablelike cabbage with currants. Substitutions are accepted. Our waitress was extremely helpful, like an obliging aunt eager to please. There are three dining rooms, pretty blue tablecloths, and a very homey atmosphere; the art displayed on the walls is by local artists and is for sale for $30 to $40.

In the Center

Hotel Polonia, Al. Jerozolimskie 45. ☎ **28-72-4.**

Cuisine: POLISH. **Directions:** Walk to the central most downtown point, the intersection of Jerozolimskie and Marszałkowska.
Prices: Salads (in season) 60¢–90¢; main courses $3.85–$5.05; garnishes 20¢–45¢; desserts 60¢–$1.60.
Open: Daily 7am–11am and 1pm–midnight.

The decor and service at this hotel dining room are undeniably superior. The dining room is splendidly spacious, done in a restrained Louis XVI style that makes having even a glass of wine or cup of coffee here an event unless some second-rate Western rock music on the sound system is ruining the effect. The waiters are old hands, yet remain attentive and graceful, without that jadedness that so often characterizes professionals in charming old-world restaurants incessantly deluged by guests.

Here you'll find moderately priced and reasonably good Polish fare: a large selection of pork and beef dishes, roast chicken, and some very good pastries.

MEALS FOR LESS THAN $10

In the Center

Restaurant Dzik, ul. Nowogrodzka 42. ☎ **21-97-28.**

Cuisine: POLISH/WILD GAME. **Directions:** Walk three blocks east of the Central Train Station, turn right on Poznańska, and go one block south.
Prices: Main courses $3–$7; wild game dishes $5.50–$9. AE.
Open: Daily 10am–11pm.

Recently renovated and stylishly decorated in red, black, and gray, this upscale restaurant claims to serve the largest selection of wild game in Warsaw for moderate prices. Venison, wild boar, moose, and elk are available in season. Dzik also serves an array of other Polish dishes like sautéed carp and salmon, pork and veal cutlets, beef Stroganoff, and chateaubriand. It's located very centrally, a few blocks from the Polonia Hotel.

WORTH THE EXTRA MONEY

In the Old Town

Świętoszek, ul. Jezuicka 6/8. ☎ **31-56-34.**

Cuisine: POLISH. **Reservations:** Required after 6pm. **Directions:** From the Old Town Marketplace, walk past Restaurant Bazyliszek on the right and take the first right.
Prices: Appetizers $4–$8; soups $1.50–$2.50; salads $1.50; main courses $8–$15.
Open: Daily 1pm–midnight.

This is a private restaurant for members of the Arts and Culture Union (artists, actors, and musicians), who have first preference for reservations. There are a few spots set aside for those ordinary mortals who make reservations for dinner. Housed in a cellar supported by Gothic barrel vaults dating from medieval times that survived World War II, Świętoszek is elegant and romantic by candlelight. You may want to dress up a bit. Live music accompanies dinner after 8pm.

The food is superb and the service attentive, if somewhat leisurely. Crab and shrimp salads make extravagant appetizers; the soups are excellent, and the green salads are generously large. Main dishes include carp with almond sauce, salmon, lobster, stuffed veal, and chateaubriand.

Many well-known Polish cultural figures frequent Świętoszek. Václav Havel, (then newly elected) president of Czechoslovakia, was invited here by former Premier Mazowiecki.

★ **Montmartre,** ul. Nowy Świat 7. ☎ **628-63-15.**

Cuisine: FRENCH. **Reservations:** Recommended. **Directions:** The restaurant is located one block south of Aleja Jerozolimskie.
Prices: Appetizers and soups $2–$8; main courses $7–$12; desserts $2.25–$4; wine $7.50–$50 a bottle, less for house wine; two-course prix-fixe menu (main course plus appetizer or dessert) served 10am–6pm, $6. AE.
Open: Mon–Sat 10am–midnight, Sun 11am–midnight.

Restaurateur Renata Bukowska lived in France for 12 years before the fall of Communism inspired her to return to her native Poland. She brought with her French chef Oliver Boudon, who expertly prepares French classics such as duck au cassis and profiteroles, tossing in a West Indian accent once in a while. The atmosphere is deeply Parisian, from the photomural of the Place de la Concorde to the natty long aprons on the waiters to the French songs played on the tape deck. The food and service are absolutely superb. My only complaint is the prices of the bottled wines seemed rather high. The house wines are quite enjoyable and inexpensive.

At Wilanów

Wilanów Restaurant, ul. Wiertnicza 27. ☎ **42-18-52.**

Cuisine: POLISH. **Reservations:** Recommended. **Directions:** Veer slightly to the right after exiting the Wilanów Palace.
Prices: Appetizers $2.50–$4; main courses $8–$10; desserts 90¢–$1.85. AE, DC, EU, JCB, MC, V.
Open: Tues–Sun noon–11pm (hot dishes until 10:30pm).

There has been a restaurant here since the days of King Jan Sobieski when he had Wilanów Palace built at the end of the 17th century. It's a splendid place to dine after admiring all that opulence at the neighboring Wilanów Palace. Still decorated with animal pelts, stuffed hunting trophies, and medieval weaponry—but in a modern updated style—the restaurant has an exclusive air about it. There's also a very elegant bar and grill section.

The game dishes include roast wild boar, quail in orange sauce, and pheasant. The roast suckling pig with buckwheat, marinated mushrooms, and cabbage salad, although not wild game, is also a delicious item.

A BOHEMIAN PUB ON A BARGE

Pub Bark[Noe's Barge], on the Vistula River. ☎ **635-62-40.**

Cuisine: POLISH PUB. **Directions:** Walk down ulica Mostowa to Wybrzeże Gdańskie, cross under, and go down to the river.
Prices: Average meal $3.70–$4.50.
Open: Summer only, daily 24 hours.

On a barge anchored on the Vistula River, the Pub Barka is the most unusual eating and drinking experience in Warsaw. Stop in and check it out. The menu changes frequently, featuring Polish and French cross-cultural favorites like stuffed crêpes, to be washed down by an imported Alsatian beer or a good French wine.

As the barge is frequented by musicians, writers, and actors, the atmosphere is informal and bohemian. On weekends in fine weather you come upon an impromptu guitar concert on the deck.

5 Attractions

Having suffered Europe's worst devastation in World War II, Warsaw is missing some of the texture of other European capitals. But if you plan an organized sightseeing program, there's plenty of interest to see.

Suggested Itineraries

If You Have 1 Day

In the morning, begin your sightseeing in Warsaw by strolling around the charming Old Town Marketplace (Rynek Starego Miasta) and the surrounding Old Town. Visit the Royal Castle, the Museum of the City of Warsaw, the Cathedral of St. John, the Barbakan fortifications, and other sights in the Old Town. After lunch in the Old Town, head up to the Wilanów Palace, and in the evening, explore some of modern Warsaw around the Royal Way.

If You Have 2 Days

Spend the first day as outlined above, and then spend your second morning visiting some of Warsaw's museums such as the National Museum and the Polish Army

Frommer's Favorite Warsaw Experiences

Old Town Horse-and-Buggy Ride Riding through Warsaw's charming reconstructed Old Town in a horse and buggy may make you feel like an aristocrat of centuries ago.

A Walk in Łazienki Park Although in a city of gray uniformity, you'll feel as if you're in the Polish countryside when you stroll through these former royal grounds.

Chopin Concerts In Lazienki Park in summer or the Chopin Museum year-round, the works of Poland's greatest composer come alive in weekly concerts.

Museum or the Marie Skłodowska–Curie Museum. In the afternoon, visit Łazienki Park.

If You Have 3 Days

Add more museums listed below to your sightseeing, and consider a trip to the Citadel or the Warsaw Ghetto or Żelazowa Wola, Chopin's birthplace, 32 miles from Warsaw.

If You Have 5 Days or More

You should probably move on to some of Poland's other sights in Kraków or Gdańsk. You might also consider a side trip from Warsaw to such towns as Łowicz, a center of folk tradition.

THE TOP ATTRACTIONS

Warsaw's top attraction is its restored Old Town (Stare Miasto) and Old Town Marketplace (Rynek Starego Miasta), completely and lovingly restored after their destruction in World War II. The top sights of this area are detailed in "Walking Tour—The Old Town," below, which should be your first sightseeing plan in town. Two of the museums and a church on the tour are also detailed below.

In the Old Town

Royal Castle [Zamek], Plac Zamkowy 4. ☎ **635-39-95.**

Dating back to the 13th century, the Royal Castle has accommodated royalty for centuries. After Warsaw became the Polish capital in 1595, Polish kings resided here, and the Polish parliament met here until the end of the 18th century. The castle survived the turbulent centuries of Polish history, but in World War II it saw its end at the hands of systematic Nazi destruction.

Until 1971, only a three-story wall fragment stood on the square, the width of only one window. Town planners began rebuilding in 1971, and by 1981 the first tourists visited the interior.

The interior decorations are a combination of period pieces donated by individuals and museums, copies of original paintings from other museums, plus works that were removed for safekeeping during the 1939 siege of Warsaw and were spared destruction.

The first section—courtiers' lodgings, parliament rooms, and paintings—consists of about two dozen rooms of various levels of decoration. The portraits of hundreds of Polish aristocrats from centuries past survey the crowds. The various restored parliament chambers suggest the tremendous pomp that attended council meetings of the Polish monarchy.

The royal apartments are more spectacular. In several rooms, it seems as though every available surface is embellished with gold paint, stucco relief, or semiprecious stones.

Admission: Courtiers' lodgings, parliament chambers, and paintings, $1 adults, 50¢ students; free for everyone Thurs. Great apartments, $2 adults, $1 students, guided tour $5.50. Exhibition 50¢. On Sun admission to the entire castle is $1.50 and no tours are given. An English-language guidebook to the castle is sold at the entrance for $1.50.

Open: Tues–Sun 10am–4pm (last entry 2:45pm).

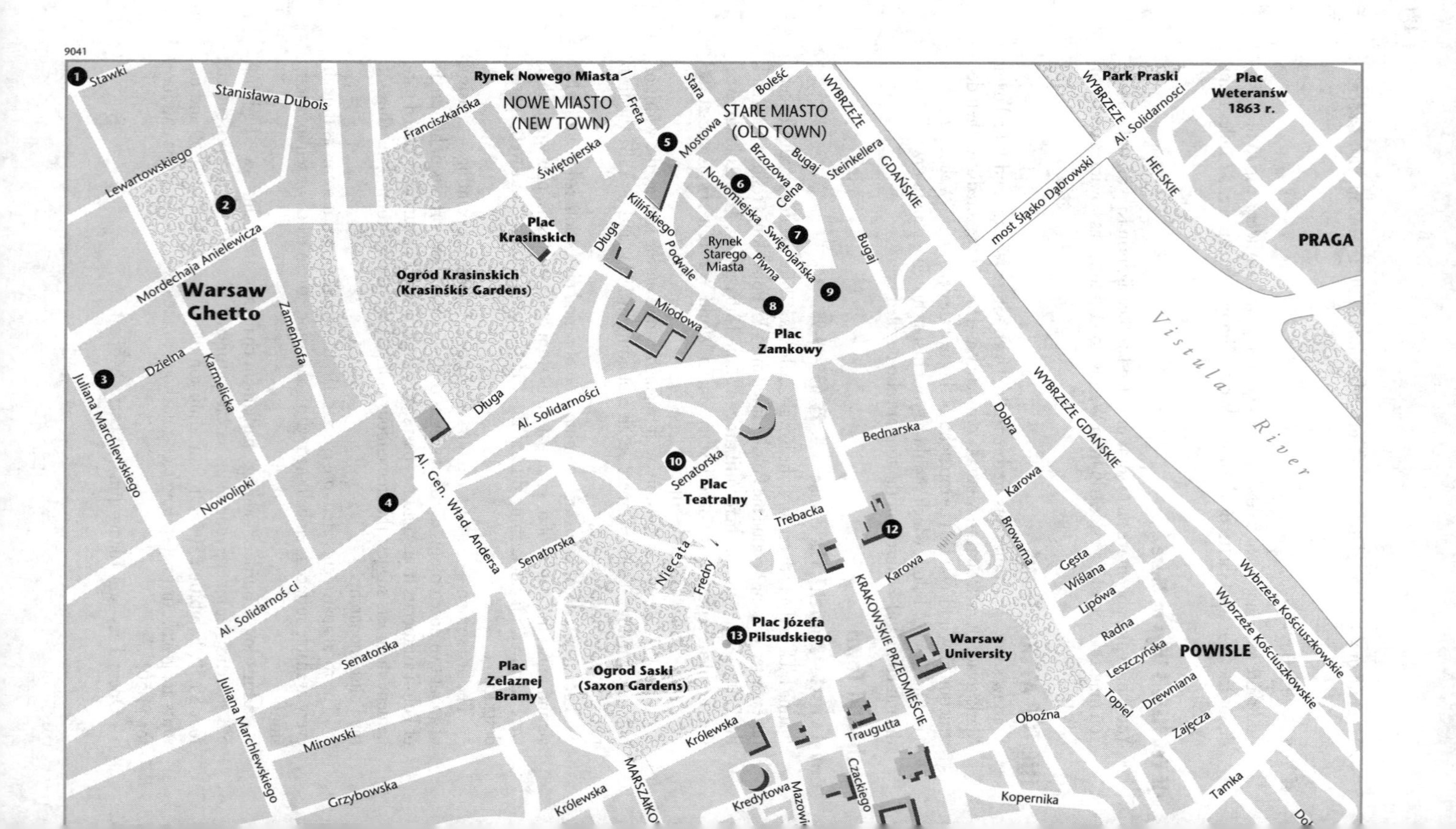
9041
Stawki
Stanisława Dubois
Rynek Nowego Miasta
NOWE MIASTO
(NEW TOWN)
Franciszkańska
Freta
Stara
Boleść
STARE MIASTO
(OLD TOWN)
WYBRZEŻE
GDAŃSKIE
Park Praski
Plac
Weteranśw
1863 r.
WYBRZEŻE
HELSKIE
Al. Solidarności
most Śląsko Dąbrowski
PRAGA
Lewartowskiego
Świętojerska
Mostowa
Brzozowa
Bugaj
Steinkellera
Nowomiejska
Celna
Kilińskiego
Podwale
Rynek
Starego
Miasta
Piwna
Świętojańska
Bugaj
Długa
Plac
Krasinskich
Ogród Krasinskich
(Krasinśkis Gardens)
Mordechaja Anielewicza
Warsaw
Ghetto
Zamenhofa
Miodowa
Plac
Zamkowy
Vistula River
Dzielna
Karmelicka
Juliana Marchlewskiego
Długa
Al. Solidarności
Bednarska
Dobra
WYBRZEŻE GDAŃSKIE
Senatorska
Plac
Teatralny
Nowolipki
Al. Gen. Wład. Andersa
Trebacka
Karowa
Browarna
Senatorska
Niecała
Fredry
Karowa
Gęsta
Wiślana
Lipówa
Radna
Leszczyńska
Wybrzeże Kościuszkowskie
Wybrzeże Kościuszkowskie
POWISLE
Al. Solidarnoś ci
Plac Józefa
Pilsudskiego
KRAKOWSKIE PRZEDMIEŚCIE
Warsaw
University
Senatorska
Plac
Zelaznej
Bramy
Ogrod Saski
(Saxon Gardens)
Topiel
Drewniana
Oboźna
Zajęcza
Mirowski
Królewska
Traugutta
Juliana Marchlewskiego
Grzybowska
Królewska
MARSZAŁKO
Kredytowa
Mazowi
Czackiego
Kopernika
Tamka
Do

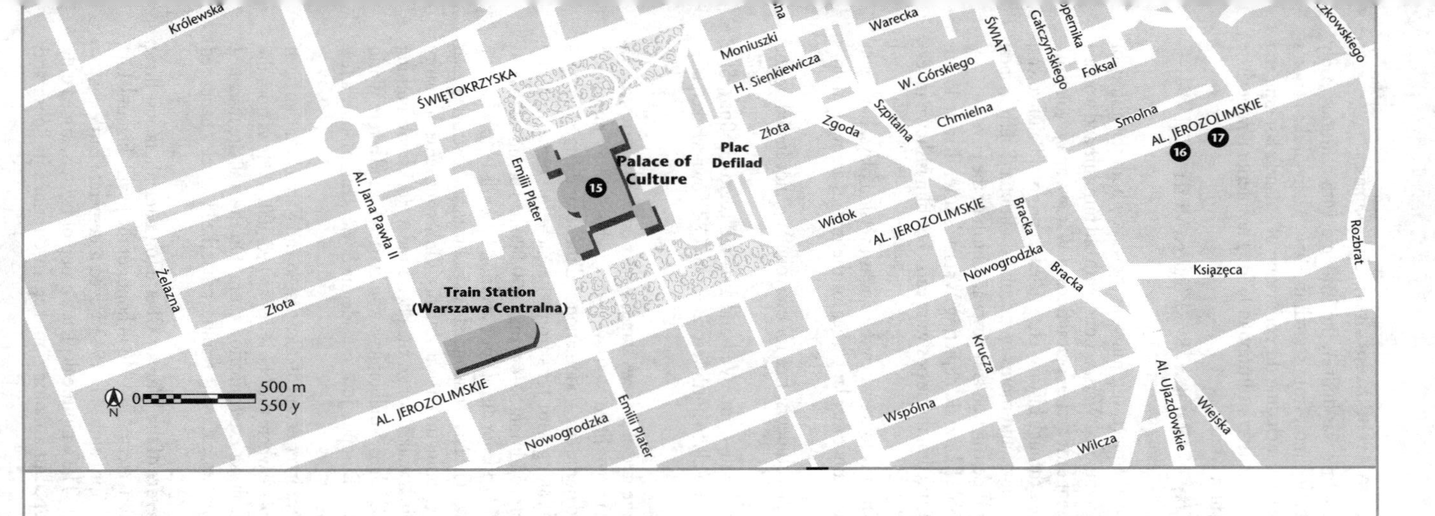

Cathedral of St. John (św. Jana Archikatedralna) 7
Chopin Museum 14
Grand Theater and Opera House 11
Historical Museum of the City of Warsaw 6
Jewish History Institute 4
Marie Skłodowska-Curie Museum 5
Memorial to the Heroes of the Warsaw Ghetto 2
Mufa Agency (it Tourist Office) 8
National Museum 16
Palace of Culture 15
Pawiak Prison (Więzienia Pawiak) 3
Polish Army Museum 17
Radziwiłł Palace 12
Royal Castle (Zamek) 9
Tomb of the Unknown Soldier 13
Umschlagplatz 1
Warsaw Nike 10

Warsaw Attractions

Cathedral of St. John [Św. Jana Archikatedralna], ul. Świętojńska.

Warsaw's oldest church, St. John's was built in the 13th and 14th centuries; badly damaged in 1944, it was rebuilt almost from scratch in 1956. Many of the nation's great events have taken place here, including the coronation of Poland's last king and the proclamation of the country's first constitution in 1791. The interior is rather bare with Gothic ribs of brick against white.

Historical Museum of the City of Warsaw, Rynek Starego Miasta 28.
☎ **635-16-25.**

Located on the Old Town Marketplace, this museum shows you both the history of Warsaw and the interior of a traditional Warsaw house with old furniture and wooden rafters. The first exhibits present early archeological finds in Warsaw, and as you work your way upstairs, you progress through history, chronicled by prints of Polish towns, old paintings, photographs, books, and rooms re-creating traditional Polish homes. It ends with the World War II destruction and postwar rebirth of the city.

A highlight is an incredible ★ **movie** depicting Warsaw's utter destruction in 1945 and its extensive reconstruction in the postwar years. The film is shown in several languages most days; check in early to see when the English version plays, but if you can't see it in English, see it in any other language, for the images are really unforgettably powerful.

Admission: 45¢ adults, 20¢ students; free for everyone Sun, not including the film showing.

Open: Tues and Thurs 11am–6pm, Wed and Fri–Sat 10am–3:30pm, Sun 10:30am–4:30pm. **Directions:** Walk to northwest side of the Old Town Marketplace.

The Warsaw Ghetto

In Warsaw's tragic history, the fate of its Jews stands out as especially sorrowful. In November 1940, the Germans confined Warsaw's Jews (who in 1939 numbered 380,000 and made up a third of the city's population and the second-largest congregation of Jews in the world) along with Jews from elsewhere in Poland to a tiny section of the city in miserable conditions. More than 400,000 had been sent to concentration camps or had perished from disease or starvation by April 1943 when the remaining rose up in resistance. The Nazis responded by systematically destroying each building in the ghetto and exterminating its inhabitants. Only your sense of history will remind you of the past in a walk through the ghetto today, for almost nothing remains from before the war. Of the 3.5 million Jews who lived in Poland before World War II (a total of two-thirds of Europe's Jews outside the Soviet Union), only a few thousand still live there today.

At **Umschlagplatz** (near the intersection of ulica Stawki and Karmelicka), an open marble memorial marks the place where the Nazis dispatched 300,000 Jews from the ghetto onto trains to the Treblinka extermination camp. On the wall are inscribed dozens of Polish-Jewish first names, a moving reminder that the Holocaust happened to real individuals.

The **Memorial to the Heroes of the Warsaw Ghetto** (on Zamenhofa, just three blocks from Umschlagplatz) was erected in 1948 in honor of the Jewish Fighting Organization (ZOB), which in April and May 1943 waged a desperate battle against heavily armed German forces. The sculpture depicts a group of fighters, armed only with sticks and stones, trapped in a flaming bunker. Inscriptions in Polish and

Hebrew quote the ZOB's final communiqué: "We are fighting for your freedom and ours, for your human and national pride—and ours."

At **Pawiak Prison,** ul. Dzielna 24/26, the Nazis imprisoned 100,000 during World War II, of which 37,000 were killed on the spot and another 60,000 were shipped off to concentration camps. In 1944 the Nazis blew up the central prison and the surrounding buildings. The 3½-acre prison first held those who resisted tsarist occupation in the 19th century. Today, in a remaining room you can see documents and exhibitions on the prison's history with descriptions in English. The admission is free. Pawiak is open for visitors on Wednesday from 9am to 5pm, Thursday 9am to 4pm, Friday from 10am to 5pm, Saturday from 9am to 4pm, and Sunday from 10am to 4pm. The last entrance is 15 minutes before closing. Pawiak is closed days after holidays.

The **Jewish Cemetery** (entrance near the corner of Okopowa and Mordechaja Anielewicza) was founded in 1806 and is the largest Jewish cemetery in Poland. It is open Monday through Thursday from 9am to 3pm and on Friday from 9am to 1pm.

The **Jewish History Institute** (at Al. Solidarności 79) explains the fate of the Jews during World War II.

The **Warsaw Nike** (on Plac Teatralny, across from the Grand Theater) is a huge statue of a rather masculine goddess with both hands raised holding a sword. The Nike (1964) pays tribute to the heroes of the 1944 Warsaw Uprising, who took arms against the Nazis and were crushed when Stalin abandoned them. After the war, the uprising was seen as an anti-Soviet act, and it wasn't until Stalin's death that a memorial could be built. During the early 1980s, many demonstrations in support of Solidarity were held on the square in front of this monument.

Outside the Center

Wilanów Palace, ul. Wiertnicza. ☎ **42-07-85** or **42-81-01.**

A fair distance outside the town center past Łazienki Park is the beautiful baroque palace of the legendary Polish King Jan III Sobieski (who is famous for helping the West finally defeat the Turks at the gates of Vienna in 1683). He spent his summers here in the late 17th century. In the 18th century King August the Strong (famous for ruling Dresden in its heyday, as well as Poland) resided here. It was originally called the Villa Nuova, later mutated to Wilanów.

The palace and park grounds are still impressive today, with the rich baroque details typical of palaces built during the time of Louis XIV. The palace was lived in until World War II, and each generation of residents left its mark, making the rooms a fascinating jumble of periods and styles. Although the Nazis plundered the estate in World War II, its great splendor and rich art have been completely restored. Distinguished foreign guests are still housed in one of the wings of the palace, but the rest of the building is open as a museum.

You can visit the palace rooms with a guide who points out the delightful frescoes, Polish portraits of the 16th through 19th centuries, and other fine interior decorations. Many rooms, such as the Green Bedchamber with its large canopied bed, have been impressively restored with period furniture.

The adjacent park is planted in the French manner, with sculpture and topiary. On the park grounds there is a small museum showing selected decorative objects—including clocks, figurines, tableware—and a few paintings and furnishings from the estate's collection. (Admission 20¢. Open daily 9:30am to 3:30pm. Follow signs to Galeria Clou.) A Poster Museum, housed in a former riding school near the palace, was closed for reconstruction at the time of writing. Call **42-26-06** or ask at the

Warsaw tourist office if it has reopened. There is also an excellent restaurant just a stone's throw from the palace entrance (see "Where to Eat," above), as well as an inexpensive bistro next to it.

Admission: Self-guided palace tour $1.50, palace tour with English-speaking guide $4. Park 50¢; with guide, $2.20.

Open: Palace, Wed–Mon 9:15am–2:30pm; park Wed–Mon 9:30am–sunset. **Closed:** Days following public holidays. **Bus:** B or 180 from the Forum Hotel, or 122 from Nowy Świat, all to last stop—the palace is across a wide boulevard and 300 yards down the road; the ride takes 20 to 25 minutes.

★ **Łazienki Park,** Al. Ujazdowskie. ☎ **21-82-12.**

Many consider this to be Poland's most beautiful palace and park complex, and you, too, may be astonished that such a place exists beyond Warsaw's monotonous urban landscape. Poland's last king, Stanisław August Poniatowski, built this romantic park in the second half of the 18th century. On the royal grounds are several ornate buildings and palaces, with large stretches of park in between. These palaces include the Orangery, which houses a sculpture garden, the 1776 White Cottage (where the king's family lived during the summer), and the neoclassical Palace on the Lake (where the king himself lived). Several of these palaces house small museums with both changing and permanent exhibitions. For example, the Palace on the Lake exhibits 18th-century furniture and paintings while a smaller pavilion displays a collection of photographs of Warsaw's destruction in 1945. A map near the entrance to the park illustrates the location of the various palaces.

Chopin concerts are held May to September on Sunday at noon at Łazienki Park's monument to the great composer (free of charge).

Admission: Palaces, $1 adults, 60¢ students; park grounds, free.

Open: Park grounds, daily 10am–sunset; Palace of the Lake and most other galleries and buildings, Tues–Sun 9:30am–3pm. **Bus:** Almost any leaving the Old Town down Krakowskie Przedmieście and Nowy Świat.

MORE ATTRACTIONS

National Museum, Al. Jerozolimskie 3. ☎ **21-10-31** or **29-50-60.**

Warsaw's central art collection, with displays of everything from ancient Egyptian, Greek, and Roman art to modern Polish art. An entire wing is devoted to medieval religious art of the 12th to the 16th century. European masters represented include Jan Brueghel the Elder, Rembrandt, Salomon van Ruysdael, and Lucas Cranach.

You can buy an English-language museum guidebook at the entrance for 75¢. Postcards and slides are also sold. The museum is currently undergoing partial reconstruction; call to check on its progress.

Admission: 50¢ adults, 25¢ students; free for everyone on Thurs.

Open: Tues and Sun 10am–5pm, Wed and Fri–Sat 10am–4pm, Thurs noon–6pm. Last entrance half an hour before closing. **Closed:** Days after public holidays. **Directions:** Any bus going east on Aleja Jerozolimskie from the Forum Hotel.

Polish Army Museum, Al. Jerozolimskie 3. ☎ **29-52-71, 29-52-72,** or **29-52-73.**

A fascinating collection of weaponry that illustrates the tragic importance war has had in Polish history. It begins with an extensive medieval armor and pageant collection; also an extensive World War II collection for history buffs. This museum is next door to the National Museum.

Admission: 75¢ adults; 50¢ students, free for everyone Fri.

Open: Wed 11am–5pm, Thurs–Fri and Sun 10am–4pm, Sat 11am–4pm. **Closed:** Jan 1, May 1, June 22, Sept 1, Dec 25, and days after public holidays. **Directions:** Walk half a block toward the river from the National Museum.

Citadel, ul. Skazańców 25 in the Żoliborz district (down the riverbank from the Old Town). ☎ **39-23-83** or **39-12-68.**

This impressive sight is often overlooked because it receives little publicity and, perhaps, because of its Russian connections. The Russians built the fortress between 1832 and 1834 to demonstrate their dominance over newly gained territory. Inside, the Russians maintained the central political prison in Poland, along with rooms for torture and execution. This prison, called Pavillion X, held 40,000 people over the 90 years it functioned. The Russians transferred many of these prisoners to exile in Siberia.

Today you can visit many of the prison cells and also see 124 fascinating paintings by Alexander Sochaczewski (1843–1923), a Polish artist exiled to Siberia for 22 years. His paintings depict the horrors of gulag internment. Without artificial lighting, the museum still feels like a gloomy prison.

The descriptions are only in Polish, but you can buy a museum guide in English at the entrance for 75¢. There's also a small machine at the entrance with a voice recording that gives an English-language description if you insert the proper change.

Incidentally, the Citadel is still used for military training.

Admission: Free.

Open: Wed–Sun 9am–4pm. **Bus:** 118 or 185 from the street on the riverbank, Wybrzeze Gdańskie, the bus stops near the museum entrance.

Św. Stanis awska Kostki, ul. Hozjusza 2 (about 10 blocks west of the Citadel). ☎ **39-45-72.**

This is the church where outspoken priest Jerzy Popiełuszko once gave his weekly Sunday sermons. Today he lies buried on the church grounds since his brutal murder (by drowning) by the Polish secret police in 1984. Many Poles visiting Warsaw come here to pay tribute to this modern-day martyr, and Solidarity symbols flourish here. The current pastor discusses the role of religion and nationalism in Poland on the last Sunday of each month at 7pm in a very popular "national" mass.

Admission: Free.

Open: Daily approx. 7am–7 or 8pm. **Tram:** 6, 15, 31, or 36 to Plac T. W. Wilsona and ask for directions. **Bus:** A, J, 116, 132, or 157 to Plac T. W. Wilsona and ask for directions.

Palace of Culture, Plac Defilad.

From the 30th floor of the city's second-tallest structure, built in 1955, you see an impressive view of a rather unimpressive urban landscape.

The palace, whose peak scrapes the sky at 777 feet, was a "gift" from the Soviet Union to the Polish people. Designed by Soviet architects, the bulky building resembles "Stalin Gothics" in Moscow. Ever since its construction, Poles have objected to the palace as both an eyesore and a symbol of Soviet oppression, and since 1989 there have been various proposals to tear it down and replace it with something else—*anything* else. But the cash-strapped government has more urgent priorities, so the landmark isn't going anywhere soon.

Admission: 75¢ adults, 35¢ students.

Open: Daily 9am–1:30pm and 2–5pm. **Directions:** Walk across from the train station to ulica Marszałkowska.

SPECIAL-INTEREST SIGHTSEEING

For the History Buff

Mausoleum of Resistance and Martyrdom[Mauzoleum Walk: Męczénstwa], Al. Armii Wojska Polskiego 25. ☎ **29-49-19.**

A few minutes from Łazienki Park, near the intersection of Aleja Armii Wojska Polskiego and Aleja Armii Ludowej, is this small museum inside the former Gestapo headquarters. In the basement, Nazis tortured many Poles prior to transferring them to Pawiak Prison. Today you'll see a few of these torture cells, as well as a re-creation of a Gestapo office, complete with a portrait of Hitler on the wall and Nazi jacket hanging in the corner of the room. The modest collection can be seen in a few minutes. An English-language guidebook is sold at the entrance.

Admission: Free.

Open: Wed 9am–5pm, Thurs 9am–4pm, Fri 10am–5pm, Sat 9am–4pm, Sun 10am–6pm. **Closed:** Days after public holidays. **Bus:** 122 or 144 from Krakowskie Przedmieście.

For Chopin Lovers

Chopin Museum, in Ostrogski Palace, ul. Okólnik 1. ☎ **27-54-71.**

A museum celebrating the life of the great Polish pianist known for his nocturnes, mazurkas, and polonaises. Displays include Chopin's piano from 1848–49 (the year of his death), portraits, copies of his letters and scores, a model of his left hand, and displays of his personal belongings such as his French passport.

There's an elegant concert hall on the third floor where the museum stages concerts costing $2.25. Consult the *Warsaw Voice* for concert times.

Admission: 35¢ adults, 20¢ students.

Open: Mon–Wed and Fri–Sat 10am–2pm, Thurs noon–6pm. **Closed:** Holidays.

For Science Buffs and Feminists

Marie Skłodowská-Curie Museum, ul. Freta 16. ☎ **31-80-92.**

The 1867 birthplace of Marie Curie, this museum celebrates the scientist famous for her research in radioactivity and discovery of radium. You'll see some of her laboratory tools, such as an electroscope, an ionization chamber, and a quadrant electrometer. The museum also displays her portraits on paintings, stamps, coins, and even the currently circulated 20,000-złoty bill. Like her fellow countryman Chopin, she spent much of her life in France, where she died in 1934. You can buy an English-language museum guide for $3.

Admission: 30¢ adults, 15¢ students.

Open: Tues–Sat 10am–4:30pm, Sun 10am–2:30pm. **Closed:** Holidays.

Directions: Walk from Barbakan down ulica Freta.

Walking Tour

The Old Town

Start Plac Zamkowy.
Finish Plac Zamkowy.
Time 1½ hours, not including museum stops.

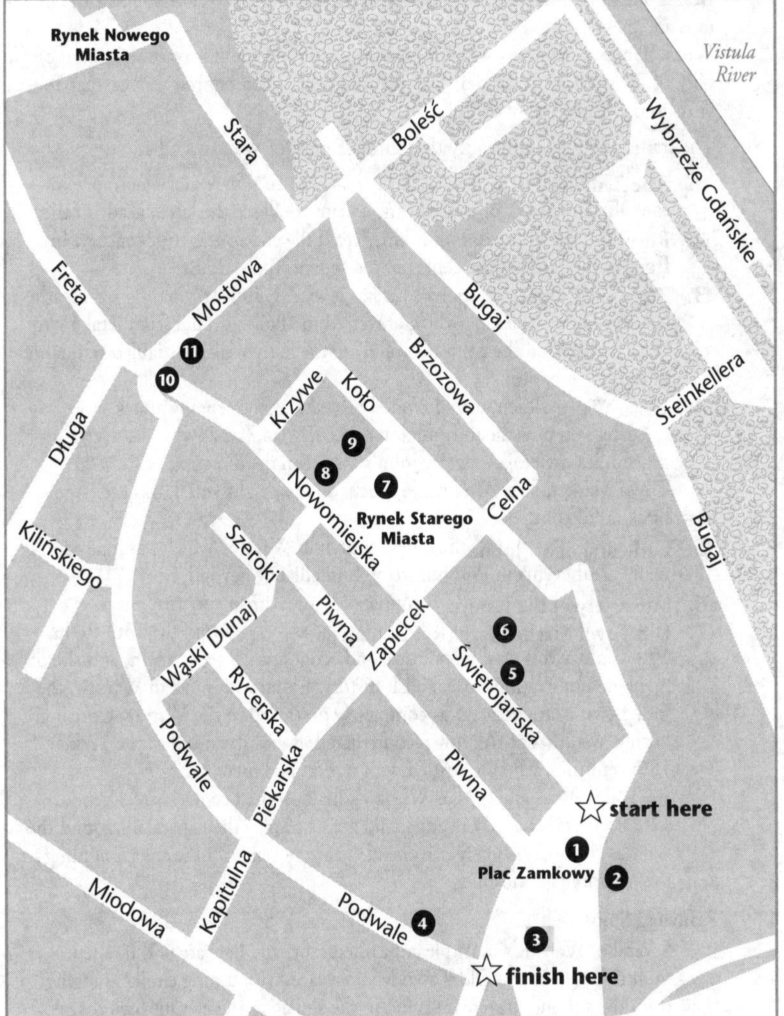

1. Plac Zamkowy (Royal Square)
2. Royal Castle
3. Zygmunt Column
4. Town Walls
5. Cathedral of St. John
6. Monastery of the Jesuits
7. Old Town Marketplace (Rynek Starego Miasta)
8. Historical Museum of the City of Warsaw
9. Negro House
10. Barbakan
11. Mermaid

Best Times Tuesday to Saturday morning, when the Royal Castle and the museums are open.

Worst Times Monday, when the Royal Castle and the Historical Museum of the City of Warsaw are closed, or Sunday morning, when church services bar tourist visits to the Cathedral of St. John.

The traffic and gray uniformity that shrouds most of Warsaw end at:

1. **Plac Zamkowy (Royal Square),** the large open square at the entrance to the Old Town. On one side of the square you'll see the large facade of the:
2. **Royal Castle,** home to Polish kings from the end of the 16th century. In front of the castle at the center of the square you'll see the:
3. **Zygmunt Column.** Topped by a statue of Zygmunt III holding a cross, the column honors the king who transferred the Polish capital from Kraków to Warsaw. Beyond the column, you'll see the fairly well-maintained remnants of the:
4. **Town Walls,** which once provided protection from enemy attack.

   After you pass the information office in Plac Zamkowy, take a left down ulica Świętojańska (St. John's Street) in the direction of the Old Town Marketplace. After half a block, on your right you'll pass the large brick facade of the:
5. **Cathedral of St. John,** the oldest church in Warsaw, which has figured in many great events in Polish history. Immediately beyond is the:
6. **Monastery of the Jesuits.** A couple of houses down you arrive at the:
7. **Old Town Marketplace (Rynek Starego Miasta).** From the 13th to the 19th century this was the political and economic center of town, and site of many demonstrations over Polish history. Along with most of Warsaw, the Old Town Marketplace was completely destroyed in the Warsaw Uprising during World War II. Now reconstructed, it looks as it did in the 17th and 18th centuries, when it bustled with traders and merchants.

   Today it has emerged as Warsaw's major tourist center. Street vendors sell cassette tapes and souvenirs, and artists display their work all around the square. Horse-and-buggy drivers queue at the center of the square, adding to the traditional atmosphere.

Refueling Stops

Several of Warsaw's most pleasant restaurants and bars are within a few minutes' walk of the Old Town Marketplace, with dining choices ranging from the summer ice-cream stand in the square to the elegant **Świętoszek.**

Along ulica Freta to the northwest of the Barbakan are several good eateries, including the rock-bottom budget **Pod Barbakanem Milk Bar** and **Pod Samsonem,** one of the best moderately priced restaurants in Old Town. See "Where to Eat," above, for listings.

An essential stop on the square is the:

8. **Historical Museum of the City of Warsaw,** where a graphic film illustrates Warsaw's wartime destruction. Next door is the:
9. **Negro House,** Rynek Starego Miasta 36. Here you'll see a statue of a black slave: The original owner of this building was a dealer in slaves.

   If you leave the square by Nowomiejska Street (the street along the left side of the Warsaw Historical Museum), you come upon the:

10. **Barbakan,** Warsaw's impressive fortified brick town walls, first built in the 16th century which include turrets and a surrounding moat. Restored after the war, the Barbakan now attracts artists and crafts vendors, who set up their works along the brick walls. On the right side of the walls, you'll notice the statue of a:
11. **Mermaid,** the symbol of Warsaw.

    If you take a left after the Barbakan on ulica Podwale, you'll walk alongside the old city walls en route back to Plac Zamkowy.

Final Refueling Stops

For a rare dining experience in Eastern Europe, have a delicious vegetarian meal at the first organic-foods restaurant in Warsaw, **Nowe Miasto,** in the Nowe Miasto Marketplace. Or if you're not hungry and just want a beer or a glass of wine, drop into the courtyard of the popular **Café Lapidarium.**

Walking Tour
The Royal Way

Start Plac Zamkowy (Royal Square).
Finish Warsaw University.
Time 30 minutes.
Best Time Weekdays, when stores are open, or Saturday morning.
Worst Times Sunday, when stores are closed.

The Royal Way begins at Plac Zamkowy and commemorates the many royal residences, manors of the nobility, and other important houses that lined this boulevard during centuries of the Polish monarchy. These reconstructed homes, painted in a variety of pastel colors, are a welcome change from the gray uniformity of Warsaw's many postwar constructions. The prewar atmosphere, as well as the many shops on the street, make it a favorite for locals and tourists. The Royal Way's name changes several times as you move farther away from the Old Town. It begins as Krakowskie Przedmieście, becomes Nowy Świat, and then it's Aleja Ujazdowskie.

As you walk along this street from the Royal Square, you can see a number of important buildings and palaces. After two blocks, on your left you'll pass the:

1. **Radziwiłł Palace,** Krakowskie Przedmieście 46/48, a large white palace with a flag on top and an equestrian statue in front. In 1955 officials from the nations of Eastern Europe and the Soviet Union met here to form a military and a political alliance, which was dubbed the Warsaw Pact. Today it houses the Council of Ministers and is closed to the public. Across the street is the:
2. **Potocki Palace,** Krakowskie Przedmieście 32, a 17th-century building now home to the Ministry of Culture and Art.

    Next to the Radziwiłł Palace is the:
3. **Bristol Hotel,** a neo-Renaissance structure once owned by Polish statesman Ignacy Paderewski.

    A block and a half farther you'll pass:
4. **Warsaw University,** Krakowskie Przedmieście 26/28, Poland's biggest university, which was established in 1816. You can walk past the school gates and have a quick look around the campus. Across the street is the:

5. **Church of the Holy Cross,** a 17th-century baroque design which contains the heart of Chopin inside an urn.

Final Refueling Stops

Stop off and have a healthful, fresh salad at the **Chic & Fit Salad Bar,** on ulica Chmielna; or meet with students and enjoy a bite at **Universytecki,** the milk bar at Krakowskie Przedmieście 20/22. Or have a beer at the popular **Pub Harenda,** with draft Guinness on tap.

If you take a bus or taxi along the Royal Way away from the center of town, you'll eventually arrive at two of Warsaw's most interesting sights: **Łazienki Park,** the loveliest area in town, with several museums, and **Wilanów Palace,** the home of the legendary King Jan III Sobieski.

6 Savvy Shopping

THE SHOPPING SCENE My favorite places to stroll and shop are ulica Marszałkowska (in front of the Palace of Culture), where you'll find the large Centrum department stores, Wars and Sawa; ulica Rutkowskiego (behind the Centrum department store), a smaller street with shops that sell used watches, a few antiques, and other goodies; Aleja Jerozolimskie, a large avenue that intersects the Royal Way; and Nowy Świat and Krakowskie Przedmieście, Warsaw's Royal Way and main shopping avenue with a wide variety of stores. A number of fancier stores selling items as such silver, amber, and art have started to appear especially along the Royal Way as Warsaw has become more popular with Western tourists.

Bazar Różyckiego Bargain-hunters will enjoy the bustling outdoor flea market at Targowa 50/52, in the Praga District. You can find a wide variety of such things as food (including Russian caviar), clothes, old coins, medals from World War II, and various odds and ends. Very few foreign tourists venture to this market, but many pickpockets do. It's open Monday through Saturday from about 10am to 6pm. To get there, take tram no. 13 or 26 from outside the Old Town.

7 Evening Entertainment

Warsaw offers frequent concerts, theater, film, a thriving jazz scene, and other cultural performances. The English-language *Warsaw Voice* prints highlights of upcoming musical events.

Chopin lovers can attend free concerts at noon on Sunday from May to September at Łazienki Park's monument to the great composer. The Chopin Museum in Ostrogski Palace, ulica Okólnik 1 (☎ **27-54-71**), also hosts concerts.

Tickets for theater, film, and music performances can be purchased at ZASP, Al. Jerozolimskie 25 (☎ **21-94-54** or **21-93-83**). It's open Monday through Friday from 11am to 6pm and on Saturday from 11am to 2pm (closed June to August). You can also ask your hotelier where to buy tickets.

MOVIES Many foreign movies are shown in their original languages with subtitles. Two Warsaw theaters that feature American movies are Relax at ul. Zlota 8 and Kultura at Krakowskie Przedmieście 21/23; the Bajka Theater at Marszałkowska 138 frequently

Walking Tour—The Royal Way

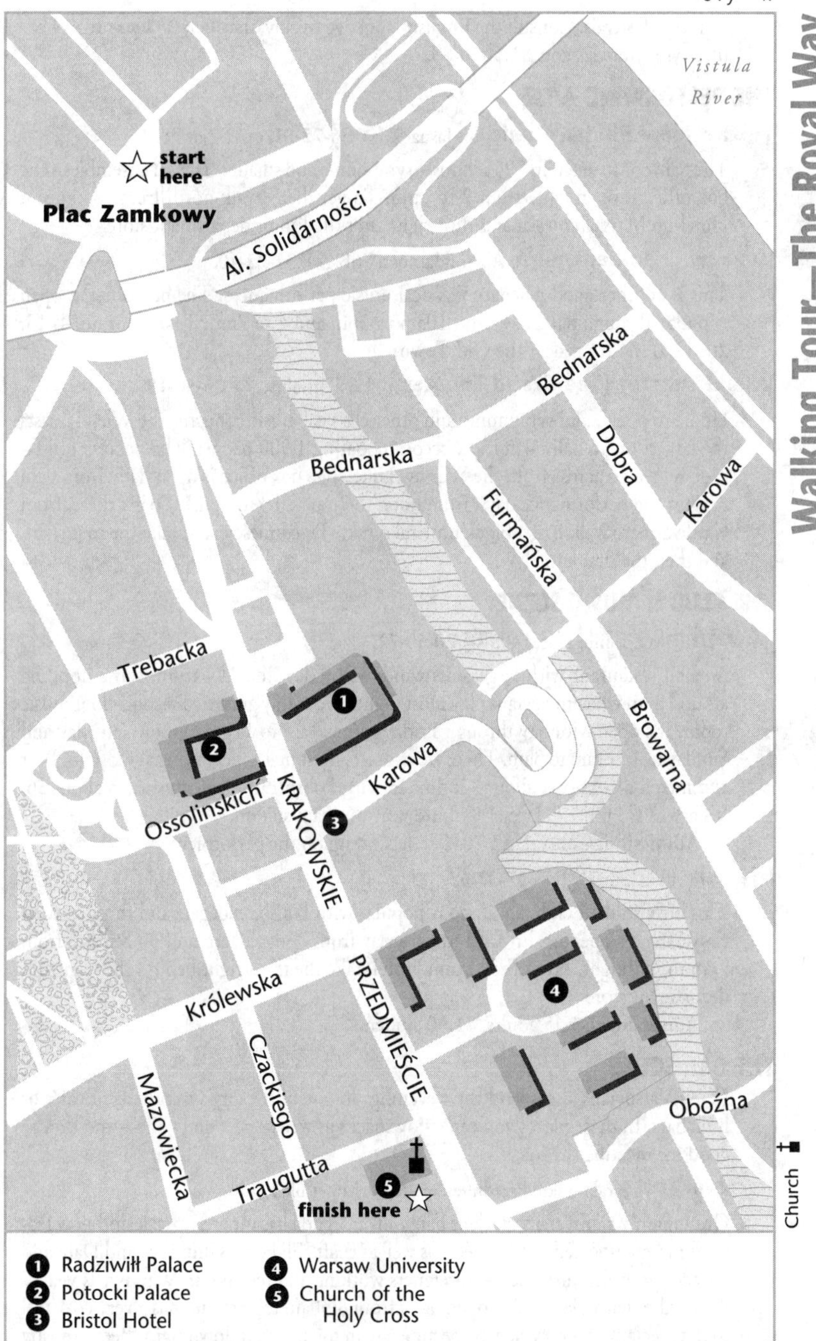

runs film festivals. Consult the English-language weekly, the *Warsaw Voice,* for schedules. Most movies cost $1.50 to $3.

THE PERFORMING ARTS

The National Philharmonic, ul. Jasna 5. ☎ **26-72-81,** ext. 37 or 38.

The hall, constructed in 1955, houses symphonic and smaller classical ensembles. The box office is open daily from 2 to 7pm. To get there, walk north from the Forum Hotel up Marszałkowska and turn right after the Junior department store.

Warsaw Chamber Opera, Al. Solidarności 76B. ☎ **31-22-40.**

This is another good place for classical music performances. The box office is open Monday through Saturday from 10am to 2pm and 4 to 7pm. Take tram no. 4, 13, 26, 32, or 34 from near the Old Town.

Wielki Theater [The Grand Theater], Plac Teatralny. ☎ **26-50-19.**

Home to opera, and symphonic and other classical music concerts, the Wielki boasts the largest opera hall in Europe, accommodating 1,900 people. The neoclassical facade is located across from the Warsaw Nike. The box office is open daily from 9am to 7pm (on performance days, from noon to 2pm and 3 to 7pm). To get there, from Castle Square walk half a block up Krakowskie Przedmieście and take the first right, and then the first left.

THE CLUB & MUSIC SCENE

Akwarium, ul. Emilii Plater 49. ☎ **20-50-72.**

A small restaurant with large glass windows by day, the Akwarium starts hopping around 8pm when musicians play most nights in a wildly grafittied second-floor music room. It's open Monday through Friday from 11am to 11pm and on Saturday and Sunday from 11am to 3am. There are concerts most nights beginning at 8:30pm. Beer and mixed drinks cost about $2; dinner, with Polish/European cuisine, is about $6. It's across from the Palace of Culture near the train station.

Admission: Concert, $3.70–$4, depending on the performer.

Hybrydy, ul. Złoto 7/9. ☎ **27-37-63.**

This busy student club and disco is popular with Polish teenagers and those in their early 20s. It's open on Friday and Saturday from 7pm to 4am and on Sunday from 7pm to midnight. From the Forum Hotel, take the third right behind the Centrum department store.

Admission: $3.35 adults, $1.50 students.

THE BAR SCENE

Many Varsovians also spend their evenings in one of the city's hundreds of cafés or milk bars. In these places you can enjoy snacks as well as beer and wine—and they're good for meeting the locals.

Harenda Pub, Krakowskie Przedmieście 4/6, at Kopernika.

Once mainly a university student hangout, Harenda has moved upscale and now features many imported bottled beers as well as draft Kilkenny, Guinness, and Dab, and attracts wealthier customers—foreigners working and residing in Warsaw, as well as die-hard billiard players. It's open daily from 8:30am to 6am and has a very cozy feel to it, especially at 4am when everything else in town is shut down tight. Beers, mostly foreign, cost $1.50 to $4.50. The pub is on the same block as the Hotel Harenda, but on the side farthest from Krakowskie Przedmieście.

GAMBLING

The democratic reforms of recent years have introduced Poland to some new capitalist vices—several casinos have opened up across town. All wagering is done in złoty.

Orbis Casino, in the Hotel Victoria Inter-Continental, ul. Królewska 11. ☎ **27-80-11.**

The largest casino in town, this was also Poland's first casino in nearly 50 years when it opened its doors in the fall of 1989. Jacket and tie are required for men. It's open daily from 1pm to 5am. It's a short walk up Królewska from Krakowskie Przedmieście.

Teren Wyścigów Konnych [Race Track], ul. Pulawska. ☎ **43-14-41.**

You can spend a Saturday or Sunday afternoon during the summer at this race track near the airport. Take tram no. 4 or bus A.

8 Easy Excursions

ŁOWICZ

This charming small town 50 miles west of Warsaw is a center of regional folk tradition. The fast train from Warsaw takes 1½ to 2 hours and costs $2 in first class, $1.35 in second class.

There's a worthwhile **Ethnographic Museum** of folk costumes and other objects at Rynek Kościuszki 4 (☎ **8201/39-28**), open Tuesday through Sunday from 9am to 6pm.

The best time to visit Łowicz is on the holiday of ★ **Corpus Christi** (which is held 10 days after Pentecost and 60 days after Easter). Townspeople put on an elaborate pageant and wear original folk costumes.

ŻELAZOWA WOLA

Fans of classical music can visit the **birthplace of Frédéric Chopin** in Żelazowa Wola, 32 miles west of Warsaw. A museum in town (☎ **828/223-00**) documents the life of the great composer. It's open May to September, Tuesday through Sunday from 10am to 5:30pm; October to April, Sunday and Tuesday through Friday from 10am to 4pm and on Saturday from 10am to 2:30pm. Each Sunday from May to September talented musicians give concerts at 11am and 3pm.

You can only reach Żelazowa Wola by bus from Warsaw. Admission to the park or a park concert is $1.50 for adults and 75¢ for students; to a museum concert, $6.

28

Kraków & Southern Poland

NO TOUR OF POLAND WOULD BE COMPLETE WITHOUT A VISIT TO KRAKÓW AND some of the cities in southern Poland. Kraków embodies everything you'd expect from a medieval capital of an important kingdom. One of the few Polish cities to escape large-scale destruction in World War II, Kraków retains much of its historic beauty and grandeur, including a large castle filled with treasures on a hill in the center of town. There's also a magnificent Gothic cathedral and a medieval university.

North of Kraków is Częstochowa, where thousands of pilgrims and tourists arrive every day to pay tribute to the Black Madonna, the second most sacred Catholic shrine in the world after the Vatican. South of Kraków, visitors ski or hike in the breathtaking Tatra Mountains around the resort town of Zakopane. To the east is Łańcut, one of the most impressive chateaux in Eastern Europe.

Lublin, also to the east of Kraków, is a good base for exploring the smaller towns of southeastern Poland.

SEEING KRAKÓW & SOUTHERN POLAND

Make Kraków your first and primary destination in this region, about three hours by express train from Warsaw. From there you can make several day trips to destinations such as Auschwitz, Łańcut, and the pope's birthplace in Wadowice.

For dramatic alpine beauty, proceed from Kraków to Zakopane by bus, in the heart of the Tatra Mountains. From there you can explore nearby lakes and mountains on day trips.

Visit Częstochowa's famous Black Madonna between Kraków and Warsaw. It's a detour off the main Warsaw–Kraków rail line, but frequent trains connect both cities. Since accommodations are fairly expensive or poor in quality in Częstochowa, you might even want to visit on a day trip and continue by evening to your next destination.

Rail connections between Warsaw and Lublin are frequent and fairly rapid, but getting to Lublin from Kraków is a bit problematic, as the rail system is somewhat sparse in southeastern Poland. Instead, consider the bus; it's also an interesting area to explore by car, for it boasts a number of picturesque villages off the main tourist path.

1 Kraków

182 miles S of Warsaw

GETTING THERE • **By Plane** Flights from Warsaw take 40 minutes and cost about $70. The airport (☎ **11-67-00**) is in Balice, 10 miles from Kraków. Take bus no. 208 to Kraków's central railroad station.

• **By Train** An express from Warsaw takes under three hours ($11.50 in first class, $7.65 in second class); "fast" trains take four to five hours ($8.50 in first class, $5.75 in second class). There are also direct connections to most Polish cities, and overnight trains to Gdańsk, Świnoujście, Szczecin, Berlin, Vienna, Budapest, and Bratislava.

Kraków's central train station (☎ **933** or **22-41-82**) is just to the northwest of the Old Town. There's an information desk (*informacja krajowa*) in the train station, next to the baggage check near the clock toward Platform 1.

If you have a lot of luggage, you might want to take a taxi to your hotel (as you exit the main terminal building, you'll see a taxi stand to the right), but keep in mind that most of the Old Town is closed to traffic, so you'll be left at a square nearby.

What's Special About Kraków & Southern Poland

Architectural Highlights

- Kraków's Old Town, astonishingly well preserved, with medieval Europe's largest Old Market Square and traditional cobblestone streets.
- Wieliczka Salt Mines, 90 miles of tunnels including a religious chapel and tennis court underground.
- Lublin's Old Town Square and Castle.
- Original Renaissance town plan in Zamość, southeast of Lublin.

Churches

- Wawel Cathedral, in Kraków, with the tombs of Poland's greatest kings and queens.
- Church of St. Mary in Kraków, with a magnificent carved wooden altar.
- Jasna Góra Monastery in Częstochowa, home to the sacred Black Madonna.

Festivals

- The Days of Kraków, in June, with music, dancing, and much merriment.

Historic Sights

- Auschwitz, outside Kraków, the most notorious death camp of World War II.
- Majdanek, in Lublin, death camp second only to Auschwitz.

Judaica

- Kraków's Kazimierz District, a historic Jewish ghetto.
- Kazimierz Dolny, a picturesque village of 3,000, once home to 30,000 Jews.

Museums

- The rich tapestry and weapons collection in the former home of Poland's royalty, Wawel Castle in Kraków.
- Leonardo da Vinci's *Lady with an Ermine* and Rembrandt's *Landscape with the Good Samaritan* in Kraków's Czartoryski Museum.
- Kraków's University Museum, with the 600-year-old Jagiellonian University's treasures.

Natural Spectacles

- The Tatra Mountains south of Kraków, perfect for hiking and skiing.

To get to the Old Town on foot (about a 15-minute walk), head slightly to the left as you exit the station. Half a block away, go down a pedestrian underpass, which leads to a small park. Continue straight ahead until you reach the medieval fortifications. A turn left into the Old Town leads straight to the Main Market Square.

The city's secondary station, Kraków Płaszow, is to the southeast of the Old Town. To get to the center from there, take tram 3 or 13.

- **By Bus** Kraków's bus terminal is just north of the main train station.
- **By Car** It typically takes about 4½ hours to drive to Kraków from Warsaw.

INFORMATION One of Poland's most helpful tourist offices is Centrum Informacji Turystycznej (C.I.T.), ul. Pawia 8 (☎ **012/22-60-91**), open Monday through Friday from 8am to 4pm, and from May to September also on the last

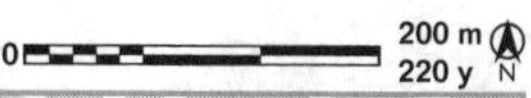
0
200 m
220 y
N

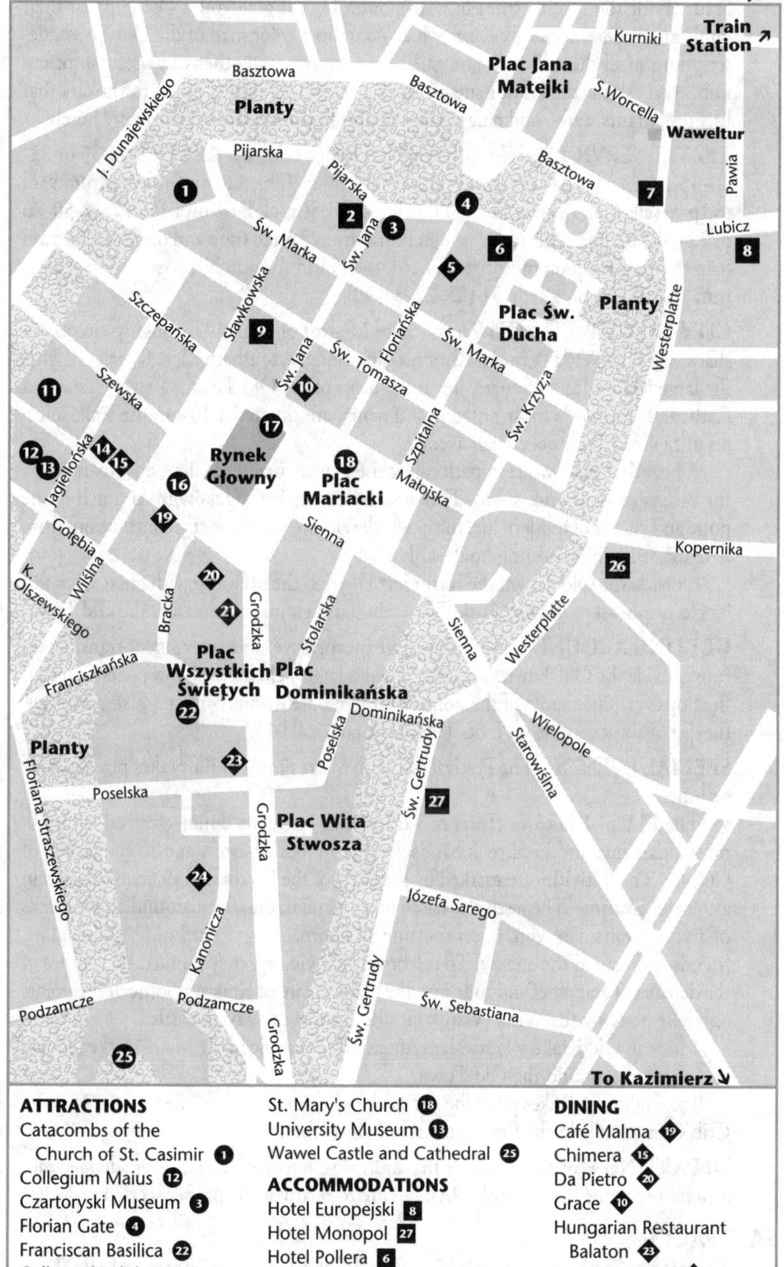
Train Station
Kurniki
Plac Jana Matejki
Basztowa
Planty
S.Worcella
Waweltur
J. Dunajewskiego
Pijarska
Pawia
Lubicz
Św. Marka
Św. Jana
Sławkowska
Szczepańska
Floriańska
Plac Św. Ducha
Westerplatte
Św. Tomasza
Szewska
Św. Krzyża
Szpitalna
Rynek Głowny
Plac Mariacki
Jagiellońska
Małojska
Gołębia
Sienna
Kopernika
Wiślna
K. Olszewskiego
Bracka
Grodzka
Stolarska
Franciszkańska
Plac Wszystkich Świętych
Plac Dominikańska
Dominikańska
Wielopole
Starowiślna
Poselska
Floriana Straszewskiego
Św. Gertrudy
Plac Wita Stwosza
Józefa Sarego
Kanonicza
Podzamcze
Św. Sebastiana
To Kazimierz
ATTRACTIONS
Catacombs of the Church of St. Casimir 1
Collegium Maius 12
Czartoryski Museum 3
Florian Gate 4
Franciscan Basilica 22
Gallery of Polish Painting (Cloth Hall) 17
Ratusz 16
St. Anne's Church 11
St. Mary's Church 18
University Museum 13
Wawel Castle and Cathedral 25
ACCOMMODATIONS
Hotel Europejski 8
Hotel Monopol 27
Hotel Pollera 6
Hotel Polonia 7
Hotel Polski 2
Hotel Saski 9
PTTK Dom Turysty 26
DINING
Café Malma 19
Chimera 15
Da Pietro 20
Grace 10
Hungarian Restaurant Balaton 23
Jama Michalika 5
Kawiarnia u Literatow 24
Restauracja Wierzynek 21

Saturday of the month from 8am to noon. They'll give you a free copy of their publication *Cracow and Environs,* which contains a color map of the Old Town, descriptions of all the museums and galleries in the city, and other very useful information. Also ask for the latest issue of *Inside Kraków,* a monthly guide to the city that lists restaurants, cafés, and clubs. You can also find *Inside Kraków* at many hotels.

TRAVEL SERVICES The Orbis office at Rynek Główny 41 (☎ **22-40-35** or **22-40-35**), open Monday through Friday from 8am to 7pm, and on Saturday from 9am to 1pm, sells train tickets. The LOT airline office is at ul. Basztowa 15 (☎ **22-50-76** or **22-70-78**), open Monday through Friday from 8am to 6pm and on Saturday from 8am to 2pm. Helping motorists in need, the Polish Automobile Association (PZM) runs an office at ul. Dietla 51 (☎ **22-34-90**).

CITY LAYOUT The Old Town (Stare Miasto) of Kraków is roughly circular in shape, with the Wisła (Vistula) River running along its southern edge. Rynek Główny, the large Main Market Square, lies at the heart of the Old Town. Wawel Castle and Cathedral, Kraków's most noted monuments, are situated a 10-minute walk south on ulica Grodzka, a pedestrian avenue.

A beautiful narrow green park called the Planty surrounds the Old Town where the defensive walls once stood. This area divides ancient Kraków from much of the noise and clutter of modern life; the newer developments of the city continue out from here for miles in broad ring boulevards.

Outside the Old Town, the Kazimierz District, the prewar Jewish ghetto, is a few blocks southeast of Wawel Castle. The train station is just northeast of the Old Town.

GETTING AROUND Public buses are inexpensive, and an excellent tram system runs outside the Old Town. The Old Town is largely closed to all but pedestrian traffic; however, since most of the points of interest are in this compact historic center, they're easily accessible on foot. To order a taxi, call 919.

SPECIAL EVENTS The Festival of Polish Short Feature Films takes place in May or June.

The ✪ **Dni-Krakówa** (Days of Kraków), in June, is a famous festival with folk music, dancing, and local rock bands, usually in local theaters and in the House of Culture. The festivities are marked by the entry of the Lajkonik (raftsman) dressed in a colorful costume. The festival is based on a legend dating from around 1240. It tells of a young raftsman who, upon spotting an approaching Tatar horde, gathered his friends and routed the enemy. To celebrate their victory, they donned the clothes of the defeated Tatar chief and rode into the main square of Kraków. Some of the events also take place by the Wisła (Vistula) in the shadow of Wawel Castle.

Music in Old Kraków Festival, in August, offers music in the Main Market Square and elsewhere around the Old Town.

Jazz Halloween takes place the last weekend in October, and the Kraków Nativity Crib Contest is held the first Thursday of December.

DEPARTING • By Train Note that individual tracks at the station are divided into different sections (for example, 2A); be sure to board at the proper section.

FAST FACTS

American Express The Orbis office in the Cracovia Hotel, Al. Focha 1 (☎ **22-46-32**), handles most American Express services. The PKO bank at Rynek Główny 31, on the corner of Szewska street, will change traveler's checks into dollars for a $1.50 commission per transaction.

Area Code Kraków's telephone area code is 012.

Bookstores There are no exclusively English-language bookstores in Kraków, but several bookstores in the Old Town have a shelf or two with English-language paperbacks.

Cameras/Film Developing There is a Kodak store on the north side of the Main Market Square that is fairly reliable.

Embassies/Consulates The American Consulate is at Stolarska 9 (☎ **22-97-64**). A library here, with American books, newspapers, and magazines, is open Monday through Friday from noon until 4:45pm.

Luggage Storage/Lockers The central train station has a baggage-storage facility by the information desk hear the clock Platform 1.

Post Office The main post office at Wiepole 2, just outside the Old Town on the corner of Westerplatte, is open Monday through Friday from 7:30am to 8:30pm, on Saturday from 8am to 2pm, and on Sunday from 9am until 11am. There is also a post office across the square from the train station on Wiepole, which is open Monday through Saturday from 7am to 8pm and on Sunday from 9am to 4pm.

Telephone/Telegraph/Telex In addition to telegraph services, the main post office has card telephones that are open 24 hours a day. The post office across from the train station on Wiepole has two card phones that are open the same hours as the office.

Water Kraków has had problems with water pollution, so this is a particularly bad place to drink from the tap.

Ancient royal capital, medieval university, modern metropolis with 750,000 inhabitants—Kraków is all these things and much more. In no other Polish city will you find so much well-preserved history and culture as you stroll the cobblestone streets, stopping at Gothic churches and well-endowed museums.

Legend says that Kraków was founded well over 1,000 years ago by Prince Krak. The excellent defensive position of Wawel Hill and Kraków's location on a main north-south trade route contributed to its growth. Merchants from southern Europe traveling to the north in search of Baltic amber and from Western Europe en route to Byzantium and Ruthenia converged on Kraków.

In 1038, during the reign of the Piast dynasty, the royal capital was transferred from Gniezno to Kraków. The city was destroyed by a Tatar invasion in 1241, but was speedily rebuilt. For over five centuries Polish kings were both crowned and laid to rest here. Their home in Wawel Castle and its cathedral, and the treasures they contain, are the two most important relics from this era in Polish history.

When the capital was moved from Kraków to Warsaw in 1596, the city walls were torn down. This, in effect, made Kraków an open city, nearly impossible to defend, thus assuring Warsaw's preeminence. After the Congress of Vienna, Kraków was briefly an independent republic before falling under Austrian rule. Like Prague and Budapest, the city thrived as part of the multiethnic Habsburg empire, and its statesmen, scholars, and artists were able to be full participants in the life of a great European state.

Kraków's university and its intellectual tradition made it an important center of a reborn Poland. Under the Nazi regime, Kraków again became a capital, this time of the German-controlled General Government. Poland's postwar Communist government tried to tame the city by shifting attention elsewhere and by building the ultraproletarian town of Nowa Huta nearby. But Kraków remained defiant, and today it shines as a dynamic center of private enterprise and a magnet for visitors.

WHAT TO SEE & DO

There are more than 1,000 buildings of historical and architectural note within Kraków's city limits. If you plan to see many museums in Kraków, you may save a little money by buying a combined admission ticket ($2.50 for adults, $1.25 for students) to the various museums, including the Czartoryski, Matejo, and Wyspiański museums and the two galleries of Polish art. The ticket is sold at the museums where it is valid.

There are many museums worth seeing in Kraków; consult the tourist office's *Cracow and Environs* for a complete list.

The best place to begin a tour of the city is in the Rynek Główny (Main Market Square) in the center of the Old Town.

The Main Market Square

The Rynek Główny (Main Market Square) is one of the largest in contemporary Europe. It's divided at the center by the huge, arcaded Sukiennice (Cloth Hall), which was built as a commercial center in the 13th century and is still used for that purpose. A row of shops running the interior length of the arcade sell a variety of souvenirs and folk art, mostly handcrafted. The second floor houses the Gallery of Polish Painting (for details, see below). Outside Cloth Hall, vendors sell flowers and other goods.

Also on the square is the Kościół Mariacki, a Gothic church dedicated to St. Mary (see below), and the tiny Romanesque Kościół św. Wojciecha, which dates back to the 11th century and shows that the square's level during medieval times was about six feet below what it is today.

On the west side of the Main Market Square, only a single tower remains of the Old Town Hall (Ratusz), most of which was destroyed in 1820. The tower is a fine example of secular medieval Gothic architecture. Inside there's an exhibition on the history of Kraków (☎ **22-53-98**), open May 15 to October 15, Wednesday and Friday through Sunday from 9am to 3pm and Thursday from 11am to 6pm. The tower's basement holds a café (see "Where to Eat," below) and a theater. Not far from the tower is a stone slab marking the spot where Tadeusz Kościuszko declared open rebellion against the Russian Empire on March 24, 1794.

Gallery of 19th-Century Polish Painting, Rynek Główny, Sukiennice (Cloth Hall), 2nd floor. ☎ **22-11-66.**

The collection, dating primarily from the 19th and 20th centuries, features works by famous Polish painters. Many show the local countryside and Polish portraits; there are also a few huge epic themes of glorious moments in Polish history. Unfortunately, the museum's modern interior gives few glimpses of the ancient origin of the building, but one room does offer attractive views of the Old Market Square below.

Admission: 75¢ adults, 35¢ students; free for everyone Thurs.

IMPRESSIONS

But what gives Cracow a sort of sharp outline of spires and turrets against the background of history is the fact that it is a seat of culture on the edge of the uncultivated wilds.

—G.K. Chesterton, *Generally Speaking,* 1928

Open: Wed and Fri–Sun 10am–3:30pm, Thurs noon–5:30pm; last entry a half hour before closing. **Directions:** Enter Cloth Hall on the side facing St. Mary's Church, just to right of the building's center.

★ **Kościół Mariacki [St. Mary's Church],** Rynek Głowny.

Built in the 13th and 14th centuries, this splendid Gothic church contains a magnificent wooden altar carved by Wit Stwosz between 1477 and 1489. The altar, besides being a work of art, is a valuable historical record: The sculptor carved the faces of the saints in the likenesses of the town fathers of his times.

Every day on the hour a single bugle is played from each side of the church tower. The call (the Hejnał) begins and then is cut short. Broadcast at noon throughout Poland by radio, this bugle call honors a bugler who sounded the alarm that saved the city from a surprise Tatar attack. The bugler kept to his post on the city walls until his clarion alarm was cut short by a Tatar arrow that pierced his throat.
Frequent organ and other concerts are also held inside.

Admission: 25¢.

Open: Church, daily 6am–8 or 9pm; altarpiece of Wit Stwosz, Mon–Sat noon–6pm, Sun and holidays 2–6pm. **Directions:** Walk to the northeast corner of the Old Market Square.

A Walk Around the Old Town

Heading one block west of the Market Square, you arrive at the Collegium Maius on ulica św. Anny. Established in 1364, this is the oldest part of the Jagiellonian University, which itself is one of Europe's most ancient universities. The stunning brick-and-stone Gothic buildings house the impressive University Museum (for details, see below). Continue down the street half a block to św. Anny 11 to the beautiful baroque St. Anne's Church. The patron saint of the university, Jan Kanty, is buried in the transept.

On the northern end of the Old Town on ulica Floriańska is the brick Florian Gate, over 110 feet tall, where local artists frequently sell their works. The core of this original town fortification was built in the 13th century and the cupola was added in the 17th century. It's the only one remaining of the seven original city gates. Another major remnant of the once-impregnable outer works is the adjacent Barbican. A circular fortification representing the pinnacle of medieval defensive architecture, the Barbican was once linked to the Florian Gate by a covered passage and surrounded by a moat. The road from the Florian Gate down ulica Floriańska, through the Rynek Główny and to ulica Grodzka, is known as the "Royal Route." Here, kings returning from war or travel held a procession before returning to Wawel Castle.

A two-minute walk from the Barbican brings you to another important stop on your Kraków itinerary, the Czartoryski Museum, on ulica św. Jana (for details, see below). From there it's another three blocks to one of Poland's most bizarre sights, the catacombs of the Church of St. Casimir (see below).

★ **University Museum,** Jagiellońska 15. ☎ **22-05-49.**

Inside the oldest building of Jagiellonian University, the university's rich history comes alive in these rooms: the *Aula,* an assembly hall with many portraits of people affiliated with the university such as past kings, rectors, and bishops of Kraków (who also served as chancellors of the university); the *Copernicus Room,* showing astronomical devices of the sort used by Jagiellonian University's most famous dropout; the *Professors' Apartments,* re-creating the elegant conditions enjoyed by university faculty in the 18th and 19th centuries; the *University Treasury,* with the rector's insignia, handcrafts, drinking vessels, and a French-made globe from 1510, one of the first in the world to include America (just 18 years after Columbus's discovery); the *Professors' Dining Hall,* from the 15th century; and the *Library,* which includes the only existing reconstructions of Copernicus's instruments such as the wooden "Triquetrum" which he used to map out the stars.

You can also pause in the beautiful medieval courtyard outside the museum. Some of the university's 60,000 present-day students gather here after class when school is in session. Incidentally, the museum rooms themselves are still used from time to time for important university functions. Off the courtyard you can also buy souvenirs at the university store, which sells "Universitas Jagellonica" T-shirts and other mementoes; open Monday through Friday from 10am to 6pm.

Admission: 75¢ adults, 35¢ students.

Open: Mon–Fri 11am–2:30pm, Sat 11am–1:30pm. **Directions:** From the Main Market Square, walk down św. Anny and turn left down Jagiellońska.

★ **Czartoryski Museum,** ul. św. Jana 19. ☎ **22-55-66.**

The oldest museum in the country, this branch of the Polish National Museum features an impressive collection of weaponry and armor, tapestries, porcelain, drinking vessels, and foreign paintings, including some gorgeous Turkish ceremonial saddles. The highlights of the picture collection are Leonardo da Vinci's portrait *Lady with an Ermine* and Rembrandt's *Landscape with the Good Samaritan,* both located on the third floor.

Admission: 75¢ adults, 35¢ students; free Fri.

Open: Mon and Sat–Sun 10am–3pm, Fri noon–5pm. **Directions:** From the Main Market Square, walk north on św. Jana three blocks.

Catacombs of the Church of St. Casimir, ul. Reformacka 4.

Beneath a wooden trapdoor of a 17th-century church are vaults containing open coffins of aristocrats and common people of 16th- to 19th-century Kraków. Since the corpses are open to viewing, you gain an eerie glimpse of the past—with clothing, hair, and some parts of the face still visible. In one of the 71 coffins displayed here, you'll see a woman who died on her wedding day, still in her wedding dress. Although the catacombs do not maintain normal working hours, you can try your luck and see if you can convince one of the monks to escort you down there.

Admission: Free, although a church donation is suggested.

Open: Upon special request only. **Directions:** From the Main Market Square, walk west on Szczepańska one block and turn right onto ulica Reformacka.

Franciscan Basilica, Plac Wszystkich Świętych. ☎ **22-71-15.**

Built in the 13th century, the church is most noteworthy for its turn-of-the-century stained-glass windows by Stanisław Wyspiański, which rival Mucha's Cyril and Methodius window in Prague's St. Vitus Cathedral and Tiffany's works as great examples of art nouveau stained glass. An explanation of the windows in English can be found by the entrance. If the windows intrigue you, check out the Wyspiański Museum at Kanonicza 9.

Wawel Castle and Cathedral

Wawel Castle and the nearby Wawel Cathedral are two of the most important historical treasures in all of Poland. Surrounded by fortified walls atop Wawel Hill just south of the Old Town, the structures here served as the religious and political center of Poland for hundreds of years beginning in the early Middle Ages. You'll need at least half a day to see these treasures. An office at the entrance to the hill provides English-language tours, starting at $10 for 90 minutes.

★ **Wawel Cathedral,** on Wawel Hill. ☎ **22-26-43** or **22-94-95.**

The eastern facade of Wawel Cathedral is clearly one of the great architectural medleys of Europe. Parts of the building survive from the 14th century, but considerable additions were made later as Poland moved from the Middle Ages into the Renaissance. Round arches compete with Gothic arches, Ionic columns set off Doric columns, and brick contrasts with both rough and smooth stone. Crowning the cathedral is the gilded dome of the Zygmunt chapel (1519–39), designed by the Florentine Bartolomeo Berrecci, which shines against the calmer bronze and brick on each side.

Inside, you can see the interiors of the many chapels, as well as several royal tombs and that of Polish poet Adam Mickiewicz. High in the tower is the church bell *Zygmunt.* Cast from captured cannon in 1520, its powerful toll echoes off the surrounding hills and far out to Kraków's suburbs. From the top of the belltower you can admire a view over Kraków, although through a mesh fence (to get to the belltower, follow the signs inside the cathedral reading DO DZWONU ZYGMUNTA). Also visit the Royal Crypt, beneath the cathedral, which contains many kings and queens, bishops, and other notables in Polish history, including Tadeusz Kościuszko, a Polish nationalist best known by Americans for his participation in their War of Independence. Most recently, Gen. Wladyslaw Sikorski, who led the Polish government-in-exile during World War II, was interred here. He died in a plane crash in 1943, but it wasn't until 50 years after his death that the anti-Communist could be buried in his native land.

To visit the belltower as well as the crypt you must buy tickets from a church building across from the cathedral. This stand also sells a useful, very detailed English-language guide of the cathedral for $1.

In another structure across from the main cathedral entrance, you can see an impressive collection of crowns, scepters, and orbs used by Polish royalty (such as the crown, scepter, and orb of King Kazimierz the Great from 1370) in the Cathedral Museum. Downstairs, you'll see a collection of robes and objects used by Pope John Paul II.

Admission: Cathedral, free; belltower and crypt, $1 adults, 50¢ students.

Open: Cathedral, Mon–Sat 9am–5:30pm, Sun 12:15–5:30pm; tower and crypt, Tues–Sun 10am–5:30pm. Oct–Apr, until 3pm. **Directions:** From the Main Market Square, walk south on Grodzka; take the fourth right onto Plac Wita Stwosza, then turn left on Kanonicza. At that street's end, a pathway continues uphill to the castle; the cathedral is the first building to the left.

★ **Wawel Castle,** on Wawel Hill. ☎ **22-51-55.**

From the cathedral, proceed to Wawel Castle, today home to the Royal Castle Rooms, entered from the southeast corner of the courtyard, and the Royal Treasury and Armory, entered from the northeast corner.

Situated around a Renaissance colonnaded courtyard, the Royal Castle Rooms were built in the 16th century by Italian masters brought in by King Zygmunt the Old of the Jagiellons. The castle suffered damage from a fire in 1702 and then by Austrian troops who occupied it during the partition period. It's been refurnished since 1905 with period pieces donated from all over Europe. Its finest treasure is a collection of Flemish tapestries, ordered expressly for the royal chambers by Zygmunt August the

Jagiellon. He supervised the work during the more than 20 years it took to complete the weaving. When Zygmunt August died, the collection numbered 356 tapestries of the highest quality. Unfortunately, only 136 pieces have survived. Canada kept the tapestries for safekeeping during World War II, and after considerable delay, returned them in 1959. Other highlights include original furniture and paintings from the castle.

Unfortunately, like many of the tapestries, much of the Royal Treasury and Armory has been plundered over the years. However, the *Szczerbiec,* the sword used for coronations since 1320, remains in the castle. Other surviving riches include an impressive array of arms and knightly armor, and a collection of Middle and Near Eastern artifacts accumulated, as one tour guide explained in a magnificent understatement, "through the years of not always peaceful contacts with the Middle East."

Admission: Royal Castle Rooms, $1 adults, 50¢ students; Treasury, $1 adults, 50¢ students. Both areas are free to all on Fri.

Open: Treasury and Armory, Tues–Sun 10am–3pm; Royal Castle Rooms, Tues, Thurs, and Sat–Sun 10am–3pm, Wed and Fri 10am–4pm. Guided tours in English (included in the price of your ticket) begin at 10:25am and 2:25pm. **Directions:** On Wawel Hill, walk past the cathedral, turn left, and proceed through the arches.

Dragon's Cave, near the Vistula River at the foot of the Wawel Hill fortifications.

Below the Wawel is a cave reputed to have been the home of a dragon that subsisted on a diet of Polish maidens. There's an actual fire-breathing dragon on view—the metal rendition spouts fiery butane jets. It's the creation of sculptor Bolesław Chromy.

Admission: 35¢.

Open: May–Sept, Tues–Sun 10am–3pm.

The Kazimierz District

Before World War II Jews made up a quarter of Kraków's population, and most lived in the Kazimierz District southeast of the Old Town. Until 1800 Kazimierz was a separate city altogether, as Jews were barred from living in Kraków proper. To get there from the Old Town, walk southeast down ulica Starowiślna, about a 10-minute walk.

The Jewish community centered around Poland's oldest Jewish temple, the Old Synagogue, ul. Szeroka 24 (☎ **22-09-62**), dating back to the 15th century. Although most of the Old Synagogue is a reconstruction—the Nazis first used the building as an army storeroom and then demolished it—it now houses a museum of the history of Jews in Poland. Upon entering, you'll see the central ribbed-vaulted room of the synagogue with two columns in the center and a brass chandelier hanging from the ceiling. Adjacent rooms have photos and objects such as scrolls in Hebrew documenting Jewish life in the city. A room upstairs chronicles the Nazi deportation of Jews from Kraków. The desk at the entrance has a few brochures on Jewish sights in the Kazimierz District. Admission to the Old Synagogue is 75¢, 25¢ for students, and it's open on Wednesday and Thursday from 9am to 3:30pm, on Saturday and Sunday from 9am to 3pm, and on Friday from 11am to 6pm (it's closed the first Saturday and Sunday of the month).

In addition to the Old Synagogue there's an old Jewish cemetery, near ul. Szeroka 40, which was used from the 16th to the 18th century, but was largely destroyed in World War II and subsequently restored. Several other synagogues remain in the area, and there are also a number of Renaissance and Gothic buildings and churches.

For details on some of the district's other sights, ask the tourist office for the pamphlet "The Kazimierz District."

Ethnographic Museum, 1 Plac Wolnica. ☎ **56-28-63.**

This small museum documents the folk traditions of various regions of Poland with displays of costumes, models, crafts, and even reconstructed peasant dwellings you can step inside. Particularly interesting are the elaborate Nativity scenes and the half-Christian/half-pagan pageant costumes. Temporary exhibits in an adjoining building display the folklife of other parts of the world.

Admission: 50¢ adults, 40¢ students.

Open: Mon 10am–6pm, Wed–Fri 10am–3pm, Sat–Sun 10am–2pm. **Directions:** From the Old Synagogue, walk west on Jozefa, then make a left on Bożego Ciała.

SHOPPING

Compared to many cities in Poland, Kraków provides a fairly fruitful destination for souvenir and gift shopping, especially in Kraków's Old Town. You'll see many silver- and gold-jewelry shops, as well as stores selling amber, books, and a wide variety of other goods. There are many stores along ulica Floriańska, and except in very cold weather, artists sell touristy paintings along the fortifications by ulica Pijarska. Wander the side streets beyond this area to make your own discoveries as well.

Inside the covered arcade in the Main Market Square you can buy folk dolls and costumes, wooden stools and carvings, blankets, sweaters, and other trinkets. There are also dozens of art galleries in the Old Town, with the most notable clusters along Floriańska and Stolarska, opposite the U.S. consulate.

EVENING ENTERTAINMENT

Start your evening with a stroll through the Main Market Square, where you're likely to find musicians and performers at various corners. During several festivals a stage is erected at the foot of the Old Town Hall for official performances.

Classical Music

Capella Cracoviensis, ul. Zwierzyniecka 1. ☎ **21-45-66.** Fax 21-96-60.

This chamber music ensemble was formed in 1970 by conductor Stanisław Gałoński, and it consists of an orchestra, a mixed vocal ensemble, and the Rotantists (an a capella male singing group). The ensemble's repertoire ranges from medieval music to contemporary works. Capella Cracoviensis has toured the United States, Japan, and most European countries, but Kraków has an especially lovely atmosphere in which to hear their music.

Kraków Philharmonic, Zwierzyniecka 1/3. ☎ **22-09-58** or **22-94-77.**

This is the only Eastern European orchestra conducted by an American, Gilbert Levine. Inquire at the tourist information center for the schedule at this and other music halls in town. The box office (☎ **22-59-00**) is open Monday through Friday from 9am to noon and 5 to 7pm; tickets cost about $2. To get there, walk one block south of the Main Market Square down Bracka and turn right on Franciszkańska, which continues into Zwierzyniecka.

Improvisational Theater/Alternative Music/Cabaret

Piwnica Pod Baranami, Rynek Główny 27. ☎ **22-32-65.**

This is the most unique club in Poland and *the* place to go in Kraków. It's owned and managed by Piotr Skrzynecki who, at 70 years young, is also the cabaret's emcee. The Piwnica is a magnet for Kraków's avant-garde community. From the west side of the

Main Square, you pass through an archway into a courtyard and descend stone steps into a cavernous private club—foreigners are permitted entry—with candles burning on the stone walls. You get the feeling that you're touring an inhabited mine as you walk through the many chambers that display art. The cabaret schedule is mid-September to June (to accommodate Kraków's students). The acts range from Marlene Dietrich–like renditions to political satire on national and international subjects. Naturally, the satire is in Polish, so bring a friend who can translate for you. Buy your tickets in advance—this is a very popular show.

From July to mid-September, the club turns into a disco, open to the public. It's worth stopping in to experience its uniqueness even though you'll miss the cabaret show.

Jazz

U Muniaka, ul. Floriańska 3.

If you succumb to the siren song of recorded jazz being piped onto Floriańska and follow it to its origin, you will find yourself in a very pleasant subterranean club with a warm atmosphere and a good selections of drinks—alcoholic and non-alcoholic. The best time to come is on Thursday, Friday, and Saturday when local jazz groups hit the stage. The club is open daily from noon until 3am.

Admission: $3.50 for live jazz.

Where to Stay

PRIVATE ROOMS If you're interested in a private room, try Waweltur (formerly the Wawel Tourist Office), at ul. Pawia 8 (☎ **12/22-19-21** or **22-16-40**), next door to the Centrum tourist office. They do a brisk business, so it's best to arrive early, especially during the summer. Single rooms go for $8, doubles are $13, and apartments are $21 to $27. Most of these rooms lie outside the Old Town, about a 10- or 15-minute walk from the center, so even if you generally stay in private rooms, you may want to opt for one of Kraków's inexpensive, central hotels. The Waweltur office is open Monday through Friday from 8am to 9pm and on Saturday from 9am to 3pm.

STUDENT ACCOMMODATIONS For student accommodations during July and August, inquire at Almatur at Rynek Główny 7 (☎ **012/22-63-52** or **22-67-08**; telex 325214). It's in the back of a courtyard entered from the Main Market Square. The office is open Monday through Saturday from 8:30am to 5:30pm.

HOTELS

Doubles for Less Than $23

Hotel Europejski, ul. Lubicz 5, 31-034 Kraków. ☎ **012/22-09-11.** Fax 012/21-30-36. 52 rms (35 with bath). TEL **Directions:** Turn left from train station and continue one block to ulica Lubicz; it's then just across street.

Rates: $15.50 single without bath, $19.25 single with bath; $21.50 double without bath, $29.50 double with bath; $34 triple with bath; $37 quad; $37.50 suite. AE, DC, EU, JCB, MC, V.

A thorough renovation—rooms, lobby, and exterior—was recently completed at this fine old hotel in a great location. The mattresses and bathrooms are in fine shape, but the redecoration was not done in quite the best taste. Lampshades are festooned with fabric roses that look like large, dead spiders, and the paintings on the walls approach in hideousness those found in American motels. But these minor flaws should not deter you from this hotel.

Hotel Monopol, ul. św. Gertrudy 6, 31-046 Kraków. ☎ **012/22-76-66** or **22-70-15.** 35 rms (13 with bath, 9 with shower but no toilet). TEL **Tram:** 10 from the train station. **Bus:** C from the train station one stop.

Rates (including breakfast): $15 single without bath, $17.50 single with shower only; $20 single with bath and toilet, $20 double without bath, $24 double with shower only, $27.50 double with bath and toilet; $25 triple without bath, $32.50 triple with bath and toilet. AE, DC, EU, JCB, MC, V.

A comfortable splurge choice in previous editions of this guidebook, the Monopol is now looking a bit tired, but prices have also fallen, increasing the hotel's appeal. The rooms feature firm mattresses, double windows that keep out noise, and desks that you can actually sit at and write on. Rooms are also well lit. All but one of the double rooms have full private bathrooms. This three-star hotel is outside the Old Town but just a five-minute walk to the Main Market Square. There's a café/bar downstairs, with a disco most evenings.

Hotel Polonia, ul. Basztowa 25, 31-156 Kraków. ☎ **012/22-12-33.** Fax 012/22-16-21. Telex 322729. 69 rms (30 with bath). TEL **Directions:** From the train station, walk across the square, toward the Old Town.

Rates: $11 single without bath, $13.50 single with bath; $16.50 double without bath, $20.50 double with bath, $22.50 double with bath and TV; $20 triple without bath, $24 triple with bath, $23.50 quad without bath; $27.50 apartment.

Aggressively promoted as only a privatized hotel could be, the Polonia has put lighted billboards in the train station and painted a trail of signs on the sidewalk leading from the tourist office to its door. Ah, capitalism! Built in 1917, the hotel retains such elegant traces of its age as intricate ironwork and capitals in the hallways. The rooms with bath are well worth the extra money—most were renovated recently, and they boast new carpeting and real stall showers. The rooms without bath are fine, but the coed hallway showers mean long walks and little privacy. The lobby is small but pleasant, with a few armchairs and tables.

Doubles for Less Than $28

Hotel Pollera, ul. Szpitalna 30, 31-204 Kraków. ☎ **012/22-10-44** or **22-11-28.** Fax 012/22-13-89 42 rms (24 with bath). TEL **Directions:** After entering the Old Town through the Barbican walls, walk left one block and take the first right.

Rates: $17.50 single without bath, $21.50 single with shower, $33.50 single with shower and toilet; $25.50 double without bath, $28.50 double with shower, $41 double with shower and toilet; $44 triple with shower and toilet.

The hotel was undergoing renovation at the time of this writing. Because the hotel often fills up, reserve as early as you can. The hotel has an attractive, dignified restaurant with large mirrors and high ceilings. It's located just three blocks from the Main Market Square.

Hotel Polski, ul. Pijarska 17, 31-015 Kraków. ☎ **012/22-11-44** or **22-15-29.** Fax 012/22-14-26. 50 rms (24 with bath). TEL **Directions:** After entering the Old Town through the Barbican walls, turn right.

Rates (including breakfast): $17.50 single without bath, $22.50 single with bath; $25 double without bath, $32.50 double with bath. AE, DC, EU, JCB, MC, V.

Attractively located across from Kraków's medieval fortifications, just three blocks from the Main Market Square, the Polski offers spacious though somewhat drab budget rooms. Rugs cover the parquet floors in some rooms and new tiling surrounds the sink areas. The public hallways are clean but could use a repainting; the attractive location here makes up for such shortcomings. The public bathrooms are very clean and in good repair, and the bathtubs are large. There's a convenience shop attached to the lobby.

Hotel Saski, ul. Slawkowska 3, 31-014 Kraków. ☎ **012/21-42-22.** Fax 012/21-48-30. Telex 325779. 60 rms (12 with bath, 18 with shower but no toilet). TEL **Directions:** After entering the Old Town through the Barbican walls, walk straight ahead two blocks, then turn right; continue two blocks and turn left.

Rates (including breakfast): $17 single without bath, $18.25 single with shower only, $20.50 single with full bath and TV; $26.50 double without bath, $29.50 double with shower only. $32.50 double with full bath; $29.50 triple without bath, $32.50 triple with shower only, $35.50 triple with full bath; $40–$50 apartment. AE, DC, EU, JCB, MC, V.

The Hotel Saski is by far the best budget buy for comfortable facilities in town—and it's just a block from the Market Square. It was renovated recently, giving it a more attractive look than most places around, with details such as deep-red bedspreads and a decorative rug in every freshly painted room. You'll ride an antique elevator (from 1903) up from the upscale-looking lobby. The hotel also has a café, a restaurant, and a lobby gift shop.

Outside the Town Center

Hotel Pod Kopcem, Al. Waszyngtona, 30-204 Kraków. ☎ **012/22-03-55** or **22-20-55.** Fax 012/22-01-29. Telex 322609. 53 rms (41 with bath). TEL **Bus:** 100 from Plac Jana Matejki just north of the Barbican fortifications in the Old Town, a 20-minute ride (runs every hour).

Rates (including breakfast): $34.50 double without bath, $42 double with bath; $42 triple without bath, $52 triple with bath; $54.50 suite. AE, DC, EU, JCB, MC, V.

Travelers with cars seeing Kraków at a slower, romantic pace may enjoy this hotel perched on a hill high above the city in a 19th-century Austrian brick fortress. Behind the fortress is a massive mound in honor of Tadeusz Kościuszko, a popular excursion for locals. The views down the valley over the towers of Kraków are magnificent. The rooms here are also very quiet and attractive, with black wood furniture, parquet floors, and stylish lamps near the beds. There's a stone-floored lobby and a friendly, English-speaking reception. Also a restaurant, bar, disco, Pewex shop, a newsstand, and a massive bronze cannon defending the door. For hikers, there are some lovely trails nearby; pick up the map *Las Wolski* from a tourist information office.

Hotel Wanda, ul. Koniewa 9, 30-150 Kraków. ☎ **012/37-16-77.**
Fax 012/37-85-18. Telex 0325507. 80 rms (all with bath). TV TEL **Directions:** The hotel lies on route E40 into town, next to the Holiday Inn. Buses 139, 173, 208, 238, and 258 connect it with the center.

Rates: $46 single; $60 double; $81 triple. Nov–Apr, $20 single; $32 double; $44 triple. AE, DC, EU, JCB, MC, V. **Parking:** $4.

With the Wanda, you trade the convenience and character of the older hotels in central Kraków for the high standards of maintenance and service that Orbis provides. The hotel is a couple of miles outside of the center of town, so you will have to take the bus in to do any sightseeing. The decor is drab, with a great deal of brown, but the rooms are spotless, and in general the Wanda resembles a good American motel, with double beds and modern bathrooms.

A Super-Budget Choice

Pttk Dom Turysty, ul. Westerplatte 15/17, 31-033 Kraków. ☎ **012/22-95-66.** Fax 012/21-27-26. 170 rms (3 with bath, 62 with toilet but no shower). **Directions:** From the train station, walk straight ahead one block, then turn left down Westerplatte four blocks.

Rates: $16 single without bath, $21 single with bath; $20 double with toilet but no shower, $28 double with bath; $34.50 triple with bath; $5 per person in an eight-bedded room. AE, DC, EU, JCB, MC, V.

PTTK is a cheap place to stay, but it's very crowded with little privacy. Though supposedly for all visitors, it's overwhelmingly patronized by young people and student groups. PTTK has a very inexpensive restaurant open from 7am to 9pm. There's also a plastic-and-glass lobby and a luggage room where you can leave your things when you go out for the day. The rooms are small but clean, and the doubles have phones. Most of the furniture is in good condition, but the mattresses are very soft and springy, offering little support. Though the place is something of a zoo in the daytime, it quiets down at night, although there's a disco Monday through Friday. There's also an exchange desk, a souvenir shop, luggage-storage service, and a bar.

Where to Eat

Meals for Less Than $3

★ $ **Chimera,** ul. Św. Anny 3.

Cuisine: SALAD. **Directions:** From the Ratusz tower in the Rynek, walk one block west on Św. Anny.

Prices: Salads 75¢ small, $1.50 large.

Open: Daily 9am–midnight.

In a country where a mixed salad generally means two colors of cabbage and some pickled carrots, Chimera offers salads that are extraordinary. A small plate (75¢) will get you large portions of four of about two dozen salads—green salads, bean salads, pasta salads, fruit salads, even some with meat and fish. A large plate entitles you to even larger portions of six salads. You can help yourself to fresh bread. Hot soup or light meals are offered, too.

The setting is one of the coziest of Kraków's many cellars. In the evenings, there is live piano music, and in winter a wood fire welcomes you inside.

Grace, ul. Św. Jana 1 and ul. Św. Anny 7.

Cuisine: PIZZA. **Directions:** From the Main Market Square, walk west on Św. Anny or north on Św. Jana.

Prices: Pizzas $1.50–$3.50.

A jazzy pizzeria with neon signs and posters of classic American cars, Grace serves pizza that is much closer to an American version than most of what goes by the name in Poland. The dough is light and chewy, and the toppings are cooked into the pizza—no raw onions piled on here. Of course, if you want bananas on your pizza or would like to douse it in ketchup (10¢), that's your prerogative.

Hungarian Restaurant Balaton, ul. Grodzka 37. ☎ **22-04-69.**

Cuisine: HUNGARIAN. **Directions:** Walk down ulica Grodzka a few blocks south of the Main Market Square.

Prices: Main courses 80¢–$2.30.

Open: Daily 9am–10pm (hot meals served 1pm–9:30pm).

For a simple and delicious sit-down meal, I like the Balaton. The decor is dark-stained paneled walls, beige vaulted ceilings, wood tables, and red and black placemats. If you're lucky you'll find the sole English-speaking waiter to translate the limited Polish- and Hungarian-language menu. It's worth the effort: The lightly spiced goulash soup, filled with chunks of meat and potatoes, is an unusually good variation for just 85¢. Other specialties of the house include *placki zemniaczane* (potato pancakes with a delicious meat and cream sauce) and the tender Budapest chicken in a rich paprika-accented sauce.

Da Pietro, Rynek Główny 17. ☎ **22-32-79.**

Cuisine: ITALIAN. **Reservations:** Recommended. **Directions:** The restaurant is opposite the small church in the Main Market Square.

Prices: Appetizers and soups $1.25–$3.50; pasta and pizza $2.50–$4; meat and fish main courses $4.50–$7.50; desserts $2.50.

Da Pietro is set in three cellar rooms with vaulted brick ceilings. The lighting is very romantic—indirect lamps and candles on the tables. Beware of the acoustics; I had no trouble eavesdropping on a conversation 30 feet away in the opposite corner of the room. The food is quite authentically Italian and simply flawless, from the ambrosial roasted red peppers to the intense tiramisu. If you're staying in Kraków for several days, come here early as you may want to come back for a second or third time.

Worth the Extra Money

Restauracja Wierzynek, Rynek Główny, 2nd floor. ☎ **22-98-96** or **22-10-35.**

Cuisine: POLISH. **Reservations:** Required in summer; call a day or two ahead. **Directions:** Walk to the south side of the Main Market Square.

Prices: Soup $1–$6; main courses $8–12; desserts $1–3; glass of wine $1.70–$5.10. AE, DC, EU, MC, V.

Open: Daily 8am–11pm (last hot dish served at 10:30pm).

You won't find a more elegant restaurant in all of Poland. Its name comes from a 14th-century city councilman who entertained a group of kings in his home during the 1364 Great Conference of monarchs in Kraków. The royal visitors included Polish King Kazimierz the Great, German Emperor Charles IV, and King Louis of Hungary. The meals served on gold and silver platters established a tradition of elegance that the restaurant strives to maintain. Today's leaders still eat here, and recent visitors have included Presidents Bush and Gorbachev.

Two shining suits of armor guard the door you enter. Upstairs in the main dining room, you sit in antique chairs beneath elegant wood ceilings and brass chandeliers. You might like to request a romantic window table for two overlooking the town square. In summer, a lute player entertains guests from 8 to 10pm.

Appetizers include *żurek polski* (a rich cream broth garnished with sausage and egg), Polish beetroot (*barszcz*) soup, or a choice of other soups. For a main course you can select one of several carp, trout, or salmon dishes, roast duck with apples, and several wild game dishes. Extensive dessert offerings include chocolate or poppy-seed cake, and ice cream.

Cafés

Cafe Malma, Rynek Główny 25. ☎ **21-98-94.**

Cuisine: DESSERT. **Directions:** Walk to the south side of the Main Market Square.
Prices: Coffee 20¢–30¢; cakes 75¢; sundaes $1.50–$1.80; salads and snacks 60¢–$2.50.
Open: Daily 11am–11pm.

Located in a convenient spot just opposite the town hall tower, this bright and cheerful café serves real cappuccino and tasty pastries. Try the mocha cake.

Jama Michalika, ul. Floriańska 45. ☎ **22-15-61.**

Cuisine: DESSERTS.
Prices: Hot drinks 35¢–$2; snacks $1–$2; desserts 35¢–$2.25.
Open: Daily 9am–10pm.

Founded in 1895 as a pastry shop, Jama Michalika has an art nouveau decor, which reflects the age when Kraków was closely tied to the movement in Vienna. Several walls are covered with drawings. And to make the café unique in Kraków and perhaps in all of Poland, no smoking is allowed.

Pod Ratuszem [Stanczyk], Rynek Główny. ☎ **21-13-26.**

Cuisine: DRINKS. **Directions:** The café is housed in the basement of the medieval town hall tower.
Prices: Drinks 25¢–$1.35; ice cream $1.25; toast and soup 35¢–$1.35.
Open: Daily 10am–1am. **Closed:** 7–9pm on days when there is a theater performance.

The brick-and-stone cellars of Kraków's Ratusz have had various uses over the years. Originally they were torture chambers, whose implements can still be seen in the Matejo museum. In the 14th century there was a bar here; in the 15th, a brothel. Now it's a café, especially renowned for its hot, spiced mead (honey wine). On Fridays and Saturdays jazz or blues starts up at 10pm. Occasionally art is exhibited on the walls.

Kawiarnia U Literatów [Polish Literary Club], ul. Kanonicza 7.

Cuisine: SNACKS. **Directions:** From the Main Market Square, walk south on Grodzka, take the third right, and then the first left.
Prices: Cakes 75¢; ice cream 65¢; coffee 60¢–75¢; mixed drinks $1.20–$3.
Open: Daily 9am–9pm.

A quiet, dignified place good for intimate conversation, with wooden ceilings and stone walls. The more public room is through the large, arched stone doorway and on the right. The larger room in the back is for club members only. The coffee and the cheesecake (*sernik domowy*) are especially good here. There's an outdoor terrace in the summer.

2 Excursions from Kraków

Auschwitz [Oświęcim]

38 miles W of Kraków

GETTING THERE • By Train The local train to Oświęcim takes about 1¼ hours ($2.65 in first class, $1.75 in second class). Once there, take a taxi or local bus from the front of the train station to the Auschwitz Museum.

• **By Bus** Buses leave several times daily from Kraków's central bus station (*dworzec autobusowy*; ☎ **936**) across from the train station; the schedule is clearly posted. They cost $1.25 and stop close to the museum.

A visit to the concentration camp at Auschwitz, just outside the industrial town of Oświęcim (pronounced Ausch-*vien*-chim) will certainly be one of the most deeply felt experiences of your Polish travels. Opened in June 1940, Auschwitz proved to be the ultimate in Nazi cruelty. At the height of its efficiency in the summer of 1944, the complex could gas and cremate more than 20,000 people in a 24-hour period. Estimates of the dead range from 1 million to 3.5 million. In addition to murdering people, the Germans used the camp to detain POWs, extract slave labor, and perform "medical" experiments that resulted in the maiming or death of its victims.

KL Auschwitz comprised Auschwitz I, in Oświęcim, two other large camps, and 40 smaller subcamps where German companies exploited the labor of prisoners.

Auschwitz I, at ul. Wiezniow Oświęcimia 20 (☎ **320-02**), has the majority of exhibits and a visitor's center. There, you may watch a graphic film shot by the Soviet army when it liberated the camp on January 27, 1944. The images are so powerful, you don't need to wait for a showing in English.

After passing through the gate with the infamous slogan, ARBEIT MACHT FREI ("work leads to freedom") written above, you will enter into a complex of surprisingly sturdy brick buildings with trees in front—these were built as Polish army barracks shortly after World War I. Used to warehouse Nazi prisoners, they now exhibit a room full of human hair, taken from corpses for use in German industry; thousands of eyeglasses; and tins of Zyklon-B, the pesticide used to kill prisoners. Throughout several of the buildings are photographs of thousands of Polish political prisoners in camp uniform, along with the dates they entered Auschwitz and perished.

The scientific slaughter of more than a million people, almost all of them Jews, took place not among these tidy barracks but at **Auschwitz II/Birkenau**, in the village of Brzezinka, about two miles from the main camp. (You can ask at the museum information desk for a map with directions and walk there or take a bus that runs four times a day.) Several times larger than Auschwitz I, Birkenau consisted mainly of wooden, stablelike barracks with dirt floors. You will enter to one side of the main gate, through which rolled trains of freight and cattle cars, packed with Jews from all over occupied Europe. Follow the rails to the selection ramp, where Jews were dragged out of the cars and paraded in front of Nazi doctors, who picked out those they thought capable of slave labor. More than 70% of the deportees, including almost all of the children and old people, were sent straight along the tracks to the crematoria, where they were stripped, gassed, and cremated within hours of their arrival. These four crematoria are now in ruins—one was destroyed by sabotage, the others by the Nazis fleeing the advancing Red Army—but they remain the most dreadful constructions in Europe.

Those prisoners not sent immediately to the chimneys lived in crowded barracks. These barracks were not made to last; most were destroyed by the fleeing Nazis, others have simply rotted slowly since the end of the war, and some of those you see have been entirely reconstructed. Still, the forest of brick chimneys and the remaining buildings show the vastness of the machine created by Hitler's Germany. Birkenau has only a few displays and plaques among the barracks, and it receives far fewer visitors than Auschwitz I. But it's easier here to be alone with one's thoughts, interrupted only by the haunting rumble of trains pulling into the nearby Oścwięcim station.

Admission to the camp is free; you'll pay 25¢ to see the film and $1.10 for parking. The camp is open daily: in June, July, and August from 8am to 7pm; in May and September from 8am to 6pm; in April and October from 8am to 5pm; in March and November and early December from 8am to 4pm; and in late December, January, and February from 8am to 3pm. Children under 13 are not admitted to Auschwitz I, but they may visit the camp at Birkenau.

Wieliczka Salt Mines

7 miles SE of Kraków

GETTING THERE • By Train From Kraków, the train to Wieliczka takes 23 minutes (90¢ in first class, 60¢ in second); from the station, follow the signs DO KOPALNI.

• By Bus Buses leave several times daily from Kraków's central bus station (*dworzec autobusowy*, ☎ **936**), across from the train station. The schedule is posted.

The Wieliczka Salt Mines (☎ **78-26-53**) were founded 700 years ago, and they still produce 60% of the salt consumed at Polish tables. Sometime in the 16th century, a miner started carving sculpture out of the salt rock, and the tradition snowballed from there. Now, amid the 90 miles of tunnels stand dozens of carved, saline figures, both religious and secular, and even whole chapels hewn out of vast pieces of salt. Unlike granite or bronze, salt is translucent, and many of the sculptures glow from electric lights placed behind them, while older sculptures have gained a Henry Moore–like smoothness from centuries of slow erosion. The mines were used as a bombproof slave-labor factory by the Nazis during World War II, and today a small sanatorium operates here in the antiseptic salt air.

The mines can be visited only by guided tours, which last about 45 minutes and take you through the chambers with the most elaborate carvings. None of the modern operations are included on the tour. The trip involves a lot of walking, including several hundred steps down, though there is an elevator to get you to the top. If you go alone, you will have to wait until enough English-speakers show up to form a tour, but you are guaranteed not to wait longer than an hour. Tickets cost $3.50 for adults, $2 for students. You can also take a tour organized by Orbis that departs from the Hotel Cracovia. The cost is $12 for transportation and a guide.

The mines are open daily: April 17 to October 15, from 7am to 7pm; October 16 to April 16, from 8am to 4pm.

Wadowice, the Pope's Birthplace

31 miles SW of Kraków

GETTING THERE • By Bus Take a bus from Kraków's central station (*dworzec autobusowy*, ☎ **936**), across from the train station.

In 1920 Karol Wojtyła was born in the small hamlet of Wadowice, and following his ascension as Poland's first pope of the Roman Catholic Church, the town started attracting pilgrims. Visitors today can see the pope's birthplace at ul. Kościelna 7, site of a small museum, and the nearby Church of the Blessed Virgin Mary, where he was baptized.

3 Częstochowa

135 miles SW of Warsaw, 72 miles NW of Kraków

GETTING THERE • By Train From Warsaw, expresses take about 3 1/3 hours ($10.50 in first class, $7.10 in second class). From Kraków, a fast train takes between 2 and 2 1/2 hours ($5.40 in first class, $3.60 in second class). Most trains arrive at Częstochowa Główna (central station), on the east side of town; a few arrive at Częstochowa Stradom, on the south side.

The city can be seen en route from Warsaw or Łódź to Kraków. Or you can do it as a day trip from Kraków (the last direct train back to Kraków departs Częstochowa at 5:21pm, but you can take a later train to Katowice and transfer from there for Kraków).

ESSENTIALS The telephone area code is 0833.

ORIENTATION The Avenue of Our Lady, Aleja Najświętszej Marii Panny ("Al. NMP" for short), bisects the town from east to west and runs from the foot of the Jasna Góra Monastery through the center of town. The main railroad station (Częstochowa Główna) is just south of Al. NMP on ulica Świerczewskiego. To reach the monastery, head north (ask to make sure) as you exit from the station and walk until you reach the first cross street; this is Aleja Najświętszej Marii Panny. Turn left (west) and the Jasna Góra Monastery is not more than a 20-minute walk away (you'll see the tall steeple in the distance).

INFORMATION Tourist Information Office, Al. NMP 65 (☎ **24-13-60, 24-34-12**), sells a couple of English-language color pamphlets about the monastery and town (20¢ to 25¢) as well as more thorough books in English and maps of Częstochowa and other cities. Some staff members speak English. It's open Monday through Friday 9am to 6pm, Saturday and Sunday 10am to 4pm. The Orbis office at Al. NMP 40/42 is open Monday, Tuesday, Thursday, and Friday 8am to 4pm and Wednesday 9am to 5pm.

SPECIAL EVENTS Any major Catholic holidays bring special celebrations—and crowds—to Częstochowa. Special Marian holidays include May 3 (Queen of Poland), August 15 (Ascension of the Virgin Mary), August 26 (Our Lady of Częstochowa), September 8 (birth of the Virgin Mary), and December 8 (Immaculate Conception of the Blessed Virgin Mary). November also brings the Jeunesses Musicales International Music Festival.

Częstochowa (pronounced "*Chenst*-a-*ho*-va") is the home of the famous Jasna Góra Monastery, which houses the sacred Black Madonna and one of Poland's most important collections of Catholic religious and historical artifacts. Jasna Góra will fascinate you not only with the beauty of the Black Madonna, but also with the intensity of worship that you witness. A million Poles a year come to Częstochowa (pop. 250,000) not as tourists, but as devout pilgrims.

WHAT TO SEE & DO

A veritable codex of different building styles, the **Jasna Góra Monastery** containing the Black Madonna was originally founded in 1382. By 1430 the monastery added a church to accommodate the growing number of pilgrims, and after a fire in 1690 destroyed much of the complex, it was again rebuilt. Since then, it has survived remarkably intact despite several adversities.

Fortified in the early 17th century, the complex withstood a Swedish siege in 1655, and a Russian assault in 1770 (the Polish commander was Count Kazimierz Pulaski, who later gained fame fighting in the American Revolution). Associated with both spiritual and temporal glory, the shrine bears great significance for Polish patriots.

Today the entirely peaceful monastery grounds are open daily from 5:45am to 9:30pm. For a detailed guidebook on the monastery, ask at the various souvenir stands for the English-language *Jasna Góra: A Companion Guide,* which costs about $2. All museums and chapels here are free, but donations are welcomed.

★ **The Black Madonna,** Jasna Góra.

Jasna Góra's greatest treasure is the Black Madonna, believed to have been painted on a cypress plank at the dawn of the Christian era in Jerusalem, perhaps by St. Luke. Later seen in Byzantium, it was offered to the Pauline Monks at Jasna Góra in the 14th century. During a fierce attack on Częstochowa by Hussites in 1430, the attackers managed to break in and slash the face of the Madonna. Desecrated, stolen, and later abandoned, it was allegedly retrieved and restored. People at the time hailed the near-perfect restoration as a miracle. However, some experts believe that the present picture is a copy ordered by King Władysław Jagiełło. According to this theory, the scars (which remain to this day) are merely burn marks carefully made to resemble the Hussite sword slashes.

You can view the Black Madonna in Jasna Góra's **Chapel of Our Lady (Kaplica Matki Bozej)** only during liturgical services when it is unveiled to the sound of trumpets. An elaborate frame covers most of the painting and shows the Madonna wearing a gold crown with jewels so splendid that they make it hard to see her facial details. Indeed, unless you go close to the altar (which is difficult because of worshiping pilgrims) you might not see the famous scars on the side of the Virgin Mary's face.

In this chapel you'll also see a collection of thousands of Virgin Mary, pope, and city pins on the walls. One wall is adorned with several dozen crutches, evidence of the many miracles attributed to the Black Madonna. The adjacent basilica is a splendid example of baroque architecture in its unrestrained gaudiness.

Admission: Free, but donations accepted.

Open: Chapel, daily 5:45am–7 or 8pm. Black Madonna visible: daily 6am–noon, 3–4:45, 6:30–7:30pm, and 9–9:30pm. During special feasts hours may be extended, including until late at night. **Directions:** After entering the monastery, walk straight ahead past the first church on the right; the Black Madonna is at the back of the second church on your right.

Sala Rycerska, in Jasna Góra.

If you're a fan of the pope, you'll enjoy this collection of photos showing him in many different settings during his world travels.

Admission: Free.

Open: Daily 5:45am–7 or 8pm. **Directions:** Walk upstairs from the Chapel of Our Lady.

Treasury [Skarbiec], in Jasna Góra.

A rich collection of monstrances, chalices, votive offerings, crosses, church vestments, and other church treasures.

Admission: Free.

Open: May–Oct, Mon–Sat 9–11:30am and 3:30–5:30pm, Sun 8am–1pm and 3–5:30pm. Nov–Apr, Mon–Sat 9–10:30am and 3:30–4:30pm, Sun 9am–12:30pm and 3:30–5pm. **Directions:** Walk to the room above the Sacristy, near the Black Madonna.

The 600 Year Museum [Muzeum Szescetiecia], in Jasna Góra.

A collection of religious paintings, Bibles, holy tracts dating back hundreds of years, musical instruments from the 17th to the 20th century, ecumenical garb, and odds and ends such as Lech Wałęsa's Nobel Peace Prize certificate.

Admission: Free.

Open: Daily 11am–4:30pm. **Directions:** Walk across the courtyard from the Chapel of Our Lady.

Arsenal, in Jasna Góra.

A collection of arms and armor used to protect the monastery against its many foreign attackers.

Admission: Free.

Open: May–Oct, Mon–Fri 9am–noon and 2:30–6pm, Sun and holidays 9am–noon and 2–6pm; Nov–Apr, Mon–Sat 9am–11:45am and 3–4:45pm, Sun and holidays 9am–11:45am and 2–4:45pm. **Directions:** Walk to the southwest corner of the monastery grounds.

Belltower [Wieza], in Jasna Góra.

For a bit of exercise and perspective over Jasna Góra, you can hike up to the top of the monastery belltower, although the view is not outstanding.

Admission: Free.

Open: May–Oct, Mon–Sat 8am–4pm, Sun and holidays 8–10:30am and 1–5pm.

WHERE TO STAY

Tourists and pilgrims often crowd Częstochowa's few hotels; during any religious festivals, accommodations are harder to get than an audience with the pope—reserve rooms ahead of time. Not only are accommodations hard to come by, but they're also uncomfortable or overpriced. Częstochowa's Orbis hotels are vastly overpriced, while offering comfort I'd expect in budget hotels. However, the cheaper pilgrim hotels are quite basic. Perhaps it's best to visit Częstochowa for a day and continue along to another, less famous (and less crowded) town to spend the night. As Częstochowa is located along the main route between Kraków and Warsaw, this is not difficult to do.

Students can arrange inexpensive summer accommodations at Almatur, ul. NMP 37 (☎ **0833/44-368;** fax 0833-44-378), open Monday through Friday from 9am to 4pm.

For those stranded in town without a reservation, there are several budget hotels on ulica Piłsudskiego just south of Aleja Najświętszej Marii Panny.

Dom Pielgrzyma [House of Pilgrims], ul. S. Wyszynskiego 1/31, Częstochowa.

☎ **0833/24-70-11.** 262 rms (75 with bath). **Directions:** The hotel is located adjacent to the monastery on the side farther from the center of town.

Rates: $15 single with bath; $4 double without bath, $15 double with bath; $7.50 triple without bath, $22.50 triple with bath; $2 for a bed in a four-person room.

Built in the early 1980s and operated by the monastery, this hotel is just what you'd expect of an inn for pilgrims: it's large, institutional, and spotlessly clean. The hostel rooms are a bit spartan but not uncomfortable, and the mattresses are excellent. The rooms with bath are carpeted. Downstairs there's a cafeteria. Reservations are suggested.

Polonia Centralny, ul. Piłsudskiego 9, 42-000 Częstochowa. ☎ **0833/440-67.** Fax 0833/65-11-05. 60 rms (27 with bath). **Directions:** Walk across from the train station.

Rates (including breakfast): $10 single without bath, $13 single with bath; $16.50 double without bath, $19 double with shower, $23 double with full bath, $23.50 triple without bath, $31.50 triple with shower, $35 triple with full bath; $31–$36.50 apartment. AE, DC, EU, JCB, MC, V. **Parking:** $2.25.

The Polonia Centralny is located at the southernmost end of ulica Piłsudskiego. Its plant-filled lobby and some of its rooms were renovated about a year ago and look fresh and new with cheerful wallpaper and pink bedspreads. The entire building has been upgraded by the addition of 27 private bathrooms. The rooms are simply furnished, but have high ceilings, nice carpets, and firm mattresses. The public bathrooms are clean and in good condition; if you take a room without a bath, get to the shower early unless you don't mind your shower lukewarm.

As the Polonia Centralny is often packed with pilgrims, make reservations early or be prepared to "tip" the clerk a few dollars to help "find" you a room. The restaurant is open daily from 7am to 1am; there's a live band that plays from 8pm to 1am.

WHERE TO EAT

Hotel Patria, ul. Starucha 1. ☎ **470-01.**

Cuisine: POLISH. **Directions:** From Jasna Góra, walk downhill past the park and turn left.
Prices: Soups 50¢–80¢; main courses $2.20–$7.55. AE, DC, EU, JCB, MC, V.
Open: Daily noon–1pm.

Though no culinary giant, the restaurant at the Hotel Patria is said to be the best in Częstochowa and many tour groups here make this a busy place. One dining room has a few token military ornaments on the walls; in another room a grand piano on a riser at one end gives it a nightclub atmosphere in the evening. The waiters don't speak English, but English menus are available. The house specialties include cucumber soup, pork cutlets for a modest $2.50, many beef dishes, and a wide selection of cold meat appetizers. For vegetarians there's an *omelet z pieczarkami* (a mushroom omelet) for $1.50, and sautéed trout and carp.

4 Łańcut

100 miles E of Kraków, 82 miles S of Lublin

GETTING THERE • By Train Łańcut lies on the line between Kraków and Przemyśl. A fast train from Kraków takes 2 1/3 hours and costs $6.50 in first class, $4.35 in second. A normal train takes 3 3/4 hours and costs $4.35 in first class, $2.90 in second. From the train station, take bus 8 or 10 (15¢) or a taxi ($1.25) to the palace (*zamek*).

• By Bus There are two afternoon buses from Lublin to Łańcut, and one morning bus from Łańcut to Lublin. There are also frequent connections between Łańcut and Rzeszow, the nearest city. The bus station is about two blocks from the entrance to the palace park.

An early morning day trip from Kraków on a stop between Kraków and Lublin, the town of Łańcut contains ★ **Łańcut Palace,** one of the great chateaux of Eastern Europe. The hill on which it stands was originally fortified in the 17th century, and the present palace was built at the end of the 18th. But its present appearance, interior and exterior, is the turn-of-the-century creation of owners Elzbieta and Roman Potocki.

Unlike so many historic Polish buildings, Łańcut was spared devastation during World War II. As a result, it's more completely furnished than Wilanów or even Wawel. Candles in the candelabra, fresh flowers on the tables, walking sticks thrust into Delft umbrella stands, and even gold-rimmed chamber pots in the bathrooms all give the impression that the Potockis have just popped out for a jaunt to Monte Carlo and can be expected back at any moment. The experience is not so much of touring a hushed museum as of visiting a house—a house owned by people with superb taste and bottomless bank accounts. There is not a great deal of flashy gold, but there is plenty of walnut, silk, and crystal. The inlaid floors alone would make the palace worth a visit.

In addition to the two dozen or so rooms in the palace (including a ballroom, a sculpture gallery, and several apartments), you can visit a tropical greenhouse and a stable with a collection of 19th-century carriages and African animals shot on safari. Surrounding the palace is a lovely park.

The palace (☎ **017/25-20-08**) is open from late April to early October from Tuesday through Saturday from 9am until 2:30pm and on Sundays and holidays from 9am until 4pm. From mid-February until late April and from mid-October through November it is open from Tuesday through Sunday from 10am until 2:30pm. It is closed from December until mid-February. Tickets, which are purchased at an office on ulica Zamkowa, across the street from the entrance to the park, cost $1.50 for adults, $1 for students. A guide can be hired for $10. In summer, a 15-minute spin in a carriage costs $6.25.

WHERE TO STAY & EAT

Hotel Zamkowy, ul. Zamkowa 1, 37-100 Łańcut. ☎ **017/25-26-71** or **25-26-72.** 23 rms (7 with bath). TEL

Rates: $6 double without plumbing, $10 double with sink, $15 double with bath; $9 triple without plumbing, $21 triple with bath. AE, DC, EU, JCB, MC, V.

Though located in a corner of Łańcut Palace, the Hotel Zamkowy cannot claim to house its guests in the manner of the Potockis. The era evoked by the drab rooms with their poor, springy mattresses is more postwar deprivation than Habsburg opulence. Nevertheless, the rooms are spacious enough for tables and chairs, and several have pleasant views of the château's park. And the location is quite convenient, especially if you want to catch an early morning bus from the nearby bus station. The restaurant Zamkowa (☎ **28-05**), in the same corner of the palace, serves a standard institutional Polish menu (a lot of pork cutlets) for about $4 a meal. Ask for the English translation of the menu. It's open daily from 9am to 9pm, serving hot meals after 1pm.

5 Zakopane & the Tatra Mountains

65 miles S of Kraków

GETTING THERE • By Train The fast train from Kraków, of which there are several per day, takes 2½ hours and costs $5.30 in first class, $3.50 in second. Zakopane is quite far from all other Polish cities, but you can take an overnight train to or from

Warsaw, Gdańsk, Poznań, Lublin, or Szczecin. Zakopane's station is at ul. Chramcówski 35 (☎ **145-04**), a 10-minute walk to the center of town down ulica Kościuszki. There's a 24-hour baggage check; knock on the wooden window if it appears closed.

• **By Bus** More than a dozen buses leave daily from Kraków's bus station, next to the train station, arriving about 2½ hours later at ul. Kościuszki 25 (☎ **146-03**), opposite the train station. To buy your return bus ticket, go to Window 1 for connections to Kraków and Warsaw. The bus to Kraków ($1.90) leaves from Bay 6.

• **By Car** The drive from Kraków takes a little under two hours.

ESSENTIALS The telephone area code is 0165. For auto emergencies in Zakopane, call PZM (☎ **127-97**) or go to their office on ulica Droga na Bystre. For emergency aid in the mountains, contact the Mountain Volunteer Rescue Team (GOPR), at ul. Pitsudskiego 63A (☎ **61-550**). For emergency service in Zakopane, call 999 or 120-21 to 120-26 at ul. Kamieniec 10. For information about hiking trails and a map of Zakopane, go to the Orbis office at ul. Kropówski 22 (☎ **150-51**), open Monday through Friday from 8am to 8pm and Saturday from 8am to 2pm. The post office, which includes a telephone office, is on ulica Zaruskiego, across from the Hotel Gazda. It's open Monday through Friday from 8am to 8pm, on Saturday from 9am to 2pm, and on Sunday and holidays from 9 to 11am.

SPECIAL EVENTS The Tatra Autumn and Festival of Highlanders' Culture is in mid-August.

At the bottom of the map of Poland, wedged between two strips of Slovakia, lies Zakopane, at the entrance to the Tatra Mountains National Park. Although it may look insignificant on a map, this is the most awesome, inspiring landscape in all of Poland. Steep peaks towering 6,000 feet into the clouds, roaring waterfalls, glassine lakes, and an animal population that includes bears, lynxes, and golden eagles make up the amazing Tatra Mountains.

The small mountain town of Zakopane (pop. 41,000) has been a popular resort area since the end of the 19th century, when some Polish scientists declared that the healthy Tatra Mountain air could cure tuberculosis, among other ailments. Today it's one of Poland's most-visited tourist spots, with some three million visitors a year. As a result, Zakopane has become a fairly cosmopolitan town dotted with hotels, restaurants, stores, and tourist offices. Yet just beyond Zakopane's hilly streets begins the wild outdoors of the Tatra Mountains. To experience the Tatras, find a hotel in Zakopane to serve as your mountain base.

WHAT TO SEE & DO

A Walk Downtown

Downtown Zakopane around the pedestrians-only ulica Krupówki is a pleasant area for an afternoon walk, where families and young couples buy ice-cream cones after a day in the mountains. You'll also enjoy shopping along these streets, as many locals sell hand-knit wool sweaters, socks, and hats at outdoor stands. You'll even see them hard at work knitting new samples as they wait for customers. Stores in the area also sell silver items.

Mountain Excursions

Morskie Oko [Eye of the Sea], Tatra Mountains.

I highly recommend a half- or full-day visit to this large, 86-acre lake high in the mountains (4,570 feet above sea level) right near the Slovak border. The view is marvelous: The jagged rock mountains, covered in snow even in the summer, reflect perfectly off a still lake.

Hikers will definitely want to continue walking around the lake and then up the hill on the left. It's a strenuous climb, but at the top you'll find another beautiful lake, Czarny Sław (Black Pond) at 5,182 feet above sea level, where you'll observe a breathtaking panorama of Morskie Oko and the surrounding mountains.

Getting there by bus from the center of Zakopane is a 22-mile journey as well as an adventure. You can get to Pałenica Białczanska by bus (one hour). The bus stops just outside the entrance to the national park. There you can hire a horsecart (or a sleigh in winter) for the $4^1/_2$ miles to the Włodienica station and walk the remaining mile to the lake. The ride costs $2.50 each way for up to four people. You can also walk the entire way along a well-marked, well-maintained, and not too steep trail.

Kasprowy Wierch, Tatra Mountains.

You'll enjoy taking the 15-minute cable-car (built in 1939) ride up and down this mountain; though close to downtown Zakopane, it's still 6,510 feet above sea level. Once at the top, you can explore the area or dine leisurely in the restaurant.

To get to the cable-car station, take a bus from Zakopane to Kuźnice on the south side of town; walk to cable-car station at the foot of the mountain. The cable car is open daily from 7:30am to 4:30pm, and there is often a long line. It is closed in May and November.

Hiking

Zakopane is separated from the Slovak Republic by the Tatrzanski Park Narodowy (the Tatra National Park). You can only enter the park at designated points, and you will have to pay 25¢ admission each time you enter. The trails are clearly blazed and in good condition, and the mountain scenery is sublime. The mountains run east–west, and the southern, Slovak faces get almost all of the sunlight.

Orbis sells a very good 1:30,000 scale map of the park ($1), including trails, contours, and lodgings, from mountain huts to hotels. This map is a handy guide on short day hikes (you may want to take a local bus to the nearest park entrance) or, with a lot of energy, you can hike all the way to the Slovak side of the mountains, where small signs delineate the border. Serious hikers can continue through the mountains for days, and eat and lodge at the various PTTK hotels scattered in the high Tatra area.

WHERE TO STAY

Visitors to Zakopane can choose to stay either in a hotel or in a small rustic pension; bargain-hunters can also rent private rooms, Zakopane's most inexpensive accommodations. Finally, the most adventurous travelers can rough it at spartan PTTK hotels in the middle of the mountains. Be sure to reserve a room in Zakopane, because all hotels are booked solid in the high season.

Doubles for Less Than $20

$ **Juventur Hotel,** ul. Słoneczna 2A, 34-500 Zakopane. ☎ **0165/66-253.** 53 rms (32 with bath). **Directions:** From the bus station, walk one block south on Kościuszki and then turn right down Słoneczna, a 10-minute walk.

Rates (including breakfast): $7.55 single without bath, $10.75 single with bath; $15.50 double without bath, $21.50 double with bath; $17 triple without bath, $32.25 triple with bath. AE, DC, EU, JCB, MC, V.

An excellent value, just a few minutes' walk from ulica Kościuszki across a large field. You'll see the hotel's name in large letters on the roof as you approach. Recent renovations have added bathrooms to many of the rooms, making the new and clean facilities a bit cramped. There's a café-bar in the lobby, and a restaurant off the lobby, open daily from 8am to 8pm. Student discounts are offered.

Doubles for Less Than $40

Hotel Gazda, ul. Zaruskiego 2, 34-500 Zakopane. ☎ **0165/150-11** to **150-16.** Fax 0165/153-30. Telex 325304. 63 rms (48 with bath, 15 with toilet but no shower). TEL TV **Directions:** From the bus station, walk down ulica Kościuszki to ulica Krupówki.

Rates (including breakfast): $20 single with toilet but no shower, $24.45 single with bath; $33.35 with bath. AE, DC, EU, JCB, MC, V.

The glass-and-wood exterior makes the Hotel Gazda somewhat modern in a town of rustic chalets. Pleasant rooms have three large windows, which bring in lots of mountain air and light. Bathrooms are small, but rooms often have a large couch. Public facilities include a lobby jewelry stand, a Pewex store, and a restaurant. Reservations are recommended in summer—the Gazda is often filled with groups.

Hotel Orbis Giewont, ul. Kościuszki 1, 34-500 Zakopane. ☎ **0165/120-11.** Telex 322270. 48 rms (37 with bath). TEL TV **Directions:** From the bus station, walk down ulica Kościuszki to ulica Krupówki.

Rates (including breakfast): Ski season $32 single with bath; $40 double without bath, $53 double with bath. Off-season $21 single with bath; $20 double without bath, $36 double with bath. AE, DC, EU, JCB, MC, V.

This three-star hotel in the center of Zakopane looks much like a New England mountain lodge with its brightly carpeted rooms, dark-stained furniture, and high ceilings. A double without bath is by far the best budget value here, for public bathrooms are well maintained. The lobby has a Pewex stand, and upstairs is a good restaurant (see "Where to Eat," below).

Pensions (Pensjonats)

I highly recommend a pensjonats for outstanding comfort at a good price. These small inns serve three meals a day in addition to housing you in quaint two- or three-story wood chalets. You can book through Orbis at ul. Krupówski 22 (☎ **0165/150-51**). The rates are $9 to $15 per person with full board. Orbis also books private rooms without board for $4 to $4.50 per person.

Super-Budget Choices

Dom Turysty Pttk, Zaruskiego 5, 34-500 Zakopane. ☎ **0165/632-81** to **632-84.** **Reservations:** ☎ **0165/632-07;** fax 0165/123-58. 57 rms (5 with bath, 7 with shower but no toilet). TEL **Directions:** From ulica Krupówki, walk past the Hotel Gazda and continue down the street.

Rates: $9 single without bath; $11 double without bath, $13 double with shower, $15.50 double with bath; $16.50 triple without bath, $19.50 triple with shower, $23.25 triple with full bath. $2.75 per person in a six- to eight-bedded room. AE, DC, EU, JCB, MC, V.

Dom Turysty is a large, sturdy, stone-and-wood chalet. You pass through a long, spacious lobby usually full of children to reach your room. The few rooms with private bathroom are quite decent, with blond-wood walls that give a convincing mountain-chalet look. The mattresses are not terrific, but they are bearable. However, rooms without private bathrooms rely on dirty, distant public bathrooms and should be used only as a last resort. Try to get a room on the third floor, which is quieter; the first two floors are filled with teenagers who jam into the TV room to cheer their favorite soccer teams or gather round practicing guitarists on floor lobbies to hear popular songs.

WHERE TO EAT

$ **Obrochtówka,** ul. Kraszewskiego 10A. ☎ **39-87.**

Cuisine: POLISH. **Directions:** From the Giewont Hotel, walk uphill on Krupówki, which leads into Zamoyskiego; ulica Kraszewskiego is third left.
Prices: Soup 50¢–$1.05; main courses $1.95–$4.
Open: Tues–Sun noon–10pm. **Closed:** Apr or May.

This small restaurant with waitresses in traditional dress, log-cabin walls on one side and cavernous stone on the other, caters to Poles and tour groups who come to eat such specialties as lamb shashlik with rice and salad for $3.85 or potato pancakes with goulash and salad for $3.25. You'll also find excellent soups, such as the white borscht served with potatoes sprinkled with sausage and parsley, and roast poultry at very moderate prices. Try their delicious homemade cheesecake "Roza" for dessert. There is taped traditional Polish folk music in the background. It's located a bit outside the town center. Enter the restaurant via the cellar stairs; it may look closed, but just pop open the door.

Hotel Giewont, ul. Kościuszki 1. ☎ **20-11.**

Cuisine: POLISH. **Directions:** Walk to the side entrance of the hotel in the town center.
Prices: Soups 60¢–90¢; main courses $2–$3.50; dessert 45¢–$1.10. AE, DC, EU, JCB, MC, V.
Open: Daily noon–10pm (last serving at 11:30pm).

The Giewont is a favorite among many locals. The attractive large dining room has high ceilings and ceramic chandeliers. Specialties include superlative mushrooms and main courses such as roast turkey, pork cutlet, or rumpsteak with butter; quite tasty french fries accompany many of these dishes. You order from an English-language menu. You can top off your dinner with a choice from a wide selection of desserts. There's live music and dancing from 8pm to 1am in the drink bar. The café is open from 8am to 9pm, the bistro from 11am to 6pm.

ONE-DAY EXCURSIONS

Nowy Sącz

This older, more picturesque town in the mountains is slightly northeast of Zakopane. Originally developed because of its importance on the "Hungarian Trade Route," Nowy Sącz, and its sister town, Stary Sącz, look as they did hundreds of years ago.

For private-room rentals and tourist information, go to the **Poprad** office at ul. Romanowskiego 4A (☎ **018/226-05** or **210-02**).

Rafting in Pieniny National Park

Those looking for more fast-paced adventure than summer hiking can ride a raft (made from a hollowed tree trunk) down the River Dunajec in the nearby Pieniny National

Park. The ride passes through beautiful, sometimes rugged, territory beneath steep rocks as high as 1,300 feet above the river. The ride is an invigorating and unforgettable experience. It lasts 2¹/₂ hours when the river is high in the beginning of the summer and 3 to 4 hours at the end of the summer. Book your excursion (from May to September only) through Orbis in Nowy Sącz, Zakopane, or Kraków.

6 Lublin

93 miles SE of Warsaw

GETTING THERE • **By Train** From Warsaw, express trains take 2³/₄ hours ($8.75 in first class, $5.75 in second class). Trains arrive at Plac Wójtowicza 1 (☎ **202-19**), about a 20- to 30-minute walk from the center. From the station, follow ulica 1 Maja and then ulica Mariana Buczka to the Old Town, a long and somewhat confusing route. Better to take trolleybus no. 150 from in front of the station to Krakowskie Przedmieście, or a taxi.

To buy tickets for your departure, go to Windows 2 to 7. Line 1 is for ticket-price information. There's also an information desk off Platform 1.

• **By Bus** Since the only direct trains from Lublin to many cities depart at inconvenient times, you may do slightly better on the bus. Try to buy your tickets as early as possible, since buses do sometimes sell out. Buses from Kraków, Częstochowa, or other cities to the southwest arrive at the main bus station (PKS Dworzec Główny) just north of the castle at Al. Tysiąclecia 9, on Nowy Plac Targowy (☎ **266-49**). You can check your bags here; look for the sign reading PRZECHOWALNIA BAGAZU.

You'll also find a colorful outdoor food market in the square in front of this station where local peasants sell their produce, so you can stock up on fruits and vegetables before your journey.

For other destinations in Poland, check at the Tourist Information Office to make sure that the bus leaves from here; there are two different bus stations in Lublin.

• **By Car** The drive from Warsaw to Lublin on the E-81 takes about two hours.

ESSENTIALS The telephone area code is 081.

ORIENTATION Once you reach Lublin's center, you'll find it very easy to get around by foot, as most sights are clustered in the pedestrians-only Old Town (Stare Miasto). The modern section of town centers around Krakowskie Przedmieście, and if you follow this street eastward you'll arrive at the Old Town's Kraków Gate. After this gate, the road continues as ulica Bramowa and then changes to ulica Grodzka and ulica Zamkowa, before arriving at Lublin's castle.

INFORMATION Tourist Information Office, Krakowskie Przedmieście 78 (☎ **081/244-12**), will provide English-language pamphlets on Lublin or sell you a guidebook to the city. Open Monday through Friday from 9am to 5pm and on Saturday from 10am to 2pm.

Lublin (pop. 300,000) is perhaps the quintessential Polish provincial city. Sitting between the Vistula and the Bug, it is squarely in the Polish heartland and has been under foreign rule for perhaps fewer years than any other Polish city. While always one of Poland's major cities, it has never been the largest. And it has never served as capital, except for a few months toward the end of World War II when the Soviets established a puppet Polish government here to compete with the government-in-exile in London. Perhaps its greatest distinction is as the only Polish city with two universities, one of them Catholic University, the only private institution of higher learning in the Poland.

Although many buildings have been erected in Lublin since World War II, the small Old Town, one of the most ancient city quarters in all of Poland, retains the picturesque atmosphere of the Middle Ages, with its Gothic castle and Renaissance houses on the main square. Just outside Lublin is the former Nazi death camp, Majdanek, a testimony to the horrors of World War II. Lublin is a small city which can be seen in a day; but if you make it this far you should probably budget some time for day trips.

WHAT TO SEE & DO

Begin your sightseeing with a walk through Lublin's Old Town (Stare Miasto). As you enter the Old Town from Krakowskie Przedmieście, you pass under the 14th-century Kraków Gate, whose interior now serves as the Museum of the History of Lublin (for details, see below).

Continuing on the main road past the gate, you'll soon arrive at the Rynek (Old Town Square), which once served as the heart of business, political, and religious affairs in Lublin. At the center of this square you can still see the 14th-century yellow Old Town Hall, which is also known as the Tribunal, in reference to its use from the 16th century onward. A number of the other buildings on this square show picturesque, if faded, painted facades.

If you turn right after passing the Old Town Hall, you reach the Dominican church and monastery (see below).

After you leave the core of the Old Town (away from the modern center), you'll come to the impressive 14th-century castle. And about two miles away from the center of Lublin, you'll find the Majdanek concentration camp (see below).

Museum of the History of Lublin, Brama Krakówska. ☎ **26-001.**

Situated inside the top of the Kraków Gate into town, this museum displays objects, prints, and paintings illustrating Lublin's long history, explained only by Polish captions. The highlight of the museum is the 360° view over Lublin from the top floor.

Admission: 40¢ adults, 25¢ students.

Open: Wed–Sat 9am–4pm, Sun 9am–5pm. **Directions:** Enter just to the right before going under the Kraków Gate into the Old Town; it's up three flights of stairs.

Dominican Church and Monastery, ulica Złota.

Built by King Kazimierz the Great, this 14th-century church boasts beautiful frescoes in its chapels dating back to the 17th and 18th centuries. Monastic buildings are connected to the church on the side.

Admission: Free.

Open: Mon–Fri 8am–7pm, Sat–Sun 3–6pm. **Directions:** Right after the Old Town Hall, walk two blocks down ulica Złota.

Lublin Castle, ul. Zamkowa 9. ☎ **25-001.**

Built by King Kazimierz the Great in the 14th century, this sizable castle on a small hilltop was greatly restored in the 19th century with a flamboyant, almost Middle Eastern facade. During the Middle Ages important political meetings were often held in the castle, and the Polish kings frequently received visitors and foreign envoys here. During World War II the Nazis used the castle as their regional headquarters, where they interrogated and tortured some 400,000 prisoners in five years.

Today the castle museum displays a varied art and history collection, starting on the first floor with an archeological collection of ceramic pots, bones, and prehistoric remains from Lublin. There's also a display of Polish coins. On the second and third floors you'll see 17th- to 20th-century Polish art, as well as 16th- to 19th-century clocks, silver plates, candlestick holders, porcelain, and guns.

Admission: 40¢ adults, 25¢ for students; free for everyone Sat.

Open: Wed–Sat 9am–4pm, Sun 9am–5pm. **Directions:** Walk northeast from the main street in the Old Town.

Majdanek Concentration Camp, Męczenników Majdanka Rd., about two miles southeast of the town center. ☎ **42-647.**

More people died at this Nazi concentration camp than at any other in Poland, except Auschwitz. Today the camp remains much as it was 50 years ago when 360,000 people from 30 countries were murdered. The visitors center at the entrance sells an English-language map (5¢) and some books in English. I especially recommend the work by Czeslaw Rajca and Anna Wisniewska, which contains testimonials of camp survivors. The center sometimes screens films in English about the camp.

Two barracks are filled with 800,000 pairs of shoes taken from prisoners here and elsewhere for use by German companies. Other barracks are filled with bunk beds, showing the cramped conditions the inmates had to endure. At the far end of the camp is a mausoleum containing ashes of the Nazis' victims. Nearby is an intact gas chamber and a crematorium that could burn up to 1,000 bodies per day.

Open: May–Sept, Tues–Sun 8am–6pm; Oct–Apr, Tues–Sun 8am–3pm. Children under 14 are not admitted. **Trolleybus:** 153 from the center of Lublin.

WHERE TO STAY

Hotel Victoria, ul. Narutowicza 56/58, 20-016 Lublin. ☎ **081/270-11.**
Fax 081/290-26. Telex 642349. 190 rms (150 with bath). TEL **Trolleybus:** 150 from the train station.

Rates: $12.50 single without bath, $20 single with bath; $35 double with bath; $50 apartment. Breakfast $3.25.

I recommend this large hotel, about a 15-minute walk from the Old Town, for its good maintenance and cleanliness, qualities not always present in Lublin's hotels. Rooms are small and somewhat cramped but pleasant; if you're lucky enough to have a room on one of the top floors, you'll get a fine view of the city. All the rooms have toilets. There are no hallway showers, so if you take a room without bath you're stuck with sponge bathing. The rooms are fresh painted and have good lighting, but a few of the mattresses are quite saggy. The reception staff speaks English.

Downstairs you'll find a Pewex store, a newsstand, and a good restaurant that many consider Lublin's best. Main courses cost $1.50 to $7.40 and it's open daily from 1pm to midnight.

Motel PZM, ul. B. Prusa 8, 20-064 Lublin. ☎ **081/34-232** or **34-372.** Telex 643192.
67 rms (23 with bath, 30 with shower but no toilet). TEL **Bus:** 1 (to the northeast) or 34 from the train station.

Rates: $9.50 single with shower but no toilet; $13 double without bath, $15–$16 double with bath. Breakfast $1.50. **Parking:** Free.

At this low-priced motel, just a 10-minute walk from the Old Town, you'll find the rooms pleasant, with a plant in each and lots of natural light. All singles have showers but no toilets—but the public bathrooms are clean. If you're getting a double, get a larger one for the extra $2 to $3—they're much less cramped. The reception is on the second floor, with a TV lounge to the side. Downstairs there's a newsstand and a decent restaurant serving simple dishes like goulash and roast chicken, open on Monday from 9am to 7pm and Tuesday through Sunday from 9am to 10pm.

The motel is only two blocks from the bus station, making it convenient if you plan to make day trips or continue on to the next city by bus.

Hotel Lubliniaka, ul. Krakowskie Przedmieście 56, 20-002 Lublin. ☎ **081/242-61.**
65 rms (2 with bath). TEL **Bus:** 13 from the train station.

Rates: $10.50 single without bath, $14 single with bath (only two rooms); $16.50 double without bath; $17 quad without bath; $18 six-person room without bath; $30 apartment. Breakfast $3.25.

Located in a turn-of-the-century building with a large dome and a clock at its center, this hotel reflects little of its earlier charms. The rooms have high ceilings, but they vary in quality. In some, the paint is decidedly ugly, while in others it is merely unattractive. The beds are generally firm. The hallway bathrooms are not in great shape and don't smell very good, but the in-room baths are no treat either.

WHERE TO EAT

Karczma Słupska, Al. Racławckie 22. ☎ **388-13.**

Cuisine: SŁUPSK-STYLE POLISH. **Trolleybus:** 153, 157, or 161 from Kraków Gate.
Prices: Soups 25¢–45¢; main courses $2.60–$3.
Open: Wed 10am–8pm, Thurs–Tues 10am–10pm.

With pleasant decor in the Baltic country style and booths of dark wood, this restaurant has everything you, as a budget traveler, seek: The food and service are good, the menu is translated into English, and the prices are low.

Baltic specialties include soups with bacon or noodles and a "hunter's pack" joint of pork (*juki mysliskie ze schabu*) for very moderate prices. There are a number of delicious vegetarian dishes like pierogi with cabbage and potato pancakes. Another feature is a daily student lunch special: soup and a main course for 75¢ (there are many students from neighboring Catholic University who come in for lunch).
There is music Thursday through Tuesday from 4:30pm to 9:30pm.

7 Excursions from Lublin

Kazimierz Dolny

25 miles NW of Lublin

GETTING THERE • By Bus The bus from Lublin to Kazimierz Dolny will leave you within a block of the Town Square (Rynek).

INFORMATION The monoglot Tourist Information Office is in the main Town Square at no. 27 (☎ **100-46**), open May to August, daily from 7:30am to 7pm; and September to April, Monday through Friday from 7:30am to 3pm.

Kazimierz Dolny (pop. 4,500) is a quaint town with cobblestone streets, few cars, and a spacious town square with a large water well in the middle. When I last visited I saw a lively farmer's market on the square, with horsecarts carrying away the goods at the end of the morning.

Small houses and narrow streets built in the late Renaissance style, along with the impressive remains of a 14th-century castle overlooking the city, all add to the charm of this picturesque town on the banks of the Vistula River. From the top of the castle (built by King Kazimierz the Great, after whom the town is named), there's a breathtaking view of the town and the surrounding lush countryside.

Previously, as many as 30,000 Jews lived in Kazimierz Dolny, but today there are none—many of them were killed in World War II. You can visit the former 18th-century synagogue just beyond an arched passageway off the east side of the main square. It now functions as a movie house.

Kazimierz Dolny is also known for its animal-shaped bread called Kazimierzowski kogut. You can buy some at Piekarnia, ul. Nadrzeczna 6 (☎ **143**), a block away from the Town Square. Here gingerbread chickens, alligators, and other animals go for 75¢ to $1.50 each.

Zamość

53 miles SE of Lublin

GETTING THERE The bus from Lublin takes 1½ hours; train connections are particularly poor and take several hours.

INFORMATION The Tourist Information Office is located at Rynek Wielki 13 (☎ **0884/22-92;** telex 0643412) and it's open Monday through Friday from 8am to 4pm and on Saturday from 10am to 2pm. It's as organized, computerized, color-coded, and English-speaking a place as you're likely to find in Eastern Europe. There's plenty of maps and other information on Zamość and the surrounding region.

In 1580 Polish nobleman Jan Zamoyski decided to found a new town to be the capital of the land under his control. To design the town—which he named after himself—Zamoyski enlisted Italian architect Bernando Morando. Ideal cities from the realm of the imagination were at the time a popular subject of paintings, and Morando seized the opportunity to actually build a real one. The centerpiece of Morando's plan is the gorgeous, central square (*rynek*). The influence of Italian Renaissance architecture can be seen in the square's tall town hall and arcaded merchants' houses.

WHAT TO SEE & DO

Morando carried out his commission well; Zamość is a wonderful place to walk through. In addition to the buildings on the square, there are several other Renaissance structures, including a 17th-century synagogue (now used as a library) and the Collegiate Church, designed by Morando himself.

Morando also designed the town's fortifications. Rebuilt in the 1820s and restored in 1976, these earthworks separate the historic center from more modern neighborhoods and can make a pleasant circuit walk. The *plan Starowski*, on sale at the tourist office, has a map and English descriptions of historic buildings.

Zamość suffered heavily under the Nazis, who planned to kill or deport the entire population of the town and surrounding region and repopulate it with Germans. Over 40% of the towns residents were killed. The Rotunda, a building south of the town center, was used as a prison and execution center; it's now a memorial to the victims. Open daily April 15 through September from 9am to 6pm; daily October to April 14 from 10am to 5pm.

WHERE TO STAY

Hotel Jubilat, Al. Wyszynskiego 52. ☎ **084/64-00.** Fax 084/62-15. 44 rms (all with bath). TEL **Directions:** The hotel is adjacent to the bus station, just past Bay 13.

Rates: $16.50 single; $22.50 double; $27 triple; $40 two-person apartment. Breakfast $2; TV. $2. AE, DC, EU, JCB, MC, V.

Built in 1980, the Hotel Jubilat is the only three-star hotel in Zamość. Everything in the spacious rooms looks brand new—from the carpets to the wallpaper to the large armchairs. The bathrooms have stall showers. The restaurant downstairs is open 7am to midnight.

Sandomierz

68 miles SW of Lublin, 100 NE of Kraków

GETTING THERE As the trains are very slow in this part of the country, it's best to take the bus from Lublin.

Anyone continuing from Lublin to Kraków should spend half a day in Sandomierz, a charming, well-preserved, historic town. Sandomierz is even older than it appears, with its earliest settlement dating back to the 8th century. As trading routes between Russia and Europe developed centuries later, Sandomierz became an important commercial town, with extensive trade in grain and wood.

Centered around a large market square, the main sights here include the brick Town Hall, which contains a small history museum (open on Tuesday from 10am to 5pm, Wednesday through Friday from 9am to 4pm, on Saturday from 9am to 3pm, and on Sunday from 10am to 2pm; 15¢ admission), several churches, and the underground storerooms, built in the 15th and 16th centuries at the height of the city's economic prosperity and used during World War II as hiding places by Jews. For only 35¢, a guide will lead you through a vast maze of winding tunnels, some almost 40 feet below ground, connecting these now-vacant storerooms, which begin at ulica Oleśnickiego right off the main square and exit some blocks away at the Town Hall (open from 10am to 6pm daily).

29

Northeast Poland & the Baltic Coast

THE LAND THAT NOW MAKES UP POLAND'S BALTIC COAST HAS BEEN ONE OF THE MOST fiercely contested areas of Europe. For the last thousand years, the coast has gone back and forth between Polish and German hands at least half a dozen times, with the Swedes making a bid for it in the 17th century. It's not incidental that the Second World War started in Gdańsk. Things have quieted since the German population of East Prussia, which had lived there for centuries, was finally expelled after the war.

Given this momentous history, visitors may overlook the great charms and beauty around Poland's Baltic Sea coast. Gdańsk preserves the picturesque atmosphere of an important seafaring town of hundreds of years ago. It also forms one part (albeit the largest and best known) of the Baltic's "Trojmiasto" or Tri-City area (a grouping of cities much like New York City's five boroughs), which includes Gdańsk, Sopot, and Gdynia. You can visit Sopot, a resort town, in just 15 to 20 minutes by car or train from Gdańsk, and Gdynia, an industrial town, in just 20 to 40 minutes by car or train, so your visit to Gdańsk combines three cities for the price of one.

In addition to Gdańsk, the Baltic coast offers attractive beaches and sleepy fishing towns. And the smaller towns in the area still have the old defensive walls and castles from the Middle Ages, as well as impressive Gothic churches.

And if you simply want to get away from it all, you can enjoy the Mazurian Lake region east of Gdańsk. There's swimming, fishing, and boating among an unspoiled chain of beautiful lakes.

SEEING NORTHEAST POLAND & THE BALTIC COAST

You can get to Gdańsk by express train from Warsaw, or by sleeper from Kraków, Zakopane, or Wrocław. Look for trains to Gdynia on the departure schedule; they all stop in Gdańsk. From either Gdańsk or the neighboring resort town of Sopot, you can explore the entire Tri-City area of Gdańsk, Sopot, and Gdynia by local transportation. From the Tri-City area you can also connect by boat, bus, or train to a number of beach villages, as well as such historic towns as Malbork and Frombork.

To visit the Mazurian Lake region, take the train to Olsztyn and make bus or train connections from there.

1 Gdańsk

212 miles NW of Warsaw, 100 miles N of Toruń, 188 miles NE of Poznań

GETTING THERE • **By Plane** Flights to Gdańsk from Warsaw take 40 to 50 minutes and cost $70. You'll fly into Rębiechowo Airport (☎ **41-52-51 or 41-31-41**), 10 miles from the center. Take bus no. 131 to the railroad station in the Main Town, or no. 110 to the suburban Wrzeszcz district.

• **By Train** An express from Warsaw takes as little as 3½ hours ($13.50 in first class, $10.50 in second class). Gdańsk's train station is on ulica Wały Jagiellońskie (☎ **31-00-51, 31-11-12,** or **38-52-60**). Inside is a 24-hour baggage-storage facility and a McDonald's. The private-room bureau is just across busy ulica Podwale Grodzkie. (The tourist office and Orbis are on ulica Heweliusza, just a bit farther in the same direction.)

To get to the Main Town on foot, turn right as you exit the station and walk about 10 minutes down ulica Podwale Grodzkie, then turn left.

• **By Car** It takes about 5½ hours to drive to Gdańsk from Warsaw, about the same time from Szczecin, and about 4½ hours from Poznań.

What's Special About Northeast Poland & the Baltic Coast

Beaches

- Sopot, Poland's lively summertime seaside resort with frequent concerts and a casino.
- Hel, Łeba, and Krynica Morska, more isolated attractive beaches good for relaxing and swimming.

Buildings

- Gdańsk's Town Hall, a 14th-century structure hosting the city's Historical Museum.
- Gdańsk's Harbor Crane, Europe's oldest wooden crane used to load cargo from ships in port.
- Malbork's massive 13th-century castle used by Teutonic Knights fighting against Poles.

Museums

- Gdańsk's Central Maritime Museum, displaying underwater archeological finds from the Bay of Gdańsk.
- Gdańsk's National Museum, with Hans Memling's *Last Judgment.*
- Medieval Frombork, Copernicus's home for three decades and host to a museum in his honor.

Great Neighborhoods

- Gdańsk's Main Town, an 18th-century seaport area of cobblestone streets and historic buildings.

Historic Sights

- The Gdańsk Shipyards, birthplace of the Solidarity movement.
- Adolf Hitler's wartime bunker complex near Kętrzyn.

Natural Spectacles

- The Mazurian Lakes, Poland's outpost of forests, lakes, natural wildlife, and summertime sports fun.

• **By Sea** Gdańsk is connected by ferry to Helsinki, Finland; Oxelösund, Sweden; and, in summer, Kaliningrad, Russia (see Chapter 26, "Planning a Trip to Poland"). The ferries dock at the terminal in the Nowy Port section of town. To get from the ferry terminal to the town center, take the commuter train from the Gdańsk Brzezno station to Gdańsk SKM, which is adjacent to the main train station.

ESSENTIALS Gdańsk's telephone area code is 058.

INFORMATION You'll find a helpful, English-speaking staff at the Tourist Information Office, at ul. Heweliusza 27, Gdańsk 80-890 (☎ **058/31-43-55**; fax 058/31-66-37; telex 0152-733). It's open Monday through Friday from 8am to 4pm and from June through September on Saturday from 10am to 3pm. They sell domestic bus and train tickets, ferry tickets, and a town map.

The Orbis office down the block at ul. Heweliusza 22 (☎ **058/31-45-44**; fax 058/31-31-10) is quite helpful. Orbis sells train and ferry tickets and acts as the representative of American Express and Thomas Cook. Orbis also arranges tours of Gdańsk, Malbork, Frombork, and the Gdańsk Shipyards. These tours are usually designed for German-speaking groups, but if you are interested, it is worth stopping by to see if any tours in English are planned. The office is open Monday through Friday from 9am to 5pm.

Another very helpful tourist office is the PTTK Tourist Travel Service, on the main town square at ul. Długa 45 (☎ **31-60-96**). Ask for English-speaking Marcin or Steve. They sell a wide selection of maps and guidebooks, give advice, and answer travel questions about the Tri-City area.

TRAVEL SERVICES • Airlines The main LOT airline office is at ul. Wały Jagiellońskie 2/4 (☎ **31-40-26**), open Monday through Friday from 8am to 6pm and on Saturday from 9am to 3pm.

• Car Problems For motoring problems, the Polish Automobile Association (PZM) runs an office at Kartuska 187 (☎ **981** or **32-35-50**).

CITY LAYOUT Several different districts make up the city of Gdańsk, though you'll spend most of your time in the Main Town (Głowne Miasto), where Gdańsk's historic buildings and sights are concentrated. The layout of streets in the Main Town (designed in medieval times) makes it easy to find your way around; all the major avenues lead to the port (a good five miles along an arm of the Vistula from the Gulf of Gdańsk), and small streets link up these major avenues. The principal avenue is Długa and then Długi Targ (The Long Market), which ends at the Motława Canal, the ancient port of Gdańsk. Just north of the Main Town are the Gdańsk Shipyards, a vast enclosed industrial area.

Other major districts in Gdańsk include Wrzeszcz and Oliwa, residential areas northwest of the Main Town on the way to Sopot.

Gdańsk's companion cities of Sopot and Gdynia lie to the northwest, easily reached by suburban rail.

SPECIAL EVENTS St. Dominic's Fair, held from the end of July to mid-August, offers a display of arts and crafts and musical events taking place in the Main Town.

The International Organ Music Festival takes place in July or August in Oliwa Cathedral.

FAST FACTS

Bookstore English Unlimited, at ul. Podmlynska 10 (☎ **31-33-73**), sells English-language paperbacks—mostly fiction—for $7 to $8. It's open Monday through Friday 10am to 6pm and Saturday 10am to 3pm.

Mail The main post office, located at Długi Targ 22, is open Monday through Friday from 8am to 8pm and on Saturday from 8am to 2pm.

Dry Cleaning For "next day" service, go to Garncarska 30 (a street parallel to ulica Wały Jagiellońskie), open Monday through Friday from 10am to 6pm and on the first and last Saturdays of the month from 10am to 3pm.

It's hard to find a more charming enclave in all of Poland than Gdańsk's Main Town, where the 18th century lives on in the tall, narrow buildings with peaked roofs and decorative facades along cobblestone streets. Church bells ring throughout the day and the city streets are filled with shoppers and strollers. Even though most of the area's Renaissance buildings were reconstructed following World War II, they look surprisingly authentic, as though they had not been touched for hundreds of years. As you walk along the old port, the houses may remind you of Amsterdam. One or two of these homes are so narrow that only one or two windows fit on each floor!

At the same time, Gdańsk (pop. 500,000) is a major Polish industrial center. The cranes of the famous Gdańsk Shipyards are visible from all parts of the city, and squalor characterizes the area near the shipyards.

A Brief History

A Polish settlement was recorded at Gdańsk as early as A.D. 999, and for hundreds of years thereafter Gdańsk served as a fishing and trading outpost. However, the city has not always been Polish; it changed hands between the Poles and Germans six times, and three times it maintained an independent "city-state" status. Gdańsk dates its importance back to the 13th century, when it joined the Hanseatic League, a group of merchants in northern Europe. In the 16th century, under Polish rule, Gdańsk expanded with astonishing rapidity and by the end of the century it was the largest city in Poland with 70,000 inhabitants, more than twice the size of Warsaw. But wars soon destroyed the city's prosperity.

When Poland was divided in 1793, the city was returned to Prussian hands and was named the German "Danzig," but its trading importance rapidly declined thereafter. After World War I and the Treaty of Versailles, Gdańsk was declared the "Free City of Danzig." Poland had limited rights to the city, such as permission to run the local post office and Customs bureau, but throughout the interwar period Polish-German relations were strained over Danzig.

In August 1939 many healthy German male "tourists" visited Danzig, and the German battleship *Schleswig-Holstein* paid a "courtesy" visit to the port. Days later on September 1, this battleship shelled the Polish garrison at Westerplatte, and World War II began. The German population of the city welcomed its realignment to the Third Reich and cheered Hitler when he visited on September 19. Gdańsk saw 90% of its center destroyed before it finally surrendered on May 9, 1945, a day after the Western VE-Day.

The Poles who repopulated the city after the Germans were pushed out proved to be fairly intolerant of Communism, and workers here led massive antigovernment protests in 1970 and 1980. The 1980 strikes at Gdańsk's Shipyards spawned the Solidarity trade union under the leadership of electrician Lech Wałęsa (pronounced Va-*wen*-sa). Although the union was banned in late 1981, it came back to official life in 1989, and later that year it was leading the first non-Communist government in Eastern Europe since World War II.

WHAT TO SEE & DO

A Stroll Around the Old Town

This stroll starts at Targ Węglowy, just a few blocks to the right of the train station, and finishes at the Church of Our Lady on ulica Piwna. Not counting museum stops, it should take about two hours. Try not to go on Monday or Friday, when the Historical Museum is closed.

Walking from Targ Węglowy toward the Renaissance port, you'll see the brick High Gate (closed to the public) and then you pass under the gray concrete Golden Gate, two historic entrances to the city. After these gates, Gdańsk's Royal Road (ulica Długa) begins, the street where the Polish king used to greet the locals during his annual visit. After a few blocks you'll arrive at the 14th-century brick ★ **Town Hall** (Ratusz Główny) and tall clock tower above, which currently houses the Gdańsk Historical Museum (see "Gdańsk's Museums and Churches," below).

Continuing past the Town Hall, you'll notice that the street widens and Długi Targ (The Long Market) begins. This area has served as the town's main center and marketplace for hundreds of years, and each year at the end of July and beginning of August the Long Market comes alive with ★ **St. Dominic's Fair.** At this fair, you can buy colorful folk crafts and artistic works, as well as enjoy theatrical and musical performances.

Immediately to the left after the Town Hall, you can photograph the famous 17th-century symbol of Gdańsk, the Neptune Fountain. Behind the fountain lies one of Gdańsk's most distinctive buildings, the Artus Manor (Dwór Artusa), built during the 15th to the 17th century in the Renaissance style. Local patricians often met here; today the manor occasionally displays modern-art exhibitions.

During Gdańsk's heyday, Długi Targ was the fashionable address, and the richest traders and nobility lived in the other 16th- to 18th-century buildings on this street. Even the king stayed on Długi Targ when he visited. His house, the Green Gate (of gray stone and brown brick), is at the end of the street just before the port (today there are offices inside).

Passing under the Green Gate, you now find yourself at the Old Port embankment. You'll probably agree that these Renaissance riverfront buildings make up one of Poland's most charming sights. In the distance, to the left, you'll notice the distinctive wooden Gothic Harbor Crane, built in 1444 and oldest of its kind in Europe. The building originally formed part of Gdańsk's fortification system; as shipping and commerce began to develop in the late Middle Ages, city planners added the wooden crane between two towers to hoist up masts and unload cargo from boats as they pulled into the Gdańsk harbor. It was used until the 19th century when town planners established the central port in deeper waters. The crane burned down in World War II, but was very convincingly reconstructed in its original form. Today it houses part of the Maritime Museum (see "Gdańsk's Museums and Churches," below).

Across the Motława River on the embankment lies Granary Island (Wyspa Spichlerze). At the height of Gdańsk's importance as a shipping power, some 175 granaries here stored grain, at a time when Ukrainian wheat—shipped down the Vistula to Gdańsk and then on to Amsterdam—fed the industrializing nations of Western Europe. Today you can still spot traces of World War II damage in the area as a number of buildings (including some old granaries) remain in rubble.

After walking along the embankment, return to the town center on ★ **ulica Mariacka,** a quiet cobblestone street with charming houses. Memorable sculptures and great ornaments adorn these homes, each of which has a large staircase leading up to the parlor floor. Be sure to see the drainpipes that end in fantastic sculptures of dragons and angry gargoyles.

At the end of ulica Mariacka, turn right and then take the first left and you'll reach the Gothic Church of Our Lady (Kościół Mariacki) on ulica Piwna. It's not only Poland's largest church but also the largest brick church in the world, holding up to 25,000 people at a time. It was erected in the 14th century but greatly reconstructed after World War II. It has a large cavernous interior of unadorned white with soaring arches leading to Gothic arches.

Gdańsk's Museums and Churches

Gdańsk Historical Museum, ul. Długa 47. ☎ 31-97-22.

There are many rooms preserving the glory of Gdańsk's medieval Town Hall, including the Red Room, with an elaborate series of ceiling paintings; the White Room, with

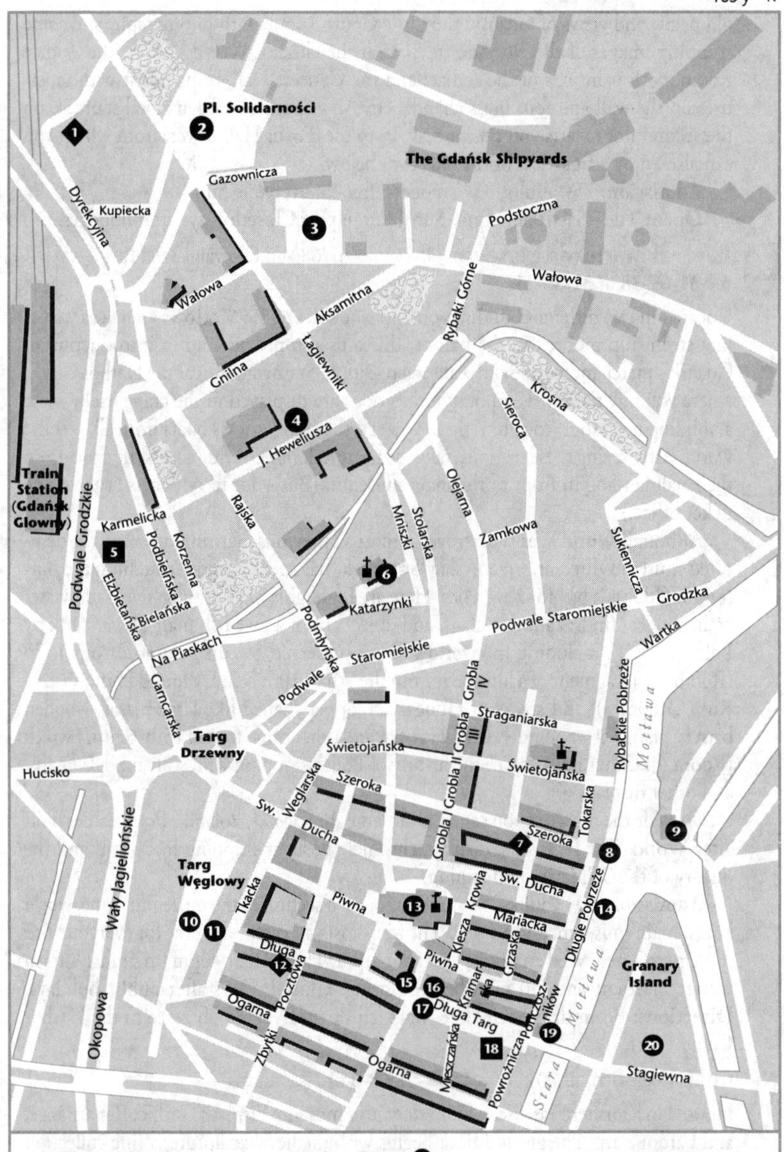

ATTRACTIONS

- Artus Manor 16
- Central Maritime Museum 9
- Church of Our Lady 13
- Tourist Information 4
- Golden Gate 11
- Granary Island 20
- Green Gate 19
- Harbor Crane 8
- High Gate 10
- Neptune Fountain 17
- Old Port Embankment 14
- Plac Solidarności 2
- Św. Brygidy Church 6
- Town Hall (Gdańsk Historical Museum) 15

ACCOMMODATIONS

- Biuro Zakwaterowańia (Private Room Bureau) 5
- Hotel Jantar 18

DINING

- Karczma Michał 1 
- Pod Łososiem 7
- Restauracja Major 12

old prints and views of Gdańsk; the Little Court Room, with photographs and some stunning images of the city's destruction at the close of World War II; the Zodiac Room, with paintings of the zodiac; and the Concert Hall, resplendent with tapestries on the wall and four brass chandeliers. An elaborate wooden spiral staircase on the second floor starts you on the way up to the Town Hall tower, from which you can also enjoy a fine view of the old town below.

Admission: 75¢ adults, 35¢ students; free for everyone Sun.

Open: Tues–Sat 10am–4pm, Sun 11am–4pm. **Closed:** Days after holidays.

★ **Central Maritime Museum,** ul. Szeroka 67/68 and Olowianka 9/11. ☎ **31-69-38** or **31-53-11.**

Located in two different buildings on opposite sides of the Motława Canal, as well as in a steamship moored in the harbor, this museum provides a fun introduction to Gdańsk's merchant marine and seafaring tradition. Start your visit at the Harbor Crane, where you buy tickets. Temporary exhibitions are displayed in the crane itself, while a building next door (to your right as you exit the crane) shows boats from all over the world. After seeing these sections, take the minute-long boat ride across the canal from the small landing in front to the main museum. (Buy your ferry tickets at the crane ticket office.)

Although World War II destroyed almost all previous maritime artifacts, the dedicated museum director, Przemysław Smolarek, has spent decades searching the bottom of Gdańsk's bay for new relics. Here are highlights of the impressive underwater archeological finds: cannons, flags, and objects from a Swedish man-of-war sunk by Poles in 1627, including the world's oldest preserved Swedish cannon from 1570 (Room 1); a fragment of a long boat from the 9th or 10th century found in the Vistula River (Room 3); and stacks of Hungarian copper shaped like large pizzas, wooden barrels, planks of wood intended for export, and other cargo from a 15th-century wreck (Room 4). Other rooms trace the history of Polish shipping with scale models, maps, and other displays.

Outside the museum you can visit the large ship *Sołdek*, Poland's first steamer built after World War II. Inside, displays chronicle postwar shipping in Poland and the history of the Solidarity trade union.

Admission: 50¢ adults, 25¢ students for each section of the museum: crane, world boats, main museum, and Sołdek. The ferry costs 5¢ each way. Free for everyone Fri.

Open: Tues–Wed and Fri–Sun 10am–4pm, Thurs 10am–6pm (to 4pm Thurs in winter); last entrance 30 min. before closing. **Closed:** Days after public holidays. **Directions:** From the Green Gate, walk left down Długie Pobrzezėe to the Harbor Crane.

National Museum, ul. Toruńska 1. ☎ **31-68-04.**

Housed in a former Franciscan monastery, this museum displays Gothic, Renaissance, and baroque art. The ground floor begins with medieval sculpture, a fine collection of silver plates and birds, 17th- and 18th-century furniture, and porcelain from all over the world. The second floor's star piece is the Flemish master Hans Memling's *Last Judgment,* located just to your right after you climb the stairs. Make sure to admire the back of the altarpiece that portrays the work's patron and his wife. Across the hall you'll see Gdańsk paintings of the 16th century, most on wood, and of 17th-century master Antoni Möller (1563–1611), whose work accurately captures the popular fashions of his day. Other artists displayed include Van Dyck, Pieter Brueghel the Younger, and Poles Andrzej Stech and Piotr Michałowski.

Admission: $1 adults, 50¢ students.

Open: May 15–Sept 14, Tues and Sat 11am–5pm, Wed–Fri 9am–3pm, Sun 9am–4pm; Sept 15–May 14, Tues and Sat 11am–3pm, Wed–Fri and Sun 9am–3pm. **Closed:** Days after holidays. **Directions:** From ulica Długa, walk south down Pocztowa and continue for four blocks.

Gothic Cathedral, in Park Oliwski, off ul. Armii Radzieckiej. ☎ **52-00-52.**

Constructed in the 13th century, this church in a residential neighborhood of Gdańsk houses one of the largest and most impressive organs in all of Europe (from the 18th century). Before the days of electricity, seven men were needed to operate the bellows that pump air into the organ's 6,300 pipes. Two thin turrets mark both sides of a very tall, narrow facade.

Open: 20-minute organ demonstrations June–Aug, Mon–Fri hourly 11am–5pm (except 2pm). Sat hourly 10am–3pm, Sun hourly 3–5pm; the rest of the year, Mon–Sat hourly 10am–3pm (except 2pm), Sun 3 and 4pm In July, there's an hour-long concert on Tues and Fri at 8pm. Check with the tourist office for the most recent schedule. **Directions:** Take tram no. 6 from in front of the train station in the direction of Sopot, or the suburban rail to the Gdańsk-Oliwa station.

Westerplatte

At Westerplatte, located at the mouth of Gdańsk's inland ports, a garrison of 182 Polish soldiers held out against 4,000 Germans for one week in September 1939. Only 15 Poles died in the futile battle, which starkly contrasts with some 400 German deaths. Today a memorial, a small exhibition, and a few burnt-out barracks stand in the area. The sight can be interesting for history buffs, but otherwise there's little to warrant a visit.

The memorial is always open. To get there, take bus no. 106 from the main railway station or, June to August, a scenic one-hour boat ride from the port at the town center's Green Gate.

On the Trail of Solidarity

In May 1989, months before the opening of the Berlin Wall and other dramatic events that brought the collapse of Communism in Eastern Europe, the trade union and political party Solidarity delivered a stinging defeat to the Communists in Poland's first free elections in 40 years. By August 1989 they led the first non-Communist government in Eastern Europe. You can visit Solidarity's birthplace at the Gdańsk Shipyards, and the union's spiritual center at the św. Brygidy Church.

The Gdańsk Shipyards [Stocznia Gdańska], Plac Solidarności Robotniczej.

An aging 340-acre plant that builds everything from cruise liners to military vessels. From August 14 to 31, 1980, 16,000 striking workers occupied the complex, forcing the Polish government to recognize Solidarity as an independent trade union. You may visit the shipyards only with an escort, which you can arrange through Orbis, ul. Heweliusza 22 (☎ **31-45-44**). You must contact Orbis several days in advance to make arrangements and you may only be able to get a tour in German.

The **Monument to Shipyard Workers,** on Plac Solidarności Robotniczej outside the shipyards, one of Gdańsk's most noted monuments, is just over a decade old. Unveiled in December 1980 after only four months of work, the immense monument (130 feet high) of three crosses and an anchor commemorates the 28 workers who died in the strikes of 1970. Constructed at the insistence of Solidarity in August

1980, it was the location of many demonstrations in the early days of the Solidarity movement from December 1980 to 1981 and again in the late 1980s when Solidarity reemerged.

Directions: Take bus no. 10 from in front of the train station, or walk for about 10 minutes from the train station.

Św. Brygidy Church, ul. Profesorska 17.

Thousands of shipyard workers and Solidarity supporters, including President Lech Wałęsa, when he's in town, attend a national mass in the name of Poland here every Sunday at 11am. Try to schedule your Gdańsk visit to fall on a Sunday in order to see and understand the intensity and blending of Poland's Catholicism and nationalism. The mass proceeds with a curious mix of religious and political sermonizing, often prompting vigorous applause. After the ceremony, a few thousand exit into the church courtyard to listen to speeches. Flags and plaques around the church honor Solidarity, and a small souvenir stand (open Monday through Saturday from 11am to 7pm) sells Solidarity mementoes. Make sure the national mass is still at 11am when you visit, and arrive as early as you can—the crowds are enormous.

Admissions: Free.

Open: Daily 7am–7pm. **Directions:** Walk one block south of the very tall Orbis Hevelius Hotel.

SHOPPING

Because amber washes up on the shores of the Baltic Sea, amber jewelry is abundant in Gdańsk: try ulica Mariacka, for example, which has many little jewelry stores, or Długi Targ for amber and silver jewelry and other souvenirs.

EVENING ENTERTAINMENT

State Opera and Baltic Philharmonic, Al. Zwycięstwa 15, in the Wrzeszcz district. ☎ **41-05-63** or **41-46-42**.

Music lovers who prefer to take in their music at a concert hall can attend performances here. You can also attend concerts in the splendid medieval Town Hall in the Main Town from time to time; inquire at the Tourist Information Office or at Orbis for all upcoming concert events. The orchestra goes on break in August or September.

To get here, take the suburban railroad toward Sopot and exit at Gdańsk Politechnika, or take most buses and trams heading toward Sopot.

Interclub Żak, Wały Jagiellonskie 1. ☎ **31-41-19** or **31-61-25.**

Gdańsk's youth center, the Żak runs a disco, pub, film club, and café in an impressive brick building that once served as the regional headquarters of the League of Nations. The disco and pub are downstairs. You can drink Okocim beer on tap and listen to live jazz or blues from 9pm to 2am or watch music videos there. Basic Polish and American food is available in the pub at low prices. Live bands occasionally play in the disco, and sometimes the stage is open to all for improvisation.

There's also a shop with helpful English-speaking salespeople who sell new age books, meditation pillows, etc.

There's a more upscale café/bar on the second floor that serves beer and mixed drinks in an attractive modern setting with rotating art exhibits on the walls and a balcony for summer sipping. A billiards room next door has three American tables.

The disco, pub, and café/bar are open Sunday through Thursday from 2pm to 2am and on Friday and Saturday from 2pm to 5am. Beer on tap in the pub costs 90¢; beer and mixed drinks in the café/bar run $1 to $2.

Admission: Disco and pub, $2.50–$3, movie, $1.25.

WHERE TO STAY

Gdańsk does not offer many budget lodgings. And many establishments have closed down in recent years, making it even more difficult to find an inexpensive room. You'll be hard-pressed to find cheaper or more pleasant accommodations than private rooms. If you can't get a private room at the agency below, try the hotel listed below or consider staying in Sopot.

PRIVATE ROOMS Go to the office that officially arranges private-room accommodations, Gdańsk Tourist, across from the central train station at ul. Heweliusza 8, 80-894 Gdańsk (☎ **058/31-26-34** or **31-38-49**), open daily from 7:30am to 7pm. The charge is a standard $7.50 for a single and $12.50 for a double, and most rooms are in homes near the center linked by bus or tram.

FOR STUDENTS In addition to the youth hostel listed below, you can inquire about other student accommodations at Almatur, ul. Długi Targ 11, 80-828 Gdańsk (☎ **058/31-20-61**), open Monday through Friday from 9am to 4pm.

Youth Hostel, ul. Walowa 21, 80-858 Gdańsk. ☎ **058/31-23-13.** 100 beds in 17 rms. **Bus:** 161 or 167 from the train station.

Rates: $2.85 per person with a youth-hostel card, $3.25 per person for others. Linen 80¢ extra.

An old brick building just a block from the Gdańsk Shipyards, the hostel charges uniform rates for all beds (rooms hold 1 to 12 beds), so you might luck out and get a single or double. The rooms are aged, but decent—with the lowest rates in town. The reception, open daily from 6 to 10am and 5 to 10pm, is on the second floor; there's a kitchen and showers in the basement.

A Hotel with a View

Hotel Jantar, ul. Długi Targ 19, 80-828 Gdańsk. ☎ **058/31-27-16.** Fax 058/31-35-29. 42 rms (13 with shower or bath but no toilet). **Bus:** 8 or 13 from the train station; get off at the fourth stop on Aleja Leningradzka and the hotel is three blocks away.

Rates (including breakfast): $18 single without bath; $27.50 double without bath, $34 double with bath but no toilet, $38.50 double with bath and TV but no toilet; $43.50 triple with bath but no toilet.

On Gdańsk's most appealing street, an area with Renaissance buildings and a king's palace nearby, the Hotel Jantar appears to be a perfect choice of accommodations. The public bathrooms are well maintained. The rooms have colorful carpets, crimson drapes, and beds with firm but slightly lumpy mattresses. If you are renting a double or a triple, ask for one facing the street as the view from the large windows is great.

WHERE TO EAT

PICNIC SUPPLIES For snacks and picnic supplies, stop by Hala Targowa, between Pańska and Lawendowska about halfway between the train station and the Main Town, a large indoor hall that spills into nearby streets with stands of fruit, vegetables, meat, fish, candy, clothes, and other goods. It's open Monday to Friday 9am to 6pm and on the first and last Saturdays of the month from 9am to 3pm.

In the Main Town

Karczma Michał, ul. Jana z Kolna 8. ☎ **311-05-35.**

Cuisine: POLISH. **Reservations:** Recommended Sat–Sun.
Prices: Soup $1; main courses $2.50–$4.50; dessert $1.50; glass of beer or wine 75¢–$1.50.
Open: Summer, daily 10am–10pm; other seasons, daily 10am–9pm.

This is a pleasant basement restaurant directly opposite the Solidarity monument with blond-wood booths and walls decorated with paintings and plants. The advertising promises "food just like Mom's." A menu in English is available, and the prices are reasonable. The house specialty is a delicious pork chop à la polonaise with potatoes, sauerkraut, beans, and a cucumber salad; the portions are large. Desserts are fresh fruit in season with cream. The service is excellent.

The personable owners, Mirosław Urbanik and Barbara Gwizda, are deservedly proud that a "famous French travel guide recommends their restaurant." They also hastened to point out that many well-known Poles have dined here. Add your own comments to their guest book.

Restauracja Major, Długa 18. ☎ **31-10-69.**

Cuisine: POLISH/EUROPEAN. **Reservations:** Recommended. **Directions:** From the Town Hall, walk west on Długa; the restaurant will be on your left.
Prices: Appetizers and soups $1.50–$7.50; main courses $7–$8; desserts $1.50–$3. AE, EU, DC, JCB, MC, V.
Open: Daily 1pm–midnight (last serving at 11:30pm).

This restaurant occupies the adjoining ground floors of several historic buildings on Długa street, with views out onto the pedestrians-only thoroughfare. The upscale decor in each room is different and gives the appearance of several different establishments when in fact there is only one. The food—with selections from several different European traditions, including Polish, German, Hungarian, and French—is uniformly good, and the service quite professional.

Worth the Extra Money

Pod Łososiem [Under the Salmon], ul. Szeroka 54. ☎ **31-76-52.**

Cuisine: POLISH. **Reservations:** Recommended. **Directions:** Walk along the canal to the Harbor Crane; go under the crane and up a block and a half.
Prices: Soup $1.50–$3; fish dishes $6.50–$20; meat and poultry dishes $7–$12. AE, DC, EU, JCB, MC, V.
Open: Daily noon–11pm; hot meals after 1pm.

A posh restaurant where the richest patricians and foreign merchants have been dining for hundreds of years, Pod Łososiem first opened as an inn in 1598 during Gdańsk's golden years; during that time the restaurant made and served its own liquor. Although it closed down in World War II, it reopened in 1976 with all its former elegance. On entering, you pass through an elegant Renaissance parlor room. Inside, brass chandeliers hang from a dark-stained wood ceiling supported by large beams, and paintings of old Gdańsk on the walls surround you. Baltic Sea fish is the specialty here, and you can choose among trout, salmon, eel, and other fish from the day's catch. Those in the mood to splurge can order the "Sailor's Plate," a selection of trout, salmon, eel, and other fish in one giant dish. But don't feel compelled to order fish; dishes like roast duck with apples, boar steak, and pheasant are excellent, too.

2 Sopot

7 miles NW of Gdańsk

GETTING THERE • **By Train** The frequent commuter trains between Gdańsk and Sopot cost only 40¢ and take 20 minutes, making the following stops: Gdańsk Gł. (main station), Gd. Stocznia (the Shipyards), Gd. Politechnika, Gd. Wrzeszcz, Gd. Lotnisko, Gd. Przymorze, Gd. Oliwa, Sopot Wyścigi, and Sopot (the main station). Buy your local commuter train ticket in the underground ticket office at the Gdańsk train station, not at the regular train ticket windows.

Note: All trains, including fast and express trains, stop at Sopot on their way to Gdynia.

• **By Boat** From Gdańsk by boat, it takes an hour and costs $2.50.

• **By Taxi** The 15-minute ride from Gdańsk costs about $6 to $7.

ESSENTIALS The telephone area code is 058.

ORIENTATION Most of Sopot's major streets run parallel to the sea; the town's foremost shopping and tourist promenade, ulica Bohaterów Monte Cassino, however, is perpendicular to the sea. From the train station, at ul. Dworcowy 7 (☎ **51-00-31**, 51-00-32, or 51-00-33), walk to your left down the small hill; when you come to Plac Konstytucji 3 Maja, turn right onto the beginning of Sopot's famous and picturesque pedestrian mall. You'll find a baggage depot at the station should you want to leave luggage behind.

INFORMATION There's a tourist bureau (Buiro Turystyczny) at ul. Chopin 10, just below the train station (open Monday through Friday from 8am to 4pm), where you can get a good map of the city.

SPECIAL EVENTS The Opera in the Woods, outdoor opera in summer, usually in August.

Poland's wealthy have visited the Polish Baltic's premier resort town since early in the last century, and until World War II visitors to Sopot enjoyed beautiful unspoiled beaches by day and an exciting nightlife that centered around a large casino. Since then, the casino burned down (in World War II) and the industrial waste from Gdańsk and Gdynia has polluted the town's sea water. Nonetheless, Sopot remains one of Poland's most lively and appealing resort towns—albeit without swimming, but in 1990 they did restore gambling. Victorian architecture lines the streets and cultural activities take place throughout the year. I recommend a visit to Sopot during your sojourn in Gdańsk; you might even stay in a budget hotel in Sopot and travel to Gdańsk by day.

WHAT TO SEE & DO

Sopot is a 20th-century resort town, and the main areas to visit are the pedestrian mall, Monte Cassino, and the Molo Park at the end of the mall (open in summer daily from 8am to 8pm for 15¢ for adults and 7¢ for students; the rest of the year 24 hours daily for free). A 1,680-foot pier extends from the park out to sea; you can catch ferries from the end of the pier (☎ **51-12-93**) to Gdańsk, Westerplatte, Gdynia, and Hel for less than $4 each way.

To see what Sopot might have looked like in its glory days before the war, wander along ulica Westerplatte, parallel to the train tracks, a few minutes' walk from Monte Cassino.

EVENING ENTERTAINMENT

In summer (usually in August), Sopot hosts such classics as *Carmen* and *Aïda* at the outdoor **Opera in the Woods** (Opera Leśna), ul. Moniuszki 10 (☎ **51-18-12**). You can get the latest program and buy tickets at the Sopot Orbis office, ul. Bohaterów Monte Cassino 49 (☎ **51-26-15**), or at the BART office, ul. Kościuszki 6 (☎ **51-44-43**). You can walk there along Monte Cassino away from the sea, but you may find it easier to take a taxi.

If the weather isn't suitable for an outdoor evening, try a film. Several theaters on Monte Cassino screen American and British films. You can also gamble at the casino in the Hotel-Orbis Grand, ul. Powstańców Warszawy 12/14 (☎ **51-00-41**).

WHERE TO STAY

You want to see Gdańsk, so why in the world should you stay in Sopot? First, Gdańsk offers very few budget hotels, which often fill up, so you may be forced to look for a hotel elsewhere. Second, the larger number of hotels in Sopot gives you a better chance to find a good budget buy. And finally, Sopot offers a more lively nightlife than Gdańsk, ranging from Opera in the Woods to punk rock, so after a day of sightseeing in Gdańsk you can enjoy an evening of fun near your hotel in Sopot.

PRIVATE ROOMS There is a private bed-and-breakfast agency in Sopot called Guide (☎ **51-69-78**), owned by a Polish woman who speaks good English. A single is $15 and a double goes for $20, and they can also place you in Gdańsk or Gdynia if you prefer.

Doubles for Less Than $18

Hotel Albatross, Pl. Konstytucji 3 Maja no. 2, 81-704 Sopot. ☎ **058/51-15-25.** 25 rms (none with bath). **Directions:** Walk left half a block from the train station.

Rates: $6.65 single; $11.10 double. Prices decrease about 50% during winter.

This hotel, across from the train station and just five minutes from the beach, offers aging, spartan rooms with sinks and small tables. Although the building is generally not well maintained, public facilities have new tile and are fairly clean (the doors don't lock!). The floors creak and groan, so get a room on the third floor if you can. Overall, it's a bargain.

Pensjonat Irena, ul. Chopina 36, 81-786 Sopot. ☎ **058/51-20-73.** 20 rms (none with bath). **Directions:** From the train station, exit down ulica Dworcowa, turn right one block down ulica Kościuszki, and take the first left down ulica Chopina; continue for two blocks.

Rates: $10 single; $15 double; $18 triple. DC, EU, JCB, M, V.

The Pensjonat Irena is a four-story boardinghouse on a quiet side street, with a good restaurant downstairs (see "Where to Eat," below), and the bathrooms fairly well kept. The carpets are thin but free of stains. The restaurant is open daily from 8am to 7pm; the bar, daily from 1 to 9pm.

Doubles for Less Than $26

Hotel Maryla, Al. Sępia 22, 81-713 Sopot. ☎ **058/51-00-34.** 18 rms (all with bath) TEL **Bus:** 122 north from Molo. **Train:** Sopot–Kamienny Potok.

Rates: $27.50 double; $32.50 triple; $45 two-person apartment with TV. Cheaper in winter.

Near Gdynia, this pensjonat has recently completed a major overhaul and is considerably more attractive than the two hotels listed above. Danuta Czerwionka, at the desk, speaks good English. Rooms have shiny new tiled bathrooms, and large balconies in two rooms. Some rooms have individualized color schemes. There's a bar on the ground floor (open from 2pm to 4am) and an attractive restaurant (open from 8am to midnight) with large windows and plants. You can dance in the disco downstairs on Friday and Saturday from 9pm to 6am, but if you prefer to sleep, you won't hear the noise from your room. The Maryla is a two-minute walk from the beach, but is far from town and is best enjoyed if you're traveling by car.

Worth the Extra Money

★ **Hotel-Orbis Grand,** ul. Powstańców Warszawy 12/14, 81-718 Sopot. ☎ **058/51-00-41.** Fax 058/51-61-24. 112 rms (all with bath). TEL **Bus:** 187 from Plac Konstytucji 3 Maja to the left of the train station; if you have little luggage, walk 10 to 15 minutes down Bohaterów Monte Cassino and then turn left before Molo.

Rates (including breakfast): May–Sept, $60 single; $84 double; $150 two-room suite, $180 three-room suite with TV and ocean view. Oct–Apr, $33 single; $45 double; $72 two-room suite; $102 three-room suite. AE, DC, EU, JCB, MC, V.

This 1926 hotel on the beach resembles a huge palace. After entering the lobby through a revolving door, you'll see elegant mirrors and pink lamps, and a circular atrium rising four stories. Turn-of-the-century details, like brass faucets and big bathtubs, as well as wood-and-mirror closets and period furniture, decorate the rooms; half have a great view over the beach and tiny balconies. Only a third of the rooms have the 1920s-style bathrooms, so specifically ask for them as they really help recall that romantic era. All the rooms are quite spacious; the doubles could pass for suites. This hotel has more character than any other in Poland, and for that reason alone I think it's worth going over your budget for a day or two. It's no wonder that visiting dignitaries, from the Shah of Iran to Charles de Gaulle, have stayed here.

Dining/Entertainment: Visitors in Sopot speak of the Grand's restaurant in superlatives. The menu includes roast turkey with delectable french fries, chateaubriand, and various fish. Main courses cost $3.65 to $8.45. Try to sit at one of the window tables overlooking the Baltic Sea. Open daily from 1pm to midnight. There's also a café in the area in front of the restaurant.

In 1990 the hotel resumed operating a casino for the first time since 1939. It's open from 1pm to 5am.

WHERE TO EAT

Pensjonat Irena, ul. Chopina 36. ☎ **51-20-73.**

Cuisine: POLISH. **Directions:** Exit the train station down ulica Dworcowa, turn right down Kościuszki one block, and take first the left down Chopina; continue for two blocks.

Prices: Soups 30¢–75¢; main courses (with fries or salad) $1.75–$2.05.

Open: Daily 8am–7pm.

For good budget fare, try the basement dining room in this hotel, where you can feast on quality home-style cooking. Every item is individually prepared when you order. Possibilities include fish, roast chicken, pork cutlet, and shashlik.

3 Gdynia & the Baltic Coast

6 miles N of Sopot, 13 miles NW of Gdańsk

GETTING THERE • **By Train** An express train from Gdańsk takes about 20 minutes ($1.10 in first class, 75¢ in second); the commuter local takes about twice as long but costs only 60¢. Trains from all over Poland terminate in Gdynia after passing through Gdańsk.

ESSENTIALS The telephone area code is 058.

ORIENTATION Gdynia is an industrial town spread out parallel to the seafront with many docks protruding out to sea. The main train station, Gdynia-Głowna (☎ **20-09-02** or **21-67-01**), lies about six blocks from the waterfront. Walk to the Chinese restaurant, make a left, then walk straight down ulica 10 Lutego toward the sea for the sights listed below.

INFORMATION The Information Office in Gdańsk should be able to answer your tourist questions on Gdynia before you arrive, but there is also a helpful private tourist bureau, Sports Tourist, at ul. Starowiejska 35 (☎ **058/21-77-34** or **22-91-64**), open Monday through Friday from 10am to 6pm and on the first and second Saturdays of the month from 9am to 2pm. They can answer questions and book tickets on the ferry to Karlskrona, Sweden.

Gydnia is the third leg of the Polish Tri-City area that includes Gdańsk and Sopot. Although Gdynia's industry plays an important role in the Polish economy, the town offers little to the average traveler. It was first built up after World War I when the Poles felt that the so-called Free City of Danzig was not serving Polish shipping interests.

WHAT TO SEE & DO

If you're especially interested in maritime history, you may enjoy a visit to one of three museums in Gdynia.

Oceanographic Museum and Aquarium, Al. Zjednoczenia 1. ☎ **21-70-21.**

This is a fairly small aquarium, with an emphasis on the marine life of the Baltic Sea. Don't miss the sea turtles, hidden away on the ground floor.

Admission: $1 adults, 50¢ students.

Open: Tues–Sun 10am–4pm. **Closed:** Holidays and days after holidays. **Directions:** From the train station, walk straight down 10 Lutego and then onto the dock platform Aleja Zjednoczenia.

The O.R.P. Błyskawica, przy Nabrzezu Pomorskim. ☎ **27-37-27.**

A warship in the harbor, which saw active duty in World War II, now houses a small ship museum.

Open: May–Oct 15, daily 10am–4pm. **Closed:** Days after holidays. **Directions:** From the train station, walk down 10 Lutego and continue straight down the dock platform.

Open Air Naval Museum, ul. Sedzickiego 3.

East of Gdynia's pier is a lovely stretch of white beach. On a street that runs parallel to the beach you'll find this small park, containing artillery from the 17th to the 20th centuries and naval aircraft of various vintages.

Admission: 30¢ adults, 15¢ students.

Open: In summer, daily 10am–5pm; in winter, daily 10am–4pm.

BALTIC COAST EXCURSIONS

To the Beach

Just because the beach in the Gdańsk area has been polluted doesn't mean that you won't be able to swim while you're in Poland. You'll find a number of beaches at the nearby Baltic Coast that are both unspoiled and relatively uncrowded.

HEL Many travelers enjoy Hel, a town at the end of a razor-thin peninsula that juts out into the Baltic Sea above the Tri-City area. Little fishing villages and small forests dot the 21-mile peninsula, so explore around a bit to find a beach to your liking. In summer, boats leave for Hel from Gdańsk, Sopot, and Gdynia every morning and return in the evening for about $3.70 each way. The ride from Gdańsk takes about 2 hours, 1¹/₂ hours from Sopot.

ŁEBA Many Gdańsk locals prefer Łeba, 62 miles west of the Tri-City area, accessible from Gdynia in 2 hours and 40 minutes by fast train ($2.85 in first class, $1.90 in second class), or by bus. It's a small fishing town with clean beaches and fewer visitors than Hel. Łeba is also noted for its shifting dunes. In World War II Rommel's Afrika Korps trained at Łeba, and V-1 and V-2 rockets were fired at London from here. Today desert movies are filmed on the beach from time to time.

KRYNICA MORSKA Perhaps the least-crowded beaches are on the Amber Coast (so named because of the rich supply of amber mined here) east of Gdańsk toward the Russian-border. The one-hour bus ride from Gdańsk is picturesque, with beautiful views of the Polish forest and lakes on one side, and the sea opposite. Along the way you'll pass the former Nazi concentration camp **Stuthoff** (Sztutowo) (☎ **83-58** or **83-59**), where 85,000 people perished.

Historic Towns

MALBORK The main reason for stopping in Malbork is to see the **Teutonic Castle,** ul. Hiberna 1 (☎ **055/33-64**). The Order of the Teutonic Knights, the persistent and mighty enemy of Poland, set up their headquarters in Malbork (called Marienburg in German) in the second half of the 13th century so that they could rule the northern Baltic territories. The knights kept expanding their fortifications until they were finally defeated by the Poles in the 15th century. Before World War II, the fortress regained its original function: Hitler set up an elite Nazi academy here.

The castle, restored at the turn of the century and after the war, consists of three large sections—the low, middle, and high castle—all divided by moats and drawbridges. Of course it's also protected by high defensive walls and watchtowers. The Malbork castle keeps an extensive collection of amber art and jewelry, as well as displays on the history of this defensive bastion, and on medieval weaponry.

The castle can be visited only with a guide. Admission with a Polish-speaking guide costs $2.25 for adults, $1.50 for students. An English-speaking guide costs an additional $22.50 per group; it is best to call ahead to arrange this, particularly in the off-season. The castle is open daily May through September 8:30am to 5pm and October to April 9am to 3pm. Last admission is 30 minutes before closing.

Most trains traveling between Gdańsk and Warsaw stop in Malbork, about 45 minutes outside Gdańsk by fast train (from Gdańsk, $2.50 in first class, $1.65 in second class). There's a BORT, PTTK Tourist Information Office near the castle at ul. Hiberna 4 (☎ **055/31-72**), open daily from 10am to 1pm.

FROMBORK Between 1512 and 1543 Copernicus made his home in this small medieval town just 10 miles from the present-day Russian border. In Frombork, Copernicus developed the heliocentric theory of the solar system, which paved the way to current astronomy, with his classic work *On the Revolutions of Celestial Bodies.*

Copernicus did his research at the Frombork cathedral, visible from all over town and just a short walk from the bus station. At the right of the entrance to the cathedral complex, you will find the **Copernicus Museum** (☎ **0506/72-18**) with portraits of the astronomer (no two look alike) and full-scale models of the instruments he used in his observations (he did not have a telescope). The **cathedral** itself is quite beautiful. Although somber and dark on the outside, inside it's filled with light and its columns and walls are decorated with gold and brilliant colors like an illuminated manuscript. Finally, you can climb a **tower** (not the one Copernicus used; that one can only be seen from the outside) for a magnificent panoramic view of the cathedral, the town, and Vislinsky Bay. In the basement of the tower, there is a **planetarium** with four shows per day. The buildings are open in summer from 9am to 4:30pm, until 3:30pm the rest of the year. The cathedral is closed to visitors not attending services on Sundays, and the museum is closed on Mondays and days after holidays. Admission to each building is 40¢ to 50¢ for adults, 20¢ to 30¢ for students. Buy all your tickets at the museum ticket office.

You can get to Frombork from Gdańsk by bus, or, in summer, by ferry from Krynica Morska, which takes 1½ hours.

A Day in Russia

KALININGRAD To add a dash of True East to your trip, spend a day in Russia. In 1945, the Prussian German port of Königsberg, once home to philosopher Immanuel Kant, came under Soviet rule. It was renamed for the president of the USSR, Mikhail Kalinin. When the Soviet Union split up in 1991, the *oblast* was left as a tiny exclave of the Russian Federation, separated from Russia proper by independent Lithuania. Soviet-era restrictions on visits by Westerners have eased. A day in Kaliningrad gives you the chance to compare Russia's climb out of Communism with that of Poland.

Orbis in Gdańsk sells the required Russian visas for $30, and in the summer they offer one-day round-trip cruises from Gdańsk to Kaliningrad. Halex in Frombork (☎ and fax **0506/75-00** or **74-80**) has a similar package: $70, including boat fare, visa, and lunch. If you feel adventurous, you can obtain a visa from Orbis and take a direct train from Gdańsk, but because of the difference between European and Russian rail gauges, the 110-mile trip takes 6 hours.

4 The Mazurian Lakes Region

If you ask Poles what section of the country they most enjoy visiting in summer, chances are they'll answer the Mazurian Lakes region in northeastern Poland. Known as the "Land of 1,000 Lakes," the area actually boasts some 3,000 lakes amid lush forests.

In July and August you can swim in clean, pure waters, but unless you grew up in the Arctic, you'll probably find it too cold during June or September. But the rest of the year you can fish for trout, crayfish, eel, or pike; you can go in the woods and hunt for bison, lynx, deer, and fox; or you can sail and canoe in the many lakes that are connected through small canals.

The Mazurian Lakes region's most attractive feature is its undeveloped natural beauty, but don't expect much in the way of tourist facilities in the area. The paucity of hotels in the region leads one Polish guidebook to conclude: "The best way to visit this area is by car with your own trailer, camper, or tent." If "roughing it" appeals to you, ask local information offices about camping sites and boat rentals. If you prefer to check into a hotel rather than pitch a tent, remember that Mazurian Lakes hotels are very basic and not as clean as most tourist facilities. However, Orbis may be able to arrange a week-long rental of a cottage in the area if you contact them ahead of time.

You're likely to pass first through Olsztyn on your way to the Mazurian Lakes. Then you can travel on to Kętrzyn and Grünwald.

5 Olsztyn

133 miles N of Warsaw, 97 SE of Gdańsk

GETTING THERE • By Train The express from Warsaw takes three hours ($13.35 in first class, $9.40 in second class); the fast train from Gdańsk takes about the same time ($7.10 in first class, $4.70 in second class).

ESSENTIALS The telephone area code is 0889.

INFORMATION The PTTK Tourist Information Office is at Wysoka Brama (the High Gate), off ulica Staromiejska (☎ **0889/27-40-58** or **27-40-59**), and Orbis is at ul. Dąbrowszczaków 1 (☎ **0889/27-57-91**). Both these offices can provide information on accommodations and sports in the Mazurian Lakes. Students should go to the Almatur office, ul. Kortowo DS 2 (☎ **0889/27-86-53**), open Monday through Friday from 8am to 4pm; they can give you information on the large student center at Lake Mamry.

You may want to pass quickly through Olsztyn. Advertised sights include the Monument of Gratitude to the Red Army and the Monument to the Heroes Who Fought for the Social Liberation of Warmia and Mazury. However, as the largest city in the Mazurian area (as well as the former capital of Prussia), it does have a few hotels for anyone with a car who can drive to the lakes during the day.

Excursions from Olsztyn

KĘTRZYN

A fast train from Olsztyn takes about 1¾ hours ($2.55 in first class, $1.70 in second).

During World War II Adolf Hitler decided that he and his highest commanders could best direct the campaign against the Soviet Union from the Wolf's Lair (Wilczy Szaniec in Polish) in the woods of what was then called East Prussia. The complex (called Wolfschanzer in German) consisted of 80 huge concrete-and-steel bunkers—one bunker per commander—camouflaged and spread out over several miles. A direct telephone line connected the complex with Berlin, and an airfield allowed quick departures. With the Russian advance of 1945 they abandoned the headquarters; the last Nazi commander to leave the premises destroyed everything except the bunkers (the thick concrete-and-steel walls were cracked and displaced by the blast). Hitler's bunker, with its 30-foot-thick ceiling, also survived.

The Wolf's Lair was also the site of the nearly successful attempt on Hitler's life during the war. On July 20, 1944, Count Claus Schenk von Stauffenberg, a General Staff colonel, left a briefcase with a bomb at a meeting attended by Hitler. Several people died in the blast, but Hitler survived.

You can reach the complex by taking the bus from Olsztyn or the resort town of Giżycko to Kętrzyn (pronounced *Kent*-chin); get off at Wilczy Szaniec (the Wolf's Lair), six miles east of the town center in the woods of Gierłoz. If the bus stops only in central Kętrzyn, you can catch a local bus to the Lair. The Wolf's Lair is open May to August, daily from 9am to 5pm; 9am to 2pm the rest of the year when there is no snow.

If you experience difficulties in Kętrzyn, the Bort PTTK office at ul. 1 Maja no. 5 (☎ **088988/29-78**), open May to September, Monday through Friday from 8am to 5pm, and the rest of the year, Monday through Friday from 8am to 3pm, can answer your questions.

GRÜNWALD

After hundreds of years of bitter struggle, the Poles finally managed to defeat the Teutonic Knights at Grünwald in 1410. Today a huge monument and a museum (☎ **088982/12-28**) commemorate this historic battle that Poles still recall; one inscription in the museum reads "Grünwald 1410, Berlin 1945."

German President Hindenburg (Hitler's predecessor as leader of Germany) was initially buried just outside Grünwald, in tribute to his role in defeating the Russians in 1914 during World War I. Later, his remains were transferred to the Rhineland. You won't find his sepulchral monument in the area, however; the Soviet Red Army destroyed it as they advanced in World War II.

You can take a bus to Grünwald from Olsztyn, a 25-mile journey.

Western Poland

30

MOST TRAVELERS TO POLAND TEND TO LEAVE WESTERN POLAND OFF THEIR TRAVEL itineraries. Yet for some visitors Western Poland also provides the very reason to visit. For example, businesspeople from both Eastern and Western Europe meet annually in Poznań at the large trade fair that promotes international commerce. Clothing manufacturers visit the textile warehouses of Łåódž, a large factory city from the 19th century. Western Poland also offers several appealing tourist destinations. I especially recommend Toruń, to the north, one of Poland's most charming medieval towns and birthplace of the astronomer Copernicus. And both Poznań and Wrocław offer attractive old town squares that illustrate what all of Europe was like centuries ago.

In between these large cities in western Poland you'll find dozens of peasant villages that have remained unaffected by the 20th century. Here, in areas that largely escaped the damage of World War II, the arrival of a Westerner is an event.

SEEING WESTERN POLAND

Train connections are extensive in western Poland and should easily accommodate any sightseeing itinerary.

1 Toruń

115 miles NW of Warsaw, 100 miles S of Gdańsk

GETTING THERE • **By Train** The Warsaw–Toruń express takes about three hours ($10.50 in first class, $7.10 in second class). An express train from Gdańsk takes about the same amount of time and costs the same but departs Gdańsk at 5:30am. There is also a slow train from Gdańsk to Toruń; it takes 4½ hours and costs $7.50 in first class, $5 in second. There are overnight trains to and from Kraków and Zakopane.

When you arrive at Toruń's Głowny (main) station (☎ **272-22**), south of the Vistula River and town center, take bus no. 22 from the square beyond Track 4 two stops and you'll arrive just three blocks from the Old Town Marketplace. Go to Windows 1 to 5 to buy tickets to your next destination after Toruń.

All trains stop at Toruń Głowny, but some also stop at Toruń Miasto, which is on the northern bank of the river, just east of the old town.

• **By Bus** From the bus station on ulica Jana Dąbrowskiego (☎ **228-42**), walk down ulica Uniwersytecka one block, turn right for one block and then left for one block, and you'll reach the Old Town Marketplace (Rynek Staromiejski).

ESSENTIALS The telephone area code is 0856.

ORIENTATION Toruń's major sights are compactly arrayed around Rynek Staromiejski, the charming, pedestrians-only Old Town Marketplace, located just north of the Vistula River. From this square you can easily walk to most of the hotels, museums, restaurants, and offices listed here.

INFORMATION For tourist information, go to the very helpful Wojewódzki Ośrodek Informacji Turystycznej (WOIT), Rynek Staromiejski 1 (☎ **0856/10-931;** fax 0856/10-930), open on Monday and Saturday from 9am to 4pm, Tuesday through Friday from 9am to 6pm, and in the summer only, also on Sunday from 9am to 1pm. Or you can go to Orbis, ul. Zeglarska 31 (☎ **0856/217-14** or **243-46**), open Monday through Friday from 9am to 5pm and Saturday from 9am to 2pm.

If Kraków charmed you and you want to visit another picturesque medieval Polish town, then include Toruń on your Polish itinerary. Like Kraków, Toruń (pop. 203,000)

What's Special About Western Poland

Architectural Highlights

- Toruń's Town Hall, a 13th-century structure that once housed kings and nobility.
- Toruń's Walls, typical defensive structures of the Middle Ages.
- Town Hall of Poznań, fine example of Renaissance architecture with a central clock tower, complemented by charming houses on a nearby square.
- Gothic Old Town Hall of Wrocław.

Museums

- Toruń's House of Copernicus, birthplace of the great Polish astronomer.
- Poznań's Museum of Musical Instruments, one of the most valuable in the world.
- Łódź's Art Museum, with Europe's second-largest collection of abstract art.

Events

- Poznań's Trade Fairs, held several times a year.

escaped World War II with very little damage, so you'll see buildings virtually untouched since the Middle Ages and the Renaissance.

Toruń was originally two separate towns, both dating from the 13th century. The first, centered around what is now the Rynek Staromiejski (the Old Town market square), was a commercial outpost, founded in 1233 to handle Poland's trade with Western Europe. A second town (1265) grew up around another rynek (on ulica Sukiennicza) and was composed of craftsmen. The two settlements, each with its own government and parish church, were separated by a wall and by a castle belonging to the Teutonic Knights. But in 1454, the knights were expelled, the towns merged, and Toruń developed into a rich and prosperous city with many special privileges granted by the king. During these golden years many ornate buildings were erected, and of these, some 350 Gothic structures still remain. The scientific work of Copernicus, who was born here in 1473, furthered the fame of Toruń throughout the world, and established an academic tradition still alive in Toruń's Kopernik University today.

WHAT TO SEE & DO

The Town Hall and Belltower (Ratusz), Rynek Staromiejski 1. ☎ **27-038.**

The Town Hall, originally built in the 13th century and rebuilt in the 16th and 17th centuries, once lodged kings and distinguished guests. Today it contains a collection of church art from the Middle Ages, including some interesting 14th-century stained-glass windows. It also houses a series of paintings of all the Polish kings from 992 to 1753. From atop the belltower, you can enjoy a panoramic view of the entire town. The Town Hall stands at the center of the charming Old Town Marketplace, Rynek Staromiejski.

Admission: Town Hall, 20¢; belltower, 75¢ adults, 35¢ students.

Open: Tues–Sun 10am–4pm.

House of Copernicus, ul. Kopernika 15/17. ☎ **267-48.**

The 1473 birthplace of Copernicus, the great astronomer who first advanced the heliocentric theory of the solar system, this museum highlights his life, with astronomical devices, paintings, prints, stamps, and coins bearing his likeness, and even boxes and cans of food named after Copernicus! Although Copernicus lived at this address for seven years, his actual house was rebuilt in the 19th century and its Gothic appearance restored in the early 1960s. In the same building to the left of the main entrance you can also visit a typical 16th-century house with furnishings and art of that era. Unfortunately, both museums offer only Polish-language descriptions, but they do screen a film about Copernicus in English upon request.

Admission: 20¢ adults, 15¢ students, 35¢ extra to see the film; free for everyone Sun.

Open: Tues–Sun 10am–4pm. **Directions:** From the Old Town Marketplace, walk one block toward the river and turn left.

Church of Our Lady [Św. Marii], ul. Panny Marii.

Just off the Old Town Marketplace is this impressive, large 13th-century Gothic brick church. The interior shows tall, soaring Gothic arches and long, thin stained-glass windows. There's also a Renaissance organ from the 17th century.

Admission: Free.

Open: Daily approx. 6:15am–7pm. **Directions:** Walk half a block west of the Old Town Marketplace.

St. John's Church [Św. Jana], ul. Żeglarska.

Two blocks south of the Old Town w Marketplace, the 12th-century St. John's Church contains a beautiful collection of Gothic frescoes. In days of old, monarchs visiting Toruń would attend service here.

Admission: Free.

Open: Variable. The most reliable time to visit is 11am–1pm.

Dom Pod Gwiazdą [House Under the Star], Rynek Staromiejski 35. ☎ **211-33.**

Inside a baroque house from 1697 you can see a collection of art from Asia, with pieces from China, Japan, India, Tibet, and Vietnam. Works include porcelain, paintings on silk and paper, sculptures, and other objects.

Admission: 20¢ adults, 15¢ students.

Open: Tues–Sun 10am–4pm.

A Stroll Along the Town Walls

After you visit Toruń's formal museums, continue down to the riverbank, where you can see the defensive walls that once protected the city, and inside them, near ulica Podmurna, the ruins of a 14th-century Teutonic castle. The walls stood undamaged until the 19th century when Prussian occupiers of Toruń deemed them ugly and tore most of them down, replacing them with a ring of forts outside the city. The walls at the river were allowed to remain, and they provide a fascinating glimpse of 13th- to 15th-century city fortifications. Of the ten or so city gates that once gave access to the walled city, three remain along the river. At the end of ulica Kopernika stands—or leans—the last of Toruń's defensive towers.

WHERE TO STAY

Toruń has a large number of super-budget hotels, thanks to its student population. A new youth hostel is scheduled to open at time of press; contact the tourist office for details.

Pod Orłem, ul. Mostowa 15/17, 87-100 Toruń. ☎ **0856/250-24.** 30 rms (6 with bath), 2 apartments. **Bus:** From Toruń Główny, take any bus one stop west to Piłsudski bridge, then take 29 to the hotel. Bus 29 runs straight from Toruń Miasto to the hotel.

Rates: $10 single without bath; $12.50 double without bath, $22.50 double with bath. Breakfast $1.50. **Parking:** $2.50.

This two-star hotel has a great location on beautiful Mostowa street in the middle of the old town. The rooms without bath are clean, with wall-to-wall industrial carpeting, and the hallway bathrooms and showers are in good shape as well. But the pride of the hotel are the six doubles with bath, these are spacious, light, and nicely furnished.

Hotel Polonia, pl. Teatralny 5, 87-100 Toruń. ☎ **0856/230-28.** 45 rms (11 with bath). **Bus:** 22 from the train station for three stops.

Rates: $7.50 single without bath, $13.50 single with bath; $10 double without bath, $17 double with bath; $15 triple without bath, $18.50 triple with bath.

The Polonia is a two-star hotel just a three-minute walk from the Old Town Marketplace. Its Victorian exterior has panache, and the interior has been nicely renovated. You'll find the hotel well maintained, with exceptionally clean bathrooms for a hotel in this category, and deep bathtubs in the private bathrooms. However, the four-story building lacks an elevator. The restaurant downstairs, with stained-glass windows and evening music, is fairly attractive.

Żajazd Staropolski, ul. Żeglarska 10/14, 87-100 Toruń. ☎ **0856/260-61** to **260-63.** Fax 0856/253-84. 36 rms (all with bath). TEL **Directions:** Walk three blocks from the Old Town Marketplace toward the river.

Rates (including breakfast): June–Sept, 45–59 DM ($26–$34) single; 68–100 DM ($39–$58) double. Oct–May, 30% less. AE, DC, EU, JCB, MC, V.

If you want more comfort in Toruń, choose this hotel just minutes from the Old Town Marketplace. This spot offers very pleasant large rooms with light-green or white walls and small, clean private bathrooms. The costlier rooms are more spacious and have better carpets, furniture, and bathroom fixtures. The rooms on the third floor seem to be the most pleasant, and the corner doubles on each floor are larger and have more windows. There's a TV room and a restaurant downstairs. Reservations required in the summer.

WHERE TO EAT

Żajazd Staropolski, ul. Żeglarska 10/14. ☎ **260-61** to **260-63.**

Cuisine: POLISH. **Reservations:** Recommended in summer. **Directions:** Walk three blocks from the Old Town Marketplace toward the river.
Prices: Soups 20¢–$2.25; main courses $1.25–$4.
Open: Daily 7am–10pm.

A charming Gothic-style restaurant with a high wooden ceiling supported by carved beams and exposed brick walls. You can enjoy good Polish and Central European specialties such as goulash soup, żurek, or the house specialty, cutlet staropolski with mushrooms. In addition to a variety of steak dishes, they serve trout, carp, and a vegetarian plate with vegetables, eggs, and potatoes. Venison is only $2.50 a portion here and wine is 80¢ to $1.25 a glass. The menu is in Polish and German.

Restaurant Orbis-Kosmos, ul. Portowa 2. ☎ **289-00.**

Cuisine: POLISH. **Directions:** Walk outside the town center, to the street near the river off Aleja 700–Lecia Toruńia.
Prices: Soups 75¢–$1.85; main courses $3–$5. AE, DC, EU, JCB, MC, V.
Open: Daily 1–11pm (last serving 30 minutes before closing).

A modern place with stained-glass windows, this restaurant in the aging Kosmos Hotel serves specialties such as beefsteak with vegetables and fries, and a tasty veal cutlet à la Suisse (with breadcrumbs on the outside and butter and cheese on the inside). The soups are quite good, especially the fruit soup; otherwise, dishes are uninspired although rather imaginatively named: beefsteak Fernando and filet Frasčatti.

The Orbis-Helios Hotel restaurant at ul. Kraszewskiego 1/3 (☎ **250-33**) offers an almost identical menu and prices; open 1 to 11pm daily.

For Dessert

Kawiarnia Relaks, ul. Szewska 4.

Cuisine: DESSERT. **Directions:** Walk one block east from the marketplace.
Prices: Tea 35¢; coffee 40¢–$1; ice cream 30¢–$1.50; Naleśniki (crêpes) $1.
Open: Daily 9am–7pm.

Modern black plastic tables and chairs have changed the Markiza's former turn-of-the-century ice-cream parlor ambience, but people still love to linger over sweets or coffee. I recommend their scrumptious lody ambrozja, which comes with a large helping of ice cream covered in nuts, a mound of fresh fruit, and whipped cream for a real treat.

2 Poznań

188 miles W of Warsaw, 106 miles N of Wrocław

GETTING THERE • **By Plane** The flight from Warsaw to Poznań takes an hour and costs $70. The Poznań airport is four miles out of town. Buses travel from the airport to the LOT office near the Old Marketplace.

• **By Train** The express train from Warsaw takes between 3¼ hours ($12.75 in first class, $8.50 in second class). A fast train from Toruń takes 2¾ hours and costs $6 in first class, $4 in second. A regular train takes 35 minutes longer and costs one-third less. From Wrocław, a fast train takes two hours and costs $6.50 in first class, $4.35 in second. From Berlin it's about five hours by train. The railroad station at Poznań is divided in two parts, connected by an underground passage. The main station building between Tracks 3 and 4 contains ticket windows, reservations, information, and the baggage check (open 24 hours, year-round). The smaller building on the west side of the tracks (past Track 6) is primarily for local trains. To reach the nearest bus and tram station and the nearby accommodations bureau listed below, exit the station past Track 6. Buy bus and tram tickets from the kiosk near the stop.

• **By Car** Poznań is about 4½ hours' driving time from Warsaw, and about 3 hours from Wrocław.

ESSENTIALS Poznań's telephone area code is 061. During the annual trade fair, many offices, museums, and restaurants extend their hours.

INFORMATION Wojewódzkie Centrum Informacji Turystyczney is located at Stary Rynek 59 (☎ **061/52-61-56**). It's open Monday through Friday from 9am to 5pm and on Saturday from 10am to 2pm; during trade fairs, daily from 9am to 6pm. The English-speaking staff will provide you with a map and answer all your questions.

An English translation of their very useful guidebook *Poznań A to Z* may be in print by the time you get to Poznań. It contains in-depth tourist information and pullout city maps marked with bus and tram lines.

TRAVEL SERVICES The **LOT airline office** is near the Old Marketplace at ul. św. Marcina 69 (☎ **52-28-47**). It is open Monday through Friday 9am to 6pm and Saturday 9am to 3pm. There's a baggage storage facility in the main train station building between Tracks 3 and 4, open 24 hours year-round.

FAST FACTS • Mail/Telephone The post and telephone office is located next to the train station and across from the accommodations bureau; it's open Monday to Saturday from 7am to 9pm.

CITY LAYOUT The center of Poznań lies to the west of the Warta River, with the town's earliest settlements on Ostrów Tumski (Cathedral Island). The large and charming Old Marketplace (Stary Rynek) lies at the center of tourist Poznań, laid out in a grid pattern; most museums and sights are only a few blocks from here. The train station and Poznań Trade Fair complex lie to the southwest of the city center about a 20-minute walk away; from the station, go north on Franklina Roosevelta and then right on ulica św. Marcin.

SPECIAL EVENTS Poznań is best known for its International Trade Fairs, held in June for industrial goods and in March and September for consumer products. St. John's Fair, with medieval stalls in the Old Town Marketplace and other events, takes place during the June fair. About a dozen various smaller trade fairs are also held annually. Every fifth year in September, Poznań hosts the Wieniawski International Composers' Contest (next held in 1996).

Poznań (pop. 600,000), the site of Poland's annual International Trade Fair and dozens of smaller fairs, suffered heavily during the war. Rebuilt, it's now one of the main business centers of Poland. With modern tall glass buildings and the beautifully reconstructed old square, Poznań is one of Poland's more cosmopolitan cities.

The city's first settlement clustered around a wooden castle on the island of Ostrów Tumski in the early 9th century and became the capital of the surrounding area. In 1253 monarch Przemsł I chartered Poznań on the left bank of the Warta River and granted the town municipal rights.

The geographical position of Poznań astride the main east-west trade routes, contributed to its early growth; the town was familiar to foreign merchants as early as the 14th century and prospered greatly during the Middle Ages and into the 16th century. Under the partition of Poland in 1793, Poznań fell to Prussia, which retained control for the next 125 years. During World War II more than half the city was destroyed. Reconstruction, especially the restoration of the Old Town, was remarkably speedy and successful considering the damage.

On June 28, 1956, workers from the enormous Cegielski manufacturing complex and other factories marched on the city center to protest poor working conditions, low standards of living, and the disparity between the promises of the Communist government and the wretched reality of postwar Poland. Once downtown, they attacked government and party buildings, then battled security forces for two days. Hundreds were killed. The "Poznań events" led to a new, milder government in Warsaw, which granted a relatively free church and private farms.

WHAT TO SEE & DO

A Stroll Through the Old Marketplace

Begin your sightseeing at the Stary Rynek (Old Marketplace), which was almost totally destroyed in World War II and reconstructed with great care. At the very center stands the Renaissance Town Hall, designed by architect Jean Baptiste Quadro of Lugano and constructed during 1550–55. The facade is adorned with a splendid three-story loggia and three turrets; the central one has a coat-of-arms and a clock. When the clock strikes noon, a bugle is heard and the heraldic goats of Poznań appear. Inside the Town Hall is the perfectly preserved Grand Lobby from 1555, with its magnificent coffered ceiling.

In front of the Town Hall is a rococo fountain of Persephone as well as a tortuous relic of the past: a 16th-century pillory where criminals were flogged.

You'll also want to admire the facades around the square, dating mostly from the 15th century. They range from floral patterns to illustrations of knights in armor; some even have reliefs. There is also a set of buildings near the pillory in the center of the square that capture the spirit of the Middle Ages. Note their narrow width—in days of old, the government taxed homeowners for each facade window.

On the square you'll also see several museums, including the Museum of Musical Instruments and the Polish Army Museum, the tourist information office, the PTTK Dom Turysty hotel, and several restaurants and cafés.

Ostrów Tumski

After exploring Poznań's Old Town, cross the Warta River to Ostrów Tumski (Cathedral Island), where Poznań was first settled. At the center you'll find the cathedral, a beautiful, tall medieval brick structure with symmetrical towers in front. Destroyed by fire during the Soviet occupation in 1946, the cathedral has been substantially rebuilt. Most of the interior appears far newer than the exterior, but in the basement you can visit relics and foundations from earlier churches dating from the 10th and 11th centuries (go down just to the left after entering the cathedral). In the main part of the cathedral, visit the ornate 19th-century neo-Byzantine Golden Chapel in the walkway behind the altar. In the chapel are the tombs of Prince Mieszko I and King Bolesław the Brave, the first leaders of Poland. You can buy an English-language description of the cathedral at the entrance for 35¢. Outside, in front of the cathedral you'll see the small brick Church of the Blessed Virgin, and to the side, the Archdiocese Museum, filled with goldsmith work and other religious mementoes, open Monday through Saturday from 9am to 3pm.

Admission to the cathedral is free. Admission to the basement is 30¢ for adults, 15¢ for students. The cathedral is open Monday through Saturday from 9am to 6pm and on Sunday from 2 to 6pm. Take tram 4, 8, 16, or 17, and get off right after the bridge over the Warta River.

Poznań's Museums

Poznań is a city of many museums, with a wide variety to choose from. Only highlights are listed here; inquire at the tourist information office for a complete listing.

Museum of Musical Instruments, Stare Rynek 45. ☎ **52-08-57.**

Another point of interest on the Old Marketplace. The museum's collection displays instruments from all over the world, including some of Chopin's pianos and Guarneri violins. This museum is one of the most valuable of its kind in the world.

Admission: 50¢ adults, 30¢ students; free for everyone Fri.

Open: Tues 11am–5pm, Wed and Fri 10am–6pm, Sat 10am–5pm, Sun 10am–3pm. **Closed:** Days after holidays.

National Museum, Al. Marcinkowskiego 9. ☎ **52-80-11.**

A gallery of 18th- to 20th-century Polish painting with a few European masters. It's especially strong in Dutch landscape painters of the 17th century such as Jan van Goyen and Saloman van Ruysdael. Other artists displayed include Van Dyck and the great painter of fantasy Hieronymus Bosch. Among the Polish artists, keep an eye out for modernist Malczewski.

Admission: 50¢ adults, 30¢ students; free for everyone Fri.

Open: Wed and Fri–Sat 10am–4pm, Tues noon–6pm, Sun 10am–3pm. **Closed:** Days after holidays. **Directions:** From Stary Rynek, walk three blocks west down Paderewskiego and turn right.

Polish Army Museum, Stary Rynek 9. ☎ **52-67-39.**

Opposite the Town Hall at the center of the Old Marketplace is this modest collection of armor, muskets, swords, World War II uniforms, and some modern guns.

Admission: 50¢ adults, 30¢ children.

Open: Tues noon–6pm, Wed and Fri–Sat 9am–4pm, Thurs 9am–3pm, Sun and holidays 10am–3pm. **Closed:** Days after holidays and the third Tues of each month.

Ethnographic Museum of Wielkopolska, ul. Grobla 25. ☎ **52-30-06** (entrance on Mostowa).

Permanent exhibitions in the former Freemasons Lodge building include regional tapestry, costumes, and embroidery, and 19th- to 20th-century Wielkopolska folk art (sculpture, glass painting, instruments, and ritual objects). Also on display are folk handcrafts from Nepal, India, and Afghanistan.

Admission: 50¢ adults, 30¢ students; free for everyone Fri.

Open: Tues–Wed and Fri–Sat 10am–4pm, Sun 10am–3pm. **Closed:** Days after holidays. **Directions:** From the Old Marketplace, walk along ulica Wodna, cross Grabary, and take a right on Mostowa.

Fara Poznańska [Poznań Parish Church of Fara], ul. Gołębia 1.

With one of the most stunningly beautiful baroque church interiors in all of Poland, this is the only building in Poznań that's registered in the UNESCO list of World Cultural Heritage sites. Fortunately, the church suffered only minor damage during World War II and was completely restored by 1949.

Admission: Free.

Open: Daily 6am–8pm. **Directions:** Two blocks south of the Old Marketplace, take a left on Gołębia.

EVENING ENTERTAINMENT

For a listing of concerts, theater, film, and other cultural events in Poznań, buy the monthly magazine *IKS*, available at newsstands for 75¢. Although it's in Polish, you may understand some of the listings, or you can ask your receptionist for assistance. You can also drop by the Poznań Philharmonic at ul. św. Marcin 81 (☎ **52-47-08** or **52-43-51**); the box office is open Monday through Friday from noon to 4pm.

WHERE TO STAY

Poznań's hotels are not particularly cheap, but budgeteers do have the option of a private room. Remember that rooms double or triple in price and are nearly impossible to get without reservations during the biggest trade fairs, especially the one in June, so note the exact date (it fluctuates) and plan accordingly. Students should inquire about inexpensive summer lodgings from Almatur, ul. Fredry 7 (☎ **61/52-36-45, 52-74-50**, or **52-74-49**), open on Monday from noon to 7pm and Tuesday through Friday from 10am to 4pm.

The easiest way to find a room upon arrival in Poznań is to stop at the Przemysław Accommodations Bureau, ul. Glogowska 16, 60-702 Poznań (☎ **061/66-35-60;** fax 061/66-51-63; telex 0413677), and ask for either a budget hotel room or a private room. If you plan to arrive in Poznań when this English-speaking bureau is closed, give them a call ahead of time. If you prefer a cheaper private room, you must stay for a minimum of two nights. During fairs, a private room costs $19 for one person, $24 for two, and apartments with kitchens cost $37.50 for one person, $61.50 for two, and $80 for three. When there is no fair, a private room for one person costs $8 and $10.70 for two people. Normally the firm does not rent out whole apartments when there is no fair, but if you really want one they can probably find one for you. This office also has a currency-exchange office offering a good rate. To get here, exit the train station past Track 6, cross the street, and look for sign HOTELE on the far left-hand side of a long white building. They're open Monday through Friday from 8am to 6pm; during minor fairs they're open Monday through Friday 8am to 10pm, and during major trade fairs they're open 24 hours.

Doubles for Less Than $30

Pttk Dom Turysty, Stary Rynek 91, 61-773 Poznań. ☎ **and fax 061/52-88-93.** 41 rms (7 with bath). **Tram:** 5 from the train station to Plac Wolności; then walk to the Old Marketplace.

Rates: $16 single without bath, $18.50 single with bath; $21.50 double without bath but with sink, $32 double with bath; $19.50 triple without bath or sink, $27 triple without bath but with sink; $5.50 per person in four- or five-bedded room; $4.25 per person in six- or seven-bedded room.

The best location in town, right on the Old Marketplace, this hotel offers unusually clean rooms for PTTK, plus it's the only place that does not hike its prices during trade fairs. Private bathrooms are tiny but clean, and beds are firm. The best things going here are the views over the square available from some rooms and a friendly desk staff that speaks English. There's a restaurant, bar, and newsstand downstairs. Enter the hotel from ulica Wroniecka just off Stary Rynek.

Hotel Wielkopolska, ul. św. Marcin 67, 61-806 Poznań. ☎ **061/52-76-31.** Fax 061/53-08-80. 112 rms (55 with bath). TEL **Tram:** 5 or 21 from the train station.

Rates (including breakfast): $14.50 single without bath, $19.50 single with bath; $28 double without bath, $31 double with bath. During fairs: $18.50 single without bath, $27.50 single with bath; $35 double without bath, $40 double with bath. AE, DC, EU, JCB, MC, V.

For more comfort than the PTTK Dom Turysty, you might choose this hotel, located about halfway between the train station and the Old Marketplace, where some rooms are quite spacious with desks, bright-red carpets, and gold curtains. Some of the mattresses here do merit replacement. The hallway baths are quite clean, although some of the tile is cracked. Rooms with bath also have black-and-white televisions. The reception is friendly and speaks German. The restaurant downstairs is quite elegant for a mid-priced hotel and has live music in the evening. There's a terrific pastry shop adjacent to the hotel, too.

Doubles for Less Than $36

Hotel Lech, ul. św. Marcin 74, 61-806 Poznań. ☎ **061/53-01-51** to **53-01-58.** Fax 061/53-08-80. Telex 413660. 80 rms (all with bath). TEL TV **Tram:** 5 or 21 from the train station.

Rates (including breakfast): $23.50 single; $35 double. During fairs: $55 single; $70–$80 double. AE, DC, EU, JCB, MC, V.

Located right across the street from the Wielkopolska, the Lech greets visitors with a brightly lit reception area and stone floors. The entire hotel has been refurbished, making the Lech one of the best-maintained budget hotels in town. The desk staff is friendly. An added convenience here is being able to make direct intercity or international calls from your room. There are good firm beds, radios, double windows, and tiny but clean bathrooms. High ceilings, colorful curtains and quilt covers, and wall-to-wall carpeting round out its attraction. There's also a tourist information office and a kantor; the breakfast room also serves as a drink bar from 7am to midnight.

Hotel Rzymski, Al. K. Marcinkowskiego 22, 61-827 Poznań. ☎ **061/52-81-21.** Fax 061/52-89-83. Telex 0413780. 100 rms (60 with bath). TEL TV

Rates (per person, including breakfast): When there is no trade fair, 27 DM ($15.50) without bath, 32 DM ($18.40) with bath; during minor fairs, 75 DM ($43) without bath, 96 DM ($55) with bath; during major fairs 118 DM ($67.60) without bath, 160 DM ($91.70) with bath. AE, DC, EU, JCB, MC, V.

Privatized in 1990, this hotel is currently undergoing a rolling renovation. The unrenovated rooms are not bad—they are quite spacious, with parquet floors and good mattresses. And the renovated rooms are superb—charcoal-gray carpeting, gleaming white stuccoed walls, and bright-red furniture create a jazzy, modern feeling. Of course, the refurbished rooms are just as huge as the older ones.

WHERE TO EAT

Be warned that, especially during the big trade fair, many restaurants in Poznań have limited menu choices, especially in the late evening. I suggest having an early dinner when you're in Poznań during any of the big conventions. The entire street of Polwiejska is a pedestrian mall packed with eateries and shops—this is where the locals shop and eat.

Meals for Less Than $3

Kujawianka Bar-Cafeteria, ul. Polwiejska 10.

Cuisine: CAFETERIA. **Directions:** From the Old Marketplace walk south down Szklona past Plac Wiosny Ludów.
Prices: Soups and salads 50¢–65¢; main courses $1–$2.
Open: Mon–Fri 10am–8pm, Sat 10am–6pm, Sun noon–6pm.

This simple cafeteria-style dining room has tables and a counter. It's clean, pleasant, and very popular due to the tasty food served in large portions for rock-bottom prices—goulash, chicken, shashlik with gobs of potatoes. Half a liter of beer is $1.30.

Bar Altum, near the Akademia Economiczna (Economics Academy), ul. Powstancow Wielkopolskich 16.

Cuisine: CAFETERIA. **Directions:** From the university, walk three long blocks south down Aleja Niepodleglosci to the tall brick building with the electronic billboard on the side.

Prices: Soups 50¢; main courses 75¢–$2.15.
Open: Mon–Fri 8am–6pm, Sat 8am–4pm.

Recommended by a local student, this is another simple cafeteria-style dining hall. It's on the mezzanine (second floor) with large windows overlooking the street and serves basic dishes like pork chops with cabbage and fries, spaghetti with meat sauce, and shashlik with rice for low prices. If you're not terribly hungry and just want a sandwich and a cup of coffee, there's also a café on the ninth floor, open Monday through Friday 8am to 4pm. One entire side of the café is windows, making it a good vantage point from which to get an overview of Poznań.

Worth the Extra Money

Smakosz [Good Eating], ul. 27 Grudnia 7. ☎ **52-33-20.**

Cuisine: POLISH. **Directions:** Walk west of the Old Marketplace, just past Plac Wolnosci.
Prices: Soups 50¢–$1.50; main courses $1.50–$4.50.
Open: Daily noon–11pm.

You'll enjoy a first-class, memorable dining experience at Smakosz with excellent food, atmosphere, and service. The lobby of this Old Polish–style restaurant has a red marble floor and dark-wood paneling; it's separated from the dining rooms with gold velour curtains. The dining rooms are quite elegant with fine paintings, good carpeting, and subdued lighting. The attentive waiters have their own stations. Main dishes here include trout, roast turkey, and a very large selection of beef dishes including steaks and chateaubriand. The soups are tasty and the house specialty—roast pork with gravy, potatoes, and salad (*Schab Wielkopolska*)—is excellent as well as reasonable at $4.

3 Łódź

82 miles SW of Warsaw, 133 miles NE of Wrocław,
150 miles N of Kraków

GETTING THERE • **By Train** Warsaw is as little as 2 hours away by express train ($8.10 in first class, $5.40 in second class). Wrocław is 3½ hours away ($9.15 in first class, $6.10 in second). Trains arrive at several stations: Łódź Fabryczna, ulica Armii Ludowej (☎ **33-98-80**), on the east side of town near the center, has connections with destinations in the south (including Lublin, Kraków, and Częstochowa) and Warsaw; this station also houses PKS, the main bus station. Łódź Kaliska, Aleja Unii (☎ **86-48-13**) on the west side of town, usually has connections with the north and west. Łódź Chojny, ulica Śląska (☎ **43-30-13**), on the south side of town, usually has connections to the north and international trains.

Orbis sells train tickets at Piotrkowska 68 (☎ **36-97-98**). Open Monday through Friday from 9am to 5pm and Saturday from 9am to 3pm.

• **By Car** The typical drive from Warsaw to Łódź takes just over two hours.

ESSENTIALS The telephone area code is 041.

ORIENTATION A large sprawling city, Łódź does have a recognizable grid pattern at its center. The long main street is ulica Piotrkowska, site of the town's primary hotel, the Orbis Grand, a number of travel bureaus, and many stores.

INFORMATION The Tourist Information Office, ul. Traugutta 18 (☎ **33-72-99**), has some friendly English-speakers who hand out some free pamphlets about the city. Maps and English-language guides are also sold. The staff books hotel rooms in

Łódź and throughout Poland. From the train station, it's to the left of the Hotel Centrum, in the rear of the Dom Kultury building. Open Monday through Friday 8:15am to 4:15pm and Saturday 10am to 2pm.

• **For Students** Almatur (called Biuro Podrozy i Turystyki here) is located at ul. Piotrkowska 59 (☎ **37-11-22** or **37-18-46**, fax 37-11-85); they're open Monday through Friday from 10am to 4pm.

SPECIAL EVENTS In March there are the Łódź Operatic Meetings and the Polish Festival of Theatrical School Productions. The Łódź Ballet Meetings are in May and June every odd year (next in 1995), and the International Textile Exhibition every July.

Łódź (pronounced Wooch), Poland's second-largest city (pop. 850,000), was the country's largest textiles and cloth-goods producer in the 19th century. Today it still serves as an important industrial center, and its neighborhoods remain a mix of both 19th- and 20th-century industrial architecture. For most people this may not be the most interesting city to include in their itinerary (Łódź's critics call it "Poland's ugliest city"). But it can be an interesting day trip from Warsaw, or a stop en route from Wrocław to Warsaw, or from Torun to Kraków. The business traveler interested in a little discount shopping or the history and architecture buff who wants to see a vintage 19th-century industrial town will find the city interesting.

WHAT TO SEE & DO

To view some of the ornate and detailed architecture of the 19th century, take a walk along ulica Piotrkowska, where merchants and politicians lived in Łódź's heyday. The buildings range from the aesthetically pleasing and even charming to those rather ugly. Ulica Zachodnia also has some impressive mansions, including one now used as a municipal building on the corner of Zielona, and another that is now the city's history museum (see below).

For a view of some typical industrial architecture, visit the Poltex Factory (from 1878) at Ogrodowa 17, or the brick factory from 1894 at Piotrkowska 242/250, about 5 minutes north by foot from the Textile Museum.

★ **Łódź Art Museum [Muzeum Sztuki],** ul. Więckowskiego 36. ☎ **33-97-90.**

Created in 1931 to house works by local artists, this museum has grown to become Europe's second-largest collection of abstract art. Starting with early icons and religious art, the collection progresses to the modern with works by Paul Klee, Max Ernst, Picasso, Victor Vasarely, Fernand Léger, and Andy Warhol. Other artists include Łódź's most important 20th-century artist, Władyslaw Strzeminski, whose *Neoplastic Room* shows art on the ceiling and walls; abstract Moscow-born sculptor Katarzyna Kobro; German Joseph Beuys, creator of "social sculpture" concerned with the environment and humans; and Californian Sam Francis.

Admission: 75¢ adults, 40¢ students; free Thurs.

Open: Tues 10am–5pm, Wed and Fri 11am–5pm, Thurs noon–7pm, Sat–Sun 10am–4pm. **Bus:** D, J, or 86; or walk three blocks west of ulica Piotrkowska.

Central Textile Museum [Centralne Muzeum Włókiennictwa], ul. Piotrkowska 282. ☎ **84-87-10.**

Inside Łódź's first modern weaving and spinning factory, which operated from 1837 to the end of World War II, this small specialized collection documents the history of textile production in Łódź. Starting with manual weaving mills of wood, it moved up to mechanized metal models, which include Łódź's first steam engine.

Admission: 15¢; free Fri.

Open: Tues and Sat 10am–4pm; Wed and Fri 9am–5pm, Thurs 10am–5pm, Sun 10am–3pm. **Tram:** 2, 6, 7, 11, 19, 20, 21.

Museum of the History of Łódź, ul. Ogrodowa 15. ☎ **57-08-81.**

Housed in a magnificent and massive palace built by Jewish cotton baron Israel Poznański, this museum displays some 19th-century period rooms, as well as a collection of memorabilia pertaining to pianist Arthur Rubinstein.

Admission: 50¢ adults, 25¢ students.

Open: Tues and Thurs–Sun 10am–2pm, Wed 2pm–6pm. **Tram:** 2, 5, 11, 21, 22, 45, 46, or 101.

WHERE TO STAY

Hotel Polonia, ul. Narutowicza 38, 90-125 Łódź. ☎ **042/33-18-96.** 112 rms (76 with bath). TEL **Directions:** Walk a block to right of the Łódź Fabryczna train station as you exit; it's just beyond an attractive small church.

Rates (including breakfast): $13.50 single without bath, $16 single with bath; $23 double without bath, $28 double with bath; $31.50–$35 apartment.

A dark gray, six-story building in the center of town, the Polonia offers fairly large rooms with aging furnishings, high ceilings, and dim lighting. Rooms overlook a well-trafficked intersection in front of the hotel or a bare interior courtyard. The public bathrooms are old and not very clean; the private ones have large tubs and old plumbing. The reception is friendly but no one speaks English. One pleasant rare feature of the hotel is the Italian pizzeria Da Mario, located to the back of the lobby.

Hotel Savoy, ul. Traugutta 6, 90-107 Łódź. ☎ **042/32-93-60.** 94 rms (48 with bath). TEL **Directions:** Walk straight ahead for two blocks from the Łódź Fabryczna.

Rates: $13.50 single without bath, $16.50 single with bath, $21 large renovated single with bath; $23 double without bath, $28 double with bath and TV; $38.50 apartment.

Ongoing renovations have left this old hotel with a bewildering range of decor, from the gorgeous art nouveau lobby to the grim concrete-floored hallway bathrooms. In good shape are rooms with bathrooms, which have spanking new fixtures and stall showers. The rooms without baths are less appealing—they have rather ugly vinyl-tiled sink areas—but are still quite clean. The large singles and apartments are quite snazzy.

Student Lodgings

International Student Hotel [Międzynarodowy Hotel Studencki], Al. Politechniki 9. ☎ **042/36-80-04.** About 300 beds. **Tram:** 27 from the Fabryczna train station, or 20 or 26 from the Kaliska train station.

Rates: About $3 per person. **Open:** July–Aug only.

Beds are in doubles and triples, and every four rooms share an aging not so clean bathroom. To make sure this is still a student hotel, contact Almatur at the back of a long courtyard at Piotrkowska 59, second floor (☎ **042/86-44-79** or **37-11-22**), open Monday through Friday from 11am to 3pm.

WHERE TO EAT

Restaurant Malinowa, in the Hotel Orbis Grand, ul. Piotrkowska 72. ☎ **33-99-20** or **32-19-95.**

Cuisine: POLISH/INTERNATIONAL. **Reservations:** Recommended. **Directions:** The Orbis Grand is at the center of town, at the corner of Piotrkowska and Traugutta. The restaurant entrance is on ulica Traugutta.
Prices: Soups $1–2; main courses $5–$8; desserts 40¢–$2.45; bottle of wine $3–6. AE, DC, EU, JCB, MC, V.
Open: Daily 1pm–1am (last serving at 11:30pm).

Inside the elegant, newly painted 1888 Orbis Grand Hotel, the Malinowa suggests an opulent ballroom with its lofty ceilings, gurgling fountains, and small cherubs crowning plaster columns. The menu is in Polish and English. You'll enjoy a good, standard selection of Polish and international specialties such as salmon sauté, shashlik, chateaubriand, veal steak, and roast turkey, served at a rather leisurely pace.

Next door, a shop sells snacks from the Malinowa's kitchen to go. It's open Monday through Friday 9am to 5pm and Saturday 10am to 4pm.

4 Wrocław

215 miles SW of Warsaw, 160 miles NW of Kraków

GETTING THERE • By Plane The flight from Warsaw takes a little over an hour and costs $70. The airport is in Strachowice (☎ **61-63-25**), six miles outside town. LOT buses usually meet arriving flights.

• By Train An express train from Warsaw takes about 5½ hours ($14.50 in first class, $9.70 in second class), 4 hours from Kraków ($9 in first class, $6 in second class). From the main Wrocław Główny train station (☎ **360-31** to **360-35**), south of the city center, walk west (left) on ulica Piłsudskiego to ulica Świdnicka. Turn right (north) and continue until you cross Plac Kościuszki; then follow the road north into the center of town. It's not more than a 20-minute walk. You can check your bags at the station 24 hours a day.

The **Orbis** office, at ul. Piłsudskiego 62 (☎ **387-45**), sells train and other transportation tickets. Open Monday through Friday from 9am to 5pm and on Saturday from 10am to 2pm.

• By Car Warsaw is about five hours away by car, and Kraków, three to four hours.

ESSENTIALS The telephone area code is 071.

ORIENTATION It's fairly easy to navigate your way across Wrocław thanks to a grid pattern of streets at its center. Rynek, the historic market square, sits at the center of town, about 15 minutes on foot north of ulica Piłsudskiego, home to a cluster of budget hotels and the train station. A few blocks north of Rynek is the Odra River, which contains several attractive islands including the large Ostrów Tumski (Cathedral Island).

INFORMATION The Centrum Informacji is at Rynek 14 (☎ **383-31** or **44-39-23**), open Monday through Friday from 9am to 5pm and on Saturday from 10am to 2pm. They can provide you with a map and information regarding museums, tours, and entertainment. They are somewhat understaffed at times, but are friendly, so be patient.

SPECIAL EVENTS In February is the Polish Contemporary Music Festival; in March, April, or May, the Jazz on the Odra festival; and in May and June, the Festival of Polish Contemporary Plays. In September, the Wratislava Cantans, Festival of Oratory and Cantata Music, is held.

As Poland regained its independence as late as 1918, every inch of it at some point in the not too distant past was ruled from a foreign capital. Wrocław (pop. 640,000) has a particularly foreign-dominated past. Although it belonged to Poland in the early Middle Ages, in 1335 it was ceded to the Czechs, who later passed it on to the Austrians, who in turn lost it to the Prussians. Until 1945 it was Breslau: a German city, populated with only a few Poles in the minority. This long German history ended in a thundering Götterdämmerung in the spring of 1945; the "fortress city" battled the Red Army for over two months, and in the end 70 percent of it was destroyed.

After the war, Wrocław became the largest German city to be transferred to Polish rule. Its former inhabitants moved west, and their places were taken by Poles, many of whom came from lands annexed by the Soviet Union. Despite this transition, Wrocław retains a distinctive character. Although it sustained heavy war damage, many late-19th and early-20th-century buildings remained intact and the medieval marketplace has been rebuilt. A tradition of architectural innovation has continued, making Wrocław a far more interesting place to walk around than most Polish cities. And the Germans themselves are back, seeking investment opportunities so close to their border. Although not as cosmopolitan as Warsaw or Kraków, Wrocław is a city with texture and grace.

WHAT TO SEE & DO

The Old Town Hall and Marketplace

Built initially in the 13th century, Wrocław's splendid Gothic Old Town Hall on Wrocław's central Marketplace (Rynek) was refinished, damaged, and rebuilt until it was finally finished in the 16th century. You can visit the brick, rib-vaulted interior, with walls lined by heraldic flags, which today hosts Wrocław's Historical Museum. Displays show off silver, pewter, some armor, paintings of past royalty, and an impressive collection of photographs of prewar Wrocław. The ground floor also has a changing exhibition. After you visit inside the museum, spend some time admiring the square outside, which is lined with Renaissance and baroque burghers' houses. Most were destroyed in the war and subsequently rebuilt.

Admission to the museum is 50¢, free on Wednesday. It's open Wednesday through Saturday from 10am to 4pm, and on Sunday from 10am to 5pm; last entrance is 30 minutes before closing. Take tram no. 6, 7, 8, 14, 31, or 36 from the intersection of ulica Świdnicka and ulica Piłsudskiego.

A Stroll from the Marketplace to Ostrów Tumski

After visiting the Town Hall, walk north from the square down ulica Kuźnicza. After four blocks you'll arrive at Wrocław University, a baroque structure built by Emperor Leopold I of Austria in 1702. Turn right and then left from the university to come to the bank of the Odra River, and then turn right again. After one long block you come to a park area parallel to the Odra River called Bulwar Xawerego Dunikowskiego, where you'll enjoy picturesque views across the river. After a few minutes' pause, cross Most Piaskowy, a bridge that leads to Wyspa Piasek (Sand Island). Here you'll see a large baroque structure once an Augustinian monastery and today the University Library.

The first right off the island leads you to Ostrów Tumski (Cathedral Island), Wrocław's most charming section, with cobblestone streets, little traffic, two- to four-story houses reconstructed in a traditional style, and several important churches. The first structure you'll see to your left is the impressive, dark brick Church of the Holy Cross, begun in 1288. The interior, open daily from 10am to noon and 1 to 3pm, has been completely rebuilt with white walls and new brick separated by modern stained glass. A block away is the reconstructed Gothic Cathedral of St. John the Baptist, begun in the 12th century and redone in the 16th century. The darkened brick exterior has two symmetrical belltowers, and an interior with brick Gothic arches and stained-glass windows. It's open daily: from 6am to 7pm September to June and 6am to 1pm and 5 to 7pm in July and August. Just one block north of the cathedral are attractive botanical gardens, open daily from 8am to 6pm ($1 for adults, 50¢ for students), with a small lake at the center and many birds.

WHERE TO STAY

PRIVATE ROOMS For a private room, drop by the Biuro Usług Turystycznych, ul. Piłsudskiego 98 (☎ **071/44-41-01** or **368-11**; telex 712766 or 712132), open Monday through Friday 8:30am to 5pm, Saturday 8:30am to 2pm. They rent singles for $8.50 and doubles for $15. Most private rooms are in the center of town, and are usually available on short notice. To get here from the train station, turn left and proceed down ulica Piłsudskiego.

Doubles for Less Than $25

Hotel Saigon, ul. Wita Stwosza 22/23, 50-148 Wrocław. ☎ **071/44-28-81** to **44-28-85**. Fax 071/330-37. 70 rms (all with bath). TEL TV **Tram:** 2, 9, 11, or 17 from the train station to Dominikanski Plac.

Rates: $24.50 single; $29.50 double.

The former Hotel Politchniki Wrocławskiej has undergone a major transformation. The Hotel Saigon since mid-1992, it now offers very modern accommodations with a Vietnamese theme at surprisingly moderate prices, and is definitely my top choice in town. The lobby is tastefully furnished with expensive, hand-carved chairs, screens, and inlaid tables and accented with lots of plants. The equally attractive hotel restaurant serves breakfast from 8 to 10am and Polish and Vietnamese food from 11am to 11pm. Large, freshly painted rooms have good beds, nice carpets, double windows, and satellite TVs. Clean bathrooms have overhead showers. Additionally, the Saigon is better located for sightseeing than other budget choices in town, just four blocks from the Rynek and five minutes from Ostrów Tumski.

The Grand Hotel, ul. Piłsudskiego 100/102, 50-014 Wrocław. ☎ **71/360-71.** Telex 712457. 181 rms (49 with bath). TEL **Directions:** Just walk across the street from the main train station.

Rates: $9 single without bath, $11 single with bath; $12 double without bath, $14.50 double with bath; $29 apartment DC, EU, JCB, MC, V.

The Grand has good, clean rooms with high ceilings, old floral wallpaper, and attractive bay windows in some rooms. The common bathrooms may not be acceptable, so consider the more expensive rooms with private bathrooms. The rooms on the south side of the hotel are sunny, but noisy as they face the train station. There's a travel bureau and a currency-exchange window in the lobby. Only Polish and German are spoken at the desk.

Doubles for Less Than $30

Europejski Hotel, ul. Piłsudskiego 88, 50-017 Wrocław. ☎ **071/310-71** to **310-77**. Telex 712381. 39 new rms, 37 old rms (all with bath). TEL **Directions:** From the train station, turn left and proceed two blocks down Piłsudskiego.

Rates (including breakfast): $13.50–$18.15 old single, $23.50 new single; $23.50 old double, $34.50 new double. AE, DC, EU, JCB, MC, V.

A modern, sharp-looking lobby with lots of marble—floors, walls, and reception counter—greets you in this hotel refurbished in 1989. Half the rooms reflect similar comfort—pristine rooms with modern (if brown) furnishings, large windows, wall-to-wall carpeting, stand-up showers, and new doors. In the older, unrefurbished wing, the halls are lit with fluorescent bulbs, the rooms are smaller (with parquet floors topped by rugs), and the bathrooms have exposed pipes and hip baths with hand-held shower hoses. These rooms, however, are still quite clean and boast good mattresses. English is spoken, and the receptionist is friendly. There's a tiny bar, as well as a café and a restaurant, open daily from 7am to 10pm.

Student Accommodations

Student Hotel "Dwudziestolatka" [The Twenty-Year-Old Female], ul. Piastowska 1–13, Wrocław. ☎ **071/22-50-31.** Fax 071/340-00. 444 rms (28 with shower). **Tram:** 4 from the train station.

Rates: $4 per person. **Open:** June to mid-Sept only.

Adjoining rooms for two and three people here share bathrooms that are always very clean. Amenities include two TV lounges with satellite reception and telephones on each floor. There's a buffet for breakfast as well as a restaurant, open Monday through Friday from 10am to 11pm and on Saturday and Sunday from 5 to 11pm.

Call ahead and check with the Almatur office at ul. Kościuszki 34a (☎ **071/44-30-03**), open June through September, Monday through Friday 8am to 5pm and Saturday 10am to 2pm; October through May, Monday and Friday 9am to 4pm, Tuesday through Thursday 9am to 5pm, and Saturday 10am to 2pm.

WHERE TO EAT

There are several inexpensive food bars like the Bar Żak on the Market Square where you can get a filling and inexpensive meal of soup and roast chicken or beef shashlik for $1.50 to $2 at a sidewalk table situated in a great historic setting.

Vega, 26 Rynek Ratusz.

Cuisine: SALADS/SANDWICHES. **Directions:** The restaurant is opposite the Feniks store.
Prices: Soups 60¢; salads $1.80 a pound.
Open: Mon–Fri 8am–7pm, Sat–Sun 9am–5pm.

This vegetarian restaurant, right in the middle of Wrocław's market square, is a step up from the standard milk bar. The atmosphere is cheerful, with live plants, halogen lights, and large photos of whales in clip frames. The salads are nicely composed, with a good selection of ingredients.

★ **Belle Epoque**, Rynek 20–21. ☎ **356-17.**

Cuisine: FRENCH. **Reservations:** Recommended.
Prices: Soups and appetizers $1.50–$9; main courses $5–$10.50; desserts $1.75–$2.50; wine 75¢ per glass, $5.50–$75 per bottle. AE, DC, EU, JCB, MC, V.
Open: Daily noon–midnight (last serving at 11:30pm).

The menu here is in French and Polish, but the waiters and most of the diners speak English. The dining room is done in shades of mauve and blue, accented by brass railings and enormous chandeliers. It's quite theatrical and a bit intense. The food is quite good, though it falls short of excellent. All is quite plausibly French—except the disappointing bread.

A Café

Dwor Wazow, Rynek 5. ☎ **44-16-33.**

Cuisine: DESSERTS. **Directions:** The café is on the west side of the main market square.
Prices: Coffee 65¢–$3.75; tea 60¢–$1; desserts $1–$4.30.

This café is part of a new luxury hotel. Whether you sit at the sidewalk tables facing the beautiful market square or in the attractive salon in colder weather, you'll have your choice of 9 varieties of coffee, 14 varieties of tea, and several desserts, including a heavenly nut cake. There is also a restaurant in the same complex.

An Excursion to Książ

Perched dramatically above a steep wooded ravine, **Książ Castle** has a fairy-tale-quality. Its strategic position earned it the name, "the key to Silesia." Its high walls and stone towers are massive yet graceful. With woods all around it, the castle makes a nice fair-weather excursion.

The castle was begun in the 13th century, when this area was under Polish rule. From 1509 to 1945, it belonged to the Hochberg family of German princes, who called it Fürstenstein and defended it against Swedish forces during the Thirty Years' War. Extensive construction was done in the baroque style in the early 18th century, followed by various styles in the early 20th.

Since its annexation in 1945 as part of recovered territories, Książ has been used for various purposes. Today the interior is part museum, with some rooms restored to their prewar splendor. Most noteworthy is **Maximillian Hall,** built between 1718 and 1732. This hall is a riot of baroque ornamentation, with gilt molding, several colors of marble, and a swarm of plaster putti. The castle also houses a conference center, art gallery, and temporary exhibition space. Outside, a path leads from the ticket office down to the **terrace,** where flower beds and fountains compete for your attention with the stunning view of the ravine.

Admission to the castle is $1 for adults, 60¢ for students; admission to the terrace is 50¢ for adults, 30¢ for students; and a combined ticket is $1.25 for adults, 75¢ for students. The castle is open in summer daily from 9am to 6pm, in spring and fall Monday through Friday 9am to 4pm and Saturday and Sunday 9am to 5pm, and in winter Tuesday through Sunday 10am to 3pm. The ticket office closes an hour before the castle itself.

Książ can be seen as a day trip from Wrocław, or you can stay in the hotel attached to the castle. To get there, first take a train from Wrocław to Wałbrzych, in the direction of Jelenia Góra. Deboard the train at Wałbrzych Miasto (both local and fast trains stop here). Fast trains take about 1½ hours and cost $2.90 in first class, $2 in second. At the station, walk through the tunnel below the tracks to get to the stop for bus 8, which will take you right to the castle, a trip of about 30 minutes.

WHERE TO STAY

Hotel Książ, ul. Piastow S1. 1, 58-306 Wałbrzych. ☎ **074/250-17** or **250-18**.
Fax 074/785-06. Telex 742484. 40 rms (all with bath). **Directions:** The hotel is clearly marked, just inside the main castle entrance.

Rates: $10 single; $12.50 double.

If you are intrigued by the idea of staying in a castle that was once home to princes or a fortress that has resisted marauding Swedish armies, the Hotel Książ, which was more or less built into the castle, is the place. The mattresses and the carpets are past their prime, but the paint is bright and fresh, and the bathrooms are even stylish. There is a restaurant and a bar in the hotel.

31

Getting to Know Slovenia

A VISIT TO SLOVENIA WILL UPSET ALL THE STEREOTYPES OF POST-COMMUNIST societies that you have formed elsewhere in Eastern Europe. The towns and the landscape are clean and unpolluted. Public transportation is comfortable and dignified. Service personnel, for the most part, smile and speak English. Tourist offices, free brochures, good signs, and posted train schedules will help you navigate your way around. Hotel and restaurant standards outpace those of Prague and Budapest, as do prices.

In fact, Slovenes right now are busy trying to make a case that they are not part of Eastern Europe at all. "We're in the Alps—on the sunny side," they proclaim. They'll remind you that at Kranjska Gora in northwestern Slovenia you can spend the day skiing from Slovenia to Austria to Italy and back. But while Slovenes *are* very Alpine, they are also very much Slavs—with linguistic and cultural affinities to the Balkans and a history of Communism. It remains to be seen whether the world will come to lump Slovenia with the developed countries of Western Europe. The Slovenes are hoping that you will.

Slovenes who desperately want to be seen as part of Western Europe are reacting quite naturally to what they feel is a conspiracy of ignorance that scares prospective visitors away from their country. Businesses and travelers who say "we wouldn't want to go anywhere in the former Yugoslavia" would probably do well to visit Ljubljana, which is no less safe than Venice, Vienna, or Budapest. The troubles in Yugoslavia are far away. Meanwhile, Slovenia is probably more ready to join the European Union than Hungary or the Czech Republic, both of which clamor for it much more loudly.

This is not to say that Slovenia is the most cosmopolitan country in this guidebook. It's a fairly conservative and provincial place. You won't find the morning's *International Herald Tribune* anywhere in Ljubljana, for example. But there are clear Alpine lakes, miles of hiking and skiing trails, brilliant Adriatic beaches, world-famous caves, and calm, dignified Ljubljana. The land of the Alpine Slavs is certainly the most overlooked success story in Eastern Europe.

1 Geography, History & Politics

GEOGRAPHY

Slovenia is an Alpine nation whose highest point and national symbol is Mount Triglav, which rises to 2,854 meters (9,396 feet). Forests and mountains dominate the landscape. Yet a short Adriatic seacoast runs from Koper to Portorož in southwestern Slovenia, and the warmth of southern Europe's climate moderates Slovenia's Alpine spirit both culturally and meteorologically. A small area at the northeastern tip of the country is an extension of the Hungarian plains.

Slovenia borders on Italy to the west, Austria to the north, Hungary to the northeast, and Croatia to the east and south. Although almost all of these borders have been at one time or another in dispute, today they are relatively uncontroversial. Even the toughest of Slovenia's ethnic questions—the future of the Slovene population around the Italian city of Trieste and of the ethnic Hungarians in northeastern Slovenia—are nonissues compared with the troubles elsewhere in the Balkans. Although they speak many different dialects, most Slovenes consider themselves a fairly homogenous and unified nation, which is one of the main reasons they have been unaffected by the ethnic violence that has swept the rest of what used to be Yugoslavia.

HISTORY

The history of Slovenia goes back to Roman times, when Ljubljana was a settlement called Emona. The ancestors of the modern-day Slovenes, however, arrived only during the great Slavic migrations of the 6th and 7th centuries A.D. They were soon conquered by Charlemagne's armies and forcibly Christianized. Charlemagne's realm was centered in Western Europe and had Slovenia as its southeasternmost point. Today Slovenes prefer to view themselves as an eastern outpost of Western Europe rather than as a Balkan outpost in Central Europe.

During the Middle Ages most of Slovenia became part of the duchies of Carniola, Carinthia, and Styria, which belonged to the Habsburg Empire. German was the language of government and commerce. The Venetians dominated a few sections of western Slovenia. For well over 500 years, the Slovenes shared their land with people who spoke German and Italian, and these two cultures influenced the language, food, architecture, and religion of Slovenia.

The Napoleonic occupation (1809–14) was a turning point for Slovenia. It brought reforms in all spheres of public administration, including roads, education, trade, and law. Most importantly, it elevated the Slovene language to official status in local affairs. This planted seeds of Slovene pride and independence that sprouted during the century of Habsburg rule after Napoléon's defeat. Slovenia benefited from the Habsburg Empire's 19th-century economic boom. The Vienna-Trieste railway, Austria's main link to the sea, was built through Ljubljana in the 1850s. Slovenia was always fortunate to be part of the more prosperous Austrian half of the empire; Croatia was part of the poorer Hungarian half, while Serbia and Bosnia were still shaking off the chaos of Turkish domination.

After Austria-Hungary's defeat in World War I, Slovenia joined the new South Slavic kingdom of Yugoslavia. After World War II and the terror of German and Italian occupation, Slovenia became part of the reborn, Communist Yugoslavia under the leadership of Marshal Tito, a Croat whose mother was Slovene.

Tito's death in 1980 loosened the charismatic glue that had kept Yugoslavia together. A difference of opinion gradually began to emerge between Serbian Communists, who favored a centralized Yugoslavia, and Slovene Communists, who wanted power to remain distributed among the different republics. By 1989, the dispute was in the open. Serbian Communists, particularly Slobodan Milošević, fulminated that the Yugoslav federation's decentralized nature had failed to spread wealth and prosperity from Slovenia and Croatia to Serbia, and wanted government decisions to be based on majority rule—meaning that populous Serbia could always outvote Slovenia.

Matters came to a head in January 1990 at a special nationwide Communist Party conference. The Slovene delegation found its proposals stymied, and they walked out. This spelled the end of Yugoslav Communist unity and the beginning of Slovenia's preparations for independence; from this point on Slovenia began to act as a sovereign state. Slovenia held Yugoslavia's first multiparty elections since 1938 in April 1990 and stopped sending recruits to the Yugoslav army. Factories began stamping products "Made in Slovenia." As negotiations aimed at saving Yugoslavia failed in early 1991, Milošević made it increasingly clear that he wanted to use the Yugoslav army to prevent Slovenia from formally seceding. The Slovenes were undaunted. On June 25, 1991, they declared independence. Yugoslav army troops in Slovenia tried to keep control of the country's border posts. But, fighting far from home, the demoralized Yugoslav troops were routed by an eager, professional Slovene army that had been preparing for just this for months. After 10 days of fighting, Yugoslav troops retreated from Slovenia.

Independent Slovenia found it had a surprisingly viable economy. Its Austrian legacy had left Slovenia the richest part of Yugoslavia, producing more than 20% of the federation's output with less than 10% of its population. The mildness of Yugoslav Communism had helped Slovenia avoid economic devastation. Even during the Communist days, the Western car makers Renault and Citroën had established plants in Slovenia. But Slovenia's most important asset was its sense of cultural and administrative separateness, even superiority, during the Communist period.

Today, Slovenia has relapsed into Alpine calm and sleepiness, while trying its best to match Western Europe in its economy and standard of living. With the highest GDP of the ex-Communist countries, Slovenia reminds visitors more of Austria, its neighbor to the north, than of Croatia, its neighbor to the east.

2 Some Cultural Notes

Slovene is a South Slavic language, related to Serbo-Croatian, but slightly influenced by German and preserving more archaic forms than other South Slavic languages. Slovenes take pride that the earliest extended texts in any Slavic language, the Freising manuscripts, were written by a Slovene bishop in the mid-10th century. Serbo-Croatian speakers often cannot understand spoken Slovene. Essentially all Slovenes understand Serbo-Croatian, but they detest having to speak it, especially on their own territory. Fortunately, many Slovenes know English well, and most know enough for basic communication and simple transactions. If English fails, try German or Italian.

Although the first book in the Slovene language was published in 1551, the greatest contribution to Slovene literature was that of the Romantic poet France Prešeren (1800–1849). Prešeren is honored with a statue at the very center of Ljubljana. Another important writer was the realist novelist Ivan Cankar (1893–1950), after whom Ljubljana's main cultural center is named.

Slovenia has always played a small part in the Central European musical and artistic tradition. Jakob Gallus was a major baroque composer, whose image now appears on the 500-tolar bill. The Slovene Philharmonic dates back to as early as 1701. Ironically, Franz Schubert was rejected for a post as teacher at the Ljubljana music school in 1816. But early in his career, Gustav Mahler spent a year as conductor in the Provincial Theater.

Early architecture in Ljubljana was much influenced by the Italian baroque. In modern times Slovenia is best known for the creations of Jože Plečnik (see Chapter 33).

Those interested in more contemporary artistic trends may be either intrigued or put off by Neue Slowenische Kunst (NSK). This movement encompasses both music and the visual arts and deals with such themes as war, fascism, science, and sovereignty.

3 Food & Drink

Slovene cuisine blends typical elements of Italian, Austrian, and Balkan dishes. The day may begin with a continental breakfast or a Vienna-style pastry. Lunch could be pizza or pasta with Italian ice cream for dessert. A *burek* (Balkan-style cheese wrapped in layers of thin-rolled dough) makes a nice afternoon snack. A meat cutlet is often served at dinner. You can also find excellent smoked and cured meats and Hungarian-style goulash and dessert pancakes. A common, tasty dessert is *gibanica,* made of poppy seeds, crushed nuts, curds, and layers of dough. Good Slovene food goes best with good Slovene wine, and you should have no trouble securing an excellent bottle.

32

Planning a Trip to Slovenia

SLOVENIA BOASTS OVER A DOZEN SKI RUNS, EXCELLENT CROSS-COUNTRY TRAILS, several lakes that freeze over in winter and are cleared for skating, challenging terrain for Alpine hiking, famous karst cave systems, the horse stables at Lipica (which formerly supplied the Spanish Riding School in Vienna), and some good beaches along its minuscule Adriatic coast. Tourist offices can give you all the details you need.

1 Information, Entry Requirements & Money

SOURCES OF INFORMATION

In the U.S., you should contact the **Slovenian Tourist Office,** 122 E. 42nd St., Suite 3006, New York, NY 10168-0092 (☎ **212/682-5896;** fax 212/661-2469), for brochures, maps, and general information. Several travel agencies also specialize in Slovenia, including Slovenia Travel in New York (☎ **212/661-2466**), Kollander World Travel in Cleveland (☎ toll free **800/800-5981**), Kompas in Florida (☎ toll free **800/233-6422),** and Sterling & Cruises in Texas (☎ toll free **800/367-2328**).

In Great Britain, you can contact the Kompas office, which doubles as a sort of Slovenian Tourist Office, at 57 Grosvenor St., London W1X 9DA (☎ **071/499-7488**).

ENTRY REQUIREMENTS

American, Canadian, British, Irish, and Australian citizens require only their passport to visit Slovenia for up to 90 days. The Slovene Embassy in Washington reports that citizens of New Zealand should be able to get a visa at the border, even when arriving by train, for $13, but it is more prudent to take care of this beforehand. Check with one of the consulates below, as requirements may change—the exemption for Americans, Canadians, and Australians is subject to annual review, though it has been consistently extended.

- **In the U.S.:** 1525 New Hampshire Ave. NW, Washington, DC 20036 (☎ **202/332-9332**).
- **In Canada:** 150 Metcalf St., Suite 2101, Ottawa, ON K2P 1P1 (☎ **613/565-5781**).
- **In the U.K.:** Suite 1, Cavendish Court, 11–15 Wigmore St., London W1H 9LA (☎ **071/495-7775**).
- **In Australia:** P.O. Box 188, Coogee, Sydney, NSW 2034 (☎ **02/314-5116**).
- **Slovenia** does not have consulates in Ireland or New Zealand.

MONEY

CASH/CURRENCY The official currency of Slovenia is the **tolar;** one one-hundredth of a tolar equals one **stotin.** You'll see coins of 50 stotins and of 1, 2, and 5 tolars, and notes of 10, 20, 50, 100, 200, 500, and 1,000 tolars. The prices quoted here reflect an exchange rate of $1 = 130 tolars.

Exchanging Money Banks, hotels, travel agencies, and tourist offices usually have exchange offices. The best rates are at banks. There is no black market.

TRAVELER'S CHECKS Most places that change money will also change traveler's checks.

CREDIT CARDS Many of Slovenia's places of business accept credit cards, including most of the places I list. MasterCard is the most widely accepted.

2 When to Go

CLIMATE

July and August can be unbearably hot in Ljubljana, though slightly more comfortable in the mountains and along the coast. May, June, September, and October are milder yet still warm. Slovenia wears snow well—Ljubljana's castle hill is a particularly peaceful sight under a white winter hat—so especially if you like to ski, you might enjoy a visit between Christmastime and the end of February, when snowfall is most assured. (The caves at Postojna are also less crowded in winter.) The down-seasons of November, late March, and April bring grayer and bleaker weather, during which some hotels lower their rates or shut down completely.

HOLIDAYS

The official holidays in Slovenia are January 1–2 (New Year's), February 8 (Culture Day), the Monday after Easter, April 27 (National Resistance Day), May 1–2 (Labor Day), June 25 (Statehood Day), August 15 (Assumption), October 31 (Reformation Day), November 1 (Remembrance Day), December 25 (Christmas), and December 26 (Independence Day).

Slovenia Calendar of Events

- **International Biennial of Graphic Art** (mid-June to Sept), in Ljubljana. International exhibition of graphic art, centered in the castle in Tivoli Park. Odd-numbered years only.
- **Summer in Old Ljubljana** (early July–early Sept), in Ljubljana. Classical music in the Old Town.
- **International Summer Festival** (mid-July to Aug), in Ljubljana. Theater and classical music in the open-air theater in Križanke.
- **Wine Fair** (early Sept), in Ljubljana. International wine fair at the Ljubljana Fairgrounds.

3 Getting There

BY PLANE Slovenia's flag carrier, Adria Airways, flies from Ljubljana to a number of European capitals, including London, Moscow, Paris, Rome, Vienna, Zürich, and Tirana. Their round-trip fares are quite competitive and they also offer a good selection of one-day-in-advance youth fares.

Austrian Airlines (☎ toll free **800/843-0002**) may have resumed flights from Vienna to Ljubljana by the time you read this. In the meantime, they will be happy to book you onto an Adria Airways flight on the same route.

BY TRAIN From Vienna to Ljubljana is a six-hour train journey with three direct trains a day. Salzburg is only 4½ hours away; trains from Venice take 5½ hours. Tickets on these routes run $30 to $50; those under 26 receive a sizable discount.

The one daily direct train from Budapest takes 7½ hours and passes through a tiny corner of Croatia; British citizens need no visa for this, but Americans, Canadians, Australians, New Zealanders, and Irish will need to stop by the Croatian Embassy in Budapest at Nógradi u. 28b (☎ **155-1522;** open Monday through Friday

9am to 2pm; take bus 21 from Moszkva tèr) for a free transit visa, issued on the spot. You can avoid this problem by going from Budapest to Ljubljana via Vienna.

4 Getting Around

BY TRAIN The Slovene train system is reliable and well organized, but because of Slovenia's mountainous terrain, stations are often distant from the most interesting sights in rural towns. Buses are equal in price and speed, and superior in comfort and convenience.

BY BUS Slovenia's buses are run by dozens of different operators, but they all use the same stations and follow the timetables posted there. Buses are much nicer than elsewhere in Eastern Europe: roomy and comfortable, with luggage space below. You can get tickets from windows at stations, but many people just buy them on board.

BY CAR Driving in Slovenia is likely to be a pleasure. Roads are well engineered, there is a useful, though incomplete, toll motorway system, and with tourists staying away right now, summer traffic jams are fairly light. Gas is cheaper than elsewhere in Eastern Europe—about 61 tolars (45¢) per liter. Speed limits are 120kmph (75 m.p.h.) on motorways, 80kmph (50 m.p.h.) on other roads, and 60kmph (35 m.p.h.) in built-up areas.

Car Rentals Several multinational firms as well as some smaller private agencies have rental offices in Ljubljana; as usual, the only affordable deals come when you reserve from outside the country, through one of the multinationals. At last report, Budget offered the best prices, with weekly unlimited-mileage rates starting at about $150 as long as you reserve from abroad.

Suggested Itineraries

If You Have 3 Days

If you want to see a city, base yourself in Ljubljana with a day trip to either Bled or Postojna. If you want to relax, base yourself in Bled and make a day trip to Ljubljana.

If You Have a Week

Spend at least three days in Ljubljana, saving one for a day trip to Postojna; spend another two or three days in Bled, and consider exploring some of the areas of the country that we don't cover, such as the Adriatic seacoast, the famous stables at Lipica, or the areas upvalley from Bled like Kranjska Gora and Lake Bohinj.

5 Enjoying Slovenia on a Budget

THE $30-A-DAY-BUDGET

It's not difficult to live on $30 a day in Slovenia; if you travel with a companion, you'll be able to afford to stay in hotels. Solo travelers will have to stay in private rooms and order carefully at restaurants to stay within the $30 budget.

ACCOMMODATIONS If you have a car, you can save money at the same time as you take advantage of a network of (at last count 77) farms across Slovenia that accommodate paying guests—many in splendid Alpine settings. They are all listed in a free brochure available from the tourist office or from VAS, the agency that manages the network, at Miklošičeva cesta 4,61000 Ljubljana (☎ **061/219-447**; fax 061/219-388). You can reserve through VAS, or directly to the farms. Prices per person per night (including breakfast) range from 18 to 28 DM ($10.55 to $16.45), depending on the category and the season. Meals are often available for 6 to 7 DM ($3.50 to $4.10) per person apiece.

TIPPING Most restaurant bills do not include service. Leave a small tip (10% is plenty), or simply round up the bill.

Fast Facts: Slovenia

American Express The Atlas travel agency at Mestni trg 6 in the old town (☎ **222-741**; fax 222-711) represents American Express in Slovenia, in a limited way. They hold mail for clients and allow you to cash personal checks, but they do not replace lost checks or sell new ones (although they can help you arrange replacement through a better-equipped AmEx office). Open Monday through Friday from 9am to 5pm, Saturday from 9am to noon.

Bookstores The best selection of foreign books is in the Mladinska Knjiga shop on the second floor of Slovenska cesta 29 (☎ **125-0196**). It's open Monday through Friday from 9am to 7:30pm and Saturday from 8am to 1pm.

Business Hours Typical business hours are Monday through Friday from 9 or 10am to 6 or 7pm, and on Saturday from 8 or 9am until noon or 1pm. Nearly everything (including many restaurants) shuts on Sundays.

Currency Exchange Banks always have the best rates. The main downtown Ljubljanska Banka office at the corner of Slovenka cesta and Subičeva ulica has excellent rates, charges no commission on traveler's checks, and stays open Monday through Friday from 8am to 6pm and Saturday from 8am to noon. At other times, head for the information office in the train station, where the rates are not outstanding, but fair.

Doctors/Dentists The Slovene health care system is better than those elsewhere in Eastern Europe. Ask your host, your hotel staff, your embassy, or the tourist office for a referral.

Drugstores Either the drugstore at Prešernov trg 5, or the one a few blocks away at Miklošičeva cesta 24, keeps someone on 24-hour duty (you must ring the bell after hours).

Electricity The electric power is 220–240 volts, 50 cycles, AC.

Embassies/Consulates Citizens of Australia, Canada, Ireland, and New Zealand can call the British Embassy, which will put them in touch with their embassies in Vienna or in the case of Ireland, with the local EC representation.

- **United Kingdom:** Trg republike 3, 4th floor. (☎ **125-7191**).
- **United States:** Pražakova ul. 4. (☎ **301-427**).

Emergencies For the police, call 92; in case of fire, call 93; for an ambulance, dial 94.

Laundry There's a friendly, modern Laundromat called "Tič" (☎ **126-3233**) in the basement of Building IX of the Ljubljana university complex. The building is between Skapinova ulica and Cesta I. To reach it, take bus 14 to the Študentsko naselje stop, then ask for Building IX. A complete load (wash and dry) costs 630 tolars ($4.80). Open Monday through Friday from 8am to 2pm and 4 to 7pm, Saturday from 8am to 2pm.

Maps The tourist office will give you a free map of central Ljubljana, as will almost any hotel or travel agency. Better maps with street indexes are on sale in bookstores for about 500 tolars ($3.80). For the country's best selection of maps, head to the Slovene cartographic institute's outlet, a tiny shop called Kod & Kam (How & Where), at Trg francoske revolucije 7 (☎ **213-537**). It's open Monday through Friday from 9am to 7pm, Saturday from 8am to 1pm.

Newspapers/Magazines Foreign papers are scarce in Slovenia. The best place to try is the newsstand of the Grand Hotel Union at Miklošičeva cesta 1 in Ljubljana, which usually has yesterday's editions of the *International Herald Tribune* and British dailies.

Post Office The main post office at Slovenska cesta 32 is open Monday through Friday from 7am to 8pm, and Saturday from 7am to 1pm. You can make phone calls and mail letters 24 hours a day at the branch at Pražakova ul. 3, near the train station.

Safety Ljubljana and Slovenia are in a quiet, sleepy corner of the Alps. You may see refugees from the troubles farther south in the Balkans, and the odd skinhead, but problems here are relatively unlikely.

Telephones Pay phones take tokens, which come in sizes A, B, and C. The small size A token, which costs 20 tolars (15¢), is enough for about a 10-minute local call. It's cheaper to call using magnetic cards, which you can buy at post offices, but very few pay phones outside of post offices accept the cards. You can also make calls from booths at most post offices; you pay when you're done. Be aware that international calls from Slovenia cost considerably more than from most of the other countries in this book—calls to America, for instance, cost 288 tolars ($2.20) per minute. At press time, there was no USA Direct service from Slovenia. Dial 901 to reach a Slovene operator, who will probably speak English.

The country code for Slovenia is 386. Remember to drop the first zero of the city code when calling from abroad.

Time Slovenia is in the same Central European time zone as Warsaw, Prague, and Budapest, one hour ahead of London and six hours ahead of New York.

Water Tap water is safe to drink.

33

Ljubljana

LJUBLJANA (PRONOUNCED *LYOOB*-LYONNA) IS A SMALL CITY OF UNDER 300,000 PEOPLE, where people dress conservatively and you always need reservations for dinner. It does not entirely feel like the first city of a fully independent nation—and there lies much of its appeal. Ljubljana's peacefulness and orderliness, its well-washed shop windows and sense of reserved prosperity, are in marked contrast to every other Eastern European capital. The city may remind you instead of a Western European provincial center, which is exactly what it was under several hundred years of Habsburg rule. The legacy of upper-middle-class civic-mindedness survives in Ljubljana's beautiful town center, divided by the Ljubljanica River and dwarfed by the hill and the castle that spawned the city in the first place.

Probably no city in Europe was so influenced by the vision of one single architect as Ljubljana was by Jože Plečnik (1872–1957). He either designed or rebuilt dozens of the city center's monuments and buildings, including the Triple Bridge at Prešernov trg, the promenade along the banks of the Ljubljanica, and Križanke, the old castle-fortress at the south end of downtown. A visit to the two branches of Ljubljana's architectural museum is a highlight of any visit to Slovenia.

1 Orientation

ARRIVING

BY PLANE Brnik Airport is about 40 minutes' drive north of Ljubljana. It's a small airport with only one level, but modern and welcoming. When you arrive, you must exit to the street and then reenter the departure hall to reach the airport information desk, airline counters, newsstands, and the Kompas office that will change money and give you a free map of the city. Both special Adria Airways buses (timed to connect with flights), and regular city buses (on an independent timetable), leave from the parking lot and cost 300 tolars ($2.30). They bring you to the square in front of Ljubljana's central train and bus stations. If you need a taxi, it's more economical to pick one up there, as the airport is very distant and the Adria buses have luggage space.

BY TRAIN OR BUS The train station and the bus station are together at the north edge of downtown. A 24-hour information and currency-exchange desk, a left-luggage office (also open 24 hours), and a photo booth are near the international ticket counter in the train station. Taxis stop outside. The tourist office and the central business district are a 10-minute walk away; turn right as you exit the station, walk about three blocks, and then make a left onto Slovenska cesta. Bus 9 follows the exact same route under motor power.

TOURIST INFORMATION

Ljubljana's **Tourist Information Center** (Turistični Informativni Center) at Slovenska cesta 35 (☎ **224-222;** fax 222-115) will give you all the information you need on Ljubljana and has limited information on the rest of Slovenia. They also change money and reserve private rooms (see "Where to Stay," below). Opening hours are Monday through Friday from 8am to 7pm, and Saturday and Sunday from 8am to noon and 4 to 7pm. You can walk here from the train station, or take bus 9 for two stops.

CITY LAYOUT

The castle hill, bounded to the west and north by the narrow, curving river Ljubljanica, is the central feature of Ljubljana. In a slim ribbon of land on its lower slopes, between the river and the line where the grade becomes too steep to build, Ljubljana's medieval inhabitants raised the oldest houses of the old town. The opposite bank of the river was built up later, and became the modern center of town. Slovenska cesta, Ljubljana's modern and uninspiring main street, bisects it from north to south. A ring of busy boulevards now circles the modern center; the train station lies along the northern section of the ring. Beyond the ring rise high-rise suburbs, which are quite nice by Eastern European standards.

The statue in Prešernov trg of France Prešeren, Slovenia's most famous poet, is a favorite meeting point before an evening out. Beside it is the Triple Bridge. Because it's too much trouble to climb to the top of the castle hill, this square and bridge is the day-to-day spiritual center of town.

The tourist office's information brochure lays out an excellent self-guided downtown walking tour route, coordinated with yellow signposts placed throughout the city. If you'd like, you might spend your first half day in Ljubljana getting acquainted with the city in this way. However, Ljubljana is small enough that you may do just as well on your own.

2 Getting Around

BY BUS Ljubljana's green-and-white buses run just about everywhere from early morning until almost midnight. You board through the front doors only, pay the driver, and exit through the rear doors only. Buses are a little nicer than in other Eastern European countries, and a little more expensive: 60 tolars (45¢) if you pay with coins as you board (no change given), or 43 tolars (30¢) if you buy a little green bus token (*žeton*) from any newsstand.

BY TAXI Taxis are easy to find in Ljubljana, but can only be an occasional luxury for the budget traveler, as prices are comparable to those in Western Europe and the Ljubljana bus system is excellent.

ON FOOT Everything I've listed in Ljubljana, with the exception of Fužine Castle, the university Laundromat, and the Austrian Airlines office, is within reasonable walking distance of the town center.

3 Where to Stay

PRIVATE ROOMS The Tourist Information Center at Slovenska cesta 35 (☎ **224-222;** fax 222-115) maintains a sensibly centralized list of people in Ljubljana who rent out private rooms, and will be happy to call and reserve for you. The cost is $10 per person per night.

HOTELS

Hotel Park, Tabor 9, 61000 Ljubljana. ☎ **061/133-1306.** Fax 061/321-352. 120 rms (60 with bath). TEL **Directions:** From the train station, walk left two blocks and then turn right down Metelkova ulica for two blocks.

Rates (including breakfast): 2,510 tolars ($19.30) single without bath, 3,110 tolars ($23.90) single with bath; 3,920 tolars ($30.15) double without bath, 4,920 tolars ($37.80) double with bath. Students receive 20% off these rates. MC.

In a 12-story socialist-era building in the center of Ljubljana, the Park gets a bad rap around town because the upper six floors are reserved for "long-term" guests—largely

Ljubljana Orientation

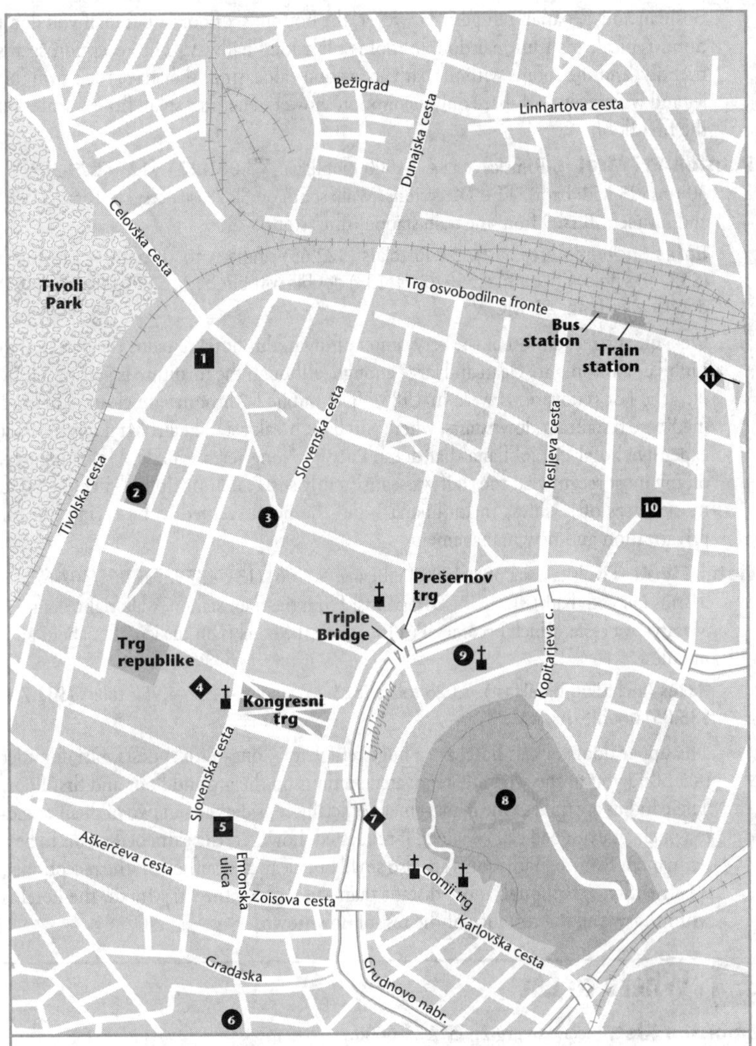

Tourist Information Office 3

ACCOMMODATIONS

Hotel Park 10

Hotel Tivoli 1

Pansion Pri Mraku 5

DINING

Emonska Klet 4

Mao-Tai 11

Romeo 7

ATTRACTIONS

Central Market 9

Ljubljana Architectural Museum (Plečnik Collection) 6

Ljubljana Castle 8

National Gallery 2

† Church

9050

Bosnian and Croatian refugees. However, the bottom six floors are fine, if you don't mind typical, institutional double rooms off a long hallway. The reception seems friendly, and the rooms without bath are a good value, since they have their own toilet and washbasin and share only a common shower. There's a small fitness center on the first floor.

Pansion Pri Mraku, Rimska cesta 4, 61000 Ljubljana. ☎ **061/223-412** or **223-387.** 30 rms (23 with bath). TEL **Directions:** Walk south on Slovenska cesta to Rimska cesta and turn left. **Bus:** 9 from the train station (three stops).

Rates (including breakfast): 2,945 tolars ($22.65) single without bath, 4,215 tolars ($32.40) single with bath; 4,290 tolars ($33) double without bath, 5,990 tolars ($46.05) double with bath. AE, MC, V.

On a quiet street almost at the very center of town, this hotel remains the best deal in Ljubljana. Rooms are clean and large enough, although the furniture is getting a little old (the last renovations were in 1980). The public bathrooms are clean. There's a mediocre restaurant downstairs, where you'll eat breakfast. The Pri Mraku is the least expensive hotel in Ljubljana that doesn't accept "long-term" guests. Unfortunately, on my most recent visit the staff was consistently surly and unhelpful—in contrast to most places of business in Ljubljana—and the hotel seemed to be crying out for privatization and new management.

Hotel Tivoli, Tivolska cesta 30, 61000 Ljubljana. ☎ **061/131-4359.** Fax 061/302-671. 31 rms (all with bath). TEL TV **Directions:** From the train station, walk right along Masarykova cesta, which becomes Tivolska cesta; the hotel is on the left after about 10 minutes.

Rates (including breakfast): 3,026 tolars ($23.25) single; 4,252–4,952 tolars ($32.70–$38.05) double. AE, MC.

The upper floors of this hotel are a huge refuge for "long-term" guests, but don't let that blind you to the separate, renovated sections on the ground floor and first floor. These rooms are tiny, so the management officially considers all but two of them singles to which an extra bed can be added if requested; however, the extra bed seems to be a permanent feature. Bathrooms are also small but clean and sufficient, the receptionist was friendly, and though more distant than the Park or the Pri Mraku, the hotel is within easy walking distance of the rest of downtown.

4 Where to Eat

Emonska Klet, Plečnikov trg 2. ☎ **125-6000.**

Cuisine: SLOVENE. **Reservations:** Recommended. **Directions:** Walk to the square on the east side of the Maximarket department store, near Trg republike.
Prices: Soups 170 tolars ($1.30); main courses 720–1,100 tolars ($5.50–$8.45). MC.
Open: Mon–Fri noon–4pm and 7pm–1am, Sat 7pm–1am.

This basement restaurant takes its name from Emona, the Roman name for Ljubljana. Inside, the arched stone ceilings do lend it a slightly ancient feel. The menu is small and traditional; locals know Emonska Klet primarily for its beef goulash, which is served with home-baked bread after midnight for 400 tolars ($3.05). Lunch specials here start at 600 tolars ($4.60). You may want to make dinner reservations for 7pm in order to avoid the musician, who plays Monday through Friday from 9pm, and on Saturday from 8pm.

Mao-Tai, Šmartinska cesta 3. ☎ **131-0259.**

Cuisine: CHINESE. **Reservations:** Recommended in the evening. **Directions:** From the train station, walk left about six blocks to where the street curves, and turn right a half block.
Prices: Soups 100–140 tolars (75¢–$1.05); main courses 420–700 tolars ($3.20–$5.35).
Open: Daily 1–10pm.

Though it's a few blocks away from the parts of town that tourists are likely to frequent, Mao-Tai is one of the few restaurants in downtown Ljubljana with a seating area large enough so that you can probably get away without reservations at dinner. Dishes also come in tremendous portions.

Romeo, Stari trg 6. ☎ **216-979.**

Cuisine: PIZZA. **Reservations:** Recommended on weekend evenings. **Directions:** Walk through the old town several blocks rightward from the Triple Bridge.
Prices: Pizzas 360–570 tolars ($2.75–$4.35); ice cream 270 tolars ($2.05). MC.
Open: Daily 11am–1am.

This small place serves succulent pizzas with excellent crusts after an amazingly short waiting time. It's also open on Sundays, unlike most restaurants in Ljubljana. The ice-cream selection vaults it over the competing pizzerias in town.

5 Attractions

Ljubljana Castle [Ljubljanski Grad]. ☎ **132-7216.**

Ljubljana's fortress-crowned castle hill towers dramatically and suddenly over the city, inviting comparison with cities like Edinburgh and Salzburg. Most of Ljubljana Castle dates from the 16th and 17th centuries, when it was the seat of government for what was then the Habsburg province of Carniola. The chapel dates from as early as 1489, however, and in fact humans have taken advantage of the natural defenses of the castle hill for at least 3,000 years. By the 20th century the complex had gotten quite run-down; Jože Plečnik, who viewed the castle hill as the spiritual center of Slovene civilization, actually wanted to tear down the castle itself and replace it with a futuristic temple in the shape of an eight-sided cone, which would house the Slovene Parliament. In the end, renovations began in the 1960s and continue today.

Begin your visit by hiking up along one of the steep paths from the old town. If you're not too winded you can continue up to the lookout tower on the cityward side of the castle, visiting the chapel on the way. By the main castle entrance, on the side away from the town, is a slightly dungeonlike café, which at least manages to stay cool in summer. Above the café is Ljubljana's main marriage hall, and adjoining it is a pentagonal tower with a modest but attractive (and free) exhibit of artifacts found during the castle renovations.

Admission: Lookout tower and chapel, 90 tolars (65¢); pentagonal tower, free.

Open: Lookout tower and chapel, daily 10am–dusk; pentagonal tower, Tues, Thurs, and Sun 11am–6pm, Wed and Fri 1–6pm; café, Tues–Sun 11am–midnight. The surrounding paths and parkland are always open.

Ljubljana Architectural Museum–Fužine Castle [Ljubljanski Arhitekturni Muzej–Grad Fužine], Studenec 2a. ☎ **140-9798.**

Opened in 1992, the main branch of the Architectural Museum occupies a lovely renovated Renaissance castle set splendidly on the banks of the Ljubljanica just outside town. The exhibition revolves around a fantastic collection of photographs of buildings designed by Jože Plečnik in Vienna, Prague, and Ljubljana, which was originally exhibited at the Pompidou Center in Paris. Also on display are scale models of some of Plečnik's Ljubljana creations, including the Triple Bridge, as well as several of his original chairs. A soon-to-open restaurant should add to the appeal of this excellent museum.

Admission: 100 tolars (75¢), 50 tolars (35¢) students.

Open: Mon–Fri 10am–3pm. **Bus:** 20 (marked "Fužine") from Kongresni trg to the last stop; then walk from the turnaround 50 meters to the white building by the river.

Ljubljana Architectural Museum–Plečnik Collection [Plečnikova Zbirka], Karunova ul. 4. ☎ **213-008.**

This is Jože Plečnik's house, which the eccentric bachelor architect designed for himself and his three bachelor brothers. Half of the house is now an architectural study center and library of Plečnik's drawings and sketches. The rest remains mostly as he left it when he died in 1957. Unlike most museums of this sort, there are no cordons in the rooms, so visitors can walk all around, enjoy the house's turrets and terraces, and peer closely at Plečnik's pencils, brushes, and drafting tools. You'll leave with a feeling of intimate acquaintance with the artistic world of early 20th-century Central Europe. The walk from downtown brings you through the attractive neighborhoods of Krakovo and Trnovo.

Admission: Free.

Open: Tues and Thurs 10am–2pm, or by arrangement (call a day in advance). **Directions:** Walk about five blocks south of Trg francoske revolucije; the museum is just past the church. **Bus:** 9 from the train station (four stops).

OTHER ATTRACTIONS

Ljubljana is the home of Slovenia's **National Museum** (Narodni Muzej), **National Gallery** (Narodna Galeria), and **Gallery of Modern Art** (Moderna Galeria). The three museums are next to each other along Prešernova cesta at the west edge of downtown. The National Museum contains mostly Roman artifacts and natural history displays; the National Gallery displays some Gothic sculptures and a few rooms of Slovene Romantic and impressionist works; the Gallery of Modern Art has only visiting exhibitions until its collection of Slovene art reopens. None of these collections is particularly impressive. Each is open Tuesday through Saturday from 10am to 6pm, and on Sunday from 10am to 1pm; admission fees range from 50 to 200 tolars (35¢ to $1.50). The **Tivoli Park,** across Tivolska cesta and the train tracks from the museums, is a nice place to walk, and the castle in the park sometimes houses exhibitions.

6 Savvy Shopping

WINE Slovenia's sunny, south-facing hillsides produce some good wines, and the place to sample them is **Vinoteka,** Dunajska cesta 10–18 (☎ **131-5015**), a wine shop, bar, and restaurant in the basement of the round building of the Ljubljana fairgrounds. The wine shop has a comprehensive selection of attractive Slovene vintages to suit every price range, and the staff to help you select one. It's open Monday through Friday from 10am to 7pm, and on Saturday from 9am to 1pm. The restaurant, which is open Monday through Friday from 10am to 11pm, has complete lunch menus for 800 tolars ($6.15)—not including wine. Reservations are strongly recommended, especially in summer and for evening meals. During fairs, the shop and restaurant are open maximum hours on weekends as well; the Wine Fair is, of course, the best time to come (in early September). To reach Vinoteka on foot from the train station (about 10 minutes), walk right to the first main intersection, then turn right under the overpass. MasterCard and VISA accepted.

SOUVENIRS A tiny one-room shop called **365,** at Mestni trg 9 (☎ **331-186**), sells Slovene handcrafts and traditional decorative and kitchen earthenware items, made by potters from different parts of Slovenia, at very reasonable prices. You can pick up small gifts here around Christmas and Eastertime. It's open Monday through Saturday from 10am to 8pm.

CENTRAL MARKET The outdoor part of the market, on Vodnikov trg, is the place to pick up fruit in summer, or a hat or scarf in winter. The covered section of the market, which stretches along the riverside Adamič-Lundrovo nabrezje between the Triple Bridge and the Zmajski (Dragon) Bridge, was designed by—you guessed it—Jože Plečnik. The best time to come is Sunday morning, when there's a flea market here as well.

7 Moving On—Travel Services

BY PLANE The Austrian Airlines office is outside the center of town, at Dunajska cesta 107 (☎ **168-4099** or **168-4373**). It's open Monday through Thursday from 8am to 5pm, and Friday from 8am to noon. You can reach it on bus 6 or 8 from Slovenska cesta in the town center.

The Adria Airways town ticket office is at Gosposvetska cesta 6 (☎ **313-312**). It's open Monday through Friday from 8am to 7pm and Saturday from 8am to 1pm. Adria Airways buses to Brnik airport leave from the Ljubljana bus station about 80 minutes before each flight; the trip takes 40 minutes and costs 300 tolars ($2.30). The airport is distant and the Adria buses have luggage space, so if you need a taxi, take it only to the bus station, and then switch to the bus. For airport information, call **064/222-700, 064/261-229,** or **061/261-981.**

BY TRAIN Most of the staff at the train information counter in the station speak English, although they are less than overwhelmingly helpful and friendly. You'll have to ask specifically for the brochure that lists timings for all international trains to and from Ljubljana (in English), or for the comprehensive timetable (*vozni red,* in Slovene only). For information over the phone, call 131-5167. The ticket windows, both for international trains (next to the information counter) and for domestic trains (in the hall outside) are open 24 hours a day; again, most staff speak English. Those under 26 receive about 30% off all international fares. For example, the one-way fare to Budapest is 3,800 tolars ($29.20); if you're under 26, it's only 2,950 tolars ($22.65). If you qualify, make sure to ask for this discount when you buy your ticket.

BY BUS Schedules are posted inside the bus station building on the square in front of the train station. You can buy tickets at the windows nearby, or on the bus. There's an information window (☎ **133-6136**) across from the ticket windows, where English is sometimes spoken.

8 Easy Excursions from Ljubljana

The Caves at Postojna

If you ever wondered what Hades is like, don't miss Postojnska Jama (the Postojna Caves), located in the town of Postojna about 32 miles southwest of Ljubljana on the highway to the coast. With about 12 miles (20km) of discovered passageways, Postojnska Jama is a vast, self-contained underground world. Unlike some of the "dry" caverns in parts of the United States, a vast, ice-cold underground river flows through the lower levels of Postojnska Jama, and water seeps down from ground level through the limestone roof of the cave, creating fantastic stalactites and stalagmites. The caves are also home to a diminutive amphibian, *Proteus anguinus,* found nowhere else in the world. Blind and about a foot long, these newts live in a small pond, which you'll see as you exit the caves.

You start the tour aboard a train that whizzes through some very narrow passageways. From the end of the tracks you walk with your group through an incredible series of caves with endless limestone formations and halls whose immense size will stagger you. In no case are visitors allowed to roam around unescorted.

No matter how hot or cold it is outside, the temperature in the caves is a very cool and damp 47°F; wear warm clothing. You can rent an overcoat for 100 tolars (75¢) at the entrance if you have forgotten. You don't need waterproof footwear if you are only going on the standard 1½ hour cave tour.

In July and August, tours leave every hour from 9am to 7pm; in May, June, and September, every hour from 9am to 6pm; in April and October, every two hours from 9am to 5pm; in March, every two hours from 9am to 3pm; and from November to February, Monday through Friday at 10am and 2pm and Saturday and Sunday every two hours from 10am to 4pm. The tours run every day. Arrive early, as the trains do fill up; the first visit of the day is usually the least crowded. You can call **067/23041** for more information. They charge a steep admission fee of 20 DM ($11.75) for adults and 10 DM ($5.85) for children, but it's certainly worth it, and there's a 20% reduction from October to March.

Cave guides discourage photography, especially during high season when the caves can be crowded and camera flashes annoying. This is partly for your own benefit, since the dim lighting makes even a strong flash useless at distances over six feet, and wider views impossible without a tripod or very high speed film (at least 800 ASA).

More adventurous travelers might prefer to visit the Pivka, Črna, or Planinska caves—smaller, wilder caverns in the Postojna system. The cave administration organizes regular tours to these in the summer, and will run tours on demand all year for groups of at least three people, costing 10 DM ($5.85) per person. You need to bring waterproof boots.

Buses to Postojna leave Ljubljana about every hour from 5am to 11pm; the trip itself takes an hour and costs 420 tolars ($3.20). From the bus station, signs guide you along the 15-minute walk to the cave entrance just outside of town. The train station is twice as far away and the trains from Ljubljana are half as frequent. There is a large tourist complex outside the cave entrance for souvenirs, changing money, eating, and spending the night (though it's better to stay in Ljubljana).

If you've come by car you can also visit the Predjamski Grad, a Renaissance castle in the mouth of another cave about five miles northwest of Postojnska Jama. Nestled against the slopes of Mount Hrušica, this old fortress was once the lair of the rebel knight Erasmus Predjamski, who was betrayed by his servants and murdered while sitting on the toilet.

LAKE BLED

GETTING THERE • By Bus Buses from Ljubljana to Bled leave every hour from 6am to 10:30pm, and take about an hour and 15 minutes for 445 tolars ($3.40). The Bled bus station is in the center of town near the church. You can also take a train, but it stops a few miles away from Bled, in the town of Lesce.

ESSENTIALS Bled's telephone code is 064.

INFORMATION The Bled Tourist Association (Turistično društvo Bled) maintains an office at cesta Svobode 15 (☎ **064/77409**), on the lakeward side of the Hotel Park, whose staff should be able to help you. It's open daily from 8am to 6pm; in November (and generally in winter when there's no snow) only from 8am to 3pm.

Nestled in the Julian Alps at a height of 1,644 feet, Lake Bled has attracted visitors since the time of the Romans. In the middle of the lake, a tiny island with a 17th-century church at its center reflects almost perfectly on the lake's emerald waters. Trees line the lakeshore and crickets chirp in the forest of this peaceful enclave, creating the perfect Alpine wonderland.

The small town of Bled (pop. 5,600) abuts the east end of the lake, and hosts several hotels, restaurants, and other tourist facilities. A medieval-looking castle (actually from 1700) on a hilltop 330 feet above draws visitors in search of the best vantage point.

WHAT TO SEE & DO

Ask at any hotel or business for a copy of the 70-page booklet *Bled Tourist News,* which lists cultural events as well as important addresses and descriptions of nearby sights and tours. Don't miss taking a **boat** to see the Church of St. Mary on Bled Island; try to get an early start in summer to avoid the tourist crush. Boats leave from docks near the Hotel Park, the Hotel Jelovica, and the Pension Mlino from 8am to 6pm in summer, and from 11am to 3pm in fall and winter until the ice freezes and again in the spring. The fare is about 750 tolars ($5.75) round-trip. You can also **swim** in the lake, but only in July and August is the water comfortable.

There are two thermal springs in town, tennis, horseback riding, rowing, bicycling, and hiking paths originally laid out in the mid-1800s, when Bled started to become a popular health resort. Or you can walk around the entire lake in about two hours. There's also an 18-hole golf course in Lesce, 1½ miles east of Bled. In the winter, you can downhill-ski at nearby Zatrnik or Straža; back at Bled, after the lake freezes, you can rent skates and glide out to the island.

Those in search of even more Alpine beauty can continue to Lake Bohinj, a less known but equally stunning lake to the southwest of Bled, underneath Mount Triglav; or northeast to Kranjska Gora, near the Italian and Austrian borders. Bohinj and Kranjska Gora boast Slovenia's highest and longest downhill and cross-country ski trails.

WHERE TO STAY

PRIVATE ROOMS Private room prices are standardized in Bled, with singles costing 34 DM ($20) and doubles 54 DM ($31.75). Breakfast is not included. Stays of at least three nights earn a 30% discount, and the basic rate also falls by about 10%

between September 1 and November 15 and again between March 15 and July 1. You must reserve rooms through one of two agencies: Globtour, at Ljubljanska cesta 7 in the Hotel Krim (☎ **064/77909**; fax 064/78185), or Kompas, at Ljubljanska cesta 4 in the shopping complex (☎ **064/77-235**). At least one of the offices is open every day until at least 7pm; if you're going to arrive later, you can call ahead.

HOTELS

Hotel Astoria, Prešernova cesta 44, 64260 Bled. ☎ **064/77871.** Fax 064/77850. 72 rms (all with bath). TEL

Rates (including breakfast): 87 DM ($51.15) double. Half board 10 DM ($5.85) per person extra. 5% off Sep–Christmas and Mar–Apr, and another 5% off for stays of at least four days. MC, V.

On the hillside a block above the bus station, this hotel was once reserved for members of the Yugoslav People's Army. It's fundamentally in typical Late Socialist Hotel style, but so well disguised that it actually feels nice: half the rooms have lake views and terraces, and there's a pleasant reception area and restaurant, modern rooms, and a reasonably attractive facade. You may find the two-room suites worth the extra money, at only about 10 DM ($5.85) more expensive than doubles.

Pension Mlino, cesta Svobode 45, 64260 Bled. ☎ **064/77321.** Fax 064/76021. 12 rms (all with bath). **Directions:** Follow the road along the south shore of the lake about 15 to 20 minutes' walk from the center of Bled.

Rates (including breakfast): July–Aug, 104 DM ($61.15) double; May–June and Sept–Oct 15, 86 DM ($50.55); Oct 16–Apr, 56 DM ($32.90). Half pension 12 DM ($7.05) per person extra. MC.

This is a small lakeside guesthouse with a restaurant on the first floor, in the village of Mlino, quite near Lake Bled's island. The room decoration feels more rural, but just as comfortable, as in the larger hotels in town, and the location is also quieter and quainter. The rates are somewhat negotiable, especially if you plan a longer stay, and you should bring the tourist office's Bled hotel price list along to increase your bargaining power if need be.

WHERE TO EAT

Okarina, Riklijeva ul. 9. ☎ **77458.**

Cuisine: INDIAN/INTERNATIONAL. **Reservations:** Recommended. **Directions:** Walk from the church away from the lake and look to the right.

Prices: Soups 200–400 tolars ($1.50–$3.05); vegetarian main courses with rice 800–950 tolars ($6.15–$7.30).

Open: Daily 11am–1am. **Closed:** For two weeks in Nov or Dec.

At Okarina, you not only dine well but eat healthily, with an emphasis on excellent Indian vegetarian dishes. Non-Indian meat dishes are more expensive, ranging from 1,000 to 1,700 tolars ($7.65 to $13.05). You can fill your plate from the well-stocked salad bar for 460 tolars ($3.50), or you can just devour the tasty rolls and crudité plate, which you receive in exchange for the obligatory 220 tolar ($1.65) cover charge. The elegant interior features a wood-beamed ceiling and foreign newspapers. On Saturdays, live Indian music starts at 8pm.

Getting to Know Romania

34

MOST AMERICANS ASSOCIATE THE MYSTERIOUS LAND OF ROMANIA WITH THE legendary vampire, Count Dracula of Transylvania, or his modern flesh-and-blood incarnation, the Communist leader Nicolae Ceauşescu. But the traveler who ventures beyond this infamous image is richly rewarded—Romania is by far the most varied in landscape and cultures of the Eastern European countries. Count Metternich once said about it: "Romania? A profusion, not a nation."

In many ways Romania (pop. 25 million) differs from Eastern Europe's other countries—everything from language (a Romance, not a Slavic, tongue) to economic development (it's Eastern Europe's least prosperous country). Progress and modernity have come slowly to parts of the country like the remote north and some medieval towns, and you'll feel like you're walking into another age when you enter them.

What to Expect

Romania is definitely worth exploring, but traveling there on your own will be quite an adventure, combining few comforts with many challenges. Forewarned is forearmed. While conditions are steadily improving, only the most experienced travelers should attempt travel there in these days of change and confusion. In return for your intrepid explorer's spirit, you'll encounter sights rarely seen by Westerners: remote villages where peasants have maintained their folk arts and a traditional way of life; unique medieval monasteries with churches richly decorated with vivid and well-preserved 400-year-old frescoes; nature reserves teeming with wildlife in the Danube Delta, the crossroads of five major bird migration routes from Europe and Asia.

You will also bear witness to one of the century's key historical events. Much of the Soviet-era political and economic apparatus in other Eastern European countries has been swept away. Not so in Romania, where reform has happened only fitfully. Thus, the visitor can witness the historical spectacle of a crumbling repressive regime yielding in places to sprouts of liberated initiative and activity.

1 Geography, History & Politics

GEOGRAPHY

Located on the Balkan Peninsula, Romania borders the newly independent state of Moldova to the east, Ukraine to the north, Hungary and the republic of Serbia to the west, and Bulgaria to the south. A country half the size of France, Romania is every bit as varied in landscape and geography as its more famous Latin cousin, Italy: alpine mountains and vineyard-covered hills, lush green valleys and flat plains, the Danube wetlands and the Black Sea coast. Much of Romania is mountainous or hilly, with the Carpathian Mountains and Transylvanian Alps stretching across about a third of the country from the north to the southwest. Romania's highest peak is Mount Moldoveanu (8,344 feet) in the Făgăras Mountains, the country's most popular hiking area.

Many of its rivers originate in these mountains, and most flow into the Dunărea (Danube). The 1776-mile-long river flows east to west through the middle of Europe past eight countries and three of their capitals—and flows through Romania for 666 of these miles. Forming Romania's border with Bulgaria, the Danube empties into the Black Sea through the vast Danube Delta.

Prey to successive waves of invaders, Romania's borders have changed countless times over the course of history. In modern times, after World War I and the breakup

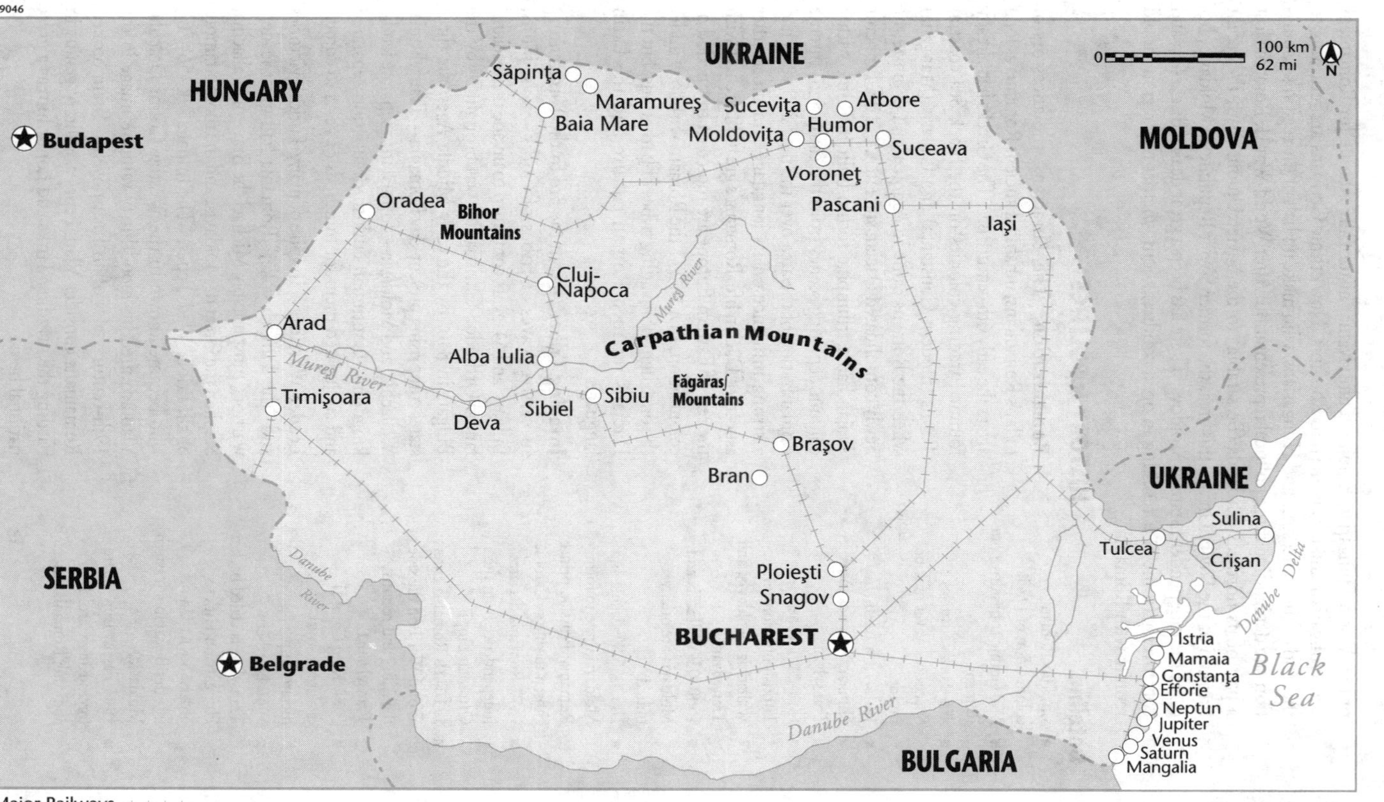
9046
HUNGARY
Budapest
UKRAINE
MOLDOVA
100 km
62 mi
0
N
Săpinţa
Maramureş
Baia Mare
Suceviţa
Arbore
Humor
Moldoviţa
Suceava
Voroneţ
Pascani
Iaşi
Oradea
Bihor Mountains
Cluj-Napoca
Mureş River
Arad
Carpathian Mountains
Alba Iulia
Făgăraş Mountains
Timişoara
Sibiel
Sibiu
Deva
Braşov
Bran
UKRAINE
Sulina
Tulcea
Crişan
Danube Delta
SERBIA
Danube River
Ploieşti
Snagov
BUCHAREST
Belgrade
Istria
Mamaia
Constanţa
Eforie
Neptun
Jupiter
Venus
Saturn
Mangalia
Black Sea
Danube River
BULGARIA
Major Railways

Romania

of the Austro-Hungarian Empire, Transylvania, historically a home for Romanians and Hungarians alike, was given to Romania. Now ethnic Germans are returning to the land of their ancestors and Hungarians, who make up half of the region's population, are demanding more political representation. After World War II, Romania lost a part of its northeastern lands (Bessarabia) to the Soviet Union. With the recent breakup of the Soviet Union, this area, the former Soviet Republic of Moldavia, became the independent state of Moldova. There has been a great deal of discussion and controversy (some of it resulting in open conflict) about whether this region should reunite with Romania.

HISTORY & POLITICS

Romanization The Thracians, the ancestors of today's Romanians, inhabited ancient Romania as long ago as the early 6th century B.C. The Greeks had already founded trading colonies on the Black Sea coast at Tomis (modern Constanţa) and Callatis (Mangalia) when the Romans came to conquer and colonize the newly consolidated Dacian state in A.D. 106. Emperor Trajan had a triumphal forum built in Rome with a column depicting scenes from the campaign. Intense Romanization of the area over the next 200 years had a strong influence on its language and most other aspects of Dacian life. Romania's great differences with the rest of Eastern Europe are rooted in this period of colonization. In A.D. 271 the Romans withdrew under the onslaught of invading tribes of barbarians, but the Dacians retained Roman culture and the Latin language.

Invading Tribes From the 3rd to the 10th century successive waves of tribes of Goths, Slavs, Huns, Bulgars, and Magyars continued to invade the Dacians' lands. Orthodox Christianity was brought in by the Bulgars in 846. By the early Middle Ages, the three states comprising present-day Romania—Transylvania, Wallachia, and Moldavia—formed into separate feudal kingdoms. Continual Turkish occupation separated and subjugated them for hundreds of years to come.

Leader-Warriors In spite of many Turkish victories and "the Turkish yoke," Romania had great leader-warriors, most notably Michael the Brave of Wallachia, Stephen the Great of Moldavia, and the most infamous of all, Prince Vlad Ţepeş, "The Impaler" (1456–76), who became known in the West as Count Dracula. Vlad acquired his bloodthirsty vampire image in the 19th-century tales of an Irish novelist, Bram Stoker. Romanians consider Vlad Ţepeş a military genius in battling the invading Turks and honor him as a great national hero.

Dateline

- A.D. 106 Roman colonization of Dacia.
- 271 Gothic tribes drive out Romans.
- 3rd–10th centuries Successive waves of tribes invade.
- 10th–13th centuries Hungary expands into Transylvania.
- 15th–16th centuries Turkish invasions of Wallachia, Moldavia, and Transylvania.
- 1600–01 Wallachia and Moldavia are briefly united.
- 1862–66 Wallachia and Moldavia unite to form Romania; Prussian prince chosen to rule as Carol I.
- 1877 Romania declares independence from the Ottoman Empire.
- 1916–18 Romania enters World War I on the side of the Allies and regains Transylvania.
- 1938 King Carol II declares a royal dictatorship.
- 1940 Northern Transylvania ceded back to Hungary on Hitler's orders: Soviet Union invades Bessarabia (eastern Moldavia).
- 1941 Fascist Iron Guard forces King Carol II to abdicate; Romania enters

➤

A National State In 1600 the three Romanian states were briefly united, but it was not until 1862 that Alexandru Ion Cuza created a national state by joining Wallachia and Moldavia. However, politicians from the newly joined states could not iron out a stable ruling coalition, and fear of Russian territorial ambitions catalyzed them to action. They chose Prussian Prince Carol I to stabilize their government and rule over them in 1866. After World War I—in the reign of King Ferdinand (Carol's nephew) and Queen Maria, when the Austro-Hungarian Empire had been defeated—Transylvania was returned to Romania and joined Wallachia and Moldavia to form a new state. During World War II, the fascist Romanian Iron Guard deposed King Carol II, and Romania entered the war alongside the Axis.

Communism In 1947 King Michael (the son of Carol II) formally abdicated and Romania became a socialist state under the rule of Gheorghe Gheorghiu-Dej. Gheorghiu-Dej differed from Soviet-supported Communist leaders in other Soviet Bloc countries by pursuing an isolationist tack that took Romania out of Moscow's direct sphere of influence. In 1962, Romania stopped participating in Warsaw Pact military maneuvers. In 1965 Nicolae Ceauçescu became president and continued Romania's maverick foreign policy, condemning the Soviet invasion of Czechoslovakia in 1968. In 1984 Romania sent athletes to the Los Angeles Olympics—even though the rest of the Warsaw Pact boycotted the games.

Despite its relative flexibility in its foreign policy, Communist Romania maintained one of Eastern Europe's most rigid, repressive societies. A vast police state grew to monitor its citizens, all forms of birth control were banned, conversations with foreigners were suspect, and a massive Ceauşescu cult was fostered.

Unlike the repressive government in East Germany, which at least achieved relative economic prosperity, Romania, once the "breadbasket of the Balkans," gradually emerged as the "basket case of the Balkans." Massive heavy-industry projects failed to bring economic prosperity, so the country exported many of its prime goods—including food and oil—in Ceauşescu's obsessive attempt to rid the country of foreign debt.

When Gorbachev's reforms offered new economic hope for Eastern Europe in the mid-1980's, Ceauşescu

Dateline

World War II by invading the Soviet Union with the Nazis.

- 1944 The Resistance captures the occupying Nazis in Romania, declares war on Germany; Soviet forces enter Romania.
- 1946 Under Soviet pressure, King Michael accedes to Communist-led government.
- 1947 King Michael abdicates; northern Transylvania is returned to Romania.
- 1958 Occupying Soviet army leaves Romania.
- 1965 Nicolae Ceauşescu becomes president of Romania.
- 1968 Government denounces Soviet invasion of Czechoslovakia.
- 1977 Major earthquake hits Bucharest and nearby areas.
- 1981 Government begins massive cutback in consumer goods and living standards to pay off foreign debt of $11 billion.
- 1987 Protest by 10,000 workers in Braşov broken up by police.
- 1988 Ceauşescu announces plan to demolish almost 8,000 small villages to make way for new housing projects.
- 1989 Massacre at Timişoara kills hundreds; revolution results in heavy fighting, finally toppling the government of Nicolae Ceauşescu; he and his wife, Elena, executed on Christmas Day.
- 1990 May election gives landslide victory to former Communist Ion Iliescu;

➤

Dateline

antigovernment protests continue; in June, government-sanctioned miners attack protesters in wild melee; protests continue throughout the year.

- 1991 Parliament adopts a new constitution.
- 1992 Political and economic reforms proceed slowly; Ion Iliescu reelected president.

remained the Bloc's staunchest opponent of change, declaring perestroika to be "in total contradiction with socialist principles."

The Revolution of 1989 After anti-Communist revolution had swept over Eastern Europe in the fall of 1989, the anger of the Romanian people finally boiled over when security forces killed hundreds of prodemocracy demonstrators in the western city of Timişoara in December 1989. Protests spread across the country and the army revolted against Ceauşescu. The bitter fighting that erupted in Bucharest and other Romanian cities was some of the worst seen in Europe since World War II. A few days after the revolution began, Ceauşescu was caught; on Christmas Day he and his wife Elena were executed.

In the first free postwar elections in May 1990, Romanians gave a commanding 89% approval to the National Salvation Front and Ion Iliescu—a former Communist and Ceauşescu ally who helped lead the revolution.

Despite a seemingly fair election, public order in the months after the revolution remained a bit shaky. Protests against the government continued through 1990, including a 53-day-long spring occupation of University Square in Bucharest; in June 1990 Interior Ministry forces cleared away these protesters, killing several demonstrators and wounding hundreds. The following day, with the sanction of the government, 7,000 miners swept through the streets to beat antigovernment protesters.

In October 1990 the government accelerated its plans to introduce a free-market economy by removing price subsidies and devaluing its currency. Popular protests and calls for the government to resign continued after these announcements. The government, in turn, showed limited tolerance for democratic freedoms at year's end—on Christmas Day—when it expelled King Michael from the country within 12 hours of his first visit since 1947.

Today Violence has eased up since the bloody days of the televised revolution, but for a great many Romanians little has improved since those wild days of great hope. Romania continues to have the lowest standard of living in Eastern Europe after Albania; and for many, change has created new economic dislocation and much new suffering: an unemployment rate of 30%, inflation of over 300%, and frozen salaries. Recovering from the consequences of Ceauşescu's maniacal policies and extravagant building projects that left economy ravaged, the country polluted, and the people destitute from exploitation and numb from years of repression may take decades. What is even more disheartening, as the fall 1992 election confirmed—many of his attitudes and institutions are likely to remain in place for some time.

Unlike in some other Eastern European countries, political and economic reform seems to be proceeding quite slowly, even stalling, in Romania. A new constitution was adopted by Parliament in December 1991, fully two years after the revolution.

IMPRESSIONS

No country is kinder to the wanderer who has good legs.
—Walter Starkie, *Raggle-Taggle,* 1933

2 Famous People

Vlad Ţepeş (1430–76) Ruling prince of Wallachia from 1456 to 1462 and in 1476, Ţepeş is still honored in Romania as a nationalist who valiantly fought invading Ottoman Turkish armies. He was infamous for slowly torturing his victims to death by impaling them on rounded wooden stakes, earning him the name "Vlad the Impaler." If that didn't suit his grisly appetite, he might lop off an arm or a leg and watch his victims slowly die, leaving the dead bodies to rot outside.

His father was given the Order of the Dragon or "dracul" for fighting the Turks. As the son of dracul, he gained the name dracula. But he was never considered a vampire until Bram Stoker characterized him as such in the 19th-century novel.

Stephen the Great (Ştefan cel Mare) (1434–1504) Prince of Moldavia from 1457 to 1504, Stephen is remembered in Romanian history for his resistance to Ottoman Turkish invaders in Moldavia. Following each victory against the Turks, he built a beautiful frescoed monastery, leaving Romania one of its greatest cultural heritages in the Bukovina region.

King Michael of Romania (1921–) The last king of Romania, Michael served from 1927 to 1930 and 1940 to 1947. During the war years he was a popular symbol of resistance to the pro-Nazi Iron Guard government, and he played an important role in the 1944 coup that ended Romania's Axis alliance. Under Soviet pressure, he abdicated in 1947. Since then he has lived in exile in Switzerland. In 1990 the new government at first barred him from making his first return visit to Romania. When they finally allowed him to visit on Christmas Day, they expelled him within 12 hours.

Nicolae Ceauşescu (1918–89) Communist leader of Romania for 24 years (1965–89), Nicolae Ceauşescu held the titles of president, general secretary of the Communist Party, supreme commander of the armed forces, and president of the State Council. He implemented a brutal, repressive society at home, but was frequently praised abroad for his strong Romanian nationalism and degree of independence from Moscow. He maintained a strong personality cult, and his likeness adorned street-corner banners, newspaper headlines, and television bulletins.

Ceauşescu's wife, Elena, served as first deputy prime minister, and many of his other relatives served in the government, leading locals to joke that while Russia proclaimed "socialism in one country" after its revolution, in Romania they saw "socialism in one family." Ceauşescu and his wife were tried by a military tribunal and executed on Christmas Day in 1989.

Constantin Brancuşi (1876–1957) A sculptor and pioneer of abstract art whose work exerted a tremendous influence on 20th-century art. He learned wood carving as a peasant boy in his native village, and after studying art in Bucharest, he left for Paris (where he spent most of the rest of his life, from 1904 on). Influenced by the interest in primitive carving and the modern art movement, he produced numerous increasingly abstract sculptures, the most famous of which is *Bird in Space.*

Nadia Comaneci (1961–) The 14-year-old gymnast who won the world's admiration by scoring the first perfect "10" score in the 1976 Montréal Olympics. She went on to win three gold medals at Montréal after earning seven perfect scores. In the 1980 Moscow Olympics she won two more gold medals and two silver medals. In late 1989, just a few weeks before the revolution, she fled Romania to Hungary, and then settled in the United States.

3 Cultural Notes

LITERATURE Like other Eastern European peoples, Romanians—dominated successively by Slavic, Greek, and French cultural influences—have had to struggle to develop an original literature. Drama, because of its public character, played a leading role; Ion Caragiale, a 19th-century writer of satiric comedies of manners, is the greatest dramatist. Other great names include poets Mihail Eminescu, Tudor Arghezi (the 20th-century poet laureate), and Mihai Beniuc, and novelists Liviu Rebreanu, Paul Goma, and Mihail Sadoveanu (perhaps the most important 20th-century Romanian writer).

Although the works of Arghezi and Caragiale are available in French and German, almost nothing in Romanian literature has ever been translated into English. The only Romanian writer of international repute is the absurdist playwright Ionesco, who wrote in French.

FOLK ART The most original and interesting aspect of Romanian art, outside of church painting, is its folk tradition. Far from dying out in the industrial age, Romanian folk art has flourished like never before, partly because of the emphasis placed upon it by the former Communist regime. The national and provincial folk museums have fine collections.

MUSIC The isolation of the Orthodox church from the music world of Western Europe—along with the centuries of Turkish domination—left Romania a musical backwater until the 1820s. Keyboard writing, chamber music, symphony, concerto, and opera—virtually the entire Western musical tradition, had to be assimilated in one fell swoop.

Folk Music The nationalism that swept Europe in the 19th century inspired a delving into native folk music in most countries. In Romania this meant digging into an extraordinarily rich tradition, with tunes based on the ancient modes and a number of exotic scales. The Hungarian composer Béla Bartók was among those who took part in compiling the massive collections of folk music that appeared toward the turn of the century (at the time, part of Transylvania was under Hungarian control); he also published piano versions of some Romanian songs and dances, introducing them to a wider European audience. The National Museum in Bucharest has a vast collection of folk music, with thousands of recordings, whose preservation has been state-subsidized since 1896.

Like Bartók in Hungary, the Romanian composers (and a number of Germans who worked in Romania) who emerged in the 19th century made great use of folk materials. This is also true of Georges Enesco (born Enescu; 1881–1955), the most famous Romanian composer and a great conductor and virtuoso violinist; his music reveals a passionate study of Romanian folk tunes.

ARCHITECTURE • Byzantine Most Byzantine churches in Romania belong to a late period, some from after the fall of Constantinople. Near Bucharest, the Snagov Monastery, on a lovely island in Lake Snagov (a holiday resort) has a fine church built in the early 1500s, but with much later paintings (from 1815). The Patriarchal

IMPRESSIONS

The bowed head avoids the sword.
—Romanian Folk Expression

Cathedral in Bucharest is among the most highly developed examples of the Byzantine style, which persisted very late in Romania—until nearly the end of the 17th century.

• **Romanesque** As in Czechoslovakia, few Romanesque buildings survived the Turkish invasion in Romania, but there is a wealth of Gothic monuments, many built in very heterogeneous styles. An ideal architectural tour runs simply from the Hungarian border through Cluj, Alba Iulia, Sibiu, Braşov, and Sinaia (and near Sighişoara and Bran)—that is, through the Carpathians—to Bucharest.

• **Gothic** Among the purest Gothic structures in the country is graceful St. Michael's in Cluj. Alba Iulia Cathedral was originally purely Romanesque, but now has many Gothic additions. Sibiu is an unusually well preserved medieval town, with a fine cathedral. The most famous of the many Gothic monuments in Braşov is the Black Church, with many odd interior details. The castles of Bran and Hunedoara are perched in impregnable Gothic isolation and moody splendor in the mountains. Sighişoara has a fortified church.

Many monasteries were also fortified in this period; the most interesting are those of Suceviţa, Putna, and Dragomirna, all in Moldavia. All three are entirely surrounded by medieval walls and towers, while the buildings inside are variously Byzantine, Gothic, or Renaissance.

• **Painted Churches** Moldavia also boasts a number of unique "painted churches," the most famous being those at Suceviţa monastery, Voronet (these two are true masterpieces), Neamţ, Moldoviţa, and Humor. These 15th- to 16th-century churches are covered entirely, inside and out, with fresco paintings, which once narrated the Bible stories to illiterate worshipers. How the exterior frescoes have survived 400 years of severe winters with their colors vividly fresh and intact is a mystery. In Iaşi, the ancient Moldavian capital, is the Church of the Three Hierarchs, an anachronistic 17th-century Gothic-Byzantine building clad in carved stone lacework.

Did You Know . . . ?

- The Romanian language is the closest descendant of ancient Latin of all European tongues.
- The real Count Dracula, Vlad Ţepeş, is a national hero in Romania, honored in history museums across the country, for his role in fighting the Turkish invaders.
- Romania is the only Eastern European country to have fully paid off its entire foreign debt.
- Trajan's column in Rome, one of the ancient Rome's most famous surviving monuments, shows reliefs of the conquest of Dacia—modern-day Romania.
- The youngest land of Europe is found at the edge of the Danube Delta—the two tons of silt deposited there add 40m (131 ft.) of new land annually.
- The Danube Delta lies in the path of five major bird migration paths. Here you can observe some 250 species of migrating birds from China, Siberia, Europe, India, and Africa.
- Romania is one of the world's major suppliers of carbon black for dyes, printing ink, and tires.

• **Neoclassical** Because of the perseverance of the Byzantine-Gothic style and the predominance of wooden architecture, Romania had almost no neoclassical structures before the 19th century. Bucharest possesses a number of these, including the Romanian Athenaeum, the Palace of Justice, the Center for Economic Development, the General Post Office, and the Central Bank. A number of buildings display the Romantic neo-Gothic and neo-Byzantine revival styles (the terminology is somewhat ironic here, given that the original styles scarcely had time to die out before they were revived), including the royal palace in Sinaia (the fairy-tale Castle Peles), the Greek Orthodox cathedral in Constanţa, and the capital's Domniţa Balasa Church.

• **Modern** The best modern buildings in the country are, of course, the least Stalinoid ones. The State Circus, for example, has a rippling concrete roof like that on Nervi's sports complex in Rome.

4 Food & Drink

Food is abundant in Romania. Supply has rebounded from the dismal situation in 1991 when Western news reported that famine was imminent. The variety may not be overwhelming (summer fruit and vegetables improve the situation considerably), but feeding oneself is not a problem.

Romanians rarely eat at restaurants, and tourism has been down since 1990, so reservations are largely unnecessary for even the most elegant establishments. Occasionally an entire restaurant will be booked by a tour group, but even then the host will usually find you seating.

Restaurant options remain limited. Some new restaurants brighten bigger cities, but in most cases hotel restaurants, many of them quite elegant with turn-of-the century trappings and starched linen settings, remain the best (and often only) option for a civilized, well-rounded meal. Hotel restaurant menus emphasize generic meat-and-potatoes-based continental fare and usually little else. Romanian national dishes are lamentably few on most menus.

THE CUISINE • **Soups** If you're ever in doubt about what to choose from the menu, order a soup—they are especially good in Romania and you can hardly go wrong. Soups come in two main varieties: *supă* (a broth- or cream-based soup, such as beef consommé or cream of mushroom), or the more common *ciorbă* (a hearty sour soup base with meat and a variety of vegetables). Romanian favorites include *ciorbă de perisoare* (with spicy meatballs), *ciorbă de văcuta tărănesca* (peasant beef soup), and *ciorbă de fasole* (bean soup). For an adventurous taste beloved by most Romanians, try *ciorbă de burta*—stomach (tripe) soup. Ciorbăs often come with a chili pepper that Romanians like to nibble on through the course.

• **Main Dishes** Grilled pork or beef is the most common main course in most Romanian restaurants. Pork is served in endless variations, such as pork cutlets, roast loin of pork, and pork schnitzel. In better restaurants, chicken and veal are offered, as is turkey breast. Chicken and turkey are usually accompanied with a portion of *mujdei* (an intense garlic sauce).

While still rare, fish is appearing more frequently on menus. When not breaded and fried to death in the Romanian version of *à la meunière*, fish (carp, perch, trout, and, in the Danube Delta, sturgeon) can be especially good. If you can communicate to your waiter that you want your fish grilled or poached, the cook will be more than obliging. Food in Romania can be quite delicious if you master the menu terms or have a friend along who can translate.

Be sure to try such Romanian traditional dishes as *sarmale* (spiced meat wrapped in cabbage or grape leaves), *tocana* (a meat stew with vegetables), *musaca* (meat, vegetable, and potato casserole), and *mamaliga cu brînză* (a cornmeal dish, like Italian polenta, with unsalted feta cheese).

• **Fruits and Vegetables** The most common vegetable garnishes in restaurants are green beans, peas, and carrots, all of which are usually cooked to death. Although summer and fall markets are full of fresh produce, vegetarians and travelers with special dietary requirements are likely to have a difficult time unless they shop in outdoor markets. From May to October, restaurants do serve pepper, eggplant, cucumber, tomato, or green salads; in the winter, it's often sauerkraut (*varza acra*). A filling vegetarian meal can be had by combining dishes of stuffed peppers and eggplant, omelets, sheep's cheese with polenta, and yogurt.

• **Yogurt** The yogurt comes under a number of names: *sana, lapte acru, kefir,* and *iaourt.* Look for it in shops if you can't get it in restaurants.

• **Cheese** The choice of cheeses tends to be limited to *kashkaval* (hard yellow cheese) and *brînză,* a sheep's milk brine cheese like feta (the best variety is *telemea*).

• **Bread** Although the bread served in many restaurants is often disappointing compared to what's available in bread shops, sometimes you'll be served delicious fresh bread. In Moldavia there's a wonderful light sourdough rye with corn.

• **Desserts** As for desserts, the pastries can vary from overly sweet to light and delicious, while the ice cream in restaurants can be terrible and watery. Instead, search out such traditional Romanian desserts as *clatite* (marvelous jam-filled crêpes) and *papanas* (delicious doughnuts drizzled with a sour-cream sauce).

DRINK • Water and Soft Drinks Outside Bucharest, Romanian tap water, especially in the mountains, is safe to drink and can be quite good. However, if you have a delicate stomach or happen to like mineral water, there are many to choose from: Borsec and Dorna are two of my favorites. On the rare occasion when there's no mineral water (it seems that some restaurants no longer want to bother recycling bottles) you might be offered *sifor,* a harsh seltzer water served from a classic '40s bottle. Soft drinks such as Coke and Pepsi are now bottled in Romania and widely available. Coffee, served Turkish style, comes at the end of the meal. Request it specially if you can't wait until the end of breakfast for your wake-up jolt.

• **Wine, Beer, and Brandy** Good local wine does wonders to enhance a Romanian meal. Some outstanding choices include Murfatlar and Merlot reds and whites like dry Rieslings, Cotnari, Tirnave, and Jidvei. Muscat Ottonel and Pinot Gris Murfatlar are delicious, aromatic, slightly sweet dessert wines especially good after dinner. Romanians usually take white wine mixed with sparkling water, an option your waiter will offer with an interrogative "*şpriţ?*" In most places wine can be ordered only by the bottle—you can try ordering it by the glass in places frequented by tourists. If you know you won't be able to finish the bottle, ask the waiter to leave the cork so you can take the bottle with you.

Beers are now more widely available. Bucegi is a potent 12% lager; Azuga trails behind at 7%. Asking for a *halba* gets you a half-liter, listed on the menu as an "h."

The Romanian national liquor is an intense plum brandy called *ţuica.* Although sometimes available at restaurants and served as an apéritif, you are more likely to have it offered you by its proud brewer in a Romanian home. Ţuica recipes are precious patrimony. "Norok" (naw-ROK) means "cheers."

35

Planning a Trip to Romania

ROMANIA STILL POSES MORE CHALLENGES FOR THE INDEPENDENT TRAVELER THAN the other countries of Eastern Europe, particularly in this time of enormous transition. This chapter will help you identify and tackle important advance-planning issues before you go. Nonetheless, while careful advance planning is very useful, only flexibility, a sense of humor, and an adventurous spirit will get you through the rigors of independent travel in Romania. Leave rigid expectations at home and be prepared for plenty of surprises.

1 Information, Entry Requirements & Money

SOURCES OF INFORMATION

IN THE U.S. The **Romanian National Tourist Office** is helpful in answering general questions about travel and can provide tourist pamphlets and group-tour brochures. Although they do not make any hotel or flight bookings, they can refer you to travel agencies that specialize in travel to Romania. They are located at 342 Madison Ave., Suite 210, New York, NY 10016 (☎ **212/697-6971;** fax 212/697-6972). Write, call, or fax well in advance, but don't give up; the office is often understaffed, but your inquiry will eventually be answered.

There are three excellent travel agencies that have been sending groups to Romania for years. True believers all, their dedication to the cause of Romanian tourism derives mostly from a love of the country and its unrealized potential. They all arrange flights, tours, custom itineraries, and are a valuable source of enthusiasm. Their contacts enable them to offer the cheapest rates on a wide range of services, and they may have valuable information about changes that have occurred after the publication of this book.

CII (Carpaţi International Inc.) was created in 1991 to meet the need for reliable and professional tourist services in Romania. CII works in close conjunction with ONT-Carpaţi, the state travel company that held a monopoly on all aspects of travel in Romania. They specialize in package tours but will arrange trips of any length and special interest. For inquiries and their glossy brochure, contact their friendly staff at 152 Madison Ave., Suite 1103, New York, NY 10016 (☎ **212/447-1534,** or toll free **800/447-8742;** fax 212/447-1434); they are open business hours weekdays.

ACTS (Academic Consulting and Travel Services), which began as an agency for booking cultural and sports exchanges to Romania, still excels in customized travel arrangements. They also arrange tours, flight tickets, and car rentals. Contact them at 144 De Forest Rd., Dix Hills, NY 11746 (☎ **516/499-7851**). Their Bucharest office is at Str. Allea Valea Villor Nr. 2, Bl. A 53, Sc. D, Apt. 46. (☎ **1/777-95-08;** fax 1/312-10-12).

Littoral Travel is the oldest of the three, founded in 1979. They are a full-service provider arranging flights, tours, rentals, translators, and other amenities at 615 Hope Rd., Eatontown, NJ 07724 (☎ **908/389-2160;** fax 908/389-1974); 310 Madison Ave., Suite 118, New York, NY 10017 (☎ **212/697-7119**); or in Bucharest as AAA of Romania, c/o ACR/Hertz, Str. Take Ionescu 27 (☎ **1/650-25-95**).

IN THE U.K. The Romanian National Tourist Office is at 17 Nottingham St., London W1M 3RD (☎ **071/584-8090**).

ENTRY REQUIREMENTS

Everyone needs a passport and visa to enter Romania. Advance purchase of a visa is recommended but not mandatory. You can obtain a visa quickly and easily at the Bucharest airport. Obtaining a visa at border crossings or on trains is more time-consuming and less convenient.

At time of press, it took three weeks from the date of application to obtain a visa from the embassy in the United States; the cost was $30, and visas are good for 30 days.

For more details contact the following embassies/consulates:

- **Australia** Romanian Consulate-General, 333 Old South Head Rd., Bondi, NSW (☎ **02/36-50-15;** fax 612/50-5714).
- **Canada** Romanian Embassy, 655 Rideau St., Ottawa, ON K1N 6A3 (☎ **613/232-5345;** fax 613/567-4365).
- **New Zealand** Romanian Embassy, Dorris Garden Crescent St., 31 Wellington (☎ 85-11-04).
- **United Kingdom** Romanian Embassy, 4 Palace Green, Kensington, London W8 BQ (☎ **937-9666** or **963-8069**).
- **United States** Romanian Embassy, 1607 23rd St. NW, Washington, DC 20008 (☎ **202/232-4747,** or **232-4749;** fax 202/232-4748). Romanian Consulate, 573 Third Ave., New York, NY 10016 (☎ **212/682-9120**).

MONEY

CASH/CURRENCY Romanian **lei** (leu in the singular), the national currency, are issued in coins and notes. Coins come in 1, 2, 5, 10, 20, and 50 lei, and banknotes are issued in denominations of 100, 500, 1,000, and 5,000 lei. A brooding Constantin Brancuşi graces the new 500-lei note, while the 1,000-lei note features the poet Eminescu. A 10,000-lei note will most likely be issued within the year. Also, 100 bani equal a leu, but most bani have been withdrawn from circulation, as have the 10-, 20-, and 50-lei notes.

During research of this section $1 = 1,300 lei and the prices quoted are based on that rate. Bear in mind when calculating prices that Romania's annual rate of inflation is over 200%, so dollar prices given in this section may prove a more stable indicator of costs.

Telephone Number Advisory

At press time, Romania was in the process of updating and changing its telephone system. Every effort was made to provide the updated telephone numbers for the establishments listed in this guide; however, some numbers will change during the lifetime of this book. Fortunately, in most cases, numbers are simply gaining a prefix of an additional one or two digits. For example, a "6" was added to most six-digit numbers in Bucharest. When the update is complete, Bucharest numbers will have seven digits, and all other numbers throughout Romania will have six. It will be relatively easy to guess the correct number if the number we list is wrong: find the new prefix for the town to which the number is connected (look at other phone numbers for that town), and append it. When calling from the United States, to check on a telephone number, you can call the Romanian National Tourist Office in New York at 212/697-6971.

What Things Cost In Romania	U.S. $
State taxi from Bucharest's airport to the city center	10.00
Metro from the train station to Bucharest's Unirii Square	.04
Local telephone call	.02
Double room, with bath, at Bucharest's Inter-Continental Hotel (deluxe)	220.00
Double room, with bath, at Bucharest's Capitol Hotel	44.00
Double room, with bath, at Succava's Hotel Arcaşul (moderate)	33.00
Lunch or dinner for one, without wine, at Casa Capşa, in Bucharest (moderate)	4.00
Lunch or dinner for one, without wine, at the Hotel Continental in Cluj (budget)	2.00
Pint of Romanian beer	.23
Coca-Cola	.30
Cup of coffee	.10
Roll of ASA 100 Kodak or Agfa film, 36 exposures	3.99
Admission to Bucharest's History Museum	.08
Concert at the Athenaeum in Bucharest	.77
Bag of popcorn	.09

Exchanging Currency You can exchange money at tourist offices, banks, most hotels, and in the many new exchange bureaus that have opened in the past five years. Exchange bureaus are the best places to exchange currency as some hotels tend to give lower rates and banks are usually very crowded. Exchange rates and commission rates are becoming somewhat more variable as half-measures toward privatization are being undertaken. Be sure to pick up a receipt for the exchange transaction—some hotels require proof of legal currency exchange. You'll also need it to change the lei back into hard currency when you leave—it's still not legal to import and export lei.

Since the legal exchange rate is so favorable now, illegal exchange on the formerly notorious "black market" is no longer the great bargain it used to be, while still entailing great risks. Some of the unscrupulous methods still used by professional thieves include shortchanging the unsuspecting traveler by wrapping new bills around wads of worthless or counterfeit ones or shouting to the police in the street after a transaction and running off with the hard currency. Needless to say, why invite the risk?

TRAVELER'S CHECKS Some exchange bureaus (especially those in hotels) will exchange traveler's checks into lei, although most prefer cash; the commission rate is 3% to 4%. You can have traveler's checks cashed into hard currency at only three locations in all Romania (see "Banks" in "Fast Facts: Bucharest" in Chapter 36).

CREDIT CARDS Some major upscale hotels accept payment by credit card, but few restaurants accept them. This will undoubtedly change when American Express opens an office in Bucharest. You can get a cash advance in lei with your AMEX card at the Bucharest American Express office (see "Fast Facts: Bucharest" in Chapter 36).

Be aware that the convenience of paying with plastic won't get you the best exchange rate.

2 When to Go

CLIMATE Romania has long, bitter winters and hot, humid summers. During the Ceauşescu years, many hotels as well as private homes lacked heating and hot water because of fuel shortages. The heating situation has improved vastly in postrevolutionary Romania, but winter is not the ideal season for travel unless you're going to the skiing resort at Poiana Braşov, one of the spas catering to foreigners taking off-season indoor water cures, or Bucharest, the capital. TAROM, the national airline, drastically curtails its domestic flight schedules off-season and there may be only one or two flights a week to some cities.

Late spring, summer, and autumn are the best times to visit. The ice on the roads has melted, the meadows and hillsides are a lush green, and fresh food is more plentiful. Fall brings the late harvest and stunning foliage. Bucharest can be very hot and humid in July and August, and air conditioning is almost nonexistent.

Average temperatures in Bucharest range from occasional highs in the 80s in July and August, through the 50s and 60s in spring and fall, to a low in the 20s in January. Generally the seacoast has warmer winters and cooler summers, while the mountains are cooler in summer and much colder in the winter.

Bucharest's Average Daytime Temperatures

	Jan	Feb	Mar	Apr	May	June	July	Aug	Sept	Oct	Nov	Dec
Temp. (°F)	27	31	40	53	63	70	74	73	65	54	42	33
Temp. (°C)	–3	–1	4	12	17	21	23	21	18	12	6	1

Holidays Official Romanian holidays are celebrated on January 1–2 (New Year), Easter, May 1–2 (Labor Day), December 1 (Romania's Unification Day), and December 25 (Christmas).

Romania Calendar of Events

May to August

- **Youth Folk Dance Festival,** Braşov (May). A 400-year-old festival with a costume parade. First Sunday in May.
- **"Golden Stag" Annual Festival of Music,** Braşov (September). Pop singers from all over the world perform in Braşov's stunning central square.
- **Mountain Crafts Fair,** Fundata, in Braşov county (June). Artisans from the counties of Braşov, Argeş, and Dimoviţa gather to sell their handmade crafts. Last Sunday in June.
- **Stejarul (The Oak Tree) Festival,** Somcuta Mare, Maramureş county (July). The biggest folklore event in the county. First Sunday in July.
- **Hora de la Prislop Festival,** Prislop Mountain, Maramureş county (August). This is an age-old traditional festival and dance contest with competing groups from Maramureş county and northern Moldavia. Second Sunday in August.

September to December

- **George Enescu Music Festival,** Bucharest (September). Held every three years (next in 1997). Music by the Romanian composer is featured at the Romanian Athenaeum.
- **Wine Harvest Folk Festival,** at the 500-year-old Odobeşti Winery in Vrancea county (September). A traditional celebration marking the beginning of the grape harvest. Last Sunday in September.
- **Jazz Festival,** in Braşov (September–October). A new annual event for jazz-lovers.

3 Alternative Travel

SPA TRAVEL Among Romania's primary attractions are its 160 spas, a few of which have operated since Roman times. Romanian spas have never been as famous as the Czech spas of Karlsbad or Marienbad, except for a brief period in the '70s when some Hollywood stars discovered Dr. Ana Aslan's Gerovital rejuvenation treatments. Among Europeans who believe in spas as sources of health and rejuvenation, Germans and Finns are the most frequent visitors to Romanian spas.

In the U.S., contact the Romanian National Tourist Office for material on spa programs, or you can also call or write CII for their latest schedules and price quotes (see "Information" above in this chapter).

HIKING There's wonderful hiking in the Carpathian Mountains, both of the nature-walk/day-hike variety and more serious mountain climbing. Sinaia, a few hours north of Bucharest, is a good place for an easy day hike in the Bucegi Mountains. The most popular hiking area in the country is north of Sibiu, in central Romania—the Făgăraş Mountains, Romania's highest and most rugged mountains. For more information on hiking and sports tours in Romania, contact **ACTS** (Academic Consulting and Travel Services), 144 De Forest Rd., Dix Hills, NY 11746 (☎ **516/499-7851**). They also have an office in Bucharest at Str. Allea Valea Villor Nr. 2 Bl. A53, Sc. D, Apt. 46 (☎ **1/777-95-08**).

FOR STUDENTS The organization **CTT** (Company for Youth Travel) will certainly not turn away the lone student traveler stranded in Bucharest, but they do prefer to deal with groups of students. If you're interested in learning more about their current programs, write them or stop by their offices in Bucharest at Str. Mendeleev 2 (☎ **614-42-00**). Every summer for one week in August, CTT sponsors the International Folklore Festival for Young People at the Black Sea coast youth resort Costineşti. Opening with a national costume parade and featuring three days of international folk dance competition, it affords a nice opportunity to buy, sell, or trade arts and crafts and schmooze with young people from all over. Groups must consist of 30 dancers and musicians and two group leaders; the age range for participants is 14 to 31. For full details and applications, write to the CTT Festival Secretariate of the Mondial Folklore Festival, Str. Mendeleev 2, 20169 Bucharest, or fax them at **612-01-26.**

4 Getting There

Romania is somewhat remote from Europe's most frequented gateway cities. Whereas all the other countries covered in this book are within a few hours of Berlin, Vienna, or Istanbul, Romania borders Eastern Europe's least-visited areas: eastern Hungary, northern Bulgaria, eastern Serbia, Moldova, and Ukraine.

BY PLANE You can fly to Bucharest from several U.S. cities on a number of different carriers, including **Lufthansa, Delta,** and **Swissair.** They offer comfortable and reliable service to Romania with frequent connections in European capitals to Bucharest. **TAROM Romanian Air Transport,** at 342 Madison Ave., Suite 213, New York, NY 10173 (☎ **212/687-6013** or **687-6104**), flies directly to Bucharest several times a week from the U.S. off-season and daily in the summer. Their service has not had the best reputation in the past, but imminent privatization ought to make a difference.

Before booking a flight, check around for bargain travel-agency deals, as normal prices can be high. U.S. travel agencies that specialize in low fares to Romania include **ACTS** (Academic Consulting and Travel Services) at 144 De Forest Rd., Dix Hills, NY 11746 (☎ **516/499-7851**), and **Littoral Travel,** 615 Hope Rd., Eatontown, NJ 07724 (☎ **908/389-2160**). The folks at CII (see above under "Sources of Information") may also be of help. Call to find out the latest fares.

BY TRAIN Getting to Bucharest by train involves a lengthy journey: Sofia is 11 hours away; Budapest, 15 hours; and both Warsaw and Istanbul, about 24 hours. You can save some time and money by planning your itinerary to include overnight travel. There are four trains daily from Sofia to Bucharest; the cost is $13 in first class, $8.50 in second class. The fare for the 15-hour Budapest–Bucharest trip is $35 in first class, $23.50 in second (40% discount for round-trip). The long journey from Warsaw to Bucharest costs $41.50 in first class, $28.25 in second; from Istanbul the cost is $45 in first class, $30 in second class.

BY CAR In past years, visitors arriving by car were subject to long lines and rigorous inspections at the frontier, particularly at the Guirgiu crossing on the Bulgarian border. These checks may ease up by the time you visit. Try to find out the border situation before leaving the country from which you're driving. Although the journey into Romania can be long and tiring, you'll enjoy the ease of getting around by car in Romania.

PACKAGE TOURS The country's tourism industry, a still-intact web of transportation and accommodation services managed by ONT-Carpaţi, is better geared to shepherding large groups than accommodating independent travelers. Package tours tend to overkill with folk dancing and Dracula lore, but they are probably the only way to see all Romania's highlights in a reasonable space of time. One felicitous approach might be to mix independent travel in areas easily accessible by rail with package tours to Romania's far-flung sites in Maramureş or Bukovina.

For a sampling of ONT-Carpaţi tour pamphlets, contact the Romanian National Tourist office (see "Information," above in this chapter). CII has a wide variety of tours from a 5-day introductory visit to more comprehensive trips of 11 days by motor coach to major cities and noteworthy sites. CII can also put together custom-tailored itineraries (see "Information," above in this chapter).

ACTS specializes in custom itineraries for special interests such as sports, business, winery, monastery, hiking and trekking, and birding in the Danube Delta. They can help you plan a tour of Romania in conjunction with Bulgaria as they work with travel agencies in Sofia (see "Information," above in this chapter). Littoral Travel specializes in Dracula tours, spa travel, and multicountry itineraries in Central and Eastern Europe (see "Information," above in this chapter).

5 Getting Around

BY PLANE The Romanian airline **TAROM** flies out of Bucharest's Baneasa Airport to most major Romanian cities, including Baie Mare, Cluj-Napoca, Constanţa, Iaşi, Sibiu, Suceava, Timişoara, and Tulcea. However, be apprised that service does not operate year-round; it's curtailed off-season, so there may be only one or two flights a week to some cities. Sporadic fuel shortages and a lack of passengers (few Romanians can afford the tickets now) keep off-season air service very erratic. When there are not enough passengers for a flight, it's canceled. If you plan to fly a lot during any season other than summer, be sure to supplement your itinerary with a fallback plan of rail travel alternatives. TAROM also flies out of Constanţa to other Romanian cities besides Bucharest, but only during July and August.

Fares are expensive for Romanians but cheap by Western standards, all costing between $30 and $48 one way. Children under 12 fly at a 50% discount. Fares must be paid in hard currency. Credit cards can be used at the airport ticket counter, but not at the agency. For current schedules and prices, check with TAROM in Bucharest at their domestic flights office at Str. Buzesti 59–61 (☎ **659-41-25** or **659-41-85**), open Monday to Friday from 7am to 7pm, Saturday from 7am to 1pm. Reserve seats two to three days in advance.

BY TRAIN No train system in all of Europe bewilders and frustrates travelers like **CFR** (Romanian State Railways). To minimize your difficulties, read the terminology and useful guidelines given below.

Types of Trains There are several types of trains: express trains are called *rapid* (the fastest) or *accelerat.* Local trains are called *personal* or *cursa* (slow, stop at every station). Express trains travel at twice the speed of local trains and require the purchase of an additional speed supplement and a seat reservation (both minimal fees). Local trains are slow and often crowded with commuters; they are not recommended for traveling distances over 50 miles. On a schedule, *rapid* trains are signified by two-digit numbers, *accelerat* trains have three, and *personal* and *cursa* trains have four.

Arrivals and Departures *Plecarea* (abbreviated "pl") means departures, and *Sosirea* (abbreviated "sos") means arrivals. On a schedule, the average entry will be two lines long. For example, the first line might say "Accel 221 Buch–Făgăras–Buzias–Timişoara"; this line gives the type of train (Accel), the number (221), and the destinations. The second line might read "12,25 17 12,42 21,04." These four numbers indicate arrival time in the station (12:25 pm), waiting time in the station (17 minutes), departure time from the station (12:42), and the arrival time at the last destination (21:04 or 9:04pm in Timişoara).

Fares The cost of a ticket consists of three items: the base fare, a speed supplement, and a seat reservation. If you miss your train, the ticket is still valid for 24 hours, but you must buy a new seat reservation.

Advance Purchase Always buy your tickets at least one day in advance from the local CFR office. Avoid buying tickets at train stations whenever possible because train stations sell tickets only one or two hours before departure. This often creates a chaotic situation as people anxiously wait in long lines and seats occasionally sell out. The Agenţia CFR (Căilor Ferate Române) offices are ticket bureaus, which are located apart from train stations (local CFR offices are listed in the city descriptions). Tickets are available up to 10 days in advance for domestic travel and a month in advance for international travel at these offices. CFR offices stop selling seat reservations five or six hours before a train is scheduled to depart. Most are open Monday through Saturday from 8am to 8pm and on Sunday from 8am to 1pm. You can also purchase tickets to depart from a city other than the one you're in, but this requires two steps: purchasing the ticket a few days in advance, then returning to pick it up.

When buying a ticket at CFR, read the schedule to find out the *number* of your train, and then look for the ticket window that has a small sign advertising sales for that specific train. CFR's town offices charge a 4% commission over the regular train-station price.

InterRail and Eurail InterRail passes are valid on Romanian trains, but EurailPasses are not. If you're going to be traveling a lot by train it's worth purchasing a train schedule (Mersul Trenurilor) for 500 lei (40¢). New schedules come out at the end of May and are on sale at most CFR ticket bureaus and railway stations in major cities.

What to Purchase Always buy first-class tickets and seat reservations on the fastest train. On the whole, Romanian trains are poorly maintained and often very crowded, making long journeys difficult and, at times, unpleasant. Travelers accustomed to Western train travel are often shocked by the state of the public facilities. Although Romanian first-class seats are less well maintained than most Western European second-class facilities, they do make a journey more bearable. Fares are incredibly low: first-class *rapid* to Braşov is $1.60; to Cluj-Napoca it costs $3.30; and to Baie Mare it's $4.10.

Seat reservations are a must for all long journeys. They cost 250 lei (19¢) for a trip less than 250km (155 miles) on rapid trains in first class. For longer rides reservations cost 500 lei (40¢) in first class. You can also reserve couchette (*cusete*) beds for night trains with a first-class ticket purchase. The cost of a bed depends on the distance traveled, starting at 750 lei (60¢) for a trip less than 150km (93 miles), increasing to 2,200 lei ($1.70) for a 600km (372-mile) trip. A private compartment for a 600km (372-mile) ride costs 5,525 lei ($4.25).

Don't Ride Without a Ticket You might think, since lines are so long, "I'll just buy my ticket on the train and pay a supplement." Unfortunately, the rules say that you must first find the conductor to do this, and since corridors are so crowded, it's often impossible to move about to look for a conductor. Furthermore, you won't have a seat reservation and probably no seat. If you do find a conductor first, you'll pay an additional supplement of about $2, plus especially high charges for the seat reservation and the ride itself. If the conductor finds you first, you'll be hit with an even stiffer fine, and even may be thrown off the train.

Food and Drink on the Train Although there are dining cars on some long-distance trains, it's best to bring along some food and drink with you, in case food supplies run out (not an impossibility when the train is crowded).

BY BUS As difficult as train travel is within Romania, you're going to want to save bus travel for the shorter routes where trains don't go. Try to book in advance, and always arrive early to get onto the bus and maybe even find a seat. It's best to check with local county tourist offices for exact details about rural and intercity buses—otherwise you might get stranded. These schedules are so erratic they seem to depend on drivers' moods; bus stops can change in response to local conditions and needs.

BY CAR • Rentals Because trains are overcrowded and poorly maintained with a Byzantine system of ticket distribution, driving is an attractive option in Romania. Also, a number of the country's most attractive lures—including the Bukovina monasteries outside Suceava and the wonderful peasant region of Maramureş—are easily accessible only by car.

• **Hertz** The least expensive car rented here is a Peugeot 205, which goes for $147 per week plus 25¢ per kilometer or for $399 with unlimited mileage. Rates for four to six and one to three days are 15% and 38% more expensive. Buying the collision damage waiver (CDW) for $15 per day reduces the damages deductible to zero from $2,500. All services add an 18% tax. Prices are liable to change at any moment, but an advance order guarantees the price for 60 days. The price is the same whether renting in Bucharest or in advance from the U.S. (☎ toll free **800/654-3001**). It's best to order three to five days in advance if you want to guarantee a category of car. All major credit cards are accepted. The Hertz desk at Otopeni Airport (☎ **633-31-37**) is open daily from 8am to 8pm. In Bucharest, the Hertz office is at the Automobile Club (ACR), at Str. Cihoschi 2 (☎ **612-94-20**); it's open Monday through Friday from 8am to 7:30pm and on Saturday and Sunday from 8am to 2pm. Hertz also has offices in Braşov and the Black Sea coast towns of Mamaia, Efforie Nord, and Neptun.

• **Europcar** (National's name abroad) The least expensive rental available here is the Romanian-made Dacia 1310. Weekly rates, including the collision damage waiver (CDW) and 18% service tax, are $182 plus 22¢ per kilometer, or $426 with unlimited mileage. Rentals for three to six days are 26% more expensive. The Dacia is available to walk-in customers only. If ordering in advance from the U.S. (☎ toll free **800/CAR-EUROPE**), the least expensive model available is a Citroën AX-10 (a significant improvement over the Dacia), at a weekly rate of $442, CDW and tax included. The daily rate is roughly 30% more expensive. The walk-in rate for the Citroën is significantly more expensive. Personal accident insurance for passenger protection adds $4.25 per day. Rates are likely to change without notice. Europcar's Bucharest office is at Bd. Magheru 7 (☎ **614-40-58**), next to ONT-Carpaţi, and at Bucharest airport 24 hours daily (☎ **633-75-01**). There are offices in Braşov, Constanţa, and Timişoara.

• **Avis** This company is planning to open several new offices in Romania and may offer competitive prices. Check with them in the U.S. (☎ toll free **800/331-1084**) for details.

• **ACTS** (see "Information," above in the chapter) This firm rents cars *with drivers* at rates comparable to those charged by Hertz and Europcar without drivers. Unlimited mileage within Bucharest costs $65 per day. Outside of Bucharest, the rate goes up to $85 per day, which includes the cost of lodging for the driver. For an eight-seat minibus, the rate is $105 per day within Bucharest, $140 without. It's best to arrange the car before your trip (☎ **516/499-7851**), although ACTS may be able to set you up from its Bucharest office (☎ **1/777-95-08**).

Travelers should be aware that the incidence of car theft and vandalism has risen dramatically in Bucharest recently. This being the case, it seems prudent to purchase car-theft insurance or rent a car outside Bucharest if you're planning on doing some major touring by car.

• **Gasoline** In late 1993 gasoline cost 330 lei per liter (25¢) or 95¢ a gallon. There has been talk that the price will double, making it comparable to Western European prices. Check with the information sources listed in "Information, Entry Requirements, and Money," above, before you leave or you may get caught drastically recalculating your budget because of the spiraling inflation. The state fuel company PECO has been joined by Western companies such as Shell, and now distances between filling stations are less heart-stopping. Still, be sure to fill up whenever you can. Most Romanian country maps mark the location of gas stations, which are usually open Monday through Saturday from 7am to 7pm. There are a few 24-hour stations on major roads leading into cities.

• **Driving Rules** Except in a few places outside of cities, Romanian roads are two-lane and not maintained to high standards. Signs are maddeningly absent, and in the rain, roads drain poorly. Furthermore, they are the primary artery for all wheeled and legged voyages. Heavily laden trucks, buses, combines, cars, horsecarts, livestock, bicyclists, pedestrians, sheep, geese, and suicidal stray dogs are just a few of the obstacles one normally encounters. Unless you're using military-issue night goggles, you'll find that these objects will be nearly invisible at twilight or night on the unlit roads. Drive by day, if at all possible.

Speed limits are 60kmph (37 m.p.h.) within cities, and 80 to 90 kmph (50 to 56 m.p.h.) outside cities (depending on the size of the car). If a driver in the oncoming lane blinks his headlights, it means police radar lies ahead. You must have either your regular driver's license or an international driver's license, as well as a Green Card for third-party insurance. Don't drink and drive.

In case of a breakdown or an accident, don't leave the scene; have someone notify the police or try to reach the **Automobil Clubul Roman (ACR)** for assistance. Their central office is at Str. Cihoschi 2 in Bucharest (☎ **611-04-08** or **611-43-65**).

HITCHHIKING Many Romanians of all ages hitchhike, but Eastern European cars tend to be small and their number on the road is limited—so you can't always be sure of getting a ride. Waving a pack of cigarettes or a foreign passport is no longer the magic wand it used to be in flagging down the infrequent traffic—although it may land you a ride in a horse-drawn wagon. However, the ongoing civil war in the former Yugoslavia has rerouted an increased number of large transport trucks through Romania and Bulgaria and you may be able to catch a ride on a main highway if a curious driver wants to meet a foreigner to share part of a long drive. It's not advisable for women to hitchhike alone; if you must hitch, travel in pairs.

Suggested Itineraries

City Highlights

Braşov A medieval trading town with an Old Town of 15th- and 16th-century merchants' houses and shops lining cobblestone streets at the foot of towering Tîmpa Mountain. One of "Dracula's castles" is at Bran, 17 miles away.

Bucharest Romania's capital has many good art and history museums; lovely parks; and Ceauşescu's Folly, the grandiose "House of the Republic," an 11-story, 1,500-room palace, the centerpiece of one of Europe's most radical "urban renewal" projects.
Cluj-Napoca An ancient city, Cluj dates back to ancient Roman times, and more recently, was the capital of Transylvania. Today it's one of Romania's foremost university towns.
Constanţa Gateway to the Black Sea coast and an important ancient Greek and Roman port town, Constanţa has a vast Roman-era mosaic floor and the country's most impressive archeological museum. It's also near the Black Sea coast beaches.
Iaşi The cultural center and capital of Moldavia for 400 years. This city is also famous for its 300 colleges, its Palace of Culture containing four museums, and its Church of the Three Hierarchs.
Sibiu A charming Transylvanian town with one of Romania's most important folk-art and painting museums, medieval fortifications, and one of Romania's most impressive outdoor folk-culture museums.
Suceava Gateway city to the Bukovina region where medieval fortress-monasteries shelter one of Eastern Europe's most unique treasures—churches adorned with vivid, remarkably well preserved 400-year-old interior and exterior frescoes.
Timişoara Romania's most culturally Western city, Timişoara contains many beautiful examples of Habsburg architecture. The 1989 revolution that brought the end of the Ceauşescu regime began here.

Planning Your Itinerary

Although most of Romania's cities can be seen in a day or two, allow yourself plenty of time for traveling between destinations. Trains are quite slow and tiring, so don't plan a rigorous schedule or you'll wear yourself out. Driving will take much longer than you expect: Steep mountain passes, lots of horse-drawn carts, farm vehicles, and pedestrians slow you down.

If You Have 1 Week

Day 1 Arrive in Bucharest and see the sights of Romania's capital.
Day 2 Travel to Sinaia, two hours north of Bucharest; see the Royal Castle and go on to nearby Braşov. Or go straight to Braşov, three hours north of Bucharest.
Days 3–5 Visit Braşov and continue west in Transylvania to Sibiu and then north to Cluj, spreading three days between these two cities full of history and museums.
Days 6 and 7 Then go to Suceava and visit the beautiful nearby medieval monasteries. To allow for travel time, spend two nights in Suceava.
Day 8: Return to Bucharest for your international flight.

If You Have 2 Weeks

Days 1 and 2 Arrive in Bucharest and see the sights of Romania's capital.
Day 3 Travel to Sinaia, two hours north of Bucharest; see the Royal Castle and go on to Braşov. Or go straight to Braşov, three hours north of Bucharest and visit Dracula's Castle in Bran, 17 miles away.
Days 4–6 Continue west in Transylvania to Sibiu, and then head north to Cluj, stopping off in Alba Iulia en route. Spend three days on these three cities full of history and museums.

Days 7–9 Go northeast and spend two days exploring the small villages and authentic traditional peasant culture of the Maramureş region (best done by driving).
Days 10–12 Continue traveling east to Suceava and visit the medieval monasteries (best done by driving or joining a local excursion).
Days 12–14 Visit Constanţa for a day and spend another day at the beach at one of the nearby resort towns.
Day 15 Return to Bucharest or travel down the coast to Varna, Bulgaria, by express bus.

If You Have More Time

Consider spending a day in Iaşi and then continue down to Tulcea to journey through the incredible nature preserves of the Danube Delta by boat. Take a day hike in the mountains outside of Sinaia, Braşov, or Sibiu. Or spend another day exploring either the Maramureş region or visiting the Bukovina monasteries. Take a day or two to rest on the Black Sea beaches or plan your trip so as to be able to attend one of the many folklore festivals or fairs held outdoors around the country.

6 Enjoying Romania on a Budget

THE $30-A-DAY BUDGET

Romania is currently the least developed and least expensive Eastern Europe country for foreigners to travel in. I say "currently" because the situation is volatile and runaway inflation could alter the picture by the time you arrive.

SAVING MONEY ON . . .

ACCOMMODATIONS • Hotels Rigid government controls have been loosened and hotel rates that were previously artificially inflated have now come down to a reasonable level. At press time, if you want to live in a decent hotel in Romania you won't have to spend more than $20 to $25 a day for food and lodging in most cities outside Bucharest, and much less—$10 to $15 a day—if you stay in private rooms. Hotel rates in Bucharest are higher and you'll spend $30 to $40 a day and up for a single in the better hotels listed.

The complex coupon system (which necessitated the advance purchase of vouchers for discounts on the terribly inflated hotel rates) seems to have been eliminated. There is no guarantee, however, that either situation will remain stable: Inflation may skyrocket and discount vouchers may be reintroduced.

Single rooms in "luxury" category hotels in Bucharest are worth paying for, while the double rooms fall within our $30-a-day budget range quite nicely. These rooms come with a substantial breakfast of an omelet or a plate of cheese and cold meats with rolls and strong Turkish coffee or sweet tea. You can also be reasonably confident of a steady supply of hot water in the mornings and evenings.

• Private Rooms Private rooms are far and away the best budget option in Romania, but as of this writing they're hard to find. During the Ceauşescu era the government banned locals from hosting all foreigners except for immediate family. Today, anybody can put you up, but few travel agencies rent private rooms.

The National Tourist Office in Bucharest no longer rents rooms, but in the future smaller travel agencies may spring up across the country. Ask around to see whether such bureaus have opened by the time you arrive, or ask locals if they know of friends who can put you up. I've listed several individuals and a travel agency that offer centrally located rooms in the Bucharest chapter and in Suceava in Chapter 37.

- **Camping** Another inexpensive choice for accommodations is camping, but keep in mind that facilities are crowded and basic—with public bathrooms only for the most intrepid travelers who are carefree to needs of comfort. For a list of Romania's 150 campsites, contact the Romanian National Tourist Office before you go.

MEALS Restaurants are extremely inexpensive in Romania. You should pay close attention to the bill, for some waiters can be unscrupulous. Liquor will bring up your tally—especially imported mixed drinks, but even an imported beer will cost more than three times as much as a good domestic beer.

SIGHTSEEING Museums are inexpensive, and sightseeing will typically cost only 50¢ to $1 a day in Bucharest, much less elsewhere.

SHOPPING Romania is not especially rich in tourist souvenirs, but you'll find folk jackets and embroidered blouses and dresses, pottery, wood carvings, and records with traditional Romanian folk music.

TRANSPORTATION Domestic public transportation is poor and hard to deal with in Romania, but it's inexpensive, so you don't have to do anything special to receive low fares.

It's quite advantageous to sightsee by car in Romania, but rentals can be very expensive—$426 a week with unlimited mileage for a Romanian Dacia. You could rent a car in a neighboring country and drive in, but very few rental companies allow their cars to cross the Romanian border, even those that rent within Romania.

TIPPING Tip waiters 15%; bartenders, 10%; bellhops, 500 lei (40¢) per piece of luggage; and state taxis, 10% to 15%.

EXCHANGING MONEY Exchange rates are so favorable that it's wise to stay away from the black market. Private exchange bureaus are the best places to exchange foreign currency into lei, offering the best rates. Some private bureaus run out of money by midafternoon, so get to them before then.

Hotels are most convenient, but have higher commission rates; banks are usually very crowded. There's a 1.5 to 3% commission charge for exchanging traveler's checks.

Fast Facts: Romania

Business Hours Banks are usually open Monday through Friday from 8am to 12:30pm. Offices usually stay open Monday through Friday from 8 or 9am (although Romanians say that no one works until they've had their morning coffee, which takes 30 to 60 minutes) until 4 or 5pm, and they close at 1pm on Saturday; most are closed Sunday. In cities and larger towns, shops are open Monday through Friday from 7 or 8am to 5 or 6pm (the larger stores stay open until 8 or 9pm). Some stores close for a few hours in the afternoon; most are open on Saturday, but close by 1pm.

Camera/Film Romania is a beautiful country, so bring a camera. Western film brands are available in most cities, but stock up in Bucharest just to be safe. There is also Fuji and Kodak one-hour film developing in Bucharest.

Cigarettes At this writing, none of the concern that some Western nations are exhibiting toward smoking as a health hazard is in evidence in Romania. In fact, privatization has made prestigious Western cigarette brands like Kent and Marlboro widely available. There are no restrictions on smoking in restaurants or other public places except the metro. In fact, you might be appalled at how much people smoke; train compartments and long-distance buses can be asphyxiating to nonsmokers.

Customs You are allowed to bring in two cameras, 10 rolls of film, two liters of alcohol, four liters of wine, one carton of cigarettes, and other personal items.

Before making any large purchases inside Romania, make sure that you can export the item. If export is permitted, you may take out a certain amount duty free; purchases above that amount are subject to customs duty. Check the latest customs rules when you visit.

Drugstores Western medications and toiletries are widely available in Bucharest, scarce elsewhere, so bring enough for the duration of your trip in Romania.

Electricity Romania's electrical sockets punch out 220 volts, 50 cycles, AC, although you may find 110 volts in Bucharest.

Embassies/Consulates Citizens of Australia, Ireland, and New Zealand should contact the British embassy for assistance.

- **Canada** The embassy is at Nicolae Iorga 36, Bucharest (☎ **650-61-40**).
- **United Kingdom** The embassy is at Str. Jules Michelet 24, Bucharest (☎ **611-16-34**).
- **United States** The embassy is located on Strada Snagov (near the Hotel Inter-Continental on the corner of Strada Batiştei) (☎ **610-40-40**).

Emergencies Dial **061** for an ambulance, **055** for the police, and **081** for the fire department.

Languages Of all the Romance languages—Italian, Portuguese, French, and Spanish—Romanian is the closest to ancient Latin. Even with its Slavic and Turkish influences, Romanian is a fairly accessible tongue for Westerners. Travelers with a smattering of French, Spanish, Portuguese, or Italian will understand some of the language, and those who speak only English will find Romanian much easier to pronounce than other Eastern European languages. Many words in Romanian are actually pronounced just as they appear. Many people dealing with tourists in the larger cities often speak some English; in smaller towns, expect these people to speak some Frenc or German.

Laundry Coin-operated laundries have not yet invaded Romania, so the easiest way to get your clothes clean is to bargain with the hotel service staff or with your private room host.

Mail Although mail service has improved since the revolution and is reportedly no longer monitored, it remains one of Eastern Europe's less reliable systems. For important letters, I suggest waiting until you get back to the West. Letters to the U.S. cost 207 lei (16¢) and postcards cost 70 lei (5¢); to Great Britain, a letter costs 180 lei (14¢) and a postcard is 45 lei (3¢).

Maps Maps, especially those in English, can be hard to find in Romania, so make sure to ask the Romanian National Tourist Office before you leave for maps of all cities you plan to visit. They, unlike most tourist offices inside Romania, are fairly well stocked.

When reading maps, searching for addresses, or navigating your way around Romania, you should know that **Strada** (abbreviated "Str.") means "street," **Calea** means "avenue," **Bulevardul** (abbreviated "Bd.") means "boulevard," Şoseaua (abbreviated "Sos.") is an even wider avenue than a boulevard, Piaţa is a square or plaza, and Drumul means "lane." Note that in Romanian addresses, street numbers follow the street name (for example, Str. Academiei 35).

When reading maps as well as listings in this guidebook, keep in mind that many street names are in the process of being changed as Romania wipes out vestiges of Communism. This may be a source of confusion as different people tell you different names for the same street. Keep an eye out for possible changes.

Movies Most English and American movies play in the original language with Romanian subtitles. Always check beforehand just to make sure. Movie tickets cost 300 to 350 lei (23¢ to 27¢).

Newspapers/Magazines You may occasionally find *Newsweek, Time,* or the *International Herald Tribune* in Bucharest, but on the whole, Western newspapers and magazines are still rare in Romania.

Photography You may now take photographs freely in Romania, with the exception of military objects with a NO PHOTOGRAPHY sign (a red slash over a black camera).

Police The national police emergency number is **055.**

Radio On the Black Sea coast, "Radio Holiday" broadcasts at 101.1 FM on the hour between 10am and 2pm and 4 to 8pm in five languages, including English, with news and information. Local non–state-controlled stations are springing up around the country, featuring Western pop music and the news. There are several in Bucharest that broadcast news bulletins in French and English.

Restrooms Always carry toilet paper with you if you plan to use public toilets. Women will also have to pay 50 lei (4¢) to an attendant at many bathrooms.

Safety With a postrevolutionary shortage of police, crime has risen in recent years. Westerners occasionally encounter petty theft and rip-offs from savvy, street-smart locals, especially in Bucharest. Be alert, especially in the most heavily touristed areas. Car theft is on the rise in the capital, so buy insurance.

I've heard from women traveling alone in Romania that some Romanians try to pick up female visitors (reading a map in public is a sure way to draw attention). A resolute "No!" and walking away will usually be enough to deter them.

Telephone For local calls, use a 50-lei coin. For long-distance or international calls, go to the international post office. The cost of a call to the U.S. from the Communications Center is 1,143 lei (90¢) per minute, minimum of three. It's difficult or impossible to make long-distance calls without assistance, even inside Romania. If you want to make hotel reservations for your next destination, for example, it's best to let your current hotelier take care of it for you. Usually it's not possible to make local calls directly from your hotel room; you have to ask the hotel receptionist for a line out.

Currently, there is only one public access point—a specially designated phone at Otopeni Airport in Bucharest—from which you can make collect calls and charge calls using an international telephone calling card. The service charge for making a collect call (person-to-person only) is $6, and using an AT&T International phone card costs $2.50; both calls cost $2.70 for the first minute and $1.50 for each additional minute. To connect to AT&T direct, dial **01-800-4288;** for MCI direct, dial **01-800-1800.**

Television Romanian TV frequently broadcasts English-language movies and melodramas with Romanian subtitles. For "Star Trek, the Next Generation," tune in Sunday at 7pm; "Dallas" titillates twice a week at 9:15pm, Thursday and Saturday; classic Hollywood films play Tuesday and Thursday at 9 or 9:15pm.

Time Official Romanian time is one hour ahead of Central Europe, two hours ahead of Greenwich mean time, and seven hours ahead of eastern standard time. Romania goes to daylight saving time the last Sunday in March and goes back to standard time the last Sunday in September.

Water Some people find the water remarkably good, especially in the mountains, and suffer no ill effects from it, while others avoid it and drink only bottled mineral water, which is plentiful and quite inexpensive.

36

Bucharest

YOU'RE NOT LIKELY TO BE INSTANTLY CHARMED BY MODERN BUCHAREST (POP. 2.4 million). It's easy to come away with the impression that this is a drab gray city filled with oppressive government buildings and blocs of ugly high-rise apartments, and wonder why it was known before World War II as the "Paris of the Balkans." But the city possesses excellent art collections, good history museums, and beautiful parks and lakes, and there's much to explore in Bucharest, too.

First mentioned by name in 1459 by the infamous Vlad Ţepeş, who built a princely court here, Bucharest was the capital of the feudal state of Wallachia in the mid-17th century and became the country's capital two centuries later. The city managed to survive centuries of Ottoman occupation, but little of its historic center has survived the ravages of this century—heavy Nazi bombing and Ceauşescu's ruthless destruction of thousands of houses and places of worship and displacement of the population for what has amounted to mere showcase urban renewal and a costly, gargantuan, and largely useless palace. The pockets here and there that have survived this demolition are some of the more fascinating parts of the city.

Bucharest has great charm and style, but it's the quiet and elusive kind, tucked away on the small side streets and discovered only if you wander off the noisy wide main boulevards. Walk east of the Inter-Continental Hotel, near the U.S. Embassy or east of the Dorobanţi Hotel near Piaţa Lahovary. Take a stroll around the northern end of Calea Victoriei where chestnut- and mansion-lined Şoseaua Kiseleff begins or along the winding streets off its southern end in the Lipscani shopping district. Wander in these old quarters and you'll soon come upon some small architectural wonder like an elegant art nouveau mansion, a tiny, elaborately decorated church, or a crumbling fin-de-siècle hotel with pleasing stucco ornament.

There are also lively markets with Gypsies hawking their wares and large parks with shady, tranquil paths and lakes with rowboats for hire. The unique open-air Village Museum brings together authentic peasant dwellings and churches from the rest of Romania to give you a glimpse of what's in store for you if you continue exploring the country. So along with the enormous downtown government buildings scarred with bullets from the December 1989 revolution and Ceauşescu's deserted Civic Center and monstrous Government Palace, take the time to find these intriguing nooks and crannies as counterpoint, to restore your soul and Bucharest's, too.

1 Orientation

ARRIVING

BY PLANE By the time you arrive at Bucharest's **Otopeni International Airport,** it may be entirely renovated and quite unlike the permanent urban-renewal project it resembled for the past few years. As of this writing, "Arrivals" was maturing nicely into a finished terminal; "Departures" was still all exposed girders and temporary corridors.

If you don't have a visa, stop at the "Visa Tax" window to purchase a visa for $30 before proceeding to passport control.

Theoretically there's supposed to be an ONT-Carpaţi desk open around the clock at the airport, so if you're disoriented and need help, try to find them; there's usually someone on the staff who speaks English and may be able to help out.

Officially, a TAROM bus leaves the airport almost every hour on the hour from 5am to 10pm, with stops at Băneasa domestic airport, Piaţa Presei Libere, Piaţa

What's Special About Bucharest

Architectural Highlights

- Bulevardul Unïrii (formerly the Boulevard of the Victory of Socialism), a massive symmetrical three-mile-long avenue created in the 1980s.
- Casa Republicii (House of the Republic), a gargantuan palace at the end of Bulevardul Unirii, an enduring monument to Communist architecture.

Churches

- Patriarchal Cathedral, dating from 1668, the seat of the patriarch of the Romanian Orthodox church.

Historic Sights

- The purported burial place of Vlad (Count Dracula) Ţepeş on an island in Lake Snagov, 22 miles north of Bucharest.

Museums

- Museum of the History of Romania, with the country's finest treasures including a 4th- or 5th-century A.D. gold table setting, and one of the largest cameos in the world.
- Bucharest Art Museum, with works by Titian, Tintoretto, El Greco, Rembrandt, Monet, and Renoir.
- Museum of Art Collections, with pre-Communist art collections of Romanian nobles and wealthy citizens, including works by Matisse, Cézanne, and Picasso.
- Village and Folk Art Museum, with a collection of peasant houses from all over the country installed in a park setting.

Parks

- Parcul Herăstrău, the largest of Bucharest's many parks, with a series of connecting lakes and the unique Village and Folk Art Museum.
- Grădina Cişmigiu, the oldest and most central of Bucharest's parks, with a lake, a zoo, and acres of flowers.

Victoriei, Piaţa Universităţii, and the main TAROM office in downtown Bucharest on the corner at Str. Brezoianu 10. You can connect to metro stations not far from each of the last three stops. The bus fare is 100 lei (8¢); you pay the driver directly.

If this bus is nowhere to be found, you can take local bus no. 131 or 331 from the main road leading to the airport to Piaţa Presei Libere. From there you can change to the metro or bus no. 49 to the center.

Alternatively, you might consider a taxi into town, which should cost about 10,000 lei ($7.70). Almost all taxi drivers will assume that you know nothing about their country and will try to inflate fares and ask for hard currency. State taxis are required to use their meters, here as elsewhere in Bucharest, but it may not be easy to convince the drivers of that.

BY TRAIN Train travelers arrive at the main station—Găra de Nord (☎ **052**), a large, chaotic mess. On the right when stepping off the platform there is an ONT-Carpaţi tourist office offering little in the way of useful services and much in the way of stench. There is, however, an exchange office there. It's open Monday through Friday from 8am to 4pm and on Saturday from 8am to 1pm. A baggage check designated for foreigners is on the right before you exit the station under the sign Bagaje de Mira. It's open 24 hours, and the charge is per day 110 lei (8¢) for small items, 220 lei (16¢) for large items. The international telephone office in the station is open 24 hours a day. It's best to order a call in advance, or allow 30 to 45 minutes to place one when there.

To get into town, take metro Line 1 or 3; both lines have their terminus at the train station. As you leave the station onto Piaţa Gării de Nord, turn left to reach the metro entrance.

TOURIST INFORMATION

For Bucharest information, as well as other tourist assistance, drop by the Carpaţi National Tourist Office, Bd. Magheru 7 (☎ **616-77-91** or **614-19-22**). Lines can be long, but service has improved somewhat here in recent years. As Romania's main tourist office, it offers all the tourist services available in the country—such as day tours of Bucharest or week-long trips across all Romania. Open Monday through Saturday from 7:30am to 8pm and on Sunday from 8am to 2pm.

CITY LAYOUT

MAIN ARTERIES & STREETS Bucharest is a huge, sprawling city with major streets radiating from Piaţa Victoriei in the north. The main downtown area begins at Piaţa Romană in the north, which connects to the city's main shopping avenue, Bulevardul Magheru. After several blocks Bulevardul Magheru changes its name to Bulevardul Bălcescu, and then to Bulevardul I. C. Brătianu; stores, shops, airline offices, and hotels line this wide street. (One easy-to-find landmark on Bulevardul Bălcescu is the 22-story Hotel Inter-Continental.) This major avenue ends at Piaţa Unirii, site of Bucharest's largest department store.

Parallel to Bulevardul Magheru/Bălcescu/Brătianu a few blocks west is Calea Victoriei, Bucharest's other major avenue of interest to tourists and home to several museums, hotels, restaurants, and government buildings. In the middle of Calea Victoriei sits Piaţa Revolutiei, also called Piaţa Palatului or Palace Square (formerly Piaţa Gheorghiu-Dej), site of the Bucharest Art Museum and the former Communist Party headquarters. Most of the hotels and sights recommended in this chapter are located on these two boulevards or on nearby side streets.

At the southern part of the city on a roughly east-west axis is Bulevardul Unirii (formerly Boulevard of the Victory of Socialism). Dozens of streets and several neighborhoods were completely leveled to make room for this Ceauşescu-inspired urban renovation, which runs parallel to Piaţa Unirii.

North of the city center is an attractive strip of parks and lakes called Parcul Herăstrău.

A Note on Street Addresses When reading maps, searching for addresses, or navigating your way around Romania, you should know that Strada (abbreviated "Str.") means "street," Calea means "avenue," Bulevardul (abbreviated "Bd.") means "boulevard," Piaţa is a square or plaza, Drumul means "lane," and Şoseaua refers to a very wide boulevard. Note that Romanian addresses follow European usage in which street numbers follow the street name (for example, Str. Academiei 35).

MAPS Many Bucharest city maps are out of date. Following the December 1989 Romanian revolution many street names have been changed to wipe away the Communist past of the city.

2 Getting Around

BY METRO One positive side to Bucharest's massive "urban renewal" in the last decade is its four-line metro system, completed in 1986. The most important line for tourists is the north/south blue line, Line 2, which makes stops in Piaţa Victoriei, Piaţa Romană, Piaţa Universităţii, and Piaţa Unirii. Two other lines service the east and west sides of the city. The orange Line 3 forms a circle over Line 2; it stops at the Găra de Nord (the train station), and connects to the main no. 2 line at Piaţa Victoriei. The red Line 1 connects Găra de Nord with Piaţa Unirii.

The system opens daily at 5am and closes at 11pm or midnight, and costs 50 lei (4¢). Put the coin into the turnstile; you can get change at the booths near the entrance. Metro maps are now available, and are posted at the entrance to all stations. In general, the metro and the new minibuses (see below) are the fastest and most convenient public transportation for tourists.

BY BUS & TRAM Except for the metro, public transportation is quite old and dilapidated. Buses and trams tend to fill up rapidly; on a bus you risk not only being hot and crowded, but also losing your wallet. Current bus and tram maps are sometimes on sale at kiosks where tickets are sold. Whenever possible I suggest sticking to the metro, although some bus numbers are offered in this chapter. Buses, trolleybuses (buses connected to electric power lines), and trams all cost 50 lei (4¢). Tickets come in pairs, and you use each half once. You must perforate your tickets in the small metal boxes on board the vehicle. Inspectors patrol often and if they catch you without a ticket they'll fine you 1,200 lei (90¢) on the spot. If you don't pay within 24 hours, the fine goes up to 10,000 lei ($7.70).

There are minibuses called "Maxi Taxi" that travel up and down Bulevarduls Magheru/Bălcescu. The driver will pick you up and drop you off wherever you like. They cost 200 lei (15¢) a ride.

BY TAXI Taxis are an option even for budget travelers! The drop rate is 80 lei (6¢), and the fare rises 400 lei (30¢) per kilometer. The fare is the same on weekends and at night. Any state taxi (any taxi with a meter) is obliged to use the meter. You might also come across a "private" taxi (especially at the airport) without a meter in which you negotiate the fare; they will always try to charge foreigners several times the normal tariff, so always try to find a state taxi if possible. All state taxis have a checkered strip marking the vehicle on its sides and usually the number 053, too. If you can't flag down a taxi on the street, it's also possible to order a cab by phone at **053.**

ON FOOT Although distances can be sizable between monuments, I suggest more walking in Bucharest than you might normally do, in order to uncover the city's hidden pleasures.

Fast Facts: Bucharest

American Express This recently opened office, at Magheru 7, 70161 (☎ and fax **312-25-96**) in the ONT-Carpaţi building, offers most AMEX services, including check issuance, emergency check cashing, and lost or stolen credit card replacement. All cash advances are in lei (and at an unfavorable rate). The office is open Monday through Friday from 8:30am to 6pm and Saturday from 9:30am to 2pm. The three banks listed below (under "Banks") are the only places in Romania that cash traveler's checks into hard currency.

Area Code Bucharest's telephone area code is **1.**

Auto Repair For repairs and information, drop by or call the Romanian Automobile Club (ACR), Str. Cihoschi 2 (☎ **611-04-08** or **611-43-65**), open Monday through Friday from 7:30am to 7:30pm, on Saturday from 7:30am to 2:30pm, and on Sunday from 8am to 2pm. This office also has a Hertz car-rental desk (☎ **612-94-20**), open Monday through Friday from 8am to 7:30pm and on Saturday and Sunday from 8am to 2pm.

Banks The following three banks are the only places in Romania to get cash traveler's checks for hard currency. They also handle wire transfers.

- **Commercial Bank of Romania,** Bd. Carol I 12–14 (☎ **614-56-80** or **615-75-60;** telex 10938 or 11998); go in through the unmarked mirrored door directly to your right as you enter the foyer. Commission is 1.5%. Hours are Monday through Friday 8:30am to 1pm.
- **Romanian Bank for Development,** Str. Doamnei 4 (☎ **614-91-04**); use windows 23 and 24. Attendants Christina and Jige speak English and are helpful. Hours are Monday through Friday 8:30am to noon.
- **Romanian Bank for Foreign Trade,** Calea Victoriei 22–24 (☎ **914-91-90**), use windows 4 or 6. The bank uses a computer system just installed by IBM. Commission is 2% for the first $100, 1.5% thereafter. Hours are Monday through Friday 8:30am to noon.

Bookstores Regular bookstores have very little to offer English speakers, aside from an occasional English-Romanian dictionary, city map (in Romanian), and pro-wrestling magazine. Libraria Mihail Sadoveanu, at Bd. Magheru 4–6, is as well stocked as any.

Currency Exchange You can exchange money at tourist offices, hotels, or the many private exchange bureaus that have opened downtown. Some private bureaus run out of money by midafternoon in Bucharest, so get to one early in the day. The exchange rate is favorable so avoid "black market" street dealers; it's too risky.

Doctors/Dentists Ask your embassy for advice in finding a competent English-speaking doctor or dentist (see "Embassies/Consulates," below). For health emergencies, have some one who speaks Romanian call an ambulance at **061** or get to the Spitalul Cinic de Urgenţǎ at Calea Floreasca 8 (☎ **679-40-80** or **679-64-90**). The Policlinica Batiştei at Str. Batiştei 27 (☎ **614-81-13** to **614-81-15**), near the U.S. Embassy, is accustomed to dealing with foreigners.

Drugstores Bucharest has several 24-hour pharmacies; the central one, Pharmacie No. 5, at Bd. Magheru 18 (☎ **659-61-15**), stocks vitamins, aspirin, ibuprofen, Biseptol (equivalent to Alka-Seltzer), Band-Aids, soap, shampoo, and other sundries. Antibiotics are reportedly available over the counter to foreigners. The Ministry of Commerce and Tourism map lists the other 24-hour pharmacies.

Embassies/Consulates Citizens of Australia, Ireland, and New Zealand should contact the British embassy for assistance.

- **Canada** The embassy is at Nicolae Iorga 36 (☎ **650-61-40**).
- **United Kingdom** The embassy is at Str. Jules Michelet 24 (☎ **611-16-34**).
- **United States** The embassy is located at the corner of Strada Snagov and Batiştei (near the Hotel Inter-Continental) (☎ **610-40-40**).

Emergencies For an ambulance dial **061,** for the police **055,** and for the fire department **081.**

Laundry The easiest and cheapest way to do laundry is to negotiate directly with the service staff of your hotel.

Luggage Storage The main train station has a 24-hour luggage check, charging 110 lei to 220 lei (8¢ to 16¢) per bag per 24 hours.

Maps New maps of Bucharest can be purchased in Bucharest at the ONT-Carpaţi office and most upscale hotels for 1,000 lei (75¢). Public transit maps are often on sale at kiosks where public transit tickets are sold.

Newspapers/Magazines The Hotel Inter-Continental sells a few copies of *Time* and *Newsweek,* usually available on Thursday or Friday, and sells out soon after. You can pick up two-week-old copies of *Newsweek* and *Time* in the open-air bookstalls near Piaţa Romană and Piaţa Universităţii and in the downtown underground metro underpasses. If not, you can read U.S. periodicals at the American Cultural Center Library, Str. Tudor Arghezi 7–9 (☎ **614-00-08**), near the American embassy.

An eight-page daily English-language newspaper called *9 O'clock News* appeared in 1990. Primarily oriented toward a business audience, it also has listings of general interest for travelers: cultural events, restaurant reviews, recommended exchange bureaus, clubs, and movie listings. Check at the Dorobanţi and Inter-Continental hotels for copies.

Police In an emergency, call the police at **055.**

Post Office In general, mail to the U.S. is slow and expensive. Ask your hotel for the nearest post office; one convenient location is inside the main train station, open Monday through Friday from 7:30am to 8pm and on Saturday from 8am to 2pm.

Radio In Bucharest, Radio Contact at 96.1 FM is a 24-hour pop and rock music station that broadcasts BBC news bulletins in English.

Restrooms In Bucharest, as elsewhere in Romania, you should carry toilet paper to use the public restrooms, and women should have a spare 50 lei (4¢) to give to the attendant.

Safety Although I haven't come across any specific statistics, locals say that crime has risen since the December 1989 revolution and reduction of the massive police presence. Be particularly alert for pickpockets and purse snatchers on public transportation, at the train station, and in other crowded areas. As is the case in other major Eastern European capitals, car theft and vandalism are on the rise in Bucharest. Take precautions and be sure to purchase car-theft insurance.

Telephones Telephone numbers within the Bucharest metropolitan area are slowly being converted from six to seven digits. In most cases, this is achieved by adding a **"6"** at the beginning of an existing number. For example, **15-33-00** becomes **615-33-00.** If a six-digit number listed here doesn't work, try adding a **"6."**

You can make international phone calls either from the 24-hour phone bureau at the train station, or at the Communications Center (Direcţia de Telecomunicaţii, sometimes called the Telephone Palace) at Calea Victoriei 37, at the corner of Strada Matei Millo, open Monday through Friday from 7:30am to 8pm and on Saturday from 8am to 2pm. The international phones are located on the right, around the corner from the main entrance. At the time of writing, the cost of making a telephone call to the U.S. from the Communications Center is 1,143 lei (90¢) per minute, with a minimum of three charged. Calling from your hotel is more convenient, but will cost from 20% more to double that rate.

Presently, there's only one public access point, a specially designated phone at Otopeni Airport in Bucharest, from which you can make collect calls and charge calls using an international telephone calling card. See "Fast Facts: Romania" in Chapter 35 for rates.

Water While drinking tap water in most unpolluted regions of Romania poses no threat to travelers except those with delicate systems, it's not recommended in Bucharest. Bottled mineral water is plentiful and inexpensive.

3 Where to Stay

PRIVATE ROOMS Although ONT-Carpaţi no longer rents any private rooms to travelers, a joint U.S.-Romanian travel agency and several individuals do offer accommodations in apartments and houses. By the time you arrive in Bucharest several more private agencies may be renting rooms.

In the U.S., you can contact ACT (Academic Consulting and Travel Services) (☎ **516/499-7851;** fax 516/499-6654) before you leave to reserve a newly renovated studio apartment with all the amenities in a fine downtown location near the American embassy. Access to a direct international phone line and transfers from/to the airport are also available, making these rooms especially suitable for the business traveler. Their Bucharest office is at Str. Allea Valea Villor Nr. 2, Bl. A 53, Sc. D, Apt. 46. (☎ **1/777-95-08;** fax 1/312-10-12).

Keep in mind that many locals would like to rent you a room in their house, often at very reasonable rates—the problem is finding them. If you meet a helpful clerk in the tourist office, a hotel receptionist, or other Romanians, ask if they know of friends who'd like to rent a room or apartment.

One helpful individual renting rooms is Aurelia Dumitrescu (☎ **675-75-58**). Aurelia is an English-speaking guide in Bucharest who has gathered together a group of friends to offer about 50 private rooms to tourists, each costing $30 to $40 per night, including breakfast. As she is often out showing tour groups around, try writing her ahead, or keep calling back to reach her.

HOTELS

Many of Bucharest's belle-époque hotels are receiving badly needed renovation, albeit at varying pace and urgency. Unfortunately, prices seem to be rising more steeply than the level of comfort. Credit cards are rarely accepted unless the booking is made through ONT-Carpaţi.

Capitol, Calea Victoriei 29, Bucharest 70101. ☎ **615-80-30.** Fax 312-41-69. 47 rms (all with bath). A/C TV TEL **Metro:** Piaţa Universităţii.

Rates (including continental breakfast): $34 single; $44 double; $60 triple. AE, DC, MC, V (credit-card payment is only possible with a Carpaţi booking).

For the moment, Capitol is a good value in Bucharest accommodations. The lobby and restaurant, sporting a new skin of mauve and violet with polished wood highlights, are considerably more modern than at other hotels. Rooms range from gracious and large with French doors for windows and marble sinks, to cramped and dim with lumpy mattresses. Cable TV in each room unfortunately carries only Romanian and Italian channels. Renovation similar to the lobby's is slated for guest rooms, accompanied by a ratings upgrade from two to three stars. Until then and the inevitable price increase, Capitol is a strong value.

★ **Hotel Manuc,** Str. Iulia Manin 62–64. ☎ **613-14-15.** Fax 312-28-11. 80 rms (all with bath). TV **Metro:** Piaţa Unirii.

Rates (including breakfast): $45 single; $60 double as single; $66 double. AE, DC, MC, V.

Gracious and free of the obsequious stuffiness common at other Bucharest hotels, this beautifully renovated inn in the center of Bucharest's old town, though on the expensive side of hotels listed here, is an excellent value. Warmth that succored 19th-century travelers is preserved in the half-timbered architecture and guest rooms that face a peaceful inner courtyard. Accessed from wooden arcaded galleries, each guest room has a huge foyer, spacious bed and bathrooms, attractive new wooden furniture, and satellite TV. Accents in brass and a floral-patterned fabric beautifully complement the whitewashed walls and high timbered ceilings. A day bar and an excellent restaurant (see "Where to Eat," below) round out some of the classiest digs in the city.

★ **Hotel Bulevard,** Bd. M. Kogălniceanu 1, 70601 Bucharest. ☎ **615-33-00.** Fax 312-39-23. Telex 10886 GHB. 89 rms (all with bath). TV TEL **Metro:** Piaţa Universităţii.

Rates (including breakfast): First floor, $46 single; $62 double. Second and third floors, $38 single; $46 double. Off-season prices are 10%–20% lower.

Among the city's best hotels, the Hotel Bulevard reflects Bucharest's turn-of-the-century heyday, when high imperial pretension and cheap artisanship produced architectural majesty. Although renovation has not attended Bulevard's relatively high prices, enough faded glory remains to quench one's thirst for pomp, and the hotel is located just minutes from all major tourist sites. Built in 1896 by King Carol I, it looks like a plain government office building on the outside, but step inside and you're surrounded by marble in many shades, marble columns, and Louis XIV–style furniture. Other referents of bygone times are the wrought-iron staircases, good carpets, and stained glass in the restaurant ceiling. The rooms vary greatly in size—some are very large and others have small bathrooms. There's a brasserie with a disco, a restaurant, and a beautifully trimmed day bar.

$ **Hotel Ambassador,** Bd. Magheru 8–10, 70156 Bucharest. ☎ **615-90-80.** 235 rms (all with bath). TV **Metro:** Piaţa Universităţii; the hotel is across the street from the ONT-Carpaţi office.

Rates (including breakfast): $34–$41 single; $53–$63 double. AE, DC, MC, V.

Another very centrally located, older hotel (built in 1937), the Ambassador is a little shabbier than others on this list. The price differential depends on room size and whether it faces the street or the back of the hotel. Most rooms facing the street are quite spacious and flooded with light, decorated with solid furniture, drapes, and

Bucharest Accommodations & Dining

ACCOMMODATIONS
- Capitol 9
- Hotel Ambassador 5
- Hotel Bulevard 13
- Hotel Dorobanţi 1
- Hotel Manuc 16

DINING
- Amzei Market 2
- Brasserie Athenée Palace 4
- Caru Cu Bere 14
- Casa Capşa 10
- Cofeteria 5
- Efes Pub 3
- Hotel Bulevard 13
- Panipat 6
- Restaurant Hotel Manuc 16
- Restaurant Pescarul (The Fisherman) 11
- Simigerie 15
- Spicul 12
- Unirea Market 17

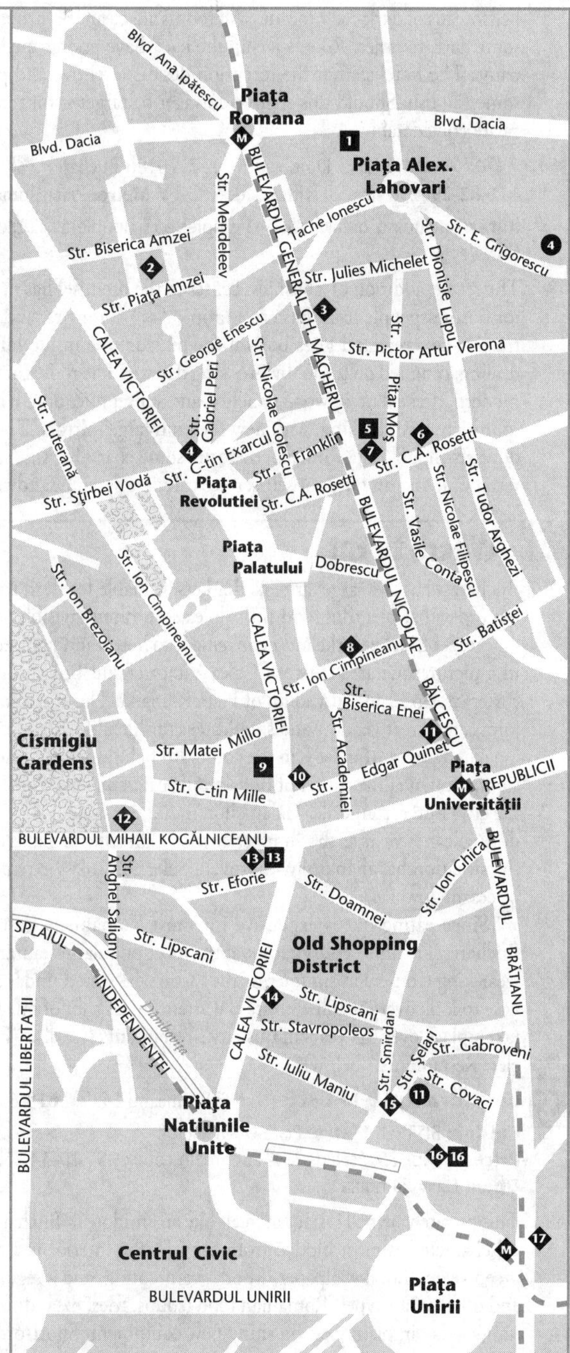

M Metro

bedspreads of dark-red brocades. All rooms are clean. Bathrooms have tubs and handsome dark-red tiles. Rooms facing the back have poorer-quality furniture and older paint. The hotel staff at the reception desk is attentive and professional and speaks some English. Should this eligible dowager be targeted for renovation, prices will escalate considerably.

Hotel Dorobanţl, Calea Dorobantilor 1–7, 70186 Bucharest. ☎ **611-08-60** or **611-82-29.** 298 rms (all with bath). A/C TV **Metro:** Piaţa Romană.

Rates (including breakfast): $41 single; $51 double as single; $63 double. AE, DC, MC, V.

The recent addition of a business center to the premises has made this hotel a favorite for businesspeople from Eastern Europe, Arab countries, and the Far East. An unattractive concrete and glass box on the outside, the inside hums with wheeling and dealing, centered on the lobby's rocking day bar. The rooms are comfortable and fairly modern, dressed up in wood paneling and sunset hues of red, brown, and gold. Bathrooms are fresh looking, with new tiles and large mirrors. The hotel is a bit north of downtown, off Piaţa Romană; there are some charming side streets nearby. There's a restaurant and an outdoor self-service cafeteria serving sandwiches and drinks.

4 Where to Eat

Bucharest has two large farmers' markets, valuable for fresh fruit, vegetables, and as a reminder that plentiful foodstuffs do exist, if often invisibly, in the city.

Amzei Market is the most convenient to hotels and sightseeing. It occupies a plaza in a picturesque area between Calea Victoriei and Bulevardul Magheru, off Strada Bisterica Amzei and just south of Piaţa Romană. The area also concentrates fast-food joints and street vendors and should see considerable urban renewal in coming years.

The **Unirea Market** is in the courtyard behind the enormous Unirea department store, located at the corner of Bulevarduls Brătianu and Unirii in the southern part of the city. Enter from Calea Călăruşilor, under the sign for supermarket Andra. Known during leaner years as the "hunger circus," reflecting its big crowds and thin displays, the situation has thankfully improved. Selection is less extensive than at Amzei, but prices are lower.

Since eating out is expensive for most Romanians, restaurant reservations in Bucharest are unnecessary except at the most popular restaurants. Men should always wear long trousers in summer or they won't be seated under any circumstances. It's wise to look over the bill with special attention, as a lot of imaginative accounting has taken place over the years in this city's restaurants (see also "Frommer's Smart Traveler: Restaurants," below).

$ **Restaurantul a la Carte,** Ion Cîmpineanu 14. ☎ **615-65-98.**

Cuisine: BISTRO. **Metro:** Piaţa Universităţii.

Prices: Soups 85¢; salads 35¢–75¢; main courses $1.10–$4.25.

Open: Daily 24 hours.

This privately owned restaurant feels like an antidote to Bucharest's often brutal physical character. Almost hidden from outside, the interior is a charming mix of plush green velvet, floral wallpaper, woody wainscoting, and a regular clientele of students and other smart types. Romanian food (soups, fries, meat dishes) is made to order 24 hours a day in plain view on shiny new equipment. Short-order cooking assures the food is fresh, if slow in coming during lunch when up to 35 diners crowd the small space. However, the people-watching is excellent—best if you've snagged a seat in one of the opera-box alcoves, and the food, once it arrives, is humble and delicious. The coffee, quite appropriately, is also good. Summer adds a bonus of air conditioning.

★ $ **Restaurant Pescarul [The Fisherman],** Bd. N. Bălcescu 9. ☎ **50-72-44.**
Cuisine: ROMANIAN. **Reservations:** Recommended for dinner.
Prices: Soups and salads 25¢–35¢; main courses $1–$1.40.
Open: Mon–Sat 10am–11pm.

The Fisherman, across the boulevard from the Inter-Continental Hotel, has the largest and most inexpensive selection of fish dishes in town, including sturgeon (*morun*), pike (*zander*), perch (*salau*), trout (*pastrav*), mackerel (*scrumbie*), and carp (*crap*). While most fish is sautéed here, it's quite tasty. For a treat, try the wonderful fish chowder (*ciorbă de peste*). This is one of the few restaurants in Bucharest popular with tourists and Romanians alike, as attests the spirited noise level and smoky atmosphere. Despite elegant starched-linen place settings and heavy flatware, the decor is more publican-funky than fancy. Velveteen drapes, framed pictures of game animals, a high ceiling lined with curved planks of dark stained wood—all contribute to the besotted feeling that one is dining inside an enormous wine cask. Beer, wine, and liquor are served and consumed in rollicksome quantities. All in all, great fun and good eating. For a quieter atmosphere and even stranger decor, try the restaurant's brasserie–day bar next door.

$ **Hotel Bulevard,** Bd. M. Kogălniceanu 1. ☎ **15-33-00.**
Cuisine: ROMANIAN. **Metro:** Piaţa Universităţii.
Prices: Soups 40¢–45¢; salads 20¢–40¢; courses $1.55–$3.85.
Open: Daily 9am–2am.

The main dining room of this hotel restaurant has lavish decor and a romantic fin-de-siècle atmosphere that recalls ghosts of a bygone era. The location couldn't be more central; the prices are reasonable and the service very attentive. There is, however, one major drawback to dining here: Whether or not you enjoy entertainment and loud music with your dinner, you can be assured that most Romanian hotel restaurants feature a floor show of one sort or another with loud music during the summer. The Hotel Bulevard is, sad to say, no exception. The cabaret floor show begins at 9pm and

Frommer's Smart Traveler: Restaurants

1. Never assume that you'll be given a menu—always ask for one before ordering to get an idea of prices.

2. Some restaurants don't have printed menus because they only offer a limited number of dishes supplemented by changing daily specials. If there is no menu, ask the waiter for prices. Write the prices down so you can compare them with the bill.

3. Ask whether dishes are priced by weight (for example, per 100 grams).

4. If the main course doesn't come with side dishes, tell the waiter which garnishes you'd like—otherwise he will decide for you and you might be surprised by the choices and the price.

5. Always check the addition.

the cover charge is about $1.50. However, you'll be able to enjoy a delicious lunch or a quiet early dinner here. The cream of mushroom soup, beef tournedos, and salad are excellent and a terrific bargain for under $2. For light meals, there are omelets and spaghetti. You can enjoy a wide selection of dishes in grand style here without demolishing your budget.

Brasserie Athenée Palace, Str. Episcopei 1–3. ☎ **614-08-99.**

Cuisine: ROMANIAN. **Directions:** Walk to the northeast side of Piaţa Revolutiei, at the corner of Calea Victoriei.
Prices: Spaghetti 50¢–80¢; main courses 90¢–$1.90; fish dishes $2.45–$3.55.
Open: Daily 10am–10pm.

This is an excellent lunch and dinner place if you don't want a long-drawn-out full-course affair. As the waiter explained to me, if you're not entertaining friends and just want a quick meal in Romania, go to the brasserie part of a restaurant. Most main courses are in the $1 to $1.50 range and include schnitzel, pork chops, beef Stroganoff, fish, and grilled meats. Vegetarians can choose from a selection of omelets and spaghetti. This is one of the few places in the Balkans where I was able to find a green salad in early March! This place has a very comfortable mix of formal and casual elements with nice old booths, starched napkins, and the quick if somewhat flustered service of young waiters in training. Menu in Romanian, French, and Chinese.

MEALS FOR LESS THAN $5

Casa Capşa, Str. Edgar Quinet 1. ☎ **13-44-82.**

Cuisine: ROMANIAN. **Reservations:** High season. **Directions:** Walk two blocks south of Piaţa Revolutiei on Calea Victoriei.
Prices: Soups 25¢–90¢; main courses $1–$3.10.
Open: Lunch daily 12:30–5:30pm; dinner daily 7:30pm–midnight (last hot serving at 11pm).

The Capşa has been serving good food in an elegant 19th-century salon since 1852; at the end of the last century it was the great favorite of poets and writers. You'll be seated at a long banquette or on brocade chairs underneath three chandeliers. The walls, as well as flowers and attentive waiters in black tie, all add to the appealing ambience. Specialties include onion soup, beef Wellington, schnitzel Cordon Bleu, venison in wine sauce, and for dessert, ice cream. Fresh caviar is often on the menu as an hors d'oeuvre. According to the manager, "Many foreigners don't even know where Romania is on the map, but they do know Casa Capşa."

Try the brasserie section for quicker, less formal service. The food is prepared in the same kitchen as the more elegant part of the restaurant.

Restaurant Hotel Manuc, in the Hotel Manuc, Str. Iulia Manin 62–64.
☎ **613-14-15.**

Cuisine: ROMANIAN/CONTINENTAL. **Reservations:** Recommended during high season. **Directions:** Follow the southern city center walking tour; it's in the Hotel Manuc.
Prices: Soups 15¢–85¢; main courses 45¢–$1.35; fish $2.85–$5.40. AE, DC, MC, V.
Open: Daily 10am–10 or 11pm.

The hotel's comforting architecture of timbered ceilings over thick arches supports an elegant and cozy dining atmosphere. The menu includes more Romanian dishes than usual in Bucharest's hotel restaurants, allowing one the opportunity to explore specialties that make the Romanian gourmand's heart beat fast. *Tochitura en mamaliga* is a heavy classic of pork and beef in gravy over polenta, crowned with a poached egg. *Pulpa de miel la tava,* a hearty piece of lamb with gravy, will subdue most appetites. A band performs a mixture of folk and pop music every night, thankfully on acoustic instruments. The attentive staff has unfortunately been known to inflate the bill. Check the tab with care, and hold your ground.

BEER HALLS/FAST FOOD

Caru Cu Bere, Str. Stavropoleos 3–5. ☎ **616-37-93.**

Cuisine: ROMANIAN. **Directions:** From the Romanian History Museum, walk north half a block and then turn right.
Prices: Beer 75¢ a mug; soups 75¢; meat platters $2.70–$3.10.
Open: Daily 10am–9:30pm.

Built in 1879 as a German-style beer house, this restaurant has an elaborate interior with neo-Gothic vaulted arches embellished with German coats of arms, stained-glass windows, decorative columns, and a wooden spiral staircase leading up to a balcony floor. They only serve a few main courses here such as grilled pork, sausages (*mititei*), or shish kebab, as well as excellent soup. The attractive decor and lively atmosphere has attracted several generations of dignitaries, including Sen. Edward Kennedy in more recent years. It's a great place to stop on the Walking Tour (see below).

Efes Pub, Bd. Magheru 3.

Cuisine: ROTISSERIE GRILL. **Directions:** Walk south one block from Piaţa Română.
Prices: Half rôtisserie chicken $2.30; sausages $1; baklava 60¢.
Open: Daily 10am–midnight.

With blue-and-yellow awnings and klieg lighting, Efes pub lights up Bulevardul Magheru like a beacon. Efes is a venture between Turkish and Romanian entrepreneurs replacing a seedy, much-loved beer hall with one bigger, cleaner, and so far, less-loved than the original. Summer months help the outdoor beer garden achieve partying critical mass, but at other times, you may find yourself enjoying very good rôtisserie chicken or bratwurst amid many empty booths. Still, Efes remains one of few places in the city for a good meal without hotel restaurant pretension. And where else west of Istanbul can one have an Efes beer and baklava in the same sitting?

PASTRIES

Cofeteria, at the Hotel Ambassador, Bd. Magheru 8–10.

Cuisine: CONFECTIONARY. **Directions:** Walk south on Magheru from Piaţa Română.
Prices: Most items 12¢–25¢.
Open: Daily 8am–10pm.

With an excellent location on Bucharest's main promenade, Cofeteria is well located to deliver a sugar boost when you need it most. The bright, clean room with screaming red walls plies teenyboppers and families with an ultra-rich assortment of tortes, roulades, éclairs, cakes, cookies, and pastries. Except for the loud Western music, the candied air of utopian cheer makes this confectionary the perfect Ceauşescu-era time capsule.

Panipat, Str. C. A. Rossetti 15, half a block from Bd. Magheru.

Cuisine: BAKED GOODS. **Directions:** Walk two blocks south of the ONT-Carpaţi office off Magheru and turn left onto C. A. Rossetti.

Prices: Portions 19¢–25¢; whole tortes and pies $2.70.
Open: Mon–Sat 8am–10pm.

This growing chain of pâtisseries drums up business with irresistible pastries and clever packaging. All over Bucharest people seem to be toting pyramid-shaped packages blazened with the company logo—a horn spilling over with bread products. The apple brioche stars in a superb cast of confections. There is a second location at the corner of Strada Orlando and Calea Victoriei, two blocks south of Piaţa Victoriei.

Simigerie, at the corner of Str. Smîrdan and Str. Selari.

Cuisine: BAKED GOODS. **Directions:** Walk two short blocks north of Stavrapoleos Church in the old shopping district.
Prices: 3¢–13¢.
Open: Mon–Fri 7am–8pm, Sat 9am–1pm.

The grim woman selling out of a decrepit doorway, the dark bustle of activity behind her, the heavenly smell—all suggest a bakery in a war zone. But the product from this implausible takeout in the heart of the old shopping district is delicious. *Covrigi* (3¢) resemble pretzels and come hot and chewy. *Meremere cu branza* (13¢) is flaky and filled with sweet cheese.

Spicul, Kogălniceanu 24–26, at the southeast corner of Cişmigiu Park.

Cuisine: BAKED GOODS. **Directions:** from Piaţa Universităţii, walk west to the corner of Cişmigiu Park.
Prices: 4¢–6¢.
Open: Mon–Fri 6am–8pm, Sat 6am–6pm.

This simple state-run establishment is one of the city's best bakeries, perpetually churning out fresh goodies to a perpetual though speedy line of customers. Rather than crowd the few stand-up tables, head for Cişmigiu Park, Bucharest's leafy oasis just next door. *Trigoane cu brínza* (6¢) is a hot flaky triangle plumped with sweet cheese and dusted in sugar. *Merisur cu mere* (4¢), also flaky, is four-sided and has apple innards.

5 Attractions

Bucharest was established in the 15th century under the rule of Vlad Ţepeş (Count Dracula) as a bulwark against invading Turks. Over the next several hundred years Bucharest thrived as an important trading post among the various states of Romania.

Despite its past economic prosperity and history, few historic structures have survived. The Germans heavily bombed the city at the end of World War II, and even in the last few years 16th- to 18th-century churches and structures have been demolished in an ambitious urban-development plan centered around the Victory of Socialism Boulevard (now renamed Bulevardul Unirii). As a result, much of Bucharest wears a Stalinist face of drab gray buildings. However, in the city's museums and older quarters you'll see many fine examples of Bucharest's art and architecture from its more stylish days.

Suggested Itineraries

If You Have 1 Day

Visit the History Museum and the Art Museum, and take the Walking Tour (see below in this chapter). Leave some time to wander in the Lipscani shopping district.

Bucharest Attractions

INFORMATION

ONT Carpaţi Tourist Office 6

ATTRACTIONS

Amzei Outdoor Market 3
Museum of Art Collections 1
Museum of Ceramics and Glassware 2
Museum of the City of Bucharest 9
Museum of the History of Romania 10
National Art Museum 7
Old Princely Court (Curtea Veche) 11
Romanian Atheneum 8
Swimming Pool (At the Hotel Bucureşti) 5
Tăndarică Puppet and Marionette Theater 4

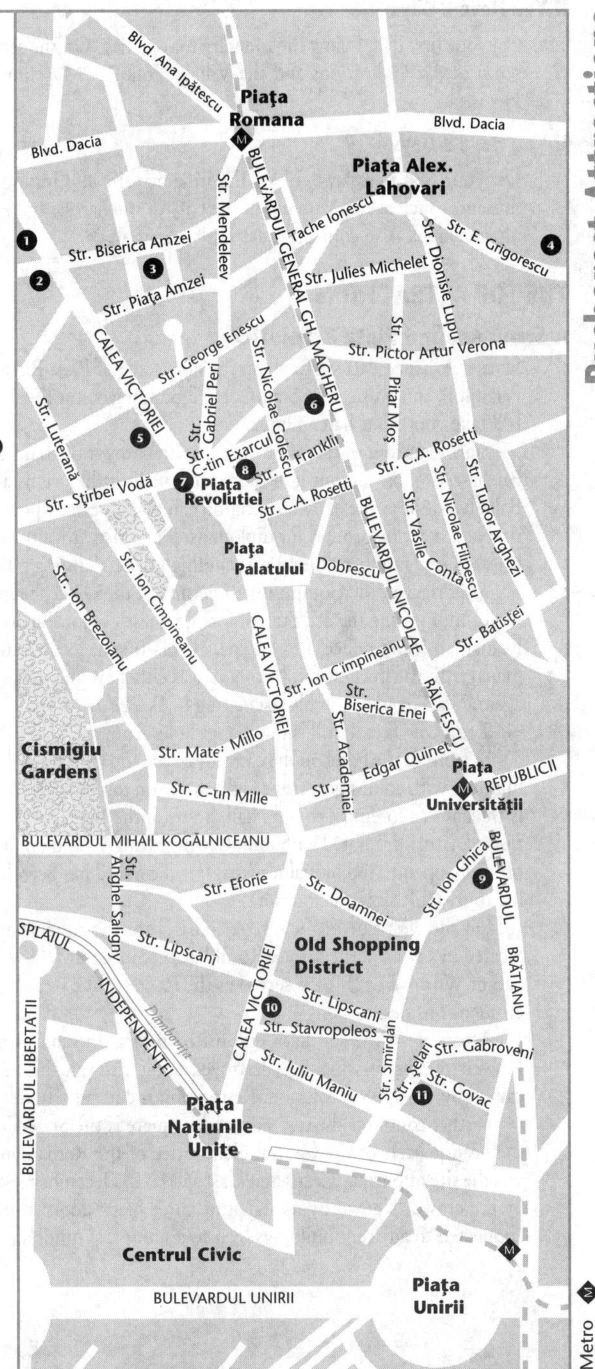

Metro

If You Have 2 Days

On your first day, follow the itinerary for one day. On the second day, visit the Museum of Art Collections and the Village Folk Art Museum and its adjacent park, Herăstrău.

If You Have 3 Days

For your first two days, follow the itinerary above. On your third day, add more museums such as the Museum of the City of Bucharest, and explore more of the city on your own. Also consider a day trip to Snagov.

THE TOP ATTRACTIONS

A Stroll Around Piaţa Revolutiei

Start at Athenée Palace Hotel, on the north side of Piaţa Revolutiei (also called Piaţa Palatului), and finish at the State Council Building on the south side of Piaţa Revolutiei. It'll take you about half an hour.

Start your tour of this large square in downtown Bucharest at the Athenée Palace, Bucharest's most famous hotel and once the most luxurious accommodations in the Balkans. Built in the early 20th century, it was especially popular in the interwar period as a meeting ground for diplomats, journalists, royalty, and adventurers. It was featured in a number of novels, including Oliva Manning's *Balkan Trilogy.*

After the war the Communist government took over the hotel and made it a center for monitoring the activities of foreign guests, according to the former head of the Romanian secret police, Ion Pacepa. "Every one of its 300 employees, from the top manager to the lowliest scrubwoman, was either an intelligence officer or a recruited agent," Pacepa writes in his fascinating book *Red Horizons.*

Today the facade still shows bullet holes from the December 1989 revolution.

In front of the hotel on the east side of the square is the Athenaeum, a neoclassical building with columns in front and a dome on top built in 1888. Today the building is Bucharest's foremost concert hall, home of the Bucharest Philharmonic. The interior is lavishly decorated with murals, winged angels, and other rococo details. It's not officially open to individual tourists, but the guard has been known to allow the polite tourist a look at the interior.

On the west side of the square across from the Athenaeum is the Art Museum, located in a wing of the former Royal Palace. Since the demise of the monarchy at the end of World War II it has served as the Palace of the Republic, and is used for government business.

Across from the southern end of the palace on Piaţa Revolutiei is the Central University Library, which was destroyed along with valuable manuscripts during a fire caused by the 1989 revolution. Restoration is currently under way.

Farther south on the east side of the square is the State Council Building. Once the headquarters of the Central Committee of the Romanian Communist Party, it was the site of Nicolae Ceauşescu's last speech in December 1989, when he was jeered by the crowd. Known by its signature three black doors, the structure is said to be connected to adjacent buildings by a series of secret tunnels.

★ **Museum of the History of Romania,** Calea Victoriei 12. ☎ **15-70-55** or **15-70-56.**

Here you'll learn about Romania's rich history, starting with the foundation of the Dacian state over 2,000 years ago. Pottery, tools, and other aspects of daily life including religious worship illustrate Dacia's early history, and coins, glass, and stone inscriptions highlight the Roman era. The collection also describes the arrival of many migratory tribes in Romania from the 7th to the 11th century, and dedicates an entire room to Vlad Ţepeş, the real Count Dracula from the 15th century. The massive collection contains medieval swords, armor, medieval religious manuscripts, and secular art.

The highlight of the museum is the ★ Lapidarium and Treasury, found straight ahead as you enter the museum. Here you'll see a section-by-section reproduction of Trajan's column in Rome, which recounts the Dacian campaign, as well as original Roman sculptures and stones found across Romania. Beneath the Lapidarium is the heavily guarded ★ Treasury, with gold and precious stones dating back to the 4th millennium B.C. Highlights include: the Orghidan Cameo from the 3rd century A.D., one of the largest cameos in the world; the Pietroasa Treasure, gold pieces dating from the 4th to 5th centuries A.D. that are from a set called the *Hen with the Golden Chickens,* with a large gold plate and several gold chickens and serving pieces; 19th- and 20th-century crowns of the former Romanian family; and valuable jewelry from private collections of the 20th century.

The massive foyer that greets you as you enter, now used for temporary exhibits, used to house the notorious "Proofs of Love" exhibit, a kitschy display of gifts presented to Ceauşescu during his 24 years in power. Notable among displayed items were gifts from the United States given during a period in the 1970s and early 1980s when Ceauşescu found favor with the West for defying the Soviets. American gifts included keys to the cities of Los Angeles, New York, and Allentown; trophies from high school sports teams; and a Mickey Mouse watch, care of Disney. The collection will rest in storage until the time when the museum directors feel comfortable revisiting this episode in Romania's history.

Admission: History museum, 100 lei (7¢); treasury, 100 lei (7¢).

Open: Tues–Sun 10am–6pm (last entry at 5:30pm). **Directions:** Walk south down Calea Victoriei for about 10 minutes from Piaţa Revolutiei. Turn right inside for the history collection or walk straight ahead for the treasury.

National Art Museum, Str. Stirbei Vodă 1.

Located in a wing of the former Royal Palace, Romania's central art museum suffered severe damage in the Romanian revolution of 1989. After Nicolae Ceauşescu fled the capital on the night of December 21, his personal Special Troop bodyguards took positions on the upper floor of the museum. When the army turned against Ceauşescu, heavy fighting ensued, smashing large holes in the museum walls and breaking the windows. Fires broke out in several rooms, destroying the museum archives and its restoration studio; 75 paintings were also destroyed.

The museum has reopened halls in the north and south wings for temporary exhibits while repairs are made.

Admission: 500 lei (40¢) foreigners, 400 lei (30¢) students.

Open: Wed–Sun 10am–6pm. **Directions:** Walk to the northwest side of Piaţa Revolutiei.

Museum of Art Collections, Calea Victoriei 111. ☎ **50-61-32.**

This is one of Bucharest's most interesting museums. It contains collections that once belonged to well-to-do locals, accumulated before and donated shortly after the arrival of socialism in Romania. Many of the collections reposed in family "home museums," until President Ceauşescu decided in 1978 they belonged under the same roof. Whether collections were donated or simply nationalized is unclear, but presently there is talk of returning them. Each collection has been left intact in the museum's galleries, preserving collectors' individual tastes as the primary organizing element. The holdings include works of Romania's greatest painters, a few examples of impressionism and postimpressionism, and a hilarious display of one collector's Orient fetish. Best of all are the Persian, Daghestani, Kazakh, Anatolyan, Uzbek, and Macedonian Oriental rugs, off the floors of private residences and onto the walls.

Other highlights include Henri Matisse's *Nude in Studio* and *Nude Indoors;* Paul Cézanne's *Portrait of a Little Girl,* Renoir's *Two Women Bathing,* Pissarro's *Portrait of a Little Girl,* and Picasso's *Corrida.*

Admission: 600 lei (45¢) adults, 300 lei (25¢) students.

Open: Wed–Sun 10am–6pm. **Metro:** Piaţa Romană. **Directions:** Walk about 10 minutes northwest on Calea Victoriei from Piaţa Revolutiei.

Old Princely Court [Curtea Veche], Ste. Iuliu Maniu 33. ☎ **14-03-75.**

When Bucharest was little more than a village, Vlad the Impaler built his residence here. Parts of his 15th-century palace and walls remain, albeit in somewhat neglected condition, showing some of Bucharest's earliest foundations. In addition to brick walls and staircases you'll see 15th-century column fragments. Additions, renovations, and foot traffic over the years have unfortunately diminished its impact.

Admission: Free.

Open: Currently under reconstruction, so may not be open.

★ **Village and Folk Art Museum,** Şoseaua Kiseleff 28–30. ☎ **617-59-20.**

One of Europe's first outdoor museums, and highly recommended as one of the capital's most noted attractions, this museum was founded by the University of Bucharest in the late 1930s. It's situated on the shore of Herăstrău Lake in Bucharest's largest park and contains more than 300 rural buildings—houses, churches, windmills, and watermills—brought from villages all over Romania. The buildings were chosen as typical of certain regions like Maramureş county, the Danube Delta, Sibiu and Braşov, etc., and many of them contain period furnishings, carpets, and decorative weavings, as well as household implements, ceramics, and costumes reflecting traditional peasant life in these regions. Some outdoor displays contain carved gates and crosses, farm tools, fountains, and well houses. There's a fine gift shop with handmade crafts and an English-language pamphlet with a map for sale at the entrance.

In addition to demonstrations of such crafts as weaving, pottery, and spinning at various times, every Sunday at 11am in the summertime there are folklore shows, music and poetry recitals, and classical-music concerts performed in the amphitheater. An International Folklore Festival and dance competition is held every two years.

Admission: 100 lei (8¢) adults, 50 lei (4¢) students.

Open: Apr–Oct 1, Mon 9am–5pm, Tues–Sun 9am–8pm; Oct 2–Mar, daily 9am–5pm. **Directions:** Bus no. 131 or 331 from the center of town, or metro to Aviatorilor, then either bus.

Patriarchal Cathedral, Aleea Patriarhiei 21.

The seat of the patriarch of the Romanian Orthodox church, this church dates back to 1668. A porch arcade with 20th-century frescoes leads into the interior of the church where a number of former Romanian bishops are buried. Unfortunately, none of the original paintings remain; much of the artwork you see dates only to a 1959–62 restoration. The wooden iconostasis dates back to the 18th century, however. The current patriarch still presides over services here on some Sundays.

Across from the church is the heavily guarded neoclassical Parliament from 1912, where sessions are held every few weeks, and the Patriarch's Palace, a 1708 structure that accommodates the patriarch and the church offices.

Admission: Free.

Open: Daily 7am–7 or 8pm. **Metro:** Piaţa Unirii; then walk southwest up Cathedral Hill.

MORE ATTRACTIONS

Museum of the City of Bucharest, Bd. I. C. Brătianu 1. ☎ **613-21-54.**

This museum (housed in the lovely 1833 neo-Gothic-style Şuţu palace) chronicles events in Bucharest from its earliest settlement to the present day with archeological finds, documents, tools, and historical objects. Wonderful old photographs and maps make a fairly convincing explanation of how the city was once known as the "Paris of the Balkans."

Admission: 500 lei (40¢).

Open: Tues–Sun 10am–5pm. **Metro:** Piaţa Universităţii.

Parcul Herăstrău, north of the city center.

Bucharest is famous for its lush parks and this one is the largest and loveliest, with a series of connecting lakes at its center. In summer you can also go boating here. Or you can go for a leisurely stroll or go swimming, or visit the Village and Folk Art Museum (see above).

Admission: Free.

Open: Daily 24 hours. **Directions:** Metro to Aviatorilor on the blue Line 2; then bus no. 131 or 331.

Swimming Pool, in the Hotel Bucureşti, Calea Victoriei 63–69. ☎ **15-45-80.**

These two large pools (one indoor, the other outdoor) are open to the public year round. There's also a sauna ($1 extra). The entrance is on the side of the hotel on Strada George Enescu.

Admission: 2,000 lei ($1.55) for one entry.

Open: Pool, Tues–Sat 8am–8pm, Sun 8am–2pm, Mon noon–8pm. Sauna, Mon–Fri 7am–7pm, Sat–Sun 7am–1pm. **Directions:** Walk several long blocks north of Piaţa Revolutiei and turn left.

Tăndarică Puppet and Marionette Theater, Str. Eremia Grigorescu 24. ☎ **15-23-77.**

For young and old alike, universal stories like *Cinderella* and *Pinocchio* are performed by the puppet-masters of this world-renowned company. No translation is necessary for these amusing puppet shows. It's located off Piaţa Lahovary.

Admission: 500 lei (40¢).

Open: Schedules vary, but performances are usually at noon or thereabouts. **Metro:** Piaţa Romană.

Grădina Cişmigiu [Cişmigiu Gardens], west of the city center, off Bd. Kogălniceanu.

This 19th-century oasis in central Bucharest is the oldest of Bucharest's many spacious and restful parks that offer respite from urban oppression and summer heat. There are 34 acres of greenery with flowers, a zoo, a restaurant (Monte Carlo), and a lake with rowboats for rent.

Rowboat rental: 560 lei (45¢) per hour, 10am–6pm.

Walking Tour

The Southern City Center

Start Museum of History.
Finish House of the Republic on Bulevardul Unirii.
Time Allow approximately three hours.
Best Times Shopping hours, when many locals make their way to Strada Lipscani.
Worst Times In the evenings, when churches are closed.

From Bucharest's most important museum on Calea Victoriei, walk down the museum steps to the right and take the first right down Strada Stavropoleos. After a block you'll arrive at the:

1. **Stavropoleos Church,** at no. 6. Built in 1724 by a Greek monk in Byzantine style fused with Renaissance elements, it's rich in wood and stone carving. A flashlight will serve you well here, as the lighting is dim. In the church courtyard are tombstones under an arcade. It's generally open from 8am to 7 or 8pm, with occasional pauses from noon to 4 or 5pm.

Refueling Stop

For a beer and a choice of a few main courses amid stunning neo-Gothic decor, drop by the **Caru cu Bere,** located just a few steps away from the church back toward the Museum of History.

From the church, continue to the end of the street and then turn left on Strada Smîrdan. The first street you immediately come upon is one of Bucharest's busiest shopping thoroughfares:

2. **Strada Lipscani.** After surveying the people and window-shopping, return to Strada Smîrdan, walk south, and take the first left onto Strada Iuliu Maniu. After a short block you'll pass the:
3. **Old Princely Court (Curtea Veche),** Count Dracula's home in Bucharest. Immediately past these ruins is:
4. **Biserica St. Anton,** a small Romanian Orthodox church with paintings on the wall and an iconostasis. Across the street is:
5. **Hanul Manuc (Manuc's Inn).** Built by an Armenian merchant and politician named Manuc Bey Mirzaian as a caravansary (inn) in 1808, it's still maintained as a unique hotel. Its 32 rooms are decorated in period style with wooden ceilings and old furniture. A long balcony with wooden pillars carved

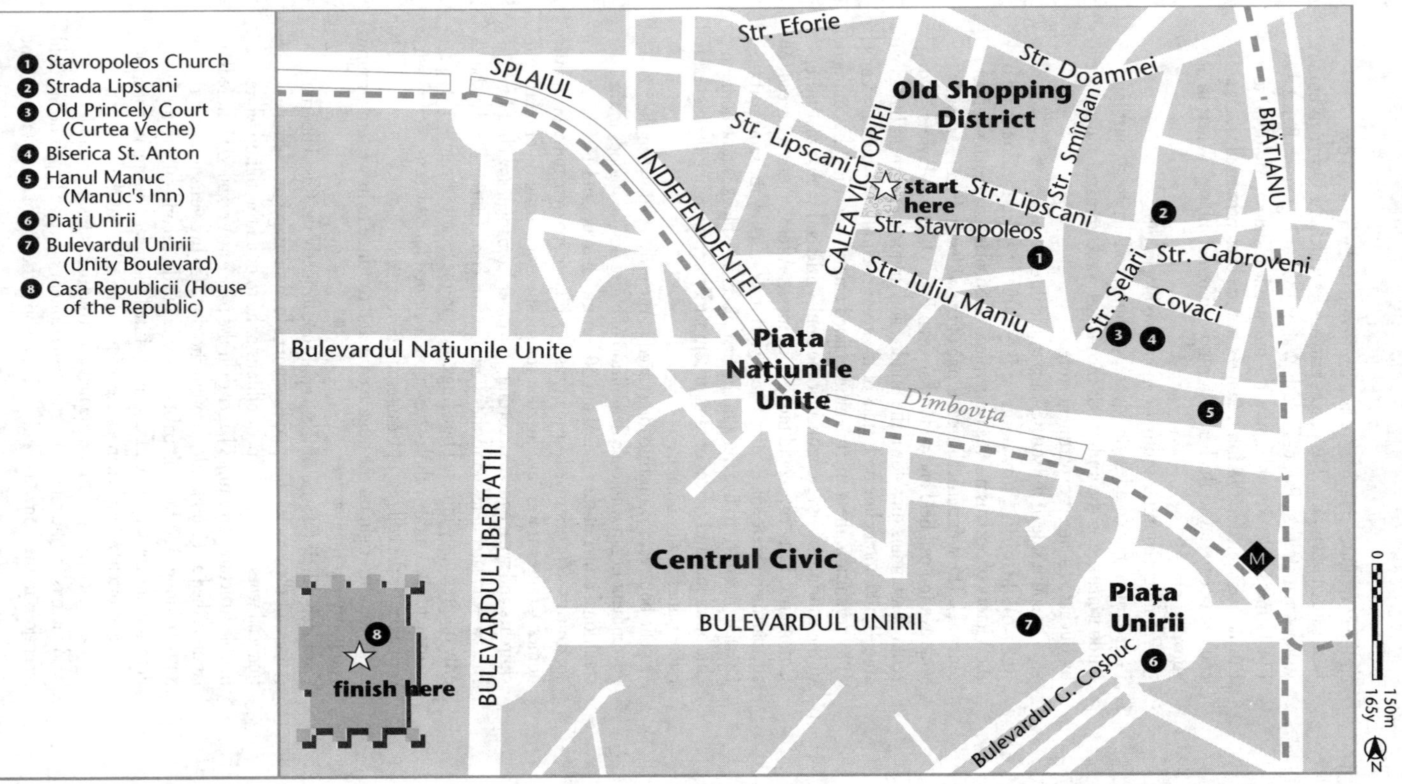

Walking Tour — The Southern City Center

in the Maramureş style overlooks a large courtyard with a rowdy beer-garden restaurant. The peace treaty under which the Ottoman Empire surrendered after the Russo-Turkish War of 1806–12, granting Bessarabia (the former Soviet Republic, now the independent state of Moldova) to Russia, was signed in this inn. Manuc's Inn has been privatized and is a choice place to stay in Bucharest (for more information, see "Where to Stay," above).

From here continue south for about two blocks to:

6. **Piaţa Unirii.** For decades this square was home to Bucharest's bustling outdoor market; in the mid-1980s the market was eliminated and replaced by Bucharest's largest department store.

The south side of the square leads to the three-mile-long:

7. **Bulevardul Unirii (Unity Boulevard)**—formerly called the Boulevard of the Victory of Socialism—the centerpiece of Nicolae Ceauşescu's "urban renewal." The symmetrical street is one of the widest in Europe, about as wide as a football field and wider than even Paris's Champs-Elysées. A long series of fountains runs down the middle, and uniform apartment blocks with some 1,500 homes line both sides of the avenue. Until Romania's December 1989 revolution, these apartments remained empty—awaiting the completion of the enormous Casa Republicii at the boulevard's end so that the entire Communist Party elite could move in en masse. After Ceauşescu's execution, all apartments were snapped up cheaply, in most cases by the same party favorites intended to live there in the first place. The block is now home to chic boutiques and offices of foreign companies, commanding the highest real estate values in all Romania.

The boulevard's construction started in the early 1980s when the government began wholesale demolition of entire neighborhoods in the traditional center of the city. About 30 historic churches and 15,000 apartments were destroyed; as many as 50,000 citizens were moved from their homes. Ceauşescu was "overjoyed at the prospect of getting rid of musty old churches and synagogues," according to former Romanian spy chief Ion Pacepa, who later defected to the West. Construction continues today, but only on previously initiated buildings. Behind the facade of completed apartments lie muddy rubble-strewn tracts cleared for new construction but orphaned by the collapse of Ceauşescu's government.

If you turn right on the huge avenue and continue to its western terminus you'll arrive at the massive:

8. **Casa Republicii (House of the Republic),** formerly the Casa Poporului (House of the People). Despite Romania's food shortages and terrible financial woes, Ceauşescu spent billions of lei to build this hilltop white marble structure three times larger than the palace at Versailles. Hundreds of laborers died as 12,000 toiled around the clock for five years to create the 840-foot-long, 300-foot-tall palace that's reputedly second only to the U.S. Pentagon in size. Ceauşescu frequently visited the palace during its construction, and often ordered changes according to his whim of the moment.

Ceauşescu planned to use the massive structure as his home and headquarters for the most important government offices. He planned to hold receptions in the Romania Hall, which is about the size of a football field and decorated with hand-carved marble and gold leaf. And to ensure against political trouble, he built miles of secret escape tunnels underneath the palace.

Although the interior was open to visitors for a few months after the revolution, it is now closed; at press time, the government is still trying to decide exactly what to do with it.

6 Savvy Shopping

Although Bucharest is no shopper's paradise, there are many interesting items available at very good prices: Crafts, antiques, and folk music are good buys.

The best places to buy Romanian crafts like embroidered towels and blouses, carved wooden items, and tooled leather goods are at "Artizanat" shops. In downtown Bucharest "Artizanat" shops can be found at Str. Academiei 35–37, Piaţa Revolutiei 12, Bd. Magheru 11, and Calea Victoriei 24. Like most shops in Romania, they're closed Sunday. All large department stores have crafts sections that are usually located on the ground floor.

The best music store for records and tapes is the "Muzica" shop at Calea Victoriei 49, open Monday through Friday from 9:30am to 7pm.

There is also a growing number of good antiques and consignment shops, the best ones at Calea Victoriei 56 and Str. Buzeşti 61 (near Piaţa Victoriei).

The best areas to window-shop are the wide thoroughfares Calea Victoriei and Bulevarduls Magheru/Bălcescu/Brătianu.

There is a more lively area of small shops and Gypsy and Turkish street stalls in the maze of narrow streets off Strada Lipscani that is the old shopping district.

A wonderful complex of eight boutiques and art galleries in a restored inn, Hanul Bazarul cu tei, is located off Lipscani (look for the signs). The items purchased there have been approved by the Ministry of Culture and can legally be taken out of the country. Some travelers have found real treasures there like antique jewelry and fountain pens, hand-painted silk dresses, and modern paintings for very good prices.

For outdoor and flea markets, visit Bucharest's central outdoor/indoor market at Piaţa Obor. Enormous and busy, this is mainly a fresh produce and flowers market, though there are some crafts and household items for sale. To get there, take the Metro to the "Obor" stop, tram no. 5 or trolleybus no. 66.

7 Evening Entertainment

Bucharest offers little in the way of Western nightlife. Unless you meet some locals to socialize with, you'll probably turn in early. Dim street lighting by night does not help the evening action. Of course, some locals stay up late, but mostly to eat and drink at a restaurant for several hours and maybe dance to the restaurant's live band. Hotels featuring a band and dance floor include the Continental, Athenée Palace, and Bucureşti, a few of these hotels also sponsor nightclub acts.

THE PERFORMING ARTS Bucharest's most distinguished cultural arena, with a lavish rococo interior, is the Romanian Athenaeum, Str. Franklin 1, on the northeast side of Piaţa Revolutiei. (☎ **615-00-26**). The local philharmonic has its headquarters here and visiting groups often perform here, but events are held only September to June. The box office is open daily from 10am to 6pm. Tickets typically cost under $1.

For information on other concerts in town, including at the Opera House at Bulevardul Kogălniceanu 70 (☎ **613-18-57**), ask a local for help in checking the listings in the newspaper. Or ask the National Tourist Office.

MOVIES The Romanian National Archive maintains two theaters in Bucharest that show, in addition to features from the Romanian cinema, an excellent repertory of classic, cult, and popular Hollywood films. Nearly all films are shown with subtitles. Cinema Eforie is at Str. Eforie 2 (☎ **613-04-83**), Cinema Union is on Strada Ion Câmpineanu (☎ **613-49-04**). Printed schedules are obtainable outside the cinemas. Tickets cost 350 lei (30¢).

Cinema Patria (Bd. Magheru 12–14) is the first cinema in Romania to get the latest Arnold Schwarzenegger and Jean-Claude Van Damme extravaganzas, usually within six weeks of U.S. release. Tickets cost 300 lei (25¢) and shows run roughly every two hours between 9am and 7pm.

8 An Easy Excursion

LAKE SNAGOV

Although Bucharest has many fine parks, a new favorite of city dwellers eager to get away for a day of swimming, picnicking, and walking in the woods is Lake Snagov, 22 miles north of the capital. The lake, private villas on its shores, and surrounding woods were the exclusive retreat of the Ceauşescu clan and their trusted friends, but the area is now open to the public and some of the villas have been turned into hotels and restaurants. It has also become an obligatory stop on the Dracula tours: Legend has it that Vlad Ţepeş is buried under the altar of a church on the island. He supposedly went into hiding in the church to escape execution after losing a battle against the Turks and then built a fortified monastery, which is still functioning as a place of worship with several monks in residence.

There are several ways to get to Snagov Lake and the monastery. You can pay for the convenience of a pricey (but infrequent) excursion with a group at ONT-Carpaţi, or you can take a bus or train on your own. Take bus no. 131 or 331 from Lahovary Square to the main North Bus Station at Piaţa Presei Libere, where you can catch buses to Snagov Lake and the zoo in Băneasa Forest (Pădurea Băneasa). To get to the monastery on the island in the middle of the lake, you'll want to catch a ferry. Follow the signs or ask locals in the village of Snagov for directions to the ferry; it's about a mile walk. The ferry runs daily from mid-May to mid-September whenever the captain determines he has enough people on board (every hour or so). The bus and boat fares cost only a few cents.

Alternatively, you can take a train from Gară de Nord or Băneasa Station, farther north. The train takes about an hour; then it's a pleasant countryside walk of a bit over a mile to the lake. You can swim in the lake and rent a rowboat, but there's no place to dock on the island, so don't try to row out to the monastery. You might like to bring a picnic lunch, although there are outdoor food stalls and a few beer gardens serving grilled meats and drinks.

9 Moving On—Travel Services

BY PLANE For international tickets and reservations, go to the TAROM office at the corner of Domiţa Anastasia and Strada Brezoianu (☎ **16-33-46** for information, **15-27-47** for reservations), open Monday through Thursday from 7:30am to 6pm and on Friday from 7:30am to 2pm.

For domestic tickets, go to TAROM's other office in Piaţa Victoriei (☎ **59-41-85**), open Monday through Friday from 8am to 5pm. Domestic flights depart from Băneasa Airport (☎ **33-53-92**), near Otopeni.

Most European air carriers have offices along Magheru.

Buses to both the domestic airport Băneasa and Otopeni International Airport depart almost hourly on the hour from 5am to 11pm from the main TAROM office on the corner at Str. Brezoianu 10, with a stop across from the ONT tourist office. The ride to Otopeni takes 40 minutes and costs 100 lei (8¢). Buy the ticket from the driver. For up-to-date bus times, either consult TAROM's international timetable (available from their New York and most domestic offices); alternatively, call TAROM (☎ **16-33-46**), Bucharest's main tourist office, or the airport (☎ **33-31-37** or **33-66-02**).

BY TRAIN Before you leave Bucharest by train, you have a substantial labor ahead—buying the tickets. For domestic train tickets, go to the CFR rail agency at Brezoianu 10 (☎ **13-26-42** to **13-26-44, 15-56-86, 13-90-21,** or **14-98-19**), located inside the TAROM international ticket office with only a TAROM sign outside. The CFR office is open Monday through Friday from 7:30am to 7pm and on Saturday from 7:30am to 1pm. Expect long lines at all hours.

You can also buy domestic tickets at the train station two hours before the train departs, a confusing and frustrating option. Go to the information desk on the right as you walk in and ask at which window you must buy your ticket. First- and second-class tickets are sold in different, adjacent halls.

For international train tickets, visit the CFR office on the second floor of Bulevardul Brătianu 44 bis (☎ **40-11-26**), with the entrance on Piaţa Unirii. Buying a ticket in the midst of the complete chaos that reigns here may prove the single most difficult task for a tourist in Eastern Europe, so if you do succeed in getting a ticket, my congratulations! You must pay for international tickets in hard currency. Open Monday through Friday from 7:30am to 6pm and on Saturday from 7:30am to noon.

BY BUS In the last few years, a few private travel agencies have begun to offer direct buses from Bucharest to Istanbul or Athens at very low fares (about $30). To find these offers, look for advertisements in hotel lobbies in the center, or ask the tourist office. Buses to Istanbul often depart from the Gară de Nord and you buy the ticket directly on board. You have to go there to find out the current schedule.

37 Transylvania & Moldavia

COUNT DRACULA LIVED IN TRANSYLVANIA, AND IN THE MINDS OF MANY HE STILL dwells in the mysterious hamlets of this remote region. Despite the gloomy reputation, Transylvania is home to Romania's most charming towns. In places like Braşov, Sibiu, and Cluj-Napoca, you'll find medieval churches and old town halls towering over two- and three-story buildings. And in the Maramureş region near the Ukrainian border, you'll see peasants in native costumes preserving traditions virtually extinct in the rest of Europe.

Museums in Transylvania chronicle its long history, which began before the Roman colonization. You'll also see Central European architecture dating from an era when Transylvania was part of Hungary. Two million Hungarians still live in this region, which remains a continuing source of diplomatic friction between Hungary and Romania.

Moldavia is not as famous in Western folklore as Transylvania, but it contains stunning medieval monasteries spread across the countryside—the most beautiful of them centered around Suceava. Their brightly colored frescoes are a moving testament to religious devotion and esthetic refinement.

The picturesque towns of Transylvania and Moldavia should be your primary destinations in Romania. After all, how many opportunities will you have to visit the painted monasteries of Bukovina or the castles of Dracula?

SEEING TRANSYLVANIA & MOLDAVIA

Distances are fairly vast and transportation slow between the cities listed in this chapter, so you'll either have to pick out just a few destinations or allow as much as two weeks to see everything.

One logical starting point from Bucharest is Braşov, three hours away by train. From there you can connect to Sibiu and then Cluj by fairly good train connections.

If you want to explore the peasant culture in Maramureş you'll need a car, which will be quite useful in seeing the Bukovina monasteries north of Suceava as well. If you want to make an extensive tour of Romania's north, drive from Cluj through Baia Mare to explore the peasant villages, and then continue to Suceava and the Bukovina monasteries. You can also visit Suceava by overnight train from Bucharest or from the major cities in Transylvania (though train routes are circuitous). It's easiest to visit Iaşi from Suceava.

1 Braşov

103 miles NW from Bucharest

GETTING THERE • By Train The express train from Bucharest takes under three hours and costs $1.60 in first class.

The train station on Piaţa Gării (☎ **11-02-33**) is in a modern part of town northeast of the historic center. To reach the Old Town, take trolley bus no. 3 or regular bus no. 4; if you prefer to walk for about 25 minutes, go straight down the wide Bulevardul Victoriei, and continue to the right down 15 Noiembre. Pass Piaţa Teatrului and enter the Old Town on Strada Republicii.

What's Special About Transylvania & Moldavia

Architectural Highlights

- Castle of Bran, near Braşov, reputedly the home of Count Dracula.
- Citadel of Alba Iulia, the largest in Transylvania, with an interior large enough to accommodate a small city.

Churches

- Black Church of Braşov, Transylvania's most important Gothic structure, with a mellifluous organ; offers summertime concerts.
- Cluj's 14th-century St. Michael's Church, with many fragments of the original medieval decorations still intact.
- Wonderfully well preserved interior and exterior religious frescoes of the Bukovina monasteries, a site often considered the tourist highlight of Romania.
- Church of the Three Hierarchs in Iaşi, from the early 17th century with an intricately carved stone exterior.

Museums

- Brukenthal Museum in Sibiu, with one of Romania's finest collections of folk art and paintings.
- Cluj's Art Museum, with a rich collection of Romanian and some European painting.
- Ethnographic Museum in Cluj, with a large collection of Romanian peasant culture.
- Art Museum and Polytechnical Museum in Iaşi's Palace of Culture, with European masters' paintings and a collection of music boxes.
- Outdoor museums re-creating typical Romanian peasant villages in Sibiu and Cluj.

Villages

- Sibiel, a peasant village outside Sibiu with a lovely church and hospitable locals who offer room and board.
- The Maramureş region near the border, where peasants live little affected by modernity, preserving their age-old culture and crafts.

Buy onward tickets from the CFR Railway Agency in the heart of the Old Town at Str. Republicii 53 (☎ **14-29-12**), open Monday through Friday from 7am to 7:30pm. Connections to Sibiu and Cluj-Napoca are good; there are four or five *rapid* trains daily.

• **By Car** The drive from Bucharest takes about three hours and passes through a region of vast pollution around Ploeşti, yielding to mountain beauty closer to Braşov.

ESSENTIALS Braşov's telephone area code is 68.

ORIENTATION Most of the sights and hotels are in the Old Town, southwest of modern Braşov. The lovely main square is Piaţa Sfatului, which connects to a lively pedestrian street, Strada Republicii. The town's principal sights all lie within walking distance of this square. Just south of the Old Town rises Timpa Mountain.

INFORMATION The company Societatea Comercială Postăvarul has replaced the ONT-Carpaţi Tourist Office in the Hotel Aro Palace at Bd. Eroilor 9 (☎ **68/14-28-40;** fax 68/14-16-48). This office, located to the right after you pass the reception desk, has lots of brochures; the helpful staff will assist you with information about Braşov and trips to Bran Castle ($28). They're open Monday through Saturday from 8am to 8pm and on Sunday from 8am to noon. When they're closed, ask for help at the Hotel Aro reception desk.

Braşov is the northernmost Romanian city with Hertz and Europcar offices. You may want to pick up a rental here for trips to the remote Maramureş and Bukovina regions. Hertz (☎ **11-89-20**) is in the Hotel Capitol, Bd. Eroilor 19; Europcar (☎ **14-28-40**) is in the Hotel Carpaţi, Bd. Eroilor 25.

You can make international phone calls at the Telephone Bureau, on the corner of the Hotel Capitol off Bulevardul Eroilor. The office is open daily from 6:30am to 9pm.

An excellent map of the city is widely available at newsstands and tourist offices. Called *Braşov—Planul Municipului,* it costs 250 lei (19¢) and comes with pullout indices for monuments, services, and public transportation routes.

SPECIAL EVENTS On the first Sunday in May Braşov hosts a 400-year-old Youth Folk Dance Festival that includes a costume parade; there are also two new festivals, the "Golden Stag" Annual Festival of Music in September and the Jazz Festival from September to October.

Romania's second-largest city, Braşov (pop. 323,000) differs markedly from the country's capital. Travelers fatigued by Bucharest's gray immensity will savor the human scale and charm of Braşov's picturesque medieval center. Nestled in the velvet lap of Mt. Timpa, the battlemented Old Town enchants. Burgher houses in cheerful pastels shape a vibrant town square; narrow cobbled streets wind off from the center, still clattering and echoing after centuries with sounds of life and commerce; and church spires and clock towers add a counterpoint of Gothic gravity.

Braşov's importance as a major trading center dates back to the 13th century when as Kronstadt it was one of seven major Transylvanian towns founded by German merchants from Saxony and the Rhineland. Many of the town's medieval and Renaissance buildings still exist, thanks to the diplomatic skill and military foresight of town leaders. During repeated Turkish attacks in the region from the 15th to the 18th century, strongly fortified Braşov escaped major war damage. Braşov remains a center of trade, but the cloth, metal, and wax production of yore has been supplanted by tractors, furniture, and fabrics.

WHAT TO SEE & DO

Black Church (Biserica Neagră), Piaţa Curtea Bisericii Neagră.

Smoke damage from a 1689 fire blackened the walls of this 14th-century Lutheran church, giving it its distinctive name. Long since cleaned up, any lingering blackness is the result of pollution. The church, which serves the 1,000 ethnic Germans still living in Braşov, represents the farthest incursion of Protestantism in the Balkans. Turkish rugs from the 17th and 18th centuries hang from carved pews and balconies, lending the church a strange Islamic touch. They were given by Saxon merchants between the 15th and 18th centuries. Notice the painted crests designating pews of specific guilds. The organ, which dates from 1839, has 4,002 pipes, making it the largest in Romania and Southern Europe. The central pews have been designed with flipping backrests to face the organ in the back of the church. Sample them yourself at a concert, given in July and August on Tuesday, Thursday, and Saturday. September concerts take place on Wednesday. All concerts cost 150 lei (12¢) and begin at 6pm.

Admission: 100 lei (8¢).

Open: July–Aug, Mon–Sat 9:30am–6pm; the rest of the year, Mon–Sat 9:30–1pm and 3–5pm. **Directions:** Walk half a block southwest from Piaţa Sfatului.

Braşov History Museum, Piaţa Sfatului 30. ☎ **14-36-85.**

You can learn about the historical past of Braşov and all of Transylvania inside the 15th-century Casa Sfatului (Council Hall), where town leaders once decided Braşov's trade and diplomatic policy. The exterior of this apricot-colored building has a clock tower at its center built in 1528.

Admission: 100 lei (8¢).

Open: Tues–Sun 10am–6pm. **Directions:** Walk to the center of Piaţa Sfatului.

Schei Gate [Porta Schei].

Until the 20th century, Romanians and Hungarians were not allowed to own land in the center of the city. In 1828, Schei Gate was erected on the boundary between Saxon Kronstadt and the Romanian Schei District, as a tollhouse and symbolic barrier to non-Saxons.

Directions: From Piaţa Sfatului, walk south and then west along Schei Gate Street for 10 minutes.

St. Nicholas Church, Piaţa Unirii 2.

This multispired Orthodox church, with an uncharacteristic Gothic steeple at its center, dates its foundations to 1400. It has served as the main church for the Romanian community of Braşov from the time Romanians were required to live outside the walls of the Kronstadt citadel. Russian tsarina Elizabeth donated funds for the clock tower in 1750. A fresco of Romania's last king, Michael, in full military dress, is up on the right as you enter. Sunday mass, featuring a gorgeous choir, is worth visiting for the intense devotion and community spirit that accompany it.

The building on the left of the church was the first school in Transylvania (1760) to teach in the Romanian language. It now contains a museum with old manuscripts, paintings, silver, and other precious objects.

The cemetery abutting the church has served the Romanian community for centuries. Its height and slope are the result of several burial strata. The view out from within the cemetery—a diorama of grave markers against the city's terra-cotta roofs with stepped grazing pastures on the horizon—is breathtaking.

Admission: Free.

Open: Church, Tues noon–6pm, Wed 8am–7pm, Thurs 8am–6pm, Fri 8am–7pm, Sat 7am–3pm, Sun 6am–7pm; museum, Tues–Sun 9am–6pm. **Directions:** Walk about 10 minutes southwest of Piaţa Sfatului.

Tîmpa Mountain, south of the Old Town.

To enjoy a panoramic view of both modern and ancient Braşov, ride to the top of this steep mountain just a few blocks south of Piaţa Sfatului. You can get to the top in a few minutes via cable car (called *Tele Cabina* in Romanian) on Strada Tiberiu Brediceanu for 500 lei (40¢). On the way to the cable car you'll see fragments of the original 15th-century town walls. If you exit the cable car to the left, you'll soon arrive at the Weaver's Bastion, the town's best-preserved 16th-century bastion and now housing a small museum with a miniature model of 17th-century Braşov.

Open: Cable-car rides, summer, Tues–Sun 9am–10pm; 10:30am–6pm winter. **Directions:** To get to the cable car, exit Piața Sfatului to the southeast, and continue to Strada Castelului. A path continues from here to Strada Tiberiu Brediceanu; then turn right to the cable car.

WHERE TO STAY

PRIVATE ROOMS There's a new private accommodations office called EXO at Str. Postăvarul 6 (☎ **68/14-45-91;** fax 14-39-75). The sign on the building says DISPECERAT CAZARE. It's open Monday through Saturday from 11am to 8pm, and Sunday from 11am to 2pm. Rooms cost $5.50 to $16 per day. All rooms are within a 15-minute walk of the Old Town. During the tourist season, it's best to call in advance from Bucharest to reserve a centrally located room.

Hotels

Hotel Coroana, Str. Republicii 62, 2200 Brașov. ☎ **68/14-43-30.** 79 rms (all with bath). TV TEL **Bus:** 4 from the train station.

Rates (including breakfast): $44.50 double as single; $56.60 double. Winter rates are 10% less. AE, DC, MC, V.

This hotel's central location—just off the Old Town's lively main street, Strada Republicii—and some recent renovations recommend it as the best place to stay in town. Chandeliers, brass fixtures, stained glass, and lots of marble give the hotel some upscale sparkle. High ceilings create a feeling of spaciousness. The staff at the desk is friendly in several languages. The hotel has a dim, high-ceilinged brasserie frequented by locals who can get loud and animated, but the food is delicious, inexpensive, and served quickly. Try their vegetable veal soup and roast chicken.

Hotel Capitol, Bd. Eroilor 19, 2200 Brașov. ☎ **68/11-89-20.** 184 rms (all with bath). TV TEL **Bus:** 4 from the train station.

Rates (including continental breakfast): $50 double as single; $57.70–$63.50 double. Highest prices May 16–Sept. AE, DC, MC, V.

This nondescript high-rise hotel has a fine location and some of the rooms on the upper floors offer really beautiful views over a nearby hill through wall-to-wall windows. The dark-wood lobby seems musty and some of the rooms are dingy with truly shocking color combinations. Be sure to ask for the more recently renovated rooms—they have new furniture and new carpets. The bathrooms are clean with large mirrors, and the service is excellent. Call early; tour groups often stay in the Capitol. The Capitol also participated in recent history, as various military forces took positions in the hotel during the December 1989 revolution and engaged in heavy fighting. There are still visible bullet marks on the hotel facade.

WHERE TO EAT

Meals for Less Than $5

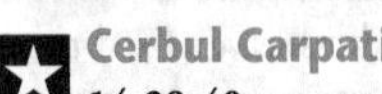

Cerbul Carpatin [Carpathian Stag], Piața Sfatului 13. ☎ **14-39-81** or **14-28-40.**

Cuisine: ROMANIAN. **Reservations:** Recommended on folklore nights. You may need to haggle with the doorman if your group is a small one. **Directions:** Walk to the south side of the main square.

Prices: Three-course meal, without wine, roughly $4. There's a $1 cover charge on folklore nights.

Open: Dinner only, Tues–Sun 7–10pm. **Closed:** Mid-Oct to mid-Dec to replenish the wine cellar.

An obligatory stop on many group tours, this restaurant is one of the best places in the country for a full-tilt evening of Romanian folklore, an experience you should have at least once (although you will be lucky to escape the country with that few). The 16th-century Renaissance building on the main town square features two long dining rooms with steeply banked walls that magnify the rollicking effect produced by energetic, talented dancers and fine singers who perform in stunning authentic costumes. Their repertoire includes many song and dance favorites from different regions of Romania. You can sit in either of the two long rooms, or in the wine cellar. Main courses include carp, sarmale, beef Stroganoff, and grilled veal and pork; the salads are quite good. Be sure to sample the restaurant's fine wine from their huge private cellar; the pinot gris murfatlar, a fragrant, faintly sweet dessert wine, is especially good after dinner.

Orient Ceai-Cafe, Str. Republicii 2.

Cuisine: DESSERT.
Prices: Hot beverages 6¢–30¢; snacks 12¢–40¢; desserts 14¢–25¢.
Open: Daily 9am–9pm.

There's no other café like this privately run day bar in all of Romania. A great place for breakfast, a light meal, or coffee and dessert, it looks like something from a stylish street in Paris. Porcelain chandeliers hang from a timbered roof, wicker panels alternate with *art moderne* lamp pillars along the walls, and marble cladding tops off the seating area. The central café branches off into separate rooms: On the left side you can order pastries with coffee or tea, liquor, and soft drinks. The right side serves snacks and light meals like omelets, ham and salami appetizers, and pizza. A beautiful ceramic tiled stove, arched windows, and fresh flowers complete the elegant decor. Just off the northeastern corner of Piaţa Sfatului, the café spills out onto an outdoor terrace in the summer.

Worth the Extra Money

Restaurant Cetate, Cetăţuia Hill. ☎ **11-76-14.**

Cuisine: ROMANIAN/INTERNATIONAL. **Reservations:** Recommended in summer.
Directions: No buses come to this hilltop location, so either walk up the hill north of the Old Town (for about 20 minutes) or take a taxi.
Prices: Average meal $8 (including cover charge for musical program).
Open: Daily 11am–10pm.

Admit it, castles connote consumption. You toured Castelul Bran and thought of tables groaning with food and flowing with wine. You thought how wonderful mead and lamb must have tasted while arrows clattered ineffectually against the outside walls. At this 15th-century fortress-cum-restaurant, you no longer need repress those Falstaffian fantasies. Amid artifacts from the Middle Ages such as axes, crossbows, and armor, waiters dressed in a modest approximation of medievel dress serve a fixed-price menu of tasty international and Romanian specialties. A small band performs, enlarged to a small orchestra when groups come to dinner. Vocalists accompany the orchestra after dinner to finish the evening in rousing song. The music begins at 7:30 or 8pm and lasts until 10pm, except Thursday. If you prefer to do without the music, you can eat in other sections of the castle and order à la carte. Lunch outside on one of the battlemented porches can be lovely in nice weather.

Easy Excursions

POIANA BRAŞOV

Romania's best-known and most popular winter ski resort, Poiana Braşov offers alpine magnificence and sweet air year-round. Only eight miles southwest of Braşov and serviced by frequent buses, the trip is an easy excursion. Skiing and sledding is from November to March on a network of a dozen ski slopes and sledding runs of various difficulty. Some of the ski lifts, which include cable chairs, tows, and a gondola, are open during the summer for hiking and general sightseeing. There's also a variety of recreational facilities for other seasonal activities like swimming, tennis, volleyball, minigolf, and horseback riding. Sports equipment can be rented at the half-dozen major hotels. For amusement in the evenings there are discos, bars, bonfire cookouts, folk performances at restaurants, and floor shows.

The sports facilities, hotels and villas, restaurants, and bars are some of the best-supplied and -equipped establishments in Romania outside Bucharest and the affordable prices in Poiana Braşov attract Europeans, especially the English and Germans, looking for inexpensive package holidays. For the latest information on prices and charter flights, contact Roman Holidays at 54 Pembroke Rd., London W8 6NX (☎ **071/602-7094**).

For the best information in Romania about Poiana Braşov, speak with Andi Gherasim, the manager of Complex Favorit at the resort (☎ **68/26-22-71**). He speaks excellent English and is very knowledgeable about the area.

To get to Poiana Braşov from the center of Braşov, take bus no. 20 from the copper-colored City Library (Biblioteca Judeteana) at the end of Bulevardul 15 Noiembre. The bus takes 20 to 30 minutes to climb uphill along a beautiful mountain road, costs 135 lei (10¢) one way, and runs every half hour from 6am to 10pm.

BRAN CASTLE

Built in 1377 by Braşov merchants to protect a strategic mountain pass and control trade between Transylvania and Wallachia, Bran Castle has been widely promoted by the tourism industry as "Dracula's Castle"—the former home of Vlad Ţepeş (better known as Count Dracula). It's doubtful that he ever lived here, but he did raid and try to destroy nearby Braşov. You may recall that in Bram Stoker's 1897 novel, Dracula's castle was located on the Tihuţa Pass in the remote north. In any case, the castle certainly is impressive, with its foreboding situation, flush walls, and 53 rooms filled with artifacts. Unfortunately, the site has been renovated a mite too thoroughly: a fresh coat of plaster covers gray stone and many original frescoes, and much of the original furniture has been removed. If you're a maven of the macabre, rumor has it that there's a collection of medievel torture instruments in the basement.

Admission to the castle is 600 lei (45¢), and includes entry into the open-air village museum near the base of the castle. An unexpected pleasure, the museum features transplanted shepherd and peasant dwellings with fully furnished interiors, demonstrations of village technology and costume, and accompanying English-language text. The whole complex is open Tuesday through Sunday from 9am to 5pm.

Private accommodations are always an option in Bran. The **Olteanu family,** well known in town, has been renting rooms to vacationers for years. A favorite of Frommer's readers, the Olteanu homestead represents years of careful buildout and loving decoration. For $10 per person per night (hard currency only), you will be pampered with attention and fed a bountiful breakfast. The Olteanus have many rooms to choose from, and if by chance they are full, they can find someone else in town to put you up. Call ahead (☎ **68/23-63-95**), or simply look for Vasile Olteanu in the parking lot of Bran Castle, where he sells crafts in the small bazaar Tuesday through Sunday from 10am to 4pm.

Unfortunately, getting to the castle of Bran on your own will be challenging. Take trolleybus no. 5 (from in front of the Aro Palace Hotel) to Braşov's Bartholomew Station and get the direct bus to Bran, a 30-minute ride. If there's no bus, you can take the train to Rîsnov, 20 minutes from Braşov; from Rîsnov, catch a bus to Bran (a 30-minute ride). At Bran, walk up the hill to the castle.

It might be easier to come here with a group or hire a guide in Poiana Braşov. There are organized half-day trips whenever there's a large enough group. The cost is about $10 and most tours depart from Poiana Braşov, the ski resort area that foreign groups stay at, located eight miles south of Braşov (see above). Check with the tourist office at the Hotel Aro Palace at Bd. Eroilor 9 (☎ **68/14-28-40**) for schedules and current prices.

SINAIA

Conveniently situated on the Bucharest–Braşov rail line and motor road, Sinaia (pop. 12,000) works well as a stopover on the way to, or day trip from, Braşov (28 miles away). The principal attractions are the Royal Palace of Peleş and the Sinaia Monastery. Soaring alpine charms and gracious accommodation options, however, may lure you for a longer stay.

The town takes its name from the monastery founded here in 1695 by Boyar Contacuzino, after his return from an evidently inspiring pilgrimage to Mt. Sinai. Sinaia's monks lived in splendid isolation, disturbed on only a few occasions by rampaging Russians and Turks, until 1870, when King Carol swooned over the sumptuous mountain scenery and decided to build his summer palace here. Within a decade, a railway line was built from Bucharest, and the landowning class girded the hills with their fanciful villas (which you can rent for reasonable prices), causing Sinaia to be known as the "Pearl of the Carpathians."

Hiking, climbing, and even skiing (there are trails and a cable car) are all excellent in Sinaia. In addition, the town boasts trappings of a small resort, with landscaped parks, restaurants with folk dancing, and discos.

Peleş Castle is the summer residence built by the "imported ruler," Carol Hohenzollern Siegmaringen, king of Romania (1866–1914). Carol studied art at the University of Heidelberg and fancied himself a connoisseur. Decorated for the most part by Carol's eccentric wife, Carmen Sylvan, the palace reflects the king's wish that it represent "all of Europe." There are more than 160 rooms furnished lushly in a dizzying number of styles—German and English Renaissance, Swiss, French, and Italian baroque, Chinese and Turkish—with every manner of exquisite material. Pure kitsch, but of the highest quality. Three Rembrandts, a passel of Italian masters, and frescoes and surface decoration by a then little-known 20-year-old Gustav Klimt highlight the collection.

Unlike Ceauşescu, who starved the populace to finance his extravagant palace, King Carol sold off personal lands in Germany to fund his castle. Such modern innovations as an elevator powered by electricity and boiler-fed radiators were introduced in 1883. In his will, King Carol left the castle "to the people." Ceauseçu closed it in

1974 for use as a private retreat for Communist officials. It was reopened in 1990 and has become a regular stop on coach tours.

You cannot see the castle without a guide, and as English-speaking visitors are few, you are likely to receive a private tour. If your guide lavishes special attention on you, compensate with a generous tip, and it might earn you a special trip to the exquisite, barred-off living quarters on the top floor. In summer, come early as lines can be long. Foreigners pay different admission (roughly $1.50) than locals. Foreigners also use a different entrance, which expedites matters somewhat. Enter a door on the right through the castle's inner courtyard. The castle is open from 9am to 3pm, Wednesday through Sunday.

Inside the walls of **Sinaia Monastery,** mountains looming above as the only outside witness, one almost senses the isolated, austere atmosphere monks used to experience here. The grounds, where seven working monks live, include several small churches and courtyards. The larger church was built by Carol in the 19th century, blending Moldavian and Wallachian styles. It was the first church in Romania to use electric lighting. There is a fresco of Carol on the immediate right as you enter. Admission to the monastery is 23¢.

If you're coming for the day, good places for lunch or a drink are the Hotel Montana or the elegant old world Hotel Palace. Better yet, take the tram up 1,400 meters (Tuesday through Sunday from 9am to 5pm; $1.38 round-trip) to Restaurant Popaşul Alpin, where a meal with a breathtaking view will come to no more than $2, *ţuica* (plum brandy) included.

If staying overnight, the **Hotel Montana** (built in 1975), at Bd. Carpaţi 24 (☎ **44/31-27-51**), has comfortable singles for $17.85, and doubles with spectacular views for $27.55. The hotel also rents ski equipment in the winter. Eclectic, delightful **Intim,** whose turret is the only external building visible from within the monastery, was built in 1917 by a Romanian general. The hotel's 32 doubles go for $14, breakfast not included. The hotel is located just off Bulevardul Carpaţi on the northern end of town. You would also do well to check your bag in the train station and wander until you find accommodation to your liking. All the major hotels are on Bulevardul Carpaţi, while villas cluster on Strada Aosta. Converted outbuildings of the palace, often more fanciful than residences themselves, proffer lodging as well.

Sinaia's train station is a five-minute walk from the town center. Walk up the steep steps and follow Bulevardul Carpaţi to the left. There are five rapid trains from Braşov and Bucharest daily. The trip from Braşov takes 45 minutes and costs 45¢. The trip from Bucharest by car, once past the Ploieşti refineries, traverses an old Turkish trade route through beautiful mountain scenery.

2 Sibiu

169 miles NW of Bucharest, 89 miles W of Braşov, 107 miles S of Cluj-Napoca

GETTING THERE • By Plane Flights from Bucharest take 50 minutes and the fare is $32. Inquire at TAROM Romanian Airlines for details of airport bus service. The local office is at Str. Bălcescu 10 (☎ **1-11-57**) and is open Monday through Friday 7am to 5pm and Saturday 8am to noon.

• **By Train** The express train from Bucharest takes about 5½ hours, for $2.65 in first class. From Braşov the express takes 2½ to 3 hours, and the fare is $2.05 in first class.

The train station is located northeast of the main square at Piaţa Gării (☎ **1-11-39**). You can leave your bags at a somewhat hard-to-find window in an underground passageway parallel to Track 1, open 24 hours; bags cost 15¢ per day. To get to the center, walk for about 10 minutes down Strada Magheru; you'll see a tower straight ahead in the distance.

The CFR Railway Ticket Agency (the easiest place to buy train tickets) is located a block from Piaţa Republicii, at N. Bălcescu 6 (☎ **1-20-85**), open Monday through Friday from 7am to 8pm and on Saturday from 7am to 2pm.

• **By Bus** Buses arrive and depart from Piaţa Gării (☎ **3-43-55**), alongside the train station, as well as from Piaţa Lemnelor (☎ **1-70-16**), west of the city center.

ESSENTIALS Sibiu's telephone area code is 69. All of Sibiu's telephone numbers are now six digits long. All five-digit numbers listed here lack a one-digit prefix. Try using a "4."

ORIENTATION The main area of interest to tourists in Sibiu is clustered around the main square, Piaţa Mare. The town's main sights, the Brukenthal Museum and the Old Town Hall Tower, are on this square. A busy pedestrian shopping street, Strada N. Bălcescu, runs southwest from the square, exiting into Piaţa Unirii.

INFORMATION For maps and tourist information, the former ONT agency at Str. N. Bălcescu 4 has been newly privatized as the Prima Ardeleana (☎ **69/41-25-59;** fax 69/41-79-33). It's open Monday through Friday from 9am to 6pm and on Saturday from 9am to 1pm. They'll help you make hotel reservations locally and in other Romanian cities.

Municipal center of the surrounding area, Sibiu is one of the oldest towns on the Transylvanian Plateau. Originally established 2,000 years ago as the Roman city of Cibinium, it has been a political and economic center ever since. Along with six other towns (Braşov, Cluj-Napoca, Mediaş, Bistriţa, Sebeş, and Sighişoara), Sibiu was founded by German merchants whom the Hungarian King Géza II invited to colonize strategic regions of Transylvania in 1143. They built Hermannstadt on the remains of the older Roman city, and in 1326 the first major series of fortifications were completed. Sibiu soon became an important center for craft items as well as a German cultural center. A library was established in the 14th century, followed in the 15th century by the Universitas Saxonum and a printing house in 1528.

Today the Old Town center of Sibiu retains its impressive and beautiful medieval character, with fine municipal buildings; churches; colorful blue-, mauve-, and apricot-colored houses with half-closed attic window "eyes" peering down from red roofs onto winding cobblestone streets; and heavy fortifications around the city that once staunchly defended it from invaders. Around the center of the Old Town are Sibiu's important industrial plants, which produce much of Romania's beer, automobiles, candy, and furniture.

WHAT TO SEE & DO

Brukenthal Museum, Piaţa Republicii 4–5. ☎ **41-76-91.**

One of Romania's oldest and most famous museums, the Brukenthal is located in the baroque palace of Baron Samuel von Brukenthal, governor of Transylvania from 1777 to 1787. Since 1817 it has served as a museum of Transylvanian history and folk culture, with Brukenthal's personal collection the core collection of the museum. The second floor shows off baroque furniture, costumes, and paintings on glass in a few rooms, and then continues with wooden tools, pottery, textiles, re-created interiors from peasant homes, and other examples of Romania's rich peasant culture. In addition to its folk-art collection, the Brukenthal Museum contains paintings from the workshops of such world-renowned masters as Titian, Raphael, and Caravaggio. Unfortunately, several original Rubenses and Van Dycks were stolen in 1968.

Admission: Painting collection, 200 lei (15¢); folk-art collection, 150 lei (12¢).

Open: Tues–Sun 10am–6pm. **Directions:** Walk to the southeast side of Piaţa Republicii.

Council Tower, Piaţa 6 Mare no. 1.

From atop this tower whose foundations date back to 1324, you have the best panoramic view in town. Inside is a small exhibition on Sibiu's history, with old maps, photos, and a town model. Only the first story of the tower is the original; the rest was reconstructed between the 16th and 19th centuries.

Admission: 100 lei (8¢).

Open: May–Sept, Tues–Sun 9am–5pm. **Closed:** Oct–Apr. **Directions:** From the Brukenthal Museum, walk across Piaţa Republicii and turn left after the large church.

Museum of the Pharmacy, Piaţa 6 Mare no. 26.

Inside a building that housed the "Black Bear" pharmacy as early as 1600, you can view a typical pharmacy of the 17th to 19th centuries with stained wooden cabinets and well-ordered collections of medicine jars.

Admission: Free.

Open: Tues–Sun 10am–6pm. **Directions:** From the Brukenthal Museum, walk across Piaţa Republicii and turn left after the large church.

★ **Museum of Folk Technology,** in Dumbrava Sibiului Forest. ☎ **42-02-15.**

Located far from the center of town to the southwest, this museum spread out across a lovely forest shows an authentically re-created peasant village complete with a lake at its center. The distances between the 200 houses are large, necessitating quite a bit of walking across a lovely park of 235 acres. It will take three or four hours to complete the circuit. You can learn about traditional Romanian folk techniques for making handcrafts, textiles, food, and other aspects of peasant life. You can even fish here for 500 lei (40¢), or go boating on the lake for 100 lei (8¢) per half hour. Make sure to buy the English-language museum map at the entrance.

Admission: 500 lei (40¢), plus 500 lei (40¢) to take photos.

Open: May–Oct, Tues–Sun 10am–6pm. **Closed:** Nov–Apr, depending on weather. **Directions:** Take Sibiu's only tram from the cemetery; or bus no. 23.

Sibiu Synagogue, on the corner of Str. General Magheru and Str. Constituţiei.

Stranded amid half-finished three-story apartment blocks is a synagogue, the last remnant of Sibiu's once considerable Jewish community. Fully 90% of Transylvania's Jewish population was delivered into Nazi hands with the collusion of the Fascist Romanian Iron Guard.

Admission: Free.

Open: Mon–Fri 11am–1pm. **Directions:** From the city center, walk northeast along Strada General Magheru toward the train station. At Strada Constituţiei, make a right. It's on the left.

Other Sights

Some of Sibiu's other sights include the huge Gothic Evangelical Church (1300–1520) and the 13th-century Defense Tower on Piaţa Grivita, built after the city was destroyed by Tartars in 1241. There are several other medieval walls and some of the 40 towers that once protected the town still intact all around the city. Off Piaţa 6 Mare you can see the Council Tower (see above), the Staircase Tower (1567) and the more recent (1859) wrought-iron Liars' Bridge. Walk behind the Evangelical Church, down the old Staircase Passage into the lower town, and lose yourself in the maze of colorful arcaded shops and houses. Visit Piaţa Cibin where there's a market selling ceramics, crafts, and produce. All the while, you'll be followed by the watchful half-closed attic "eyes" peering down from red-tiled roofs.

WHERE TO STAY

PRIVATE ROOMS The enterprising folks of Sibiu were the first in post-Ceauşescu Romania to open a private-room agency, called Exo. Their centrally located "office" is off the main square inside the courtyard at N. Bălcescu 1 (☎ **69/41-79-71**), open from 2 to 8pm daily; it's really just the apartment of a charming elderly gentleman named Filip Copanceanu. As he speaks only Romanian and Russian, you may want to call his colleague, Gheorghe Belet (☎ **69/48-21-96**), who speaks English. Rooms cost about $15, although you can try to negotiate.

Hotels

Împăratul Romanilor, Str. N. Bălcescu 4, 2400 Sibiu. ☎ **69/41-76-25.** Fax 69/413-2-78. 102 rms (all with bath). TV TEL A/C **Directions:** Walk two blocks south of the Old Town Square, Piaţa Mare.

Rates: $27.90–$37.50 single; $48.30–$54.10 double.

Long Sibiu's most eminent hotel (an inscription in the entryway states that there has been an inn here since 1542), it has always hosted the city's most important guests. Heavy baroque syle within and without once pleased the likes of Franz Liszt and Johann Strauss. Newly privatized and renovated, this delightful hotel is elegant, comfortable, and clean. The furniture is new and the beds are comfortable; the bathrooms, however, are quite small. You'll enjoy its ambience, its proximity to the historic Piaţa Republicii, and the attentive service from the reception desk. There are two restaurants and an exchange office in the lobby (see "Where to Eat," below).

Hotel Bulevard, Piaţa Unirii 10, 2400 Sibiu. ☎ **69/41-21-40.** Telex 49240. 122 rms (all with bath). TV TEL **Trolleybus:** 1 or 2 from the train station.

Rates (including breakfast): $13.65–$17.90 single; $23.90–$25.65 double (higher price for rooms with a bathtub or facing the street).

If you don't want to splurge on the Împăratul Romanilor and don't enjoy staying in private rooms, you might have to settle for a room in this historic 150-year-old building facing the main town square. Although the building's exterior and its large lobby are attractive, the rooms and elevators are quite shabby, and hallway lighting is almost nonexistent. The carpets and furniture are worn, and the plumbing old. But don't be discouraged; on the whole, the place is clean, though some rooms are better than others—with more space, better lighting, and newer beds. The woman at the reception desk said she'd help travelers find good rooms. There's a brasserie and large outdoor terrace café where many young people congregate.

Hotel Continental, Calea Dumbrăvii 2–4, 2400 Sibiu. ☎ **69/41-69-10.** Fax 69/41-56-24. 180 rms (all with bath). TV TEL **Trolleybus:** 1 or 2 from the train station.

Rates (including breakfast): $20.20 single; $31.40 double.

This 14-floor concrete monolith, only a five-minute walk from the old town, represents a good value among Sibiu's frequently occupied hotels. Piecemeal renovation has produced a curious though not uncomfortable mishmash of fresh and faded decor. The fixtures, bathrooms, and wallpaper are more recent, while the furniture and carpeting show serious wear. A cheerful, chaotic blend of colors with high ceilings and good maintenance results in a pleasant, livable atmosphere. By the time you arrive, at least one-quarter of the rooms should be fully renovated (although available at a slightly higher rate). The hotel restaurant is one of Sibiu's better ones (see "Where to Eat," below).

WHERE TO EAT

Hotel Împăratul Romanilor, Str. N. Bălcescu 4. ☎ **41-64-90.**

Cuisine: ROMANIAN. **Reservations:** Recommended. **Directions:** Walk two blocks south of Piața Republicii on Strada N. Bălcescu.

Prices: Soups 20¢–55¢; main courses 85¢–$1.80; desserts 17¢–45¢. Cover charge 2,000 lei ($1.55).

Open: Breakfast/lunch daily 7am–4pm; dinner daily 6pm–midnight.

The "unparalleled dining experience" that this plummy restaurant aims to provide falls a little on the kitschy side of classy, but the experience is very enjoyable nonetheless. Such offerings as tomato or cream of mushroom soup, beef Stroganoff, grilled chicken, and a variety of desserts are well prepared and served elegantly. The large dining room features lavender walls, plants, and wood-glass partitions separating the tables. A sliding glass roof lets in light by day and cool air on a summer's night.

Much of the fun comes from watching locals out for a night on the town enjoying the live music, the floor show, and dancing from 7pm to midnight. There's also music from noon to 2pm. The special "White Hall" is for group banquets.

Hotel Continental, Calea Dumbravii 2–4. ☎ **41-69-10.**

Cuisine: ROMANIAN. **Reservations:** Recommended. **Directions:** Walk three blocks south of Piața Republicii on Strada N. Bălcescu.

Prices: Soups 7¢–35¢; main courses 50¢–$1.30.

Open: Daily noon–midnight.

Located in one of Sibiu's two high-rise hotels, this large second-floor restaurant with retro-futuristic decor from the 1960s will, fortunately, soon be undergoing renovation. The menu is very large and quite varied, although the quality of dishes can vary. The soups and salads are excellent. Try the spicy spring salad soup in season for an unusual treat. We enjoyed chicken breast with mushrooms and grilled pork, but the side dishes were disappointing—overcooked peas and pasty rice. To cool off in the summer, try the local beer, called 3 Stejari (Three Oaks).

Restaurant Bufnița [The Owl], Str. N. Bălcescu 45. ☎ **41-41-33.**

Cuisine: ROMANIAN. **Directions:** Walk several blocks south of Piața Republicii past the Împăratul Romanilor.

Prices: Lunch or dinner $2–$3.

Open: Sun–Thurs 8am–midnight, Fri–Sat 8am–3am.

The Bufniţa is a popular spot for Romanian pub grub on this main street full of shops, shoppers, and places to eat. Drop in for a quick lunch or for some wine and late-night weekend entertainment. Smoky and dark, the atmosphere can get quite bawdy. The large dining hall in the back is decorated with deer antlers and an enormous ceramic stove. Late-night disco after 10pm.

Easy Excursions

★ SIBIEL

One of my most rewarding experiences in Romania was a small side trip to Sibiel, a tiny peasant town 12 miles west of Sibiu. It's the kind of place where ox carts go down the dirt road running alongside the village houses and children run about without fearing cars; a single hand-cranked telephone at the village post office connects Sibiel to the outside world.

Sibiel also possesses one of Romania's best-preserved 18th-century churches, **St. Holy Trinity,** with interior frescoes from 1774. The frescoes were covered up until only 1965, and today they're remarkably well preserved. Next to the church is a small **museum** featuring 17th- to 19th-century icons painted on glass, a popular Romanian folk-art form. The museum sells modern paintings on glass. Both the museum and church are open daily from 8am to 8pm, and cost 50 lei (4¢) to see.

For a first-hand experience of what life is like in a Romanian village you can stay with a family in Sibiel. Museum guide Cristina Banciu and her family welcome you into their country house, offering room and full board for about 20,000 lei ($15) a night. She doesn't speak much English, but she's hospitable and serves good, plain, homegrown and home-cooked food. If her house is full, she'll find you a room with a neighbor.

To get to Sibiel, take the 30-minute train from Sibiu, and then walk down a bumpy dirt road for over a mile. One bus a day also connects from Sibiu's bus terminal on Strada Lemnelor.

RĂŞINARI & PĂLTINIŞ

Much of Sibiu's popularity with tourists is due to its close proximity to the Făgăraş mountains in the Carpathian Plateau. Hikers, skiers, and walkers all use the city as a base to enjoy Romania's most accommodating natural resource. A gorgeous way to see what the fuss is about is to take a day trip on a nice day to Păltiniş, stopping midway at the town of Răşinari. The hour-long drive or bus ride, 20 miles over a snaking road through breathtaking scenery, is worth the trip alone.

The village of Răşinari sits couched in a majestic bowl where the Făgăraş mountains begin to ascend. Long one of the richest traditional villages in Romania, the source of Răşinari's livelihood is visible in the cottony tufts that dot the surrounding hillsides (they register as sheep after a moment's concentration). The architecture of the town represents a superior example of Transylvanian village style. Adjoining homestead walls crowd up along the edges of narrow winding streets, presenting a formidable barricade to would-be invaders. Passing through, one experiences visual deprivation that lends the sensation of being in a maze. Romania's greatest living philosopher, Emile Cioran, now living in Paris, is a native of these labyrinthine streets.

From Răşinari, the road threads up into the foothills, and the scenery becomes voluptuous. In places, the arrangement of soft grassy slopes in the foreground, steeply pitched folds midway, and sharply creased peaks on the horizon form so perfect a diorama as to look prearranged. Areas cropped close and velvety by grazing are marked by crude huts that shepherds use for months at a time before they return with their flocks to the village.

Păltiniş is not nearly a town so much as a widening of the road in a crook of the mountain. The resort is likewise minimal, with a lone chair lift hanging over a cleft in the evergreen wall. This is the sleepy sort of hamlet where all inhabitants appear to know and recognize each other as fellow citizens. Lounging cats and dogs, an occasional cow munching grass on the side of the road, a lone women in the bus depot ticket office, all seem to have an allotted place in the unhurried life of the town. Several hiking trails begin where the chair lift lets off. If you desire to spend a night, Johan March (☎ **69/41-50-77** or **41-79-51**) rents beds in rustic dorm-style rooms redolent with the smell of pine for 1,500 lei ($1.15). There are a total of 16 beds in 5 rooms a short distance from the bus depot.

Buses make the round-trip from Sibiu to Păltiniş with a stop in Răşinari on Tuesday, Friday, Saturday, and Sunday. The bus departs from Sibiu's train station and costs 300 lei (23¢). Răşinari is the last stop on Sibiu's only tram line, which also serves the Sibiu Museum of Folk Technology (see above). Buses T1 or no. 23 go as far as the cemetery. From there, you can pick up the tram.

ALBA IULIA

Alba Iulia's historical importance goes back to ancient times when as Apulum it was the capital of the large province of Dacia. The capital of Transylvania from 1542 to 1690, Alba Iulia has become a symbol of unity for Romanians: For it was here in 1600 that Michael the Brave succeeded in briefly uniting the principalities of Wallachia, Moldavia, and Transylvania, and was proclaimed ruler of Romania by the head of the church.

Today Alba Iulia (pop. 65,000) is worth visiting for its ★ **Citadel,** which was originally constructed in the 13th century, then rebuilt several times before it took its present form in the 18th century. Solidly constructed of red brick in the star-shaped style of the French military engineer Vauban, it has seven bastions and six gates, and is surrounded by a moat. It took 20,000 serfs almost 30 years to complete the structure, and it's so immense that it contains a small town within its walls.

Highlights within the Citadel include the 13th-century Romanesque-Gothic **St. Mihail's Catholic Cathedral** with the tomb of the famous Magyar prince, János Hunyadi (Ioan Hunedoara), who led his Christian forces to victory over the Ottoman armies near Belgrade in 1456; the immense Orthodox **Cathedral of Reunification,** nearby, built to commemorate the return of Transylvania to Romania, where Ferdinand and Marie were crowned king and queen of Romania in 1914; and the **Union Museum** (open Tuesday through Sunday) with its extensive exhibit of Transylvanian history (unfortunately, the captions are only in Romanian).

Of recent interest is the new section of Alba Iulia: blocks of high-rise apartments built in the 1980s during Ceauşescu's feverish campaign of urban renewal.

If you have trouble finding lodgings in Sibiu and are headed to Cluj-Napoca, you can visit Alba Iulia and overnight there. Have someone help you call ahead to the **Hotel Cetate** at **58/82-38-04** (no English spoken) to reserve a room there. The Hotel Cetate is a relatively new 10-story generic high-rise with 125 rooms with great views of the Citadel at Str. Unirii 3. It's nothing special, but the rooms are decent and have good beds. Singles with baths are $14; doubles, $22. There are buses from the train and bus stations (about a mile away) every half hour to a stop nearby.

According to locals, "the best place in town" to eat is the privately run **Astoria** at Str. Tudor Vladimirescu 11 (☎ **58/82-64-68**). You'll have a long wait until one of the overworked waitresses dressed in orange military jackets serves you, but the fixed-price menu, soup and grilled pork chop (*cotlet de porc gratar*), was good and cheap at $1.10. The place turned out to be an ideal spot for surveying the local people scene.

You can get to Alba Iulia in about two hours by express train from Sibiu if connections are good. As it's on the way between Sibiu (44 miles away) and Cluj (58 miles away), it's a good place to break up the journey. There are also several direct buses from Sibiu which connect on to Cluj.

3 Timişoara

350 miles NW of Bucharest, 180 miles W of Sibiu

GETTING THERE • By Plane The flight from Bucharest to Timişoara costs $48. TAROM has its local office at Bulevardul 16 Decembrie no. 3–5 (☎ **13-68-65**).

• By Train The express from Bucharest takes about eight or nine hours for 4,825 lei ($3.70) in first class. There are a number of night trains with couchette beds in addition to day trains. From Sibiu, take the train to Arad, about a 4½-hour journey; then change trains to Timişoara, not more than 1 hour away. You can connect to Arad from Budapest, Hungary, in under five hours.

The main station is Timişoara North Station, at Strada Gării 3 (☎ **11-25-52**). Trolleybus no. 11 or 14 or tram no. 1 connect with most downtown hotels.

To buy departure tickets, stop by the CFR ticket office, located inside the main post office at Bulevardul 16 Decembrie no. 2 (☎ **11-35-50**); turn to the left as you enter the main post office hall. Open Monday through Friday from 8am to 8pm.

• By Bus The long-distance bus terminal is at Strada Reşiţa 54 (☎ **11-36-30**).

ESSENTIALS Timişoara's telephone area code is 56.

ORIENTATION Historic Timişoara, site of most hotels and sights, is contained within the oval-shaped boundary of the old fortified citadel. Although trams run through frequently, the area is easily appreciated on foot. There are three major modes of urban activity, arrayed on a south-north axis through the center of the old town. The broad pedestrian-only Bulevardul 16 Decembrie 1989, where crowds gathered and sparked the 1989 revolution, leads from the Metropolitan Cathedral in the south to Piaţa Libertaţii at the city's geographical center. Due north from here, the street opens onto Piaţa Unirii, site of many beautiful Habsburg-era structures.

INFORMATION Newly privatized S.C.T. Cardinal, on Bd. Republicii 6 (☎ **19-03-58**), is working hard to provide services at the level of a Western travel agency. They have maps, information on tours, and can arrange accommodations. Open from Monday to Friday 8am to 6pm and Saturday 9am to 1pm, they hope to soon offer services 24 hours a day.

Timişoara is not as good a point as Braşov from which to explore Romania's remote northern areas in a rented car, although it may serve as an ideal drop-off point. Europcar (☎ **13-65-32**) shares office space with S.C.T. Cardinal (see above). Hertz (☎ **13-33-33**) is at Str. Hector 31.

On December 15, 1989, about 200 people gathered outside the home of Lászlo Tökes, an outspoken Hungarian-Romanian priest, to prevent his impending arrest by the *Securitate.* By the next day this group had swelled to 50,000 people, many of them teenagers, chanting slogans such as "Down with Ceauşescu." The following day, the Romanian dictator himself acted without hesitation. "I want that calm should be restored in Timişoara in one hour," Ceauşescu ordered according to a closed-circuit TV recording government meetings.

Troops responded with machine guns and tanks as well as with clubs and water cannons. Hundreds were massacred and then secretly buried in mass graves. When news of the tragedy spread, anger overcame fear to inspire the Romanian revolution; on Christmas Day, dictator Ceauşescu and his wife, Elena, were executed.

But while the rest of Romania still seems haunted by the bloody memory of the revolution, Timişoara has responded to the exorcism with a flurry of economic activity that is restoring some of its historical stature as Romania's most culturally Western city. Markets and stores here are glitzier and better stocked than anywhere outside of Bucharest, and the street culture of outdoor cafés and beer patios fueled by the considerable student population—many of whom are veterans of 1989—is vibrant.

Founded in the early 13th century as a Hungarian border fortress, Ottoman Turks froze the city's evolution from 1552 until Habsburg liberation in 1712. The Habsburgs lavished considerable largesse on the city, marked by many fine examples of baroque architecture visible today. Although the city passed into Romanian hands in 1920, it remained thoroughly cosmopolitan, with sizable German, Hungarian, and Romanian communities living in harmony unique among Romanian cities.

WHAT TO SEE & DO

Banat Museum, Piaţa Huniade 1. ☎ **13-48-18.**

Located inside a castle built in the 14th century and restored in the 19th century, this museum offers four distinct sections: history (on the second floor), flora and fauna (third floor), coins, and temporary exhibitions.

Admission: History, Flora and Fauna, Numismatic Cabinet, and Temporary Exhibits, 50 lei (4¢).

Open: Tues–Sun 10am–5pm. **Directions:** From the north side of Bulevardul 30 Decembrie, walk a block east.

The Bastion of the Citadel, Str. 4 Popa Şapcă.

Located in part of Timişoara's 18th-century town fortifications, this museum normally hosts two collections, one on folk art and traditions, and the other on modern technology.

Admission: Free.

Open: Mon–Sat 9am–4:30pm. **Directions:** From the Hotel Continental, walk two blocks north on Strada Hector.

Metropolitan Cathedral, Bulevardul 16 Decembrie 1989.

Anchoring the southern end of Bulevardul 16 Decembrie 1989 is Timişoara's impressive main Orthodox church. Rising 268 feet in brick and wood, it synthesizes Byzantine and native Romanian folk elements. The intricately carved wood door frames, as well as the freestanding memorial crosses in front of the church, are a preview of what you'll see decorating gateways to peasant homesteads if you venture north into the Maramureş region. Built in 1936–46, the church interior accommodates 5,000 under its tiled domed roof. There is an interesting display of 16th- to 19-century icons on wood and glass in the basement, open upon request.

Admission: Free.

Open: Cathedral, daily 10am–7pm; basement icon collection, Tues–Sun 10am–4pm. **Directions:** Walk to the south side of Bulevardul 16 Decembrie 1989.

Hungarian Reform Church, Timotei Cipariu 1.

This is the headquarters of the Rev. Lászlo Tökes, the Hungarian-Romanian pastor whose defiance of the regime of Nicolae Ceauşescu sparked the violent December 1989 Romanian revolution. On the street in front of the church you'll see wall plaques honoring the first victims of the revolution.

Admission: Free.

Open: Tues and Fri 9am–1pm and 3–5pm, Wed–Thurs and Sat 9am–1pm. Services, sometimes led by the Reverend Tökes, are held on Sun. **Directions:** From the south end of the Bulevardul 16 Decembrie 1989, continue straight over the canal on Bulevardul 6 Mare and take the second or third left.

WHERE TO STAY

Hotel Banatul, Bd. Republicii 5, 1900 Timişoara. ☎ **56/13-60-30.** 240 rms (60 for foreigners, with bath). TV TEL **Directions:** Walk to the northern end of Bulevardul 16 Decembrie 1989 and look left.

Rates (for foreigners, including breakfast): $26 single; $33.20 double. AE, DC, MC, V.

The sparse lobby with reception desk enclosed in fiberglass like a ticket window is little more than a way-station between the street and your room. Foreigners pay twice as much as Romanians but stay in rooms renovated for the purpose (be sure you are given the correct room). Rooms are utilitarian but not uncomfortable, featuring nice wallpaper, new bed coverings, and very clean bathrooms.

Hotel Continental, Bd. Revolutiei 2, 1900 Timişoara. ☎ **56/13-41-44** or **56/19-41-44.** Fax 56/13-04-81. All rooms with bath. TV TEL **Directions:** Take tram no. 1 one stop from the train station.

Rates (including breakfast): $40.20 single; $48.70 single as double (adds couch-bed); $62.40 double. AE, DC, MC, V.

This 13-floor concrete high-rise is upholstered nicely enough to be the best hotel in town. While a little pricey, the single-as-double rooms represent good value. The staff is helpful, if you can find them in a lobby vivid with burlesque textures. Dark woodgrain paneling, vibrant medallion-patterned carpeting, and velvety overstuffed thrones studded with brass rivets simulate the excesses of a traditional grand European hotel. Rooms display similar attention to detail with rich-looking fabrics on the walls and good-quality furniture. There is a restaurant on the premises serving the typical menu of pork and beef dishes, albeit prepared well.

4 Cluj-Napoca

276 miles NW of Bucharest, 107 miles N of Sibiu

GETTING THERE • By Plane Flights from Bucharest to Cluj-Napoca take a little over an hour and cost $44. The airport is northeast of the city center at Str. Aurel Vlaicu 149 (☎ **64/14-24-26**). Inquire about airport bus connections at TAROM, Piaţa Mihai Viteazul 11 (☎ **13-02-34**).

• **By Train** Express trains from Bucharest take about 7½ to 8 hours, and the fare is 4,264 lei ($3.30) in first class. Consider sleeping away these hours on one of several night trains with couchettes. The ride from Braşov takes five hours and costs 2,868 lei ($2.20) in first class. From Sibiu, connect to Copşa Mică, a 45-minute express ride for 981 lei (75¢) in first class, then north to Cluj, 2½ hours away.

The train station is at Piaţa Gării (☎ **11-60-60**), north of the city center. Here you'll find a 24-hour luggage check near a small bank of telephones. To get to the town center, take either tram no. 101 to the second stop, or trolleybus no. 9, both of which leave from in front of the station. You can also walk to the city center in about 15 to 20 minutes; go straight ahead (south) on Strada Horea, cross the bridge, and continue until you reach Piaţa Unirii.

• **By Bus** The local bus station is at Str. Budai Nagy Antal 131–133 (☎ **14-24-26**), northeast of the city center toward the airport.

ESSENTIALS The telephone area code is 64.

INFORMATION The local ONT office is at Str. 30 Decembrie (☎ **64/11-23-44**), two blocks west of the main square, Piaţa Unirii. The office and the street may have new names by the time you arrive; it's open Monday through Friday from 9am to 4pm. Some of the staff have been known to help travelers get private rooms. KM.0 (Kilometer Zero), at Piaţa Unirii 10 (☎ **64/11-65-57**), is a private tourist agency offering a variety of services such as accommodations booking, tours, money exchange, and car rentals. Their hours are Monday through Friday 9am to 8pm, Saturday 10am to 5pm.

There is an excellent, if dated, map available at tourist offices and newsstands along Piaţa Unirii.

You can call home at the telephone bureau at Piaţa Unirii 5, open daily from 7am to 9pm.

CITY LAYOUT Cluj is divided by the Someşul Mic River, which flows west to northeast. The large and lively Piaţa Unirii—site of the Cathedral of St. Mihail and the baroque Banffy Palace Art Museum, as well as shops and eateries—centers the old historic part of Cluj. Several major avenues originate from the square. Bulevardul 22 Decembrie and Strada Gh. Doja originate at the northeastern corner: Doja shoots north toward the river, and 22 Decembrie continues east. Strada Petru Groza begins at the southeast corner and also runs east. From the northwest corner of Piaţa Unirii, Strada 30 Decembrie runs west and turns into Calea Moţilor. Strada Universităţii begins in the southwest corner and heads south. Also originating in the southwest corner and heading west is Strada Napoca, a narrow promenade lined with cafés and art galleries that spills into Piaţa Pacii, the center of student life. Strada Victor Babeş heads uphill from Piaţa Pacii past several pubs and eateries before hitting the boundary of Cluj's Botanical Gardens.

GETTING AROUND Like all major Romanian cities, Cluj has both a cheap trolleybus and a tram system. But the buses tend to be very crowded and sites that you'll want to explore are centrally located, so it's more rewarding to get around on foot.

Car Rental If you plan to see the Maramureş area at your own pace, try to rent one of three cars available at KM.0, Piaţa Unirii 10 (☎ **64/11-65-57**). They are open Monday through Friday 9am to 8pm, Saturday 10am to 5pm. Europcar and Hertz used to maintain Cluj offices and may yet reestablish themselves in this market.

DEPARTING • By Train You can buy train tickets for your departure at the CFR agency at Piaţa Mihai Viteazul 21 (☎ **11-22-12**), open Monday through Friday 8am to 7pm and Saturday 8am to 1pm.

Romania's third city, Cluj (pop. 400,000) is also one of its most charming. Tidy Habsburg boulevards and squared-off plazas are cross-cut with meandering alleys left from Cluj-Napoca's medieval era. Romania's highest student ratio (there are more than 24,000 in the city) results, predictably, in Romania's highest concentration of cafés, bookstores, and antic youthful behavior. But what appears in the architecture to be a genteel shingling of historical epochs actually conceals a very present and unresolved tension between Hungarians and Romanians. Cluj was the city's name during Hungarian and Habsburg rule. By adding the ancient Dacian name of Napoca to Cluj, the Romanians stress their historic claim to the city. Due to the great number of Hungarians living here (40% of the population by some estimates), and perhaps also due to the city's relatively provincial situation, Cluj has become a flash-point for Hungarian-Romanian tension. Cluj-Napoca is referred to here as Cluj—not for any political reasons, but to keep things simple.

The Transylvanian plateau has been prized for its mineral wealth for thousands of years, and from the time Roman emperor Hadrian granted the town of Napoca municipal status in the 2nd century A.D., Cluj has been its principal city. German merchants arrived in the 12th century, and by the 16th century, the city was commonly a site for markets and fairs. Cluj hit its golden age with Habsburg and Hungarian control from the late 17th century to the 20th.

Swank restaurants, art galleries, and beautifully renovated shopping areas in portions of the city center seem to indicate that another golden age is upon Cluj. In truth, Cluj has been the beneficiary of an investment scheme that has bilked the rest of Romania of estimated billions in lei. Founded by little-known businessman Ioan Stoica in February 1992, the scheme, called Caritas (unrelated to the Vatican-sponsored charity organization of the same name), promised investors 800% interest on investments of over 20,000 lei ($15) after three months. The "game," as it was called in Cluj, kept up payments for over 20 months before tailing off drastically.

Known as a pyramid scheme because it operates by continually widening the investor base to pay off earlier investors, Caritas was aided by Cluj's mayor Gheorghe Funar in publicizing it. Funar published the names of Caritas "winners" in his nationalist anti-Hungarian newspaper *Mesagerul Transilvan.* As the paper's daily circulation shot up from 3,000 to 250,000 and began distribution throughout Romania, Funar's virulent right-wing message went with it. Cluj acquired the moniker "Caritas-Napoca" and a reputation as the "city of millionaires." Several million people from all over Romania streamed in to lay down their money; an estimated three in eight Romanian families participated. While authorities sort out how to deal with nearly bankrupt Caritas and the legions who almost certainly will not get their money back, one thing is clear: a massive redistribution of the nation's wealth took place, and residents of Cluj were the prime benefactors.

WHAT TO SEE & DO

St. Michael's Cathedral, at the center of Piaţa Unirii.

Cluj's Catholic cathedral, right in the heart of town, St. Michael's dates back to 1349. Although the building has suffered numerous disasters, such as a fire in 1489 and an earthquake in 1764, it has been well restored over the years and today is the only structure in Cluj that still has fragments of its original medieval decorations. The interior is large and bare, with Gothic vaults, stained-glass windows, and some original paintings. The exterior is marked by a 260-foot-tall tower.

In front of the church on Piaţa Unirii is the gargantuan **Statue of Matei Corvin** (Matthias Corvinus) accepting homage from great statesmen. An ethnic Hungarian, Matei Corvin was born in Cluj in 1443 and ruled as Hungary's great Renaissance king from 1458 to 1490. Dedicated in 1902 during Hungarian rule, it was rededicated after a fashion in December 1992 in a gesture that provoked and angered Cluj's Hungarian community. A new bronze plaque describes the king's warmongering in Moldavia as an attack on people "of the same blood." Presumably, the statement claims Corvin as an ethnic Romanian who betrayed his own.

Admission: Free.

Open: Sat–Thurs 6am–8pm. **Directions:** Walk to the center of Piaţa Unirii.

Art Museum, Piaţa Unirii 30. ☎ **12-69-52.**

Across from the church on the piaţa is one of the most important baroque buildings in Romania, the Banffy Palace, built from 1774 to 1785. Magyar nobility once lived in it, but now it contains Cluj's art collection featuring mostly Romanian artists with a sprinkling of other Europeans and displays of weapons, icons, and rugs. Special exhibitions are held here from time to time.

Admission: 100 lei (8¢) adults, 50 lei (4¢) students.

Open: Wed–Sun 9am–5pm (last entrance at 4:30pm). **Directions:** Exit the church to the east side of the square.

★ **Ethnographic Museum of Transylvania,** Str. 30 Decembrie 21. ☎ **11-23-44** or **11-21-48.**

One of Romania's most interesting ethnographical museums, this collection holds 65,000 museum pieces: a vast historical assortment of authentic clothing worn by the diverse population from the different regions of Transylvania, embroidery, weavings and rugs, ceramics, musical instruments, and agricultural tools. The collection of regional costumes and rugs is considered the finest in Romania. Although many pieces are in storage, there's certainly enough here to entertain and educate you on local Transylvanian ways. Fortunately, you'll be helped along with some English-language exhibition descriptions.

Admission: 100 lei (8¢).

Open: Tues–Sun 9am–5pm. **Directions:** From Piaţa Unirii, walk two blocks west on Strada 30 Decembrie.

★ **Ethnographic Museum in the Open,** in Hoia Forest. ☎ **18-67-76.**

A reconstructed peasant village with 150 typical dwellings and wooden churches spread over 185 acres, this open-air museum has an air of real authenticity and is quite captivating. If you can't get to the Maramureş area, come here. With few signs on the houses and few other tourists around, this museum really makes you feel as though you're exploring a typical Transylvanian hamlet. If you ask the porter at the entrance desk, he or she will open a few of the houses for you.

Admission: 100 lei (8¢) adults, 50 lei (4¢) students.

Open: May–Oct, Tues–Sun 9am–5pm. **Closed:** Nov–Apr. **Bus:** 28 from Piaţa Mihai Viteazul, a few blocks north of Piaţa Unirii. **Directions:** Walk 15 minutes up Strada Grigonescu across the river heading northwest.

History Museum of Transylvania, Str. Daicovicin 2. ☎ **11-86-77.**

A chronicle of the region's history starting with early fossils—the usual collections of pottery shards, and Bronze Age weapons and tools—and then moving up to relics of the Dacian and Roman eras. Highlights include a marble statue of Dionysus from Alba lulia and small heads and statues of other Roman gods. Displays of medieval armor and weaponry are evidence of the turbulence of life in the Middle Ages in Transylvania.

Make sure you visit the museum **Lapidarium,** on the ground floor off the courtyard. Here you'll see Dacian, Roman, and medieval Transylvanian inscriptions on stone and funerary markers.

Admission: 100 lei (8¢).

Open: Tues–Sun 9am–5pm. **Directions:** From Piaţa Unirii, walk about three blocks north up Strada Roosevelt and then turn west.

History of the Pharmacy Museum, Str. Gh. Doja 1.

Located inside what some historians believe was the first pharmacy in Cluj, from 1573, this small collection shows the three typical rooms of a late 19th-century pharmacy: the area where medicines were sold, the medicine storerooms, and the basement laboratory. Jars for herbs, spices, and even aphrodisiacs are displayed on the ground floor, and test tubes and other lab equipment are displayed in the basement.

Admission: 75 lei (6¢).

Open: Mon–Sat 9am–4pm. **Directions:** Walk to the north side of Piaţa Unirii to the intersection with Strada Gh. Doja.

Tailor's Bastion, Str. Sandór Petőfi.

For a glimpse of the town's medieval defenses and fortifications, visit this bastion built in 1405. This last surviving tower is named for the guild that was obligated to maintain and defend it. In the 15th century there were many such towers, each maintained by a different guild, such as the cobblers, the butchers, etc. It's viewed from the outside only.

Admission: Free.

Directions: From Piaţa Unirii, walk two blocks east on Strada Petru Groza, then two blocks to the right.

Botanical Gardens, Str. Republicii 42. ☎ **11-21-52.**

For a relaxing change of pace, visit the botanical gardens and botanical museum of Babeş-Bolyai University. At one time this garden was one of the largest collections of flora (10,000 species) in the Balkans, but neglect has taken its toll. There are exhibits on the use of plants in industry and a Japanese garden as well.

Admission: 100 lei (8¢).

Open: Gardens, daily 9am–7pm; greenhouse, daily 9am–5pm; botanic museum, Mon–Sat 9am–2pm. **Directions:** From Piaţa Unirii, walk west on Strada Napoca and turn left on Strada Republicii.

WHERE TO STAY

★ $ **Hotel Continental,** Str. Napoca 1,3400 Cluj-Napoca. ☎ **64/11-14-41.** 51 rms (24 with bath). TV TEL **Bus:** 35 from the train station.

Rates (including continental breakfast): $14.15 single without bath, $21.15 single with bath; $22 double without bath, $25–$28 double with bath; $34–$43 one- and two-room suites.

This gracious landmark has anchored the corner of Piata Unirii since 1906, when it was called the Hotel New York. As that rare species of Romanian hotel combining elegance, good facilities, and very reasonable rates, it should be your first choice in Cluj accommodations. Although well worn, the hotel is neither dingy nor depressing. Original paintings, parquet floors and rugs, high ceilings, and chandeliers have stood the test of time. Rooms have rather narrow beds but good mattresses and lovely floor-to-ceiling windows. Bathrooms are old but clean. The concierge said a thorough renovation is planned. Hopefully, it will not result in drastically escalated prices. For a treat, eat in the first-rate hotel restaurant (see below).

Hotel Napoca, Str. Jozsa Bela 1–3, 3400 Cluj-Napoca. ☎ **64/18-07-15.**
Fax 64/18-56-27. 156 rms (all with bath). TV TEL **Bus:** 27 from the train station.

Rates: $28 single; $40–$43.90 double.

Built in 1969, there has been little investment since then and it shows. The lobby of this concrete-and-glass structure has something of the sweep and vastness of an airport terminal. A 10-minute walk over a small bridge and through a park to the center of town makes it an alternative to the Continental if it's full. The hallways are quite run-down, but the furniture in the rooms is new. Single rooms are large and have radios. The clientele is mostly Eastern Europeans, businessmen and groups. There's nonstop satellite TV in the lobby. The receptionist, Doina Oprea, is a savvy and helpful woman who loves to practice her already exceptional English; she is a real asset to the local tourist industry. There's an exchange office, a gift shop, and a restaurant in the lobby.

Hotel Sport, Str. George Coşbuc 15. ☎ **64/19-39-21** or **64/19-37-62.** Telex 31397.
136 rms (all with bath). TV TEL **TRAM:** From the train station take no. 101 or 102 and get off at the stadium or sports complex.

Rates (including breakfast): $32.30 single; $41.55 double; $50.80 triple.

This concrete high-rise, in a leafy part of Cluj a 10-minute walk from the city center, used to serve sports teams exclusively. (The cheery, beefy fellows at the pennant-bedecked reception could be former athletes who came and never left.) Instead of the tattered, fading grandeur of other hotels listed here, Sport is essentially an upgraded dormitory. Rooms have solid new furniture, wall-to-wall windows, and bathrooms with very tidy groutwork. Half of the rooms have TVs, and most enjoy wonderful views. This is basic but very appealing accommodation.

WHERE TO EAT

Cluj's unusually wide range of eating establishments is the product of a hungry student population and the infusion of new money. Many cluster around Strada Napoca, Piaţa Pacii, and Strada Victor Babeş.

Hotel Continental, Str. Napoca 1. ☎ **11-14-41.**

Cuisine: ROMANIAN. **Bus:** 35 from the train station.

$ **Prices:** Salads 18¢–75¢; soups; 40¢–65¢; main courses 25¢–$1.35.

Open: Thurs–Tues 7am–7pm and 10pm–midnight.

You'll find good variety and daily specials at this hotel restaurant, and especially good soups and main courses. I give it highest marks—if the cook stays on until you visit, you'll enjoy some of the best hotel food for the most reasonable prices in the country. The service is also first-rate. For a memorable lunch, try the soup with fresh vegetables and meatballs (*ciorbâ de perişoare*) and roast chicken, or the *tocanită piperatață* (spicy pork stew).

At one time a glamorous casino, the deep-rose dining room has a bit too many tables and red plush chairs cramming its interior, but the napkins are freshly starched and the waiters very attentive. Its clientele is well-to-do locals and foreign travelers. Lunch is best here, since the hours are a bit erratic and there may be a noisy evening cabaret show with a small cover charge during the late dinner hours.

★ **Napoca 15,** Str. Napoca 15. No phone.

Cuisine: ITALIAN. **Reservations:** Recommended evenings. **Directions:** Exit Piaţa Unirii onto Strada Napoca at its southwestern corner.
Prices: Pizza $1.30–$1.55; pasta $1.10; grilled meats $2–$2.55.
Open: Daily 9am–midnight.

This trattoria is one of Cluj's first fully private establishments, and much care has gone into making it distinctive and special. There are three eating areas, each tinctured with its own unique flavor. The outdoor patio is a superb venue for a drink, a midday meal, and people-watching on Strada Napoca. For quiet romance or contemplation, take a table in nice weather on the balcony that overlooks the leafy inner courtyard. And the small dining room, decorated with what might be Romania's first postmodern lighting fixtures, is sleek and urbane. The food is simple, tasty, and fresh, with a nice array of pastas and pizzas to choose from. Service is attentive without being obsequious. They do not yet have a phone, so drop by if you want to make a reservation.

Expres Restaurant Autoservice, Piaţa Pacii, facing the back of St. Michael's Cathedral.

Cuisine: CAFETERIA.
Prices: Soups and salads 10¢–15¢; main courses 30¢–60¢.
Open: Mon–Fri 8am–8pm, Sat 8am–midnight.

A no-frills self-service cafeteria with cheap meals frequented by Cluj's large student population. It's one of many eateries on the busy central square, but it's undoubtedly the cheapest one and the only one where you'll find a marble-top table at which to sit. The large turnover of many students and locals keeps the place bustling and the food fresh. Main courses include sausage with mashed potatoes, roast chicken with fries, spaghetti and meatballs; side dishes like carrot salad or sauerkraut come in the glass-encased display. Some beer and soft drinks, even wine is available.

Excursions to the Maramureş Region

Several hours' drive north of Cluj (95 miles) or three hours by express train to Baia Mare brings you to the heart of ★ **Maramureş,** a unique region not only in Romania but in all Eastern Europe. Never conquered by the Romans and only recently made accessible by roads, people in this remote northwestern area have preserved their traditional peasant culture and way of life intact to this day. Fortunately the region is as yet not self-conscious and barely exploited commercially by tourism.

Set in the pristine countryside are villages with wooden structures—churches, houses and their porches, barns, gates, and wells—that are elaborately carved with intricate symbols like the coiled rope, the sun and moon, the tree of life, and other geometric and floral patterns.

Women spin as they walk with their flocks of sheep or sit and gossip in front of their high carved gates. Ducks, goats, and chickens wander out of front yards onto the roads as small children with their grandmothers watch from their perches on benches.

In the summer you'll see people in the fields hoeing their crops or bringing in huge mounds of hay on carts. Local women, both young and old, show off sturdy legs in the surprisingly short skirts and boldly striped aprons. "Folk costumes" are items of clothing worn daily here.

Carts and wagons drawn by horses and sometimes oxen provide much of the transportation. Many people walk, often pulling small wagons behind them; a few ride bicycles; and occasionally an ancient motorcycle with a sidecar drives by.

The infrequent transportation here is both a blessing and a curse: It keeps away hordes of visitors from trampling the very things they're coming to see and brings the dedicated few willing to brave the discomfort. Bus and train service are erratic and require in-depth local knowledge to negotiate. The best way to travel through this isolated rural country is to rent a car—either on your own or with a driver—and explore slowly, stopping at the small villages along the way.

THE TOWNS The most elaborate gates and porches begin appearing in the village of Vadu Izei. The towns of Rozavlea and Bogdan Vodă have magnificent 16th- and 17th-century wooden churches with interior frescoes and fishscale shingle spires at least 100 feet high. The church in Surdeşti with its 150-foot steeple is one of the tallest wooden structures of its kind in the world. Sighetu Marmaţiei is the northernmost Romanian city and dates back to the early 14th century. It's a wonderful town to explore, has several small museums, arts and crafts cooperatives, and an award-winning folk-dance ensemble.

BAIA MARE

You might want to rent a car in Cluj or take a train or bus from Cluj to Baia Mare (pop. 150,000), a mining town some 100 miles north. It's a few hours' drive and you can decide whether to spend the night in Baia Mare or farther north, in Sighetu Marmaţiei.

INFORMATION & TOURS You can get a very good map of Maramureş county in English and book a tour at the International Travel Agency, the former county ONT office, located at Bd. Unirii 5 (☎ **62/41-67-41**), across from the large department store Maramureş in downtown Baia Mare. It's open Monday through Friday from 8am to 2pm. Call in advance to book a hotel and plan an excursion. Be sure to ask for Daniela Grigorescu, who speaks English. Depending on the demand, they arrange a variety of one- and two-day trips through Maramureş, including a circular tour which follows the route Baia Mare, Surdeşti, Mara, Vadu, Sighetu Marmatieţi, Săpînţa, Seini, Baia Mare. A one-day trip around the county (125 miles) costs about $65 per car with a guide; for a bit less per day, you can join a small group of six to eight people for a two-day trip by van with an overnight stay in a peasant house in one of the villages.

Another place to call ahead in Baia Mare to book a trip is Viki and Mi, a local private travel agency run by Viki Lăcătus. She is very friendly and energetic, but doesn't speak English, so have your hotelier help out. Her number is **62/42-80-59,** and she's available Monday through Friday from 9am to 6pm and on Saturday from 9am to 1pm. She offers one- or two-day excursions by private car or minivan with meals and a guide. A one-day tour of Maramureş through numerous towns and villages, including Sighetu, Vama, and Săpînţa (where the "Merry Cemetery" is located) with an English-speaking guide and lunch at a peasant's house costs about $60 per car. A more comprehensive two-day tour of the area with a guide and overnight accommodations at the Borşa health resort with meals costs $100 per car. Pickup and delivery in Baia Mare at your hotel or the train station by car are included.

ACCOMMODATIONS If you're stopping off in Baia Mare, a single with bath at the Hotel Mara, Bd. Unirii 11 (☎ **62/43-66-60**), will cost you about $18, including breakfast; a double runs $27. For a provincial town, their restaurant menu is quite extensive and the food excellent.

SIGHETU MARMAŢIEI

Farther north of Baia Mare is the town of Sighetu Marmaţiei. You can cross north into Ukraine across the Tisa River from here.

There are several hotels in old-fashioned Sighetu Marmaţiei. The most appealing is the lodge-style Hotel Marmatia, at Str. M. Eminescu 74 (☎ **62/1-22-41**), near a park with wonderful old trees. Their rates run about $27 for a single and $41 for a double, and their food is decent Romanian fare. For the cash-poor and adventurous, there's the Ardealul Hotel opposite the railway station with very worn-out, spartan doubles with shared baths for about $18.

SĂPÎNŢA

A favorite destination in the area is Săpînţa, 52 miles from Baia Mare and 11 miles west of Sighetu Marmaţiei. It's notable for its handcrafts and the "Merry Cemetery" (Cimitrul Vesel) near its church. You can also purchase handmade rugs, blankets, men's hats, and folk costumes for sale by local weavers along the road into Săpînţa at very low prices.

Local wood-carver and artist Ioan Stan Pătras began a tradition of carving and painting graveyard crosses back in 1935. What makes these crosses unique is not only the carved relief sculpture illustrating the life of the deceased, but the epitaphs in verse commenting on that life. Carved floral and geometric patterns decorate the predominantly bright-blue crosses; the naïve-style relief sculpture painted in bold primary colors at the base depicts the deceased's occupation (woodsman, priest, mother, weaver, farmer, barber), the cause of death (a miner killed in a blast, a small girl hit by a taxi, a tractor mishap), and a rhyme describing the traits of the deceased. It's a unique art form and a fascinating chronicle of local history. Try to bring along a Romanian companion to translate the obituaries to get a real sense of the local "merry" attitude of poking fun at life and death. Admission to the cemetery is 100 lei (8¢).

Pătras's own obituary and large cross are directly in front of the entrance to St. Mary's Church. Take a left when you leave the churchyard and walk through the village where women do their weaving and the men their chores in their yards. At the end of the street, the only house with a pine tree growing next to it and decorated with brightly painted carving is Pătras's house. Now a museum of the master's life, it is administered by his apprentice, Dimitru Pop. Designated since the age of 8 to follow in Patras's footsteps, the teenage Pop rebelled and left the town to seek a different destiny. With the death of Patras in 1977, Pop experienced a change of heart, and he returned to Săpînţa to carry on the tradition. He occupies the house next door to Patras's and keeps his workshop in a nearby shed. Just knock on his door and he will let you into the museum, which contains many beautiful examples of Patras's craft.

5 Suceava

271 miles N of Bucharest

GETTING THERE • By Plane Flights from Bucharest take about an hour and the fare is $44.

The TAROM office is at Str. Nicolae Bălcescu 2 (☎ **71-46-86**), open Monday through Saturday from 7am to 8pm.

• By Train Express trains from Bucharest to Suceava take about six hours, and the fare is 4,264 lei ($3.30) in first class.

For train tickets, go to the CFR bureau at Str. N. Bălcescu 8 (☎ **71-43-35**), open Monday through Friday from 7am to 8pm.

• By Bus Suceava's long-distance bus station is at Str. V. Alecsandri 2 (☎ **71-62-39**), just two blocks north of the Hotel Arcaşul. From here you can walk to most hotels in town within 10 minutes.

ESSENTIALS Suceava's telephone area code is 30.

INFORMATION The Suceava County Tourist Office is at Str. N. Bălcescu 2 (☎ **30/72-12-97** or **71-09-44**), off Piaţa Revoluţie. This office offers one- and two-day tours and can rent you a car with a private driver (you cannot, however, get a car without the driver).

The one-day tour, to Moldoviţa, Suceaviţa, and Voroneţ, includes lunch at the Rădăuţi restaurant and costs $100 (plus a $10 to $15 tip for the guide) for up to two people. The two-day tour adds monasteries in Humor, Putna, and Dragomirna and costs $152 for two people, $164 for three, including lodging for the right.

The car and driver rental rate of 260 lei per kilometer (20¢) plus 10% commission for the driver is far cheaper than what Hertz and Europcar charge. The cars are Romanian Dacias with seating for three plus the driver. Minivans with nine seats are available for slightly more money. Open Monday through Saturday from 9am to 6pm.

ORIENTATION Suceava is not large but its layout is unusual: The city center is on one hill and is flanked to the east and west by hills, with ruins of once-imposing castles and fortifications crowning each hill. Piaţa Revoluţie lies at the center of town; you'll find several travel offices just off this square on Strada Nicolae Bălcescu. The major hotels and museums are all within walking distance of here.

Most trains from Bucharest stop at both stations north of town: Suceava Station and then Suceava Nord. To reach the city center from Suceava Nord at Strada Gării 4 (☎ **71-00-37**), take bus no. 1 or 19 for about 10 to 15 minutes. To get to the center of town from Suceava Station at Str. N. Iorga 7 (☎ **71-38-97**), take bus no. 3, 4, 26, or 29 for about 15 minutes. Between 5am and 8pm the buses run every 30 minutes or so, but in the evening the bus service slows down, and stops about 10 or 11pm.

Suceava, with a population of 140,000, is not a particularly exciting tourist destination, but it serves as an excellent base to see the surrounding 500-year-old monasteries famous for their bold red-and-blue religious frescoes.

The first traces of civilized habitation in the Suceava region were left by Dacian tribes free of Roman domination in the 2nd to 3rd centuries A.D. In the 15th and 16th centuries when the monasteries were built, Suceava was a major commercial and cultural center. During these years the city was repeatedly damaged by enemy attacks and fire, culminating with the destruction of most of the town by the Turks in 1675.

In 1775 Suceava was occupied by the Habsburgs. Since its return to Romania in 1918, the city has become increasingly important as a commercial center; the most important industries are paper and wood pulp, furniture, and textiles.

WHAT TO SEE & DO

The monasteries far outshadow any sight or museum in Suceava, but you may be interested in a half day of sightseeing here.

Princely Citadel [Cetatea de Scaun], Parcul Cetății 3/14. ☎ **71-11-21.**

Located on a high plateau in an enormous eight-square-mile park on the east edge of town, these medieval fortifications surrounded by a moat were originally built in 1388 as the fortified home of Prince Petru Muşat I, the man who moved Moldavia's capital from Siret to Suceava. About 25 years later King Alexandru began to improve the fortifications, a process later continued by Stefan the Great (1457–1504). It withstood many Turkish raids, but its walls were weakened by earthquakes and local treachery, and it finally fell during the Ottoman invasion in 1675. During Habsburg rule, from 1775 to the 19th century, the Citadel itself served as a stone quarry for new buildings and further damage was inflicted.

Most of Suceava's other fortifications are in similar condition—primarily just in ruins. The one complete set of structures is the Zamca buildings, erected in 1606. On the west side of the city on Strada Zamcii, they offer a glimpse of what the huge fortified city looked like.

Admission: 100 lei (8¢).

Open: Tues–Sun 10am–6pm. **Directions:** From Piaţa Revoluţie, walk east for 10 to 15 minutes into Parcul Cetății.

Folk Art Museum (Hanul Domesc), Str. Ciprian Porumbescu 5. ☎ **71-37-75.**

An inn during the 16th century, this is the oldest civil structure in Suceava county, now housing an impressive collection of peasant and folk artifacts. The first floor shows typical rooms of a peasant house with a stone stove and the colorful fabrics the region is famous for. Other displays include costumes, silver jewelry, masks, and painted Easter eggs. The second floor has more peasant costumes, a weaving mill, and more handmade fabrics. It's quite a well-arranged collection.

Admission: 100 lei (8¢).

Open: Tues–Sun 10am–6pm. **Directions:** From Piaţa Revoluţie, walk a block west and then turn left.

County History Museum, Ştefan cel Mare 33. ☎ **71-64-39.**

A typical Romanian history museum starting with prehistoric artifacts, chronicling the county's growth up to the 20th century. Most interesting is the section devoted to Ştefan cel Mare's life. One room shows the royal reception room with life-size models of the king and his court. Unfortunately, here, as in most Romanian history museums, descriptions are only in Romanian. After World War II displays, the collection abruptly turns into a display of 19th- and 20th-century paintings, replacing works once dedicated to the glory of the Communist era.

Admission: 100 lei (8¢) adults, 50 lei (4¢) students.

Open: Tues–Sun 10am–6pm. **Directions:** From Piaţa Revoluţie, walk three blocks south on Ştefan cel Mare.

WHERE TO STAY

PRIVATE ROOMS As of this writing, Suceava has no private accommodations office, but local journalist and disc jockey **Doru Popovici** says he can help travelers find private rooms for as little as $8 to $12 a night. He speaks excellent English and runs the independent radio station "Uniplus" Radio Suceava, Bd. 1 Decembrie 1918 no. 10. You can try to reach him at **30/71-33-51** during the day. He can also find someone to drive you to the monasteries for $60 to $70 (in hard currency) a day. Or write him in advance at the above address, 5800 Suceava.

Prof. Michaela Iliescu (☎ **30/71-71-13**) can also help you find a room in Suceava or accommodations in peasant homes for $20 to $25 per night, breakfast included. Call her after 8pm a few days in advance; ask about beds in the monasteries and local country inns as well.

Hotels

Arcaşul, Str. Mihai Viteazul 4–6, 5800 Suceava. ☎ **30/71-09-44.** 100 rms (all with bath). TEL **Bus:** 1, 11, or 26 from Suceava Nord. **Trolleybus:** Take the town's only trolleybus from Suceava train station.

Rates: $21.50 single; $33.50 double.

Although the lobby is dim, you'll be welcomed by the earnest and helpful Aurora Ţintilá at reception desk with an admirable command of English, French, and German. There are nice touches like fresh flowers and heavy velvet drapes, but the rooms are spoiled by sagging mattresses and very dim lighting. The Arcaşul used to be the center of local nightlife, but now all the young people go to the Hotel Bucovina for a heavy disco scene. The staff here arranges tours to the monasteries. The hotel also has one of the better restaurants in a town not particularly distinguished by its cuisine (see "Where to Eat," below).

Hotel Suceava, Str. Nicolae Bălcescu, 5800 Suceava. ☎ **30/72-24-97** or **72-28-38.** 103 rms (all with bath). TEL **Bus:** 1 or 19 from Suceava Nord. **Trolleybus:** Take the town's only trolleybus from Suceava train station.

Rates (including continental breakfast): $14.10 single; $20–$22.70 double; $25.40 triple.

Located right off Piaţa Revoluţie, Suceava's main square, and just across from the tourism office, this hotel is slightly more pleasant than others in town. You've seen the folksy furniture before, the medallion-patterned rugs, the chintzy neo-Victorian wall-lamps, but somehow, here at the Suceava, it all just adds up better. Decorated in nonoffensive shades of orange, amber, brown, and rust, the rooms are clean and have good mattresses. Best of all, each bed is covered with a luxurious heavy quilted duvet. The first floor is reserved for Western tourists, while the second and third floors are for Eastern Europeans (and cost less). There's a restaurant downstairs, open daily from 7am to 10pm.

WHERE TO EAT

Hotel Arcaşul, Str. Mihai Viteazul 4/6. ☎ **71-09-44.**

Cuisine: ROMANIAN. **Directions:** From Piaţa Revoluţie, walk three blocks west down Strada Bălcescu, then turn left half a block.
Prices: Soups 21¢–30¢; main courses 40¢–$1.20.
Open: Daily 7am–11pm.

By local reputation one of Suceava's two best restaurants (the other is in the Hotel Bucovina), the Arcaşul still has a somewhat limited menu, but it's the most lively diner spot in town. Try the house specialty, the *techitură bucoviniană* (a savory local concoction of beef, pork, and gravy over polenta). The restaurant is part of a local experiment in privatization: It's being managed on a trial basis by hotel staff members who pooled their money in a limited partnership. We wish them success—they're doing their best in very tough times.

Hotel Bucovina, Str. Ana Ipătescu 5. ☎ **71-70-48.**

Cuisine: ROMANIAN. **Directions:** From Piaţa Revoluţie, walk two blocks south on Strada Ana Ipătescu.
Prices: Soups 10¢–60¢; main courses 55¢–$1.50.
Open: Breakfast daily 7–9am; lunch daily noon–3pm; dinner daily 6–10pm.

Decorated in a classic socialist-hotel decor of red curtains, wood paneling, and a dance floor at the center, the Bucovina offers passable cuisine, as well as excruciatingly loud disco music six nights a week from 8 to 11pm. A bonus, however, is an English-language menu, with such offerings as chicken breast with mushrooms, roast beef, and stuffed peppers. The clientele is mostly young people with a sprinkling of local rural folks, shady underworld characters, and during the tourist season, groups of foreigners. The dining room is filled with noise and clouds of thick cigarette smoke—quite unappetizing.

Excursions to the Bukovina Monasteries

Nestled in tranquil velvety green meadows deep in the Carpathian foothills of Bukovina, in the remote northeast corner of the country, are Romania's greatest artistic treasures: ★ **15th century monastery churches** with remarkably well preserved frescoes on their exterior walls. The entire area has been designated a national monument. If you are interested in art, these incomparable monastery churches with their elaborately painted frescoes are undeniably worth the journey.

As remote and difficult to access as Maramureş, the Bukovina region is not well known or heavily visited by tourists (see "Getting There," below). Of the fourteen monasteries scattered throughout the region, the five considered most outstanding are Voroneţ, Humor, Moldoviţa, Suceviţa, and Arbore.

A great many churches and monasteries were built during the reign of Prince Stefan the Great (1457–1504) to celebrate his victories in battles with the encroaching Ottoman Turks. This tumultuous period of hard-won autonomy and cultural flowering is considered Moldavia's Golden Age. Altogether, the warrior prince and his son Petru Rareş erected a total of 44 churches and monasteries.

The monastery churches were built as monuments to political and military achievements, but they testify as well to the considerable artistic acumen of Moldavian society during the period. Their distinctive architecture defined what later came to be called the Moldavian style, essentially a blend of local building techniques (octagonal towers with peaked roofs that spread out to form very broad eaves) with imported Gothic and Byzantine styles.

But it is the fresco work, interior and exterior, that qualifies these churches as world treasures. Biblical stories, folk legends, and customs are rendered with exquisite detail and palette in purely pictorial form, for the devotional benefit of the illiterate. How the vivid colors have withstood more than four centuries of exposure to sun, snow, and wind is a mystery that experts have not yet solved. Although the paints have been chemically analyzed, neither the longevity of the pigments nor the color tones (especially the Voroneţ blue) have ever been duplicated with any success. The damage caused by candle smoke, earthquakes, and vandalism is currently being restored with the help of UNESCO.

GETTING THERE The monasteries are situated within a radius of 50 miles west and northeast of Suceava; visiting all five in less than two days will take some serious hoofing. Lamentably, they're difficult to reach by public transportation (suggestions are given below in the individual destination descriptions); renting a car or joining an organized tour is the best way to visit them. If you're going to venture out on your own, be prepared: few locals speak any English, assuring quite an adventure should you run out of gas or get lost.

Tours The prices and conditions of tours listed here are likely to change at any moment, and the future should bring more choices. Check around before deciding.

The Suceava County Tourist Office (see "Information," above) offers one- and two-day tours to the Bukovina monasteries. The one-day tour goes to Moldoviţa, Suceviţa, and Voroneţ and includes lunch in a Rădăuţi restaurant for $100 (plus a $10 to $15 tip for the guide) for up to two people. The two-day tour adds monasteries in Humor, Putna, and Dragomirna and costs $152 for two people, $164 for three.

The Hotel Arcaşul in Suceava (see "Where to Stay," above) also organizes trips to the Bukovina monasteries. Arcaşul's one-day trip to Suceviţa, Moldoviţa, and Voroneţ costs $65 during the high season. The two-day tour includes three additional monasteries (Putna, Humor, and Arbore), an overnight at the Hotel Cimpulung Moldovenesc, and a superb lunch at the Hotel Nordic in Rădăuţi—all for $110.

Hiring a Local Driver For those who'd prefer a less packaged visit, the Suceava County Tourist Office (see "Information," above) rents cars with drivers for 260 lei per kilometer (20¢) plus 10% commission for the driver—far cheaper than what Hertz and Europcar charge. The cars are Romanian Dacias with seating for three plus the driver. Minivans with nine seats are available for slightly more money. Or call local journalist and radio disc jockey **Doru Popovici.** He can find drivers willing to take people to the monasteries for about $60 to $70 (in hard currency) a day. He works at "Uniplus" Radio Suceava, Bd. 1 Decembrie 1918 no. 10, and can be reached there during the day by calling **30/71-33-51.** You can also try your own luck at finding a local taxi driver or private individual.

HOURS All monasteries maintain the same hours: daily from 7am until sundown, which means as late as 8pm in summer, to as early as 4pm in winter. Each charges a mere 500 lei (40¢) entrance fee, usually collected by a resident nun.

VORONEŢ

The oldest and most famous monastery is Voroneţ. Located in the middle of a small whitewashed village, set against the green rolling Moldavian hills, it was built in three months and three weeks by Prince Stefan the Great in 1488. The frescoes inside were added later in 1496–97, during the reign of his son, Prince Petru Rareş; the extraordinary exterior ones were painted in 1547. Although the magnificent colors are the hallmark of all the monasteries, the Voroneţ Monastery is especially famous for its stunning Voroneţ blue, a color unlike any other in the world.

The western facade is covered with frescoes of scenes from the Last Judgment, with wild animals carrying pieces of people who have been torn apart by beasts. The sinners broiling in the coals at Jesus' feet present a veritable Moldavian rogues' gallery, filled with Turks and fierce Tartars. At the top, angels roll up the signs of the zodiac, ending the procession of time, as archangels blow a bucium, the favorite horn of Moldavian shepherds to this day. The souls being carried heavenward are wrapped in embroidered Moldavian towels; those doomed to hell wear turbans like the Ottomans, the most hated of Moldavia's foes. On the south wall is the genealogy of Christ in the form of the Tree of Jesse, set against a background of wondrous Voroneţ blue.

To get here from Suceava, take the train to Gura Humorului (on an express train the trip lasts 55 minutes); once in Gura Humorului, buses to Voroneţ (4 miles away) meet arriving trains all day—though on Sunday they run less often.

HUMOR

The small church at Humor (☎ **Humor 170**) was founded by Petru Rareş and Chancellor Theodor in 1530. About four miles from the village of Gura Humorului, the monastery site had been a workshop for some of Romania's most gifted calligraphers as early as the 15th century.

Many of the characteristic Moldavian details found at Voroneţ can be found here also. Of note is the somewhat-faded southern facade covered with a composition of 24 scenes based on a poem written by Patriarch Serghie. The poem is dedicated to the Virgin Mary who, it was felt, saved Constantinople from a Persian attack in 626. The Moldavians equated this intervention with their own desire for victory over the Ottomans. So fervent was the artist's hatred of the Turks that the representations of victory are imagined scenes of good and evil that bear little relation to actual historical events. In another scene the devil is represented as a fat, jocular old woman (ask one of the groundkeepers to point it out; it can be hard to spot). The predominant color is rose red.

Walls once surrounded the monastery, but the Austrian Habsburg emperors removed them in the 18th century. A sole tower and a few wall fragments remain. Today the monastery serves only as a museum.

To get here from Suceava, take the train to Gura Humorului, which takes 55 minutes on an express; buses to both Voroneţ and Humor should meet arriving trains, though few buses run on Sunday.

MOLDOVIŢA

The largest of the five best-known monasteries is Moldoviţa (☎ **30/83-63-48**), built in 1532 and painted five years later. The church is enclosed behind stone fortress walls and covered with hundreds of pictures. On the southern wall is the *Prayer to the Virgin* and the genealogy of Christ painted in the form of a Tree of Jesse against a dark-blue background. One side of the fresco has been worn away over time. In the open porch there's a memorable *Last Judgment.* You'll notice graffiti scratched into it that dates from the middle of the 19th century, the destructive legacy of Habsburg soldiers who were stationed here.

Perhaps the most unusual scene here is the panoramic A.D. 626 *Siege of Constantinople,* in which the Persians fought the Byzantines. The artist portrayed the Persians as Turks, Moldaviţa's enemy when the work was rendered, and the brave defending Byzantines as the Moldavians at the Citadel of Suceava.

There's also a small museum displaying the original throne of Prince Petru Rareş (son of Stefan the Great) as well as an excellent collection of 16th-century ornamental art, books, and icons.

There are nine nuns who live at Moldoviţa now, and they're possibly in need of funds to complete the construction of new living quarters for incoming novices. Visit with them; though poor, like the Romanian country people, they are friendly and hospitable. Leave them a donation and they'll pray for you and your family.

To get here from Suceava, take the express train to Vama (about 1 hour and 15 minutes). From there you can connect by train to Moldoviţa in about 45 minutes, or by bus.

SUCEVIŢA

Hidden high up in the hills, the Suceviţa Monastery looks more like a citadel than a monastery—it has a thick stone wall with several imposing towers and a stout gatehouse guarding the monastery entrance. There are several legends connected with this monastery; one involves a woman who, for 30 years, hauled stone in her ox-drawn wagon for the monastery construction. In memory of her faithful toil a likeness of her head was carved in black stone and set under the eaves. The western wall remains undecorated because, according to legend, a workman fell and died of injuries here. On the northern wall is the fantastic *Ladder of Virtues,* depicting the 30 steps to heaven, and on the southern wall is, again, a Tree of Jesse with Christ's genealogy. It includes *The Procession of the Philosophers,* with Pythagoras, Sophocles, Plato, and Aristotle clad in beautiful Byzantine robes. To the right is the Virgin, depicted as a Byzantine princess. The rest of the building depicts the hierarchy of heaven in intricate detail and sumptuous color.

To the left after entering the monastery grounds, which are still run by the nuns who live there, you'll find a museum, which displays 17th- and 18th-century Moldavian icons, bibles, church vestments, crosses, and other sacred objects.

To get here from Suceava, you can take the train to Rădăuţi, 11 miles away, in over an hour, from which buses connect to Suceviţa six to eight times a day.

Lunch in Rădăuţi

Hotel Nordic, Piaţa Unirii 67, Rădăuţi. ☎ **30/96-28-03.**

Cuisine: ROMANIAN. **Directions:** Take Route 17A toward the Suceviţa Monastery; the hotel is in the main town square.
Prices: Four-course meal with wine under $2.
Open: Daily 8am–midnight.

If you're anywhere near Rădăuţi (and you'll pass through it if you're headed northwest to the Suceviţa Monastery from Suceava), stop here for a truly memorable meal. Simply put, you'll get the best home-cooked food in all of Romania for the least money here. While the decor isn't much and the dining room is filled with smoke, small gracious touches like an embroidered tablecloth with sprigs of cedar or rosebuds and a rudimenary ice bucket for wine are winning. Best of all is the superb and astonishingly cheap food. Daily specials might include pickled mushrooms (20¢), vegetable soup or sarmale (10¢), roast pork slices with gravy or roast chicken with onions (30¢), and clatite with jam (10¢). You'll come away sorry you ever doubted that Romanians could prepare food well. The restaurant is run privately and the manager, Mr. Rado, will gladly accept your appreciation through an interpreter.

ARBORE

The smallest and simplest of the monasteries, Arbore is dimly lit, without a cupola, and was built by a lesser noble called a boyar. Green is the predominant color at Arbore; five shades of green are blended with reds, yellows, and blues. The western wall displays numerous miniature scenes from the Book of Genesis and the lives of saints. The figures are animated, their faces glow a healthy pink, and they wear elegant cloaks and gowns—everything is done with the attention to detail and the delicacy that's usually seen in miniatures. In the courtyard you can still see the heavy stone slabs with 15 small hollows in which the pigments were mixed.

6 Iaşi

254 miles NE of Bucharest, 87 SE of Suceava

GETTING THERE • By Plane For flight and airport-bus information, inquire at TAROM (☎ **11-52-39**), Str. Arcu 3, just off Piaţa Unirii. You can fly from Bucharest to Iaşi's airport (☎ **14-29-53**) in slightly more than an hour for $44.

• **By Train** The express train from Bucharest to Iaşi takes about seven hours, making the ride a good candidate for an overnight couchette (for example, as of this writing, a train with sleeper compartments leaves Bucharest at 11:20pm, arriving at 5:55am in Iaşi). The fare is 4,264 lei ($3.30) in first class. The train from Suceava, with a change in Pascani, takes about two hours.

There's a 24-hour baggage check in a building adjacent to the station; exit the platform on the far right and look for the window.

To find out train schedules and to buy tickets, drop by the CFR Railway Ticket Agency, Piaţa Unirii 9–11 (☎ **11-36-73**), open Monday through Friday from 8am to 8pm and on Saturday from 8am to 2pm.

• **By Car** As I have mentioned, it's easiest to explore the north of the country by car. If you're visiting Suceava by car, you can continue to Iaşi by car in about three hours.

ESSENTIALS Iaşi's telephone area code is 32.

ORIENTATION Iaşi runs roughly along a north-south line with the Bahlui River cutting through its southern edge. The main square is Piaţa Unirii, site of two hotels, the tourist office, and several other travel agencies. From this square begins Strada Ştefan cel Mare, which leads to the symbol of Iaşi, the massive Palace of Culture, after about a 15-minute walk. Most sights and services are on or near this main drag.

To get to town from the train station on Piaţa Gării (☎ **13-60-90** or **11-33-33**), walk up the main street (east) as you leave the station to Strada Arcu, not more than a 5- or 10-minute walk away, and then turn right (south) to Piaţa Unirii. Tram nos. 2 and 9 traverse the same route.

INFORMATION Iaşi's main tourist office for dealing with foreigners is the **Agenţia de Turism International,** Piaţa Unirii 12 (☎ **32/14-30-37**). The wonderfully obliging English-speaking manager will answer questions and help set you up with accommodations. The office will also rent a car with a driver ($65 a day for 250km, plus 20¢ for each additional kilometer), and it stocks a good supply of brochures and maps. The office is open Monday through Friday, 8:30am to 5:30pm, Saturday 9am to 1pm. You can also check out the Moldova Travel Agency (☎ **32/11-43-64**), around the corner from the Moldova Hotel, or Edmond, which shares an office with TAROM (see "Getting There by Plane," above). Both are private agencies dealing mostly with Romanians and speaking little English, but they may still be able to satisfy your touristic needs.

Set among rolling hills on the Moldavian Plateau between the river valleys of the Prut to the east and the Moldova to the west, Iaşi (pronounced "ee-ahsh"; pop. 430,000) served as the capital of Moldavia and its leading cultural center for three centuries, from 1565 to 1859. Here in 1859 Alexander Ioan Cuza united Moldavia and Wallachia, an act that established the Romanian state and scuttled the designs of three competing empires—Russian, Ottoman, and Habsburg.

Iaşi has been a leading intellectual center since Prince Vasile Lupu in the early 1600s established Romania's first institution of higher learning, the Vasilian Academy. Some 50,000 students attending Iaşi's 30 technical universities and colleges, many from Arab and African countries, carry on the tradition of learning. Alexander Cuza University, built in the last decade of the 19th century, is the oldest in Romania.

Vasile Lupu was an imposing figure in Moldavia's cultural development. His 20-year reign saw the building of many churches (including the Church of the Three Hierarchs) and printing houses. Iaşi has also long been a center of book publishing, earning it the sobriquet of "City of Books and Poetry." The first important poetic work in Romanian was printed here by Metropolitan Dosoftei in 1673.

Other prominent figures of Romanian history to have lived and worked in Iaşi were poets Mihail Eminescu and Vasile Alecsandri, the composer Georges Enesco, and statesmen like Alexander Cuza and Michael Kogălniceanu.

There is much evidence of Iaşi's illustrious past in its many museums, churches, and monasteries. Its rich traditions and active cultural, scientific, and political life are carried on in the truly impressive national theater, the scores of colleges, and numerous flourishing political organizations. Today, in addition to its great concentration of institutions of higher learning, it's the center of the movement seeking to unite the newly independent state of Moldova (formerly the Soviet Republic of Moldavia and before that, Bessarabia, the eastern half of Moldavia) with Romania.

WHAT TO SEE & DO

Palace of Culture, Str. Palatului 1. ☎ **11-41-36.**

Iaşi's massive neo-Gothic palace in the southern part of town was built in 1906–25 at the location of the first Princely Court of the Moldavian Vovoides (1437). Today the palace is an important museum complex, with four separate collections. The Polytechnical Museum is the best of the lot. Perhaps misnamed, as it is devoted entirely to the technology of recorded sound, it begins with platen-driven music boxes and concludes somewhat hilariously with a garden-variety cassette-playing boom box. In between, there are pianolas, mechanical pianos, an amazing mechanical piano-violin, and gramophones. If you plead sweetly, the attendent might crank them up for you. The Art Museum, Romania's oldest national collection, contains a few works by Veronese, Tintoretto, Van Dyck, and Caravaggio, as well as many landscapes by

Romanian artists. The Ethnographic Museum has a mediocre collection of rugs, furniture, household objects, and tools. The History Collection recounts Moldavia's history through uninspired archeological and other displays.

Admission: History, Ethnographic, or Polytechnical Museum, 75 lei (6¢); Art Museum, 120 lei (9¢).

Open: All museums, Tues–Sun 10am–5pm. **Tram:** 9 from the train station.

Biserica Trei Ierarhi (Church of the Three Hierarchs), Ştefan cel Mare 62.

Built by Vasile Lupu in 1635–39, this church was an important preserve of culture during the Middle Ages, containing a school and a printing press. It is most noteworthy for its facade embroidered with intricately carved stonework and its rich golden interior decoration. The stonework portrays popular Moldavian patterns influenced by Islamic art brought by the marauding Ottomans. Legend has it that gold once covered the exterior, but invading Turks surrounded the church with hay and lit a fire, melting off the precious metal.

Inside, paintings with rich gold backgrounds cover all corners of the church. Many of these were restored at the end of the last century in local Renaissance style. To the left of the entrance inside you'll see the tomb of Prince Vasile Lupu, son of Stefan the Great and Iaşi's greatest medieval cultural figure.

Admission: 75 lei (6¢).

Open: Daily 8am–8pm. **Directions:** From Piaţa Unirii, walk south down Ştefan cel Mare for about 10 minutes.

Golia Monastery, Str. Cuza Voda 51.

This brooding monastery tucked in the middle of Iaşi's old town provides refuge and sanctuary today much as it did from invading Turks in the 17th century. Built between 1650 and 1660, it was decorated in late Renaissance style with elements that mark the architectural transition to the baroque. Entry is achieved through a gateway under the 30-meter Golia Tower, which rises incongruously out of a lattice of narrow streets. Despite high-rise apartment blocks that rise beyond the walls, the surprisingly expansive space and landscaping within shape a tranquil sanctum. The monastery church, built in 1660, features frescoes reminiscent of those in the Bukovina monasteries and a gorgeous carved iconostasis.

Admission: Free.

Open: Daily 9am–6pm. **Directions:** From Piaţa Unirii, walk south on Strada Cuza Voda for 15 minutes.

WHERE TO STAY

Hotel Traian, Piaţa Unirii 1, 6600 Iaşi. ☎ **32/14-33-30.** Telex 22270. 137 rms (all with bath). TEL TV **Tram:** 3, 9, or 11 one stop from the train station.

Rates (including continental breakfast): $20 single; $30 double; $45 triple. Rooms without TV, $3 less.

Traian has been Iaşi's most impressive hotel since 1882, and with all that has happened since then, you will forgive and probably enjoy its additional cachet as Iaşi's most kitschy hotel. Guest rooms feature a color scheme right out of an Easter egg hunt: pink and lavender walls, purple carpets, and white furniture garlanded heavily with doilies. The overall effect, however, is charming and fun right down to the blinking neon sign on the front facade. Elements of luxury left over from bygone days include ornate moldings, high ceilings, and the liberal use of marble on the stairwells and in the lobby.

The bathrooms have aged less gracefully and could use renovation, but they deliver the goods nevertheless. If you take a room facing Piaţa Unirii you can see the statue of Prince Alexander Ioan Cuza, who was elected by the Bucharest parliament that united Moldavia with Muntenia (Wallachia) in 1859. If traffic and tram noise disturb you, the rooms toward the back are much quieter.

Hotel Moldova, Str. Anastase Panu 21–29, 6600 Iaşi. ☎ **98/14-22-25.** 156 rms (all with bath). TV TEL **Tram:** 9 from the train station.

Rates (including breakfast): $26.15–$28.50 single; $42.30–$46.15 double. Lower-priced rooms are on the first and 12th floors and suffer respectively from disco noise and inadequate heating. Doubles without TV, subtract $1.55.

The exterior is yet another uninspired generic 12-story concrete-and-glass building, and the lobby is rather dull, but in general, this is a clean and well-maintained hotel. After the dimly lit hallways, the rooms accost you with a wild and cheerful combination of purple carpets and orange bedspreads and drapes. The lighting and beds are good, and the bathrooms are enlivened by handsome orange-brown tiles and new plumbing fixtures. Try to get a room with a view of Iaşi's oldest and most charming church, St. Nicholas, which was founded by Stefan the Great in 1492.

Facilities: Swimming pool (open Tuesday through Sunday 5 to 7pm and 8pm to midnight, for 750 lei (58¢).

WHERE TO EAT

As Iaşi is a big college town, there is a proliferation of restaurants that cater to those with little patience for the pretension of a hotel dining room. Look for them—diners and pizza pads and cafés—below Piaţa Unirii on Strada Ştefan cel Mare, Strada 14 Decembrie 1989, and by the National Theater on Strada Dobrogeanu.

Restaurant Select, Piaţa 14 Decembrie 1989. ☎ **14-73-93.**

Cuisine: ROMANIAN/ITALIAN. **Directions:** Walk south two minutes from Piaţa Unirii.
Prices: Soups 45¢–55¢; pizza 55¢–$1; main courses 35¢–$1.35.
Open: 24 hours, with a short break in the early morning.

A handsome turn-of-the century baroque pleasure palace, Select has recently been reconstructed as an end-of-the century post-Communist pleasure palace. On the premises are a restaurant, pâtisserie, bingo room, and casino. The plush decor and mostly female staff flitting about in miniskirt-with-black-tie uniforms give the complex an air of unreconstructed naughtiness. This is the new Eastern Europe, making up for years of missed indulgence. Far more subtle is the food at the restaurant. In addition to all your continental favorites, the menu features tangy, chewy pizza that is as good as you will find in all of Romania. The ciorbás are top-notch as well, and bread made from pizza dough comes warm. Save space for dessert at the Cofeteria across the hall. The crowd of high rollers the restaurant draws provides people-watching at its best.

Hotel Traian, Piaţa Unirii 1. ☎ **14-33-30.**

Cuisine: ROMANIAN. **Tram:** 3, 9, or 11 from the train station.
Prices: Salads 21¢; soups 23¢–45¢; main courses 35¢–75¢.
Open: Daily 7am–midnight.

A dark-green dining hall in the grand manner, with marble floors, high ceilings, velvet drapes, and lace curtains covering huge windows—but too shabby to be pretentious. The menu is extensive and multilingual (with some hilarious translation errors), the food tasty and quite inexpensive, and the local dry white Feteasca wine excellent.

Try the *mamaliga* (polenta) or the chicken for a fail-safe meal. Electro-folk musical accompaniment makes for interesting seasoning.

Fast Food, Cuza Vodă II.

Cuisine: ROMANIAN TAKE-OUT **Directions:** From Piaţa Unirii, walk one block east to the middle of Cuza Vodă.

Prices: Sandwiches 15¢; main courses 90¢–$1.20.

Open: Daily 6am–4pm and 5pm–4:30am (holidays 10am–4pm).

This tiny private place, with very limited seating, is mostly for take-out. Sandwiches like grilled cheese or smoked pork, portions of grilled pork or beef with fries, along with beer, coffee, cigarettes, soft drinks, and whiskey are offered. The menu board changes daily, so things are fresh. The service is fast and they work almost around the clock, so you'll never go hungry in this town. The prices are a bit higher here, but the convenience, cleanliness, and novelty are worth it.

38

Romania's Black Sea Coast

THE LANDSCAPE ON ROMANIA'S BLACK SEA COAST RANGES FROM UNSPOILED NATURE rich in birds and wildlife north in the Danube Delta, to miles of high-rise beach resorts on the shore, to a sad and ugly petrochemical wasteland in the central part of the coast. The industrial area ends near Constanţa, an ancient town founded by Greeks in the 5th century B.C. and later settled by the Romans. Here you'll see impressive Roman ruins in the heart of town as well as the Dacian, Greek, and Roman artifacts inside its fine museums. South of Constanţa are beach resorts—although they're not the most attractive in Europe, they make for a refreshing summer afternoon's swim or some invigorating water sports.

SEEING THE BLACK SEA COAST

The main rail line and roads from Bucharest go through Constanţa, which serves as a hub for the Black Sea coast. From there, you can continue to the various beach resorts by either bus or train, or continue north to the Danube Delta area.

1 Constanţa

140 miles E of Bucharest

GETTING THERE • By Plane The TAROM flight from Bucharest to Constan$a takes about 40 minutes and costs $30.

Your flight will land at Constanţa's Aeroportul International Mihail Kogălniceanu (☎ **61-52-76** or **61-64-46**). An airport bus meets arriving flights and travels the 22 miles to downtown Constanţa in about 40 minutes for 125 lei (10¢). Buses from downtown Constanţa to the airport leave from the TAROM Airlines office at Str. Ştefan cel Mare 15 (☎ **66-26-32, 66-05-08,** or **66-15-91**) one hour and 20 minutes before departure; be sure to double-check the time.

• By Train The express train from Bucharest to Constanţa makes unusually good time for Romania: about three hours, at a fare of $1.95 in first class. Note that tickets for the express train on this route frequently sell out in summer, so buy the tickets as soon as you possibly can—or you may be forced to take the local train, which travels at a snail's pace, without a seat reservation.

Constanţa's train station, Gara Feroviară, at Piaţa Victoriei 1 (☎ **61-67-25**), is more than a 20-minute walk from the Old Town along Bulevardul Republicii. If you don't feel like the two-kilometer (1.2 miles) walk, take trolleybus no. 40 or 43 (150 lei/12¢ for a two-way ticket—cross the parking lot and look left for the depot). The staff at the train station information counters speak a little English.

• By Bus Due to excellent rail connections, a bus to the Black Sea Coast should be a secondary or tertiary choice. The primary station is Constanţa Sud, just one block north of the train station at Teodor Burada 1 (☎ **6-00-40**). Constanţa Nord is north of the city center at the intersection of Strada Soveja and Bulevardul Tomis.

• By Car Bucharest and Constanţa are connected by two-lane Route 3, passing through some very interesting scenery, which is just as well since traffic can be heavy. At the two-thirds point, the pretty poplar-lined agricultural route becomes a superhighway in honor of a pair of Ceauçescu follies. Cernavodă, unmistakable from its five reactor shells, will be Romania's only nuclear power plant if ever finished. The Danube Canal, built at tremendous human and financial expense, extends over 50 miles to the Black Sea. Opened in 1984, it is rarely used, an example of the deluded schemes of the Ceauçescu era. The drive takes three or four hours.

What's Special About Romania's Black Sea Coast

Beaches

- A series of fairly modern resorts across wide stretches of beach north and south of Constanţa.

Ancient Monuments

- Ancient Roman mosaic floor in Constanţa, an astonishingly well preserved colored mosaic from the 3rd or 4th century A.D.

Spas

- Eforie Nord, Romania's best-known health spa, where you can take cold mud packs on the beach.

Wineries

- Murfatlar vineyards, where some of Romania's best wines are produced.

Nature

- The Danube Delta, swampy marshlands at the terminus of the mighty Danube, home to many birds and other wildlife.

Museums

- National History and Archeological Museum in Constanţa, with an excellent collection of antiquities.
- Constanţa's Museum of the Romanian Navy, with a look at maritime navigation since antiquity.

ESSENTIALS Constanţa's telephone area code is 41.

INFORMATION There are two tourist offices in the city center that provide information, hotel bookings, and somewhat pricey tours for all Black Sea Coast resorts. ONT-Carpaţi, at Bd. Tomis 66 (☎ **61-48-00**), is open during the summer from 8am to 7pm Monday through Saturday, and on Sunday from 8am to 1pm. Off-season closing is an hour earlier. In addition to reservations and tours, they rent poky Romanian Dacias for $40 per day plus 20¢ per kilometer. The S.A. Litoral Travel Agency in the Hotel Continental, Bd. Republicii 20 (☎ **61-56-60**), holds longer hours—open year-round daily from 9am to 9pm—but has fewer resources than ONT.

CITY LAYOUT Constanţa's *centru* (center) and Old Town, which contain all the sights and hotels listed here, lie at the city's easternmost point on a small peninsula rimmed by a seafront promenade and flanked to the south by the facilities of the port. Bulevardul Republicii leads from the train station and hits Bulevardul Tomis at a right angle. Tomis spills into the Old Town and concludes at scenic Piaţa Ovidiu where the city's museums, mosques, and churches lie. Trolleybus nos. 40, 41, and 43 tootle along the major boulevards but do not enter the picturesque tangle of Old Town streets.

DEPARTING • **By Train** To avoid the especially long lines at the train station for departing trains, buy your rail tickets at the Agenţia CFR, at Str. Vasile Canarache 4 (☎ **61-49-60**), open Monday through Friday from 7am to 7pm and on Saturday from 7am to 1pm. The agency is conveniently located near Piaţa Ovidiu behind the Archeological Museum.

Constanţa (pop. 350,000) is the oldest city in Romania. Founded in the 5th century B.C. by Greek traders, Constanţa has been the site of uninterrupted habitation for over 26 centuries. First called Tomis by its Grecian founders, it was renamed in the 4th century A.D. in honor of Constantine the Great and probably called Constantiana. The city belonged to the Ottoman Empire from 1413 until 1878, when the burgeoning Romanian state annexed it. Constanţa's most significant historical resident, the Roman poet Ovid, was exiled here in A.D. 9 by Caesar Augustus, who was offended by Ovid's racy *Art of Love.* Tomis was then a rather primitive outpost on the periphery of the Roman empire, and Ovid lived out the remainder of his days in an elegiac misery of longing for Rome. His literary output from the period is considered one of the earliest examples of exile literature.

The city's cultural charms may have left Ovid cold, but its strategic location on the Black Sea, midway between Istanbul and Odessa, has been an irresistible lure for Greek, Roman, Turkish, and Romanian occupants. The huge commercial port—Romania's largest—and the new industrial development north and west of the city are rather unsightly, but the old historic part of town displays a first-rate selection of remnants from the city's historical eras. From the distinctly Arabic bustle of the narrow streets off Piaţa Ovidiu to the belle-époque elegance of the Cazino restaurant that anchors Constanţa's seaside promenade, modern Constanţa is a compendium of history as well as a gateway to Romania's beach resorts.

WHAT TO SEE & DO

National History and Archeological Museum, Piaţa Ovidiu 12. ☎ **61-45-83.**

Artifacts from the Stone Age to the present are highlighted by an excellent collection of antiquities from the Dacian, Greek, and Roman eras. It starts on the second floor with mammoth tusks found at Poarta Alba, and has pieces such as a 5th-century B.C. granite sculpture of a Thracian-Scythian fighter. The collection also contains stone inscriptions of the Roman Empire in the region.

On the ground floor, the museum treasury boasts an impressive array of Greek statuary (primarily busts) from the 4th through the 2nd century B.C. The jewel of this room, and the entire museum collection, is the *Glykon,* the Goddess of Fortune and protector of the city, a marvelously disturbing composite of a male figure, serpent, lion, and wild antelope, sculpted in the 2nd or 3rd century A.D. Other pieces in the treasury include busts of Roman emperors Constantine and Antoninus Pius, 2nd-century A.D. Roman armor, and blown glass from the Roman era. A guide to the museum holdings in English is worth purchasing for its preinflation cost of 8 lei (1/2¢) and its gonzo Marxist discussion of archeological history.

In front of the museum you'll see another important historical figure in the statue of Ovid, designed by Italian sculptor Ettore Ferrari in 1887.

Admission: 100 lei (8¢).

Open: June–Sept, daily 9am–8pm; Oct–May, Wed–Sun 9am–5pm. **Bus:** 40, 41, or 43 from the train station to the intersection of Bulevardul Republicii and Bulevardul Tomis; then walk 10 minutes southeast.

Roman Warehouses and Bath Complex, Piaţa Ovidiu. ☎ **61-45-83.**

These impressive Roman ruins, highlighted by a massive colored mosaic floor, were discovered only in 1959 as construction workers bulldozed the area to lay foundations for a new building. The 3rd- or 4th-century A.D. mosaic floor, at a commercial center of the ancient Roman colony, once covered more than 2,000 square yards, of which 850 square yards remain. The tiny mosaic tiles portray geometrical shapes and floral patterns. Around the mosaic floors you'll also see ancient Roman jars and marble fragments.

Down the hill from the mosaic hall are more Roman remains including the city's bath complex from the 4th–5th centuries A.D. made of stone and brick. These remains were discovered in 1964.

History buffs may also want to visit a small garden of ruins a few blocks away off Bulevardul Carpaţi; fragments remaining include a few columns and a carved marble slab. On Bulevardul Republicii you can also see fragments of 3rd-century A.D. Roman walls.

Admission: 100 lei (8¢) to view mosaic floor; the other Roman ruins are free.

Open: June–Dec, Tues–Sun 9am–8pm; Jan–May, Tues–Sun 9am–6pm.
Directions: Walk just left of the entrance to the National History and Archeology Museum.

Museum of the Romanian Navy, Str. Traian 53. ☎ **61-39-42.**

This collection chronicles Romania's episodic naval history, starting with displays on navigation in antiquity and moving quickly to artifacts from recent history, such as an aqualung suit, modern torpedoes, and officers' uniforms. You'll also see a model of the Danube Canal located north of Constanţa. Built partially with prison labor and opened in 1984, it is little-used—yet another monument to the dictator's megalomania. A courtyard of the museum shows off modern anchors and battleship guns.

Admission: 200 lei (16¢).

Open: June–Sept 14, daily 9am–8pm; the rest of the year, Tues–Sun 9am–5pm.
Directions: From Piaţa Ovidiu, walk along Strada Traian and veer left with the street.

Cool for Kids

Acvariu (Aquarium), on the Faleza Promenade across from the Cazino restaurant. ☎ **1-12-77.**

This admittedly limited museum, stocked mostly with hobbyists' tropical fish, deserves notice for its thrilling exhibit on the incomparably ugly sturgeon. The central tank is stuffed to the gills with millions of dollars of potential caviar. Beluga and sterlet are the featured varieties. Other exhibits include a display depicting the migration patterns of eels and a tank of lumpy Romanian carp, a warning of what the strict diet of pork and cheese will do to you long-term.

Admission: 200 lei (16¢).

Open: Daily 9am–4pm.

Complex of Museums of Natural Science, Bd. Mamaia 255–265. ☎ **64-70-55.**

Located near an amusement park, this collection of museums is especially fun for children. Here you watch live dolphin shows in an indoor/outdoor Delfinarium; ponder the skies in the Planetarium; see live fish in the Aquarium; or learn about the wonders of the deep in the Sea Museum.

Admission: Delfinarium, 100 lei (8¢); Planetarium, 50 lei (4¢); Sea Museum, 75 lei (6¢); Aquarium, 75 lei (6¢).

Open: Summer, shows at the indoor Delfinarium, daily at 10am, noon, and 2pm; shows at the outdoor Delfinarium, daily at 11am, 3pm, 5pm, and 7pm; Planetarium shows, daily at 11:45am and every subsequent 2 hours until 7:45pm; Sea

Museum and Aquarium, summer daily 9am–8pm; winter, daily 8:30am–3:30pm. **Trolleybus:** 40.

WHERE TO STAY

Constanţa suffers from overcrowding and scarce accommodations during the summer, and prices can climb steeply. If you have trouble finding a room in one of the hotels listed below, drop by ONT-Carpaţi or the tourist information desk in the Hotel Continental and ask for help in getting a reservation elsewhere.

Casa Tineretului, Bd. Tomis 20–26, 8700 Constanţa. ☎ **41/61-35-90.** 69 rms (all with bath). TV TEL **Bus:** Airport bus to the TAROM office, or 40 or 43 from the train station to the intersection of Bulevarduls Tomis and Republicii, then walk down Tomis a few blocks.

Rates (including breakfast): $21.20 double.

This is a good choice for a clean, inexpensive double if the Hotel Intim (see below) is full. Centrally located in the middle of Old Town, this four-story hotel run by CTT, the Romanian youth tourism organization, is open to the general public. The desk staff speaks a bit of English. There's a gift shop and public telephone in the bright white marble lobby, but no sitting room. The rooms, mostly doubles, were recently painted and are fresh-looking, with pale-pink walls, red carpets, white furniture, and lace curtains. Try to get a good mattress—they tend to be worn-out. Bathrooms have enclosed showers and the shared baths have an extra toilet and sink. There are food shops and a fresh fruit and vegetable stand across the street. The best thing about the hotel is its terrific restaurant and outdoor café (see "Where to Eat," below).

Hotel Intim, Str. N. Titulescu 7–9, 8700 Constanţa. ☎ **41/61-82-85.** Telex 14243. 21 rms (all with bath). **Directions:** From Casa Cu Lei (two blocks west of Piaţa Ovidiu), turn right and walk half a block.

Rates: $13.30–$20.80 single; $22.90–$31.90 double; some apartments available.

Highly recommended—this is one of my best buget-hotel finds in Romania. Small, as its name implies, this place did its first tour of duty as an exclusive Communist Party inn. Labels change but fond memories of superlative accommodation must have lingered as it's often booked solid by business and government people. Make an effort to reserve a room well in advance. Unlike most hotels in this price range, it's extremely well maintained. Recently renovated, it has beautifully appointed, color-coordinated rooms with elegant matching furniture and good beds. There's a doorman (rare for Romania) and some of the loveliest bathroom tiles I've seen in Eastern Europe.

The hotel restaurant harmonizes with the rest of the hotel in decor, and its pale walls are gracefully scrawled with elaborate floral patterns. Dining here is more a feast for the eyes than a gourmet experience. The offerings are standard, albeit well cooked. Serving hours are 7am to 10pm. The staff is very efficient and accustomed to VIPs, and will try to accommodate your wishes. There's a pleasant outdoor garden terrace with a fountain, which is locked at times and then accessible only through the lobby.

Hotel Palace, Str. Remus Opreanu 5–7, 8700 Constanţa. ☎ **41/61-46-96.** 132 rms (all with shower). TV TEL **Bus:** Airport bus to the TAROM office, or 40 or 43 from the train station to the intersection of Bulevarduls Tomis and Republicii, then walk or get a taxi for a short distance.

Rates: $32 single; $41.10 double; $54.20 triple.

This well-situated older hotel in the lumbering "grand style" has two pink marble staircases gracing its entrance: left leads to the hotel lobby, right goes to the restaurant. The receptionists are especially helpful, but the lobby, though redolent with old-world charm, is also redolent with kitchen odors. Rooms feel spacious, featuring high ceilings, plenty of interior lighting, and French doors that open onto a terrace—many overlooking the sea. Furniture is oldish and the black-and-white TVs antediluvian, but the color palette thankfully refrains from retina-scorching combinations. Check the beds, as their condition varies greatly. Bathrooms have showers and are clean but worn-out looking. The restaurant is one of Constanţa's most popular, and the oompah music can get quite loud, so choose your room with this in mind. Food at the restaurant is quite good, if a little expensive, and the crowd is a colorful lot, consisting of regulars from Constanţa's business community.

WHERE TO EAT

Casa Cu Lei (House with the Lions), Str. Dianei 1. ☎ **61-80-50.**

Cuisine: ROMANIAN. **Reservations:** Recommended. **Directions:** Walk two blocks west of Piaţa Ovidiu.

Rates: Salads 25¢; main courses $1.55–$2.45.

Open: Daily 10am–1am.

One of Romania's most elegant restaurants, Casa cu Lei, built in 1907 with four lions atop columns on the facade, was once a private villa. Today the two-story structure is a mix of a bar, salon, and eclectically decorated restaurant. The most alluring dining room, the Salon Brîncovenesc on the second floor, features paneled walls, hanging wooden lamps, large wool and wood seats, and elaborate place settings. The other two are Spanish and Venetian style and quite ornate. Main dishes include beef tournedos, pork filet "surprise," and beef Stroganoff. The waiters in black tie don't speak English, but the menu isn't hard to read if you bring your dictionary. As prices are fairly high for Romania, monitor the bill closely.

Frankly, I'd put this place more in the category of a visual experience since the food was fairly mediocre when I ate there, but some people rave about it. Perhaps you'll catch it on a good day. In any case, its curious ambience, so fitting in this ancient polygot port, is definitely worth experiencing.

Casa Tineretului, Bd. Tomis 20–26. ☎ **61-35-90.**

Cuisine: ROMANIAN. **Bus:** To the corner of Bulevarduls Republicii and Tomis, then walk down Tomis several blocks.

Prices: Soups and salads 20¢–40¢; main courses 70¢–$1.25.

Open: Breakfast/lunch daily 6:30am–4pm; dinner daily 6pm–midnight.

Expect to pay rock-bottom prices for very fresh and very good food. The menu changes daily and is posted in the hotel lobby at the restaurant entrance. It's a long and otherwise dull dining hall separated by feeble partitions and tired-looking houseplants into sections of four tables, but then, it's the food you've come here for and you can sit and eat on the outdoor patio. The clientele is mixed: young people and older regulars. Prices are all low, but bear in mind that portions of meat and fish are priced by the gram here, so indicate how much you'd like (or your waiter will decide that for you). Also notice the prices and number of garnishes—a quartered lemon doubled the price of the fish that I ordered. Especially good here: the chicken soup with lots of fresh vegetables, the pike-perch (salau), generous salads, roast chicken legs, and filling mamaliga with feta and sour cream.

For a Glass of Wine or Dessert, With a View

Cazino Restaurant, on the Faleza sea promenade across from the Aquarium.

Cuisine: ROMANIAN.
Prices: Coffee and dessert 75¢–$1; bottle of wine $1–$4.
Open: Daily 11am–midnight (patios).

This palatial-looking art nouveau confection was built in 1910 on the shore promenade as a casino. Lush velvet drapes and valances within, ecstatic ribbing whooshing up to staunch caryatids without, the building speaks volumes about a moment of affluence long past. Set a little back from the promenade on the seawall, one wonders why the last regime didn't just push it in. Such a building places unfair demands on proprietors to provide service requisite with its splendor, and the current crew, not surprisingly, isn't up to the task. The food, consisting of the usual grilled and fried items, is pedestrian. Instead, come to share a bottle of wine from the excellent selection of Romanian vintages, or have coffee and dessert, while enjoying the sea breeze on one of the outdoor terraces or from the colonnaded arcade facing the park and Aquarium.

To get here, walk down toward the sea past the Palace Hotel along the promenade the locals call "Faleza."

AN EXCURSION TO HISTRIA (ISTRIA)

If you're interested in ancient history and archeology, visit Histria (Istria), 43 miles north of Constanţa. Your tour of the country's oldest ancient settlement could be one of your sightseeing highlights of Romania. Intrepid Greek merchants settled in Histria in 657 B.C. and built a small colony. These Greek pioneers thrived on importing wine, olive oil, and weapons. Later the Romans gained control of this port, and the city flourished until the 7th century A.D.

On an excursion to Histria today, you can visit a small museum filled with Greek and Roman relics, and see the impressive remains of the town wall with towers and gates, different residences, and religious temples, such as one to Aphrodite. Histria is open Tuesday through Sunday from 10am to 6pm.

The easiest way to see Histria is on an ONT half-day tour. The entire outing from Constanţa takes 4 hours—1½ hour's driving time, 2 hours to visit the museum, and a half-hour stop for refreshments at a restaurant in Constanţa; it costs about $20. Unfortunately, tours have been curtailed of late due to lack of interest. Inquire at the ONT-Carpaţi office in Constanţa. Alternately, you can also go by bus on your own, but be forewarned that the bus stops seven miles from the actual site—a long walk. The bus runs a few times a day from the North bus station in Constanţa. Finally, you can haggle a trip with a taxi. You should be able to find one willing to make the two-way jaunt for $20.

2 The Black Sea Beaches

Mangalia: 27 miles S of Constanţa; Neptun: 23 miles S of Constanţa; Mamaia: 2 miles N of Constanţa

GETTING THERE • **By Train** The main train line from Bucharest turns south along the coast after Constanţa, making stops in the resorts of Eforie Nord, Eforie Sud, Neptun, and last, 27 miles south, Mangalia, near the Bulgarian border. The express ride from Constanţa to Mangalia takes just over an hour and costs about 95¢ in first class.

• **By Bus** If you want to continue north to Mamaia from Constanţa, take trolleybus no. 40 for 300 lei (23¢) from Constanţa's train station. There are many different buses, public and private, that run between resorts south of Constanţa, including one that runs from Mangalia to Constanţa with stops at all the resorts along the way.

• **By Car** One of Romania's best roads runs between Bucharest and Constanţa and continues to Mangalia, making it easy to get around by car along the coast. Hotels have ample parking.

ESSENTIALS The telephone area code for the beach resorts south of Constanţa is 91; the area code for Mamaia is 41.

ORIENTATION Nine of Romania's Black Sea resorts stretch in a continuous string south of Constanţa: Eforie Nord and Eforie Sud, Costineşti (the youth resort), Neptun-Olimp, Jupiter, Venus, Cap Aurora, Saturn, and Mangalia (the ancient port of Callatis). The 10th and largest one, Mamaia, lies two miles north of Constanţa.

SPECIAL EVENTS From the end of July until the first Sunday in August, several resorts jointly co-host the Miss Litoral Contest, which selects the most fetching beauty in the region. Both Romanian and foreign women are said to compete in the contest, vying for a prize of two weeks' holiday in Romania.

CTT, the Company for Youth Travel that arranges student travel in Romania, sponsors a week-long International Folklore Festival for Young People at the youth resort of Costineşti during the last week in August. There's a national costume parade, three days of international folk-dance competition, and an opportunity to buy, sell, or trade authentic arts and crafts. Age range for participants is 14 to 31. For full details and applications, write to the CTT Festival Secretariate of the Mondial Folklore Festival, Str. Mendeleev 2, 20169 Costineşti, or inquire at the Casa Tineretului in Constanţa (see "Where to Stay," above).

While it lacks the dramatic cliffs, secluded coves, and charming fishing villages that make the Bulgarian coast so beautiful and romantic, the Romanian Black Sea coast offers clean and wide beaches with fine white sand, resorts with good amenities, summer sports facilities, and evening entertainment. In short, all you and thousands of East Europeans need for a holiday on the seashore.

It was in the 1960s Romania created a "Riviera" by developing some 30 miles of wide white-sand beaches along its 152-mile-long Black Sea coast. Resorts with high-rise modern hotels, apartments, restaurants, nightclubs, and discos were established.

Nine resorts stretch in a string south of Constanţa: Eforie Nord and Eforie Sud (also called Carmen Silva, after King Carol's wife); Costineşti (the youth resort); the "antiquity belt" named in honor of Greek and Roman deities that were once worshiped here—Neptun-Olimp, Jupiter, Venus, Cap Aurora, and Saturn; and Mangalia (the ancient port of Callatis). The 10th and largest one, Mamaia, lies just two miles north of Constanţa.

The resorts are nominally open from May through September. High-season, from mid-July through August, brings a groaning density to the region's beaches and hotels. All but a few of the hotels close down after September, and prices then are often negotiable. Although water and weather are too cold for swimming at this time of year, the resorts achieve a ghost-town stillness that may be interesting to some.

EFORIE NORD

This quiet turn-of-the-century spa is my favorite resort on the Romanian coast. Its calm atmosphere, shady tree-lined streets, and well-established art deco hotels and villas, some of which date from the 1930s, lend it a Mediterranean charm. Unlike most of the coastal resorts where miles of sterile-looking modern hotels are deserted off-season, people live here year-round.

Eforie Nord and its twin, Eforie Sud, are situated between the Black Sea and Lake Techirgiol, a saltwater lake that is known for its therapeutic mud. Eforie Nord is located about 10 miles south of Constanţa, and can be reached from Constanţa by bus no. 10 or 11 (for 300 lei; 23¢.), which run four times a day. Bus no. 12, which also runs along the coast from Mangalia to Constanţa, also stops here.

Eforie Nord's central shopping district runs along the main boulevard, Cel Mare, which is parallel to the seashore. Here you'll find the post office, bus station, hotels, restaurants, and produce markets. Private accommodations, rare for the Romanian coast, can also be found here.

Accommodations • **Litoral S.A.** has a branch office here. They can help you find accommodations as well as tell you how to get a good caking in Eforie Nord's famous sapropelic mud, if you so desire. The office is at Str. Brizei 6 (☎ **72-22-45**). The **Meduza Hotel** (☎ **41/74-27-70**), one of three towers at the resort's northernmost point, is open year-round and offers simple, clean doubles for $21.20.

What to See and Do

Eforie Nord is better known for the lake mud baths than for its beaches. Lake Techirgiol's shores are rich in healing black sapropelic mud and its salt content is five times that of the sea. Many people come here to treat their arthritis; there's a sanitorium on the shore, Şanitoriul Balnea, which specializes in treating rheumatic problems. If you'd like to try a mud bath (costs about 12¢) and bathe in the salt lake, walk along the promenade a little past the sanitorium to the Baile Reci (Cold Baths) on the lakeshore.

Eforie Nord's beaches lie below six-foot cliffs along the eastern edge of the town. To get there, walk down any street east of Ştefan Cel Mare and find a path down the cliffs. A favorite bathing spot is the very warm Lake Belona, beyond the beach at the south end of town.

NEPTUN-OLIMP

Considered the chicest of Romania's Black Sea resorts since it opened in 1960, Neptun-Olimp was open only to foreign tourists and select Romanians prior to the 1989 revolution. But now its hotels, restaurants, and nightspots can be enjoyed by all. The area has two artificial lakes for yachting and pleasant gardens for strolling, and you can take a horse and buggy ride.

The former Ceauşescu villa, Nufar, was open to the public after the revolution but then was closed in 1991 due to a theft—it's unclear when it will reopen; check locally. Double apartments in luxury villas, once the playground of the party elite, now rent for more than $150 a night.

A large shopping center has a good selection of folk crafts and tourist souvenirs; above the shopping arcade on the second floor, there are a number of travel agencies and an **ONT-Carpaţi** tourist office. **Hotel Doina** (☎ **41/73-18-18** or **73-16-50**) in Neptun, open year-round, is the resort's premier hotel offering "exotic remedies" to those who dare. Rooms have a shrunken fairy-tale quaintness and bear the marks of many a holiday maker, but they are clean and well maintained, with new bathrooms. Doubles go for $16.35.

If you're in the mood to find a quiet, deserted place, there are small villages in the 13 or so miles between Neptun and Eforie Sud where the beaches are wild and undeveloped.

MAMAIA

With more than 60 hotels, Mamaia is the largest Romanian resort town on the Black Sea coast and the only one north of Constanţa. Mamaia is a narrow four-mile strip of land between the tideless saltwater Black Sea and freshwater Lake Siutghiol (also called Lake Mamaia). The town is lined with hotels and restaurants and planted with lots of greenery and shady trees. It's the best equipped of Romania's Black Sea resorts and, because it's only two miles from Constanţa, tends to be the most crowded.

Information There are two tourist information offices in Mamaia: the **Societatea Comerciala Mamaia** desk at the Hotel Bucuresti (☎ **91/83-17-80** or **83-11-52**), which is open summer only, and the **International Tourism Agency Litoral,** adjacent to the Hotel Perla (open daily, 8am to 9pm in summer and 8am to 4pm in winter). To get to the latter from Constanţa, take trolleybus no. 40 to the last stop and walk or transfer to trolleybus no. 47 or bus no. 23, then get off immediately past the amusement park, near the Perla Hotel. They didn't speak much English when I visited, but give them a try.

Accommodations Mamaia has a wide range of accommodations, from basic camping, simple cottages, and two-story mini-hotels (misnomered villas) to well-appointed deluxe hotels with bars, discos, and private beaches. Most of Mamaia's hotels were built in the 1960s and '70s, and some have not been well maintained. Sadly, there are far fewer Eastern European tourists now because of the economic hard times—many of these facilities are quite deserted these days.

You can try at the above listed tourist agencies to arrange for a place to stay, but you may do just as well leaving your things in a locker at the train station or in Constanţa and wandering down the main boulevard lined with different types of lodgings to see what strikes your fancy. The prices are quite reasonable, ranging from $15 to $40 for a double (much less if you're a group of three or four or if you know how to bargain).

What to See and Do

There are a wide variety of recreational and sports activities, especially water sports, available in Mamaia: sailing, waterskiing, scuba diving, rowing pedal boats, windsurfing, etc. There's a casino (the first in Romania) near the Hotel Albatros. You can take a half-hour excursion boat across Lake Mamaia to Ovidiu Island—there's a reputedly good seafood restaurant there. All in all, plenty to keep you busy if you get bored relaxing on the beach.

Tours The above listed tourist agencies also arrange sightseeing tours. Although they usually serve prebooked groups, you may be able to squeeze in on one. A four-hour wine-tasting tour to the renowned Murfatlar vineyards, about 20 miles away, costs $10. Trips to the ancient historic sites of Histria or Adamclisi cost about $20. If you're not planning on traveling to other parts of Romania on your own, you might look into going on a tour from here. Among other trips to choose from, there's a two-day weekend trip to the Danube Delta, with an overnight at the Hotel Lebǎda, trips on small boats through small channels, and lunch and dinner in Tulcea for about $125.

3 Tulcea & the Danube Delta

163 miles NE of Bucharest, 76 miles N of Constanţa

GETTING THERE • By Plane TAROM flies from Bucharest. Buses shuttle between the airport and the TAROM office (☎ **51-12-27**), at Strada Isaccei, open 10am to 5pm Monday to Friday. The office is just across the street from the Hotel Delta. Flight time is about 45 minutes and tickets cost $38.

• By Train Trains to Tulcea connect through the town of Medgidia on the main Bucharest–Constanţa rail line. The express from Medgidia to Tulcea takes about 2½ hours. The ride from Bucharest to Tulcea takes a total of 5 hours and costs roughly $3.35; it's just half an hour from Constanţa.

• By Car The drive from Constanţa, much of it through a petrochemical wasteland, takes at least 2 to 2½ hours.

ESSENTIALS • Information/Trip Planning One of the county tourist agencies where some English is spoken is the DELTAROM Agency, Str. Isaccei 4 (☎ **40/51-16-07**), directly opposite the Hotel Delta. It's open daily in summer from 8am to 8pm and in winter from 8am to 5pm. They offer daily trips down the delta and tours of local wineries (see below).

An excellent contact if you have any specific questions about the region is Maria Elena Apolon, public relations manager for Atbad Ltd. Trade and Travel, at Str. Babadag 11 (☎ **40/51-41-14;** fax 40/51-76-25). She's had a decade of experience in Romanian travel and will try to answer any questions you have. Atbad also provides tours and accommodations (see below).

• Mail/Telephone The telephone area code is 40. All of Tulcea's local phone numbers now have six digits. Try prefixing five-digit numbers listed here with a "5." There's a post and telegraph station at Str. Păcii 20.

CITY LAYOUT The center of Tulcea is located on the south bank of the Dunărea Canal, and the main streets and hotels are within just a block or two of the canal. If you arrive at Tulcea's train station, just off the canal promenade, walk straight ahead with the Dunărea Canal on your left. You'll reach the town's largest hotel, the Hotel Delta, in about 10 minutes. The docks for the Navrom line boats departing into the Danube Delta are right in front of the hotel.

DEPARTING • By Train For your departure tickets, drop by Tulcea's CFR Railway Office at Str. Progresului 28 (☎ **1-13-60**), near the Danube Delta Museum. In summer it's open Monday through Friday from 9am to 6pm and some Saturdays from 9am to 1pm; in winter, Monday through Friday from 9am to 4pm.

Tulcea, a small port at the center of Romania's canned-fish industry, is the best launching point for a trip into the Danube Delta. Here the mighty Danube concludes its 1,776-mile trip from the Black Forest mountains of Germany through eight countries, fanning out into a 1,660-square mile alluvial reserve before trickling into the Black Sea. The entire region is a dynamic ecosystem fed continually by Danube silt. Smaller discrete ecosystems with running water, stagnant water, wetland, and terrestrial characteristics support an astonishing array of flora and fauna.

Cavorting by the delta's riverbanks, lakes, streamlets, and marshes are 280 species of birds, 177 of which are hatching. A major migratory nexus, the Danube Delta provides shelter for a seasonal convergence of birds from West Africa, the Nile River, the Persian Gulf, and Russia. Flamingos, Dalmatian pelicans, pygmy cormorants, spoonbills, and squacco herons are among the species you might glimpse. Nonavian residents include otters, minks, foxes, wild boars, and sturgeon—source of caviar coveted throughout the world.

WHAT TO SEE & DO

Before you go to the delta, stop by the Danube Delta Museum, Str. Progresului 32 (☎ **1-58-66**), the region's natural-history museum, for a preview of the local wildlife. The diorama of a white stoat weasel hissing over the body of a gray mouse is . . . stirring. It's open Tuesday through Sunday from 9am to 5pm, and in summer, also on some Mondays. To get there, from the Hotel Egreta, walk southwest on Strada Babadag, and turn right after several blocks onto Strada Progresului.

Touring the Danube Delta

The DELTAROM Agency, Str. Isaccei 4 (☎ **915/1-16-07**), is a county tourist agency that offers daily one- and two-day trips down the Danube Delta for groups of 4 to 18 people at reasonable prices. Both tours depart at 10:30am.

On the one-day trip, you travel by hydrofoil along the Sulina Channel to visit several lakes and some small villages; you'll see how delta people live and fish. Lunch is taken either on board or in the town of Crisan and the boat returns by 6:30pm. The cost is $30 per person. The drawback to this organized tour is that the motors of the large boat often scare away the very birds and animals that you're hoping to see.

The two-day trips include explorations of lakes, islands, and smaller riverways in small boats along with hiking in protected wildlife areas such as the C. A. Rosetti Nature Reserve, all meals, and an overnight stay at the Hotel Lebȧda in Crisan. You return by 7pm second day. The all-inclusive trip is $70. Tours run between April 1 and November 1.

Specialized Delta Trips Atbad Ltd. Trade & Travel (☎ **40/51-41-14;** fax 40/51-76-25) was the first private tourist agency in the delta, founded in 1990. They can arrange specialized and custom tours for ecologists, biologists, and birdwatchers, fishermen, and hunters. For birdwatchers, the best season is late August through September; the hunting season lasts October through March; the fishing season is roughly mid-June to the end of March. For best results, inquire well in advance.

For a splurge, you may want to stay at one of the company's two "flotels"—deluxe accommodations on barges moored in Murighiol, a settlement out in the delta. For $75 per person per day, you will get great service and food. The fee includes touring through the delta in small boats, a meal, and a night in the flotel. While tours are not officially offered to small groups or for less than two days, Atbad is flexible and may be open to negotiation. Or if you're weary of hotel life and would like the unique experience of staying with a family in a village on the delta, Atbad can also help you find private accommodations with full board in remote delta villages. The price will vary, depending on such variables as location and transportation costs. Atbad also arranges wine-tasting trips, trips to nearby cities such as Iaši, or the resorts and Black Sea coast cities like Constanţa.

On Your Own If you prefer to avoid group travel and see the area independently, look for a fisherman you can pay to take you out on a small boat through the channels and waterways. You're not likely to find anyone who speaks English, so use your best sign language and negotiate with someone you feel you can trust until you reach an equitable price. Aside from a custom tour arranged by Atbad, this is your best chance to actually see some of the wildlife in the region.

But don't venture out on your own in a boat unless you're with someone who knows the area well. Recent ecological consciousness in Romania has resulted in new wildlife-protection rules barring tourists from many areas of the delta. In addition, travelers unfamiliar with the endless channels that all look the same have been known to get lost for days.

WHERE TO STAY & EAT

Hotel Delta, Str. Isaccei 2, 8800 Tulcea. ☎ **40/51-47-20.** 117 rms (all with bath) TV TEL **Bus:** 1, 2, 4, or 5 from the train station.

Rates (including breakfast): $34.20 single; $43.85 double.

Tulcea's biggest hotel is by far its nicest. The grand lobby, designed to accommodate the elbows of large tour groups, is a paragon of 1970s socialist-realist chic. Hard angles, absurd chandeliers, ocher-tone coloring, and mosaic murals all around typify the style. The rooms have solid furniture and good beds, bright lighting, cable television (EuroChannel and MTV), and balconies with screen doors (there are plenty of mosquitoes in summer). Bathrooms are a pleasure, with marble counters and big mirrors.

The hotel is also the town's only reasonable eatery. The large main dining room, low-ceilinged and clad predominantly in varnished wood with views out into the harbor, suggests the below-deck environs of an oceangoing vessel. The food is very good, with fresh fish nearly always available. The usual pork and beef dishes abound, but salads and soups are quite above par—try the superlative *ciorbă de peste* (fish soup). The bill can add up, however, as prices are quoted per 100g (about 4 ounces) of meat or fish. Expect a tab between $1.50 and $3.85 per person. Though the restaurant is understaffed, the servers are nonetheless cheerful.

As befits its role as a Tulcea cultural epicenter, the restaurant atmosphere can get quite festive, especially when the house band Rosu Sii Alb (Black and White) kicks out with its fusion of jazz and folk.

Hotel Egreta, Str. Păcii 1, Tulcea 8800. ☎ **40/51-71-03.** 116 rms (all with bath). TV TEL **Bus:** 1, 2, 4, 5, or 6 from the train station.

Rates (including continental breakfast): $20.90 single; $25.70 double.

The single rooms here are quite small, very basic, and somewhat stuffy. The bathrooms are clean but bare bulbs give them a depressing and worn look; some single rooms share bathrooms and showers with other singles. Located around the corner from the Hotel Delta, this hotel can save you a bit of money, but the Delta is definitely the better choice for a double room.

APPENDIX

A Bulgarian Language Guide

Bulgarian Vocabulary

The Bulgarian language is written in the Cyrillic alphabet, not the Latin characters familiar to those who speak English or the other Western European languages. The Bulgarian letters and their pronunciation are roughly as follows:

А, а	f*a*ther
Б, б	*b*oy
В, в	*v*ery
Г, г	*g*ood
Д, д	*d*ead
Е, е	n*e*ver
Ж, ж	a*z*ure, plea*s*ure
З, з	*z*ebra
И, и	n*ee*d
Й, й	*y*es
К, к	o*k*ay
Л, л	*l*eave
М, м	*m*other
Н, н	*n*othing
О, о	*o*pen
П, п	*p*ortrait
Р, р	slightly trilled *r*
С, с	*s*ilk
Т, т	*t*ap
У, у	r*oo*m
Ф, ф	*f*ather
Х, х	slightly harder than the *h* in *h*ark
Ц, ц	ge*ts*
Ч, ч	*ch*icken
Ш, ш	*sh*ip
Щ, щ	*shch*, as in fre*sh ch*eese

Ъ, ъ	like "*uh*," but shorter and more guttural
Ь, ь	much like a fleeting *y* inserted between a consonant and a vowel
Ю, ю	*u*nion
Я, я	Y*a*lta

In addition to these individual letters, certain vowel combinations have specialized pronunciations:

ай	*a*isle
ей	fr*ei*ght
ий	as in *feet*, but more elongated
ой	b*oy*
***v*й**	as in g*ooey*, but shorter

Everyday Expressions

English	Bulgarian	Pronounced
Hello	**Здравейте**	zdra-*vay*-teh
Good morning	**Добро утро**	*do*-bro *oo*-tro
Good evening	**Добър вечер**	*do*-bar *veh*-cher
How are you?	**Как сте?**	kak steh?
Very well	**Добре съм**	do-*breh* sahm
Thank you	**Мерсн; Ълагодаря**	mer-*see;* blah-go-dar-*yah*
You're welcome	**Моля**	*mol*-yah
Please	**Моля**	*mol*-yah
Yes	**Да**	dah
No	**Не**	neh
Excuse me	**Извинявам се, Извинете**	eez-veen-*yah*-vahm seh, eez-vee-*neh*-teh
How much does it cost?	**Колко струва?**	*kol*-ko *stroo*-vah?
I don't understand.	**Не разбирам**	neh rahz-*bee*-rahm.
Just a moment.	**Момент само**	mo-*ment* sah-mo.
Good-bye	**Довиждане**	do-*veezh*-dah-neh
I am sorry.	**Извинявам се, Простите**	eez-veen-*yah*-vam seh, pro-*stee*-teh.

Traveling

Where is the? . . .	**Къде е? . . .**	kuh-*deh* eh? . . .
bus station	**автобусната гара**	ahv-to-*booss*-nah-tah *gah*-rah
train station	**гарата**	*gah*-rah-tah
airport	**аерогарата**	ah-*eh*-ro-gah-rah-ta
baggage check	**багажната каса**	bah-*gazh*-nah-tah *kah*-sah
check-in counter	**штанд за проверка на билетите**	shtand zah pro-*vehr*-kah na bee-*leh*-tee-teh
Where can I find a taxi?	**Къле се намира такси?**	kuh-*deh* seh nah-*mee*-rah *taks*-see?
How much is the fare?	**Колко струва билет?**	*kol*-ko *stroo*-vah bee-*let?*
I am going to . . .	**Аз пътувам до . . .**	ahz pah-*too*-vahm do . . .
one-way ticket	**Ьилет в една посока**	bee-*let* vuh ed-*nah* po-*so*-kah
round-trip ticket	**Ьилет в дво посоки**	bee-*let* vuh dveh po-*so*-kee
Sleeping berth	**спалнья места**	*spal*-na *myes*-ta

English	Bulgarian	Pronounced
car-rental office	**Бюро за наемане на колите**	byoo-*ro* zah nah-*yem*-ah-neh na ko-*lee*-teh
Where can I find a gas station?	**Къде е бензинна станця?**	kuh-*deh* eh ben-*zee*-nah *stahn*-tsee-yah?
How much is gas?	**Колко струва бензин?**	*kol*-ko *stroo*-vah ben-*zeen?*
Please fill the tank.	**Пълн резервоар, моля**	pah-lun reh-zehr-vo-*ahr*, *mol*-yah.

Accommodations

I am looking for . . .	**Аз търся . . .**	ahz *tur*-syah . . .
a hotel	**хотея**	ho-*tel*
private room	**Частна квартира**	*chast*-na kvar-*teer*-na
accommodations office	**Квартирно Бюро**	kvar-*teer*-no byu-*ro*
a youth hostel	**студентското обшежитие**	stoo-*den*-sko-to ob-shteh-*zhee*-tee-yeh
I am staying . . .	**Аз живея тук . . .**	ahz zhee-*vay*-ah toohk . . .
a few days	**няколко дена**	*nyah*-kol-ko *deh*-nah
two weeks	**Две седмици**	dveh *sed*-mee-tsee
a month	**един месец**	eh-*deen meh*-sets
I have a reservation.	**Имам резервация**	*ee*-mahm reh-zehr-*vah*-tsee-yah.
My name is . . .	**Казвам се . . .**	*kahz*-vahm seh . . .
Do you have a room? . . .	**Имате лн стая? . . .**	*ee*-mah-teh lee *stah*-yah? . . .
for tonight	**за една нощ**	zah ed-*nah* nozht
for three nights	**за три нощи**	zah tree *nozh*-tee
for a week	**за една седмица**	zah ed-*nah sehd*-mee-tsah
I would like . . .	**Иекам . . .**	*eez*-kahm . . .
a single	**с едно легло**	suh ed-*no* leg-*lo*
a double	**с две легла**	suh dveh leg-*lah*
I want a room . . .	**Искам стая . . .**	*eez*-kahm *stah*-yah . . .
with a bath/shower	**с баня/душ**	suh *bahn*-yan/doosh
without a bath/shower	**без баня/душ**	bez *bahn*-yah/doosh
with a view	**с хубава гледка**	suh *khoo*-bah-vah *gled*-kah
How much is the room?	**Колко струва стаята?**	*kol*-ko *stroo*-vah *stah*-yah-tah?
with breakfast	**със закуска**	suh zah-*koo*-skah
May I see the room?	**Мога ли да видя стаята?**	*mo*-gah lee dah *vee*-dyah *stah*-yah-tah?
The key	**Ключ**	klyooch
The bill, please	**Сметка, моля**	*smet*-kah *mol*-yah

Getting Around

I am looking for . . .	**Аз търся . . .**	ahz *tuhr*-syah . . .
a bank	**Банка**	*bahn*-kah
the church	**черква**	*chehrk*-vah
the city center	**центъра на града**	*tsen*-tah-rah na grah-*dah*
the museum	**музей**	moo-*zay*
a pharmacy	**аптека**	ahp-*teh*-kah
the park	**парк**	pahrk
the theater	**театър**	teh-*ah*-tahr
the tourist office	**туристическое бюро**	too-ree-*stee*-chess-ko byoo-*ro*
the embassy	**легация**	leh-*gah*-tsyah

English	Bulgarian	Pronounced
Where is the nearest telephone?	**Къде е най-близкия телефон?**	kuh-*deh* eh nah-ee-*bleez*-kee-yah tel-eh-*fohn?*
I would like to buy . . .	**Искам да купя . . .**	*eez*-kahm dah *koo*-pyah . . .
a stamp	**марка**	*mahr*-kah
a postcard	**пощенска карта**	*pohsh*-ten-skah *kar*-tah
a map	**карта**	*kar*-tah

Signs

Open	**Отворено**	ot-vo-*re*-no
Closed	**Затворено**	zat-vo-*re*-no
No Trespassing	**Не се влиза!; Входа забранен!**	
No Parking	**Не се паркира; паркирането забранено**	
Entrance	**Вход**	
Exit	**Изход**	
Information	**Справки**	
No Smoking	**Не се пуши**	
Arrivals	**Кацане; иядване**	
Departures	**Излети; тръгване**	
Toilets	**Тоалети**	
Danger	**Опасно!**	

Numbers

1 **един** (eh-*deen*)
2 **два** (dvah)
3 **три** (tree)
4 **четнри** (*cheh*-tir-ee)
5 **пет** (pet)
6 **шест** (shest)
7 **седем** (*seh*-dem)
8 **осем** (*o*-sem)
9 **девет** (*deh*-vet)
10 **десет** (*deh*-set)
11 **единадесет** (eh-dee-*nahd*-ee-set)
12 **дванадесет** (dvah-*nahd*-ee-set)
13 **тринадесет** (tree-*nahd*-ee-set)
14 **четиринадесет** (cheh-tir-ee-*nahd*-ee-set)
15 **петнадесет** (pet-*nahd*-ee-set)
16 **шестнадесет** (shest-*nahd*-ee-set)
17 **седемнадесет** (seh-dem-*nahd*-ee-set)
18 **осемнадесет** (o-sem-*nahd*-ee-set)
19 **деветнадесет** (deh-vet-*nahd*-ee-set)
20 **двадесет** (*dvah*-deh-set)
30 **тридесет** (*tree*-deh-set)
40 **четирийсет** (cheh-*tir*-ee-deh-set)
50 **петдесет** (pet-deh-*set*)
60 **шестдесет** (shest-deh-*set*)
70 **седемдесет** (seh-dem-deh-*set*)
80 **осемдесет** (o-sem-deh-*set*)
90 **деветдесет** (deh-veht-deh-*set*)
100 **сто** (sto)
500 **петсотин** (*pet*-sto-teen)
1,000 **хиляда** (kheel-*yah*-dah)

Eating

English	Bulgarian	Pronounced
Restaurant	**Ресторант**	res-to-*rahnt*
Breakfast	**Закуска**	zah-*koo*-skah
Lunch	**Овед**	o-*bed*
Dinner	**Вечеря**	veh-*cheh*-ryan
A table for two, please.	**Моля маса за двама**	*mol*-yah *mah*-sah zah *dvah*-mah.
Waiter	**Сервитьор**	sehr-vee-*tyor*
Waitress	**Сервитьорка**	sehr-vee-*tyor*-kah

English	Bulgarian	Pronounced
I would like . . .	**Искам . . .**	*eez*-kahm . . .
a menu	**меню**	men-*yoo*
a fork	**вилица**	*vee*-lee-tsah
a knife	**нож**	nozh
a spoon	**льжица**	*lah*-zhee-tsah
a napkin	**салфетка**	sohl-*fet*-kah
a glass (of water)	**чашка (вода)**	*chash*-kah (vo-*dah*)

Bulgarian Menu Terms

General Terms

English	Bulgarian	Pronounced
Soup	**чорба, супа**	chor-*bah*, soopa
Eggs	**яйца**	yah-ee-*tsah*
Meat	**месо**	meh-*so*
Fish	**риба**	*ree*-bah
Vegetables	**Зеленчуци**	zeh-len-*choo*-tsee
Fruit	**Плодове**	plo-do-*veh*
Desserts	**Десерти**	deh-*sehr*-tee
Beverages	**Напитки**	nah-*peet*-kee
Salt	**Сол**	sohl
Pepper	**Пипер**	*pee*-pehr
Mustard	**Горчица**	gor-*chee*-tsah
Vinegar	**Оцет**	o-*tset*
Oil	**Масло**	*mah*-slo
Sugar	**Захар**	*zah*-khar
Tea	**Чай**	*chah*-ee
Coffee	**Кафе**	kah-*feh*
Bread	**Хляб**	khlyab
Butter	**Краве масло**	*krah*-veh mah-*slo*
Wine	**Вино**	vee-*no*
Vodka	**Ракня**	rah-*kee*-yah

Note: Ordering in a Bulgarian restaurant that has no English translation is a special challenge, since the menu is written in the Cyrillic alphabet. The following is listed as a guide to asking for the most popular Bulgarian dishes:

Cold Appetizers

Haiver caviar
Kashkaval yellow cheese
Lukanka dried sausage
Shunka ham
Shpekov salam smoked sausage
Sirene cheese

Soups

Chorba gulash goulash soup
Chorba ot leshta lentil soup
Chorba ot riba fish soup
Pileshka supa chicken soup

Salads

Domati presni fresh tomatoes
Krastavitsi presni fresh cucumbers
Meshana salata mixed salad
Pecheni chushki roasted red peppers
Shopska salad mixed salad with grated cheese
Zelena salata green lettuce

Eggs

Omlet omelet
Yatsa birkani scrambled eggs
Yatsa na ochi fried eggs

Meats

Agneshko lamb
Biftek beefsteak
Kievski kotlett chicken Kiev
Kyufteta meatballs
Meshana skapa mixed grill
Pilye chicken
Ramstek rumpsteak
Schnitzel schnitzel
Shashlik shish kebab
Stek steak
Svinsko pork
Teleshko veal

Fish

Byala riba perch
Lefer blue fish
Moruna codfish
Pirzhena riba fried fish
Skumriya mackerel

Vegetables

Domati tomatoes
Gibi mushrooms
Grah peas
Kartofi potatoes
Morkovi carrots
Oriz rice

Desserts

Kicelo mlyako yogurt
Kompot asorti mixed compote
Palachinka crêpe
Sladoled ice cream
Torta cake

Fruits

Grozde grapes
Kryshi pears
Limon lemon
Plodove fruits
Portokali oranges
Praskova peach
Yabilka apple

Beverages

Chai tea
Pryasno mlyako milk
Kafe coffee
Mineralna voda mineral water
Shveps Schweppes (lemon or orange soda)
Beli vina white wine
Cherveni vina red wine
Shumyaschi vina sparkling wine
Pivo beer

Condiments

Chlyab bread
Konfitur jam
Maslo butter
Med honey
Zahar sugar

Cooking Terms

File filet
Na gril grilled
Natyur plain
Pecheno roast
Pirzheni fried
Shishcheta shish kebab
S limanov sos with lemon sauce

B Czech & Slovak Language Guide

Czech Vocabulary

There are 32 vowels and consonants in the Czech alphabet, and most of the consonants are pronounced about as they are in English. Accent marks over vowels lengthen the sound of the vowel, as does the *kroužek*, or little circle ("°"), which appears only over "o" and "u."

A, a	f*a*ther
B, b	*b*oy
C, c	ge*ts*
Č, č	*ch*oice
D, d	*d*ay
D', d'	*Di*or
E, e	n*e*ver
F, f	*f*ood
G, g	*g*oal

H, h	un*h*and
Ch, ch	Lo*ch* Lomond
I, i	n*ee*d
J, j	*y*es
K, k	*k*ey
L, l	*l*ord
M, m	*m*ama
N, n	*n*o
N', n'	Ta*ny*a
O, o	a*w*ful
P, p	*p*en
R, r	slightly trilled *r*
Ř, ř	slightly trilled *r* + *sh* as in cru*sh*
S, s	*s*eat
Š, š	cru*sh*
T, t	*t*oo
T', t'	no*t y*et
U, u	r*oo*m
V, v	*v*ery
W, w	*v*ague
Y, y	funn*y*
Z, z	*z*ebra
Ž, ž	a*z*ure, plea*s*ure

Everyday Expressions

English	**Czech**	Pronounced
Hello	**Dobrý den**	*daw*-bree den
Good morning	**Dobré jitro**	*daw*-breh *yee*-traw
Good evening	**Dobrý večer**	*daw*-bree *veh*-chair
How are you?	**Jak se máte?**	*yahk* seh *mah*-teh
Very well	**Velmi dobře**	*vel*-mee *daw*-brsheh
Thank you	**Děkuji vam**	*dyek*-ooee vahm
You're welcome	**Prosím**	*praw*-seem
Please	**Prosím**	*praw*-seem
Yes	**Ano**	*ah*-no
No	**Ne**	neh
Excuse me	**Promiňte**	*praw*-min-teh
How much does it cost?	**Kolik to stojí?**	*kaw*-leek taw *staw*-ee
I don't understand.	**Nerozumím.**	*neh*-raw-zoo-meem
Just a moment.	**Moment, prosím.**	*maw*-ment, *praw*-seem
Good-bye	**Na shledanou**	*nah* skleh-dah-noh-oo

Traveling

Where is the? . . .	**Kde je? . . .**	*gde* yeh? . . .
bus station	**autobusové nádraží**	*ahoo*-taw-boos-oh-veh *nah*-drah-shee
train station	**nádraží**	*nah*-drah-shee
airport	**letiště**	*leh*-tyish-tyeh
baggage check	**úschovna zavazadel**	*oo*-skohv-nah *zah*-vahz-ah-del
Where can I find a taxi?	**Kde najdu taxi?**	*gde nai*-doo *tahks*-eh

Traveling

English	Czech	Pronounced
Where can I find a gas station?	**Kde najdu benzínovou pumpu?**	*gde nai*-doo *ben*-zeen-oh-voh *poomp*-oo
How much is gas?	**Kolik stojí benzín?**	*koh*-leek *stoh*-yee *ben*-zeen
Please fill the tank.	**Naplňte mi nádrž, prosím**	*nah*-puln-teh mee *nah*-dursh, *praw*-seem
How much is the fare?	**Kolik je jízdné?**	*koh*-leek yeh yeesd-neh
I am going to . . .	**Pojedu do . . .**	*poh*-yeh-doo doh . . .
One-way ticket	**Jízdenka**	*yeez*-den-kah
Round-trip ticket	**Zpáteční jízdenka**	*zpah*-tech-nee *jeez*-den-kah
Car-rental office	**Půjčovna aut**	*poo*-eech-awv-nah ah-oot

Accommodations

English	Czech	Pronounced
I'm looking for . . .	**Hledám . . .**	*hleh*-dahm . . .
a hotel	**hotel**	*haw*-tel
a youth hostel	**studentskou ubytovnu**	*stoo*-dent-skoh *oo*-beet-ohv-noo
I am staying . . .	**Zůstanu . . .**	*zoo*-stah-noo . . .
a few days	**několik dnů**	*nyeh*-koh-leek dnoo
two weeks	**dva týdny**	dvah tid-*neh*
a month	**jeden měsíc**	*yeh*-den *myeh*-seets
I have a reservation.	**Mám zamluvený nocleh.**	mahm *zah*-mloo-veh-ni *nawts*-leh.
My name is . . .	**Jmenují se . . .**	*meh*-noo-yee seh . . .
Do you have a room? . . .	**Máte pokoj? . . .**	*mah*-teh *poh*-koy? . . .
for tonight	**na dnešek**	*nah* dneh-sheck
for three nights	**na tři dny**	*nah* trshee dnee
for a week	**na tyden**	*nah* tee-den
I would like . . .	**Chci . . .**	khtsee . . .
a single	**jednolůžkový pokoj**	*jed*-noh-loosh-koh-vee *poh*-koy
a double	**dvojlůžkovy pokoj**	*dvoy*-loosh-koh-vee *poh*-koy
I want a room . . .	**Chci pokoj . . .**	khtsee *poh*-koy . . .
with a bath	**s koupelnou**	*skoh*-pehl-noh
without a bath	**bez koupelny**	*behz* koh-pehl-nee
with a shower	**se sprchou**	*seh* spur-choh
without a shower	**bez sprchy**	*bez* sprech-*eh*
with a view	**s pohledem**	*spoh*-hlehd-ehm
How much is the room? . . .	**Kolik stojí pokoj? . . .**	*koh*-leek *stoh*-yee *paw*-koy? . . .
with breakfast	**se snídaní**	*seh* snee-dan-nyee
May I see the room?	**Mohu vidět ten pokoj?**	*moh*-hoo *vee*-dyet ten *paw*-koy
The key	**Klíč**	kleech
The bill, please.	**Dejte mi učet, prosím.**	*day*-teh mee *oo*-cheht, *praw*-seem.

Getting Around

English	Czech	Pronounced
I'm looking for . . .	**Hledám**	*hleh*-dahm . . .
a bank	**banku**	*bahnk*-oo
the church	**kostel**	*kaws*-tell
the city center	**centrum**	*tsent*-room
the museum	**muzeum**	*moo*-zeh-oom
a pharmacy	**lekarnu**	*lek*-ahr-noo
the park	**park**	pahrk
the theater	**divadlo**	*dee*-vahd-loh

English	Czech	Pronounced
the tourist office	**cestovní kancelář**	*tses*-tohv-nee *kahn*-tseh-larsh
the embassy	**velvyslanectví**	*vehl*-vee-slahn-ets-tvee
Where is the nearest telephone?	**Kde je nejbližší telefon?**	gde yeh *nay*-bleesh-ee *tel*-oh-fohn
I would like to buy . . .	**Chci koupit . . .**	khtsee *koh*-peet . . .
a stamp	**známku**	*znahm*-koo
a postcard	**pohlednici**	*poh*-hlehd-nit-seh
a map	**mapu**	*mahp*-oo

Signs

English	Czech
No Trespassing	**Cizím vstup zakázán**
No Parking	**Neparkovat**
Entrance	**Vchod**
Exit	**Východ**
Information	**Informace**
No Smoking	**Kouření zakázáno**
Arrivals	**Příjezd**
Departures	**Odjezd**
Toilets	**Toalety**
Danger	**Pozor, nebezpečí**

Numbers

1 **jeden** (*yeh*-den)
2 **dva** (dvah)
3 **tři** (trshee)
4 **čtyři** (*chtee*-rshee)
5 **pět** (pyet)
6 **šest** (shest)
7 **sedm** (*seh*-duhm)
8 **osm** (*aw*-suhm)
9 **devět** (*deh*-vyet)
10 **deset** (*deh*-set)
11 **jedenáct** (*yeh*-deh-nahtst)
12 **dvanáct** (*dvah*-nahtst)
13 **třináct** (*trshee*-nahtst)
14 **čtrnáct** (*chtur*-nahtst)
15 **patnáct** (*paht*-nahtst)
16 **šestnáct** (*shest*-nahtst)
17 **sedmnáct** (*seh*-doom-nahtst)
18 **osmnáct** (*aw*-soom-nahtst)
19 **devatenáct** (*deh*-vah-teh-nahtst)
20 **dvacet** (*dvah*-tset)
30 **třicet** (*trshee*-tset)
40 **čtyřicet** (*chti*-rshee-tset)
50 **padesát** (*pah*-deh-saht)
60 **šedesát** (*she*-deh-saht)
70 **sedmdesát** (*seh*-duhm-deh-saht)
80 **osmdesát** (*aw*-suhm-deh-saht)
90 **devadesát** (*deh*-vah-deh-saht)
100 **sto** (staw)
500 **pět set** (*pyet* set)
1,000 **tisíc** (*tyee*-seets)

Eating

English	Czech	Pronounced
Restaurant	**Restaurace**	*rehs*-tow-rah-tseh
Breakfast	**Snídaně**	*snee*-dah-nyeh
Lunch	**Oběd**	*oh*-byed
Dinner	**Večeře**	*veh*-chair-sheh
A table for two, please. (Lit.: There are two of us)	**Jsme dva.**	*ees*-meh dvah
Waiter	**Číšník**	*cheess*-neek
Waitress	**Servírka**	ser-*veer*-ka

Eating

English	Czech	Pronounced
I would like . . .	**Chci . . .**	khtsee . . .
a menu	**jídelní lístek**	*yee*-del-nee *lees*-teck
a fork	**vidličku**	*veed*-leech-koo
a knife	**nůž**	noosh
a spoon	**lžičku**	lu-*shich*-koo
a napkin	**ubrousek**	*oo*-broh-seck
a glass (of water)	**skleničku (vody)**	*sklehn*-ich-koo (vod-*deh*)
the check, please	**účet, prosím**	*oo*-cheht, *praw*-seem
Is the tip included?	**Je v tom zahrnuto spropitné?**	yeh *ftohm*-zah *hur*-noo-toh *sproh*-peet-neh?

Czech Menu Terms

General Terms

Soup	**Polévka**	*poh*-lehv-kah
Eggs	**Vejce**	*vayts*-eh
Meat	**Maso**	*mahs*-oh
Fish	**Ryba**	*ree*-bah
Vegetables	**Zelenina**	*zehl*-eh-nee-nah
Fruit	**Ovoce**	*oh*-voh-tseh
Desserts	**Moučníky**	*mohch*-nee-kee
Beverages	**Nápoje**	*nah*-poy-yeh
Salt	**Sůl**	sool
Pepper	**Pepř**	*peh*-prsh
Mayonnaise	**Majonéza**	*mai*-o-neza
Mustard	**Hořčice**	*hohrsh*-chee-tseh
Vinegar	**Ocet**	*oh*-tseht
Oil	**Olej**	*oh*-lay
Sugar	**Cukr**	*tsoo*-ker
Tea	**Čaj**	chye
Coffee	**Káva**	*kah*-vah
Bread	**Chléba**	*khlehb*-ah
Butter	**Máslo**	*mahs*-loh
Wine	**Víno**	*vee*-noh
Fried	**Smažený**	*smah*-sheh-nee
Roasted	**Pečený**	*pech*-eh-nee
Boiled	**Vařený**	*vah*-rsheh-nee
Grilled	**Grilováný**	*gree*-loh-vah-nee

Soups

Bramborová potato
Čočková lentil
Gulášová goulash
Rajská tomato
Slepičí chicken
Zeleninová vegetable

Meats

Biftek steak
Guláš goulash
Hovězi beef
Játra liver
Jehněčí lamb
Kachna duck
Klobása sausage
Králík rabbit
Skopové mutton
Telecí veal
Telecí kotleta veal cutlet
Vepřové pork

Fish

Karp carp
Kaviár caviar
Rybí filé fish filet
Sled herring
Štika pike
Treska cod
Úhoř eel
Ústřice oysters

Eggs

Míchaná vejce scrambled eggs
Smažená vejce fried eggs
Vařená vejce boiled eggs
Vejce na měkko soft-boiled eggs
Vejce se slaninou bacon and eggs
Vejce se šunkou ham and eggs

Salads

Fazolový salát bean salad
Hlávkový salát mixed green salad
Okurkový salát cucumber salad
Salát z červené řepy beet salad

Vegetables

Brambory potatoes
Celer celery
Chřest asparagus
Cibule onions
Houby mushrooms
Květák cauliflower
Mrkev carrots
Paprika peppers
Rajská jablíčka tomatoes
Zelí cabbage

Desserts

Koláč cake
Cukroví cookies
Čokoládová zmrzlina chocolate ice cream
Jablkový závin apple strudel
Palačinky pancakes
Vanilková zmrzlina vanilla ice cream

Fruits

Citrón lemon
Hruška pears
Jablko apple
Švestky plums

Beverages

Čaj tea
Káva coffee
Mléko milk
Víno wine
  červené red
  bílé white
Voda water

Slovak Vocabulary

The Slav language is the national language of Slovakia. The Czech and Slav languages evolved similarly from the Old Slav language, and today Czechs and Slavs can generally understand each other.

In the Slovak language, vowels are both short (a, ä, e, i, y, o, u) and long (á, é, í, ó, u). Vowels are pronounced the same as in Czech, but the Slav language does not have ů and ě. The ä is unique to the Slav language; it's pronounced like the *a* in *act.*

The Slav diphthongs ia, ie, iu, and ou are best pronounced by running the vowel sounds together as one syllable.

Slav consonants are similar to Czech consonants. Unique to the Slovak language are d' (a soft palatel sound pronounced like *dy*), l' (*ly*), ň (*ny*), t' (*ty*), dz (like *th* in *that*), dž (like the *j* in *jean*), and *ov* (like *oh* when a final syllable).

Everyday Expressions

English	**Slovak**	Pronounced
Good morning	**Dobré ráno**	*do*-brair *raa*-no
Good evening	**Dobrý večer**	*do*-bree *veh*-chehr
Good night	**Dobrú noc**	*do*-broo nots
How are you?	**Jako sa máte?**	*yah*-ko-sah *maa*-tyeh?

English	Slovak	Pronounced
I'm pleased to meet you	**Teší mňa že som Vás poznal**	*teh*-shee-mnyah *zheh*-sahm vaas *po*-znahl
Thank you	**D'akujem Vám**	*dyah*-ku-yem-vaam
You're welcome	**Ste vítaný**	slyeh *vee*-tah-nee
Please	**Prosím**	*pro*-seem
Yes	**Áno**	*aa*-no
No	**Nie**	nyieh
Excuse me (I'm sorry)	**Prepáčte mi**	*preh*-paach-tyeh-mi
Do you speak English?	**Hovoríte anglicky?**	*ho*-vo-ree-tyeh *ahn*-glits-ki?
Does anyone speak English?	**Hovorí tu niekto anglicky?**	*ho*-vo-ree-tu *nyi*-eh-kto *ahn*-glits-ki?
I don't understand	**Nerozumiem Vám**	*neh*-ro-zu-mi-ehm vaam
Please write it down	**Prosím napíšte mi to**	*Pro*-seem *nah*-pish-tyeh *mi*-to

Accommodations

English	Slovak	Pronounced
What is the address?	**Jaká je adresa?**	*yah*-kaa yeh *ah*-dreh-sah?
How much is it per night?	**Kol'ko stojí na noc?**	*Koly*-ko *sto*-yee nah nots?
How much is it per person?	**Kol'ko stojí na osobu?**	*Koly*-ko *sto*-yee nah *o*-so-bu?
Does it include breakfast?	**Raňajky sú započítané?**	*rah*-nyay-ki soo *zah*-po-chee-tah-nair?
Can I see the room?	**Môžem vidieť isbu?**	*mou*-zhehm *vi*-dyety *is*-bu?
Where is the toilet?	**Kde je záchod?**	*gdeh*-yeh *zaa*-khod?
Do you have a single room available?	**Máte volnú jednopostel'ová?**	*Maa*-teh *vol*-ynoo *yeh*-dno-po-slyeh-lyo-vaa?
Do you have a double room available?	**Máte volnú dvojpostel'ová isba?**	*Maa*-teh *vol*-ynoo *dvoy*-po-slyeh-lyo-vaa *is*-bah?

Getting Around

English	Slovak	Pronounced
Where is a . . . ?	**Kde je** . . . ?	*gdyeh*-yeh . . . ?
bank	**banka**	*bahn*-kah
post office	**pošta**	*posh*-tah
telephone center	**telefónna ústredňa**	*te*-le-faw-nah *oo*-streh-dnyah
the tourist information office	**turistická informačná kancelária**	*tu*-ris-tits-kaa *in*-for-mach-naa *kahn*-tseh-laa-riah
What time does the bus leave?	**Kedy odchádza autobus?**	*keh*-di *ot*-khaa-dzah *ow*-to-bus?
I want to go to . . .	**Chcem ist' do** . . .	*khtsehm* isty do . . .

Numbers

1 **jeden** (*yeh*-dehn)
2 **dva** (dvah)
3 **tri** (tri)
4 **štyri** (*shti*-ri)
5 **pät'** (paty)
6 **šest'** (shehsty)
7 **sedem** (*seh*-dehm)
8 **osem** (*o*-sehm)
9 **devät'** (*deh*-vaty)
10 **desat'** (*deh*-sahty)
20 **dvadsat'** (*dvahd*-sahty)
30 **tridsat'** (*trid*-sahty)
100 **sto** (sto)

Eating

English	Slovak	Pronounced
breakfast	**raňajky**	*rah*-nyahy-ki
lunch	**obed**	*o*-behd
dinner	**večera**	*veh*-cheh-rah

C Hungarian Language Guide

Hungarian Vocubulary

My transcription of the Hungarian language used here is of necessity approximate. Your best bet is to mimic the pronunciation of Hungarians whenever possible.

a	*taut*
á	b*ah*
e	*ever*
é	d*ay*
i	*teen*
í	*teen*
o	b*o*ne
ó	b*o*ne (but slightly shorter)
ö	sub*ur*b or French p*eu*r (shown phonetically below as "ur")
ő	sub*ur*b or French p*eu*r (shown phonetically below as "ur")
u	*moon*
ú	*moon*
ü	*teen*
ű	*teen*

Most Hungarian consonants are pronounced approximately as they are in English, including the following: *b, d, f, h, k, l, m, n, p, t, v,* and *y.* There are some differences, however, particularly in the consonant combinations, as follows:

c	ge*ts*
cs	*ch*ill
g	*g*ill
gy	he*dg*e
j	*y*outh
ny	as in Russian *ny*et
r	slightly trilled *r*, as in Spanish
s	*sh*eet
sz	*s*ix
z	*z*ero
zs	a*z*ure, plea*s*ure

Everyday Expressions

English	Hungarian	Pronounced
Hello	**Jó napot**	*yoh* naw-poht
Good morning	**Jó reggelt**	*yoh* rej-jelt
Good evening	**Jó estét**	*yoh* esh-tayt
How are you?	**Hogy van?**	*hoj* vawn?
Very well	**Nagyon jól**	*naw*-jon *yohl*
Thank you	**Köszönöm**	*kur*-sur-nurm
You're welcome	**Kérem**	*kay*-rem
Please	**Legyen szíves**	*leh*-jen see-vesh
Yes	**Igen**	*ee*-gen
No	**Nem**	*nem*
Excuse me.	**Bocsánat.**	*boh*-chah-nawt.
How much does it cost?	**Mennyibe kerül?**	*men*-yee-beh keh-reel?

English	**Hungarian**	Pronounced
I don't understand.	**Nem értem.**	*nem* ayr-tem.
Just a moment.	**Egy pillanat**	*ej* peel-law-nawt
Good-bye	**Viszontlátásra**	*vee*-sont-lah-tahsh-raw

Traveling

English	Hungarian	Pronounced
Where is the? . . .	**Hol van? . . .**	*hohl* vawn? . . .
bus station	**az autóbusz-állomás**	awz *ow*-toh-boos-ah-loh-mahsh
train station	**a vasútállomás**	aw *vah*-shoot-ah-loh-mahsh
airport	**a repülőtér**	aw *reh*-pee-lur-tayr
baggage check	**a csomag-megőrző**	aw *choh*-mawg-meg-ur-zur
Where can I find a taxi?	**Hol kaphatok taxit?**	*hohl* kawp-haw-tok *tawk*-seet?
How much is the fare?	**Mennyi a viteldíj?**	*men*-yee aw *vee*-tel-dee
I am going to . . .	**. . . -ig akarnék menni**	. . . -eeg aw-kawr-nayk men-ee
One-way ticket	**egy útra**	*ej* oot-raw
Round-trip ticket	**oda-vissza**	*oh*-daw-*vees*-saw
Car-rental office	**autókölcsönző**	*ow*-toh-kurl-churn-zur
Where can I find a gas station?	**Merre van egy töltőállomás?**	*meh*-reh vawn ej *turl*-tur-ah-loh-mahsh
How much is gas?	**Mennyi a benzin?**	*men*-yee aw *ben*-zeen
Please fill the tank.	**Tele kérem**	*teh*-leh kay-rem

Accommodations

English	Hungarian	Pronounced
I'm looking for a hotel.	**Egy szállodát keresek.**	ej *sah*-loh-daht keh-reh-shek.
I'm looking for a pension.	**Egy penziót keresek.**	ej *pen*-zee-oht keh-reh-shek.
I'm looking for a youth hostel.	**Egy ifjúsági szállót keresek.**	ej *eef*-yoo-shah-gee *sah*-loht keh-reh-shek.
I am staying . . .	**Néhány . . .**	*nay*-hahn . . .
a few days	**napig leszek itt**	*naw*-peeg leh-sek eet
two weeks	**két hétig leszek itt**	*kayt hayt*-eeg leh-sek eet
a month	**egy hónapig leszek itt**	*ej hoh*-naw-peeg leh-sek eet
I have a reservation.	**Foglaltam már szobát.**	*fohg*-lawl-tawm mahr soh-baht.
My name is . . .	**A nevem . . .**	aw *neh*-vem . . .
Do you have a room? . . .	**Van egy szobája? . . .**	*vawn* ej soh-bah-yaw? . . .
for tonight	**ma éjszakára**	*maw* ay-saw-kah-raw
for three nights	**három éjszakára**	*hah*-rom ay-saw-kah-raw
for a week	**egy hétre**	*ej hayt*-reh
I would like . . .	**Kérek . . .**	*kay*-rek . . .
a single	**egy egyágyas szobát**	*ej ej*-ah-jawsh sho-baht
a double	**egy kétágyas szobát**	*ej kayt*-ah-jawsh soh-baht
with bath	**fürdővel**	*feer*-dur-vel
without bath	**fürdő nélkül**	*feer*-dur *nayl*-keel
with shower	**zuhanyozóval**	*zoo*-hawn-yoh-zoh-vawl
without shower	**zuhanyozó nélkül**	*zoo*-hawn-yoh-zoh *nayl*-keel
with a view	**szép kilátással**	*sayp kee*-lah-tahsh-shawl
How much is the room?	**Mennyibe kerül a szoba?**	*men*-yee-beh keh-reel aw *soh*-baw?
with breakfast	**a reggelit beszámítva**	aw *reg*-geh-leet beh-sah-meet-vaw
May I see the room?	**Megnézhetem a szobát?**	*meg*-nayz-hem-tem aw *soh*-baht?
The key	**A kulcs**	aw *koolch*
The bill, please	**Kérem a számlámat**	*kay*-rem aw *sahm*-lah-mawt

Getting Around

English	Hungarian	Pronounced
I'm looking for a . . .	**Keresek egy . . .**	*keh*-reh-shek ej . . .
I'm looking for the . . .	**Keresem a . . .**	*keh*-reh-shem aw . . .
bank	**bankot**	*bawn*-koht
church	**tamplomot**	*tem*-ploh-moht
city center	**belvárost**	*bel*-vah-rosht
museum	**múzeumot**	*moo*-zeh-oo-moht
pharmacy	**patikát**	*paw*-tee-kaht
park	**parkot**	*pawr*-koht
theater	**színházat**	*seen*-hah-zawt
tourist office	**turista ügynökséget**	*too*-reesh-taw eej-nurk-shay-get
embassy	**nagykövetséget**	*nawj*-kur-vet-shay-get
Where is the nearest telephone?	**Hol van a legközelebbi telefon?**	*hohl* vawn aw *leg*-jur-zeh-leb-bee *teh*-leh-fohn?
I would like to buy . . .	**Kérek . . .**	*kay*-rek . . .
a stamp	**egy bélyeget**	ej *bay*-eh-get
a postcard	**egy levelezólapot**	ej *leh*-veh-leh-zur-law-poht
a map	**egy térképet**	ej *tayr*-kay-pet

Signs

English	Hungarian
No Trespassing	**Átlépni tilos; Belépni tilos**
No Parking	**A parkolás tilos**
Entrance	**Bejárat**
Exit	**Kijárat**
Information	**Tudakozó**
No Smoking	**Tilos a dohányzás**
Arrivals	**Érkezések**
Departures	**Indulások**
Toilets	**Toalettek**
Danger	**Vigyázat**

Numbers

1 **egy** (*ej*)
2 **kettó** (*ket*-tur)
3 **három** (*hah*-rohm)
4 **négy** (*nayj*)
5 **öt** (*urt*)
6 **hat** (*hawt*)
7 **hét** (*hayt*)
8 **nyolc** (*nyohlts*)
9 **kilenc** (*kee*-lents)
10 **tíz** (*teez*)
11 **tizenegy** (*teez*-en-ej)
12 **tizenkettó** (*teez*-en-ket-tur)
13 **tizenhárom** (*teez*-en-hah-rohm)
14 **tizennégy** (*teez*-en-nayj)
15 **tizenöt** (*teez*-en-urt)
16 **tizenhat** (*teez*-en-hawt)
17 **tizenhét** (*teez*-en-hayt)
18 **tizennyolc** (*teez*-en-nyohlts)
19 **tizenkilenc** (*teez*-en-kee-lents)
20 **húsz** (*hoos*)
30 **harminc** (*hawr*-meents)
40 **negyven** (*nej*-ven)
50 **ötven** (*urt*-ven)
60 **hatvan** (*hawt*-vawn)
70 **hetven** (*het*-ven)
80 **nyolcvan** (*nyohlts*-vawn)
90 **kilencven** (*kee*-lents-ven)
100 **száz** (*sahz*)
500 **ötszáz** (*urt*-sahz)
1,000 **ezer** (*eh*-zer)

Eating

English	**Hungarian**	Pronounced
Restaurant	**Vendéglő**	*ven*-dayg-lur
Breakfast	**Reggeli**	*reg*-geh-lee
Lunch	**Ebéd**	*eh*-bayd
Dinner	**Vacsora**	*vaw*-choh-raw
A table for two, please.	**Kérek egy asztalt két személyre.**	*kay*-rek ej aws-tawlt *kayt* seh-may-reh.
Waiter	**Pincér**	*peent*-sayr
Waitress	**Pincérnó**	*peent*-sayr-nur
I would like . . .	**Kérnék . . .**	*kayr*-nayk . . .
a menu	**egy étlapot**	ej *ayt*-law-poht
a fork	**egy villát**	ej *veel*-laht
a knife	**egy kést**	ej *kaysht*
a spoon	**egy kanalat**	ej *kaw*-naw-lawt
a napkin	**egy szalvétát**	ej *sawl*-vay-taht
a glass (of water)	**egy pohár (vizet)**	ej poh-hahr (*vee*-zet)
the check, please	**fizetek**	*fee*-zeh-tek
Is the tip included?	**A borravaló szerepel a számlában?**	aw *bohr*-raw-vaw-loh seh-reh-pel aw sahm-lah-bawn?

Hungarian Menu Terms

General Terms

Soups	**Levesek**	*leh*-veh-shek
Eggs	**Tojás**	*toh*-yahsh
Salads	**Saláták**	*shaw*-lah-tahk
Meats	**Hús**	*hoosh*
Meat dishes	**Húsételek**	*hoosh*-ay-teh-lek
Fish	**Halak**	*haw*-lawk
Vegetables	**Főzelék**	*fur*-zeh-layk
Desserts	**Tészták**	*tays*-tahk
Fruits	**Gyümölcs**	*jee*-murlch
Beverages	**Italok**	*ee*-taw-lohk
Bread	**Kenyér**	*ken*-yayr
Butter	**Vaj**	*vaw*-ee

Condiments

Mayonnaise	**Majonéz**	*maw*-yoh-nayz
Mustard	**Mustár**	*moosh*-tahr
Oil	**Olaj**	*oh*-law-ee
Vinegar	**Ecet**	*eh*-tset
Salt	**Só**	*shoh*
Black pepper	**Bors**	*borsh*
Paprika	**Paprika**	*paw*-pree-kaw

Cooking Terms

Fresh	**Friss**	*freesh*
Raw	**Nyers**	*nyersh*
Spicy	**Fűszerezve**	*fee*-seh-rez-veh
Salty	**Sós**	*shosh*

English	**Hungarian**	Pronounced
Baked/fried	**Sütve**	*sheet*-veh
Deep-fried	**Zsírban sütve**	*zheer*-bawn sheet-ve
Steamed	**Párolva**	*pah*-rohl-vaw
Braised	**Dinsztelve**	*deen*-stel-veh
Stuffed	**Töltve**	*turlt*-veh
Toasted	**Pirítva**	*pee*-reet-vaw
Boiled	**Főzve**	*furz*-veh
Rare	**Félig nyersen**	*fay*-leeg nyer-shen
Medium	**Közepesen kisütve**	*kur*-zeh-peh-shen *kee*-sheet-veh
Well done	**Agyonsütve**	*aw*-john sheet-veh
Hot (peppery)	**Csípős**	*chee*-pursh
Hot (in temperature)	**Forró**	*fohr*-roh
Cold	**Hideg**	*hee*-deg

Soups

Húsleves bouillon
Zöldborsóleves pea soup
Zöldségleves vegetable soup
Paradicsomleves tomato soup
Gulyásleves goulash soup
Gombaleves mushroom soup

Eggs

Tükörtojás fried eggs
Rántotta scrambled eggs
Omlett omelet
Gombás omlett mushroom omelet
Lágy tojás soft-boiled eggs
Kemény tojás hard-boiled eggs
Szalonnával with bacon
Kolbásszal with sausage
Sonkával with ham

Salads

Fejes saláta green salad
Paprikasaláta pepper salad
Uborkasaláta cucumber salad
Vegyes saláta mixed salad

Meats

Marhahús beef
Borjúhús veal
Disznóhús pork
Csirke chicken
Kacsa duck
Liba goose
Bárány lamb

Meat Dishes

Pörkölt goulash
Bécsi szelet wienerschnitzel
Tokány ragoût
Nyársonsült shish kebab
Kotlett cutlet
Pecsenye roast
Paprikáscsirke chicken paprikash
Malacsült roast piglet

Fish

Ponty carp
Csuka pike
Fogas Balaton pike-perch
Pisztráng trout
Tonhal tuna
Halászlé fish stew
Csuka tejfölben pike with sour cream

Vegetables

Burgonya potato
Káposzta cabbage
Rizs rice
Gomba mushrooms
Spenót spinach
Lecsó pickled vegetables
Bab beans
Zöldbab green beans
Paradicsom tomato

Desserts

Almás rétes apple strudel
Cseresznyes retes cherry strudel
Túrós rétes cheese strudel
Csokoládé torta chocolate cake
Lekváros palacsinta palacsinta with preserves
Fagylalt ice cream

Fruits

Barack apricot
Cseresznye cherries
Dinnye melon
Körte pears
Narancs oranges
Szőlő grapes

Beverages

Víz water
Tej milk
Narancslé orange juice
Kávé coffee
Tea tea
Kakaó cocoa
Fehér bor white wine
Vörös bor red wine
Koktél cocktail
Pálinka brandy
Sör beer
Barna sör dark beer
Pezsgő champagne

D Polish Language Guide

Polish Vocabulary

The Polish alphabet has a few more letters than English—a total of 33. Most (the letters *b, d, f, g, h, k, l, m, n, p, r, s, t, x, z*) are pronounced as they are in English; some letters are pronounced somewhat differently, as shown below:

a	*a*lmost (never as in lace)
ą	maiso*n* (nasal pronunciation as in French)
b	*b*oy
c	lo*ts*
d	*d*ay
e	g*e*t
ę	str*e*ngth (nasal when precedes a consonant)
f	*f*ool
g	*g*irl
h	*h*ello
i	mar*i*ne
j	*y*oung
k	*k*ey
l	*l*ord
m	*m*om
n	*n*o
o	n*o*r
ó	n*u*clear
p	*p*en
r	*r*un
s	*s*un
t	*t*op
u	n*u*clear (like ó)
w	*v*ery
x	o*x*
y	d*i*d
z	*z*ero

Additional letters and consonant clusters are as follows:

ć	*ch*eese
ch	lo*ch* (Scottish pronunciation)
cz	*ch*oice

dz	a*dz*e
dź	*j*erk
dż	bri*dg*e
ł	*w*eek
ń	o*n*ion
sz	*sh*ore
ś	*sh*eer
ź	gara*g*e
rz	plea*s*ure
ż	a*z*ure

Note: Polish distinguishes between genders, hence adjective and verb endings differ for male and female, as in the expression "I would like": *chciałbym* (male) or *chciałbym* (female). Polish expressions with slashes between them indicate first the male and then the female form.

Everyday Expressions

English	Polish	Pronounced
Hello, Greetings	**Witam, cześć**	*vee*-tam, cheshch
Good morning	**Dzień dobry**	dzheyn *do*-bri
Good evening	**Dobry wieczór**	*do*-bri *vyeh*-choor
How are you?	**Jak się masz?**	yak sheh mash?
Very well	**Bardzo dobrze**	*bar*-dzo *do*-bzheh
Thank you	**Dziękuję**	dzhyen-*koo*-yeh
You're welcome	**Proszę**	*pro*-sheh
Please	**Proszę**	*pro*-sheh
Yes	**Tak**	tak
No	**Nie**	nyeh
Excuse me	**Przepraszam**	psheh-*pra*-sham
How much does it cost?	**Ile kosztuje?**	*ee*-leh kosh-*too*-yeh?
I don't understand.	**Nie rozumiem.**	nyeh roz-*oom*-yem.
Just a moment.	**Chwileczkę.**	khvi-*lech*-keh.
Good-bye	**Do widzenia**	do vee-*dzen*-ya

Traveling

Where is the? . . .	**Gdzie jest? . . .**	gdzhyeh yest? . . .
bus station	**dworzec autobusowy**	*dvo*-zhets ow-to-bu-*so*-vi
train station	**dworzec kolejowy**	*dvo*-zhets ko-ley-*o*-vi
airport	**lotnisko**	lot-*nee*-sko
baggage check	**przechowalnia bagażu**	psheh-ho-*val*-nya ba-*ga*-zhoo
Where can I find a taxi?	**Gdzie mogę znaleźć taksówke?**	gdzhyeh *mo*-geh *zna*-leshch tak-*soof*-keh?
How much is the fare?	**Ile kosztuje przejazd?**	*ee*-leh kosh-*too*-yeh *psheh*-yazd?
I am going to . . .	**Idę do [walking] . . .**	*ee*-deh do . . .
	Jadę do [riding] . . .	ya-deh do . . .
One-way ticket	**Bilet w jedną stronę**	*bee*-let w *yed*-no *stro*-neh
Round-trip ticket	**Bilet tam i z powrotem**	*bee*-let tam i spo-*vro*-tem
Car-rental office	**Wypożyczalnia samochodów**	vi-po-zhi-*chal*-nya sa-mo-*ho*-doof

English	**Polish**	Pronounced
Where can I find a gas station?	**Gdzie mogę znaleźć stacje benzynową?**	gdzhyeh *mo*-geh *zna*-leshch *sta*-tsyeh ben-zi-*no*-vo?
Please fill the tank.	**Proszę napelnić bak.**	*pro*-sheh na-*pel*-neech bak.

Accommodations

English	Polish	Pronounced
I'm looking for . . .	**Szukam . . .**	*shoo*-kam . . .
a hotel	**hotel**	*ho*-tel
a pension	**pensjonatu**	pen-syo-*na*-too
a youth hostel	**schronisko młodżiezowe**	skhro-*nee*-sko mlo-dzheh-*zho*-weh
I am staying . . .	**Będę przebywać . . .**	*ben*-deh psheh-*bi*-vach . . .
a few days	**kilka dni**	*keel*-ka dnee
two weeks	**dwa tygodnie**	dva ti-*god*-nyeh
I have a reservation.	**Mam rezerwację**	mam reh-zer-*va*-tsyeh
My name is . . .	**Moje nazwisko . . .**	*mo*-yeh naz-*vee*-sko . . .
Do you have a room? . . .	**Czy ma Pan/Pani pokój? . . .**	tchi ma pan/*pa*-nee *po*-kooy? . . .
for tonight	**na dzisiejszą noc**	na dzhee-*shey*-shon nots
for three nights	**na trzy doby**	na tchi *do*-bi
for a week	**na tydzień**	na *ti*-dzheyn
I would like . . .	**Chciałbym/chciałabym . . .**	*khchow*-bim/ *khchow*-a-bim . . .
a single	**jedynke, na jedną osobę**	yeh-*din*-keh, na *yed*-no o-*so*-beh
a double	**dwójke, na dwie osoby**	*dvooy*-keh, na dvyeh o-*so*-bi
I want a room . . .	**Chciałbym/chciałabym . . .**	*khchow*-bim/ *khchow*-a-bim
with a shower	**z prysznicem**	sprish-*nee*-tsem
without a shower	**bez prysznica**	bez prish-*nee*-tsa
with bath	**z łazienka**	z wa-*zhen*-ko
without a bath	**bez łazienka**	bez wa-*zhen*-kee
How much is the room?	**Ile kosztuje pokój?**	*ee*-leh kosh-*too*-yeh *po*-kooy?
with breakfast?	**z śniadaniem?**	s shnya-*da*-nyem?
May I see the room?	**Czy mogę zobaczyć pokój?**	tchi *mo*-geh zo-*ba*-chich *po*-kooy?
The key	**Klucz**	klooch
The bill, please	**Poproszę rachunek**	po-*pro*-sheh ra-*hoo*-nek

Getting Around

English	Polish	Pronounced
I'm looking for . . .	**Szukam . . .**	*shoo*-kam . . .
a bank	**bank**	bank
the church	**kościół**	*kosh*-chyoo
the city center	**śródmieście**	shrood-*myesh*-chyehh
the museum	**muzeum**	moo-*zeh*-oom
a pharmacy	**aptekę**	ap-*teh*-keh
the park	**park**	park
the theater	**teatr**	*teh*-atr
the tourist office	**biuro podrózy**	*byoo*-ro po-*droo*-zhi
the embassy	**ambasadę**	am-ba-*sa*-deh
Where is the nearest telephone?	**Gdzie jest najbliższy telefon?**	gdzhyeh yest nay-*blizh*-shi te-*leh*-fon?
I would like to buy . . .	**Chciałbym/chciałabym kupić . . .**	*khchow*-bim/ *khchow*-a-bim *koo*-peech . . .
a stamp	**znaczek**	*zna*-chek
a postcard	**pocztówkę**	po-*chtoo*-fkeh
a map	**mapę**	*ma*-pe

Signs

English	Polish	Pronounced
No Trespassing	**Wstęp wzbroniony**	
No Parking	**Nie parkować**	
Entrance	**Wejście**	
Exit	**Wyjście**	
Information	**Informacja**	
Sightseeing Route	**Kierunek Zwiedzania**	
No Smoking	**Nie palić, palenie wzbronione**	
Arrivals (air)	**Przyjazdy (Przyloty)**	
Departures (air)	**Odjazdy (Odloty)**	
Toilets	**Toalety**	
Danger	**Niebezpieczeństwo**	

Numbers

1 **jeden** (*yeh*-den)
2 **dwa** (dva)
3 **trzy** (tchi)
4 **cztery** (*tchteh*-ri)
5 **pięć** (pyench)
6 **sześć** (sheshch)
7 **siedem** (*sheh*-dem)
8 **osiem** (*o*-shyem)
9 **dziewięć** (*dzhyeh*-vyench)
10 **dziesięć** (*dzeh*-shyench)
11 **jedenaście** (yeh-den-*a*-shchyeh)
12 **dwanaście** (dva-*na*-shchyeh)
13 **trzynaście** (tchi-*na*-shchyeh)
14 **czternaście** (tchter-*na*-shchyeh)
15 **piętnaście** (pyent-na-shchyeh)
16 **szesnaście** (shesh-*na*-shchyeh)
17 **siedemnaście** (she-dem-*na*-shchyeh)
18 **osiemnaście** (o-shem-*na*-shchyeh)
19 **dziewiętnaście** (dzheh-vyent-*na*-shchyeh)
20 **dwadzieścia** (dva-*dzhyeh*-shchya)
30 **trzydzieści** (tchi-*dzhyeh*-shchee)
40 **czterdzieści** (tchter-*dzhyeh*-shchee)
50 **pięćdziesiąt** (pyen-*dzhyeh*-shont)
60 **sześćdziesiąt** (shesh-*dzhyeh*-shont)
70 **siedemdziesiąt** (sheh-dem-*dzhyeh*-shont)
80 **osiemdziesiąt** (o-shem-*dzhyeh*-shont)
90 **dziewięćdziesiąt** (dzhye-vyen-*dzyeh*-shont)
100 **sto** (sto)
500 **pięćset** (*pyench*-set)
1,000 **tysiąc** (*ti*-shonts)

Eating

English	Polish	Pronounced
Restaurant	**Restauracja**	res-tau-*ra*-tsya
Breakfast	**Śniadanie**	shnya-*da*-nyeh
Lunch	**Obiad**	*o*-byad
Supper	**Kolacja**	ko-*la*-tsya
A table for two, please.	**Proszę o stołik na dwie osoby.**	pro-*sheh* o *sto*-leek na dvyeh o-*so*-bi.
Waiter	**Kelner**	*kel*-ner
Waitress	**Kelnerka**	kel-*ner*-ka
I would like . . .	**Poproszę . . .**	po-*pro*-sheh . . .
a menu	**karte**	*kar*-teh
a fork	**widelec**	wi-*del*-ets
a knife	**nóż**	noozh
a spoon	**łyżke**	*wizh*-keh
a napkin	**serwetkę**	ser-*vet*-keh
a glass (of water)	**szklankę (wody)**	*shklan*-ken (*vo*-di)
The check, please	**Poproszę o rachunek**	po-*pro*-sheh o ra-*hoo*-nek
Is the tip included?	**Czy napiwek jest wliczony?**	tchi na-*pee*-vek yest vlee-*cho*-ni?

Polish Menu Terms

General Terms

English	Polish	Pronounced
Soups	**Zupy**	*zoo*-pi
Eggs	**Jajka**	*yay*-ka
Salads	**Sałaty**	sa-*wa*-ti
Meats	**Mięso**	*mien*-so
Fish	**Ryba**	*ri*-ba
Vegetables	**Warzywa**	va-*zhy*-va
Desserts	**Desery**	deh-*seh*-ri
Fruits	**Owoce**	o-*vo*-tseh
Beverages	**Napoje**	na-*po*-yeh

Condiments

Salt	**Sól**	sool
Pepper	**Pieprz**	pyepsh
Mustard	**Musztarda**	moo-*shtar*-da
Vinegar	**Ocet**	*o*-tset
Oil	**Olej**	*o*-ley
Sugar	**Cukier**	*tsoo*-kyer

Soups

Barszcz Polish beet soup
Botwina beet soup with beet greens
Chlodnik cold beet soup with vegetables
Grzybowa mushroom soup
Jarzynowa vegetable soup
Kapusniak cabbage soup
Krem pomidorowy tomato soup
Rybna fish soup
Zalewajka onion soup
Zurek Polski farmer's soup, a sour-tasting broth with sausages or egg

Meats

Baranina lamb
Befsztyk Tatarski steak tartare
Bigos sausages and sauerkraut
Cielęcina veal
Comber sarni venison
Dziczyzna game
Escalopki veal or pork schnitzel
Flaki tripe with seasoning
Gęs goose
Golonka boiled pork shank
Gulasz wołowy beef goulash
Indyk turkey
Kaczka pieczona roast duck
Kotlet schabowy breaded pork cutlet
Kułduny dumplings filled with meat
Kurczę chicken
Pieczeń z dzika roast wild boar
Pierogi large dumplings with meat
Sarnina roast venison
Stek steak
Szynka ham
Wątroba liver
Wieprzowina pork
Wołowina beef

Fish

Dorsz cod
Karp carp
Łosos salmon
Pstrąg trout
Raki crayfish
Sandacz pike-perch
Sledż herring
Węgorz eel

Eggs

Jaja gotowane boiled eggs
Jaja sadzone fried eggs
Jajecznica scrambled eggs
Omlet omelet
  z groszkiem konserwowym with green peas
  z pieczarkami with mushrooms

Salads

Mizeria ze śmietaną cucumber salad
Sałata mieszana mixed salad
Sałatka z czerwonej kapusty red cabbage salad
Sałatka zielona green salad
Sałatka z pomidorów tomato salad

Vegetables
Ćwikła red beets
Frytki french fries
Groszek peas
Grzyby mushrooms
Kapusta cabbage
Kluski z ziemniakow dumplings
Marchewka carrots
Pieczarki mushrooms
Pomidory tomatoes
Ryż rice
Szpinak spinach
Ziemniaki potatoes

Desserts
Kompot mieszany mixed compote
Lody ice cream
Kakaowe chocolate
Kawowe coffee (flavor)
Waniliowe vanilla
Tort czekoladowy chocolate cake
Tort makowy poppyseed cake

Fruits
Cytryna lemon
Gruszki pears
Jabłka apples
Owoce fruit

Beverages
Herbata tea
Kawa coffee
Mleko milk
Piwo beer
Śmietanka cream
Sok juice
Szampan champagne
Wino wine
Białe white
Czerwone red
Woda mineralna mineral water

Condiments and Others
Bułki rolls
Chleb bread
Chrzan horse radish
Lód ice
Masło butter

Cooking Terms
Dobrze upieczone well done
Faszerowany stuffed
Gotowany boiled
Krwiste rare
Smażona fried
Wędzona smoked
Zapiekana baked
Z rusztu grilled
Z wody boiled

E Romanian Language Guide

Romanian Vocabulary

Romanian vowels are pronounced somewhat differently from the same letters in English:

a	f*a*ther
ă	*a*go
â	[same as î; see below]
e	m*e*t
i	b*e*
î	like *a*go, but shorter and tenser
o	g*o* (but slightly shorter)
u	b*oo*t

Most Romanian consonants are pronounced quite similarly to their English equivalents, with the following exceptions:

c	*c*at [except in "ce" or "ci" combinations]
ce	*ch*eck
ci	*ch*eap

g	*g*oat [except in "ge" or "gi" combinations]
ge	*j*et
gi	*J*eep
ş	*sh*eep
ţ	ge*ts*

Everyday Expressions

English	Romanian	Pronounced
Hello	**Salut**	sah-*loot*
Good morning	**Bună dimineata**	*boo*-nah dee-mee-*nah*-tsah
Good evening	**Bună seara**	*boo*-nah seh-ah-*rah*
How are you?	**Ce mai faci?**	cheh mye fahch?
Very well	**Foarte bine**	fo-*ahr*-teh *bee*-neh
Thank you	**Mulţumesc**	mool-tsoo-*mesk*
You're welcome	**Sinteţ bine venit**	*sin*-tets *bee*-neh veh-*neet*
Please	**Vă rog; Te rog**	vah rohg; teh rohg
Yes	**Da**	dah
No	**Nu**	noo
Excuse me	**Scuză-mă; Pardon**	*skoo*-zah mah; par-*dohn*
How much does it cost?	**Cit costă?**	kit *ko*-stah?
I don't understand.	**Nu inţeleg.**	noo oon-tseh-*leg*.
Just a moment.	**Numai cun moment.**	*noo*-mye oon mo-*ment*.
Good-bye	**La revedere**	lah reh-veh-*deh*-reh
I am sorry.	**Imi pare rău.**	oom pah-*reh* ro.
Where is the? . . .	**Unde este? . . .**	*oon*-deh *yes*-teh? . . .
bus station	**staţia de autobuz**	*stah*-tsee-yah deh ow-toh-*booss*
train station	**staţia de tren; gara**	*stah*-tsee-yah deh tren; *gah*-rah
airport	**aeroportul**	ah-eh-ro-*por*-tool
baggage check	**controlul bagajelor**	kohn-*trol*-ool bah-*gah*-zheh-lor
check-in counter	**casa de bilete**	*kah*-sah deh bee-*leh*-teh
Where can I find a taxi?	**Unde pot gąsi un taxiu?**	*oon*-deh poht gah-see oon tak-*syoo*
How much is the fare?	**Cit este taxa? Cit este costul unei calţatori?**	kit *yess*-teh *tahk*-sah; kit *yess*-tess *koss*-tool *oo*-nay kah-lah-*toh*-ree
I am going to . . .	**Merg la . . .**	mehrg lah . . .
One-way ticket	**Bilet numai dus**	bee-let *noo*-mye dooss
Round-trip ticket	**Bilet in circuit**	bee-let in cheer-*kweet*
Car-rental office	**Oficiu de inchiriat maşini**	o-*fee*-chyoo deh een-kee-ree-*yat* mah-*sheen*
Where can I find a gas station?	**Unde pot găsi o benzinărie?**	*oon*-deh poht gah-*see* o ben-zee-nah-*ree*-yeh?
How much is gas?	**Cit costă benzina?**	kit *kos*-tah ben-*zee*-nah?
Please fill the tank.	**Te rog umple rezervorul.**	teh rohg *oom*-pleh reh-zeh-*vo*-rool.

Accommodations

I am looking for . . .	**Caut . . .**	kowt . . .
a hotel	**hotel**	ho-*tel*
a youth hostel	**cămin studenţesc**	kah-*meen* stoo-den-*tsesk*
I am staying . . .	**Stau . . .**	*stah*-oo . . .
a few days	**citeva zile**	kit-eh-*vah* zee-*leh*
two weeks	**două săptămini**	*do*-ah sep-tah-*moon*-ee
a month	**o lună**	o *loo*-nah

Accommodations

English	Romanian	Pronounced
I have a reservation.	**Am o rezervare de loc.**	ahm o reh-zehr-*vah*-reh deh lohk.
My name is . . .	**Mă numesc . . .**	mah noo-*mesk* . . .
Do you have a room? . . .	**Aveţi o cameră? . . .**	ah-*veh*-tee o *kah*-meh-rah? . . .
for tonight	**pentru o noapte**	*pen*-troo o no-*ahp*-teh
for three nights	**pentru trei nopţi**	*pen*-troo tray *nopts*
for a week	**pentru o săptămina**	*pen*-troo o sep-tah-*muh*-nah
I would like . . .	**Aş dori . . .**	ash do-*ree* . . .
a single	**cameră pentru o persoana**	*kah*-meh-rah *pen*-troo o pehr-so-*ah*-nah
a double	**cameră pentru două persoane**	*kah*-meh-rah *pen*-troo *do*-o per-so-*ah*-neh
I want a room . . .	**Aş dori o cameră . . .**	ash do-*ree* o *kah*-meh-rah
with a bath/shower	**cu baie/duş**	koo *bah*-yeh/doosh
without a bath/shower	**fărabaie/duş**	*fuh*-rah *bah*-yeh/doosh
with a view	**cu vedere**	koo veh-*deh*-reh
How much is the room?	**Cit costă cameră?**	kit *kos*-tah *kah*-meh-rah?
with breakfast	**cu micul dejun**	koo *mee*-kool deh-*zhoon*
May I see the room?	**Pot să văd cameră?**	poht sah vud *kah*-meh-rah?
The key	**cheia**	*kay*-ah
The bill, please	**Nota vă rog**	*no*-tah vah rohg

Getting Around

English	Romanian	Pronounced
I am looking for . . .	**Eu caut . . .**	*yeh*-oo kowt . . .
a bank	**o bancă**	o *bahn*-kah
the church	**biserica**	bee-*seh*-ree-kah
the city center	**centrul oraşului**	*chen*-trool o-*rah*-shoo-lui
the museum	**muzeul**	moo-*zeh*-ool
a pharmacy	**farmacia**	far-mah-*chee*-ah
the park	**parcul**	*pahr*-kool
the theater	**teatrul**	teh-*ah*-trool
the tourist office	**oficiul de turism**	o-*fee*-chool deh too-*reezm*
the embassy	**ambasada**	ahm-bah-*sah*-dah
Where is the nearest telephone?	**Unde este cel mai apropiat telefon?**	*oon*-deh *yes*-teh chel *mah*-ee ah-pro-*pyat* teh-leh-*fohn?*
I would like to buy . . .	**Aş vrea să cumpar . . .**	ash vrah sah *koom*-por . . .
a stamp	**timbru postal**	*teem*-broo po-*shtal*
a postcard	**o carte poştala**	o *kar*-teh po-*shtah*-luh
a map	**o hartă**	o *har*-tuh

Signs

English	Romanian
No trespassing	**Nu se trece**
No parking	**Parcarea interzisă**
Entrance	**Intrare**
Exit	**Ieşire**
Information	**Informaţii**
No smoking	**Fumatul interzis**
Arrivals	**Sosiri**
Departures	**Plecări**
Toilets (WC)	**Toaleta (WC)**
Danger	**Pericol**

Numbers

1 **unu** (*oo*-noo)
2 **doi** (doy)
3 **trei** (tray)
4 **patru** (*pah*-troo)
5 **cinci** (cheench)
6 **şase** (*shah*-say)
7 **şapte** (*shap*-tay)
8 **opt** (ohpt)
9 **nouă** (*no*-uh)
10 **zece** (*zeh*-chay)
11 **unsprezece** (*oon*-spreh-zeh-cheh)
12 **doisprezece** (*doy*-spreh-zeh-cheh)
13 **treisprezece** (*tray*-spreh-zeh-cheh)
14 **patrusprezece** (*pah*-troo-spreh-zeh-cheh)
15 **cincisprezece** (*cheench*-spreh-zeh-cheh)
16 **şasesprezece** (*shah*-say-spreh-zeh-cheh)
17 **şaptesprezece** (*shap*-tay-spreh-zeh-cheh)
18 **optsprezece** (*ohpt*-spreh-zeh-cheh)
19 **nouăsprezece** (*no*-uh-spreh-zeh-cheh)
20 **două zeci** (*do*-uh zech)
30 **tre zeci** (trey zech)
40 **patru zeci** (*pah*-troo zech)
50 **cinci zeci** (cheench zech)
60 **şase zeci** (*shah*-seh zech)
70 **şapte zeci** (*shap*-teh zech)
80 **opt zeci** (ohpt zech)
90 **nouă zeci** (*no*-uh zech)
100 **o sută** (o *soo*-tuh)
500 **cinci sute** (cheench *soo*-teh)
1,000 **o mie** (o *mee*-eh)

Eating

English	**Romanian**	Pronounced
Restaurant	**Restaurant**	res-tau-*rahnt*
Breakfast	**Micul dejun**	*mee*-kool deh-*zhoon*
Lunch	**Prinzul**	*prin*-zool
Dinner	**Cina**	*chee*-nah
A table for two, please.	**O masă cu două locuri.**	o *mah*-sah koo *do*-ah *lo*-koo-ree.
Waiter	**Chelner**	*kel*-nehr
Waitress	**Chelnariţa**	*kel*-nah-ree-tsah
I would like . . .	**Aş dori . . .**	ash doh-*ree* . . .
a menu	**un meniu**	oon men-*yoo*
a fork	**o furculită**	o foor-koo-*lee*-tsah
a knife	**un cuţit**	oon koo-*tseet*
a spoon	**o lingură**	o *leen*-goo-rah
a napkin	**şerveţel**	*shehr*-veh-tsel
a glass (of water)	**un pahar (de apa)**	oon pah-*har* (deh *ah*-puh)
the check, please	**nota de plată**	*no*-tah deh *plah*-tah

Romanian Menu Terms

General Terms

English	**Romanian**	Pronounced
Soup	**Supa**	*soo*-pah
Eggs	**Ouă**	*o*-ah
Meat	**Carne**	*kar*-neh
Fish	**Peşte**	*pesh*-teh
Vegetables	**Vegetale**	veh-jeh-*tah*-leh
Fruits	**Fructe**	*frook*-teh
Dessert	**Desert**	deh-*sehr*-teh
Beverages	**Băuturi**	buh-oo-*too*-reh
Salt	**Sare**	*sah*-reh
Pepper	**Piper**	pee-*pehr*
Mustard	**Mustar**	moo-*shtar*

General Terms

English	Romanian	Pronounced
Vinegar	**Oţet**	o-tset
Oil	**Ulei**	oo-*leh*-eey
Sugar	**Zahăr**	*zah*-har
Tea	**Ceai**	chah-ee
Coffee	**Kafea**	kah-*feh*-ah
Bread	**Pîine**	*puh*-ee-neh
Butter	**Unt**	oont
Wine	**Vin**	veen
Vodka	**Vodka**	*vod*-kah

Soups

Ciorbă de perişoare meatball soup
Ciorbă taraneasca peasant-style soup with vegetables
Supa cu taitei noodle soup
Supa de pasare chicken soup

Meats

Cirnaţi sausage
Creier brains
Curcan turkey
Ficat liver
Mititei grilled meat rolls
Miel lamb
Porc pork
Pui chicken
Raţa duck
Rinichi kidneys
Sarmale meat rolled in cabbage
Snitel pork schnitzel
Şunca ham
Vită beef

Fish

Morun sturgeon
Pastrav trout
Plachie de crap carp cooked in the oven with spices
Şalău sturgeon
Zander pike-perch

Eggs

Ouă fierte boiled eggs
Ouă jumări scrambled eggs
Ouă ochiuri fried eggs
Ochiuri romanesti poached eggs
Cu şunca with ham
Omletá omelet

Salads

Salata de castraveţi cucumber salad
Salata de cartofi potato salad
Salata de cruditati mixed salad
Salata de roşii tomato salad
Salata verde green salad

Vegetables

Cartofi prajiţi fried potatoes
Cartofi fiertí boiled potatoes
Castraveti cucumbers
Ciuperci mushrooms
Conopida cauliflower
Fasole beans
Fasole verde string beans
Mamaliga polenta
Mazare peas
Morcovi carrots
Orez rice
Puré de cartofi mashed potatoes
Roşii tomatoes
Sfecla rosie beets
Spanac spinach
Sparanghel asparagus
Varza cabbage
Varza acră sauerkraut
Varza rosie red cabbage

Desserts

Baclava sweet baklava pastry
Clătite crêpes
Cozonac Moldavian pound cake
Frişca whipped cream
Ingheţată ice cream
de ciocolata chocolate
de vanilie vanilla
Plăcintă pie
Papanaş doughnuts with sour cream sauce
cu brinza with cheese

Fruits

Căpsuni strawberries
Cirese cherries
Lámpie lemons
Mere apples
Pere pears
Piersici peaches
Portocale oranges

Beverages

Apa minerala mineral water
Bere beer
  neagra dark
  blonda light
Cafea coffee
Coniac brandy
Lapte milk
Sifon soda
Ţuica plum brandy
Vin wine
  roşu red
  alb white

Condiments and Others

Brinza cheese
Caşcaval hard cheese
Chifle rolls
Gheaţă ice
Mustăr mustard
Oţet vinegar
Pîne bread
Piper pepper
Sare salt
Telemea feta cheese
Unt butter
Zahăr sugar

Cooking Terms

Copt baked
Fiert boiled
Fript broiled
La gratar grilled
Prajit fried
Umplut stuffed

Index

Please send me the books checked below:

FROMMER'S COMPREHENSIVE GUIDES

(Guides listing facilities from budget to deluxe, with emphasis on the medium-priced)

	Retail Price	Code
☐ Acapulco/Ixtapa/Taxco, 2nd Edition	$13.95	C157
☐ Alaska '94-'95	$17.00	C131
☐ Arizona '95 (Avail. 3/95)	$14.95	C166
☐ Australia '94-'95	$18.00	C147
☐ Austria, 6th Edition	$16.95	C162
☐ Bahamas '94-'95	$17.00	C121
☐ Belgium/Holland/Luxembourg '93-'94	$18.00	C106
☐ Bermuda '94-'95	$15.00	C122
☐ Brazil, 3rd Edition	$20.00	C111
☐ California '95	$16.95	C164
☐ Canada '94-'95	$19.00	C145
☐ Caribbean '95	$18.00	C148
☐ Carolinas/Georgia, 2nd Edition	$17.00	C128
☐ Colorado, 2nd Edition	$16.00	C143
☐ Costa Rica '95	$13.95	C161
☐ Cruises '95-'96	$19.00	C150
☐ Delaware/Maryland '94-'95	$15.00	C136
☐ England '95	$17.95	C159
☐ Florida '95	$18.00	C152
☐ France '94-'95	$20.00	C132
☐ Germany '95	$18.95	C158
☐ Ireland, 1st Edition (Avail. 3/95)	$16.95	C168
☐ Italy '95	$18.95	C160

	Retail Price	Code
☐ Jamaica/Barbados, 2nd Edition	$15.00	C149
☐ Japan '94-'95	$19.00	C144
☐ Maui, 1st Edition	$13.95	C153
☐ Nepal, 2nd Edition	$18.00	C126
☐ New England '95	$16.95	C165
☐ New Mexico, 3rd Edition (Avail. 3/95)	$14.95	C167
☐ New York State, 4th Edition	$19.00	C133
☐ Northwest, 5th Edition	$17.00	C140
☐ Portugal '94-'95	$17.00	C141
☐ Puerto Rico '95-'96	$14.00	C151
☐ Puerto Vallarta/Manzanillo/ Guadalajara '94-'95	$14.00	C028
☐ Scandinavia, 16th Edition (Avail. 3/95)	$19.95	C169
☐ Scotland '94-'95	$17.00	C146
☐ South Pacific '94-'95	$20.00	C138
☐ Spain, 16th Edition	$16.95	C163
☐ Switzerland/Liechtenstein '94-'95	$19.00	C139
☐ Thailand, 2nd Edition	$17.95	C154
☐ U.S.A., 4th Edition	$18.95	C156
☐ Virgin Islands '94-'95	$13.00	C127
☐ Virginia '94-'95	$14.00	C142
☐ Yucatan, 2nd Edition	$13.95	C155

FROMMER'S $-A-DAY GUIDES

(Guides to low-cost tourist accommodations and facilities)

	Retail Price	Code
☐ Australia on $45 '95-'96	$18.00	D122
☐ Costa Rica/Guatemala/Belize on $35, 3rd Edition	$15.95	D126
☐ Eastern Europe on $30, 5th Edition	$16.95	D129
☐ England on $60 '95	$17.95	D128
☐ Europe on $50 '95	$17.95	D127
☐ Greece on $45 '93-'94	$19.00	D100
☐ Hawaii on $75 '95	$16.95	D124

	Retail Price	Code
☐ Ireland on $45 '94-'95	$17.00	D118
☐ Israel on $45, 15th Edition	$16.95	D130
☐ Mexico on $45 '95	$16.95	D125
☐ New York on $70 '94-'95	$16.00	D121
☐ New Zealand on $45 '93-'94	$18.00	D103
☐ South America on $40, 16th Edition	$18.95	D123
☐ Washington, D.C. on $50 '94-'95	$17.00	D120

FROMMER'S CITY $-A-DAY GUIDES

	Retail Price	Code
☐ Berlin on $40 '94-'95	$12.00	D111
☐ London on $45 '94-'95	$12.00	D114

	Retail Price	Code
☐ Madrid on $50 '94-'95	$13.00	D119
☐ Paris on $45 '94-'95	$12.00	D117

FROMMER'S FAMILY GUIDES

	Retail Price	Code
☐ California with Kids	$18.00	F100
☐ Los Angeles with Kids	$17.00	F103
☐ New York City with Kids	$18.00	F101
☐ San Francisco with Kids	$17.00	F104
☐ Washington, D.C. with Kids	$17.00	F102

FROMMER'S CITY GUIDES

(Pocket-size guides to sightseeing and tourist accommodations and facilities in all price ranges)

	Retail Price	Code
☐ Amsterdam '93-'94	$13.00	S110
☐ Athens, 10th Edition (Avail. 3/95)	$12.95	S174
☐ Atlanta '95	$12.95	S161
☐ Atlantic City/Cape May, 5th Edition	$13.00	S130
☐ Bangkok, 2nd Edition	$12.95	S147
☐ Barcelona '93-'94	$13.00	S115
☐ Berlin, 3rd Edition	$12.95	S162
☐ Boston '95	$12.95	S160
☐ Budapest, 1st Edition	$13.00	S139
☐ Chicago '95	$12.95	S169
☐ Denver/Boulder/Colorado Springs, 3rd Edition	$12.95	S154
☐ Dublin, 2nd Edition	$12.95	S157
☐ Hong Kong '94-'95	$13.00	S140
☐ Honolulu/Oahu '95	$12.95	S151
☐ Las Vegas '95	$12.95	S163
☐ London '95	$12.95	S156
☐ Los Angeles '95	$12.95	S164
☐ Madrid/Costa del Sol, 2nd Edition	$12.95	S165
☐ Mexico City, 1st Edition	$12.95	S170
☐ Miami '95-'96	$12.95	S149
☐ Minneapolis/St. Paul, 4th Edition	$12.95	S159
☐ Montreal/Quebec City '95	$11.95	S166
☐ Nashville/Memphis, 1st Edition	$13.00	S141
☐ New Orleans '95	$12.95	S148
☐ New York '95	$12.95	S152
☐ Orlando '95	$13.00	S145
☐ Paris '95	$12.95	S150
☐ Philadelphia, 8th Edition	$12.95	S167
☐ Prague '94-'95	$13.00	S143
☐ Rome, 10th Edition	$12.95	S168
☐ San Diego '95	$12.95	S158
☐ San Francisco '95	$12.95	S155
☐ Santa Fe/Taos/Albuquerque '95	$12.95	S172
☐ Seattle/Portland '94-'95	$13.00	S137
☐ St. Louis/Kansas City, 2nd Edition	$13.00	S127
☐ Sydney, 4th Edition	$12.95	S171
☐ Tampa/St. Petersburg, 3rd Edition	$13.00	S146
☐ Tokyo '94-'95	$13.00	S144
☐ Toronto '95 (Avail. 3/95)	$12.95	S173
☐ Vancouver/Victoria '94-'95	$13.00	S142
☐ Washington, D.C. '95	$12.95	S153

FROMMER'S WALKING TOURS

(With routes and detailed maps, these companion guides point out the places and pleasures that make a city unique)

	Retail Price	Code
☐ Berlin	$12.00	W100
☐ Chicago	$12.00	W107
☐ England's Favorite Cities	$12.00	W108
☐ London	$12.00	W101
☐ Montreal/Quebec City	$12.00	W106
☐ New York	$12.00	W102
☐ Paris	$12.00	W103
☐ San Francisco	$12.00	W104
☐ Washington, D.C.	$12.00	W105

SPECIAL EDITIONS

	Retail Price	Code
☐ Bed & Breakfast Southwest	$16.00	P100
☐ Bed & Breakfast Great American Cities	$16.00	P104
Caribbean Hideaways	$16.00	P103
☐ National Park Guide, 29th Edition	$17.00	P106
☐ Where to Stay U.S.A., 11th Edition	$15.00	P102

FROMMER'S TOURING GUIDES

(Color-illustrated guides that include walking tours, cultural and historic sites, and practical information)

	Retail Price	Code
☐ Amsterdam	$11.00	T001
☐ Barcelona	$14.00	T015
☐ Brazil	$11.00	T003
☐ Hong Kong/Singapore/Macau	$11.00	T006
☐ Kenya	$14.00	T018
☐ London	$13.00	T007
☐ New York	$11.00	T008
☐ Rome	$11.00	T010
☐ Scotland	$10.00	T011
☐ Sicily	$15.00	T017
☐ Tokyo	$15.00	T016
☐ Turkey	$11.00	T013
☐ Venice	$ 9.00	T014

Please note: If the availability of a book is several months away, we may have back issues of guides to that particular destination. Call customer service at (815) 734-1104.

010 36 11663401 Mark Robertson